ADVANCED DIGITAL SIGNAL PROCESSING

ADVANCED DIGITAL SIGNAL PROCESSING

John G. Proakis

Northeastern University

Charles M. Rader

Massachusetts Institute of Technology, Lincoln Laboratories

Fuyun Ling

Codex Corporation

Chrysostomos L. Nikias

University of Southern California

Macmillan Publishing Company
NEW YORK

Maxwell Macmillan Canada
TORONTO

Maxwell Macmillan International
NEW YORK OXFORD SINGAPORE SYDNEY

Editor(s): John Griffin
Production Supervisor: John Travis
Production Manager: Valerie Sawyer
Cover Designer: Eileen Burke
Illustrations by Vantage Art, Inc.

This book was set in 10/12 Times Roman by Monotype Composition Company, and printed and bound by Quinn-Woodbine, Incorporated. The cover was printed by Quinn-Woodbine, Incorporated.

Printed in the United States of America

Macmillan Publishing Company
866 Third Avenue, New York, New York 10022

Macmillan Publishing Company is part of the
Maxwell Communication Group of Companies.

Collier Macmillan Canada, Inc.
1200 Eglinton Avenue, E.
Suite 200
Don Mills, Ontario M3C 3N1

Library of Congress Cataloging in Publication Data

Advanced digital signal processing / J. Proakis . . . [et al.].
p. cm.
Includes bibliographical references and index.
ISBN 0-02-396841-9
1. Signal processing—Digital techniques. I. Proakis, John G.
TK5102.5.A325 1992
621.382'2—dc20 91-28104
CIP

Printing: 1 2 3 4 5 6 7 8 Year: 2 3 4 5 6 7 8 9 0 1

PREFACE

The field of digital signal processing (DSP) has expanded rapidly over the past two decades. During the late sixties and seventies we witnessed the development of the basic theory for digital filter design and the development of computationally efficient algorithms for evaluating the Fourier transform, convolution, and correlation. During the decade of the eighties we experienced an explosion in DSP applications spurred by significant advances in digital computer technology and integrated-circuit fabrication. In the last ten years the basic DSP theory has expanded to include parametric signal modeling, with applications to power spectrum estimation and system modeling, adaptive signal processing algorithms, multirate signal processing, multi dimensional signal processing and higher-order statistical methods for signal processing.

With the expansion of the basic DSP theory and the rapid growth in applications of DSP that has been spurred by the development of fast and inexpensive digital signal processors there is a growing interest in advanced courses in DSP, covering a variety of topics. As a consequence, there has developed a need for textbooks covering these advanced topics. This book was written with the goal of satisfying, in part, this need.

The material treated in this book may be grouped into four major topics. The first topic deals with computationally efficient algorithms for convolution and correlation. This topic is covered in Chapter 2. The second major topic is multirate signal processing. This topic is treated in Chapter 3. The remaining six chapters deal with statistical signal processing. Chapters 4 through 7 constitute a comprehensive treatment of optimum filter design methods and adaptive filtering. Chapter 4 treats linear prediction and optimum Wiener filters. Included in this chapter is a description of the Levinson-Durbin and Schur algorithms. Chapter 5 considers the filter design problem based on the least-squares method and describes several methods for solving least squares problems, including the Givens transformation, the Householder transformation and singular-value decomposition. In Chapter 6 we treat single-channel adaptive filters based on the LMS algorithm and on recursive least-squares algorithms. Finally, in Chapter 7 we describe computationally efficient recursive least-squares algorithms for multi-channel signals. The last two chapters constitute the fourth major topic of the book. Chapter 8 deals with power spectrum estimation, including both parametric and nonparametric methods. In Chapter 9 we describe the use of higher-order statistical methods for signal modeling and system identification.

Although the material in this book was written by four different authors, we have tried very hard to maintain common notation throughout the book. We believe we have succeeded in developing a coherent treatment of the major topics indicated above. Chapter 1 provides an introduction to selected basic DSP material that is typically found in a first level DSP book and also serves to establish some of the notation used throughout the book.

In our treatment of the various topics, we generally assume that the reader has had a prior course on the fundamentals of digital signal processing. The fundamental topics assumed as background include the z-transform, the analysis and characterization of discrete-time systems, the Fourier transform, the discrete Fourier transform (DFT), and the design of FIR and IIR digital filters.

We believe that the topics covered in the book are sufficiently broad to provide some choice for the instructor and the students. Chapters 2 and 3 are to a large extent self-contained and independent of the other chapters. Chapters 4 through 7 constitute another self-contained unit. Finally, Chapters 8 and 9 may be considered as a self-contained unit. However, the treatment of parametric spectrum estimation methods in Chapter 8 relies heavily on the material in Chapter 4.

The authors wish to thank Prof. Eric M. Dowling, University of Texas at Dallas, and Prof. David Munson, University of Illinois at Urbana, for reviewing the manuscript; Gloria Proakis for typing the major part of the manuscript for this book; and Evangelos Zervas for proofreading.

John G. Proakis
Charles M. Rader
Fuyun Ling
Chrysostomos L. Nikias

CONTENTS

Chapter 2 ALGORITHMS FOR CONVOLUTION AND DFT 76

Chapter 3 MULTIRATE DIGITAL SIGNAL 141

CHAPTER 1

INTRODUCTION

In this chapter we review some basic topics in digital signal processing, and in the process, we establish notation that is used throughout the book. We begin with the characterization of deterministic and random signals in Section 1.1. Then in Section 1.2, we describe the characterization of linear time-invariant systems, in both the time domain and the frequency domain. Included in this treatment are definitions of basic properties of systems, such as causality, stability, minimum phase, maximum phase, mixed phase, all-pass, and bandpass. The response of linear time-invariant systems to random inputs signals is also derived.

The third major topic of this chapter is concerned with the sampling of signals in the time and frequency domains. Conditions are derived for alias-free sampling of continuous-time signals. Also treated in this section is the discrete Fourier transform (DFT) for finite-duration sequences.

Linear filtering methods based on the use of the DFT is the fourth major topic of this chapter. The final topic of this chapter is a description of the complex cepstrum of a signal. The use of the complex cepstrum in performing signal deconvolution is also treated briefly.

The foregoing topics are usually covered in a first course in digital signal processing. Consequently, its treatment is intended to serve as a brief review. Our choice of review topics was influenced by the advanced topics treated in this book. However, we should emphasize that many other important topics have been omitted. We assume that the reader is familiar with z-transforms and Fourier transforms, and their use in the analysis of linear time-invariant systems. We also assume that the reader is familiar with filter design methods and design tools and algorithms for both analog and digital filters. The introductory books by DeFatta et al. (1988), Oppenheim and Schafer (1989), Proakis and Manolakis (1992), and Roberts and Mullis (1987) provide the necessary background material for the topics treated in this book.

1.1 CHARACTERIZATION OF SIGNALS

A signal is defined as any physical quantity that varies with time, space, or any other independent variable or variables. Mathematically, we describe a signal as a function of one or more independent variables. If the signal is a function of a single independent variable, the signal is said to be *one-dimensional*. On the other hand, a signal is called *M-dimensional* (multidimensional) if it is a function of M independent variables.

In some applications signals are generated by multiple sources or multiple sensors. Such signals can be represented in vector form, where each element of the vector is a signal from a single source or a single sensor. The signal vector is called a *multichannel signal.*

In this book we deal mainly with one-dimensional, either single-channel or multichannel signals for which the independent variable is time. When the independent variable is continuous, the signal is called a *continuous-time signal* or an *analog signal*. On the other hand, when the independent variable is discrete, the signal is called a *discrete-time signal.*

1.1.1 Deterministic Signals

Let us consider a deterministic continuous-time signal $x(t)$ that may be real- or complex-valued. We assume that the signal has finite energy, defined as

$$\mathscr{E} = \int_{-\infty}^{\infty} |x(t)|^2 \, dt \tag{1.1.1}$$

Such a signal is represented in the frequency domain by its Fourier transform

$$X(F) = \int_{-\infty}^{\infty} x(t)e^{-j2\pi Ft} \, dt \tag{1.1.2}$$

where F is the frequency in cycles per second or hertz (Hz). From Parseval's theorem we have

$$\mathscr{E} = \int_{-\infty}^{\infty} |x(t)|^2 \, dt = \int_{-\infty}^{\infty} |X(F)|^2 \, dF \tag{1.1.3}$$

The quantity $|X(F)|^2$ represents the distribution of signal energy as a function of frequency, and hence it is called the *energy density spectrum.* It is denoted as

$$S_{xx}(F) = |X(F)|^2 \tag{1.1.4}$$

$S_{xx}(F)$ may also be viewed as the Fourier transform of another function, $r_{xx}(\tau)$, called the *autocorrelation function* of the finite-energy signal $x(t)$, which is defined as

$$r_{xx}(\tau) = \int_{-\infty}^{\infty} x^*(t)x(t + \tau)\, dt \tag{1.1.5}$$

Indeed, it easily follows that

$$S_{xx}(F) = \int_{-\infty}^{\infty} r_{xx}(\tau)e^{-j2\pi F\tau}\, d\tau \tag{1.1.6}$$

so that $S_{xx}(F)$ and $r_{xx}(\tau)$ are a Fourier transform pair.

Similar relationships hold for discrete-time signals, which often are the result of uniformly sampling continuous-time signals. To be specific, suppose that $x(n)$ is a real- or complex-valued sequence, where n takes integer values. If $x(n)$ is deterministic and has finite energy, that is,

$$\mathscr{E} = \sum_{n=-\infty}^{\infty} |x(n)|^2 \tag{1.1.7}$$

then $x(n)$ has the frequency-domain representation

$$X(\omega) = \sum_{n=-\infty}^{\infty} x(n)e^{-j\omega n} \tag{1.1.8}$$

or equivalently,

$$X(f) = \sum_{n=-\infty}^{\infty} x(n)e^{-j2\pi fn} \tag{1.1.9}$$

where $\omega = 2\pi f$. The units for the frequency variables ω and f are radians and cycles, respectively [or radians per sample interval and cycles per sample interval if the sequence $x(n)$ is obtained by sampling a continuous-time signal $x(t)$ at a rate of $F_s = 1/T$ samples per second, where T is the sample interval; then $\omega = \Omega T = 2\pi FT$ and $f = FT$].

We note that $X(\omega)$ is periodic with period $\omega_p = 2\pi$ and $X(f)$ is periodic with period $f_p = 1$. In fact, the Fourier transform relationship in (1.1.9) may be interpreted as a Fourier series representation of the periodic function $X(f)$, where the sequence $\{x(n)\}$ constitutes the set of Fourier coefficients. Thus

$$\begin{aligned} x(n) &= \int_{-1/2}^{1/2} X(f)e^{j2\pi fn}\, df \\ &= \frac{1}{2\pi}\int_{-\pi}^{\pi} X(\omega)e^{j\omega n}\, d\omega \end{aligned} \tag{1.1.10}$$

This relationship may also be viewed as the inverse Fourier transform, which yields the sequence $x(n)$ from $X(f)$ or, equivalently, from $X(\omega)$.

By applying Parseval's theorem, the energy of the discrete-time sequence is also given as

$$\mathscr{E} = \int_{-1/2}^{1/2} |X(f)|^2\, df \tag{1.1.11}$$

The quantity $|X(f)|^2$ represents the distribution of signal energy as a function of frequency, and hence it is called the *energy density spectrum* of the discrete-time signal. It is denoted as

$$S_{xx}(f) = |X(f)|^2 \tag{1.1.12}$$

The energy density spectrum $S_{xx}(f)$ is related to the autocorrelation sequence

$$r_{xx}(m) = \sum_{n=-\infty}^{\infty} x^*(n)x(n+m) \tag{1.1.13}$$

via the Fourier transform. That is,

$$S_{xx}(f) = \sum_{m=-\infty}^{\infty} r_{xx}(m)e^{-j2\pi fm} \tag{1.1.14}$$

Two elementary deterministic signals that will be used frequently are the unit impulse and the unit step functions. In the continuous-time domain the unit impulse may be defined by the property

$$\int_{-\infty}^{\infty} \delta(t)g(t)dt = g(0) \tag{1.1.15}$$

where $g(t)$ is an arbitrary function continuous at $t = 0$. Hence, its area is

$$\int_{-\infty}^{\infty} \delta(t)\,dt = 1 \tag{1.1.16}$$

The unit step function is defined as

$$u(t) = \begin{cases} 1, & t \geq 0 \\ 0, & t < 0 \end{cases} \tag{1.1.17}$$

In discrete time, the unit sample, or unit impulse sequence, is defined as

$$\delta(n) = \begin{cases} 1, & n = 0 \\ 0, & n \neq 0 \end{cases} \tag{1.1.18}$$

The unit step sequence is denoted as $u(n)$ and defined as

$$u(n) = \begin{cases} 1, & n \geq 0 \\ 0, & n < 0 \end{cases} \tag{1.1.19}$$

A continuous-time signal $x(t)$ may be represented in general as the convolution of itself with a unit impulse,

$$x(t) = \int_{-\infty}^{\infty} x(\tau)\delta(t-\tau)\,d\tau \tag{1.1.20}$$

for all t. Similarly, a sequence $x(n)$ may be represented as

$$x(n) = \sum_{k=-\infty}^{\infty} x(k)\delta(n-k) \tag{1.1.21}$$

The expression in (1.1.21) is basically a convolution of the sequence $x(n)$ with the unit sample sequence $\delta(n)$. Equivalently, (1.1.21) may be viewed as the superposition (sum over k) of unit sample sequences $\delta(n - k)$ scaled in amplitude by the corresponding values, $x(k)$, of the sequence $x(n)$.

1.1.2 Random Signals, Correlation Functions, and Power Spectra

In this section we provide a brief review of the characterization of random signals in terms of statistical averages expressed in both the time and frequency domains. The reader is assumed to have a background in probability theory and random processes at least at the level given in the books of Helstrom (1984), Peebles (1987), Papoulis (1984), and Davenport (1970).

Random Processes. Many physical phenomena encountered in nature are best characterized in statistical terms. For example, meteorological phenomena such as air temperature and air pressure fluctuate randomly as a function of time. Thermal noise voltages generated in the resistors of electronic devices, such as a radio or television receiver, are also randomly fluctuating phenomena. These are just a few examples of random signals. Such signals are usually modeled as infinite-duration, infinite-energy signals.

Suppose that we take the set of waveforms corresponding to the air temperature in different cities around the world. For each city there is a corresponding waveform that is a function of time, as illustrated in Fig. 1.1. The set of all possible waveforms is called an *ensemble* of time functions or, equivalently, a *random process*. The waveform for the temperature in any particular city is a *single realization* or a *sample function* of the random process. Similarly, the thermal noise voltage generated in a resistor is a single realization or a sample function of the random process which consists of all noise voltage waveforms generated by the set of all resistors.

The set (ensemble) of all possible noise waveforms of a random process is denoted as $X(t,S)$, where t represents the time index and S represents the set (sample space) of all possible sample functions. A single waveform in the ensemble is denoted by $x(t,s)$. Usually, we drop the variable s (or S) for notational convenience, so that the random process is denoted as $X(t)$ and a single realization is denoted as $x(t)$.

Having defined a random process $X(t)$ as an ensemble of sample functions, let us consider the values of the process for any set of time instants $t_1 > t_2 > t_3 > \cdots > t_n$, where n is any positive integer. In general, the samples $X_{t_i} \equiv X(t_i)$, $i = 1, 2, \ldots, n$, are n random variables characterized statistically by their joint probability density function (pdf) denoted as $p(x_{t_1}, x_{t_2}, \ldots, x_{t_n})$ and any n.

Stationary Random Processes. Suppose that we have n samples of the random process $X(t)$ at $t = t_i$, $i = 1, 2, \ldots, n$, and another set of n samples

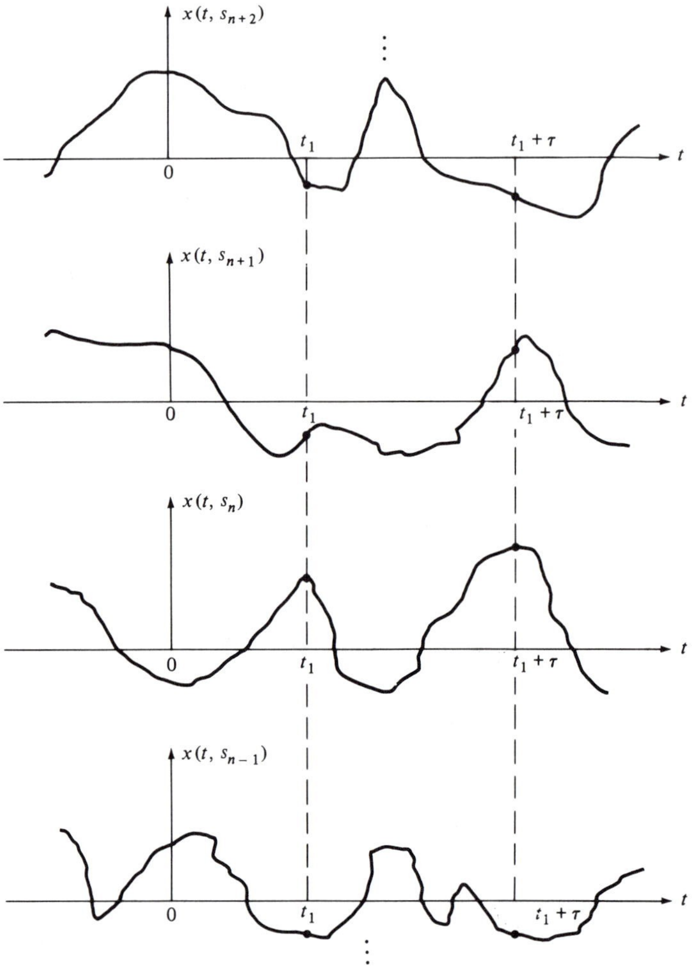

FIGURE 1.1 Sample functions of a random process.

displaced in time from the first set by an amount τ. Thus the second set of samples are $X_{t_i+\tau} \equiv X(t_i + \tau)$, $i = 1, 2, \ldots, n$, as shown in Fig. 1.1. This second set of n random variables is characterized by the joint probability density function $p(x_{t_i+\tau}, \ldots, x_{t_n+\tau})$. The joint pdf's of the two sets of random variables may or may not be identical. When they are identical, that is, when

$$p(x_{t_1}, x_{t_2}, \ldots, x_{t_n}) = p(x_{t_1+\tau}, x_{t_2+\tau}, \ldots, x_{t_n+\tau}) \tag{1.1.22}$$

for all τ and all n, the random process is said to be *stationary in the strict sense*. In other words, the statistical properties of a stationary random process are invariant to a translation of the time axis. On the other hand, when the joint pdf's are different, the random process is nonstationary.

Statistical (Ensemble) Averages. Let us consider a random process $X(t)$ sampled at time instant $t = t_i$. Thus $X(t_i)$ is a random variable with pdf $p(x_{t_i})$. The lth *moment* of the random variable is defined as the *expected value* of $X^l(t_i)$,

$$E[X_{t_i}^l] = \int_{-\infty}^{\infty} x_{t_i}^l p(x_{t_i})\, dx_{t_i} \tag{1.1.23}$$

In general, the value of the lth moment will depend on the time instant t_i if the pdf of X_{t_i} depends on t_i. When the process is stationary, however, $P(x_{t_i+\tau}) = p(x_{t_i})$ for all τ. Hence the pdf is independent of time and, consequently, the lth moment is independent of time (a constant).

Next let us consider the two random variables $X_{t_i} = X(t_i)$, $i = 1, 2$, corresponding to samples of $X(t)$ taken at $t = t_1$ and $t = t_2$. The statistical (ensemble) correlation between X_{t_1} and X_{t_2} is measured by the joint moment

$$E[X_{t_1}X_{t_2}] = \int_{-\infty}^{\infty}\int_{-\infty}^{\infty} x_{t_1}x_{t_2}\, p(x_{t_1},x_{t_2})\, dx_{t_1}\, dx_{t_2} \tag{1.1.24}$$

Since the joint moment depends on the time instants t_1 and t_2, it is denoted as $\gamma_{xx}(t_1,t_2)$ and is called the *autocorrelation function* of the random process. When the process $X(t)$ is stationary, the joint pdf of the pair (X_{t_1},X_{t_2}) is identical to the joint pdf of the pair $(X_{t_1+\tau},X_{t_2+\tau})$ for any arbitrary τ. This implies that the autocorrelation function of $X(t)$ depends on the time difference $t_1 - t_2 = \tau$. Hence for a stationary random process the autocorrelation function is

$$\gamma_{xx}(\tau) = E[X_{t_1+\tau}X_{t_1}] \tag{1.1.25}$$

On the other hand,

$$\gamma_{xx}(-\tau) = E[X_{t_1-\tau}X_{t_1}] = E[X_{t_1}X_{t_1+\tau}] = \gamma_{xx}(\tau) \tag{1.1.26}$$

Therefore, $\gamma_{xx}(\tau)$ is an even function. We also note that $\gamma_{xx}(0) = E[X_{t_1}^2]$ is the *average power* of the random process.

There exist nonstationary processes with the property that the mean value of the process is a constant and the autocorrelation function satisfies the property $\gamma_{xx}(t_1,t_2) = \gamma_{xx}(t_1 - t_2)$. Such a process is called *wide-sense stationary*. Clearly, wide-sense stationarity is a less stringent condition than strict-sense stationarity. In our treatment we shall only require that the processes be wide-sense stationary.

Related to the autocorrelation function is the *autocovariance function*, which is defined as

$$\begin{aligned} c_{xx}(t_1,t_2) &= E\{[X_{t_1} - m(t_1)][X_{t_2} - m(t_2)]\} \\ &= \gamma_{xx}(t_1,t_2) - m(t_1)m(t_2). \end{aligned} \tag{1.1.27}$$

where $m(t_1) = E[X_{t_1}]$ and $m(t_2) = E[X_{t_2}]$ are the mean values of X_{t_1} and X_{t_2}, respectively. When the process is stationary,

$$c_{xx}(t_1,t_2) = c_{xx}(t_1 - t_2) = c_{xx}(\tau) = \gamma_{xx}(\tau) - m_x^2 \tag{1.1.28}$$

where $\tau = t_1 - t_2$. Furthermore, the variance of the process is $\sigma^2 = c_{xx}(0) = \gamma_{xx}(0) - m_x^2$.

Statistical Averages for Joint Random Processes. Let $X(t)$ and $Y(t)$ be two random processes and let $X_{t_i} \equiv X(t_i)$, $i = 1, 2, \ldots, n$, and $Y_{t_j}' \equiv Y(t_j')$, $j = 1, 2, \ldots, m$, represent the random variables at times $t_1 > t_2 > \cdots > t_n$ and $t_1' > t_2' > \cdots > t_m'$, respectively. The two sets of random variables are characterized statistically by the joint pdf

$$p(x_{t_1}, x_{t_2}, \ldots, x_{t_n}, y_{t'_1}, y_{t'_2}, \ldots, y_{t'_m})$$

for any set of time instants t_i and t_j' and for any positive integer values of m and n.

The *cross-correlation function* of $X(t)$ and $Y(t)$, denoted as $\gamma_{xy}(t_1,t_2)$, is defined by the joint moment

$$\gamma_{xy}(t_1,t_2) \equiv E[X_{t_1} Y_{t_2}] = \int_{-\infty}^{\infty}\int_{-\infty}^{\infty} x_{t_1} y_{t_2} p(x_{t_1}, y_{t_2})\, dx_{t_1}\, dy_{t_2} \tag{1.1.29}$$

and the cross-covariance is

$$c_{xy}(t_1,t_2) = \gamma_{xy}(t_1,t_2) - m_x(t_1)m_y(t_2) \tag{1.1.30}$$

When the random processes are jointly and individually stationary we have $\gamma_{xy}(t_1,t_2) = \gamma_{xy}(t_1 - t_2)$ and $c_{xy}(t_1,t_2) = c_{xy}(t_1 - t_2)$. In this case

$$\gamma_{xy}(-\tau) = E[X_{t_1} Y_{t_1+\tau}] = E[X_{t_1-\tau} Y_{t_1}] = \gamma_{yx}(\tau) \tag{1.1.31}$$

The random processes $X(t)$ and $Y(t)$ are said to be *statistically independent* if and only if

$$p(x_{t_1}, x_{t_2}, \ldots, x_{t_n}, y_{t'_1}, y_{t'_2}, \ldots, y_{t'_m}) = p(x_{t_1}, \ldots, x_{t_n}) p(y_{t'_1}, \ldots, y_{t'_m})$$

for all choices of t_i, t_j' and for all positive integers n and m. The processes are said to be *uncorrelated* if

$$\gamma_{xy}(t_1,t_2) = E[X_{t_1}]E[Y_{t_2}] \tag{1.1.32}$$

so that $c_{xy}(t_1,t_2) = 0$.

A complex-valued random process $Z(t)$ is defined as

$$Z(t) = X(t) + jY(t) \tag{1.1.33}$$

where $X(t)$ and $Y(t)$ are random processes. The joint pdf of the complex-valued random variables $Z_{t_i} \equiv Z(t_i)$, $i = 1, 2, \ldots, n$ is given by the joint pdf of the components (X_{t_i}, Y_{t_i}), $i = 1, 2, \ldots, n$. Thus the pdf that characterizes, Z_{t_i}, $i = 1, 2, \ldots, n$, is

$$p(x_{t_1}, x_{t_2}, \ldots, x_{t_n}, y_{t_1}, y_{t_2}, \ldots, y_{t_n})$$

A complex-valued random process $Z(t)$ is encountered in the representation of the in-phase and quadrature components of the lowpass equivalent of a narrowband random signal or noise. An important characteristic of such a process is its autocorrelation function, which is defined as

$$\begin{aligned}\gamma_{zz}(t_1,t_2) &= E[Z_{t_1}Z_{t_2}^*] \\ &= E[(X_{t_1} + jY_{t_1})(X_{t_2} - jY_{t_2})] \\ &= \gamma_{xx}(t_1,t_2) + \gamma_{yy}(t_1,t_2) + j[\gamma_{yx}(t_1,t_2) - \gamma_{xy}(t_1,t_2)]\end{aligned} \tag{1.1.34}$$

When the random processes $X(t)$ and $Y(t)$ are jointly and individually stationary, the autocorrelation function of $Z(t)$ becomes

$$\gamma_{zz}(t_1, t_2) = \gamma_{zz}(t_1 - t_2) = \gamma_{zz}(\tau)$$

where $\tau = t_1 - t_2$. The complex conjugate of $\gamma_{zz}(\tau)$ is

$$\gamma_{zz}^*(\tau) = E[Z_{t_1}^* Z_{t_2}] = E[Z_{t_1}^* Z_{t_1-\tau}] = \gamma_{zz}(-\tau) \tag{1.1.35}$$

Now suppose that $Z(t) = X(t) + jY(t)$ and $W(t) = U(t) + jV(t)$ are two complex-valued random processes. Their cross-correlation function is defined as

$$\begin{aligned}\gamma_{zw}(t_1,t_2) &= E[Z_{t_1}W_{t_2}^*] \\ &= E[(X_{t_1} + jY_{t_1})(U_{t_2} - jV_{t_2})] \\ &= \gamma_{xu}(t_1,t_2) + \gamma_{yv}(t_1,t_2) + j[\gamma_{yu}(t_1,t_2) - \gamma_{xv}(t_1,t_2)]\end{aligned} \tag{1.1.36}$$

When $X(t)$, $Y(t)$, $U(t)$, and $V(t)$ are pairwise stationary, the cross-correlation functions in (1.1.36) become functions of the time difference $\tau = t_1 - t_2$. In addition, we have

$$\gamma_{zw}^*(\tau) = E[Z_{t_1}^* W_{t_1-\tau}] = E[Z_{t_1+\tau}^* W_{t_1}] = \gamma_{wz}(-\tau) \tag{1.1.37}$$

Power Density Spectrum. A stationary random process is an infinite energy signal and hence its Fourier transform does not exist. The spectral characteristic of a random process is obtained according to the Wiener–Khinchine theorem by computing the Fourier transform of the autocorrelation function. That is, the distribution of power with frequency is given by the function

$$\Gamma_{xx}(F) = \int_{-\infty}^{\infty} \gamma_{xx}(\tau)e^{-j2\pi F\tau}\, d\tau \tag{1.1.38}$$

The inverse Fourier transform is given as

$$\gamma_{xx}(\tau) = \int_{-\infty}^{\infty} \Gamma_{xx}(F)e^{j2\pi F\tau}\, dF \tag{1.1.39}$$

We observe that

$$\begin{aligned}\gamma_{xx}(0) &= \int_{-\infty}^{\infty} \Gamma_{xx}(F)\, dF \\ &= E[X_t^2] \geq 0\end{aligned} \tag{1.1.40}$$

Since $E(X_t^2) = \gamma_{xx}(0)$ represents the average power of the random process, which is the area under $\Gamma_{xx}(F)$, it follows that $\Gamma_{xx}(F)$ is the distribution of power as a function of frequency. For this reason, $\Gamma_{xx}(F)$ is called the *power density spectrum* of the random process.

If the random process is real, $\gamma_{xx}(\tau)$ is real and even and hence $\Gamma_{xx}(F)$ is real and even. If the random process is complex valued, $\gamma_{xx}(\tau) = \gamma_{xx}^*(-\tau)$ and hence

$$\Gamma_{xx}^*(F) = \int_{-\infty}^{\infty} \gamma_{xx}^*(\tau)e^{j2\pi F\tau}\, d\tau = \int_{-\infty}^{\infty} \gamma_{xx}^*(-\tau)e^{-j2\pi F\tau}\, d\tau$$
$$= \int_{-\infty}^{\infty} \gamma_{xx}(\tau)e^{-j2\pi F\tau}\, d\tau = \Gamma_{xx}(F)$$

Therefore, $\Gamma_{xx}(F)$ is always real.

The definition of the power density spectrum can be extended to two jointly stationary random processes $X(t)$ and $Y(t)$, which have a cross-correlation function $\gamma_{xy}(\tau)$. The Fourier transform of $\gamma_{xy}(\tau)$ is

$$\Gamma_{xy}(F) = \int_{-\infty}^{\infty} \gamma_{xy}(\tau)e^{-j2\pi F\tau}\, d\tau \tag{1.1.41}$$

which is called the *cross-power density spectrum*. It is easily shown that $\Gamma_{xy}^*(F) = \Gamma_{yx}(-F)$. For real random processes, the condition is $\Gamma_{yx}(F) = \Gamma_{xy}(-F)$.

Discrete-Time Random Signals. The characterization of continuous-time random signals given above can easily be carried over to discrete-time signals. Such signals are usually obtained by uniformly sampling a continuous-time random process. A discrete-time random process $X(n)$ consists of an ensemble of sample sequences $x(n)$. The statistical properties of $X(n)$ are similar to the characterization of $X(t)$, with the restrictions that n is now an integer (time) variable. To be specific, we state the form for the important moments that we will use in this book.

The lth moment of $X(n)$ is defined as

$$E[X_n^l] = \int_{-\infty}^{\infty} x_n^l p(x_n)\, dx_n \tag{1.1.42}$$

and the autocorrelation sequence is

$$\gamma_{xx}(n,k) = E[X_n X_k] = \int_{-\infty}^{\infty}\int_{-\infty}^{\infty} x_n x_k p(x_n,x_k)\, dx_n\, dx_k \tag{1.1.43}$$

Similarly, the autocovariance is

$$c_{xx}(n,k) = \gamma_{xx}(n,k) - E[X_n]E[X_k] \tag{1.1.44}$$

For a stationary process, we have the special forms

$$\begin{aligned} \gamma_{xx}(n-k) &= \gamma_{xx}(m) \\ c_{xx}(n-k) &= c_{xx}(m) = \gamma_{xx}(m) - m_x^2 \end{aligned} \tag{1.1.45}$$

where $m_x = E[X_n]$ is the mean of the random process and $m = n - k$. The variance is defined as $\sigma^2 = c_{xx}(0) = \gamma_{xx}(0) - m_x^2$.

For a complex-valued stationary process $Z(n) = X(n) + jY(n)$ we have

$$\gamma_{zz}(m) = \gamma_{xx}(m) + \gamma_{yy}(m) + j[\gamma_{yx}(m) - \gamma_{xy}(m)] \tag{1.1.46}$$

and the cross-correlation sequence of two complex-valued stationary sequences $Z(n) = X(n) + jY(n)$ and $W(n) = U(n) + jV(n)$ is

$$\gamma_{zw}(m) = \gamma_{xu}(m) + \gamma_{yv}(m) + j[\gamma_{yu}(m) - \gamma_{xv}(m)] \tag{1.1.47}$$

As in the case of a continuous-time random process, a discrete-time random process has infinite energy but a finite average power, which is given as

$$E[X_n^2] = \gamma_{xx}(0) \tag{1.1.48}$$

By use of the Wiener–Khinchine theorem, we obtain the spectral characteristic of the discrete-time random process by computing the Fourier transform of the autocorrelation sequence $\gamma_{xx}(m)$,

$$\Gamma_{xx}(f) = \sum_{m=-\infty}^{\infty} \gamma_{xx}(m)e^{-j2\pi fm} \tag{1.1.49}$$

The inverse transform relationship is

$$\gamma_{xx}(m) = \int_{-1/2}^{1/2} \Gamma_{xx}(f)e^{j2\pi fm}\, df \tag{1.1.50}$$

We observe that the average power is

$$\gamma_{xx}(0) = \int_{-1/2}^{1/2} \Gamma_{xx}(f)\, df \tag{1.1.51}$$

so that $\Gamma_{xx}(f)$ is the distribution of power as a function of frequency [i.e., $\Gamma_{xx}(f)$ is the power density spectrum of the random process $X(n)$]. The properties we have stated for $\Gamma_{xx}(F)$ also hold for $\Gamma_{xx}(f)$.

Time Averages for a Discrete-Time Random Process. Although we have characterized a random process in terms of statistical averages, such as the mean and the autocorrelation sequence, in practice we usually have available a single realization of the random process. Let us consider the problem of obtaining the averages of the random process from a single realization. To accomplish this, the random process must be *ergodic*.

By definition, a random process $X(n)$ is ergodic if, with probability 1, all the statistical averages can be determined from a single sample function of the process. In effect, the random process is ergodic if time averages obtained from a single realization are equal to the statistical (ensemble) averages. Under this condition, we can attempt to estimate the ensemble averages by use of time averages from a single realization.

To illustrate this point, let us consider the estimation of the mean and the autocorrelation of the random process from a single realization $x(n)$. Since we are interested in only these two moments, we will define ergodicity with respect to these parameters. For additional details on the requirements for mean ergodicity and autocorrelation ergodicity which are given below, the reader is referred to the book by Papoulis (1984).

Mean-Ergodic Process. Given a stationary random process $X(n)$ with mean

$$m_x = E[X_n]$$

let us form the *time average*

$$\hat{m}_x = \frac{1}{2N+1} \sum_{n=-N}^{N} x(n) \tag{1.1.52}$$

In general, we view $\hat{m}_x$ in (1.1.52) as an estimate of the statistical mean whose value will vary with the different realizations of the random process. Hence $\hat{m}_x$ is a random variable with a pdf $p(\hat{m}_x)$. Let us compute the expected value of $\hat{m}_x$ over all possible realizations of $X(n)$. Since the summation and the expectation are linear operations we may interchange them, so that

$$E[\hat{m}_x] = \frac{1}{2N+1} \sum_{n=-N}^{N} E[x(n)] = \frac{1}{2N+1} \sum_{n=-N}^{N} m_x = m_x \tag{1.1.53}$$

Since the mean value of the estimate is equal to the statistical mean, we say that the estimate $\hat{m}_x$ is *unbiased*.

Next we compute the variance of m_x. We have

$$\operatorname{var}(\hat{m}_x) = E[|\hat{m}_x|^2] - |m_x|^2$$

But

$$\begin{aligned} E[|\hat{m}_x|^2] &= \frac{1}{(2N+1)^2} \sum_{n=-N}^{N} \sum_{k=-N}^{N} E[x^*(n)x(k)] \\ &= \frac{1}{(2N+1)^2} \sum_{n=-N}^{N} \sum_{k=-N}^{N} \gamma_{xx}(k-n) \\ &= \frac{1}{2N+1} \sum_{m=-2N}^{2N} \left(1 - \frac{|m|}{2N+1}\right) \gamma_{xx}(m) \end{aligned}$$

Therefore,

$$\begin{aligned} \operatorname{var}(\hat{m}_x) &= \frac{1}{2N+1} \sum_{m=-2N}^{2N} \left(1 - \frac{|m|}{2N+1}\right) \gamma_{xx}(m) - |m_x|^2 \\ &= \frac{1}{2N+1} \sum_{m=-2N}^{2N} \left(1 - \frac{|m|}{2N+1}\right) c_{xx}(m) \end{aligned} \tag{1.1.54}$$

If var $(\hat{m}_x) \to 0$ as $N \to \infty$, the estimate converges with probability 1 to the statistical mean m_x. Therefore, the process $x(n)$ is mean ergodic if

$$\lim_{N\to\infty} \frac{1}{2N+1} \sum_{m=-2N}^{2N} \left(1 - \frac{|m|}{2N+1}\right) c_{xx}(m) = 0 \tag{1.1.55}$$

Under this condition, the estimate $\hat{m}_x$ in the limit as $N \to \infty$ becomes equal to the statistical mean,

$$m_x = \lim_{N\to\infty} \frac{1}{2N+1} \sum_{n=-N}^{N} x(n) \tag{1.1.56}$$

Thus the time-averaged mean, in the limit as $N \to \infty$, is equal to the ensemble mean.

A sufficient condition for (1.1.55) to hold is if

$$\sum_{m=-\infty}^{\infty} |c_{xx}(m)| < \infty \tag{1.1.57}$$

which implies that $c_{xx}(m) \to 0$ as $m \to \infty$. This condition holds for most zero-mean processes encountered in the physical world.

Correlation-Ergodic Process. Now let us consider the estimate of the autocorrelation $\gamma_{xx}(m)$ from a single realization of the process. Following our previous notation, we denote the estimate (for a complex-valued signal, in general) as

$$r_{xx}(m) = \frac{1}{2N+1} \sum_{n=-N}^{N} x^*(n)x(n+m) \tag{1.1.58}$$

Again, we regard $r_{xx}(m)$ as a random variable for any given lag m, since it is a function of the particular realization. The expected value (mean value over all realizations) is

$$\begin{aligned} E[r_{xx}(m)] &= \frac{1}{2N+1} \sum_{n=-N}^{N} E[x^*(n)x(n+m)] \\ &= \frac{1}{2N+1} \sum_{n=-N}^{N} \gamma_{xx}(m) = \gamma_{xx}(m) \end{aligned} \tag{1.1.59}$$

Therefore, the expected value of time-averaged autocorrelation is equal to the statistical average. Hence we have an unbiased estimate of $\gamma_{xx}(m)$.

To determine the variance of the estimate $r_{xx}(m)$, we compute the expected value of $|r_{xx}(m)|^2$ and subtract the square of the mean value. Thus

$$\text{var}[r_{xx}(m)] = E[|r_{xx}(m)|^2] - |\gamma_{xx}(m)|^2 \tag{1.1.60}$$

But

$$E[|r_{xx}(m)|^2] = \frac{1}{(2N+1)^2} \sum_{n=-N}^{N} \sum_{k=-N}^{N} E[x^*(n)x(n+m)x(k)x^*(k+m)] \tag{1.1.61}$$

The expected value of the term $x^*(n)x(n + m)x(k)x^*(k + m)$ is just the autocorrelation sequence of a random process defined as

$$v_m(n) = x^*(n)x(n + m)$$

Hence (1.1.61) may be expressed as

$$\begin{aligned} E[|r_{xx}(m)|^2] &= \frac{1}{(2N+1)^2} \sum_{n=-N}^{N} \sum_{k=-N}^{N} \gamma_{vv}^{(m)}(n-k) \\ &= \frac{1}{2N+1} \sum_{n=-2N}^{2N} \left(1 - \frac{|n|}{2N+1}\right) \gamma_{vv}^{(m)}(n) \end{aligned} \tag{1.1.62}$$

and the variance is

$$\operatorname{var}[r_{xx}(m)] = \frac{1}{2N+1} \sum_{n=-2N}^{2N} \left(1 - \frac{|n|}{2N+1}\right) \gamma_{vv}^{(m)}(n) - |\gamma_{xx}(m)|^2 \tag{1.1.63}$$

If $\operatorname{var}[r_{xx}(m)] \to 0$ as $N \to \infty$, the estimate $r_{xx}(m)$ converges with probability 1 to the statistical autocorrelation $\gamma_{xx}(m)$. Under these conditions, the process is *correlation ergodic* and the time-averaged correlation is identical to the statistical average,

$$\lim_{N\to\infty} \frac{1}{2N+1} \sum_{n=-N}^{N} x^*(n)x(n + m) = \gamma_{xx}(m) \tag{1.1.64}$$

In our treatment of random signals we assume that the random processes are mean ergodic and correlation ergordic, so that we can deal with time averages of the mean and autocorrelation obtained from a single realization of the process.

1.2 CHARACTERIZATION OF LINEAR TIME-INVARIANT SYSTEMS

In this section we review briefly the characteristics of linear time-invariant systems in both the time and frequency domains.

1.2.1 Time-Domain Characterization

The input–output relationship of any system is denoted as

$$y(t) = H[x(t)] \tag{1.2.1}$$

where $x(t)$ is the input to the system, $y(t)$ the output of the system, and $H[\cdot]$ denotes the transformation performed by the system. A system is *linear* if and only if

$$H[a_1x_1(t) + a_2x_2(t)] = a_1H[x_1(t)] + a_2H[x_2(t)] \tag{1.2.2}$$

where a_1 and a_2 are arbitrary constants. A system is *time invariant* if and only if

$$y(t) = H[x(t)]$$

implies that

$$y(t - t_0) = H[x(t - t_0)] \tag{1.2.3}$$

where t_0 is any real number.

Now suppose that a linear time-invariant (LTI) system H, when excited by an impulse $\delta(t)$, produces the output $y(t) \equiv h(t)$, where $h(t)$ is called the *impulse response* of the system. Since an arbitrary finite-energy signal $x(t)$ can be represented as a superposition of impulses as given by (1.1.20), it follows that the response of the system $x(t)$ may be expressed as

$$y(t) = \int_{-\infty}^{\infty} x(\tau)h(t - \tau)\, d\tau \tag{1.2.4}$$

This is the convolution integral, which relates the output of the system to the input $x(t)$ and the impulse response $h(t)$.

For a subclass of LTI systems, there is an equivalent alternative relationship between the input and the output of the system, which is given by the linear differential equation with constant coefficients

$$\sum_{k=0}^{N} a_k \frac{d^k y(t)}{dt^k} = \sum_{k=0}^{M} b_k \frac{d^k x(t)}{dt^k}, \qquad a_0 = 1 \tag{1.2.5}$$

where the a_k and b_k are the coefficients that characterize the system. The relationship between these system parameters and the impulse response may easily be established by use of the Laplace transform. Specifically, the Laplace transform relationship obtained from the convolution integral in (1.2.4) is

$$\frac{Y(s)}{X(s)} = H(s) \tag{1.2.6}$$

where $Y(s)$, $X(s)$, and the $H(s)$ are the two-sided Laplace transforms of $y(t)$, $x(t)$, and $h(t)$, respectively,

$$H(s) = \int_{-\infty}^{\infty} h(t)e^{-st}\, dt \tag{1.2.7}$$

Similarly, the Laplace transform of the differential equation in (1.2.5) yields

$$\frac{Y(s)}{X(s)} = \frac{\sum_{k=0}^{M} b_k s^k}{\sum_{k=0}^{N} a_k s^k} \tag{1.2.8}$$

From (1.2.6) and (1.2.8) it follows that

$$H(s) = \frac{\sum_{k=0}^{M} b_k s^k}{\sum_{k=0}^{N} a_k s^k} \tag{1.2.9}$$

Hence $H(s)$, which is called the *system function* of the LTI system, is a rational function when the input $x(t)$ and the output $y(t)$ are related through the differential equation given in (1.2.5). The roots of the numerator polynomial depend on the coefficients b_k and are called the *zeros* of the system. The roots of the denominator polynomial depend on the coefficients a_k and are called the *poles* of the system. The impulse response $h(t)$ is simply the inverse Laplace transform of $H(s)$.

A discrete-time system may be characterized in the time domain in a similar manner. Specifically, a discrete-time system is linear if and only if

$$H[a_1x_1(n) + a_2x_2(n)] = a_1H[x_1(n)] + a_2H[x_2(n)] \qquad (1.2.10)$$

where a_1 and a_2 are arbitrary constants. A system is time invariant (also called *shift invariant*) if and only if

$$y(n) = H[x(n)]$$

implies that

$$y(n - n_0) = H[x(n - n_0)] \qquad (1.2.11)$$

where n_0 is any arbitrary (positive or negative) integer.

Now suppose that the response of the LTI system to the unit sample sequence $\delta(n)$ is $y(n) = H[\delta(n)] \equiv h(n)$. Then since any arbitrary sequence $x(n)$ may be represented as a linear superposition of unit sample sequences as given by (1.1.21), it follows that the response of the LTI system to the input sequence $x(n)$ may be expressed as

$$y(n) = \sum_{k=-\infty}^{\infty} x(k)h(n - k) \qquad (1.2.12)$$

This is the convolution sum that expresses the output $y(n)$ of the system as a function of the input sequence $x(n)$ and the unit sample response $h(n)$.

For a subclass of discrete-time LTI systems, the input–output relationship is expressed in terms of the difference equation

$$\sum_{k=0}^{N} a_k y(n - k) = \sum_{k=0}^{M} b_k x(n - k), \qquad a_0 = 1 \qquad (1.2.13)$$

where a_k and b_k are the coefficients that characterize the system.

For discrete-time systems, the z-transform provides the means for relating the unit sample response of the system to the coefficients a_k and b_k in the difference equation. First, the two-sided z-transform of the convolution sum given by (1.2.12) yields

$$Y(z) = X(z)H(z) \qquad (1.2.14)$$

where $Y(z)$, $X(z)$, and $H(z)$ are the z-transforms of $y(n)$, $x(n)$, and $h(n)$, respectively,

$$H(z) = \sum_{n=-\infty}^{\infty} h(n)z^{-n} \qquad (1.2.15)$$

$H(z)$ is called the *system function* for the discrete-time system. Similarly, the z-transform of the difference equation given in (1.2.13) is

$$Y(z) \sum_{k=0}^{N} a_k z^{-k} = X(z) \sum_{k=0}^{M} b_k z^{-k} \tag{1.2.16}$$

or equivalently,

$$Y(z) = X(z) \frac{\sum_{k=0}^{M} b_k z^{-k}}{\sum_{k=0}^{N} a_k z^{-k}} \tag{1.2.17}$$

By comparing (1.2.14) with (1.2.17) we observe that the system function for the LTI system characterized by the difference equation in (1.2.13) is

$$H(z) = \frac{\sum_{k=0}^{M} b_k z^{-k}}{\sum_{k=0}^{N} a_k z^{-k}} \tag{1.2.18}$$

We note that the system function given by (1.2.18) is rational. The coefficients b_k determine the values of the zeros of $H(z)$ and the coefficients a_k determine the values of the poles of $H(z)$. Clearly, the inverse z-transform of $H(z)$ yields the unit sample response of the LTI system. This relationship is given as

$$h(n) = \frac{1}{2\pi j} \oint_C H(z) z^{n-1}\, dz \tag{1.2.19}$$

where the integral is a contour integral over a closed path C that encircles the origin and lies within the region of convergence of $H(z)$.

1.2.2 Frequency-Domain Characterization

Let us consider a continuous-time LTI system with an exponential input signal of the form

$$x(t) = e^{j\Omega t} = e^{j2\pi F t}$$

where Ω is the angular frequency of the signal in radians per second and F is the frequency in hertz (Hz). From the convolution integral in (1.2.4) we determine the response of the system to this exponential signal as

$$\begin{aligned} y(t) &= \int_{-\infty}^{\infty} e^{j\Omega\tau} h(t - \tau)\, d\tau \\ &= \left[\int_{-\infty}^{\infty} h(\tau) e^{-j\Omega\tau}\, d\tau \right] e^{j\Omega t} \end{aligned} \tag{1.2.20}$$

First, we note that the output of the system is also an exponential of the same frequency as the input signal, scaled by the term in brackets, which is a complex number that depends on the characteristics of the LTI system at the frequency Ω. This term, denoted as $H(\Omega)$,

$$H(\Omega) = \int_{-\infty}^{\infty} h(t)e^{-j\Omega t}\,dt \tag{1.2.21}$$

or equivalently, as $H(F)$,

$$H(F) = \int_{-\infty}^{\infty} h(t)e^{-j2\pi Ft}\,dt \tag{1.2.22}$$

is the Fourier transform of the impulse response $h(t)$. $H(\Omega)$ or $H(F)$ is called the *frequency response* of the LTI system. Since $H(F)$ [or $H(\Omega)$] is a complex-valued function of the frequency variable, it may be expressed as

$$H(F) = H_r(F) + jH_i(F) \tag{1.2.23}$$

where $H_r(F) = \text{Re}[H(F)]$ and $H_i(F) = \text{Im}[H(F)]$. Usually, the frequency response is represented by the magnitude and phase of $H(F)$, defined as

$$\begin{aligned} |H(F)| &= \sqrt{H_r^2(F) + H_i^2(F)} \\ \Theta(F) &= \tan^{-1}\frac{H_i(F)}{H_r(F)} \end{aligned} \tag{1.2.24}$$

Similarly, a discrete-time LTI system is characterized in the frequency domain by its frequency response. It may be obtained by exciting the system with the discrete-time exponential sequence

$$x(n) = e^{j\omega n} = e^{j2\pi fn} \tag{1.2.25}$$

If we substitute this exponential sequence into the convolution sum formula given by (1.2.12), we obtain the response

$$\begin{aligned} y(n) &= \sum_{k=-\infty}^{\infty} e^{j\omega k}h(n-k) \\ &= \left[\sum_{k=-\infty}^{\infty} h(k)e^{-j\omega k}\right]e^{j\omega n} \end{aligned} \tag{1.2.26}$$

Therefore, the response $y(n)$ is an exponential sequence of the same frequency as the input sequence and scaled by the frequency response of the system, which is defined as

$$H(\omega) = \sum_{k=-\infty}^{\infty} h(k)e^{-j\omega k} \tag{1.2.27}$$

or equivalently, as

$$H(f) = \sum_{k=-\infty}^{\infty} h(k)e^{-2\pi fk} \tag{1.2.28}$$

$H(\omega)$ [or $H(f)$] is simply the Fourier transform of the unit sample response of the discrete-time system.

We observe that the frequency response $H(\omega)$ [or $H(f)$] is periodic with period $\omega_p = 2\pi$ ($f_p = 1$). In fact, the expressions for $H(\omega)$ and $H(f)$, given by (1.2.27) and (1.2.28), respectively, are in the form of a Fourier series, where the sequence $\{h(n)\}$ represents the Fourier series coefficients,

$$\begin{aligned} h(n) &= \frac{1}{2\pi}\int_{-\pi}^{\pi} H(\omega)e^{j\omega n}\, d\omega \\ &= \int_{-1/2}^{1/2} H(f)e^{j2\pi fn}\, dt \end{aligned} \tag{1.2.29}$$

Since $H(f)$ is a complex-valued function of frequency, it may be expressed as

$$H(f) = H_r(f) + jH_i(f) \tag{1.2.30}$$

where $H_r(f) = \text{Re}[H(f)]$ and $H_i(f) = \text{Im}[H(f)]$. Alternatively, we may express $H(f)$ in terms of its magnitude and phase, where

$$\begin{aligned} |H(f)| &= \sqrt{H_r^2(f) + H_i^2(f)} \\ \Theta(f) &= \tan^{-1}\frac{H_i(f)}{H_r(f)} \end{aligned} \tag{1.2.31}$$

1.2.3 Causality and Stability

A system is said to be *causal* if its output at any time instant depends only on present and past inputs. In mathematical terms, the output of a causal discrete-time system satisfies an equation of the form

$$y(n) = G[x(n), x(n - 1), \ldots] \tag{1.2.32}$$

where $G[\cdot]$ is an arbitrary function. If the system does not satisfy this condition, it is called *noncausal.*

In the case of a linear time-invariant system, the necessary and sufficient condition for causality is that the impulse response $h(n) = 0$ for $n < 0$ [$h(t) = 0$ for $t < 0$, in the case of a continuous linear time-invariant system].

Stability is another important property of a system. By definition, a system is said to be *bounded input–bounded output* (BIBO) *stable* if and only if every bounded input produces a bounded output. Hence if the input $x(n)$ is bounded, there exists a constant M_x such that $|x(n)| \le M_x < \infty$. Similarly, if the output $y(n)$ is bounded, there exists a constant M_y such that $|y(n)| \le M_y < \infty$. In the case of a linear time-invariant system, the condition $|y(n)| \le M_y < \infty$ for every $|x(n)| \le M_x < \infty$ implies that

$$\sum_{k=-\infty}^{\infty} |h(k)| < \infty \tag{1.2.33}$$

The converse is also true, so that (1.2.33) is both a necessary and sufficient condition for stability of a linear time-invariant system. The equivalent condition for a continuous linear time-invariant system is

$$\int_{-\infty}^{\infty} |h(t)|\, dt < \infty \tag{1.2.34}$$

Finally, if an LTI system has a rational system function and is stable, it follows that all the poles of the system are inside the unit circle in the z-plane (left-half s-plane for continuous-time LTI systems). The *Schur–Cohn test* provides a simple method for determining if all the poles of the system lie inside the unit circle. Suppose that the denominator polynomial is expressed in the form

$$A_m(z) = \sum_{k=0}^{m} a_m(k) z^{-k}, \qquad a_m(0) = 1$$

[Note that the coefficient $a_m(0)$ is normalized to unity.] Then we form the *reverse polynomial* of degree m as

$$\begin{aligned} B_m(z) &= \sum_{k=0}^{m} a_m(m-k) z^{-k} \\ &= z^{-m} A_m(z^{-1}) \end{aligned}$$

To determine if the polynomial $A_m(z)$ has all its roots inside the unit circle, we compute the coefficients of all lower-degree polynomials $A_n(z)$, $n = m - 1, m - 2, \ldots, 1$, according to the recursive equation

$$A_{n-1}(z) = \frac{A_n(z) - a_n(n) B_n(z)}{1 - |a_n(n)|^2}, \qquad n = m, m-1, \ldots, 1$$

Then the Schur–Cohn stability test states that $A_m(z)$ has all its roots inside the unit circle if and only if $|a_n(n)| < 1$ for $n = m, m - 1, \ldots, 1$. We shall encounter this type of recursive equation in conjunction with the treatment of lattice filters in Chapter 4.

1.2.4 Bandpass Systems and Signals

A bandpass filter or a bandpass system is a system that passes frequency components of a signal in some narrow frequency band above zero frequency. By direct analogy, we define a bandpass signal as a signal with frequency content concentrated in a narrow band of frequencies above zero frequency. Bandpass signals and systems arise frequently in practice, most notably in communications where information-bearing bandpass signals are transmitted over bandpass channels, such as satellites, telephone channels, and radio channels. In this section we describe the characteristics of bandpass signals and systems.

Representation of Bandpass Signals. An analog signal $x(t)$ with frequency content concentrated in a narrow band of frequencies around some frequency F_c is called a *bandpass signal* and is represented in general as

$$x(t) = A(t) \cos[2\pi F_c t + \phi(t)] \tag{1.2.35}$$

where $A(t)$ is called the *amplitude* or *envelope* of the signal and $\phi(t)$ is called the phase of the signal. The frequency F_c may be selected to be any frequency within the frequency band occupied by the signal. Usually, it is the frequency at the center of the frequency band and, in amplitude modulation, it is called the *carrier frequency,* as we shall observe below.

By expanding the cosine function in (1.2.35), we obtain an alternative representation of the bandpass signal, namely,

$$\begin{aligned} x(t) &= A(t) \cos \phi(t) \cos 2\pi F_c t - A(t) \sin \phi(t) \sin 2\pi F_c t \\ &= u_c(t) \cos 2\pi F_c t - u_s(t) \sin 2\pi F_c t \end{aligned} \tag{1.2.36}$$

where, by definition,

$$\begin{aligned} u_c(t) &= A(t) \cos \phi(t) \\ u_s(t) &= A(t) \sin \phi(t) \end{aligned} \tag{1.2.37}$$

Since the sinusoids $\cos 2\pi F_c t$ and $\sin 2\pi F_c t$ differ by 90° and are usually represented as two rotating phasors, as shown in Fig. 1.2, we say that they are in phase quadrature (i.e., they are perpendicular). In turn, the signal components $u_c(t)$ and $u_s(t)$ that multiply $\cos 2\pi F_c t$ and $\sin 2\pi F_c t$, respectively, are called the *in-phase* and *quadrature components* or, simply, the quadrature components of the signal $x(t)$.

Finally, a third representation for the bandpass signal $x(t)$ is obtained by defining the *complex envelope*

$$u(t) = u_c(t) + ju_s(t) \tag{1.2.38}$$

so that

$$x(t) = \text{Re}[u(t)e^{j2\pi F_c t}] \tag{1.2.39}$$

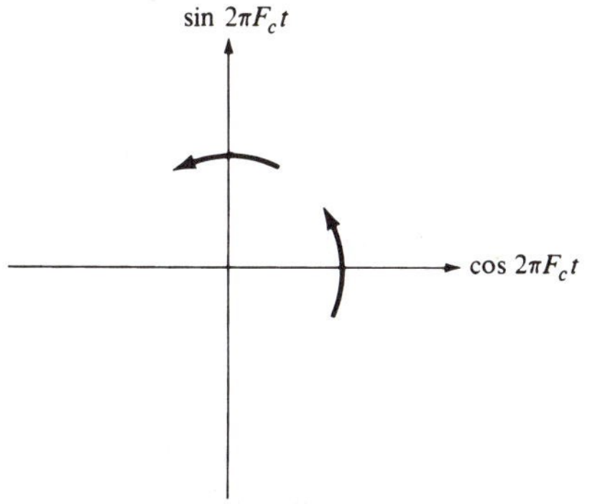

FIGURE 1.2 Sine and cosine signals in phase quadrature.

In the frequency domain, the signal $x(t)$ is represented by its Fourier transform. That is,

$$X(F) = \int_{-\infty}^{\infty} x(t)e^{-j2\pi Ft}\,dt \tag{1.2.40}$$

If we substitute from (1.2.39) into (1.2.40) for $x(t)$ and use the identity

$$\text{Re}(q) = \tfrac{1}{2}(q + q^*) \tag{1.2.41}$$

we obtain

$$\begin{aligned} X(F) &= \tfrac{1}{2}\int_{-\infty}^{\infty} [u(t)e^{j2\pi F_c t} + u^*(t)e^{-j2\pi F_c t}]e^{-j2\pi Ft}\,dt \\ &= \tfrac{1}{2}\int_{-\infty}^{\infty} u(t)e^{-j2\pi(F-F_c)t}\,dt + \tfrac{1}{2}\int_{-\infty}^{\infty} u^*(t)e^{-j2\pi(F+F_c)t}\,dt \end{aligned} \tag{1.2.42}$$

Now if $U(F)$ denotes the Fourier transform of the complex signal $u(t)$, (1.2.42) may be expressed as

$$X(F) = \tfrac{1}{2}[U(F - F_c) + U^*(-F - F_c)] \tag{1.2.43}$$

It is apparent from (1.2.43) that the spectrum of the bandpass signal $x(t)$ can be obtained from the spectrum of the complex signal $u(t)$ by a frequency translation. To be more precise, suppose that the spectrum of the signal $u(t)$ is as shown in Fig. 1.3. Then the spectrum of $X(F)$ for positive frequencies is simply $U(F)$ translated in frequency to the right by F_c and scaled in amplitude by $\frac{1}{2}$. The spectrum of $X(F)$ for negative frequencies is obtained by first folding $U(F)$ about $F = 0$ to obtain $U(-F)$, conjugating $U(-F)$ to obtain $U^*(-F)$, translating $U^*(-F)$ in frequency to the left by F_c, and scaling the result by $\frac{1}{2}$. Thus we obtain the signal spectrum shown in Fig. 1.3. The folding and conjugation of $U(F)$ for the negative-frequency component of the spectrum result in a magnitude spectrum $|X(F)|$ that is even and a phase spectrum $\measuredangle X(F)$ that is odd. These symmetry properties must hold since the signal $x(t)$ is real valued. However, they do not apply to the spectrum of the complex signal $u(t)$.

The development above implies that *any bandpass signal $x(t)$ can be represented by an equivalent lowpass signal $u(t)$*. In general, the equivalent lowpass signal $u(t)$ is complex valued, whereas the bandpass signal $x(t)$ is real. The latter can be obtained from the former through the time-domain relation in (1.2.39) or through the frequency-domain relation in (1.2.43).

Representation of Bandpass Systems. The representation of a bandpass signal in terms of an equivalent lowpass signal conveniently carries over to analog bandpass filters. To be specific, suppose that we have a bandpass filter with a frequency-response characteristic $H(F)$, as illustrated in Fig. 1.4. Clearly, we can define an equivalent lowpass filter with frequency

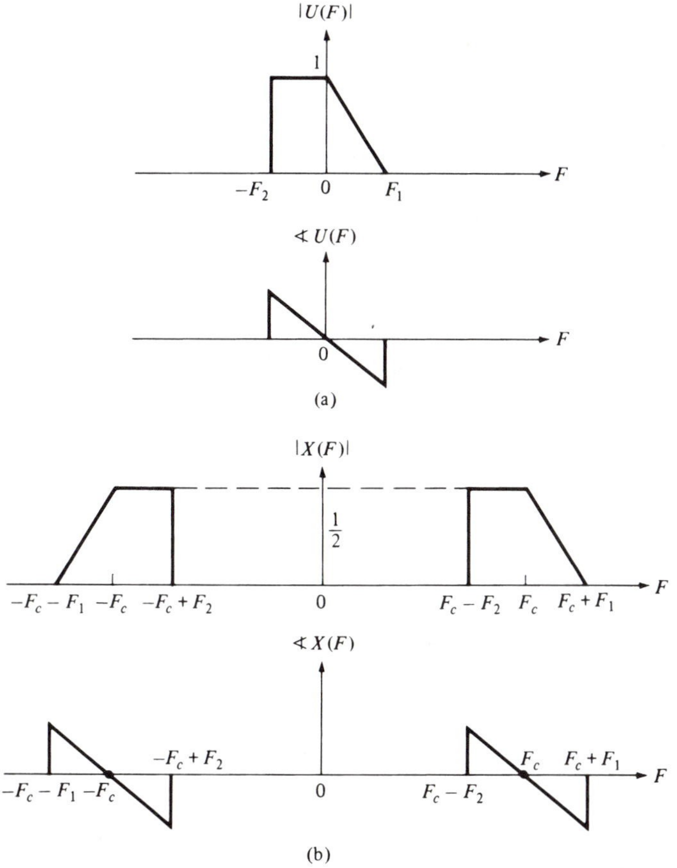

FIGURE 1.3 (a) Spectrum of the lowpass signal and (b) the corresponding spectrum for the bandpass signal.

response $C(F)$, as illustrated in Fig. 1.4b, such that $H(F)$ is related to $C(F)$ through a frequency translation. Specifically,

$$H(F) = C(F - F_c) + C^*(-F - F_c) \tag{1.2.44}$$

This expression resembles (1.2.43) except for the scale factor of $\frac{1}{2}$ that appears in (1.2.43). We deliberately defined $C(F)$ without this scale factor for a reason that will become apparent below.

Now the inverse transform of $H(F)$ yields the impulse response $h(t)$ of the bandpass filter. If $c(t)$ denotes the inverse Fourier transform of $C(F)$, then

$$c(t)e^{j2\pi F_c t} \xleftrightarrow{F} C(F - F_c)$$

and

$$c^*(t)e^{-j2\pi F_c t} \xleftrightarrow{F} C^*(-F - F_c)$$

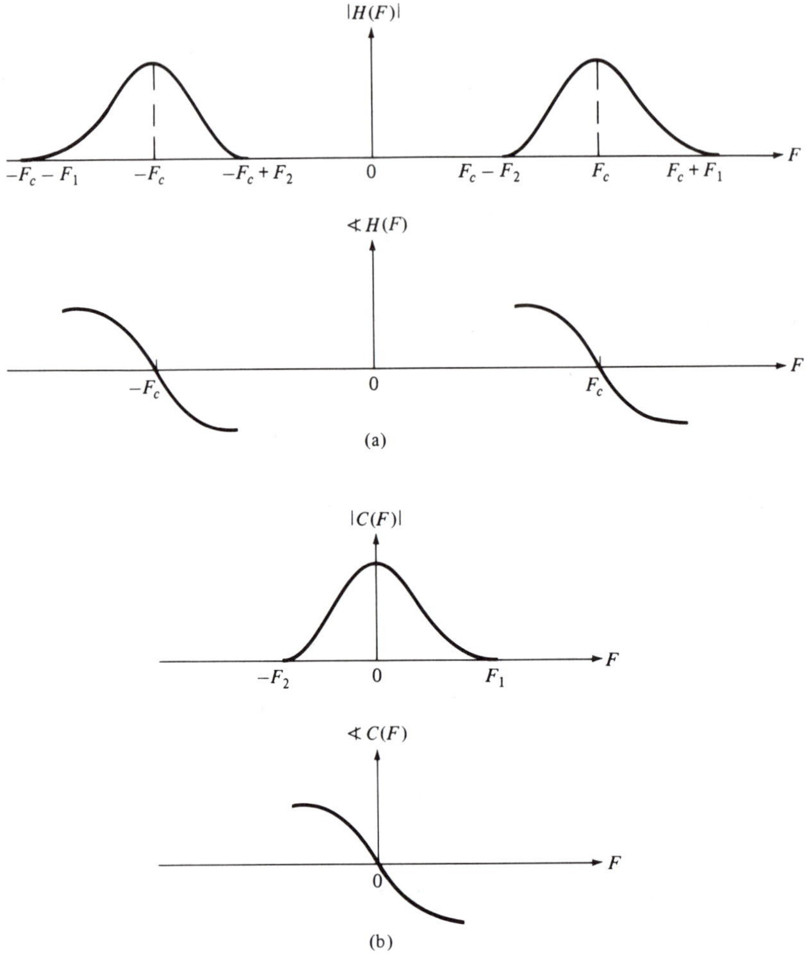

FIGURE 1.4 (a) Bandpass filter and (b) its equivalent lowpass filter.

Consequently, the time-domain relation corresponding to (1.2.44) has the form

$$\begin{aligned} h(t) &= c(t)e^{j2\pi F_c t} + c^*(t)e^{-j2\pi F_c t} \\ &= 2\,\mathrm{Re}[c(t)e^{j2\pi F_c t}] \end{aligned} \tag{1.2.45}$$

Thus the bandpass filter with impulse response $h(t)$ may be represented by an equivalent lowpass filter with impulse response $c(t)$, or $2c(t)$ if we wish to include the scale factor.

Response of a Bandpass System to a Bandpass Signal. Let us consider the response of a bandpass system with frequency response $H(F)$ to a bandpass input signal $x(t)$ having the spectrum $X(F)$. In terms of frequency-domain quantities, the spectrum of the filter output $Y(F)$ is simply the product of $H(F)$ with $X(F)$,

$$Y(F) = H(F)X(F) \tag{1.2.46}$$

Now if we use (1.2.43) and (1.2.44) to substitute for $X(F)$ and $H(F)$ in (1.2.46), we obtain

$$\begin{aligned} Y(F) &= [C(F - F_c) + C^*(-F - F_c)][\tfrac{1}{2} U(F - F_c) + \tfrac{1}{2} U^*(-F - F_c)] \\ &= \tfrac{1}{2} [C(F - F_c)U(F - F_c) + C^*(-F - F_c)U^*(-F - F_c)] \end{aligned} \tag{1.2.47}$$

where the cross terms $C(F - F_c)U^*(-F - F_c)$ and $C^*(-F - F_c)U(F - F_c)$ vanish because the spectra do not overlap. By defining an equivalent lowpass spectrum $V(F)$ as

$$V(F) = C(F)U(F) \tag{1.2.48}$$

it follows that $Y(F)$ can be expressed as

$$Y(F) = \tfrac{1}{2} [V(F - F_c) + V^*(-F - F_c)] \tag{1.2.49}$$

which is the desired result. In turn, the inverse Fourier transform of $V(F)$ is simply the convolution of the equivalent lowpass input signal $u(t)$ with the equivalent lowpass impulse response $c(t)$,

$$v(t) = \int_{-\infty}^{\infty} c(\tau)u(t - \tau)\, d\tau \tag{1.2.50}$$

where $v(t)$ is related to the real bandpass signal input $y(t)$ according to the formula

$$y(t) = \text{Re}[v(t)e^{j2\pi F_c t}] \tag{1.2.51}$$

We note that the spectrum of the output signal given in (1.2.49) resembles the form of the spectrum in the input signal given by (1.2.43). Both expressions have the scale factor $\frac{1}{2}$, which is made possible as a result of our definition in (1.2.44). The results above indicate that it is possible to model bandpass signals and systems by their equivalent lowpass counterparts. Analysis and synthesis of such signals can be performed entirely at low frequencies and the desired bandpass signals and systems can be obtained easily from their equivalent lowpass counterparts by a simple frequency translation. Figure 1.5 summarizes these relationships.

1.2.5 Inverse Systems, Minimum-Phase Systems, and All-Pass Systems

A system is said to be invertible if there is a one-to-one correspondence between its input and output signals. This definition implies that if we know the output sequence $y(n)$, for all n, of an invertible system, we can uniquely

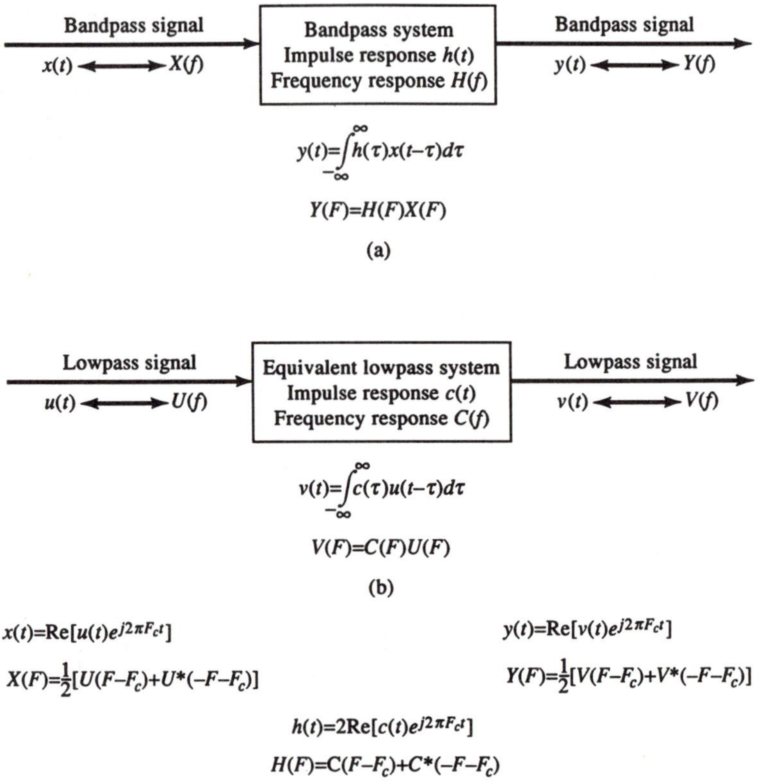

FIGURE 1.5 Equivalent lowpass representation of bandpass signals and systems.

determine its input $x(n)$ for all n. Clearly, the cascade connection of a system and its inverse are equivalent to the identity system.

Now let us consider a linear time-invariant system with system function $H(z)$ and impulse response $h(n)$. Let $H_I(z)$ and $h_I(n)$ denote the system function and the impulse response, respectively, of the inverse system. Then $H_I(z)$ and $h_I(n)$ must satisfy the respective conditions

$$H(z)H_I(z) = 1 \tag{1.2.52}$$

$$h(n) * h_I(n) = \delta(n) \tag{1.2.53}$$

If $H(z)$ is rational,

$$H(z) = \frac{B(z)}{A(z)} \tag{1.2.54}$$

then

$$H_I(z) = \frac{A(z)}{B(z)} \tag{1.2.55}$$

Thus the zeros of $H(z)$ become the poles of the inverse system, and vice versa.

The invertibility of a linear time-invariant system is intimately related to the characteristics of the phase spectral function of the system. To illustrate this point, let us consider an all-zero system with system function

$$H(z) = b_0(1 - z_1 z^{-1})(1 - z_2 z^{-1}) \cdots (1 - z_M z^{-1}) \tag{1.2.56}$$

where all $|z_i| < 1$ and $b_0 > 0$. If we compute the phase angle $\theta_k(\omega) = \measuredangle (1 - z_k e^{-j\omega})$ of the kth factor in $H(z)$, we find that $\theta_k(0) = 0$ and $\theta_k(\pi) = 0$, when z_k is real and $|z_k| < 1$. Furthermore, the net phase change in $\theta_k(\omega)$ as ω varies from $\omega = 0$ to $\omega = \pi$ is zero. Consequently, $\measuredangle H(\pi) = \measuredangle H(0) = 0$ and the net phase change between $\omega = 0$ and $\omega = \pi$ is

$$\measuredangle H(\pi) - \measuredangle H(0) = 0 \tag{1.2.57}$$

On the other hand, consider the all-zero system

$$H_a(z) \equiv H(z^{-1}) = b_0(1 - z_1 z)(1 - z_2 z) \cdots (1 - z_M z) \tag{1.2.58}$$

which has all its zeros (assumed to be real) outside the unit circle. In this case each factor in $H(z)$ contributes a net phase change of π radians between $\omega = 0$ and $\omega = \pi$. Hence

$$\measuredangle H_a(\pi) - \measuredangle H_a(0) = M\pi \tag{1.2.59}$$

Now if we take any other M-zero system with system function $H_b(z)$ of the form given in (1.2.56), where M_1 of the zeros are outside the unit circle, then

$$\measuredangle H_b(\pi) - \measuredangle H_b(0) = M_1\pi \tag{1.2.60}$$

The relationships (1.2.57), (1.2.59) and (1.2.60) are easily generalized to a system having complex-valued zeros, that occur in complex-conjugate pairs.

Thus we observe that when all the zeros are inside the unit circle, the net phase change is a minimum (i.e., zero), and when all the zeros are outside the unit circle, the net phase change is a maximum (i.e., $M\pi$). We call the first system a *minimum-phase system* and the second system a *maximum-phase system.* A system with some of the zeros inside and the others outside the unit circle is called a *mixed-phase system.*

The minimum-phase property of all-zero systems carries over to LTI systems with rational system functions. Specifically, a *stable* and *causal* LTI system with system function

$$H(z) = \frac{B(z)}{A(z)}$$

is minimum phase if all the zeros of $H(z)$ are inside the unit circle. If some of the zeros are outside the unit circle, the system is called mixed phase, and when all the zeros are outside the unit circle, the system is called maximum phase.

From the discussion we conclude that a minimum phase causal and stable pole–zero system has a causal and stable inverse that is minimum phase. The inverse system has the system function

$$H_I(z) = H^{-1}(z) = \frac{A(z)}{B(z)}$$

Hence the minimum-phase property of $H(z)$ ensures the stability of the inverse system $H^{-1}(z)$, and the stability and causality of $H(z)$ implies the minimum-phase property of $H^{-1}(z)$. Mixed-phase causal systems and maximum-phase causal systems result in unstable inverse systems.

Finally, let us consider an all-pass system, which is defined as an LTI system that satisfies the condition

$$|H(\omega)| = 1, \qquad 0 \leq \omega \leq \pi \tag{1.2.61}$$

If a stable and causal LTI system with a rational system function $H(z) = B(z)/A(z)$ is all-pass, then for every pole p_i there is a zero at $z = 1/p_i^*$. This condition is necessary to preserve the all-pass property given by (1.2.61). Hence $B(z) = z^{-N}A(z^{-1})$ and all the zeros of the all-pass system are outside the unit circle. Consequently, a stable and causal all-pass system is a maximum-phase system.

1.2.6 Response of Linear Systems to Random Input Signals

Let us consider a discrete-time linear time-invariant system with unit sample response $h(n)$ and frequency response $H(f)$. For this development we assume that $h(n)$ is real. Let $x(n)$ be a sample function of a stationary random process $X(n)$ that excites the system and let $y(n)$ denote the response of the system to $x(n)$.

From the convolution summation that relates the output to the input we have

$$y(n) = \sum_{k=-\infty}^{\infty} h(k)x(n-k) \tag{1.2.62}$$

Since $x(n)$ is a random input signal, the output is also a random sequence. In other words, for each sample sequence $x(n)$ of the process $X(n)$ there is a corresponding sample sequence $y(n)$ of the output random process $Y(n)$. We wish to relate the statistical characteristics of the output random process $Y(n)$ to the statistical characterization of the input process and the characteristics of the system.

The expected value of the output $y(n)$ is

$$\begin{aligned} m_y &\equiv E[y(n)] = E\left[\sum_{k=-\infty}^{\infty} h(k)x(n-k)\right] \\ m_y &= m_x \sum_{k=-\infty}^{\infty} h(k) \end{aligned} \tag{1.2.63}$$

From the Fourier transform relationship

$$H(f) = \sum_{k=-\infty}^{\infty} h(k)e^{-2\pi fk} \tag{1.2.64}$$

we have

$$H(0) = \sum_{k=-\infty}^{\infty} h(k) \tag{1.2.65}$$

which is the direct-current (dc) gain of the system. The relationship in (1.2.65) allows us to express the mean value in (1.2.63) as

$$m_y = m_x H(0) \tag{1.2.66}$$

The autocorrelation sequence for the output random process is

$$\begin{aligned}
\gamma_{yy}(m) &= E[y^*(n)y(n+m)] \\
&= E\left[\sum_{k=-\infty}^{\infty} h(k)x^*(n-k) \sum_{j=-\infty}^{\infty} h(j)x(n+m-j)\right] \\
&= \sum_{k=-\infty}^{\infty}\sum_{j=-\infty}^{\infty} h(k)h(j)E[x^*(n-k)x(n+m-j)] \\
&= \sum_{k=-\infty}^{\infty}\sum_{j=-\infty}^{\infty} h(k)h(j)\gamma_{xx}(k-j+m)
\end{aligned} \tag{1.2.67}$$

This is the general form for the autocorrelation of the output in terms of the autocorrelation of the input and the impulse response of the system.

A special form of (1.2.67) is obtained when the input random process is white (i.e., when $m_x = 0$) and

$$\gamma_{xx}(m) = \sigma_x^2 \delta(m) \tag{1.2.68}$$

where $\sigma_x^2 \equiv \gamma_{xx}(0)$ is the input signal power. Then (1.2.67) reduces to

$$\gamma_{yy}(m) = \sigma_x^2 \sum_{k=-\infty}^{\infty} h(k)h(k+m) \tag{1.2.69}$$

Under this condition the output process has the average power

$$\gamma_{yy}(0) = \sigma_x^2 \sum_{k=-\infty}^{\infty} h^2(k) = \sigma_x^2 \int_{-1/2}^{1/2} |H(f)|^2\, df \tag{1.2.70}$$

where we have applied Parseval's theorem.

The relationship in (1.2.67) can be transformed into the frequency domain by determining the power density spectrum of $\gamma_{yy}(m)$. We have

$$\begin{aligned}\Gamma_{yy}(f) &= \sum_{m=-\infty}^{\infty} \gamma_{yy}(m)e^{-j2\pi fm}\\ &= \sum_{m=-\infty}^{\infty}\left[\sum_{k=-\infty}^{\infty}\sum_{l=-\infty}^{\infty} h(k)h(l)\gamma_{xx}(k-l+m)\right]e^{-j2\pi fm}\\ &= \sum_{k=-\infty}^{\infty}\sum_{l=-\infty}^{\infty} h(k)h(l)\left[\sum_{m=-\infty}^{\infty}\gamma_{xx}(k-l+m)e^{-j2\pi fm}\right]\\ &= \Gamma_{xx}(f)\left[\sum_{k=-\infty}^{\infty} h(k)e^{j2\pi fk}\right]\left[\sum_{l=-\infty}^{\infty} h(l)e^{-j2\pi fl}\right]\\ &= |H(f)|^2\Gamma_{xx}(f)\end{aligned} \tag{1.2.71}$$

This is the desired relationship for the power density spectrum of the output process in terms of the power density spectrum of the input process and the frequency response of the system.

The equivalent expression for continuous-time systems with random inputs is

$$\Gamma_{yy}(F) = |H(F)|^2\Gamma_{xx}(F) \tag{1.2.72}$$

where the power density spectra $\Gamma_{yy}(F)$ and $\Gamma_{xx}(F)$ are the Fourier transforms of the autocorrelation functions $\gamma_{yy}(\tau)$ and $\gamma_{xx}(\tau)$, respectively, and $H(F)$ is the frequency response of the system, which is related to the impulse response by the Fourier transform,

$$H(F) = \int_{-\infty}^{\infty} h(t)e^{-j2\pi Ft}\,dt \tag{1.2.73}$$

As a final exercise, we determine the cross-correlation of the output $y(n)$ with the input signal $x(n)$. If we multiply both sides of (1.2.62) by $x^*(n - m)$ and take the expected value, we obtain

$$\begin{aligned}E[y(n)x^*(n-m)] &= E\left[\sum_{k=-\infty}^{\infty} h(k)x^*(n-m)x(n-k)\right]\\ \gamma_{yx}(m) &= \sum_{k=-\infty}^{\infty} h(k)E[x^*(n-m)x(n-k)]\\ &= \sum_{k=-\infty}^{\infty} h(k)\gamma_{xx}(m-k)\end{aligned} \tag{1.2.74}$$

Since (1.2.74) has the form of a convolution, the frequency-domain equivalent expression is

$$\Gamma_{yx}(f) = H(f)\Gamma_{xx}(f) \tag{1.2.75}$$

In the special case where $x(n)$ is white noise, (1.2.75) reduces to

$$\Gamma_{yx}(f) = \sigma_x^2 H(f) \tag{1.2.76}$$

where σ_x^2 is the input noise power. This result forms the basis for a system identification method. Simply, it means that an unknown system with frequency response $H(f)$ can be identified by exciting the input with white noise, cross-correlating the input sequence with the output sequence to obtain $\gamma_{yx}(m)$, and finally, computing the Fourier transform of $\gamma_{yx}(m)$. The result of these computations is proportional to $H(f)$.

1.3 SAMPLING OF SIGNALS IN TIME AND FREQUENCY

Sampling is a basic prerequisite for digital processing of continuous-time signals. Usually, the continuous-time signal is sampled uniformly (constant sampling rate) and thus converted into a discrete-time sequence of numbers. After the sequence is processed, the resulting sequence may be converted back to a continuous-time signal, as, for example, in speech signal processing. Alternatively, when the objective of the signal processing is to extract signal parameters or other relevant information from the signal, as in sonar or radar signal processing, there is no need to reconvert the signal to analog form.

Sampling may also be performed on the spectrum of the signal. For example, if the signal is an aperiodic finite-energy signal, its spectrum is continuous, and hence its computation is possible, in practice, only at a set of discrete frequencies. Since we are computing the spectrum at a set of discrete frequencies, we refer to such a computation as *frequency-domain sampling*. Below we consider uniform time-domain sampling of continuous-time signals and uniform frequency-domain sampling of continuous spectra.

1.3.1 Time-Domain Sampling of Analog Signals

To process a continuous-time signal by digital signal processing techniques, it is necessary to convert the signal into a sequence of numbers. This is usually done by sampling the analog signal, say $x_a(t)$, uniformly every T seconds to produce a discrete-time signal $x(n)$ given by

$$x(n) = x_a(nT), \qquad -\infty < n < \infty \tag{1.3.1}$$

The samples must then be quantized to a discrete set of amplitude levels, and the resulting digital signal is passed to the digital processor. Figure 1.6 illustrates a typical configuration of a system for processing an analog signal digitally. In the following discussion we neglect the quantization errors that are inherent in the analog-to-digital (A/D) conversion process.

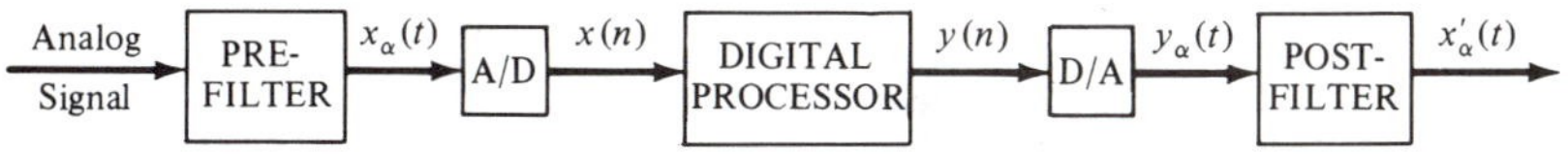

FIGURE 1.6 Configuration of system for digital processing of an analog signal.

The relationship (1.3.1) describes the sampling process in the time domain. The sampling frequency $F_s = 1/T$ must be selected large enough such that the sampling process will not result in any loss of spectral information (no aliasing). Indeed, if the spectrum of the analog signal can be recovered from the spectrum of the discrete-time signal, there is no loss of information. Consequently, we investigate the sampling process by finding the relationship between the spectra of signals $x_a(t)$ and $x(n)$.

If $x_a(t)$ is an aperiodic signal with finite energy and $X_a(F)$ is its (voltage) spectrum, the Fourier transform relationships are

$$X_a(F) = \int_{-\infty}^{\infty} x_a(t)e^{-j2\pi Ft}\,dt \tag{1.3.2}$$

$$x_a(t) = \int_{-\infty}^{\infty} X_a(F)e^{j2\pi Ft}\,dF \tag{1.3.3}$$

Note that utilization of all frequency components in the infinite frequency range $-\infty < F < \infty$ is necessary to recover the signal $x_a(t)$ if it is not bandlimited.

The spectrum of a discrete-time signal $x(n)$ obtained by sampling $x_a(t)$ is given by the Fourier transform relation

$$X(f) = \sum_{n=-\infty}^{\infty} x(n)e^{-j2\pi fn} \tag{1.3.4}$$

The sequence $x(n)$ can be recovered from its spectrum $X(\omega)$ or $X(f)$ by the inverse transform

$$x(n) = \int_{-1/2}^{1/2} X(f)e^{j2\pi fn}\,df \tag{1.3.5}$$

To determine the relationship between the spectra of the discrete-time signal and the analog signal, we use the relationship between the independent variables t and n in the signals $x_a(t)$ and $x(n)$, namely,

$$t = nT = \frac{n}{F_s} \tag{1.3.6}$$

This relationship in the time domain implies a corresponding relationship between the frequency variables F and f in $X_a(F)$ and $X(f)$, respectively.

Indeed, substitution of (1.3.6) into (1.3.3) yields

$$x(n) \equiv x_a(nT) = \int_{-\infty}^{\infty} X_a(F)e^{j2\pi nF/F_s}\,dF \tag{1.3.7}$$

If we compare (1.3.5) with (1.3.7), we conclude that

$$\int_{-1/2}^{1/2} X(f)e^{j2\pi fn}\,df = \int_{-\infty}^{\infty} X_a(F)e^{j2\pi nF/F_s}\,dF \tag{1.3.8}$$

But uniform sampling imposes a relationship between the frequency variables F and f of the corresponding analog and discrete-time signals, namely, $\omega = \Omega T$, or equivalently,

$$f = \frac{F}{F_s} \tag{1.3.9}$$

With the aid of (1.3.9), we may make a simple change in variable in (1.3.8), and thus we obtain the result

$$\frac{1}{F_s}\int_{-F_s/2}^{F_s/2} X\left(\frac{F}{F_s}\right)e^{j2\pi nF/F_s}\,dF = \int_{-\infty}^{\infty} X_a(F)e^{j2\pi nF/F_s}\,dF \tag{1.3.10}$$

Now we turn our attention to the integral on the right-hand side of (1.3.10). The integration range of this integral can be divided into an infinite number of intervals of width F_s. Thus the integral over the infinite range can be expressed as a sum of integrals,

$$\int_{-\infty}^{\infty} X_a(F)e^{j2\pi nF/F_s}\,dF = \sum_{k=-\infty}^{\infty}\int_{(k-1/2)F_s}^{(k+1/2)F_s} X_a(F)e^{j2\pi nF/F_s}\,dF \tag{1.3.11}$$

We observe that $X_a(F)$ in the frequency interval $(k - \frac{1}{2})F_s$ to $(k + \frac{1}{2})F_s$ is identical to $X_a(F - kF_s)$ in the interval $-F_s/2$ to $F_s/2$. Consequently,

$$\begin{aligned}\sum_{k=-\infty}^{\infty}\int_{(k-1/2)F_s}^{(k+1/2)F_s} X_a(F)e^{j2\pi nF/F_s}\,dF &= \sum_{k=-\infty}^{\infty}\int_{-F_s/2}^{F_s/2} X_a(F - kF_s)e^{j2\pi nF/F_s}\,dF \\ &= \int_{-F_s/2}^{F_s/2}\left[\sum_{k=-\infty}^{\infty} X_a(F - kF_s)\right]e^{j2\pi nF/F_s}\,dF\end{aligned} \tag{1.3.12}$$

where we have used the periodicity of the exponential, namely,

$$e^{j2\pi n(F+kF_s)/F_s} = e^{j2\pi nF/F_s}$$

Upon comparison of (1.3.12), (1.3.11), and (1.3.10), we conclude that

$$X\left(\frac{F}{F_s}\right) = F_s\sum_{k=-\infty}^{\infty} X_a(F - kF_s) \tag{1.3.13}$$

or equivalently,

$$X(f) = F_s\sum_{k=-\infty}^{\infty} X_a[(f - k)F_s] \tag{1.3.14}$$

This is the desired relationship between the spectrum $X(F/F_s)$ or $X(f)$ of the discrete-time signal and the spectrum $X_a(F)$ of the analog signal. The right-hand side of (1.3.13) or (1.3.14) consists of a periodic repetition of the scaled spectrum $F_sX_a(F)$ with period F_s. This periodicity is necessary because the spectrum $X(f)$ or $X(F/F_s)$ of the discrete-time signal is periodic with period $f_p = 1$ or $F_p = F_s$.

For example, suppose that the spectrum of a bandlimited analog signal is as shown in Fig. 1.7a. The spectrum is zero for $|F| \geq B$. Now, if the sampling frequency F_s is selected to be greater than $2B$, the spectrum $X(F/F_s)$ of the discrete-time signal will appear as shown in Fig. 1.7b. Thus if the sampling frequency F_s is selected such that $F_s \geq 2B$, where $2B$ is the Nyquist rate, then

$$X\left(\frac{F}{F_s}\right) = F_s X_a(F), \qquad |F| \leq \frac{F_s}{2} \tag{1.3.15}$$

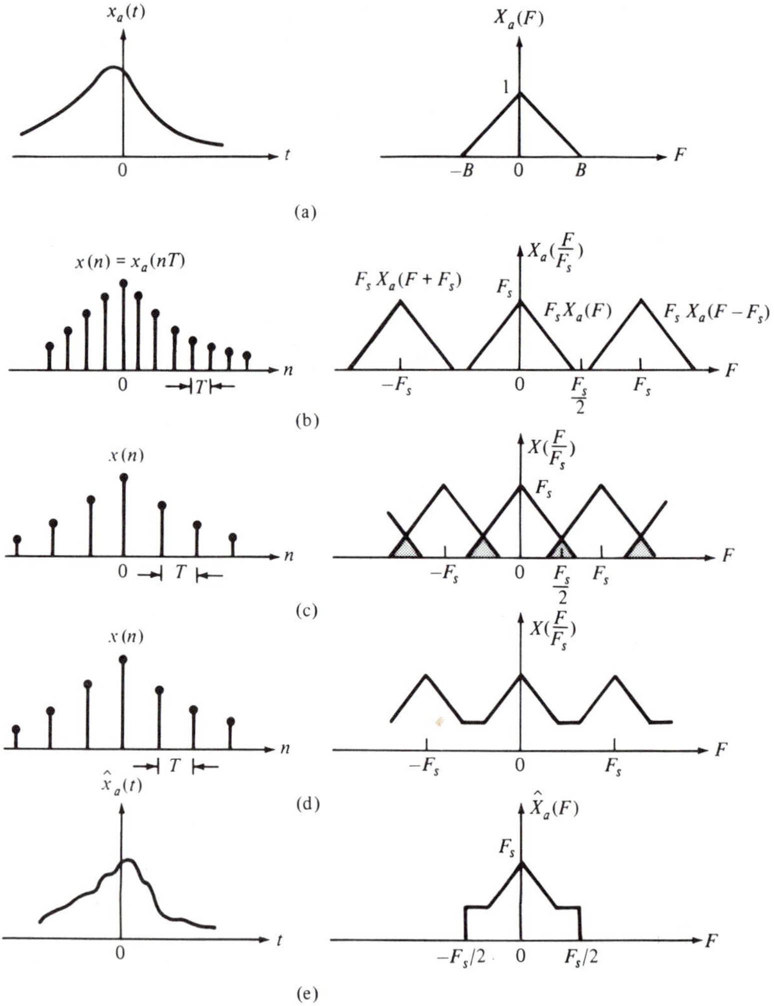

FIGURE 1.7 Sampling of an analog bandlimited signal and aliasing of spectral components.

In this case there is no aliasing, and hence the spectrum of the discrete-time signal is identical (within the scale factor F_s) to the spectrum of the analog signal, within the fundamental frequency range $|F| \le F_s/2$ or $|f| \le \frac{1}{2}$.

On the other hand, if the sampling frequency F_s is selected such that $F_s < 2B$, the periodic continuation of $X_a(F)$ results in spectral overlap, as illustrated in Fig. 1.7c and d. Thus the spectrum $X(F/F_s)$ of the discrete-time signal contains aliased frequency components of the analog signal spectrum $X_a(F)$. The end result is that the aliasing that occurs prevents us from recovering the original signal $x_a(t)$ from the samples.

Given the discrete-time signal $x(n)$ with the spectrum $X(F/F_s)$, as illustrated in Fig. 1.7b, with no aliasing, it is now possible to reconstruct the original analog signal from the samples $x(n)$. Since in the absence of aliasing

$$X_a(F) = \begin{cases} \dfrac{1}{F_s} X\left(\dfrac{F}{F_s}\right), & |F| \le \dfrac{F_s}{2} \\ 0, & |F| > \dfrac{F_s}{2} \end{cases} \tag{1.3.16}$$

and by the Fourier transform relationship (1.3.4),

$$X\left(\frac{F}{F_s}\right) = \sum_{n=-\infty}^{\infty} x(n) e^{-j2\pi F n/F_s} \tag{1.3.17}$$

then the inverse Fourier transform of $X_a(F)$ is

$$x_a(t) = \int_{-F_s/2}^{F_s/2} X_a(F) e^{j2\pi F t}\, dF \tag{1.3.18}$$

For concreteness we may assume that $F_s = 2B$. With the substitution of (1.3.16) into (1.3.18) we have

$$\begin{aligned} x_a(t) &= \frac{1}{F_s} \int_{-F_s/2}^{F_s/2} \left[\sum_{n=-\infty}^{\infty} x(n) e^{-j2\pi F n/F_s} \right] e^{j2\pi F t}\, dF \\ &= \frac{1}{F_s} \sum_{n=-\infty}^{\infty} x(n) \int_{-F_s/2}^{F_s/2} e^{j2\pi F(t - n/F_s)}\, dF \\ &= \sum_{n=-\infty}^{\infty} x_a(nT) \frac{\sin (\pi/T)(t - nT)}{(\pi/T)(t - nT)} \end{aligned} \tag{1.3.19}$$

where $x(n) = x_a(nT)$ and where $T = 1/F_s = 1/2B$ is the sampling interval. This is the reconstruction formula for the bandlimited signal $x_a(t)$.

The reconstruction formula in (1.3.19) involves the function

$$g(t) = \frac{\sin (\pi/T)t}{(\pi/T)t} \tag{1.3.20}$$

appropriately shifted by nT, $n = 0, \pm 1, \pm 2, \ldots$, and multiplied or weighted by the corresponding samples $x_a(nT)$ of the signal. We call (1.3.19) an interpolation formula for reconstructing $x_a(t)$ from its samples and $g(t)$, given in (1.3.20), is the interpolation function. We note that at $t = kT$ the interpolation function $g(t - nT)$ is zero except at $k = n$. Consequently, $x_a(t)$ evaluated at $t = kT$ is simply the sample $x_a(kT)$. At all other times the weighted sum of the time-shifted versions of the interpolation function combine to yield exactly $x_a(t)$. This combination is illustrated in Fig. 1.8.

The formula in (1.3.19) for reconstructing the analog signal $x_a(t)$ from its samples is called the *ideal interpolation formula*. It forms the basis for the *sampling theorem,* which states that a bandlimited continuous-time signal, with highest-frequency (bandwidth) B hertz, can be recovered uniquely from its samples provided that the sampling rate $F_s \geq 2B$ samples per second.

According to the sampling theorem and the reconstruction formula in (1.3.19), the recovery of $x_a(t)$ from its samples $x(n)$ requires an infinite number of samples. However, in practice, we deal with a finite number of samples of the signal and finite-duration signals. As a consequence, we are concerned only with reconstructing a finite-duration signal from a finite number of samples.

When aliasing occurs due to too low a sampling rate, this effect can be described by a multiple folding of the frequency axis of the frequency variable F for the analog signal. Figure 1.9a shows the spectrum $X_a(F)$ of an analog signal. According to (1.3.13), sampling of the signal with a sampling frequency F_s results in a periodic repetition of $X_a(F)$ with period F_s. If $F < 2B$, the shifted replicas of $X_a(F)$ overlap. The overlap that occurs within the fundamental frequency range $-F_s/2 \leq F \leq F_s/2$ is illustrated in Fig. 1.9b. The corresponding spectrum of the discrete-time signal within the fundamental frequency range is obtained by adding all the shifted portions within the range $|f| \leq \frac{1}{2}$, to yield the spectrum shown in Fig. 1.9c.

A careful inspection of Fig. 1.9a and b reveals that the aliased spectrum in Fig. 1.9c can be obtained by folding the original spectrum like an accordion with pleats at every odd multiple of $F_s/2$. Consequently, the frequency $F_s/2$ is called the *folding frequency*. Clearly, then, uniform sampling automatically forces a folding of the frequency axis of an analog signal at odd multiples of $F_s/2$ and results in the relationship $F = fF_s$ between the frequencies for continuous- and discrete-time signals. Due to the folding of the frequency

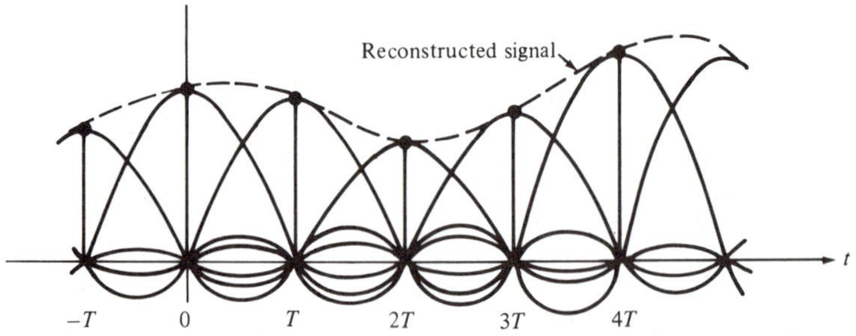

FIGURE 1.8 Reconstruction of continuous-time signal using ideal interpolation.

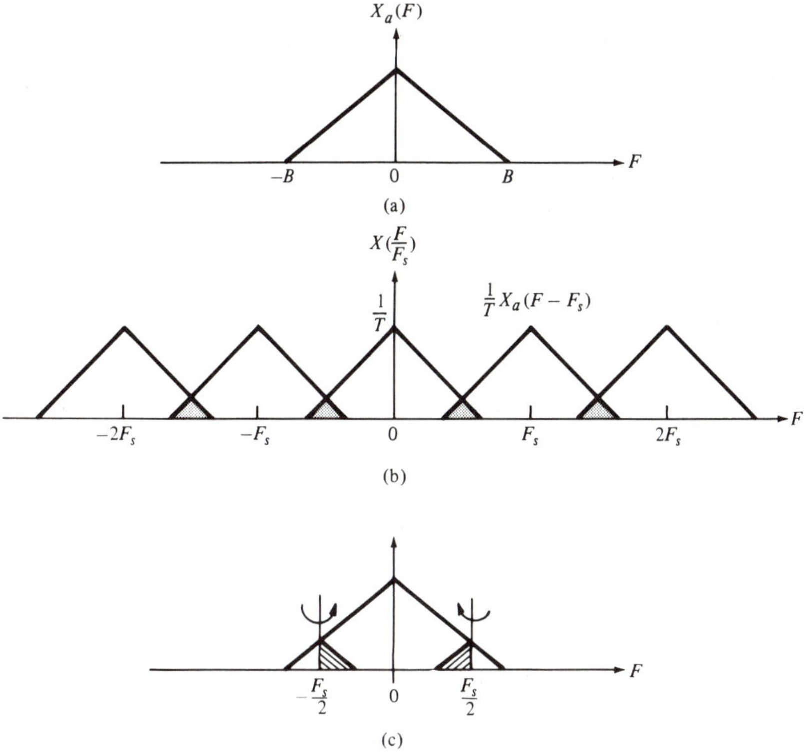

FIGURE 1.9 Illustration of aliasing around the folding frequency.

axis, the relationship $F = fF_s$ is not truly linear, but piecewise linear, to accommodate for the aliasing effect. This relationship is illustrated in Fig. 1.10.

If the analog signal is bandlimited to $B \leq F_s/2$, the relationship between f and F is linear and one-to-one. In other words, there is no aliasing. In practice, prefiltering is usually employed prior to sampling to ensure that

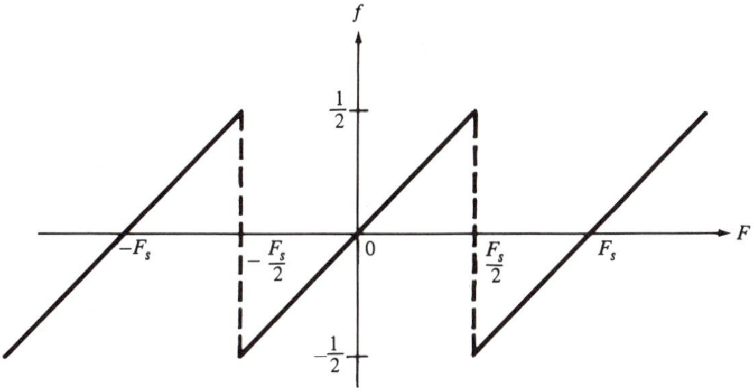

FIGURE 1.10 Relationship between frequency variables F and f.

frequency components of the signal above $F \geq B$ are sufficiently attenuated so that, if aliased, they cause negligible distortion on the desired signal.

The following examples serve to illustrate the problem of aliasing of frequency components.

EXAMPLE 1.3.1 Aliasing in Sinusoidal Signals

The continuous-time signal

$$x_a(t) = \cos 2\pi F_0 t = \tfrac{1}{2} e^{j2\pi F_0 t} + \tfrac{1}{2} e^{-j2\pi F_0 t}$$

has a discrete spectrum with spectral lines at $F = \pm F_0$, as shown in Fig. 1.11a. The process of sampling this signal with a sampling frequency F_s

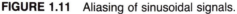

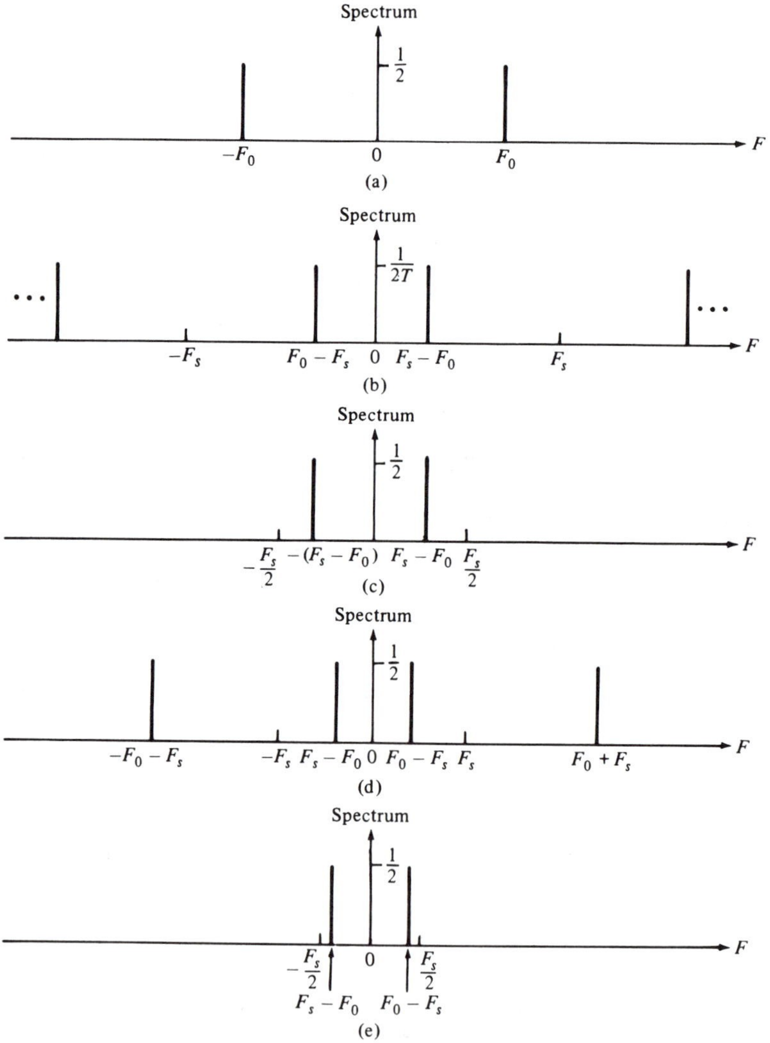

FIGURE 1.11 Aliasing of sinusoidal signals.

introduces replicas of the spectrum about multiples of F_s. This is illustrated in Fig. 1.11b for $F_s/2 < F_0 < F_s$.

To reconstruct the continuous-time signal, we should select the frequency components inside the fundamental frequency range $|F| \le F_s/2$. The resulting spectrum is shown in Fig. 1.11c. The reconstructed signal is

$$x_a(t) = \cos 2\pi(F_s - F_0)t$$

Now if F_s is selected such that $F_s < F_0 < 3F_s/2$, the spectrum of the sampled signal is shown in Fig. 1.11d. The reconstructed signal is

$$x_a(t) = \cos 2\pi(F_0 - F_s)t$$

In both cases aliasing has occurred, so that the frequency of the reconstructed signal is an aliased version of the frequency of the original signal.

EXAMPLE 1.3.2 Sampling a Nonbandlimited Signal

Consider the continuous-time signal

$$x_a(t) = e^{-A|t|}, \qquad A > 0$$

whose spectrum is given by

$$X_a(F) = \frac{2A}{A^2 + (2\pi F)^2}$$

Let us determine the spectrum of the sampled signal $x(n) \equiv x_a(nT)$. If we sample $x_a(t)$ with a sampling frequency $F_s = 1/T$, we have

$$x(n) = x_a(nT) = e^{-AT|n|} = (e^{-AT})^{|n|}, \qquad -\infty < n < \infty$$

The spectrum of $x(n)$ can be easily found if we use a direct computation of the Fourier transform. We find that

$$X\left(\frac{F}{F_s}\right) = \frac{1 - e^{-2AT}}{1 - 2e^{-AT}\cos 2\pi FT + e^{-2AT}}, \qquad T = \frac{1}{F_s}$$

Clearly, since $\cos 2\pi FT = \cos 2\pi(F/F_s)$ is periodic with period F_s, so is $X(F/F_s)$.

Since $X_a(F)$ is not bandlimited, aliasing cannot be avoided. The spectrum of the reconstructed signal $x_a(t)$ is

$$X_a(F) = \begin{cases} TX\left(\dfrac{F}{F_s}\right), & |F| \le \dfrac{F_s}{2} \\ 0, & |F| > \dfrac{F_s}{2} \end{cases}$$

Figure 1.12a shows the original signal $x_a(t)$ and its spectrum $X_a(F)$ for $A = 1$. The sampled signal $x(n)$ and its spectrum $X(F/F_s)$ are shown in Fig. 1.12b for $F_s = 1$ Hz. The aliasing distortion is clearly noticeable in the frequency domain. The reconstructed signal $\hat{x}_a(t)$ is shown in Fig.

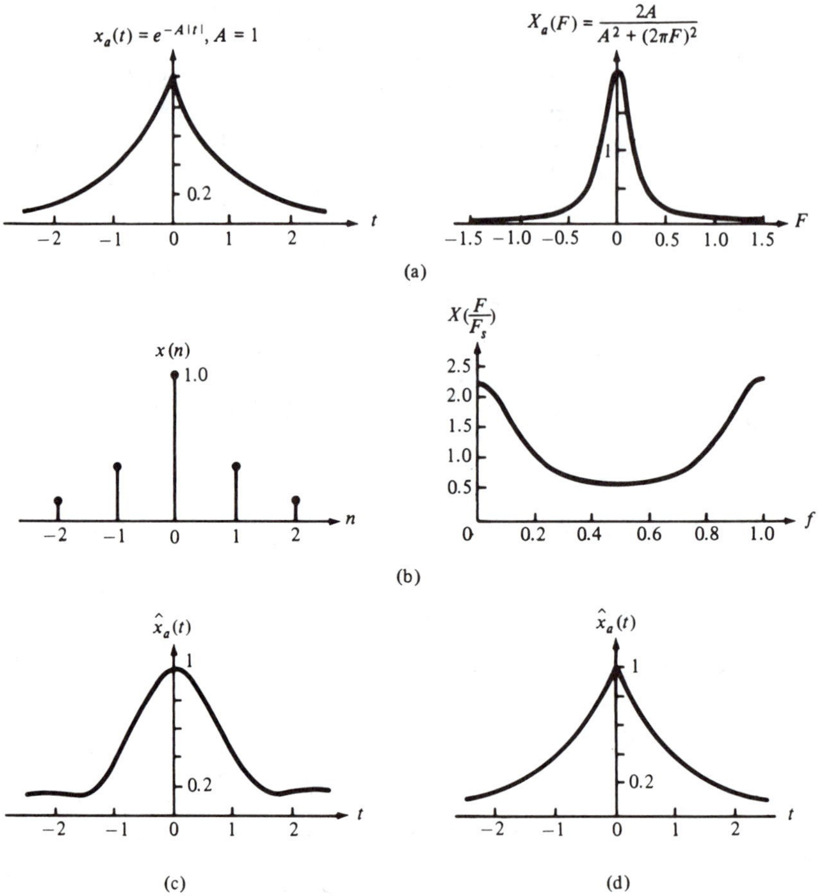

FIGURE 1.12 (a) Analog signal $x_a(t)$ and its spectrum $X_a(F)$; (b) $x(n) = x_a(nT)$ and the spectrum of $x(n)$ for $A = 1$ and $F_s = 1$: (c) reconstructed signal $\hat{x}_a(t)$ for $F_s = 1$: (d) reconstructed signal $\hat{x}_a(t)$ for $F_s = 20$.

1.12c. The distortion due to aliasing can be reduced significantly by increasing the sampling rate. For example, Fig. 1.12d illustrates the reconstructed signal corresponding to a sampling rate $F_s = 20$ Hz. It is interesting to note that in every case $x_a(nT) = \hat{x}_a(nT)$, but $x_a(t) \neq \hat{x}_a(t)$ at other values of time.

Up to this point in our discussion of sampling we have demonstrated that any analog signal with highest frequency B can be uniquely represented by samples taken at the minimum rate (Nyquist rate) of $2B$ samples per second. However, if the analog signal is a bandpass signal with frequency contents in the band $B_1 \leq F \leq B_2$, as shown in Fig. 1.13, a blind application of the sampling theorem would have us sampling the signal at a rate of $F_s \geqslant 2B_2$ samples per second. However, such a high sampling rate is not necessary.

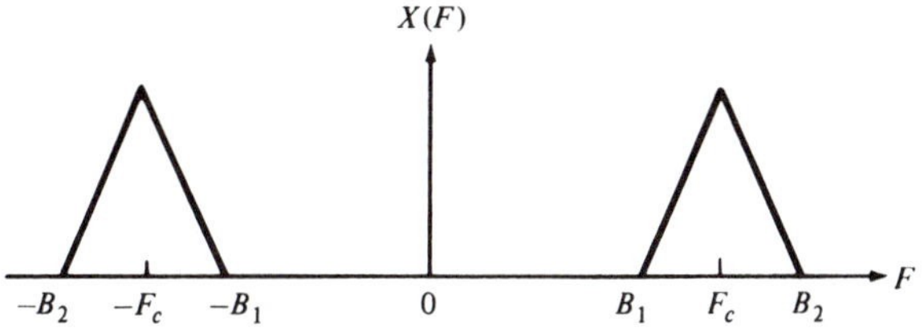

FIGURE 1.13 Bandpass signal with frequency components in the range $B_1 \le F \le B_2$.

As shown below, it is possible to sample a bandpass signal at a rate of twice its bandwidth without loss of information.

Recall that an analog bandpass signal has a frequency content concentrated in a narrow band of frequencies around some frequency F_c and is represented in general as

$$\begin{aligned} x_a(t) &= A(t)\cos[2\pi F_c t + \phi(t)] \\ &= u_c(t)\cos 2\pi F_c t - u_s(t)\sin 2\pi F_c t \end{aligned} \tag{1.3.21}$$

where $A(t)$ is the amplitude or envelope of the signal, $\phi(t)$ is the phase of the signal, and $u_c(t)$ and $u_s(t)$ are the quadrature components, defined as

$$\begin{aligned} u_c(t) &= A(t)\cos\phi(t) \\ u_s(t) &= A(t)\sin\phi(t) \end{aligned} \tag{1.3.22}$$

Instead of sampling the bandpass signal it is always possible to perform a frequency shift of the bandpass signal by an amount

$$F_c = \frac{B_1 + B_2}{2}$$

and sample the equivalent lowpass signal. Such a frequency shift can be achieved by multiplying the bandpass signal as given in (1.3.21) by the quadrature carriers $\cos 2\pi F_c t$ and $\sin 2\pi F_c t$ and lowpass filtering the products to eliminate the signal components centered at the double frequency $2F_c$. Clearly, the multiplication and the subsequent filtering are performed in the analog domain and the outputs of the filters are then sampled. The resulting equivalent lowpass signal has a bandwidth $B/2$, where $B = B_2 - B_1$; hence it can be represented uniquely by samples taken at the rate of B samples per second for each of the quadrature components. Thus the sampling can be performed on each of the lowpass filter outputs at the rate of B samples per second, as indicated in Fig. 1.14. Hence the resulting sampling rate is $2B$ samples per second.

In view of the fact that frequency conversion to lowpass allows us to reduce the sampling rate to $2B$ samples per second, it should be possible to sample the bandpass signal at a comparable rate. In fact, it is. Suppose that the upper frequency $F_c + B/2$ is a multiple of the bandwidth B (i.e., $F_c +$

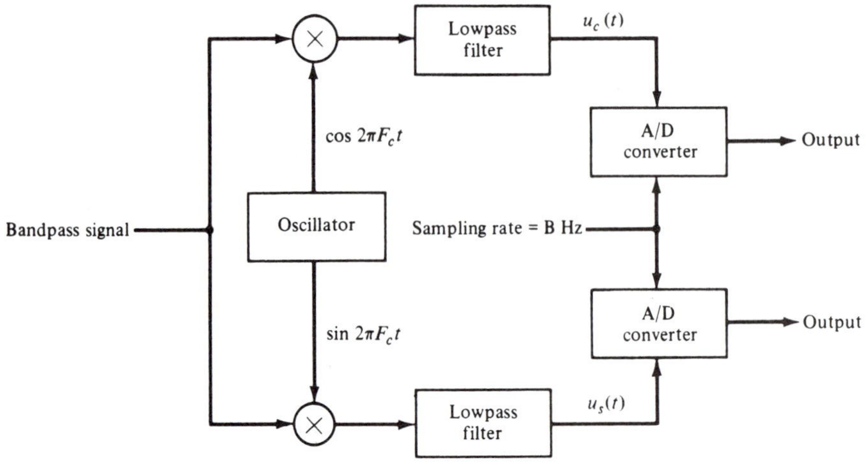

FIGURE 1.14 Sampling of a bandpass signal by first converting to an equivalent lowpass signal.

$B/2 = kB$, where k is a positive integer). If we sample $x_a(t)$ at the rate $2B = 1/T$ samples per second, we have

$$x_a(nT) = u_c(nT) \cos 2\pi F_c nT - u_s(nT) \sin 2\pi F_c nT \tag{1.3.23}$$
$$x_a(nT) = u_c(nT) \cos \frac{\pi n(2k - 1)}{2} - u_s(nT) \sin \frac{\pi n(2k - 1)}{2}$$

where the last step is obtained by substituting $F_c = kB - B/2$ and $T = 1/2B$.

For n even, say $n = 2m$, (1.3.23) reduces to

$$x_a(2mT) \equiv x(mT_1) = u_c(mT_1) \cos \pi m(2k - 1) = (-1)^m u_c(mT_1) \tag{1.3.24}$$

where $T_1 = 2T = 1/B$. For n odd, say $n = 2m - 1$, (1.3.23) reduces to

$$x_a(2mT - T) \equiv x\left(mT_1 - \frac{T_1}{2}\right) = u_s\left(mT_1 - \frac{T_1}{2}\right)(-1)^{m+k+1} \tag{1.3.25}$$

Therefore, the even-numbered samples of $x_a(t)$, which occur at the rate of B samples per second, produce samples of the lowpass signal component $u_c(t)$, while the odd-numbered samples of $x_a(t)$, which also occur at the rate of B samples per second, produce samples of the lowpass signal component $u_s(t)$.

Now the samples $u_c(mT_1)$ and the samples $u_s(mT_1 - T_1/2)$ can be used to reconstruct the equivalent lowpass signals. Thus, according to the sampling theorem for lowpass signals with $T_1 = 1/B$,

$$u_c(t) = \sum_{m=-\infty}^{\infty} u_c(mT_1) \frac{\sin(\pi/T_1)(t - mT_1)}{(\pi/T_1)(t - mT_1)} \tag{1.3.26}$$

$$u_s(t) = \sum_{m=-\infty}^{\infty} u_s\left(mT_1 - \frac{T_1}{2}\right) \frac{\sin(\pi/T_1)(t - mT_1 + T_1/2)}{(\pi/T_1)(t - mT_1 + T_1/2)} \tag{1.3.27}$$

Furthermore, the relations in (1.3.24) and (1.3.25) allow us to express $u_c(t)$ and $u_s(t)$ directly in terms of samples of $x_a(t)$. Now since $x_a(t)$ is expressed as

$$x_a(t) = u_c(t) \cos 2\pi F_c t - u_s(t) \sin 2\pi F_c t \tag{1.3.28}$$

substitution from (1.3.27), (1.3.26), (1.3.25), and (1.3.24) into (1.3.28) yields

$$\begin{aligned} x_a(t) = \sum_{m=-\infty}^{\infty} \Bigg[&(-1)^m x(2mT) \frac{\sin(\pi/2T)(t - 2mT)}{(\pi/2T)(t - 2mT)} \cos 2\pi F_c t \\ &+ (-1)^{m+k} x((2m-1)T) \frac{\sin(\pi/2T)(t - 2mT + T)}{(\pi/2T)(t - 2mT + T)} \Bigg] \end{aligned} \tag{1.3.29}$$

But $(-1)^m \cos 2\pi F_c t = \cos 2\pi F_c(t - 2mT)$ and $(-1)^{m+k} \sin 2\pi F_c t = \cos 2\pi F_c(t - 2mT + T)$. With these substitutions, (1.3.29) reduces to

$$x_a(t) = \sum_{m=-\infty}^{\infty} x(mT) \frac{\sin(\pi/2T)(t - mT)}{(\pi/2T)(t - mT)} \cos 2\pi F_c(t - mT) \tag{1.3.30}$$

where $T = 1/2B$. This is the desired reconstruction formula for the bandpass signal $x_a(t)$, with samples taken at the rate of $2B$ samples per second, for the special case in which the upper band frequency $F_c + B/2$ is a multiple of the signal bandwidth B.

In the general case where only the condition $F_c \geq B/2$ is assumed to hold, let us define the integer part of the ratio $F_c + B/2$ to B as

$$r = \left\lfloor \frac{F_c + B/2}{B} \right\rfloor \tag{1.3.31}$$

While holding the upper cutoff frequency $F_c + B/2$ constant, we increase the bandwidth from B to B', such that

$$\frac{F_c + B/2}{B'} = r \tag{1.3.32}$$

Furthermore, it is convenient to define a new center frequency for the increased bandwidth signal as

$$F_c' = F_c + \frac{B}{2} - \frac{B'}{2} \tag{1.3.33}$$

Clearly, the increased signal bandwidth B' includes the original signal spectrum of bandwidth B.

Now the upper cutoff frequency $F_c + B/2$ is a multiple of B'. Consequently, the signal reconstruction formula in (1.3.30) holds with F_c replaced by F_c' and T replaced by T', where $T' = 1/2B'$,

$$x_a(t) = \sum_{n=-\infty}^{\infty} x(nT') \frac{\sin(\pi/2T')(t - mT')}{(\pi/2T')(t - mT')} \cos 2\pi F_c'(t - mT') \tag{1.3.34}$$

This proves that $x(t)$ can be represented by samples taken at the uniform rate $1/T' = 2Br'/r$, where r' is the ratio

$$r' = \frac{F_c + B/2}{B} = \frac{F_c}{B} + \frac{1}{2} \tag{1.3.35}$$

and $r = \lfloor r' \rfloor$.

We observe that when the upper cutoff frequency $F_c + B/2$ is not an integer multiple of the bandwidth B, the sampling rate for the bandpass signal must be increased by the factor r'/r. However, note that as F_c/B increases, the ratio r'/r tends toward unity. Consequently, the percent increase in sampling rate tends to zero.

The derivation given above also illustrates the fact that the lowpass signal components $u_c(t)$ and $u_s(t)$ may be expressed in terms of samples of the bandpass signal. Indeed, from (1.3.24), (1.3.25), (1.3.26), and (1.3.27), we obtain the result

$$u_c(t) = \sum_{n=-\infty}^{\infty} (-1)^n x(2nT') \frac{\sin(\pi/2T')(t - 2nT')}{(\pi/2T')(t - 2nT')} \tag{1.3.36}$$

and

$$u_s(t) = \sum_{n=-\infty}^{\infty} (-1)^{n+r} x(2nT' - T') \frac{\sin(\pi/2T')(t - 2nT' + T')}{(\pi/2T')(t - 2nT' + T')} \tag{1.3.37}$$

where $r = \lfloor r' \rfloor$.

In conclusion, we have demonstrated that a bandpass signal can be represented uniquely by samples taken at a rate

$$2B \leq F_s < 4B$$

where B is the bandwidth of the signal. The lower limit applies when the upper frequency $F_c + B/2$ is a multiple of B. The upper limit on F_s is obtained under worst-case conditions, when $r = 1$ and $r' \approx 2$.

1.3.2 Frequency-Domain Sampling of Analog Signals

In general, continuous-time finite energy signals have continuous spectra. In this section we consider the sampling of such signals uniformly and the reconstruction of the signals from samples of their spectra. Consider an analog signal $x_a(t)$ with a continuous spectrum $X_a(F)$, which is the Fourier transform of $x_a(t)$. Now suppose that we obtain samples of $X_a(F)$ every δF hertz as shown in Fig. 1.15. Is it possible to recover $X_a(F)$ or, equivalently, $x_a(t)$ from its samples, $X_a(k\,\delta F)$, $-\infty < k < \infty$?

This problem is mathematically the dual to that of sampling a continuous-time signal in the time domain. Indeed, if we begin with (1.1.2) and sample the spectrum every δF hertz, we obtain

$$X_a(k\,\delta F) = \int_{-\infty}^{\infty} x_a(t) e^{-j2\pi k \delta F t}\, dt \tag{1.3.38}$$

It is convenient to define the reciprocal of δF as

$$T_s = \frac{1}{\delta F} \tag{1.3.39}$$

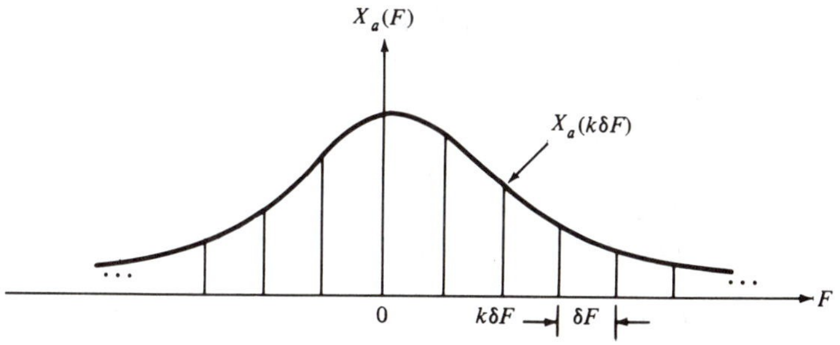

FIGURE 1.15 Evaluating the Fourier transform at a set of equally spaced discrete frequencies.

Then (1.3.38) can be expressed as

$$X_a(k\,\delta F) = \int_{-\infty}^{\infty} x_a(t)e^{-j2\pi kt/T_s}\,dt \tag{1.3.40}$$

which is analogous to (1.3.7) for time-domain sampling. Proceeding as in the case of time-domain sampling, we subdivide the integration range of the integral in (1.3.40) into an infinite number of intervals of width T_s and change the variable of integration so as to translate each integral into the fundamental range $-T_s/2 \le t \le T_s/2$. These steps lead to the result

$$X_a(k\,\delta F) = \int_{-T_s/2}^{T_s/2} \left[\sum_{n=-\infty}^{\infty} x_a(t - nT_s)\right] e^{-j2\pi kt/T_s}\,dt \tag{1.3.41}$$

which is the dual of (1.3.12).

The signal

$$x_p(t) \equiv \sum_{n=-\infty}^{\infty} x_a(t - nT_s) \tag{1.3.42}$$

is clearly periodic with fundamental period $T_s = 1/\delta F$. Hence it can be expanded into a Fourier series

$$x_p(t) = \sum_{k=-\infty}^{\infty} c_k e^{j2\pi k\delta Ft} \tag{1.3.43}$$

where

$$c_k = \frac{1}{T_s}\int_{-T_s/2}^{T_s/2} x_p(t)e^{-j2\pi k\delta Ft}\,dt \tag{1.3.44}$$

Comparison of (1.3.44) with (1.3.41) gives the result

$$\begin{aligned} c_k &= \frac{1}{T_s}X_a(k\,\delta F) \\ &= \delta F\, X_a(k\,\delta F), \qquad -\infty < k < \infty \end{aligned} \tag{1.3.45}$$

We conclude from (1.3.45) that the samples of the spectrum $X_a(F)$ correspond (within the scale factor δF) to the Fourier coefficients of a periodic signal $x_p(t)$ with period $T_s = 1/\delta F$. The periodic signal $x_p(t)$ consists of the sum of periodically extended versions of the analog signal $x_a(t)$ as given by (1.3.42) and illustrated in Fig. 1.16.

It is apparent from Fig. 1.16 that recovery of the signal $x_a(t)$ from its periodic extension $x_p(t)$ is possible if $x_a(t)$ is time limited to $|t| \le \tau$ [i.e., $x_a(t) = 0$ for $|t| > \tau$, where $\tau < T_s/2$]. If $\tau > T_s/2$, exact reconstruction of $x_a(t)$ is not possible due to "time-domain aliasing."

If the analog signal $x_a(t)$ is time limited to τ seconds and T_s is selected such that $T_s > 2\tau$, there is no aliasing and the signal spectrum $X_a(F)$ can be perfectly reconstructed from the samples $X_a(k\,\delta F)$ by using the interpolation formula

$$X_a(F) = \sum_{k=-\infty}^{\infty} X_a(k\,\delta F)\frac{\sin[(\pi/\delta F)(F - k\,\delta F)]}{(\pi/\delta F)(F - k\,\delta F)} \tag{1.3.46}$$

which is the dual of (1.3.19).

The development given above is important primarily for conceptual purposes. Although frequency sampling of continuous-time signals is encountered in practical frequency analysis applications, in many applications of this type, the analog signal is converted to a discrete-time signal and the frequency sampling is performed on the spectrum of the discrete-time signal. Frequency sampling of discrete-time signal spectra is considered below.

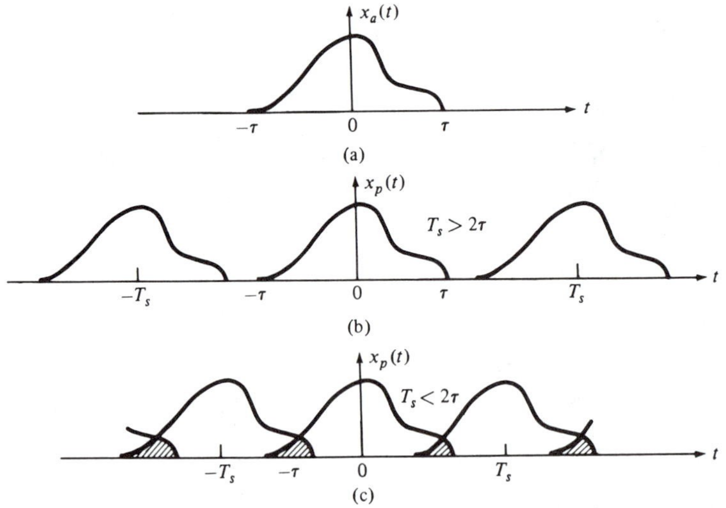

FIGURE 1.16 Periodic signal resulting from sampling a finite energy, time-limited signal in the frequency domain. Aliasing in the time domain is illustrated in (c).

1.3.3 Frequency-Domain Sampling of Discrete-Time Signals

We recall that aperiodic finite-energy signals have continuous spectra. Let us consider such an aperiodic discrete-time signal $x(n)$ with Fourier transform

$$X(\omega) = \sum_{n=-\infty}^{\infty} x(n)e^{-j\omega n} \tag{1.3.47}$$

Suppose that we sample $X(\omega)$ uniformly in frequency at a spacing of $\delta\omega$ radians between successive samples. Since $X(\omega)$ is periodic with period 2π, only samples in the fundamental frequency range are necessary. For convenience, we take N equidistant samples in the interval $0 \le \omega < 2\pi$ with spacing $\delta\omega = 2\pi/N$, as shown in Fig. 1.17. First, we consider the selection of N, the number of samples in the frequency domain.

If we evaluate (1.3.47) at $\omega = 2\pi k/N$, we obtain

$$X\left(\frac{2\pi}{N}k\right) = \sum_{n=-\infty}^{\infty} x(n)e^{-j2\pi kn/N}, \qquad k = 0, 1, \ldots, N-1 \tag{1.3.48}$$

The summation in (1.3.48) can be subdivided into an infinite number of summations, where each sum contains N terms. Thus

$$X\left(\frac{2\pi}{N}k\right) = \cdots + \sum_{n=-N}^{-1} x(n)e^{-j2\pi kn/N} + \sum_{n=0}^{N-1} x(n)e^{-j2\pi kn/N} + \sum_{n=N}^{2N-1} x(n)e^{-j2\pi kn/N}$$

$$+ \cdots = \sum_{l=-\infty}^{\infty} \sum_{n=lN}^{lN+N-1} x(n)e^{-j2\pi kn/N}$$

If we change the index in the inner summation from n to $n - lN$ and interchange the order of the summation, we obtain the result

$$X\left(\frac{2\pi}{N}k\right) = \sum_{n=0}^{N-1} \left[\sum_{l=-\infty}^{\infty} x(n - lN)\right] e^{-j2\pi kn/N} \tag{1.3.49}$$

for $k = 0, 1, 2, \ldots, N-1$.

The signal

$$x_p(n) = \sum_{l=-\infty}^{\infty} x(n - lN) \tag{1.3.50}$$

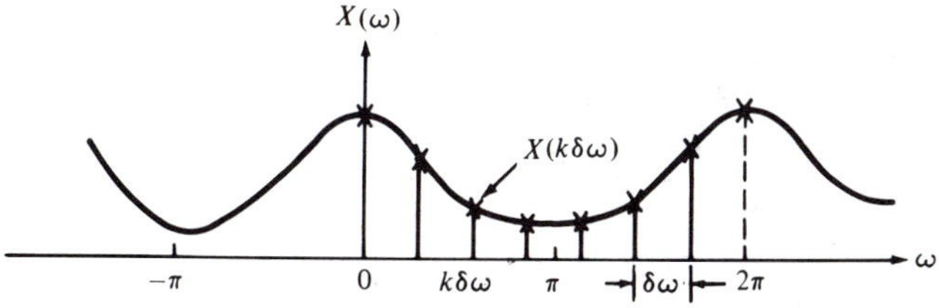

FIGURE 1.17 Frequency-domain sampling of the Fourier transform.

obtained by the periodic repetition of $x(n)$ every N samples, is clearly periodic with fundamental period N. Consequently, it can be expanded in a Fourier series as

$$x_p(n) = \sum_{k=0}^{N-1} c_k e^{j2\pi kn/N}, \qquad n = 0, 1, \ldots, N-1 \tag{1.3.51}$$

with Fourier coefficients

$$c_k = \frac{1}{N} \sum_{n=0}^{N-1} x_p(n) e^{-j2\pi kn/N}, \qquad k = 0, 1, \ldots, N-1 \tag{1.3.52}$$

Upon comparing (1.3.52) with (1.3.49) we conclude that

$$c_k = \frac{1}{N} X\left(\frac{2\pi}{N} k\right), \qquad k = 0, 1, \ldots, N-1 \tag{1.3.53}$$

Therefore,

$$x_p(n) = \frac{1}{N} \sum_{k=0}^{N-1} X\left(\frac{2\pi}{N} k\right) e^{j2\pi kn/N}, \qquad n = 0, 1, \ldots, N-1 \tag{1.3.54}$$

The relationship in (1.3.54) provides the reconstruction of the periodic signal $x_p(n)$ from the samples of the spectrum $X(\omega)$. However, it does not imply that we can recover $X(\omega)$ or $x(n)$ from the samples. To accomplish this we need to consider the relationship between $x_p(n)$ and $x(n)$.

Since $x_p(n)$ is the periodic extension of $x(n)$ as given by (1.3.50), it is clear that $x(n)$ can be recovered from $x_p(n)$ if there is no aliasing in the time domain [i.e., if $x(n)$ is time-limited to less than the period N of $x_p(n)$]. This situation is illustrated in Fig. 1.18, where without loss of generality, we

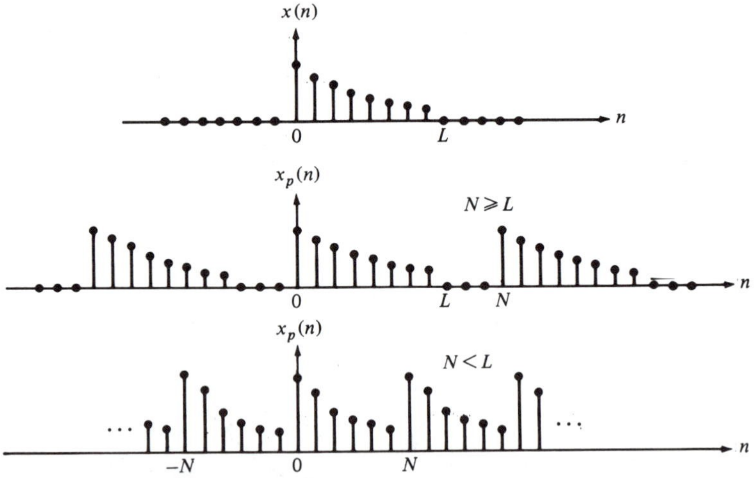

FIGURE 1.18 Aperiodic sequence $x(n)$ of length L and its periodic extension for $N \geq L$ (no aliasing) and $N < L$ (aliasing).

consider a finite-duration sequence $x(n)$, which is nonzero in the interval $0 \le n \le L - 1$. We observe that when $N \ge L$,

$$x(n) = x_p(n), \qquad 0 \le n \le N - 1$$

so that $x(n)$ can be recovered from $x_p(n)$ without ambiguity. On the other hand, if $N < L$, it is not possible to recover $x(n)$ from its periodic extension due to *time-domain aliasing*. Thus we conclude that the spectrum of an aperiodic discrete-time signal with finite-duration L can be exactly recovered from its samples at frequencies $\omega_k = 2\pi k/N$, if $N \ge L$. The procedure is to compute $x_p(n)$, $n = 0, 1, \ldots, N - 1$ from (1.3.54), then

$$x(n) = \begin{cases} x_p(n), & 0 \le n \le N - 1 \\ 0, & \text{elsewhere} \end{cases} \tag{1.3.55}$$

and finally, $X(\omega)$ can be computed from (1.3.47).

As in the case of continuous-time signals it is possible to express the spectrum $X(\omega)$ directly in terms of its samples $X(2\pi k/N)$, $k = 0, 1, \ldots, N - 1$. To derive such an interpolation formula from $X(\omega)$, we assume that $N \ge L$ and begin with (1.3.54). Since $x(n) = x_p(n)$ for $0 \le n \le N - 1$,

$$x(n) = \frac{1}{N} \sum_{k=0}^{N-1} X\left(\frac{2\pi}{N} k\right) e^{j2\pi kn/N}, \qquad 0 \le n \le N - 1 \tag{1.3.56}$$

If we use (1.3.47) and substitute for $x(n)$, we obtain

$$\begin{aligned} X(\omega) &= \sum_{n=0}^{N-1} \left[\frac{1}{N} \sum_{k=0}^{N-1} X\left(\frac{2\pi}{N} k\right) e^{j2\pi kn/N} \right] e^{-j\omega n} \\ &= \sum_{k=0}^{N-1} X\left(\frac{2\pi}{N} k\right) \left[\frac{1}{N} \sum_{n=0}^{N-1} e^{-j(\omega - 2\pi k/N)n} \right] \end{aligned} \tag{1.3.57}$$

The inner summation term in the brackets of (1.3.57) represents the basic interpolation function shifted by $2\pi k/N$ in frequency. Indeed, if we define

$$\begin{aligned} P(\omega) &= \frac{1}{N} \sum_{n=0}^{N-1} e^{-j\omega n} = \frac{1}{N} \frac{1 - e^{-j\omega N}}{1 - e^{-j\omega}} \\ &= \frac{\sin(\omega N/2)}{N \sin(\omega/2)} e^{-j\omega(N-1)/2} \end{aligned} \tag{1.3.58}$$

then (1.3.57) can be expressed as

$$X(\omega) = \sum_{k=0}^{N-1} X\left(\frac{2\pi}{N} k\right) P\left(\omega - \frac{2\pi}{N} k\right) \tag{1.3.59}$$

The interpolation function $P(\omega)$ is not the familiar $\sin(\theta)/\theta$, but instead, it is a periodic counterpart of it, due to the periodic nature of $X(\omega)$. The phase shift in (1.3.58) reflects the fact that the signal $x(n)$ is a causal finite-duration sequence of length N. The function $\sin(\omega N/2)/N \sin(\omega/2)$ is plotted in Fig. 1.19 for $N = 5$. We observe that the function $P(\omega)$ has the property

$$P\left(\frac{2\pi}{N}k\right) = \begin{cases} 1, & k = 0 \\ 0, & k = 1, 2, \ldots, N-1 \end{cases} \tag{1.3.60}$$

Consequently, the interpolation formula in (1.3.59) gives exactly the sample values $X(2\pi k/N)$ for $\omega = 2\pi k/N$. At all other frequencies, the formula provides a properly weighted linear combination of the original spectral samples.

The following example illustrates the frequency-domain sampling of a discrete-time signal and the time-domain aliasing that results.

EXAMPLE 1.3.3

Consider the signal

$$x(n) = a^n u(n), \qquad 0 < a < 1$$

The spectrum of this signal is sampled at frequencies $\omega_k = 2\pi k/N$, $k = 0, 1, \ldots, N-1$. Determine the reconstructed spectra for $a = 0.8$ when $N = 5$ and $N = 50$.

Solution: The Fourier transform of the sequence $x(n)$ is

$$X(\omega) = \sum_{n=0}^{\infty} a^n e^{-j\omega n} = \frac{1}{1 - ae^{-j\omega}}$$

When evaluated for $a = 0.8$ at the N frequencies, we obtain

$$X\left(\frac{2\pi}{N}k\right) = \frac{1}{1 - 0.8e^{-j2\pi k/N}}$$

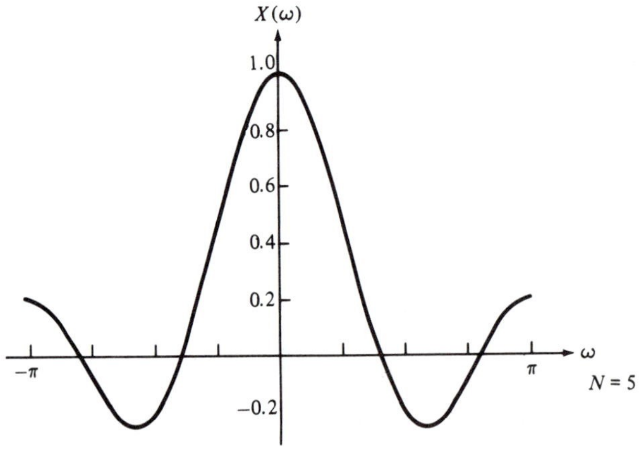

FIGURE 1.19 Plot of the function [sin (ωN/2)]/[N sin (ω/2)].

The periodic sequence $x_p(n)$ corresponding to the frequency samples $X(2\pi k/N)$, $k = 0, 1, \ldots, N - 1$, is obtained from (1.3.54). Thus

$$x(n) \equiv x_p(n) = \frac{1}{N}\sum_{k=0}^{N-1} X\left(\frac{2\pi k}{N}\right)e^{j2\pi kn/N}, \qquad n = 0, 1, \ldots, N-1$$

The results of this computation are illustrated in Fig. 1.20 for $N = 5$ and $N = 50$. For comparison, the original sequence $x(n)$ and its spectrum are also shown. The effect of aliasing is clearly evident for $N = 5$. However, for $N = 50$, the aliased components are very small, and consequently, $\hat{x}(n) \approx x(n)$, for $n = 0, 1, \ldots, N - 1$.

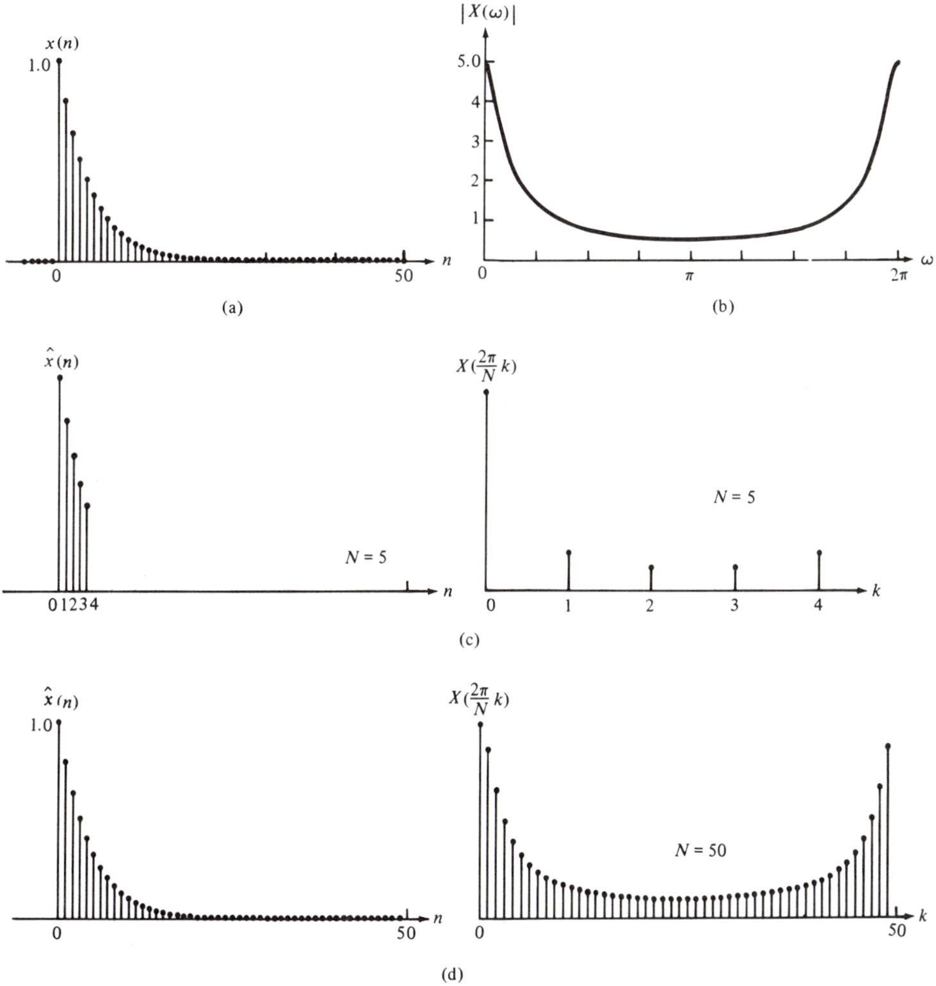

FIGURE 1.20 (a) Plot of sequence $x(n) = (0.8)^n u(n)$; (b) its Fourier transform (magnitude only); (c) effect of aliasing with $N = 5$; (d) reduced effect of aliasing with $N = 50$.

1.3.4 The Discrete Fourier Transform for Finite-Duration Sequences

The development in the preceding section was concerned with the frequency-domain sampling of an aperiodic finite energy sequence $x(n)$. In general, the equally spaced frequency samples $X(2\pi k/N)$, $k = 0, 1, \ldots, N - 1$, do not represent the original sequence $x(n)$ uniquely when $x(n)$ has infinite duration. Instead, the frequency samples $X(2\pi k/N)$, $k = 0, 1, \ldots, N - 1$, correspond to a periodic sequence $x_p(n)$ of period N, where $x_p(n)$ is an aliased version of $x(n)$, as indicated by the relation in (1.3.50),

$$x_p(n) = \sum_{l=-\infty}^{\infty} x(n - lN) \tag{1.3.61}$$

When the sequence $x(n)$ has a finite duration of length $L \leq N$, then $x_p(n)$ is simply a periodic repetition of $x(n)$, where $x_p(n)$ over a single period is given as

$$x_p(n) = \begin{cases} x(n), & 0 \leq n \leq L - 1 \\ 0, & L \leq n \leq N - 1 \end{cases} \tag{1.3.62}$$

Consequently, the frequency samples $X(2\pi k/N)$, $k = 0, 1, \ldots, N - 1$ uniquely represent the finite-duration sequence $x(n)$. Since $x(n) \equiv x_p(n)$ over a single period (padded by $N - L$ zeros), the original finite-duration sequence $x(n)$ can be obtained from the frequency samples $X(2\pi k/N)$ by means of the formula in (1.3.54).

In summary, a finite-duration sequence $x(n)$ of length L [i.e., $x(n) = 0$ for $n < 0$ and $n \geq L$] has a Fourier transform

$$X(\omega) = \sum_{n=0}^{L-1} x(n)e^{-j\omega n}, \qquad 0 \leq \omega \leq 2\pi \tag{1.3.63}$$

where the upper and lower indices in the summation reflect the fact that $x(n) = 0$ outside the range $0 \leq n \leq L - 1$. When we sample $X(\omega)$ at equally spaced frequencies $\omega_k = 2\pi k/N$, $k = 0, 1, 2, \ldots, N - 1$, where $N \geq L$, the resulting samples are

$$\begin{aligned} X(k) \equiv X\left(\frac{2\pi k}{N}\right) &= \sum_{n=0}^{L-1} x(n)e^{-j2\pi kn/N} \\ X(k) &= \sum_{n=0}^{N-1} x(n)e^{-j2\pi kn/N}, \qquad k = 0, 1, 2, \ldots, N - 1 \end{aligned} \tag{1.3.64}$$

where for convenience, the upper index in the sum has been increased from $L - 1$ to $N - 1$ since $x(n) = 0$ for $n \geq L$.

The relation in (1.3.64) is a formula for transforming a sequence $\{x(n)\}$ of length $L \leq N$ into a sequence of frequency samples $X(k)$ of length N. Since the frequency samples are obtained by evaluating the Fourier transform $X(\omega)$ at a set of N (equally spaced) discrete frequencies, the relation in (1.3.64) is called the *discrete Fourier transform* (DFT) of $x(n)$. In turn, the relation given by (1.3.54), which allows us to recover the sequence $x(n)$ from the frequency samples,

$$x(n) = \frac{1}{N}\sum_{k=0}^{N-1} X(k)e^{j2\pi kn/N}, \qquad n = 0, 1, \ldots, N-1 \qquad (1.3.65)$$

is called the *inverse DFT* (IDFT). Clearly, when $x(n)$ has length $L \le N$, the N-point IDFT will yield $x(n) = 0$ for $L \le n \le N - 1$. To summarize, the formulas for the DFT and IDFT are:

DFT	$X(k) = \sum_{n=0}^{N-1} x(n)e^{-j2\pi kn/N}, \qquad k = 0, 1, 2, \ldots, N-1$	(1.3.64)
IDFT	$x(n) = \frac{1}{N}\sum_{k=0}^{N-1} X(k)e^{j2\pi kn/N}, \qquad n = 0, 1, 2, \ldots, N-1$	(1.3.65)

EXAMPLE 1.3.4

A finite-duration sequence of length L is given as

$$x(n) = \begin{cases} 1, & 0 \le n \le L-1 \\ 0, & \text{otherwise} \end{cases}$$

Determine the N-point DFT of this sequence for $N \ge L$.

Solution: The Fourier transform of this sequence is

$$X(\omega) = \sum_{n=0}^{L-1} x(n)e^{-j\omega n}$$

$$= \sum_{n=0}^{L-1} e^{-j\omega n} = \frac{1 - e^{-j\omega L}}{1 - e^{-j\omega}} = \frac{\sin(\omega L/2)}{\sin(\omega/2)} e^{-j\omega(L-1)/2}$$

The magnitude and phase of $X(\omega)$ are illustrated in Fig. 1.21 for $L = 10$. The N-point DFT of $x(n)$ is simply $X(\omega)$ evaluated at the set of N equally spaced frequencies $\omega_k = 2\pi k/N$, $k = 0, 1, \ldots, N-1$. Hence

$$X(k) = \frac{1 - e^{-j2\pi kL/N}}{1 - e^{-j2\pi k/N}}, \qquad k = 0, 1, \ldots, N-1$$

$$= \frac{\sin(\pi kL/N)}{\sin(\pi k/N)} e^{-j\pi k(L-1)/N}$$

If N is selected such that $N = L$, the DFT becomes

$$X(k) = \begin{cases} L, & k = 0 \\ 0, & k = 1, 2, \ldots, L-1 \end{cases}$$

Thus there is only one nonzero value in the DFT. This is apparent from observation of $X(\omega)$, since $X(\omega) = 0$ at the frequencies $\omega_k = 2\pi k/L$, $k \neq$

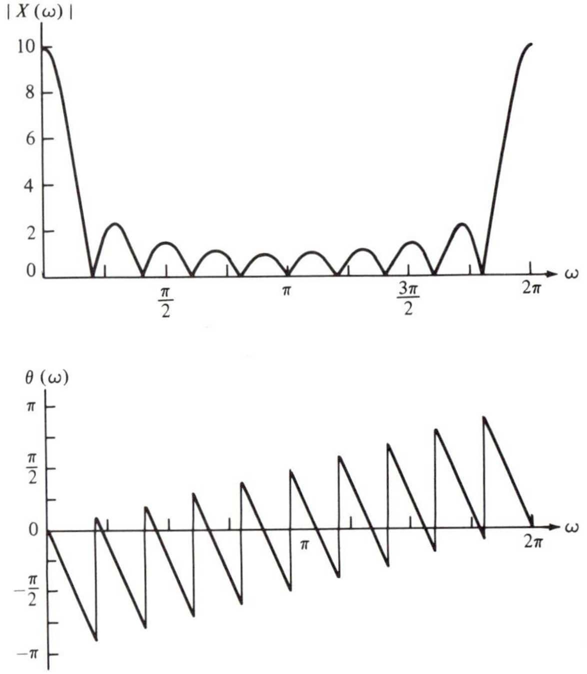

FIGURE 1.21 Magnitude and phase characteristics of the Fourier transform for signal in Example 1.3.4.

0. The reader should verify that $x(n)$ can be recovered from $X(k)$ by performing an L-point IDFT.

Although the L-point DFT is sufficient to represent uniquely the sequence $x(n)$ in the frequency domain, it is apparent that it does not provide sufficient resolution to yield a good picture of the spectral characteristics of $x(n)$. If we wish to have better resolution, we must evaluate (interpolate) $X(\omega)$ at closer spaced frequencies, say $\omega_k = 2\pi k/N$, where $N > L$. In effect, we may view this computation as expanding the size of the sequence from L points to N points by appending $N - L$ zeros to the sequence $x(n)$. This is usually called *zero padding* the sequence $x(n)$. Thus the N-point DFT provides higher resolution than the L-point DFT.

Figure 1.22 provides a plot of the N-point DFT, in magnitude and phase, for $L = 10$, $N = 50$, and $N = 100$. Now the spectral characteristics of the sequence are more clearly evident, as one will conclude by comparing these spectra to the continuous spectrum $X(\omega)$.

It is instructive to view the DFT and IDFT as linear transformations on sequences $x(n)$ and $X(k)$, respectively. Let us define an N-point vector $\mathbf{x}_N$ of the signal sequence $x(n)$, $n = 0, 1, \ldots, N - 1$, an N-point vector $\mathbf{X}_N$ of frequency samples, and an $N \times N$ matrix $\mathbf{W}_N$ as

$$\mathbf{x}_N = \begin{bmatrix} x(0) \\ x(1) \\ \vdots \\ x(N-1) \end{bmatrix}, \quad \mathbf{X}_N = \begin{bmatrix} X(0) \\ X(1) \\ \vdots \\ X(N-1) \end{bmatrix}$$

$$\mathbf{W}_N = \begin{bmatrix} 1 & 1 & 1 & \cdots & 1 \\ 1 & W_N & W_N^2 & \cdots & W_N^{N-1} \\ & W_N^2 & W_N^4 & \cdots & W_N^{2(N-1)} \\ \vdots & \vdots & \vdots & \vdots & \vdots \\ 1 & W_N^{N-1} & W_N^{2(N-1)} & \cdots & W_N^{(N-1)(N-1)} \end{bmatrix} \tag{1.3.66}$$

where, by definition,

$$W_N = e^{-j2\pi/N}$$

which is an Nth root of unity.

With these definitions, the N-point DFT may be expressed in matrix form as

$$\mathbf{X}_N = \mathbf{W}_N \mathbf{x}_N \tag{1.3.67}$$

where $\mathbf{W}_N$ is the matrix of the linear transformation. We observe that $\mathbf{W}_N$ is a symmetric matrix. If we assume that the inverse of $\mathbf{W}_N$ exists, (1.3.67) can be inverted by premultiplying both sides by $\mathbf{W}_N^{-1}$. Thus we obtain

$$\mathbf{x}_N = \mathbf{W}_N^{-1} \mathbf{X}_N \tag{1.3.68}$$

But this is just an expression for the IDFT.

In fact, the IDFT as given by (1.3.65) may be expressed in matrix form as

$$\mathbf{x}_N = \frac{1}{N} \mathbf{W}_N^* \mathbf{X}_N \tag{1.3.69}$$

where $\mathbf{W}_N^*$ denotes the complex conjugate of the matrix $\mathbf{W}_N$. Comparison of (1.3.68) with (1.3.69) leads us to conclude that

$$\mathbf{W}_N^{-1} = \frac{1}{N} \mathbf{W}_N^* \tag{1.3.70}$$

which, in turn, implies that

$$W_N W_N^* = N I_N \tag{1.3.71}$$

where I_N is an $N \times N$ identity matrix. Therefore, the matrix W_N in the transformation is an orthogonal matrix. Furthermore, its inverse exists and is given as W_N^*/N. Of course, the existence of the inverse of W_N was established from our derivation of the IDFT.

The DFT and IDFT play a very important role in many digital signal-processing applications, such as frequency analysis (spectrum analysis) of

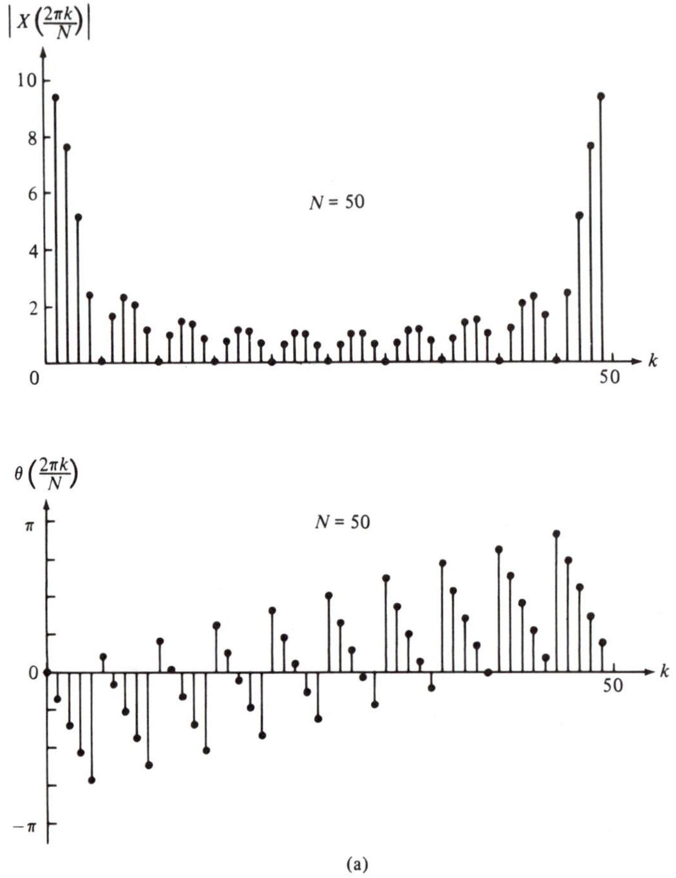

FIGURE 1.22 Magnitude and phase of an N-point DFT in Example 4.5.4: (a) $L = 10$, $N = 50$; (b) $L = 10$, $N = 100$.

signals, power spectrum estimation, and linear filtering. The importance of the DFT and IDFT in such practical applications is due to a large extent on the existence of computationally efficient algorithms, known collectively as fast Fourier transform (FFT) algorithms, for computing the DFT and IDFT.

1.4 LINEAR FILTERING METHODS BASED ON THE DFT

In Section 1.3.4 we defined the discrete Fourier transform (DFT) as the sampled version of the Fourier transform $X(\omega)$ for a finite-duration sequence $x(n)$. The sampling is performed at N equally spaced frequencies $\omega_k = 2\pi k/N$, $k = 0, 1, \ldots, N - 1$, yielding the result

$$X(k) \equiv X(\omega)\big|_{\omega_k = 2\pi k/N}, \qquad k = 0, 1, \ldots, N - 1 \tag{1.4.1}$$

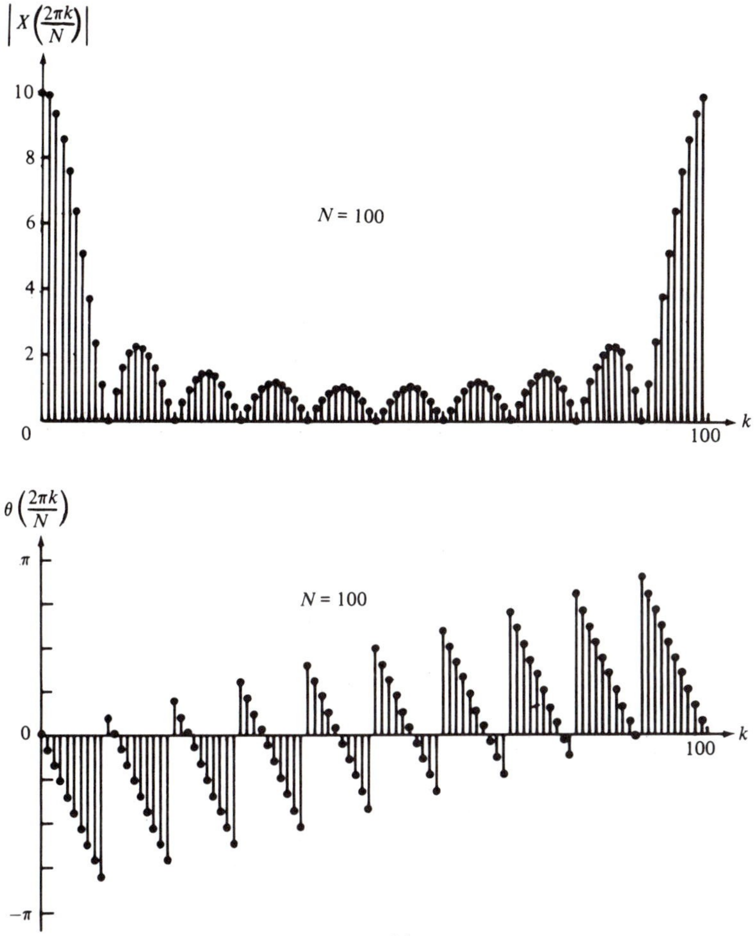

(b)

We demonstrated that the set of N complex numbers $X(k)$ provides a frequency-domain representation that uniquely characterizes a finite-duration sequence $x(n)$ of length $L \leq N$. In other words, if the DFT of $x(n)$ is

$$X(k) = \sum_{n=0}^{N-1} x(n)e^{-j2\pi kn/N}, \qquad k = 0, 1, \ldots, N-1 \tag{1.4.2}$$

the sequence $x(n)$ can be recovered via the inverse DFT (IDFT),

$$x(n) = \frac{1}{N}\sum_{k=0}^{N-1} X(k)e^{j2\pi kn/N}, \qquad n = 0, 1, \ldots, N-1 \tag{1.4.3}$$

as demonstrated in Section 1.3.4.

Since the DFT provides a discrete frequency representation of a finite-duration sequence in the frequency domain, it can be used as a computational tool for linear system analysis and, especially, for linear filtering. We know that when a system with frequency response $H(\omega)$ is excited with an input signal that has a spectrum $X(\omega)$, the output of the system has the spectrum

$$Y(\omega) = X(\omega)H(\omega) \tag{1.4.4}$$

The output sequence $y(n)$ is determined from its spectrum via the inverse Fourier transform

$$y(n) = \frac{1}{2\pi}\int_{-\pi}^{\pi} Y(\omega)e^{j\omega n}\, d\omega \tag{1.4.5}$$

The expressions in (1.4.4) and (1.4.5) provide an alternative means to convolution for determining the output $y(n)$ of a system to a given input sequence $x(n)$. In this approach the input signal $x(n)$ is Fourier transformed to yield $X(\omega)$ and the system is represented by the frequency response $H(\omega)$. Since convolution of $x(n)$ with $h(n)$ is equivalent to multiplication of $X(\omega)$ with $H(\omega)$, we obtain $Y(\omega) = X(\omega)H(\omega)$. Finally, the output sequence $y(n)$ is obtained from its spectrum by computing the inverse Fourier transform given by (1.4.5). The problem encountered with this frequency-domain approach is that $X(\omega)$, $H(\omega)$, and $Y(\omega)$ are functions of the continuous variable ω. As a consequence, the computations implied by (1.4.4) and (1.4.5) cannot be done on a digital computer, since the computer can store and perform computations on quantities only at discrete frequencies.

On the other hand, the DFT does lend itself to computation on a digital computer. In the discussion that follows, we describe how the DFT can be used to perform linear filtering in the frequency domain. In particular, we present a computational procedure that serves as an alternative to time domain convolution. The frequency-domain approach based on the DFT is computationally more efficient than time-domain convolution due to the existence of efficient algorithms for computing the DFT, such as the fast Fourier transform (FFT) algorithms.

1.4.1 Multiplication of Two DFTs and Circular Convolution

Suppose that we have two finite-duration sequences of length N, $x_1(n)$ and $x_2(n)$. Their respective N-point DFTs are

$$X_1(k) = \sum_{n=0}^{N-1} x_1(n)e^{-j2\pi nk/N}, \qquad k = 0, 1, \ldots, N-1 \tag{1.4.6}$$

$$X_2(k) = \sum_{n=0}^{N-1} x_2(n)e^{-j2\pi nk/N}, \qquad k = 0, 1, \ldots, N-1 \tag{1.4.7}$$

If we multiply the two DFTs together, the result is a DFT, say $X_3(k)$, of a sequence $x_3(n)$ of length N. Let us determine the relationship between $x_3(n)$ and the sequences $x_1(n)$ and $x_2(n)$.

We have

$$X_3(k) = X_1(k)X_2(k), \qquad k = 0, 1, \ldots, N-1 \tag{1.4.8}$$

The IDFT of $X_3(k)$ is

$$\begin{aligned} x_3(m) &= \frac{1}{N}\sum_{k=0}^{N-1} X_3(k)e^{j2\pi km/N} \\ &= \frac{1}{N}\sum_{k=0}^{N-1} X_1(k)X_2(k)e^{j2\pi km/N} \end{aligned} \tag{1.4.9}$$

If we substitute for $X_1(k)$ and $X_2(k)$ in (1.4.9), using the DFTs given in (1.4.6) and (1.4.7), we obtain

$$\begin{aligned} x_3(m) &= \frac{1}{N}\sum_{k=0}^{N-1}\left[\sum_{n=0}^{N-1} x_1(n)e^{-j2\pi kn/N}\right]\left[\sum_{l=0}^{N-1} x_2(l)e^{-j2\pi kl/N}\right]e^{j2\pi km/N} \\ &= \frac{1}{N}\sum_{n=0}^{N-1} x_1(n)\sum_{l=0}^{N-1} x_2(l)\left[\sum_{k=0}^{N-1} e^{j2\pi k(m-n-l)/N}\right] \end{aligned} \tag{1.4.10}$$

The inner sum in the brackets in (1.4.10) has the form

$$\sum_{k=0}^{N-1} a_k = \begin{cases} N, & a = 1 \\ \dfrac{1-a^N}{1-a}, & a \neq 1 \end{cases} \tag{1.4.11}$$

where a is defined as

$$a = e^{j2\pi(m-n-l)/N}$$

We observe that $a = 1$ when $m - n - l$ is a multiple of N. On the other hand, $a^N = 1$ for any value of $a \neq 0$. Consequently, (1.4.11) reduces to

$$\sum_{k=0}^{N-1} a_k = \begin{cases} N, & l = m - n + pN = m - n \pmod{N},\ p \text{ an integer} \\ 0, & \text{otherwise} \end{cases} \tag{1.4.12}$$

If we substitute the result in (1.4.12) into (1.4.10) we obtain the desired expression for $x_3(m)$ in the form

$$x_3(m) = \sum_{n=0}^{N-1} x_1(n)x_2((m-n))_N, \qquad m = 0, 1, \ldots, N-1 \tag{1.4.13}$$

where $x\ ((m))_N$ denotes the sequence $x(m \pmod{N})$.

The expression in (1.4.13) has the form of a convolution sum. However, it is not the ordinary linear convolution, which relates the output sequence $y(n)$ of a linear system to the input sequence $x(n)$ and the impulse response $h(n)$. Instead, the convolution sum in (1.4.13) involves the index $(m - n)$ (mod N) and is called *circular convolution*. Thus we conclude that multiplication of the DFTs of two sequences is equivalent to the circular convolution of the two sequences in the time domain.

The following example illustrates the operations involved in circular convolution.

EXAMPLE 1.4.1

Perform the circular convolution of the following two sequences:

$$x_1(n) = \begin{cases} 2, & n = 0 \\ 1, & n = 1 \\ 2, & n = 2 \\ 1, & n = 3 \end{cases} \qquad x_2(n) = \begin{cases} 1, & n = 0 \\ 2, & n = 1 \\ 3, & n = 2 \\ 4, & n = 3 \end{cases}$$

Solution: Each sequence consists of four nonzero points. For purposes of illustrating the operations involved in circular convolution it is desirable to graph each sequence as points on a circle. Thus the sequences $x_1(n)$ and $x_2(n)$ are graphed as illustrated in Fig. 1.23a. We note that the sequences are graphed in a counterclockwise direction on a circle. This establishes the reference direction in rotating one of the sequences relative to the other.

Now $x_3(m)$ is obtained by circularly convolving $x_1(n)$ with $x_2(n)$ as specified by (1.4.13). Beginning with $m = 0$, we have

$$x_3(0) = \sum_{n=0}^{3} x_1(n)x_2((-n))_4$$

But $x_2((-n))_4$ is simply the sequence $x_2(n)$ folded and graphed on a circle as illustrated in Fig. 1.23b. In other words, the folded sequence is simply $x_2(n)$ graphed in a clockwise direction. Another way to view this folding operation is to note that

$$x_2((0))_4 = x_2(0)$$

$$x_2((-1))_4 = x_2(3)$$

$$x_2((-2))_4 = x_2(2)$$

$$x_3((-3))_4 = x_2(1)$$

which is consistent with the graph in Fig. 1.23b.

The product sequence is obtained by multiplying $x_1(n)$ with $x_2((-n))_4$, point by point. This sequence is also illustrated in Fig. 1.23b. Finally, we sum the values in the product sequence to obtain

$$x_3(0) = 14$$

For $m = 1$, we have

$$x_3(1) = \sum_{n=0}^{3} x_1(n)x_2((1 - n))_4$$

It is easily verified that $x_2((1 - n))_4$ is simply the sequence $x_2((-n))_4$ rotated counterclockwise by one unit in time as illustrated in Fig. 1.23c. This rotated sequence multiplies $x_1(n)$ to yield the product sequence, also

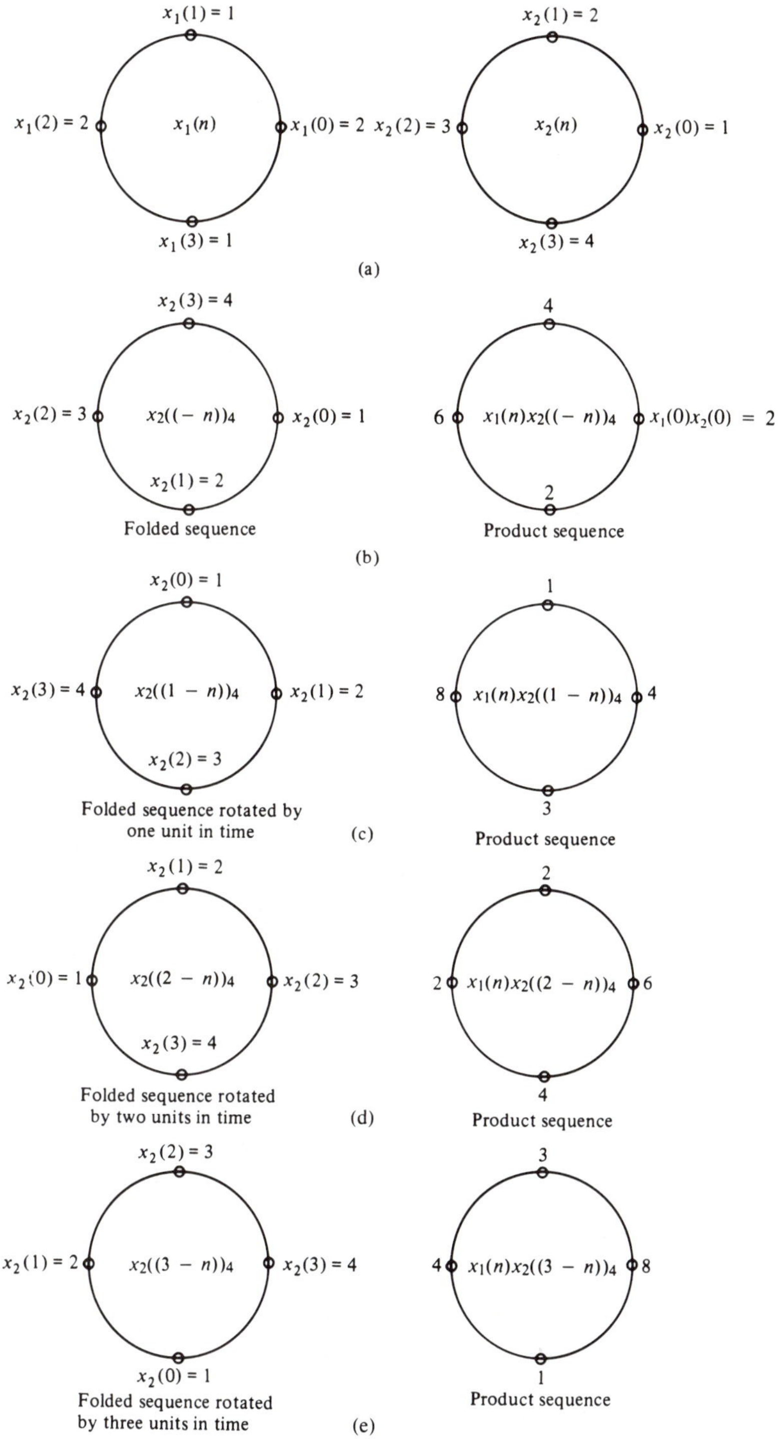

FIGURE 1.23 Circular convolution of two sequences.

illustrated in Fig. 1.23(d). Finally, we sum the values in the product sequence to obtain $x_3(1)$. Thus

$$x_3(1) = 16$$

For $m = 2$ we have

$$x_3(2) = \sum_{n=0}^{3} x_1(n)x_2((2 - n))_4$$

Now $x_2((2 - n))_4$ is the folded sequence in Fig. 1.23b rotated two units of time in the counterclockwise direction. The resultant sequence is illustrated in Fig. 1.23d along with the product sequence $x_1(n)x_2((2 - n))_4$. By summing the four terms in the product sequence, we obtain

$$x_3(2) = 14$$

For $m = 3$ we have

$$x_3(3) = \sum_{n=0}^{3} x_1(n)x_2((3 - n))_4$$

The folded sequence $x_2((-n))_4$ is now rotated by three units in time to yield $x_2((3 - n))_4$ and the resultant sequence is multiplied by $x_1(n)$ to yield the product sequence as illustrated in Fig. 1.23e. The sum of the values in the product sequence is

$$x_3(3) = 16$$

We observe that if the computation above is continued beyond $m = 3$, we simply repeat the sequence of four values obtained above. Therefore, the circular convolution of the two sequences $x_1(n)$ and $x_2(n)$ yields the sequence

$$x_2(n) = \begin{cases} 14, & n = 0 \\ 16, & n = 1 \\ 14, & n = 2 \\ 16, & n = 3 \end{cases}$$

The reader may easily show that this same result for $x_3(n)$ is obtained by computing the 4-point DFTs of $x_1(n)$ and $x_2(n)$, multiplying the 4-point DFTs to obtain $X_3(k) = X_1(k)X_2(k)$, $k = 0, 1, 2, 3$, and then computing the 4-point IDFT.

From the example above, we observe that circular convolution involves basically the same four steps as the ordinary *linear convolution: folding* one sequence, *shifting* the folded sequence, *multiplying* the two sequences to obtain a product sequence, and finally, *summing* the values of the product sequence. The basic difference between these two types of convolutions is that, in circular convolution, the folding and shifting (rotating) operations are performed in a circular fashion by computing the index of one of the sequences modulo N. In linear convolution, there is no modulo N operation.

The reader may easily show from our previous development that either one of the two sequences may be folded and rotated without changing the result of the circular convolution. Thus

$$x_3(m) = \sum_{n=0}^{N-1} x_2(n)x_1((m - n))_N \qquad m = 0, 1, \ldots, N - 1 \qquad (1.4.14)$$

1.4.2 Use of the DFT in Linear Filtering

In the preceding section it was demonstrated that the product of two DFTs is equivalent to the circular convolution of the corresponding time-domain sequences. Unfortunately, circular convolution is of no use to us if our objective is to determine the output of a linear filter to a given input sequence. In this case we seek a frequency-domain methodology that is equivalent to linear convolution.

Suppose that we have a finite-duration sequence $x(n)$ of length L which excites an FIR filter of length M. Without loss of generality, let

$$x(n) = 0, \qquad n < 0 \text{ and } n \geq L$$

$$h(n) = 0, \qquad n < 0 \text{ and } n \geq M$$

where $h(n)$ is the impulse response of the FIR filter.

The output sequence $y(n)$ of the FIR filter may be expressed in the time domain as the convolution of $x(n)$ and $h(n)$,

$$y(n) = \sum_{k=0}^{M-1} h(k)x(n - k) \qquad (1.4.15)$$

Since $h(n)$ and $x(n)$ are finite-duration sequences, their convolution is also finite in duration. In fact, the duration of $y(n)$ is $L + M - 1$.

The frequency-domain equivalent to (1.4.15) is

$$Y(\omega) = X(\omega)H(\omega) \qquad (1.4.16)$$

If the sequence $y(n)$ is to be represented uniquely in the frequency domain by samples of its spectrum $Y(\omega)$ at a set of discrete frequencies, the number of distinct samples must equal or exceed $L + M - 1$. Therefore, a DFT of size $N \geq L + M - 1$ is required to represent $y(n)$ in the frequency domain.

Now if

$$Y(k) \equiv Y(\omega)|_{\omega=2\pi k/N}, \qquad k = 0, 1, \ldots, N - 1$$

$$= X(\omega)H(\omega)|_{\omega=2\pi k/N}, \qquad k = 0, 1, \ldots, N - 1$$

then

$$Y(k) = X(k)H(k), \qquad k = 0, 1, \ldots, N - 1 \qquad (1.4.17)$$

where $X(k)$ and $H(k)$ are the N-point DFTs of the corresponding sequences $x(n)$ and $h(n)$, respectively. Since the sequences $x(n)$ and $h(n)$ have a duration less than N, we simply pad these sequences with zeros to increase their length to N. This increase in the size of the sequences does not alter their spectra $X(\omega)$ and $H(\omega)$, which are continuous spectra, since the sequences are aperiodic. However, by sampling their spectra at N equally spaced points in frequency (computing the N-point DFTs) we have increased the number of samples that represent these sequences in the frequency domain beyond the minimum number (L or M, respectively).

Since the $N = L + M - 1$ point DFT of the output sequence $y(n)$ is sufficient to represent $y(n)$ in the frequency domain, it follows that the multiplication of the N-point DFTs $X(k)$ and $H(k)$, according to (1.4.17), followed by the computation of the N-point IDFT will yield the sequence $y(n)$. In turn, this implies that the N-point circular convolution of $x(n)$ with $h(n)$ must be equivalent to the linear convolution of $x(n)$ with $h(n)$. In other words, by increasing the length of the sequences $x(n)$ and $h(n)$ to N points (by appending zeros), and then circularly convolving the resulting sequences, we obtain the same result as would be obtained with linear convolution. Thus, with zero padding, the DFT can be used to perform linear filtering.

The following example illustrates the methodology in the use of the DFT in linear filtering.

EXAMPLE 1.4.2

By means of the DFT and IDFT, determine the response of the FIR filter with impulse response

$$h(n) = \begin{cases} 1, & n = 0 \\ 2, & n = 1 \\ 3, & n = 2 \end{cases}$$

to the input sequence

$$x(n) = \begin{cases} 1, & n = 0 \\ 2, & n = 1 \\ 2, & n = 2 \\ 1, & n = 3 \end{cases}$$

Solution: The input sequence has length $L = 4$ and the impulse response has length $M = 3$. Linear convolution of these two sequences produces a sequence of length $N = 6$. Consequently, the size of the DFTs must be at least six. Hence the two sequences become

$$h(n) = \{1, 2, 3, 0, 0, 0\}$$

$$x(n) = \{1, 2, 2, 1, 0, 0\}$$

Computation of the 6-point DFTs yields $H(k)$ and $X(k)$, $k = 0, 1, 2, \ldots, 6$, from which we obtain $Y(k) = H(k)X(k)$. The 6-point IDFT of $Y(k)$ yields

$$y(n) = \{1, 4, 9, 11, 8, 3\}$$

It is important for the reader to understand the aliasing that results in the time domain when the size of the DFTs is smaller than $L + M - 1$. The following example focuses on the aliasing problem, which has been described in Section 1.3.3.

EXAMPLE 1.4.3

Determine the sequence $y(n)$, $n = 0, 1, 2, 3$, that results from the 4-point circular convolution of $h(n)$ and $x(n)$ given in Example 1.4.2 or, equivalently, from the use of the 4-point DFT of $h(n)$ and $x(n)$.

Solution: The 4-point DFTs of $h(n)$ and $x(n)$ are

$$H(k) = 1 + 2e^{-j\pi k/2} + 3e^{-j\pi k}, \qquad k = 0, 1, 2, 3$$

$$X(k) = 1 + 2e^{-j\pi k/2} + 2e^{-j\pi k} + 3e^{-j3\pi k/2}, \qquad k = 0, 1, 2, 3$$

The product of these 4-point DFTs yields $\hat{Y}(k) = H(k)X(k)$, from which we obtain the 4-point IDFT

$$\hat{y}(n) = \{9, 7, 9, 11\}$$

If we compare the result $\hat{y}(n)$ with the sequence $y(n)$ obtained in Example 1.4.2, we note that $\hat{y}(n)$ is an aliased version of $y(n)$, where

$$\hat{y}(n) = \sum_{k=-\infty}^{\infty} y(n + 4k), \qquad 0 \le n \le 3$$

Since $y(n) = 0$ except for $0 \le n \le 5$, we see that

$$\hat{y}(0) = y(0) + y(4) = 9$$

$$\hat{y}(1) = y(1) + y(5) = 7$$

$$\hat{y}(2) = y(2) = 9$$

$$\hat{y}(3) = y(3) = 11$$

Therefore, only the first two points of $y(n)$ are corrupted by the effect of aliasing. This observation has important ramifications in the following section, in which we treat the filtering of long sequences.

1.4.3 Filtering of Long Data Sequences

In practical applications involving linear filtering of signals, the input sequence $x(n)$ is often a very long sequence. This is especially true in some real-time signal processing applications concerned with signal monitoring and analysis. Since linear filtering performed via the DFT involves operations on a block of data, which by necessity must be limited in size due to limited memory of a digital computer, a long input signal sequence must be segmented to fixed-size blocks prior to processing. Since the filtering is linear, successive blocks may be processed one at a time via the DFT and the output blocks are fitted together to form the overall output signal sequence.

Below we describe two methods for linear FIR filtering of a long sequence on a block-by-block basis using the DFT. The input sequence is segmented into blocks and each block is processed via the DFT and IDFT to produce a block of output data. The output blocks are fitted together to form an overall output sequence that is identical to the sequence obtained if the long block has been processed via time-domain convolution.

The two methods to be described are called the *overlap-save method* and the *overlap-add method*. For both methods we assume that the FIR filter has duration M. The input data sequence is segmented into blocks of L points, where, by assumption, $L \gg M$ without loss of generality.

Overlap-Save Method. In this method the size of the input data blocks is $N = L + M - 1$ and the size of the DFTs and IDFT are of length N. Each data block consists of the last $M - 1$ data points of the previous data block followed by L new data points to form a data sequence of length $N = L + M - 1$. An N-point DFT is computed for each data block. The impulse response of the FIR filter is increased in length by appending $L - 1$ zeros and an N-point DFT of the sequence is computed once and stored. The multiplication of the two N-point DFTs $H(k)$ and $X_m(k)$ for the mth block of data yields

$$\hat{Y}_m(k) = H(k)X_m(k), \qquad k = 0, 1, \ldots, N - 1 \tag{1.4.18}$$

Then the N-point IDFT yields the result

$$\hat{\mathbf{Y}}_m(n) = \{\hat{y}_m(0) \quad \hat{y}_m(1) \quad \cdots \quad \hat{y}_m(M-1) \quad \hat{y}_m(M) \quad \cdots \quad \hat{y}_m(N-1)\} \tag{1.4.19}$$

Since the data record is of length N, the first $M - 1$ points of $y_m(n)$ are corrupted by aliasing and must be discarded. The last L points of $y_m(n)$ are exactly the same as the result from linear convolution, and as a consequence,

$$\hat{y}_m(n) = y_m(n), \qquad n = M, M + 1, \ldots, N - 1 \tag{1.4.20}$$

To avoid loss of data due to aliasing, the last $M - 1$ points of each data record are saved and these points become the first $M - 1$ data points of the subsequent record, as indicated above. To begin the processing, the first $M - 1$ points of the first record are set to zero. Thus the blocks of data sequences are

$$x_1(n) = \{\underbrace{0, 0, \ldots, 0}_{M-1 \text{ points}}, x(0), x(1), \ldots, x(L-1)\} \tag{1.4.21}$$

$$x_2(n) = \{\underbrace{x(L-M+1), \ldots, x(L-1)}_{\substack{M-1 \text{ data points} \\ \text{from } x_1(n)}}, \underbrace{x(L), \ldots, x(2L-1)}_{L \text{ new data points}}\} \tag{1.4.22}$$

$$x_3(n) = \{\underbrace{x(2L-M+1), \ldots, x(2L-1)}_{\substack{M-1 \text{ data points} \\ \text{from } x_2(n)}}, \underbrace{x(2L), \ldots, x(3L-1)}_{L \text{ new data points}}\} \tag{1.4.23}$$

and so on. The resulting data sequences from the IDFT are given by (1.4.19), where the first $M-1$ points are discarded due to aliasing and the remaining L points constitute the desired result from linear convolution. The segmentation of the input data and the fitting of the output data blocks together to form the output sequence are illustrated graphically in Fig. 1.24.

Overlap-Add Method. In this method the size of the input data block is L points and the size of the DFTs and IDFT is $N = L + M - 1$. To each

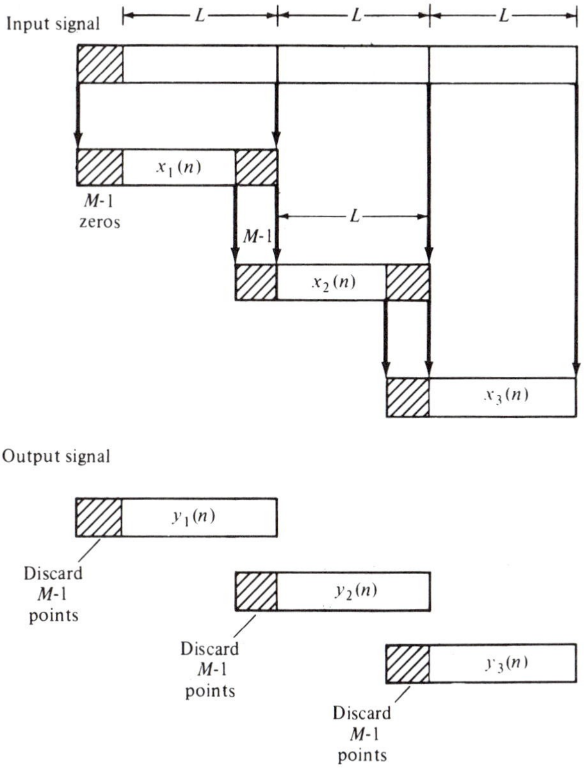

FIGURE 1.24 Linear FIR filtering by the overlap-save method.

data block we append $M - 1$ zeros and compute the N-point DFT. Thus the data blocks may be represented as

$$x_1(n) = \{x(0), x(1), \ldots, x(L-1), \underbrace{0, 0, \ldots, 0}_{M-1 \text{ zeros}}\} \tag{1.4.24}$$

$$x_2(n) = \{x(L), x(L+1), \ldots, x(2L-1), \underbrace{0, 0, \ldots, 0}_{M-1 \text{ zeros}}\} \tag{1.4.25}$$

$$x_3(n) = \{x(2L), \ldots, x(3L-1), \underbrace{0, 0, \ldots, 0}_{M-1 \text{ zeros}}\} \tag{1.4.26}$$

and so on. The two N-point DFTs are multiplied together to form

$$Y_m(k) = H(k)X_m(k), \qquad k = 0, 1, \ldots, N-1 \tag{1.4.27}$$

The IDFT yields data blocks of length N that are free of aliasing since the size of the DFTs and IDFT is $N = L + M - 1$ and the sequences are increased to N points by appending zeros to each block.

Since each data block is terminated with $M - 1$ zeros, the last $M - 1$ points from each output block must be overlapped and added to the first $M - 1$ points of the succeeding block. Hence this method is called the overlap-add method. This overlapping and adding yields the output sequence.

$$\begin{aligned} y(n) = \{&y_1(0), y_1(1), \ldots, y_1(L-1), y_1(L) + y_2(0), \\ &y_1(L+1) + y_2(1), \ldots, y_1(N-1) + y_2(M-1), y_2(M), \ldots\} \end{aligned} \tag{1.4.28}$$

The segmentation of the input data into blocks and the fitting of the output data blocks to form the output sequence are illustrated in Fig. 1.25.

1.5 THE CEPSTRUM

Let us consider a sequence $x(n)$ having a z-transform $X(z)$. We assume that $x(n)$ is a stable sequence so that $X(z)$ converges on the unit circle. The *complex cepstrum* of the sequence $x(n)$ is defined as the sequence $c_x(n)$, which is the inverse z-transform of $C_x(z)$, where

$$C_x(z) = \ln X(z) \tag{1.5.1}$$

The complex cepstrum exists if $C_x(z)$ converges in the annular region $r_1 < |z| < r_2$, where $0 < r_1 < 1$ and $r_2 > 1$. Within this region of convergence, $C_x(z)$ may be represented by the Laurent series

$$C_x(z) = \ln X(z) = \sum_{n=-\infty}^{\infty} c_x(n)z^{-n} \tag{1.5.2}$$

where

$$c_x(n) = \frac{1}{2\pi j} \oint_C \ln X(z) z^{n-1}\, dz \tag{1.5.3}$$

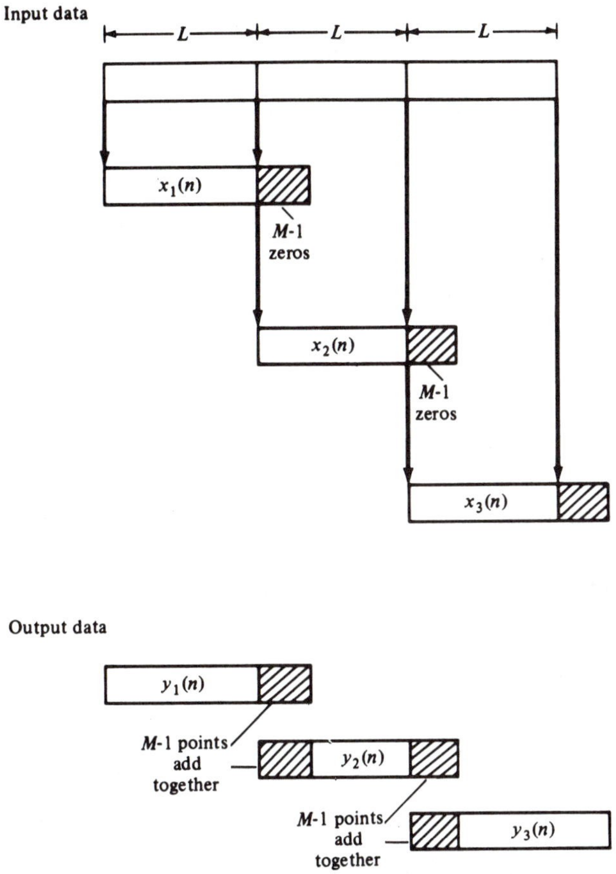

FIGURE 1.25 Linear FIR filtering by the overlap-add method.

C is a closed contour encircling the origin and lies within the region of convergence. Clearly, if $C_x(z)$ can be represented as in (1.5.2), the complex cepstrum sequence $c_x(n)$ is stable. Furthermore, if the complex cepstrum exists, $C_x(z)$ converges on the unit circle, and hence we have

$$C_x(\omega) = \ln X(\omega) = \sum_{n=-\infty}^{\infty} c_x(n)e^{-j\omega n} \tag{1.5.4}$$

where $c_x(n)$ is the sequence obtained from the inverse Fourier transform of $\ln X(\omega)$,

$$c_x(n) = \frac{1}{2\pi}\int_{-\pi}^{\pi} \ln X(\omega)e^{j\omega n}\, d\omega \tag{1.5.5}$$

If we express $X(\omega)$ in terms of its magnitude and phase, say

$$X(\omega) = |X(\omega)|e^{j\theta(\omega)} \tag{1.5.6}$$

then

$$\ln X(\omega) = \ln |X(\omega)| + j\theta(\omega) \tag{1.5.7}$$

By substituting (1.5.7) into (1.5.5) we obtain the complex cepstrum in the form

$$c_x(n) = \frac{1}{2\pi}\int_{-\pi}^{\pi} [\ln |X(\omega)| + j\theta(\omega)]e^{j\omega n}\, d\omega \tag{1.5.8}$$

Clearly, the real and imaginary parts of $c_x(n)$ are the inverse Fourier transforms of $\ln |X(\omega)|$ and $\theta(\omega)$,

$$\mathrm{Re}[c_x(n)] = \frac{1}{2\pi}\int_{-\pi}^{\pi} \ln |X(\omega)|e^{j\omega n}\, d\omega \tag{1.5.9}$$

$$\mathrm{Im}[c_x(n)] = \frac{1}{2\pi}\int_{-\pi}^{\pi} \theta(\omega)e^{j\omega n}\, d\omega \tag{1.5.10}$$

In some applications, such as speech signal processing, only the real part of the complex cepstrum is computed. In such a case the phase of $X(\omega)$ is ignored. Therefore, the sequence $x(n)$ cannot be recovered from $\mathrm{Re}[c_x(n)]$ [i.e., the transformation from $x(n)$ to $\mathrm{Re}[c_x(n)]$ is not invertible].

Homomorphic Deconvolution. The cepstrum is often a useful tool for performing deconvolution. To elaborate, let us suppose that $y(n)$ is the output sequence of a linear time-invariant system that is excited by the input sequence $x(n)$. Then

$$Y(z) = X(z)H(z) \tag{1.5.11}$$

where $H(z)$ is the system function. The logarithm of $Y(z)$ is

$$\begin{aligned} C_y(z) &= \ln Y(z) \\ &= \ln X(z) + \ln H(z) \\ &= C_x(z) + C_h(z) \end{aligned} \tag{1.5.12}$$

Consequently, the complex cepstrum of the output sequence $y(n)$ is expressed as the sum of the cepstrum of $x(n)$ and $h(n)$,

$$c_y(n) = c_x(n) + c_h(n) \tag{1.5.13}$$

Thus we observe that convolution of the two sequences in the time domain corresponds to summation of the cepstrum sequences in the cepstral domain. The system for performing these transformations is called a *homomorphic system* and is illustrated in Fig. 1.26.

In some applications such as seismic signal processing and speech signal processing, the characteristics of the cepstral sequences $c_x(n)$ and $c_h(n)$ are sufficiently different so that they can be separated in the cepstral domain. Specifically, suppose that $c_h(n)$ has its main components (main energy) in the vicinity of small values of n, whereas $c_x(n)$ has its components concen-

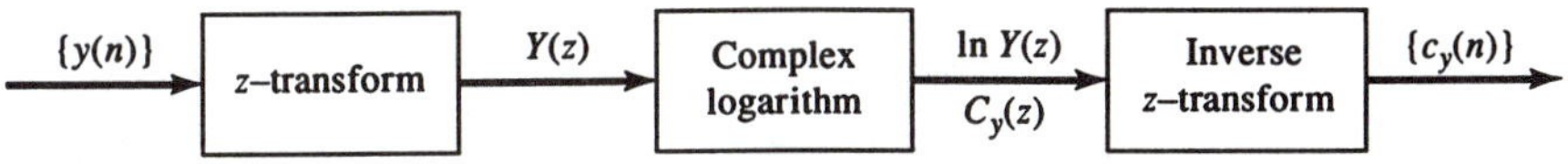

FIGURE 1.26 Homomorphic system for obtaining the cepstrum $\{c_y(n)\}$ of the sequence $\{y(n)\}$.

trated at large values of n. We may say that $c_h(n)$ is "lowpass" and $c_x(n)$ is "highpass." Then we can separate $c_h(n)$ from $c_x(n)$ by use of appropriate "lowpass" and "highpass windows," as illustrated in Fig. 1.27. Thus

$$\hat{c}_h(n) = c_y(n)w_{lp}(n) \tag{1.5.14}$$

and

$$\hat{c}_x(n) = c_y(n)w_{hp}(n) \tag{1.5.15}$$

where

$$\begin{aligned} w_{lp}(n) &= \begin{cases} 1, & |n| \leq N_1 \\ 0, & \text{otherwise} \end{cases} \\ w_{hp}(n) &= \begin{cases} 0, & |n| \leq N_1 \\ 1, & |n| > N_1 \end{cases} \end{aligned} \tag{1.5.16}$$

Once we have separated the cepstrum sequences $\hat{c}_h(n)$ and $\hat{c}_x(n)$ by windowing, the sequences $\hat{x}(n)$ and $\hat{h}(n)$ are obtained by passing $\hat{c}_h(n)$ and $\hat{c}_x(n)$ through the inverse homomorphic system, shown in Fig. 1.28.

In practice, a digital computer would be used to compute the cepstrum of the sequence $y(n)$, perform the windowing functions, and implement the inverse homomorphic system shown in Fig. 1.28. The DFT is the computationally efficient tool (implemented via the fast Fourier transform algorithm)

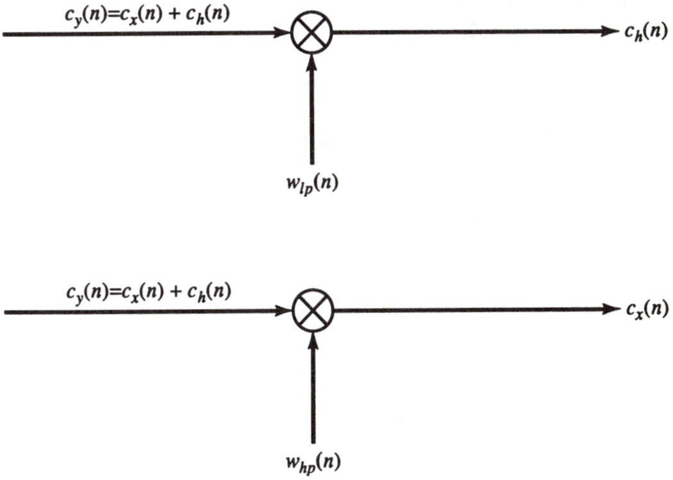

FIGURE 1.27 Separating the two cepstral components by "lowpass" and "highpass" windows.

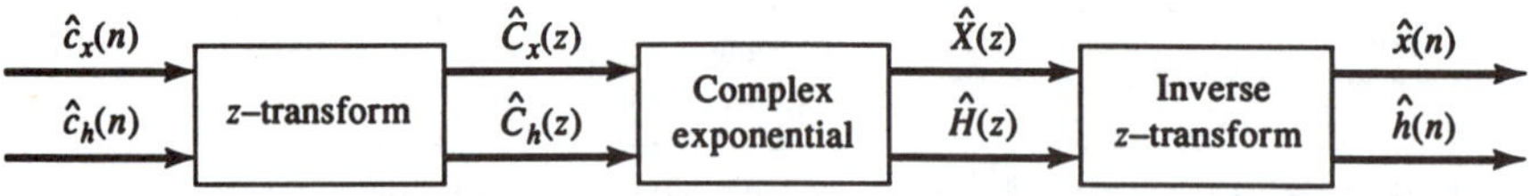

FIGURE 1.28 Inverse homomorphic system for recovering the sequences $\{\hat{x}(n)\}$ and $\{\hat{h}(n)\}$ from the corresponding cepstra.

for performing the Fourier transform and inverse Fourier transform operations. Hence, in place of the z-transform and inverse z-transform indicated in Figs. 1.26 and 1.28, we substitute the Fourier transform and inverse Fourier transform, respectively. We will encounter the complex cepstrum and its generalizations in our treatment of higher-order spectral methods in Chapter 9.

1.6 SUMMARY AND REFERENCES

In this chapter we have reviewed several topics that serve as background material for the advanced topics covered in subsequent chapters. Our coverage of the DFT and its use in linear filtering serves as background for the material covered in Chapter 2. The treatment of sampling of signals serves as background for our discussion of multirate signal processing in Chapter 3. The complex cepstrum is generally used in several signal analysis and synthesis applications and serves as background for the more advanced signal analysis methods treated in Chaper 9, which are based on higher-order spectral methods. Finally, the introductory material in Sections 1.1 and 1.2 serves as general background to the topics covered in Chapters 2 through 9.

There are several introductory-level textbooks that provide sufficient background for the topics treated in this book. In particular, we cite the books by DeFatta et al. (1988), Oppenheim and Schafer (1989), Proakis and Manolakis (1992), and Roberts and Mullis (1987).

PROBLEMS

1.1 An analog signal contains frequencies up to 10 kHz.
- **(a)** What range of sampling frequencies will allow exact reconstruction of this signal from its samples?
- **(b)** Suppose that we sample this signal with a sampling frequency $F_s = 8$ kHz. Determine the frequency of the discrete-time signal corresponding to the analog signal frequency $F_1 = 5$ kHz.
- **(c)** Repeat part (b) for a frequency $F_2 = 9$ kHz.

1.2 Two discrete-time systems H_1 and H_2 are connected in cascade, with H_2 following H_1, to form a new system H. Prove or disprove the following statements.

(a) If H_1 and H_2 are linear, H is linear.
(b) If H_1 and H_2 are time invariant, H is time-invariant.
(c) If H_1 and H_2 are LTI, the cascade of H_1 and H_2 yields the same system as the cascade of H_2 and H_1.

1.3 Compute the convolution $y(n) = x(n) * h(n)$, where $x(n) = a^n u(n)$ and $h(n) = b^n u(n)$ when $a \neq b$ and when $a = b$.

1.4 Determine the impulse response and the unit step response of the system described by the difference equations:
(a) $y(n) = 0.6y(n-1) - 0.08y(n-2) + x(n)$
(b) $y(n) = 0.7y(n-1) - 0.1y(n-2) + 2x(n) - x(n-2)$

1.5 Determine the response of the system characterized by the impulse response

$$h(n) = (\tfrac{1}{2})^n u(n)$$

when the input $x(n)$ is

(a) $x(n) = 2^n u(n)$
(b) $x(n) = u(-n)$

1.6 Determine the response $y(n)$, $n \geq 0$, of the system described by the second-order difference equation

$$y(n) - 4y(n-1) + 4y(n-2) = x(n) - x(n-1)$$

when the input is $x(n) = (-1)^n u(n)$ and the initial conditions are $y(-1) = y(-2) = 0$.

1.7 Determine the causal signal $x(n)$ having the z-transform

$$X(z) = \frac{1}{(1 - 2z^{-1})(1 - z^{-1})^2}$$

1.8 Let $x(n)$ be a sequence with z-transform $X(z)$. Determine, in terms of $X(z)$, the z-transforms of the following signals.

(a) $$x_1(n) = \begin{cases} x\left(\dfrac{n}{2}\right), & n \text{ even} \\ 0, & n \text{ odd} \end{cases}$$

(b) $x_2(n) = x(2n)$

1.9 Determine the stability region in the a_1a_2-plane for the causal system with system function

$$H(z) = \frac{1}{1 + a_1 z^{-1} + a_2 z^{-2}}$$

1.10 An LTI filter has an impulse response $h(n)$ that is real valued, even, and has a finite duration of length $2N + 1$. Show that if $z_1 = r_1 e^{j\omega_1}$ is a zero of the filter, $(1/r_1)e^{j\omega_1}$ is also a zero.

1.11 Determine the periodic sequences $x(n)$, with fundamental period $N = 8$, if their Fourier coefficients are given by

(a) $c_k = \cos \frac{k\pi}{4} + \sin \frac{3k\pi}{4}$

(b) $c_k = \begin{cases} \sin \frac{k\pi}{3}, & 0 \le k \le 6 \\ 0, & k = 7 \end{cases}$

1.12 **(a)** Show that the Fourier transform of the signal sequence

$$x(n) = \begin{cases} 1, & -M \le n \le M \\ 0, & \text{otherwise} \end{cases}$$

is

$$X(\omega) = 1 + 2 \sum_{n=1}^{M} \cos \omega n$$

(b) By expressing $x(n)$ as a sum of a causal sequence and an anticausal sequence and evaluating the Fourier transform of each sequence, show that $X(\omega)$ can also be expressed as

$$X(\omega) = \frac{\sin(M + \frac{1}{2})\omega}{\sin(\omega/2)}$$

1.13 Determine the N-point DFTs of the sequences

(a) $x(n) = e^{j2\pi n k_0/N}, \quad -\infty < n < \infty$

(b) $x(n) = \cos \frac{2\pi}{N} n k_0, \quad -\infty < n < \infty$

1.14 Consider the system described by the difference equation

$$y(n) = \tfrac{1}{4}y(n - 1) + x(n) + \tfrac{1}{2}x(n - 1)$$

(a) Determine the impulse response of the system.
(b) Determine its frequency response.
(c) Determine its response to the input sequence

$$x(n) = \cos\left(\frac{\pi}{2}n + \frac{\pi}{4}\right), \qquad -\infty < n < \infty$$

1.15 Determine the coefficients $h(n)$ of a highpass linear-phase FIR filter of length $M = 4$ that has an antisymmetric unit sample response and a frequency response that satisfies the conditions

$$H_r\left(\frac{\pi}{4}\right) = \frac{1}{2}, \qquad H_r\left(\frac{3\pi}{4}\right) = 1$$

1.16 Consider an ideal lowpass filter with impulse response $h(n)$ and frequency response

$$H(\omega) = \begin{cases} 1, & |\omega| \le \omega_c \\ 0, & \omega_c < |\omega| \le \pi \end{cases}$$

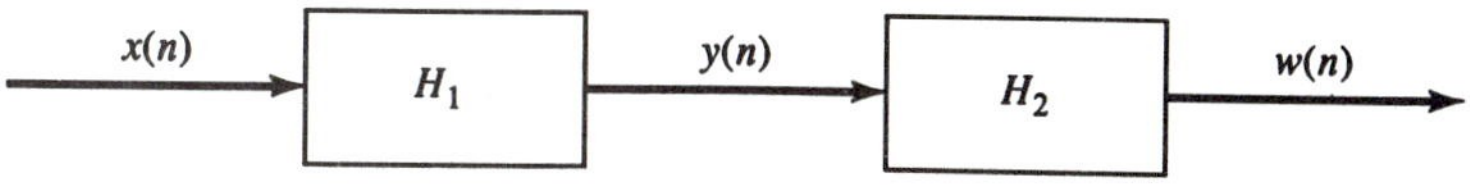

FIGURE P1.18

Determine the frequency response of the filter with impulse response

$$g(n) = \begin{cases} h\left(\frac{n}{2}\right), & n \text{ even} \\ 0, & n \text{ odd} \end{cases}$$

1.17 Consider a system with a real-valued impulse response $h(n)$ and frequency response $H(\omega) = |H(\omega)|e^{j\Theta(\omega)}$. The quantity

$$D = \sum_{n=-\infty}^{\infty} n^2h^2(n)$$

provides a measure of the "effective duration" of $h(n)$.

(a) Express D in terms of $H(\omega)$.

(b) Show that D is minimized for $\Theta(\omega) = 0$.

1.18 Two LTI systems H_1 and H_2 are connected in cascade as shown in Fig. P1.18. The system H_1 is characterized by the difference equation

$$y(n) = \tfrac{7}{12}y(n-1) - \tfrac{1}{12}y(n-2) + x(n-1) - \tfrac{1}{2}x(n-2)$$

(a) Determine the system function $H_2(z)$ so that $w(n) = x(n)$. Is the inverse system H_2 causal?

(b) Determine the system function $H_2(z)$ so that $w(n) = x(n-1)$. Is the system H_2 causal? Explain.

(c) Determine the difference equations for the systems in parts (a) and (b).

1.19 Consider a sequence of samples $x(n)$, $0 \le n \le N$, from a wide-sense stationary, zero-mean Gausian random process. An estimate of the autocorrelation sequence is

$$r(k) = \frac{1}{N - |k|} \sum_{n=0}^{N} x(n)x^*(n-k)$$

Determine the mean and variance of $r(k)$.

1.20 The impulse response of an LTI system is given by $h(n) = \delta(n) - \frac{1}{4}\,\delta(n - k_0)$. To determine the impulse response $g(n)$ of the inverse system, an engineer computes the N-point DFT $H(k)$ for $N = 4k_0$ of $h(n)$ and then defines $g(n)$ as the inverse DFT $G(k) = 1/H(k)$, $k = 0, 1, \ldots, N-1$. Determine $g(n)$ and the convolution $h(n) * g(n)$ and comment on whether the system with impulse response $g(n)$ is the inverse of the system with impulse response $h(n)$.

CHAPTER 2

ALGORITHMS FOR CONVOLUTION AND DFT

Techniques for computing the discrete Fourier transform and discrete convolutions have long been central to the science of digital signal processing. The fast Fourier transform is a fundamental algorithm for computing the discrete Fourier transform, well known since 1965. It is also widely used as a step in computing discrete convolutions.

More recently, other algorithms have been developed for computing both convolutions and discrete Fourier transforms. Although these algorithms are not of the overwhelming importance of the FFT, the fundamentally new principles on which they are based should be understood. In this chapter we use the theory of polynomial congruences to explain some of the new convolution algorithms, and we use elementary number theory to explain Winograd's Fourier transform algorithm. We also explain number-theoretic transforms based on computation in a finite ring, which can be used to compute convolutions and correlations. We discuss a method of writing efficient computer programs for some common digital signal-processing algorithms, called the *autogen* technique. Finally, we introduce a significant advanced version of the FFT algorithm called *split-radix* and show how it is synergistic with autogen.

2.1 MODULO POLYNOMIALS

Suppose that $M(u)$ is a given Nth-order polynomial and suppose that the leading coefficient, m_N, is unity.

$$M(u) = u^N + m_{N-1}u^{N-1} + \cdots + m_1 u + m_0 \tag{2.1.1}$$

A polynomial with a leading coefficient of unity is called *monic*.

Now let $P(u)$ by any other polynomial. To avoid a trivial case, assume that the degree of $P(u)$ is not less than the degree of $M(u)$. Then we can

This work was sponsored by the Department of the Air Force

determine two more polynomials, the *quotient* $Q(u)$ and the *remainder* $R(u)$, such that

$$P(u) = Q(u)M(u) + R(u) \tag{2.1.2}$$

where

$$\deg[R(u)] < \deg[M(u)] = N \tag{2.1.3}$$

The restriction on $\deg[R]$ makes $Q(u)$ and $R(u)$ unique. If the degree of $P(u)$ is less than the degree of $M(u)$ then $Q(u) = 0$ and $R(u) = P(u)$. We call $R(u)$ the *residue* of $P(u)$ with respect to the modulus $M(u)$. We also say that $P(u)$ is *congruent* to $R(u)$ modulo $M(u)$. In this regard we can think of $M(u)$ as congruent to zero, and therefore we can subtract any constant multiple or polynomial multiple of $M(u)$ from $P(u)$ and leave the residue $R(u)$ unchanged.

Given $P(u)$ and $M(u)$, there are usually several good ways to find $Q(u)$ and $R(u)$. We can always find both $Q(u)$ and $R(u)$ by polynomial (synthetic) division.

EXAMPLE 2.1.1

Let

$$M(u) = u^2 + 3u + 2 \tag{2.1.4}$$

$$P(u) = u^5 + u^2 \tag{2.1.5}$$

Then

$$
\begin{array}{r|rrrrrr}
 & u^3 & -3u^2 & +7u & -14 & & \\
\hline
u^2 + 3u + 2 & u^5 & & & +u^2 & & \\
 & u^5 & 3u^4 & 2u^3 & & & \\
\cline{2-4}
 & & -3u^4 & -2u^3 & +u^2 & & \\
 & & -3u^4 & -9u^3 & -6u^2 & & \\
\cline{3-5}
 & & & 7u^3 & +7u^2 & & \\
 & & & 7u^3 & +21u^2 & +14u & \\
\cline{4-6}
 & & & & -14u^2 & -14u & \\
 & & & & -14u^2 & -42u & -28 \\
\cline{5-7}
 & & & & & 28u & +28
\end{array}
$$

$$R(u) = 28u + 28 \tag{2.1.6}$$

$$Q(u) = u^3 - 3u^2 + 7u - 14 \tag{2.1.7}$$

But we will generally only be interested in $R(u)$ and we will discard $Q(u)$ or avoid computing it in the first place.

EXAMPLE 2.1.2

Find the residue of $3u^2 + 5u + 2$ with respect to modulus $u^2 + 2u + 1$. If we subtract three times the modulus, we get $-u - 1 = R(u)$.

EXAMPLE 2.1.3

Find the residue of $3u^2 + 5u + 1$ with respect to modulus $u + 1$. If we subtract $3u(u + 1) = 3u^2 + 3u$, we get $2u + 1$. This is not the residue because it is of degree 1, the same as the modulus. If we further subtract $2(u + 1) = 2u + 2$, we get $R(u) = -1$.

Note that if the modulus is of the form $(u - a)$, the residue of $P(u)$ is a constant, and the constant is $R(u) = r_0 = P(u)|_{u=a} = P(a)$.

2.2 CIRCULAR CONVOLUTION AS POLYNOMIAL MULTIPLICATION MOD $u^N - 1$

We are well used to representing sequences by their z-transforms, which are polynomials, and representing the convolution of sequences by a product of z-transforms, which is polynomial multiplication. Let the N-point sequences x_n and h_n have z-transforms $X(z)$ and $H(z)$, respectively. Solely to eliminate the negative exponents, define the u-transform of x_n by

$$X(u) = \sum_n x_n u^n \tag{2.2.1}$$

which is trivially related to its z-transform, and similarly for $H(u)$. The convolution $x_n * h_n$ has the u-transform $Y(u) = X(u)H(u)$.

Let us consider what is meant by

$$\hat{Y}(u) \equiv X(u)H(u) \bmod u^N - 1 \tag{2.2.2}$$

Explicitly, $\hat{Y}(u)$ is congruent to $Y(u)$ modulo $M(u)$, where $M(u) = u^N - 1$. Therefore, $\hat{Y}(u)$ is congruent to a polynomial of degree $2N - 1$,

$$y_0 + y_1 u + y_2 u^2 + \cdots + y_{N-1}u^{N-1} + y_N u^N + \cdots + y_{2N-2}u^{2N-2} + y_{2N-1}u^{2N-1}$$

We have seen in the preceding section that we can manipulate this expression while preserving the congruence. Let us therefore subtract

$$M(u) \sum_{n=N}^{2N-1} y_n u^{n-N}$$

leaving an expression of the form

$$\sum_{n=0}^{N-1} (y_n + y_{n+N})u^n$$

which must still be congruent to $\hat{Y}(u)$. But the degree of this expression is less than the degree of $M(u)$, so we know that it is not just congruent to $\hat{Y}(u)$ but equal to $\hat{Y}(u)$.

It is also equal to the u-transform of the circular convolution of x_n and h_n. We see that the operation of residue reduction modulo $u^N - 1$ accomplishes the circular wraparound that characterizes circular convolution.

Of course, this is, so far, only a mathematical description of circular convolution, not an algorithm for carrying it out. The direct approach to computing $\hat{Y}(u)$ just amounts to computing the circular convolution and hence offers no saving. However, we shall soon see another approach to computing the product of two polynomials modulo a third polynomial, and it will allow us to develop a number of algorithms for circular convolution.

2.3 A CONTINUED FRACTION OF POLYNOMIALS

Suppose that we start with two polynomials, $A_0(u)$ and $A_1(u)$, and we use synthetic division to form quotient and remainder:

$$A_0(u) = Q_1(u)A_1(u) + A_2(u) \tag{2.3.1}$$

and then if $\deg[A_2] \neq 0$, we repeat the process

$$A_1(u) = Q_2(u)A_2(u) + A_3(u) \tag{2.3.2}$$

and again and again,

$$A_2(u) = Q_3(u)A_3(u) + A_4(u)$$

$$A_3(u) = Q_4(u)A_4(u) + A_5(u)$$

$$A_4(u) = Q_5(u)A_5(u) + A_6(u)$$

Because

$$\deg[A_1(u)] > \deg[A_2(u)] > \deg[A_3(u)] \cdots \tag{2.3.3}$$

we must ultimately arrive at a polynomial whose degree is 0 and the process terminates. For example, suppose that A_6 were the first remainder to have degree 0. Then

$$A_4(u) = Q_5(u)A_5(u) + k \tag{2.3.4}$$

Take the ith equation and write it in the form

$$\frac{A_i(u)}{A_{i+1}(u)} = Q_{i+1}(u) + \frac{A_{i+2}(u)}{A_{i+1}(u)} = Q_{i+1}(u) + \frac{1}{A_{i+1}(u)/A_{i+2}(u)} \tag{2.3.5}$$

and plug these equations successively into one another to give

$$\frac{A_0}{A_1} = Q_1 + \cfrac{1}{Q_2 + \cfrac{1}{Q_3 \cdots + \cfrac{1}{Q_5 + \cfrac{1}{k}}}} \tag{2.3.6}$$

Students of electrical engineering may have encountered continued fractions in network synthesis. Here we have in mind a very different application. Define the first *convergent* as

$$\frac{C_1}{D_1} = Q_1 \tag{2.3.7}$$

and explicitly

$$C_1 = Q_1$$

$$D_1 = 1$$

Define the second convergent as

$$\frac{C_2}{D_2} = Q_1 + \frac{1}{Q_2} \tag{2.3.8}$$

and explicitly

$$C_2 = Q_1Q_2 + 1$$

$$D_2 = Q_2$$

Next define the third convergent as

$$\frac{C_3}{D_3} = Q_1 + \frac{1}{Q_2 + 1/Q_3} \tag{2.3.9}$$

and explicitly

$$C_3 = Q_3C_2 + C_1 \tag{2.3.10}$$

$$D_3 = Q_3D_2 + D_1 \tag{2.3.11}$$

The general relationship between the convergents is

$$C_i = Q_iC_{i-1} + C_{i-2} \tag{2.3.12}$$

$$D_i = Q_iD_{i-1} + D_{i-2} \tag{2.3.13}$$

Note that

$$D_1C_2 - D_2C_1 = 1 \tag{2.3.14}$$

By mathematical induction we can easily show that

$$D_iC_{i+1} - C_iD_{i+1} = (-1)^{i+1} \tag{2.3.15}$$

This means that *each ratio of convergents is in lowest terms*. To say the same thing another way, C_i and D_i have no common factor. Therefore,

$$D_5C_6 - D_6C_5 = 1 \tag{2.3.16}$$

But for the last convergents the ratio of convergents is the original ratio of polynomials

$$\frac{C_6}{D_6} = \frac{A_0(u)}{A_1(u)} \tag{2.3.17}$$

It would be tempting, but not always valid, to assume that $C_6 = A_0(u)$ and $D_6 = A_1(u)$. This would be valid if and only if $A_0(u)$ and $A_1(u)$ have no common factor.

2.4 CHINESE REMAINDER THEOREM FOR POLYNOMIALS

Suppose that we have several modulus polynomials $M_1(u)$, $M_2(u)$, . . . , $M_\mu(u)$ and we know the residues of $P(u)$ for each of these moduli:

$$P(u) \equiv R_1(u) \mod M_1(u) \tag{2.4.1}$$

$$P(u) \equiv R_2(u) \mod M_2(u) \tag{2.4.2}$$

$$\vdots \qquad \vdots \qquad \vdots \tag{2.4.3}$$

$$P(u) \equiv R_\mu(u) \mod M_\mu(u) \tag{2.4.4}$$

Further suppose that none of the $M_i(u)$ have any common factors. Let the product of all these moduli be

$$M(u) = \prod_{i=1}^{\mu} M_i(u) \tag{2.4.5}$$

a modulus whose degree is the sum of the degrees of the individual polynomial moduli. Then we can determine the residue of $P(u)$ with respect to a $M(u)$ using the Chinese remainder theorem, explained below.

$$P(u) \equiv A_1(u)R_1(u) + A_2(u)R_2(u) + \cdots + A_\mu(u)R_\mu(u) \mod M_\mu(u) \tag{2.4.6}$$

where the construction polynomials $A_i(u)$ satisfy the relationships

$$A_i(u) \equiv 1 \mod M_i(u) \tag{2.4.7}$$

$$A_i(u) \equiv 0 \mod M_j(u) \qquad i \neq j \tag{2.4.8}$$

In a moment we shall see how the construction polynomials may be predetermined. They depend only on the moduli and not on the given residues. Note that if we know that the degree of $P(u)$ is less than or equal to the degree of $M(u)$, the Chinese remainder theorem enables us to determine $P(u)$ from its residues.

The Chinese remainder theorem is obvious from its statement if we can only find the construction polynomials. To see this, simply reduce both sides of the defining equation by each modulus in turn. Therefore, the proof of the theorem will be established by the construction given below. We show how to find $A_1(u)$ and the same approach will work for the other $A_i(u)$.

As a first step, construct

$$B_1(u) = \prod_{i \neq 1} M_i(u) \tag{2.4.9}$$

We then have

$$B_1(u) \equiv 0 \quad \bmod M_j(u) \qquad 1 \neq j \tag{2.4.10}$$

If we were lucky enough, we might have $B_1(u) \equiv 1 \bmod M_1(u)$ and not have to go any further to construct $A_1(u)$. Generally, however, we will not be so lucky and we will need to do some extra work. $A_1(u)$ will be some multiple of $B_1(u)$:

$$A_1(u) = \alpha_1(u)B_1(u) \tag{2.4.11}$$

This form of construction of $A_1(u)$ guarantees that

$$A_1(u) \equiv 0 \quad \bmod M_j(u) \qquad 1 \neq j \tag{2.4.12}$$

but we still require a determination of $\alpha_1(u)$ so as to make

$$\alpha_1(u)B_1(u) \equiv 1 \quad \bmod M_1(u) \tag{2.4.13}$$

Fortunately, in the development of the continued fraction we have the mathematical tool to determine $\alpha_1(u)$. By its construction, $B_1(u)$ cannot have any factor in common with $M_1(u)$. Therefore, if we expand $M_1(u)/B_1(u)$ in a continued fraction and evaluate the convergents, the last convergents (C_ν and D_ν) are, respectively, $M_1(u)$ and $B_1(u)$. But we have

$$D_{\nu-1}C_\nu - C_{\nu-1}D_\nu = (-1)^\nu \tag{2.4.14}$$

$$D_{\nu-1}M_1(u) - C_{\nu-1}B_1(u) = (-1)^\nu \tag{2.4.15}$$

$$(-1)^{\nu+1}C_{\nu-1}B_1(u) \equiv 1 \quad \bmod M_1(u) \tag{2.4.16}$$

Hence we can associate $(-1)^{\nu+1}C_{\nu-1}$ with $\alpha_1(u)$. This completes the construction of $A_1(u)$. By the same method we can construct all $A_i(u)$. Therefore, the Chinese remainder theorem for polynomials is proved.

2.5 ALGORITHMS FOR SHORT CIRCULAR CONVOLUTIONS

Since circular convolution may be expressed by

$$\hat{Y}(u) \equiv X(u)H(u) \quad \bmod u^N - 1 \tag{2.5.1}$$

let $M(u) = u^N - 1$. Now if we can factor $u^N - 1$ we can use the Chinese remainder theorem for polynomials to derive relationships which suggest convolution algorithms. We illustrate this with $N = 6$, for six-point circular convolution.

A factorization of $u^6 - 1$ is

$$u^6 - 1 = (u - 1)(u + 1)(u^2 + u + 1)(u^2 - u + 1) \tag{2.5.2}$$

so we can assign

$$M_1(u) = u - 1$$

$$M_2(u) = u + 1$$

$$M_3(u) = u^2 + u + 1$$

$$M_4(u) = u^2 - u + 1$$

From

$$X(u) = x_0 + x_1u + x_2u^2 + x_3u^3 + x_4u^4 + x_5u^5$$

we define

$$X_1(u) = X(u) \quad \bmod u - 1 \tag{2.5.3}$$

$$X_2(u) = X(u) \quad \bmod u + 1 \tag{2.5.4}$$

$$X_3(u) = X(u) \quad \bmod u^2 + u + 1 \tag{2.5.5}$$

$$X_4(u) = X(u) \quad \bmod u^2 - u + 1 \tag{2.5.6}$$

We represent $X(u)$ as the sequence of coefficients of powers of u, namely $x_0, \ldots, x_5$. To represent $X_i(u)$, we similarly want to know the coefficients of these polynomials.

$$X_1(u) = x_{10}$$

$$X_2(u) = x_{20}$$

$$X_3(u) = x_{31}u + x_{30}$$

$$X_4(u) = x_{41}u + x_{40}$$

This takes some calculations. Since $X_1(u)$ and $X_2(u)$ are zeroth-order polynomials, these constants become

$$x_{10} = X(u)|_{u=1} = x_0 + x_1 + x_2 + x_3 + x_4 + x_5$$

$$x_{20} = X(u)|_{u=-1} = x_0 - x_1 + x_2 - x_3 + x_4 - x_5$$

To find $X_3(u)$, we divide $(u^2 + u + 1)$ into $x_0 + x_1u + x_2u^2 + x_3u^3 + x_4u^4 + x_5u^5$ by synthetic division, giving the remainder $(x_1 - x_2 + x_4 - x_5)u + (x_0 - x_2 + x_3 - x_5)$. Thus

$$x_{31} = (x_1 - x_2 + x_4 - x_5)$$

$$x_{30} = (x_0 - x_2 + x_3 - x_5)$$

and in a similar manner, to find $X_3(u)$, we divide $(u^2 - u + 1)$ into $X(u)$, giving the remainder $(x_1 + x_2 - x_4 + x_5)u + (x_0 - x_2 - x_3 + x_5)$. Thus

$$x_{41} = (x_1 + x_2 - x_4 + x_5)$$

$$x_{40} = (x_0 - x_2 - x_3 + x_5)$$

Overall, to go from the vector of coefficients $[x_0, x_1, x_2, x_3, x_4, x_5]^t$ to the vector of coefficients $[x_{10}, x_{20}, x_{31}, x_{30}, x_{41}, x_{40}]^t$ we can abbreviate the description of the work as a matrix multiplication:

$$\begin{bmatrix} x_{10} \\ x_{20} \\ x_{31} \\ x_{30} \\ x_{41} \\ x_{40} \end{bmatrix} = \begin{bmatrix} 1 & 1 & 1 & 1 & 1 & 1 \\ 1 & -1 & 1 & -1 & 1 & -1 \\ 0 & 1 & -1 & 0 & 1 & -1 \\ 1 & 0 & -1 & 1 & 0 & -1 \\ 0 & 1 & 1 & 0 & -1 & 1 \\ 1 & 0 & -1 & -1 & 0 & 1 \end{bmatrix} \begin{bmatrix} x_0 \\ x_1 \\ x_2 \\ x_3 \\ x_4 \\ x_5 \end{bmatrix} \tag{2.5.7}$$

In a similar manner we can determine

$$H_1(u) = H(u) \mod u - 1$$

$$H_2(u) = H(u) \mod u + 1$$

$$H_3(u) = H(u) \mod u^2 + u + 1$$

$$H_4(u) = H(u) \mod u^2 - u + 1$$

and we can determine the coefficients of $H_i(u)$ just as we determined the coefficients of $X_i(u)$.

Let us also define

$$\hat{Y}_1(u) = \hat{Y}(u) \mod u - 1$$

$$\hat{Y}_2(u) = \hat{Y}(u) \mod u + 1$$

$$\hat{Y}_3(u) = \hat{Y}(u) \mod u^2 + u + 1$$

$$\hat{Y}_4(u) = \hat{Y}(u) \mod u^2 - u + 1$$

However, we cannot get coefficients of $\hat{Y}_i(u)$ from coefficients of $\hat{Y}(u)$ because we do not yet know $\hat{Y}(u)$. We go the other way around. We determine each of the $\hat{Y}_i(u)$ and then use the $\hat{Y}_i(u)$ to determine $\hat{Y}(u)$.

Because the $\hat{Y}_i$ are residues, we can determine them as follows:

$$\hat{Y}_i(u) = X_i(u)H_i(u) \mod M_i(u) \tag{2.5.8}$$

$$\hat{y}_{10} = x_{10}h_{10}$$

$$\hat{y}_{20} = x_{20}h_{20}$$

$$\hat{y}_{31}u + \hat{y}_{30} = (x_{31}u + x_{30})(h_{31}u + h_{30}) \mod u^2 + u + 1$$

$$\hat{y}_{41}u + \hat{y}_{40} = (x_{41}u + x_{40})(h_{41}u + h_{40}) \mod u^2 - u + 1$$

It is trivial to see that computing $\hat{y}_{10}$ requires one multiplication, and similarly for $\hat{y}_{20}$. Let us look at the work in computing $\hat{y}_{31}u + \hat{y}_{30}$.

$$\hat{y}_{31}u + \hat{y}_{30} \equiv (x_{31}u + x_{30})(h_{31}u + h_{30}) \mod u^2 + u + 1$$

$$\equiv x_{31}h_{31}u^2 + (x_{31}h_{30} + x_{30}h_{31})u + x_{30}h_{30}$$

Because we can substitute $-u - 1$ for u^2 wherever it appears, while still preserving a congruence modulo $u^2 + u + 1$,

$$\hat{y}_{31}u + \hat{y}_{30} = x_{31}h_{31}(-u - 1) + (x_{31}h_{30} + x_{30}h_{31})u + x_{30}h_{30}$$

$$= (x_{31}h_{30} + x_{30}h_{31} - x_{31}h_{31})u + x_{30}h_{30} - x_{31}h_{31}$$

Therefore, we compute $\hat{y}_{31}$ and $\hat{y}_{30}$ using four multiplications and a few additions and subtractions.

The similar work for computing $\hat{y}_{41}u + \hat{y}_{40}$ uses the substitution $u^2 = u - 1 \mod u^2 - u + 1$. Thus

$$\hat{y}_{41}u + \hat{y}_{40} = (x_{41}h_{40} + x_{40}h_{41} + x_{41}h_{41})u + x_{40}h_{40} - x_{41}h_{41}$$

The total number of multiplications needed to obtain all the coefficients of all four $\hat{Y}_i(u)$ is 10. This is related to the factorization of $u^N - 1$. Linear factors led to one multiplication apiece. Quadratic factors led to four multiplications apiece (although we will later see how to lower this to three multiplications).

At this point we have $\hat{Y}_1(u), \ldots, \hat{Y}_4(u)$ and we may use the Chinese remainder theorem to determine $\hat{Y}(u)$. Recall that this theorem says that

$$\hat{Y}(u) = A_1(u)\hat{Y}_1(u) + A_2(u)\hat{Y}_2(u) + A_3(u)\hat{Y}_3(u) + A_4(u)\hat{Y}_4(u) \mod u^6 - 1 \tag{2.5.9}$$

We can determine $A_1(u), \ldots, A_4(u)$ before any data from X or H are given.

$$A_1(u) = \tfrac{1}{6}(u^5 + u^4 + u^3 + u^2 + u + 1)$$

$$A_2(u) = -\tfrac{1}{6}(u^5 - u^4 + u^3 - u^2 + u - 1)$$

$$A_3(u) = -\tfrac{1}{6}(u^5 - u^4 + 2u^3 - u^2 - u + 2)$$

$$A_4(u) = \tfrac{1}{6}(u^5 - u^4 - 2u^3 - u^2 + u + 2)$$

These construction polynomials have rational coefficients that are independent of the two sequences being convolved.

When we substitute the expressions for $A_i(u)$ and $\hat{Y}_i(u)$ into the Chinese remainder theorem reconstruction we get a sixth-degree polynomial modulo $u^6 - 1$.

$$\begin{aligned}\hat{Y}(u) \equiv \tfrac{1}{6}[&\hat{y}_{10}(u^5 + u^4 + u^3 + u^2 + u + 1)\\ &- \hat{y}_{20}(u^5 - u^4 + u^3 - u^2 + u - 1)\\ &- (\hat{y}_{31}u + \hat{y}_{30})(u^5 - u^4 + 2u^3 - u^2 - u + 2)\\ &+ (\hat{y}_{41}u + \hat{y}_{40})(u^5 - u^4 - 2u^3 - u^2 + u + 2)] \mod u^6 - 1\end{aligned}$$

and by making the substitution $u^6 = 1$ we get a fifth-degree polynomial whose coefficients are the coefficients of $\hat{Y}(u)$.

$$
\begin{aligned}
\hat{Y}(u) = \tfrac{1}{6}[&u^5(\hat{y}_{10} - \hat{y}_{20} + \hat{y}_{31} - \hat{y}_{30} + \hat{y}_{40} - \hat{y}_{41}) \\
&+ u^4(\hat{y}_{10} + \hat{y}_{20} - 2\hat{y}_{31} + \hat{y}_{30} - 2\hat{y}_{41} - \hat{y}_{30}) \\
&+ u^3(\hat{y}_{10} - \hat{y}_{20} + \hat{y}_{31} - 2\hat{y}_{30} - 2\hat{y}_{40} - \hat{y}_{41}) \\
&+ u^2(\hat{y}_{10} + \hat{y}_{20} + \hat{y}_{31} + \hat{y}_{30} + \hat{y}_{41} - \hat{y}_{40}) \\
&+ u(\hat{y}_{10} - \hat{y}_{20} + \hat{y}_{30} - 2\hat{y}_{31} + \hat{y}_{40} + 2\hat{y}_{41}) \\
&+ (\hat{y}_{10} + \hat{y}_{20} - \hat{y}_{31} - 2\hat{y}_{30} + \hat{y}_{41} + 2\hat{y}_{40})]
\end{aligned}
$$

This accomplishes the circular convolution. If we examine the work we must do to carry out the reconstruction, it involves multiplying the vector of coefficients $[\hat{y}_{10}, \ldots, \hat{y}_{40}]^t$ by a fixed matrix containing small rational constants, to obtain the vector $[\hat{y}_0, \ldots, \hat{y}_5]^t$.

The overall computation can be broken into four steps as follows:

- Compute coefficients of $X_i(u)$ from coefficients of $X(u)$. This requires a multiplication of a vector by a constant matrix. We may think of this step as taking some kind of transform of the input sequence.
- Compute coefficients of $H_i(u)$ from coefficients of $H(u)$. We may think of this step as taking the transform of the other input sequence.
- Compute the products required to multiply $X_i(u)$ by $H_i(u)$. These were of the form $x_{ij}h_{ik}$ in the example we just worked out. In general, they will be products of x data by h data.
- Compute the coefficients of the $\hat{Y}(u)$ as a multiplication of the vector of products by a fixed matrix containing only rational numbers independent of the data. We may think of this as an inverse transform.

In the example of six-point circular convolution, we needed 10 products,

$$
\begin{gathered}
x_{10}h_{10} \\
x_{20}h_{20} \\
x_{31}h_{31} \\
x_{30}h_{31} \\
x_{31}h_{30} \\
x_{30}h_{30} \\
x_{41}h_{41} \\
x_{40}h_{41} \\
x_{41}h_{40} \\
x_{40}h_{40}
\end{gathered}
$$

The matrix displayed in (2.5.7) for computing coefficients of $X_i(u)$ from $X(u)$ and computing coefficients of $H_i(u)$ from $H(u)$ is square, 6×6. We will find it helpful to rewrite that matrix for X and rewrite it differently for H, as matrices with 10 rows and six columns, so that the vectors they compute become

$$\begin{bmatrix} x_{10} \\ x_{20} \\ x_{31} \\ x_{30} \\ x_{31} \\ x_{30} \\ x_{41} \\ x_{40} \\ x_{41} \\ x_{40} \end{bmatrix} \qquad \begin{bmatrix} h_{10} \\ h_{20} \\ h_{31} \\ h_{31} \\ h_{30} \\ h_{30} \\ h_{41} \\ h_{41} \\ h_{40} \\ h_{40} \end{bmatrix}$$

although we would surely not repeat the redundant computations. Similarly, the additions and subtractions of products $x_{ij}h_{ik}$ to get the coefficients of $\hat{Y}_i(u)$ can be combined with the output matrix multiplication. Once we have done this, our algorithm for six-point circular convolution takes the form of first multiplying the input sequences X and H by fixed (data independent) 10×6 matrices, then computing 10 term-by-term products, and finally operating on the resulting length-10 vector by another fixed matrix with 10 columns and 6 rows. A diagram of such an algorithm is shown in Fig. 2.1.

The way that we constructed this circular convolution algorithm is fairly general. We can use it to find an algorithm for circular convolution of any length. The key idea is that by factoring $u^N - 1$ into factors of low degree, computation of a long convolution is reduced to several computations of short bilinear forms, which are then combined using the Chinese remainder theorem to give the desired result. The general form of a circular convolution algorithm constructed using these principles can be expressed as three successive matrix multiplications. We first multiply the vector $\mathbf{X}$, made up of original data, by a matrix A which gives us the coefficients of the residue polynomials $X_i(u)$. The term-by-term products may be viewed as multiplying $A\mathbf{X}$ by a diagonal matrix D whose elements are computed from $H(u)$. Finally, the reconstruction of $\hat{\mathbf{Y}}$, the vector of results, is also a matrix multiplication, and we may call this matrix B.

$$\hat{\mathbf{Y}} = BDA\mathbf{X} \tag{2.5.10}$$

We will refer to such an algorithm, whether it is used to compute circular convolution or something else, as a BDA-type algorithm.

The construction may not be optimum. For the example we worked out, six-point circular convolution, the number of multiplications of data $\times$ data can be reduced from 10 to 8. For example, to compute the two coefficients of $\hat{Y}_3(u)$ we can use the following three-multiply procedure:

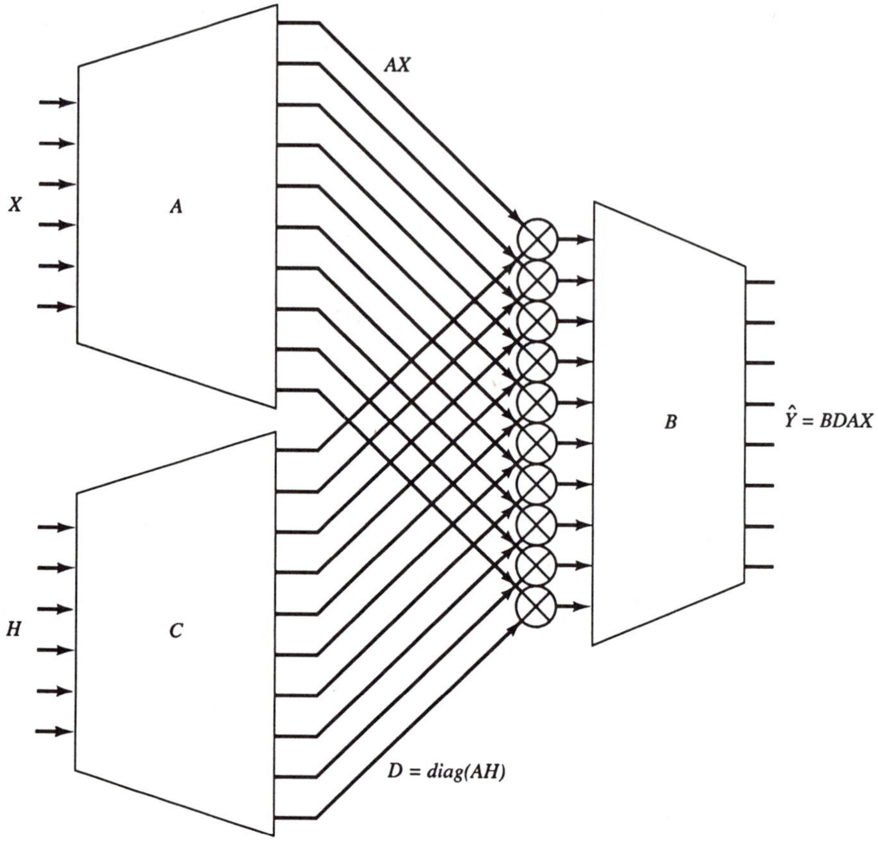

FIGURE 2.1 Form of a Circular Convolution Algorithm Derived from the Theory of Polynomial Congruences.

$$\beta_1 = x_{31}h_{31}$$

$$\beta_2 = x_{30}h_{30}$$

$$\beta_3 = (x_{30} - x_{31})(h_{30} - h_{31})$$

$$\hat{y}_{30} = \beta_2 - \beta_1$$

$$\hat{y}_{31} = \beta_2 - \beta_3$$

A similar procedure can be used to compute $\hat{Y}_4(u)$ with three multiplications. We can easily incorporate these ideas into the derivation of a six-point circular convolution algorithm and the general form of the algorithm will not change. The 10×6 transformation matrices become 8×6 transformation matrices and the Chinese remainder theorem reconstruction matrix will become a 6×8 matrix, but these matrices are still composed of data-independent rational numbers. It happens that eight is the theoretical minimum number of real multiplications of data × data for general $N = 6$ circular convolution.

2.6 HOW WE COUNT MULTIPLICATIONS

In the preceding section, we discussed, using the example of a six-point circular convolution, an algorithm for computing such a convolution with eight multiplications. We did not count among these eight multiplications such products as

$$\tfrac{1}{6}\hat{y}_{ij}$$

where the multiplier or multiplicand is a rational constant. We can actually distinguish several different kinds of multiplications and their relative cost in algorithms, to justify counting them differently.

data × rational constant If all the output multipliers are expressed as rational numbers p_i/q with a common denominator q, we may choose to compute $q\hat{y}_n$ instead of $\hat{y}_n$. Then all the output multiplications become multiplications by integers. These can be reduced to additions and hence removed from the count of multiplications.

data × general constant When the H data are available in advance, all the quantities h_{ij} may be precomputed. Any subsequent output multiplications by constants could be absorbed into the precomputed h_{ij}. But only if the word length of either multiplicand or multiplier is short can we reduce the multiplications by h_{ij} to additions.

data × data Generally, these multiplications must be counted and are the most costly.

A very important use of circular convolution is in FIR digital filtering, using the overlap-add or overlap-save approaches of Stockham to stitch together finite-length pieces of an essentially infinite-length filter output. In this application we may consider H as given once and for all, whereas X arrives at our processor a little bit at a time. Therefore, we can invest substantially in precomputing anything depending only on H in exchange for minimizing computations that depend on X. Stockham's application of overlap-save or overlap-add to convolution was motivated by the desire to adapt the FFT algorithm to computing ordinary convolutions, although the FFT is more naturally used to compute circular convolutions. But overlap-add and overlap-save methods can be used to apply any algorithm for computing a circular convolution to the computation of an ordinary convolution.

Another common issue is the difference between multiplications over different fields. Consider the six-point convolution algorithm derived in the preceding section. We found that it took the form of a pretransform and a posttransform in which all the multiplications were either absent or explained away, and a central stage of data × data using eight multiplications. We said that this was optimum. But consider an algorithm based on the Fourier transform. The pretransformations and postransformations would use only constants of the form $e^{j(2\pi k/6)}$. Only the central multiplications are of the data × data type. Yet we would not feel as comfortable in minimizing the significance of multiplications by complex transcendental constants, at least not to the same extent as multiplications by integers, rational numbers, or real numbers. We have identified a sensitivity to the *field of constants* when we agree to count or not count certain kinds of multiplications in an algorithm. That is:

1. Data × data multiplications are always counted.
2. Constant × data multiplications are not counted if the constants belong to an allowed field (e.g., rationals, complex numbers).

The allowed field should be specified when an algorithm is claimed to be optimum with regard to number of multiplications. The six-point convolution algorithm derived above is optimum when the field of allowed constants is the rational numbers.

It will be interesting to explore the implications of changing the allowed field of constants. Suppose that the constants may be complex numbers. The first step of our algorithm derivation was to display a factorization of $u^6 - 1$. Let us now use the factorization

$$u^6 - 1 = \prod_{i=0}^{5} M_i(u) \tag{2.6.1}$$

where

$$M_i(u) = u - e^{j(2\pi i/6)} \tag{2.6.2}$$

If we define $X_i(u)$ and $H_i(u)$ formally as before,

$$X_i(u) = X(u) \quad \text{mod}\,(u - e^{j(2\pi i/6)})$$

$$x_{i0} = X(u)\big|_{e^{j(2\pi i/6)}}$$

we find that we have computed the six-point discrete Fourier transforms of x_n and h_n. Similarly, when we determine reconstruction polynomials for $\hat{Y}(u)$, they will be

$$A_i(u) = \tfrac{1}{6} \sum_{k=0}^{5} e^{-j(2\pi ik/6)} u^k$$

In other words, if the field of constants allowed is the complex numbers, a derivation of the form taken in the preceding section would lead to an algorithm with six central multiplications of data × data, in which the pretransformations and posttransformation are forward and inverse discrete Fourier transforms.

2.7 CYCLOTOMIC POLYNOMIALS

Let us define the following important polynomials, which we call the *cyclotomic* polynomials:

$$C_1(u) = u - 1 \tag{2.7.1}$$

$$C_2(u) = u + 1 \tag{2.7.2}$$

$$C_3(u) = u^2 + u + 1 \tag{2.7.3}$$

$$C_4(u) = u^2 + 1 \tag{2.7.4}$$

$$C_5(u) = u^4 + u^3 + u^2 + u + 1 \tag{2.7.5}$$

$$C_6(u) = u^2 - u + 1 \tag{2.7.6}$$

$$\vdots = \vdots \tag{2.7.7}$$

$$C_k(u) = \prod_{\substack{i \le k \\ (i,k)=1}} (u - e^{j(2\pi i/k)}) \tag{2.7.8}$$

The form of the general term $C_k(u)$ is clarified by Fig. 2.2, where we show a unit circle (drawn for $k = 6$) and the roots $(e^{j(2\pi i/k)}; i = 1, 2, 4, 5)$.

The cyclotomic polynomials usually have very simple coefficients, 0 and ± 1. The lowest-ordered cyclotomic polynomial with a more complicated coefficient is $C_{105}(u)$.

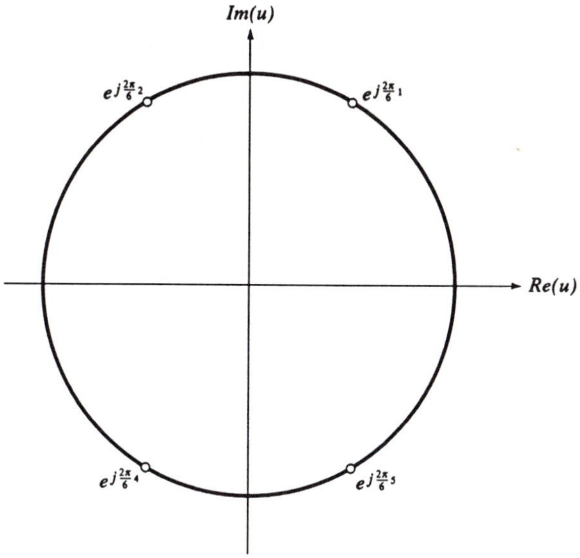

FIGURE 2.2 Roots of $C_6(u)$.

Our interest in the cyclotomic polynomials comes from their role in the factorization of $u^N - 1$.

$$u^N - 1 = \prod_{k|N} C_k(u) \tag{2.7.9}$$

where $k|N$ reads "k divides N." Thus since the divisors of $N = 6$ are 1, 2, 3, 6,

$$u^6 - 1 = C_1(u)C_2(u)C_3(u)C_6(u)$$

The simple form of the factors $C_k(u)$ guarantees the simple form of the pretransformations in any algorithms we derive for circular convolution based on the cyclotomic factorization of $u^N - 1$.

2.8 ELEMENTARY NUMBER THEORY

Many of the results in the remainder of this chapter rely on a knowledge of elementary number theory. In this section we give a brief introduction to the major theorems and procedures needed. The reader for whom this material is new is urged to acquire a more rigorous background using any of the standard textbooks in number theory.

2.8.1 Greatest Common Divisors and Euler's Totient Function

Any integer can be factored in a standard way into a product of powers of primes

$$a = p_1^{\alpha_1} p_2^{\alpha_2} \cdots p_k^{\alpha_k} \tag{2.8.1}$$

Its divisors are all the integers of the form

$$d = p_1^{\beta_1} p_2^{\beta_2} \cdots p_k^{\beta_k} \tag{2.8.2}$$

where $\beta_i \leq \alpha_i$.

We use the notation $a|b$ to indicate that the integer a is a divisor of the integer b. We use the symbol (a,b) to designate the greatest common divisor of a and b. If

$$a = \prod_i p_i^{\alpha_i}$$

$$b = \prod_i p_i^{\beta_i}$$

then

$$(a,b) = \prod_i p_i^{\min(\alpha_i,\beta_i)}$$

1 is always a divisor of any integer. If a and b have no other common divisor, then naturally $(a,b) = 1$. Then we say that a and b are mutually prime.

The Euler totient function, $\phi(a)$, defined for positive integers a, is the count of the number of positive integers less than a and mutually prime to a. Thus for $a = 6$ the integers less than 6 are 1, 2, 3, 4, 5. Of these, 1 and 5 are mutually prime to 6, so $\phi(6) = 2$. For any prime p_i we have $\phi(p_i) = p_i - 1$. We can also deduce that $\phi(p_i^{\alpha_i}) = p_i^{\alpha_i - 1}(p_i - 1)$.

A general formula for $\phi(a)$ with a given bv (2.8.1) is

$$\phi(a) = \prod_i p_i^{\alpha_i - 1}(p_i - 1) = \prod_i \phi(p_i^{\alpha_i})$$

2.8.2 The Equation *ax* + *by* = 1

The equation

$$ax + by = c \tag{2.8.3}$$

with the proviso that all quantities a, b, c, x, y must be integers, has no solution unless (a,b) is a divisor of c.

If we limit our attention to equations of the same form as (2.8.3) but with $(a,b) = 1$, we can construct solutions from solutions to the still simpler equation

$$ax + by = 1 \tag{2.8.4}$$

If (2.8.4) has the solution pair x_0, y_0 then (2.8.3) must have the corresponding solution cx_0, cy_0. Equation (2.8.4) always has solutions when a and b are mutually prime. In any such solutions we must have x and y mutually prime. A general method of solving (2.8.3) is based on the concept of a continued fraction, which we explain here. Start with any pair, a, b, both positive, not necessarily mutually prime, and assume that $a > b$ (otherwise, the procedure we are about to describe will quickly interchange their roles). We start by dividing a by b, giving

$$\frac{a}{b} = r_0 + \frac{s_0}{b} = r_0 + \frac{1}{b/s_0}, \qquad 0 \le s_0 < b$$

Then we divide b by s_0, giving

$$\frac{b}{s_0} = r_1 + \frac{s_1}{s_0} = r_1 + \frac{1}{s_0/s_1}, \qquad 0 \le s_1 < s_0$$

We continue this procedure until on the μth step we get a zero remainder, s_μ, at which point the process terminates and we have

$$\frac{a}{b} = r_0 + \frac{1}{r_1 + 1/(r_2 + 1/(r_3 + \cdots + 1/r_\mu)\cdots)}$$

The process must terminate because each s_i is nonnegative and is smaller than the one before it.

Along the way we have generated a set of equalities

$$
\begin{aligned}
a &= br_0 + s_0 \\
b &= s_0 r_1 + s_1 \\
s_0 &= s_1 r_2 + s_2 \\
s_1 &= s_2 r_3 + s_3 \\
&\vdots \qquad \vdots \\
s_{\mu-3} &= s_{\mu-2} r_{\mu-1} + s_{\mu-1} \\
s_{\mu-2} &= s_{\mu-1} r_\mu + 0
\end{aligned}
$$

$s_{\mu-1}$ is (a,b), a result known as *Euclid's algorithm.*

Returning to the continued fraction and we define a series of *convergents* as follows:

$$
\begin{aligned}
\frac{a_0}{b_0} &= r_0 \\
\frac{a_1}{b_1} &= r_0 + 1/r_1 \\
\frac{a_2}{b_2} &= r_0 + 1/(r_1 + 1/r_2) \\
&\vdots \qquad \vdots \\
\frac{a_\mu}{b_\mu} &= r_0 + 1/(r_1 + 1/r_2 + 1/(r_3 + \cdots + 1/r_\mu)\cdots)
\end{aligned}
$$

As a consequence of the preceding equation,

$$\frac{a_\mu}{b_\mu} = \frac{a}{b}$$

These convergents are all ratios of integers a_i and b_i. A procedure for specifying a_i and b_i separately and uniquely, consistent with the definition of the convergents, is

$$
\begin{aligned}
a_0 &= r_0, & b_0 &= 1 \\
a_1 &= r_0 r_1 + 1, & b_1 &= r_1 \\
a_2 &= r_2(r_0 r_1 + 1) + r_0, & b_2 &= r_2 r_1 + 1 \\
a_3 &= r_3(r_2(r_0 r_1 + 1) + r_0) + (r_0 r_1 + 1), & b_3 &= r_3(r_2 r_1 + 1) + r_1
\end{aligned}
$$

and in general for $n > 1$,

$$
\begin{aligned}
a_n &= r_n a_{n-1} + a_{n-2} \\
b_n &= r_n b_{n-1} + b_{n-2}
\end{aligned}
$$

When a_i and b_i are computed separately in this manner, the convergents have remarkable properties:

$$b_n a_{n+1} - a_n b_{n+1} = (-1)^n \tag{2.8.5}$$

This tells us that the convergents as we compute them will always be in lowest terms. Otherwise, if a_n and b_n had some common factor, it would divide the left side of (2.8.5), while we can see that the right side has no such divisor.

Now we are ready to solve (2.8.4). By hypothesis, a and b are mutually prime,† so a/b is a fraction in lowest terms. We have just shown that a_μ/b_μ is equal to it and is also in lowest terms. So

$$a_\mu = a$$

$$b_\mu = b$$

and we also have

$$b_{\mu-1}a_\mu - a_{\mu-1}b_\mu = b_{\mu-1}\,a - a_{\mu-1}b = (-1)^{\mu-1}$$

Therefore, if μ is odd, we have an immediate solution to (2.8.4), namely

$$x = b_{\mu-1}, \qquad y = -a_{\mu-1}$$

If μ is even, we must change the signs to find the solution

$$x = -b_{\mu-1}, \qquad y = a_{\mu-1}$$

2.8.3 Modulo Arithmetic

In the following discussion there is a special positive integer, M, called the *modulus*. Any two integers whose difference is an exact multiple of M are said to be *congruent*. We write

$$a \equiv b \mod M$$

We can designate any M consecutive integers as a fundamental set which we call the *residue set*. Now whatever integer we are given, of either sign, we can always find another integer congruent to the first but in the residue set. We call the resulting integer the *residue* of the first integer. When we replace an integer by its residue, we call the operation residue *reduction*.

We will use the notation

$$\langle x \rangle_M$$

to indicate the residue of x. Where M is clear we may omit it and just use $\langle x \rangle$.

† Note that if $(a,b) \neq 1$ we would discover this by the Euclid algorithm, so we would know that (2.8.4) cannot be solved.

Since any consecutive set of M integers can serve as a residue set, we must make a choice. Often in digital signal processing computations, the most convenient choice for the residue set will be

$$\left(-\left\lfloor\frac{M}{2}\right\rfloor, \ldots, \left\lfloor\frac{M-1}{2}\right\rfloor\right)$$

But in hand computations and in expressing the results in this chapter, we will usually use the residue set

$$(0, \ldots, M - 1)$$

which has the virtue that all the residues are positive. There is no problem with choosing one residue set and then changing the choice in midstream.

We will only work with integers, although they can be of either sign. Whenever we combine two or more integers to give a result which, by the nature of the operation, is guaranteed to be an integer, we can always follow that operation by residue reduction, thus defining a new but related operation. Thus the basic operations of addition, multiplication, and subtraction lead us to modulo M addition, modulo M multiplication, and modulo M subtraction.

If we start with a set of integers and carry out any chain of additions, subtractions or multiplications to produce a result, and if we start with the same set of integers and carry out the corresponding chain of modulo M additions, subtractions, or multiplications to produce another result, the two results must be congruent modulo M.

In any algorithm *that uses only these three basic operations,* if we are content with congruence instead of equality, we can substitute modulo operations for ordinary operations at will. Whenever we use a modulo operation, we are guaranteed that the result is an element in the residue set, which means that we know it can be stored in any register of at least $\lfloor\log_2 M\rfloor$ bits.

The integers making up the residue set, along with the two binary operations—addition modulo M and multiplication modulo M—form an algebraic structure called a *ring*. More precisely, there are a *commutative ring*. There are a short list of "laws" that hold for any ring, and therefore these laws hold for modulo M arithmetic. They are:

closure $a + b$ is a valid element.
$a \cdot b$ is a valid element.

commutative law $a + b = b + a$
$a \cdot b = b \cdot a$

associative law $(a + b) + c = a + (b + c)$
$a \cdot (b \cdot c) = (a \cdot b) \cdot c$

identity There is an element, denoted 0, such that $0 + a = a$
There is an element, denoted 1, such that $1 \cdot a = a$.

inverse For any element a, there is an element $(-a)$ such that $a + (-a) = 0$.

distributive law $a \cdot (b + c) = (a \cdot b) + (a \cdot c)$

The relation of congruence is very similar to equality except that it is weaker. If two integers are equal, they must be congruent. If they are congruent, they may or not be equal. However, if they are congruent and known to be not too far apart, they must be equal. For example, in daily life we use congruence in the mod 12 arithmetic of a clock. As long as we know what time it is within half a day, if we know the time modulo 12, we know the time completely.

In digital signal processing, a convolution requires only addition and multiplication. If we can restrict our raw data to integers, and if we also can be sure that the result of a computation must be within the residue set, then instead of computing with equalities, it is sufficient to compute with congruences—the final answer must be correct. But we can certainly choose our modulus so that all the inputs and also the final answer are sure to be within the residue set, so it will always be sufficient to compute each sum or product in our algorithm modulo M, *even though the true intermediate results might well not be within the basic range.*

It would seem intuitive that modulo arithmetic is more complex to perform than ordinary arithmetic. The usual mathematics textbook presents modulus arithmetic as a by-product of a division operation. But in fact, for most choices of modulus there are simple procedures for computing the residue of a sum or product. Sometimes they are a little more complicated than ordinary arithmetic. Sometimes they are even a little bit simpler.

The properties of the equation $ax + by = c$ apply directly to the modulus equation:

$$ax \equiv c \mod M$$

Thus we can solve it only if (a,M) is a divisor of c. In that case we can solve the related equation $ax + My = 1$ for x and y and then use cx, cy as the solution to the equation, and thus cx as the solution to the original congruence. In other words, we can solve any congruence of the form $\langle ax \rangle_M = c$, or else prove that it cannot be solved, using continued fractions.

The set of all residues *except* those which are not mutually prime to M is called a *reduced residue set*. For example, with $M = 10$ the reduced residue set would be

$$1, 3, 7, 9$$

Designate these reduced residues as r_i, for $i = 1, \ldots, \phi(M)$.

Now pick any a, mutually prime to M, and let $q_i = \langle ar_i \rangle_M$. We know that each q_i will, itself, be a member of the reduced residue set. All the q_i must be distinct, and since there are $\phi(M)$ of them, they must be the same $\phi(M)$ residues as r_i, albeit permuted.

Now define

$$D \equiv \prod_{i=1}^{\phi(M)} r_i \mod M$$

and of course

$$D \equiv \prod_{i=1}^{\phi(M)} (ar_i) \mod M$$

Therefore,

$$a^{\phi(M)} D \equiv D \mod M$$

Since $(D,M) = 1$ we can cancel D from both sides of the congruence, giving

$$a^{\phi(M)} \equiv 1 \mod M$$

which is known as *Euler's theorem.*

2.8.4 The Sino Representation of Integers Modulo M

Within this section we will assume that M is a composite number and that its factorization is

$$M = M_1 \times \cdots \times M_\mu$$

where

$$M_i = p_i^{\alpha_i}$$

and where the p_i are distinct primes. This implies, of course, that $(M_i,M_j) = 1$ for $i \neq j$.

If we specify the residues of some integer with respect to each modulus M_i, that is sufficient to determine the residue of that integer with respect to M. That is, if the integer is x and its residues are

$$x_i = \langle x \rangle_{M_i}$$

we can determine $\langle x \rangle_M$ uniquely. This statement is known as the *Chinese remainder theorem*. It is completely analogous to the Chinese remainder theorem for polynomials, introduced earlier. We shall not only prove the Chinese remainder theorem, but we shall do it by construction. However, rather than give a general proof, we limit ourselves to a demonstration of the construction when M is a product of three mutually prime factors. This contains all the elements of a complete proof, but it is a little easier to follow.

Therefore, we have $M = M_1M_2M_3$ and $(M_1,M_2) = (M_1,M_3) = (M_2,M_3) = 1$. We must find a set of three quantities, a_1, a_2, a_3, that obey these congruences:

$$\langle a_1 \rangle_{M_1} = 1, \qquad \langle a_2 \rangle_{M_1} = 0, \qquad \langle a_3 \rangle_{M_1} = 0$$

$$\langle a_1 \rangle_{M_2} = 0, \qquad \langle a_2 \rangle_{M_2} = 1, \qquad \langle a_3 \rangle_{M_2} = 0$$

$$\langle a_1 \rangle_{M_3} = 0, \qquad \langle a_2 \rangle_{M_3} = 0, \qquad \langle a_3 \rangle_{M_3} = 1$$

If we can find these a_i, we can construct x from its three residues $x_i = \langle x \rangle_{M_i}$ as follows:

$$x = \langle a_1 x_1 + a_2 x_2 + a_3 x_3 \rangle_{M_1 M_2 M_3} \tag{2.8.6}$$

In (2.8.6), try to compute $t_1 \equiv \langle x \rangle_{M_1}$. The second term drops out because $a_2 \equiv 0 \bmod M_1$. The third term drops out similarly. This leaves the first term:

$$t_1 = \langle a_1 x_1 \rangle_{M_1} = \langle \langle a_1 \rangle_{M_1} x_1 \rangle_{M_1} = x_1$$

Therefore, any x constructed from (2.8.6) has the proper residue modulo M_1. In a similar way, we can compute t_2 and t_3 and we see that x constructed from (2.8.6) has the right residues for all three moduli. This shows that we can construct x from its three residues if we can find a_1, a_2, a_3.

Let us show how to construct a_1. We introduce an intermediate unknown quantity b_1 with

$$a_1 = b_1 M_2 M_3 \tag{2.8.7}$$

and we must now find b_1. When we construct a_1 in this manner we are assured that $\langle a_1 \rangle_{M_2} = \langle a_1 \rangle_{M_3} = 0$. We therefore choose b_1 in such a way as to force

$$\langle b_1 \times M_2 M_3 \rangle_{M_1} = 1$$

$$b_1 \times (M_2 M_3) + c \times M_1 = 1$$

This equation can be solved for b_1 and c, as we have already seen, because M_1 and $M_2 M_3$ are mutually prime. If necessary, we can use the continued fraction method to solve for b_1, or the solution may be determined in some other way. Once we have b_1 we can find a_1 and we can use the same approach to find a_2 and a_3. This completes the proof of the Chinese remainder theorem.

An important use of the Chinese remainder theorem is in number representation. Suppose that we consider x_1, x_2, and x_3 as three digits used to represent x, but not using the familiar radix representation. Instead, the computation of value x from digits x_i, $x = [x_1, x_2, \ldots]$, is given by (2.8.6). In this number system, any computation that is a string of additions, subtractions, and multiplications modulo M may be carried out independently digit by digit.

EXAMPLE 2.8.1

Let $M = 4 \times 5 \times 7 = 140$. Let $A = 21 = [1,1,0]$ and let $B = 33 = [1,3,5]$. First we compute $C = \langle A + B \rangle_{140}$.

$$c_1 = \langle 1 + 1 \rangle_4 = 2$$

$$c_2 = \langle 1 + 3 \rangle_5 = 4$$

$$c_3 = \langle 0 + 5 \rangle_7 = 5$$

and we note that 54 is indeed represented as [2,4,5]. Next let us compute $D = \langle C^2 \rangle_{140}$.

$$d_1 = \langle 2 \times 2 \rangle_4 = 0$$

$$d_2 = \langle 4 \times 4 \rangle_5 = 1$$

$$d_3 = \langle 5 \times 5 \rangle_7 = 4$$

$54^2 = 2916$ is indeed congruent to $116 = [0,1,4]$.

Finally, look at the congruence $\langle 8x \rangle_{140} = 18$. In the Sino representation this becomes three congruences:

$$\langle 0x_1 \rangle_4 = 2$$

$$\langle 3x_2 \rangle_5 = 3$$

$$\langle 1x_3 \rangle_7 = 4$$

Many of the properties of the original congruence are revealed by the three congruences implied by the Sino representation. Indeed, here we see that the first congruence has no solutions, which disposes of the original congruence immediately. Using the Sino representation, we can use whatever we know about the properties of a congruence when the modulus is a power of a prime, to work with congruences with any modulus.

2.8.5 Exponentials Modulo *M*

Choose any integer x. Start with $x_0 = 1$ and repeatedly multiply it by x modulo M, giving

$$x_n = \langle x^n \rangle_M$$

Using ordinary arithmetic, this procedure would rapidly become impractical because x^n grows without bound. In modulus arithmetic this does not happen—the numbers never get bigger than $\pm M/2$.

Therefore, the experiment above is a finite-state machine and it must eventually produce a periodic process. We can imagine two distinct kinds of behavior of the sequence $\{x^n\}$:

1. The sequence might be periodic, from the start, with period N. This means that $x_N = 1$ and that it is the first member of the sequence after x_0 which equals 1. For example, with $M = 7$, $x = 2$ we have

$$\begin{aligned} x_0 &= 1 \\ x_1 &= 2 \\ x_2 &= 4 \\ x_3 &= 1 \\ &\vdots \\ x_n &= x_{n-3} \end{aligned}$$

2. The sequence might begin with a one-time preamble and then settle into a periodic state that does not include 1. For example, with $M = 45$, $x = 5$ we have

$$\begin{aligned} x_0 &= 1 \\ x_1 &= 5 \\ x_2 &= 25 \\ x_3 &= 35 \\ x_4 &= 40 \\ x_5 &= 20 \\ x_6 &= 10 \\ x_7 &= 5 \\ \vdots & \quad \vdots \\ x_n &= x_{n-6} \end{aligned}$$

Such a sequence might even quench itself by generating a zero. Example: $M = 8$, $x = 2$.

We find the first type of behavior most interesting because of the analogy of $\langle x^n \rangle_M$ to $(\exp [j2\pi/N])^n$ in complex arithmetic. Later in this chapter we build this analogy into an analogy of the DFT and even the FFT. But first we need to see what connections exist between M, x and the period N.

Consider the iteration that produces $x_N = 1$, if any.

$$\langle x \times x_{N-1} \rangle_M = 1$$

$$x \times x_{N-1} + b \times M = 1$$

This is an equation of the form $ax + by = 1$. We know that such an equation has solutions only if $(a,b) = 1$. Therefore, a necessary condition for immediate periodicity of the iteration is

$$(x,M) = 1$$

This is also a sufficient condition. Since we have periodicity eventually, for n sufficiently large we have

$$\langle x^n \rangle = \langle x^{n+N} \rangle$$

The difference between right and left sides in ordinary arithmetic must be a multiple of M, so we have

$$x^{N+n} - x^n = kM$$

$$(x^n)(x^N - 1) = kM$$

Both sides of this equation are partly factored. But since $(x,M) = 1$, x cannot supply any of the divisors of M. Therefore, $(x^N - 1)$ must supply all the factors of M, which means that it is some multiple of M. Thus

$$x^N = 1 + k' M$$

or in terms of residues

$$\langle x^N \rangle_M = 1$$

This is an important result of number theory. If $(x,M) = 1$, there is some smallest positive integer N for which $\langle x^N \rangle_M$ is 1, the period of the sequence $\langle x^n \rangle$. We call *N the order of x with respect to modulus M.*

There is an intimate connection between the period of the sequence $\langle x^n \rangle_M$ and the Euler totient function $\phi(M)$. The order of x with respect to M is a divisor of $\phi(M)$.

$$N | \phi(M)$$

For a few moments, let us consider the case of exponential sequences modulo a prime, p. In the residue set for modulus p, every x except 0 is in the reduced residue set and hence it has some order N. Since $\phi(p) = p - 1$ we know that the order of every x must be a divisor of $p - 1$. But which divisors of $p - 1$ are possible orders? In particular, is there any x for which the order of x is equal to $p - 1$? In fact, there is always such a choice of x, which we shall designate as g and which we call a primitive root.

$$g^t \not\equiv 1 \mod p \qquad 0 < t < p - 1$$

$$g^{p-1} \equiv 1 \mod p$$

Furthermore, there are generally several different primitive roots for any prime.

Beginning with a primitive root, we can construct the entire reduced residue set g^i, $i = 0, 1, \ldots, p - 2 = 1, 2, \ldots, p - 1$, where, of course, the elements of these two representations of the same set are in permuted order.

Now suppose that N is a divisor of $p - 1$ but is not equal to $p - 1$. We can construct an element x of order N from a primitive root:

$$x = \langle g^{(p-1)/N} \rangle_p$$

There is a more general definition of primitive roots, covering some cases other than M prime. g is a primitive root with respect to the modulus M if and only if the sequence

$$\langle g^i \rangle_M, \qquad 0 \le i < \phi(M)$$

gives the entire reduced residue set. Not every modulus M permits primitive roots—in fact, the cases that do permit primitive roots are

$$M = 2$$

$$M = 4$$

$$M = p^k$$

$$M = 2p^k$$

where p is an odd prime and k is a positive integer. Of these, the cases of greatest current interest to us are all of the form $M = p^k$. Actually, it is not very hard to find primitive roots for the primes and powers of primes that have them. For the primes, there are extensive tables of primitive roots, usually listing the smallest primitive root for each prime.

If we want a primitive root for p^k, we can go to the tables and look up a primitive root g for the prime p. Probably this will be a primitive root for p^k. Compute $d = g^{p-1} \bmod p^2$. If $d \neq 1$, g is our desired primitive root for p^k. In the rare instances where $d = 1$, $(g + p)$ is a primitive root for p^k. Once we have one primitive root, we can easily find others. If g is a primitive root for M, it is only one of a set of $\phi(\phi(M))$ primitive roots for M. Let $h = g^a$, where $(a,\phi(M)) = 1$. Then h is another primitive root. [See Problem 2.1: If x has order N with respect to modulus M, prove there are $\phi(d)$ numbers in the reduced residue set which have order N.]

Let us now look at the points of analogy between the sequence of powers of the complex exponential $W = \exp\,[j(2\pi/N)]$ and the sequence of residues of powers of x modulo M. Both $\{W^n\}$ and $\{\langle x^n\rangle\}$ are periodic. Both sequences begin with a 1 at $n = 0$ and there is a smallest N such that the Nth member of the sequence is 1. For both sequences, every member of the sequence *except 1* can be the multiplier for another sequence with the periodic property. $y = \langle x^k\rangle$ is mutually prime to M and hence satisfies $\langle y^N\rangle = 1$, so it gives rise to a sequence whose period is either N or some divisor of N.

2.9 CONVOLUTION LENGTH AND DIMENSION

In this section we will apply the Sino representation to circular convolution. The result will be that a length-N one-dimensional convolution, where N has mutually prime factors $N_1, N_2, \ldots, N_\mu$, is isomorphic to a multi-dimensional circular convolution whose lengths in the several dimensions are the mutually prime factors.

Therefore, let $x(n)$ and $h(n)$ be the two sequences that are to be convolved and let

$$y(n) = \prod_{m=0}^{N-1} x(m)h(\langle n - m\rangle_N), \qquad N = N_1 \times N_2 \times \cdots \times N_\mu \tag{2.9.1}$$

The Sino respresentations of n and m are

$$n = [n_1, n_2, \ldots, n_\mu], \qquad n_i = \langle n\rangle_{N_i} \tag{2.9.2}$$

$$m = [m_1, m_2 \ldots, m_\mu], \qquad m_i = \langle m\rangle_{N_i} \tag{2.9.3}$$

where $[n_1, n_2, \ldots, n_\mu]$ is the number n, in a representation emphasizing its Sino digits.

But in the Sino representation, the difference $\langle n - m\rangle_N$ is represented by the separate residues mod N_i,

$$\langle n - m\rangle_N = [\langle n_1 - m_1\rangle_{N_1}, \langle n_2 - m_2\rangle_{N_2}, \ldots, \langle n_\mu - m_\mu\rangle_{N_\mu}] \tag{2.9.4}$$

Now let us consider the one-dimensional N-point sequence $x(n)$ as a μ-dimensional sequence $\tilde{x}(n_1, n_2, \ldots, n_\mu)$,

$$\tilde{x}(n_1, n_2, \ldots, n_\mu) = x([n_1, n_2, \ldots, n_\mu]) \tag{2.9.5}$$

and similarly for $h(n)$ and $y(n)$. If we express the one-dimensional convolution in terms of these multidimensional indices, we get

$$\tilde{y}(n_1, \ldots, n_\mu) = \sum_{m_1=0}^{N_1-1} \cdots \sum_{m_\mu=0}^{N_\mu-1} \tilde{x}(m_1, \ldots, m_\mu)\tilde{h}(\langle n_1 - m_1\rangle_{N_1}, \ldots, \langle n_\mu - m_\mu\rangle_{N_\mu}) \tag{2.9.6}$$

In other words, we have shown that a one-dimensional circular convolution can be exactly isomorphic to a multidimensional circular convolution *when the length of the one-dimensional convolution can be factored into mutually prime factors*. Of course, the lengths N_i in the individual dimensions are dramatically less than the original length N. Since multidimensional circular convolution can be viewed as a series of one-dimensional convolutions applied to the several dimensions in turn, it is useful to have available a collection of small-N BDA-type circular convolution algorithms, derived using the techniques of Section 2.5, and carefully optimized. In Table 2.1 we give an abbreviated collection of such short convolution algorithms. A more complete table of short convolution algorithms of the BDA-type has been given in Agarwal and Cooley (1977).

Now let us consider the example of a 3×5 convolution of the newly available sequence $x(n,m)$ with a previously available sequence $h(n,m)$. We have already set up the matrices A_3, A_5, B_3, B_5, and the diagonal matrices D_3 and D_5, the D matrices being computed from the previously available $h(n,m)$. A natural formulation is

$$y(r,s) = \sum_i b_{ri}^{(3)} d_i^{(3)} \sum_n a_{in}^{(3)} \sum_j b_{sj}^{(5)} d_j^{(5)} \sum_m a_{jm}^{(5)} x(n,m) \tag{2.9.7}$$

In this formulation, the products involving A and B are cheap, involving only very small integers. The only nontrivial multiplications involve D. $D^{(5)}$ involves 10 multiplications on each of three columns, hence 30 multiplications. $D^{(3)}$ involves four multiplications on each of five columns, hence 20 multiplications. It seems, therefore, that 50 multiplications are required in all.

There is a competing formulation, however, if we interchange operations in (2.9.7):

$$y(r,s) = \sum_i b_{ri}^{(3)} \sum_j b_{sj}^{(5)} d_i^{(3)} d_j^{(5)} \sum_n a_{in}^{(3)} \sum_m a_{jm}^{(5)} x(n,m) \tag{2.9.8}$$

Now the products $d_i^{(3)} d_j^{(5)}$ may be precomputed and stored as constants e_{ij}. There are 40 different e_{ij} and each is used only once, so 40 multiplications suffice instead of 50.†

† The theoretical minimum number of multiplications needed for a length-five circular convolution is 8, whereas we have given an algorithm that uses 10. Therefore, an algorithm could be devised for 3×5 circular convolution which requires as few as 32 multiplications.

TABLE 2.1 Abbreviated Table of BDA-Type Algorithms for Circular Convolution

$$A_3 = \begin{bmatrix} 1 & 1 & 1 \\ 1 & -1 & 0 \\ 0 & 1 & -1 \\ 1 & 1 & -2 \end{bmatrix}, \quad D_3 = \text{diag}\begin{bmatrix} \frac{1}{3}(h_0 + h_1 + h_2) \\ (h_0 - h_2) \\ (h_1 - h_2) \\ \frac{1}{3}(h_0 + h_1 - 2h_2) \end{bmatrix}$$

$$B_3 = \begin{bmatrix} 1 & 1 & 0 & -1 \\ 1 & -1 & -1 & 2 \\ 1 & 0 & 1 & -1 \end{bmatrix}$$

$$A_4 = \begin{bmatrix} 1 & 1 & 1 & 1 \\ 1 & -1 & 1 & -1 \\ 1 & 1 & -1 & -1 \\ 1 & 0 & -1 & 0 \\ 0 & 1 & 0 & -1 \end{bmatrix}, \quad D_4 = \text{diag}\begin{bmatrix} \frac{1}{4}(h_0 + h_1 + h_2 + h_3) \\ \frac{1}{4}(h_0 - h_1 + h_2 - h_3) \\ \frac{1}{2}(h_0 - h_2) \\ \frac{1}{2}(h_0 - h_1 - h_2 + h_3) \\ \frac{1}{2}(h_0 + h_1 - h_2 - h_3) \end{bmatrix}$$

$$B_4 = \begin{bmatrix} 1 & 1 & 1 & 0 & -1 \\ 1 & -1 & 1 & -1 & 0 \\ 1 & 1 & -1 & 0 & 1 \\ 1 & -1 & -1 & 1 & 0 \end{bmatrix}$$

$$A_5 = \begin{bmatrix} 1 & 1 & 1 & 1 & 1 \\ 1 & 0 & 0 & 0 & -1 \\ 0 & 1 & 0 & 0 & -1 \\ 0 & 0 & 1 & 0 & -1 \\ 0 & 0 & 0 & 1 & -1 \\ 1 & 1 & 0 & 0 & -2 \\ 0 & 0 & 1 & 1 & -2 \\ 1 & 0 & 1 & 0 & -2 \\ 0 & 1 & 0 & 1 & -2 \\ 1 & 1 & 1 & 1 & -4 \end{bmatrix}$$

$$D_5 = \text{diag}\begin{bmatrix} \frac{1}{5}(h_0 + h_1 + h_2 + h_3 + h_4) \\ h_0 - h_4 \\ h_1 - h_4 \\ h_2 - h_4 \\ h_3 - h_4 \\ h_0 + h_1 - 2h_4 \\ h_2 + h_3 - 2h_4 \\ h_0 + h_2 - 2h_4 \\ h_1 + h_3 - 2h_4 \\ \frac{1}{5}(h_0 + h_1 + h_2 + h_3 - 4h_4) \end{bmatrix}$$

$$B_5 = \begin{bmatrix} 1 & 1 & 0 & -1 & -1 & 0 & 1 & 0 & 0 & -1 \\ 1 & -1 & -1 & 0 & 1 & 1 & 0 & 0 & 0 & -1 \\ 1 & -1 & 1 & -1 & 0 & 0 & 0 & 1 & 0 & -1 \\ 1 & 1 & 1 & 1 & 1 & -1 & -1 & -1 & -1 & 4 \\ 1 & 0 & -1 & 1 & -1 & 0 & 0 & 0 & 1 & -1 \end{bmatrix}$$

Although this saving appears modest, the principle behind it is quite powerful. Consider a μ-dimensional convolution of size $N_1 \times N_2 \times \cdots \times N_\mu$. Let the short convolution algorithms of the BDA type for length N_i require M_i multiplications. Then the formulation analogous to (2.9.7) would use

$$\left(\prod_{k=1}^{\mu} N_k\right) \sum_{i=1}^{\mu} \frac{M_i}{N_i}$$

multiplications while the formulation analogous to (2.9.8) would use only

$$\prod_{k=1}^{\mu} M_k$$

The simple trick of rearranging the order of sums in a multidimensional convolution, allowing us to premultiply the $d_i^{(k)}$, can therefore be quite effective as long as the number of multiplications needed in each short convolution BDA-type algorithm is not much longer than the length of the short convolution. Winograd has proved that the minimum number of multiplications for a length-N convolution is $2N - f_N$, where f_N is the number of factors in the cyclotomic polynomial factorization of $u^N - 1$. A method for finding an algorithm using this minimum number of multiplications can always be worked out using the Toom–Cook algorithm (Knuth (1969)).‡

So far we have seen that when the length of a one-dimensional circular convolution may be factored into mutually prime factors, the one-dimensional circular convolution may be rewritten as a multidimensional circular convolution where the lengths in the various dimensions are those mutually prime factors. It follows that certain multidimensional convolutions may be rewritten as one-dimensional convolutions, and so on. But we have also seen that there is a computational advantage to considering any circular convolution to have as many dimensions as possible, with as short as possible a length in each dimension, since we can combine small-N BDA-type algorithms for the different dimensions and by changing the order of the sums we can gather together the central multiplications into a single "layer" of central multiplications.

Note that when several small-N BDA-type algorithms are combined by interchanging the order of the sums and collecting together the central multipliers, the resulting algorithm is also of the BDA type. Therefore, it is only strictly necessary to have a catalog of efficient BDA-type algorithms for lengths that are powers of primes—algorithms for all other lengths may be constructed from these relatively few small-N BDA-type algorithms.

‡ Unfortunately, when the Toom–Cook algorithm is used to develop a convolution algorithm, the matrices A and B, which are guaranteed to contain only integers, often contain integers that are impractically complicated. Therefore, we may choose to use small-N BDA-type algorithms which are not optimum in the number of required multiplications. However, using the methods of derivation in Section 2.5 we get small-N algorithms that come close to optimum in Winograd's sense and yet have rather simple integers in the A and B matrices. A number of authors have tabulated such algorithms, so they do not have to be rederived.

2.10 THE DFT AS A CIRCULAR CONVOLUTION

Suppose that we have to compute the DFT of a sequence x_n whose length N is a prime. To emphasize that N is prime, call it p.

$$X_k = \sum_{n=0}^{p-1} x_n W^{nk}, \qquad k = 0, \ldots, p-1 \tag{2.10.1}$$

For the $k = 0$ term, the DFT is a simple sum:

$$X_0 = \sum_{n=0}^{p-1} x_n \tag{2.10.2}$$

For $k \neq 0$ let us separate the $n = 0$ term out of the sum, to give

$$X_k = x_0 + \sum_{n=1}^{p-1} x_k W^{nk}, \qquad k = 1, \ldots, p-1 \tag{2.10.3}$$

Now let g be any primitive root of p. The entire reduced residue set is congruent to the collection of powers of g,

$$1, 2, 3, \ldots, p-1 \leftrightarrow g^0, g^1, g^2, \ldots, g^{p-2}$$

in some order. This can be the basis of a pair of mappings:

$$n \rightarrow \langle g^r \rangle_p, \qquad r = 0, 1, \ldots, p-2 \tag{2.10.4}$$

$$k \rightarrow \langle g^s \rangle_p, \qquad s = 0, 1, \ldots, p-2 \tag{2.10.5}$$

so that

$$X_{\langle g^s \rangle} = x_0 + \sum_{r=0}^{p-2} x_{\langle g^r \rangle} W^{\langle g^r \rangle \langle g^s \rangle}, \qquad s = 0, \ldots, p-2 \tag{2.10.6}$$

But W has the property that $W^m = W^{\langle m \rangle_p}$. Hence

$$X_{\langle g^s \rangle} - x_0 = \sum_{r=0}^{p-2} x_{\langle g^r \rangle} W^{g^{r+s}}, \qquad s = 0, \ldots, p-2 \tag{2.10.7}$$

$x\langle g^r \rangle$ is the original sequence except for one point x_0, but permuted. Let us name the permuted sequence $\hat{x}_s$. It is a $(p-1)$-point sequence. Similarly, we can rename the permuted output sequence (less its zeroth point)

$$\hat{X}_s \equiv X_{\langle g^s \rangle} - x_0$$

another $(p-1)$-point sequence. But now we have to recognize a third sequence,

$$h_n = W^{\langle g^{-n} \rangle_p}$$

Note that

$$\langle g^{-n} \rangle_p = \langle g^{\langle -n \rangle_{p-1}} \rangle_p \tag{2.10.8}$$

The result is the recognition of a $(p - 1)$-point circular convolution

$$\hat{X}_s = \sum_{r=0}^{p-2} \hat{x}_r h_{\langle s-r \rangle_{p-1}} \tag{2.10.9}$$

hidden in the discrete Fourier transform computation for a prime number of points.

We can extend this idea to the case of a DFT with $N = p^q$ points. The DFT for indices divisible by p is

$$X_{pk} = \sum_{n=0}^{p^q-1} x_n W^{npk} \tag{2.10.10}$$

and after making the substitution $n = p^{q-1}r + s$, we obtain

$$X_{pk} = \sum_{s=0}^{p^{q-1}-1} \sum_{r=0}^{p-1} x_{p^{q-1}r+s} W^{(p^{q-1}r+s)pk} \tag{2.10.11}$$

$$X_{pk} = \sum_{s=0}^{p^{q-1}-1} \left(\sum_{r=0}^{p-1} x_{p^{q-1}r+s} \right) (W^p)^{sk} \tag{2.10.12}$$

In other words, a subset of the DFT is a length p^{q-1} DFT of sums of input points taken p at a time. Let us put (2.10.12) aside for a while and consider the other DFT points.

$$X_k = \sum_{p|n} x_n W^{nk} + \sum_{(n,p)=1} x_n W^{nk} \tag{2.10.13}$$

$$X_k = \sum_{n=0}^{p^{q-1}-1} x_{pn} W^{pnk} + \sum_{(n,p)=1} x_n W^{nk} \tag{2.10.14}$$

We see that (2.10.14) also contains a length p^{q-1} DFT, but this time there is another term. This other term will be shown to be a circular convolution. Let g be any primitive root for p^q. As before, we will use mappings based on the primitive root:

$$n \to \langle g^r \rangle_{p^q}, \qquad r = 0, 1, \ldots, p^q - p^{q-1} - 1 \tag{2.10.15}$$

$$k \to \langle g^s \rangle_{p^q}, \qquad s = 0, 1, \ldots, p^q - p^{q-1} - 1 \tag{2.10.16}$$

and we get

$$X_{\langle g^s \rangle} - \sum_{n=0}^{p^{q-1}-1} x_{pn} W^{pnk} = \sum_{r=0}^{p^q-p^{q-1}-1} x_{\langle g^r \rangle} W^{g^r g^s} \tag{2.10.17}$$

We now rename the permuted subsets of points whose index is prime to p:

$$x_{\langle g^r \rangle} = \hat{x}_r$$

$$X_{\langle g^s \rangle} = \hat{X}_s$$

$$W^{g^{-t}} = h_t$$

revealing the circular convolution of length $p^{q-1}(p - 1)$.

Whereas in the case of a prime number of points we found that the DFT reduced to a single circular convolution and a trivial additional correction term, here the additional correction term is two other DFTs, both of the same length, p^{q-1}. But these may be reduced iteratively to circular convolutions with correction terms that are DFTs of length p^{q-2}, and so on.

If the number of points in the DFT is a power of 2, the development above is not possible because there are no primitive roots for 2^ν, $\nu > 2$. Yet all is not lost. All the odd numbers $(1, 3, \ldots, 2^\nu - 1)$ have another representation close enough for our purpose:

$$n \equiv -1^a 3^b \mod 2^\nu \tag{2.10.18}$$

where $\quad a = 0, 1; \quad b = 0, 1, \ldots, 2^{\nu-2} - 1$

and similarly, for k odd,

$$k \equiv -1^\alpha 3^\beta \mod 2^\nu$$

where $\quad \alpha = 0,1; \quad \beta = 0, 1, \ldots, 2^{\nu-2} - 1$

Then for a DFT of length 2^ν we write separate expressions for k even

$$X_{2k} = \sum_{n=0}^{2^{\nu-2}-1} \left(\sum_{i=0}^{1} x_{n+2^{\nu-2}i} \right) W^{2kn} \tag{2.10.19}$$

which is a half-length DFT, and for k odd

$$X_{-1^\alpha 3^\beta} = \sum_{n \text{ even}} x_n W^{nk} + \sum_{a=0}^{1} \sum_{b=0}^{2^{\nu-2}-1} x_{-1^a 3^b} W^{-1^{(a+\alpha)} 3^{(b+\beta)}} \tag{2.10.20}$$

In (2.10.20) the first term is a half-length DFT and the second term is a *two-dimensional* circular convolution whose lengths in the two dimensions are 2 and $2^{\nu-2}$. Therefore, the work in computing a DFT for 2^ν points reduces to two half-length DFTs and a *two-dimensional* circular convolution. Each of the half-length DFTs may be reduced recursively, and hence the entire computation can be reduced to two-dimensional circular convolutions.

Here we have a fascinating set of relationships. For a long time we have been able to exploit the more familiar relationship between DFTs and circular convolution, for example,

$$x_n * y_n \leftrightarrow \mathrm{DFT}\{x\} \times \mathrm{DFT}\{y\}$$

Now we can additionally say that

$$\mathrm{DFT}\{x\} = \hat{x} * \hat{h} + \text{correction terms}$$

The first relationship has long been used as the basis of a way to compute convolutions. Not too surprisingly, the new relationship can be used as the basis of a fast way to compute some DFTs. The connection is by means of the BDA-type algorithms for short convolutions, introduced in the preceding section.

2.11 WINOGRAD'S DFT ALGORITHM

By expressing DFTs whose lengths are powers of a prime in terms of circular convolution, we can build up a collection of BDA-type algorithms for short-length DFTs. For example, when $N = 5$, we get the following BDA-type algorithm:

$$\begin{bmatrix} X_0 \\ X_1 \\ X_2 \\ X_3 \\ X_4 \end{bmatrix} = \mathcal{B}_5 \mathcal{D}_5 \mathcal{A}_5 \begin{bmatrix} x_0 \\ x_1 \\ x_2 \\ x_3 \\ x_4 \end{bmatrix} \tag{2.11.1}$$

$$\mathcal{A}_5 = \begin{bmatrix} 1 & 1 & 1 & 1 & 1 \\ 0 & 1 & 1 & 1 & 1 \\ 0 & 1 & -1 & -1 & 1 \\ 0 & 1 & 0 & 0 & -1 \\ 0 & 1 & -1 & 1 & -1 \\ 0 & 0 & -1 & 1 & 0 \end{bmatrix} \tag{2.11.2}$$

$$\mathcal{D}_5 = \operatorname{diag} \begin{bmatrix} 1 \\ -1 + \frac{1}{2}\left(\cos\frac{2\pi}{5} + \cos\frac{4\pi}{5}\right) \\ \frac{1}{2}\left(\cos\frac{2\pi}{5} - \cos\frac{4\pi}{5}\right) \\ j\left(\sin\frac{2\pi}{5} + \sin\frac{4\pi}{5}\right) \\ j\left(\sin\frac{4\pi}{5}\right) \\ j\left(\sin\frac{2\pi}{5} - \sin\frac{4\pi}{5}\right) \end{bmatrix} \tag{2.11.3}$$

$$\mathcal{B}_5 = \begin{bmatrix} 1 & 0 & 0 & 0 & 0 & 0 \\ 1 & 1 & 1 & 1 & -1 & 0 \\ 1 & 1 & -1 & 0 & 1 & 1 \\ 1 & 1 & -1 & 0 & -1 & -1 \\ 1 & 1 & 1 & -1 & 1 & 0 \end{bmatrix} \tag{2.11.4}$$

The $\mathcal{B}\mathcal{D}\mathcal{A}$-type algorithm above requires five multiplications by nontrivial quantities, but we shall also take note of the multiplication by $\mathcal{D}_{11}$ even though it is trivial to multiply by unity. The reason we count this last multiplication will become clear shortly. Thus a five-point DFT uses six multiplications. It is not a coincidence that all the $\mathcal{D}_{ii}$ are either purely real or purely imaginary. Table 2.2 gives multiplication counts for $\mathcal{BDA}$-type algorithms for a few short-length DFTs whose lengths are either prime or prime power.

In the case of circular convolution, we were able to show how a one-dimensional circular convolution of any length was exactly equivalent to a multidimensional circular convolution whose lengths in each dimension are the mutually prime factors of the one-dimensional length. We will now show that this is also true of the DFT.

Consider a DFT of $N = N_1N_2 \cdots N_\mu$ where $(N_i, N_j) = 1$ for all $i \neq j$.

$$X_k = \sum_{n=0}^{N-1} x_n e^{-j2\pi(nk/N_1N_2\cdots N_\mu)} \tag{2.11.5}$$

Now rewrite n and k in the Sino representations, as in (2.9.2), and substitute these in (2.11.5):

$$X_{[k_1,k_2,\ldots,k_\mu]} = \sum_{n_1=0}^{N_1-1} \cdots \sum_{n_\mu=0}^{N_\mu-1} x_{[n_1,n_2,\ldots,n_\mu]} e^{-j2\pi \frac{[\langle n_1k_1\rangle_{N_1}, \langle n_2k_2\rangle_{N_2},\ldots,\langle n_\mu k_\mu\rangle_{N_\mu}]}{N_1N_2\cdots N_\mu}}$$

We may abbreviate the exponent expression as

$$-j2\pi \frac{[\langle n_1k_1\rangle_{N_1}, \langle n_2k_2\rangle_{N_2}, \ldots, \langle n_\mu k_\mu\rangle_{N_\mu}]}{N_1N_2\cdots N_\mu} = -j2\pi \frac{[r_1, r_2, \ldots, r_\mu]}{N_1N_2\cdots N_\mu}$$

In other words, the exponent term nk is abbreviated as r and r is written in its Sino representation. But we can recover r from its Sino representation using (2.8.6):

$$r = \langle a_1r_1 + a_2r_2 + \cdots + a_\mu r_\mu\rangle_N \tag{2.11.6}$$

where each a_i is constructed so that $a_i \equiv \delta_{ij} \bmod N_j$. This allows us to simplify the exponential into a product:

$$e^{-j2\pi(nk/N_1N_2\cdots N_\mu)} = \prod_{i=1}^{\mu} e^{j2\pi \frac{a_ir_i}{N_1N_2\cdots N_\mu}}$$

TABLE 2.2 Multiplication Counts for Short-Length DFTs

N	Nontrivial	Trivial	Total
2	0	2	2
3	2	1	3
4	0	4	4
5	5	1	6
7	8	1	9
8	2	6	8
9	10	1	11
16	10	8	18

Now remember that a_i was constructed from b_i by (2.8.7):

$$a_i = b_i \prod_{j \neq i} N_j$$

$$\left(\prod_{j \neq i} N_j\right) b_i \equiv 1 \mod N_i, \qquad (b_i, N_i) = 1$$

Define the constants

$$c_i \equiv \left(\prod_{j \neq i} N_j\right) \mod N_i$$

Now let

$$k_i \rightarrow c_i s_i$$

Thus

$$s_i \equiv b_i k_i \mod N_i$$

We know that as k_i ranges over $0, 1, \ldots, N_i - 1$, s_i covers the same range since $(b_i, N_i) = 1$.

Therefore, the full expression for the DFT becomes

$$X_{[c_1k_1, c_2k_2, \ldots, c_\mu k_\mu]} = \sum_{n_1=0}^{N_1-1} \cdots \sum_{n_\mu=0}^{N_\mu-1} x_{[n_1, n_2, \ldots, n_\mu]} \prod_{i=1}^{\mu} e^{j2\pi \frac{s_i n_i}{N_i}} \qquad (2.11.7)$$

But this is nothing more than a multidimensional DFT. In other words, if we treat the one-dimensional input x_n as a multidimensional input, indexed by the digits of its Sino representation, its multidimensional DFT is a *permutation* of the one-dimensional DFT of the original input sequence.

Now a multidimensional DFT may be computed by computing one-dimensional DFTs successively along the dimensions. Therefore, if we use a $\mathcal{BDA}$-type algorithm for the one-dimensional DFTs along each dimension, we may use the reordered form of (2.9.8) to combine the central multiplications originating from each dimension into a single set of central multiplications.

The implications of this combination can be quite dramatic. If we refer to Table 2.2, we see that, for example, a 5-point DFT requires six multiplications (one trivial) and a 9-point DFT requires 11 multiplications (two trivial). Therefore, we can construct a DFT algorithm for 45 points requiring only 66 multiplications (two of which are trivial). Or, we can use short-length DFTs of lengths 3, 5, and 8 to construct a DFT of length 120 using 144 multiplications (of which six are trivial). When the number of multiplications needed by the component short-length DFTs in $\mathcal{BDA}$ form is not much more than their length, the multiplication count of the entire DFT derived by Winograd's algorithm is not much more than its length. This is in contrast to the number of multiplications required for the classical FFT, which tends to be proportional to N times the sum of its factors.

Unfortunately, the number of additions required for Winograd's DFT algorithms does not show the same behavior and is usually somewhat more than is required for a conventional DFT algorithm of comparable length. Furthermore, the matrices $\mathcal{A}_i$ and $\mathcal{B}_i$, although composed of simple entries, are not as regularly ordered as are the additions and subtractions required in an FFT algorithm, so that programs and/or hardware for the Winograd algorithm must devote a relatively large part of resources to moving data around, in comparison to the resources devoted to multiplication and addition.

Note that if the original problem is to compute a multidimensionl DFT, the Winograd trick of reordering operations in a $\mathcal{B}\mathcal{D}\mathcal{A}$-type algorithm can be applied separately for each dimension and then again across the natural dimensions for still further savings.

2.12 NUMBER-THEORETIC ANALOGY OF DFT

In previous sections we have shown how we can convolve sequences x and h by first "transforming" x and h, then multiplying the transforms together point by point, and finally inverse transforming the product. The transform chosen was often a rectangular transform, leading to a BDA-type algorithm. Alternatively, the transform chosen can be the more traditional DFT, which is also in the class of BDA-type algorithms. The rectangular transforms use the fewest possible multiplications but have a generally irregular structure and make no claim of minimizing the required number of additions. The DFT method is popular because the transform can be computed quickly by FFT and the algorithm is rather regular.

But the approach using the FFT does have a few drawbacks, slight nuisances even though well worth the savings over a direct method. Here are a few of the drawbacks:

- The FFT is formulated for complex sequences. Some tricks are available to convolve real sequences without paying the penalty for complex arithmetic, but these tricks lead to complications in procedure. It would be nice if a transform existed that had both the speed and simplicity of the FFT but worked with real arithmetic.
- The FFT uses computations involving irrational numbers, the powers of W. There is an inherent need to tolerate approximate results and to estimate the loss in accuracy due to round-off.
- Most of the multiplications needed in computing the FFT are not by "easy" numbers. An example of an easy multiplier is a power of 2, for which the product can be obtained with only a shift of the bits of the multiplicand.

It turns out that there is a way to devise a family of transforms with the desired convolution property, which overcomes these three drawbacks.

Such transforms are based on elementary number theory. They have, of course, a few drawbacks of their own, but there are cases in which they would clearly be of value.

An example is the *Fermat number transform*, introduced here and explained in more detail later. Let M, a modulus, be a Fermat number, defined as

$$M = 2^{2^{\mu}} + 1 \tag{2.12.1}$$

Thus if $\mu = 3$, $M = 2^8 + 1 = 257$. Consider what happens when we raise 2 to successive powers modulo M.

$$\begin{aligned} 2^0 &= 1 \\ 2^1 &= 2 \\ 2^2 &= 4 \\ &\vdots \\ 2^{2^{\mu}} &\equiv -1 \mod M \\ 2^{2^{\mu}+1} &\equiv -2 \mod M \\ 2^{2^{\mu}+2} &\equiv -4 \mod M \\ &\vdots \\ 2^{2^{\mu+1}} &\equiv 1 \mod M \\ &\vdots \\ 2^n &\equiv 2^{n-2^{\mu+1}} \mod M \end{aligned}$$

We see that $2^n \bmod M$ is a periodic sequence whose period is $2^{\mu+1}$. In the terminology of Section 8.5, the order of 2 with respect to modulus 257 is 16.

In general, the order of 2 with respect to modulus $M = 2^{2^{\mu}} + 1$ is $N = 2^{\mu+1}$. The sequences we transform will have length N. Let a_n be a typical sequence. We assume that every datum is a nonnegative integer (although this is not necessary).

The Fermat number transform of a_n is defined as

$$A_k = \sum_{n=0}^{N-1} a_n 2^{nk} \mod M, \qquad k = 0, 1, \ldots, N-1 \tag{2.12.2}$$

We note that the only multiplications needed to carry out this transform are multiplications by powers of 2. But furthermore, we do not intend to compute A_k, only something that is congruent to A_k modulo M. This allows us to keep all our results in registers whose word length is no more than N bits.

The Fermat number transformation can be carried out by an algorithm like the FFT. In place of multiplications of complex data by $e^{j2\pi(nk/N)}$ we multiply integer-valued data by 2^{nk}. The resulting A_k may be inverted to restore a_n. Like the DFT, the formula for an inverse Fermat number transform is very similar to that for the forward transform:

$$a_n = 2^{N-\mu-1} \sum_{k=0}^{N-1} A_k 2^{\langle -nk \rangle_N} \tag{2.12.3}$$

Unlike the DFT, a Fermat number transform does not reveal very much about the spectral composition of the sequence that was transformed.

However, if we transform two sequences a_n and b_n to get A_k and B_k and if we define C_k as the product $A_k B_k$, we can inverse transform C_k to give c_n. Then

$$c_n \equiv \sum_{m=0}^{N-1} a_m b_{n-m \bmod N} \mod M$$

In other words, c_n is the congruence equivalent of an N-point circular convolution of a_n with b_n. This enables us to compute the convolution of two sequences of integers, using a procedure in which the only nontrivial multiplications (by other than powers of 2) are the N multiplications used to compute $C_k = A_k \times B_k$. *Within* the transformation we use only easy multiplications by powers of 2. Since no irrational numbers, or even noninteger numbers, arise, the result will always be exact, without any rounding error whatsoever. There is also no need to deal with complex numbers to accomplish a convolution of real data.

The modulo M arithmetic, contrary to naive expectation, is not much more complicated than ordinary binary arithmetic. Therefore, as a tool for computing circular convolution, the Fermat number transform has great potential value. The Fermat number transform is one of a whole class of number-theoretic transforms, and related transforms.

2.13 NUMBER-THEORETIC TRANSFORM

Now let us construct an analogy to a DFT, which we shall call a *number-theoretic transform* (NTT). We will be given a modulus M and a kernel x with $(x, M) = 1$. The data to be transformed are integers $a_0, a_1, \ldots, a_{N-1}$, where N is the order of x with respect to modulus M. The transform is a set of integers $A_0, A_1, \ldots, A_{N-1}$ computed by the formula

$$A_k = \left\langle \sum_{n=0}^{N-1} a_n x^{nk} \right\rangle_M \tag{2.13.1}$$

In constructing this analogy, we imply (but have not proven) that at least some of the properties of the ordinary DFT have their counterparts in the number-theoretic DFT. So far, the main fact we have in support of our analogy is the property of x,

$$\langle x^{nk}\rangle_M = \langle x^{\langle nk\rangle_N}\rangle_M$$

(The reader must be careful to distinguish the modulus M, in the residue reductions in calculating the transform, from the modulus N, which has to do with the periodicity of the exponential sequence and the length of the transformed sequence.) But DFTs have other properties and we shall have to restrict the definition of the number-theoretic transform in order to capture these other properties. Let us therefore build up the final definition of the number-theoretic transform by going from more restrictive to less restrictive definitions. We shall first assume that M is an odd prime, then that it is a power of an odd prime, and finally that it is a product of powers of odd primes. There will not be a definition of a number-theoretic transform when M is even.

The DFT property that is elusive is the inverse transform property. We would like A_k and a_n to obey the second relationship,

$$a_n = \left\langle\left\langle\frac{1}{N}\right\rangle\left\langle\sum_{k=0}^{N-1} A_k x^{-nk}\right\rangle\right\rangle$$

but we cannot even begin to satisfy this relationship until we define some new usages. Modulo arithmetic is a ring, and division, the inverse of multiplication, is undefined. What do we mean by x^{-m} in arithmetic modulo M? And what do we mean by $1/N$ in the same arithmetic system?

The former case is relatively easy. x^{-m} must be that residue, y, of M which is the solution to $\langle x^m y\rangle_M = 1$. By the periodicity of x^m we have

$$y = \langle x^{\langle N-m\rangle_N}\rangle_M$$

We will take x^{-m} to mean $\langle x^{\langle N-m\rangle_N}\rangle_M$.

This still leaves us with the problem of $1/N$. We cannot simply assume the existence of a residue $\hat{N}$ with the property that

$$\langle \hat{N}N\rangle_M = 1$$

In fact, in many cases there is no possible $\hat{N}$.

Take the example of $M = 21$ and $x = 2$: $(2, 21) = 1$, so x^n is a periodic sequence. The powers of x are 1, 2, 4, 8, 16, 11, 1, . . . and hence $N = 6$. Can we solve $\langle 6\hat{N}\rangle_{21} = 1$? Note that this could also be written as

$$6\hat{N} + 21b = 1$$

and we know that $(6, 21) \neq 1$. So there is no solution and the DFT analogy for $M = 21$ breaks down when we try to write an expression for an inverse transform with $M = 21$ and $N = 6$.

We will say that a number-theoretic transform exists and is defined by

$$A_k = \left\langle\sum_{n=0}^{N-1} a_n x^{nk}\right\rangle_M$$

whenever the order of x with respect to modulus M is N and N has an inverse with respect to modulus M. *All that we mean when we say that a number-theoretic transform exists is that we can assign a meaning to the formulas for the transform and its inverse. It is a separate matter to decide whether the inverse transform formula actually computes the sequence that was transformed by the transform formula.*

Example With $M = 7$ and $x = 3$. The sequence of powers of x is 1, 3, 2, 6, 4, 5, 1, . . ., so $N = 6$. We can solve $6\hat{N} = 1 \bmod 7$, giving $\hat{N} = 6$. Hence we define the number-theoretic transform for $M = 7$ and $x = 3$ as

$$A_k = \left\langle \sum_{n=0}^{5} a_n 3^{nk} \right\rangle_7$$

and the inverse transform is

$$a_n = \left\langle 6 \sum_{k=0}^{5} A_k 3^{-nk} \right\rangle_7$$

The proof of the inverse property, when it holds, follows as a special case of the proof of the convolution property, which is our next subject.

For given M, if the sequences a_n and b_n have the number-theoretic transforms A_k and B_k and if

$$C_k \equiv \langle A_k B_k \rangle_M$$

we can compute a sequence c_n by using the inverse number-theoretic transform. Let us see what that gives us:

$$c_n \equiv \hat{N} \sum_{k=0}^{N-1} \left(\sum_{r=0}^{N-1} a_r x^{rk} \right) \left(\sum_{s=0}^{N-1} b_s x^{sk} \right) x^{-nk} \quad \bmod M$$

We can rewrite the inverse transform above as

$$c_n \equiv \sum_{r=0}^{N-1} \sum_{s=0}^{N-1} a_r b_s \left(\hat{N} \sum_{k=0}^{N-1} x^{(r+s-n)k} \right) \quad \bmod M$$

and we see that c_n is congruent to the circular convolution of a_n with b_n if

$$\hat{N} \sum_{k=0}^{N-1} x^{mk} \quad \bmod M = \begin{cases} 1, & \text{if } m \equiv 0 \quad \bmod N \\ 0, & \text{otherwise} \end{cases} \tag{2.13.2}$$

First, let M be a prime, p. Since $N|\phi(M)$ we have $N|(p - 1)$. Hence $N < p$, which is enough to show that it is mutually prime to p. Therefore, $\hat{N}$ exists. In (2.13.2), for $m \equiv 0 \bmod N$, each power x^{mk} is 1, the sum is N, and the product $\hat{N}N$ is unity. For $m \not\equiv 0 \bmod N$, write the sum as

$$t \equiv 1 + x^m + x^{2m} + \cdots + x^{(N-1)m} \quad \bmod M \tag{2.13.3}$$

Then

$$x^m t \equiv x^m + x^{2m} + \cdots + x^{(N-1)m} + 1 \quad \bmod M \tag{2.13.4}$$

Subtracting (2.13.3) from (2.13.4), we have

$$t(x^m - 1) \equiv 0 \mod M \tag{2.13.5}$$

Since M is prime, we have $(x^m - 1, M) = 1$. Thus $(x^m - 1)$ has an inverse and we can conclude that $t \equiv 0 \mod M$. Therefore, (2.13.2) holds and from it we see that the convolution theorem holds for a number-theoretic transform defined when M is a prime.

When M is an odd prime p, we can pick anything as x (except a multiple of p), and N, the order of x, will follow from the choice of x. The number-theoretic transform will exist, its inverse transform will be computable, and the inverse number-theoretic transform of a product of number-theoretic transforms will be congruent mod p to the N-point circular convolution of the original sequences.

Now consider $M = p^k$, a power of an odd prime. Let us suppose that we can choose x (mutually prime to p) and that it leads to N, the order of x with respect to modulus p^k, and to a number-theoretic transform for that order. Let a_n, b_n, and c_n be the three sequences in the convolution

$$c_n \equiv \sum_{m=0}^{N-1} a_m b_{\langle n-m \rangle_N} \mod p^k$$

Suppose that we write the numbers making up the sequence a_n in the radix p number system, and do the same for b_n, c_n, x, and $\hat{N}$. Now take all the equations modulo p. This will lead us to recognize that we have carried out length-N number-theoretic transforms and circular convolutions for sequences $\langle a_n \rangle_p$, and so on, modulus p. Since we know that only lengths N that divide $p - 1$ are possible, these are also the only lengths that are allowable for modulus p^k. We can define a number-theoretic transform for other lengths and we can compute according to the inverse transform expression, but it will not invert the transform.

In a similar vein, suppose that M is a product of several prime powers, $M = p_1^{k_1} p_2^{k_2} \ldots$. Choose x mutually prime to all the primes that divide M, and determine N, the order of x with respect to M. Assume that a number-theoretic transform exists with length N and that it has a computable inverse and a convolution property. Now let us write a_n in the Sino number system and do the same for b_n, c_n, x, and $\hat{N}$. If we write the equations for the transforms and convolution modulo $p_i^{k_i}$, all the operations are segregated to involve only the corresponding digit in the Sino representation. This will lead us to recognize that we have carried out a length-N number-theoretic transform for modulus $p_i^{k_i}$. Since we know that only lengths N that divide $p_i - 1$ are possible, these are also the only lengths that are allowable for moduli divisible by these primes.

Theorem: The only number-theoretic transforms that are invertible and support a circular convolution theorem for modulus M have length N, where N is a divisor of $p_i - 1$ for every prime p_i that divides M.

Corollary: There are no number-theoretic transforms of interest when M is even.

The theorem above asserts that transform lengths do not exist. It might be of interest to have the complementary statement about which transform lengths do exist.

Theorem: Number-theoretic transforms exist for modulus M and length N if and only if $N|(p_i - 1)$ for every p_i that divides M.

We do not and will not prove this theorem here. However, we will demonstrate some useful number-theoretic transforms. Although we have already seen something of the Fermat number transform, we will first introduce a simpler and less well known Mersenne number transform.

2.13.1 Mersenne Number Transform

Let $M = M_p \equiv 2^p - 1$, where p is prime. M_p is called a *Mersenne number*. M_p need not be prime.† Let $x = 2$.

The order of x with respect to M_p is exactly p. This is easy to see. $2^p \equiv 1 \bmod 2^p - 1$, and $2^n < M_p$ if $n < p$. In fact, it is worth looking at the powers of 2, modulo M_p, in binary notation. We illustrate for $p = 7$, $M_p = 127$. M_p in binary would be

$$2^7 - 1 = 1111111$$

$$\begin{aligned}
2^0 &= 0000001 \\
2^1 &= 0000010 \\
2^2 &= 0000100 \\
2^3 &= 0001000 \\
2^4 &= 0010000 \\
2^5 &= 0100000 \\
2^6 &= 1000000 \\
2^7 &= 0000001 \\
2^8 &= 0000010 \\
&\vdots
\end{aligned}$$

Note that $2^m \bmod M_p$, written in binary, is a word with $p - 1$ zeros and a 1 in bit position $\langle m \rangle_p$.

† If M_p is prime, it is called a *Mersenne prime*. Mersenne primes have a long history in recreational number theory. They are related to "perfect" numbers, which are defined as numbers that are equal to the sum of their divisors. For example, $6 = 1 + 2 + 3$. $2^{p-1}(2^p - 1)$ is perfect if $2^p - 1$ is prime. There is a surprisingly simple procedure called Lucas's test for determining whether, for a given prime p, M_p is prime or composite. Lucas's test can be carried out for Mersenne numbers with thousands of digits, and the primes that have been discovered in this way are the largest known primes.

We define the Mersenne number transform of the sequence $\{a_0, a_1, \ldots, a_{p-1}\}$ as

$$A_k = \left\langle \sum_{n=0}^{p-2} a_n 2^{nk} \right\rangle_{M_p}$$

The inverse Mersenne number transform can be defined if we can find $\hat{N}$ where

$$p\hat{N} \equiv 1 \mod 2^p - 1$$

Such an $\hat{N}$ is

$$\hat{N} = \frac{1 - M_p}{p} = \frac{2 - 2^p}{p}$$

where we are guaranteed that $\hat{N}$ is an integer by Euler's theorem. Therefore, to prove that a Mersenne number transform has the convolution property, we have only to prove that

$$t = 1 + 2^m + 2^{2m} + \cdots + 2^{(p-1)m}$$

is congruent to 0 mod M_p when $1 \leq m \leq p - 1$. We have

$$t \equiv \sum_{k=0}^{p-1} 2^{\langle mk \rangle p} \mod M_p$$

but note that because $(m, p) = 1$, the set of exponents $\langle mk \rangle_p$, $k = 0, 1, \ldots, p - 1$ is just a permutation of the integers $0, 1, \ldots, p - 1$. Thus $t = 1 + 2 + 4 + \cdots + 2^{p-1} = M_p$. This proves that the Mersenne transform is a full-fledged number-theoretic transform with the convolution property.

Since the length of the sequence being transformed is not composite, there is no FFT-like algorithm for computing the Mersenne transform. However, the arithmetic involved is easy. Suppose that we have a datum a in a p-bit word and we want to multiply a by 2^r. The ith bit of a signifies $a_i 2^i$ and after the multiplication it will signify $a_i 2^{r+i}$ in the product. We have seen that 2^n is congruent to $2^{n \bmod p}$, so we put the original bit into the result register in bit position $i + r \bmod p$—in other words, we multiply by rotating the bits in the word containing a by r bit positions. By comparison, for ordinary binary arithmetic we would shift a by r bit positions.

Modulo M_p addition is almost as easy. Suppose that a and b, which are to be added, are in p-bit registers. Their ordinary arithmetic sum giving a result c will occupy a $(p + 1)$-bit register. The most significant bit of this sum has value $c_p 2^p$, and since $2^p \equiv 1 \mod M_p$, we can also say that the sum has value $c_p 2^0$. Therefore, it can be added into bit position 0. Since c_p is just the carry bit generated at the most significant end of the p-bit adder, the Mersenne number arithmetic logic for addition simplifies to ordinary addition with the carry from the pth bit injected into the least significant bit position. This is called *end-around carry*. In the early days of digital computers, before two's-complement arithmetic became standardized, some computers were designed to use a number representation called *one's complement*. Mersenne number transform addition uses one's-complement arithmetic.

When we multiply the two transforms together, $C_k = A_k \times B_k$, we get products C_k, which each may have $2p$ bits. If we call a the word made up from the p least significant bits of C_k and we call b the word made up from the p remaining bits of C_k, then

$$C_k \equiv a + b \mod M_p$$

Therefore, the mod M_p multiplications called for to multiply together the two Mersenne number transforms are not significantly more logically complex than ordinary multiplications.

In summary, a Mersenne number transform is a number-theoretic transform that can be used to compute circular convolutions of integer sequences. The length of sequences that can be convolved must be the same as the word length used to represent the data. Furthermore, because there is no FFT-type algorithm for the Mersenne transform, each transform will require about p^2 rotate-and-add steps, in contrast to the $N \log_2 N$ complex multiplications and additions required for an FFT-based circular convolution (when N is a power of 2).

2.13.2 Fermat Number Transform

Let $M = F_\mu = 2^{2^\mu} + 1$, a Fermat number. Let $x = 2$. The order of 2 is $N = 2^{\mu+1}$. In fact, $2^{N/2}$ is trivially equal to -1, so 2^N is certainly congruent to 1. Using the example of $\mu = 3$, let us write the 16 powers of 2, modulo $F_3 = 257$, as sign-and-magnitude binary numbers with 8 bits and a sign:

$$\begin{aligned}
2^0 &= +00000001 & 2^8 &= -00000001 \\
2^1 &= +00000010 & 2^9 &= -00000010 \\
2^2 &= +00000100 & 2^{10} &= -00000100 \\
2^3 &= +00001000 & 2^{11} &= -00001000 \\
2^4 &= +00010000 & 2^{12} &= -00010000 \\
2^5 &= +00100000 & 2^{13} &= -00100000 \\
2^6 &= +01000000 & 2^{14} &= -01000000 \\
2^7 &= +10000000 & 2^{15} &= -10000000
\end{aligned}$$

So $2^m \bmod F_\mu$, written in sign-and-magnitude binary, has only a single bit and is an easy multiplier.

We have already defined the Fermat number transform of a discrete sequence $\{a_0, a_1, \ldots, a_{2N-1}\}$ in (2.12.2) and the inverse Fermat number transform in (2.12.3). The existence of $\hat{N}$ is obvious. Let us show that the inverse expression truly inverts the transform. As usual, this requires us to show that

$$t = 1 + 2^m + 2^{2m} + \cdots + 2^{(N-1)m}$$

is congruent to 0 mod F_μ when $1 \leq m \leq N - 1$. Write t as

$$t = \sum_{i=0}^{N-1} 2^{im} = \sum_{i=0}^{N/2-1} 2^{im}(1 + (2^{N/2})^m)$$

But $2^{N/2}$ is congruent to -1. Thus, when m is odd, the term $(1 + (2^{N/2})^m)$ is congruent to 0. If m is even, that same term becomes 2, can be taken outside the sum, and we can concentrate on showing that

$$\sum_{i=0}^{N/2-1} 2^{im}$$

is congruent to zero. Let $m = 2\hat{m}$ and said sum becomes

$$\sum_{i=0}^{N/4-1} 2^{i2\hat{m}}(1 + (2^{N/2})^{\hat{m}})$$

The term $(1 + (2^{N/2})^{\hat{m}})$ is congruent to 0 when $\hat{m}$ is odd and congruent to 2 when $\hat{m}$ is even. Therefore, we are only left to consider the case when $\hat{m}$ is even. But we can continue this reduction as many times as we require to dispose of all cases of m up to $m = N - 1$. Therefore, $t \equiv 0 \bmod F_\mu$ if $m \not\equiv 0 \bmod N$, as required. This proves that the Fermat number transform can be inverted and supports a convolution theorem.

We showed that the modulus arithmetic needed for Mersenne number transforms was rather simple because of the form of the modulus. Arithmetic modulo a Fermat number is also relatively simple. Suppose that we have a number a in a word with 2^μ bits:

$$a = \sum_{i=0}^{2^\mu-1} a_i 2^i$$

If we double the number, we get

$$2a = \sum_{i=0}^{2^\mu-1} a_i 2^{i+1} = \sum_{i=0}^{2^\mu-2} a_i 2^{i+1} + a_{2^\mu-1} 2^{2^\mu}$$

$$2a \equiv \sum_{i=0}^{2^\mu-2} a_i 2^{i+1} - a_{2^\mu-1} \quad \bmod F_\mu$$

This tells us that we can double a number by shifting its bits left one position, and if the bit lost to the left is a 1, subtracting 1 from the result. By induction, to multiply a by 2^r we shift left by r bit positions and subtract from the result the r-bit word fragment that spills off the left end. Similarly, addition is easy because the sum of a and b can be carried out with ordinary arithmetic except that if a carry is generated in the leftmost position, the result should be reduced by 1.

There is a complication, however. There is one possible value which cannot be represented in a word with 2^{μ} bits. An additional bit must be carried, set to 1 for this special case and zero for all other cases, and the arithmetic rules must take this special case into account. It is natural to assign the special case to the number $2^{2^{\mu}}$, which is congruent to -1. McClellan (1976) and Leibowitz (1976) have taken a different approach which permits a more convenient use of standard integrated circuits for arithmetic, in exchange for using a less familiar number system.

2.13.3 Considerations for Use of Number-Theoretic Transforms to Perform Circular Convolution

Using the number-theoretic transform to compute a convolution is an example of the use of a surrogate field (or ring). The quantities input to a computation (the numbers making up the sequences to be convolved) are put in one-to-one correspondence to elements in a finite field or ring (or in general elements of any algebraic system for which suitable laws of algebra apply), the computation is carried out in the arithmetic of the finite ring, and the results of the finite ring computations are put into one-to-one correspondence with the results in the desired system.

Note, however, that the number-theoretic transform itself cannot be put into any correspondence with a DFT. Points of analogy exist, but this is not sufficient to give number-theoretic transforms any use except as a tool for computing convolutions.

The ability to replace multiplications by complex transcendental quantities such as exp $(j2\pi/N)$ by multiplication by powers of 2 is of great value in either designing special-purpose hardware or for use in very small computers without hardware multipliers. The other often quoted advantage of the NTT approach is that the result of the computed convolution is exact without possibility of round-off. However, this second "advantage" may actually be a disadvantage in disguise. The input sequences might be quantized to perhaps 10 bits each, but a convolution of two such sequences could easily require 30 bits for exact representation. This in turn can force the use of an inconveniently large modulus. The user will pay a price in extra-long word length, with all of its attendant costs. A more conventional approach to computing a convolution would permit rounding the partial results of a computation to the accuracy really required.

The other significant disadvantage of number-theoretic transforms is the rigid relationship of the transform length to the modulus. For any given requirement this may be no problem, but small changes in the signal-processing requirements might threaten to force a complete redesign of a system.

2.13.4 Use of Surrogate Fields for Complex Arithmetic

In this section we show how complex multiplication, normally requiring four real multiplications, can sometimes be accomplished using only two.

The data are

$$A = a_r + ja_i$$

$$B = b_r + jb_i$$

and the result is to be

$$C = c_r + jc_i$$

where

$$c_r = a_r b_r - a_i b_i$$

$$c_i = a_r b_i + a_i b_r$$

First, we should remind the reader of an old trick permitting a complex multiplication using three real multiplications.

$$a_s = a_r + a_i$$

$$b_s = b_r - b_i$$

$$c_s = a_s b_s$$

$$c_u = a_r b_i$$

$$c_v = a_i b_r$$

$$c_r = c_s - c_v + c_u$$

$$c_i = c_u + c_v$$

Although this trick is occasionally useful, it sometimes costs more in extra additions than it saves in multiplications.

However, when we are working in the surrogate field or ring of modulo M, a quite different trick may be available. It requires that there be a number I in the ring for which

$$I^2 \equiv -1 \mod M \tag{2.13.6}$$

For example, if M is a Fermat number $F_\mu = 2^{2^\mu} + 1$, we can use $I = 2^{2^{\mu-1}}$. Note that I has the same algebraic property as j—it is the square root of -1—with the difference that in the modulo M ring, the complex quantities $A = a_r + ja_i$ and $B = b_r + jb_i$ can be represented as a single component modulo M elements:

$$\tilde{A} = a_r + Ia_i$$

$$\tilde{B} = b_r + Ib_i$$

and the representation of the product $C = c_r + jc_i$,

$$\tilde{C} = c_r + Ic_i = \tilde{A}\tilde{B} \mod M$$

is found with one modulo M multiplication.

But in this representation, the real and imaginary parts of a number are mixed together inextricably. There is no unambiguous way to recover c_r and c_i. We must use a double-component representation. Therefore, let us represent A by the pair $(\tilde{A}, \tilde{A}^*)$, where

$$\tilde{A} = a_r + Ia_i \tag{2.13.7}$$

$$\tilde{A}^* = a_r - Ia_i \tag{2.13.8}$$

and similarly represent B by the pair $(\tilde{B}, \tilde{B}^*)$, where $B^* = b_r - Ib_i$. Then the equivalent two-component representation for C is $(\tilde{C}, \tilde{C}^*)$ with

$$C^* \equiv \tilde{A}^*\tilde{B}^*$$

Proof:

$$\tilde{C}^* = (a_r - Ia_i)(b_r - Ib_i) = a_rb_r - I(a_rb_i + a_ib_r) + I^2a_ib_i$$

$$\tilde{C}^* \equiv (a_rb_r - a_ib_i) - I(a_rb_i + a_ib_r) \quad \text{mod } M$$

$$\tilde{C}^* \equiv c_r - Ic_i \quad \text{mod } M$$

Then

$$c_r = (2^{-1})(\tilde{C} + \tilde{C}^*) \tag{2.13.9}$$

and

$$c_i = (2I)^{-1}(\tilde{C} - \tilde{C}^*) \tag{2.13.10}$$

We see that in the case of modulo M arithmetic, the effect of complex multiplication can be achieved by a three-step process:

1. Transform from the (a_r, a_i) representation to the $(\tilde{A}, \tilde{A}^*)$ representation.
2. Carry out the multiplications separately for the two components.
3. Transform back to the (c_r, c_i) representation from the $(\tilde{C}, \tilde{C}^*)$ representation.

This makes sense only if the quantity I whose square is -1 exists in the ring. But furthermore, the multiplications by I in steps 1 and 3 should be cheap operations or there is no advantage to the method.

If two complex sequences are to be convolved using the Fermat number transform, it is legitimate to convert from one representation to the other either before or after transformation. Another application of the method is to allow direct implementation of complex FIR filters with half the expected number of real multiplications.

2.14 SPLIT-RADIX FFT

One of the most important techniques for computing lagged products is based on the efficiency with which we can compute the discrete Fourier transform. There are a great many algorithms, all of which are called the *fast Fourier transform*, whose common features are a timing and structure that depend on the way in which the number of points being transformed can be factored. When our interest in the DFT is as a step on the way to computing a convolution, we are usually free to choose the lengths of the sequences being transformed so as to optimize the FFT efficiency, and this will almost always mean that we choose a transform length that is a power of 2.

Although the history of the FFT algorithm is quite long, it became well known only in 1965. Since that time there has been surprisingly steady incremental progress in developing better and better FFT algorithms. At present, the most practical algorithms for general-purpose computer computation of the DFT when the sequence length is a power of 2 are called *split-radix* algorithms (Duhamel and Hollmann (1984)). In this section we explain the split-radix concept and show how to estimate the number of arithmetic operations needed for a given sequence length.

Once the algorithm has been specified, someone must write a program to carry out the algorithm. In the next section we introduce the *autogen* technique, which allows us to write a nearly optimum program for an algorithm like the FFT with the help of a computer.

We will introduce the split-radix concept by reviewing the standard FFT derivation, assuming that N is a power of 2. It proceeds as follows:

$$F(k) = \sum_{n=0}^{N-1} f(n) W^{nk} \tag{2.14.1}$$

We split the sum into two parts:

$$F(k) = \sum_{n=0}^{N/2-1} \left[f(n) + f\left(\frac{N}{2} + n\right) W^{(N/2)k} \right] W^{nk} \tag{2.14.2}$$

Then we write separate equations for the even and odd values of k:

$$F(2k) = \sum_{n=0}^{N/2-1} \left[f(n) + f\left(\frac{N}{2} + n\right) \right] (W^2)^{nk} \tag{2.14.3}$$

$$F(2k+1) = \sum_{n=0}^{N/2-1} \left[f(n) - f\left(\frac{N}{2} + n\right) W^n \right] (W^2)^{nk} \tag{2.14.4}$$

The first of these two equations is an $(N/2)$-point DFT on a sequence $[f(n) + f(N/2 + n)]$, which we can obtain without any multiplications. The second equation is also an $(N/2)$-point DFT, but we must compute that sequence, $[f(n) - f(N/2 + n)W^n]$, using a complex multiplication per point. The FFT algorithm is based on a recursive reduction of DFTs into combinations of shorter-length DFTs. Therefore, the typical stage of the FFT developed using the radix-2 approach will require a multiplication per point for half the sequences subsequently processed, $N/2$ multiplications for the stage.

It will pay us to pause long enough to show how to count the required number of multiplications for a radix-2 FFT. Suppose that $\mathscr{C}(N)$ is the number of complex multiplications needed to carry out a complete radix-2 DFT computation. We have seen that such a computation reduces to $N/2$ multiplications plus two shorter DFTs:

$$\mathscr{C}(N) = \frac{N}{2} + 2\mathscr{C}\left(\frac{N}{2}\right)$$

Note that this equation is pessimistic since it makes no allowance for the fact that some of the multiplications needed for the smaller transforms are trivial—this is more and more significant as the transform lengths get shorter and shorter.

Now if we replace $\mathscr{C}(N)$ by c_k, where $N = 2^k$, the previous equation becomes

$$c_k = 2^{k-1} + 2c_{k-1}$$

This is a difference equation. Its initial condition comes from the cost of a 2-point DFT (e.g., $c_1 = 1$). The solution is $c_k = \frac{1}{2}k2^k$. Hence $\mathscr{C}(N) = \frac{1}{2}N \log_2 N$.

Next we consider the radix-4 derivation. We have

$$F(k) = \sum_{n=0}^{N/4-1} \left[\sum_{l=0}^{3} f\left(n + l\frac{N}{4}\right) W^{(N/4)lk} \right] W^{nk} \tag{2.14.5}$$

We now write four separate equations for point sets of the form $4k + r$, $r = 0, 1, 2, 3$. For $r = 0$ we have

$$F(4k) = \sum_{n=0}^{N/4-1} \left[\sum_{l=0}^{3} f\left(n + l\frac{N}{4}\right) \right] (W^4)^{nk} \tag{2.14.6}$$

while for the general r we have

$$F(4k + r) = \sum_{n=0}^{N/4-1} \left[\sum_{l=0}^{3} f\left(n + l\frac{N}{4}\right) W^{(N/4)lr} W^{nr} \right] (W^4)^{nk} \tag{2.14.7}$$

In (2.14.7) we can replace $W^{(N/4)lr}$ by $(-j)^{lr}$, giving

$$F(4k + r) = \sum_{n=0}^{N/4-1} \left[\sum_{l=0}^{3} (-j)^{lr} f\left(n + l\frac{N}{4}\right) W^{nr} \right] (W^4)^{nk} \tag{2.14.8}$$

Thus we have reduced the computation of a length-N DFT to four shorter (length-$N/4$) DFTs of shorter sequences which we need to compute from the original length-N sequence. Of these four $N/4$-length sequences, one comes without multiplications and the other three require one complex multiplication per point. This uses three $N/4$ multiplications per stage, in contrast to the $N/2$ multiplications per stage needed by the radix-2 development. However, the subsequent DFTs needed are ($N/4$)-point DFTs, so a radix-4 algorithm requires half as many stages as a radix-2 algorithm. Using our difference equation approach, we have

$$\mathscr{C}(N) = \frac{3}{4}N + 4\mathscr{C}\left(\frac{N}{4}\right)$$

$$c_k = \tfrac{3}{4}2^k + 4c_{k-2}$$

with initial conditions $c_2 = 3$, so that $c_k = \frac{3}{8}k2^k$, for k even. The reader should work out the slightly more complicated expression for general k using the initial condition $c_k = 1$. The asymptotic cost of a radix-4 FFT, counting only complex multiplications, is $\frac{3}{8}N \log_2 N$ multiplications per transform.

The idea of the split-radix algorithm is simple. Use the radix-2 decomposition to create one sequence of values for further processing as an $(N/2)$-point DFT for even frequencies. From the radix-4 development, use $r = 1, 3$ to define two length-$(N/4)$ subsequences that will each yield half of the odd frequencies. These each require multiplications but push us ahead by two stages. In sizing the number of multiplications needed overall, the reduction is seen to be greater than for a radix-4 algorithm. Again let $\mathscr{C}(N)$ be the number of multiplications required for an N-point DFT using the split-radix idea. Then, because we use $N/2$ multiplications to reduce the N-point problem to an $(N/2)$-point problem plus two $(N/4)$-point problems,

$$\mathscr{C}(N) = \frac{N}{2} + \mathscr{C}\left(\frac{N}{2}\right) + 2\mathscr{C}\left(\frac{N}{4}\right) \tag{2.14.9}$$

$$c_k = 2^{k-1} + c_{k-1} + 2c_{k-2} \tag{2.14.10}$$

To see how the split-radix idea saves computation, let us try a quick solution for $\mathscr{C}(N)$. Since we expect the form of $\mathscr{C}(N)$ to be $\alpha N \log_2 N$, we can use

$$c_k = k\alpha 2^k$$

and substituting this hypothesized solution, we get

$$k\alpha 2^k = 2^{k-1} + (k - 1)\alpha 2^{k-1} + 2(k - 2)\alpha 2^{k-2}$$

$$2^{-1} = \alpha\tfrac{3}{2}$$

$$\alpha = \tfrac{1}{3}$$

Again, this is pessimistic because we have not taken any special account of the trivial multiplications. Therefore, it appears that the split-radix approach will reduce the number of complex multiplications needed for an FFT to below $\frac{1}{3}N \log_2 N$.

Now let us be a little bit more careful. First, we know that a 1-point DFT requires no multiplications. Thus $\mathscr{C}(1) = c_0 = 0$. For a 2-point transform, $\mathscr{C}(2) = c_1 = 0$. Neither of these fit the formula above, which we know to be pessimistic. Furthermore, we know that trivial multiplications by unity can be omitted. Thus

$$\mathscr{C}(N) = \frac{N}{2} - 1 + \mathscr{C}\left(\frac{N}{2}\right) + 2\mathscr{C}\left(\frac{N}{4}\right) \tag{2.14.11}$$

$$c_k = 2^{k-1} - 1 + c_{k-1} + 2c_{k-2} \tag{2.14.12}$$

$$c_0 = c_1 = 0 \tag{2.14.13}$$

This is a second-order linear difference equation with two initial conditions. Therefore, we can solve it using z-transform techniques.† The solution is

$$c_k = \frac{1}{2} + \left(\frac{3k-5}{9}\right)2^k + \frac{1}{18}(-1)^k \tag{2.14.14}$$

which has the asymptotic behavior of $\frac{1}{3}N \log_2 N$.

A similar set of calculations can be used to count complex additions or to account for the differing cost of multiplications by some special powers of W, such as $W^{mN/4}$. Returning to our decomposition for $F(4k + r)$, when r is odd (say, $r = 2s + 1$), we have

$$F(4k+r) = \sum_{n=0}^{N/4-1}\left[\sum_{l=0}^{3} f\left(n + l\frac{N}{4}\right)W^{(N/4)l(2s+1)}W^{nr}\right](W^4)^{nk}$$

$$F(4k+r) = \sum_{n=0}^{N/4-1}\left\{\sum_{l=0}^{3}\left[f\left(n + l\frac{N}{4}\right)(-1)^{ls}(-j)^l\right]W^{nr}\right\}(W^4)^{nk}$$

If we expand the sum over l, we find

$$f(n) - jf\left(n + \frac{N}{4}\right)(-1)^s - f\left(n + \frac{N}{2}\right) + jf\left(n + 3\frac{N}{4}\right)(-1)^s$$

which we may rewrite as

$$\left[f(n) - f\left(n + \frac{N}{2}\right)\right] - j(-1)^s\left[f\left(n + \frac{N}{4}\right) - f\left(n + 3\frac{N}{4}\right)\right]$$

But note that $f(n) - f(n + N/2)$ and $f(n + N/4) - f(n + 3N/4)$ are differences which naturally pair with the sums that we already compute as part of the preparation for the $(N/2)$-point transform resulting from $r = 0$, 2. There is a sharing of the "indexing" work. If we sketch a split-radix "butterfly," it will take the form of Fig. 2.3. A complete assemblage of these butterflies is shown in Fig. 2.4, in which we have shown a 16-point DFT reduced to an 8-point DFT and two 4-point DFTs, with the 8-point DFT further reduced to a 4-point DFT and two 2-point DFTs, and with each 4-point DFT reduced to a 2-point DFT and two final DFT outputs. Note that if we were to delete the rectangles that show how each reduced order DFT, we could not distinguish the *topology* of the split-radix FFT diagram from the topology of the classical radix-2 FFT. But the coefficients

† We must be cautious since this is not a stable system. The region of convergence of the z-transform must be outside $|z| = 2$.

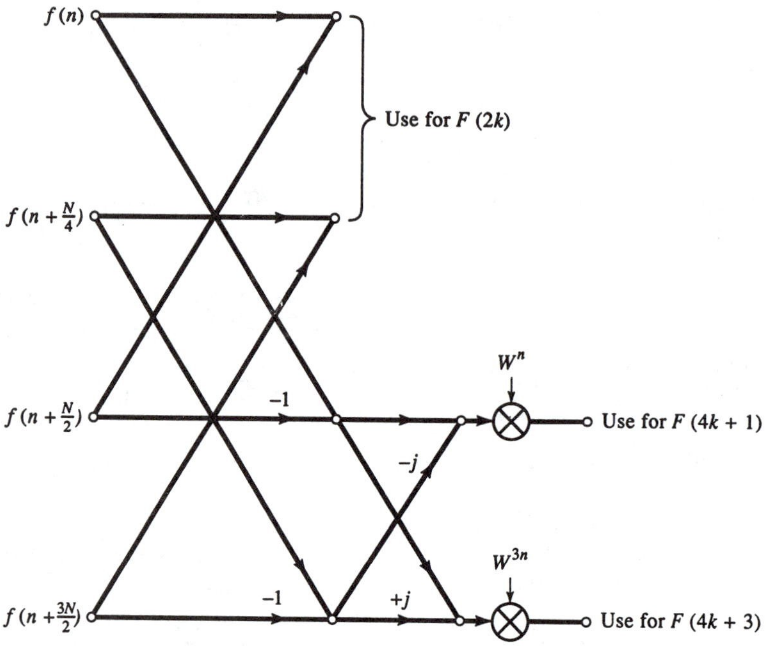

FIGURE 2.3 'Butterfly' for split radix DFT.

are different. Therefore, we see that whereas the split-radix scheme reduces the required number of complex multiplications, the number of required *complex* additions is the same for split-radix or radix-2 FFTs—but if we count real additions, the split-radix algorithm gives a reduction because each complex multiplication saved would have required some real operations, both additions and multiplications.

2.15 AUTOGEN TECHNIQUE

In the preceding section we showed how to count additions and multiplications for a given FFT algorithm, although we found that it was more and more difficult to take account of more and more special cases. We did not even attempt to consider the other operations that use up cycles in a computer program: indexing, initialization of loops, and moving data around. The arithmetic cost is, of course, most fundamental. There might be many ways to control program flow and achieve exactly the same arithmetic. In the extreme case, we might dispense entirely with nested loops and indexing and write a very efficient computer program using "straight-line" code (e.g., we can have a very long computer subroutine that codes each addition or multiplication separately). Writing such a program is quite practical by using the AUTOGEN programming method (Morris (1977)), described in

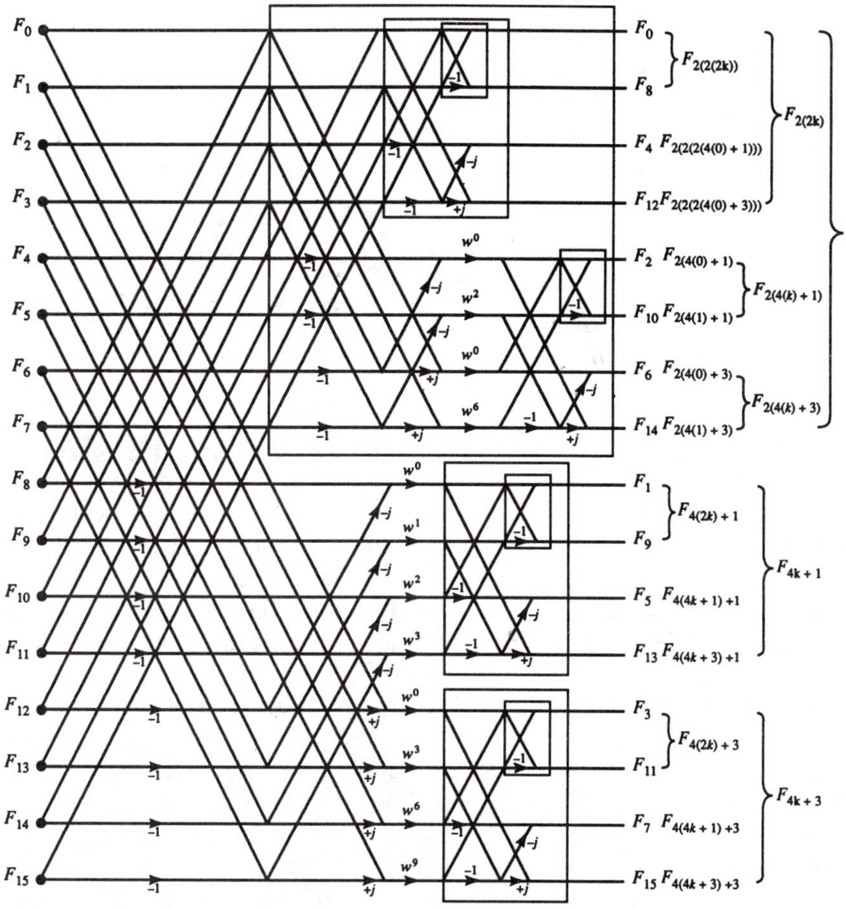

FIGURE 2.4 16 Point Split Radix DFT.

this section, which allows a computer program written with indexed loops to write another "unwrapped" program for the same purpose.

To explain the autogen technique, consider the simple FORTRAN program to add a list of 100 numbers in Fig. 2.5. Now consider the modified FORTRAN program in Fig. 2.6.

```
C  PROGRAM 1
         DIMENSION X(100)
C       S IS THE SUM and X(I) IS THE ORIGINAL DATA
         S=X(1)
         DO 1 I=2,100
           S=S+X(I)
1          CONTINUE
         END
```

FIGURE 2.5 FORTRAN Program to sum 100 numbers.

```
C  PROGRAM 2
         WRITE(6,50)
         WRITE(6,51)
         DO 1 I=2,100
           WRITE(6,52) I
1          CONTINUE
         WRITE(6,53)
50       FORMAT('      DIMENSION  X(100)')
51       FORMAT('      S=X(1)')
52       FORMAT('      S=S+X(',I3,')')
53       FORMAT('      END')
        END
```

FIGURE 2.6 Modified Form of Summing Program.

The result of running the second program is to write a character stream to unit 6. That character stream is a third FORTRAN program, which will look like Fig. 2.7. When we compile and run the third program, it will give the same result as the first program. This is a simple example of the AUTOGEN technique.

Suppose that we want to compute $\Sigma_i X(i) \cos 2\pi(I - 1)/100$. Now our elementary FORTRAN program might be as in Fig. 2.8, and the AUTOGEN program could be as in Fig. 2.9.

The result of running PROGRAM 5 is to create an AUTOGEN program in which the constants $\cos 2\pi(I - 1)/100$, which must be computed at run time in the original program, have been precomputed. The AUTOGEN program will run faster than the original program for two reasons: there is no looping or indexing, and the constants are not computed at run time.

Now consider a third issue. Some constants are special. In the example of Fig. 2.9, when $I = 26, 76$, the constant is 0. The AUTOGEN program will produce the code "S= 0.00000000*X(25)+S", the effect of which is to do nothing. But we can check for this case and avoid it. A suitably modified original program is given in Fig. 2.10. But this modification would only make the PROGRAM 6 run more slowly because of all the need for checking. One hundred tests to save two multiplications is not a good trade-off. A major difference between AUTOGEN program creation and conven-

```
DIMENSION X(100)
S=X(1)
S=S+X(  2)
S=S+X(  3)
  :
  :
S=S+X( 99)
S=S+X(100)
END
```

FIGURE 2.7 Result of Running Program 2.

```
C PROGRAM 4
      DIMENSION X(100)
      TWOPIN = 2.*3.14159265/100.
      S=0
      DO 1 I=1,100
        S=S+X(I)*COS((I-1)*TWOPIN)
1       CONTINUE
      END
```

FIGURE 2.8 Another Elementary FORTRAN Program.

```
C PROGRAM 5
      WRITE(6,50)
      TWOPIN = 2.*3.14159265/100.
      WRITE(6,51)
      DO 1 I=1,100
        T=COS((I-1)*TWOPIN)
        WRITE(6,52) T,I
1       CONTINUE
      WRITE(6,53)
50    FORMAT('      DIMENSION(X(100)')
51    FORMAT('      S=0')
52    FORMAT('      S='F10.7,'*X(',I3,')+S ')
53    FORMAT('      END')
      END
```

FIGURE 2.9 AUTOGEN Version of Program 4.

```
C PROGRAM 6
      DIMENSION X(100)
      TWOPIN = 2.*3.14159265/100.
      S=0
      DO 1 I=1,100
        T=COS((I-1)*TWOPIN)
        IF (T .NE. 0.)  THEN
          S=S+X(I)*T
        ENDIF
1       CONTINUE
      END
```

FIGURE 2.10 Program Checking for Simple Constants.

tional programming is this difference between the cost of a test at run time and a test at compile time. In the AUTOGEN version, Fig. 2.11, all the testing is to be carried out before run time. The modified AUTOGEN program created by running PROGRAM 7 will run a little bit faster than the original AUTOGEN version because it is a little shorter. It is also easy to test for other special cases, such as $I = 1, 51$, for which $T = \pm 1$. Again, in the AUTOGEN version this is worthwhile, but in a standard program the test can cost more than it saves.

An extreme example of the AUTOGEN principle is to write an FFT using a self-recursive subroutine, a subroutine that can call itself. Some computer languages do not permit this, including FORTRAN. But the AUTOGEN technique can be used across languages. An FFT written in, say, APL can be converted to an AUTOGEN program which, when run, creates a straight-line FORTRAN program.

For purposes of illustration, *let us pretend that FORTRAN would allow a subroutine to call itself.* Let us first write the standard FFT as such a recursive subroutine and then show how we might create an AUTOGEN version of it. The FFT subroutine must account for the memory management as well as the arithmetic. Figure 2.12 is a simple self-recursive subroutine that computes a length-N DFT. The use of this program for a 64-point DFT would be

CALL DFT(64,X,0)

The program above uses the flow diagram of Figs. 9.17 to 9.19 of Proakis and Manolakis (1992) for its memory management scheme. Since we have ignored the fact that FORTRAN does not allow self-recursive subroutines, there is no point in testing our purely tutorial program. Of course, even

```
C PROGRAM 7
      WRITE(6,50)
      TWOPIN = 2.*3.14159265/100.
      WRITE(6,51)
      DO 1 I=1,100
        T=COS((I-1)*TWOPIN)
        IF (T .NE. 0.)  THEN
           WRITE(6,52) T,I
        ENDIF
1       CONTINUE
      WRITE(6,53)
53    FORMAT('        END')
50    FORMAT('        DIMENSION(X(100)')
51    FORMAT('        S=0')
52    FORMAT('        S='F10.7,'*X(',I3,')+S ')
      END
```

FIGURE 2.11 AUTOGEN Program Checking for Simple Constants.

```
      SUBROUTINE DFT(N,X,MX)
C     N IS DATA LENGTH
C     INPUT SEQUENCE IS       X(MX+1), ... ,X(MX+N)
C     OUTPUT SEQUENCE IS IN PLACE, PERMUTED ORDER
      COMPLEX X,W,TEMP,T
C
      IF (N .EQ. 1) THEN
        RETURN
      ELSE
        W = CEXP(-2.*3.1415926535/N)
        M=N/2
        DO 2 J = 1,M
          TEMP = X(MX+J) + X(MX+J+M)
          T=W**(J-1)
          X(MX+M+J)=( X(MX+J)-X(MX+M+J) )*T
          X(MX+J)=TEMP
2         CONTINUE
        CALL DFT(M,X,MX)
        CALL DFT(M,X,MX+M)
        RETURN
      ENDIF
      END
```

FIGURE 2.12 Self-recursive DFT Subroutine.

within the constraints of FORTRAN, it is possible to program the equivalent of a self-recursive procedure without using subroutine calls at all, but if we were to do so here, it would hide the true idea we are trying to explain.

The self-recursive program above uses the essential idea of the FFT and the special structure of the butterfly but does not directly display any of the special structure of the resulting complete FFT algorithm. But we are going to use the program of Fig. 2.12 as the skeleton of an AUTOGEN program to write code for a DFT. Running the AUTOGEN program of Fig. 2.13 generates a straight-line program, which has no structure anyway. Therefore, such a simple skeleton can be used and a very efficient FFT program can still result.

In Fig. 2.13, note the parentheses and comma needed in format statement 52 to specify writing T as the character stream for a complex "constant" (T1,T2). We can still include checks for special cases of interest, generally the cases where T = W**(J-1) is either ± 1 or $\pm j$, and have the AUTOGEN program generate the appropriately simple code for those cases.

Next, let us consider programming a split-radix FFT. Before we were armed with the AUTOGEN technique and recursive DFT subroutines, programming a split-radix FFT would have presented a special difficulty. We could not easily arrange the computation in stages in the manner of a constant radix FFT. The basic repetitive butterfly of the split-radix algorithm extends over only one "stage" for the top half of its outputs and over two

```
      SUBROUTINE DFT(N,X,MX)
C     N IS DATA LENGTH
C     INPUT SEQUENCE IS      X(MX+1), ... ,X(MX+N)
C     OUTPUT SEQUENCE IS IN PLACE, PERMUTED ORDER
C
C  CONVERTED TO AUTOGEN FORM
C
      IF (N .NE. 1) THEN
       RETURN
      ELSE
       W = CEXP(-2.*3.1415926535/N)
       M=N/2
       DO 2 J = 1,M
        IK1 = MX+J
        IK2 = MX+J+M
        WRITE(6,51)IK1,IK2
C       TEMP = X(MX+J) + X(MX+J+M)
        T=W**(J-1)
        T1 = REAL(T)
        T2 = AIMAG(T)
        WRITE(6,52)IK2,IK1,IK2,T1,T2
C       X(MX+M+J) = ( X(MX+J)-X(MX+M+J) )*T
        WRITE (6,53) IK1
C       X(MX+J) = TEMP
2       CONTINUE
       CALL DFT(M,X,MX)
       CALL DFT(M,X,MX+M)
       RETURN
      ENDIF
51    FORMAT('      TEMP = X(',I3,')+X(',I3,')')
52    FORMAT('      X(',I3,')=(X(',I3,')-X(',I3,'))*(',F10.7,',',
     +      F10.7,')')
53    FORMAT('      X(',I3,')=TEMP)')
      END
```

FIGURE 2.13 AUTOGEN Program for FFT.

stages for the bottom half. This complicates the standard programming task enormously. But a self-recursive program for a split-radix FFT is not terribly complicated. Such an self-recursive subroutine is shown in Fig. 2.14. (The reader is reminded, however, that FORTRAN does not permit a subroutine to call itself.) The recursive form for the split-radix FFT program is almost as close to the defining equations as is the recursive form for the radix-2 FFT. It would run very slowly indeed, what with computing all the powers of W at run time, passing parameters from subroutine to subroutine, and so on. But it can be the skeleton of an AUTOGEN program that writes a very efficient split-radix FFT.

```
      SUBROUTINE DFT(N,X,MX)
C     N IS DATA LENGTH
C     INPUT SEQUENCE IS       X(MX+1), ... ,X(MX+N)
C     OUTPUT SEQUENCE IS IN PLACE, PERMUTED ORDER
C
C   USING SPLIT RADIX
      COMPLEX X,W,TEMP,T
C
      IF (N .EQ. 1) THEN
        RETURN
      ELSE IF (N .EQ. 2) THEN
       TEMP   = X(MX+1) + X(MX+2)
       X(MX+2) = X(MX+1) - X(MX+2)
       X(MX+1) = TEMP
       RETURN
      ELSE
        W = CEXP(-2.*3.1415926535/N)
        M=N/2
        DO 2 J = 1,M
          TEMP = X(MX+J) + X(MX+J+M)
          X(MX+J+M) = X(MX+J) - X(MX+J+M)
          X(MX+J) = TEMP
2         CONTINUE
        CALL DFT(M,X,MX)
C  F(4k) COMPUTED ABOVE
C
C  F(4k+1), F(4k+3) COMPUTED BELOW
        MMX = MX+M
        M=N/4
        DO 3 J=1,M
          S=0
C  FOR F(4K+1)
          T = W**((2*S+1)*(J-1))
          TEMP = (X(MMX+J) - (0.,1.)* X(MMX+M+J))*T
          S=1
C  FOR F(4k+3)
          T = W**((2*S+1)*(J-1))
          X(MMX+M+J) = (X(MMX+J) + (0.,1.)* X(MMX+J+M))*T
          X(MMX+J) = TEMP
3         CONTINUE
       CALL DFT(M,X,MMX)
       CALL DFT(M,X,MMX+M)
       RETURN
      ENDIF
      END
```

FIGURE 2.14 Self-recursive Split-radix FFT Subroutine.

2.16 SUMMARY

In this chapter we studied several novel and important techniques for computing such lagged products as convolutions and correlations. The first of these techniques was derived based on the theory of polynomial congruences. The derivation of convolution algorithms is guided by algebraic manipulation of polynomials. Treating the two sequences to be convolved as column vectors, such algorithms begin by multiplying the two vectors by predetermined matrices with simple entries, then multiplying together the resulting vectors term by term, and finally multiplying the resulting vector by another fixed matrix. When one of the input sequences is known in advance, as in the case of FIR filtering, the process reduces to a BDA-type algorithm. In the case of multidimensional circular convolutions, the "central" multiplications can be collected together, so that BDA-type algorithms for multidimensional convolution are unusually efficient in terms of multiplications per datum.

Using some results of elementary theory of numbers, we saw that most of the computation for a DFT of a sequence can usually be rearranged into the form of a sum of simple fixed multidimensional circular convolutions. When these are computed by the BDA-type algorithms, Winograd's Fourier transform algorithm results. The efficacy of the Winograd Fourier transform algorithm depends on the sequence length in a complex way (as is also the case for the classical FFT algorithm).

Also using number theory, we explored a different direction. We mapped the data to be convolved onto a surrogate ring or field within which we could find an efficient analog to the DFT which we could compute without relying on multiplications by messy trigonometric quantities. These number-theoretic transforms are of no obvious value themselves, but when there is a convolution theorem in the field or ring, the number-theoretic transforms can be the basis of a rapid computation of the desired convolution.

Finally, we introduced a further computational simplification of the classical radix-2 FFT algorithm, known as the split-radix technique. Split-radix algorithms have the topology of the classical radix-2 algorithms, but use different multiplying factors. We introduced the autogen programming technique and strongly suggested that it be applied to the programming of a split-radix FFT algorithm for maximum speed on a given computer.

PROBLEMS

2.1 Find the residue of $3u^3 + 5u^2 - 2u + 1$ with respect to the modulus $u - 2$. Find its residue with respect to modulus $2u - 4$ using synthetic division. Why did we restrict attention to modulus polynomials that were monic?

2.2 Find two polynomials $A_0(u)$ and $A_1(u)$ for which the continued fraction A_0/A_1 terminates with $A_6 = k$, with degree 0.

2.3 If $A_0(u)$ and $A_1(u)$ of Problem 2.2 have a common factor, divide both polynomials by that common factor to get $\tilde{A}_0$ and $\tilde{A}_1$. Find polynomials B_0 and B_1 that solve

$$\tilde{A}_0 B_0 + \tilde{A}_1 B_1 = 1$$

2.4 Find an algorithm of the BDA type for a short 6-point skew-circular convolution.

$$\hat{Y}(u) = X(u)H(u) \mod u^6 + 1$$

2.5 Prove, from the definition, the following properties of cyclotomic polynomials:
(a) $C_p(u) = 1 + u + u^2 + \cdots + u^{p-1}$ for p prime.
(b) $C_{p^2}(u) = C_p(u^2)$ for p prime.
(c) $C_{pq}(u) = C_q(u^p)/C_q(u)$ for p and q distinct primes.

2.6 Let $M_1 = 15$, $M_2 = 16$, $M_3 = 17$. In the Sino representation of integers modulo $M_1M_2M_3$, what three constants a_1, a_2, and a_3 let us reconstruct arbitrary x from its three residues?

2.7 How many numbers in $1 < g < 113$ are primitive roots of the prime 113?

2.8 In the DFT of p points we found a circular convolution of length $p - 1$ where one of the two sequences is predetermined.

$$h_n = W^{\langle g^{-n} \rangle_p}$$

Show that the $(p - 1)$-point DFT of h_n has $H_0 = -1$ while all its other points H_k have constant magnitude. What is that magnitude?

2.9 Derive the short-length $\mathcal{BDA}$-type algorithm for $N = 16$ using the approach suggested by (2.10.18–2.10.20). Your algorithm should use 18 multiplications in $\mathcal{D}$, of which eight are nontrivial.

2.10 Extend the Mersenne number transform to length $2p$ using -2 as the kernel.

2.11 Using the Mersenne number $M_5 = 31$, consider the number-theoretic transform of length 30 using $x = 12$. Show that this is a valid number-theoretic transform with a valid inverse. Devise a length 30 transform which has a three-stage FFT decomposition based on factors 2, 3, and 5, such that only one stage has need for multiplications that are other than cyclic shifts.

2.12 211 is a prime with 2 as a primitive root. Therefore,

$$A_k = \sum_{n=0}^{209} a_n 2^{nk} \mod 211$$

is a number-theoretic transform of length $2 \times 3 \times 5 \times 7$. Since all the multiplications required are by powers of 2, why is this number-theoretic transform not of special computational interest?

2.13 The Fermat number transform $F_\mu = 2^{2^\mu} + 1$ has length $N = 2^{\mu+1}$ using kernel $x = 2$. Find a kernel of the form $x = 2^a + 2^b$ for which x^2 is congruent to 2 modulo F_μ. This leads to a Fermat number transform with length $N = 2^{\mu+2}$. How many of the cyclic shifts with end-around complement are needed to realize this double-length Fermat number transform?

2.14 Assume that complex data are to be convolved. Complex addition, subtraction, and multiplication modulo M are defined naturally. Consider a transform using a complex kernel x, where $N = \text{order}(x)$ is the first power of x that is congruent to $(1,0)$. Find sufficient conditions for this transform to have an inverse. Find sufficient conditions for this transform to have a convolution property.

2.15 Modify the AUTOGEN program, Program 7, to write, at the end of the program it produces, a comment line telling how many multiplications and additions are carried out.

CHAPTER 3

MULTIRATE DIGITAL SIGNAL PROCESSING

In many practical applications of digital signal processing, one is faced with the problem of changing the sampling rate of a signal, either increasing it or decreasing it by some amount. For example, in telecommunication systems that transmit and receive different types of signals (e.g., teletype, facsimile, speech, video, etc.) there is a requirement to process the various signals at different rates that are commensurate with the corresponding bandwidths of the signals. The process of converting a signal from a given rate to a different rate is called *sampling-rate conversion*. In turn, systems that employ multiple sampling rates in the processing of digital signals are called *multirate digital signal-processing systems*.

Sampling-rate conversion of a digital signal can be accomplished in one of two general methods. One method is to pass the digital signal through a D/A converter, filter it if necessary, and then resample the resulting analog signal at the desired rate (i.e., to pass the analog signal through an A/D converter). The second method is to perform the sampling-rate conversion entirely in the digital domain.

One apparent advantage of the first method is that the new sampling rate can be selected arbitrarily and need not have any special relationship to the old sampling rate. A major disadvantage, however, is the signal distortion introduced by the D/A in the signal reconstruction and by the quantization effects in the A/D conversion. Sampling-rate conversion performed in the digital domain avoids this major disadvantage.

In this chapter we describe sampling-rate conversion and multi-rate signal processing in the digital domain. First we describe sampling-rate conversion by a rational factor and present several methods for implementation of the rate converter, including single-stage and multistage implementations. Then we describe a method for sampling-rate conversion by an arbitrary factor and its implementation. Finally, we present several applications of sampling-rate conversion in multi-rate signal processing systems, including the implementation of narrowband filters, digital filter banks, quadrature mirror filters and their use in subband coding, and transmultiplexing.

3.1 INTRODUCTION

The process of sampling rate conversion in the digital domain can be viewed as a linear filtering operation, as illustrated in Fig. 3.1a. The input signal $x(n)$ is characterized by the sampling rate $F_x = 1/T_x$ and the output signal $y(m)$ is characterized by the sampling rate $F_y = 1/T_y$, where T_x and T_y are the corresponding sampling intervals. In the main part of our treatment, the ratio F_y/F_x is constrained to be rational, i.e.,

$$\frac{F_y}{F_x} = \frac{U}{D}$$

where D and U are relatively prime integers. We shall show that the linear filter is characterized by a time-variant impulse response, denoted as $h(n,m)$. Hence, the input $x(n)$ and the output $y(m)$ are related by the convolution summation for time-variant systems.

The sampling-rate conversion process can also be understood from the point of view of digital resampling of the same analog signal. Let $x(t)$ be the analog signal which is sampled at the first rate F_x to generate $x(n)$. The goal of rate conversion is to obtain another sequence $y(m)$ directly from $x(n)$ which is equal to the sampled values of $x(t)$ at a second rate F_y. As is depicted in Figure 3.1b, $y(n)$ is a time shifted version of $x(n)$. Such a time shift can be realized by using a linear filter that has a flat magnitude response and a linear phase response, i.e., it has a frequency response of $e^{-j\omega\tau_i}$, where τ_i is the time delay generated by the filter. If the two sampling rates are not equal, the required amount of time shifting will vary from sample to sample, as shown in Fig. 3.1b. Thus, the rate converter can be implemented

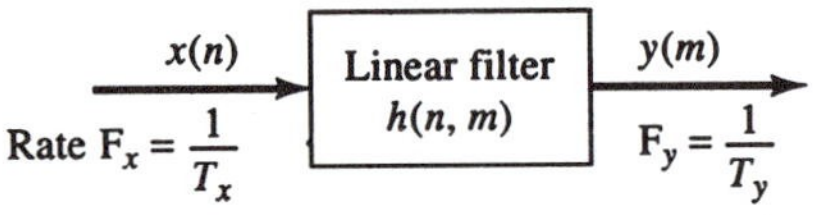

(a)

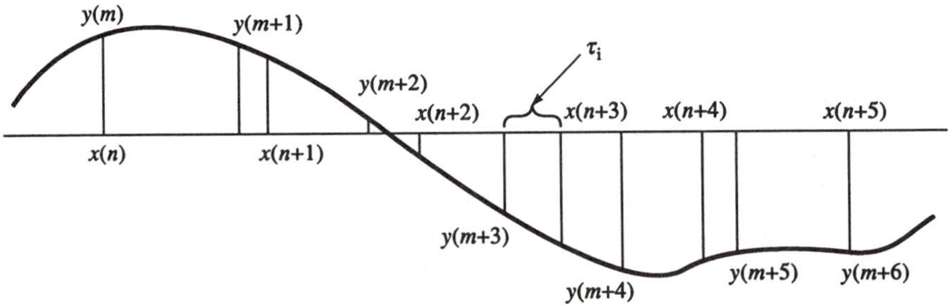

(b)

FIGURE 3.1 Sampling rate conversion viewed as a linear filtering process.

using a set of linear filters which have the same flat magnitude response but generate different time delays.

Before considering the general case of sampling-rate conversion, we shall consider two special cases. One is the case of sampling-rate reduction by an integer factor D and the second is the case of a sampling-rate increase by an integer factor U. The process of reducing the sampling rate by a factor D (down-sampling by D) is called *decimation*. The process of increasing the sampling rate by an integer factor U (up-sampling by U) is called *interpolation*.

3.2 DECIMATION BY A FACTOR *D*

Let us assume that the signal $x(n)$ with spectrum $X(\omega)$ is to be down-sampled by an integer factor D. The spectrum $X(\omega)$ is assumed to be nonzero in the frequency interval $0 \le |\omega| \le \pi$ or, equivalently, $|F| \le F_x/2$. We know that if we reduce the sampling rate by simply selecting every Dth value of $x(n)$, the resulting signal will be an aliased version of $x(n)$, with a folding frequency of $F_x/2D$. To avoid aliasing, we must first reduce the bandwidth of $x(n)$ to $F_{\max} = F_x/2D$ or, equivalently, to $\omega_{\max} = \pi/D$. Then we may down-sample by D and thus avoid aliasing.

The decimation process is illustrated in Fig. 3.2. The input sequence $x(n)$ is passed through a lowpass filter characterized by the impulse response $h(n)$ and a frequency response $H_D(\omega)$, which ideally satisfies the condition

$$H_D(\omega) = \begin{cases} 1, & |\omega| \le \dfrac{\pi}{D} \\ 0, & \text{otherwise} \end{cases} \tag{3.2.1}$$

Thus the filter eliminates the spectrum of $X(\omega)$ in the range $\pi/D < \omega < \pi$. Of course, the implication is that only the frequency components of $x(n)$ in the range $|\omega| \le \pi/D$ are of interest in further processing of the signal.

The output of the filter is a sequence $v(n)$ given as

$$v(n) = \sum_{k=0}^{\infty} h(k)x(n-k) \tag{3.2.2}$$

which is then down-sampled by the factor D to produce $y(m)$. Thus

$$\begin{aligned} y(m) &= v(mD) \\ &= \sum_{k=0}^{\infty} h(k)x(mD-k) \end{aligned} \tag{3.2.3}$$

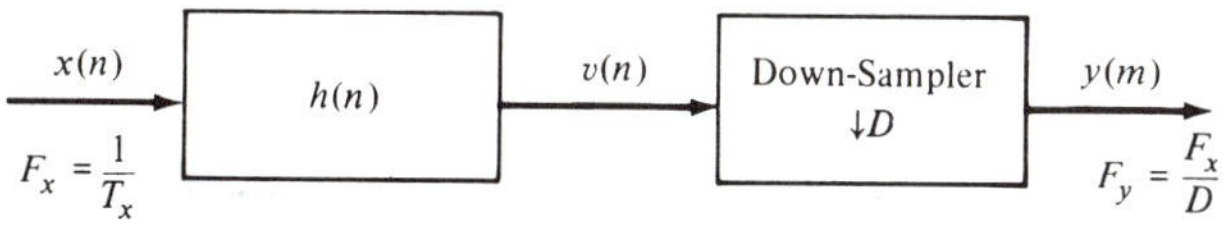

FIGURE 3.2 Decimation by a factor D.

Although the filtering operation on $x(n)$ is linear and time invariant, the down-sampling operation in combination with the filtering results in a time-variant system. This is easily verified. Given the fact that $x(n)$ produces $y(m)$, we note that $x(n - n_0)$ does not imply $y(n - n_0)$ unless n_0 is a multiple of D. Consequently, the overall linear operation (linear filtering followed by down-sampling) on $x(n)$ is not time invariant.

The frequency-domain characteristics of the output sequence $y(m)$ may be obtained by relating the spectrum of $y(m)$ to the spectrum of the input sequence $x(n)$. First, it is convenient to define a sequence $\tilde{v}(n)$ as

$$\tilde{v}(n) = \begin{cases} v(n), & n = 0, \pm D, \pm 2D, \ldots \\ 0, & \text{otherwise} \end{cases} \tag{3.2.4}$$

Clearly, $\tilde{v}(n)$ may be viewed as a sequence obtained by multiplying $v(n)$ with a periodic train of impulses $p(n)$, with period D, as illustrated in Fig. 3.3. The discrete Fourier series representation of $p(n)$ is

$$p(n) = \frac{1}{D} \sum_{k=0}^{D-1} e^{j2\pi kn/D} \tag{3.2.5}$$

Hence

$$\tilde{v}(n) = v(n)p(n) \tag{3.2.6}$$

and

$$y(m) = \tilde{v}(mD) = v(mD)p(mD) = v(mD) \tag{3.2.7}$$

Now the z-transform of the output sequence $y(m)$ is

$$\begin{aligned} Y(z) &= \sum_{m=-\infty}^{\infty} y(m)z^{-m} \\ &= \sum_{m=-\infty}^{\infty} v(mD)z^{-m} \\ Y(z) &= \sum_{m=-\infty}^{\infty} \tilde{v}(m)z^{-m/D} \end{aligned} \tag{3.2.8}$$

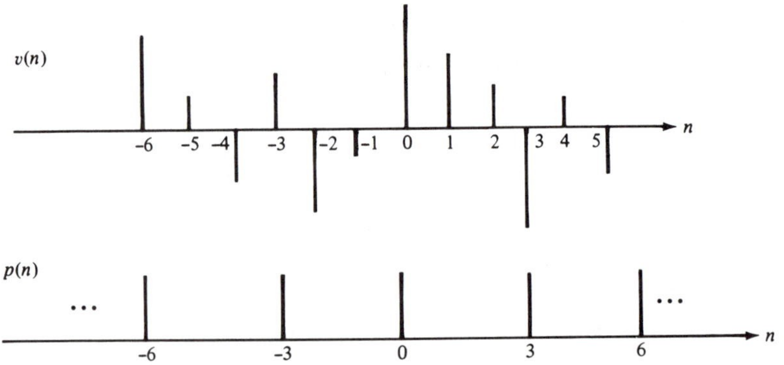

FIGURE 3.3 Multiplication of $v(n)$ with a periodic impulse train $p(n)$ with period $D = 3$.

where the last step follows from the fact that $\tilde{v}(m) = 0$ except at multiples of D. By making use of the relations in (3.2.5) and (3.2.6) in (3.2.8), we obtain

$$\begin{aligned} Y(z) &= \sum_{m=-\infty}^{\infty} v(m)\left[\frac{1}{D}\sum_{k=0}^{D-1} e^{j2\pi mk/D}\right] z^{-m/D} \\ &= \frac{1}{D}\sum_{k=0}^{D-1}\sum_{m=-\infty}^{\infty} v(m)(e^{-j2\pi k/D}z^{1/D})^{-m} \\ &= \frac{1}{D}\sum_{k=0}^{D-1} V(e^{-j2\pi k/D}z^{1/D}) \\ &= \frac{1}{D}\sum_{k=0}^{D-1} H_D(e^{-j2\pi k/D}z^{1/D})X(e^{-j2\pi k/D}z^{1/D}) \end{aligned} \tag{3.2.9}$$

where the last step follows from the fact that $V(z) = H_D(z)X(z)$.

By evaluating $Y(z)$ in the unit circle, we obtain the spectrum of the output signal $y(m)$. Since the rate of $y(m)$ is $F_y = 1/T_y$, the frequency variable, which we denote as ω_y, is in radians relative to the sampling rate F_y,

$$\omega_y = \frac{2\pi F}{F_y} = 2\pi F T_y \tag{3.2.10}$$

Since the sampling rates are related by the expression

$$F_y = \frac{F_x}{D} \tag{3.2.11}$$

it follows that the frequency variables ω_y and

$$\omega_x = \frac{2\pi F}{F_x} = 2\pi F T_x \tag{3.2.12}$$

are related by

$$\omega_y = D\omega_x \tag{3.2.13}$$

Thus the frequency range $0 \le |\omega_x| \le \pi/D$ is stretched into the corresponding frequency range $0 \le |\omega_y| \le \pi$ by the down-sampling process as expected.

We conclude that the spectrum $Y(\omega_y)$, which is obtained by evaluating (3.2.9) on the unit circle, may be expressed as

$$Y(\omega_y) = \frac{1}{D}\sum_{k=0}^{D-1} H_D\left(\frac{\omega_y - 2\pi k}{D}\right)X\left(\frac{\omega_y - 2\pi k}{D}\right) \tag{3.2.14}$$

With a properly designed filter $H(\omega)$ the aliasing is eliminated and consequently, all but the first term in (3.2.14) vanish. Hence

$$\begin{aligned} Y(\omega_y) &= \frac{1}{D} H_D\left(\frac{\omega_y}{D}\right)X\left(\frac{\omega_y}{D}\right) \\ &= \frac{1}{D} X\left(\frac{\omega_y}{D}\right) \end{aligned} \tag{3.2.15}$$

for $0 \le |\omega_y| \le \pi$. The spectra for the sequences $x(n)$, $v(n)$, and $y(m)$ are illustrated in Fig. 3.4.

3.3 INTERPOLATION BY A FACTOR *U*

An increase in the sampling rate by an integer factor of U can be accomplished by interpolating $U - 1$ new samples between successive values of the signal. The interpolation process may be accomplished in a variety of ways. We shall describe a process that preserves the spectral shape of the signal sequence $x(n)$.

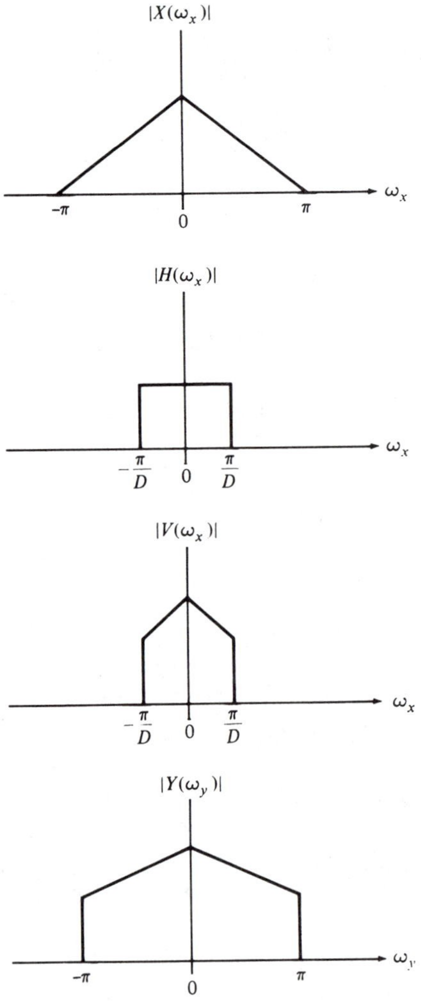

FIGURE 3.4 Spectra of signals in the decimation of $x(n)$ by a factor D.

Let $v(m)$ denote a sequence with a rate $F_y = UF_x$, which is obtained from $x(n)$ by adding $U - 1$ zeros between successive values of $x(n)$. Thus

$$v(m) = \begin{cases} x\left(\dfrac{m}{U}\right), & m = 0, \pm U, \pm 2U, \ldots \\ 0, & \text{otherwise} \end{cases} \tag{3.3.1}$$

and its sampling rate is identical to the rate of $y(m)$. This sequence has a z-transform

$$\begin{aligned} V(z) &= \sum_{m=-\infty}^{\infty} v(m)z^{-m} \\ &= \sum_{m=-\infty}^{\infty} x(m)z^{-mU} \\ &= X(z^U) \end{aligned} \tag{3.3.2}$$

The corresponding spectrum of $v(m)$ is obtained by evaluating (3.3.2) on the unit circle. Thus

$$V(\omega_y) = X(\omega_y U) \tag{3.3.3}$$

where ω_y denotes the frequency variable relative to the new sampling rate F_y (i.e., $\omega_y = 2\pi F/F_y$). Now the relationship between sampling rates is $F_y = UF_x$, and hence the frequency variables ω_x and ω_y are related according to the formula

$$\omega_y = \frac{\omega_x}{U} \tag{3.3.4}$$

The spectra $X(\omega_x)$ and $V(\omega_y)$ are illustrated in Fig. 3.5. We observe that the sampling-rate increase obtained by the addition of $U - 1$ zero samples between successive values of $x(n)$ results in a signal whose spectrum $V(\omega_y)$ is a U-fold periodic repetition of the input signal spectrum $X(\omega_x)$.

Since only the frequency components of $x(n)$ in the range $0 \le \omega_y \le \pi/U$ are unique, the images of $X(\omega)$ above $\omega_y = \pi/U$ should be rejected by passing the sequence $v(m)$ through a lowpass filter with frequency response $H_U(\omega_y)$, which ideally has the characteristic

$$H_U(\omega_y) = \begin{cases} C, & 0 \le |\omega_y| \le \pi/U \\ 0, & \text{otherwise} \end{cases} \tag{3.3.5}$$

where C is a scale factor that is required to properly normalize the output sequence $y(m)$. Consequently, the output spectrum is

$$Y(\omega_y) = \begin{cases} CX(\omega_y U), & 0 \le |\omega_y| \le \pi/U \\ 0, & \text{otherwise} \end{cases} \tag{3.3.6}$$

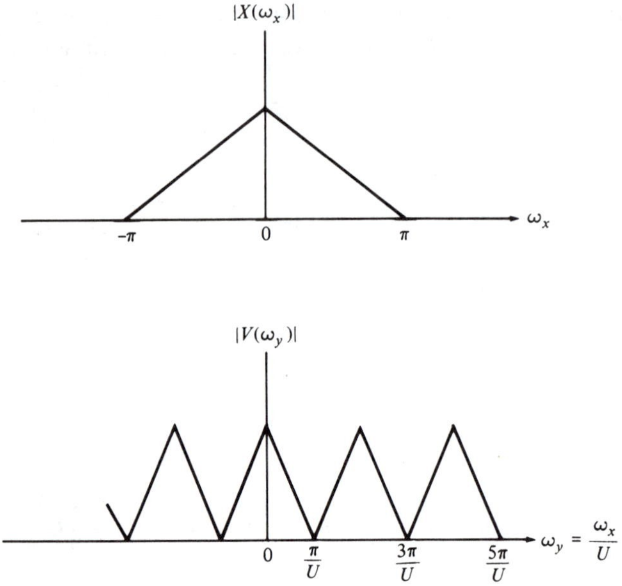

FIGURE 3.5 Spectra of $x(n)$ and $v(n)$ where $V(\omega_y) = X(\omega_y U)$.

The scale factor C is selected so that the output $y(m) = x(m/U)$ for $m = 0, \pm U, \pm 2U, \ldots$. For mathematical convenience, we select the point $m = 0$. Thus

$$\begin{aligned} y(0) &= \frac{1}{2\pi}\int_{-\pi}^{\pi} Y(\omega_y)\, d\omega_y \\ &= \frac{C}{2\pi}\int_{-\pi/U}^{\pi/U} X(\omega_y U)\, d\omega_y \end{aligned} \tag{3.3.7}$$

Since $\omega_y = \omega_x/U$, (3.3.7) may be expressed as

$$\begin{aligned} y(0) &= \frac{C}{U}\frac{1}{2\pi}\int_{-\pi}^{\pi} X(\omega_x)\, d\omega_x \\ &= \frac{C}{U}x(0) \end{aligned} \tag{3.3.8}$$

Therefore, $C = U$ is the desired normalization factor.

Finally, we indicate that the output sequence $y(m)$ can be expressed as a convolution of the sequence $v(n)$ with the unit sample response $h(n)$ of the lowpass filter. Thus

$$y(m) = \sum_{k=-\infty}^{\infty} h(m-k)v(\mathrm{k}) \tag{3.3.9}$$

Since $v(k) = 0$ except at multiples of U, where $v(kU) = x(k)$, (3.3.9) becomes

$$y(m) = \sum_{k=-\infty}^{\infty} h(m - kU)x(k) \tag{3.3.10}$$

3.4 SAMPLING-RATE CONVERSION BY A RATIONAL FACTOR *U/D*

Having discussed the special cases of decimation (down-sampling by a factor D) and interpolation (up-sampling by a factor U), we now consider the general case of sampling-rate conversion by a rational factor U/D. Basically, we can achieve this sampling-rate conversion by first performing interpolation by the factor U and then decimating the output of the interpolator by the factor D. In other words, a sampling-rate conversion by the rational factor U/D is accomplished by cascading an interpolator with a decimator, as illustrated in Fig. 3.6.

We emphasize the importance of performing the interpolation first and the decimation second, to preserve the desired spectral characteristics of $x(n)$. Furthermore, with the cascade configuration illustrated in Fig. 3.6, the two filters with impulse response $h_u(l)$ and $h_d(l)$ are operated at the same rate, UF_x, and hence can be combined into a single lowpass filter with impulse response $h(l)$ as illustrated in Fig. 3.7. The frequency response $H(\omega_v)$ of the combined filter must incorporate the filtering operations for both interpolation and decimation, and hence it should ideally possess the frequency response characteristic

$$H(\omega_v) = \begin{cases} U, & 0 \le |\omega_v| \le \min\left(\dfrac{\pi}{D}, \dfrac{\pi}{U}\right) \\ 0, & \text{otherwise} \end{cases} \tag{3.4.1}$$

where $\omega_v = 2\pi F/F_v = 2\pi F/UF_x = \omega_x/U$.

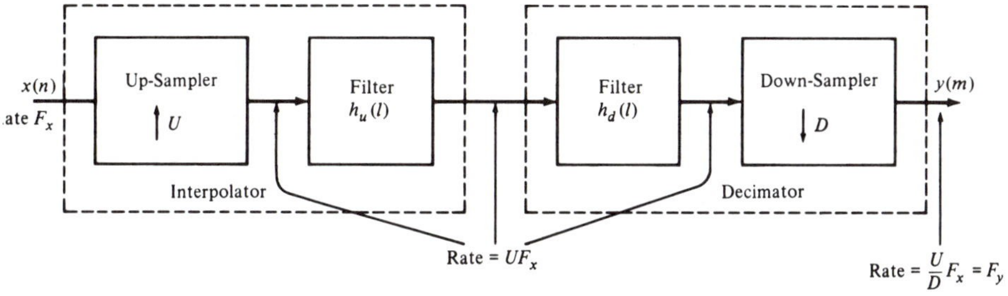

FIGURE 3.6 Method for sampling rate conversion by a factor *U/D*.

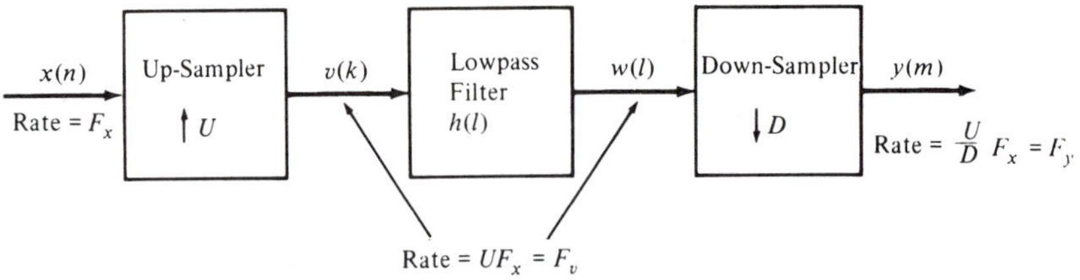

FIGURE 3.7 Method for sampling rate conversion by a factor U/D.

In the time domain, the output of the up-sampler is the sequence

$$v(l) = \begin{cases} x\left(\dfrac{l}{U}\right), & l = 0, \pm U, \pm 2U, \ldots \\ 0, & \text{otherwise} \end{cases} \tag{3.4.2}$$

and the output of the linear time-invariant filter is

$$\begin{aligned} w(l) &= \sum_{k=-\infty}^{\infty} h(l-k)v(k) \\ &= \sum_{k=-\infty}^{\infty} h(l-kU)x(k) \end{aligned} \tag{3.4.3}$$

Finally, the output of the sampling-rate converter is the sequence $y(m)$, which is obtained by down-sampling the sequence $w(l)$ by a factor of D. Thus

$$\begin{aligned} y(m) &= w(mD) \\ &= \sum_{k=-\infty}^{\infty} h(mD-kU)x(k) \end{aligned} \tag{3.4.4}$$

It is illuminating to express (3.4.4) in a different form by making a change in variable. Let

$$k = \left\lfloor \frac{mD}{U} \right\rfloor - n \tag{3.4.5}$$

where the notation $\lfloor r \rfloor$ denotes the largest integer contained in r. With this change in variable, (3.4.4) becomes

$$y(m) = \sum_{n=-\infty}^{\infty} h\left(mD - \left\lfloor \frac{mD}{U} \right\rfloor U + nU\right) x\left(\left\lfloor \frac{mD}{U} \right\rfloor - n\right) \tag{3.4.6}$$

We note that

$$\begin{aligned} mD - \left\lfloor \frac{mD}{U} \right\rfloor U &= mD \mod U \\ &= (mD)_U \end{aligned}$$

Consequently, (3.4.6) may be expressed as

$$y(m) = \sum_{n=-\infty}^{\infty} h\left(nU + (mD)_U\right)x\left(\left\lfloor \frac{mD}{U} \right\rfloor - n\right) \tag{3.4.7}$$

It is apparent from this form that the output $y(m)$ is obtained by passing the input sequence $x(n)$ through a time-variant filter with impulse response

$$g(n,m) = h(nU + (mD)_U), \qquad -\infty < m, \quad n < \infty \tag{3.4.8}$$

where $h(k)$ is the impulse response of the time-invariant lowpass filter that is operating at the sampling rate UF_x. We observe further that for any integer k,

$$\begin{aligned} g(n, m + kU) &= h(nU + (mD + kDU)_U) \\ &= h(nU + (mD)_U) \\ &= g(n,m) \end{aligned} \tag{3.4.9}$$

Hence $g(n,m)$ is periodic in the variable m with period U.

The frequency-domain relationships may be obtained by combining the results of the interpolation and decimation processes. Thus the spectrum at the output of the linear filter with impulse response $h(l)$ is

$$\begin{aligned} V(\omega_v) &= H(\omega_v)X(\omega_v U) \\ &= \begin{cases} UX(\omega_v U), & 0 \le |\omega_v| \le \min\left(\dfrac{\pi}{D}, \dfrac{\pi}{U}\right) \\ 0, & \text{otherwise} \end{cases} \end{aligned} \tag{3.4.10}$$

The spectrum of the output sequence $y(m)$, which is obtained by decimating the sequence $v(n)$ by a factor of D, is

$$Y(\omega_y) = \frac{1}{D}\sum_{k=0}^{D-1} V\left(\frac{\omega_y - 2\pi k}{D}\right) \tag{3.4.11}$$

where $\omega_y = D\omega_v$. Since the linear filter prevents aliasing as implied by (3.4.10), the spectrum of the output sequence given by (3.4.11) reduces to

$$Y(\omega_y) = \begin{cases} \dfrac{U}{D}X\left(\dfrac{\omega_y}{D}\right), & 0 \le |\omega_y| \le \min\left(\pi, \dfrac{\pi D}{U}\right) \\ 0, & \text{otherwise} \end{cases} \tag{3.4.12}$$

3.5 FILTER DESIGN AND IMPLEMENTATION FOR SAMPLING-RATE CONVERSION

As indicated in the discussion above, sampling-rate conversion by a factor U/D can be achieved by first increasing the sampling rate by U, which is accomplished by inserting $U - 1$ zeros between successive values of the input signal $x(n)$, followed by linear filtering of the resulting sequence to eliminate the unwanted images of $X(\omega)$, and finally, down-sampling the filtered signal by the factor D. In this section we consider the design and implementation of the linear filter.

3.5.1 Direct-Form FIR Filter Structures

In principle, the simplest realization of the filter is the direct-form FIR structure with system function

$$H(z) = \sum_{k=0}^{M-1} h(k)z^{-k} \tag{3.5.1}$$

where $h(k)$ is the unit sample response of the FIR filter. The lowpass filter can be designed to have linear phase and a specified passband ripple and stopband attenuation. Any of the standard, well-known FIR filter design techniques (e.g., window method, frequency sampling method) may be used to carry out this design. Thus we will have the filter parameters $h(k)$, which allow us to implement the FIR filter directly as shown in Fig. 3.8.

Although the direct-form FIR filter realization illustrated in Fig. 3.8 is simple, it is also very inefficient. The inefficiency results from the fact that the up-sampling process introduces $U - 1$ zeros between successive points of the input signal. If U is large, most of the signal components in the FIR filter are zero. Consequently, most of the multiplications and additions result in zeros. Furthermore, the down-sampling process at the output of the filter

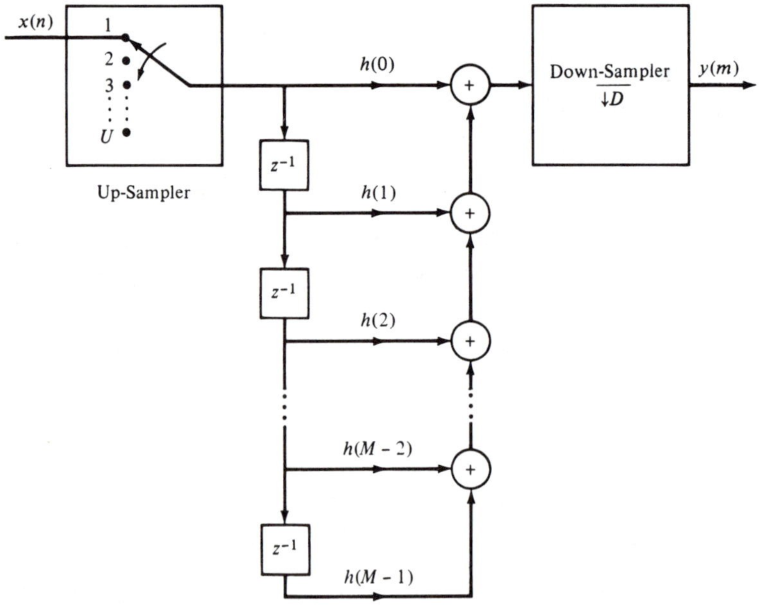

FIGURE 3.8 Direct-form realization of FIR filter in sampling rate conversion by factor *U/D*.

implies that only one out of every D output samples is required at the output of the filter. Consequently, only one out of every D possible values at the output of the filter should be computed.

To develop a more efficient filter structure, let us begin with a decimator that reduces the sampling rate by an integer factor D. From our previous discussion, the decimator is obtained by passing the input sequence $x(n)$ through an FIR filter and then down-sampling the filter output by a factor D, as illustrated in Fig. 3.9a. In this configuration, the filter is operating at

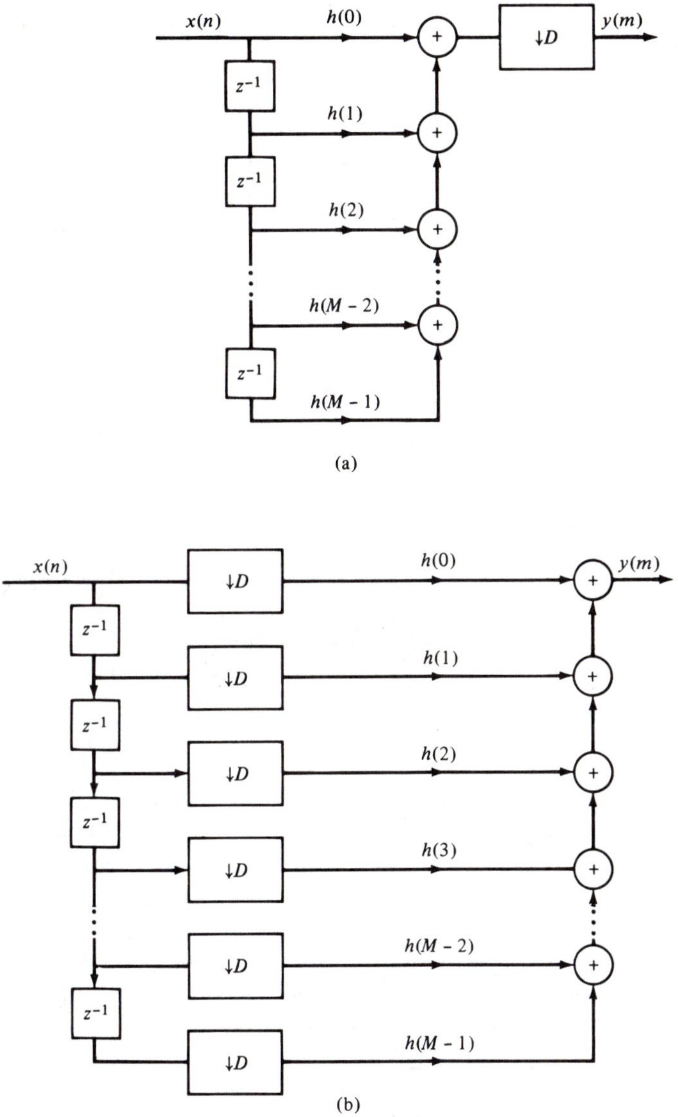

FIGURE 3.9 Decimation by a factor D.

the high sampling rate F_x, while only one out of every D output samples is actually needed. The logical solution to this inefficiency problem is to embed the down-sampling operation within the filter, as illustrated in the filter realization given in Fig. 3.9b. In this filter structure, all the multiplications and additions are performed at the lower sampling rate F_x/D. Thus we have achieved the desired efficiency. Additional reduction in computation can be achieved by exploiting the symmetry characteristics of $h(k)$. Figure 3.10

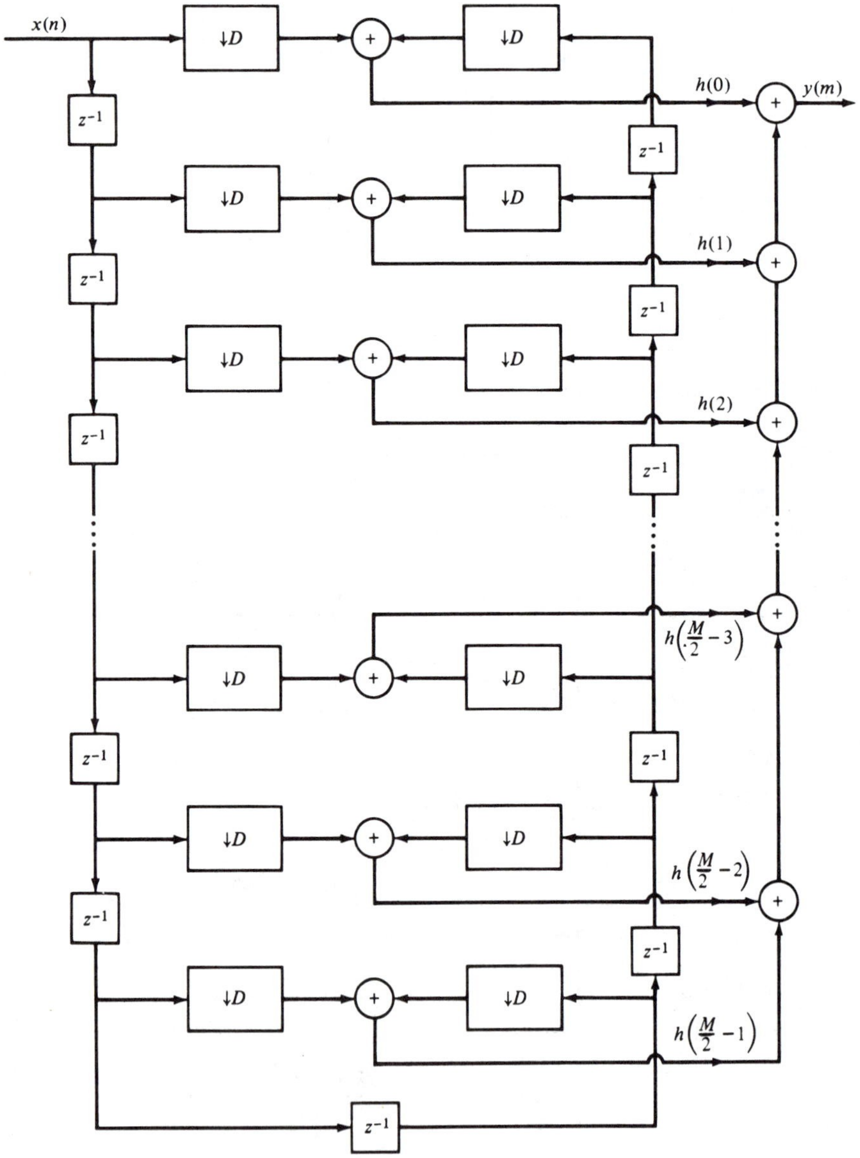

FIGURE 3.10 Efficient realization of a decimator that exploits the symmetry in the FIR filter.

illustrates an efficient realization of the decimator in which the FIR filter has linear phase and hence $h(k)$ is symmetric.

Let us consider next the efficient implementation of an interpolator, which is realized by first inserting $U - 1$ zeros between samples of $x(n)$ and then filtering the resulting sequence. The direct-form realization is illustrated in Fig. 3.11. The major problem with this structure is that the filter computations are performed at the high sampling rate UF_x. The desired simplification is achieved by first using the transposed form of the FIR filter, as illustrated in Fig. 3.12a and then embedding the up-sampler within the filter, as shown in Fig. 3.12b. Thus all the filter multiplications are performed at the low rate F_x, while the up-sampling process introduces $U - 1$ zeros in each of the filter branches of the structure shown in Fig. 3.12b. The reader may easily verify that the two filter structures in Fig. 3.12 are equivalent.

It is interesting to note that the structure of the interpolator shown in Fig. 3.12b can be obtained by transposing the structure of the decimator shown in Fig. 3.9. We observe that the transpose of a decimator is an interpolator, and vice versa. These relationships are illustrated in Fig. 3.13, where (b) is obtained by transposing (a), and (d) is obtained by transposing (c). Consequently, a decimator is the dual of an interpolator, and vice versa. From these relationships it follows that there is an interpolator whose structure is the dual of the decimator shown in Fig. 3.10, which exploits the symmetry in $h(n)$.

3.5.2 Polyphase Filter Structures

The computational efficiency of the filter structure above can also be achieved by reducing the large FIR filter of length M into a set of smaller filters of length $K = M/U$, where M is selected to be a multiple of U. To demonstrate this point, let us consider the interpolator given in Fig. 3.11.

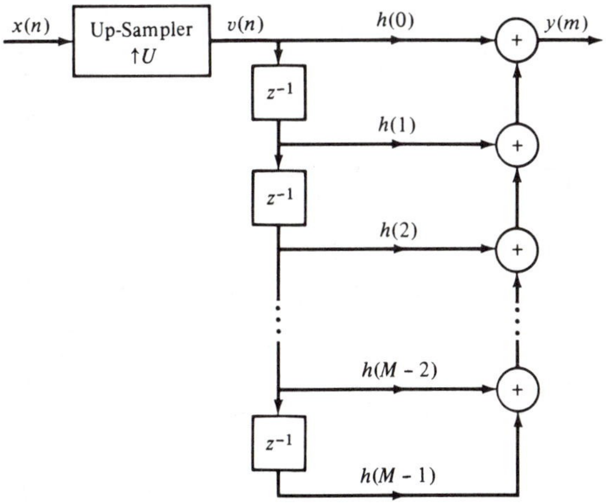

FIGURE 3.11 Direct-form realization of FIR filter in interpolation by a factor U.

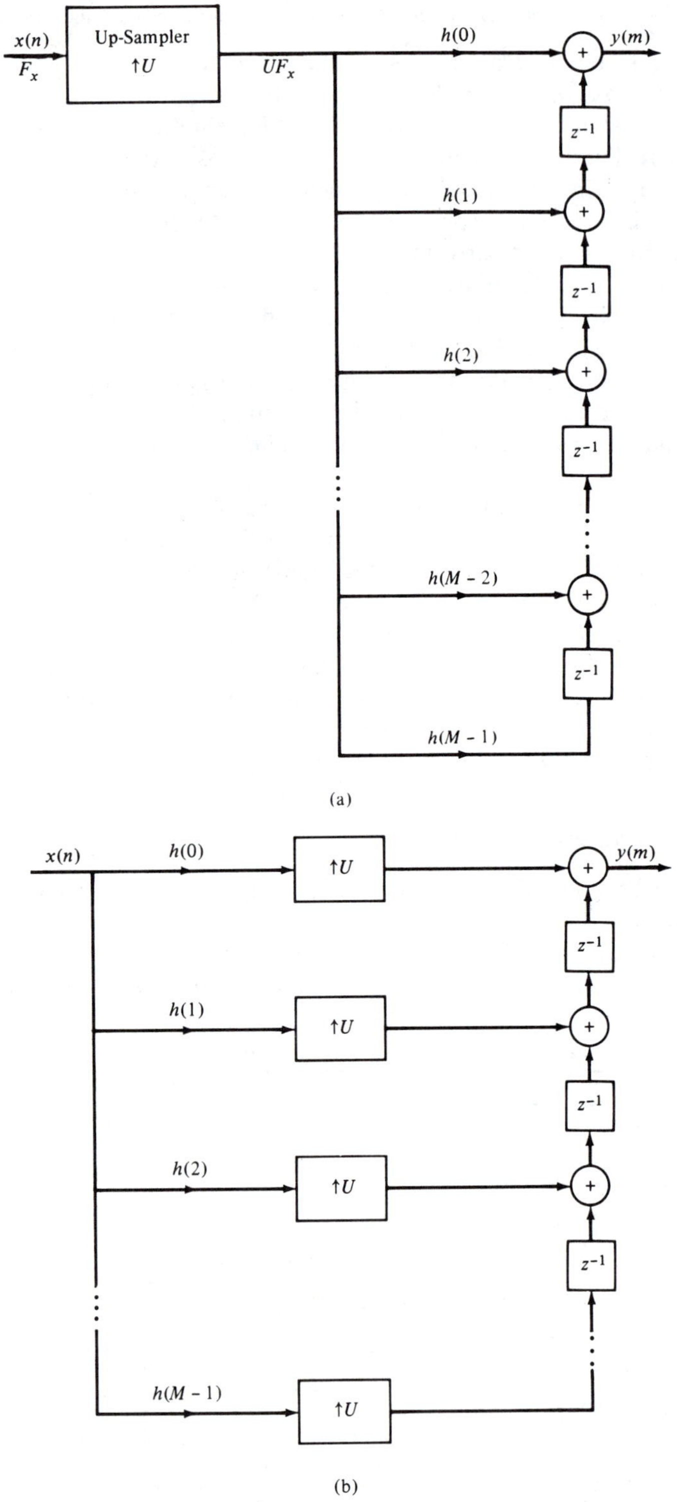

FIGURE 3.12 Efficient realization of an interpolator.

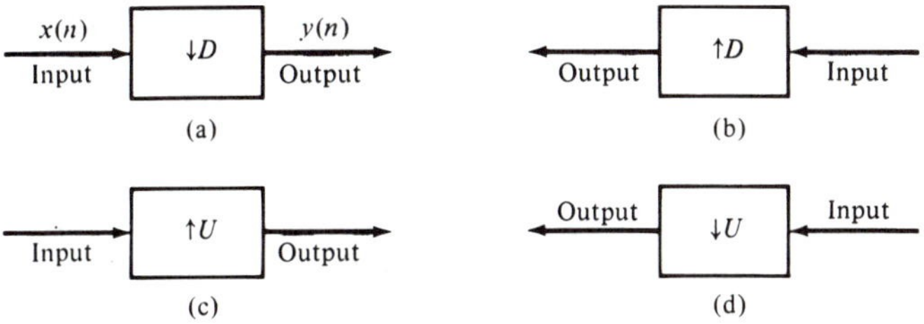

FIGURE 3.13 Duality relationships obtained through transposition.

Since the up-sampling process inserts $U - 1$ zeros between successive values of $x(n)$, only K of the M input values stored in the FIR filter at any one time are nonzero. At one time instant these nonzero values coincide and are multiplied by the filter coefficients $h(0)$, $h(U)$, $h(2U)$, . . . , $h(M - U)$. In the following time instant, the nonzero values of the input sequence coincide and are multiplied by the filter coefficients $h(1)$, $h(U + 1)$, $h(2U + 1)$, . . . , $h(M - U + 1)$, and so on. This observation leads us to define a set of smaller filters, called *polyphase filters*, with unit sample responses.

$$p_k(n) = h(k + nU), \qquad \begin{array}{l} k = 0, 1, \ldots, U - 1 \\ n = 0, 1, \ldots, K - 1 \end{array} \tag{3.5.2}$$

where $K = M/U$ is an integer.

From the discussion above it follows that the set of U polyphase filters can be arranged as a parallel realization, and the output of each filter can be selected by a commutator as illustrated in Fig. 3.14. The rotation of the commutator is in the counterclockwise direction beginning with the point at $m = 0$. Thus the polyphase filters perform computations at the low sampling rate F_x and the rate conversion results from the fact that U output samples are generated, one from each of the filters, for each input sample.

The decomposition of $h(k)$ into the set of U subfilters with impulse response $p_k(n)$, $k = 0, 1, \ldots, U - 1$, is consistent with our previous

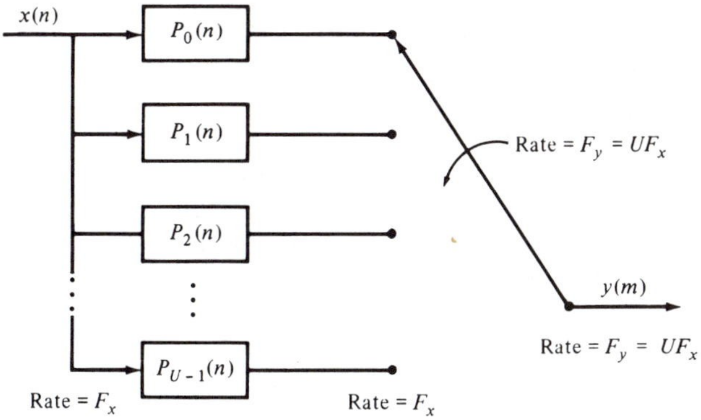

FIGURE 3.14 Interpolation by use of polyphase filters.

observation that the input signal was being filtered by a periodically time-variant linear filter with impulse response

$$g(n,m) = h(nU + (mD)_U) \tag{3.5.3}$$

where $D = 1$ in the case of the interpolator. We noted previously that $g(n,m)$ varies periodically with period U. Consequently, a different set of coefficients are used to generate the set of U output samples $y(m)$, $m = 0, 1, \ldots, U - 1$.

Additional insight can be gained about the characteristics of the set of polyphase subfilters by noting that $p_k(n)$ is obtained from $h(n)$ by decimation with a factor U. Consequently, if the original filter frequency response $H(\omega)$ is flat over the range $0 \leq |\omega| \leq \pi/U$, each of the polyphase subfilters will possess a relatively flat response over the range $0 \leq |\omega| \leq \pi$ (i.e., the polyphase subfilters are basically all-pass filters and differ primarily in their phase characteristics). This explains the reason for the term *polyphase* in describing these filters.

The polyphase filter can also be viewed as a set of U subfilters connected to a common delay line. Ideally, the kth subfilter will generate a forward time shift of $(k/U)T_x$, for $k = 0, 1, 2, \ldots, U - 1$, relative to the zeroth subfilter. Therefore, if the zeroth filter generates zero delay, the frequency response of the kth subfilter is

$$p_k(\omega) = e^{j\omega k/U}$$

A time shift of an integer number of input sampling intervals (e.g., lT_x) can be generated by shifting the input data in the delay line by l samples and using the same subfilters. By combining these two methods, we can generate an output that is shifted forward by an amount $(l + i/U)T_x$ relative to the previous output.

By transposing the interpolator structure in Fig. 3.14, we obtain a commutator structure for a decimator that is based on the parallel bank of polyphase filters, as illustrated in Fig. 3.15. The unit sample responses of the polyphase filters are now defined as

$$p_k(n) = h(k + nD), \qquad \begin{array}{l} k = 0, 1, \ldots, D - 1 \\ n = 0, 1, \ldots, K - 1 \end{array} \tag{3.5.4}$$

where $K = M/D$ is an integer when M is selected to be a multiple of D. The commutator rotates in a counterclockwise direction starting with the filter $p_0(n)$ at $m = 0$.

Although the two commutator structures for the interpolator and the decimator described above rotate in a counterclockwise direction, it is also possible to derive an equivalent pair of commutator structures having a clockwise rotation. In this alternative formulation, the sets of polyphase filters are defined to have impulse responses

$$p_k(n) = h(nU - k), \qquad k = 0, 1, \ldots, U - 1 \tag{3.5.5}$$

$$p_k(n) = h(nD - k), \qquad k = 0, 1, \ldots, D - 1 \tag{3.5.6}$$

for the interpolator and decimator, respectively.

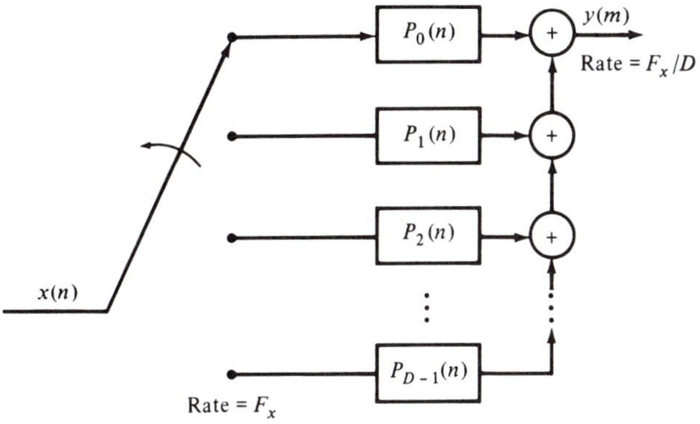

FIGURE 3.15 Decimination by use polyphase filters.

3.5.3 Time-Variant Filter Structures

Having described the filter implementation for a decimator and an interpolator, let us now consider the general problem of sampling-rate conversion by the factor U/D.

In the general case of sampling-rate conversion by a factor U/D, the filtering can be accomplished by means of the linear time-variant filter described by the response function

$$g(n,m) = h(nU + (mD)_U) \tag{3.5.7}$$

where $h(n)$ is the impulse response of the low-pass FIR filter, which, ideally, has the frequency response specified by (3.4.1). For convenience we select the length of the FIR filter $h(n)$ to a multiple of U (i.e., $M = KU$). As a consequence, the set of coefficients $g(n,m)$ for each $m = 0, 1, 2, \ldots, U - 1$, contains K elements. Since $g(n,m)$ is also periodic with period U, as demonstrated in (3.4.9), it follows that the output $y(m)$ may be expressed as

$$y(m) = \sum_{n=0}^{K-1} g\left(n, m - \left\lfloor \frac{m}{U} \right\rfloor U\right) x\left(\left\lfloor \frac{mD}{U} \right\rfloor - n\right) \tag{3.5.8}$$

Conceptually, we can think of performing the computations specified by (3.5.8) by processing blocks of data of length K by a set of K filter coefficients $g\left(n, m - \left\lfloor \frac{m}{U} \right\rfloor U\right)$, $n = 0, 1, \ldots, K - 1$. There are U such sets of coefficients, one set for each block of U output points of $y(m)$. For each block of U output points, there is a corresponding block of D input points of $x(n)$ that enter in the computation.

The block processing algorithm for computing (3.5.8) can be visualized as illustrated in Fig. 3.16. A block of D input samples is buffered and shifted into a second buffer, of length K, one sample at a time. The shifting from the input buffer to the second buffer occurs at a rate of one sample each

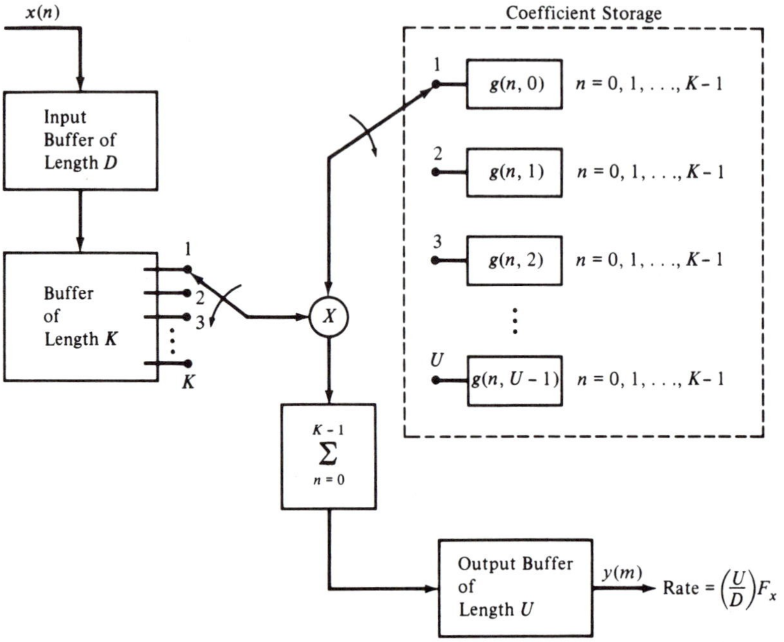

FIGURE 3.16 Efficient implementation of sampling-rate conversion by block processing.

time the quantity $\lfloor mD/U \rfloor$ increases by one. For each output sample $y(l)$, the samples from the second buffer are multiplied by the corresponding set of filter coefficients $g(n, l)$ for $n = 0, 1, \ldots, K - 1$, and the K products are accumulated to give $y(l)$, for $l = 0, 1, \ldots, U - 1$. Thus U outputs result from this computation, which is then repeated for a new set of D input samples, and so on.

An alternative method for computing the output of the sample rate converter specified by (3.5.8) is by means of an FIR filter structure with periodically varying filter coefficients. Such a structure is illustrated in Fig. 3.17. The input samples $x(n)$ are passed into a shift register that operates at the sampling rate F_x and is of length $K = M/U$, where M is the length of the time-invariant FIR filter, specified by the frequency response given by (3.4.1). Each stage of the register is connected to a hold-and-sample device that serves to couple the input sample rate F_x to the output sample rate $F_y = (U/D)F_x$. The sample at the input to each hold-and-sample device is held until the next input sample arrives and then discarded. The output samples of the hold-and-sample device are taken at times mD/U, $m = 0, 1, 2, \ldots$. When both the input and output sampling times coincide (i.e., when mD/U is an integer), the input to the hold-and-sample is changed first and then the output samples the new input. The K outputs from the K hold-and-sample devices are multiplied by the periodically time-varying coefficients $g(n, m - \lfloor m/U \rfloor U)$, for $n = 0, 1, \ldots, K - 1$, and the resulting

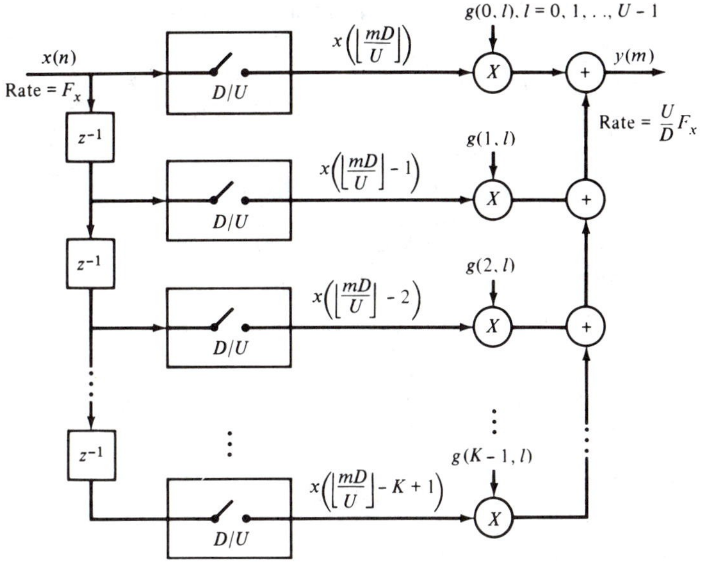

FIGURE 3.17 Efficient realization of sampling-rate conversion by a factor *U/D*.

products are summed to yield $y(m)$. The computations at the output of the hold-and-sample devices are repeated at the output sampling rate of $F_y = (U/D)F_x$.

Finally, rate conversion by a rational factor U/D can also be performed by use of a polyphase filter having U subfilters. If we assume that the mth sample $y(m)$ is computed by taking the output of the i_mth subfilter with input data $x(n), x(n-1), \ldots, x(n-K+1)$ in the delay line, the next sample, $y(m+1)$, is taken from the (i_{m+1})st subfilter, after shifting l_{m+1} new samples in the delay lines where $i_{m+1} = (i_m + D)_{\text{mod } U}$ and l_{m+1} is the integer part of $(i_m + D)/U$. The integer i_{m+1} should be saved to be used in determining the subfilter from which the next sample is taken.

Let us now demonstrate the filter design procedure, first in the design of a decimator, second in the design of an interpolator, and finally, in the design of a rational sample-rate converter.

EXAMPLE 3.5.1

Design a decimator that down-samples an input signal $x(n)$ by a factor $D = 2$. Use the Remez algorithm to determine the coefficients of the FIR filter that has a 0.1-dB ripple in the passband and is down by at least 30 dB in the stopband. Also determine the polyphase filter structure in a decimator realization that employs polyphase filters.

Solution: A filter of length $M = 30$ achieves the design specifications given above. The impulse response of the FIR filter is given in Table 3.1

TABLE 3.1 Coefficients of Linear-Phase FIR Filter in Example 3.5.1

FINITE IMPULSE RESPONSE (FIR)
LINEAR-PHASE DIGITAL FILTER DESIGN
REMEZ EXCHANGE ALGORITHM

FILTER LENGTH = 30

***** IMPULSE RESPONSE *****

H(1)	=	0.60256165E−02	=	H(30)
H(2)	=	−0.12817143E−01	=	H(29)
H(3)	=	−0.28582066E−02	=	H(28)
H(4)	=	0.13663346E−01	=	H(27)
H(5)	=	−0.46688961E−02	=	H(26)
H(6)	=	−0.19704415E−01	=	H(25)
H(7)	=	0.15984623E−01	=	H(24)
H(8)	=	0.21384886E−01	=	H(23)
H(9)	=	−0.34979440E−01	=	H(22)
H(10)	=	−0.15615522E−01	=	H(21)
H(11)	=	0.64006113E−01	=	H(20)
H(12)	=	−0.73451772E−02	=	H(19)
H(13)	=	−0.11873185E+00	=	H(18)
H(14)	=	0.98047845E−01	=	H(17)
H(15)	=	0.49225068E+00	=	H(16)

	BAND 1	BAND 2
LOWER BAND EDGE	0.0000000	0.3100000
UPPER BAND EDGE	0.2500000	0.5000000
DESIRED VALUE	1.0000000	0.0000000
WEIGHTING	2.0000000	1.0000000
DEVIATION	0.0107151	0.0214302
DEVIATION IN DB	0.0925753	−33.3794746

EXTREMAL FREQUENCIES—MAXIMA OF THE ERROR CURVE

0.0000000	0.0416667	0.0791667	0.1166666	0.1520833
0.1854166	0.2145832	0.2395832	0.2500000	0.3100000
0.3225000	0.3495833	0.3808333	0.4141666	0.4474999
0.4829165				

and the frequency response is illustrated in Fig. 3.18. Note that the cutoff frequency is $\omega_c = \pi/2$.

The polyphase filters obtained from $h(n)$ have impulse responses

$$p_k(n) = h(2n + k), \qquad k = 0, 1, \quad n = 0, 1, \ldots, 14$$

Note that $p_0(n) = h(2n)$ and $p_1(n) = h(2n + 1)$. Hence one filter consists of the even-numbered samples of $h(n)$ and the other filter consists of the odd-numbered samples of $h(n)$.

EXAMPLE 3.5.2

Design an interpolator that increases the input sampling rate by a factor of $U = 5$. Use the Remez algorithm to determine the coefficients of the FIR filter that has 0.1-dB ripple in the passband and is down by at least

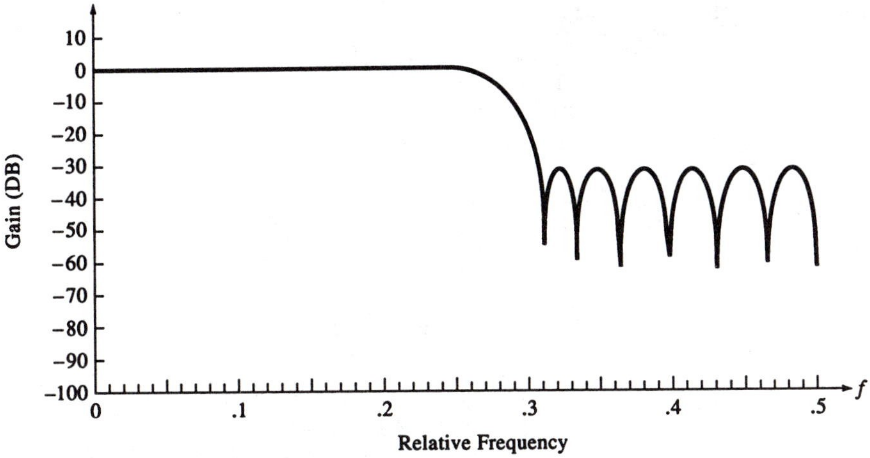

FIGURE 3.18 Magnitude response of linear-phase FIR filter of length $M = 30$ in Example 3.5.1.

30 dB in the stopband. Also, determine the polyphase filter structure in an interpolator realization based on polyphase filters.

Solution: A filter of length $M = 30$ achieves the design specifications given above. The frequency response of the FIR filter is illustrated in Fig. 3.19 and its coefficients are given in Table 3.2. The cutoff frequency is $\omega_c = \pi/5$.

The polyphase filters obtained from $h(n)$ have impulse responses

$$p_k(n) = h(5n + k), \qquad k = 0, 1, 2, 3, 4$$

Consequently, each filter has length six.

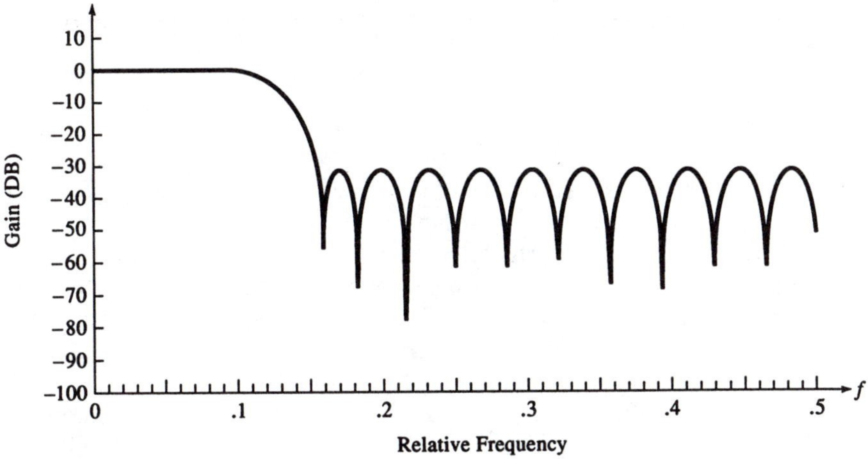

FIGURE 3.19 Magnitude response of linear-phase FIR filter of length $M = 30$ in Example 3.5.2.

TABLE 3.2 Coefficients of Linear-Phase FIR Filter in Example 3.5.2

FINITE IMPULSE RESPONSE (FIR)
LINEAR-PHASE DIGITAL FILTER DESIGN
REMEZ EXCHANGE ALGORITHM

FILTER LENGTH = 30

***** IMPULSE RESPONSE *****

H(1)	=	0.63987216E−02	=	H(30)
H(2)	=	−0.14761304E−01	=	H(29)
H(3)	=	−0.10886577E−02	=	H(28)
H(4)	=	−0.28714957E−02	=	H(27)
H(5)	=	0.10486430E−01	=	H(26)
H(6)	=	0.21477142E−01	=	H(25)
H(7)	=	0.19479362E−01	=	H(24)
H(8)	=	−0.31067431E−03	=	H(23)
H(9)	=	−0.30053033E−01	=	H(22)
H(10)	=	−0.49877029E−01	=	H(21)
H(11)	=	−0.37371285E−01	=	H(20)
H(12)	=	0.18482896E−01	=	H(19)
H(13)	=	0.10747141E+00	=	H(18)
H(14)	=	0.19951098E+00	=	H(17)
H(15)	=	0.25794828E+00	=	H(16)

	BAND 1	BAND 2
LOWER BAND EDGE	0.0000000	0.1600000
UPPER BAND EDGE	0.1000000	0.5000000
DESIRED VALUE	1.0000000	0.0000000
WEIGHTING	3.0000000	1.0000000
DEVIATION	0.0097524	0.0292572
DEVIATION IN DB	0.0842978	−30.6753349

EXTREMAL FREQUENCIES—MAXIMA OF THE ERROR CURVE

0.0000000	0.0333333	0.0645834	0.0895833	0.1000000
0.1600000	0.1745833	0.2016666	0.2370833	0.2704166
0.3058332	0.3412498	0.3766665	0.4120831	0.4474997
0.4829164				

EXAMPLE 3.5.3

Design a sample-rate converter that increases the sampling rate by a factor 2.5. Use the Remez algorithm to determine the coefficients of the FIR filter that has 0.1-dB ripple in the passband and is down by at least 30 dB in the stopband. Specify the sets of time-varying coefficients $g(n,m)$ used in the realization of the sampling-rate converter according to the structure shown in Fig. 3.17.

Solution: The FIR filter that meets the specifications of this problem is exactly the same as the filter designed in Example 3.5.2. Its bandwidth is $\pi/5$.

The coefficients of the filter are given by (3.4.8) as

$$g(n,m) = h(nU + (mD)_U)$$
$$= h\left(nU + mD - \left\lfloor \frac{mD}{U} \right\rfloor U\right)$$

By substituting $U = 5$ and $D = 2$, we obtain

$$g(n,m) = h\left(5n + 2m - 5\left\lfloor \frac{2m}{5} \right\rfloor\right)$$

By evaluating $g(n,m)$ for $n = 0, 1, \ldots, 5$ and $m = 0, 1, \ldots, 4$ we obtain the following coefficients for the time-variant filter:

$$g(0,m) = \{h(0) \quad h(2) \quad h(4) \quad h(1) \quad h(3)\}$$
$$g(1,m) = \{h(5) \quad h(7) \quad h(9) \quad h(6) \quad h(8)\}$$
$$g(2,m) = \{h(10) \quad h(12) \quad h(14) \quad h(11) \quad h(13)\}$$
$$g(3,m) = \{h(15) \quad h(17) \quad h(19) \quad h(16) \quad h(18)\}$$
$$g(4,m) = \{h(20) \quad h(22) \quad h(24) \quad h(21) \quad h(23)\}$$
$$g(5,m) = \{h(25) \quad h(27) \quad h(29) \quad h(26) \quad h(28)\}$$

A polyphase filter implementation would employ five subfilters, each of length six. To decimate the output of the polyphase filters by a factor of $D = 2$ means simply that we take every other output from the polyphase filters. Thus the first output $y(0)$ is taken from $p_0(n)$, the second output $y(1)$ is taken from $p_2(n)$, the third from $p_4(n)$, the fourth from $p_1(n)$, the fifth from $p_3(n)$, and so on.

3.6 MULTISTAGE IMPLEMENTATIONS OF SAMPLING-RATE CONVERSION

In practical applications of sampling-rate conversion we often encounter decimation factors and interpolation factors that are much larger than unity. For example, suppose that we are given the task of altering the sampling rate by the factor $U/D = 130/63$. Although in theory this rate alteration can be achieved exactly, the implementation would require a bank of 130 polyphase filters and may be computationally inefficient. In this section we consider methods for performing sampling-rate conversion for either $D \gg 1$ and/or $U \gg 1$ in multiple stages.

First, let us consider interpolation by a factor $U \gg 1$ and let us assume that U can be factored into a product of positive integers as

$$U = \prod_{i=1}^{L} U_i \tag{3.6.1}$$

Then interpolation by a factor U can be accomplished by cascading L stages of interpolation and filtering, as shown in Fig. 3.20. Note that the filter in each of the interpolators eliminates the images introduced by the up-sampling process in the corresponding interpolator.

In a similar manner, decimation by a factor D, where D may be factored into a product of positive integers as

$$D = \prod_{i=1}^{J} D_i \tag{3.6.2}$$

may be implemented as a cascade of J stages of filtering and decimation as illustrated in Fig. 3.21. Thus the sampling rate at the output of the ith stage is

$$F_i = \frac{F_{i-1}}{D_i}, \qquad i = 1, 2, \ldots, J \tag{3.6.3}$$

where the input rate for the sequence $x(n)$ is $F_0 = F_x$.

To ensure that no aliasing occurs in the overall decimation process, we may design each filter stage to avoid aliasing within the frequency band of interest. To elaborate, let us define the desired passband and the transition band in the overall decimator as

$$\begin{aligned} &\text{passband:} && 0 \le F \le F_{pc} \\ &\text{transition band:} && F_{pc} \le F \le F_{sc} \end{aligned} \tag{3.6.4}$$

where $F_{sc} \le F_x/2D$. Then aliasing in the band $0 \le F \le F_{sc}$ is avoided by selecting the frequency bands of each filter stage as follows:

$$\begin{aligned} &\text{passband:} && 0 \le F \le F_{pc} \\ &\text{transition band:} && F_{pc} \le F \le F_i - F_{sc} \\ &\text{stopband:} && F_i - F_{sc} \le F \le \frac{F_{i-1}}{2} \end{aligned} \tag{3.6.5}$$

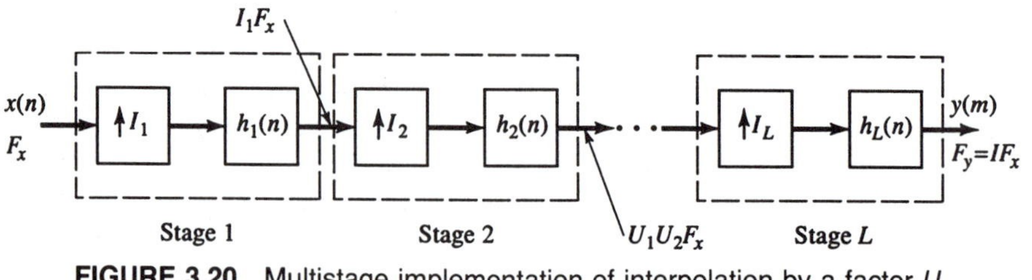

FIGURE 3.20 Multistage implementation of interpolation by a factor U.

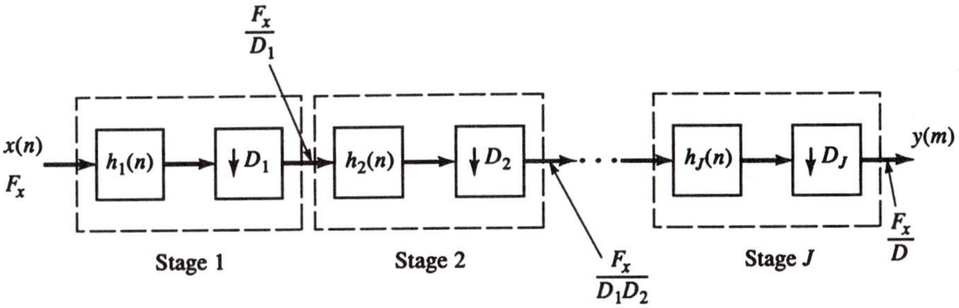

FIGURE 3.21 Multistage implementation of decimation by a factor D.

For example, in the first filter stage we have $F_1 = F_x/D_1$, and the filter is designed to have the following frequency bands:

$$\begin{aligned} &\text{passband:} && 0 \le F \le F_{pc} \\ &\text{transition band:} && F_{pc} \le F \le F_1 - F_{sc} \qquad (3.6.6) \\ &\text{stopband:} && F_1 - F_{sc} \le F \le \frac{F_0}{2} \end{aligned}$$

After decimation by D_1, there will be aliasing from the signal components that fall in the filter transition band, but the aliasing will occur at frequencies above F_{sc}. Thus there is no aliasing in the frequency band $0 \le F \le F_{sc}$. By designing the filters in the subsequent stages to satisfy the specifications given in (3.6.5), we ensure that no aliasing occurs in the primary frequency band $0 \le F \le F_{sc}$.

EXAMPLE 3.6.1

Consider an audio-band signal with a nominal bandwidth of 4 kHz that has been sampled at a rate of 8 kHz. Suppose that we wish to isolate the frequency components below 80 Hz with a filter that has a passband $0 \le F \le 75$ and a transition band $75 \le F \le 80$. Hence $F_{pc} = 75$ Hz and $F_{sc} = 80$. The signal in the band $0 \le F \le 80$ may be decimated by the factor $D = F_x/2F_{sc} = 50$. We also specify that the filter have a passband ripple $\delta_1 = 10^{-2}$ and a stopband ripple of $\delta_2 = 10^{-4}$.

The length of the linear phase FIR filter required to satisfy the specifications above may be estimated from one of the well-known formulas given in the literature. A particularly simple formula for approximating the length M, attributed to Kaiser is

$$\hat{M} = \frac{-10 \log_{10} \delta_1\delta_2 - 13}{14.6\,\Delta f} + 1 \qquad (3.6.7)$$

where Δf is the normalized (by the sampling rate) width of the transition region [i.e., $\Delta f = (F_{sc} - F_{pc})/F_s$]. A more accurate formula proposed by Herrmann et al. (1973) is

$$\hat{M} = \frac{D_\infty(\delta_1, \delta_2) - f(\delta_1, \delta_2)(\Delta f)^2}{\Delta f} + 1 \tag{3.6.8}$$

where $D_\infty(\delta_1, \delta_2)$ and $f(\delta_1, \delta_2)$ are defined as

$$\begin{aligned} D_\infty(\delta_1, \delta_2) &= [0.005309(\log_{10}\delta_1)^2 + 0.07114(\log_{10}\delta_1) - 0.4761]\log_{10}\delta_2 \\ &\quad - [0.00266(\log_{10}\delta_1)^2 + 0.5941\log_{10}\delta_1 + 0.4278] \end{aligned} \tag{3.6.9}$$

$$f(\delta_1, \delta_2) = 11.012 + 0.51244(\log_{10}\delta_1 - \log_{10}\delta_2) \tag{3.6.10}$$

Now a single FIR filter followed by a decimator would require (using the Kaiser formula) a filter of (approximate) length

$$\hat{M} = \frac{-10\log_{10}10^{-6} - 13}{14.6(5/8000)} + 1 \approx 5152$$

As an alternative, let us consider a two-stage decimation process with $D_1 = 25$ and $D_2 = 2$. In the first stage we have the specifications $F_1 = 320$ Hz and

passband: $0 \leq F \leq 75$

transition band: $75 < F \leq 240$

$$\Delta f = \frac{165}{8000}$$

$$\delta_{11} = \frac{\delta_1}{2}, \qquad \delta_{21} = \delta_2$$

Note that we have reduced the passband ripple δ_1 by a factor of 2 so that the total passband ripple in the cascade of the two filters does not exceed δ_1. On the other hand, the stopband ripple is maintained at δ_2 in both stages. Now the Kaiser formula yields an estimate of M_1 as

$$\hat{M} = \frac{-10\log_{10}\delta_{11}\delta_{21} - 13}{14.6\,\Delta f} + 1 \approx 167$$

For the second stage, we have $F_2 = F_1/2 = 160$ and the specifications

passband: $0 \leq F \leq 75$

transition band: $75 < F \leq 80$

$$\Delta f = \frac{5}{320}$$

$$\delta_{12} = \frac{\delta_1}{2}, \qquad \delta_{22} = \delta_2$$

Hence the estimate of the length M_2 of the second filter is

$$\hat{M}_2 \approx 220$$

Therefore, the total length of the two FIR filters is approximately $\hat{M}_1 + \hat{M}_2 = 387$. This represents a reduction in the filter length by a factor of more than 13.

The reader is encouraged to repeat the computation above with $D_1 = 10$ and $D_2 = 5$.

It is apparent from the computations in Example 3.6.1 that the reduction in the filter length results from increasing Δf, which appears in the denominator in (3.6.7) and (3.6.8). By decimating in multiple stages, we are able to increase the width of the transition region through a reduction in the sampling rate.

In the case of a multistage interpolator having L stages, the sampling rate at the output of the ith stage is

$$F_{i-1} = U_i F_i, \qquad i = L, L-1, \ldots, 1$$

and the output rate is $F_o = UF_L$ when the input sampling rate is F_L. The corresponding frequency band specifications are

$$\text{passband:} \qquad 0 \le F \le F_{pc}$$

$$\text{transition band:} \quad F_{pc} < F \le F_i - F_{sc}$$

The following example illustrates the advantages of multistage interpolation.

EXAMPLE 3.6.2

Let us reverse the filtering problem described in Example 3.6.1 by beginning with a signal having a passband $0 \le F \le 75$ and a transition band of $75 \le F \le 80$. We wish to interpolate by a factor of 50. By selecting $U_1 = 2$ and $U_2 = 25$, we have basically a transposed form of the decimation problem considered in Example 3.6.1. Thus we may simply transpose the two-stage decimator to achieve the two-stage interpolator with $U_1 = 2$, $U_2 = 25$, $\hat{M}_1 \approx 220$, and $\hat{M}_2 \approx 167$.

3.7 SAMPLING-RATE CONVERSION OF BANDPASS SIGNALS

A bandpass signal is a signal with frequency content concentrated in a narrow band of frequencies above zero frequency. The center frequency F_c of the signal is generally much larger than the bandwidth B (i.e., $F_c \gg B$). Bandpass signals arise frequently in practice, most notably in communications, where information-bearing signals such as speech and video are translated in frequency for transmission over such channels as wire lines, microwave radio, and satellites.

In this section we consider the decimation and interpolation of bandpass signals. As shown in Section 1.2.4, any bandpass signal has an equivalent lowpass representation, which is obtained by a simple frequency translation of the bandpass signal. For example, the bandpass signal with spectrum $X(F)$ shown in Fig. 3.22(a) can be translated to lowpass by means of a frequency translation of F_c, where F_c is some appropriate choice of frequency (usually, the center frequency) within the bandwidth occupied by the bandpass signal. Thus we obtain the equivalent lowpass signal as illustrated in Fig. 3.22(b).

Mathematically, an analog bandpass signal may be represented as

$$\begin{aligned} x(t) & A(t) \cos [2\pi F_c t + \phi(t)] \\ &= A(t) \cos \phi(t) \cos 2\pi F_c t - A(t) \sin \phi(t) \sin 2\pi F_c t \\ &= u_c(t) \cos 2\pi F_c t - u_s(t) \sin 2\pi F_c t \\ &= \mathrm{Re}[u(t) e^{j2\pi F_c t}] \end{aligned} \tag{3.7.1}$$

where, by definition,

$$u_c(t) = A(t) \cos \phi(t) \tag{3.7.2}$$

$$u_s(t) = A(t) \sin \phi(t) \tag{3.7.3}$$

$$u(t) = u_c(t) + j u_s(t) \tag{3.7.4}$$

$A(t)$ is called the *amplitude* or *envelope* of the signal, $\phi(t)$ is the phase, and $u_c(t)$ and $u_s(t)$ are called the *quadrature components* of the signal.

Physically, the translation of $x(t)$ to lowpass involves multiplying (mixing) $x(t)$ by the quadrature carriers $\cos 2\pi F_c t$ and $\sin 2\pi F_c t$ and lowpass filtering the two products to eliminate the frequency components that are generated around the frequency $2F_c$ (the double-frequency terms). Thus all the information content contained in the bandpass signal is preserved in the lowpass signal and hence the latter is equivalent to the former. This fact is obvious from the spectral representation of the bandpass signal, which may be written as

$$X(F) = \tfrac{1}{2} [U(F - F_c) + U^*(-F - F_c)] \tag{3.7.5}$$

where $U(F)$ is the Fourier transform of the equivalent lowpass signal $u(t)$ and $X(F)$ is the Fourier transform of $x(t)$.

It was shown in Section 1.3 [see also Brown (1980)] that a bandpass signal of bandwidth B may be uniquely represented by samples taken at a rate of $2B$ samples per second, provided that the upper band (highest) frequency is a multiple of the signal bandwidth B. On the other hand, if the upper band frequency is not a multiple of B, the sampling rate must be increased by a small amount to avoid aliasing. In any case, the sampling rate for the bandpass signal is bounded from above and below as

$$2B \le F_s \le 4B \tag{3.7.6}$$

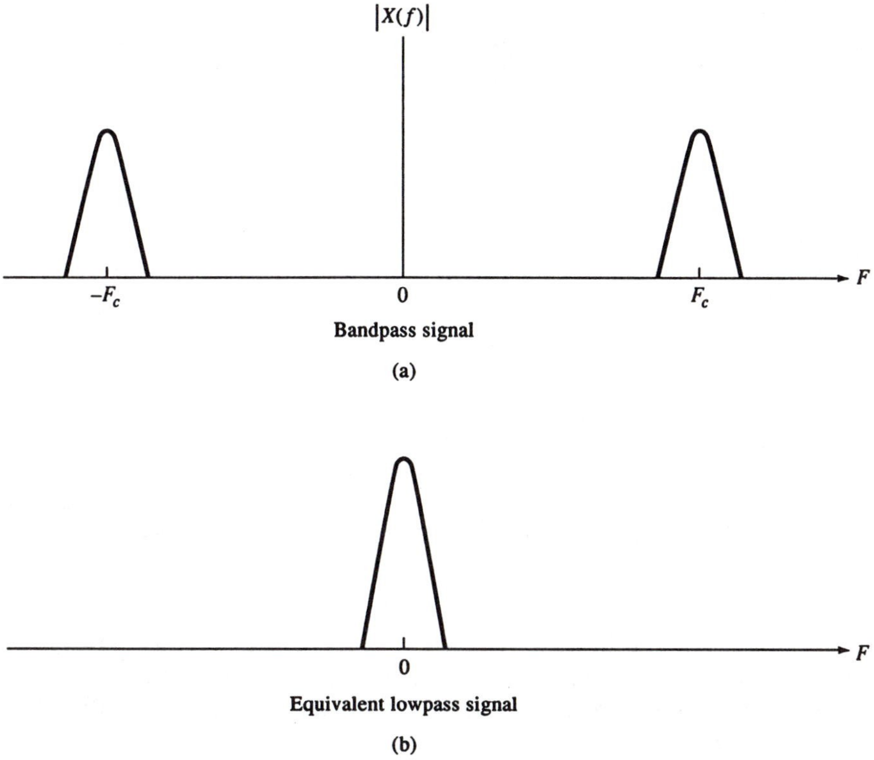

FIGURE 3.22 Bandpass signal and its equivalent lowpass representation.

The representation of discrete-time bandpass signals is basically the same as that for analog signals given by (3.7.1) with the substitution of $t = nT$, where T is the sampling interval.

3.7.1 Decimation and Interpolation by Frequency Conversion

The mathematical equivalence between the bandpass signal $x(t)$ and its equivalent lowpass representation $u(t)$ provides one method for altering the sampling rate of the signal. Specifically, we may take the bandpass signal which has been sampled at rate F_x, convert it to lowpass through the frequency-conversion process illustrated in Fig. 3.23, and perform the sampling-rate conversion on the lowpass signal using the methods described previously. The lowpass filters for obtaining the two quadrature components may be designed to have linear phase within the bandwidth of the signal and to approximate the ideal frequency response characteristic.

$$H(\omega) = \begin{cases} 1, & |\omega| \leq \dfrac{\omega_B}{2} \\ 0, & \text{otherwise} \end{cases} \tag{3.7.7}$$

where ω_B is the bandwidth of the discrete-time bandpass signal ($\omega_B \leq \pi$).

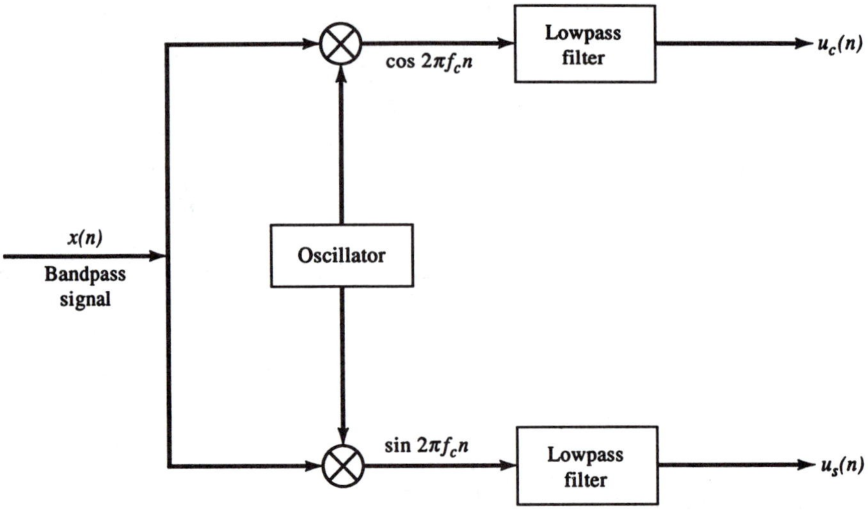

FIGURE 3.23 Conversion of a bandpass signal to lowpass.

If decimation is to be performed by an integer factor D, the antialiasing filter preceding the decimator may be combined with the lowpass filter used for frequency conversion into a single filter that approximates the ideal frequency response

$$H_D(\omega) = \begin{cases} 1, & |\omega| \leq \dfrac{\omega_D}{D} \\ 0, & \text{otherwise} \end{cases} \tag{3.7.8}$$

where ω_D is any desired frequency in the range $0 \leq \omega_D \leq \pi$. For example, we may select $\omega_D = \omega_B/2$ if we are interested only in the frequency range $0 \leq \omega \leq \omega_B/2D$ of the original signal.

If interpolation is to be performed by an integer factor U on the frequency-translated signal, the filter used to reject the images in the spectrum should be designed to approximate the lowpass filter characteristic

$$H_U(\omega) = \begin{cases} U, & |\omega| \leq \dfrac{\omega_B}{2U} \\ 0, & \text{otherwise} \end{cases} \tag{3.7.9}$$

We note that in the case of interpolation, the lowpass filter that is normally used to reject the double-frequency components is redundant and may be omitted. Its function is essentially served by the image rejection filter $H_U(\omega)$.

Finally, we indicate that sampling rate conversion by any rational factor U/D can be acomplished on the bandpass signal as illustrated in Fig. 3.24. Again, the lowpass filter for rejecting the double-frequency components generated in the frequency conversion process can be omitted. Its function

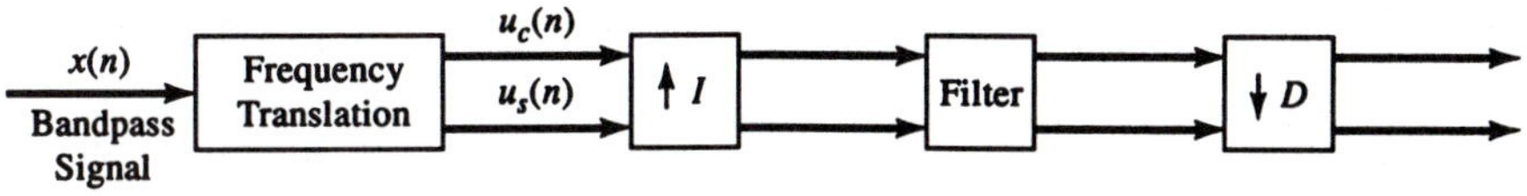

FIGURE 3.24 Sampling rate conversion of a bandpass signal.

is simply served by the image-rejection/antialiasing filter following the interpolator, which is designed to approximate the ideal frequency response characteristic

$$H(\omega) = \begin{cases} U, & 0 \le |\omega| \le \min\left(\dfrac{\omega_B}{2D}, \dfrac{\omega_B}{2U}\right) \\ 0, & \text{otherwise} \end{cases} \tag{3.7.10}$$

Once the sampling rate of the quadrature signal components has been altered by either decimation or interpolation or both, a bandpass signal may be regenerated by amplitude modulating the quadrature carriers $\cos \omega_c n$ and $\sin \omega_c n$ by the corresponding signal components and adding the two signals. The center frequency ω_c is any desirable frequency in the range

$$\min\left(\frac{\omega_B}{2D}, \frac{\omega_B}{2U}\right) \le \omega_c \le \pi \tag{3.7.11}$$

3.7.2 Modulation-Free Method for Decimation and Interpolation

By restricting the frequency range for the signal whose frequency is to be altered, it is possible to avoid the carrier modulation process and to achieve frequency translation directly. In this case we exploit the frequency translation property that is inherent in the process of decimation and interpolation.

To be specific, let us consider the decimation of the sampled bandpass signal whose spectrum is shown in Fig. 3.25. Note that the signal spectrum is confined to the frequency range

$$\frac{m\pi}{D} \le \omega \le \frac{(m+1)\pi}{D} \tag{3.7.12}$$

where m is a positive integer. A bandpass filter would normally be used to eliminate signal frequency components outside the desired frequency range.

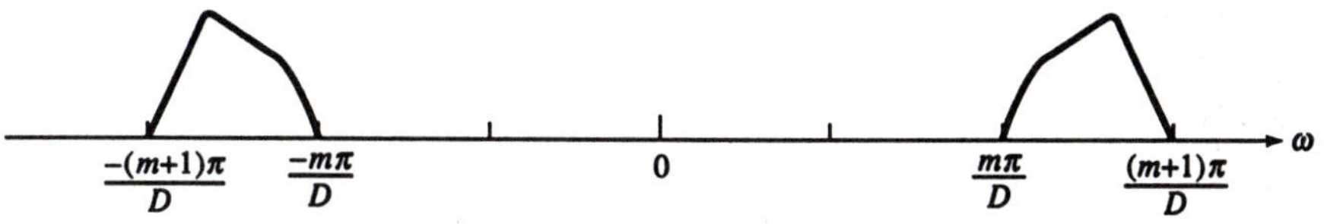

FIGURE 3.25 Spectrum of a bandpass signal.

Then, direct decimation of the bandpass signal by the factor D results in the spectrum shown in Fig. 3.26(a) for m odd and in Fig. 3.26(b) for m even. In the case where m is odd, there is an inversion of the spectrum of the signal. This inversion can be undone by multiplying each sample of the decimated signal by $(-1)^n$, $n = 0, 1, \ldots$. Note that violation of the bandwidth constraint given by (3.7.12) results in signal aliasing.

Modulation-free interpolation of a bandpass signal by an integer factor U can be accomplished in a similar manner. The process of up-sampling by inserting zeros between samples of $x(n)$ produces U images in the band $0 \le \omega \le \pi$. The desired image can be selected by bandpass filtering. Note that the process of interpolation also provides us with the opportunity to achieve frequency translation of the spectrum.

Finally, modulation-free sampling rate conversion for a bandpass signal by a rational factor U/D can be accomplished by cascading a decimator with an interpolator in a manner that depends on the choice of the parameters D and U. A bandpass filter preceding the sampling converter is usually required to isolate the signal frequency band of interest. Note that this approach provides us with a modulation-free method for achieving frequency translation of a signal by selecting $D = U$.

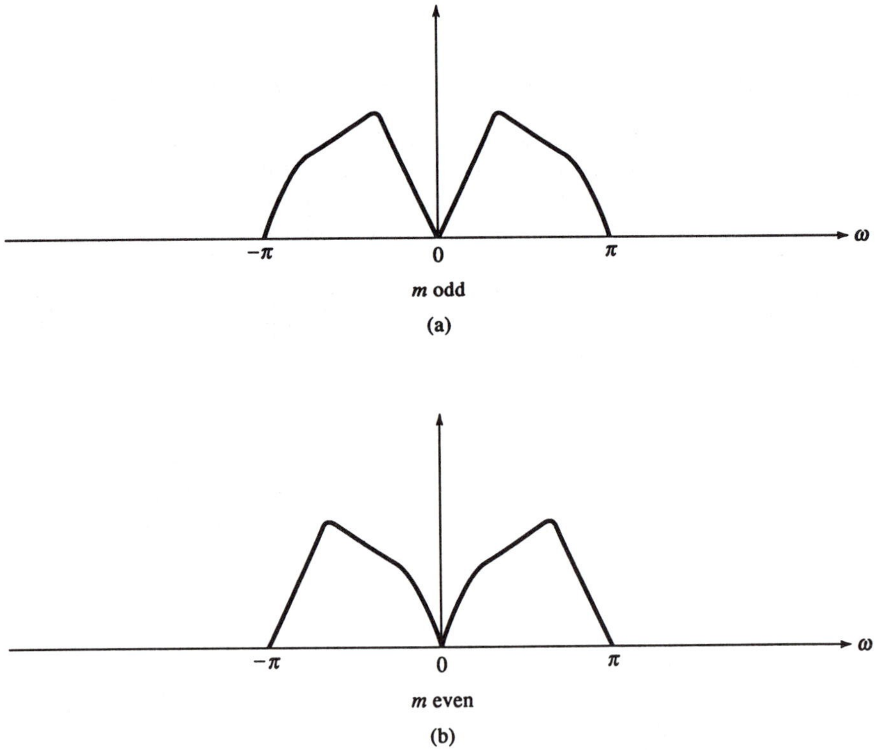

FIGURE 3.26 Spectrum of decimated bandpass signal.

3.8 SAMPLING-RATE CONVERSION BY AN ARBITRARY FACTOR

In the previous sections of this chapter, we have shown how to perform sampling-rate conversion exactly by a rational number U/D. In some applications it is either inefficient or, sometimes, impossible to use such an exact rate conversion scheme. We first consider the following two cases.

Case 1. We need to perform rate conversion by the rational number U/D, where U is a large integer (e.g., $U/D = 1023/511$). Although we can achieve exact rate conversion by this number, we would need a polyphase filter with 1023 subfilters. Such an exact implementation is obviously inefficient in memory usage because we need to store a large number of filter coefficients.

Case 2. In some applications, the exact conversion rate is not known when we design the rate converter, or the rate is continuously changing during the conversion process. For example, we may encounter the situation where the input and output samples are controlled by two independent clocks. Even though it is still possible to define a nominal conversion rate that may be a rational number, the actual rate would be slightly different, depending on the frequency difference between the two clocks. Obviously, it is not possible to design an exact rate converter in this case.

To implement sampling-rate conversion for applications similar to these cases, we resort to nonexact rate-conversion schemes. Unavoidably, such a nonexact scheme will introduce some distortion in the converted output signal. (It should be noted that distortion exists even in an exact rational rate converter because the polyphase filter is never ideal.) Such a converter will be adequate, as long as the total distortion does not exceed the specification required in the application.

Depending on the application requirements and implementation constraints, we can use first-order, second-order, or higher-order approximations. We shall describe first-order and second-order approximation methods and provide an analysis of the resulting timing errors.

3.8.1 First-Order Approximation

Let us denote the arbitrary conversion rate by r and suppose that the input to the rate converter is the sequence $x(n)$. We need to generate a sequence of output samples which are separated in time by T_x/r, where T_x is the sample interval for $x(n)$. By constructing a polyphase filter with a large number of subfilters as described above, we can approximate such a sequence with a nonuniformly spaced sequence. Without loss of generality, we may express $1/r$ as

$$\frac{1}{r} = \frac{k}{U} + \beta$$

where k and U are positive integers and β is a number in the range

$$0 < \beta < \frac{1}{U}$$

Consequently, $1/r$ is bounded from above and below as

$$\frac{k}{U} < \frac{1}{r} < \frac{k+1}{U}$$

U corresponds to the interpolation factor that will be determined to satisfy the specification on the amount of tolerable distortion introduced by rate conversion. U is also equal to the number of polyphase filters.

For example, suppose that $r = 2.2$ and that we have determined, as we demonstrate below, that $U = 6$ polyphase filters are required to meet the distortion specification. Then

$$\frac{k}{U} \equiv \frac{2}{6} < \frac{1}{r} < \frac{3}{6} \equiv \frac{k+1}{U}$$

so that $k = 2$. The time spacing between samples of the interpolated sequence is T_x/U. However, the desired rate $r = 2.2$ corresponds to a decimation rate of 2.727, which falls between $k = 2$ and $k = 3$. In the first-order approximation, we achieve the desired decimation rate by selecting the output sample from the polyphase filter that is closest in time to the desired sampling time. This is illustrated in Fig. 3.27 for $U = 6$.

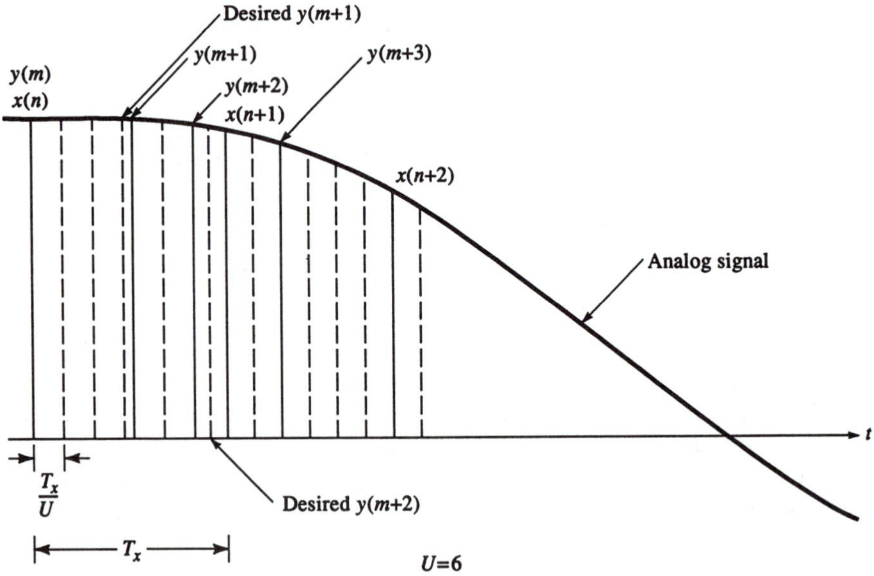

FIGURE 3.27 Sample rate conversion by use of first-order approximation.

In general, to perform rate conversion by a factor r, we employ a polyphase filter to perform interpolation and thus increase the frequency of the original sequence of a factor of U. The time spacing between the samples of the interpolated sequence is equal to T_x/U. If the ideal sampling time of the mth sample, $y(m)$, of the desired output sequence is between the sampling times of two samples of the interpolated sequence, we select the sample closer to $y(m)$ as its approximation.

Let us assume that the mth selected sample is generated by the i_mth subfilter using the input samples $x(n), x(n-1), \ldots, x(n-K+1)$ in the delay line. The normalized sampling timing error (i.e., the time difference between the selected sampling time and the desired sampling time normalized by T_x) is denoted by t_m. The sign of t_m is positive if the desired sampling time leads the selected sampling time, and negative otherwise. It is easy to show that $|t_m| \leq 0.5/U$. The normalized time advance from the mth output $y(m)$ to the $(m+1)$st output $y(m+1)$ is equal to $1/r + t_m$.

To compute the next output, we first determine a number that is closest to $i_m/U + 1/r + t_m + k_m/U$ and is of the form $l_{m+1} + i_{m+1}/U$, where both l_{m+1} and i_{m+1} are integers and $i_{m+1} < U$. Then the $(m+1)$st output $y(m+1)$ is computed using the (i_{m+1})th subfilter after shifting the signal in the delay line by l_{m+1} input samples. The normalized timing error for the $(m+1)$th sample is $t_{m+1} = (i_m/U + 1/r + t_m) - (l_{m+1} + i_{m+1}/U)$. It is saved for the computation of the next output sample.

By increasing the number of subfilters used, we can arbitrarily increase the conversion accuracy. However, we also need to use more memory to store the large number of filter coefficients. Hence it is desirable to use as few subfilters as possible while keeping the distortion in the converted signal below the specification. The distortion introduced due to the sampling-time approximation is most conveniently evaluated in the frequency domain.

Suppose that the input data sequence $x(n)$ has a flat spectrum from $-\omega_x$ to ω_x, where $\omega_x < \pi$, with a magnitude A. Its total power can be computed using Parseval's theorem, namely,

$$P_s = \frac{1}{2\pi}\int_{-\omega_x}^{\omega_x} |X(\omega)|^2\, d\omega = \frac{A^2\omega_x}{\pi} \tag{3.8.1}$$

From the discussion given above, we know that for each output $y(m)$, the time difference between the desired filter and the filter actually used is t_m, where $|t_m| \leq 0.5/U$. Hence the frequency response of these filters can be written as $e^{j\omega\tau}$ and $e^{j\omega(\tau - t_m)}$, respectively. When U is large ωt_m is small. By ignoring high-order errors, we can write the difference between the frequency responses as

$$\begin{aligned} e^{j\omega\tau} - e^{j\omega(\tau - t_m)} &= e^{j\omega\tau}(1 - e^{-j\omega t_m}) \\ &= e^{j\omega\tau}(1 - \cos\omega t_m + j\sin\omega t_m) \approx je^{j\omega\tau}\,\omega t_m \end{aligned} \tag{3.8.2}$$

By using the bound $|t_m| \leq 0.5/U$, we obtain an upper bound for the total error power as

$$P_e = \frac{1}{2\pi}\int_{-\omega_x}^{\omega_x} |X(\omega)e^{j\omega\tau} - X(\omega)e^{j\omega(\tau - t_m)}|^2 \, d\omega$$

$$\approx \frac{1}{2\pi}\int_{-\omega_x}^{\omega_x} |X(\omega)je^{j\omega\tau}\,\omega t_m|^2 \, d\omega$$

$$\leq \frac{1}{2\pi}\int_{-\omega_x}^{\omega_x} A^2\left(\frac{0.5}{U}\right)^2 \omega^2 \, d\omega = \frac{A^2\omega_x^3}{12\pi U^2} \qquad (3.8.3)$$

This bound shows that the error power is inversely proportional to the square of the number of subfilters U. Therefore, the error magnitude is inversely proportional to U. Hence we call the approximation of the rate-conversion method described above a *first-order approximation*. By using (3.8.3) and (3.8.1), the signal-to-distortion ratio due to a sampling-time error for the first-order approximation, denoted as SD_tR1 is lower bounded as

$$SD_tR1 = \frac{P_s}{P_e} \geq \frac{12U^2}{\omega_x^2} \qquad (3.8.4)$$

It can be seen from (3.8.4) that the signal-to-distortion ratio is proportional to the square of the number of subfilters.

EXAMPLE 3.8.1

Suppose that the input signal has a flat spectrum between -0.8π and 0.8π. Determine the number of subfilters to achieve a signal-to-distortion ratio of 50 dB.

Solution: To achieve an $SD_tR > 10^5$, we set $SD_1R1 = 12U^2/\omega_x^2$ equal to 10^5. Thus we find that

$$U \approx \omega_x\sqrt{\frac{10^5}{12}} \approx 230 \text{ subfilters}$$

3.8.2 Second-Order Approximation (Linear Interpolation)

The disadvantage of the first-order approximation method is the large number of subfilters needed to achieve a specified distortion requirement. Below we describe a method that uses linear interpolation to achieve the same performance with a reduced number of subfilters.

The implementation of the linear interpolation method is very similar to the first-order approximation discussed above. Instead of using the sample from the interpolating filter that is closest to the desired conversion output as the approximation, we compute two adjacent samples with the desired sampling time falling between their sampling times, as illustrated in Figure 3.28. The normalized time spacing between these two samples is $1/U$. Assuming that the sampling time of the first sample lags the desired sampling

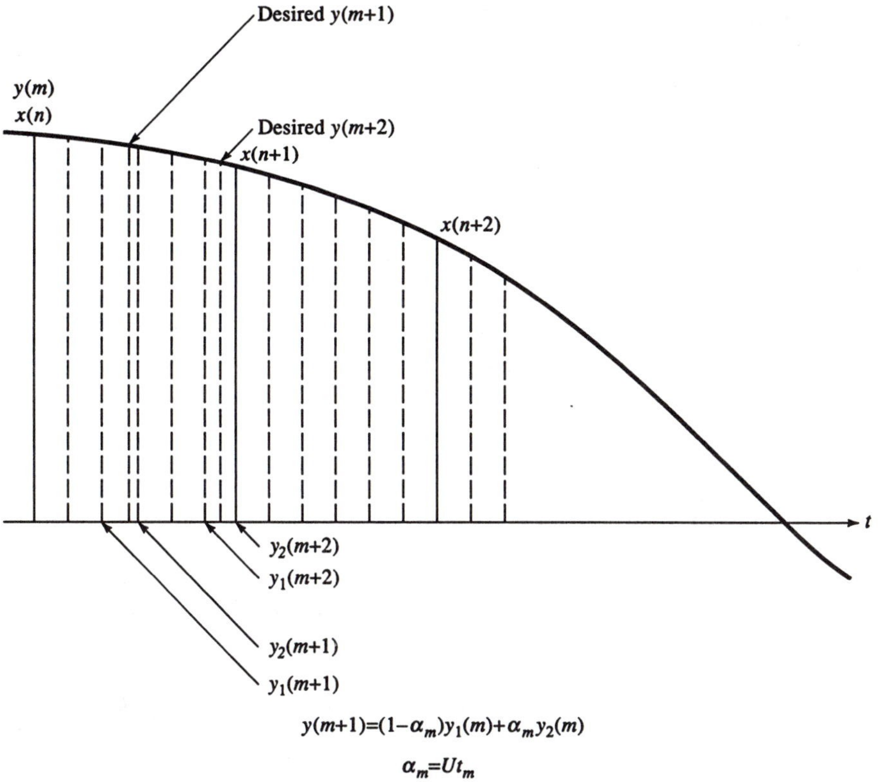

FIGURE 3.28 Sample rate conversion by use of linear interpolation.

time by t_m, the sampling time of the second sample is then leading the desired sampling time by $(1/U) - t_m$. If we denote these two samples by $y_1(m)$ and $y_2(m)$ and use linear interpolation, we can compute the approximation to the desired output as

$$y(m) = (1 - \alpha_m)y_1(m) + \alpha_m y_2(m) \tag{3.8.5}$$

where $\alpha_m = Ut_m$. Note that $0 \le \alpha_m \le 1$.

The implementation of linear interpolation is similar to that for the first-order approximation. Normally, both $y_1(m)$ and $y_2(m)$ are computed using the ith and $(i + 1)$th subfilters, respectively, with the same set of input data samples in the delay line. The only exception is in the boundary case, where $i = U - 1$. In this case we use the $(U - 1)$th subfilter to compute $y_1(m)$, but the second sample $y_2(m)$ is computed using the zeroth subfilter after new input data are shifted into the delay line.

To analyze the error introduced by the second-order approximation, we first write the frequency responses of the desired filter and the two subfilters used to compute $y_1(m)$ and $y_2(m)$ as $e^{j\omega\tau}$, $e^{j\omega(\tau - t_m)}$, and $e^{j\omega(\tau - t_m + 1/U)}$, respectively. Because linear interpolation is a linear operation, we can also use linear interpolation to compute the frequency response of the filter that generates $y(m)$ as

$$\begin{aligned}
&(1 - Ut_m)e^{j\omega(\tau - t_m)} + Ut_m e^{j\omega(\tau - t_m + 1/U)} \\
&= e^{j\omega\tau}[(1 - \alpha_m)e^{-j\omega t_m} + \alpha_m e^{j\omega(-t_m + 1/U)}] \\
&= e^{j\omega\tau}(1 - \alpha_m)(\cos \omega t_m - j \sin \omega t_m) \\
&\quad + e^{j\omega\tau}\alpha_m [\cos \omega (-t_m + 1/U) + j \sin \omega (-t_m + 1/U)]
\end{aligned} \tag{3.8.6}$$

By ignoring high-order errors, we can write the difference between the desired frequency responses and the one given by (3.8.6) as

$$\begin{aligned}
&e^{j\omega\tau} - (1 - \alpha_m)e^{j\omega(\tau - t_m)} - \alpha_m e^{j\omega(\tau - t_m + 1/U)} \\
&= e^{j\omega\tau}\{[1 - (1 - \alpha_m) \cos \omega t_m - a_m \cos \omega(-t_m + 1/U)] \\
&+ j[(1 - \alpha_m) \sin \omega t_m - \alpha_m \sin \omega(-t_m + 1/U)]\} \\
&\approx e^{j\omega\tau}\left[\omega^2(1 - \alpha_m)\frac{\alpha_m}{U^2}\right]
\end{aligned} \tag{3.8.7}$$

Using $(1 - \alpha_m)\, \alpha_m \leq \frac{1}{4}$, we obtain an upper bound for the total error power as

$$\begin{aligned}
P_e &= \frac{1}{2\pi}\int_{-\omega_x}^{\omega_x} |X(\omega)[e^{j\omega\tau} - (1 - \alpha_m)e^{j\omega(\tau - t_m)} - \alpha_m e^{j\omega(\tau - t_m + 1/U)}]|^2\, d\omega \\
&\approx \frac{1}{2\pi}\int_{-\omega_x}^{\omega_x} \left| X(\omega)e^{j\omega\tau}\left[\omega^2(1 - \alpha_m)\frac{\alpha_m}{U^2}\right]\right|^2 d\omega \\
&\leq \frac{1}{2\pi}\int_{-\omega_x}^{\omega_x} A^2\left(\frac{0.25}{U^2}\right)^2 \omega^4\, d\omega = \frac{A^2\omega_x^5}{80\pi U^4}
\end{aligned} \tag{3.8.8}$$

This result indicates that the error magnitude is inversely proportional to U^2. Hence we call the approximation using linear interpolation a *second-order approximation*. Using (3.8.8) and (3.8.1), the signal-to-distortion ratio due to a sampling-time error for the second-order approximation, denoted by $\mathrm{SD_tR2}$, is bounded from below as

$$\mathrm{SD_tR2} = \frac{P_s}{P_e} \geq \frac{80U^4}{\omega_x^4} \tag{3.8.9}$$

Therefore, the signal-to-distortion ratio is proportional to the fourth power of the number of subfilters.

EXAMPLE 3.8.2

Determine the number of subfilters required to meet the specifications given in Example 3.8.1. when linear interpolation is employed.

Solution: To achieve $SD_1R > 10^5$, we set $SD_1R2 = 80U^4/\omega_x^4$ equal to 10^5. Thus we obtain

$$U \approx \omega_x^4 \sqrt{\frac{10^5}{80}} \approx 15 \text{ subfilters}$$

From this example we see that the required number of subfilters for the second-order approximation is reduced by a factor of about 15 compared to the first-order approximation. However, we now need to compute two interpolated samples in this case, instead of one for the first-order approximation. Hence we have doubled the computational complexity.

Linear interpolation is the simplest case of the class of approximation methods based on Lagrange polynomials. It is also possible to use higher-order Lagrange polynomial approximations (interpolation) to further reduce the number of subfilters required to meet specifications. However, the second-order approximation seems sufficient for most practical applications. The interested reader is referred to the paper by Ramstad (1984) for higher-order Lagrange interpolation methods.

3.9 APPLICATIONS OF MULTIRATE SIGNAL PROCESSING

There are numerous practical applications of multirate signal processing. In this section we describe a few of these applications.

3.9.1 Design of Phase Shifters

Suppose that we wish to design a network that delays the signal $x(n)$ by a fraction of a sample. Let us assume that the delay is a rational fraction of a sampling interval T_x [i.e., $d = (k/U)T_x$, where k and U are relatively prime positive integers]. In the frequency domain, the delay corresponds to a linear-phase shift of the form

$$\Theta(\omega) = -\frac{k\omega}{U} \tag{3.9.1}$$

The design of an all-pass, linear-phase filter is relatively difficult. However, we may use the methods of sample-rate conversion to achieve a delay of $(k/U)T_x$, exactly, without introducing any significant distortion in the signal. To be specific, let us consider the system shown in Fig. 3.29. The sampling rate is increased by a factor U using a standard interpolator. The lowpass filter eliminates the images in the spectrum of the interpolated signal, and its output is delayed by k samples at the sampling rate UF_x. The delayed signal is decimated by a factor $D = U$. Thus we have achieved the desired delay of k/U.

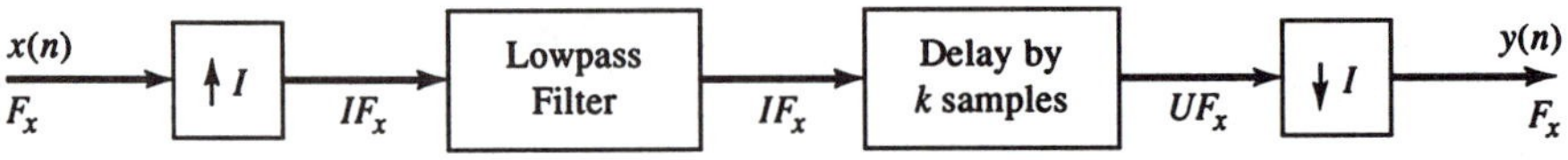

FIGURE 3.29 Method for generating a delay in a discrete-time signal.

An efficient implementation of the interpolator is the polyphase filter illustrated in Fig. 3.30. The delay of k samples is achieved by placing the initial position of the commutator at the output of the kth subfilter. Since decimation by $D = U$ means that we take one out of every U samples from the polyphase filter, the commutator position may be fixed to the output of the kth subfilter. Thus a delay a k/U can be achieved by using only the kth subfilter of the polyphase filter. We note that the polyphase filter introduces an additional delay of $(M - 1)/2$ samples, where M is the length of its impulse response.

Finally, we mention that if the desired delay is a nonrational factor of the sample interval T_x, either the first- or second-order approximation method described in Section 3.8 can be used to obtain the delay.

3.9.2 Interfacing of Digital Systems with Different Sampling Rates

In practice we frequently encounter the problem of interfacing two digital systems that are controlled by independently operating clocks. An analog

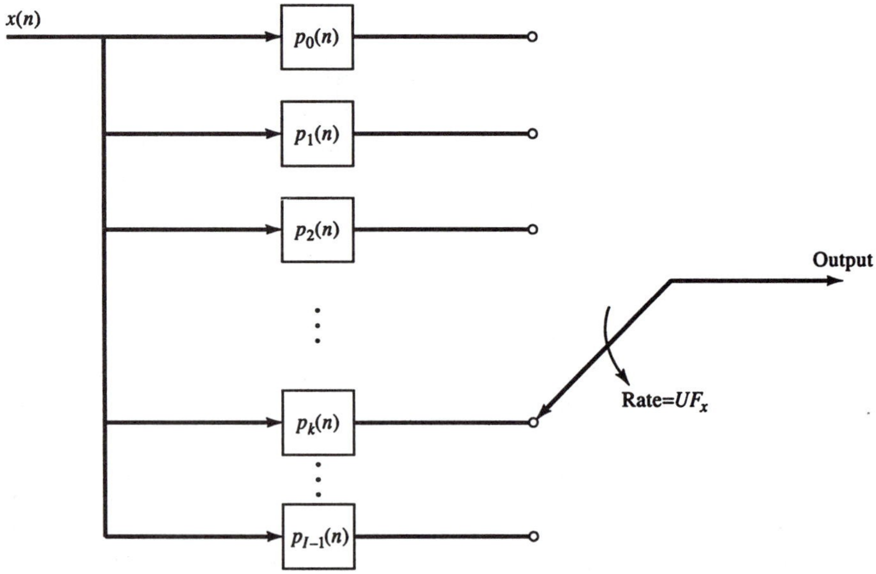

FIGURE 3.30 Polyphase filter structure for implementing the system shown in Fig. 3.29.

solution to this problem is to convert the signal from the first system to analog form and resample it at the input to the second system using the clock in this system. However, a simpler approach is one where the interfacing is done by a digital method using the basic sample-rate conversion methods described in this chapter.

To be specific, let us consider interfacing the two systems with independent clocks as shown in Fig. 3.31. The output of system A at rate F_x is fed to an interpolator which increases the sampling rate by U. The output of the interpolator is fed at the rate UF_x to a digital sample-and-hold which serves as the interface to system B at the high sampling rate UF_x. Signals from the digital sample-and-hold are read out into system B at the clock rate DF_y of system B. Thus the output rate from the sample-and-hold is not synchronized with the input rate.

In the special case where $D = U$ and the two clock rates are comparable but not identical, some samples at the output of the sample-and-hold may be repeated or dropped at times. The amount of signal distortion resulting from this method can be kept small if the interpolator–decimator factor is large. By using linear interpolation in place of the digital sample-and-hold, as we described in Section 3.8, we may further reduce the distortion and thus reduce the size of the interpolator factor.

3.9.3 Implementation of Narrowband Lowpass Filters

In section 3.6 we demonstrated that a multistage implementation of sampling-rate conversion often provides for a more efficient realization, especially when the filter specifications are very tight (e.g., a narrow passband and a narrow transition band). Under similar conditions, a lowpass, linear-phase FIR filter may be more efficiently implemented in a multistage decimator–interpolator configuration. To be more specific, we may employ a multistage implementation of a decimator of size D, followed by a multistage implementation of an interpolator of size U, where $U = D$.

We demonstrate the procedure by means of an example for the design of a lowpass filter that has the same specifications as the filter in Example 3.6.1.

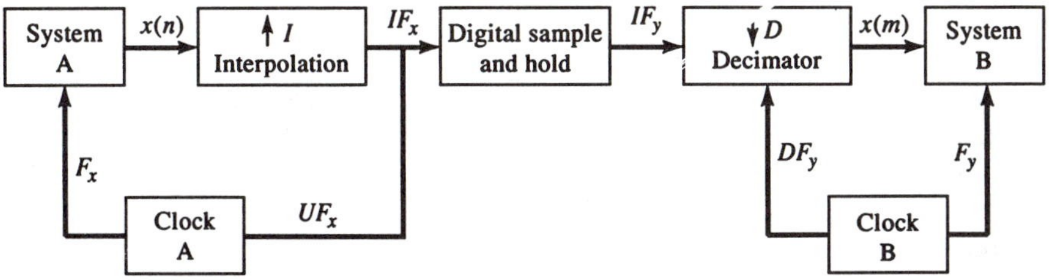

FIGURE 3.31 Interfacing of two digital systems with different sampling rates.

EXAMPLE 3.9.1

Design a linear-phase FIR filter that satisfies the following specifications:

sampling frequency:	8000 Hz
passband:	$0 \leq F \leq 75$
transition band:	$75 \leq F \leq 80$
stopband:	$80 \leq F \leq 4000$
passband ripple:	$\delta_1 = 10^{-2}$
stopband ripple:	$\delta_2 = 10^{-4}$

Solution: If this filter were designed as a single-rate linear-phase FIR filter, the length of the filter required to meet the specifications is (from Kaiser's formula)

$$\hat{M} \approx 5152$$

Now suppose that we employ a multirate implementation of the lowpass filter based on a decimation and interpolation factor of $D = U = 100$. A single-stage implementation of the decimator–interpolator requires an FIR filter of length

$$\hat{M}_1 = \frac{-10 \log_{10}(\delta_1\delta_2/2) - 13}{14.6\,\Delta f} + 1 \approx 5480$$

However, there is a significant savings in computational complexity by implementing the decimator and interpolator filters by their corresponding polyphase filters. If we employ linear-phase (symmetric) decimation and interpolation filters, the use of polyphase filters reduces the multiplication rate by a factor of 100.

A significantly more efficient implementation is obtained by using two stages of decimation followed by two stages of interpolation. For example, suppose that we select $D_1 = 50$, $D_2 = 2$, $U_1 = 2$ and $U_2 = 50$. Then the required filter lengths are

$$\hat{M}_1 = \frac{-10 \log(\delta_1\delta_2/4) - 13}{14.6\,\Delta f} + 1 \approx 177$$

$$\hat{M}_2 = \frac{-10 \log_{10}(\delta_1\delta_2/4) - 13}{14.6\,\Delta f} + 1 \approx 233$$

Thus we obtain a reduction in the overall filter length of $2(5480)/2(177 + 233) \approx 13.36$. In addition, we obtain further reduction in the multiplication rate by using polyphase filters. For the first stage of decimation the reduction in multiplication rate is 50, while for the second stage the reduction in multiplication rate is 100. Further reductions can be obtained by increasing the number of stages of decimation and interpolation.

3.9.4 Implementation of Digital Filter Banks

Filter banks are generally categorized as two types, *analysis filter banks* and *synthesis filter banks*. An analysis filter bank consists of a set of filters, with system functions $H_k(z)$, arranged in a parallel bank as illustrated in Fig. 3.32a. The frequency response characteristics of this filter bank splits the signal into a corresponding number of subbands. On the other hand, a synthesis filter bank consists of a set of filters with system functions $G_k(z)$, arranged as shown in Fig. 3.32b, with corresponding inputs $y_k(n)$. The outputs of the filters are summed to form the synthesized signal $x(n)$.

Filter banks are often used for performing spectrum analysis and signal synthesis. When a filter bank is employed in the computation of the discrete Fourier transform (DFT) of a sequence $x(n)$, the filter bank is called a *DFT filter bank*. An analysis filter bank consisting of N filters $[H_k(z), k = 0, 1,$

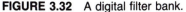

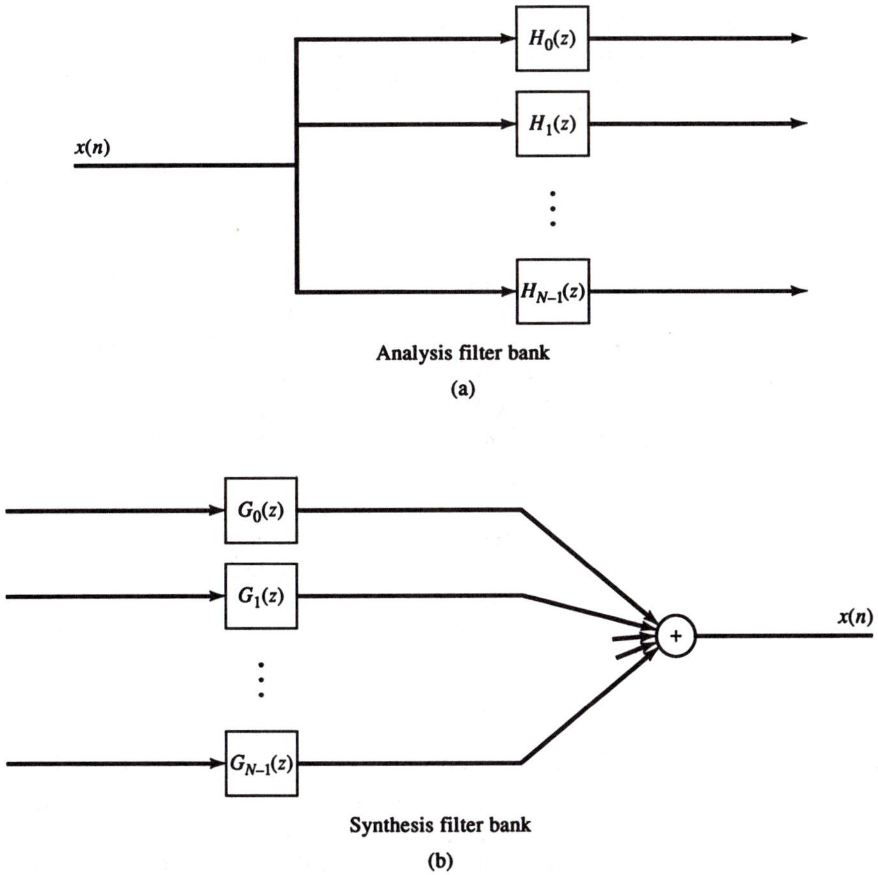

FIGURE 3.32 A digital filter bank.

$\ldots, N-1]$ is called a *uniform DFT filter bank* if $H_k(z)$, $k = 1, 2, \ldots, N-1$, are derived from a prototype filter $H_0(z)$, where

$$H_k(\omega) = H_0\left(\omega - \frac{2\pi k}{N}\right), \qquad k = 1, 2, \ldots, N-1 \tag{3.9.2}$$

Hence the frequency response characteristics of the filters $H_k(z)$, $k = 0, 1, \ldots, N-1$ are simply obtained by uniformly shifting the frequency response of the prototype filter by multiples of $2\pi/N$. In the time domain the filters are characterized by their impulse responses, which may be expressed as

$$h_k(n) = h_0(n)e^{j2\pi nk/N}, \qquad k = 0, 1, \ldots, N-1 \tag{3.9.3}$$

where $h_0(n)$ is the impulse response of the prototype filter.

The uniform DFT analysis filter bank may be realized as shown in Fig. 3.33(a), where the frequency components in the sequence $x(n)$ are translated in frequency to lowpass by multiplying $x(n)$ with the complex exponentials $\exp(-j2\pi nk/N)$, $k = 1, \ldots, N-1$, and the resulting product signals are passed through a lowpass filter with impulse response $h_0(n)$. Since the output of the lowpass filter is relatively narrow in bandwidth, the signal may be decimated by a factor $D \leq N$. The resulting decimated output signal may be expressed as

$$X_k(m) = \sum_n h_0(mD - n)x(n)e^{-j2\pi nk/N}, \qquad \begin{array}{l} k \doteq 0, 1, \ldots, N-1 \\ m = 0, 1, \ldots \end{array} \tag{3.9.4}$$

where $X_k(m)$ are samples of the DFT at frequencies $\omega_k = 2\pi k/N$.

The corresponding synthesis filter for each element in the filter bank may be viewed as shown in Fig. 3.33b, where the input signal sequences $Y_k(m)$, $k = 0, 1, \ldots, N-1$, are up-sampled by a factor of $U = D$, filtered to remove the images, and translated in frequency by multiplication with the complex exponentials $\exp(j2\pi nk/N)$, $k = 0, 1, \ldots, N-1$. The resulting frequency-translated signals from the N filters are then summed. Thus we obtain the sequence

$$\begin{aligned} v(n) &= \frac{1}{N}\sum_{k=0}^{N-1} e^{j2\pi nk/N}\left[\sum_m Y_k(m)g_0(n - mU)\right] \\ &= \sum_m g_0(n - mU)\left[\frac{1}{N}\sum_{k=0}^{N-1} Y_k(m)e^{j2\pi nk/N}\right] \\ &= \sum_m g_0(n - mU)y_n(m) \end{aligned} \tag{3.9.5}$$

where the factor $1/N$ is a normalization factor, $y_n(m)$ represent samples of the inverse DFT sequence corresponding to $Y_k(m)$, $g_0(n)$ is the impulse response of the interpolation filter, and $U = D$.

The relationship between the output $X_k(m)$ of the analysis filter bank and the input $Y_k(m)$ to the synthesis filter bank depends on the application.

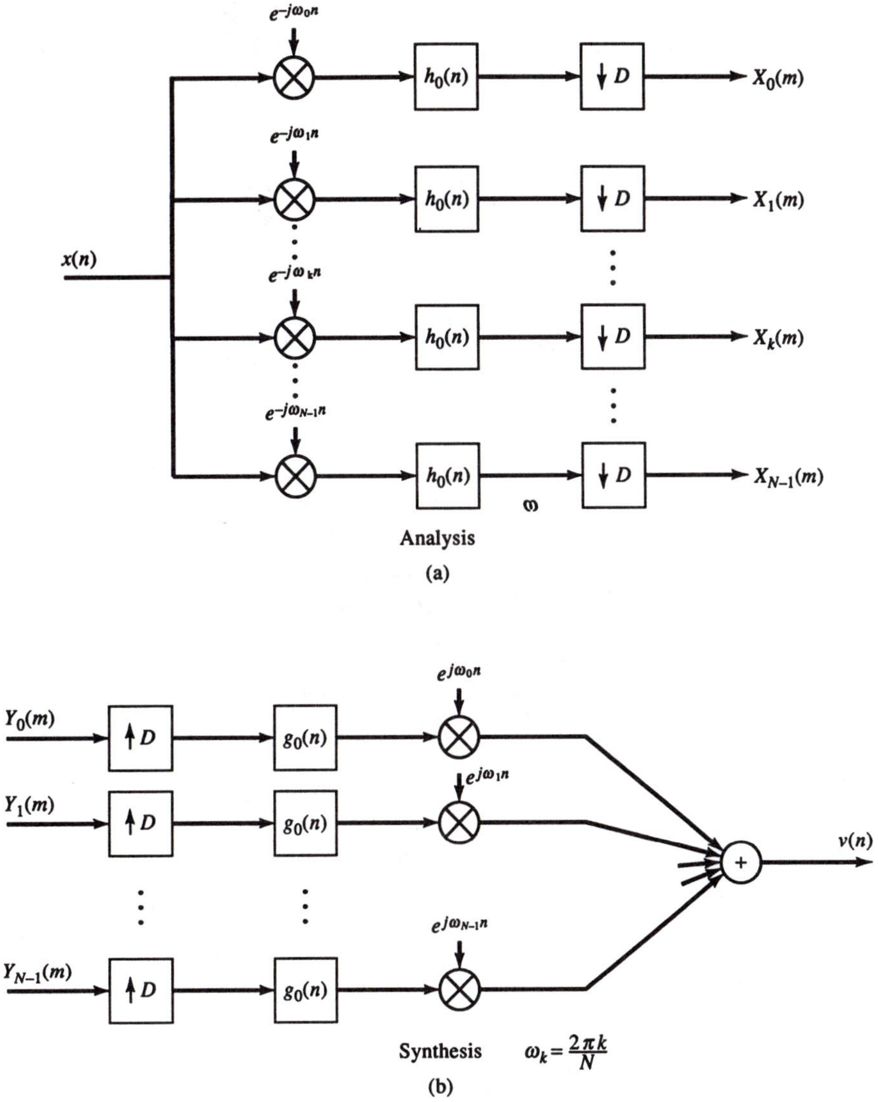

FIGURE 3.33 A uniform DFT filter bank.

Usually, $Y_k(m)$ is a modified version of $X_k(m)$, where the specific modification is determined by the application.

An alternative realization of the analysis and synthesis filter banks is illustrated in Fig. 3.34. The filters are realized as bandpass filters with impulse responses

$$h_k(n) = h_0(n)e^{j2\pi nk/N}, \qquad k = 0, 1, \ldots, N-1 \tag{3.9.6}$$

The output of each bandpass filter is decimated by a factor D and multiplied by $\exp(-j2\pi mk/N)$ to produce the DFT sequence $X_k(m)$. The modulation

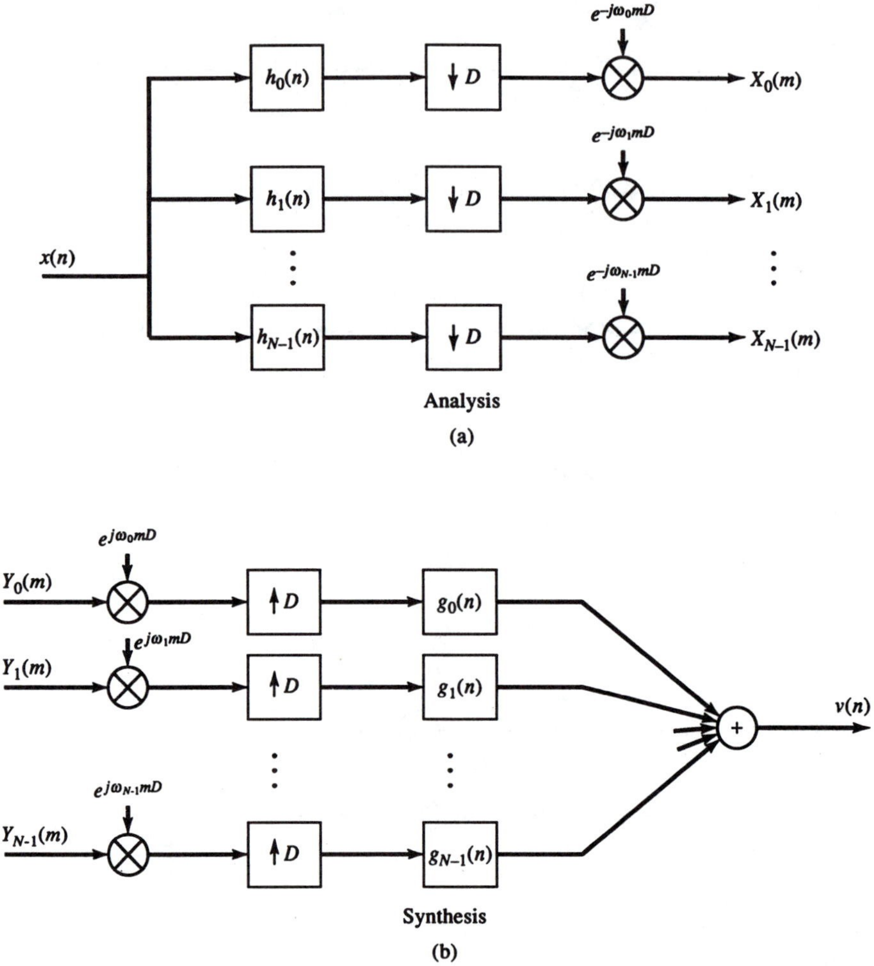

FIGURE 3.34 Alternative realization of a uniform DFT filter bank.

by the complex exponential allows us to shift the spectrum of the signal from $\omega_k = 2\pi k/N$ to $\omega_0 = 0$. Hence this realization is equivalent to the realization given in Fig. 3.33. The filter bank output may be written as

$$X_k(m) = \left[\sum_n x(n)h(mD - n)e^{j2\pi k(mD-n)/N} \right] e^{-j2\pi mkD/N} \tag{3.9.7}$$

The corresponding filter bank synthesizer may be realized as shown in Fig. 3.34(b), where the input sequences are first multiplied by the exponential factors $\exp(j2\pi kmD/N)$, up-sampled by the factor $U = D$, and the resulting sequences are filtered by the bandpass interpolation filters with impulse responses

$$g_k(n) = g_0(n)e^{j2\pi nk/N} \tag{3.9.8}$$

where $g_0(n)$ is the impulse response of the prototype filter. The outputs of these filters are then summed to yield

$$v(n) = \frac{1}{N}\sum_{k=0}^{N-1}\left\{\sum_{m}\left[Y_k(m)e^{j2\pi kmU/N}\right]g_k(n - mU)\right\} \qquad (3.9.9)$$

where $U = D$.

In the implementation of digital filters banks computational efficiency can be achieved by use of polyphase filters for decimation and interpolation. Of particular interest is the case where the decimation factor D is selected to be equal to the number N of frequency bands. When $D = N$, we say that the filter bank is *critically sampled.*

For the analysis filter bank, let us define a set of $N = D$ polyphase filters with impulse responses

$$p_k(n) = h_0(nN - k), \qquad k = 0, 1, \ldots, N - 1 \qquad (3.9.10)$$

and the corresponding set of decimated input sequences

$$x_k(n) = x(nN + k), \qquad k = 0, 1, \ldots, N - 1 \qquad (3.9.11)$$

Note that the definition of $p_k(n)$ as given above implies that the commutator for the decimator rotates clockwise.

The structure of the analysis filter bank based on the use of polyphase filters can be obtained by substituting (3.9.10) and (3.9.11) into (3.9.7) and rearranging the summation into the form

$$X_k(m) = \sum_{n=0}^{N-1}\left[\sum_{l} p_n(l)x_n(m - l)\right]e^{-j2\pi nk/N}, \quad k = 0, 1, \ldots, D - 1 \qquad (3.9.12)$$

where $N = D$. Note that the inner summation represents the convolution of $p_n(l)$ with $x_n(l)$. The outer summation represents the N-point DFT of the filter outputs. The filter structure corresponding to this computation is illustrated in Fig. 3.35. Each sweep of the commutator results in N outputs, denoted as $r_n(m)$, $n = 0, 1, \ldots, N - 1$ from the N polyphase filters. The N-point DFT of this sequence yields the spectral samples $X_k(m)$. For large values of N, the FFT algorithm provides an efficient means for computing the DFT.

Now suppose that the spectral samples $X_k(m)$ are modified in some manner, prescribed by the application, to produce $Y_k(m)$. A filter bank synthesis filter based on a polyphase filter structure can be realized in a similar manner. First, we define the impulse response of the N ($D = U = N$) polyphase filters for the interpolation filter as

$$q_k(n) = g_0(nN + k), \qquad k = 0, 1, \ldots, N - 1 \qquad (3.9.13)$$

and the corresponding set of output signals as

$$v_k(n) = v(nN + k), \qquad k = 0, 1, \ldots, N - 1 \qquad (3.9.14)$$

Note that the definition of $q_k(n)$ as given above implies that the commutator for the interpolator rotates counterclockwise.

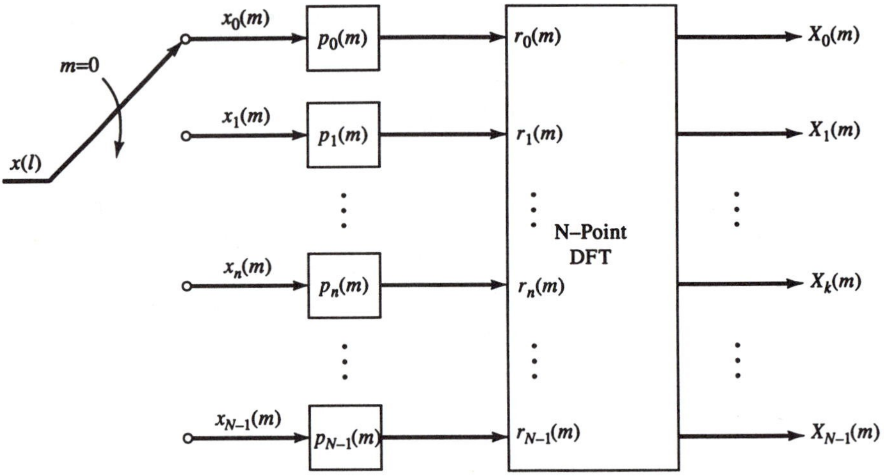

FIGURE 3.35 Digital filter bank structure for the computation of (3.9.12).

By substituting (3.9.13) into (3.9.5), we can express the output $v_l(n)$ of the lth polyphase filter as

$$v_l(n) = \sum_m q_l(n-m)\left[\frac{1}{N}\sum_{k=0}^{N-1} Y_k(m)e^{j2\pi kl/N}\right], \quad l = 0, 1, \ldots, N-1 \qquad (3.9.15)$$

The term in brackets is the N-point inverse DFT of $Y_k(m)$, which we denote as $y_l(m)$. Hence

$$v_l(n) = \sum_m q_l(n-m)y_l(m), \qquad l = 0, 1, \ldots, N-1 \qquad (3.9.16)$$

The synthesis structure corresponding to (3.9.16) is shown in Fig. 3.36. It is interesting to note that by defining the polyphase interpolation filter as in (3.9.13), the structure in Fig. 3.36 is the transpose of the polyphase analysis filter shown in Fig. 3.35.

In our treatment of digital filter banks we considered the important case of critically sampled DFT filter banks, where $D = N$. Other choices of D and N may be employed in practice, but the implementation of the filters becomes more complex. Of particular importance is the oversampled DFT filter bank, where $N = KD$; D denotes the decimation factor and K is an integer that specifies the oversampling factor. In this case it can be shown that the polyphase filter bank structures for the analysis and synthesis filters may be implemented by use of N subfilters and N-point DFTs and inverse DFTs.

3.9.5 Subband Coding of Speech Signals

A variety of techniques have been developed to represent speech signals efficiently in digital form for either transmission or storage. Since most of

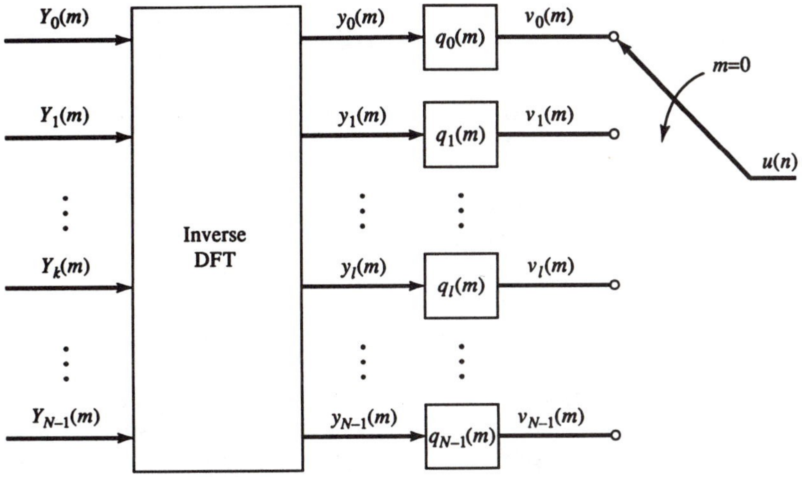

FIGURE 3.36 Digital filter bank structure for the computation of (3.9.16).

the speech energy is contained in the lower frequencies, we would like to encode the lower-frequency band with more bits than the high-frequency band. Subband coding is a method whereby the speech signal is subdivided into several frequency bands and each band is digitally encoded separately.

An example of a frequency subdivision is shown in Fig. 3.37a. Let us assume that the speech signal is sampled at a rate F_s samples per second.

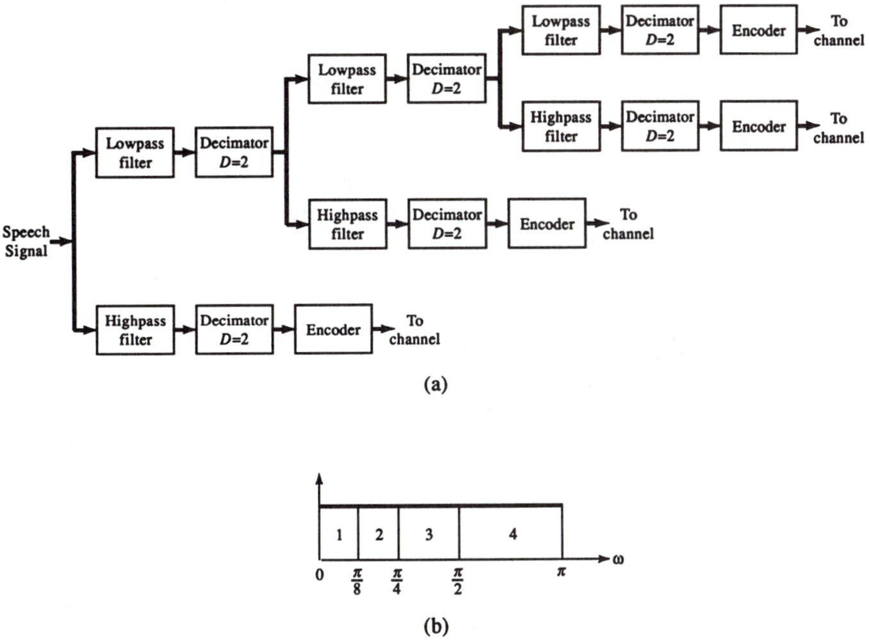

FIGURE 3.37 Block diagram of a subband speech coder.

The first frequency subdivision splits the signal spectrum into two equal-width segments, a lowpass signal ($0 \le F \le F_s/4$) and a highpass signal ($F_s/4 \le F \le F_s/2$). The second frequency subdivision splits the lowpass signal from the first stage into two equal bands, a lowpass signal ($0 < F \le F_s/8$) and a highpass signal ($F_s/8 \le F \le F_s/4$). Finally, the third frequency subdivision splits the lowpass signal from the second stage into two equal bandwidth signals. Thus the signal is subdivided into four frequency bands, covering three octaves, as shown in Fig. 3.37b.

Decimation by a factor of 2 is performed after frequency subdivision. By allocating a different number of bits per sample to the signal in the four subbands, we can achieve a reduction in the bit rate of the digitalized speech signal.

Filter design is particularly important in achieving good performance in subband coding. Aliasing resulting from decimation of the subband signals must be negligible. It is clear that we cannot use brickwall filter characteristics as shown in Fig. 3.38a, since such filters are physically unrealizable. A particularly practical solution to the aliasing problem is to use *quadrature mirror filters* (QMF), which have the frequency response characteristics shown in Fig. 3.38b. These filters are described in the following section.

The synthesis method for the subband-encoded speech signal is basically the reverse of the encoding process. The signals in adjacent lowpass and highpass frequency bands are interpolated, filtered, and combined as shown in Fig. 3.39. A pair of QMF is used in the signal synthesis for each octave of the signal.

Subband coding is also an effective method to achieve data compression in image signal processing. By combining subband coding with vector quantization for each subband signal, Safranek et al. (1988) have obtained coded images with approximately $\frac{1}{2}$ bit per pixel, compared with 8 bits per pixel for the uncoded image.

In general, subband coding of signals is an effective method for achieving bandwidth compression in a digital representation of the signal when the signal energy is concentrated in a particular region of the frequency band. Multirate signal-processing provides efficient implementations of the subband encoder.

3.9.6 Quadrature Mirror Filters

The basic building block in applications of quadrature mirror filters (QMF) is the two-channel QMF bank shown in Fig. 3.40. This is a multirate digital filter structure that employs two decimators in the "signal analysis" section and two interpolators in the "signal synthesis" section. The lowpass and highpass filters in the analysis section have impulse responses $h_0(n)$ and $h_1(n)$, respectively. Similarly, the lowpass and highpass filters contained in the synthesis section have impulse responses $g_0(n)$ and $g_1(n)$, respectively.

The Fourier transforms of the signals at the outputs of the two decimators are

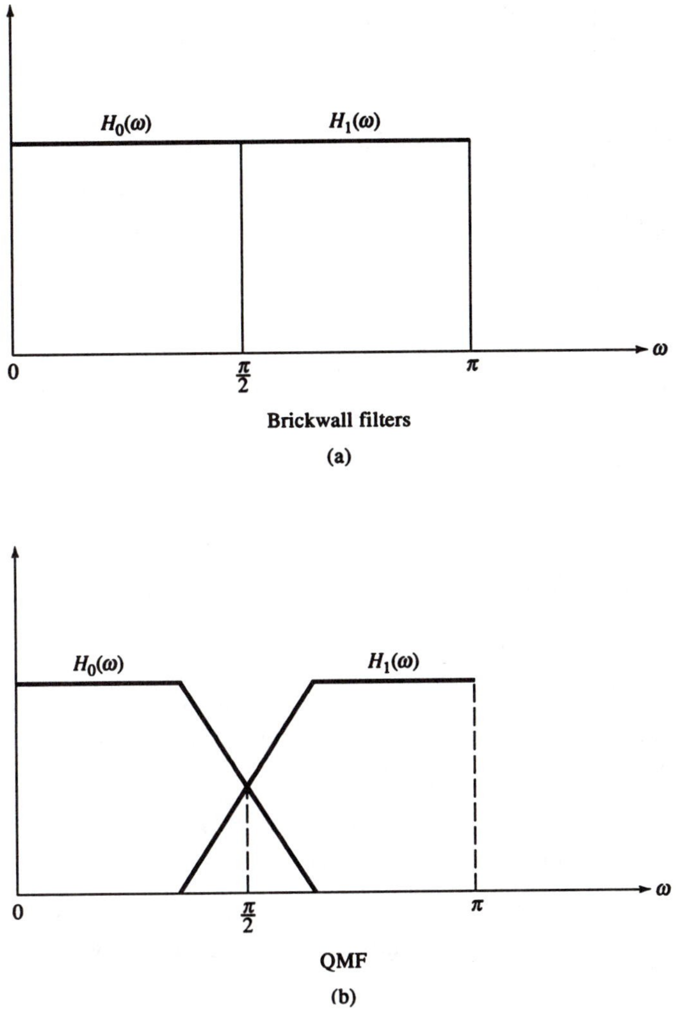

FIGURE 3.38 Filter characteristics for subband coding.

$$X_{a0}(\omega) = \frac{1}{2}\left[X\left(\frac{\omega}{2}\right)H_0\left(\frac{\omega}{2}\right) + X\left(\frac{\omega - 2\pi}{2}\right)H_0\left(\frac{\omega - 2\pi}{2}\right)\right]$$
$$X_{a1}(\omega) = \frac{1}{2}\left[X\left(\frac{\omega}{2}\right)H_1\left(\frac{\omega}{2}\right) + X\left(\frac{\omega - 2\pi}{2}\right)H_1\left(\frac{\omega - 2\pi}{2}\right)\right] \quad (3.9.17)$$

If $X_{s0}(\omega)$ and $X_{s1}(\omega)$ represent the two inputs to the synthesis section, the output is simply

$$\hat{X}(\omega) = X_{s0}(2\omega)G_0(\omega) + X_{s1}(2\omega)G_1(\omega) \quad (3.9.18)$$

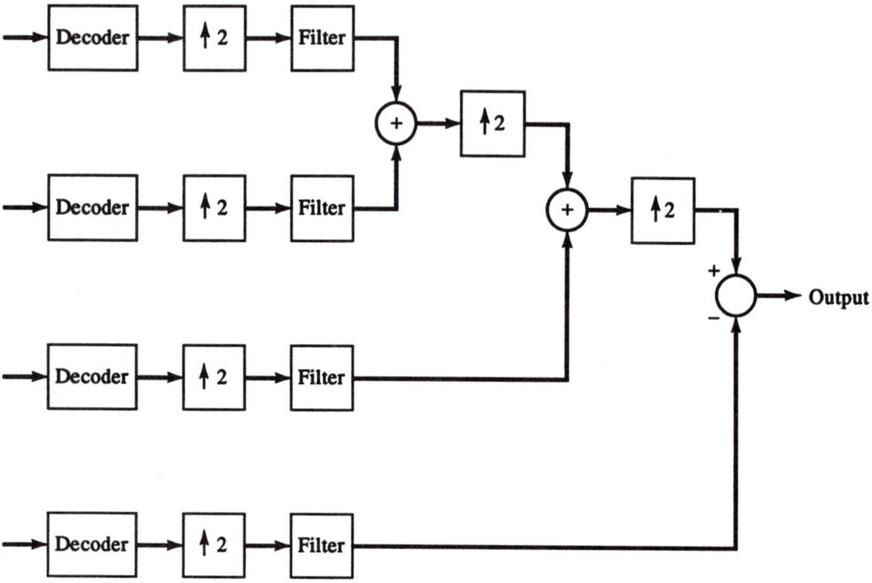

FIGURE 3.39 Synthesis of subband-encoded signals.

Now suppose that we connect the analysis filter to the corresponding synthesis filter, so that $X_{a0}(\omega) = X_{s0}(\omega)$ and $X_{a1}(\omega) = X_{s1}(\omega)$. Then, by substituting from (3.9.17) into (3.9.18), we obtain

$$\begin{aligned}\hat{X}(\omega) &= \tfrac{1}{2}[H_0(\omega)G_0(\omega) + H_1(\omega)G_1(\omega)]X(\omega) \\ &\quad + \tfrac{1}{2}[H_0(\omega - \pi)G_0(\omega) + H_1(\omega - \pi)G_1(\omega)]X(\omega - \pi)\end{aligned} \qquad (3.9.19)$$

The first term in (3.9.19) is the desired signal output from the QMF bank. The second term represents the effect of aliasing, which we would like to eliminate. Hence we require that

$$H_0(\omega - \pi)G_0(\omega) + H_1(\omega - \pi)G_1(\omega) = 0 \qquad (3.9.20)$$

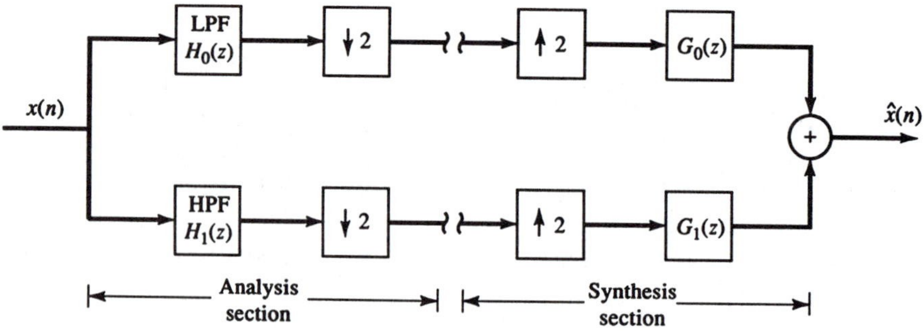

FIGURE 3.40 Two-channel QMF bank.

This condition can be simply satisfied by selecting $G_0(\omega)$ and $G_1(\omega)$ as

$$G_0(\omega) = H_1(\omega - \pi), \qquad G_1(\omega) = -H_0(\omega - \pi) \tag{3.9.21}$$

Thus the second term in (3.9.19) vanishes.

To elaborate, let us assume that $H_0(\omega)$ is a lowpass filter and $H_1(\omega)$ is a mirror image highpass filter. Then we may express $H_0(\omega)$ and $H_1(\omega)$ as

$$\begin{aligned} H_0(\omega) &= H(\omega) \\ H_1(\omega) &= H(\omega - \pi) \end{aligned} \tag{3.9.22}$$

where $H(\omega)$ is the frequency response of a lowpass filter. In the time domain, the corresponding relations are

$$\begin{aligned} h_0(n) &= h(n) \\ h_1(n) &= (-1)^n h(n) \end{aligned} \tag{3.9.23}$$

As a consequence, $H_0(\omega)$ and $H_1(\omega)$ have mirror-image symmetry about the frequency $\omega = \pi/2$, as shown in Fig. 3.38(b). To be consistent with the constraint in (3.9.21), we select the lowpass filter $G_0(\omega)$ as

$$G_0(\omega) = 2H(\omega) \tag{3.9.24}$$

and the highpass filter $G_1(\omega)$ as

$$G_1(\omega) = -2H(\omega - \pi) \tag{3.9.25}$$

In the time domain, these relations become

$$\begin{aligned} g_0(n) &= 2h(n) \\ g_1(n) &= -2(-1)^n h(n) \end{aligned} \tag{3.9.26}$$

The scale factor of 2 in $g_0(n)$ and $g_1(n)$ corresponds to the interpolation factor that is used to normalize the overall frequency response of the QMF. With this choice of the filter characteristics, the component due to aliasing vanishes. Thus the aliasing resulting from decimation in the analysis section of the QMF bank is perfectly canceled by the image signal spectrum that arises due to interpolation. As a result, the two-channel QMF behaves as a linear time-invariant system.

If we substitute for $H_0(\omega)$, $H_1(\omega)$, $G_0(\omega)$, and $G_1(\omega)$ into the first term of (3.9.19), we obtain

$$\hat{X}(\omega) = [H^2(\omega) - H^2(\omega - \pi)]X(\omega) \tag{3.9.27}$$

Ideally, the two-channel QMF bank should have unity gain,

$$|H^2(\omega) - H^2(\omega - \pi)| = 1 \qquad \text{for all } \omega \tag{3.9.28}$$

where $H(\omega)$ is the frequency response of a lowpass filter. Furthermore, it is also desirable for the QMF to have linear phase.

Now let us consider the use of a linear-phase filter $H(\omega)$. Hence $H(\omega)$ may be expressed in the form

$$H(\omega) = H_r(\omega)e^{-j\omega(N-1)/2} \tag{3.9.29}$$

where N is the filter length. Then

$$\begin{aligned} H^2(\omega) &= H_r^2(\omega)e^{-j\omega(N-1)} \\ &= |H(\omega)|^2 e^{-j\omega(N-1)} \end{aligned} \tag{3.9.30}$$

and

$$\begin{aligned} H^2(\omega - \pi) &= H_r^2(\omega - \pi)e^{-j(\omega-\pi)(N-1)} \\ &= (-1)^{N-1}|H(\omega - \pi)|^2 e^{-j\omega(N-1)} \end{aligned} \tag{3.9.31}$$

Therefore, the overall transfer function of the two-channel QMF that employs linear-phase FIR filters is

$$\frac{\hat{X}(\omega)}{X(\omega)} = [|H(\omega)|^2 - (-1)^{N-1}|H(\omega - \pi)|^2]e^{-j\omega(N-1)} \tag{3.9.32}$$

Note that the overall filter has a delay of $N - 1$ samples and a magnitude characteristic

$$A(\omega) = |H(\omega)|^2 - (-1)^{N-1}|H(\omega - \pi)|^2 \tag{3.9.33}$$

We also note that when N is odd, $A(\pi/2) = 0$, because $|H(\pi/2)| = |H(3\pi/2)|$. This is an undesirable property for a QMF design. On the other hand, when N is even,

$$A(\omega) = |H(\omega)|^2 + |H(\omega - \pi)|^2 \tag{3.9.34}$$

which avoids the problem of a zero at $\omega = \pi/2$. For N even, the ideal two-channel QMF should satisfy the condition

$$A(\omega) = |H(\omega)|^2 + |H(\omega - \pi)|^2 = 1 \qquad \text{for all } \omega \tag{3.9.35}$$

which follows from (3.9.33). Unfortunately, the only filter frequency response function that satisfies (3.9.35) is the trivial function $|H(\omega)|^2 = \cos^2 a\omega$. Consequently, any nontrivial linear-phase FIR filter $H(\omega)$ will introduce some amplitude distortion.

The amount of amplitude distortion introduced by a nontrivial linear-phase FIR filter in the QMF can be minimized by optimizing the FIR filter coefficients. A particularly effective method is to select the filter coefficients of $H(\omega)$ such that $A(\omega)$ is made as flat as possible while simultaneously minimizing (or constraining) the stopband energy of $H(\omega)$. This approach leads to the minimization of the integral squared error

$$J = w\int_{\omega_s}^{\pi} |H(\omega)|^2\, d\omega + (1 - w)\int_0^{\pi/2} [A(\omega) - 1]^2\, d\omega \tag{3.9.36}$$

where w is a weighting factor in the range $0 < w < 1$. In performing the optimization, the filter impulse response is constrained to be symmetric (linear phase). This optimization is easily done numerically on a digital computer. This approach has been used by Johnston (1980) and Jain and Crochiere (1983) to design two-channel QMFs. Tables of optimum filter coefficients have been tabulated by Johnston (1980).

As an alternative to the use of linear-phase FIR filters, we may design an IIR filter that satisfies the all-pass constraint given by (3.9.28). For this purpose, elliptic filters provide especially efficient designs. Since the QMF would introduce some phase distortion, the signal at the output of the QMF can be passed through an all-pass phase equalizer which is designed to minimize phase distortion.

In addition to the two methods for QMF design described above, one can also design the two-channel QMFs to eliminate completely both amplitude and phase distortion as well as canceling aliasing distortion. Smith and Barnwell (1984) have shown that such *perfect reconstruction QMF* can be designed by relaxing the linear-phase condition of the FIR lowpass filter $H(\omega)$. To achieve perfect reconstruction, we begin by designing a linear-phase FIR half-band filter of length $2N - 1$.

A half-band filter is defined as a zero-phase FIR filter whose impulse response $b(n)$ satisfies the condition

$$b(2n) = \begin{cases} \text{constant}, & n = 0 \\ 0, & n \neq 0 \end{cases} \tag{3.9.37}$$

Hence, all the even-numbered samples are zero except at $n = 0$. The zero-phase requirement implies that $b(n) = b(-n)$. The frequency response of such a filter is

$$B(\omega) = \sum_{n=-K}^{K} b(n) e^{-j\omega n} \tag{3.9.38}$$

where K is odd. Furthermore, $B(\omega)$ satisfies that the condition $B(\omega) + B(\pi - \omega)$ is equal to a constant for all frequencies. The typical frequency response characteristic of a half-band filter is shown in Fig. 3.41. We note that the filter response is symmetric with respect to $\pi/2$, the band-edge frequencies ω_p and ω_s are symmetric about $\omega = \pi/2$, and the peak passband

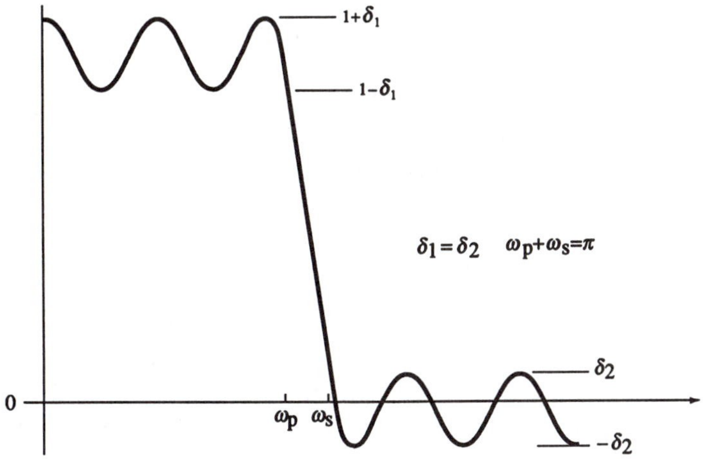

FIGURE 3.41 Frequency response characteristic of FIR half-band filter.

and stopband errors are equal. We also note that the filter can be made causal by introducing a delay of K samples.

Now, suppose that we design an FIR half-band filter of length $2N - 1$, where N is even, with frequency response as shown in Fig. 3.42a. From $B(\omega)$ we construct another half-band filter with frequency response

$$B_+(\omega) = B(\omega) + \delta e^{-j\omega(N-1)} \tag{3.9.39}$$

as shown in Fig. 3.42b. Note that $B_+(\omega)$ is nonnegative, and hence it has the spectral factorization

$$B_+(z) = H(z)H(z^{-1})z^{-(N-1)} \tag{3.9.40}$$

or equivalently,

$$B_+(\omega) = |H(\omega)|^2 e^{-j\omega(N-1)} \tag{3.9.41}$$

where $H(\omega)$ is the frequency response of an FIR filter of length N with real coefficients. Due to the symmetry of $B_+(\omega)$ with respect to $\omega = \pi/2$, we also have

$$B_+(z) + (-1)^{N-1}B_+(-z) = \alpha z^{-(N-1)} \tag{3.9.42}$$

or equivalently,

$$B_+(\omega) + (-1)^{N-1}B_+(\omega - \pi) = \alpha e^{-j\omega(N-1)} \tag{3.9.43}$$

where α is a constant. Thus by substituting (3.9.40) into (3.9.42) we obtain

$$H(z)H(z^{-1}) + H(-z)H(-z^{-1}) = \alpha \tag{3.9.44}$$

Since $H(z)$ satisfies (3.9.44) and since aliasing is eliminated when we have $F_0(z) = H_1(-z)$ and $F_1(z) = -H_0(-z)$, it follows that these conditions are satisfied by choosing $H_1(z)$, $G_0(z)$, and $G_1(z)$ as

$$\begin{aligned}
H_0(z) &= H(z) \\
H_1(z) &= -z^{-(N-1)}H_0(-z^{-1}) \\
F_0(z) &= z^{-(N-1)}H_0(z^{-1}) \\
F_1(z) &= z^{-(N-1)}H_1(z^{-1}) = -H_0(-z)
\end{aligned} \tag{3.9.45}$$

Thus aliasing distortion is eliminated and, since $\hat{X}(\omega)/X(\omega)$ is a constant, the QMF performs perfect reconstruction so that $x(n) = \alpha x(n - N + 1)$. However, we note that $H(z)$ is not a linear-phase filter.

The FIR filters $H_0(z)$, $H_1(z)$, $G_0(z)$, and $G_1(z)$ in the two-channel QMF bank are efficiently realized as polyphase filters. Since $U = D = 2$, two polyphase filters are implemented for each decimator and two for each interpolator. However, when we employ linear-phase FIR filters, the symmetry properties of the analysis filters and synthesis filters allow us to simplify the structure and reduce the number of polyphase filters in the analysis section to two filters and in the synthesis section to another two filters.

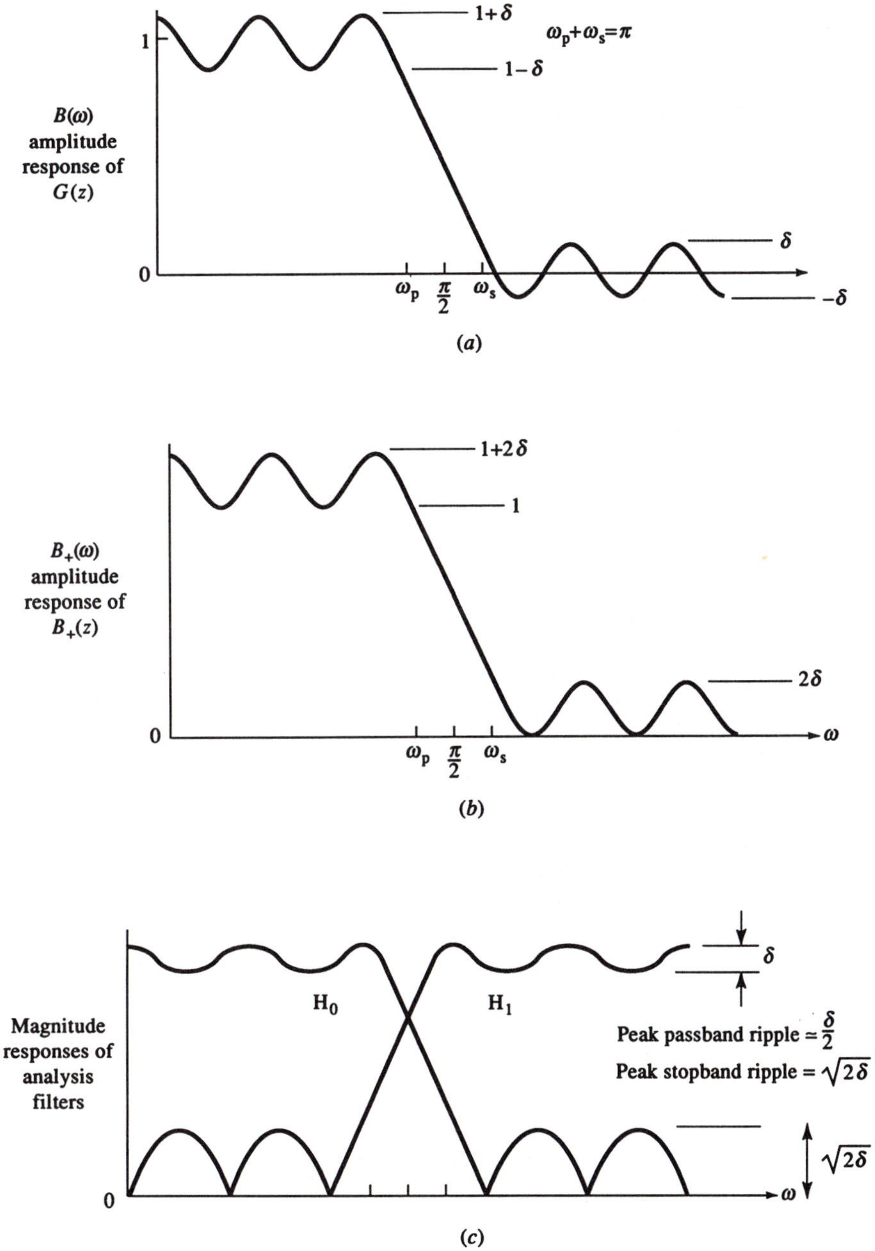

FIGURE 3.42 Frequency response characteristics of half-band filters $B(\omega)$ and $B_+(\omega)$. (From Vaidyanathan (1987))

To demonstrate this construction, let us assume that the filters are linear-phase FIR filters of length N (N even), which have impulse responses given by (3.9.23). Then the outputs of the analysis filter pair, after decimation by a factor of 2, may be expressed as

$$\begin{aligned} X_{ak}(m) &= \sum_{n=-\infty}^{\infty} (-1)^{kn} h(n) x(2m - n), \qquad k = 0, 1 \\ &= \sum_{i=0}^{1} \sum_{l=-\infty}^{\infty} (-1)^{k(2l+i)} h(2l + i) x(2m - 2l - i) \qquad (3.9.46) \\ &= \sum_{l=0}^{N-1} h(2l) x(2m - 2l) + (-1)^k \sum_{l=0}^{N-1} h(2l + 1) x(2m - 2l - 1) \end{aligned}$$

Now, let us define the impulse response of two polyphase filters of length $N/2$ as

$$p_i(m) = h(2m + i), \qquad i = 0, 1 \qquad (3.9.47)$$

Then (3.9.46) may be expressed as

$$\begin{aligned} X_{ak}(m) = &\sum_{l=0}^{N/2-1} p_0(m) x(2(m - l)) \\ &+ (-1)^k \sum_{l=0}^{N/2-1} p_1(m) x(2m - 2l - 1), \qquad k = 0, 1 \end{aligned} \qquad (3.9.48)$$

This expression corresponds to the polyphase filter structure for the analysis section that is shown in Fig. 3.43. Note that the commutator rotates counterclockwise and that the filter with impulse response $p_0(m)$ processes the even-numbered samples of the input sequence, and the filter with impulse response $p_1(m)$ processes the odd-numbered samples of the input signal.

In a similar manner, by using (3.9.26), we can obtain the structure for the polyphase synthesis section, which is also shown in Fig. 3.43. This derivation is left as an exercise for the reader (Problem 3.14). Note that the commutator also rotates counterclockwise.

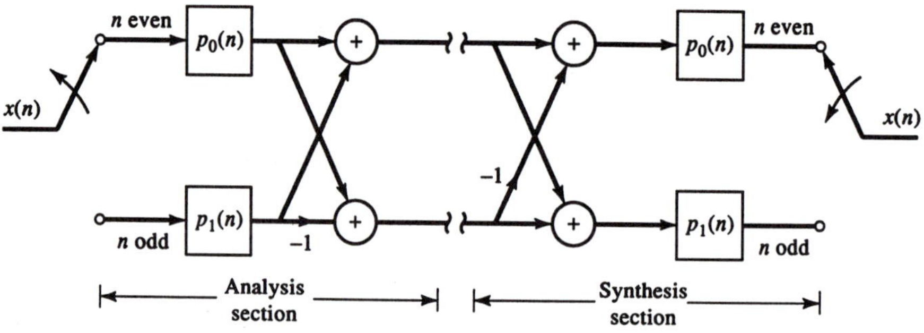

FIGURE 3.43 Polyphase filter structure for the QMF bank.

Finally, we observe that the polyphase filter structure shown in Fig. 3.43 is approximately four times more efficient than the direct-form FIR filter realization.

3.9.7 Transmultiplexers

Another application of multirate signal processing is in the design and implementation of digital transmultiplexers, which are devices for converting between time-division-multiplexed (TDM) signals and frequency-division-multiplexed (FDM) signals. In a transmultiplexer for TDM-to-FDM conversion, the input signal, $x(n)$, is a time-division-multiplexed signal consisting of L signals, which are separated by a commutator switch. Each of these L signals is then modulated on different carrier frequencies to obtain an FDM signal for transmission. In a transmultiplexer for FDM-to-TDM conversion, the composite signal is separated by filtering into the L signal components, which are then time-division multiplexed.

In telephony, single-sideband transmission is used with channels spaced at a nominal 4-kHz bandwidth. Twelve channels are usually stacked in frequency to form a basic group channel, which has a bandwidth of 48 kHz. Larger-bandwidth FDM signals are formed by frequency translation of multiple groups into adjacent frequency bands. We shall confine our discussion to digital transmultiplexers for 12-channel FDM and TDM signals.

Let us first consider FDM-to-TDM conversion. The analog FDM signal is passed through an A/D converter as shown in Fig. 3.44a. The digital signal is then demodulated to baseband by means of single-sideband demodulators. The output of each demodulator is decimated and fed to the commutator of the TDM system.

To be specific, let us assume that the 12-channel FDM signal is sampled at the Nyquist rate of 96 kHz and passed through a filter-bank demodulator. The basic building block in the FDM demodulator consists of a frequency converter, a lowpass filter, and a decimator, as illustrated in Fig. 3.44b. Frequency conversion may be efficiently implemented by the DFT filter bank described previously. The lowpass filter and decimator are efficiently implemented by use of the polyphase filter structure. Thus the basic structure for the FDM-to-TDM converter has the form of a DFT filter bank analyzer. Since the signal in each channel occupies a 4-kHz bandwidth, its Nyquist rate is 8 kHz, and hence the polyphase filter output may be decimated by a factor of 12. Consequently, the TDM commutator is operating at a rate of 12×8 kHz, or 96 kHz.

In TDM-to-FDM conversion, the 12-channel TDM signal is demultiplexed into 12 individual signals, where each signal has a rate of 8 kHz. The signal in each channel is interpolated by a factor of 12 and is frequency-converted by a single-sideband modulator as shown in Fig. 3.45. The signal outputs from the 12 single-sideband modulators are summed and fed to the D/A converter. Thus we obtain the analog FDM signal for transmission. As in the case of FDM-to-TDM conversion, the interpolator and the modulator

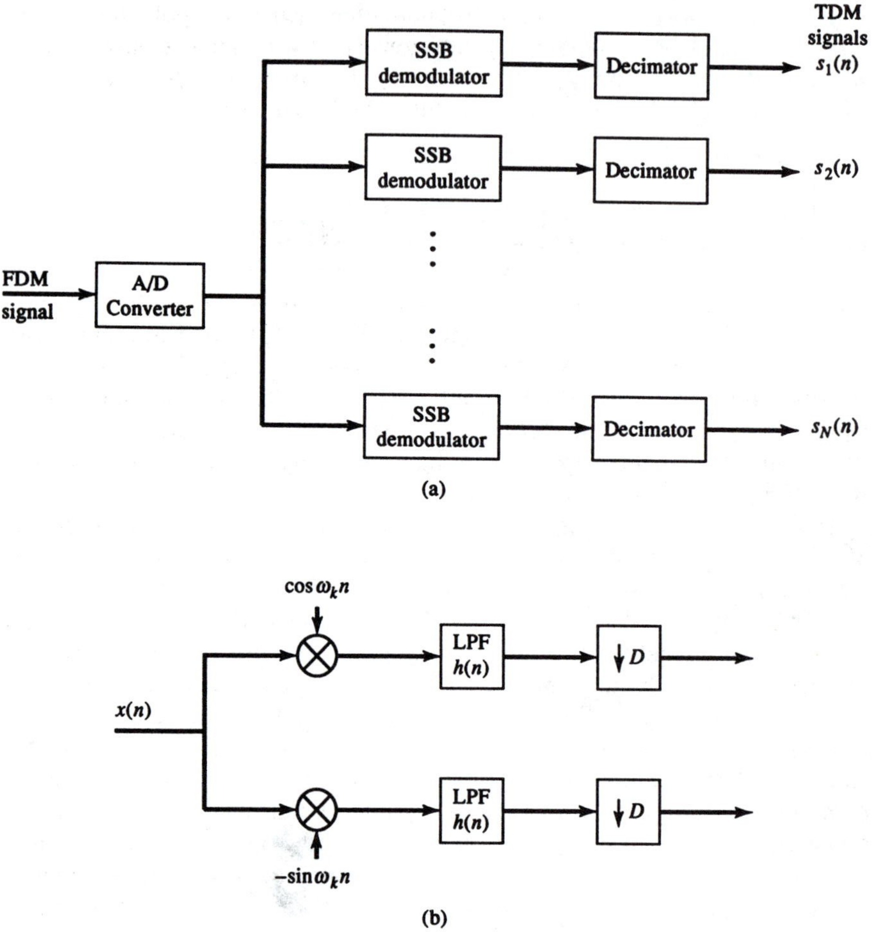

FIGURE 3.44 Block diagram of FDM-to-TDM transmultiplexer.

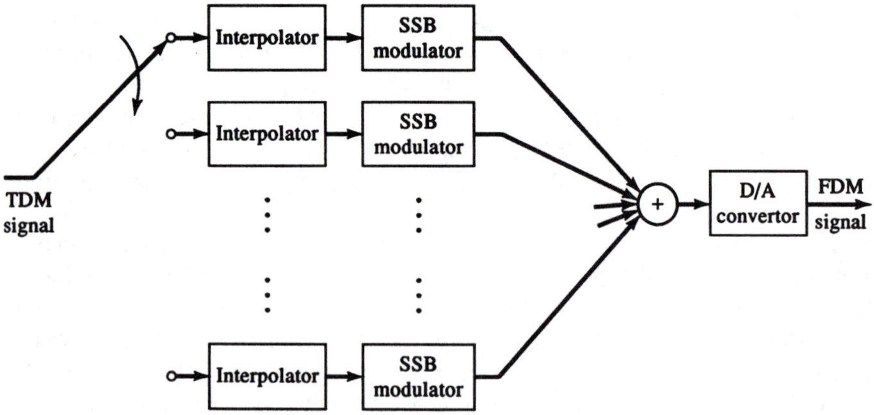

FIGURE 3.45 Block diagram of TDM-to-FDM transmultiplexer.

filter are combined and efficiently implemented by use of a polyphase filter. The frequency translation may be accomplished by the DFT. Consequently, the TDM-to-FDM converter encompasses the basic principles introduced previously in our discussion of DFT filter bank synthesis.

3.10 SUMMARY AND REFERENCES

The need for sampling-rate conversion arises frequently in digital signal processing applications. In this chapter we first treated sampling-rate reduction (decimation) and sampling-rate increase (interpolation) by integer factors and then demonstrated how the two processes can be combined to obtain sampling-rate conversion by any rational factor. Later, in Section 3.8, we described a method to achieve sampling-rate conversion by an arbitrary factor.

In general, the implementation of sampling-rate conversion requires the use of a linear time-variant filter. We described methods for implementing such filters, including the class of polyphase filter structures, which are especially simple to implement. We also described the use of multistage implementations of multirate conversion as a means for simplifying the complexity of the filter required to meet the specifications.

In the special case where the signal to be resampled is a bandpass signal, we described two methods for performing the sampling-rate conversion, one of which involves frequency conversion, while the second is a direct conversion method that does not employ modulation.

Finally, we described a number of applications that employ multirate signal processing, including the implementation of narrowband filters, phase shifters, filter banks, subband speech coders, and transmultiplexers. These are just a few of the many applications encountered in practice where multirate signal processing is used.

The first comprehensive treatment of multirate signal processing was given in the book by Crochiere and Rabiner (1983). The use of interpolation methods to achieve sampling-rate conversion by an arbitrary factor is treated in a paper by Ramstad (1984). A thorough tutorial treatment of multirate digital filters and filter banks, including quadrature mirror filters, is given in the papers by Vaidyanathan (1987, 1990), where many references on various applications are cited, and by Vetterli (1987). A comprehensive survey of digital transmultiplexing methods is given in the paper by Scheuermann and Gockler (1981). Subband coding of speech has been considered in many publications. The pioneering work on this topic was done by Crochiere (1977, 1981) and by Garland and Esteban (1980). Subband coding has also been applied to coding of images. We mention the papers by Vetterli (1984), Woods and O'Neil (1986), Smith and Eddins (1988), and Safranek et al. (1988) as just a few examples. In closing, we wish to emphasize that multirate signal processing continues to be a very active research area.

PROBLEMS

3.1 An analog signal $x_a(t)$ is bandlimited to the range $900 \le F \le 1100$ Hz. It is used as an input to the system shown in Fig. P3.1. In this system, $H(F)$ is an ideal lowpass filter with cutoff frequency $F_c = 125$ Hz.

(a) Determine and sketch the spectra for the signals $x(n)$, $w(n)$, $v(n)$, and $y(n)$.

(b) Show that it is possible to obtain $y(n)$ by sampling $x_a(t)$ with period $T = 4$ milliseconds.

3.2 Consider the signal $x(n) = a^n u(n)$, $|a| < 1$.

(a) Determine the spectrum $X(\omega)$.

(b) The signal $x(n)$ is applied to a decimator that reduces the rate by a factor of 2. Determine the output spectrum.

(c) Show that the spectrum in part (b) is simply the Fourier transform of $x(2n)$.

3.3 The sequence $x(n)$ is obtained by sampling an analog signal with period T. From this signal a new signal is derived having the sampling period $T/2$ by use of a linear interpolation method described by the equation

$$y(n) = \begin{cases} x\left(\frac{n}{2}\right), & n \text{ even} \\ \frac{1}{2}\left[x\left(\frac{n-1}{2}\right) + x\left(\frac{n+1}{2}\right)\right], & n \text{ odd} \end{cases}$$

(a) Show that this linear interpolation scheme can be realized by basic digital signal-processing elements.

(b) Determine the spectrum of $y(n)$ when the spectrum of $x(n)$ is

$$X(\omega) = \begin{cases} 1, & 0 \le |\omega| \le 0.2\pi \\ 0, & \text{otherwise} \end{cases}$$

(c) Determine the spectrum of $y(n)$ when the spectrum of $x(n)$ is

$$X(\omega) = \begin{cases} 1, & 0.7\pi \le |\omega| \le 0.9\pi \\ 0, & \text{otherwise} \end{cases}$$

3.4 Design a decimator that down-samples an input signal $x(n)$ by a factor $D = 5$. Use the Remez algorithm to determine the coefficients of the FIR filter that has 0.1 dB ripple in the passband ($0 \le \omega \le \pi/5$) and is down by at least 30 dB in the stopband. Also determine the corresponding polyphase filter structure for implementing the decimator.

3.5 Design an interpolator that increases the input sampling rate by a factor of $U = 2$. Use the Remez algorithm to determine the coefficients of the FIR filter that has a 0.1-dB ripple in the passband ($0 \le \omega \le \pi/2$) and is down by at least 30 dB in the stopband. Also, determine the corresponding polyphase filter structure for implementing the interpolator.

3.6 Design a sample-rate converter that reduces the sampling rate by a factor $\frac{2}{5}$. Use the Remez algorithm to determine the coefficients of the FIR filter that has a 0.1-dB ripple in the passband and is down by at least 30 dB in the stopband. Specify the sets of time-variant coefficients $g(n,m)$ and the corresponding coefficients in the polyphase filter realization of the sample-rate converter.

3.7 Consider the two different ways of cascading a decimator with an interpolator shown in Fig. P3.7.

(a) If $D = U$, show that the outputs of the two configurations are different. Hence, in general, the two systems are not identical.

(b) Show that the two systems are identical if and only if D and U are relatively prime.

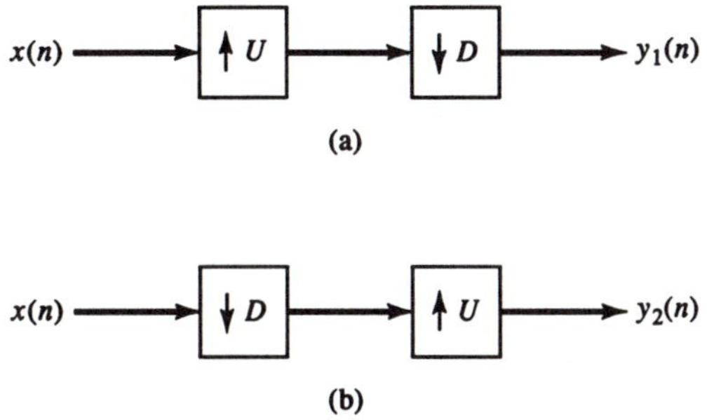

FIGURE P3.7

3.8 Prove the equivalence of the two decimator and interpolator configurations shown in Fig. P3.8. These equivalent relations are called the "noble identities" [see Vaidyanathan (1990)].

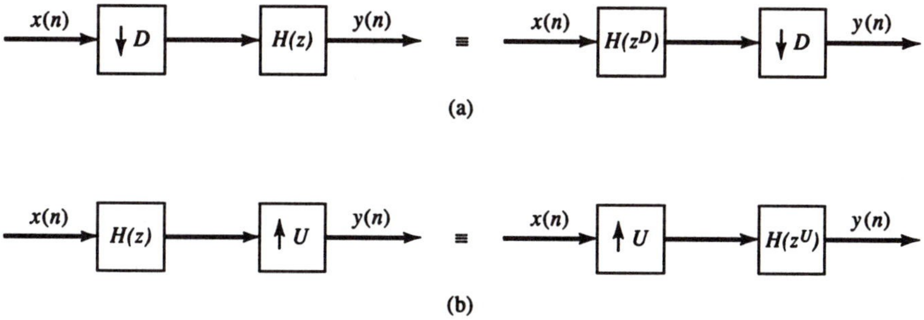

FIGURE P3.8

3.9 Consider an arbitrary digital filter with transfer function

$$H(z) = \sum_{n=-\infty}^{\infty} h(n)z^{-n}$$

(a) Perform a two-component polyphase decomposition of $H(z)$ by grouping the even-numbered samples $h_0(n) = h(2n)$ and odd-numbered samples $h_1(n) = h(2n + 1)$. Thus show that $H(z)$ may be expressed as

$$H(z) = H_0(z^2) + z^{-1}H_1(z^2)$$

and determine $H_0(z)$ and $H_1(z)$.

(b) Generalize the result in part (a) by showing that $H(z)$ can be decomposed into an D-component polyphase filter structure with transfer function

$$H(z) = \sum_{k=0}^{D-1} z^{-k}H_k(z^D)$$

Determine $H_k(z)$.

(c) For the IIR filter with transfer function

$$H(z) = \frac{1}{1 - az^{-1}}$$

determine $H_0(z)$ and $H_1(z)$ for the two-component decomposition.

3.10 Design a two-stage decimator for the following specifications:

$$D = 100$$

passband:	$0 \le F \le 50$
transition band:	$50 \le F \le 55$
input sampling rate:	10,000 Hz
ripple:	$\delta_1 = 10^{-1}, \delta_2 = 10^{-3}$

3.11 Design a linear-phase FIR filter that satisfies the following specifications based on a single-stage and a two-stage multirate structure:

sampling rate:	10,000 Hz
passband:	$0 \le F \le 60$
transition band:	$60 \le F \le 65$
ripple:	$\delta_1 = 10^{-1}, \delta_2 = 10^{-3}$

3.12 Prove that the half-band filter that satisfies (3.9.43) is always odd and that the even coefficients are zero.

3.13 Design a one- and a two-stage interpolator to meet the following specification:

$$U = 20$$

input sampling rate:	10,000 Hz
passband:	$0 \le F \le 90$
transition band:	$90 \le F \le 100$
ripple:	$\delta_1 = 10^{-2}, \delta_2 = 10^{-3}$

3.14 By using (3.9.26) derive the equations corresponding to the structure for the polyphase synthesis section shown in Fig. 3.43.

3.15 Show that the transpose of an L-stage interpolator for increasing the sampling rate by an integer factor U is equivalent to an L-stage decimator that decreases the sampling rate by a factor $D = U$.

3.16 Sketch the polyphase filter structure for achieving a time advance of $(k/U)T_x$ in a sequence $x(n)$.

3.17 Prove the following expressions for an interpolator of order U.

(a) The impulse response $h(n)$ can be expressed as

$$h(n) = \sum_{k=0}^{U-1} p'_k(n - k)$$

where

$$p'_k(n) = \begin{cases} p_k\left(\dfrac{n}{U}\right), & n = 0, \pm U, \pm 2U, \ldots \\ 0, & \text{otherwise} \end{cases}$$

(b) $H(z)$ may be expressed as

$$H(z) = \sum_{k=0}^{U-1} z^{-k} p_k(z)$$

(c)

$$p_k(z) = \frac{1}{U} \sum_{n=-\infty}^{\infty} \sum_{l=0}^{U-1} h(n) e^{j2\pi l(n-k)/U} z^{-(n-k)/U}$$

$$p_k(\omega) = \frac{1}{U} \sum_{l=0}^{U-1} H\left(\omega - \frac{2\pi l}{U}\right) e^{j(\omega - 2\pi l)k/U}$$

CHAPTER 4

LINEAR PREDICTION AND OPTIMUM LINEAR FILTERS

The design of filters to perform signal estimation is a problem that frequently arises in the design of communication systems, control systems, in geophysics, and in many other disciplines. In this chapter we treat the problem of optimum filter design from a statistical viewpoint. The filters are constrained to be linear and the optimization criterion is based on the minimization of the mean-square error. As a consequence, only the second-order statistics (autocorrelation and cross-correlation functions) of a stationary process are required in the determination of the optimum filters.

Included in this treatment is the design of optimum filters for linear prediction. Linear prediction is a particularly important topic in digital signal processing with applications in a variety of areas, such as speech signal processing, image processing, and noise suppression in communication systems. As we shall observe, the determination of the optimum linear filter for prediction requires the solution of a set of linear equations that have some special symmetry. To solve these linear equations, we describe two algorithms, the Levinson–Durbin algorithm and the Schur algorithm, which provide the solution to the equations through computationally efficient procedures that exploit the symmetry properties.

In the last section of this chapter we treat an important class of optimum filters called Wiener filters. Wiener filters are widely used in many applications involving the estimation of signals corrupted with additive noise.

4.1 INNOVATIONS REPRESENTATION OF A STATIONARY RANDOM PROCESS

In this section we demonstrate that a wide-sense stationary random process may be represented as the output of a causal and causally invertible linear system excited by a white noise process. The condition that the system is causally invertible also allows us to represent the wide-sense stationary random process by the output of the inverse system, which is a white noise process.

Let us consider a wide-sense stationary process $x(n)$ with autocorrelation sequence $\gamma_{xx}(m)$ and power spectral density $\Gamma_{xx}(f)$, $|f| \leq \frac{1}{2}$. We assume that $\Gamma_{xx}(f)$ is real and continuous for all $|f| \leq \frac{1}{2}$. The z-transform of the autocorrelation sequence $\gamma_{xx}(m)$ is

$$\Gamma_{xx}(z) = \sum_{m=-\infty}^{\infty} \gamma_{xx}(m) z^{-m} \tag{4.1.1}$$

from which we obtain the power spectral density by evaluating $\Gamma_{xx}(z)$ on the unit circle [i.e., by substituting $z = \exp(j2\pi f)$].

Now, let us assume that $\log \Gamma_{xx}(z)$ is analytic (possesses derivatives of all orders) in an annular region in the z-plane that includes the unit circle (i.e., $r_1 < |z| < r_2$, where $r_1 < 1$ and $r_2 > 1$). Then $\log \Gamma_{xx}(z)$ may be expanded in a Laurent series of the form

$$\log \Gamma_{xx}(z) = \sum_{m=-\infty}^{\infty} v(m) z^{-m} \tag{4.1.2}$$

where the $v(m)$ are the coefficients in the series expansion. We may view $v(m)$ as the sequence with z-transform $V(z) = \log \Gamma_{xx}(z)$. Equivalently, we may evaluate $\log \Gamma_{xx}(z)$ on the unit circle,

$$\log \Gamma_{xx}(f) = \sum_{m=-\infty}^{\infty} v(m) e^{-j2\pi fm} \tag{4.1.3}$$

so that the $v(m)$ are the Fourier coefficients in the Fourier series expansion of the periodic function $\log \Gamma_{xx}(f)$. Hence

$$v(m) = \int_{-1/2}^{1/2} [\log \Gamma_{xx}(f)] e^{j2\pi fm} df, \qquad m = 0, \pm 1, \ldots \tag{4.1.4}$$

We observe that $v(m) = v(-m)$, since $\Gamma_{xx}(f)$ is a real and even function of f.

From (4.1.2) it follows that

$$\begin{aligned} \Gamma_{xx}(z) &= \exp\left[\sum_{m=-\infty}^{\infty} v(m) z^{-m}\right] \\ &= \sigma_w^2 H(z) H(z^{-1}) \end{aligned} \tag{4.1.5}$$

where, by definition, $\sigma_w^2 = \exp[v(0)]$ and

$$H(z) = \exp\left[\sum_{m=1}^{\infty} v(m) z^{-m}\right], \qquad |z| > r_1 \tag{4.1.6}$$

If (4.1.5) is evaluated on the unit circle, we have the equivalent representation of the power spectral density as

$$\Gamma_{xx}(f) = \sigma_w^2 |H(f)|^2 \tag{4.1.7}$$

We note that

$$\log \Gamma_{xx}(f) = \log \sigma_w^2 + \log H(f) + \log H^*(f)$$

$$= \sum_{m=-\infty}^{\infty} v(m) e^{-j2\pi f m}$$

From the definition of $H(z)$ given by (4.1.6), it is clear that the causal part of the Fourier series in (4.1.3) is associated with $H(z)$ and the anticausal part is associated with $H(z^{-1})$. The Fourier series coefficients $v(m)$ are the *cepstral coefficients* and the sequence $v(m)$ is called the *cepstrum* of the sequence $\gamma_{xx}(m)$, as defined in Section 1.5.

The filter with system function $H(z)$ given by (4.1.6) is analytic in the region $|z| > r_1 < 1$. Hence in this region it has a Taylor series expansion as a causal system of the form

$$H(z) = \sum_{m=0}^{\infty} h(n) z^{-n} \tag{4.1.8}$$

The output of this filter to a white noise input sequence $w(n)$ with power spectral density σ_w^2 is a stationary random process $x(n)$ with power spectral density $\Gamma_{xx}(f) = \sigma_w^2 |H(f)|^2$. Conversely, the stationary random process $x(n)$ with power spectral density $\Gamma_{xx}(f)$ may be transformed into a white noise process by passing $x(n)$ through a linear filter with system function $1/H(z)$. We call this filter a *noise whitening filter*. Its output, denoted as $w(n)$ is called the *innovations process* associated with the stationary random process $x(n)$. These two relationships are illustrated in Fig. 4.1.

The representation of the stationary stochastic process $x(n)$ as the output of an IIR filter with system function $H(z)$ given by (4.1.8) and excited by a white noise sequence $w(n)$ is called the *Wold representation*.

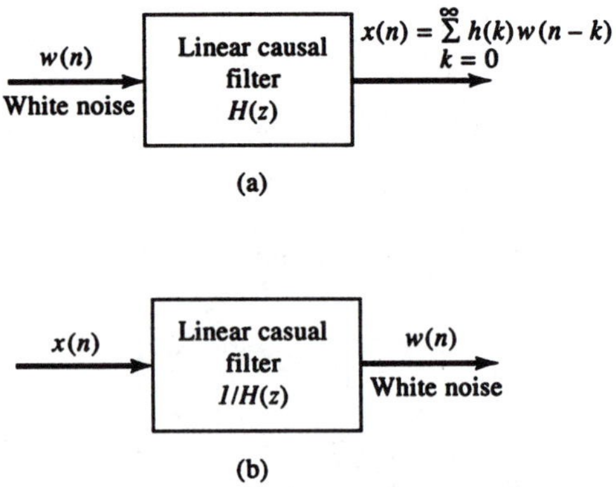

FIGURE 4.1 Filters for generating (a) the random process $x(n)$ from white noise and (b) the inverse filter.

4.1.1 Rational Power Spectra

Let us now restrict our attention to the case where the power spectral density of the stationary random process $x(n)$ is a rational function, expressed as

$$\Gamma_{xx}(z) = \sigma_w^2 \frac{B(z)B(z^{-1})}{A(z)A(z^{-1})}, \qquad r_1 < |z| < r_2 \tag{4.1.9}$$

where the polynomials $B(z)$ and $A(z)$ have roots that fall inside the unit circle in the z-plane. Then the linear filter $H(z)$ for generating the random process $x(n)$ from the white noise sequence $w(n)$ is also rational and is expressed as

$$H(z) = \frac{B(z)}{A(z)} = \frac{\sum_{k=0}^{q} b_k z^{-k}}{1 + \sum_{k=1}^{p} a_k z^{-k}}, \qquad |z| > r_1 \tag{4.1.10}$$

where b_k and a_k are the filter coefficients that determine the location of the zeros and poles of $H(z)$, respectively. Thus $H(z)$ is causal, stable, and minimum phase. Its reciprocal $1/H(z)$ is also a causal, stable, minimum-phase linear system. Therefore, the random process $x(n)$ uniquely represents the statistical properties of the innovations process $w(n)$, and vice versa.

For the linear system with the rational system function $H(z)$ given by (4.1.10), the output $x(n)$ is related to the input $w(n)$ by the difference equation

$$x(n) + \sum_{k=1}^{p} a_k x(n-k) = \sum_{k=0}^{q} b_k w(n-k) \tag{4.1.11}$$

We will distinguish among three specific cases.

Autoregressive (AR) Process: $b_0 = 1,\ b_k = 0,\ k > 0$

In this case the linear filter $H(z) = 1/A(z)$ is an all-pole filter and the difference equation for the input–output relationship is

$$x(n) + \sum_{k=1}^{p} a_k x(n-k) = w(n) \tag{4.1.12}$$

In turn, the noise-whitening filter for generating the innovations process is an all-zero filter.

Moving Average (MA) Process: $a_k = 0,\ k \geq 1$

In this case the linear filter $H(z) = B(z)$ is an all-zero filter and the difference equation for the input–output relationship is

$$x(n) = \sum_{k=0}^{q} b_k w(n-k) \tag{4.1.13}$$

The noise-whitening filter for the MA process is an all-pole filter.

Autoregressive, Moving Average (ARMA) Process. In this case the linear filter $H(z) = B(z)/A(z)$ has both finite poles and zeros in the z-plane and the corresponding difference equation is given by (4.1.11). The inverse system for generating the innovation process from $x(n)$ is also a pole–zero system of the form $1/H(z) = A(z)/B(z)$.

4.1.2 Relationships Between the Filter Parameters and the Autocorrelation Sequence

When the power spectral density of the stationary random process is a rational function, there is a basic relationship that exists between the autocorrelation sequence $\gamma_{xx}(m)$ and the parameters a_k and b_k of the linear filter $H(z)$ that generates the process by filtering the white noise sequence $w(n)$. This relationship may be obtained by multiplying the difference equation in (4.1.11) by $x^*(n-m)$ and taking the expected value of both sides of the resulting equation. Thus we have

$$\begin{aligned} E[x(n)x^*(n-m)] = &-\sum_{k=1}^{p} a_k E[x(n-k)x^*(n-m)] \\ &+ \sum_{k=0}^{q} b_k E[w(n-k)x^*(n-m)] \end{aligned} \tag{4.1.14}$$

Hence

$$\gamma_{xx}(m) = -\sum_{k=1}^{p} a_k \gamma_{xx}(m-k) + \sum_{k=0}^{q} b_k \gamma_{wx}(m-k) \tag{4.1.15}$$

where $\gamma_{wx}(m)$ is the cross-correlation sequence between $w(n)$ and $x(n)$.

The cross-correlation $\gamma_{wx}(m)$ is related to the filter impulse response. That is,

$$\begin{aligned} \gamma_{wx}(m) &= E[x^*(n)w(n+m)] \\ &= E\left[\sum_{k=0}^{\infty} h(k)w^*(n-k)w(n+m)\right] \\ &= \sigma_w^2 h(-m) \end{aligned} \tag{4.1.16}$$

where, in the last step, we have used the fact that the sequence $w(n)$ is white. Hence

$$\gamma_{wx}(m) = \begin{cases} 0, & m > 0 \\ \sigma_w^2 h(-m), & m \le 0 \end{cases} \tag{4.1.17}$$

By combining (4.1.17) with (4.1.14) we obtain the desired relationship

$$\gamma_{xx}(m) = \begin{cases} -\sum_{k=1}^{p} a_k \gamma_{xx}(m-k), & m > q \\ -\sum_{k=1}^{p} a_k \gamma_{xx}(m-k) + \sigma_w^2 \sum_{k=0}^{q-m} h(k) b_{k+m}, & 0 \le m \le q \\ \gamma_{xx}^*(-m), & m < 0 \end{cases} \tag{4.1.18}$$

This represents a nonlinear relationship between $\gamma_{xx}(m)$ and the parameters a_k and b_k.

The relationship in (4.1.18) applies, in general, to the ARMA process. For an AR process, (4.1.18) simplifies to

$$\gamma_{xx}(m) = \begin{cases} -\sum_{k=1}^{p} a_k \gamma_{xx}(m-k), & m > 0 \\ -\sum_{k=1}^{p} a_k \gamma_{xx}(m-k) + \sigma_w^2, & m = 0 \\ \gamma_{xx}^*(-m), & m < 0 \end{cases} \tag{4.1.19}$$

Thus we have a linear relationship between $\gamma_{xx}(m)$ and the a_k parameters. These equations are called the *Yule–Walker equations* and may be expressed in the matrix form

$$\begin{bmatrix} \gamma_{xx}(0) & \gamma_{xx}(-1) & \gamma_{xx}(-2) & \cdots & \gamma_{xx}(-p) \\ \gamma_{xx}(1) & \gamma_{xx}(0) & \gamma_{xx}(-1) & \cdots & \gamma_{xx}(-p+1) \\ \vdots & \vdots & \vdots & & \vdots \\ \gamma_{xx}(p) & \gamma_{xx}(p-1) & \gamma_{xx}(p-2) & \cdots & \gamma_{xx}(0) \end{bmatrix} \begin{bmatrix} 1 \\ a_1 \\ a_2 \\ \vdots \\ a_p \end{bmatrix} = \begin{bmatrix} \sigma_w^2 \\ 0 \\ 0 \\ \vdots \\ 0 \end{bmatrix} \tag{4.1.20}$$

This correlation matrix is Toeplitz and hence it can be efficiently inverted by use of the algorithms described in Section 4.3.

Finally, by setting $a_k = 0$, $1 \le k \le p$, and $h(k) = b_k$, $0 \le k \le q$, in (4.1.18), we obtain the relationship for the autocorrelation sequence in the case of a MA process, namely,

$$\gamma_{xx}(m) = \begin{cases} \sigma_w^2 \sum_{k=0}^{q} b_k b_{k+m}, & 0 \le m \le q \\ 0, & m > q \\ \gamma_{xx}^*(-m), & m < 0 \end{cases} \tag{4.1.21}$$

4.2 FORWARD AND BACKWARD LINEAR PREDICTION

Linear prediction is an important topic in digital signal processing that has many practical applications. In this section we consider the problem of linearly predicting the value of a stationary random process either forward in time or backward in time. This formulation leads to lattice filter structures and to some interesting connections to parametric signal models.

4.2.1 Forward Linear Prediction

Let us begin with the problem of predicting a future value of a stationary random process from observation of past values of the process. In particular, we consider the *one-step forward linear predictor*, which forms the prediction of the value $x(n)$ by a weighted linear combination of the past values $x(n - 1), x(n - 2), \ldots, x(n - p)$. Hence the linearly predicted value of $x(n)$ is

$$\hat{x}(n) = -\sum_{k=1}^{p} a_p(k)x(n - k) \tag{4.2.1}$$

where the $-a_p(k)$ represent the weights in the linear combination. These weights are called the *prediction coefficients* of the one-step forward linear predictor of *order p*. The negative sign in the definition of $x(n)$ is for mathematical convenience and conforms with current practice in the technical literature.

The difference between the value $x(n)$ and the predicted value $\hat{x}(n)$ is called the *forward prediction error*, denoted as $f_p(n)$,

$$\begin{aligned} f_p(n) &= x(n) - \hat{x}(n) \\ &= x(n) + \sum_{k=1}^{p} a_p(k)x(n - k) \end{aligned} \tag{4.2.2}$$

We view linear prediction as being equivalent to linear filtering where the predictor is embedded in the linear filter, as shown in Fig. 4.2. This is called a *prediction-error filter* with input sequence $x(n)$ and output sequence $f_p(n)$. An equivalent realization for the prediction-error filter is shown in Fig. 4.3. This realization is a direct-form FIR filter with system function

$$A_p(z) = \sum_{k=0}^{p} a_p(k)z^{-k} \tag{4.2.3}$$

where, by definition, $a_p(0) = 1$.

There is another realization of the prediction-error filter which takes the form of a lattice structure. To describe this structure and to relate it to the direct-form FIR filter structure, let us begin with a predictor of order $p = 1$. The output of such a filter is

$$f_1(n) = x(n) + a_1(1)x(n - 1) \tag{4.2.4}$$

This output can be obtained from the single-stage lattice filter, illustrated in Fig. 4.4, by exciting both inputs by $x(n)$ and selecting the output from the top branch. Thus the output is exactly that given by (4.2.4) if we select $K_1 = a_1(1)$. The parameter K_1 in the lattice filter is called a *reflection coefficient*.

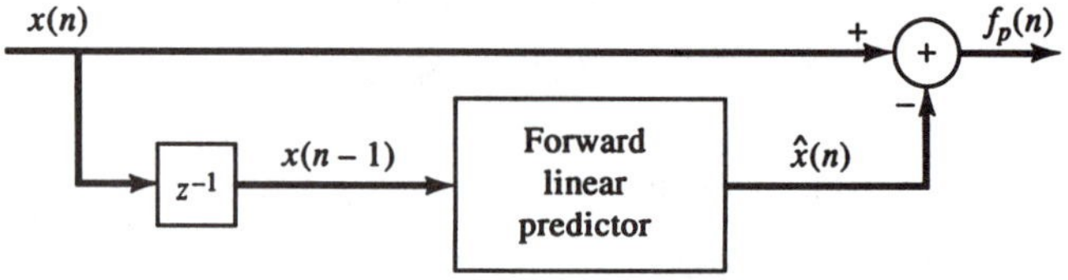

FIGURE 4.2 Forward linear prediction.

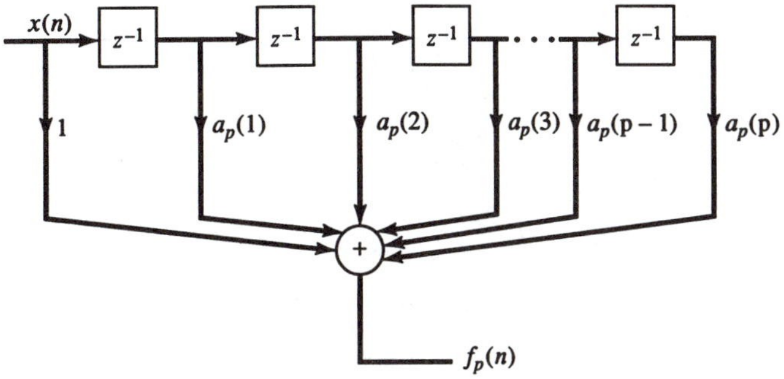

FIGURE 4.3 Prediction-error filter.

Next, let us consider a predictor of order $p = 2$. In this case the output of the direct-form FIR filter is

$$f_2(n) = x(n) + a_2(1)x(n-1) + a_2(2)x(n-2) \tag{4.2.5}$$

By cascading two lattice stages as shown in Fig. 4.5, it is possible to obtain the same output as (4.2.5). Indeed, the two outputs from the first stage are

$$\begin{aligned} f_1(n) &= x(n) + K_1x(n-1) \\ g_1(n) &= K_1^*x(n) + x(n-1) \end{aligned} \tag{4.2.6}$$

The two outputs from the second stage are

$$\begin{aligned} f_2(n) &= f_1(n) + K_2g_1(n-1) \\ g_2(n) &= K_2^*f_1(n) + g_1(n-1) \end{aligned} \tag{4.2.7}$$

If we focus our attention on $f_2(n)$ and substitute for $f_1(n)$ and $g_1(n-1)$ from (4.2.6) into (4.2.7), we obtain

$$\begin{aligned} f_2(n) &= x(n) + K_1x(n-1) + K_2[K_1^*x(n-1) + x(n-2)] \\ &= x(n) + (K_1 + K_1^*K_2)x(n-1) + K_2x(n-2) \end{aligned} \tag{4.2.8}$$

Now (4.2.8) is identical to the output of the direct-form FIR filter given by (4.2.5) if we equate the coefficients. Thus

$$a_2(2) = K_2, \qquad a_2(1) = K_1 + K_1^*K_2 \tag{4.2.9}$$

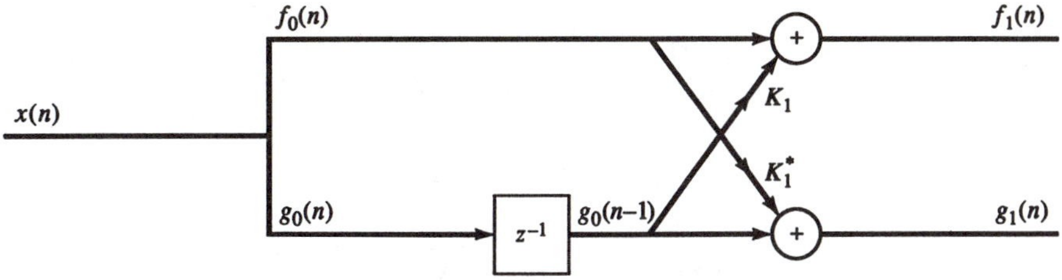

FIGURE 4.4 Single-stage lattice filter.

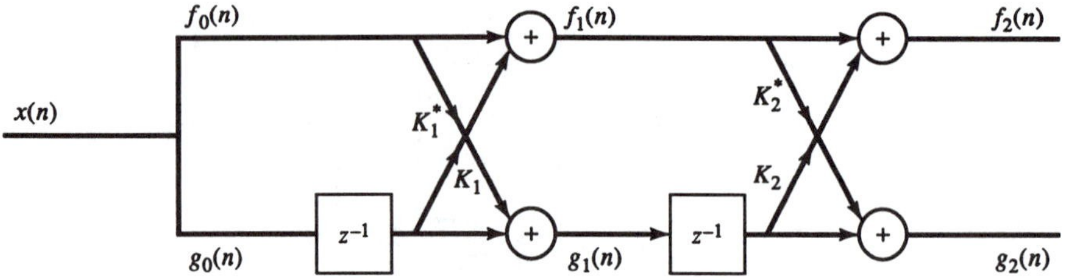

FIGURE 4.5 Two-stage lattice filter.

or equivalently,

$$K_2 = a_2(2), \qquad K_1 = a_1(1) \tag{4.2.10}$$

By continuing this process one can easily demonstrate by induction the equivalence between an mth-order direct-form FIR filter and an mth-order or m-stage lattice filter. The lattice filter is generally described by the following set of *order-recursive equations*:

$$\begin{aligned} f_0(n) &= g_0(n) = x(n) \\ f_m(n) &= f_{m-1}(n) + K_m g_{m-1}(n-1), \qquad m = 1, 2, \ldots, p \\ g_m(n) &= K_m^* f_{m-1}(n) + g_{m-1}(n-1), \qquad m = 1, 2, \ldots, p \end{aligned} \tag{4.2.11}$$

Then the output of the p-stage lattice filter is identical to the output of a p-order direct-form FIR filter. Figure 4.6 illustrates a p-stage lattice filter in block diagram form along with a typical stage that shows the computations given by (4.2.11).

As a consequence of the equivalence between the direct-form prediction-error FIR filter and the FIR lattice filter, the output of the p-stage lattice filter is expressed as

$$f_p(n) = \sum_{k=0}^{p} a_p(k)x(n-k), \qquad a_p(0) = 1 \tag{4.2.12}$$

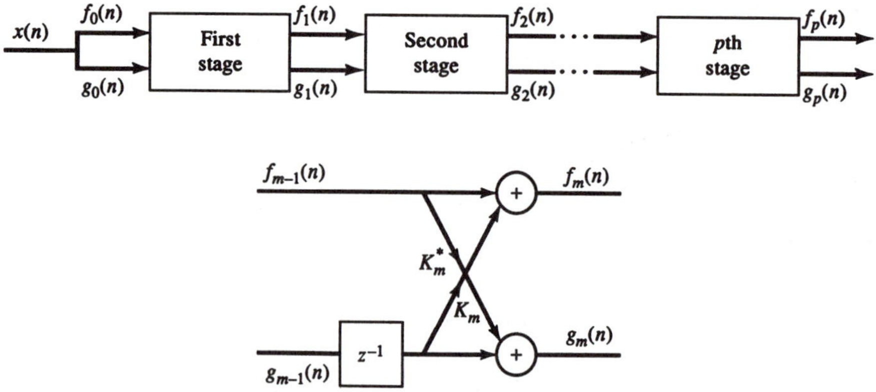

FIGURE 4.6 p-stage lattice filter.

Since (4.2.12) is a convolution sum, the z-transform relationship is

$$F_p(z) = A_p(z)X(z) \tag{4.2.13}$$

or equivalently,

$$A_p(z) = \frac{F_p(z)}{X(z)} = \frac{F_p(z)}{F_0(z)} \tag{4.2.14}$$

The mean-square value of the forward linear prediction error $f_p(n)$ is

$$\begin{aligned} \mathscr{E}_p^f &= E[|f_p(n)|^2] \\ &= \gamma_{xx}(0) + 2\,\mathrm{Re}\left[\sum_{k=1}^{p} a_p^*(k)\gamma_{xx}(k)\right] + \sum_{k=1}^{p}\sum_{l=1}^{p} a_p^*(l)a_p(k)\gamma_{xx}(l-k) \end{aligned} \tag{4.2.15}$$

$\mathscr{E}_p^f$ is a quadratic function of the predictor coefficients, and its minimization leads to the set of linear equations

$$\gamma_{xx}(l) = -\sum_{k=1}^{p} a_p(k)\gamma_{xx}(l-k), \qquad l = 1, 2, \ldots, p \tag{4.2.16}$$

These are called the *normal equations* for the coefficients of the linear predictor. The minimum mean-square prediction error is simply

$$\min[\mathscr{E}_p^f] \equiv E_p^f = \gamma_{xx}(0) + \sum_{k=1}^{p} a_p(k)\gamma_{xx}(-k) \tag{4.2.17}$$

In the following section we extend the development above to the problem of predicting the value of a time series in the opposite direction, namely, backward in time.

4.2.2 Backward Linear Prediction

Let us assume that we have the data sequence $x(n)$, $x(n-1), \ldots, x(n-p+1)$ from a stationary random process and we wish to predict the value $x(n-p)$ of the process. In this case we employ a *one-step backward linear predictor* of order p. Hence

$$\hat{x}(n-p) = -\sum_{k=0}^{p-1} b_p(k)x(n-k) \tag{4.2.18}$$

The difference between the value $x(n-p)$ and the estimate $\hat{x}(n-p)$ is called the *backward prediction error*, denoted as $g_p(n)$,

$$\begin{aligned} g_p(n) &= x(n-p) + \sum_{k=0}^{p-1} b_p(k)x(n-k) \\ &= \sum_{k=0}^{p} b_p(k)x(n-k), \qquad b_p(p) = 1 \end{aligned} \tag{4.2.19}$$

The backward linear predictor may be realized either by a direct-form FIR filter structure similar to the structure shown in Fig. 4.2 or as a lattice structure. The lattice structure shown in Fig. 4.6 provides the backward linear predictor as well as the forward linear predictor. To prove this point, let us consider the output of this lattice filter from the lower branch. This output is given as

$$g_1(n) = K_1^* x(n) + x(n-1) \tag{4.2.20}$$

Hence the weighting coefficient of the backward predictor is $b_1(0) = K_1^*$.

In the two-stage lattice shown in Fig. 4.5, the output of the second stage from the bottom branch is

$$g_2(n) = K_2^* f_1(n) + g_1(n-1) \tag{4.2.21}$$

If we substitute from (4.2.6) for $f_1(n)$ and $g_1(n - 1)$, we obtain

$$g_2(n) = K_2^* x(n) + (K_1^* + K_1 K_2^*) x(n-1) + x(n-2) \tag{4.2.22}$$

Hence the weighting coefficients in the backward linear predictor are identical to the coefficients for the forward linear predictor, but they occur in reverse order. Thus we have

$$b_p(k) = a_p^*(p-k), \qquad k = 0, 1, \ldots, p \tag{4.2.23}$$

In the z-domain, the convolution sum in (4.2.19) becomes

$$G_p(z) = B_p(z) X(z) \tag{4.2.24}$$

or equivalently,

$$B_p(z) = \frac{G_p(z)}{X(z)} = \frac{G_p(z)}{G_0(z)} \tag{4.2.25}$$

where $B_p(z)$ represents the system function of the FIR filter with coefficients $b_p(k)$.

Since $b_p(k) = a_p^*(p - k)$, $G_p(z)$ is related to $A_p(z)$ as follows:

$$\begin{aligned} B_p(z) &= \sum_{k=0}^{p} b_p(k) z^{-k} \\ &= \sum_{k=0}^{p} a_p^*(p-k) z^{-k} \\ &= z^{-p} \sum_{k=0}^{p} a_p^*(k) z^{k} \\ &= z^{-p} A_p^*(z^{-1}) \end{aligned} \tag{4.2.26}$$

The relationship in (4.2.26) implies that the zeros of the FIR filter with system function $B_p(z)$ are simply the (conjugate) reciprocals of the zeros of $A_p(z)$. Hence $B_p(z)$ is called the reciprocal or *reverse polynomial* of $A_p(z)$.

Now that we have established these interesting relationships between the direct-form FIR filter and the FIR lattice filter, let us return to the recursive lattice equations in (4.2.11) and transform them to the z-domain. Thus we have

$$F_0(z) = G_0(z) = X(z)$$

$$F_m(z) = F_{m-1}(z) + K_m z^{-1} G_{m-1}(z), \qquad m = 1, 2, \ldots, p \tag{4.2.27}$$

$$G_m(z) = K_m^* F_{m-1}(z) + z^{-1} G_{m-1}(z), \qquad m = 1, 2, \ldots, p$$

If we divide each equation by $X(z)$, we obtain the desired results in the form

$$A_0(z) = B_0(z) = 1$$

$$A_m(z) = A_{m-1}(z) + K_m z^{-1} B_{m-1}(z), \qquad m = 1, 2, \ldots, p \tag{4.2.28}$$

$$B_m(z) = K_m^* A_{m-1}(z) + z^{-1} B_{m-1}(z), \qquad m = 1, 2, \ldots, p$$

Thus a lattice filter is described in the z-domain by the matrix equation

$$\begin{bmatrix} A_m(z) \\ B_m(z) \end{bmatrix} = \begin{bmatrix} 1 & K_m z^{-1} \\ K_m^* & z^{-1} \end{bmatrix} \begin{bmatrix} A_{m-1}(z) \\ B_{m-1}(z) \end{bmatrix} \tag{4.2.29}$$

The relations in (4.2.28) for $A_m(z)$ and $B_m(z)$ allow us to obtain the direct-form FIR filter coefficients $a_m(k)$ from the reflection coefficients K_m, and vice versa. We illustrate the procedure in the following example.

EXAMPLE 4.2.1

Given a three-state lattice filter with coefficients $K_1 = \frac{1}{4}$, $K_2 = \frac{1}{2}$, $K_3 = \frac{1}{3}$, determine the FIR filter coefficients for the direct-form structure.

Solution: We solve the problem recursively, beginning with (4.2.28) for $m = 1$. Thus we have

$$A_1(z) = A_0(z) + K_1 z^{-1} B_0(z)$$
$$= 1 + K_1 z^{-1} = 1 + \tfrac{1}{4} z^{-1}$$

Hence the coefficients of an FIR filter corresponding to the single-stage lattice are $\alpha_1(0) = 1$, $\alpha_1(1) = K_1 = \frac{1}{4}$. Since $B_m(z)$ is the reverse polynomial of $A_m(z)$, we have

$$B_1(z) = \tfrac{1}{4} + z^{-1}$$

Next we add the second stage to the lattice. For $m = 2$, (4.2.28) yields

$$A_2(z) = A_1(z) + K_2 z^{-1} B_1(z)$$
$$= 1 + \tfrac{3}{8} z^{-1} + \tfrac{1}{2} z^{-2}$$

Hence the FIR filter parameters corresponding to the two-stage lattice are $\alpha_2(0) = 1$, $\alpha_2(1) = \frac{3}{8}$, and $\alpha_2(2) = \frac{1}{2}$. Also,

$$B_2(z) = \tfrac{1}{2} + \tfrac{3}{8} z^{-1} + z^{-2}$$

Finally, the addition of the third stage to the lattice results in the polynomial

$$A_3(z) = A_2(z) + K_3 z^{-1} B_2(z)$$
$$= 1 + \tfrac{13}{24} z^{-1} + \tfrac{5}{8} z^{-2} + \tfrac{1}{3} z^{-3}$$

Consequently, the desired direct-form FIR filter is characterized by the coefficients

$$\alpha_3(0) = 1, \qquad \alpha_3(1) = \tfrac{13}{24}, \qquad \alpha_3(2) = \tfrac{5}{8}, \qquad \alpha_3(3) = \tfrac{1}{3}$$

As this example illustrates, the lattice structure with parameters K_1, K_2, . . . , K_p corresponds to a class of p direct-form FIR filters with system functions $A_1(z)$, $A_2(z)$, . . . , $A_p(z)$. It is interesting to note that a characterization of this class of p FIR filters in direct form requires $p(p + 1)/2$ filter coefficients. In contrast, the lattice-form characterization requires only the p reflection coefficients K_i. The reason that the lattice provides a more compact representation for the class of p FIR filters is because appending stages to the lattice does not alter the parameters of the previous stages. On the other hand, appending the pth stage to a lattice with $(p - 1)$ stages results in a FIR filter with system function $A_p(z)$ that has coefficients totally different from the coefficients of the lower-order FIR filter with system function $A_{p-1}(z)$.

A formula for determining the filter coefficients $a_p(k)$ recursively can be easily derived from polynomial relationships (4.2.28). We have

$$A_m(z) = A_{m-1}(z) + K_m z^{-1} B_{m-1}(z)$$
$$\sum_{k=0}^{m} a_m(k) z^{-k} = \sum_{k=0}^{m-1} a_{m-1}(k) z^{-k} + K_m \sum_{k=0}^{m-1} a^*_{m-1}(m - 1 - k) z^{-(k+1)} \tag{4.2.30}$$

By equating the coefficients of equal powers of z^{-1} and recalling that $a_m(0) = 1$ for $m = 1, 2, \ldots, p$, we obtain the desired recursive equation for the FIR filter coefficients in the form

$$\begin{aligned} a_m(0) &= 1 \\ a_m(m) &= K_m \\ &\vdots \\ a_m(k) &= a_{m-1}(k) + K_m a^*_{m-1}(m - k) \\ &= a_{m-1}(k) + a_m(m) a^*_{m-1}(m - k), \\ &\quad 1 \le k \le m - 1, \quad m = 1, 2, \ldots, p \end{aligned} \tag{4.2.31}$$

The conversion formula from the direct-form FIR filter coefficients $a_p(k)$ to the lattice reflection coefficients K_i is also very simple. For the p-stage lattice we immediately obtain the reflection coefficient $K_p = a_p(p)$. To obtain

$K_{p-1}, \ldots, K_1$, we need the polynomials $A_m(z)$ for $m = p - 1, \ldots, 1$. From (4.2.29) we obtain

$$A_{m-1}(z) = \frac{A_m(z) - K_m B_m(z)}{1 - |K_m|^2}, \qquad m = p, \ldots, 1 \tag{4.2.32}$$

which is just a step-down recursion. Thus we compute all lower-degree polynomials $A_m(z)$ beginning with $A_{p-1}(z)$ and obtain the desired lattice reflection coefficients from the relation $K_m = a_m(m)$. We observe that the procedure works as long as $|K_m| \neq 1$ for $m = 1, 2, \ldots, p - 1$. From this step-down recursion for the polynomials, it is relatively easy to obtain a formula for recursively and directly computing K_m, $m = p - 1, \ldots, 1$. For $m = p - 1, \ldots, 1$, we have

$$\begin{aligned} K_m &= a_m(m) \\ a_{m-1}(k) &= \frac{a_m(k) - K_m b_m(k)}{1 - |K_m|^2} \\ &= \frac{a_m(k) - a_m(m)a_m^*(m - k)}{1 - |a_m(m)|^2} \end{aligned} \tag{4.2.33}$$

which is just the recursion in the Schur–Cohn stability test for the polynomial $A_m(z)$.

As indicated above, the recursive equation in (4.2.33) breaks down if any of the lattice parameters $|K_m| = 1$. If this occurs, it is indicative that the polynomial $A_{m-1}(z)$ has a root located on the unit circle. Such a root may be factored out from $A_{m-1}(z)$ and the iterative process in (4.2.33) can be carried out for the reduced-order system.

Finally, let us consider the minimization of the mean-square error in a backward linear predictor. The backward prediction error is

$$\begin{aligned} g_p(n) &= x(n - p) + \sum_{k=0}^{p-1} b_p(k)x(n - k) \\ &= x(n - p) + \sum_{k=1}^{p} a_p^*(k)x(n - p + k) \end{aligned} \tag{4.2.34}$$

and its mean-square value is

$$\mathscr{E}_p^b = E[|g_p(n)|^2] \tag{4.2.35}$$

The minimization of $\mathscr{E}_p^b$ with respect to the prediction coefficients yields the same set of linear equations as in (4.2.16). Hence the minimum mean-square error is

$$\min[\mathscr{E}_p^b] \equiv E_p^b = E_p^f \tag{4.2.36}$$

which is given by (4.2.17).

4.2.3 Optimum Reflection Coefficients for the Lattice Forward and Backward Predictors

In Sections 4.2.1 and 4.2.2 we derived the set of linear equations that provide the predictor coefficients that minimize the mean-square value of the prediction error. In this section we consider the problem of optimizing the reflection coefficients in the lattice predictor.

The forward prediction error in the lattice filter is expressed as

$$f_m(n) = f_{m-1}(n) + K_m g_{m-1}(n-1) \tag{4.2.37}$$

The minimization of $E[|f_m(n)|^2]$ with respect to the reflection coefficient K_m yields the result

$$K_m = \frac{-E[f_{m-1}(n)g^*_{m-1}(n-1)]}{E[|g_{m-1}(n-1)|^2]} \tag{4.2.38}$$

or equivalently,

$$K_m = \frac{-E[f_{m-1}(n)g^*_{m-1}(n-1)]}{\sqrt{E^f_{m-1}E^b_{m-1}}} \tag{4.2.39}$$

where

$$E^f_{m-1} = E^b_{m-1} = E[|g_{m-1}(n-1)|^2] = E[|f_{m-1}(n)|^2]$$

We observe that the optimum choice of the reflection coefficients in the lattice predictor is the negative of the (normalized) cross-correlation coefficients between the forward and backward errors in the lattice.† Since it is apparent from (4.2.38) that $|K_m| \leq 1$, it follows that the minimum mean-square value of the prediction error, which may be expressed recursively as

$$E^f_m = (1 - |K_m|^2)E^f_{m-1} \tag{4.2.40}$$

is a monotonically decreasing sequence.

4.2.4 Relationship of an AR Process to Linear Prediction

The parameters of an AR(p) process are intimately related to a predictor of order p for the same process. To see the relationship, we recall that in an AR(p) process, the autocorrelation sequence $\gamma_{xx}(m)$ is related to the parameters a_k by the Yule–Walker equations given in (4.1.19) or (4.1.20). The corresponding equations for the predictor of order p are given by (4.2.16) and (4.2.17).

A direct comparison of these two sets of relations reveals that there is a one-to-one correspondence between the parameters a_k of the AR(p) process and the predictor coefficients $a_p(k)$ of the pth-order predictor. In fact, if the

† The normalized cross-correlation coefficients between the forward and backward error in the lattice (i.e., $-K_m$) are often called the *partial correlation* (PARCOR) *coefficients*.

underlying process $x(n)$ is AR(p), the prediction coefficients of the pth-order predictor will be identical to a_k. Furthermore, the minimum MSE in the pth-order predictor E_p^f will be identical to σ_w^2, the variance of the white noise process. In this case the prediction-error filter is a noise-whitening filter that produces the innovations sequence $w(n)$.

4.3 SOLUTION OF THE NORMAL EQUATIONS

In the preceding section we observed that the minimization of the mean-square value of the forward prediction error resulted in a set of linear equations for the coefficients of the predictor given by (4.2.16). These equations, called the *normal equations*, may be expressed in the compact form

$$\sum_{k=0}^{p} a_p(k)\gamma_{xx}(l-k) = 0, \qquad l = 1, 2, \ldots, p, \quad a_p(0) = 1 \qquad (4.3.1)$$

The resulting minimum MSE (MMSE) is given by (4.2.17). If we augment (4.2.17) to the normal equations given by (4.3.1), we obtain the set of *augmented normal equations*, which may be expressed as

$$\sum_{k=0}^{p} a_p(k)\gamma_{xx}(l-k) = \begin{cases} E_p^f, & l = 0 \\ 0, & l = 1, 2, \ldots, p \end{cases} \qquad (4.3.2)$$

We also noted that if the random process is an AR(p) process, the MMSE $E_p^f = \sigma_w^2$.

In this section we describe two computationally efficient algorithms for solving the normal equations. One algorithm, originally due to Levinson (1947) and modified by Durbin (1959), is called the *Levinson–Durbin algorithm*. This algorithm is suitable for serial processing and has a computation complexity of $O(p^2)$. The second algorithm, due to Schur (1917), also computes the reflection coefficients in $O(p^2)$ operations but with parallel processors the computations can be performed in $O(p)$ time. Both algorithms exploit the Toeplitz symmetry property inherent in the autocorrelation matrix. We begin by describing the Levinson–Durbin algorithm.

4.3.1 Levinson–Durbin Algorithm

The Levinson–Durbin algorithm is a computationally efficient algorithm for solving the normal equations in (4.3.1) for the prediction coefficients. This algorithm exploits the special symmetry in the autocorrelation matrix

$$\mathbf{\Gamma}_p = \begin{bmatrix} \gamma_{xx}(0) & \gamma_{xx}^*(1) & \cdots & \gamma_{xx}^*(p-1) \\ \gamma_{xx}(1) & \gamma_{xx}(0) & \cdots & \gamma_{xx}^*(p-2) \\ \vdots & \vdots & & \\ \gamma_{xx}(p-1) & \gamma_{xx}(p-2) & \cdots & \gamma_{xx}(0) \end{bmatrix} \qquad (4.3.3)$$

Note that $\Gamma_p(i,j) = \Gamma_p(i - j)$, so that the autocorrelation matrix is a *Toeplitz matrix*. Since $\Gamma_p(i,j) = \Gamma_p^*(j,i)$, the matrix is also Hermitian.

The key to the Levinson–Durbin method of solution that exploits the Toeplitz property of the matrix is to proceed recursively, beginning with a predictor of order $m = 1$ (one coefficient) and to increase the order recursively, using the lower-order solutions to obtain the solution to the next higher order. Thus the solution to the first-order predictor obtained by solving (4.3.1) is

$$a_1(1) = -\frac{\gamma_{xx}(1)}{\gamma_{xx}(0)} \tag{4.3.4}$$

and the resulting MMSE is

$$\begin{aligned} E_1^f &= \gamma_{xx}(0) + a_1(1)\gamma_{xx}(-1) \\ &= \gamma_{xx}(0)[1 - |a_1(1)|^2] \end{aligned} \tag{4.3.5}$$

Recall that $a_1(1) = K_1$, the first reflection coefficient in the lattice filter.

The next step is to solve for the coefficients $a_2(1)$ and $a_2(2)$ of the second-order predictor and express the solution in terms of $a_1(1)$. The two equations obtained from (4.3.1) are

$$\begin{aligned} a_2(1)\gamma_{xx}(0) + a_2(2)\gamma_{xx}^*(1) &= -\gamma_{xx}(1) \\ a_2(1)\gamma_{xx}(1) + a_2(2)\gamma_{xx}(0) &= -\gamma_{xx}(2) \end{aligned} \tag{4.3.6}$$

By using the solution in (4.3.4) to eliminate $\gamma_{xx}(1)$, we obtain the solution

$$\begin{aligned} a_2(2) &= -\frac{\gamma_{xx}(2) + a_1(1)\gamma_{xx}(1)}{\gamma_{xx}(0)[1 - |a_1(1)|^2]} \\ &= -\frac{\gamma_{xx}(2) + a_1(1)\gamma_{xx}(1)}{E_1^f} \\ a_2(1) &= a_1(1) + a_2(2)a_1^*(1) \end{aligned} \tag{4.3.7}$$

Thus we have obtained the coefficients of the second-order predictor. Again, we note that $a_2(2) = K_2$, the second reflection coefficient in the lattice filter.

Proceeding in this manner, we may express the coefficients of the mth-order predictor in terms of the coefficients of the $(m - 1)$st-order predictor. Thus we may write the coefficient vector $\mathbf{a}_m$ as the sum of two vectors, namely,

$$\mathbf{a}_m = \begin{bmatrix} a_m(1) \\ a_m(2) \\ \vdots \\ a_m(m) \end{bmatrix} = \begin{bmatrix} \mathbf{a}_{m-1} \\ \cdots \\ 0 \end{bmatrix} + \begin{bmatrix} \mathbf{d}_{m-1} \\ \cdots \\ K_m \end{bmatrix} \tag{4.3.8}$$

where $\mathbf{a}_{m-1}$ is the predictor coefficient vector of the $(m - 1)$st-order predictor and the vector $\mathbf{d}_{m-1}$ and the scalar K_m are to be determined. Let us also partition the $m \times m$ autocorrelation matrix Γ_{xx} as

$$\mathbf{\Gamma}_m = \begin{bmatrix} \mathbf{\Gamma}_{m-1} & \boldsymbol{\gamma}_{m-1}^{b*} \\ \boldsymbol{\gamma}_{m-1}^{bt} & \gamma_{xx}(0) \end{bmatrix} \tag{4.3.9}$$

where $\boldsymbol{\gamma}_{m-1}^{bt} = [\gamma_{xx}(m-1) \quad \gamma_{xx}(m-2) \quad \cdots \quad \gamma_{xx}(1)] = (\boldsymbol{\gamma}_{m-1}^{b})^t$, the asterisk (*) denotes the complex conjugate and $\boldsymbol{\gamma}_m^t$ denotes the transpose of $\boldsymbol{\gamma}_m$. The superscript b on $\boldsymbol{\gamma}_{m-1}$ denotes the vector $\boldsymbol{\gamma}_{m-1}^t = [\gamma_{xx}(1) \quad \gamma_{xx}(2) \quad \cdots \quad \gamma_{xx}(m-1)]$ with elements taken in reverse order.

The solution to the equation $\mathbf{\Gamma}_m \mathbf{a}_m = -\boldsymbol{\gamma}_m$ may be expressed as

$$\begin{bmatrix} \mathbf{\Gamma}_{m-1} & \boldsymbol{\gamma}_{m-1}^{b*} \\ \boldsymbol{\gamma}_{m-1}^{bt} & \gamma_{xx}(0) \end{bmatrix} \left(\begin{bmatrix} \mathbf{a}_{m-1} \\ 0 \end{bmatrix} + \begin{bmatrix} \mathbf{d}_{m-1} \\ K_m \end{bmatrix} \right) = - \begin{bmatrix} \boldsymbol{\gamma}_{m-1} \\ \gamma_{xx}(m) \end{bmatrix} \tag{4.3.10}$$

This is the key step in the Levinson–Durbin algorithm. From (4.3.10) we obtain two equations,

$$\mathbf{\Gamma}_{m-1}\mathbf{a}_{m-1} + \mathbf{\Gamma}_{m-1}\mathbf{d}_{m-1} + K_m \boldsymbol{\gamma}_{m-1}^{b*} = -\boldsymbol{\gamma}_{m-1} \tag{4.3.11}$$

$$\boldsymbol{\gamma}_{m-1}^{bt}\mathbf{a}_{m-1} + \boldsymbol{\gamma}_{m-1}^{bt}\mathbf{d}_{m-1} + K_m \gamma_{xx}(0) = -\gamma_{xx}(m) \tag{4.3.12}$$

Since $\mathbf{\Gamma}_{m-1}\mathbf{a}_{m-1} = -\boldsymbol{\gamma}_{m-1}$, (4.3.11) yields the solution

$$\mathbf{d}_{m-1} = -K_m \mathbf{\Gamma}_{m-1}^{-1} \boldsymbol{\gamma}_{m-1}^{b*} \tag{4.3.13}$$

But $\boldsymbol{\gamma}_{m-1}^{b*}$ is just $\boldsymbol{\gamma}_{m-1}$ with elements taken in reverse order and conjugated. Therefore, the solution in (4.5.13) is simply

$$\mathbf{d}_{m-1} = K_m \mathbf{a}_{m-1}^{b*} = K_m \begin{bmatrix} a_{m-1}^*(m-1) \\ a_{m-1}^*(m-2) \\ \vdots \\ a_{m-1}^*(1) \end{bmatrix} \tag{4.3.14}$$

The scalar equation (4.3.12) can now be used to solve for K_m. If we eliminate $\mathbf{d}_{m-1}$ in (4.3.12) by using (4.3.14), we obtain

$$K_m[\gamma_{xx}(0) + \boldsymbol{\gamma}_{m-1}^{bt}\mathbf{a}_{m-1}^{b*}] + \boldsymbol{\gamma}_{m-1}^{bt}\mathbf{a}_{m-1} = -\gamma_{xx}(m)$$

Hence

$$K_m = -\frac{\gamma_{xx}(m) + \boldsymbol{\gamma}_{m-1}^{bt}\mathbf{a}_{m-1}}{\gamma_{xx}(0) + \boldsymbol{\gamma}_{m-1}^{bt}\mathbf{a}_{m-1}^{b*}} \tag{4.3.15}$$

Therefore, by substituting the solutions in (4.3.14) and (4.3.15) into (4.3.8), we obtain the desired recursion for the predictor coefficients in the Levinson–Durbin algorithm as

$$a_m(m) = K_m = -\frac{\gamma_{xx}(m) + \boldsymbol{\gamma}_{m-1}^{bt}\mathbf{a}_{m-1}}{\gamma_{xx}(0) + \boldsymbol{\gamma}_{m-1}^{bt}\mathbf{a}_{m-1}^{b*}} = -\frac{\gamma_{xx}(m) + \boldsymbol{\gamma}_{m-1}^{bt}\mathbf{a}_{m-1}}{E_m^f} \tag{4.3.16}$$

$$\begin{aligned} a_m(k) &= a_{m-1}(k) + K_m a_{m-1}^*(m-k) \\ &= a_{m-1}(k) + a_m(m) a_{m-1}^*(m-k), \qquad \begin{aligned} k &= 1, 2, \ldots, m-1 \\ m &= 1, 2, \ldots, p \end{aligned} \end{aligned} \tag{4.3.17}$$

The reader should note that the recursive relation in (4.3.17) is identical to the recursive relation in (4.2.31) for the predictor coefficients, which was obtained from the polynomials $A_m(z)$ and $B_m(z)$. Furthermore, K_m is the reflection coefficient in the mth-stage of the lattice predictor. This development clearly illustrates that the Levinson–Durbin algorithm produces the reflection coefficients for the optimum lattice predictor as well as the coefficients of the optimum direct-form FIR predictor.

Finally, let us determine the expression for the MMSE. For the mth-order predictor, we have

$$\begin{aligned} E_m^f &= \gamma_{xx}(0) + \sum_{k=1}^{m} a_m(k)\gamma_{xx}(-k) \\ &= \gamma_{xx}(0) + \sum_{k=1}^{m} [a_{m-1}(k) + a_m(m)a_{m-1}^*(m-k)]\gamma_{xx}(-k) \qquad (4.3.18) \\ &= E_{m-1}^f[1 - |a_m(m)|^2] = E_{m-1}^f(1 - |K_m|^2), \qquad m = 1, 2, \ldots, p \end{aligned}$$

where $E_0^f = \gamma_{xx}(0)$. Since the reflection coefficients satisfy the property that $|K_m| \leq 1$, the MMSE for the sequence of predictors satisfies the condition

$$E_0^f \geq E_1^f \geq E_2^f \geq \cdots \geq E_p^f \qquad (4.3.19)$$

This concludes the derivation of the Levinson–Durbin algorithm for solving the linear equations $\mathbf{\Gamma}_m \mathbf{a}_m = -\boldsymbol{\gamma}_m$, for $m = 0, 1, \ldots, p$. We observe that the linear equations have the special property that the vector on the right-hand side also appears as a vector in $\mathbf{\Gamma}_m$. In the more general case where the vector on the right-hand side is some other vector, say $\mathbf{c}_m$, the set of linear equations can be solved recursively by introducing a second recursive equation to solve the more general linear equations $\mathbf{\Gamma}_m \mathbf{b}_m = \mathbf{c}_m$. The result is a *generalized Levinson–Durbin* algorithm (see Problem 4.12).

The Levinson–Durbin recursion given by (4.3.17) requires $O(m)$ multiplications and additions (operations) to go from stage m to stage $m + 1$. Therefore, for p stages it will take on the order of $1 + 2 + 3 + \cdots + p = (p + 1)/2$, or $O(p^2)$ operations to solve for the prediction filter coefficients, or the reflection coefficients, compared with $O(p^3)$ operations if we did not exploit the Toeplitz property of the correlation matrix.

If the Levinson–Durbin algorithm is implemented on a serial computer or signal processor, the required computation time is on the order of $O(p^2)$ time units. On the other hand, if the processing is performed on a parallel processing machine utilizing as many processors as necessary to exploit the full parallelism in the algorithm, the multiplications as well as the additions required to compute (4.3.17) can be carried out simultaneously. Therefore, this computation can be performed in $O(p)$ time units. However, the computation in (4.3.16) for the reflection coefficients takes additional time. Certainly, the inner products involving the vectors $\mathbf{a}_{m-1}$ and $\boldsymbol{\gamma}_{m-1}^b$ can be computed simultaneously by employing parallel processors. However, the addition of these products cannot be done simultaneously but, instead, require $O(\log p)$ time units. Hence the computations in the Levinson–Durbin algorithm, when performed by p parallel processors, can be accomplished in $O(p \log p)$ time.

In the following section we describe another algorithm, due to Schur (1917), that avoids the computation of inner products, and hence it is more suitable for parallel computation of the reflection coefficients.

4.3.2 The Schur Algorithm

The Schur algorithm is intimately related with a recursive test for determining the positive definiteness of a correlation matrix. To be specific, let us consider the autocorrelation matrix $\mathbf{\Gamma}_{p+1}$ associated with the augmented normal equations given by (4.3.2). From the elements of this matrix we form the function

$$R_0(z) = \frac{\gamma_{xx}(1)z^{-1} + \gamma_{xx}(2)z^{-2} + \cdots + \gamma_{xx}(p)z^{-p}}{\gamma_{xx}(0) + \gamma_{xx}(1)z^{-1} + \cdots + \gamma_{xx}(p)z^{-p}} \tag{4.3.20}$$

and the sequence of functions $R_m(z)$ defined recursively as

$$R_m(z) = \frac{R_{m-1}(z) - R_{m-1}(\infty)}{z^{-1}[1 - R^*_{m-1}(\infty)R_{m-1}(z)]}, \qquad m = 1, 2, \ldots \tag{4.3.21}$$

Schur's theorem states that a necessary and sufficient condition for the correlation matrix to be positive definite is that $|R_m(\infty)| < 1$ for $m = 1, 2, \ldots, p$.

Let us demonstrate that the condition for positive definiteness of the autocorrelation matrix $\mathbf{\Gamma}_{p+1}$ is equivalent to the condition that the reflection coefficients in the equivalent lattice filter satisfy the condition $|K_m| < 1$, $m = 1, 2, \ldots, p$.

First, we note that $R_0(\infty) = 0$. Then from (4.3.21) we have

$$R_1(z) = \frac{\gamma_{xx}(1) + \gamma_{xx}(2)z^{-1} + \cdots + \gamma_{xx}(p)z^{-p+1}}{\gamma_{xx}(0) + \gamma_{xx}(1)z^{-1} + \cdots + \gamma_{xx}(p)z^{-p}} \tag{4.3.22}$$

Hence $R_1(\infty) = \gamma_{xx}(1)/\gamma_{xx}(0)$. We observe that $R_1(\infty) = -K_1$.

Second, we compute $R_2(z)$ according to (4.3.21) and evaluate the result at $z = \infty$. Thus we obtain

$$R_2(\infty) = \frac{\gamma_{xx}(2) + K_1\gamma_{xx}(1)}{\gamma_{xx}(0)(1 - |K_1|^2)}$$

Again, we observe that $R_2(\infty) = -K_2$. By continuing this procedure, we find that $R_m(\infty) = -K_m$ for $m = 1, 2, \ldots, p$. Hence the condition $|R_m(\infty)| < 1$ for $m = 1, 2, \ldots, p$ is identical to the condition $|K_m| < 1$ for $m = 1, 2, \ldots, p$, and ensures the positive definiteness of the autocorrelation matrix $\mathbf{\Gamma}_{p+1}$.

Since the reflection coefficients can be obtained from the sequence of functions $R_m(z)$, $m = 1, 2, \ldots, p$, we have another method for solving the normal equations. We call this method the *Schur algorithm*.

Schur Algorithm. Let us first rewrite $R_m(z)$ as

$$R_m(z) = \frac{P_m(z)}{Q_m(z)}, \qquad m = 0, 1, \ldots, p \tag{4.3.23}$$

where

$$\begin{aligned} P_0(z) &= \gamma_{xx}(1)z^{-1} + \gamma_{xx}(2)z^{-2} + \cdots + \gamma_{xx}(p)z^{-p} \\ Q_0(z) &= \gamma_{xx}(0) + \gamma_{xx}(1)z^{-1} + \cdots + \gamma_{xx}(p)z^{-p} \end{aligned} \tag{4.3.24}$$

Since $K_0 = 0$ and $K_m = -R_m(\infty)$ for $m = 1, 2, \ldots, p$, the recursive equation (4.3.21) implies the following recursive equations for the polynomials $P_m(z)$ and $Q_m(z)$:

$$\begin{bmatrix} P_m(z) \\ Q_m(z) \end{bmatrix} = \begin{bmatrix} 1 & K_{m-1} \\ K^*_{m-1}z^{-1} & z^{-1} \end{bmatrix} \begin{bmatrix} P_{m-1}(z) \\ Q_{m-1}(z) \end{bmatrix}, \qquad m = 1, 2, \ldots, p \tag{4.3.25}$$

Thus we have

$$\begin{aligned} P_1(z) &= P_0(z) = \gamma_{xx}(1)z^{-1} + \gamma_{xx}(2)z^{-2} + \cdots + \gamma_{xx}(p)z^{-p} \\ Q_1(z) &= z^{-1}Q_0(z) = \gamma_{xx}(0)z^{-1} + \gamma_{xx}(1)z^{-2} + \cdots + \gamma_{xx}(p-1)z^{-p} \end{aligned} \tag{4.3.26}$$

and

$$K_1 = -\left.\frac{P_1(z)}{Q_1(z)}\right|_{z=\infty} = -\frac{\gamma_{xx}(1)}{\gamma_{xx}(0)} \tag{4.3.27}$$

Next the reflection coefficient K_2 is obtained by determing $P_2(z)$ and $Q_2(z)$ from (4.3.25), dividing $P_2(z)$ by $Q_2(z)$ and evaluating the result at $z = \infty$. Thus we find that

$$\begin{aligned} P_2(z) &= P_1(z) + K_1Q_1(z) \\ &= [\gamma_{xx}(2) + K_1\gamma_{xx}(1)]z^{-2} + \cdots + [\gamma_{xx}(p) + K_1\gamma_{xx}(p-1)]z^{-p} \\ Q_2(z) &= z^{-1}[Q_1(z) + K_1^*P_1(z)] \\ &= [\gamma_{xx}(0) + K_1^*\gamma_{xx}(1)]z^{-2} + \cdots \\ &\quad + [\gamma_{xx}(p-2) + K_1^*\gamma_{xx}(p-1)]z^{-p} \end{aligned} \tag{4.3.28}$$

Thus we observe that the recursive equation in (4.3.25) is equivalent to (4.3.21).

Based on these relationships the Schur algorithm is described by the following recursive procedure:

Initialization. Form the $2 \times (p + 1)$ generator matrix

$$\mathbf{G}_0 = \begin{bmatrix} 0 & \gamma_{xx}(1) & \gamma_{xx}(2) & \cdots & \gamma_{xx}(p) \\ \gamma_{xx}(0) & \gamma_{xx}(1) & \gamma_{xx}(2) & \cdots & \gamma_{xx}(p) \end{bmatrix} \tag{4.3.29}$$

where the elements of the first row are the coefficients of $P_0(z)$ and the elements of the second row are the coefficients of $Q_0(z)$.

Step 1. Shift the second row of the generator matrix to the right one place and discard the last element of this row. A zero is placed in the vacant position. Thus we obtain a new generator matrix

$$\mathbf{G}_1 = \begin{bmatrix} 0 & \gamma_{xx}(1) & \gamma_{xx}(2) & \cdots & \gamma_{xx}(p) \\ 0 & \gamma_{xx}(0) & \gamma_{xx}(1) & \cdots & \gamma_{xx}(p-1) \end{bmatrix} \tag{4.3.30}$$

The (negative) ratio of the elements in the second column yields the reflection coefficient $K_1 = -\gamma_{xx}(1)/\gamma_{xx}(0)$.

Step 2. Multiply the generator matrix by the 2×2 matrix

$$\mathbf{V}_1 = \begin{bmatrix} 1 & K_1 \\ K_1^* & 1 \end{bmatrix} \tag{4.3.31}$$

Thus we obtain

$$\mathbf{V}_1\mathbf{G}_1 = \begin{bmatrix} 0 & 0 & \gamma_{xx}(2) + K_1\gamma_{xx}(1) & \cdots & \gamma_{xx}(p) + K_1\gamma_{xx}(p-1) \\ 0 & \gamma_{xx}(0) + K_1^*\gamma_{xx}(1) & \cdots\cdots\cdots\cdots & \cdots & \gamma_{xx}(p-1) + K_1^*\gamma_{xx}(p) \end{bmatrix} \tag{4.3.32}$$

Step 3. Shift the second row $\mathbf{V}_1\mathbf{G}_1$ by one place to the right and thus form the new generator matrix

$$\mathbf{G}_2 = \begin{bmatrix} 0 & 0 & \gamma_{xx}(2) + K_1\gamma_{xx}(1) & \cdots & \gamma_{xx}(p) + K_1\gamma_{xx}(p-1) \\ 0 & 0 & \gamma_{xx}(0) + K_1^*\gamma_{xx}(1) & \cdots & \gamma_{xx}(p-2) + K_1^*\gamma_{xx}(p-1) \end{bmatrix} \tag{4.3.33}$$

The negative ratio of the elements in the third column of $\mathbf{G}_2$ yields K_2.

Steps 2 and 3 are repeated until we have solved for all p reflection coefficients. In general, the 2×2 matrix in step m is

$$\mathbf{V}_m = \begin{bmatrix} 1 & K_m \\ K_m^* & 1 \end{bmatrix} \tag{4.3.34}$$

and multiplication of $\mathbf{V}_m$ by $\mathbf{G}_m$ yields $\mathbf{V}_m\mathbf{G}_m$. In step 3 we shift the second row of $\mathbf{V}_m\mathbf{G}_m$ one place to the right and thus we obtain the new generator matrix $\mathbf{G}_{m+1}$.

We observe that the shifting operation of the second row in each iteration is equivalent to multiplication by the delay operator z^{-1} in the second recursive equation in (4.3.25). We also note that the division of the polynomial $P_m(z)$ by the polynomial $Q_m(z)$ and the evaluation of the quotient at $z = \infty$ is equivalent to dividing the elements in the $(m + 1)$st column of $\mathbf{G}_m$. The computation of the p reflection coefficients can be accomplished by use of parallel processors in $O(p)$ time units. Below we describe a pipelined architecture for performing these computations.

Another way of demonstrating the relationship of the Schur algorithm to the Levinson–Durbin algorithm and the corresponding lattice predictor is to determine the output of the lattice filter obtained when the input sequence is the correlation sequence $\{\gamma_{xx}(m), m = 0, 1, \ldots\}$. Thus the first input to the lattice filter is $\gamma_{xx}(0)$, the second input is $\gamma_{xx}(1)$, and so on [i.e., $f_0(n) = \gamma_{xx}(n)$]. After the delay in the first stage, we have $g_0(n-1) = \gamma_{xx}(n-1)$. Hence for $n = 1$, the ratio $f_0(1)/g_0(0) = \gamma_{xx}(1)/\gamma_{xx}(0)$, which is the negative of the reflection coefficient K_1. Alternatively, we may express this relationship as

$$f_0(1) + K_1 g_0(0) = \gamma_{xx}(1) + K_1\gamma_{xx}(0) = 0$$

Furthermore, $g_0(0) = \gamma_{xx}(0) = E_0^f$. At time $n = 2$, the input to the second stage is, according to (4.2.11),

$$f_1(2) = f_0(2) + K_1 g_0(1) = \gamma_{xx}(2) + K_1\gamma_{xx}(1)$$

and after the unit of delay in the second stage, we have

$$g_1(1) = K_1^* f_0(1) + g_0(0) = K_1^*\gamma_{xx}(1) + \gamma_{xx}(0)$$

Now the ratio $f_1(2)/g_1(1)$ is

$$\frac{f_1(2)}{g_1(1)} = \frac{\gamma_{xx}(2) + K_1\gamma_{xx}(1)}{\gamma_{xx}(0) + K_1^*\gamma_{xx}(1)} = \frac{\gamma_{xx}(2) + K_1\gamma_{xx}(1)}{E_1^f} = -K_2$$

Hence

$$f_1(2) + K_2 g_1(1) = 0$$

$$g_1(1) = E_1^f$$

By continuing in this way, we can show that at the input to the mth lattice stage, the ratio $f_{m-1}(m)/g_{m-1}(m-1) = -K_m$ and $g_{m-1}(m-1) = E_{m-1}^f$. Consequently, the lattice filter coefficients obtained from the Levinson algorithm are identical to the coefficients obtained in the Schur algorithm. Furthermore, the lattice filter structure provides a method for computing the reflection coefficients in the lattice predictor.

A Pipelined Architecture for Implementing the Schur Algorithm. Kung and Hu (1983) developed a pipelined lattice-type processor for implementing the Schur algorithm. The processor consists of a cascade of p lattice-type stages, where each stage consists of two processing elements (PEs), which we designate as upper PEs, denoted as $A_1, A_2, \ldots, A_p$, and lower PEs, denoted as $B_1, B_2, \ldots, B_p$, as shown in Fig. 4.7. The PE designated as A_1 is assigned the task of performing divisions. The remaining PEs perform one multiplication and one addition per iteration (one clock cycle).

Initially, the upper PEs are loaded with the elements of the first row of the generator matrix $\mathbf{G}_0$, as illustrated in Fig. 4.7. The lower PEs are loaded with the elements of the second row of the generator matrix $\mathbf{G}_0$. The computational process begins with the division PE, A_1, which computes the first reflection coefficient as $K_1 = -\gamma_{xx}(1)/\gamma_{xx}(0)$. The value of K_1 is sent simultaneously to all the PEs in the upper branch and lower branch.

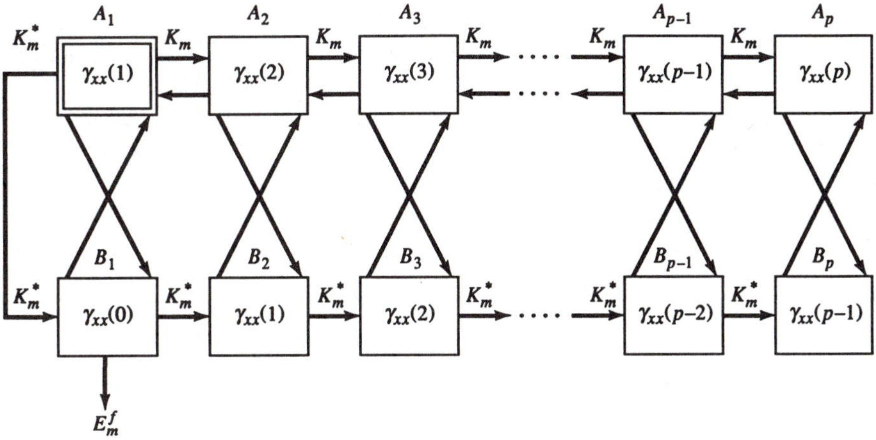

FIGURE 4.7 Pipelined parallel processor for computing the reflection coefficients.

The second step in the computation is to update the contents of all processing elements simultaneously. The contents of the upper and lower PEs are updated as follows:

$$\text{PE } A_m\text{:} \quad A_m \leftarrow A_m + K_1 B_m, \qquad m = 2, 3, \ldots, p$$

$$\text{PE } B_m\text{:} \quad B_m \leftarrow B_m + K_1^* A_m, \qquad m = 1, 2, \ldots, p$$

The third step involves the shifting of the contents of the upper PEs one place to the left. Thus we have

$$\text{PE } A_m\text{:} \quad A_{m-1} \leftarrow A_m, \qquad m = 2, 3, \ldots, p$$

At this point PE A_1 contains $\gamma_{xx}(2) + K_1\gamma_{xx}(1)$ while PE B_1 contains $\gamma_{xx}(0) + K_1^*\gamma_{xx}(1)$. Hence the processor A_1 is ready to begin the second cycle by computing the second reflection coefficient $K_2 = -A_1/B_1$. The three computational steps beginning with the division A_1/B_1 are repeated until all p reflection coefficients are computed. Note that PE B_1 provides the minimum mean-square error E_m^f for each iteration.

If τ_d denotes the time for PE A_1 to perform a (complex) division and τ_{ma} is the time required to perform a (complex) multiplication and an addition, the time required to compute all p reflection coefficients is $p(\tau_d + \tau_{ma})$ for the Schur algorithm.

4.4 PROPERTIES OF THE LINEAR PREDICTION-ERROR FILTERS

Linear prediction filters possess several important properties, which are described below. We begin by demonstrating that the forward prediction-error filter is minimum phase.

Minimum-Phase Property of the Forward Prediction-Error Filter. We have already demonstrated that the reflection coefficients K_i are correlation coefficients, and consequently, $|K_i| \le 1$ for all i. This condition and the relation $E_m^f = (1 - |K_m|^2)E_{m-1}^f$ may be used to show that the zeros of the prediction-error filter are either all inside the unit circle or they are all on the unit circle.

First, we show that if $E_p^f > 0$, the zeros $|z_i| < 1$ for every i. The proof is by induction. Clearly, for $p = 1$ the system function for the prediction-error filter is

$$A_1(z) = 1 + K_1 z^{-1} \tag{4.4.1}$$

Hence $z_1 = -K_1$ and $E_1^f = (1 - |K_1|^2)E_0^f > 0$. Now suppose that the hypothesis is true for $p - 1$. Then if z_i is a root of $A_p(z)$, we have from (4.2.26) and (4.2.28)

$$\begin{aligned} A_p(z_i) &= A_{p-1}(z_i) + K_p z_i^{-1} B_{p-1}(z_i) \\ &= A_{p-1}(z_i) + K_p z_i^{-p} A_{p-1}^*\left(\frac{1}{z_i}\right) = 0 \end{aligned} \tag{4.4.2}$$

Hence

$$\frac{1}{K_p} = -\frac{z_i^{-p} A_{p-1}^*\left(\dfrac{1}{z_i}\right)}{A_{p-1}(z_i)} \equiv Q(z_i) \tag{4.4.3}$$

We note that the function $Q(z)$ is all pass. In general, an all-pass function of the form

$$P(z) = \prod_{k=1}^{N} \frac{z z_k^* + 1}{z + z_k}, \qquad |z_k| < 1 \tag{4.4.4}$$

satisfies the property that $|P(z)| > 1$ for $|z| < 1$, $|P(z)| = 1$ for $|z| = 1$, and $|P(z)| < 1$ for $|z| > 1$. Since $Q(z) = -P(z)/z$, it follows that $|z_i| < 1$ if $|Q(z)| > 1$. Clearly, this is the case since $Q(z_i) = 1/K_p$ and $E_p^f > 0$.

On the other hand, suppose that $E_{p-1}^f > 0$ and $E_p^f = 0$. In this case $|K_p| = 1$ and $|Q(z_i)| = 1$. Since the MMSE is zero, the random process $x(n)$ is called *predictable* or *deterministic*. Specifically, a purely sinusoidal random process of the form

$$x(n) = \sum_{k=1}^{M} \alpha_k e^{j(n\omega_k + \theta_k)} \tag{4.4.5}$$

where the phases θ_k are statistically independent and uniformly distributed over $(0,2\pi]$, has the autocorrelation

$$\gamma_{xx}(m) = \sum_{k=1}^{M} \alpha_k^2 e^{jm\omega_k} \tag{4.4.6}$$

and the power density spectrum

$$\Gamma_{xx}(f) = \sum_{k=1}^{M} \alpha_k^2 \delta(f - f_k), \qquad f_k = \frac{\omega_k}{2\pi} \tag{4.4.7}$$

This process is predictable with a predictor of order $p \geq M$.

To demonstrate the validity of the statement, consider passing this process through a prediction-error filter of order $p \geq M$. The MSE at the output of this filter is

$$\begin{aligned} \mathscr{E}_p^f &= \int_{-1/2}^{1/2} \Gamma_{xx}(f)\, |A_p(f)|^2\, df \\ &= \int_{-1/2}^{1/2} \left[\sum_{k=1}^{M} \alpha_k^2 \delta(f - f_k) \right] |A_p(f)|^2\, df \\ &= \sum_{k=1}^{M} \alpha_k^2\, |A_p(f_k)|^2 \end{aligned} \tag{4.4.8}$$

By choosing M of the p zeros of the prediction-error filter to coincide with the frequencies f_k, the MSE $\mathscr{E}_p^f$ can be forced to zero. The remaining $p - M$ zeros can be selected arbitrarily to be anywhere inside the unit circle.

Finally, the reader may prove that if a random process consists of a mixture of a continuous power spectral density and a discrete spectrum, the prediction-error filter must have all its roots inside the unit circle.

Maximum-Phase Property of the Backward Prediction-Error Filter. The system function for the backward prediction error filter of order p is

$$B_p(z) = z^{-p} A_p^*(z^{-1}) \tag{4.4.9}$$

Consequently, the roots of $B_p(z)$ are the reciprocals of the roots of the forward prediction-error filter with system function $A_p(z)$. Hence if $A_p(z)$ is minimum phase, $B_p(z)$ is maximum phase. However, if the process $x(n)$ is predictable, all the roots of $B_p(z)$ lie on the unit circle.

Whitening Property. Suppose that the random process $x(n)$ is an AR(p) stationary random process that is generated by passing white noise with variance σ_w^2 through an all-pole filter with system function

$$H(z) = \frac{1}{1 + \sum_{k=1}^{p} a_k z^{-1}} \tag{4.4.10}$$

Then the prediction-error filter of order p has the system function

$$A_p(z) = 1 + \sum_{k=1}^{p} a_p(k) z^{-k} \tag{4.4.11}$$

where the predictor coefficients $a_p(k) = a_k$. The response of the prediction-error filter is a white noise sequence $w(n)$. In this case the prediction-error filter whitens the input random process $x(n)$ and is called a whitening filter, as indicated in Section 4.2.

More generally, even if the input process $x(n)$ is not an AR process, the prediction-error filter attempts to remove the correlation among the signal samples of the input process. As the order of the predictor is increased, the predictor output $\hat{x}(n)$ becomes a closer approximation to $x(n)$ and hence the difference $f(n) = \hat{x}(n) - x(n)$ approaches a white noise sequence.

Orthogonality of the Backward Prediction Errors. The backward prediction errors $g_m(k)$ from different stages in the FIR lattice filter are orthogonal. That is,

$$E[g_m(n)g_l^*(n)] = \begin{cases} 0, & 0 \le l \le m-1 \\ E_m^b, & l = m \end{cases} \tag{4.4.12}$$

This property is easily proved by substituting for $g_m(n)$ and $g_l^*(n)$ into (4.4.12) and carrying out the expectation. Thus

$$\begin{aligned} E[g_m(n)g_l^*(n)] &= \sum_{k=0}^{m} b_m(k) \sum_{j=0}^{l} b_l^*(j) E[x(n-k)x^*(n-j)] \\ &= \sum_{j=0}^{l} b_l^*(j) \sum_{k=0}^{m} b_m(k)\gamma_{xx}(j-k) \end{aligned} \tag{4.4.13}$$

But the normal equations for the backward linear predictor require that

$$\sum_{k=0}^{m} b_m(k)\gamma_{xx}(j-k) = \begin{cases} 0, & j = 1, 2, \ldots, m-1 \\ E_m^b, & j = m \end{cases} \tag{4.4.14}$$

Therefore,

$$E[g_m(n)g_l^*(n)] = \begin{cases} E_m^b = E_m^f, & m = l \\ 0, & 0 \le l \le m-1 \end{cases} \tag{4.4.15}$$

Additional Properties. There are a number of other interesting properties regarding the forward and backward prediction errors in the FIR lattice filter. These are given below for real-valued signals. Their proof is left as an exercise for the reader.

(a) $E[f_m(n)x(n-i)] = 0, \quad 1 \le i \le m$

(b) $E[g_m(n)x(n-i)] = 0, \quad 0 \le i \le m-1$

(c) $E[f_m(n)x(n)] = E[g_m(n)x(n-m)] = E_m$

(d) $E[f_i(n)f_j(n)] = E_{\max(i,j)}$

(e) $E[f_i(n)f_j(n-t)] = 0, \quad \text{for} \begin{cases} 1 \le t \le i-j, & i > j \\ -1 \ge t \ge i-j, & i < j \end{cases}$

(f) $E[g_i(n)g_j(n-t)] = 0, \quad \text{for} \begin{cases} 0 \le t \le i-j, & i > j \\ 0 \ge t \ge i-j+1, & i < j \end{cases}$

(g) $E[f_i(n+i)f_j(n+j)] = \begin{cases} E_i, & i = j \\ 0, & i \ne j \end{cases}$

(h) $E[g_i(n+i)g_j(n+j)] = E_{\max(i,j)}$

(i) $E[f_i(n)g_j(n)] = \begin{cases} K_j E_i, & i \ge j, \quad i,j \ge 0, \quad K_0 = 1 \\ 0, & i < j \end{cases}$

(j) $E[f_i(n)g_i(n-1)] = -K_{i+1}E_i$

(k) $E[g_i(n-1)x(n)] = E[f_i(n+1)x(n-i)] = -K_{i+1}E_i$

(l) $E[f_i(n)g_j(n-1)] = \begin{cases} 0, & i > j \\ -K_{j+1}E_i, & i \le j \end{cases}$

4.5 AR LATTICE AND ARMA LATTICE-LADDER FILTERS

In Section 4.2 we developed the all-zero FIR lattice structure and showed its relationship to linear prediction. The linear predictor with transfer function

$$A_p(z) = 1 + \sum_{k=1}^{p} a_p(k)z^{-k} \tag{4.5.1}$$

when excited by an input random process $x(n)$ produces an output that approaches a white noise sequence as $p \to \infty$. On the other hand, if the input process is an AR(p), the output of $A_p(z)$ is white. Since $A_p(z)$ generates a MA(p) when excited with a white noise sequence, the all-zero lattice is sometimes called a *MA lattice*. Below we develop the lattice structure for the inverse filter $1/A_p(z)$, which we call the *AR lattice*, and the lattice-ladder structure for an ARMA process.

4.5.1 AR Lattice Structure

Let us consider an all-pole system with system function

$$H(z) = \frac{1}{1 + \sum_{k=1}^{p} a_p(k)z^{-k}} \tag{4.5.2}$$

The difference equation for this IIR system is

$$y(n) = -\sum_{k=1}^{p} a_p(k)y(n-k) + x(n) \tag{4.5.3}$$

Now suppose that we interchange the roles of the input and output [i.e., interchange $x(n)$ with $y(n)$, in (4.5.3)]. Thus we obtain the difference equation

$$x(n) = -\sum_{k=1}^{p} a_p(k)x(n-k) + y(n)$$

or equivalently,

$$y(n) = x(n) + \sum_{k=1}^{p} a_p(k)x(n-k) \tag{4.5.4}$$

We observe that (4.5.4) is a difference equation for an FIR system with system function $A_p(z)$. Thus an all-pole IIR system can be converted to an all-zero system by interchanging the roles of the input and output.

Based on this observation, we can obtain the structure of an AR(p) lattice from a MA(p) lattice by interchanging the input with the output. Since the MA(p) lattice has $y(n) = f_p(n)$ as its output and $x(n) = f_0(n)$ is the input, we let

$$\begin{aligned} x(n) &= f_p(n) \\ y(n) &= f_0(n) \end{aligned} \tag{4.5.5}$$

These definitions dictate that the quantities $f_m(n)$ be computed in descending order. This computation can be accomplished by rearranging the recursive equation for $f_m(n)$ in (4.2.11) and solving for $f_{m-1}(n)$ in terms of $f_m(n)$. Thus we obtain

$$f_{m-1}(n) = f_m(n) - K_m g_{m-1}(n-1), \qquad m = p, p-1, \ldots, 1$$

The equation for $g_m(n)$ remains unchanged. The result of these changes is the set of equations

$$\begin{aligned} x(n) &= f_p(n) \\ f_{m-1}(n) &= f_m(n) - K_m g_{m-1}(n-1) \\ g_m(n) &= K_m^* f_{m-1}(n) + g_{m-1}(n-1) \\ y(n) &= f_0(n) = g_0(n) \end{aligned} \tag{4.5.6}$$

The corresponding structure for the AR(p) lattice is shown in Fig. 4.8. Note that the all-pole lattice structure has an all-zero path with input $g_0(n)$ and output $g_p(n)$ which is identical to the all-zero path in the MA(p) lattice structure. This is not surprising, since the equation for $g_m(n)$ is identical in the two lattice structures.

We also observe that the AR(p) and MA(p) lattice structures are characterized by the same parameters, namely, the reflection coefficients, K_i. Consequently, the equations given in (4.2.31) and (4.2.33) for converting between the system parameters $a_p(k)$ in the direct-form realizations of the all-zero system $A_p(z)$ and the lattice parameters, K_i, of the MA(p) lattice structure, apply as well to the all-pole structures.

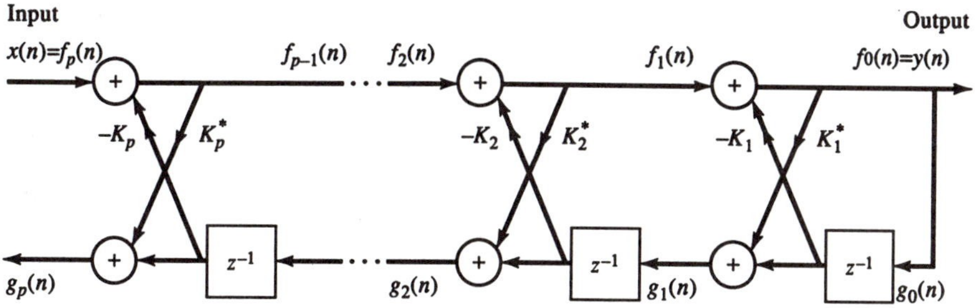

FIGURE 4.8 Lattice structure for an all-pole (AR(p)) system.

4.5.2 ARMA Processes and Lattice-Ladder Filters

The all-pole lattice provides the basic building block for lattice-type structures that implement IIR systems that contain both poles and zeros. To construct the appropriate structure, let us consider an IIR system with system function

$$H(z) = \frac{\sum_{k=0}^{q} c_q(k) z^{-k}}{1 + \sum_{k=1}^{p} a_p(k) z^{-k}} = \frac{C_q(z)}{A_p(z)} \tag{4.5.7}$$

Without loss of generality, we assume that $p \geq q$.

This system is described by the difference equations

$$\begin{aligned} v(n) &= -\sum_{k=0}^{p} a_p(k) v(n-k) + x(n) \\ y(n) &= \sum_{k=0}^{q} c_q(k) v(n-k) \end{aligned} \tag{4.5.8}$$

which are obtained by viewing the system as a cascade of an all-pole system followed by an all-zero system. From (4.5.8) we observe that the output $y(n)$ is simply a linear combination of delayed outputs from the all-pole system.

Since zeros will result from forming a linear combination of previous outputs, we may carry over this observation to construct a pole–zero system by using the all-pole lattice structure as the basic building block. We have clearly observed that $g_m(n)$ in the all-pole lattice may be expressed as a linear combination of present and past outputs. In fact, the system

$$H_b(z) \equiv \frac{G_m(z)}{Y(z)} = B_m(z) \tag{4.5.9}$$

in an all-zero system. Therefore, any linear combination of $g_m(n)$ is also an all-zero filter.

Let us begin with an all-pole lattice filter with coefficients K_m, $1 \leq m \leq p$, and add a *ladder* part by taking as the output a weighted linear combination of $g_m(n)$. The result is a pole–zero filter that has the *lattice-ladder* structure shown in Fig. 4.9. Its output is

$$y(n) = \sum_{k=0}^{q} \beta_k g_k(n) \tag{4.5.10}$$

where β_k are the parameters that determine the zeros of the system. The system function corresponding to (4.5.10) is

$$H(z) = \frac{Y(z)}{X(z)} = \sum_{k=0}^{q} \beta_k \frac{G_k(z)}{X(z)} \tag{4.5.11}$$

Since $X(z) = F_p(z)$ and $F_0(z) = G_0(z)$, (4.5.11) may be expressed as

$$\begin{aligned} H(z) &= \sum_{k=0}^{q} \beta_k \frac{G_k(z)}{G_0(z)} \frac{F_0(z)}{F_p(z)} \\ &= \frac{1}{A_p(z)} \sum_{k=0}^{q} \beta_k B_k(z) \end{aligned} \tag{4.5.12}$$

Therefore,

$$C_q(z) = \sum_{k=0}^{q} \beta_k B_k(z) \tag{4.5.13}$$

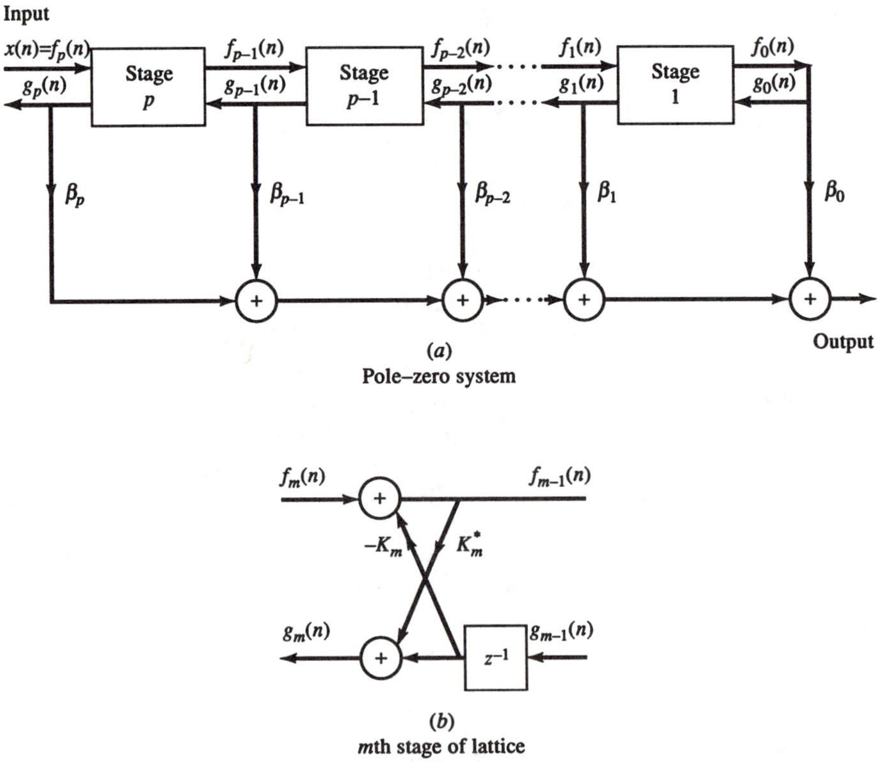

FIGURE 4.9 Lattice-ladder structure for pole-zero system.

This is the desired relationship that can be used to determine the weighting coefficients β_k.

Given the polynomials $C_q(z)$ and $A_p(z)$, where $p \geq q$, the reflection coefficients K_i are determined first from the coefficients $a_p(k)$. By means of the step-down recursive relation given by (4.2.32) we also obtain the polynomials $B_k(z)$, $k = 1, 2, \ldots, p$. Then the ladder parameters can be obtained from (4.5.13), which can be expressed as

$$\begin{aligned} C_m(z) &= \sum_{k=0}^{m-1} \beta_k B_k(z) + \beta_m B_m(z) \\ &= C_{m-1}(z) + \beta_m B_m(z) \end{aligned} \tag{4.5.14}$$

or equivalently,

$$C_{m-1}(z) = C_m(z) - \beta_m B_m(z), \qquad m = p, p-1, \ldots, 1 \tag{4.5.15}$$

By running this recursive relation backward, we can generate all the lower-degree polynomials, $C_m(z)$, $m = p - 1, \ldots, 1$. Since $b_m(m) = 1$, the parameters β_m are determined from (4.5.15) by setting

$$\beta_m = c_m(m), \qquad m = p, \quad p-1, \ldots, 1,0 \tag{4.5.16}$$

This lattice-ladder filter structure, when excited by a white noise sequence, generates an ARMA(p,q) process which has a power density spectrum

$$\Gamma_{xx}(f) = \sigma_w^2 \frac{|C_q(f)|^2}{|A_p(f)|^2} \tag{4.5.17}$$

and an autocorrelation function that satisfies (4.1.18), where σ_w^2 in the variance of the input white noise sequence.

4.6 WIENER FILTERS FOR FILTERING AND PREDICTION

In many practical applications we are given an input signal, $x(n)$, which consists of the sum of a desired signal, $s(n)$, and an undesired noise or interference, $w(n)$, and we are asked to design a filter that will suppress the undesired interference component. In such a case the objective is to design a system that filters out the additive interference while preserving the characteristics of the desired signal, $s(n)$.

In this section we treat the problem of signal estimation in the presence of an additive noise disturbance. The estimator is constrained to be a linear filter with impulse response $h(n)$, which is designed so that its output approximates some specified desired signal sequence $d(n)$. Figure 4.10 illustrates the linear estimation problem.

The input sequence to the filter is $x(n) = s(n) + w(n)$, and its output sequence is $y(n)$. The difference between the desired signal and the filter output is the error sequence $e(n) = d(n) - y(n)$. We distinguish three special cases:

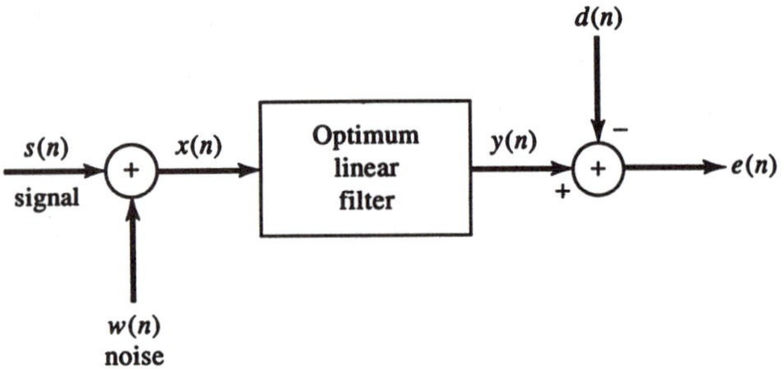

FIGURE 4.10 Model for linear estimation problem.

1. If $d(n) = s(n)$, the linear estimation problem is referred to as *filtering*.
2. If $d(n) = s(n + D)$, where $D > 0$, the linear estimation problem is referred to as signal *prediction*. Note that this problem is different from the prediction considered in Chapter 3, where $d(n) = x(n + D)$, $D \geq 0$.
3. If $d(n) = s(n - D)$, where $D > 0$, the linear estimation problem referred to as signal *smoothing*.

Our treatment will concentrate on filtering and prediction.

The criterion selected for optimizing the filter impulse response $h(n)$ is the minimization of the mean-square error. This criterion has the advantages of simplicity and mathematical tractability. The basic assumptions are that the sequences $s(n)$, $w(n)$, and $d(n)$ are zero mean and wide-sense stationary. The linear filter will be assumed to be either FIR or IIR. If it is IIR, we assume that the input data $x(n)$ is available over the infinite past. We begin with the design of the optimum FIR filter. The optimum linear filter, in the sense of minimum mean-square error (MMSE), is called a *Wiener filter*.

4.6.1 FIR Wiener Filter

Suppose that the filter is constrained to be of length M with coefficients $h(k)$, $0 \leq k \leq M - 1$. Hence its output $y(n)$ depends on the finite data record $x(n), x(n - 1), \ldots, x(n - M + 1)$,

$$y(n) = \sum_{k=0}^{M-1} h(k)x(n - k) \tag{4.6.1}$$

The mean-square value of the error between the desired output $d(n)$ and $y(n)$ is

$$\begin{aligned} \mathscr{E}_M &= E[|e(n)|^2] \\ &= E\left[\left|d(n) - \sum_{k=0}^{M-1} h(k)x(n - k)\right|^2\right] \end{aligned} \tag{4.6.2}$$

Since this is a quadratic function of the filter coefficients, the minimization of $\mathscr{E}_M$ yields the set of linear equations

$$\sum_{k=0}^{M-1} h(k)\gamma_{xx}(l-k) = \gamma_{dx}(l), \qquad l = 0, 1, \ldots, M-1 \tag{4.6.3}$$

where $\gamma_{xx}(k)$ is the autocorrelation of the input sequence $x(n)$ and $\gamma_{dx}(k) = E[d(n)x^*(n-k)]$ is the cross-correlation between the desired sequence $d(n)$ and the input sequence, $x(n)$, $0 \le n \le M-1$. This set of linear equations that specify the optimum filter is called the *Wiener–Hopf equation*. These equations are also called the normal equations, which we encountered earlier in this chapter in the context of linear one-step prediction.

In general, the equations in (4.6.3) can be expressed in matrix form as

$$\mathbf{\Gamma}_M \mathbf{h}_M = \boldsymbol{\gamma}_d \tag{4.6.4}$$

where $\mathbf{\Gamma}_M$ is an $M \times M$ (Hermitian) Toeplitz matrix with elements $\Gamma_{lk} = \gamma_{xx}(l-k)$ and $\boldsymbol{\gamma}_d$ is the $M \times 1$ cross-correlation vector with elements $\gamma_{dx}(l)$, $l = 0, 1, \ldots, M-1$. The solution for the optimum filter coefficients is

$$\mathbf{h}_{\text{opt}} = \mathbf{\Gamma}_M^{-1}\boldsymbol{\gamma}_d \tag{4.6.5}$$

and the resulting minimum MSE achieved by the Wiener filter is

$$\text{MMSE}_M = \min_{\mathbf{h}_M} \mathscr{E}_M = \sigma_d^2 - \sum_{k=0}^{M-1} h_{\text{opt}}(k)\gamma_{dx}^*(k) \tag{4.6.6}$$

or equivalently,

$$\text{MMSE}_M = \sigma_d^2 - \boldsymbol{\gamma}_d^{*t}\mathbf{\Gamma}_M^{-1}\boldsymbol{\gamma}_d \tag{4.6.7}$$

where $\sigma_d^2 = E[|d(n)|^2]$.

Let us consider some special cases of (4.6.3). If we are dealing with filtering, $d(n) = s(n)$. Furthermore, if $s(n)$ and $w(n)$ are uncorrelated random sequences, as it is usually the case in practice,

$$\begin{aligned} \gamma_{xx}(k) &= \gamma_{ss}(k) + \gamma_{ww}(k) \\ \gamma_{dx}(k) &= \gamma_{ss}(k) \end{aligned} \tag{4.6.8}$$

and the normal equations in (4.6.3) become

$$\sum_{k=0}^{M-1} h(k)[\gamma_{ss}(l-k) + \gamma_{ww}(l-k)] = \gamma_{ss}(l), \qquad l = 0, 1, \ldots, M-1 \tag{4.6.9}$$

If we are dealing with prediction, then $d(n) = s(n + D)$ where $D > 0$. Assuming that $s(n)$ and $w(n)$ are uncorrelated random sequences, we have

$$\gamma_{dx}(k) = \gamma_{ss}(k + D) \tag{4.6.10}$$

Hence the equations for the Wiener prediction filter become

$$\sum_{k=0}^{M-1} h(k)[\gamma_{ss}(l-k) + \gamma_{ww}(l-k)] = \gamma_{ss}(l + D), \qquad l = 0, 1, \ldots, M-1 \tag{4.6.11}$$

In all these cases, the correlation matrix to be inverted is Toeplitz. Hence the (generalized) Levinson–Durbin algorithm may be used to solve for the optimum filter coefficients.

EXAMPLE 4.6.1

Let us consider a signal $x(n) = s(n) + w(n)$, where $s(n)$ is an AR(1) process that satisfies the difference equation

$$s(n) = 0.6s(n-1) + v(n)$$

where $v(n)$ is a white noise sequence with variance $\sigma_v^2 = 0.64$ and $w(n)$ is a white noise sequence with variance $\sigma_w^2 = 1$. We design a Wiener filter of length $M = 2$ to estimate $s(n)$.

Since $s(n)$ is obtained by exciting a single-pole filter by white noise, the power spectral density of $s(n)$ is

$$\begin{aligned}\Gamma_{ss}(f) &= \sigma_v^2|H(f)|^2\\ &= \frac{0.64}{|1 - 0.6e^{-j2\pi f}|^2}\\ &= \frac{0.64}{1.36 - 1.2\cos 2\pi f}\end{aligned}$$

The corresponding autocorrelation sequence $\gamma_{ss}(m)$ is

$$\gamma_{ss}(m) = (0.6)^{|m|}$$

The equations for the filter coefficients are

$$2h(0) + 0.6h(1) = 1$$

$$0.6h(0) + 2h(1) = 0.6$$

Solution of these equations yields the result

$$h(0) = 0.451, \qquad h(1) = 0.165$$

The corresponding minimum MSE is

$$\begin{aligned}\text{MMSE}_2 &= 1 - h(0)\gamma_{ss}(0) - h(1)\gamma_{ss}(1)\\ &= 1 - 0.451 - (0.165)(0.6)\\ &= 0.45\end{aligned}$$

This error can be reduced further by increasing the length of the Wiener filter (see Problem 4.27).

4.6.2 Orthogonality Principle in Linear Mean-Square Estimation

The normal equations for the optimum filter coefficients given by (4.6.3) can be obtained directly by applying the orthogonality principle in linear mean-square estimation. Simply stated, the mean-square error $\mathscr{E}_M$ in (4.6.2) is a minimum if the filter coefficients $h(k)$ are selected such that the error is orthogonal to each of the data points in the estimate,

$$E[e(n)x^*(n-l)] = 0, \qquad l = 0, 1, \ldots, M-1 \tag{4.6.12}$$

where

$$e(n) = d(n) - \sum_{k=0}^{M-1} h(k)x(n-k) \tag{4.6.13}$$

Conversely, if the filter coefficients satisfy (4.6.12), the resulting MSE is a minimum.

When viewed geometrically, the output of the filter, which is the estimate

$$\hat{d}(n) = \sum_{k=0}^{M-1} h(k)x(n-k) \tag{4.6.14}$$

is a vector in the subspace spanned by the data, $x(k)$, $0 \le k \le M-1$. The error $e(n)$ is a vector from $d(n)$ to $\hat{d}(n)$ [i.e., $d(n) = e(n) + \hat{d}(n)$], as shown in Fig. 4.11. The orthogonality principle states that the length $\mathscr{E}_M = E[|e(n)|^2]$ is a minimum when $e(n)$ is perpendicular to the data subspace [i.e., $e(n)$ is orthogonal to each data point $x(k)$, $0 \le k \le M-1$].

We note that the solution obtained from the normal equations in (4.6.3) is unique if the data $x(n)$ in the estimate $\hat{d}(n)$ are *linearly independent*. In this case the correlation matrix $\mathbf{\Gamma}_M$ is nonsingular. On the other hand, if the data are linearly dependent, the rank of $\mathbf{\Gamma}_M$ is less than M and hence the solution is not unique. In this case the estimate $\hat{d}(n)$ can be expressed as a linear combination of a reduced set of linearly independent data points equal to the rank of $\mathbf{\Gamma}_M$.

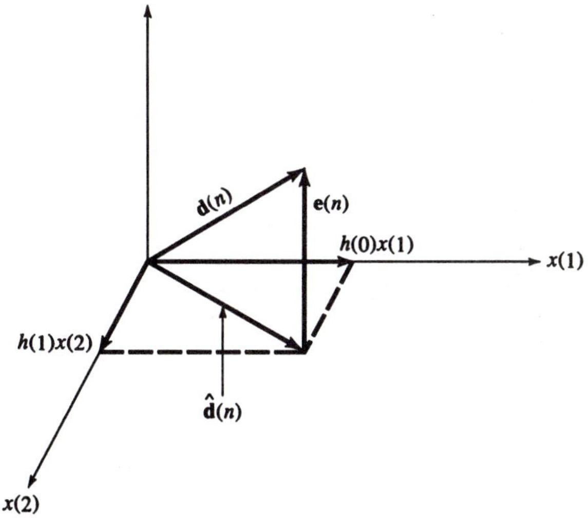

FIGURE 4.11 Geometric interpretation of linear MSE problem.

Since the MSE is minimized by selecting the filter coefficients to satisfy the orthogonality principle, the residual minimum MSE is simply

$$\text{MMSE}_M = E[e(n)d^*(n)] \tag{4.6.15}$$

which yields the result given in (4.6.6).

4.6.3 IIR Wiener Filter

In the preceding section we constrained the filter to be FIR and obtained a set of M linear equations for the optimum filter coefficients. In this section we allow the filter to be infinite in duration (IIR) and the data sequence will also be infinite. Hence the filter output is

$$y(n) = \sum_{k=0}^{\infty} h(k)x(n-k) \tag{4.6.16}$$

The filter coefficients are selected to minimize the mean-square error between the desired output $d(n)$ and $y(n)$,

$$\begin{aligned} \mathscr{E}_\infty &= E[|e(n)|^2] \\ &= E\left[\left|d(n) - \sum_{k=0}^{\infty} h(k)x(n-k)\right|^2\right] \end{aligned} \tag{4.6.17}$$

Application of the orthogonality principle leads to the Wiener–Hopf equation

$$\sum_{k=0}^{\infty} h(k)\gamma_{xx}(l-k) = \gamma_{dx}(l), \qquad l \geq 0 \tag{4.6.18}$$

The residual MMSE is simply obtained by application of the condition given by (4.6.15). Thus we obtain

$$\text{MMSE}_\infty = \min_{\mathbf{h}} \mathscr{E}_\infty = \sigma_d^2 - \sum_{k=0}^{\infty} h_{\text{opt}}(k)\gamma_{dx}^*(k) \tag{4.6.19}$$

The Wiener–Hopf equation given by (4.6.18) cannot be solved directly with z-transform techniques because the equation holds only for $l \geq 0$. We shall solve for the optimum IIR Wiener filter based on the innovations representation of the stationary random process $x(n)$.

Recall that a stationary random process $x(n)$ with autocorrelation $\gamma_{xx}(k)$ and power spectral density $\Gamma_{xx}(f)$ may be represented by an equivalent innovations process $i(n)$ by passing $x(n)$ through a noise-whitening filter with system function $1/G(z)$, where $G(z)$ is the minimum-phase part obtained from the spectral factorization of $\Gamma_{xx}(z)$,

$$\Gamma_{xx}(z) = \sigma_i^2 G(z)G(z^{-1}) \tag{4.6.20}$$

Hence G(z) is analytic in the region $|z| > r_1$, where $r_1 < 1$.

Now, the optimum Wiener filter may be viewed as the cascade of the whitening filter $1/G(z)$ with a second filter, say $Q(z)$, whose output $y(n)$ is identical to the output of the optimum Wiener filter. Since

$$y(n) = \sum_{k=0}^{\infty} q(k)i(n-k) \tag{4.6.21}$$

and $e(n) = d(n) - y(n)$, application of the orthogonality principle yields the new Wiener–Hopf equation as

$$\sum_{k=0}^{\infty} q(k)\gamma_{ii}(l-k) = \gamma_{di}(l), \qquad l \geq 0 \tag{4.6.22}$$

But since $i(n)$ is white, it follows that $\gamma_{ii}(l-k) = 0$, unless $l = k$. Thus we obtain the solution as

$$q(l) = \frac{\gamma_{di}(l)}{\gamma_{ii}(0)} = \frac{\gamma_{di}(l)}{\sigma_i^2}, \qquad l \geq 0 \tag{4.6.23}$$

The z-transform of the sequence $q(l)$ is

$$\begin{aligned} Q(z) &= \sum_{k=0}^{\infty} q(k)z^{-k} \\ &= \frac{1}{\sigma_i^2}\sum_{k=0}^{\infty} \gamma_{di}(k)z^{-k} \end{aligned} \tag{4.6.24}$$

If we denote the z-transform of the two-sided cross-correlation sequence $\gamma_{di}(k)$ by $\Gamma_{di}(z)$,

$$\Gamma_{di}(z) = \sum_{k=-\infty}^{\infty} \gamma_{di}(k)z^{-k} \tag{4.6.25}$$

and define $[\Gamma_{di}(z)]_+$ as

$$[\Gamma_{di}(z)]_+ = \sum_{k=0}^{\infty} \gamma_{di}(k)z^{-k} \tag{4.6.26}$$

then

$$Q(z) = \frac{1}{\sigma_i^2}[\Gamma_{di}(z)]_+ \tag{4.6.27}$$

To determine $[\Gamma_{di}(z)]_+$, we begin with the output of the noise-whitening filter, which may be expressed as

$$i(n) = \sum_{k=0}^{\infty} v(k)x(n-k) \tag{4.6.28}$$

where $v(k)$, $k \geq 0$, is the impulse response of the noise-whitening filter,

$$\frac{1}{G(z)} \equiv V(z) = \sum_{k=0}^{\infty} v(k)z^{-k} \tag{4.6.29}$$

Then

$$\begin{aligned}\gamma_{di}(k) &= E[d(n)i^*(n-k)] \\ &= \sum_{m=0}^{\infty} v(m)E[d(n)x^*(n-m-k)] \\ &= \sum_{m=0}^{\infty} v(m)\gamma_{dx}(k+m)\end{aligned} \tag{4.6.30}$$

The z-transform of the cross-correlation $\gamma_{di}(k)$ is

$$\begin{aligned}\Gamma_{di}(z) &= \sum_{k=-\infty}^{\infty}\left[\sum_{m=0}^{\infty} v(m)\gamma_{dx}(k+m)\right]z^{-k} \\ &= \sum_{m=0}^{\infty} v(m) \sum_{k=-\infty}^{\infty} \gamma_{dx}(k+m)z^{-k} \\ &= \sum_{m=0}^{\infty} v(m)z^{m} \sum_{k=-\infty}^{\infty} \gamma_{dx}(k)z^{-k} \\ &= V(z^{-1})\Gamma_{dx}(z) = \frac{\Gamma_{dx}(z)}{G(z^{-1})}\end{aligned} \tag{4.6.31}$$

Therefore,

$$Q(z) = \frac{1}{\sigma_i^2}\left[\frac{\Gamma_{dx}(z)}{G(z^{-1})}\right]_+ \tag{4.6.32}$$

Finally, the optimum IIR Wiener filter has the system function

$$\begin{aligned}H_{\text{opt}}(z) &= \frac{Q(z)}{G(z)} \\ &= \frac{1}{\sigma_i^2 G(z)}\left[\frac{\Gamma_{dx}(z)}{G(z^{-1})}\right]_+\end{aligned} \tag{4.6.33}$$

In summary, the solution for the optimum IIR Wiener filter requires that we perform a spectral factorization of $\Gamma_{xx}(z)$ to obtain $G(z)$, which is the minimum-phase component, and then we solve for the causal part of $\Gamma_{dx}(z)/G(z^{-1})$. The following example illustrates the procedure.

EXAMPLE 4.6.2

Let us determine the optimum IIR Wiener filter for the signal given in Example 4.6.1. For this signal we have

$$\Gamma_{xx}(z) = \Gamma_{ss}(z) + 1 = \frac{1.8(1-\frac{1}{3}z^{-1})(1-\frac{1}{3}z)}{(1-0.6z^{-1})(1-0.6z)}$$

where $\sigma_i^2 = 1.8$ and

$$G(z) = \frac{1-\frac{1}{3}z^{-1}}{1-0.6z^{-1}}$$

The z-transform of the cross-correlation $\gamma_{dx}(m)$ is

$$\Gamma_{dx}(z) = \Gamma_{ss}(z) = \frac{0.64}{(1 - 0.6z^{-1})(1 - 0.6z)}$$

Hence

$$\left[\frac{\Gamma_{dx}(z)}{G(z^{-1})}\right]_+ = \left[\frac{0.64}{(1 - \frac{1}{3}z)(1 - 0.6z^{-1})}\right]_+$$

$$= \left[\frac{0.8}{1 - 0.6z^{-1}} + \frac{0.266z}{1 - \frac{1}{3}z}\right]_+$$

$$= \frac{0.8}{1 - 0.6z^{-1}}$$

The optimum IIR filter has the system function

$$H_{\text{opt}}(z) = \frac{1}{1.8}\left(\frac{1 - 0.6z^{-1}}{1 - \frac{1}{3}z^{-1}}\right)\left(\frac{0.8}{1 - 0.6z^{-1}}\right)$$

$$= \frac{\frac{4}{9}}{1 - \frac{1}{3}z^{-1}}$$

and an impulse response

$$h_{\text{opt}}(n) = \tfrac{4}{9}(\tfrac{1}{3})^n, \qquad n \geq 0$$

We conclude this section by expressing the minimum MSE given by (4.6.19) in terms of the frequency-domain characteristics of the filter. First we note that $\sigma_d^2 \equiv E[|d(n)|^2]$ is simply the value of the autocorrelation sequence $\gamma_{dd}(k)$ evaluated at $k = 0$. Since

$$\gamma_{dd}(k) = \frac{1}{2\pi j}\oint_C \Gamma_{dd}(z)z^{k-1}\,dz \tag{4.6.34}$$

it follows that

$$\sigma_d^2 = \gamma_{dd}(0) = \frac{1}{2\pi j}\oint_C \frac{\Gamma_{dd}(z)}{z}\,dz \tag{4.6.35}$$

where the contour integral is evaluated along a closed path encircling the origin in the region of convergence of $\Gamma_{dd}(z)$.

The second term in (4.6.19) is also easily transformed to the frequency domain by application of Parseval's theorem. Since $h_{\text{opt}}(k) = 0$ for $k < 0$, we have

$$\sum_{k=-\infty}^{\infty} h_{\text{opt}}(k)\gamma_{dx}^*(k) = \frac{1}{2\pi j}\oint_C H_{\text{opt}}(z)\Gamma_{dx}(z^{-1})z^{-1}\,dz \tag{4.6.36}$$

where C is a closed contour encircling the origin that lies within the common region of convergence of $H_{\text{opt}}(z)\Gamma_{dx}(z^{-1})$.

By combining (4.6.35) with (4.6.36), we obtain the desired expression for the MMSE_∞ in the form

$$\text{MMSE}_\infty = \frac{1}{2\pi j}\oint_C [\Gamma_{dd}(z) - H_{\text{opt}}(z)\Gamma_{dx}(z^{-1})]z^{-1}\,dz \tag{4.6.37}$$

EXAMPLE 4.6.3

For the optimum Wiener derived in Example 4.6.2, the minimum MSE is

$$\text{MMSE}_\infty = \frac{1}{2\pi j}\oint_C \left[\frac{0.3555}{(z - \frac{1}{3})(1 - 0.6z)}\right] dz$$

There is a single pole inside the unit circle at $z = \frac{1}{3}$. By evaluating the residue at the pole, we obtain

$$\text{MMSE}_\infty = 0.444$$

We observe that this MMSE is only slightly smaller than that for the optimum two-tap Wiener filter in Example 4.6.1.

4.6.4 Noncausal Wiener Filter

In the preceding section we constrained the optimum Wiener filter to be causal [i.e., $h_{\text{opt}}(n) = 0$ for $n < 0$]. In this section we drop this condition and allow the filter to include both the infinite past and the infinite future of the sequence $\{x(n)\}$ in forming the output $y(n)$,

$$y(n) = \sum_{k=-\infty}^{\infty} h(k)x(n - k) \tag{4.6.38}$$

The resulting filter is physically unrealizable. It may also be viewed as a *smoothing filter* in which the infinite future signal values are used to smooth the estimate $\hat{d}(n) = y(n)$ of the desired signal $d(n)$.

Application of the orthogonality principle yields the Wiener–Hopf equation for the noncausal filter in the form

$$\sum_{k=-\infty}^{\infty} h(k)\gamma_{xx}(l - k) = \gamma_{dx}(l), \qquad -\infty < l < \infty \tag{4.6.39}$$

and the resulting MMSE_{nc} as

$$\text{MMSE}_{\text{nc}} = \sigma_d^2 - \sum_{k=-\infty}^{\infty} h(k)\gamma_{dx}^*(k) \tag{4.6.40}$$

Since (4.6.39) holds for $-\infty < l < -\infty$, this equation can be transformed directly to yield the optimum noncausal Wiener filter as

$$H_{\text{nc}}(z) = \frac{\Gamma_{dx}(z)}{\Gamma_{xx}(z)} \tag{4.6.41}$$

The MMSE_{nc} can also be simply expressed in the z-domain as

$$\text{MMSE}_{\text{nc}} = \frac{1}{2\pi j}\oint_C [\Gamma_{dd}(z) - H_{\text{nc}}(z)\Gamma_{dx}(z^{-1})]z^{-1}\,dz \qquad (4.6.42)$$

The following example serves to compare the form of the optimal noncausal filter with the optimal causal filter obtained in the preceding section.

EXAMPLE 4.6.4

The optimum noncausal Wiener filter for the signal characteristics given in Example 4.6.1 is given by (4.6.41), where

$$\Gamma_{dx}(z) = \Gamma_{ss}(z) = \frac{0.64}{(1 - 0.6z^{-1})(1 - 0.6z)}$$

and

$$\begin{aligned}\Gamma_{xx}(z) &= \Gamma_{ss}(z) + 1 \\ &= \frac{2(1 - 0.3z^{-1} - 0.3z)}{(1 - 0.6z^{-1})(1 - 0.6z)}\end{aligned}$$

Then

$$H_{\text{nc}}(z) = \frac{0.3555}{(1 - \frac{1}{3}z^{-1})(1 - \frac{1}{3}z)}$$

This filter is clearly noncausal.

The minimum MSE achieved by this filter is determined from evaluating (4.6.42). The integrand is

$$\frac{1}{z}\Gamma_{ss}(z)\,[1 - H_{\text{nc}}(z)] = \frac{0.3555}{(z - \frac{1}{3})(1 - \frac{1}{3}z)}$$

The only pole inside the unit circle is $z = \frac{1}{3}$. Hence the residue is

$$\left.\frac{0.3555}{1 - \frac{1}{3}z}\right|_{z=1/3} = \frac{0.3555}{\frac{8}{9}} = 0.40$$

Hence the minimum-achievable MSE obtained with the optimum noncausal Wiener filter is

$$\text{MMSE}_{\text{nc}} = 0.40$$

Note that this is lower than the MMSE for the causal filter, as expected.

4.7 SUMMARY AND REFERENCES

The major focal point in this chapter was the design of optimum linear systems for linear prediction and filtering. The criterion for optimality was the minimization of the mean-square error between a specified desired filter output and the actual filter output.

In the development of linear prediction we demonstrated that the equations for the forward and backward prediction errors specified a lattice filter whose parameters, the reflection coefficients K_m, were simply related to the filter coefficients $a_m(k)$ of the direct-form FIR linear predictor and the associated prediction error filter. The optimum filter coefficients K_m and $a_m(k)$ are obtained easily from the solution of the normal equations.

We described two computationally efficient algorithms for solving the normal equations, the Levinson–Durbin algorithm and the Schur algorithm. Both algorithms are suitable for solving a Toeplitz system of linear equations and have a computational complexity of $O(p^2)$ when executed on a single processor. However, with full parallel processing, the Schur algorithm solves the normal equations in $O(p)$ time, whereas the Levinson–Durbin algorithm requires $O(p \log p)$ time.

In addition to the all-zero lattice filter which resulted from linear prediction, we also derived the AR lattice (all-pole) filter structure and the ARMA lattice-ladder (pole–zero) filter structure. Finally, we described the design of the class of optimum linear filters, called Wiener filters.

Linear estimation theory has had a long and rich history of development over the past four decades. Kailath (1974) presents a historical account of the first three decades. The pioneering work of Wiener (1949) on optimum linear filtering for statistically stationary signals is especially significant. The generalization of the Wiener filter theory to dynamical systems with random inputs was developed by Kalman (1960) and Kalman and Bury (1961). Kalman filters are treated in the books by Meditch (1969), Brown (1983), and Chui and Chen (1987). The monograph by Kailath (1981) treats both Wiener and Kalman filters.

There are numerous references on linear prediction and lattice filters. Tutorial treatments on these subjects have been published in the journal papers by Makhoul (1975, 1978), and Friedlander (1982). The books by Haykin (1991), Markel and Gray (1976), and Tretter (1976) provide comprehensive treatments of these subjects. Applications of linear prediction to spectral analysis are found in the books by Kay (1988) and Marple (1987), to geophysics in the book Robinson and Treitel (1980), and to adaptive filtering in the book by Haykin (1991).

The Levinson–Durbin algorithm for solving the normal equations recursively was given by Levinson (1947) and later modified by Durbin (1959). Variations of this classical algorithm, called *split-Levinson algorithms,* have been developed by Delsarte and Genin (1986) and by Krishna (1988). These algorithms exploit additional symmetries in the Toeplitz correlation matrix and save about a factor of 2 in the number of multiplications.

The Schur algorithm was originally described by Schur (1917) in a paper published in German. An English translation of this paper appears in the book edited by Gohberg (1986). The Schur algorithm is intimately related to the polynomials $A_m(z)$, which may be interpreted as orthogonal polynomials. A treatment of orthogonal polynomials is given in the books by Szegö

(1958), Grenander and Szegö (1958), and Geronimus (1958). The thesis of Vieira (1977) and the papers by Kailath, Vieira, and Morf (1978), Delsarte, Genin, and Kamp (1980), and Youla and Kazanjian (1978) provide additional results on orthogonal polynomials. Kailath (1985, 1986) provides tutorial treatments of the Schur algorithm and its relationship to orthogonal polynomials and the Levinson–Durbin algorithm. The pipelined parallel processing structure for computing the reflection coefficients based on the Schur algorithm and the related problem of solving Toeplitz systems of linear equations is described in the paper by Kung and Hu (1983). Finally, we should mention that some additional computational efficiency can be achieved in the Schur algorithm, by further exploiting symmetry properties of Toeplitz matrices, as described by Krishna (1988). This leads to the so-called split-Schur algorithm, which is analogous to the split-Levinson algorithm.

PROBLEMS

4.1 The power density spectrum of an AR process $x(n)$ is given as

$$\Gamma_{xx}(\omega) = \frac{\sigma_w^2}{|A(\omega)|^2} = \frac{25}{|1 - e^{-j\omega} + \frac{1}{2}e^{-j2\omega}|^2}$$

where σ_w^2 is the variance of the input sequence.

(a) Determine the difference equation for generating the AR process when the excitation is white noise.

(b) Determine the system function for the whitening filter.

4.2 An ARMA process has an autocorrelation $\gamma_{xx}(m)$ whose z-transform is given as

$$\Gamma_{xx}(z) = 9\frac{(z - \frac{1}{3})(z - 3)}{(z - \frac{1}{2})(z - 2)}, \qquad \tfrac{1}{2} < |z| < 2$$

(a) Determine the filter $H(z)$ for generating $x(n)$ from a white noise input sequence. Is $H(z)$ unique? Explain.

(b) Determine a stable linear whitening filter for the sequence $x(n)$.

4.3 Consider the ARMA process generated by the difference equation

$$x(n) = 1.6x(n-1) - 0.63x(n-2) + w(n) + 0.9w(n-1)$$

(a) Determine the system function of the whitening filter and its poles and zeros.

(b) Determine the power density spectrum of $x(n)$.

4.4 Determine the lattice coefficients corresponding to the FIR filter with system function

$$H(z) = A_3(z) = 1 + \tfrac{13}{24}z^{-1} + \tfrac{5}{8}z^{-2} + \tfrac{1}{3}z^{-3}$$

4.5 Determine the reflection coefficients K_m of the lattice filter corresponding to the FIR filter described by the system function

$$H(z) = A_2(z) = 1 + 2z^{-1} + \tfrac{1}{3}z^{-2}$$

4.6 **(a)** Determine the zeros and sketch the zero pattern for the FIR lattice filter with reflection coefficients

$$K_1 = \tfrac{1}{2}, \qquad K_2 = -\tfrac{1}{3}, \qquad K_3 = 1$$

(b) Repeat part (a) but with $K_3 = -1$.

(c) You should have found that the zeros lie on the unit circle. Can this result be generalized? Explain.

4.7 Determine the impulse response of the FIR filter that is described by the lattice coefficients $K_1 = 0.6$, $K_2 = 0.3$, $K_3 = 0.5$, and $K_4 = 0.9$.

4.8 In Section 4.2.4 we indicated that the noise-whitening filter $A_p(z)$ for a causal AR(p) process is a forward linear prediction-error filter of order p. Show that the backward linear prediction-error filter of order p is the noise-whitening filter of the corresponding anticausal AR(p) process.

4.9 Use the orthogonality principle to determine the normal equations and the resulting minimum MSE for a forward predictor of order p that predicts m samples ($m > 1$) into the future (m-step forward predictor). Sketch the prediction error filter.

4.10 Repeat Problem 4.9 for an m-step backward predictor.

4.11 Determine a Levinson–Durbin recursive algorithm for solving for the coefficients of a backward prediction-error filter. Use the result obtained to show that coefficients of the forward and backward predictors may be expressed recursively as

$$\mathbf{a}_m = \begin{bmatrix} \mathbf{a}_{m-1} \\ 0 \end{bmatrix} + K_m \begin{bmatrix} \mathbf{b}_{m-1} \\ 1 \end{bmatrix}$$

$$\mathbf{b}_m = \begin{bmatrix} \mathbf{b}_{m-1} \\ 0 \end{bmatrix} + K_m^* \begin{bmatrix} \mathbf{a}_{m-1} \\ 1 \end{bmatrix}$$

4.12 The Levinson–Durbin algorithm described in Section 4.3.1 solved the linear equations

$$\mathbf{\Gamma}_m \mathbf{a}_m = -\boldsymbol{\gamma}_m$$

where the right-hand side of this equation has elements of the autocorrelation sequence that are also elements of the matrix $\mathbf{\Gamma}_m$. Let us consider the more general problem of solving the linear equations

$$\mathbf{\Gamma}_m \mathbf{b}_m = \mathbf{c}_m$$

where $\mathbf{c}_m$ is an arbitrary vector. (The vector $\mathbf{b}_m$ is *not* related to the coefficients of the backward predictor.) Show that the solution to

$\mathbf{\Gamma}_m \mathbf{b}_m = \mathbf{c}_m$ can be obtained from a *generalized Levinson–Durbin* algorithm which is given recursively as

$$b_m(m) = \frac{c(m) - \boldsymbol{\gamma}_{m-1}^{bt} \mathbf{b}_{m-1}}{E_{m-1}^f}$$

$$b_m(k) = b_{m-1}(k) - b_m(m) a_{m-1}^*(m-k), \qquad \begin{aligned} k &= 1, 2, \ldots, m-1 \\ m &= 1, 2, \ldots, p \end{aligned}$$

where $b_1(1) = c(1)/\gamma_{xx}(0) = c(1)/E_0^f$ and $a_m(k)$ is given by (4.3.17). Thus a second recursion is required to solve the equation $\mathbf{\Gamma}_m \mathbf{b}_m = \mathbf{c}_m$.

4.13 Use the generalized Levinson–Durbin algorithm to solve the normal equations recursively for the m-step forward and backward predictors.

4.14 Show that the transformation

$$V_m = \begin{bmatrix} 1 & K_m \\ K_m^* & 1 \end{bmatrix}$$

in the Schur algorithm satisfies the special property

$$\mathbf{V}_m \mathbf{J} \mathbf{V}_m^t = \mathbf{J}$$

where

$$\mathbf{J} = \begin{bmatrix} 1 & 0 \\ 0 & -1 \end{bmatrix}$$

Thus $\mathbf{V}_m$ is called a *J-rotation matrix*. Its role is to rotate or hyperbolate the row of $\mathbf{G}_m$ to lie along the first coordinate direction [Kailath (1985)].

4.15 Prove the additional properties (a) through (l) of the prediction-error filters given in Section 4.4.

4.16 Extend the additional properties (a) through (l) of the prediction-error filters given in Section 4.4 to complex-valued signals.

4.17 Determine the reflection coefficient K_3 in terms of the autocorrelations $\gamma_{xx}(m)$ from the Schur algorithm and compare your result with the expression for K_3 obtained from the Levinson–Durbin algorithm.

4.18 Consider an infinite-length ($p = \infty$) one-step forward predictor for a stationary random process $x(n)$ with power density spectrum $\Gamma_{xx}(f)$. Show that the mean-square error of the prediction-error filter may be expressed as

$$E_\infty^f = 2\pi \exp\left\{ \int_{-1/2}^{1/2} \ln \Gamma_{xx}(f)\, df \right\}$$

4.19 Determine the output of an infinite-length ($p = \infty$) m-step forward predictor and the resulting mean-square error when the input signal is a first-order autoregressive process of the form

$$x(n) = ax(n-1) + w(n)$$

4.20 An AR(3) process $x(n)$ is characterized by the autocorrelation sequence $\gamma_{xx}(0) = 1$, $\gamma_{xx}(1) = \frac{1}{2}$, $\gamma_{xx}(2) = \frac{1}{8}$, and $\gamma_{xx}(3) = \frac{1}{64}$.

(a) Use the Schur algorithm to determine the three reflection coefficients K_1, K_2, and K_3.

(b) Sketch the lattice filter for synthesizing $x(n)$ from a white noise excitation.

4.21 The purpose of this problem is to show that the polynomials $A_m(z)$, which are the system functions of the forward prediction-error filters of order m, $m = 0, 1, \ldots, p$, may be interpreted as orthogonal on the unit circle. Toward this end, suppose that $\Gamma_{xx}(f)$ is the power spectral density of a zero-mean random process $x(n)$ and let $A_m(z)$, $m = 0, 1, \ldots, p$, be the system functions of the corresponding prediction-error filters. Show that the polynomials $A_m(z)$ satisfy the orthogonality property

$$\int_{-1/2}^{1/2} \Gamma_{xx}(f) A_m(f) A_n^*(f)\, df = E_m^f \delta_{mn}, \qquad m, n = 0, 1, \ldots, p$$

4.22 Determine the system function of the all-pole filter that is described by the lattice coefficients $K_1 = 0.6$, $K_2 = 0.3$, $K_3 = 0.5$, and $K_4 = 0.9$.

4.23 Determine the parameters and sketch the lattice-ladder filter structure for the system with system function

$$H(z) = \frac{1 - 0.8z^{-1} + 0.15z^{-2}}{1 + 0.1z^{-1} - 0.72z^{-2}}$$

4.24 Consider a signal $x(n) = s(n) + w(n)$, where $s(n)$ is an AR(1) process that satisfies the difference equation

$$s(n) = 0.8s(n - 1) + v(n)$$

where $v(n)$ is a white noise sequence with variance $\sigma_v^2 = 0.49$ and $w(n)$ is a white noise sequence with variance $\sigma_w^2 = 1$. The processes $v(n)$ and $w(n)$ are uncorrelated.

(a) Determine the autocorrelation sequences $\gamma_{ss}(m)$ and $\gamma_{xx}(m)$.

(b) Design a Wiener filter of length $M = 2$ to estimate $s(n)$.

(c) Determine the MMSE for $M = 2$.

4.25 Determine the optimum causal IIR Wiener filter for the signal given in Problem 4.24 and the corresponding MMSE_∞.

4.26 Determine the system function for the noncausal IIR Wiener filter for the signal given in Problem 4.24 and the corresponding MMSE_{nc}.

4.27 Determine the optimum FIR Wiener of length $M = 3$ for the signal in Example 4.6.1 and the corresponding MMSE_3. Compare MMSE_3 with MMSE_2 and comment on the difference.

4.28 An AR(2) process is defined by the difference equation

$$x(n) = x(n-1) - 0.6x(n-2) + w(n)$$

where $\{w(n)\}$ is a white noise process with variance σ_w^2. Use the Yule–Walker equations to solve for the values of the autocorrelation $\gamma_{xx}(0)$, $\gamma_{xx}(1)$, and $\gamma_{xx}(2)$.

4.29 An observed random process $x(n)$ consists of the sum of an AR(p) process of the form

$$s(n) = -\sum_{k=1}^{p} a_p(k)s(n-k) + v(n)$$

and a white noise process $w(n)$ with variance σ_w^2. The random process $v(n)$ is also white with variance σ_v^2. The sequences $v(n)$ and $w(n)$ are uncorrelated. Show that the observed process $x(n) = s(n) + w(n)$ is ARMA(p,p) and determine the coefficients of the numerator polynomial (MA component) in the corresponding system function.

CHAPTER 5

LEAST-SQUARES METHODS FOR SYSTEM MODELING AND FILTER DESIGN

Least-squares methods find widespread use in all scientific disciplines where data are obtained by measurement of some physical process. In this chapter we apply the least-squares method in estimation of the parameters of linear system models for unknown systems. Thus a linear system model with a finite set of parameters is postulated for the unknown system and the least-squares method is used to estimate the model parameters. This is a problem in *system identification*.

Least-squares methods also find use in another class of practical problems in which we are given an output signal from a system whose characteristics are unknown and we are asked to determine the input signal. For example, in the transmission of digital information at high data rates over telephone channels, it is well known that the channel distorts the signal and causes intersymbol interference among the data symbols. The intersymbol interference may cause errors when we attempt to recover the data. If the data are transmitted over the direct-dial network, the channel characteristics that cause the distortion vary considerably from one telephone call to another. Therefore, it is appropriate to assume that the channel, which is well modeled as a linear system, is unknown to the receiver that must recover the digital information. In such a case the problem is to design a corrective system which, when cascaded with the original system, produces an output that, in some sense, corrects for the distortion caused by the channel and thus yields a replica of the desired transmitted signal. In digital communications such a corrective system is called an *equalizer*. In the general context of linear systems theory, however, we call the corrective system an *inverse system,* because it has a frequency response that is basically the reciprocal of the frequency response of the system that caused the distortion. Furthermore, since the distortive system yields an output $y(n)$ that is the convolution of the input $x(n)$ with the impulse response $h(n)$, the operation that takes $y(n)$ and produces $x(n)$ is called *deconvolution*.

The term *deconvolution* is often used in seismic signal processing and, more generally, in geophysics to describe the operation of separating the input signal from the characteristics of the system that are being measured.

The deconvolution operation is actually intended to identify the characteristics of the system, in this case the earth. The "inverse system" in this case has a frequency response that is the reciprocal of the input signal spectrum that has been used to excite the system.

System modeling and system identification are treated in Section 5.1. The use of least-squares methods in the design of linear predictive filters and FIR inverse filters for deconvolution are described in Section 5.2. Finally, in Section 5.3 we present several different methods for solving least-squares estimation problems.

5.1 SYSTEM MODELING AND IDENTIFICATION

Suppose that we have a linear time-invariant system whose characteristics are unknown. By probing the system with an input sequence $x(n)$ and observing the output sequence $y(n)$, we wish to determine its time-domain or frequency-domain characteristics. This is a problem in *system identification*.

We shall constrain the system identification problem further by modeling the unknown system either as an all-zero filter, an all-pole filter, or as a system containing both poles and zeros. Then the problem reduces to estimating the parameters of the model. These models are called MA, AR, and ARMA models, respectively, which is consistent with the terminology introduced in Chapter 4. We shall use the method of least squares for performing parameter estimation and thus system identification.

5.1.1 System Identification Based on FIR (MA) System Model

Let us begin with an FIR or MA(q) model for an unknown system $H(z)$. The model has a system function

$$\hat{H}(z) = \sum_{k=0}^{q} b_k z^{-k} \tag{5.1.1}$$

Both the unknown system and the model are excited by the same input sequence $x(n)$, as shown in Fig. 5.1. Let $y(n)$ be the observed output of the unknown system and $\hat{y}(n)$ be the output for the model.

$$\hat{y}(n) = \sum_{k=0}^{q} b_k x(n-k), \qquad n = 1, 2, \ldots, N \tag{5.1.2}$$

where $N \gg q$.

The difference between the output $y(n)$ of the unknown system and the output $\hat{y}(n)$ of the model is defined as the error sequence, $e(n)$. In the method of least squares, the parameters b_k of the model are selected to minimize the sum of the squared-error sequence $e(n)$,

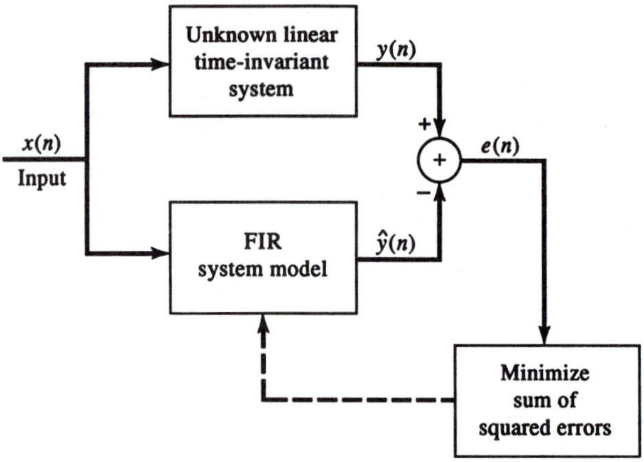

FIGURE 5.1 System identification based on FIR system model.

$$\begin{aligned}\mathscr{E}(q) &= \sum_{n=1}^{N} |e(n)|^2 \\ &= \sum_{n=1}^{N} \left| y(n) - \sum_{k=0}^{q} b_k x(n-k) \right|^2\end{aligned} \tag{5.1.3}$$

By differentiating $\mathscr{E}(q)$ with respect to each of the model coefficients, we obtain the set of linear equations

$$\sum_{k=0}^{q} b_k r_{xx}(l-k) = r_{yx}(l), \qquad l = 0, 1, \ldots, q \tag{5.1.4}$$

where, by definition,

$$r_{xx}(l, k) = \sum_{n=1}^{N} x(n-k)x^*(n-l) = r_{xx}(l-k) \tag{5.1.5}$$

$$r_{yx}(l) = \sum_{n=1}^{N} y(n)x^*(n-l) \tag{5.1.6}$$

The reader should note that (5.1.4) is identical in form to the Wiener–Hopf equation for the optimum FIR Wiener filter given by (4.6.3).

The minimum (least-squares) error is

$$\mathscr{E}_{\min}(q) = \sum_{n=1}^{N} |y(n)|^2 - \sum_{k=0}^{q} b_k r_{yx}^*(k) \tag{5.1.7}$$

The optimum filter model parameters b_k can be determined for different filter lengths q, and the resulting minimum error $\mathscr{E}_{\min}(q)$ can be computed and used as a criterion for selecting an appropriate filter length.

The least-squares optimization problem can be formulated in matrix form as follows. From (5.1.3) we have the error $e(n)$ expressed as

$$e(n) = y(n) - \sum_{k=0}^{q} b_k x(n-k), \qquad n = 1, 2, \ldots, N \tag{5.1.8}$$

We define the N-dimensional vector $\mathbf{e}$ as $\mathbf{e} = [e(1), e(2), \ldots, e(N)]^t$, the output vector $\mathbf{y}$ as $\mathbf{y} = [y(1), y(2), \ldots, y(N)]^t$, the coefficient vector $\mathbf{b}$ as $\mathbf{b} = [b_0, b_1, \ldots, b_q]^t$, and an $N \times (q + 1)$ input data matrix $\mathbf{X}$ as

$$\mathbf{X} = \begin{bmatrix} x(1) & 0 & \cdots\cdots & 0 \\ x(2) & x(1) & 0 \;\cdots & 0 \\ \vdots & \vdots & \vdots & \vdots \\ x(q+1) & x(q) & \cdots\cdots & x(1) \\ \vdots & \vdots & & \vdots \\ x(N) & x(N-1) & \cdots\cdots & X(N-q) \end{bmatrix} \tag{5.1.9}$$

Then (5.1.8) may be expressed in matrix form as

$$\mathbf{e} = \mathbf{y} - \mathbf{X}\mathbf{b} \tag{5.1.10}$$

The least-squares optimization involves the minimization of $\mathscr{E}(q)$,

$$\mathscr{E}(q) = \mathbf{e}^H\mathbf{e} = (\mathbf{y} - \mathbf{X}\mathbf{b})^H(\mathbf{y} - \mathbf{X}\mathbf{b}) \tag{5.1.11}$$

which yields the result

$$\mathbf{b} = (\mathbf{X}^H\mathbf{X})^{-1}\mathbf{X}^H\mathbf{y} \tag{5.1.12}$$

The resulting least-squares error is

$$\mathscr{E}_{\min}(q) = \mathbf{y}^H\mathbf{y} - \mathbf{y}^H\mathbf{X}\mathbf{b} \tag{5.1.13}$$

The exponent H denotes the conjugate transpose (Hermitian) of the vector or matrix. We note that $\mathbf{X}^H\mathbf{X}$ corresponds to the autocorrelation matrix of the data with elements given by (5.1.5) and $\mathbf{X}^H\mathbf{y}$ corresponds to a cross-correlation vector with elements given by (5.1.6). In fact, we may define the data autocorrelation matrix as $\mathbf{R}_{xx} = \mathbf{X}^H\mathbf{X}$ and the data cross-correlation vector as $\mathbf{r}_{yx} = \mathbf{X}^H\mathbf{y}$. Then the least-squares solution given by (5.1.12) may be expressed as $\mathbf{b} = \mathbf{R}_{xx}^{-1}\mathbf{r}_{yx}$.

Given the input data sequence $x(n)$ and the observed output sequence $y(n)$, the least-squares solution for the model coefficients can be obtained numerically by one of the methods described in Section 5.3.

An extension of this problem formulation is to consider sequential estimation of the model parameters as additional data become available. For example, suppose that we have estimated the model parameters on the basis of data received up to time n, and let us denote the optimal least-squares estimate as $\mathbf{b}(n)$. Now suppose that new data $[x(n + 1)]$ have been observed. How can we efficiently update this estimate recursively so that the new coefficient vector $\mathbf{b}(n + 1)$ is the least-squares estimate, based on the data record $[x(k), y(k), 0 \leq k \leq n + 1]$? This is a problem that falls in the broad category of adaptive filtering (or adaptive system identification) and its solution leads to recursive least-squares (RLS) estimation, which is described in Chapters 6 and 7.

5.1.2 System Identification Based on an All-Pole (AR) System Model

Let us take as the model for the unknown system an all-pole filter of the form

$$\hat{H}(z) = \frac{b_0}{1 + \sum_{k=1}^{p} a_k z^{-k}} \tag{5.1.14}$$

Of course, the unknown system may differ from the model. The problem is to estimate the parameters b_0 and a_k of this model.

Suppose that we place an FIR system with system function $1/\hat{H}(z)$ in cascade with the unknown system, as shown in Fig. 5.2. If the unknown system is indeed all-pole, the cascade of the two systems results in an identity system.

Now suppose that the unknown system is excited by an arbitrary (nonzero) sequence $x(n)$, and let $y(n)$ denote its response. Then the output of the inverse system is

$$\begin{aligned}\hat{x}(n) &= \frac{1}{b_0}\left[y(n) + \sum_{k=1}^{p} a_k y(n-k)\right] \\ &= \sum_{k=0}^{p} a'_k y(n-k), \qquad n = 1, 2, \ldots, N\end{aligned} \tag{5.1.15}$$

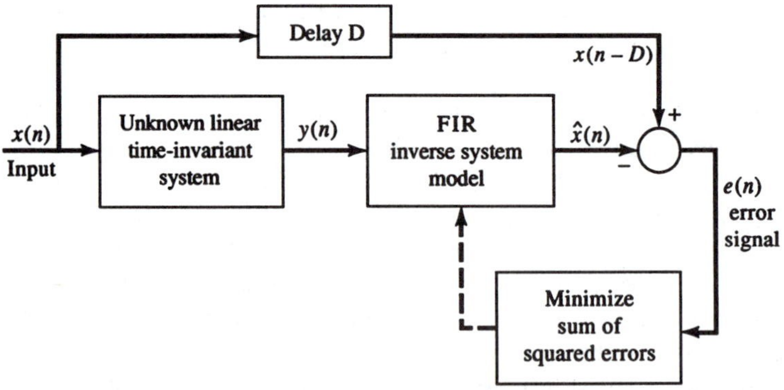

FIGURE 5.2 System identification based on an all-pole system model.

where $N \gg p$ and, by definition,

$$a'_k = \begin{cases} \dfrac{1}{b_0}, & k = 0 \\ \dfrac{a_k}{b_0}, & 1 \le k \le p \end{cases} \tag{5.1.16}$$

The difference between the desired output $x(n)$ and the actual output $\hat{x}(n)$ constitutes the error $e(n)$, which may be minimized in the least-squares sense. It may also be desirable to introduce a delay, say D, in the desired signal to account for a nominal delay in the signal through the cascade of the unknown system and the inverse system. Hence we minimize

$$\begin{aligned} \mathscr{E}(p,D) &= \sum_{n=1}^{N} |x(n-D) - \hat{x}(n)|^2 \\ &= \sum_{n=1}^{N} \Big|x(n-D) - \sum_{k=0}^{p} a'_k y(n-k)\Big|^2 \end{aligned} \tag{5.1.17}$$

with respect to the filter coefficients a'_k.

The differentiation of $\mathscr{E}(p,D)$ results in the set of linear equations

$$\sum_{k=0}^{p} a'_k r_{yy}(l-k) = r_{xy}(l-D), \qquad l = 1, 2, \ldots, p \tag{5.1.18}$$

where, by definition,

$$r_{yy}(l-k) = \sum_{n=1}^{N} y(n-k)y^*(n-l) \tag{5.1.19}$$

$$r_{xy}(l) = \sum_{n=1}^{N} x(n)y^*(n-l) \tag{5.1.20}$$

This set of linear equations is similar in form to the set given in (5.1.14).

The minimum (least-squares) error is

$$\mathscr{E}_{\min}(p,D) = \sum_{n=1}^{N} |x(n-D)|^2 - \sum_{k=0}^{p} a'_k r^*_{xy}(k-D) \tag{5.1.21}$$

By solving (5.1.18) for different values of D and substituting the resulting optimum coefficients a'_k in (5.1.21), we can determine an appropriate value of the delay for a given choice of filter length p. The length of the inverse filter can also be selected by solving (5.1.18) for different values of p and using (5.1.21) as a criterion for selecting an appropriate value for p.

Finally, we should indicate that the least-squares estimation of the model parameters a_k can also be formulated in matrix form, and the resulting least-squares solution has the general form given by (5.1.12).

As in the case of the FIR model, we can consider extending the least-squares estimation problem to sequential estimation of the model parameters as new data become available. Such an extension leads to recursive least-squares methods for estimating the model parameters and is described in general in Chapters 6 and 7.

5.1.3 System Identification Based on Pole–Zero (ARMA) System Model

Now, let us consider a pole–zero model for an unknown system of the form

$$\hat{H}(z) = \frac{\sum_{k=0}^{q} b_k z^{-k}}{1 + \sum_{k=1}^{p} a_k z^{-k}} \tag{5.1.22}$$

$$= \sum_{k=0}^{\infty} h(k) z^{-k} \tag{5.1.23}$$

where $h(k)$ is its unit sample response. The model has $p + q + 1$ parameters, namely, the coefficients a_k and b_k.

If the unknown system is excited by the input sequence $x(n)$, its response is the sequence $y(n)$. If we attempt to use the least-squares method to optimize the model parameters, we find that the optimization leads to a set of nonlinear equations, which, in general, are difficult to solve. As an alternative we consider several suboptimum methods that yield tractable solutions.

The first method that we consider is not based on the least-squares method. Instead, it is based on exact matching of the impulse response of the unknown system to that of the model.

Padé Approximation Method. Suppose that we excite the unknown system and the model by an impulse [i.e., $x(n) = \delta(n)$]. Let the response of the unknown system be $h_d(n)$, the desired impulse response. In this case the response of the model is

$$y(n) = h(n) = -\sum_{k=1}^{p} a_k h(n-k) + \sum_{k=1}^{q} b_k \delta(n-k), \qquad n \geq 0 \tag{5.1.24}$$

Since $\delta(n - k) = 0$, except at $n = k$, (5.1.24) may be expressed as

$$h(n) = -\sum_{k=1}^{p} a_k h(n-k) + b_n, \qquad 0 \leq n \leq q \tag{5.1.25}$$

$$h(n) = -\sum_{k=1}^{p} a_k h(n-k), \qquad n > q \tag{5.1.26}$$

The two sets of equations in (5.1.25) and (5.1.26) can be used to solve for the model parameters by exactly matching the impulse response of the model to that of the unknown system for $0 \leq n \leq p + q$. Beginning with (5.1.26), we set $h(n) = h_d(n)$ for $q < n < q + p$ and solve for the a_k. Then we set $h(n) = h_d(n)$ for $0 \leq n \leq q$ and solve (5.1.25) for the b_k. Thus we have obtained estimates of the parameters a_k and b_k by exactly matching the model impulse response to that of the unknown system for $0 \leq n \leq q + p$. Hence the error $e(n) = h_d(n) - h(n) = 0$ for $0 \leq n \leq q + p$. This design technique is usually called the *Padé approximation procedure*.

EXAMPLE 5.1.1

Suppose that the unknown system is a fourth-order Butterworth filter with system function

$$H_d(z) = \frac{4.8334 \times 10^{-3}(z + 1)^4}{(z^2 - 1.3205z + 0.6326)(z^2 - 1.0482z + 0.2959)}$$

The unit sample response corresponding to $H_d(z)$ is shown in Fig. 5.3. Let us use the Padé approximation method to approximate $H_d(z)$.

Solution: We observe that the system has $q = 4$ zeros and $p = 4$ poles. It is instructive to determine the coefficients of the model when the number of zeros and/or poles in the model is different from $H_d(z)$.

In Fig. 5.4 we plot the frequency response of the model with parameters obtained by the Padé approximation method. We have considered four cases for the model: $q = 3, p = 5$; $q = 3, p = 4$; $q = 4, p = 4, q = 4$; $p = 5$. We observe that when $q = 3$, the resulting frequency response is a relatively poor approximation to the desired response. However, an increase in the number of poles from $p = 4$ to $p = 5$ appears to

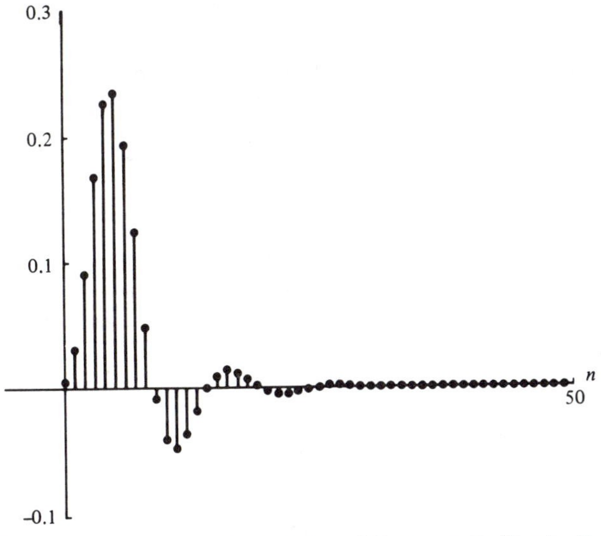

FIGURE 5.3 Impulse response $h_d(n)$ of digital Butterworth filter in Example 5.1.1.

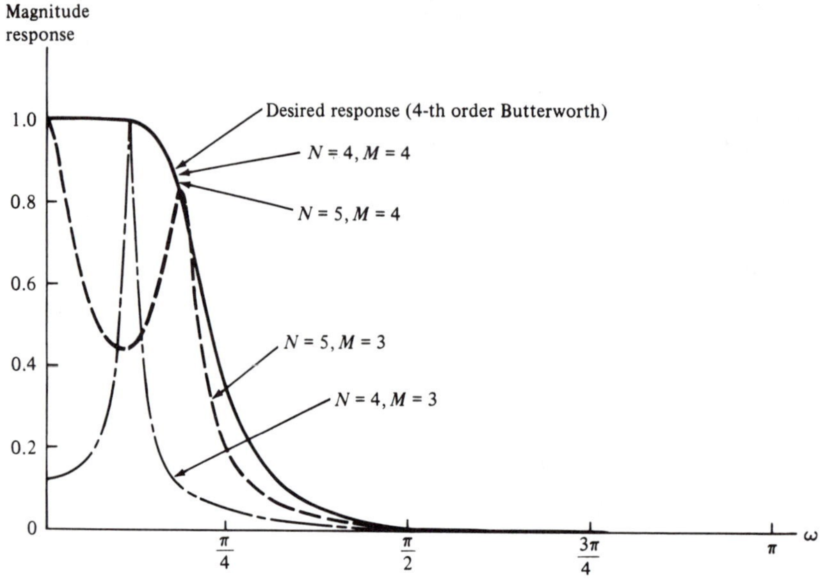

FIGURE 5.4 Filter designs based on Pade approximation (Example 5.1.1).

compensate in part for the lack of the one zero. When q is increased from three to four, we obtain a perfect match with $H_d(z)$, not only for $p = 4$ but for $p = 5$.

The degree to which the Padé approximation method produces an acceptable match to the unknown system depends in part on the number of filter coefficients that are selected. Since the design method matches $h_d(n)$ only up to the number of model parameters, the more complex the model, the better the approximation to $h_d(n)$, for $0 \leq n \leq p + q$. However, this is also the major limitation with the Padé approximation method; namely, the model must contain a large number of poles and zeros. For this reason the Padé approximation method has found limited use in practice.

Prony's Method. The least-squares method can be used to identify the pole parameters a_k of the model. Suppose that we observe $h_d(n)$ by exciting the unknown system by $x(n) = \delta(n)$. Then we may use linear prediction to form the estimate

$$\hat{h}_d(n) = -\sum_{k=1}^{p} a_k h_d(n-k), \qquad n > q \tag{5.1.27}$$

as illustrated in Fig. 5.5. Then, for $n > q$, we may select the pole parameters a_k that minimize the least-squares error

$$\mathscr{E}(p,q) = \sum_{n=q+1}^{N} [h_d(n) - \hat{h}_d(n)]^2 = \sum_{n=q+1}^{N} \left[h_d(n) + \sum_{k=1}^{p} a_k h_d(n-k) \right]^2 \tag{5.1.28}$$

where N is selected to satisfy the condition $N \gg p$. The minimization of $\mathscr{E}(p,q)$ with respect to the pole parameters a_k leads to the set of linear equations

$$\sum_{k=1}^{p} a_k r_{dd}(k,l) = -r_{dd}(k,0), \qquad l = 1, 2, \ldots, p \tag{5.1.29}$$

where $r_{dd}(k,l)$ is defined as

$$r_{dd}(k,l) = \sum_{n=q+1}^{N} h_d(n-k) h_d(n-l) \tag{5.1.30}$$

Thus we obtain the filter parameters a_k.

Once the pole parameters are determined, the parameters b_k may be determined simply by substituting the solution $\hat{a}_k$ into (5.1.25). Thus

$$b_n = h_d(n) + \sum_{k=1}^{p} \hat{a}_k h_d(n-k), \qquad 0 \leq n \leq q \tag{5.1.31}$$

This method is usually called *Prony's method.* Unfortunately, Prony's method does not provide accurate estimates for b_k, especially when there is measurement noise associated with the observed signal.

Shanks's Method. A much better approach is to estimate the b_k by employing a least-squares criterion. To describe this method, suppose that the pole parameters a_k are determined from (5.1.29), which were obtained

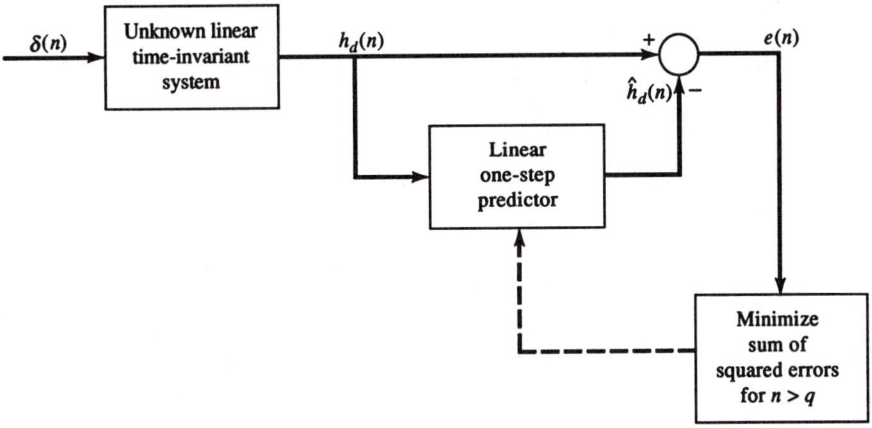

FIGURE 5.5 Method for determining the pole parameters in a pole-zero model.

by minimizing the squared-error function $\mathscr{E}(p,q)$ given in (5.1.28). From the estimate of a_k, we can synthesize the all-pole filter

$$H_p(z) = \frac{1}{1 + \sum_{k=1}^{p} \hat{a}_k z^{-k}} \tag{5.1.32}$$

The response of this filter to the unit sample sequence $\delta(n)$ is

$$v(n) = -\sum_{k=1}^{p} \hat{a}_k v(n-k) + \delta(n), \qquad n \geq 0 \tag{5.1.33}$$

If the sequence $v(n)$ is used to excite an all-zero filter with system function

$$H_q(z) = \sum_{k=0}^{q} b_k z^{-k} \tag{5.1.34}$$

as illustrated in Fig. 5.6, its response is

$$\hat{h}_d(n) = \sum_{k=0}^{q} b_k v(n-k) \tag{5.1.35}$$

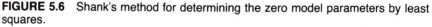

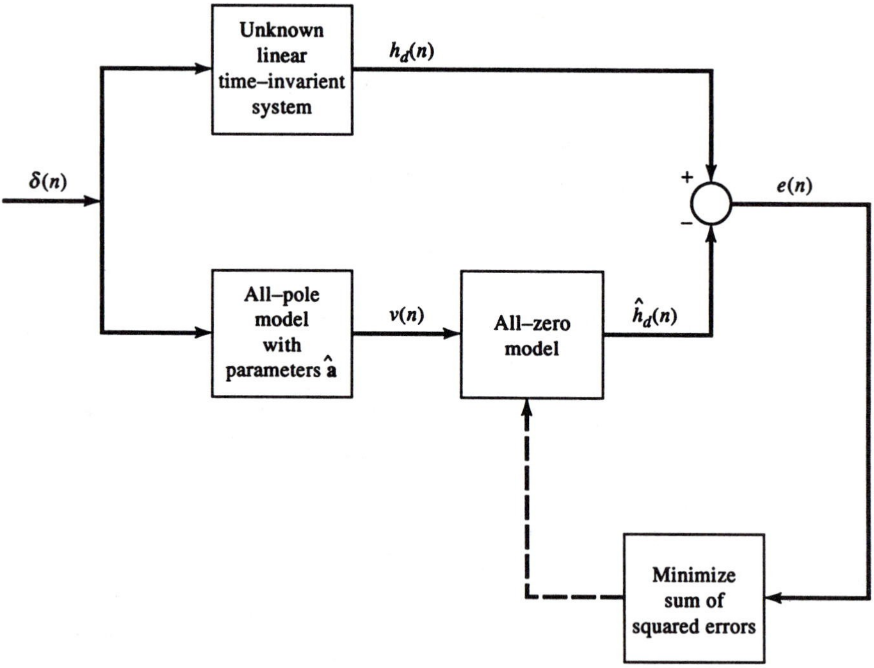

FIGURE 5.6 Shank's method for determining the zero model parameters by least squares.

Now, we can define an error sequence $e(n)$ as

$$\begin{aligned} e(n) &= h_d(n) - \hat{h}_d(n) \\ &= h_d(n) - \sum_{k=0}^{q} b_k v(n-k) \end{aligned} \tag{5.1.36}$$

and consequently, the parameters b_k can also be determined by means of the least-squares criterion, that is, from the minimization of

$$\mathscr{E}(q) = \sum_{n=0}^{N} \left[h_d(n) - \sum_{k=0}^{q} b_k v(n-k) \right]^2 \tag{5.1.37}$$

Thus we obtain a set of linear equations for the parameters b_k, in the form

$$\sum_{k=0}^{q} b_k r_{vv}(k,l) = r_{vd}(l), \qquad l = 0, 1, \ldots, q \tag{5.1.38}$$

where, by definition,

$$r_{vv}(k,l) = \sum_{n=0}^{N} v^*(n-k)v(n-l) \tag{5.1.39}$$

$$r_{vd}(k) = \sum_{n=0}^{N} h_d(n)v^*(n-k) \tag{5.1.40}$$

This method for estimating the model parameters b_k is due to Shanks (1967).

EXAMPLE 5.1.2

Suppose that the unknown system is a three-pole and three-zero type II lowpass Chebyshev digital filter that has the system function

$$H_d(z) = \frac{0.3060(1 + z^{-1})(0.2652 - 0.09z^{-1} + 0.2652z^{-2})}{(1 - 0.3880z^{-1})(1 - 1.1318z^{-1} + 0.5387z^{-2})}$$

Its unit impulse response is shown in Fig. 5.7. The estimates of the parameters of several models obtained by the three least-squares methods—least-squares inverse method, Prony's method, and Shanks's method—are given in Table 5.1. Note that both Prony's and Shanks's method give good estimates when the model order is as large as the order of the unknown system.

5.2 LEAST-SQUARES FILTER DESIGN FOR PREDICTION AND DECONVOLUTION

In Chapter 4 we treated the design of linear prediction filters based on minimization of the MSE. This approach requires that we know the second-

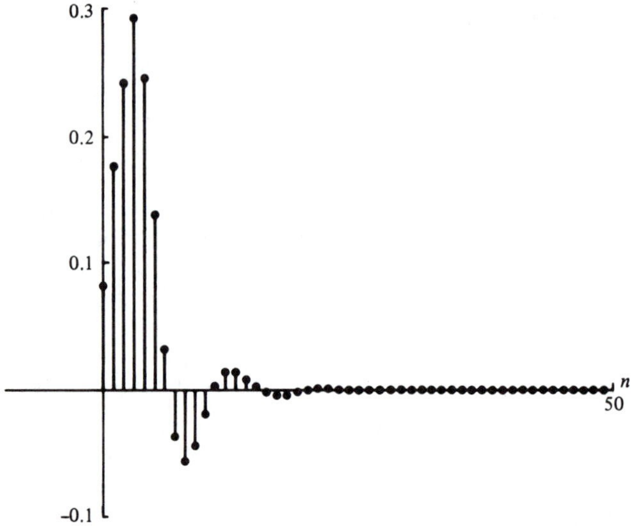

FIGURE 5.7 Impulse response $h_d(n)$ of type II Chebyshev digital filter given in Example 5.1.2.

TABLE 5.1 Pole—Zero Locations for Filter Designs in Example 8.4.5

Chebyshev Filter:

Zeros: -1, $0.1738311 \pm j0.9847755$
Poles: 0.3880, $0.5659 \pm j0.467394$

Filter Order	Poles in Least Squares Inverse
$N = 3$	0.8522 $0.6544 \pm j0.6224$
$N = 4$	$0.7959 \pm j0.3248$ $0.4726 \pm j0.7142$

Filter Order	Prony's Method		Shanks' Method	
	Poles	Zeros	Poles	Zeros
$N = 3$ $M = 2$	0.5332 $0.6659 \pm j0.4322$	$-0.1497 \pm j0.4925$	0.5348 $0.6646 \pm j0.4306$	$-0.2437 \pm j0.5918$
$N = 4$ $M = 2$	0.7092 -0.2919 $0.6793 \pm j0.4863$	$-0.1982 \pm j0.37$	0.7116 -0.2921 $0.6783 \pm j0.4855$	$0.306 \pm j0.4482$
$N = 3$ $M = 3$	0.3881 $0.5659 \pm j0.4671$	-1 $0.1736 \pm j0.9847$	0.3881 $0.5659 \pm j0.4671$	-1 $0.1738 \pm j0.9848$
$N = 4$ $M = 3$	-0.00014 0.388 $0.5661 \pm j0.4672$	-1 $0.1738 \pm j0.9848$	-0.00014 0.388 $0.566 \pm j0.4671$	-1 $0.1738 \pm j0.9848$

order statistics of the signals (i.e., the means and correlation functions). In this section we consider the same filter design problem based on least-squares optimization. We also consider the design of FIR Wiener filters based on the least-squares criterion.

Least-squares filter design methods find widespread use in many practical applications, including digital communication system design and in seismic signal processing. Common to these two areas is the requirement to perform signal deconvolution. In deconvolution, the objective is to recover either the input signal $x(n)$ or the system impulse response $h(n)$ from the output $y(n)$. In general, the roles of the sequences $x(n)$ and $h(n)$ are interchangeable. Hence any method for estimating $x(n)$ from $y(n)$ may also be applied to the estimation of $h(n)$ from $y(n)$, and vice versa.

In the context of digital communications, the input signal $x(n)$ is an information-bearing signal which is transmitted over a channel. The channel distorts the signal and produces $y(n)$ at its output. The process of deconvolution involves the design of a linear system or filter that corrects for the channel distortion and produces an output that is a replica of the channel input $x(n)$. The linear filter employed for this purpose is called a *channel equalizer*. This filter may be viewed as an approximation of the inverse filter to the channel response.

In seismic signal processing the deconvolution process involves the estimation of the impulse response $h(n)$ of the system—in this case, the characteristics of the earth. In this application the excitation $x(n)$ is known.

We begin by considering the design of linear prediction filters by the least-squares method. Then we describe a method for designing FIR approximations to the inverse of a linear system, also based on a least-squares criterion. The resulting filter is a Wiener filter that is applicable for channel equalization in digital communications and for deconvolution, in general.

Another method for deconvolution, based on linear prediction, is described in Section 5.2.2. This method is also based on the least-squares criterion and is particularly applicable to seismic signal processing.

5.2.1 Least-Squares Linear Prediction Filter

In Section 4.2 we treated the design of forward and backward linear predictive filters from a statistical viewpoint. In this subsection we demonstrate that linear prediction filters can also be designed based on the method of least squares. Only forward linear prediction is considered at this point. In Chapter 6 we shall encounter both forward and backward linear prediction based on a least-squares error criterion in the context of adaptive filtering.

Suppose that we have observed a sequence of data $x(n)$, $n \geq 0$. Let us form a linearly predicted value of $x(n)$ as

$$\hat{x}(n) = -\sum_{k=1}^{p} a_p(k)x(n-k), \qquad n \geq p \tag{5.2.1}$$

where $a_p(k)$ are the predictor coefficients to be determined. For each value of $n \geq p$, we may define an error signal $e(n) = x(n) - \hat{x}(n)$. Then the predictor coefficients $a_p(k)$ are selected to minimize the sum of squared errors

$$\begin{aligned}\mathscr{E}(p) &= \sum_{n=p}^{N} |e(n)|^2 \\ &= \sum_{n=p}^{N} \left| x(n) + \sum_{k=1}^{p} a_p(k)x(n-k) \right|^2\end{aligned} \tag{5.2.2}$$

where $N \gg p$. Minimization of $\mathscr{E}(p)$ yields the set of linear equations

$$\sum_{k=1}^{p} a_p(k) r_{xx}(m,k) = -r_{xx}(m,0), \qquad m = 1, 2, \ldots, p \tag{5.2.3}$$

where $r_{xx}(m,k)$ is the time-averaged autocorrelation of $x(n)$, defined as

$$r_{xx}(m,k) = \sum_{n=p}^{N} x(n-k)x^*(n-m) \tag{5.2.4}$$

Thus we observe that the least-squares predictor with coefficients given by (5.2.3) is similar in form to the optimum MSE predictor derived in Chapter 4. However, there is a basic difference. The data autocorrelation matrix with elements $r_{xx}(m,k)$ is no longer Toeplitz.

The least-squares optimization problem described above can also be formulated in matrix form by defining an error vector $\mathbf{e}$ with components $e(n)$ for $p \leq n \leq N$, a data vector $\mathbf{x}$ with elements $x(n)$, $p \leq n \leq N$, a coefficient vector $\mathbf{a}$ with elements $a_p(k)$, and an $(N - p + 1) \times p$ matrix $\mathbf{X}$ with elements $x(n - k)$. Then

$$\mathbf{e} = \mathbf{x} + \mathbf{X}\mathbf{a} \tag{5.2.5}$$

Minimization of $\mathscr{E}(p) = \mathbf{e}^H\mathbf{e}$ results in the matrix equation

$$\mathbf{X}^H\mathbf{X}\mathbf{a} + \mathbf{X}^H\mathbf{x} = 0$$

Hence the optimum solution is

$$\mathbf{a} = -(\mathbf{X}^H\mathbf{X})^{-1}\mathbf{X}^H\mathbf{x} \tag{5.2.6}$$

We note that $\mathbf{X}^H\mathbf{X}$ represents the autocorrelation matrix for the data and $\mathbf{X}^H\mathbf{x}$ represents a p-dimensional vector with elements $r_{xx}(m,0)$, $m = 1, 2, \ldots, p$.

Methods for solving (5.2.6) efficiently are described in Section 5.3. Extensions to sequential linear prediction as new data become available is treated in Chapter 6, where we introduce recursive least-squares predictors and where we obtain the associated lattice filter structures.

5.2.2 FIR Least-Squares Inverse (Wiener) Filters

Recall that the inverse to a linear time-invariant system with impulse response $h(n)$ and system function $H(z)$ is defined as the system whose impulse response $h_I(n)$ and system function $H_I(z)$ satisfy the respective equations

$$h(n) * h_I(n) = \delta(n) \tag{5.2.7}$$

$$H(z)H_I(z) = 1 \tag{5.2.8}$$

In general, $H_I(z)$ will be IIR unless $H(z)$ is an all-pole system, in which case $H_I(z)$ will be FIR.

In many practical applications it is desirable to restrict the inverse filter to be FIR. Thus $H_I(z)$ is usually an approximation to the inverse filter. Obviously, one simple method for restricting the inverse to be FIR is to truncate $h_I(n)$. In so doing, we incur a total squared approximation error equal to

$$\mathscr{E}_t = \sum_{n=M}^{\infty} h_I^2(n) \tag{5.2.9}$$

where M is the length of the truncated filter and $\mathscr{E}_t$ represents the energy in the tail of the impulse response $h_I(n)$.

Alternatively, we may use the least-squares error criterion to optimize the M coefficients of the FIR filter. First, let $d(n)$ denote the *desired output sequence* of the FIR filter of length M and let $h(n)$ be the input sequence. Then if $y(n)$ is the output sequence of the filter, as illustrated in Fig. 5.8, the error sequence between the desired output and the actual output is

$$e(n) = d(n) - \sum_{k=0}^{M-1} b_k h(n-k), \qquad n = 0, 1, \ldots, N \tag{5.2.10}$$

where the b_k are the FIR filter coefficients.

The sum of squares of the error sequence is

$$\mathscr{E}(M) = \sum_{n=0}^{N} \left[d(n) - \sum_{k=0}^{M-1} b_k h(n-k) \right]^2 \tag{5.2.11}$$

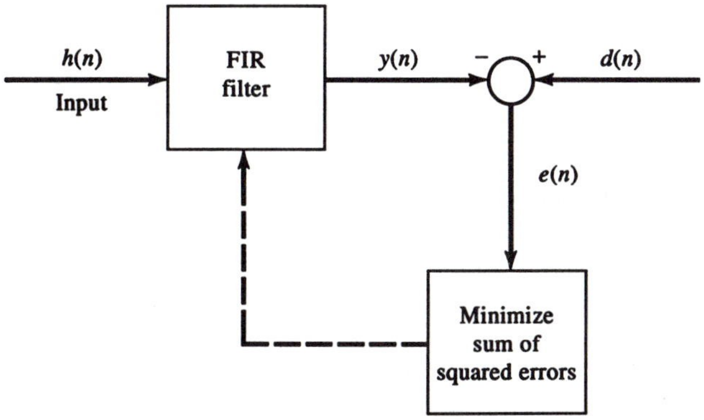

FIGURE 5.8 Least squares design of FIR filter.

When $\mathscr{E}(M)$ is minimized with respect to the filter coefficients, we obtain the set of linear equations

$$\sum_{k=0}^{M-1} b_k r_{hh}(k - l) = r_{dh}(l), \qquad l = 0, 1, \ldots, M - 1 \tag{5.2.12}$$

where $r_{hh}(l)$ is the autocorrelation of $h(n)$, defined as

$$r_{hh}(l) = \sum_{n=0}^{N} h(n)h(n - l) \tag{5.2.13}$$

and $r_{dh}(n)$ is the cross-correlation between the desired output $d(n)$ and the input sequence $h(n)$, defined as

$$r_{dh}(l) = \sum_{n=0}^{N} d(n)h(n - l) \tag{5.2.14}$$

The basic formulation of the FIR inverse filter is similar in form to the system identification problem based on an FIR (MA) system model. Consequently, the set of linear equations for the coefficients of the FIR inverse filter is similar to the set of equations given in (5.1.4) for the FIR model parameters. Furthermore, the linear equations in (5.2.12) are (the least-squares) equivalent to the equations in (4.6.3) for the finite-length Wiener filter. Consequently, the FIR least-squares inverse filter with coefficients specified by (5.2.12) is a (least-squares) Wiener filter.

If the optimum least-squares FIR filter is to be an approximate inverse filter, the desired response is

$$d(n) = \delta(n) \tag{5.2.15}$$

Then the cross-correlation between $d(n)$ and $h(n)$ reduces to

$$r_{dh}(l) = \begin{cases} h(0), & l = 0 \\ 0, & \text{otherwise} \end{cases} \tag{5.2.16}$$

The minimum value of the least-squares error obtained with the optimum FIR filter is

$$\begin{aligned} \mathscr{E}_{\min}(M) &= \sum_{n=0}^{N} \left[d(n) - \sum_{k=0}^{M-1} b_k h(n - k) \right] d(n) \\ &= \sum_{n=0}^{N} d^2(n) - \sum_{k=0}^{M} b_k r_{dh}(k) \end{aligned} \tag{5.2.17}$$

In the case where the FIR filter is the least-squares inverse filter, $d(n) = \delta(n)$ and $r_{dh}(n) = h(0)\delta(n)$. Therefore,

$$\mathscr{E}_{\min} = 1 - h(0)b_0$$

EXAMPLE 5.2.1

Determine the least-squares FIR inverse filter of length 2 to the system with impulse response

$$h(n) = \begin{cases} 1, & n = 0 \\ -\alpha, & n = 1 \\ 0, & \text{otherwise} \end{cases}$$

where $|\alpha| < 1$. Compare the least-squares solution with the approximate inverse obtained by truncating $h_I(n)$.

Solution: Since the system has a system function $H(z) = 1 - \alpha z^{-1}$, the exact inverse is IIR and is given by

$$H_I(z) = \frac{1}{1 - \alpha z^{-1}}$$

or equivalently,

$$h_I(n) = \alpha^n u(n)$$

If this is truncated after n terms, the residual energy in the tail is

$$\mathscr{E}_t = \sum_{k=n}^{\infty} \alpha^{2k}$$

$$\mathscr{E}_t = \alpha^{2n}(1 + \alpha^2 + \alpha^4 + \cdots)$$

$$\mathscr{E}_t = \frac{\alpha^{2n}}{1 - \alpha^2}$$

From (5.2.12) the least-squares FIR filter of length 2 satisfies the equations

$$\begin{bmatrix} 1 + \alpha^2 & -\alpha \\ -\alpha & 1 + \alpha^2 \end{bmatrix} \begin{bmatrix} b_0 \\ b_1 \end{bmatrix} = \begin{bmatrix} 1 \\ 0 \end{bmatrix}$$

which have the solution

$$b_0 = \frac{1 + \alpha^2}{1 + \alpha^2 + \alpha^4}$$

$$b_1 = \frac{\alpha}{1 + \alpha^2 + \alpha^4}$$

For purposes of comparison, the truncated inverse filter of length 2 has the coefficients $b_0 = 1$, $b_1 = \alpha$.

The minimum (least-squares) error is

$$\mathscr{E}_{\min} = \frac{\alpha^4}{1 + \alpha^2 + \alpha^4}$$

which compares with

$$\mathscr{E}_t = \frac{\alpha^4}{1 - \alpha^2}$$

for the truncated approximate inverse. Clearly, $\mathscr{E}_t > \mathscr{E}_{\min}$, so that the least-squares FIR inverse filter is superior.

In Example 5.2.1 the impulse response $h(n)$ of the system was minimum phase. In such a case we selected the desired response to be $d(0) = 1$ and $d(n) = 0$, $n \geq 1$. On the other hand, if the system is nonminimum phase, a delay should be inserted in the desired response in order to obtain a good filter design. The value of the appropriate delay depends on the characteristics of $h(n)$. In any case we can compute the least-squares error filter for different delays and select the filter with a delay that produces a small least-squares error. The following example illustrates the effect of the delay.

EXAMPLE 5.2.2

Determine the least-squares FIR inverse of length 2 to the system with impulse response

$$h(n) = \begin{cases} -\alpha, & n = 0 \\ 1, & n = 1 \\ 0, & \text{otherwise} \end{cases}$$

where $|\alpha| < 1$.

Solution: This is a maximum-phase system. If we select $d(n) = \delta(n)$, we obtain the same solution as in Example 5.2.1, with a minimum least-squares error

$$\begin{aligned} \mathscr{E}_{\min} &= 1 - h(0)b_0 \\ &= 1 + \alpha\frac{1 + \alpha^2}{1 + \alpha^2 + \alpha^4} \end{aligned}$$

If $0 < \alpha < 1$, $\mathscr{E}_{\min} > 1$, which represents a poor inverse filter. If $-1 < \alpha < 0$, $\mathscr{E}_{\min} < 1$. In particular, for $\alpha = \frac{1}{2}$, we obtain $\mathscr{E}_{\min} = 1.57$. For $\alpha = -\frac{1}{2}$, $\mathscr{E}_{\min} = 0.81$, which is still a very large value for the squared error.

Now suppose that the desired response is specified as $d(n) = \delta(n - 1)$. Then the set of equations for the filter coefficients, obtained from (5.2.12), is the solution to the equations

$$\begin{bmatrix} 1 + \alpha^2 & -\alpha \\ -\alpha & 1 + \alpha^2 \end{bmatrix} \begin{bmatrix} b_0 \\ b_1 \end{bmatrix} = \begin{bmatrix} h(1) \\ h(0) \end{bmatrix} = \begin{bmatrix} 1 \\ -\alpha \end{bmatrix}$$

The solution of these equations is

$$b_0 = \frac{1}{1 + \alpha^2 + a^4}$$

$$b_1 = \frac{-\alpha^3}{1 + \alpha^2 + \alpha^4}$$

The least-squares error, given by (5.2.17), is

$$\mathscr{E}_{\min} = 1 - b_0 r_{dh}(0) - b_1 r_{dh}(1)$$
$$= - b_0 h(1) - b_1 h(0)$$

$$\mathscr{E}_{\min} = 1 - \frac{1}{1 + \alpha^2 + \alpha^4} + \frac{\alpha^4}{1 + \alpha^2 + \alpha^4}$$

$$\mathscr{E}_{\min} = 1 - \frac{1 - \alpha^4}{1 + a^2 + \alpha^4}$$

In particular, suppose that $\alpha = \pm\frac{1}{2}$. Then $\mathscr{E}_{\min} = 0.29$. Consequently, the desired response $d(n) = \delta(n - 1)$ results in a significantly better inverse filter. Further improvement is possible by increasing the length of the inverse filter and the delay.

In general, when the desired response is specified to contain a delay D, then $d(n) = \delta(n - D)$ and the cross-correlation $r_{dh}(l)$, defined in (5.2.14), becomes

$$r_{dh}(l) = h(D - l), \qquad l = 0, 1, \ldots, M - 1$$

The set of linear equations for the coefficients of the least-squares FIR inverse filter, given by (5.2.12), reduce to

$$\sum_{k=0}^{M-1} b_k r_h(k - l) = h(D - l), \qquad l = 0, 1, \ldots, M - 1 \qquad (5.2.18)$$

Then the expression for the corresponding least-squares error, given in general by (5.2.17), becomes

$$\mathscr{E}_{\min} = 1 - \sum_{k=0}^{M-1} b_k h(D - k) \qquad (5.2.19)$$

In general, the least-squares solution for the FIR inverse filter parameters given by (5.2.12) can be obtained by the methods described in Section 5.3. Adaptive inverse filters are widely used in digital communication systems to compensate for channel distortion and are called *adaptive equalizers*. A recursive least squares formulation for such filters is given in Chapter 6.

5.2.3 Predictive Deconvolution

Least-squares methods have found widespread use in the field of geophysics and, in particular, in seismic signal processing for oil exploration. Below we describe deconvolution by means of the least-squares method to remove the reverberation and signal excitation effects in seismograms.

In seismic exploration of the earth's subsurface, an acoustic source is used to emit a signal waveform which can be represented in sampled form as a discrete time sequence $x(n)$. As this short pulse of acoustic energy propagates through the earth, some of the energy is reflected back to the surface. The reflections result from discontinuities in the composition of the earth subsurface. These observations have led to mathematical models of the earth subsurface as a layered medium, where each layer has a different composition and hence different propagation characteristics. Reflections of the signal occur at the boundaries of the different layers.

Figure 5.9 illustrates a very simple model to account for signal reflections. With such a model, the signal $y(n)$ received and recorded at a seismometer can be expressed as

$$y(n) = \sum_{i=1}^{L} k_i x(n - D_i) \tag{5.2.20}$$

where the k_i are the reflection coefficients at the interfaces between the various layers of the earth and the D_i represent the corresponding propagation delays. The number L of reflection coefficients is usually large.

The received signal $y(n)$ is viewed as the convolution of the excitation $x(n)$ with the sequence

$$\epsilon(n) = \sum_{i=1}^{L} k_i \delta(n - D_i) \tag{5.2.21}$$

where $\epsilon(n)$ represents the characteristics of the medium. The geophysicist is interested in recovering the sequence $\epsilon(n)$ from $y(n)$ and thus in extracting the information contained in $\epsilon(n)$ concerning the composition of the earth. Consequently, this is a problem in deconvolution or inverse filtering to remove the effects of the excitation $x(n)$.

A more complex signal propagation model is obtained when there is a layer of water between the signal source and the earth layers. It is well known that large amounts of oil and gas lie in the rock formations below

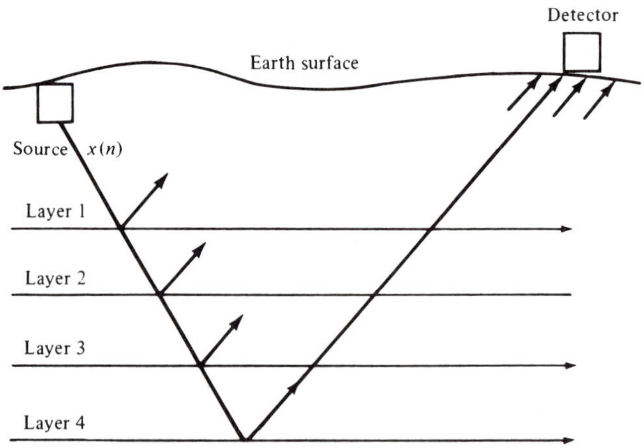

FIGURE 5.9 Signal propagation in a layered medium.

the bottom of the sea. In seismic exploration to identify the location of these deposits, a short signal pulse is imparted into the water by a seismic source. The bottom of the sea reflects a portion of the pulse energy back to the surface, while the remaining energy propagates into the rock formations and is reflected back to the surface from the various layers in the rock formations of the earth. The pulse energy that remains in the water is reflected from the surface back to the bottom. Some of this energy from the second bounce is reflected back to the surface while the remaining energy propagates through into the rock formation, and so on. The received signal $y(n)$ is recorded at the surface by a seismic detector. A model for this rather complex signal propagation is illustrated in Fig. 5.10.

The signal energy that propagates within the water is called a *reverberation signal*. It is relatively strong and tends to mask the reflections from the rock formations in the earth. In general, we can represent the received signal sequence at the detector as

$$y(n) = x(n) * c(n) * \epsilon(n) \tag{5.2.22}$$

where $\epsilon(n)$ represents the response of the layered earth to a unit impulse, $c(n)$ is an impulse train representing the reflectivity properties of the water, and $x(n)$ is the input signal pulse. The signal

$$p(n) = x(n) * c(n) \tag{5.2.23}$$

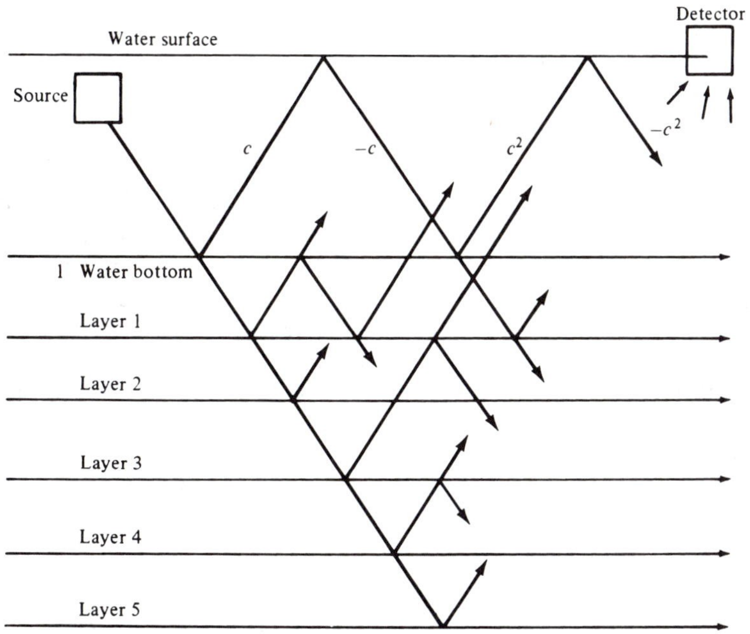

FIGURE 5.10 Reverberation of signal in water.

represents the undesirable reverberation component that we wish to eliminate through deconvolution.

The reverberation signal corresponding to a signal path may be expressed as

$$p_1(n) = x(n) - c_1x(n - D) + c_1^2x(n - 2D) - c_1^3x(n - 3D) + \cdots$$

and in the z-transform domain as

$$P_1(z) = (1 - c_1z^{-D} + c_1^2z^{-2D} - c_1^3z^{-3D} + \cdots)X(z) \tag{5.2.24}$$
$$= \frac{1}{1 - c_1z^{-D}}X(z)$$

where D is the delay in propagation from the surface to the bottom of the sea. Therefore, the system function for the propagation of the reverberating signal in the water is

$$C(z) = \frac{1}{1 - c_1z^{-D}} \tag{5.2.25}$$

Since $c_1 < 1$, on physical grounds, the system is stable. Its inverse is FIR and minimum phase. Below, we describe the method for deconvolving $y(n)$ with respect to the excitation $x(n)$ and the reverberating medium $c(n)$ to obtain $\epsilon(n)$. The deconvolution to remove the effects of both $x(n)$ and $c(n)$ is performed simultaneously in one step. Thus the inverse filter is the combined inverse to $p(n) = x(n) * c(n)$.

In order to derive the inverse system, let us assume that the desired sequence $\epsilon(n)$ is a sequence of uncorrelated reflections. Consequently, $\epsilon(n)$ resembles white noise with an autocorrelation sequence

$$r_{\epsilon\epsilon}(l) = \begin{cases} E_\epsilon, & l = 0 \\ 0, & l \neq 0 \end{cases} \tag{5.2.26}$$

where E_ϵ is some arbitrary constant. On the other hand, the sequence $p(n) = x(n) * c(n)$ is highly correlated. In other words, successive samples of $p(n)$ do not change much. We take advantage of this correlation or slow variation in $p(n)$ to estimate $p(n)$ from past samples and then to subtract the estimate from $y(n)$.

To proceed, suppose that we form an estimate of $p(n)$ by forming a weighted linear combination of the past M samples of $y(n)$ [i.e., the samples, $y(n - 1), y(n - 2), \ldots, y(n - M)$]. Thus we are using one-step forward linear prediction to estimate $y(n)$. Let $\hat{y}(n)$ be the predicted value. It is expressed as

$$\hat{y}(n) = \sum_{k=1}^{M} b_ky(n - k) \tag{5.2.27}$$

where the b_k are the prediction coefficients. The filter coefficients are selected to minimize the sum of the squared error sequence $e(n)$,

$$\mathscr{E}(M) = \sum_{n=0}^{N} |e(n)|^2$$
$$\mathscr{E}(M) = \sum_{n=0}^{N} \left| y(n) - \sum_{k=1}^{M} b_k y(n-k) \right|^2 \tag{5.2.28}$$

The minimization of $\mathscr{E}(M)$ with respect to the coefficients b_k leads to the set of linear equations of the form

$$\sum_{k=1}^{M} b_k r_{yy}(k-l) = r_{yy}(l), \qquad l = 1, 2, \ldots, M \tag{5.2.29}$$

where $r_{yy}(l)$ is the autocorrelation of the sequence $y(n)$, defined as

$$r_{yy}(l) = \sum_{n=0}^{N} y(n)y^*(n-l) \tag{5.2.30}$$

We express the equations given by (5.3.29) in the matrix form

$$\begin{bmatrix} r_{yy}(0) & r_{yy}(1) & \cdots & r_{yy}(M-1) \\ r_{yy}(1) & r_{yy}(0) & \cdots & r_{yy}(M-2) \\ \vdots & & & \\ r_{yy}(M-1) & r_{yy}(M-2) & \cdots & r_{yy}(0) \end{bmatrix} \begin{bmatrix} b_1 \\ b_2 \\ \vdots \\ b_M \end{bmatrix} = \begin{bmatrix} r_{yy}(1) \\ r_{yy}(2) \\ \vdots \\ r_{yy}(M) \end{bmatrix} \tag{5.2.31}$$

or equivalently, as

$$\mathbf{R_{yy}b} = \mathbf{r}_{yy} \tag{5.2.32}$$

These equations are the normal equations, previously encountered in the context of linear prediction. We observe that the matrix $\mathbf{R}_{yy}$ is a Toeplitz matrix, and hence it lends itself to an efficient solution by use of the Levinson–Durbin algorithm or the Schur algorithm.

Now, the autocorrelation sequence $r_{yy}(l)$ can be expressed in the spectral domain as

$$S_{yy}(\omega) = S_{pp}(\omega)S_{\epsilon\epsilon}(\omega) \tag{5.2.33}$$

where $S_{yy}(\omega)$ is the Fourier transform of $r_{yy}(l)$, $S_{pp}(\omega)$ is the Fourier transform of the autocorrelation $r_{pp}(l)$, and $S_{\epsilon\epsilon}(\omega)$ is the Fourier transform of the autocorrelation $r_{\epsilon\epsilon}(l)$. Alternatively, in the correlation domain, the relationship is

$$r_{yy}(l) = r_{pp}(l) * r_{\epsilon\epsilon}(l) \tag{5.2.34}$$

Since the correlation sequence $r_{\epsilon\epsilon}(l)$ is an impulse (a unit sample) it follows that

$$r_{yy}(l) = E_\epsilon r_{pp}(l) \tag{5.2.35}$$

Therefore, except for the proportionality factor E_ϵ, the autocorrelation sequence for $y(n)$ is identical to the autocorrelation of the sequence $p(n)$.

This implies that the coefficients of the FIR linear prediction filter depend only on the correlation properties of the sequence $p(n)$. There is no dependence in the sequence $\epsilon(n)$.

In view of the foregoing correlation properties of the signals, the FIR filter predicts the sequence $p(n)$ from past values of $y(n)$, as indicated in (5.2.27). The predicted value $\hat{y}(n)$ is basically an estimate of $p(n)$, which is subtracted from the observed value $y(n)$ to yield an estimate of the desired sequence $\epsilon(n)$, as illustrated in Fig. 5.11.

The overall system in Fig. 5.11 is an FIR *prediction error filter* with coefficients

$$g_k = \begin{cases} 1, & k = 0 \\ -b_k, & k = 1, 2, \ldots, M \end{cases} \tag{5.2.36}$$

It remains to be shown that this FIR filter with system function

$$G(z) = \sum_{k=0}^{M} g_k z^{-k} \tag{5.2.37}$$

is the least-squares inverse filter to the sequence $p(n)$, which represents the combined reverberation and signal excitation as defined by (5.2.23). Toward this end, we write the linear equation in (5.2.32) in the form

$$\mathbf{r}_{pp} - \mathbf{R}_{pp}\mathbf{b} = 0 \tag{5.2.38}$$

where the autocorrelation matrix $\mathbf{R}_{pp}$ and vector $\mathbf{r}_{pp}$ are related to $\mathbf{R}_{yy}$ and $\mathbf{r}_{yy}$ by (5.2.35). Equivalently, (5.2.38) may be written as a set of M linear equations of the form

$$\sum_{k=0}^{M} g_k r_{pp}(k - l) = 0, \qquad l = 1, 2, \ldots, M \tag{5.2.39}$$

where the g_k are defined by (5.2.36).

Let us augment the set of linear equations in (5.2.39) with the equation

$$\sum_{k=0}^{M} g_k r_{pp}(k) = \beta \tag{5.2.40}$$

where β is a scale factor. Then the combination of (5.2.40) with (5.2.39) results in a set of $M + 1$ linear equations of the form

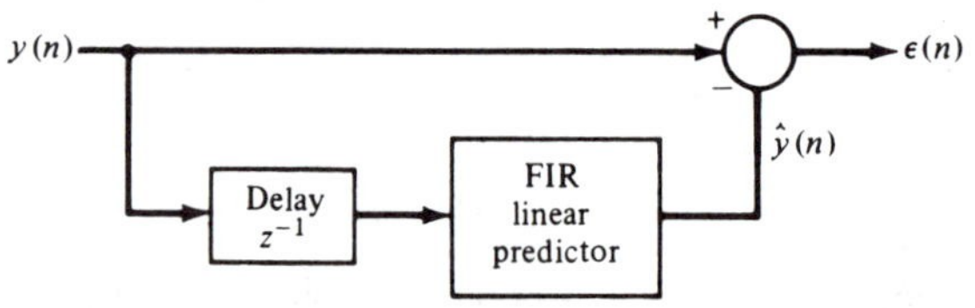

FIGURE 5.11 Deconvolution by linear prediction.

$$\begin{bmatrix} r_{pp}(0) & r_{pp}(1) & \cdots\cdots & r_{pp}(M) \\ r_{pp}(1) & r_{pp}(0) & \cdots\cdots & r_{pp}(M-1) \\ \vdots & \vdots & & \vdots \\ r_{pp}(M) & r_{pp}(M-1) & \cdots\cdots & r_{pp}(0) \end{bmatrix} \begin{bmatrix} g_0 \\ g_1 \\ \vdots \\ g_M \end{bmatrix} = \begin{bmatrix} \beta \\ 0 \\ \vdots \\ 0 \end{bmatrix} \tag{5.2.41}$$

Clearly, this set of equations is identical in form to the set of equations for the least-squares FIR inverse filter given by (5.2.12). Therefore, the coefficients obtained by solving the set of $M + 1$ equations given by (5.2.41) or, equivalently, by solving the reduced set of M equations given by (5.2.38), are the coefficients of the least-squares FIR inverse filter. The least-squares method described in this section for deconvolution based on linear prediction is called *predictive deconvolution*.

5.3 SOLUTION OF LEAST-SQUARES ESTIMATION PROBLEMS

In this section we present several methods for solving the least-squares estimation problems described in the preceding two sections. These methods will be used again in Chapters 6 and 7, in the development of time-recursive least-squares estimation algorithms. The methods treated are most easily developed with the aid of matrix notation. We begin by stating some basic definitions and concepts from linear algebra.

5.3.1 Definition and Basic Concepts

In this section we introduce the vector and matrix notation and necessary terminology to treat least-squares estimation problems. We assume that the reader is familiar with basic concepts in linear algebra.

Vectors and Matrices. An N-dimensional *vector* $\mathbf{v}$ is an ordered N-tuple of real or complex numbers $v_1, v_2, \ldots, v_N$, called the *elements* of $\mathbf{v}$. A vector is understood to be a column vector.

A *matrix* is a rectangular array of real or complex numbers called the elements of the matrix. An $N \times M$ matrix has N rows and M columns. If $M = N$, the matrix is called a *square matrix*. An N-dimensional vector may be viewed as an $N \times 1$ matrix. An $N \times M$ matrix may be viewed as having N M-dimensional vectors as its rows or M N-dimensional vectors as its columns.

The *complex conjugate* and the *transpose* of a matrix $\mathbf{A}$ are denoted as $\mathbf{A}^*$ and $\mathbf{A}^t$, respectively. The conjugate transpose of a matrix with complex elements is denoted as $\mathbf{A}^H$ (i.e., $\mathbf{A}^H = [\mathbf{A}^*]^t = [\mathbf{A}^t]^*$).

A square matrix $\mathbf{A}$ is said to be *symmetric* if $\mathbf{A}^t = \mathbf{A}$. A square matrix $\mathbf{A}$ with complex-valued elements is said to be *Hermitian* if $\mathbf{A}^H = \mathbf{A}$.

Vector and Matrix Norms. The *inner product* or dot product of two N-dimensional vectors $\mathbf{u}$ and $\mathbf{v}$ is defined as

$$\mathbf{u}^H\mathbf{v} = \sum_{k=1}^{N} u_k^* v_k$$

If $\mathbf{u}^H\mathbf{v} = 0$, the vectors are said to be *orthogonal.*

The *Euclidean norm,* or L_2-norm of a vector $\mathbf{v}$, is denoted by $\|\mathbf{v}\|$ and defined as

$$\|\mathbf{v}\| = (\mathbf{v}^H\mathbf{v})^{1/2} = \left(\sum_{k=1}^{N} |v_k|^2\right)^{1/2}$$

The *Euclidean norm* of a matrix $\mathbf{A}$, denoted as $\|A\|$, is defined as

$$\|\mathbf{A}\| = \max_{v \neq 0} \left(\frac{\|\mathbf{A}\mathbf{v}\|}{\|\mathbf{v}\|}\right)$$

for any vector $\mathbf{v}$. It is easy to verify that the norm of a square matrix is equal to the magnitude of its largest eigenvalue.

Another useful quality associated with a matrix $\mathbf{A}$ is the nonzero minimum value of $\|\mathbf{A}\mathbf{v}\|/\|\mathbf{v}\|$. It is easy to verify that when $\mathbf{A}$ is a nonsingular square matrix, this minimum value is equal to the magnitude of the smallest eigenvalue.

A set of vectors $\mathbf{v}_1, \mathbf{v}_2, \ldots, \mathbf{v}_M$ is *linearly independent* if and only if

$$\sum_{i=1}^{M} c_i \mathbf{v}_i = \mathbf{0}$$

implies that $c_1 = c_2 = \cdots = c_M = 0$.

Condition Number. The *condition number* of a matrix $\mathbf{A}$ is defined as the ratio of the maximum value to the minimum value of $\|\mathbf{A}\mathbf{v}\|/\|\mathbf{v}\|$. If $\mathbf{A}$ is a nonsingular square matrix, the condition number is equal to the product of the norm of $\mathbf{A}$ and the norm of $\mathbf{A}^{-1}$,

$$\text{condition number of } \mathbf{A} = \|\mathbf{A}\| \cdot \|\mathbf{A}^{-1}\|$$

In this case the condition number is equal to the ratio $|\lambda_{\max}/\lambda_{\min}|$, where $\lambda_{\max}$ is the largest eigenvalue of $\mathbf{A}$ and $\lambda_{\min}$ is the smallest eigenvalue. Clearly, the condition number of a matrix is greater than or equal to unity.

Linear Spaces, Subspaces, and Their Basis. The set $\mathbb{A}^N$ of *all* N-dimensional vectors is an N-dimensional vector space. A linear space must satisfy the following conditions: if $\mathbf{u}$ and $\mathbf{v}$ are members of a linear space, denoted by $\mathbf{u} \in \mathbb{A}^N$ and $\mathbf{v} \in \mathbb{A}^N$, $\mathbf{u} + \mathbf{v}$ and $\alpha\mathbf{u}$ are also the members of the space, where α is a complex number. If a subset $\mathbb{P}$ of $\mathbb{A}^N$ is also a linear space (i.e., it satisfies the conditions above), $\mathbb{P}$ is called a *subspace* of $\mathbb{A}^N$. There exists a maximum number of vectors in a subspace that can be linearly independent. This maximum number M is called the *dimension* of the subspace.

Any vector in an M-dimensional subspace $\mathbb{P}$ can be expressed as a linear combination of M linearly independent vectors in the subspace. Any set of such M linearly independent vectors is called *a basis* of the subspace $\mathbb{P}$. We also say that this set of vectors *spans* $\mathbb{P}$. A set of M mutually orthogonal vectors $\mathbf{v}_i$ forms a basis of $\mathbb{P}$ and is called an *orthogonal basis*. Furthermore, if the vectors in the set have unit length (i.e., $\|\mathbf{v}_i\| = 1$ for all i), we call the set an *orthonormal basis*.

Orthogonality of Vectors and Subspaces, Orthogonal Decomposition, and Projection. A vector $\mathbf{v}$ is *orthogonal to a subspace* $\mathbb{P}$ if it is orthogonal to every vector in $\mathbb{P}$ or, equivalently, if $\mathbf{v}$ is orthogonal to every vector in a basis of $\mathbb{P}$. Let $\mathbb{Q}$ and $\mathbb{P}$ be subspaces of $\mathbb{A}^N$. $\mathbb{Q}$ *is orthogonal to* $\mathbb{P}$ if every vector in $\mathbb{Q}$ is orthogonal to every vector in $\mathbb{P}$, or, equivalently, every vector in a basis of $\mathbb{Q}$ is orthogonal to every vector in a basis of $\mathbb{P}$.

If two subspaces $\mathbb{P}$ and $\mathbb{Q}$ of $\mathbb{A}^N$ are orthogonal to each other, the *direct sum* of $\mathbb{P}$ and $\mathbb{Q}$, denoted by $\mathbb{P} \oplus \mathbb{Q}$ is the subspace consisting of all vectors $\mathbf{v}$ that satisfy $\mathbf{v} = \mathbf{u} + \mathbf{w}$, $\mathbf{u} \in \mathbb{P}$ and $\mathbf{w} \in \mathbb{Q}$. The dimension of $\mathbb{P} \oplus \mathbb{Q}$ is equal to sum of the dimensions of $\mathbb{P}$ and $\mathbb{Q}$. If $\mathbb{P} \oplus \mathbb{Q} = \mathbb{A}^N$, we call $\mathbb{P}$ and $\mathbb{Q}$ the *orthogonal complements* of each other. This is denoted by $\mathbb{P} = \mathbb{Q}\perp$ and $\mathbb{Q} = \mathbb{P}\perp$.

Given any vector $\mathbf{v} \in \mathbb{A}^N$ and $\mathbb{P}$ is a subspace of $\mathbb{A}^N$, there exists a unique representation of $\mathbf{v}$ as $\mathbf{v} = \mathbf{u} + \mathbf{w}$, where $\mathbf{u} \in \mathbb{P}$, $\mathbf{w} \in \mathbb{P}\perp$. The vector $\mathbf{u}$ is the vector in $\mathbb{P}$ that is nearest to $\mathbf{v}$ (i.e., $\|\mathbf{v} - \mathbf{u}\| \leq \|\mathbf{t} - \mathbf{v}\|$ for any vector $\mathbf{t} \in \mathbb{P}$). The vector $\mathbf{u}$ is called the (orthogonal) *projection* of $\mathbf{v}$ onto $\mathbb{P}$ and the difference $\mathbf{e} = \mathbf{v} - \mathbf{u}$ is called the *residual* of the projection $\mathbf{u}$.

5.3.2 Matrix Formulation of Least-Squares Estimation

In the least-squares estimation problems treated in Sections 5.1 and 5.2, we were dealing with a single time series. However, in many signal-processing applications, such as in sonar and radar, signals are received by an array of sensors. The output of each sensor is a time series and the composite signal from all the sensors is represented as a signal vector with components corresponding to the time series from each of the sensors. The signal vector received is called a *multichannel signal*.

In this section we formulate the least-squares estimation problem in the general case of multichannel signals. The more restrictive case of a single time series, which was treated in Sections 5.1 and 5.2, also fits this formulation.

The methods for solving least-squares estimation problems presented in this section form the basis for the time-recursive adaptive filtering algorithms described in Chapters 6 for a single time series, and in Chapter 7 for multichannel time series.

Let $\mathbf{X}_M(n)$ denote the received signal vector, which is defined as

$$\mathbf{X}_M(n) = [x_1(n), x_2(n), \ldots, x_M(n)]^t \tag{5.3.1}$$

From the sequence of received vectors $\mathbf{X}_M(0)$, $\mathbf{X}_M(1)$, . . . , $\mathbf{X}_M(n)$, we construct an $(n + 1) \times M$ data matrix $\mathbf{A}_M(n)$ defined as

$$\mathbf{A}_M(n) = [\mathbf{X}_M(0), \mathbf{X}_M(1), \ldots, \mathbf{X}_M(n)]^t$$

$$\begin{bmatrix} x_1(0) & x_2(0) & \cdots x_M(0) \\ x_1(1) & x_2(1) & \cdots x_M(1) \\ \vdots & \vdots & \vdots \\ x_1(n) & x_2(n) & \cdots x_M(n) \end{bmatrix} = [\mathbf{a}_1(n), \mathbf{a}_2(n), \ldots, \mathbf{a}_M(n)] \tag{5.3.2}$$

where the vectors $\mathbf{a}_i(n)$, $i = 1, 2, \ldots, M$, are the column vectors of $\mathbf{A}_M(n)$, (i.e., $\mathbf{a}_i(n) = [x_i(0), x_i(1), \ldots, x_i(n)]^t$). We also define the desired signal vector as $\mathbf{d}(n) = [d(0), d(1), \ldots, d(n)]^t$.

An estimate of the desired signal $d(l)$ is formed by forming a weighted linear combination of the signal vector $\mathbf{X}_M(l)$. Thus

$$\hat{d}(l,n) = \mathbf{X}_M^t(l)\mathbf{h}_M(n), \qquad 0 \le l \le n \tag{5.3.3}$$

where $\mathbf{h}_M(n) = [h(1,n), h(2,n), \ldots, h(M,n)]^t$ is the coefficient vector for an Mth-order linear combiner. The difference between the desired signal $d(l)$ and the estimate $\hat{d}(l,n)$ is defined as the error

$$e(l,n) = d(l) - \hat{d}(l,n), \qquad 0 \le l \le n \tag{5.3.4}$$

The least-squares estimation problem may be stated as follows. Given the set of observation vectors $\mathbf{X}_M(l)$, $l = 0, 1, \ldots, n$, determine the coefficient vector $\mathbf{h}_M(n)$ that minimizes the weighted sum of magnitude-squared errors

$$\mathscr{E}_M(n) = \sum_{l=0}^{n} w^{n-l}|e(l,n)|^2 \tag{5.3.5}$$

where w is a weighting factor selected in the range $0 < w \le 1$.

The exponential weighting incorporated in the expression for the weighted squared error $\mathscr{E}_M(n)$ is often used to deemphasize the effect of older data on the estimation of the filter coefficients. If a rectangular weighting factor is desired for the block of data, we may set $w = 1$. Such weighting would be appropriate if the data in the observation interval are statistically stationary.

In matrix form, the least-squares estimation problem can be formulated more compactly. The error vector $\mathbf{e}(n) = [e(0,n), e(1,n), \ldots, e(n,n)]^t$ may be expressed as

$$\mathbf{e}(n) = \mathbf{d}(n) - \mathbf{A}_M(n)\mathbf{h}_M(n) \tag{5.3.6}$$

where $\mathbf{d}(n) = [d(0), d(1), \ldots, d(n)]^t$, and the weighted sum of magnitude squared errors is simply the squared norm of $\mathbf{W}(n)\mathbf{e}(n)$. That is,

$$\mathscr{E}_M(n) = \mathbf{e}^H(n)\mathbf{W}^2(n)\mathbf{e}(n) \equiv \|\mathbf{W}(n)\mathbf{e}(n)\|^2 \tag{5.3.7}$$

where $\mathbf{W}(n)$ denotes the diagonal weighting matrix

$$\mathbf{W}(n) = \text{diag}\,(\sqrt{w^n}, \sqrt{w^{n-1}}, \ldots, \sqrt{w}, 1) \tag{5.3.8}$$

If we substitute (5.3.6) into (5.3.7) and perform the minimization of $\mathscr{E}_M(n)$ with respect to the coefficient vector $\mathbf{h}_M(n)$, we obtain the set of *normal equations,* which are expressed in matrix form as

$$\mathbf{A}_M^H(n)\mathbf{W}^2(n)\mathbf{A}_M(n)\mathbf{h}_M(n) - \mathbf{A}_M^H(n)\mathbf{W}^2(n)\mathbf{d}(n) = \mathbf{0}_M \tag{5.3.9}$$

Hence the solution for the optimum coefficient vector is

$$\mathbf{h}_M(n) = [\mathbf{A}_M^H(n)\mathbf{W}^2(n)\mathbf{A}_M(n)]^{-1}\mathbf{A}_M^H(n)\mathbf{W}^2(n)\mathbf{d}(n) \tag{5.3.10}$$

It is interesting to note that the $M \times M$ matrix $\mathbf{A}_M^H(n)\mathbf{W}^2(n)\mathbf{A}_M(n)$ is simply the (weighted) autocorrelation matrix for the data. That is,

$$\begin{aligned}\mathbf{R}_M(n) &= \mathbf{A}_M^H(n)\mathbf{W}^2(n)\mathbf{A}_M(n) \\ &= \sum_{l=0}^{n} w^{n-l}\mathbf{X}_M(l)\mathbf{X}_M^H(l)\end{aligned} \tag{5.3.11}$$

and hence

$$\mathbf{h}_M(n) = \mathbf{R}_M^{-1}(n)\mathbf{A}_M^H(n)\mathbf{W}^2(n)\mathbf{d}(n) \tag{5.3.12}$$

The corresponding estimate of the desired signal vector is

$$\begin{aligned}\hat{\mathbf{d}}(n) &= \mathbf{A}_M(n)\mathbf{h}_M(n) \\ &= \mathbf{A}_M(n)\mathbf{R}_M^{-1}(n)\mathbf{A}_M^H(n)\mathbf{W}^2(n)\mathbf{d}(n)\end{aligned} \tag{5.3.13}$$

Geometrically, we view $\hat{\mathbf{d}}(n)$ as the projection of $\mathbf{d}(n)$ onto the linear subspace spanned by the column vectors $\mathbf{a}_i(n)$, $i = 1, 2, \ldots, M$, of $\mathbf{A}_M(n)$. If the column vectors of $\mathbf{A}_M(n)$ are linearly independent, the $M \times M$ correlation matrix $\mathbf{R}_M(n)$ is nonsingular and hence the normal equations have a unique solution given by (5.3.10). We assume that this condition holds.

Now let us define the matrix $\mathscr{P}(n)$ as

$$\mathscr{P}(n) = \mathbf{A}_M(n)\mathbf{R}_M^{-1}(n)\mathbf{A}_M^H(n)\mathbf{W}^2(n) \tag{5.3.14}$$

Then the estimate $\hat{\mathbf{d}}(n)$ is simply expressed as

$$\hat{\mathbf{d}}(n) = \mathscr{P}(n)\mathbf{d}(n) \tag{5.3.15}$$

Since $\hat{\mathbf{d}}(n)$ is a projection of $\mathbf{d}(n)$ onto the linear subspace spanned by the column vector of $\mathbf{A}_M(n)$, we call $\mathscr{P}(n)$ the *projection matrix* or *projection operator*.

The projection operator has two important properties. First, it possesses Hermitian symmetry [i.e., $\mathscr{P}^H(n) = \mathscr{P}(n)$]. Second, it is idempotent [i.e., $\mathscr{P}^2(n) = \mathscr{P}(n)$].

Finally, we state that $\mathscr{P}(n)$ provides an *orthogonal projection* of $\mathbf{d}(n)$ onto the linear subspace spanned by $\mathbf{A}_M(n)$. The proof of this property is straightforward. We may write the error vector $\mathbf{e}(n)$ for the optimum choice of $\mathbf{h}_M(n)$ as

$$\begin{aligned} \mathbf{e}(n) &= \mathbf{d}(n) - \hat{\mathbf{d}}(n) \\ &= [\mathbf{I} - \mathcal{P}(n)]\mathbf{d}(n) \end{aligned} \tag{5.3.16}$$

Then

$$\begin{aligned} \mathbf{A}_M^H(n)\mathbf{e}(n) &= (\mathbf{A}_M^H(n) - \mathbf{A}_M^H(n)\mathcal{P}(n))\mathbf{d}(n) \\ &= (\mathbf{A}_M^H(n) - \mathbf{A}_M^H(n)\mathbf{W}^2(n)\mathbf{A}_M(n)\mathbf{R}_{\bar{M}}^{-1}(n)\mathbf{A}_M^H(n))\,\mathbf{d}(n) = \mathbf{0}_M \end{aligned} \tag{5.3.17}$$

for the optimum choice of the coefficient vector $\mathbf{h}_M(n)$. Therefore, the column vectors $\mathbf{a}_i(n)$, $i = 1, 2, \ldots, M$, are orthogonal to the error vector $\mathbf{e}(n)$. This demonstrates the *orthogonality principle* in least-squares estimation, which may be stated as follows:

Orthogonality Principle. To minimize the weighted squared error given by (5.3.7), the coefficient vector $\mathbf{h}_M(n)$ should be selected such that the error vector $\mathbf{e}(n)$ is *orthogonal* to the linear subspace spanned by $\mathbf{A}_M(n)$ [i.e., $\mathbf{a}_i^H(n)\mathbf{e}(n) = 0$ for $i = 1, 2, \ldots, M$].

Since the error vector $\mathbf{e}(n)$ is orthogonal to the data vectors $\mathbf{a}_i(n)$, $i = 1, 2, \ldots, M$, it follows that the minimum value of the weighted squared error is

$$\begin{aligned} E_M(n) &\equiv \min_{\mathbf{h}_M(n)} \mathcal{E}_M(n) \\ &= \mathbf{d}^H(n)[\mathbf{d}(n) - \hat{\mathbf{d}}(n)] \\ &= \|\mathbf{d}(n)\|^2 - \mathbf{d}^H(n)\mathcal{P}(n)\mathbf{d}(n) \end{aligned} \tag{5.3.18}$$

The geometric relationships $\hat{\mathbf{d}}(n)$, $\mathbf{d}(n)$, $\mathbf{e}(n)$, and $\mathbf{A}_M(n)$ are illustrated in Fig. 5.12.

Finally, we observe that the effect of the exponential weighting matrix $\mathbf{W}(n)$ that is used in the minimization of the vector error norm may be incorporated into the signal and error quantities as follows. We define a weighted error vector as

$$\begin{aligned} \mathbf{e}^w(n) &= \mathbf{W}(n)\mathbf{e}(n) \\ &= \mathbf{W}(n)\mathbf{d}(n) - \mathbf{W}(n)\mathbf{A}_M(n)\mathbf{h}_M(n) \\ &= \mathbf{d}^w(n) - \mathbf{A}_M^w(n)\mathbf{h}_M(n) \end{aligned} \tag{5.3.19}$$

where $\mathbf{d}^w(n)$ and $\mathbf{A}_M^w(n)$ are the weighted desired signal vector and data matrix, respectively,

$$\begin{aligned} \mathbf{d}^w(n) &= \mathbf{W}(n)\mathbf{d}(n) \\ \mathbf{A}_M^w(n) &= \mathbf{W}(n)\mathbf{A}_M(n) \end{aligned} \tag{5.3.20}$$

Thus the weighting matrix $\mathbf{W}(n)$ is incorporated into the data, and the least-squares minimization problem is now based on minimizing the squared norm $\|\mathbf{e}^w(n)\|^2$. Hence the solution for the optimum coefficient vector $\mathbf{h}_M(n)$

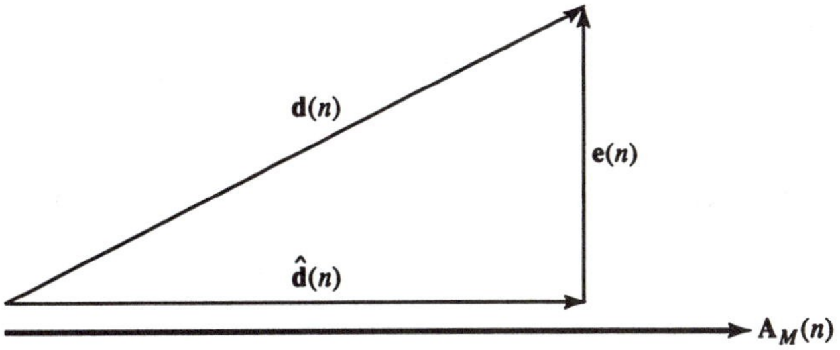

FIGURE 5.12 Geometric relationships among $\mathbf{d}(n)$, $\hat{\mathbf{d}}(n)$, $\mathbf{e}(n)$, and $\mathbf{A}_M(n)$.

given by (5.3.10) may be expressed in terms of the modified (weighted) vector $\mathbf{d}^w(n)$ and matrix, $\mathbf{A}_M^w(n)$.

In the following sections we describe several methods for solving the normal equations. To simplify the notation, we set $\mathbf{W}(n)$ to the identity matrix $\mathbf{I}$. We also drop the time index n.

5.3.3 Cholesky Decomposition

Let us consider the solution for the normal equations given by (5.3.9) as

$$\mathbf{R}_M \mathbf{h}_M = \mathbf{A}_M^H \mathbf{d} \tag{5.3.21}$$

where, for convenience, we have dropped the time index n and have set the diagonal weighting matrix to the identity matrix. $\mathbf{R}_M$ is the signal autocorrelation matrix defined by (5.3.11) as $\mathbf{R}_M = \mathbf{A}_M^H \mathbf{A}_M$. The product $\mathbf{A}_M^H \mathbf{A}_M$ is called a *squaring operation* and the data matrix $\mathbf{A}_M$ may be called the *square root* of $\mathbf{R}_M$. As a result of the squaring operation, the condition number of $\mathbf{R}_M$ is equal to the square of the condition number of the data matrix $\mathbf{A}_M$. From numerical analysis we know that for a specified round-off error introduced in computations, the accuracy of the solution $\mathbf{h}_M$ is inversely proportional to the condition number of the matrix $\mathbf{R}_M$. In addition, the dynamic range of the elements $\mathbf{R}_M$ is increased (exponentially) by the squaring operation. For these reasons it is often preferable when solving for $\mathbf{h}_M$ to avoid directly inverting the autocorrelation matrix $\mathbf{R}_M$.

In this section we describe one method for factoring the autocorrelation matrix $\mathbf{R}_M$ into a product of two square matrices, a lower triangular matrix and an upper triangular matrix,

$$\mathbf{R}_M = \mathbf{L}_M \mathbf{L}_M^H \tag{5.3.22}$$

where $\mathbf{L}_M$ is defined as

$$\mathbf{L}_M = \left[\begin{array}{cccc} \diagdown & 0 & 0 \cdots & 0 \\ & \diagdown & & 0 \cdots 0 \\ & & \diagdown & \cdot \\ & & & \cdot \end{array}\right] \tag{5.3.23}$$

This factorization of $\mathbf{R}_M$ is called a *Cholesky decomposition*.

For the moment, let us assume that we have obtained such a decomposition. Then the normal equations given by (5.3.21) may be expressed as

$$\mathbf{L}_M \mathbf{L}_M^H \mathbf{h}_M = \mathbf{b}_M \tag{5.3.24}$$

where, by definition, $\mathbf{b}_M = \mathbf{A}_M^H \mathbf{d}$. Let us now define the vector $\mathbf{y}_M$ as

$$\mathbf{y}_M = \mathbf{L}_M^H \mathbf{h}_M \tag{5.3.25}$$

Hence the equation

$$\mathbf{L}_M \mathbf{y}_M = \mathbf{b}_M \tag{5.3.26}$$

can easily be solved for $\mathbf{y}_M$ without direct matrix inversion, because $\mathbf{L}_M$ is a (lower) triangular matrix. Thus we have

$$\begin{aligned} y_1 &= \frac{b_1}{l_{11}} \\ y_i &= \frac{1}{l_{ii}}\left[b_i - \sum_{j=1}^{i-1} l_{ij} y_j\right], \qquad 2 \le i \le M \end{aligned} \tag{5.3.27}$$

where l_{ij} are the elements of $\mathbf{L}_M$.

Once we have solved for $\mathbf{y}_M$ we may use back substitution to solve for $\mathbf{h}_M$. Thus we have

$$\mathbf{L}_M^H \mathbf{h}_M = \mathbf{y}_M \tag{5.3.28}$$

Since $\mathbf{L}_M^H$ is an upper triangular matrix, we begin with the solution for h_M, which is given by

$$h_M = \frac{y_M}{l_{MM}} \tag{5.3.29}$$

Then

$$h_i = \frac{1}{l_{ii}}\left(y_i - \sum_{j=i+1}^{M} h_j l_{ji}^*\right), \qquad M-1 \geqslant i \geqslant 1 \tag{5.3.30}$$

Thus we have obtained the solution to the normal equations from the Cholesky factors $\mathbf{L}_M$ and $\mathbf{L}_M^H$.

Now let us consider the factorization of $\mathbf{R}_M$. We have

$$r_{ij} = \sum_{k=1}^{\min(i,j)} l_{ik} l_{jk}^* \tag{5.3.31}$$

where the diagonal elements l_{ii} are real valued. Thus

$$r_{11} = l_{11}^2$$

and hence $l_{11} = \sqrt{r_{11}}$. For the first column of $\mathbf{R}_M$ we have

$$r_{i1} = l_{i1} l_{11}$$

Hence

$$l_{i1} = \frac{r_{i1}}{l_{11}}, \qquad 1 \le i \le M \tag{5.3.32}$$

In general, (5.3.31) may be expressed as

$$r_{ij} = l_{ij}l_{jj} + \sum_{k=1}^{j-1} l_{ik}l_{jk}^*, \qquad i > j \tag{5.3.33}$$

which can be rearranged to yield the desired recursion for the elements of $\mathbf{L}_M$, in the form

$$l_{ij} = \frac{1}{l_{jj}}\left(r_{ij} - \sum_{k=1}^{j-1} l_{ik}l_{jk}^*\right), \qquad i > j \tag{5.3.34}$$

and

$$l_{jj} = \left(r_{jj} - \sum_{k=1}^{j-1} |l_{jk}|^2\right)^{1/2} \tag{5.3.35}$$

Thus we obtain the elements of the lower triangular matrix $\mathbf{L}_M$ for the factorization of $\mathbf{R}_M$.

Although we have shown how to evaluate the Cholesky factors from the data autocorrelation matrix, this approach requires high-precision arithmetic, first in forming $\mathbf{R}_M$ and then in factoring it. Consequently, this method is not generally used in practice. Instead, the Cholesky factors are obtained directly from the data matrix $\mathbf{A}_M$ by use of the QR decomposition described in Section 5.3.5.

5.3.4 LDU Decomposition

Another type of square-root factorization of the autocorrelation matrix $\mathbf{R}_M$ is an LDU decomposition, where $\mathbf{L}$ is a lower triangular matrix with unity diagonal elements, $\mathbf{U} = \mathbf{L}^H$ is an upper triangular matrix, and $\mathbf{D}$ is a diagonal matrix. Thus we have

$$\mathbf{R}_M = \mathbf{L}_M\mathbf{D}_M\mathbf{L}_M^H \tag{5.3.36}$$

where $\mathbf{D}_M$ is a diagonal matrix with diagonal elements δ_k. Although we have used the same symbol, $\mathbf{L}_M$, to denote the lower triangular matrix in the LDU and Cholesky decompositions, the reader should note that the two decompositions yield different triangular matrices.

The factorization of $\mathbf{R}_M$ may be expressed by the set of linear equations

$$r_{ij} = \sum_{k=1}^{j} l_{ik}\delta_k l_{jk}^*, \qquad 1 \le j \le i-1, \qquad i \ge 2 \tag{5.3.37}$$

where r_{ij} are elements of $\mathbf{R}_M$. Then the elements l_{ik} and δ_k are determined from (5.3.37) as follows:

$$\begin{aligned} \delta_1 &= r_{11} \\ l_{ij}\delta_j &= r_{ij} - \sum_{k=1}^{j-1} l_{ik}\delta_k l_{jk}^*, \qquad \begin{array}{l} 1 \le j \le i-1 \\ 2 \le i \le M \end{array} \\ \delta_i &= r_{ii} - \sum_{k=1}^{j-1} |l_{ik}|^2\delta_k, \qquad 2 \le i \le M \end{aligned} \tag{5.3.38}$$

As in the case of the Cholesky decomposition, the LDU decomposition of $\mathbf{R}_M$ according to (5.3.38) requires high-precision arithmetic in forming $\mathbf{R}_M$ and in factoring it. Consequently, this approach is not generally used in practice. Instead, the LDU decomposition is obtained directly from the data matrix $\mathbf{A}_M$ by use of the QR decomposition described in Section 5.3.5.

Once the elements of $\mathbf{L}_M$ and $\mathbf{D}_M$ are determined, the solution of the linear equations for the coefficients of the optimum filter is obtained by the same two-step procedure used in the preceding section, where we used the Cholesky factors. Thus we have

$$\mathbf{L}_M \mathbf{D}_M \mathbf{L}_M^H \mathbf{h}_M = \mathbf{b}_M \tag{5.3.39}$$

First, we define

$$\mathbf{y}_M = \mathbf{D}_M \mathbf{L}_M^H \mathbf{h}_M \tag{5.3.40}$$

and solve the triangular system $\mathbf{L}_M \mathbf{y}_M = \mathbf{b}_M$. This solution yields

$$\begin{aligned} y_1 &= b_1 \\ y_{ii} &= b_i - \sum_{j=1}^{i-1} l_{ij} y_j, \qquad 2 \le i \le M \end{aligned} \tag{5.3.41}$$

Having obtained $\mathbf{y}_M$, the last step is to compute $\mathbf{h}_M$. We have the upper triangular system

$$\mathbf{D}_M \mathbf{L}_M^H \mathbf{h}_M = \mathbf{y}_M \tag{5.3.42}$$

or equivalently,

$$\mathbf{L}_M^H \mathbf{h}_M = \mathbf{D}_M^{-1} \mathbf{y}_M \tag{5.3.43}$$

By beginning with the solution for h_M we obtain the desired solution, which is

$$\begin{aligned} h_M &= \frac{y_M}{\delta_M} \\ h_i &= \frac{y_i}{\delta_i} - \sum_{j=i+1}^{M} l_{ji}^* h_j, \qquad 1 \le i \le M-1 \end{aligned} \tag{5.3.44}$$

5.3.5 QR Decomposition

The Cholesky and LDU decompositions perform square-root decompositions of the data autocorrelation matrix $\mathbf{R}_M$ and thus provide a means for solving the normal equations given by (5.3.9). However, there exist methods for factoring $\mathbf{A}_M$ directly without having to compute $\mathbf{R}_M$ first. We show below that $\mathbf{A}_M$ can be decomposed into an orthogonal matrix $\mathbf{Q}$ and an upper triangular matrix, which we denote as $\mathcal{R}$. Such a decomposition is called a *QR decomposition* (QRD). In general, algorithms for solving the normal equations based on the QRD provide better numerical accuracy than square-root algorithms, which are based on the decomposition of the autocorrelation matrix $\mathbf{R}_M$.

For any arbitrary $N \times M$ matrix $\mathbf{A}$, where $N > M$, there always exists an $N \times N$ orthogonal matrix $\mathbf{Q}$, such that

$$\mathbf{QA} = \begin{bmatrix} \mathcal{R} \\ \mathbf{O} \end{bmatrix} \tag{5.3.45}$$

where $\mathcal{R}$ is an upper triangular square matrix and $\mathbf{O}$ is a null matrix. Hence $\mathcal{R}$ has the form

$$\mathcal{R} = \begin{bmatrix} 0 & \diagdown & & & \\ \cdot & 0 & & & \\ \cdot & \cdot & \cdot & & \\ 0 & 0 & 0 & 0 & 0 \end{bmatrix} \tag{5.3.46}$$

Before we demonstrate the construction of such a decomposition, we make the following remarks:

1. The triangular matrix $\mathcal{R}$ in a QR decomposition of matrix $\mathbf{A}$ is a Cholesky factor of the matrix $\mathbf{A}^H\mathbf{A}$.
2. Each row of the triangular matrix $\mathcal{R}$ is unique up to a complex scale factor with unit magnitude. Hence if $\mathcal{R}_1$ and $\mathcal{R}_2$ are two different $\mathcal{R}$-factors in a QR decomposition of the matrix $\mathbf{A}$, we can always find a complex-valued diagonal matrix Δ whose complex-valued diagonal elements have unit magnitude, so that $\mathcal{R}_1 = \Delta\mathcal{R}_2$.
3. For any matrix $\mathbf{A}$ there exists a unique $\mathcal{R}$ whose diagonal elements are all real and nonnegative.
4. If $N > M$, the orthogonal matrix $\mathbf{Q}$ in a QR decompositions of $\mathbf{A}$ is not unique for the same $\mathcal{R}$-factor.
5. Since the condition number of the orthogonal matrix $\mathbf{Q}$ is unity, it follows that the condition number of $\mathcal{R}$ is equal to the condition number of $\mathbf{A}$ when using a Euclidean norm.

To obtain the solution to the normal equations using the QR decomposition, let us begin with the equation (5.3.9), which we may write as [with $\mathbf{W}(n) = \mathbf{I}$]

$$\mathbf{A}_M^H\mathbf{A}_M\mathbf{h}_M = \mathbf{A}_M^H\mathbf{d} \tag{5.3.47}$$

Now if $\mathbf{Q}$ and $\mathcal{R}$ form a QRD of the data matrix $\mathbf{A}_M$, we may express (5.3.47) as

$$\begin{bmatrix} \mathcal{R}_M \\ \mathbf{O}_{N-M} \end{bmatrix}^H \mathbf{Q}^H\mathbf{Q} \begin{bmatrix} \mathcal{R}_M \\ \mathbf{O}_{N-M} \end{bmatrix} \mathbf{h}_M = \begin{bmatrix} \mathcal{R}_M \\ \mathbf{O}_{N-M} \end{bmatrix}^H \mathbf{Q}^H\mathbf{d} \tag{5.3.48}$$

where

$$\mathcal{R}_M = \begin{bmatrix} r'_{11} & r'_{12} & \cdots & r'_{1M} \\ 0 & r'_{22} & r'_{23} & r'_{2M} \\ \vdots & \vdots & \vdots & \vdots \\ 0 & 0 & 0 & r'_{MM} \end{bmatrix} \tag{5.3.49}$$

Let us define the partitioned vector $\mathbf{Q}^H\mathbf{d}$ as

$$\mathbf{Q}^H\mathbf{d} = \begin{bmatrix} \hat{\mathbf{d}}_M \\ \mathbf{c}_{N-M} \end{bmatrix} \tag{5.3.50}$$

Then

$$\begin{bmatrix} \mathfrak{R}_M \\ \mathbf{O}_{N-M} \end{bmatrix}^H \begin{bmatrix} \hat{\mathbf{d}}_M \\ \mathbf{c}_{N-M} \end{bmatrix} = \mathfrak{R}_M^H\hat{\mathbf{d}}_M + \mathbf{O}_{N-M}\mathbf{c}_{N-M} = \mathfrak{R}_M^H\hat{\mathbf{d}}_M \tag{5.3.51}$$

The left-hand side of (5.3.48) reduces to $\mathfrak{R}_M^H\mathfrak{R}_M\mathbf{h}_M$. Therefore, the QR decomposition reduces the normal equations to the equivalent form

$$\mathfrak{R}_M\mathbf{h}_M = \hat{\mathbf{d}}_M \tag{5.3.52}$$

Since $\mathfrak{R}_M$ is an upper triangular matrix, the solution of (5.3.52) is easily obtained. Hence the computational burden of solving for the optimum least-squares coefficient vector $\mathbf{h}_M$ is dominated by the computation of $\mathfrak{R}_M$ and the top M elements of $\mathbf{Q}^H\mathbf{d}$. Note that the explicit computation of $\mathbf{Q}$ is not required. We also observe that the condition number of $\mathfrak{R}_M$ is the same as that of $\mathbf{A}_M$, which is equal to the square root of the condition number of the data autocorrelation matrix $\mathbf{R}_M$. Consequently, (5.3.52) is not as sensitive to round-off errors as the solution obtained from (5.3.12).

The relationships among the QR, the Cholesky, and the LDU decomposition are easily established. From the definition of the QR decomposition, it is easily seen that

$$\mathbf{R}_m = \mathfrak{R}_M^H\mathfrak{R}_M \tag{5.3.53}$$

The $\mathfrak{R}_M$ is the Cholesky factor of the data autocorrelation matrix $\mathcal{R}_M$, as indicated previously (Remark 1).

The relationship between the QRD and LDU decompositions may be established by expressing the upper triangular matrix $\mathcal{R}_M$ as

$$\mathfrak{R}_M = \mathbf{D}_M^{1/2}\tilde{\mathfrak{R}}_M \tag{5.3.54}$$

where $\mathbf{D}_M^{1/2}$ is a diagonal matrix with elements r'_{ii}, $1 \le i \le M$, and $\tilde{\mathfrak{R}}_M$ is an upper triangular matrix with diagonal elements equal to unity and off-diagonal elements r'_{ij}/r'_{ii}. By substituting (5.3.54) into (5.3.53) we obtain

$$\mathbf{R}_M = \mathfrak{R}_M^H\mathfrak{R}_M = \tilde{\mathfrak{R}}_M^H\mathbf{D}_M^{1/2}\mathbf{D}_M^{1/2}\tilde{\mathfrak{R}}_M = \tilde{\mathfrak{R}}_M^H\mathbf{D}_M\tilde{\mathfrak{R}}_M \tag{5.3.55}$$

Since $\tilde{\mathfrak{R}}_M^H$ is a lower triangular matric with unity diagonal and $\mathbf{D}_M$ is a diagonal matrix, this decomposition of $\mathbf{R}_M$ is an LDU decomposition. From the uniqueness of the Cholesky factor $\mathfrak{R}_M$, it follows that $\mathbf{D}_M$ and $\tilde{\mathfrak{R}}_M$ are uniquely defined and hence this factorization of $\mathbf{R}_M$ is unique.

Finally, we note that the coefficient vector can also be expressed as the solution to the equation

$$\tilde{\mathfrak{R}}_M\mathbf{h}_M = \mathbf{D}_M^{-1/2}\hat{\mathbf{d}}_M \tag{5.3.56}$$

which follows directly by substituting (5.3.54) into (5.3.52). In the next three sections we describe three methods for computing the matrices $\mathbf{Q}$ and $\mathcal{R}$ from the data matrix $\mathbf{A}_M$.

5.3.6 Gram–Schmidt Orthogonalization

The Gram–Schmidt orthogonalization is a classical mathematical technique for constructing mutually orthogonal vectors from a set of linearly independent vectors. This procedure is well known in the field of linear algebra. It is often used to form an orthogonal basis in a linear space.

The application of the Gram–Schmidt orthogonalization to solving least-squares problems has been known for a long time. However, it was found [Rice (1966)] that the classical Gram–Schmidt algorithm has significantly less numerical stability than another mathematically equivalent algorithm called the *modified Gram–Schmidt (MGS) algorithm*. As a result the MGS algorithm is more widely used in practice. Below we present the classical and modified Gram–Schmidt algorithms for solving least-squares estimation problems.

The Gram–Schmidt orthogonalization procedure, or Gram–Schmidt algorithm, can be described as follows. We wish to construct a set of M mutually orthogonal vectors, $\{\mathbf{q}_1, \mathbf{q}_2, \ldots, \mathbf{q}_M\}$ from a given set of M linearly independent vectors $\{\mathbf{v}_1, \mathbf{v}_2, \ldots, \mathbf{v}_M\}$, such that for $k = 1, 2, \ldots, M$, the set $\{\mathbf{q}_1, \mathbf{q}_2, \ldots, \mathbf{q}_k\}$ spans the same k-dimensional subspace as the set $\{\mathbf{v}_1, \mathbf{v}_2, \ldots, \mathbf{v}_k\}$.

The classical Gram–Schmidt algorithm determines $\mathbf{q}_j$ in terms of $\mathbf{v}_j$ and the previously determined vectors $\mathbf{q}_1, \mathbf{q}_2, \ldots, \mathbf{q}_{j-1}$ as follows:

$$\mathbf{q}_1 = \mathbf{v}_1 \tag{5.3.57}$$

$$\mathbf{q}_j = \mathbf{v}_j - \sum_{i=1}^{j-1} \tilde{r}_{ij}\mathbf{q}_i, \qquad j = 2, 3, \ldots, M$$

where

$$\tilde{r}_{ij} = \frac{\mathbf{q}_i^H \mathbf{v}_j}{\mathbf{q}_i^H \mathbf{q}_i}, \qquad i<j \tag{5.3.58}$$

It is easily verified that $\mathbf{q}_i$ and $\mathbf{q}_j$ are orthogonal,

$$\mathbf{q}_i^H \mathbf{q}_j = 0, \qquad i \neq j \tag{5.3.59}$$

Thus the basic procedure is to form $\mathbf{q}_j$ from $\mathbf{v}_j$ by subtracting from $\mathbf{v}_j$ any components in the space spanned by $\mathbf{q}_i$, $i = 1, 2, \ldots, j-1$. What is left must be orthogonal to $\mathbf{q}_i$ and in the space spanned by $\mathbf{v}_i$, $i = 1, 2, \ldots, j-1$, and $\mathbf{v}_j$.

Since $\mathbf{q}_i$ does not have unity length, the $\mathbf{q}_i$'s are not normalized vectors. We can construct an orthonormal vector set ($\hat{\mathbf{q}}_i$, $i = 1, 2, \ldots, k$) from the set ($\mathbf{q}_i$, $i = 1, 2, \ldots, k$) by dividing each vector by its length,

$$\hat{\mathbf{q}}_i = \frac{\mathbf{q}_i}{\sqrt{\mathbf{q}_i^H \mathbf{q}_i}} \tag{5.3.60}$$

As has been mentioned above, there exists a modified version of the classical Gram–Schmidt algorithm which has better numerical behavior than the classical one. The modified Gram–Schmidt (MGS) algorithm is given below.

First, we note that the value of the inner product $k_{ij} = \mathbf{v}_j^H \mathbf{q}_i$ does not change if $\mathbf{v}_j$ is replaced by any vector of the form $\tilde{\mathbf{v}}_j = \mathbf{v}_j - \sum_{k=1}^{j-1} a_k \mathbf{q}_k$, $j > i$, because $\mathbf{q}_i$ and $\mathbf{q}_k$ are orthogonal for $k \neq i$. Our approach is to modify the set of remaining vectors $\mathbf{v}_j$ iteratively each time a new orthogonal vector is formed. Hence, in the first iteration we modify the vectors $\mathbf{v}_j$, $j = 2, 3, \ldots, M$, by subtracting $\tilde{r}_{1j}\mathbf{q}_1$ from $\mathbf{v}_j$. Thus we obtain $\mathbf{q}_j^{(1)} = \mathbf{v}_j - \tilde{r}_{1j}\mathbf{q}_1$ for $j = 2, 3, \ldots, M$. These now replace the vectors $\mathbf{v}_j$, $j = 2, 3, \ldots, M$. Then we set $\mathbf{q}_2 = \mathbf{q}_2^{(1)}$ and proceed to modify the remaining vectors $\mathbf{q}_j^{(1)}$ by replacing them with $\mathbf{q}_j^{(2)} = \mathbf{q}_j^{(1)} - \tilde{r}_{2j}\mathbf{q}_2$. In general, we have

$$\mathbf{q}_j^{(i)} = \mathbf{q}_j^{(i-1)} - \tilde{r}_{ij}\mathbf{q}_i \tag{5.3.61}$$

Thus the inner product in (5.3.58) is replaced by

$$\tilde{r}_{ij} = \frac{k_{ij}}{d_i} = \frac{\mathbf{q}_i^H \mathbf{q}_j^{(i)}}{\mathbf{q}_i^H \mathbf{q}_i} \tag{5.3.62}$$

In summary, the MGS algorithm is given by the following recursive equations:

$$\mathbf{q}_j^{(1)} = \mathbf{v}_j, \qquad j = 1, 2, \ldots, \mathrm{M} \tag{5.3.63}$$

loop $i = 1, 2, \ldots, M$:

$$\mathbf{q}_i = \mathbf{q}_i^{(1)} \tag{5.3.64}$$

$$\delta_i = k_{ii} = \mathbf{q}_i^H \mathbf{q}_i \tag{5.3.65}$$

loop $j = i + 1, \ldots, M$:

$$k_{ij} = \mathbf{q}_i^H \mathbf{q}_j^{(i)} \tag{5.3.66}$$

$$\tilde{r}_{ij} = \frac{k_{ij}}{\delta_i} \tag{5.3.67}$$

$$\mathbf{q}_j^{(i+1)} = \mathbf{q}_j^{(i)} - \tilde{r}_{ij}\mathbf{q}_i \tag{5.3.68}$$

To solve the LS problem by use of the Gram–Schmidt orthogonalization, we let the vector set $\{\mathbf{v}_k, k = 1, 2, \ldots, M\}$ be the column vectors of the data matrix $\mathbf{A}_M$ (i.e., $\{\mathbf{a}_k, k = 1, 2, \ldots, M\}$). From (5.3.63) through (5.3.68), it can be shown that the vector sets $\mathbf{q}_i$ and $\mathbf{v}_i \equiv \mathbf{a}_i$ are related by the matrix equation

$$[\mathbf{a}_1, \mathbf{a}_2, \ldots, \mathbf{a}_M] = [\mathbf{q}_1, \mathbf{q}_2, \ldots, \mathbf{q}_M]\tilde{\mathcal{R}} \tag{5.3.69}$$

where

$$\tilde{\mathcal{R}} = \begin{bmatrix} 1 & \tilde{r}_{12} & \cdots & \tilde{r}_{1M} \\ & 1 & \cdots & \tilde{r}_{2M} \\ & & \ddots & \vdots \\ \mathbf{0} & & & 1 \end{bmatrix} \tag{5.3.70}$$

By using the normalized (orthonormal) vectors $\hat{\mathbf{q}}_i^H$, $i = 1, \ldots, M$, as the first M row vectors, we construct an orthogonal matrix **Q**. The choice of the rest of the row vectors of **Q** are rather arbitrary (actually, they are never used) as long as they are mutually orthogonal and orthogonal to $\mathbf{q}_i$, $i = 1, \ldots, M$. The orthogonal matrix **Q** can be expressed as

$$\mathbf{Q} = [\hat{\mathbf{q}}_1, \hat{\mathbf{q}}_2, \ldots, \hat{\mathbf{q}}_M, *, \ldots, *]^H \tag{5.3.71}$$

where the * denotes vectors that are orthogonal to $\hat{\mathbf{q}}_i$, $i = 1, \ldots, M$.

By premultiplying **Q** on both sides of (5.3.69) and noticing that $\mathbf{q}_i$'s are mutually orthogonal, and the bottom $N - M$ row vectors of **Q** are orthogonal to $\mathbf{a}_i$, we have

$$\mathbf{Q}[\mathbf{a}_1, \mathbf{a}_2, \ldots, \mathbf{a}_M] = \begin{bmatrix} \mathbf{D}^{1/2}\tilde{\mathcal{R}} \\ \mathbf{0} \end{bmatrix} = \begin{bmatrix} \mathcal{R} \\ \mathbf{0} \end{bmatrix} \tag{5.3.72}$$

where $\mathbf{D}^{1/2}$ is a diagonal matrix whose ith element is $\mathbf{q}_i^H \mathbf{q}_i / \sqrt{\delta_i} = \sqrt{\delta_i}$, for $i = 1, 2, \ldots, M$. Equation (5.3.72) clearly shows that the Gram–Schmidt algorithm, either classical or modified, indeed provides a QRD of the data matrix $\mathbf{A}_M$.

5.3.7 Givens Rotation

In this section we describe a method for constructing a QR decomposition based on a series of plane rotations, called *Givens rotations*. Let us consider a two-component vector $\mathbf{v} = [v_1, v_2]^t$, where for the moment, we assume that v_1 and v_2 are real. The vector has length $r = \sqrt{v_1^2 + v_2^2}$ and angle $\theta = \tan^{-1}(v_2/v_1)$. Hence

$$\mathbf{v} = \begin{bmatrix} v_1 \\ v_2 \end{bmatrix} = \begin{bmatrix} r\cos\theta \\ r\sin\theta \end{bmatrix} \tag{5.3.73}$$

Suppose that we wish to construct an angle-rotated vector **v** as shown in Fig. 5.13. It is easily verified that by selecting an orthogonal transformation matrix **G** as

$$\mathbf{G} = \begin{bmatrix} \cos\phi & \sin\phi \\ -\sin\phi & \cos\phi \end{bmatrix} \tag{5.3.74}$$

the vector $\mathbf{v}' = \mathbf{G}\mathbf{v}$ is

$$\mathbf{v}' = \begin{bmatrix} r\cos(\theta - \phi) \\ r\sin(\theta - \phi) \end{bmatrix} \tag{5.3.75}$$

Note that $\mathbf{G}^t\mathbf{G} = \mathbf{I}$, so that the column vectors in **G** are normalized to unit length.

Now, suppose that we choose an angle rotation matrix such that the second component of $\mathbf{v}'$ is zero (i.e., $v_2' = 0$). Then

$$-v_1\sin\phi + v_2\cos\phi = 0 \tag{5.3.76}$$

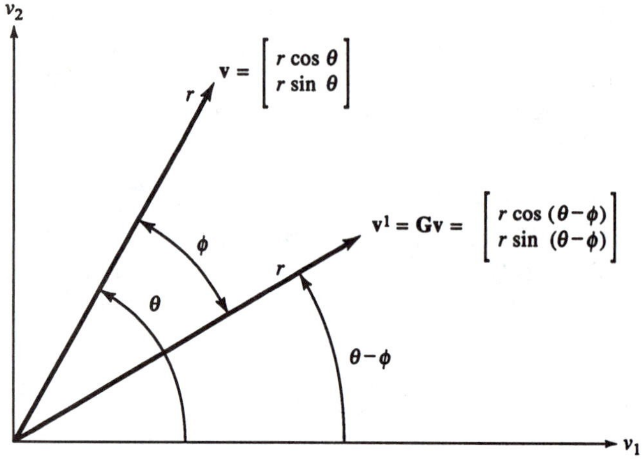

FIGURE 5.13 Angle rotation of a vector.

and

$$\phi = \tan^{-1}\frac{v_2}{v_1} \tag{5.3.77}$$

Thus the elements of **G** become

$$\mathbf{G} = \begin{bmatrix} c & s \\ -s & c \end{bmatrix} \tag{5.3.78}$$

where

$$\begin{aligned} c = \cos\phi &= \frac{v_1}{\sqrt{v_1^2 + v_2^2}} \\ s = \sin\phi &= \frac{v_2}{\sqrt{v_1^2 + v_2^2}} \end{aligned} \tag{5.3.79}$$

This procedure is easily extended to vectors with complex-valued elements. Thus for any given vector $\mathbf{v} = [\, v_1, v_2]$, where v_1 and v_2 are complex, the 2×2 orthogonal matrix **G**, which results in

$$\mathbf{G}\mathbf{v} = \begin{bmatrix} r \\ 0 \end{bmatrix} \tag{5.3.80}$$

is given by

$$\mathbf{G} = \begin{bmatrix} c & s \\ -s^* & c \end{bmatrix} \tag{5.3.81}$$

where $r = \sqrt{|v_1|^2 + |v_2|^2}$, $c = v_1/r$, and $s = v_2^*/r$. It is easily verified that $\mathbf{G}^H\mathbf{G} = \mathbf{I}$.

The development above demonstrates that it is possible to annihilate an element in a two-dimensional vector by using a Givens rotation. We can extend the elementary Givens rotation to annihilate an element in a vector with n elements. This can be done as follows: For an N-dimensional vector $\mathbf{v}_N = [v_1, \ldots, v_j, \ldots, v_k, \ldots, v_N]^t$, with either $v_j \neq 0$ or $v_k \neq 0$, we can construct an $N \times N$ orthogonal matrix $\mathbf{G}_N$ such that

$$\mathbf{G}_N = \begin{bmatrix} I & & & & 0 \\ & c & \mathbf{0}^t & s & \\ & \mathbf{0} & I & \mathbf{0} & \\ & -s^* & \mathbf{0}^t & c & \\ 0 & & & & I \\ \cdot & j & \cdots & k & \cdot \end{bmatrix} \begin{matrix} : \\ i \\ : \\ j \\ : \\ \end{matrix} \tag{5.3.82}$$

where $c = v_i/\sqrt{|v_i|^2 + |v_j|^2}$ and $s = v_j^*/\sqrt{|v_i|^2 + |v_j|^2}$. It can be shown that

$$\mathbf{G}_N\mathbf{v}_N = [v_1, \ldots \sqrt{|v_i|^2 + |v_j|^2}, \ldots, 0, \ldots, v_n]^t \tag{5.3.83}$$

It is easy to verify that $\mathbf{G}_N$ is an orthogonal matrix (i.e., $\mathbf{G}_N^H\mathbf{G}_N = \mathbf{I}$). Since all the other elements of $\mathbf{v}_N$ except v_j and v_k do not change, we say that such a Givens rotation operates on the jth and kth elements of $\mathbf{v}_N$. If it is operating on a matrix with N rows, it will modify only the ith and jth rows, and we say that it operates on the ith and jth rows of the matrix.

By applying another Givens rotation operating on two elements of the vector $\mathbf{G}_N\mathbf{v}_N$ obtained in (5.3.83), we can generate one more zero in this vector. Thus we can annihilate all but one of the elements of vector $\mathbf{v}_N$, leaving only one nonzero element, by using at most $N - 1$ Givens rotations. As a consequence of the length-preserving property of orthogonal transformations, it can be shown that the residual element is equal to the length of $\mathbf{v}_N$ (square root of the sum of all the squared elements of the vector $\mathbf{v}_N$).

Let us now consider the use of Givens rotation to perform a QRD of the data matrix $\mathbf{A}_M$. First, by annihilating the elements in the second row through the Nth row of the first column of $\mathbf{A}_M$ using $N - 1$ Givens rotations as described above, we are left with the elements in the top row unannihilated. Then, without touching the first row, we construct $N - 2$ Givens rotations to eliminate the third through Nth elements in the second column. These Givens rotations do not affect the first column because all the elements in the second through the Nth rows of this column have already been set to zero. By continuing this procedure, we can convert the matrix $\mathbf{A}_M$ into an upper triangular matrix and thus realize its QR decomposition. The orthogonal matrix $\mathbf{Q}$ is the product of the $M \times (2N - M + 1)/2$ Givens rotation matrices. Note that $\mathbf{Q}$ is not computed explicitly.

To solve the exponentially weighted LS problem using the Givens rotations, we first combine the matrix $\mathbf{A}_M$ and vector $\mathbf{d}$ into an augmented matrix $\bar{\mathbf{A}}_M = [\mathbf{A}_M \;\; \mathbf{d}]$. By applying a series of Givens rotations to $\mathbf{A}_M$ to perform the QR decomposition of $\mathbf{A}_M(n)$, we also obtain the rotated vector $\underline{\mathbf{d}}$, which is the last column of matrix $\mathbf{Q}\bar{\mathbf{A}}_M$. Then the coefficient vector $\mathbf{h}_M$ can be solved as described previously by solving (5.3.52).

As described above, the Givens transformation involves the computation of square roots, which, in general, is a time-consuming operation for conventional multiply–add digital computers. In Chapter 7 we present a specially configured processor called a CORDIC which performs Givens rotations efficiently. Alternatively, we may devise *square-root-free* Givens transformations. This topic is also treated in Chapter 7.

5.3.8 Householder Reflection

In this section we describe another type of orthogonal transformation, called a *Householder reflection,* to perform a QR decomposition. Unlike the Givens transformation, the Householder transformation is a reflection rather than a rotation. As a consequence, the determinant of the Householder transformation matrix is equal to -1.

The Householder transformation $\mathbf{H}$ is usually expressed as

$$\mathbf{H} = \mathbf{I} - 2\mathbf{b}_0\mathbf{b}_0^H \tag{5.3.84}$$

where $\mathbf{b}_0$ is a vector whose elements are to be determined and which has unit length (i.e., $\mathbf{b}_0^H\mathbf{b}_0 = 1$). It is interesting to note that $\mathbf{H}^H = \mathbf{H}$. Consequently,

$$\begin{aligned}\mathbf{H}^H\mathbf{H} = \mathbf{H}\mathbf{H} &= [\mathbf{I} - 2\mathbf{b}_0\mathbf{b}_0^H]\,[\mathbf{I} - 2\mathbf{b}_0\mathbf{b}_0^H] \\ &= \mathbf{I} - 4\mathbf{b}_0\mathbf{b}_0^H + 4\mathbf{b}_0\mathbf{b}_0^H\mathbf{b}_0\mathbf{b}_0^H \\ &= \mathbf{I} - 4\mathbf{b}_0\mathbf{b}_0^H + 4\mathbf{b}_0\mathbf{b}_0^H = \mathbf{I}\end{aligned}$$

Hence $\mathbf{H}$ is orthogonal.

We also observe that if $\mathbf{b}_0 = \mathbf{x}$, then $\mathbf{Hx} = -\mathbf{x}$. From this relationship we deduce that the transformation matrix $\mathbf{H}$ is a projection operator that results in a reflected image of any arbitrary vector $\mathbf{z}$ with respect to the orthogonal subspace of $\mathbf{b}_0$. This geometrical interpretation is shown in Fig. 5.14.

To use the Householder transformation to perform the QR decomposition, we first consider the problem of using a Householder transformation to zero all the elements of a vector except one. Assuming that we have an N-

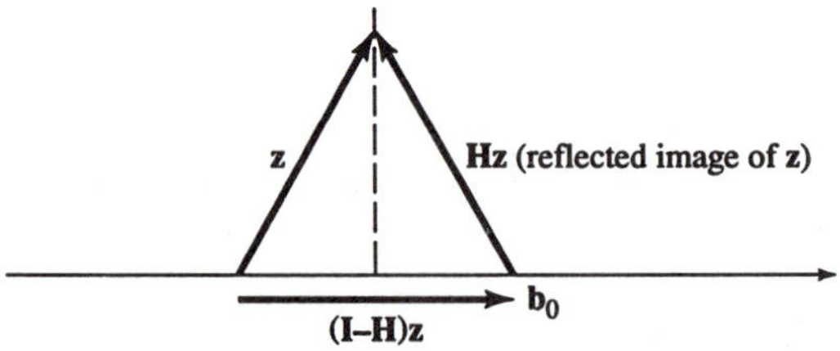

FIGURE 5.14 Geometrical interpretation of the Householder transformation.

dimensional vector $\mathbf{v} = [v_1, \ldots, v_i, \ldots, v_N]^t$, let us define the (unnormalized) vector $\mathbf{b}$ for a Householder transformation $\mathbf{H}_b = \mathbf{I} - 2\mathbf{b}\mathbf{b}^H/\mathbf{b}^H\mathbf{b}$ as

$$\mathbf{b} = \mathbf{v} + \sigma \|\mathbf{v}\| \, \mathbf{E}_i \qquad (5.3.85)$$

where $\sigma = v_i/|v_i|$ and $\|\mathbf{v}\|$ is the Euclidian norm, or length, of the vector $\mathbf{v}$,

$$\|\mathbf{v}\| = \sqrt{\mathbf{v}^H\mathbf{v}} = \sqrt{\sum_{k=1}^{N} |v_k|^2} \qquad (5.3.86)$$

and $\mathbf{E}_i$ is an n-dimensional vector that has $N - 1$ zeros and one element equal to 1 at the ith location. Applying the Householder transformation to $\mathbf{v}$, based on the vector $\mathbf{b}$ given by (5.3.85) we have

$$\mathbf{H}_b\mathbf{v} = \mathbf{v} - \frac{2\mathbf{b}\mathbf{b}^H\mathbf{v}}{\mathbf{b}^H\mathbf{b}} = \mathbf{v} - 2(\mathbf{v} + \sigma\|\mathbf{v}\|\mathbf{E}_i)\frac{(\mathbf{v}^H + \sigma^*\|\mathbf{v}\|\mathbf{E}_i^t)\mathbf{v}}{\|\mathbf{b}\|^2} \qquad (5.3.87)$$

The squared norm of vector $\mathbf{b}$ is

$$\begin{aligned} \|\mathbf{b}\|^2 = \mathbf{b}^H\mathbf{b} &= (\mathbf{v}^H + \sigma^*\|\mathbf{v}\|\mathbf{E}_i^t)\,(\mathbf{v} + \sigma\|\mathbf{v}\|\mathbf{E}_i) \\ &= \mathbf{v}^H\mathbf{v} + 2\,\mathrm{Re}\,[\sigma^*\|\mathbf{v}\|\mathbf{E}_i^t\mathbf{v}] + |\sigma|^2\|\mathbf{v}\|^2\mathbf{E}_i^t\mathbf{E}_i \end{aligned} \qquad (5.3.88)$$

Since $\mathbf{E}_i^t\mathbf{v} = v_i$ we have

$$\sigma^*\mathbf{E}_i^t\mathbf{v} = \frac{v_i^*}{|v_i|}v_i = \frac{|v_i|^2}{|v_i|} = |v_i| \qquad (5.3.89)$$

By using the relations $\mathbf{E}_i^t\mathbf{E}_i = 1$, $\mathbf{E}_i^t\mathbf{v} = \mathrm{v}_i$, $|\sigma|^2 = |v_i|^2/|v_i|^2 = 1$, and (5.3.88) we obtain

$$\|\mathbf{b}\|^2 = \mathbf{b}^H\mathbf{b} = 2\|\mathbf{v}\|^2 + 2\|\mathbf{v}\|\,\mathrm{Re}[\sigma^*\mathbf{E}_i^t\mathbf{v}] = 2(\|\mathbf{v}\|^2 + |v_i|\|\mathbf{v}\|) \qquad (5.3.90)$$

Then, by using (5.3.88) and (5.3.89), we can rewrite (5.3.87) as

$$\begin{aligned} \mathbf{H}_b\mathbf{v} &= \mathbf{v} - \frac{2\mathbf{b}\mathbf{b}^H\mathbf{v}}{\|\mathbf{b}\|^2} = \mathbf{v} - 2(\mathbf{v} + \sigma\|\mathbf{v}\|\mathbf{E}_i)\frac{(\mathbf{v}^H + \sigma^*\|\mathbf{v}\|\mathbf{E}_i^t)\mathbf{v}}{\|\mathbf{b}\|^2} \\ &= \mathbf{v} - 2(\mathbf{v} + \sigma\|\mathbf{v}\|\mathbf{E}_i)\left[\frac{\|\mathbf{v}\|^2 + \sigma^*\|\mathbf{v}\|\mathbf{E}_i^t\mathbf{v}}{\|\mathbf{b}|^2}\right] \\ &= \mathbf{v} - 2(\mathbf{v} + \sigma\|\mathbf{v}\|\mathbf{E}_i)\frac{\|\mathbf{v}\|^2 + |v_i|\|\mathbf{v}\|}{2(\|\mathbf{v}\|^2 + |v_i|\|\mathbf{v}\|)} \\ &= \mathbf{v} - (\mathbf{v} + \sigma\|\mathbf{v}\|\mathbf{E}_i) = -\sigma\|\mathbf{v}\|\mathbf{E}_i = -\frac{\mathrm{v}_i}{|v_i|}\|\mathbf{v}\|\mathbf{E}_i \end{aligned} \qquad (5.3.91)$$

Equation (5.3.91) shows that the Householder transformation given by (5.3.84) transforms vector $\mathbf{v}$ into another vector with only one nonzero element, $-(v_i / |v_i|)\|\mathbf{v}\|$ at the ith location. We can also view this process as a transformation that compresses the total energy of $\mathbf{v}$ into the single ith element. It is also possible to let $\sigma = -(v_i/|v_i|)$. However, from (5.3.88) and (5.3.90) we note that the expression with the plus sign is more desirable because we can avoid loss of precision due to subtraction in the computation of $\|\mathbf{b}\|^2$ in the denominator.

Now, let us apply the Householder transformation to perform the QR decomposition of the augmented data matrix $\overline{\mathbf{A}}$. First we denote the kth column vector $\mathbf{a}_k$ as

$$\mathbf{a}_k = [x_{k1}^{(1)}, x_{k2}^{(1)}, \ldots, x_{kN}^{(1)}]^t, \qquad k = 1, 2, \ldots, M$$

The elements of the column vector $\mathbf{e}$ are denoted by $e_k^{(1)}$, $k = 1, 2, \ldots, N$.

The first Householder transformation is constructed based on the vector $\mathbf{b}_1$, defined by

$$\mathbf{b}_1 = \mathbf{p}_1 + \sigma_1 \|\mathbf{p}_1\| \mathbf{E}_1 \tag{5.3.92}$$

where $\mathbf{p}_1 = \mathbf{a}_1$ and $\sigma_1 = x_{11}^{(1)}/|x_{11}^{(1)}|$. The Householder matrix $\mathbf{H}_1$ based on $\mathbf{b}_1$ is

$$\mathbf{H}_1 = \mathbf{I} - \frac{2\mathbf{b}_1\mathbf{b}_1^H}{\mathbf{b}_1^H\mathbf{b}_1} \tag{5.3.93}$$

By applying $\mathbf{H}_1$ to $\overline{\mathbf{A}}$, we annihilate all the elements in the first column except its first element. All other columns are also transformed and the transformed matrix can be expressed as

$$\mathbf{H}_1\overline{\mathbf{A}} = \begin{bmatrix} r_{11} & r_{12} & \cdots & r_{1M} & r_{1z} \\ 0 & x_{22}^{(2)} & \cdots & x_{M2}^{(2)} & e_2^{(2)} \\ \vdots & \vdots & \cdots & \vdots & \vdots \\ 0 & x_{2N}^{(2)} & \cdots & x_{MN}^{(2)} & e_N^{(2)} \end{bmatrix} \tag{5.3.94}$$

Note that the computational complexity of multiplying $\overline{\mathbf{A}}$ by the Householder matrix $\mathbf{H}_1$ is much less than that required for multiplying it by a general $M \times M$ matrix. The total number of complex multiplications and accumulations (CMACs) required to compute $\mathbf{H}_1\overline{\mathbf{A}}$ is approximately equal to $2NM$. In addition, we also need a division and a square-root operation. By comparison, to multiply by a general $M \times M$ matrix would have required NM^2 CMACs.

In the second step, we construct a second Householder matrix $\mathbf{H}_2$, as

$$\mathbf{H}_2 = \mathbf{I} - \frac{2\mathbf{b}_2\mathbf{b}_2^H}{\mathbf{b}_2^H\mathbf{b}_2} \tag{5.3.95}$$

which is based on the vector $\mathbf{b}_2$ defined as

$$\mathbf{b}_2 = \mathbf{p}_2 + \sigma_2\|\mathbf{p}_2\|\mathbf{E}_2 \tag{5.3.96}$$

where

$$\mathbf{p}_2 = [0, x_{22}^{(2)}, x_{23}^{(2)}, \ldots x_{2N}^{(2)}]^t \tag{5.3.97}$$

and $\sigma_2 = [x_{22}^{(2)}/|x_{22}^{(2)}|]$. The zero in the first element of $\mathbf{p}_2$ occurs because we wish not to modify the first row of the matrix $\mathbf{H}_1\overline{\mathbf{A}}$, which has already been placed in the desired form. By applying $\mathbf{H}_2$ to matrix $\mathbf{H}_1\overline{A}$, we have

$$\mathbf{H}_2\mathbf{H}_1\overline{\mathbf{A}} = \begin{bmatrix} r_{11} & r_{12} & \cdots & r_{1M} & r_{1z} \\ 0 & r_{22} & \cdots & r_{2M} & r_{2z} \\ 0 & 0 & \cdots & x_{M3}^{(3)} & e_3^{(3)} \\ \vdots & \vdots & \cdots & & \\ 0 & & \cdots & x_{MN}^{(3)} & e_N^{(3)} \end{bmatrix} \tag{5.3.98}$$

Applying $\mathbf{H}_2$ to matrix $\mathbf{H}_1\overline{\mathbf{A}}$ requires a $2 \times (M - 1) \times (N - 1)$ CMACs plus one division and one square-root operation.

Similarly, we can annihilate the bottom $N - 3$ elements of the third column of the matrix $\mathbf{H}_2\mathbf{H}_1\overline{\mathbf{A}}$. By continuing this process, after applying $M + 1$ Householder transformations, we have transformed the matrix $\overline{\mathbf{A}}$ into an upper triangular matrix,

$$\mathbf{H}_{M+1}\mathbf{H}_M \cdots \mathbf{H}_1\overline{\mathbf{A}} = \begin{bmatrix} \mathcal{R} & \tilde{\mathbf{d}}_M \\ 0 & * \\ \mathbf{0} & \mathbf{0} \end{bmatrix} \tag{5.3.99}$$

Then the LS coefficient vector $\mathbf{h}_M$ can be obtained by solving

$$\mathcal{R}\,\mathbf{h}_M = \tilde{\mathbf{d}}_M \tag{5.3.100}$$

It should be noted that unlike the R-factors generated by the Givens algorithm or the Gram–Schmidt algorithm, the diagonal elements of the upper triangular matrix $\mathcal{R}$ generated by the Householder transformation are, in general, neither real nor positive. However, it is always possible to multiply each row of $\begin{bmatrix} \mathcal{R} & \tilde{\mathbf{d}}_M \\ 0 & * \end{bmatrix}$ by a complex number with unity magnitude to make the diagonal elements become real and positive. From the uniqueness of the R-factor in the QRD it can be shown that the converted matrix problem is identical to the R-factor matrix generated by the Givens algorithm.

The computational complexity of the LS estimation problem using the Householder transformation can be obtained as follows. In the ith step of the Householder transformation of the signal matrix $\mathbf{W}\overline{\mathbf{A}}$, we need about $2 \times (M - i + 1) \times (N - i + 1)$ complex multiplications and additions plus one square-root operation and one division [Rader and Steinhardt (1986)]. For a total of M steps, we need about $(M^2 \times N - M^3/3)$ CMACs plus M square-root operations and M divisions.

5.3.9 Singular-Value Decomposition

In this section we present another orthogonal decomposition of a rectangular matrix that is practically useful in solving least-squares problems. We begin by considering the eigenvalue–eigenvector decomposition of a positive definite symmetric $M \times M$ autocorrelation matrix $\mathbf{R}_M$. Such a matrix has a decomposition of the form

$$\mathbf{R}_M = \mathbf{V}_M\mathbf{\Lambda}_M\mathbf{V}_M^H \tag{5.3.101}$$

where $\mathbf{V}_M$ is the $M \times M$ orthogonal matrix consisting of the eigenvectors of $\mathbf{R}_M$ and $\mathbf{\Lambda}_M = \text{diag}(\lambda_1, \lambda_2, \ldots, \lambda_M)$, where the diagonal elements are the eigenvalues of $\mathbf{R}_M$. For convenience, we arrange the eigenvalues as a nonincreasing sequence (i.e., $\lambda_1 \geq \lambda_2 \geq \lambda_3, \ldots \geq \lambda_M$).

Singular-Value Decomposition of a Square Matrix. The eigenvalue–eigenvector decomposition of $\mathbf{R}_M$ is simply related to the singular-value decomposition of a matrix. Suppose that $\mathbf{A}$ is restricted to be a nonsingular square $M \times M$ data matrix and let $\mathbf{R}_M = \mathbf{A}^H\mathbf{A}$. Then there exists an $M \times M$ orthogonal matrix $\mathbf{U}_M$, an $M \times M$ orthogonal matrix $\mathbf{V}_M$, and an $M \times M$ diagonal matrix $\mathbf{\Sigma}$ with diagonal elements σ_i such that

$$\mathbf{A} = \mathbf{U\Sigma V}^H \tag{5.3.102}$$

The diagonal elements of $\mathbf{\Sigma}$ are positive and are arranged in nonincreasing order (i.e., $\sigma_1 \geq \sigma_2 \geq \cdots \geq \sigma_M > 0$). These elements are called the *singular values* of the matrix $\mathbf{A}$ and are related to the eigenvalues of $\mathbf{R}_M = \mathbf{A}^H\mathbf{A}$.

The relationship between σ_i and λ_i is established by substituting (5.3.102) in $\mathbf{R}_M = \mathbf{A}^H\mathbf{A}$ and comparing the result with (5.3.101). Thus we obtain

$$\mathbf{\Sigma\Sigma} = \mathbf{\Sigma}^2 = \mathbf{\Lambda} \tag{5.3.103}$$

where $\sigma_i = \sqrt{\lambda_i}$. Consequently, the singular values of the matrix $\mathbf{A}_M$ are the positive square roots of the eigenvalues of $\mathbf{A}^H\mathbf{A}$.

Now let us define an $M \times M$ matrix $\mathbf{U}$ as

$$\mathbf{U} = \mathbf{AV\Sigma}^{-1} \tag{5.3.104}$$

where $\mathbf{V}$ is the $M \times M$ orthogonal matrix obtained from the eigenvalue–eigenvector decomposition of $\mathbf{A}^M\mathbf{A}$. Then

$$\begin{aligned}\mathbf{U}^H\mathbf{U} &= \mathbf{\Sigma}^{-1}\mathbf{V}^H\mathbf{A}^H\mathbf{AV\Sigma}^{-1} \\ &= \mathbf{\Sigma}^{-1}\mathbf{V}^H\mathbf{V\Lambda V}^H\mathbf{V\Sigma}^{-1} \\ &= \mathbf{\Sigma}^{-1}\mathbf{\Lambda\Sigma}^{-1} = \mathbf{I}_M\end{aligned}$$

Hence $\mathbf{U}$ is an orthogonal matrix. Thus we have demonstrated that a nonsingular, square data matrix $\mathbf{A}$ has a singular-value decomposition (SVD) as indicated by (5.3.102), where $\mathbf{U}$ and $\mathbf{V}$ are orthogonal matrices and $\mathbf{\Sigma}$ is a diagonal matrix with elements σ_i, which are the positive square roots of the eigenvalues of $\mathbf{A}^H\mathbf{A}$.

Singular-Value Decomposition of a Rectangular Matrix. Now let us assume that $\mathbf{A}$ is an $N \times M$ matrix of rank k. Then there exists an $N \times N$ orthogonal matrix $\mathbf{U}$, an $M \times M$ orthogonal matrix $\mathbf{V}$, and an $N \times M$ diagonal matrix $\mathbf{\Sigma}$ such that

$$\mathbf{A} = \mathbf{U\Sigma V}^H \tag{5.3.105}$$

where $\mathbf{\Sigma}$ is defined as

$$\mathbf{\Sigma} = \begin{bmatrix} \mathbf{S} & \mathbf{0} \\ \mathbf{0} & \mathbf{0} \end{bmatrix} \tag{5.3.106}$$

and

$$\mathbf{S} = \text{diag}(\sigma_1, \sigma_2, \ldots, \sigma_k)$$

The first k singular values in $\boldsymbol{\Sigma}$ are strictly positive (i.e., $\sigma_1 \geq \sigma_2 \geq \cdots \geq \sigma_k > 0$). The remaining $N - k$ singular values are zero.

The SVD of $\mathbf{A}$ may also be expressed as

$$\mathbf{A} = \sum_{i=1}^{k} \sigma_i \mathbf{u}_i \mathbf{v}_i^H \tag{5.3.107}$$

where $\mathbf{u}_i$ are the column vectors of $\mathbf{U}$, which are called the *left singular vectors of* $\mathbf{A}$, and $\mathbf{v}_i$ are the column vectors of $\mathbf{A}$, which are called the *right singular vectors of* $\mathbf{A}$.

The singular values σ_i are the nonnegative square roots of the eigenvalues of $\mathbf{A}^H\mathbf{A}$. To demonstrate this point, we postmultiply (5.3.105) by $\mathbf{V}$. Thus we obtain

$$\mathbf{AV} = \mathbf{U\Sigma} \tag{5.3.108}$$

or equivalently,

$$\mathbf{A}\mathbf{v}_i = \begin{cases} \sigma_i \mathbf{u}_i, & 1 \leq i \leq k \\ \mathbf{0}, & k < i \leq M \end{cases} \tag{5.3.109}$$

Similarly, we may postmultiply $\mathbf{A}^H = \mathbf{V\Sigma U}^H$ by $\mathbf{U}$. Thus we obtain

$$\mathbf{A}^H\mathbf{U} = \mathbf{V\Sigma} \tag{5.3.110}$$

or equivalently,

$$\mathbf{A}^H\mathbf{u}_i = \begin{cases} \sigma_i \mathbf{v}_i, & 1 \leq i \leq k \\ \mathbf{0}, & k < i \leq N \end{cases} \tag{5.3.111}$$

Then, by premultiplying both sides of (5.3.109) with $\mathbf{A}^H$ and using (5.3.111), we obtain

$$\mathbf{A}^H\mathbf{A}\mathbf{v}_i = \begin{cases} \sigma_i^2 \mathbf{v}_i, & 1 \leq i \leq k \\ \mathbf{0}, & k < i \leq M \end{cases} \tag{5.3.112}$$

This demonstrates that the M eigenvalues of $\mathbf{A}^H\mathbf{A}$ are the squares of the singular values of $\mathbf{A}$ and the corresponding M eigenvectors $\mathbf{v}_i$ are the right singular vectors of $\mathbf{A}$.

Next, we premultiply both sides of (5.3.111) by $\mathbf{A}$ and use (5.3.109) to obtain

$$\mathbf{A}\mathbf{A}^H\mathbf{u}_i = \begin{cases} \sigma_i^2 \mathbf{u}_i, & 0 \leq i \leq k \\ \mathbf{0}, & k < i \leq N \end{cases} \tag{5.3.113}$$

This demonstrates that the N eigenvalues of $\mathbf{AA}^H$ are the squares of the singular values of $\mathbf{A}^H$ and the corresponding N eigenvectors $\mathbf{u}_i$ of $\mathbf{AA}^H$ are the left singular vectors of $\mathbf{A}$.

We also observe that the number of positive singular values of $\mathbf{A}$ is equal to the rank of $\mathbf{A}$. This number is simply the number of linearly independent columns of **A**. Furthermore, it can be shown that the norm of **A** is equal to the largest singular value of **A**,

$$\|\mathbf{A}\| = \sigma_1 \tag{5.3.114}$$

The SVD from the QR Decomposition. The SVD of a rectangular $N \times M$ matrix **A** can also be obtained from the QR decomposition. Recall that any $N \times M$ matrix **A**, where $N > M$, can be decomposed as

$$\mathbf{A} = \mathbf{Q}\begin{bmatrix} \mathcal{R} \\ \mathbf{0} \end{bmatrix} \tag{5.3.115}$$

where **Q** is an N × N orthogonal matrix, $\mathcal{R}$ is an M × M upper triangular matrix, and **0** is the $(N - M) \times M$ null matrix.

Suppose that we perform the SVD of the $M \times M$ matrix $\mathcal{R}$. Thus we obtain

$$\mathcal{R} = \mathbf{W}\mathbf{\Sigma}_M\mathbf{V}^H \tag{5.3.116}$$

where **W** and **V** are $M \times M$ orthogonal matrices. Now we may define an $N \times N$ orthogonal matrix **U** and an $N \times M$ diagonal matrix $\mathbf{\Sigma}$ as

$$\begin{aligned} \mathbf{U} &= \mathbf{Q}\begin{bmatrix} \mathbf{W} & \mathbf{0} \\ \mathbf{0} & \mathbf{I} \end{bmatrix} \\ \mathbf{\Sigma} &= \begin{bmatrix} \mathbf{\Sigma}_M \\ \mathbf{0} \end{bmatrix} \end{aligned} \tag{5.3.117}$$

where **I** is the identity matrix of dimension $N - M$. Thus we obtain the SVD of **A** as

$$\mathbf{A} = \mathbf{U}\mathbf{\Sigma}\mathbf{V}^H \tag{5.3.118}$$

In summary, the SVD of **A** may be computed by first performing a QR decomposition of **A**. For this computation we may use either Givens transformations or Householder transformations. Once **Q** and $\mathcal{R}$ are obtained, we must decompose $\mathcal{R}$. This may be accomplished by using one of several existing SVD algorithms that are designed for square matrices, such as the Jacobi method, which is based on Givens rotations [see Golub and Van Loan (1989)]. A particularly straightforward method is to work with $\mathcal{R}^H$, where

$$\mathcal{R}^H = (\mathbf{W}\mathbf{\Sigma}_M\mathbf{V}^H)^H = \mathbf{V}\mathbf{\Sigma}_M\mathbf{W}^H \tag{5.3.119}$$

and to diagonalize $\mathcal{R}^H$ by performing a series of plane (Givens) rotations or Householder reflections. Thus we may apply a form of the QR decomposition on the lower triangular matrix $\mathcal{R}^H$. Lawson and Hanson (1974) describe such a method based on the use of a sequence of Householder transformations and special plane rotations to obtain the decomposition given by (5.3.119). A FORTRAN subroutine is provided in their text for the computation of the SVD. Other methods for computing the SVD of a square matrix directly, based on the use of Jacobi transformations, have been described by Luk (1986), Brent and Luk (1985), and Brent, Luk, and Van Loan (1985) and implemented efficiently on parallel processing computers.

The Moore–Penrose Pseudoinverse. When a rectangular $N \times M$ matrix $\mathbf{A}$ has a SVD as $\mathbf{A} = \mathbf{U\Sigma V}^H$, its Moore–Penrose pseudoinverse, denoted by $\mathbf{A}^+$, is an $M \times N$ matrix defined as

$$\mathbf{A}^+ = \mathbf{V\Sigma}^+\mathbf{U}^H \tag{5.3.120}$$

where $\mathbf{\Sigma}^+$ is an $M \times N$ matrix defined as

$$\mathbf{\Sigma}^+ = \begin{bmatrix} \mathbf{S}^{-1} & \mathbf{0} \\ \mathbf{0} & \mathbf{0} \end{bmatrix} \tag{5.3.121}$$

and $\mathbf{S}^{-1}$ is a $k \times k$ diagonal matrix with elements equal to the reciprocals of the singular values of $\mathbf{A}$,

$$\mathbf{S}^{-1} = \text{diag}\left(\frac{1}{\sigma_1}, \frac{1}{\sigma_2}, \ldots, \frac{1}{\sigma_k}\right) \tag{5.3.122}$$

We may also express the right-hand side of (5.3.120) in terms of the right and left singular vectors of $\mathbf{A}$,

$$\mathbf{A}^+ = \sum_{i=1}^{k} \frac{1}{\sigma_i} \mathbf{v}_i\mathbf{u}_i^H$$

Thus we observe that the rank of $\mathbf{A}^+$ is equal to the rank of $\mathbf{A}$.

The Moore–Penrose pseudoinverse $\mathbf{A}^+$ plays an important role in the solution of the least-squares problem, as we observe below.

When the rank $k = M$ or $k = N$, the pseudoinverse $\mathbf{A}^+$ can be expressed in terms of $\mathbf{A}$. To be specific,

$$\begin{aligned} \mathbf{A}^+ &= \mathbf{A}^H(\mathbf{AA}^H)^{-1}, && k = N \\ \mathbf{A}^+ &= (\mathbf{A}^H\mathbf{A})^{-1}\mathbf{A}^H, && k = M \\ \mathbf{A}^+ &= \mathbf{A}^{-1}, && k = M = N \end{aligned} \tag{5.3.123}$$

The relations are equivalent to

$$\begin{aligned} \mathbf{AA}^+ &= \mathbf{I}_M, && k = M \\ \mathbf{A}^+\mathbf{A} &= \mathbf{I}_N, && k = N \\ \mathbf{AA}^+ = \mathbf{A}^+\mathbf{A} &= \mathbf{I}_M, && k = M = N \end{aligned} \tag{5.3.124}$$

which are easily established from the SVDs of $\mathbf{A}$ and $\mathbf{A}^+$.

Use of the SVD in Computing the Least-Squares Solution. Let us return to the least-squares problem, in which the error vector $\mathbf{e}$ is defined as

$$\mathbf{e} = \mathbf{d} - \mathbf{A}_M\mathbf{h}_M \tag{5.3.125}$$

where $\mathbf{d}$ is the desired signal vector and $\mathbf{A}_M\mathbf{h}_M$ is the estimate $\hat{\mathbf{d}}$. The problem is to determine the vector $\mathbf{h}_M$ that minimizes the squared norm (i.e., $\|\mathbf{e}\|^2$).

By using the SVD of $\mathbf{A}_M$ in (5.3.125), we obtain

$$\mathbf{e} = \mathbf{d} - \mathbf{U}\mathbf{\Sigma}\mathbf{V}^H\mathbf{h}_M \tag{5.3.126}$$

or equivalently,

$$\mathbf{U}^H\mathbf{e} = \mathbf{U}^H\mathbf{d} - \mathbf{\Sigma}\mathbf{V}^H\mathbf{h}_M \tag{5.3.127}$$

Since $\mathbf{U}$ is an orthogonal matrix, $\|\mathbf{e}\|^2 = |\mathbf{U}^H\mathbf{e}\|^2$. Hence the vector $\mathbf{h}_M$ that minimizes $\|\mathbf{e}\|^2$ also minimizes $\|\mathbf{U}^H\mathbf{e}\|^2$.

Let us partition the orthogonal matrices $\mathbf{U}$ and $\mathbf{V}$ as

$$\begin{aligned}\mathbf{U} &= [\mathbf{U}_1 \quad \mathbf{U}_2] \\ \mathbf{V} &= [\mathbf{V}_1 \quad \mathbf{V}_2]\end{aligned} \tag{5.3.128}$$

where $\mathbf{U}_1$ and $\mathbf{V}_1$ contain the column vectors for the left and right singular values associated with the nonzero singular values of $\mathbf{A}_M$, and $\mathbf{U}_2$ and $\mathbf{V}_2$ contain the column vectors associated with the zero singular values of $\mathbf{A}_M$, respectively. If we substitute (5.3.128) into (5.3.127), we obtain

$$\begin{aligned}\mathbf{U}^H\mathbf{e} &= \begin{bmatrix}\mathbf{U}_1^H \\ \mathbf{U}_2^H\end{bmatrix}\mathbf{d} - \begin{bmatrix}\mathbf{S} & \mathbf{0} \\ \mathbf{0} & \mathbf{0}\end{bmatrix}\begin{bmatrix}\mathbf{V}_1^H \\ \mathbf{V}_2^H\end{bmatrix}\mathbf{h}_M \\ &= \begin{bmatrix}\mathbf{U}_1^H\mathbf{d} \quad \mathbf{S}\mathbf{V}_1^H\mathbf{h}_M \\ \mathbf{U}_2^H\mathbf{d}\end{bmatrix}\end{aligned} \tag{5.3.129}$$

Hence

$$\mathscr{E}_M = \|\mathbf{U}^H\mathbf{e}\|^2 = \|\mathbf{U}_1^H\mathbf{d} - \mathbf{S}\mathbf{V}_1^H\mathbf{h}_M\|^2 + \|\mathbf{U}_2^H\mathbf{d}\|^2 \tag{5.3.130}$$

Clearly, the minimum of $\mathscr{E}_M$ with respect to $\mathbf{h}_M$ is

$$E_M = \min_{\mathbf{h_M}} \mathscr{E}_M = \|\mathbf{U}_2^H\mathbf{d}\|^2 \tag{5.3.131}$$

which occurs when

$$\mathbf{S}\mathbf{V}_1^H\mathbf{h}_M = \mathbf{U}_1^H\mathbf{d} \tag{5.3.132}$$

or equivalently,

$$\mathbf{V}_1^H\mathbf{h}_M = \mathbf{S}^{-1}\mathbf{U}_1^H\mathbf{d} \tag{5.3.133}$$

Therefore, the optimum coefficient vector may be expressed as

$$\mathbf{h}_M = \sum_{i=1}^{k} \frac{\mathbf{u}_i^H\mathbf{d}}{\sigma_i}\mathbf{v}_i \tag{5.3.134}$$

where k is the rank of $\mathbf{A}_M$. The solution vector $\mathbf{h}_M$ is unique and is the minimum norm solution to the least-squares problem.

Another form for the solution is obtained by observing that $\mathbf{V}_2^H\mathbf{h}_M$ does not affect $\mathscr{E}_M$ and hence may be set to zero. By combining this condition with (5.3.133), we obtain

$$\begin{aligned}\mathbf{V}^H\mathbf{h}_M &= \begin{bmatrix}\mathbf{S}^{-1} & \mathbf{0}\\ \mathbf{0} & \mathbf{0}\end{bmatrix}\begin{bmatrix}\mathbf{U}_1^H\\ \mathbf{U}_2^H\end{bmatrix}\mathbf{d}\\ &= \boldsymbol{\Sigma}^+\mathbf{U}^H\mathbf{d}\end{aligned} \tag{5.3.135}$$

Therefore,

$$\begin{aligned}\mathbf{h}_M &= \mathbf{V}\boldsymbol{\Sigma}^+\mathbf{U}^H\mathbf{d}\\ &= \mathbf{A}_M^+\mathbf{d}\end{aligned} \tag{5.3.136}$$

Now, recall that $\mathbf{h}_M$ is an M-dimensional coefficient vector and $\mathbf{A}_M$ is an $(n + 1) \times M$ data matrix. Assuming that $\mathbf{A}_M$ has rank M, the pseudoinverse can be expressed as

$$\mathbf{A}_M^+ = (\mathbf{A}_M^H\mathbf{A}_M)^{-1}A_M^H \tag{5.3.137}$$

as indicated in (5.3.123). By substituting (5.3.137) into (5.3.136), we obtain

$$\mathbf{h}_M = (\mathbf{A}_M^H\mathbf{A}_M)^{-1}\mathbf{A}_M^H\mathbf{d} \tag{5.3.138}$$

which is our familiar result for the optimum least-squares coefficient vector.

In conclusion, the SVD provides the solution to the least-squares optimization problem in the form given by (5.3.134) or (5.3.136), where $k \leq M$ is the rank of the data matrix $\mathbf{A}_M$. The resulting minimum least-squares error is given by (5.3.131), which may also be expressed in terms of the left singular vectors as

$$E_M = \min_{h_M} \mathscr{E}_M = \sum_{i=k+1}^{M} \mathbf{u}_i^H\mathbf{d} \tag{5.3.139}$$

Least-Squares Estimation of Rank-Deficient Signals Based on SVD. Above, we have described the SVD method and its application to least-squares estimation. In particular, we have shown in (5.3.138) that if the rank of the data matrix $\mathbf{A}_M$ is equal to M, the SVD method yields a LS estimate that is identical to the LS estimate obtained by conventional methods based on the QRD. However, the SVD method is capable of providing a better estimate of the coefficient vector $\mathbf{h}_M$ when there is additive noise corrupting the observed data. In many practical applications, the autocorrelation matrix of the noise corrupted data is almost always full rank, while the signal component in the observed data has an autocorrelation matrix of lower rank. The conventional LS estimation methods yield the LS estimate based on the full rank of the observed data matrix. On the other hand, the SVD method allows us to separate the signal subspace from the noise subspace and thus we obtain a better LS estimate of the coefficient vector $\mathbf{h}_M$.

Let us assume that the data vector $\mathbf{X}_M(n)$ has the form

$$\mathbf{X}_M(n) = \mathbf{s}_M(n) + \mathbf{n}_M(n) \tag{5.3.140}$$

where $\mathbf{n}_M(n)$ represents the noise component in $\mathbf{X}_M(n)$ and $\mathbf{s}_M(n)$ represents the signal component. Obviously, if there is no noise [i.e., the signal-to-noise ratio (SNR)] is infinite, we have $\mathbf{X}_M(n) = \mathbf{s}_M(n)$. We define the rank of the autocorrelation matrix of $\mathbf{s}_M(n)$ to be the rank of the signal component in $\mathbf{X}_M(n)$, which is equal to the rank of the matrix $\mathbf{A}_M$ for SNR $= \infty$. If the rank of the autocorrelation matrix of $\mathbf{s}_M(n)$ is less than M, we say that the signal correlation matrix is rank deficient. For example, in spectrum estimation problems involving the estimation of multiple sinusoids in noise, the rank of the autocorrelation matrix of the signal vector is equal to the number of sinusoids and is independent of the dimension of the data vectors. It is desirable to choose the dimension of the data vector to be much larger than the number of sinusoids in order to improve the resolution of the signal estimate. This spectrum estimation problem is treated in Chapter 8. As a second example, the data vectors of a fractionally spaced equalizer (FSE) used in data communications is always rank deficient ([Gitlin and Weinstein, 1981)]. The application of SVD to frequency estimation of sinusoids was described by Tufts and Kumaresan (1982), and its application to FSE was given by Long et al. (1988).

To apply the SVD method to LS estimation of rank-deficient signals, we first determine the rank of the signal. The rank is known in some applications. For example, the rank of the FSE data autocorrelation matrix is known to be equal to the number of data symbol intervals that the FSE spans. On the other hand, in the estimation of the frequencies of multiple sinusoids in noise, the number of sinusoids in the signal may not be known. In such a case, the rank is estimated from the data. For example, if the number of sinusoids is not known, we can estimate the rank of the signal by examining the magnitudes of the eigenvalues of the autocorrelation matrix $\mathbf{R}_M(n)$. The eigenvalues with larger magnitudes are contributed by the signal and the smaller ones are due to noise. If the power level of the sinusoids is well above the noise power, this method provides a reliable estimate of the rank.

Once the rank of the signal is determined, we can apply the SVD method to the LS estimation of rank-deficient signals. The estimation procedure is very similar to the one given (5.3.125) through (5.3.136). Let us assume that the rank of the signal is determined to be equal to k and the SVD of the data matrix $\mathbf{A}_M(n)$ is given by (5.3.118). The singular value matrix $\mathbf{\Sigma}$ is arranged so that the magnitudes of its elements are in a nonincreasing order. We then construct a new matrix $\tilde{\mathbf{\Sigma}}$ by setting the $M - k$ smaller elements of $\mathbf{\Sigma}$ to zero. Then the optimal estimate of the coefficient vector $\mathbf{h}_M(n)$ is computed according to (5.3.136) by using $\tilde{\mathbf{\Sigma}}$ in place of $\mathbf{\Sigma}$.

As shown by Long et al. (1988), when we use the SVD-based method described above, the excess MSE is M/k times smaller than the excess MSE obtained by using conventional LS estimation, provided that k is equal to or larger than the true rank of the signal. The improvement is significant if the ratio M/k is large. An improvement in the LS estimate can still be achieved even when we overdetermine the rank of the signal (i.e., k is larger than the true signal rank), provided that $k < M$. Consequently, the estimation error in the LS coefficient vector $\mathbf{h}_M(n)$ is also reduced accordingly.

5.4 SUMMARY AND REFERENCES

Least-squares methods were discovered by Gauss in the early nineteenth century and are widely used in diverse fields of science and engineering today. In general, the attractive features of least-squares estimation methods are (1) their mathematical tractability, (2) the existence of numerically efficient algorithms for their solution, and (3) the fact that they provide optimum or near-optimum solutions.

In this chapter we have used least-squares methods for system modeling and parameter estimation, for deconvolution, and for filter design. In these estimation problems, the least-squares criterion leads to a set of normal equations for the parameters to be estimated.

Several methods for solving the normal equations were presented. The Cholesky and LDU decompositions were presented as factorizations of the data autocorrelation matrix $\mathbf{R}_M = \mathbf{A}_M^H\mathbf{A}_M$, where $\mathbf{A}_M$ is the data matrix. In practice, however, the "squaring operation" implied in the formation of the autocorrelation matrix from $\mathbf{A}_M$ requires high-precision arithmetic, and consequently, the direct decomposition of $\mathbf{R}_M$ is usually avoided except, perhaps, in cases where M is small and the amount of data is large. Instead, the decomposition can be obtained by directly operating on the data matrix $\mathbf{A}_M$ using the QR decomposition. We demonstrated that the Givens and Householder transformations provide computationally efficient algorithms for performing the QRD.

Singular value decomposition (SVD) was also introduced as a method for solving least-squares problems. In particular, we demonstrated that the SVD, which provides the singular values of the data matrix $\mathbf{A}_M$, allows us to obtain the LS solution as given by (5.3.134) or (5.3.136), for a rank-deficient matrix. This method is particularly useful in estimating the parameters of signals embedded in noise, where the rank of the autocorrelation matrix of the signal is smaller than the rank of the data autocorrelation matrix $\mathbf{R}_M$. By separating out the singular values of $\mathbf{A}_M$ due to noise only from those of the rank-deficient signal, we obtain less noisy LS estimates of the signal parameters.

All of the numerical methods described in Section 5.3 for solving least-squares estimation problems are well known and in some sense are classical. In the next two chapters we extend these methods to sequential least-squares estimation, which applies to the case where the LS estimate is updated recursively in time as new data become available.

There are numerous references dealing with linear filtering and least-squares estimation. Kailath (1974) provides a historical perspective of linear filter theory up to the early 1970s, including the work of Wiener (1949) and Kalman (1960). The solution of least-squares estimation problems are treated in several books [e.g., Golub and Van Loan (1989), Lawson and Hanson (1974), Stewart (1973), Forsythe and Moler (1967), and Wilkinson (1965)].

Computational methods for the SVD are given by Luk (1986), Brent and Luk (1985), Brent, Luk, and Van Loan (1985), and Lawson and Hanson (1974).

PROBLEMS

5.1 Determine the least-squares FIR inverse system of length $M = 3$ to the system with impulse response

$$h(n) = \begin{cases} 2, & n = 0 \\ 1, & n = 1 \\ 0, & \text{otherwise} \end{cases}$$

Also, determine the least-squares error for the optimum length $M = 3$ system.

5.2 Determine the least-squares FIR inverse filter of length $M = 3$ for the system with impulse response

$$h(n) = \begin{cases} -\frac{1}{2}, & n = 0 \\ 1, & n = 1 \\ 0, & \text{otherwise} \end{cases}$$

and the desired response is specified as $d(n) = \delta(n - 2)$. Also compute the value of the least-squares error for $M = 3$.

5.3 Consider a radio communication system in which the signal transmitted over the channel propagates over two different paths as shown in Fig. P5.3. The direct path has an unknown gain (attenuation) factor b_0 and the reflected path is characterized by a gain factor $b_1 < b_0$. The received signal is modeled as

$$y(n) = b_0 x(n) + b_1 x(n - D), \qquad D \text{ an integer}$$

where $x(n)$ is the transmitted sequence. Determine the parameters b_0 and b_1 of the model

$$H(z) = b_0 + b_1 z^{-D}$$

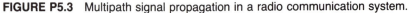

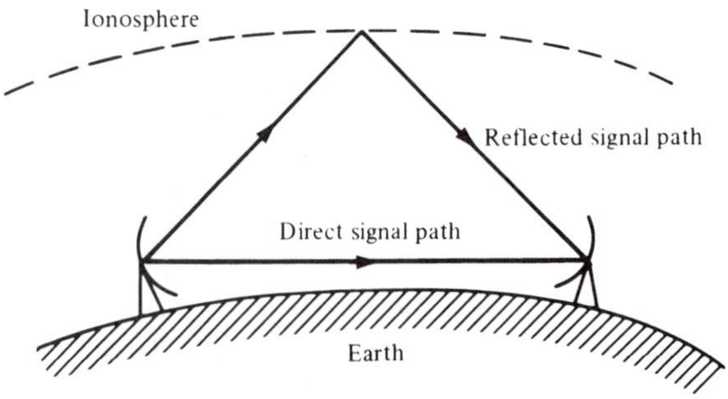

FIGURE P5.3 Multipath signal propagation in a radio communication system.

which provides the least-squares fit to the channel response. You may assume that D is known.

5.4 A linear system $C(z)$ is characterized by the system function

$$C(z) = \frac{1}{1 - 0.9z^{-1}}$$

Determine the optimum coefficients of an FIR filter with system function $B(z) = b_0 + b_1 z^{-1}$ which minimizes the least-squares error for the configuration shown in Fig. P5.4. The additive noise is white with variance $\sigma_w^2 = 0.1$.

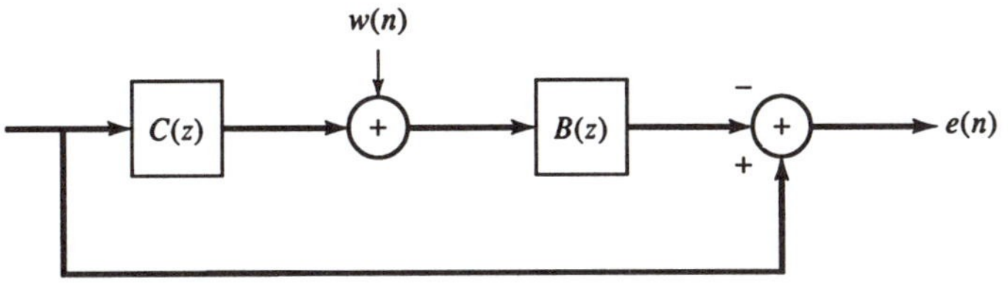

5.5 Two methods for estimating the parameters of an unknown linear system modeled as a pole–zero system are shown in Fig. P5.5. Using the least-squares criterion, determine the equations for the two different configurations. Comment on the difference in these two approaches.

5.6 An $M \times M$ autocorrelation matrix $\mathbf{\Gamma}$ has eigenvalues $\lambda_1 > \lambda_2 > \cdots > \lambda_M > 0$ and corresponding eigenvectors $\mathbf{v}_1, \mathbf{v}_2, \ldots, \mathbf{v}_M$. Such a matrix can be represented as

$$\mathbf{\Gamma} = \sum_{i=1}^{M} \lambda_i \mathbf{v}_i \mathbf{v}_i^H$$

(a) If $\mathbf{\Gamma} = \mathbf{\Gamma}^{1/2}\mathbf{\Gamma}^{1/2}$, where $\mathbf{\Gamma}^{1/2}$ is the square root of $\mathbf{\Gamma}$, show that $\mathbf{\Gamma}^{1/2}$ can be represented as

$$\mathbf{\Gamma}^{1/2} = \sum_{i=1}^{M} \lambda_i^{1/2} \mathbf{v}_i \mathbf{v}_i^H$$

(b) Using this representation, determine a procedure for computing $\mathbf{\Gamma}^{1/2}$.

5.7 Show that the eigenvalues of a lower or upper triangular matrix are equal to its diagonal elements.

5.8 In the text we described an LDU decomposition of the data autocorrelation matrix $\mathbf{R}$. Determine the equations for a UDL decomposition where $\mathbf{U}$ is an upper triangular matrix, $\mathbf{D}$ is a diagonal matrix, and $\mathbf{L}$ is a lower triangular matrix.

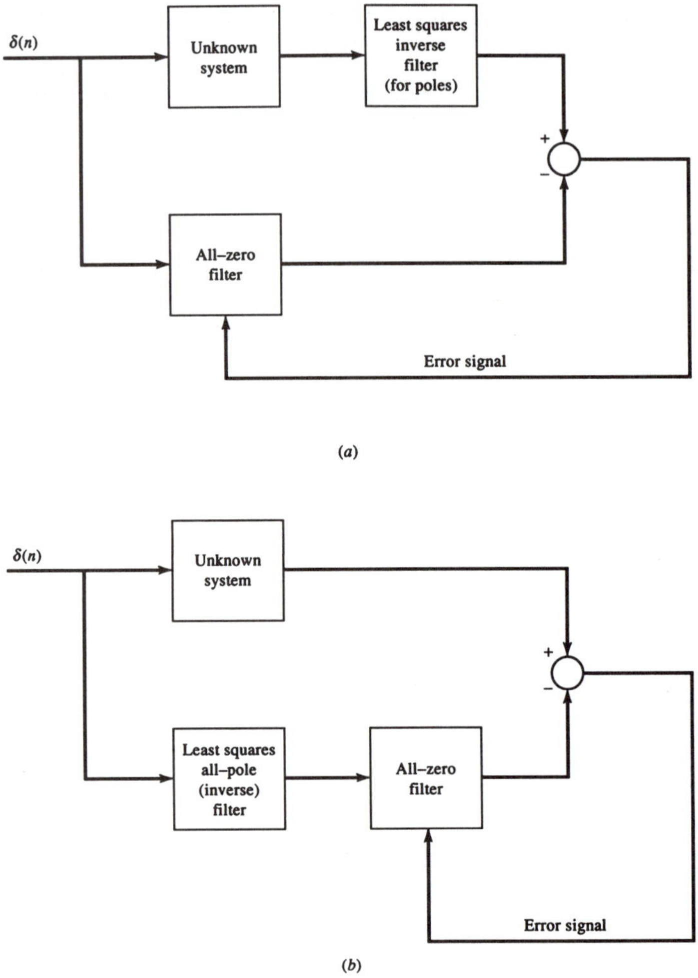

FIGURE P5.5

5.9 An unknown system is excited by a white noise sequence. From its output response $y(n)$ we have obtained the autocorrelation sequence

$$r_{yy}(m) = \begin{cases} 38, & m = 0 \\ 5, & m = \pm 1 \\ -6, & m = \pm 2 \\ 0, & \text{otherwise} \end{cases}$$

Determine the system function corresponding to the minimum-phase system.

5.10 Perform the Cholesky and the LDU decompositions of the correlation matrix

$$\mathbf{R} = \begin{bmatrix} 3 & 2 & 1 \\ 2 & 3 & 2 \\ 1 & 2 & 3 \end{bmatrix}$$

5.11 Let $\mathbf{X}_M(n)$ be an $M \times 1$ (nonzero) data matrix. Demonstrate that the $M \times M$ matrix $\mathbf{X}_M(n)\mathbf{X}_M^H(n)$ has rank 1.

5.12 Let $\mathbf{x}$ be an arbitrary $M \times 1$ nonzero vector and $\mathbf{Q}$ be an $M \times M$ orthogonal matrix. Show that the Euclidean norm of $\mathbf{x}$ is invariant under an orthogonal transformation $\mathbf{Q}$.

5.13 Show that the norm of a square matrix $\mathbf{A}$ is equal to the magnitude of its largest eigenvalue.

5.14 Let $\mathbf{A}$ be an arbitrary (nonzero) $M \times N$ matrix, $\mathbf{P}$ an $N \times N$ orthogonal matrix, and $\mathbf{Q}$ an $M \times M$ orthogonal matrix. Show that the Euclidean norm of $\mathbf{A}$ is invariant to the transformation $\mathbf{QAP}$.

5.15 Let $\mathbf{A}$ be a square matrix. From the definition of the condition number of $\mathbf{A}$, show that

$$\text{condition number of } \mathbf{A} = \left|\frac{\lambda_{\max}}{\lambda_{\min}}\right|$$

This ratio is usually called the *eigenvalue spread*. Note that if $|\lambda_{\max}|/|\lambda_{\min}| \gg 1$, round-off errors in the numerical computation of $\mathbf{A}^{-1}$ cause large errors in the elements of $\mathbf{A}^{-1}$. In such a case we say that the matrix $\mathbf{A}$ is ill-conditioned.

5.16 Let $\mathbf{\Gamma}_M$ be an $M \times M$ autocorrelation matrix of a wide-sense stationary random process. Prove that

$$\det(\mathbf{\Gamma}_M) = \prod_{i=1}^{M} \lambda_i$$

5.17 Let $x(n)$ be an AR(1) process described by the difference equation

$$x(n) = 0.8x(n - 1) + w(n)$$

where $w(n)$ is a white noise process with variance $\sigma_w^2 = 0.1$.

(a) Determine the eigenvalues of the 2×2 autocorrelation matrix $\mathbf{\Gamma}_{xx}$ of $x(n)$.

(b) Determine the eigenvalues of the 3×3 autocorrelation matrix $\mathbf{\Gamma}_{xx}$ of $x(n)$.

(c) Evaluate the eigenvalue spread for the eigenvalues obtained in parts (a) and (b).

5.18 Prove that $\mathbf{A}$ and $\mathbf{A}^H$ have the same set of nonzero singular values but different numbers of zero singular values.

5.19 Prove that the Euclidean norm of $\mathbf{A}$ is equal to its largest singular value.

5.20 Prove the relations in (5.3.123).

5.21 Prove the relations in (5.3.124).

5.22 Prove that the least-squares estimate $\mathbf{h}_M$ obtained by use of the SVD of $\mathbf{A}$, given by (5.3.134), is orthogonal to the right singular vectors corresponding to the zero singular values.

5.23 Prove the expression in (5.3.139) for the least-squares error corresponding to the optimum least-squares solution for $\mathbf{h}_M$.

5.24 Consider the partition of $\mathbf{U}$ and $\mathbf{V}$ as given by (5.3.128). Prove that:

(a) $\mathbf{U}_1\mathbf{U}_1^H = \mathbf{A}\mathbf{A}^+$

(b) $\mathbf{V}_1\mathbf{V}_1^H = \mathbf{A}^+\mathbf{A}$

(c) $\mathbf{U}_2\mathbf{U}_2^H = \mathbf{I}_N - \mathbf{A}\mathbf{A}^+$

(d) $\mathbf{V}_2\mathbf{V}_2^H = \mathbf{I}_M - \mathbf{A}^+\mathbf{A}$

5.25 Prove that the condition number of the data matrix $\mathbf{A}$ is equal to the ratio of the largest to the smallest nonzero singular values.

5.26 Prove that the projection operator $\mathcal{P}(n)$ is Hermitian symmetric and idempotent.

CHAPTER 6

ADAPTIVE FILTERS

In contrast to filter design techniques described in Chapter 4, which were based on knowledge of the second-order statistics of the signals, there are many digital signal processing applications in which these statistics cannot be specified a priori. We have already encountered such applications in Chapter 5, where we described the use of least-squares methods in the design of Wiener filters for channel equalization and for the removal of reverberation effects through deconvolution in seismic signal processing. In these examples the filter coefficients depend on the characteristics of the medium and cannot be specified a priori. Instead, they are determined by the method of least squares, from measurements performed by transmitting signals through the physical media. Such filters, with adjustable parameters, are usually called *adaptive filters,* especially when they incorporate some algorithm that allows the filter coefficients to adapt to changes in the signal statistics.

Adaptive filters have received considerable attention by many researchers over the past 20 years. As a result, many computationally efficient algorithms for adaptive filtering have been developed during this period. In this chapter we describe two basic algorithms, the least-mean-square (LMS) algorithm, which is based on a gradient optimization for determining the coefficients, and the class of recursive least-squares algorithms, which include both direct form FIR and lattice realizations. Before we describe the algorithms, we present several practical applications in which adaptive filters have been used successfully in the estimation of signals corrupted by noise and other interference.

6.1 APPLICATIONS OF ADAPTIVE FILTERS

Adaptive filters have been widely used in communication systems, control systems, and various other systems in which the statistical characteristics of the signals to be filtered are either unknown a priori or, in some cases, slowly time variant (nonstationary signals). Numerous applications of adaptive filters have been described in the literature. Some of the more noteworthy applications include (1) adaptive antenna systems in which adaptive filters are used for beam steering and for providing nulls in the beam pattern to remove undesired interference [see the paper by Widrow et al. (1967)]; (2) digital communication receivers in which adaptive filters are used to provide equalization of intersymbol interference and for channel identification [see the papers by Lucky (1965), Proakis and Miller (1969), Gersho (1969), George et at. (1971), Proakis (1970, 1975), Magee and Proakis (1973), Picinbono (1977), and Nichols et al. (1977)]; (3) adaptive noise canceling techniques in which an adaptive filter is used to estimate and eliminate a noise component in a desired signal [see the papers by Widrow et al. (1975), Hsu and Giordano (1978), and Ketchum and Proakis (1982)]; (4) system modeling, in which an adaptive filter is used as a model to estimate the characteristics of an unknown system. These are just a few of the best known examples on the use of adaptive filters.

Although both IIR and FIR filters have been considered for adaptive filtering, the FIR filter is by far the most practical and widely used. The reason for this preference is quite simple. The FIR filter has only adjustable zeros, and hence it is free of stability problems associated with adaptive IIR filters that have adjustable poles as well as zeros. We should not conclude, however, that adaptive FIR filters are always stable. On the contrary, the stability of the filter depends critically on the algorithm for adjusting its coefficients, as will be demonstrated in Sections 6.2 and 6.3.

Of the various FIR filter structures that are possible, the direct form and the lattice form are the ones used in adaptive filtering applications. The direct-form FIR filter structure with adjustable coefficients $h(n)$, is illustrated in Fig. 6.1. On the other hand, the adjustable parameters in an FIR lattice structure are the reflection coefficients K_n.

As important consideration in the use of an adaptive filter is the criterion for optimizing the adjustable filter parameters. The criterion must not only provide a meaningful measure of filter performance but must also result in a practically realizable algorithm.

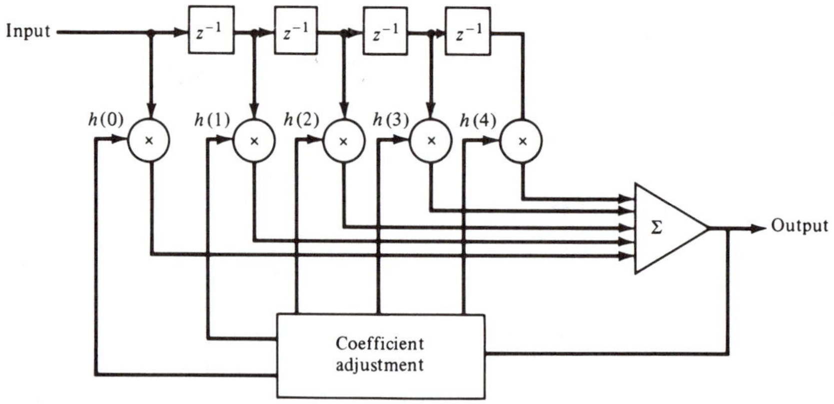

FIGURE 6.1 Direct-form adaptive FIR filter.

For example, a desirable performance index in a digital communication system is the average probability of error. Consequently, in implementing an adaptive equalizer, we might consider the selection of the equalizer coefficients to minimize the average probability of error as the basis for our optimization criterion. Unfortunately, however, the performance index (average probability of error) for this criterion is a highly nonlinear function of the filter coefficients and the signal statistics. As a consequence, the implementation of an adaptive filter that optimizes such a performance index is complex and impractical.

In some cases a performance index that is a nonlinear function of the filter parameters possesses many relative minima (or maxima), so that one is not certain whether the adaptive filter has converged to the optimum solution or to one of the relative minima (or maxima). For these reasons, some desirable performance indices, such as the average probability of error in a digital communication system, must be rejected on the grounds that they are impractical to implement.

Two criteria that provide good measures of performance in adaptive filtering applications are the least-squares criterion and its counterpart in a statistical formulation of the problem, the mean-square-error (MSE) criterion. The least-squares and MSE criteria result in a quadratic performance index as a function of the filter coefficients and hence possess a single minimum. The resulting algorithms for adjusting the coefficients of the filter are relatively easy to implement, as we demonstrate in Sections 6.2 and 6.3.

Below we describe several applications of adaptive filters that serve as a motivation for the mathematical development of algorithms derived in Sections 6.2 and 6.3. We find it convenient to use the direct-form FIR structure in these examples. Although we will not develop the recursive algorithms for automatically adjusting the filter coefficients in this section, it is instructive to formulate the optimization of the filter coefficients as a least-squares optimization problem. This development will serve to establish a common framework for the algorithms derived in the next two sections.

6.1.1 System Identification or System Modeling

The formulation of the problem has been given in Section 5.1 and illustrated in Fig. 5.1. We have an unknown system, called a *plant,* that we wish to identify. The system is modeled by an FIR filter with adjustable coefficients. Both the plant and model are excited by an input sequence $x(n)$. If $y(n)$ denotes the output of the plant and $\hat{y}(n)$ denotes the output of the model,

$$\hat{y}(n) = \sum_{k=0}^{M-1} h(k)x(n-k) \tag{6.1.1}$$

we may form the error sequence

$$e(n) = y(n) - \hat{y}(n), \qquad n = 0, 1, \ldots \tag{6.1.2}$$

and select the coefficients $h(k)$ to minimize

$$\mathscr{E}_M = \sum_{n=0}^{\infty} \left[y(n) - \sum_{k=0}^{M-1} h(k)x(n-k) \right]^2 \tag{6.1.3}$$

For convenience, we have assumed that the sequences $x(n)$ and $y(n)$ are infinite in duration.

The least-squares criterion leads to the set of linear equations, previously derived in Section 5.1, for determining the filter coefficients,

$$\sum_{k=0}^{M-1} h(k)r_{xx}(l-k) = r_{yx}(l), \qquad l = 0, 1, \ldots, M-1 \tag{6.1.4}$$

In (6.1.4), $r_{xx}(l)$ is the autocorrelation of the sequence $x(n)$ and $r_{yx}(l)$ is the cross-correlation of the system output with the input sequence.

By solving (6.1.4) we obtain the filter coefficients for the model. Since the filter parameters are obtained directly from measurement data at the input and output of the system, without prior knowledge of the plant, we call the FIR filter model an adaptive filter.

If our only objective is to identify the system by use of the FIR model, the solution of (6.1.4) would suffice. In control systems applications, however, the system being modeled may be time variant, changing slowly with time, and ultimately, our purpose for having a model is to use it for designing a controller that controls the plant. Furthermore, measurement noise is usually present at the output of the plant. This noise introduces uncertainty in the measurements and corrupts the estimates of the filter coefficients in the model. Such a scenario is illustrated in Fig. 6.2. Now, the adaptive filter must identify and track the time-variant characteristics of the plant in the presence of measurement noise at the output of the plant. The algorithms described in Sections 6.2 and 6.3 are applicable to this system identification problem.

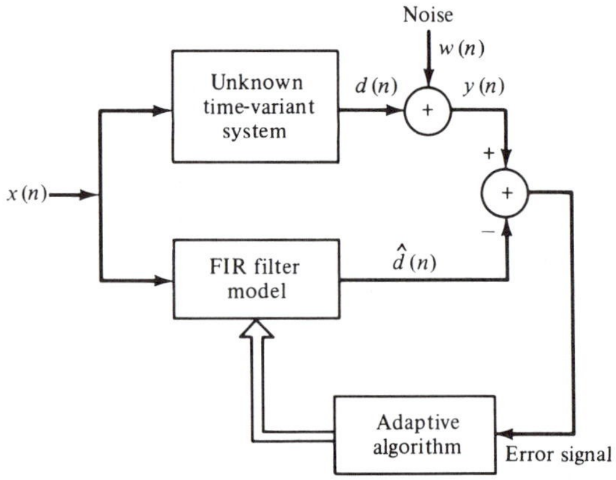

FIGURE 6.2 Application of adaptive filtering to system identification.

6.1.2 Adaptive Channel Equalization

Figure 6.3 shows a block diagram of a digital communication system in which an adaptive equalizer is used to compensate for the distortion caused by the transmission medium (channel). The digital sequence of information symbols $a(n)$ is fed to the transmit filter, whose output is

$$s(t) = \sum_{k=0}^{\infty} a(k)p(t - kT_s) \tag{6.1.5}$$

where $p(t)$ is the impulse response of the filter at the transmitter and T_s is the time interval between information symbols (i.e., $1/T_s$ is the symbol rate). For purposes of this discussion we may assume that $a(n)$ is a multilevel sequence that takes on values from the set $\pm 1, \pm 3, \pm 5, \ldots, \pm(M - 1)$, where M is the number of possible symbol values.

Typically, the pulse $p(t)$ is designed to have the characteristics illustrated in Fig. 6.4. Note that $p(t)$ has amplitude $p(0) = 1$ at $t = 0$ and $p(nT_s) = 0$ at $t = nT_s$, $n = \pm 1, \pm 2, \ldots$. As a consequence, a series of successive pulses transmitted sequentially every T_s seconds do not interfere with one another when sampled at the time instants $t = nT_s$. Thus $a(n) = s(nT_s)$.

The channel, which is usually well modeled as a linear filter, distorts the pulse and thus causes intersymbol interference. For example, in telephone channels, filters are used throughout the system to separate signals in different frequency ranges. These filters cause phase and amplitude distortion. Figure 6.5 illustrates the effect of channel distortion on the pulse $p(t)$ as it might appear at the output of a telephone channel. Now we observe that the samples taken every T_s seconds are corrupted by interference from several adjacent symbols. The distorted signal is also corrupted by additive noise, which is usually wideband.

At the receiving end of the communication system the signal is first passed through a filter that is designed primarily to eliminate the noise outside the frequency band occupied by the signal. We may assume that

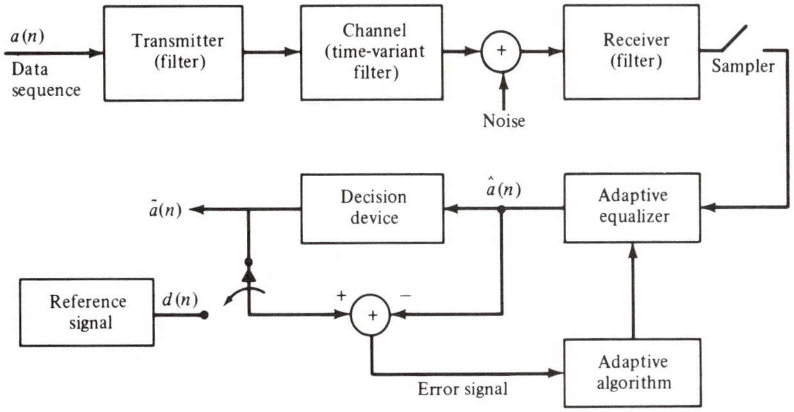

FIGURE 6.3 Application of adaptive filtering to adaptive channel equalization.

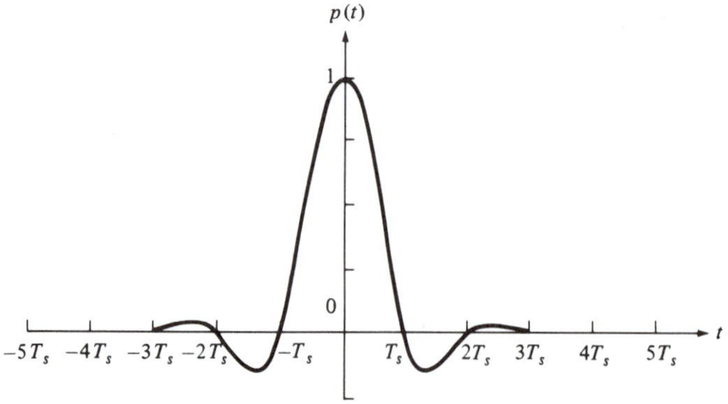

FIGURE 6.4 Pulse shape for digital transmission of symbols at a rate of $1/T_s$ symbols per second.

this filter is a linear-phase FIR filter that limits the bandwidth of the noise but causes negligible additional distortion on the channel-corrupted signal.

Samples of the received signal at the output of this filter reflect the presence of intersymbol interference and additive noise. If we ignore the possible time variations in the channel for the moment, we may express the sampled output at the receiver as

$$\begin{aligned} x(nT_s) &= \sum_{k=0}^{\infty} a(k)q(nT_s - kT_s) + w(nT_s) \\ &= a(n)q(0) + \sum_{\substack{k=0 \\ k \neq n}}^{\infty} a(k)q(nT_s - kT_s) + w(nT_s) \end{aligned} \tag{6.1.6}$$

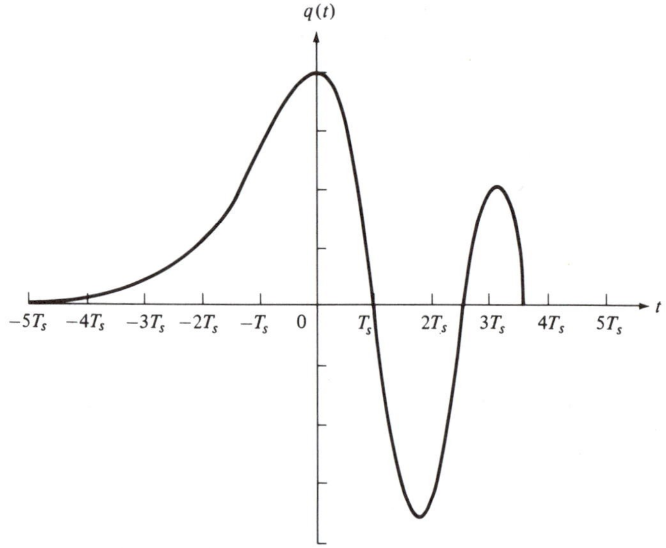

FIGURE 6.5 Effect of channel distortion on the signal pulse in Fig. 6.4.

where $w(t)$ represents the additive noise and $q(t)$ represents the distorted pulse at the output of the receiver filter.

To simplify our discussion, we assume that the sample $q(0)$ is normalized to unity by means of an automatic gain control (AGC) contained in the receiver. Then the sampled signal given in (6.1.6) may be expressed as

$$x(n) = a(n) + \sum_{\substack{k=0 \\ k\neq n}}^{\infty} a(k)q(n-k) + w(n) \tag{6.1.7}$$

where $x(n) \equiv x(nT_s)$, $q(n) \equiv q(nT_s)$, and $w(n) \equiv w(nT_s)$. The term $a(n)$ in (6.1.7) is the desired symbol at the nth sampling instant. The second term

$$\sum_{\substack{k=0 \\ k\neq n}}^{\infty} a(k)q(n-k)$$

constitutes the intersymbol interference due to the channel distortion, and $w(n)$ represents the additive noise in the system.

In general, the channel distortion effects embodied through the sampled values $q(n)$ are unknown at the receiver. Furthermore, the channel may vary slowly with time so that the intersymbol interference effects are time variant. The purpose of the adaptive equalizer is to compensate the signal for the channel distortion so that the resulting signal can be detected reliably.

Let us assume that the equalizer is an FIR filter with M adjustable coefficients $h(n)$. Its output may be expressed as

$$\hat{a}(n-D) = \sum_{k=0}^{M-1} h(k)x(n-k) \tag{6.1.8}$$

where D is a nominal delay in processing the signal through the filter and $\hat{a}(n)$ represents an estimate of the nth information symbol. Initially, the equalizer is trained by transmitting a known data sequence $d(n)$. Then the equalizer output, say $\hat{d}(n)$, is compared with $d(n)$ and an error is generated that is used to optimize the filter coefficients.

If we again adopt the least-squares error criterion, we select the coefficients $h(k)$ to minimize the quantity

$$\begin{aligned} \mathcal{E}_M &= \sum_{n=0}^{\infty} [d(n) - \hat{d}(n)]^2 \\ &= \sum_{n=0}^{\infty} \left[d(n) - \sum_{k=0}^{\infty} h(k)x(n+D-k) \right]^2 \end{aligned} \tag{6.1.9}$$

The results of the optimization is a set of linear equations of the form

$$\sum_{k=0}^{M-1} h(k)r_{xx}(l-k) = r_{dx}(l+D), \qquad l = 0, 1, 2, \ldots, M-1 \tag{6.1.10}$$

where $r_{xx}(l)$ is the autocorrelation of the sequence $x(n)$ and $r_{dx}(l)$ is the crosscorrelation between the desired sequence $d(n)$ and the received sequence $x(n)$.

Although the solution of (6.1.10) is obtained recursively in practice, as will be demonstrated in the following two sections, in principle, we observe that these equations result in values of the coefficients for the initial adjustment of the equalizer. After the short training period, which lasts less than 1 second for most channels, the transmitter begins to transmit the information sequence $a(n)$. To track the possible time variations in the channel, the equalizer coefficients must continue to be adjusted in an adaptive manner while receiving data. As illustrated in Fig. 6.3, this is usually accomplished by treating the decisions at the output of the decision device as correct, and using the decisions in place of the reference $d(n)$ to generate the error signal. This approach works quite well when decision errors occur infrequently (e.g., less than one decision error per 100 symbols). The occasional decision errors cause only small misadjustments in the equalizer coefficients. In Sections 6.2 and 6.3 we describe the adaptive algorithms for recursively adjusting the equalizer coefficients.

6.1.3 Echo Cancellation in Data Transmission Over Telephone Channels

In the transmission of data over telephone channels, modems (modulator/demodulator) are used to provide an interface between the digital data sequence and the analog channel. Shown in Fig. 6.6 is a block diagram of a communication system in which two terminals, labeled A and B, transmit data by using modems A and B to interface to a telephone channel. As shown, a digital sequence $a(n)$ is transmitted from terminal A to terminal B while another digital sequence $b(n)$ is transmitted from terminal B to A. This simultaneous transmission in both directions is called *full-duplex transmission*.

As described above, the two transmitted signals may be represented as

$$S_A(t) = \sum_{k=0}^{\infty} a(k)p(t - kT_s) \tag{6.1.11}$$

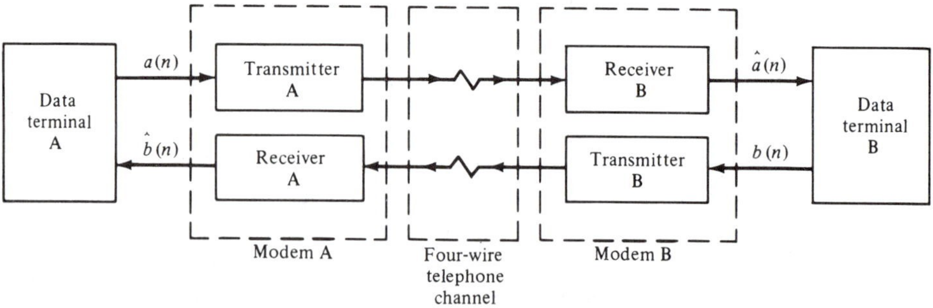

FIGURE 6.6 Full-duplex data transmission over telephone channels.

and

$$S_B(t) = \sum_{k=0}^{\infty} b(k)p(t - kT_s) \qquad (6.1.12)$$

where $p(t)$ is a pulse, as shown in Fig. 6.4.

When a subscriber leases a private line from a telephone company for the purpose of transmitting data between terminals A and B, the telephone line provided is a four-wire line, which is equivalent to having two dedicated telephone (two-wire) channels, one (pair of wires) for transmitting data in one direction and one (pair of wires) for receiving data from the other direction. In such a case the two transmission paths are isolated, and consequently, there is no "crosstalk" or mutual interference between the two signal paths. Channel distortion is compensated by use of an adaptive equalizer, as described above, at the receiver of each modem.

The major problem with the system shown in Fig. 6.6 is the cost of leasing a four-wire telephone channel. If the volume of traffic is high and the telephone channel is used either continuously or frequently, as in banking transactions systems or airline reservation systems, the system pictured in Fig. 6.6 may be cost-effective; otherwise, it is not.

An alternative solution for low-volume, infrequent transmission of data is to use the dial-up switched telephone network. In this case the local communication link between the subscriber and the local central telephone office is a two-wire line, called the *local loop*. At the central office, the subscriber two-wire line is connected to the main four-wire telephone channels that interconnect different central offices, called *trunk lines,* by a device called a *hybrid*. By using transformer coupling, the hybrid is tuned to provide isolation between the transmit and receive channels in full-duplex operation. However, due to impedance mismatch between the hybrid and the telephone channel, the level of isolation is often insufficient and, consequently, some of the signal on the transmit side leaks back and corrupts the signal on the receiver side, causing an "echo" that is often heard in voice communications over telephone channels.

To mitigate the echoes in voice transmission, telephone companies employ a device called an *echo suppressor*. In data transmission the solution is to use an *echo canceler* within each modem. Echo cancelers are implemented as adaptive filters with automatically adjustable coefficients, just as in the case of transversal equalizers.

With the use of hybrids to couple a two-wire channel to a four-wire channel and echo cancelers at each modem to estimate and subtract out the echoes, the data communication system for the dial-up switched network takes the form shown in Fig. 6.7. A hybrid is needed at each modem to isolate the transmitter from the receiver and to couple to the two-wire local loop. Hybrid A is physically located at the central office of subscriber A, while hybrid B is located at the central office to which subscriber B is connected. The two central offices are connected by a four-wire line, one pair used for transmission from A to B and the other pair used for transmission

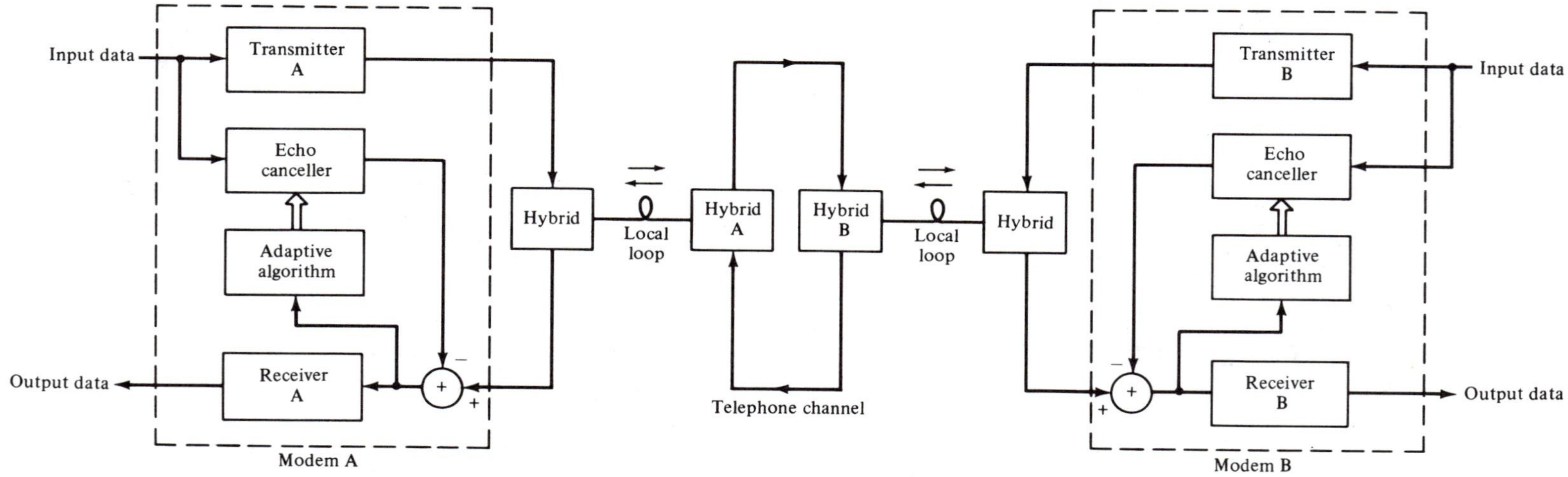

FIGURE 6.7 Block diagram model of a digital communication system that used echo cancellers in the modems.

in the reverse direction, from B to A. An echo at terminal A due to the hybrid A is called a *near-end echo,* while an echo at terminal A due to the hybrid B is termed a *far-end echo.* Both types of echoes are usually present in data transmission and must be removed by the echo canceler.

Suppose that we neglect the channel distortion for purposes of this discussion; let us deal with the echoes only. The signal received at modem A may be expressed as

$$s_{RA}(t) = A_1 s_B(t) + A_2 s_A(t - d_1) + A_3 s_A(t - d_2) \qquad (6.1.13)$$

where $s_B(t)$ is the desired signal to be demodulated at modem A; $s_A(t - d_1)$ is the near-end echo due to hybrid A; $s_A(t - d_2)$ is the far-end echo due to hybrid B; A_i, $i = 1, 2, 3$, are the corresponding amplitudes of the three signal components; and d_1 and d_2 are the delays associated with the echo components. A further disturbance that corrupts the received signal is additive noise, so that the received signal at modem A is

$$r_A(t) = s_{RA}(t) + w(t) \qquad (6.1.14)$$

where $w(t)$ represents the additive process.

The adaptive echo canceler attempts to estimate adaptively the two echo components. If its coefficients are $h(n)$, $n = 0, 1, \ldots, M - 1$, its output is

$$\hat{s}_A(n) = \sum_{k=0}^{M-1} h(k)a(n - k) \qquad 6.1.15)$$

which is an estimate of the echo signal components. This estimate is subtracted from the sampled received signal and the resulting error signal can be minimized in the least-squares sense for optimal adjustment of the coefficients of the echo canceler. There are several possible configurations for placement of the echo canceler in the modem and for forming the corresponding error signal. Figure 6.8 illustrates one configuration in which

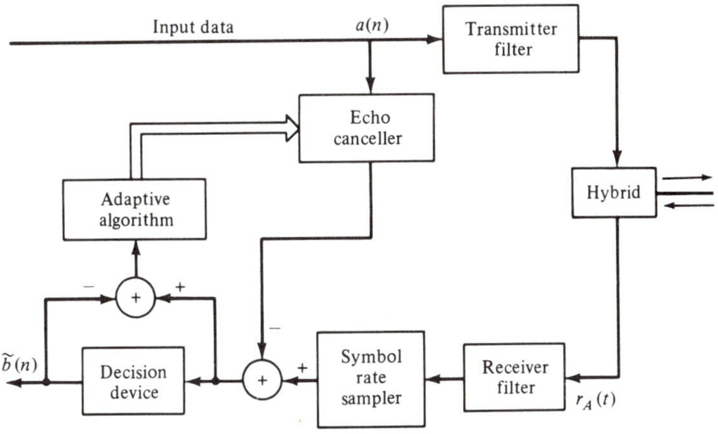

FIGURE 6.8 Symbol-rate echo canceller.

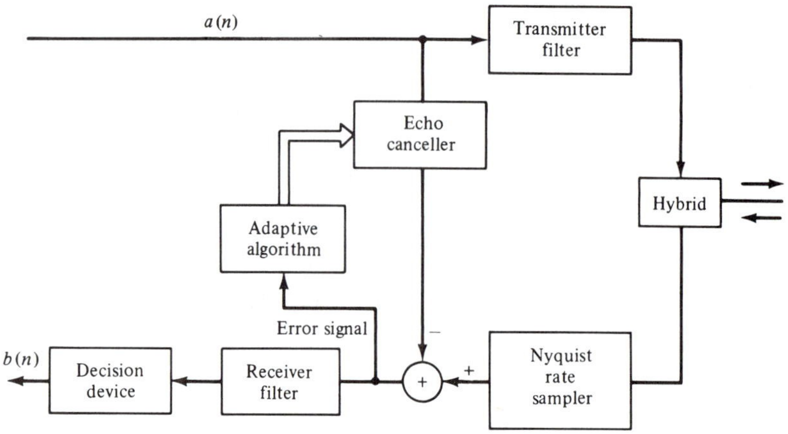

FIGURE 6.9 Nyquist rate echo canceller.

the canceler output is subtracted from the sampled output of the receiver filter with input $r_A(t)$. Figure 6.9 illustrates a second configuration, in which the echo canceler is generating samples at the Nyquist rate instead of the symbol rate. In this case the error signal used to adjust the coefficients is simply the difference between $r_A(n)$, the sampled received signal, and the canceler output. Finally, Fig. 6.10 illustrates the canceler operating in combination with an adaptive equalizer.

Application of the least-squares criterion in any of the configurations shown in Fig. 6.8, 6.9, or 6.10 leads to a set of linear equations for the

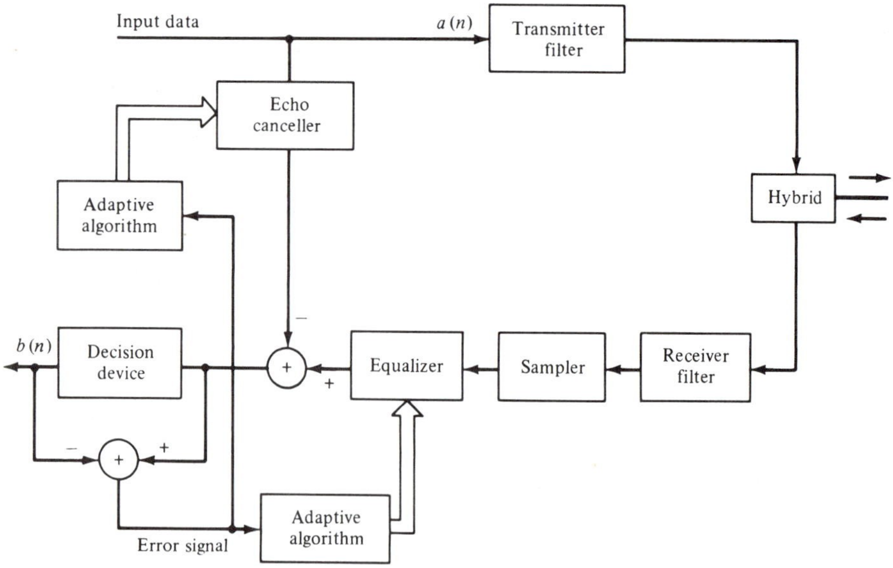

FIGURE 6.10 Modem with adaptive equalizer and echo canceller.

coefficients of the echo canceler. The reader is encouraged to derive these equations corresponding to the configurations above.

6.1.4 Suppression of Narrowband Interference in a Wideband Signal

We now discuss a problem that arises in practice, especially in signal detection and in digital communications. Let us assume that we have a signal sequence $v(n)$ that consists of a desired wideband signal sequence $w(n)$ corrupted by an additive narrowband interference sequence $x(n)$. The two sequences are uncorrelated. These sequences result from sampling an analog signal $v(t)$ at the Nyquist rate (or faster) of the wideband signal $w(t)$. Figure 6.11 illustrates the spectral characteristics of $w(n)$ and $x(n)$. Usually, the interference $|X(f)|$ is much larger than $|W(f)|$ within the narrow frequency band that it occupies.

In digital communications and in signal detection problems that fit the foregoing model, the desired signal sequence $w(n)$ is often a *spread-spectrum signal,* while the narrowband interference represents a signal from another user of the frequency band or intentional interference from a jammer trying to disrupt the communications or detection system.

Our objective from a filtering viewpoint is to employ a filter that suppresses the narrowband interference. In effect, such a filter will have a notch in the frequency band occupied by $|X(f)|$. In practice, the band occupied by $|X(f)|$ is unknown. Moreover, if the interference is nonstationary, its frequency band occupancy may vary with time. Hence an adaptive filter is desired.

From another viewpoint, the narrowband characteristics of the interference allows us to estimate $x(n)$ from past samples of the sequence $v(n)$ and to subtract the estimate from $v(n)$. Since the bandwidth of $x(n)$ is narrow compared to the bandwidth of the sequence $w(n)$, the samples $x(n)$ are highly correlated, due to the high sampling rate. On the other hand, the samples $w(n)$ are not highly correlated, since the samples are taken at the

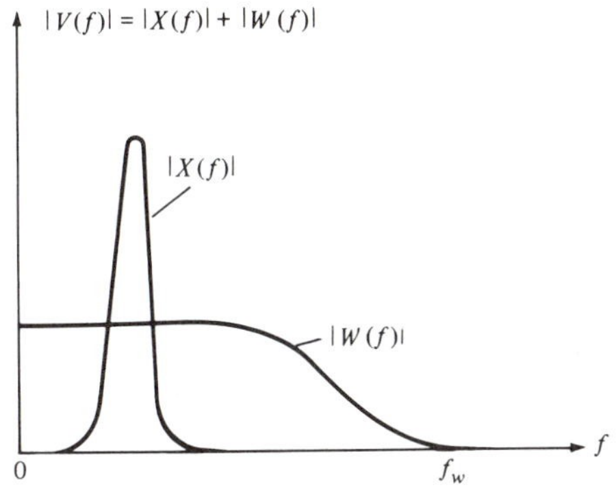

FIGURE 6.11 Strong narrowband interference $X(f)$ in a wideband signal $W(f)$.

Nyquist rate of $w(n)$. By exploiting the high correlation between $x(n)$ and past samples of the sequence $v(n)$, it is possible to obtain an estimate of $x(n)$, which can be subtracted from $v(n)$.

The general configuration is illustrated in Fig. 6.12. The signal $v(n)$ is delayed by D samples, where D is selected sufficiently large so that the wideband signal components $w(n)$ and $w(n - D)$ contained in $v(n)$ and $v(n - D)$, respectively, are uncorrelated. Usually, a choice of $D = 1$ or 2 is adequate. The delayed signal sequence $v(n - D)$ is passed through an FIR filter, which is best characterized as a linear predictor of the value $x(n)$ based on M samples $v(n - D - k)$, $k = 0, 1, \ldots, M - 1$. The output of the linear predictor is

$$\hat{x}(n) = \sum_{k=0}^{M-1} h(k)v(n - D - k) \tag{6.1.16}$$

This predicted value of $x(n)$ is subtracted from $v(n)$ to yield an estimate of $w(n)$, as illustrated in Fig. 6.12. Clearly, the quality of the estimate $\hat{x}(n)$ determines how well the narrowband interference is suppressed. It is also

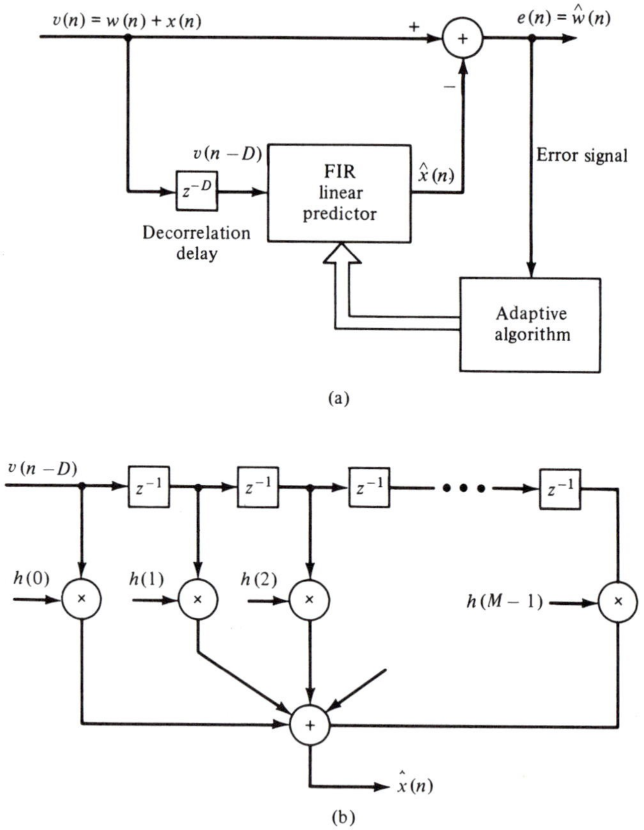

FIGURE 6.12 Adaptive filter for estimating and suppressing a narrowband interference in a wideband signal.

apparent that the delay D must be kept as small as possible to obtain a good estimate of $x(n)$, but must be sufficiently large so that $w(n)$ and $w(n - D)$ are uncorrelated.

Let us define the error sequence

$$\begin{aligned} e(n) &= v(n) - \hat{x}(n) \\ &= v(n) - \sum_{k=0}^{M-1} h(k)v(n - D - k) \end{aligned} \tag{6.1.17}$$

If we apply the least-squares criterion to select the prediction coefficients optimally, we obtain the set of linear equations

$$\sum_{k=0}^{M-1} h(k)r_{vv}(l - k) = r_{vv}(l + D), \qquad l = 0, 1, \ldots, M - 1 \tag{6.1.18}$$

where $r_{vv}(l)$ is the autocorrelation sequence of $v(n)$. Note, however, that the right-hand side of (6.1.18) may be expressed as

$$\begin{aligned} r_{vv}(l + D) &= \sum_{n=0}^{\infty} v(n)v(n - l - D) \\ &= \sum_{n=0}^{\infty} [w(n) + x(n)][w(n - l - D) + x(n - l - D)] \\ &= r_{ww}(l + D) + r_{xx}(l + D) + r_{wx}(l + D) + r_{xw}(l + D) \end{aligned} \tag{6.1.19}$$

The correlations in (6.1.19) are time-averaged correlation sequences. The expected value of $r_{ww}(l + D)$ is

$$E[r_{ww}(l + D)] = 0, \qquad l = 0, 1, \ldots, M - 1 \tag{6.1.20}$$

because $w(n)$ is wideband and D is large enough so that $w(n)$ and $w(n - D)$ are uncorrelated. Also,

$$E[r_{xw}(l + D)] = E[r_{wx}(l + D)] = 0 \tag{6.1.21}$$

by assumption. Finally,

$$E[r_{xx}(l + D)] = \gamma_{xx}(l + D) \tag{6.1.22}$$

Therefore, the expected value of $r_{vv}(l + D)$ is simply the statistical autocorrelation of the narrowband signal $x(n)$. Furthermore, if the wideband signal is weak relative to the interference, the autocorrelation $r_{vv}(l)$ in the left-hand side of (6.1.18) is approximately $r_{xx}(l)$. The major influence of $w(n)$ is to the diagonal elements of $r_{vv}(l)$. Consequently, the values of the filter coefficients determined from the linear equations in (6.1.18) are a function of the statistical characteristics of the interference $x(n)$.

The overall filter structure in Fig. 6.12 is an adaptive FIR prediction error filter with coefficients

$$h'(k) = \begin{cases} 1, & k = 0 \\ -h(k - D), & k = D, D + 1, \ldots, D + M - 1 \\ 0, & \text{otherwise} \end{cases} \tag{6.1.23}$$

and a frequency response

$$H(\omega) = \sum_{k=0}^{D+M-1} h'(k)e^{-j\omega k} \tag{6.1.24}$$

This overall filter acts as a notch filter for the interference. For example, Fig. 6.13 illustrates the magnitude of the frequency response of an adaptive filter with $M = 15$ coefficients, which attempts to suppress a narrowband interference that occupies 20% of the frequency band of a desired spread-spectrum signal sequence. The data were generated pseudorandomly by adding a narrowband interference consisting of 100 randomly phased, equal-amplitude sinusoids to a pseudonoise spread-spectrum signal. The coefficients of the filter were obtained by solving the equations in (6.1.18), with $D = 1$, where the correlation $r_{vv}(l)$ was obtained from the data. We observe that the overall interference suppression filter has the characteristics of a notch filter. The depth of the notch depends on the relative power of the interference to the wideband signal. The stronger the interference, the deeper the notch. The algorithms presented in Sections 6.2 and 6.3 are appropriate for estimating the predictor coefficients continuously in order to track a nonstationary narrowband interference signal.

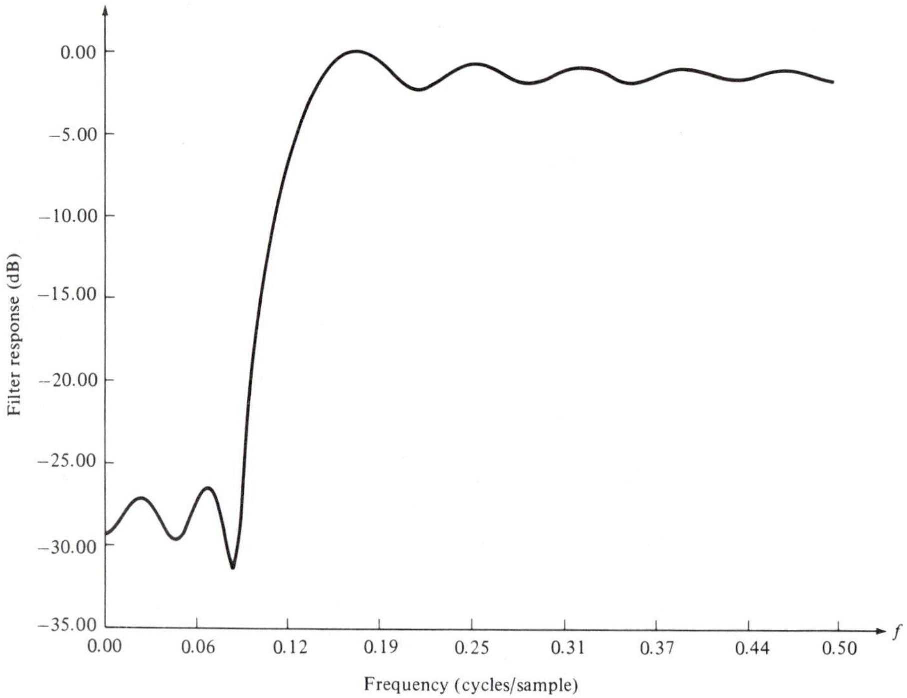

FIGURE 6.13 Frequency response characteristics of an adaptive notch filter.

6.1.5 Adaptive Line Enhancer

In the preceding example, the adaptive linear predictor was used to estimate the narrowband interference for the purpose of suppressing the interference from the input sequence $v(n)$. An adaptive line enhancer (ALE) has the same configuration as the interference suppression filter in Fig. 6.12, except that the objective is different.

In the adaptive line enhancer $x(n)$ is the desired signal and $w(n)$ represents a wideband noise component that masks $x(n)$. The desired signal $x(n)$ is either a spectral line or a relatively narrowband signal. The linear predictor shown in Fig. 6.12(b) operates in exactly the same fashion as in Fig. 6.12(a) and provides an estimate of the narrowband signal $x(n)$. It is apparent that the ALE (i.e., the FIR prediction filter) is a self-tuning filter that has a peak in its frequency response at the frequency of the sinusoid or, equivalently, in the frequency band of the narrowband signal $x(n)$. By having a narrow bandwidth, the noise $w(n)$ outside the band is suppressed, and thus the spectral line is enhanced in amplitude relative to the noise power in $w(n)$. This explains why the FIR predictor is called an ALE. Its coefficients are determined by the solution of (6.1.18).

6.1.6 Adaptive Noise Canceling

Echo cancellation, the suppression of narrowband interference in a wideband signal, and the ALE are related to another form of adaptive filtering, called *adaptive noise canceling*. A model for the adaptive noise canceler is illustrated in Fig. 6.14.

The primary input signal consists of a desired signal sequence $x(n)$ corrupted by an additive noise sequence $w_1(n)$ and an additive interference (noise) $w_2(n)$. The additive interference (noise) is also observable after it has been filtered by an unknown linear system that yields $v_2(n)$ and is further corrupted by an additive noise sequence $w_3(n)$. Thus we have available a secondary signal sequence, which may be expressed as $v(n) = v_2(n) +$

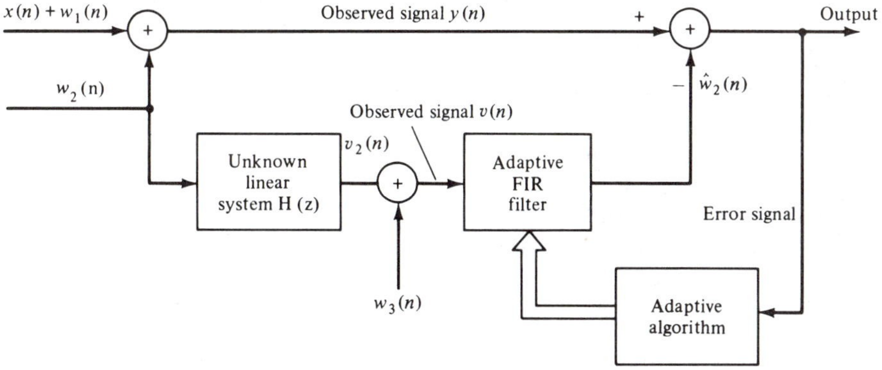

FIGURE 6.14 Example of an adaptive noise-cancelling system.

$w_3(n)$. The sequences $w_1(n)$, $w_2(n)$, and $w_3(n)$ are assumed to be mutually uncorrelated and zero mean.

As shown in Fig. 6.14, an adaptive FIR filter is used to estimate the interference sequence $w_2(n)$ from the secondary signal $v(n)$ and subtract the estimate $\hat{w}_2(n)$ from the primary signal. The output sequence, which represents an estimate of the desired signal $x(n)$, is the error signal

$$\begin{aligned} e(n) &= y(n) - \hat{w}_2(n) \\ &= y(n) - \sum_{k=0}^{M-1} h(k)v(n-k) \end{aligned} \tag{6.1.25}$$

This error sequence is used to adaptively adjust the coefficients of the FIR filter.

If the least-squares criterion is used to determine the filter coefficients, the result of the optimization is the set of linear equations

$$\sum_{k=0}^{M-1} h(k)r_{vv}(l-k) = r_{yv}(l), \qquad l = 0, 1, \ldots, M-1 \tag{6.1.26}$$

where $r_{vv}(l)$ is the sample (time-averaged) autocorrelation of the sequence $v(n)$ and $r_{yv}(l)$ is the sample cross-correlation of the sequences $y(n)$ and $v(n)$. Clearly, the noise-canceling problem is similar to the last three adaptive filtering applications described above.

6.1.7 Linear Predictive Coding of Speech Signals

Various methods have been developed over the past four decades for digital encoding of speech signals. In the telephone system, for example, two commonly used methods for speech encoding are pulse code modulation (PCM) and differential PCM (DPCM). These are examples of *waveform coding* methods. Other waveform coding methods have also been developed, such as delta modulation (DM) and adaptive DPCM, but these methods are not widely used in telephone communication systems today.

Since the digital speech signal is ultimately transmitted from the source to a destination, a primary objective in devising speech encoders is to minimize the number of bits required to represent the speech signal, while maintaining speech intelligibility. This objective has led to the development of a class of low-bit-rate (2400 bits per second and below) speech encoding methods, which are based on constructing a model of the speech source and transmitting the model parameters. Adaptive filtering finds application in these model-based speech coding systems. We shall describe a very effective method called *linear predictive coding (LPC)*.

In LPC the vocal tract is modeled as a linear all-pole filter having the system function

$$H(z) = \frac{G}{1 - \sum_{k=1}^{p} a_k z^{-k}} \tag{6.1.27}$$

where p is the number of poles, G the filter gain, and a_k the parameters that determine the poles. There are two mutually exclusive excitation functions to model voiced and unvoiced speech sounds. On a short-time basis, voiced speech is periodic with a fundamental frequency F_0, or a pitch period $1/F_0$, which depends on the speaker. Thus voiced speech is generated by exciting the all-pole filter model by a periodic impulse train with a period equal to the desired pitch period. Unvoiced speech sounds are generated by exciting the all-pole filter model by the output of a random-noise generator. This model is shown in Fig. 6.15.

Given a short-time segment of a speech signal, the speech encoder at the transmitter must determine the proper excitation function, the pitch period for voiced speech, the gain parameter G, and the coefficients a_k. A block diagram that illustrates the source encoding system is given in Fig. 6.16. The parameters of the model are determined adaptively from the data. Then the speech samples are synthesized by using the model, and an error signal sequence is generated as shown in Fig. 6.15 by taking the difference between the actual and the synthesized sequence. The error signal and the model parameters are encoded into a binary sequence and transmitted to the destination. At the receiver, the speech signal is synthesized from the model and the error signal.

The parameters of the all-pole filter model are easily determined from the speech samples by means of linear prediction. To be specific, consider the system shown in Fig. 6.17 and assume that we have N signal samples. The output of the FIR filter is

$$\hat{x}(n) = \sum_{k=1}^{p} a_k x(n-k) \tag{6.1.28}$$

and the corresponding error between the observed sample $x(n)$ and the estimate $\hat{x}(n)$ is

$$e(n) = x(n) - \sum_{k=1}^{p} a_k x(n-k) \tag{6.1.29}$$

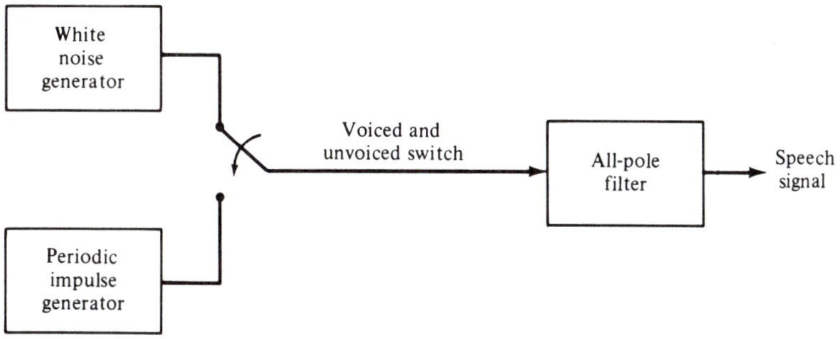

FIGURE 6.15 Block diagram model for the generation of a speech signal.

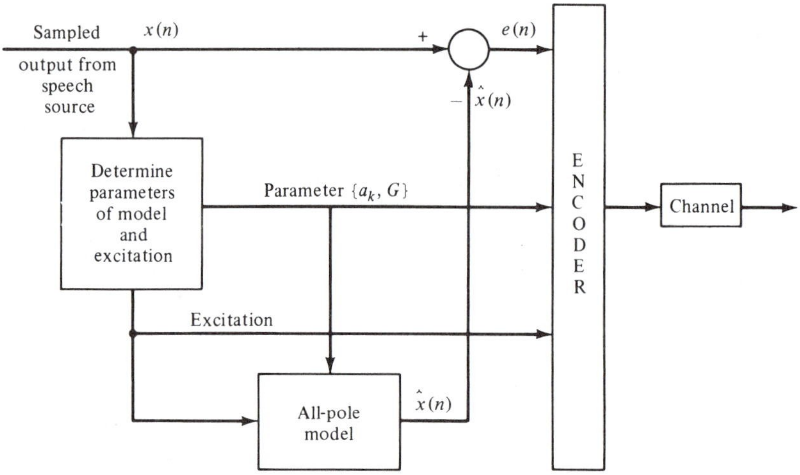

FIGURE 6.16 Source encoder for a speech signal.

By applying the least-squares criterion, we can determine the model parameters a_k. The result of this optimization is a set of linear equations

$$\sum_{k=1}^{p} a_k r_{xx}(l-k) = r_{xx}(l), \qquad l = 1, 2, \ldots, p \tag{6.1.30}$$

where $r_{xx}(l)$ is the time-averaged autocorrelation of the sequence $x(n)$. The gain parameter for the filter can be obtained by noting that its input–output equation is

$$x(n) = \sum_{k=1}^{p} a_k x(n-k) + Gv(n) \tag{6.1.31}$$

where $v(n)$ is the input sequence. Clearly,

$$\begin{aligned} Gv(n) &= x(n) - \sum_{k=1}^{p} a_k x(n-k) \\ &= e(n) \end{aligned}$$

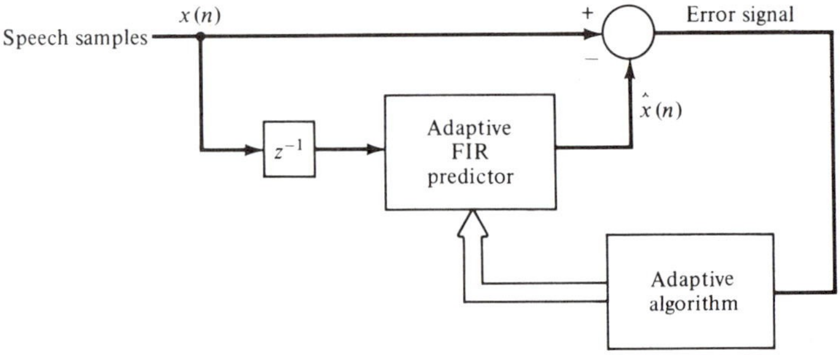

FIGURE 6.17 Estimation of pole parameters in LPC.

Then,

$$G^2 \sum_{n=0}^{N-1} v^2(n) = \sum_{n=0}^{N-1} e^2(n) \tag{6.1.32}$$

If the input excitation is normalized to unit energy by design, then

$$\begin{aligned} G^2 &= \sum_{n=0}^{N-1} e^2(n) \\ &= r_{xx}(0) - \sum_{k=1}^{p} a_k r_{xx}(k) \end{aligned} \tag{6.1.33}$$

Thus G^2 is set equal to the residual energy resulting from the least-squares optimization.

In this development we have described the use of linear prediction to adaptively determine the pole parameters and the gain of an all-pole filter model for speech generation. In practice, due to the nonstationary character of speech signals, this model is applied to short-time segments (10 to 20 milliseconds) of a speech signal. Usually, a new set of parameters is determined for each short time segment. However, it is often advantageous to use the model parameters measured from previous segments to smooth out sharp discontinuities that usually exist in estimates of model parameters obtained from segment to segment. Although our discussion was totally in terms of the FIR filter structure, we should mention that speech synthesis is usually performed by using the FIR lattice structure and the reflection coefficients K_i. Since the dynamic range of the K_i is significantly smaller than that of the a_k, the reflection coefficients require fewer bits to represent them. Hence the K_i are transmitted over the channel. Consequently, it is natural to synthesize the speech at the destination using the all-pole lattice structure described in Section 4.5.

In our treatment of LPC for speech coding, we have not considered algorithms for the estimation of the excitation and the pitch period. A discussion of appropriate algorithms for these parameters of the model would take us too far afield. The interested reader is referred to the book by Rabiner and Schafer (1978) for a detailed treatment of speech analysis and synthesis methods.

6.1.8 Adaptive Arrays

In the previous examples we considered adaptive filtering performed on a single data sequence. However, adaptive filtering has also been widely applied to multiple data sequences that result from antenna arrays and seismometer arrays, where the sensors (antennas or seismometers) are arranged in some spatial configuration. Each element of the array of sensors provides a signal sequence. By properly combining the signals from the various sensors it is possible to change the directivity pattern of the array.

For example, consider the linear antenna array consisting of five elements, as shown in Fig. 6.18a. If the signals are simply linearly summed, we obtain the sequence

$$x(n) = \sum_{k=1}^{5} x_k(n) \tag{6.1.34}$$

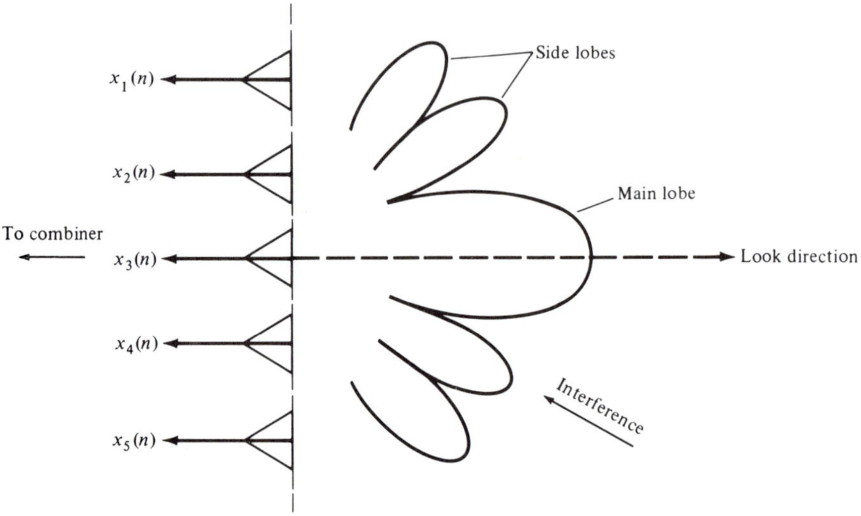

(a) Linear antenna array with antenna pattern

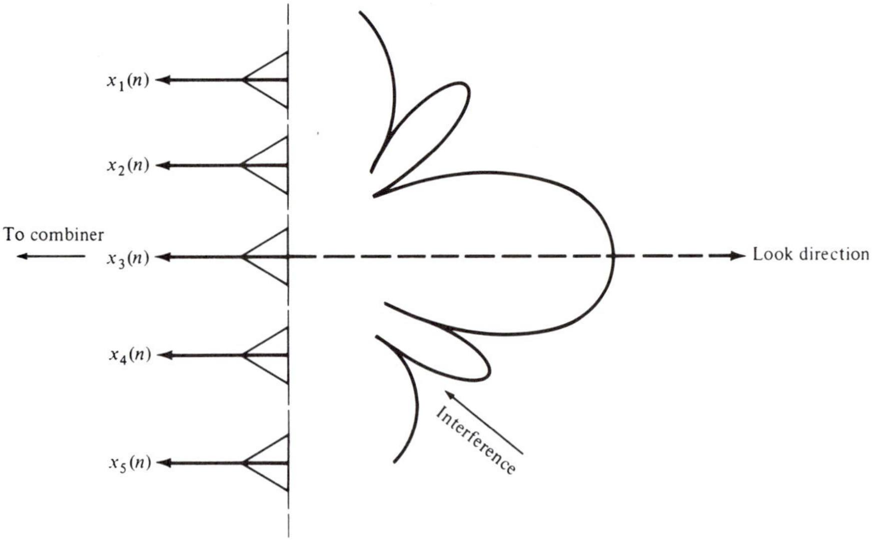

(b) Linear antenna array with a null placed in the direction of the interference

FIGURE 6.18 Linear antenna array: (a) linear antenna array with antenna pattern; (b) linear antenna array with a null placed in the direction of the interference.

which results in the antenna directivity pattern shown in Fig. 6.18a. Now suppose that an interference signal is received from a direction corresponding to one of the sidelobes in the array. By properly weighting the sequences $x_k(n)$ prior to combining, it is possible to alter the sidelobe pattern such that the array contains a null in the direction of the interference as shown in Fig. 6.18b. Thus we obtain

$$x(n) = \sum_{k=1}^{5} h_k x_k(n) \tag{6.1.35}$$

where h_k are the weights.

We may also change or steer the direction of the main antenna lobe by simply introducing delays in the output of the sensor signals prior to combining. Hence from N sensors we have a combined signal of the form

$$x(n) = \sum_{k=1}^{N} h_k x_k(n - n_k) \tag{6.1.36}$$

where h_k are the weights and n_k corresponds to an n_k-sample delay in the signal $x(n)$. The choice of weights may be used to place nulls in specific directions.

More generally, we may simply filter each sequence prior to combining. In such a case the output sequence has the general form

$$\begin{aligned} y(n) &= \sum_{k=1}^{N} y_k(n) \\ &= \sum_{k=1}^{N} \sum_{l=0}^{M-1} h_k(l) x_k(n - n_k - l) \end{aligned} \tag{6.1.37}$$

where $h_k(l)$ is the impulse response of the filter for processing the kth sensor output and n_k are the delays that steer the beam pattern.

The LMS algorithm described in Section 6.2.2 is frequently used in adaptively selecting the weights h_k or the impulse responses $h_k(l)$. The more powerful recursive least-squares algorithms described in Chapter 7 can also be applied to the multisensor (multichannel) data problem.

In the treatment given in this chapter, we deal with single-channel (sensor) signals. We treat least-squares adaptive filtering of multichannel signals in Chapter 7.

6.2 ADAPTIVE DIRECT-FORM FIR FILTERS

From the examples of the preceding section we have observed that there is a common framework in all adaptive filtering applications. The least-squares criterion that we have adopted leads to a set of linear equations for the filter coefficients, which may be expressed as

$$\sum_{k=0}^{M-1} h(k) r_{xx}(l - k) = r_{dx}(l + D), \qquad l = 0, 1, 2, \ldots, M - 1 \tag{6.2.1}$$

where $r_{xx}(l)$ is the autocorrelation of the sequence $x(n)$ and $r_{dx}(l)$ is the cross-correlation of the sequences $d(n)$ and $x(n)$. The delay parameter D is zero in some cases and nonzero in others.

We observe that the autocorrelation $r_{xx}(l)$ and the cross-correlation $r_{dx}(l)$ are obtained from the data and hence represent estimates of the true (statistical) autocorrelation and cross-correlation sequences. As a result, the coefficients $h(k)$ obtained from (6.2.1) are estimates of the true coefficients. The quality of the estimates depend on the length of the data record that is available for estimating $r_{xx}(l)$ and $r_{dx}(l)$. This is one problem that must be considered in the implementation of an adaptive filter.

A second problem that must be considered is that the underlying random process $x(n)$ is usually nonstationary. For example, in channel equalization, the frequency response characteristics of the channel may vary with time. As a consequence, the statistical autocorrelation and cross-correlation sequences, and hence their estimates, vary with time. This implies that the coefficients of the adaptive filter must change with time to reflect the time-variant statistical characteristics of the signal into the filter. This also implies that the quality of the estimates cannot be made arbitrarily high simply by increasing the number of signal samples used in the estimation of the autocorrelation and cross-correlation sequences.

There are several ways by which the coefficients of the adaptive filter can be varied with time to track the time-variant statistical characteristics of the signal. The most popular method is to adapt the filter recursively on a sample-by-sample basis as each new signal sample is received. A second approach is to estimate $r_{xx}(l)$ and $r_{dx}(l)$ on a block-by-block basis, with no attempt to maintain continuity in the values of the filter coefficients from one block of data to another. In such a scheme the block size must be relatively small, encompassing a time interval that is short compared to the time interval over which the statistical characteristics of the data change significantly. In addition to this block processing method, other block processing schemes can be devised that incorporate some continuity in the filter coefficients from block to block.

In our treatment of adaptive filtering algorithms, we consider only time-recursive algorithms that update the filter coefficients on a sample-by-sample basis. In particular, we consider two types of algorithms, the LMS algorithm, which is based on a gradient-type search for tracking the time-variant signal characteristics, and the class of recursive least-squares algorithms, which are significantly more complex than the LMS algorithm, but which provide faster convergence to changes in signal statistics.

6.2.1 Minimum Mean-Square-Error (MMSE) Criterion

The LMS algorithm, described in the following subsection, is most easily obtained by formulating the optimization of the FIR filter coefficients as an estimation problem based on the minimization of the mean-square error (MSE). Let us assume that we have available the (possibly complex-valued) data sequence $x(n)$, which are samples from a stationary random process with autocorrelation sequence

$$\gamma_{xx}(m) = E[x(n)x^*(n - m)] \tag{6.2.2}$$

From these samples we form an estimate of the desired sequence $d(n)$ by passing the observed data $x(n)$ through an FIR filter with coefficients $h(n)$, $0 \le n \le M - 1$. The filter output may be expressed as

$$\hat{d}(n) = \sum_{k=0}^{M-1} h(k)x(n - k) \tag{6.2.3}$$

where $\hat{d}(n)$ represents an estimate of $d(n)$. The estimation error is defined as

$$\begin{aligned} e(n) &= d(n) - \hat{d}(n) \\ &= d(n) - \sum_{k=0}^{M-1} h(k)x(n - k) \end{aligned} \tag{6.2.4}$$

The mean-square error as a function of the filter coefficients is

$$\begin{aligned} J(\mathbf{h}_M) &= E[|e(n)|^2] \\ &= E\left[\left|d(n) - \sum_{k=0}^{M-1} h(k)x(n - k)\right|^2\right] \\ &= E\left\{|d(n)|^2 - 2\,\mathrm{Re}\left[\sum_{l=0}^{M-1} h^*(l)d(n)x^*(n - l)\right]\right. \\ &\quad \left. + \sum_{k=0}^{M-1}\sum_{l=0}^{M-1} h^*(l)h(k)x^*(n - l)x(n - k)\right\} \\ &= \sigma_d^2 - 2\,\mathrm{Re}\left[\sum_{l=0}^{M-1} h^*(l)\gamma_{dx}(l)\right] \\ &\quad + \sum_{k=0}^{M-1}\sum_{k=0}^{M} h^*(l)h(k)\gamma_{xx}(l - k) \end{aligned} \tag{6.2.5}$$

where, by definition, $\sigma_d^2 = E[|d(n)|^2]$ and $\mathbf{h}_M$ denotes the vector of coefficients. The complex conjugate of $\mathbf{h}_M$ is denoted as $\mathbf{h}_M^*$ and the transpose as $\mathbf{h}_M^t$.

We observe that the MSE is a quadratic function of the filter coefficients. Consequently, the minimization of $J(\mathbf{h}_M)$ with respect to the coefficients leads to the set of M linear equations,

$$\sum_{k=0}^{M-1} h(k)\gamma_{xx}(l - k) = \gamma_{dx}(l), \qquad l = 0, 1, \ldots, M - 1 \tag{6.2.6}$$

The filter with coefficients obtained from (6.2.6), which is the Wiener-Hopf equation previously derived in section 4.6.1., is called the *Wiener filter*.

If we compare (6.2.6) with (6.2.1), it is apparent that these equations are similar in form. In (6.2.1) we use estimates of the autocorrelation and cross-correlation to determine the filter coefficients, whereas in (6.2.6) the statistical autocorrelation and cross-correlation are employed. Hence (6.2.6) yields the optimum (Wiener) filter coefficients in the MSE sense, whereas (6.2.1) yields estimates of the optimum coefficients.

The equations in (6.2.6) may be expressed in matrix form as

$$\mathbf{\Gamma}_M \mathbf{h}_M = \boldsymbol{\gamma}_d \tag{6.2.7}$$

where $\mathbf{\Gamma}_M$ is an $M \times M$ (Hermitian) Toeplitz matrix with elements $\Gamma_{lk} = \gamma_{xx}(l - k)$ and $\boldsymbol{\gamma}_d$ is an $M \times 1$ cross-correlation vector with elements $\gamma_{dx}(l)$, $l = 0, 1, \ldots, M - 1$. The solution for the optimum filter coefficients

$$\mathbf{h}_{\text{opt}} = \mathbf{\Gamma}_M^{-1} \boldsymbol{\gamma}_d \tag{6.2.8}$$

and the resulting minimum MSE achieved with the optimum coefficients given by (6.2.8) is

$$\begin{aligned} J_{\min} \equiv J(\mathbf{h}_{\text{opt}}) &= \sigma_d^2 - \sum_{k=0}^{M-1} h_{\text{opt}}(k) \gamma_{dx}^*(k) \\ &= \sigma_d^2 - \boldsymbol{\gamma}_d^H \mathbf{\Gamma}_M^{-1} \boldsymbol{\gamma}_d \end{aligned} \tag{6.2.9}$$

where the exponent H denotes the conjugate transpose.

Recall that the set of linear equations in (6.2.6) can also be obtained by invoking the *orthogonality principle* in mean-square estimation (see Chapter 4). According to the orthogonality principle, the mean-square estimation error is minimized when the error $e(n)$ is orthogonal, in the statistical sense, to the estimate $\hat{d}(n)$,

$$E[e(n)\hat{d}^*(n)] = 0 \tag{6.2.10}$$

But the condition in (6.2.10) implies that

$$E\left[\sum_{k=0}^{M-1} h(k)e(n)x^*(n-k)\right] = \sum_{k=0}^{M-1} h(k)E[e(n)x^*(n-k)] = 0$$

or, equivalently,

$$E[e(n)x^*(n-l)] = 0, \qquad l = 0, 1, \ldots, M - 1 \tag{6.2.11}$$

If we substitute for $e(n)$ in (6.2.11) using the expression for $e(n)$ given in (6.2.4) and perform the expectation operation, we obtain the equations given in (6.2.6).

Since $\hat{d}(n)$ is orthogonal to $e(n)$, the residual (minimum) mean-square error is

$$\begin{aligned} J_{\min} &= E[e(n)d^*(n)] \\ &= E[|d(n)|^2] - \sum_{k=0}^{M-1} h_{\text{opt}}(k) \gamma_{dx}^*(k) \end{aligned} \tag{6.2.12}$$

which is the result given in (6.2.9).

The optimum filter coefficients given by (6.2.8) can be solved efficiently by using the Levinson–Durbin algorithm. However, we shall consider the use of a gradient method for solving for $\mathbf{h}_{\text{opt}}$, iteratively. This development leads to the LMS algorithm for adaptive filtering.

6.2.2 The Widrow LMS Algorithm

There are various numerical methods that can be used to solve the set of linear equations given by (6.2.6) or (6.2.7) for the optimum FIR filter coefficients. Below, we consider recursive methods that have been devised for finding the minimum of a function of several variables. In our problem the performance index is the MSE given by (6.2.5), which is a quadratic function of the filter coefficients. Hence this function has a unique minimum, which we shall determine by an iterative search.

For the moment, let us assume that the autocorrelation matrix $\mathbf{\Gamma}_M$ and the cross-correlation vector $\boldsymbol{\gamma}_d$ are known. Hence $J(\mathbf{h}_M)$ is a known function of the coefficients $h(n)$, $0 \le n \le M - 1$. Algorithms for recursively computing the filter coefficients, and thus searching for the minimum of $J(\mathbf{h}_M)$, have the form

$$\mathbf{h}_M(n + 1) = \mathbf{h}_M(n) + \tfrac{1}{2}\Delta(n)\mathbf{S}(n), \qquad n = 0, 1, \ldots \tag{6.2.13}$$

where $\mathbf{h}_M(n)$ is the vector of filter coefficients at the nth iteration, $\Delta(n)$ is a step size at the nth iteration, and $\mathbf{S}(n)$ is a direction vector for the nth iteration. The initial vector $\mathbf{h}_M(0)$ is chosen arbitrarily. In this treatment we exclude methods that require the computations of $\mathbf{\Gamma}_M^{-1}$, such as Newton's method. We shall only consider search methods based on the use of gradient vectors.

The simplest method for finding the minimum of $J(\mathbf{h}_M)$ recursively is based on a steepest-descent search [see Murray (1972)]. In the method of steepest descent, the direction vector $\mathbf{S}(n) = -\mathbf{g}(n)$, where $\mathbf{g}(n)$ is the gradient vector at the nth iteration, defined as

$$\begin{aligned} \mathbf{g}(n) &= \frac{dJ(\mathbf{h}_M(n))}{d\mathbf{h}_M(n)} \\ &= 2[\mathbf{\Gamma}_M\mathbf{h}_M(n) - \boldsymbol{\gamma}_d], \qquad n = 0, 1, 2, \ldots \end{aligned} \tag{6.2.14}$$

Hence we compute the gradient vector at each iteration and change the values of $\mathbf{h}_M(n)$ in a direction opposite the gradient. Thus the recursive algorithm based on the method of steepest descent is

$$\mathbf{h}_M(n + 1) = \mathbf{h}_M(n) - \tfrac{1}{2}\Delta(n)\mathbf{g}(n) \tag{6.2.15}$$

or equivalently,

$$\mathbf{h}_M(n + 1) = [\mathbf{I} - \Delta(n)\mathbf{\Gamma}_M]\mathbf{h}_M(n) + \Delta(n)\boldsymbol{\gamma}_d \tag{6.2.16}$$

We state without proof that the algorithm leads to the convergence of $\mathbf{h}_M(n)$ to $\mathbf{h}_{\text{opt}}$ in the limit as $n \to \infty$, provided that the sequence of step sizes $\Delta(n)$

is absolutely summable, with $\Delta(n) \to 0$ as $n \to \infty$. It follows that $n \to \infty$, $\mathbf{g}(n) \to \mathbf{0}$.

Other candidate algorithms that provide faster convergence are the conjugate-gradient algorithm and the Fletcher–Powell algorithm. In the *conjugate-gradient algorithm,* the direction vectors are given as

$$\mathbf{S}(n) = \beta(n-1)\mathbf{S}(n-1) - \mathbf{g}(n) \tag{6.2.17}$$

where $\beta(n)$ is a scalar function of the gradient vectors [see Beckman (1962)]. In the *Fletcher–Powell algorithm,* the direction vectors are given as

$$\mathbf{S}(n) = -\mathbf{H}(n)\mathbf{g}(n) \tag{6.2.18}$$

where $\mathbf{H}(n)$ is an $M \times M$ positive definite matrix, computed iteratively, that converges to the inverse of $\mathbf{\Gamma}_M$ [see Fletcher and Powell (1963)]. Clearly, the three algorithms differ in the manner in which the direction vectors are computed.

The three algorithms described above are appropriate when $\mathbf{\Gamma}_M$ and $\boldsymbol{\gamma}_d$ are known. However, this is not the case in adaptive filtering applications, as we indicated previously. In the absence of knowledge of $\mathbf{\Gamma}_M$ and $\boldsymbol{\gamma}_d$ we may substitute estimates $\hat{\mathbf{S}}(n)$ of the direction vectors in place of the actual vectors $\mathbf{S}(n)$. Below we consider this approach for the steepest-descent algorithm.

First, we note that the gradient vector given by (6.2.14) may also be expressed in terms of the orthogonality conditions given by (6.2.10). In fact, the conditions in (6.2.10) are equivalent to the expression

$$E[e(n)\mathbf{X}_M^*(n)] = \boldsymbol{\gamma}_d - \mathbf{\Gamma}_M\mathbf{h}_M(n) \tag{6.2.19}$$

where $\mathbf{X}_M(n)$ is the vector with elements $x(n-l)$, $l = 0, 1, \ldots, M-1$. Therefore, the gradient vector is simply

$$\mathbf{g}(n) = -2E[e(n)\mathbf{X}_M^*(n)] \tag{6.2.20}$$

Clearly, the gradient vector $\mathbf{g}(n) = \mathbf{0}$ when the error is orthogonal to the data in the estimate $\hat{d}(n)$.

An unbiased estimate of the gradient vector at the nth iteration is simply obtained from (6.2.20) as

$$\hat{\mathbf{g}}(n) = -2e(n)\mathbf{X}_M^*(n) \tag{6.2.21}$$

where $e(n) = d(n) - \hat{d}(n)$ and $\mathbf{X}_M(n)$ is the set of M signal samples in the filter at the nth iteration. Thus with $\hat{\mathbf{g}}(n)$ substituted for $\mathbf{g}(n)$ we have the algorithm

$$\mathbf{h}_M(n+1) = \mathbf{h}_M(n) + \Delta(n)e(n)\mathbf{X}_M^*(n) \tag{6.2.22}$$

This is called a *stochastic-gradient-descent algorithm.* As given by (6.2.22), it has a variable step size.

It has become common practice in adaptive filtering to use a fixed-step-size algorithm, for two reasons. One is that a fixed-step-size algorithm is easily implemented in either hardware or software. Second, a fixed step size is appropriate for tracking time-variant signal statistics, whereas if $\Delta(n) \to 0$ as $n \to \infty$, adaptation to signal variations cannot occur. For these reasons, (6.2.22) is modified to the algorithm

$$\mathbf{h}_M(n + 1) = \mathbf{h}_M(n) + \Delta e(n)\mathbf{X}_M^*(n) \tag{6.2.23}$$

where Δ is now the fixed step size. This algorithm was first proposed by Widrow and Hoff (1960) and is now widely known as the *LMS (least-mean-squares) algorithm*. Clearly, it is a stochastic-gradient algorithm.

The LMS algorithm is a relatively simple algorithm to implement. For this reason it has been widely used in many adaptive filtering applications. Its properties and limitations have also been thoroughly investigated. In the following section we provide a brief treatment of its important properties concerning convergence, stability, and the noise resulting from the use of estimates of the gradient vectors. Later, we compare its properties with the more complex recursive least-squares algorithms.

Several variations of the basic LMS algorithm have been proposed in the literature and implemented in some adaptive filtering applications. One variation is obtained if we average the gradient vectors over several iterations prior to making adjustments of the filter coefficients. For example, the average over K gradient vectors is

$$\bar{\hat{\mathbf{g}}}(nK) = -\frac{2}{K}\sum_{k=0}^{K-1} e(nK + k)\mathbf{X}_M^*(nK + k) \tag{6.2.24}$$

and the corresponding recursive equation for updating the filter coefficients once every K iterations is

$$\mathbf{h}_M((n + 1)K) = \mathbf{h}_M(nK) - \tfrac{1}{2}\Delta\bar{\hat{\mathbf{g}}}(nK) \tag{6.2.25}$$

In effect, the averaging operation performed in (6.2.24) reduces the noise in the estimate of the gradient vector, as shown by Gardner (1984).

An alternative approach is to filter the gradient vectors by a lowpass filter and use the output of the filter as an estimate of the gradient vector. For example, a simple lowpass filter for the gradients yields as an output

$$\hat{\mathbf{S}}(n) = \beta\hat{\mathbf{S}}(n - 1) - \hat{\mathbf{g}}(n), \qquad \mathbf{S}(0) = -\hat{\mathbf{g}}(0) \tag{6.2.26}$$

where the choice of $0 \le \beta < 1$ determines the bandwidth of the lowpass filter. When β is close to unity, the filter bandwidth is small and the effective averaging is performed over many gradient vectors. On the other hand, when β is small, the lowpass filter has a large bandwidth and hence provides little averaging of the gradient vectors. With the filtered gradient vectors given by (6.2.26) in place of $\hat{\mathbf{g}}(n)$, we obtain the filtered version of the LMS algorithm given by

$$\mathbf{h}_M(n + 1) = \mathbf{h}_M(n) + \tfrac{1}{2}\Delta\hat{\mathbf{S}}(n) \tag{6.2.27}$$

An analysis of the filtered-gradient LMS algorithm is given in the paper by Proakis (1974).

6.2.3 Properties of the LMS Algorithm

In this section we consider the basic properties of the LMS algorithm given by (6.2.23). In particular, we focus on its convergence properties, its stability, and the excess noise generated as a result of using noisy gradient vectors in place of the actual gradient vectors. The use of noisy estimates of the gradient vectors implies that the filter coefficients will fluctuate randomly, and hence an analysis of the characteristics of the algorithm should be performed in statistical terms.

The convergence and stability of the LMS algorithm may be investigated by determining how the mean value of $\mathbf{h}_M(n)$ converges to the optimum coefficients $\mathbf{h}_{\text{opt}}$. If we take the expected value of (6.2.23), we obtain

$$\begin{aligned}\bar{\mathbf{h}}_M(n+1) &= \bar{\mathbf{h}}_M(n) + \Delta E[e(n)\mathbf{X}_M^*(n)] \\ &= \bar{\mathbf{h}}_M(n) + \Delta[\boldsymbol{\gamma}_d - \boldsymbol{\Gamma}_M\bar{\mathbf{h}}_M(n)] \\ &= (\mathbf{I} - \Delta\boldsymbol{\Gamma}_M)\bar{\mathbf{h}}_M(n) + \Delta\boldsymbol{\gamma}_d\end{aligned} \tag{6.2.28}$$

where $\bar{\mathbf{h}}_M(n) = E[\mathbf{h}_M(n)]$ and $\mathbf{I}$ is the identity matrix.

The recursive relation in (6.2.28) may be represented as a closed-loop control system, as shown in Fig. 6.19. The convergence rate and the stability of this closed-loop system are governed by our choice of the step size parameter Δ. To determine the convergence behavior, it is convenient to decouple the M simultaneous difference equations given in (6.2.28) by performing a linear transformation of the mean coefficient vector $\bar{\mathbf{h}}_M(n)$. The appropriate transformation is obtained by noting that the autocorrelation matrix $\boldsymbol{\Gamma}_M$ is Hermitian and hence can be represented as [see Gantmacher (1960)]

$$\boldsymbol{\Gamma}_M = \mathbf{U}\boldsymbol{\Lambda}\mathbf{U}^H \tag{6.2.29}$$

where $\mathbf{U}$ is the normalized modal matrix of $\boldsymbol{\Gamma}_M$ and $\boldsymbol{\Lambda}$ is a diagonal matrix with diagonal elements λ_k, $0 \le k \le M-1$, equal to the eigenvalues of $\boldsymbol{\Gamma}_M$.

When (6.2.29) is substituted into (6.2.28), the latter may be expressed as

$$\bar{\mathbf{h}}_M^0(n+1) = (\mathbf{I} - \Delta\boldsymbol{\Lambda})\bar{\mathbf{h}}_M^0(n) + \Delta\boldsymbol{\gamma}_d^0 \tag{6.2.30}$$

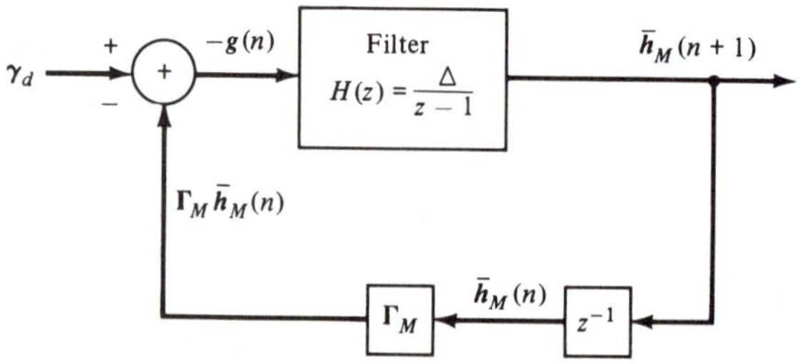

FIGURE 6.19 Closed-loop control system representation of recursive equation (6.2.28).

where the transformed (orthogonalized) vectors are $\bar{\mathbf{h}}_M^0(n) = \mathbf{U}^H\bar{\mathbf{h}}_M(n)$ and $\boldsymbol{\gamma}_d^0 = \mathbf{U}^H\boldsymbol{\gamma}_d$. The set of M first-order difference equations in (6.2.30) are now decoupled. Their convergence and their stability is determined from the homogeneous equation

$$\bar{\mathbf{h}}_M^0(n+1) = (\mathbf{I} - \Delta\mathbf{\Lambda})\bar{\mathbf{h}}_M^0(n) \tag{6.2.31}$$

If we focus our attention on the solution of the kth equation in (6.2.31), we observe that

$$\bar{h}^0(k,n) = C(1 - \Delta\lambda_k)^n u(n), \qquad k = 0, 2, \ldots, M-1 \tag{6.2.32}$$

where C is some arbitrary constant and $u(n)$ is the unit step sequence. Clearly, $h^0(k,n)$ converges to zero exponentially provided that

$$|1 - \Delta\lambda_k] < 1$$

or, equivalently,

$$0 < \Delta < \frac{2}{\lambda_k}, \qquad k = 0, 1, \ldots, M-1 \tag{6.2.33}$$

The fastest convergence rate is obtained when $\Delta = 1/\lambda_k$.

The condition given by (6.2.33) for convergence of the homogeneous difference equation for the kth normalized filter coefficient (kth mode of the closed-loop system) must be satisfied for all $k = 0, 1, \ldots, M-1$. Therefore, the range of values of Δ that ensures the convergence of the mean of the coefficient vector in the LMS algorithm is

$$0 < \Delta < \frac{2}{\lambda_{\max}} \tag{6.2.34}$$

where $\lambda_{\max}$ is the largest eigenvalue of $\mathbf{\Gamma}_M$.

Since $\mathbf{\Gamma}_M$ is an autocorrelation matrix, its eigenvalues are nonnegative. Hence an upper bound on $\lambda_{\max}$ is

$$\lambda_{\max} < \sum_{k=0}^{M-1} \lambda_k = \text{trace}\,\mathbf{\Gamma}_M = M\gamma_{xx}(0) \tag{6.2.35}$$

where $\gamma_{xx}(0)$ is the input signal power that is easily estimated from the received signal. Therefore, an upper bound on the step size Δ is $2/M\gamma_{xx}(0)$.

From (6.2.32) we observe that rapid convergence of the LMS algorithm occurs when $|1 - \Delta\lambda_k|$ is small (i.e., when the poles of the closed-loop system in Fig. 6.19 are far from the unit circle). However, we cannot achieve this desirable condition and still satisfy the upper bound in (6.2.33) when there is a large difference between the largest and smallest eigenvalues of $\mathbf{\Gamma}_M$. In other words, even if we select Δ to be $1/\lambda_{\max}$, the convergence rate of the LMS algorithm will be determined by the decay of the mode corresponding to the smallest eigenvalue $\lambda_{\min}$. For this mode, with $\Delta = 1/\lambda_{\max}$ substituted in (6.2.32), we have

$$\bar{\mathbf{h}}_M^0(k,n) = C\left(1 - \frac{\lambda_{\min}}{\lambda_{\max}}\right)^n u(n)$$

Consequently, the ratio $\lambda_{min}/\lambda_{max}$ ultimately determines the convergence rate. If $\lambda_{min}/\lambda_{max}$ is small (much smaller than unity), the convergence will be slow. On the other hand, if $\lambda_{min}/\lambda_{max}$ is close to unity, the convergence rate of the algorithm is fast.

The other important characteristic of the LMS algorithm is the noise resulting from the use of estimates of the gradient vectors. The noise in the gradient vector estimates causes random fluctuations in the coefficients about their optimal values and thus leads to an increase in the minimum MSE at the output of the adaptive filter. Hence the total MSE is $J_{min} + J_\Delta$, where J_Δ is called the *excess mean-square error.*

For any given set of filter coefficients $\mathbf{h}_M(n)$, the total MSE at the output of the adaptive filter may be expressed as

$$J(\mathbf{h}_M(n)) = J_{min} + (\mathbf{h}_M(n) - \mathbf{h}_{opt})^t \mathbf{\Gamma}_M (\mathbf{h}_M(n) - \mathbf{h}_{opt})^* \tag{6.2.36}$$

where $\mathbf{h}_{opt}$ represents the optimum filter coefficients defined by (6.2.8). A plot of $J(\mathbf{h}_M(n))$ as a function of the iteration n is called a *learning curve.* If we substitute (6.2.29) for $\mathbf{\Gamma}_M$ and perform the linear orthogonal transformation used previously, we obtain

$$J(\mathbf{h}_M(n)) = J_{min} + \sum_{k=0}^{M-1} \lambda_k \, |h^0(k,n) - h^0_{opt}(k)|^2 \tag{6.2.37}$$

where the term $h^0(k,n) - h^0_{opt}(k)$ represents the error in the kth filter coefficient (in the orthogonal coordinate system). The excess mean-square error is defined as the expected value of the second term in (6.2.37),

$$J_\Delta = \sum_{k=0}^{M-1} \lambda_k E[|h^0(k,n) - h^0_{opt}(k)|^2] \tag{6.2.38}$$

To derive an expression for the excess mean-square error J_Δ, we assume that the mean values of the filter coefficients $\mathbf{h}_M(n)$ have converged to their optimum values $\mathbf{h}_{opt}$. Then the term $\Delta e(n)\mathbf{X}^*_M(n)$ in the LMS algorithm given by (6.2.23) is a zero-mean noise vector. Its covariance is

$$\text{cov}[\Delta e(n)\mathbf{X}^*_M(n)] = \Delta^2 E[|e(n)|^2 \, \mathbf{X}_M(n)\mathbf{X}^H_M(n)] \tag{6.2.39}$$

To a first approximation, we assume that $|e(n)|^2$ is uncorrelated with the signal vector. Although this assumption is not strictly true, it simplifies the derivation and yields useful results. [The reader may refer to the papers by Mazo (1979), Jones et al. (1982), and Gardner (1984) for further discussion on this assumption.] Then

$$\begin{aligned} \text{cov}[\Delta e(n)\mathbf{X}^*_M(n)] &= \Delta^2 E[|e(n)|^2] \, E[\mathbf{X}_M(n)\mathbf{X}^H_M(n)] \\ &= \Delta^2 J_{min} \mathbf{\Gamma}_M \end{aligned} \tag{6.2.40}$$

For the orthogonalized coefficient vector $\mathbf{h}^0_M(n)$, with additive noise, we have the equation

$$\mathbf{h}^0_M(n + 1) = (\mathbf{I} - \Delta\mathbf{\Lambda})\mathbf{h}^0_M(n) + \Delta\boldsymbol{\gamma}^0_d + \mathbf{w}^0(n) \tag{6.2.41}$$

where $\mathbf{w}^0(n)$ is the additive noise vector, which is related to the noise vector $\Delta e(n)\mathbf{X}_M^*(n)$ through the transformation

$$\begin{aligned} \mathbf{w}^0(n) &= \mathbf{U}^H[\Delta e(n)\mathbf{X}_M^*(n)] \\ &= \Delta e(n)\mathbf{U}^H\mathbf{X}_M^*(n) \end{aligned} \tag{6.2.42}$$

It is easily seen that the covariance matrix of the noise vector is

$$\begin{aligned} \text{cov}[\mathbf{w}^0(n)] &= \Delta^2 J_{\min}\mathbf{U}^H\mathbf{\Gamma}_M\mathbf{U} \\ &= \Delta^2 J_{\min}\mathbf{\Lambda} \end{aligned} \tag{6.2.43}$$

Therefore, the M components of $\mathbf{w}^0(n)$ are uncorrelated and each component has the variance $\sigma_k^2 = \Delta^2 J_{\min}\lambda_k$, $k = 0, 1, \ldots, M-1$.

Since the noise components of $\mathbf{w}^0(n)$ are uncorrelated, we may consider the M uncoupled difference equations in (6.2.41) separately. Each first-order difference equation represents a filter with impulse response $(1 - \Delta\lambda_k)^n$. When such a filter is excited with a noise sequence $w_k^0(n)$, the variance of the noise at the output of the filter is

$$E[|h^0(k,n) - h_{\text{opt}}^0(k)|^2] = \sum_{n=0}^{\infty}\sum_{m=0}^{\infty}(1 - \Delta\lambda_k)^n(1 - \Delta\lambda_k)^m E[w_k^0(n)w_k^{0*}(m)] \tag{6.2.44}$$

We make the simplifying assumption that the noise sequence $w_k^0(n)$ is white. Then (6.2.44) reduces to

$$E[|h^0(k,n) - h_{\text{opt}}^0(k)|^2] = \frac{\sigma_k^2}{1 - (1 - \Delta\lambda_k)^2} = \frac{\Delta^2 J_{\min}\lambda_k}{1 - (1 - \Delta\lambda_k)^2} \tag{6.2.45}$$

If we substitute the result of (6.2.45) into (6.2.38), we obtain the expression for the excess mean-square error as

$$J_\Delta = \Delta^2 J_{\min}\sum_{k=0}^{M-1}\frac{\lambda_k^2}{1 - (1 - \Delta\lambda_k)^2} \tag{6.2.46}$$

This expression can be simplified if we assume that Δ is selected such that $\Delta\lambda_k \ll 1$ for all k. Then

$$\begin{aligned} J_\Delta &\approx \Delta^2 J_{\min}\sum_{k=0}^{M-1}\frac{\lambda_k^2}{2\Delta\lambda_k} \\ &\approx \frac{1}{2}\Delta J_{\min}\sum_{k=0}^{M-1}\lambda_k \\ &\approx \frac{\Delta M J_{\min}\gamma_{xx}(0)}{2} \end{aligned} \tag{6.2.47}$$

where $\gamma_{xx}(0)$ is the power of the input signal.

The expression for J_Δ indicates that the excess mean-square error is proportional to the step size parameter Δ. Hence our choice of Δ must be based on a compromise between fast convergence and a small excess mean-square error. In practice, it is desirable to have $J_\Delta < J_{\min}$. Hence

$$\frac{J_\Delta}{J_{\min}} \approx \frac{\Delta M \gamma_{xx}(0)}{2} < 1$$

or equivalently,

$$\Delta < \frac{2}{M\gamma_{xx}(0)} \tag{6.2.48}$$

But this is just the upper bound that we had obtained previously for $\lambda_{\max}$. In steady-state operation, Δ should satisfy the upper bound in (6.2.48); otherwise, the excess mean-square error causes significant degradation in the performance of the adaptive filter.

The analysis given above on the excess mean-square error is based on the assumption that the mean value of the filter coefficients have converged to the optimum solution $\mathbf{h}_{\text{opt}}$. Under this condition, the step size Δ should satisfy the bound in (6.2.48). On the other hand, we have determined that convergence of the mean coefficient vector requires that $\Delta < 2/\lambda_{\max}$. While a choice of Δ near the upper bound $2/\lambda_{\max}$ may lead to initial convergence of the deterministic (known) gradient algorithm, such a large value of Δ will usually result in instability of the stochastic LMS gradient algorithm.

The initial convergence or transient behavior of the LMS algorithm has been investigated by several researchers. Their results clearly indicate that the step size must be reduced in direct proportion to the length of the adaptive filter, as in (6.2.48). The upper bound given (6.2.48) is necessary to ensure the initial convergence of the stochastic-gradient LMS algorithm. In practice, a choice of $\Delta < 1/M\gamma_{xx}(0)$ is usually made. The papers by Gitlin and Weinstein (1979) and Ungerboeck (1972) contain an analysis of the transient behavior and the convergence properties of the LMS algorithm.

In a digital implementation of the LMS algorithm, the choice of the step size parameter becomes even more critical. In an attempt to reduce the excess mean-square error, it is possible to reduce the step size parameter to the point where the total output mean-square error actually increases. This condition occurs when the estimated gradient components $e(n)x^*(n - l)$, $l = 0, 1, M - 1$, after multiplication by the small step size parameter Δ are smaller than one-half of the least significant bit in the fixed-point representation of the filter coefficients. In such a case, adaptation ceases. Consequently, it is important for the step size to be large enough to bring the filter coefficients in the vicinity of $\mathbf{h}_{\text{opt}}$. If it is desired to decrease the step size significantly, it is necessary to increase the precision in the filter coefficients. Typically, 16 bits of precision may be used for the filter coefficients, with the 8 to 12 most significant bits used for arithmetic operations in the filtering of the data. The 4 to 8 least significant bits are required to provide the necessary precision for the adaptation process. Thus the scaled, estimated gradient components $\Delta e(n)x^*(n - l)$ usually affect only the least significant bits. In effect, the added precision also allows for the noise to be averaged out, since many incremental changes in the least significant bits are required before any change occurs in the upper more significant bits used in arithmetic operations for filtering of the data. For an analysis of round-off errors in a digital implementation of the LMS algorithm, the reader is referred to the papers by Gitlin and Weinstein (1979), Gitlin et al. (1982), and Caraiscos and Liu (1984).

As a final point, we should indicate that the LMS algorithm is appropriate for tracking slowly time-variant signal statistics. In such a case, the minimum MSE and the optimum coefficient vector will be time variant. In other words, $J_{\min}(n)$ is a function of time and the M-dimensional error surface is moving with the time index n. The LMS algorithm attempts to follow the moving minimum $J_{\min}(n)$ in the M-dimensional space, but it is always lagging behind due to its use of (estimated) gradient vectors. As a consequence, the LMS algorithm incurs another form of error, called the *lag error,* whose mean-square value decreases with an increase in the step size Δ. The total MSE error can now be expressed as

$$J_{\text{total}} = J_{\min}(n) + J_\Delta + J_l \tag{6.2.49}$$

where J_l denotes the mean-square error due to the lag.

In any given nonstationary adaptive filtering problem, if we plot the J_Δ and J_l as a function of Δ, we expect these errors to behave as illustrated in Fig. 6.20. We observe that J_Δ increases with an increase in Δ while J_l decreases with an increase in Δ. The total error will exhibit a minimum, which will determine the optimum choice of the step size parameter.

When the statistical time variations of the signals occur rapidly, the lag error will dominate the performance of the adaptive filter. In such a case, $J_l \gg J_{\min} + J_\Delta$, even when the largest possible value of Δ is used. When this condition occurs, the LMS algorithm is inappropriate for the application

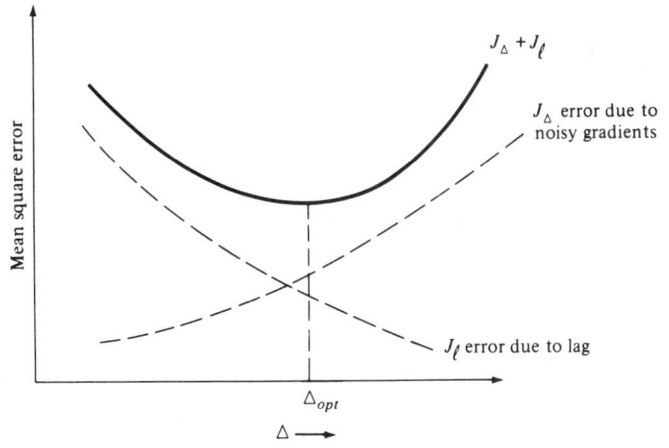

FIGURE 6.20 Excess mean-square error J_Δ and lag error J_l as a function of the step size Δ.

and one must rely on the more complex recursive least-squares algorithms described in Sections 6.2.4 and 6.3, to obtain faster convergence and tracking.

EXAMPLE 6.2.1

Learning curves for the LMS algorithm, when used to equalize a communication channel adaptively, are illustrated in Fig. 6.21. The FIR equalizer was realized in direct form and had length $M = 11$. The autocorrelation matrix $\mathbf{\Gamma}_M$ has an eigenvalue spread of $\lambda_{max}/\lambda_{min} = 11$. These three learning curves have been obtained with step sizes $\Delta = 0.045, 0.09$, and 0.115, by averaging the (estimated) MSE in 200 simulation runs. The input signal power was normalized to unity. Hence the upper bound in (6.2.48) is equal to 0.18. By selecting $\Delta = 0.09$ (one-half of the upper bound) we obtain a fast-decaying learning course, as shown in Fig. 6.21. If we divide Δ by 2 to 0.045, the convergence rate is reduced but the excess mean-square error is also reduced, so the algorithm performs better in the time-invariant signal environment. Finally, we note that a choice of $\Delta = 0.115$ causes large undesirable fluctuations in the output MSE of the algorithm. Note that $\Delta = 0.115$ is significantly lower than the upper bound given in (6.2.48).

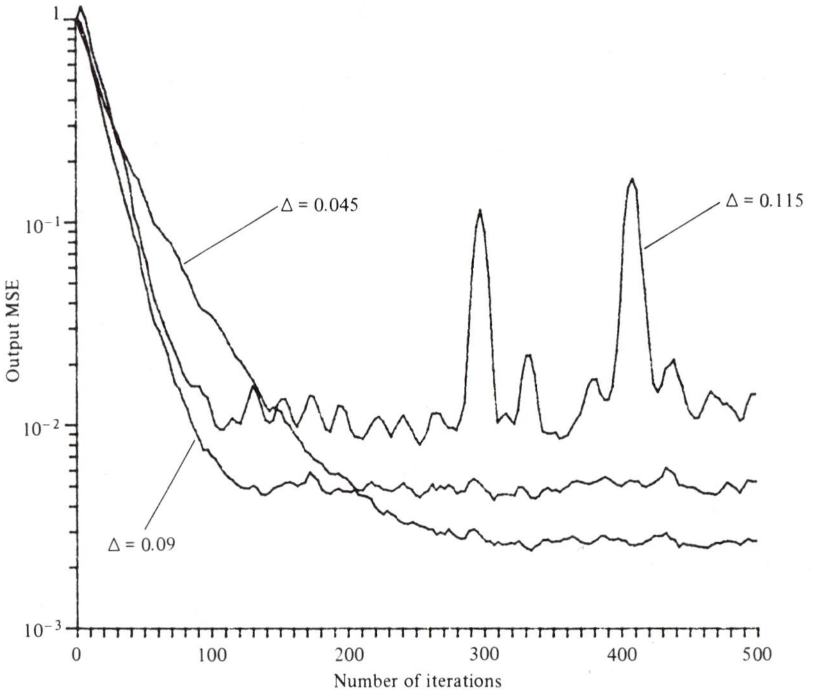

FIGURE 6.21 Learning curves for the LMS algorithm applied to an adaptive equalizer of length $M = 11$ and a channel with eigenvalue spread $\lambda_{max}/\lambda_{min} = 11$.

6.2.4 Recursive Least-Squares Algorithms for Direct-Form FIR Filters

The major advantage of the LMS algorithm lies in its computational simplicity. However, the price paid for this simplicity is slow convergence, especially when the eigenvalues of the autocorrelation matrix $\mathbf{\Gamma}_M$ have a large spread (i.e., $\lambda_{max}/\lambda_{min} \gg 1$). From another point of view, the LMS algorithm has only a single adjustable parameter for controlling the convergence rate, namely, the step size parameter Δ. Since Δ is limited for purposes of stability to be less than the upper bound in (6.2.48), the modes corresponding to the smaller eigenvalues converge very slowly.

To obtain faster convergence, it is necessary to devise more complex algorithms that involve additional parameters. In particular, if the correlation matrix $\mathbf{\Gamma}_M$ has unequal eigenvalues $\lambda_0, \lambda_1, \ldots \lambda_{M-1}$, we should use an algorithm that contains M parameters, one for each of the eigenvalues.

In deriving faster-converging adaptive filtering algorithms, we shall adopt the least-squares criterion instead of the statistical approach based on the MSE criterion. Thus we deal directly with the data sequence $x(n)$ and obtain estimates of correlations from the data.

It is convenient to express the least-squares algorithms in matrix form, to simplify the notation. Since the algorithms will be recursive in time, it is also necessary to introduce a time index in the filter-coefficient vector and in the error sequence. Hence we define the filter-coefficient vector at time n as

$$\mathbf{h}_M(n) = \begin{bmatrix} h(0,n) \\ h(1,n) \\ h(2,n) \\ \vdots \\ h(M-1, n) \end{bmatrix} \tag{6.2.50}$$

where the subscript M denotes the length of the filter. Similarly, the input signal vector to the filter at time n is denoted as

$$\mathbf{X}_M(n) = \begin{bmatrix} x(n) \\ x(n-1) \\ x(n-2) \\ \vdots \\ x(n-M+1) \end{bmatrix} \tag{6.2.51}$$

We assume that $x(n) = 0$ for $n < 0$. This is usually called *prewindowing* of the input data.

The recursive least-squares problem may now be formulated as follows. Suppose that we have observed the vectors $\mathbf{X}_M(l)$, $l = 0, 1, \ldots, n$ and we wish to determine the filter-coefficient vector $\mathbf{h}_M(n)$ that minimizes the weighted sum of magnitude-squared errors

$$\mathscr{E}_M = \sum_{l=0}^{n} w^{n-l}|e_M(l,n)|^2 \tag{6.2.52}$$

where the error is defined as the difference between the desired sequence $d(l)$ and the estimate $\hat{d}(l,n)$,

$$\begin{aligned} e_M(l,n) &= d(l) - \hat{d}(l,n) \\ &= d(l) - \mathbf{h}_M^t(n)\mathbf{X}_M(l) \end{aligned} \tag{6.2.53}$$

and w is a weighting factor in the range $0 < w \leq 1$.

The purpose of the factor w is to weight the most recent data points more heavily and thus allow the filter coefficients to adapt to time-varying statistical characteristics of the data. This is accomplished by using the exponential weighting factor with the past data. Alternatively, we may use a finite-duration sliding window with uniform weighting over the window length. We find the exponential weighting factor more convenient, both mathematically and practically. For comparison, an exponentially weighted window sequence has an effective memory of

$$\overline{N} = \frac{\sum_{n=0}^{\infty} n w^n}{\sum_{n=0}^{\infty} w^n} = \frac{w}{1 - w} \tag{6.2.54}$$

and hence should be approximately equivalent to a sliding window of length $\overline{N}$.

The minimization of $\mathscr{E}_M$ with respect to the filter coefficient vector $\mathbf{h}_M(n)$ yields the set of linear equations

$$\mathbf{R}_M(n)\mathbf{h}_M(n) = \mathbf{D}_M(n) \tag{6.2.55}$$

where $\mathbf{R}_M(n)$ is the signal (estimated) correlation matrix defined as

$$\mathbf{R}_M(n) = \sum_{l=0}^{n} w^{n-l}\mathbf{X}_M^*(l)\mathbf{X}_M^t(l) \tag{6.2.56}$$

and $\mathbf{D}_M(n)$ is the (estimated) cross-correlation vector

$$\mathbf{D}_M(n) = \sum_{l=0}^{n} w^{n-l}\mathbf{X}_M^*(l)d(l) \tag{6.2.57}$$

The solution of (6.2.55) is

$$\mathbf{h}_M(n) = \mathbf{R}_M^{-1}(n)\mathbf{D}_M(n) \tag{6.2.58}$$

Clearly, the matrix $\mathbf{R}_M(n)$ is akin to the statistical autocorrelation matrix $\mathbf{\Gamma}_M$, while the vector $\mathbf{D}_M(n)$ is akin to the cross-correlation vector $\boldsymbol{\gamma}_d$, defined previously. We emphasize, however, that $\mathbf{R}_M(n)$ is not a Toeplitz matrix, whereas $\mathbf{\Gamma}_M$ is. We should also mention that for small values of n, $\mathbf{R}_M(n)$ may be ill-conditioned, so that its inverse is not computable. In such a case it is customary initially to add the matrix $\delta\mathbf{I}_M$ to $\mathbf{R}_M(n)$, where $\mathbf{I}_M$ is an identity matrix and δ is a small positive constant. With exponential weighting into the past, the effect of adding $\delta\mathbf{I}_M$ dissipates with time.

Now, suppose that we have the solution of (6.2.58) at time $n - 1$ [i.e., we have $\mathbf{h}_M(n - 1)$ and we wish to compute $\mathbf{h}_M(n)$]. It is inefficient, and hence impractical, to solve the set of M linear equations for each new signal component. Instead, we may compute the matrix and vectors recursively. First, $\mathbf{R}_M(n)$ may be computed recursively as

$$\mathbf{R}_M(n) = w\mathbf{R}_M(n - 1) + \mathbf{X}_M^*(n)\mathbf{X}_M^t(n) \tag{6.2.59}$$

We call (6.2.59) the *time-update equation* for $\mathbf{R}_M(n)$.

Since the inverse of $\mathbf{R}_M(n)$ is needed, we use the matrix inversion lemma [see Householder (1964)]

$$\mathbf{R}_M^{-1}(n) = \frac{1}{w}\left[\mathbf{R}_M^{-1}(n - 1) - \frac{\mathbf{R}_M^{-1}(n - 1)\,\mathbf{X}_M^*(n)\mathbf{X}_M^t(n)\mathbf{R}_M^{-1}(n - 1)}{w + \mathbf{X}_M^t(n)\mathbf{R}_M^{-1}(n - 1)\mathbf{X}_M^*(n)}\right] \tag{6.2.60}$$

Thus $\mathbf{R}_M^{-1}(n)$ may be computed recursively.

For convenience we define $\mathbf{P}_M(n) = \mathbf{R}_M^{-1}(n)$. It is also convenient to define an M-dimensional vector $\mathbf{K}_M(n)$, sometimes called the *Kalman gain vector,* as

$$\mathbf{K}_M(n) = \frac{1}{w + \mu_M(n)}\mathbf{P}_M(n - 1)\mathbf{X}_M^*(n) \tag{6.2.61}$$

where $\mu_M(n)$ is a scalar defined as

$$\mu_M(n) = \mathbf{X}_M^t(n)\mathbf{P}_M(n - 1)\mathbf{X}_M^*(n) \tag{6.2.62}$$

With these definitions, (6.2.60) becomes

$$\mathbf{P}_M(n) = \frac{1}{w}[\mathbf{P}_M(n - 1) - \mathbf{K}_M(n)\mathbf{X}_M^t(n)\mathbf{P}_M(n - 1)] \tag{6.2.63}$$

Let us postmultiply (6.2.63) by $\mathbf{X}_M^*(n)$. Then

$$\begin{aligned}\mathbf{P}_M(n)\mathbf{X}_M^*(n) &= \frac{1}{w}[\mathbf{P}_M(n - 1)\mathbf{X}_M^*(n) - \mathbf{K}_M(n)\mathbf{X}_M^t(n)\mathbf{P}_M(n - 1)\mathbf{X}_M^*(n)] \\ &= \frac{1}{w}\{[w + \mu_M(n)]\mathbf{K}_M(n) - \mathbf{K}_M(n)\mu_M(n)\} = \mathbf{K}_M(n)\end{aligned} \tag{6.2.64}$$

Therefore, the Kalman gain vector may also be defined as $\mathbf{P}_M(n)\mathbf{X}_M^*(n)$.

Now we may use the matrix inversion lemma to derive an equation for computing the filter coefficients recursively. Since

$$\mathbf{h}_M(n) = \mathbf{P}_M(n)\mathbf{D}_M(n) \tag{6.2.65}$$

and

$$\mathbf{D}_M(n) = w\mathbf{D}_M(n - 1) + d(n)\mathbf{X}_M^*(n) \tag{6.2.66}$$

we have, upon substitution of (6.2.63) and (6.2.66) into (6.2.58),

$$
\begin{aligned}
\mathbf{h}_M(n) &= \frac{1}{w}[\mathbf{P}_M(n-1) - \mathbf{K}_M(n)\mathbf{X}_M^t(n)\mathbf{P}_M(n-1)] \\
&\quad \times [w\mathbf{D}_M(n-1) + d(n)\mathbf{X}_M^*(n)] \\
&= \mathbf{P}_M(n-1)\mathbf{D}_M(n-1) + \frac{1}{w}d(n)\mathbf{P}_M(n-1)\mathbf{X}_M^*(n) \\
&\quad -\mathbf{K}_M(n)\mathbf{X}_M^t(n)\mathbf{P}_M(n-1)\mathbf{D}_M(n-1) \\
&\quad - \frac{1}{w}d(n)\mathbf{K}_M(n)\mathbf{X}_M^t(n)\mathbf{P}_M(n-1)\mathbf{X}_M^*(n) \\
&= \mathbf{h}_M(n-1) + \mathbf{K}_M(n)[d(n) - \mathbf{X}_M^t(n)\mathbf{h}_M(n-1)]
\end{aligned}
\tag{6.2.67}
$$

We observe that $\mathbf{X}_M^t(n)\mathbf{h}_M(n-1)$ is the output of the adaptive filter at time n based on use of the filter coefficients at time $n - 1$. Since

$$\mathbf{X}_M^t(n)\mathbf{h}_M(n-1) = \hat{d}(n, n-1) \equiv \hat{d}(n) \tag{6.2.68}$$

and

$$e_M(n, n-1) = d(n) - \hat{d}(n, n-1) \equiv e_M(n) \tag{6.2.69}$$

it follows that the time-update equation for $\mathbf{h}_M(n)$ may be expressed as

$$\mathbf{h}_M(n) = \mathbf{h}_M(n-1) + \mathbf{K}_M(n)e_M(n) \tag{6.2.70}$$

or equivalently,

$$\mathbf{h}_M(n) = \mathbf{h}_M(n-1) + \mathbf{P}_M(n)\mathbf{X}_M^*(n)e_M(n) \tag{6.2.71}$$

To summarize, suppose that we have the optimum filter coefficients $\mathbf{h}_M(n-1)$, the matrix $\mathbf{P}_M(n-1)$, and the vector $\mathbf{X}_M(n-1)$. When the new signal component $x(n)$ is obtained, we form the vector $\mathbf{X}_M(n)$ by dropping the term $x(n-M)$ from $\mathbf{X}_M(n-1)$ and adding the term $x(n)$ as the first element. Then the recursive computation for the filter coefficients proceeds as follows:

1. Compute the filter output:

$$\hat{d}(n) = \mathbf{X}_M^t(n)\mathbf{h}_M(n-1) \tag{6.2.72}$$

2. Compute the error:

$$e_M(n) = d(n) - \hat{d}(n) \tag{6.2.73}$$

3. Compute the Kalman gain vector:

$$\mathbf{K}_M(n) = \frac{\mathbf{P}_M(n-1)\mathbf{X}_M^*(n)}{w + \mathbf{X}_M^t(n)\mathbf{P}_M(n-1)\mathbf{X}_M^*(n)} \tag{6.2.74}$$

4. Update the inverse of the correlation matrix:

$$\mathbf{P}_M(n) = \frac{1}{w}[\mathbf{P}_M(n-1) - \mathbf{K}_M(n)\mathbf{X}_M^t(n)\mathbf{P}_M(n-1)] \tag{6.2.75}$$

5. Update the coefficient vector of the filter:

$$\mathbf{h}_M(n) = \mathbf{h}_M(n-1) + \mathbf{K}_M(n)e_M(n) \tag{6.2.76}$$

The recursive algorithm specified by (6.2.72) through (6.2.76) is called the direct-form *recursive least-squares (RLS) algorithm*. It is initialized by setting $\mathbf{h}_M(-1) = \mathbf{0}$ and $\mathbf{P}_M(-1) = 1/\delta \mathbf{I}_M$, where δ is a small positive number.

The residual mean-square error resulting from the optimization above is

$$\mathscr{E}_{M\,\min} = \sum_{l=0}^{n} w^{n-l}|d(l)|^2 - \mathbf{h}_M^t(n)\mathbf{D}_M^*(n) \tag{6.2.77}$$

From (6.2.76) we observe that the filter coefficients vary with time by an amount equal to the error $e_M(n)$ multiplied by the Kalman gain vector $\mathbf{K}_M(n)$. Since $\mathbf{K}_M(n)$ is an M-dimensional vector, each filter coefficient is controlled by one of the elements of $\mathbf{K}_M(n)$. Consequently, rapid convergence is obtained. In contrast, the time-update equation for the coefficients of the filter adjusted by use of the LMS algorithm is

$$\mathbf{h}_M(n) = \mathbf{h}_M(n-1) + \Delta \mathbf{X}_M^*(n)e_M(n) \tag{6.2.78}$$

which has only the single parameter Δ for controlling the adjustment rate of the coefficients.

LDU Factorization and Square-Root Algorithms. The RLS algorithm given above is very susceptible to round-off noise in an implementation of the algorithm with finite-precision arithmetic. The major problem with round-off errors occurs in the updating of $\mathbf{P}_M(n)$. To remedy this problem, we may perform a decomposition of either the correlation matrix $\mathbf{R}_M(n)$ or its inverse $\mathbf{P}_M(n)$. Any of the decompositions described in Section 5.3 (i.e., Cholesky, LDU, or QRD) would reduce the sensitivity to round-off noise.

To be specific, let us consider an LDU decomposition of $\mathbf{P}_M(n)$. We may write

$$\mathbf{P}_M(n) = \mathbf{L}_M(n)\tilde{\mathbf{D}}_M(n)\mathbf{L}_M^H(n) \tag{6.2.79}$$

where $\mathbf{L}_M(n)$ is a lower triangular matrix with elements l_{ik}, $\tilde{\mathbf{D}}_M(n)$ is a diagonal matrix with elements δ_k, and $\mathbf{L}_M^H(n)$ is an upper triangular matrix. The diagonal elements of $\mathbf{L}_M(n)$ are set to unity (i.e., $l_{ii} = 1$). Now, instead of computing $\mathbf{P}_M(n)$ recursively, we can determine a formula for updating the factors $\mathbf{L}_M(n)$ and $\tilde{\mathbf{D}}_M(n)$ directly, thus avoiding computation of $\mathbf{P}_M(n)$.

The desired update formula is obtained by substituting the factored form of $\mathbf{P}_M(n)$ into (6.2.75). Thus we have

$$\begin{aligned}\mathbf{L}_M(n)\mathbf{D}_M(n)\mathbf{L}_M^H(n) &= \frac{1}{w}\mathbf{L}_M(n-1) \\ &\times \left[\tilde{\mathbf{D}}_M(n-1) - \frac{1}{w+\mu_M(n)}\mathbf{V}_M(n-1)\mathbf{V}_M^H(n-1)\right]\mathbf{D}_M^H(n-1)\end{aligned} \tag{6.2.80}$$

where, by definition,

$$\mathbf{V}_M(n-1) = \tilde{\mathbf{D}}_M(n-1)\mathbf{L}_M^H(n-1)\mathbf{X}_M^*(n) \tag{6.2.81}$$

The term inside the brackets in (6.2.80) is a Hermitian matrix and may be expressed in an LDU factored form as

$$\begin{aligned} &\overline{\mathbf{L}}_M(n-1)\overline{\mathbf{D}}_M(n-1)\overline{\mathbf{L}}_M^H(n-1) \\ &\qquad = \tilde{\mathbf{D}}_M(n-1) - \frac{1}{w + \mu_M(n)}\mathbf{V}_M(n-1)\mathbf{V}_M^H(n-1) \end{aligned} \tag{6.2.82}$$

Then, if we substitute (6.2.82) into (6.2.80), we obtain

$$\mathbf{L}_M(n)\tilde{\mathbf{D}}_M(n)\mathbf{L}_M^H(n) = \frac{1}{w}\mathbf{L}_M(n-1)\overline{\mathbf{L}}_M(n-1)\overline{\mathbf{D}}_M(n-1)\overline{\mathbf{L}}_M^H(n-1)\mathbf{L}_M^H(n-1)] \tag{6.2.83}$$

Consequently, the desired update relations are

$$\begin{aligned} \mathbf{L}_M(n) &= \mathbf{L}_M(n-1)\overline{\mathbf{L}}_M(n-1) \\ \tilde{\mathbf{D}}_M(n) &= \frac{1}{w}\overline{\mathbf{D}}_M(n-1) \end{aligned} \tag{6.2.84}$$

The procedure described in Section 5.3.6 may now be used to obtain the factors $\overline{\mathbf{L}}_M(n-1)$ and $\overline{\mathbf{D}}_M(n-1)$.

The resulting algorithm obtained from the time-update equations in (6.2.84) depends directly on the data vector $\mathbf{X}_M(n)$ and not on the "square" of the data vector. Thus the squaring operation of the data vector is avoided and, consequently, the effect of round-off errors is significantly reduced.

The RLS algorithms obtained from an LDU decomposition of either $\mathbf{R}_M(n)$ or $\mathbf{P}_M(n)$ are called *square-root RLS algorithms*. The book by Bierman (1977) and the papers by Carlson and Culmone (1979) and Hsu (1982) treat these types of algorithms.

A square-root RLS algorithm based on the LDU decomposition of $\mathbf{P}_M(n)$, as described above, is given in Table 6.1. Its computational complexity is proportional to M^2.

Fast RLS Algorithms. The RLS direct-form algorithm and the square-root algorithms have a computational complexity proportional to M^2, as indicated above. On the other hand, the RLS lattice algorithms derived in Section 6.3 have a computational complexity proportional to M. Basically, the lattice algorithms avoid the matrix multiplications involved in computing the Kalman gain vector $\mathbf{K}_M(n)$.

By using the forward and backward prediction formulas derived in Section 6.3 for the RLS lattice, it is possible to obtain time-update equations for the Kalman gain vector that completely avoid matrix multiplications. The resulting algorithms have a complexity that is proportional to M (multiplications and divisions), and hence they are called *fast RLS algorithms* for direct-form FIR filters.

TABLE 6.1 LDU Form of Square-Root RLS Algorithm

for $j = 1, \ldots, 2, \ldots, M$ do
  $f_j = x_j^*(n)$
end loop j

for $j = 1, 2, \ldots, M - 1$ do
  for $i = j + 1, j + 2, \ldots, M$ do
    $f_j = f_j + l_{ij}(n - 1)f_i$
end loop j

for $j = 1, 2, \ldots, M$ do
    $\bar{d}_j(n) = d_j(n - 1)/w$
    $v_j = \bar{d}_j(n)f_j$
end loop j

$\alpha_M = 1 + v_M f_M^*$
$d_M(n) = \bar{d}_M(n)/\alpha_M$
$\bar{k}_M = v_M$

for $j = M - 1, M - 2, \ldots, 1$ do
  $\bar{k}_j = v_j$
  $\alpha_j = \alpha_{j+1} + v_j f_j^*$
  $\lambda_j = f_j/\alpha_{j+1}$
  $d_j(n) = \bar{d}_j(n)\alpha_{j+1}/\alpha_1$
  for $i = M, M - 1, \ldots, j + 1$ do
    $l_{ij}(n) = l_{ij}(n - 1) + \bar{k}_i^*\lambda_j$
    $\bar{k}_i = \bar{k}_i + v_j l_{ij}^*(n - 1)$ down to $j = 2$)
  end loop i
end loop j

$\bar{\mathbf{K}}_M(n) = [\bar{k}_1, \bar{k}_2, \ldots, \bar{k}_M]^t$
$e_M(n) = d(n) - \hat{d}(n)$
$\mathbf{h}_M(n) = \mathbf{h}_M(n - 1) + [e_M(n)/\alpha_1]\bar{\mathbf{K}}_M(n)$

There are several versions of fast algorithms that differ in minor ways. Two versions are given in Tables 6.2 and 6.3 for complex-valued signals. The variables used in the fast algorithms listed in Tables 6.2 and 6.3 are defined in Section 6.3. The computational complexity for the algorithm in Table 6.2 is $9M - 5$ (complex) multiplications and divisions, whereas the one in Table 6.3 has a complexity of $8M + 6$ multiplications and divisions. Further reduction of computational complexity to $7M$ is possible. For example, Carayannis et al. (1983) describe a fast RLS algorithm, termed the *FAEST* (fast a posteriori error sequential technique) *algorithm,* with a computational complexity of $7M$. This algorithm is given in Section 6.3. Other versions of these algorithms with a complexity of $7M$ have been proposed, but many of these algorithms are extremely sensitive to round-off noise and exhibit instability problems [see papers by Falconer and Ljung

TABLE 6.2 Fast RLS Algorithm: Version A

$$f_{M-1}(n) = x(n) + \mathbf{a}^t_{M-1}(n-1)\mathbf{X}_{M-1}(n-1)$$

$$g_{M-1}(n) = x(n-M+1) + \mathbf{b}^t_{M-1}(n-1)\mathbf{X}_{M-1}(n)$$

$$\mathbf{a}_{M-1}(n) = \mathbf{a}_{M-1}(n-1) - \mathbf{K}_{M-1}(n-1)f_{M-1}(n)$$

$$f_{M-1}(n,n) = x(n) + \mathbf{a}^t_{M-1}(n)\mathbf{X}_{M-1}(n-1)$$

$$E^f_{M-1}(n) = wE^f_{M-1}(n-1) + f_{M-1}(n)f^*_{M-1}(n,n)$$

$$\begin{bmatrix} \mathbf{C}_{M-1}(n) \\ c_{MM}(n) \end{bmatrix} \equiv \mathbf{K}_M(n) = \begin{bmatrix} 0 \\ \mathbf{K}_{M-1}(n-1) \end{bmatrix} + \frac{f^*_{M-1}(n,n)}{E^f_{M-1}(n)} \begin{bmatrix} 1 \\ \mathbf{a}_{M-1}(n) \end{bmatrix}$$

$$\mathbf{K}_{M-1}(n) = \frac{\mathbf{C}_{M-1}(n) - c_{MM}(n)\mathbf{b}_{M-1}(n-1)}{1 - c_{MM}(n)g_{M-1}(n)}$$

$$\mathbf{b}_{M-1}(n) = \mathbf{b}_{M-1}(n-1) - \mathbf{K}_{M-1}(n)g_{M-1}(n)$$

$$\hat{d}(n) = \mathbf{h}^t_M(n-1)\mathbf{X}_M(n)$$

$$e_M(n) = d(n) - \hat{d}(n)$$

$$\mathbf{h}_M(n) = \mathbf{h}_M(n-1) + \mathbf{K}_M(n)e_M(n)$$

Initialization

$$\mathbf{a}_{M-1}(-1) = \mathbf{b}_{M-1}(-1) = \mathbf{0}$$

$$\mathbf{K}_{M-1}(-1) = \mathbf{0}$$

$$\mathbf{h}_{M-1}(-1) = \mathbf{0}$$

$$E^f_{M-1}(-1) = \epsilon, \quad \epsilon > 0$$

(1978), Carayannis et al. (1983, 1986) and Cioffi and Kailath (1984)]. Slock and Kailath (1988, 1991) have shown how to stabilize these fast ($7M$) algorithms with a relatively small increase in the number of computations. Two stabilized fast RLS algorithms are given in Section 6.3.

6.2.5 Properties of the Direct-Form RLS Algorithms

A major advantage of the direct-form RLS algorithms over the LMS algorithm is their faster convergence rate. This characteristic behavior is illustrated in Fig. 6.22, which shows the convergence rate of the LMS algorithm and the direct-form RLS algorithm for an adaptive FIR channel equalizer of length $M = 11$. The statistical autocorrelation matrix $\mathbf{\Gamma}_M$ for the received signal has an eigenvalue ratio of $\lambda_{max}/\lambda_{min} = 11$. All the equalizer coefficients were initially set to zero. The step size for the LMS algorithm was selected as $\Delta = 0.02$, which represents a good compromise between convergence rate and excess mean-square error.

The superiority of the RLS algorithm in achieving faster convergence is clearly evident. The algorithm converges in fewer than 70 iterations (70

TABLE 6.3 Fast RLS Algorithm: Version B

$$f_{M-1}(n) = x(n) + \mathbf{a}'_{M-1}(n-1)\mathbf{X}_{M-1}(n-1)$$

$$g_{M-1}(n) = x(n-M+1) + \mathbf{b}'_{M-1}(n-1)\mathbf{X}_{M-1}(n)$$

$$\mathbf{a}_{M-1}(n) = \mathbf{a}_{M-1}(n-1) - \mathbf{K}_{M-1}(n-1)f_{M-1}(n)$$

$$f_{M-1}(n, n) = \alpha_{M-1}(n-1)f_{M-1}(n)$$

$$E^f_{M-1}(n) = wE^f_{M-1}(n-1) + \alpha_{M-1}(n-1)|f_{M-1}(n)|^2$$

$$\begin{bmatrix} \mathbf{C}_{M-1}(n) \\ c_{MM}(n) \end{bmatrix} \equiv \mathbf{K}_M(n) = \begin{bmatrix} 0 \\ \mathbf{K}_{M-1}(n-1) \end{bmatrix} + \frac{f^*_{M-1}(n,n)}{E^f_{M-1}(n)} \begin{bmatrix} 1 \\ \mathbf{a}_{M-1}(n) \end{bmatrix}$$

$$\mathbf{K}_{M-1}(n) = \frac{\mathbf{C}_{M-1}(n) - c_{MM}(n)\mathbf{b}_{M-1}(n-1)}{1 - c_{MM}(n)g_{M-1}(n)}$$

$$\mathbf{b}_{M-1}(n) = \mathbf{b}_{M-1}(n-1) - \mathbf{K}_{M-1}(n)g_{M-1}(n)$$

$$\alpha_{M-1}(n) = \alpha_{M-1}(n-1)\left[\frac{1 - \dfrac{f_{M-1}(n)f^*_{M-1}(n, n)}{E^f_{M-1}(n)}}{1 - c_{MM}(n)g_{M-1}(n)}\right]$$

$$\hat{d}(n) = \mathbf{h}'_M(n-1)\mathbf{X}_M(n)$$

$$e_M(n) = d(n) - \hat{d}(n)$$

$$\mathbf{h}_M(n) = \mathbf{h}_M(n-1) + \mathbf{K}_M(n)e_M(n)$$

Initialization

$$\mathbf{a}_{M-1}(-1) = \mathbf{b}_{M-1}(-1) = \mathbf{0}$$

$$\mathbf{K}_{M-1}(-1) = \mathbf{0}, \quad \mathbf{h}_{M-1}(-1) = \mathbf{0}$$

$$\mathbf{E}^f_{M-1}(-1) = \epsilon > 0$$

signal samples), while the LMS algorithm has not converged in over 600 iterations. This rapid rate of convergence of the RLS algorithm is extremely important in applications where the signal statistics vary rapidly with time. For example, the time variations of the characteristics of an ionospheric high-frequency (HF) radio channel are too rapid to be adaptively followed by the LMS algorithm. However, the RLS algorithm adapts sufficiently fast to track such rapid variations [see the paper by Hsu (1982)].

Despite their superior tracking performance, the RLS algorithms for FIR adaptive filtering described in the preceding section have two important disadvantages. One is their computational complexity. The square-root algorithms have a complexity proportional to M^2. The fast RLS algorithms have a computational complexity proportional to M, but the proportionality factor is four to five times that of the LMS algorithm.

The second disadvantage of the algorithms is their sensitivity to round-off errors that accumulate as a result of the recursive computations. In some cases, the round-off errors cause these algorithms to become unstable.

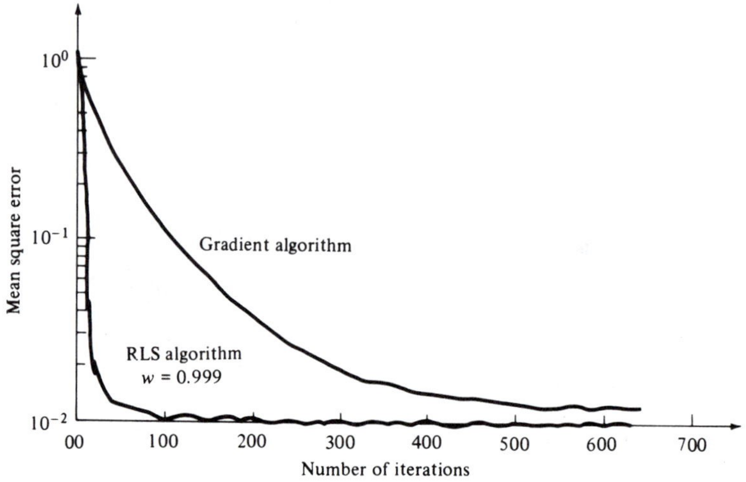

FIGURE 6.22 Learning curves for RLS algorithm and LMS algorithm for adaptive equalizer of length $M = 11$. The eigenvalue spread of the channel is $\lambda_{max}/\lambda_{min} = 11$. The step size for the LMS algorithm is $\Delta = 0.02$. (From *Digital Communication* by John G. Proakis, © 1983 by McGraw-Hill Book Company. Reprinted with permission of the publisher.)

The numerical properties of the RLS algorithms have been investigated by several researchers, including Ling and Proakis (1984a), Ljung and Ljung (1985), and Cioffi (1987). For illustrative purposes, Table 6.4 includes simulation results on the steady-state (time-averaged) square error for the RLS square-root algorithm, the fast RLS algorithm in Table 6.2, and the LMS algorithm for different word lengths. The simulation was performed with a linear adaptive equalizer having $M = 11$ coefficients. The channel had an eigenvalue ratio of $\lambda_{max}/\lambda_{min} = 11$. The exponential weighting factor used in the RLS algorithms was $w = 0.975$ and the step size for the LMS algorithm was $\Delta = 0.025$. The additive noise has a variance of 0.001. The output MSE with infinite precision is 2.1×10^{-3}.

TABLE 6.4 Numerical Accuracy of FIR Adaptive Filtering Algorithms (Least-Squares Error $\times 10^{-3}$)

	Algorithm		
Number of bits (including sign)	RLS square root	Fast RLS	LMS
16	2.17	2.17	2.30
13	2.33	2.21	2.30
11	6.14	3.34	19.0
10	17.6	[a]	77.2
9	75.3	[a]	311.0
8	[a]	[a]	1170.0

[a] Algorithm does not converge to optimum coefficients.

We should indicate that the direct-form RLS algorithm becomes unstable and hence does not work properly with 16-bit fixed-point arithmetic. For this algorithm, we found experimentally that approximately 24 bits of precision are needed for the algorithm to work properly. On the other hand, the square-root algorithm works down to about 9 bits, but the degradation in performance below 11 bits is significant. The fast RLS algorithm works well down to 11 bits for short time durations, on the order of 500 iterations. For a much larger number of iterations, the algorithm becomes unstable due to the accumulation of round-off errors. In such a case several methods have been proposed to restart the algorithm in order to prevent overflow in the coefficients. The interested reader may refer to the papers of Eleftheriou and Falconer (1987), Cioffi and Kailath (1984), and Hsu (1982). Alternatively, one may modify the algorithm as proposed by Slock and Kailath (1988, 1991) and thus stabilize it.

We also observe from the results of Table 6.4 that the LMS algorithm is quite robust to round-off noise. It deteriorates, as expected, with a decrease in the precision of the filter coefficients, but no catastrophic failure (instability) occurs with 8 or 9 bits of precision. However, the degradation in performance below 12 bits is significant.

6.3 ADAPTIVE LATTICE-LADDER FILTERS

In Chapter 4 we demonstrated that an FIR filter may also be realized as a lattice structure in which the lattice parameters, called the *reflection coefficients,* are related to the filter coefficients in the direct-form FIR structure. The method for converting the FIR filter coefficients into the reflection coefficients, and vice versa, was also described.

In this section we derive adaptive filtering algorithms in which the filter structure is a lattice or a lattice ladder. Adaptive lattice-ladder filter algorithms based on the method of least squares are derived that have several desirable properties, including computational efficiency and robustness to round-off errors.

From the development of the RLS lattice-ladder algorithms, we obtain the fast Kalman algorithms that were described in Section 6.2. We also develop a gradient-type lattice-ladder algorithm that possesses a number of desirable properties that are described in this section.

6.3.1 Recursive Least-Squares Lattice-Ladder Algorithms

We have already shown in Chapter 4 the relationship between the lattice filter structure and a linear predictor and have derived the equations that relate the predictor coefficients to the reflection coefficients of the lattice, and vice versa. We have also established the relationship between the Levinson–Durbin recursions for the linear predictor coefficients and the reflection coefficients in the lattice filter. From these developments we would expect to obtain the recursive least-squares lattice filter by formulating the least-squares estimation problem in terms of linear prediction. This is the approach that we take below.

The recursive least-squares algorithms for the direct-form FIR structures described in Section 6.2.4 are recursive in time only. The length of the filter is fixed. A change (increase or decrease) in the filter length results in a new set of filter coefficients that are totally different from those of the previous set.

In contrast, the lattice filter is order recursive. As a consequence, the number of sections that it contains can be easily increased or decreased without affecting the reflection coefficients of the remaining sections. This and several other advantages described in this and subsequent sections make the lattice filter very attractive for adaptive filtering applications.

To begin, suppose that we observe the signal $x(n - l)$, $l = 1, 2, \ldots, n$ and let us consider the linear prediction of $x(n)$. Let $f_M(l,n)$ denote the forward prediction error for an mth-order predictor, defined as

$$f_M(l,n) = x(l) + \mathbf{a}_m^t(n)\mathbf{X}_m(l - 1) \tag{6.3.1}$$

where the vector $-\mathbf{a}_M(n)$ consists of the forward prediction coefficients,

$$\mathbf{a}_m^t(n) = [a_m(1,n)\; a_m(2,n) \cdots a_m(m,n)] \tag{6.3.2}$$

and the data vector $\mathbf{X}_m(l - 1)$ is

$$\mathbf{X}_m^t(l - 1) = [x(l - 1) \quad x(l - 2) \cdots x(l - m)] \tag{6.3.3}$$

The predictor coefficients $\mathbf{a}_m(n)$ are selected to minimize the time-averaged weighted squared error

$$\mathscr{E}_m^f(n) = \sum_{l=0}^{n} w^{n-l} |f_m(l,n)|^2 \tag{6.3.4}$$

The minimization of $\mathscr{E}_m^f(n)$ with respect to $\mathbf{a}_m(n)$ leads to the following set of linear equations:

$$\mathbf{R}_m(n - 1)\mathbf{a}_m(n) = -\mathbf{Q}_m(n) \tag{6.3.5}$$

where $\mathbf{R}_m(n)$ is defined by (6.2.56) and $\mathbf{Q}_m(n)$ is defined as

$$\mathbf{Q}_m(n) = \sum_{l=0}^{n} w^{n-l} x(l)\mathbf{X}_m^*(l - 1) \tag{6.3.6}$$

The solution of (6.3.5) is

$$\mathbf{a}_m(n) = -\mathbf{R}_m^{-1}(n - 1)\mathbf{Q}_m(n) \tag{6.3.7}$$

The minimum value of $\mathscr{E}_m^f(n)$, obtained with the linear predictor specified by (6.3.7), is denoted as $E_m^f(n)$ and is given by

$$\begin{aligned} E_m^f(n) &= \sum_{l=0}^{n} w^{n-l} x^*(l)\, [x(l) + \mathbf{a}_m^t(n)\mathbf{X}_m(l - 1)] \\ &= q(n) + \mathbf{a}_m^t(n)\mathbf{Q}_m^*(n) \end{aligned} \tag{6.3.8}$$

where $q(n)$ is defined as

$$q(n) = \sum_{l=0}^{n} w^{n-l} |x(l)|^2 \tag{6.3.9}$$

The linear equations in (6.3.5) and the equation for $E_m^f(n)$ in (6.3.8) can be combined in a single matrix equation of the form

$$\begin{bmatrix} q(n) & \mathbf{Q}_m^H(n) \\ \mathbf{Q}_m(n) & \mathbf{R}_m(n-1) \end{bmatrix} \begin{bmatrix} 1 \\ \mathbf{a}_m(n) \end{bmatrix} = \begin{bmatrix} E_m^f(n) \\ \mathbf{O}_m \end{bmatrix} \tag{6.3.10}$$

where $\mathbf{O}_m$ is the m-dimensional null vector. It is interesting to note that

$$\begin{aligned} \mathbf{R}_{m+1}(n) &= \sum_{l=0}^{n} w^{n-l} \mathbf{X}_{m+1}^*(l) \mathbf{X}_{m+1}^t(l) \\ &= \sum_{l=0}^{n} w^{n-l} \begin{bmatrix} x^*(l) \\ \mathbf{X}_m^*(l-1) \end{bmatrix} [x(l)\ \mathbf{X}_m^t(l-1)] \\ &= \begin{bmatrix} q(n) & \mathbf{Q}_m^H(n) \\ \mathbf{Q}_m(n) & \mathbf{R}_m(n-1) \end{bmatrix} \end{aligned} \tag{6.3.11}$$

which is the matrix in (6.3.10).

In a completely parallel development to (6.3.1) through (6.3.11), we minimize the backward time-averaged weighted squared error for an mth-order backward predictor defined as

$$\mathscr{E}_m^b(n) = \sum_{l=0}^{n} w^{n-l} |g_m(l,n)|^2 \tag{6.3.12}$$

where the backward error is defined as

$$g_m(l,n) = x(l-m) + \mathbf{b}_m^t(n) \mathbf{X}_m(l) \tag{6.3.13}$$

and $\mathbf{b}_m^t(n) = [b_m(1,n)\ \ b_m(2,n)\ \ \cdots\ \ b_m(m,n)]$ is the vector of coefficients for the backward predictor. The minimization of $\mathscr{E}_m^b(n)$ leads to the equation

$$\mathbf{R}_m(n)\mathbf{b}_m(n) = -\mathbf{V}_m(n) \tag{6.3.14}$$

and hence to the solution

$$\mathbf{b}_m(n) = -\mathbf{R}_m^{-1}(n)\mathbf{V}_m(n) \tag{6.3.15}$$

where

$$\mathbf{V}_m(n) = \sum_{l=0}^{n} w^{n-l} x(l-m) \mathbf{X}_m^*(l) \tag{6.3.16}$$

The minimum value of $\mathscr{E}_m^b(n)$, denoted as $E_m^b(n)$, is

$$\begin{aligned} E_m^b(n) &= \sum_{l=0}^{n} w^{n-l} [x(l-m) + \mathbf{b}_m^t(n)\mathbf{X}_m(l)] x^*(l-m) \\ &= v(n) + \mathbf{b}_m^t(n) \mathbf{V}_m^*(n) \end{aligned} \tag{6.3.17}$$

where the scalar quantity $v(n)$ is defined as

$$v(n) = \sum_{l=0}^{n} w^{n-l}|x(l-m)|^2 \tag{6.3.18}$$

If we combine (6.3.14) and (6.3.17) into a single equation, we obtain

$$\begin{bmatrix} \mathbf{R}_m(n) & \mathbf{V}_m(n) \\ \mathbf{V}_m^H(n) & v(n) \end{bmatrix} \begin{bmatrix} \mathbf{b}_m(n) \\ 1 \end{bmatrix} = \begin{bmatrix} \mathbf{O}_m \\ E_m^b(n) \end{bmatrix} \tag{6.3.19}$$

We also note that the (estimated) autocorrelation matrix $\mathbf{R}_{m+1}(n)$ can be expressed as

$$\begin{aligned} \mathbf{R}_{m+1}(n) &= \sum_{l=0}^{n} w^{n-l} \begin{bmatrix} \mathbf{X}_m^*(l) \\ x^*(l-m) \end{bmatrix} [\mathbf{X}_m^t(l)\ x(l-m)] \\ &= \begin{bmatrix} \mathbf{R}_m(n) & \mathbf{V}_m(n) \\ \mathbf{V}_m^H(n) & v(n) \end{bmatrix} \end{aligned} \tag{6.3.20}$$

Thus we have obtained the equations for the forward and backward least-squares predictors of order m.

Next, we derive the order-update equations for these predictors, which will lead us to the lattice filter structure. In deriving the order-update equations for $\mathbf{a}_m(n)$ and $\mathbf{b}_m(n)$, we will make use of the two matrix inversion identities for a matrix of the form

$$\mathbf{A} = \begin{bmatrix} \mathbf{A}_{11} & \mathbf{A}_{12} \\ \mathbf{A}_{21} & \mathbf{A}_{22} \end{bmatrix} \tag{6.3.21}$$

where $\mathbf{A}$, $\mathbf{A}_{11}$, and $\mathbf{A}_{22}$ are square matrices. The inverse of $\mathbf{A}$ is expressible in two different forms,

$$\mathbf{A}^{-1} = \begin{bmatrix} \mathbf{A}_{11}^{-1} + \mathbf{A}_{11}^{-1}\mathbf{A}_{12}\tilde{\mathbf{A}}_{22}^{-1}\mathbf{A}_{21}\mathbf{A}_{11}^{-1} & -\mathbf{A}_{11}^{-1}\mathbf{A}_{12}\tilde{\mathbf{A}}_{22}^{-1} \\ -\tilde{\mathbf{A}}_{22}^{-1}\mathbf{A}_{21}\mathbf{A}_{11}^{-1} & \tilde{\mathbf{A}}_{22}^{-1} \end{bmatrix} \tag{6.3.22}$$

and

$$\mathbf{A}^{-1} = \begin{bmatrix} \tilde{\mathbf{A}}_{11}^{-1} & -\tilde{\mathbf{A}}_{11}^{-1}\mathbf{A}_{12}\mathbf{A}_{22}^{-1} \\ -\mathbf{A}_{22}^{-1}\mathbf{A}_{21}\tilde{\mathbf{A}}_{11}^{-1} & \mathbf{A}_{22}^{-1}\mathbf{A}_{21}\tilde{\mathbf{A}}_{11}^{-1}\mathbf{A}_{12}\mathbf{A}_{22}^{-1} + \mathbf{A}_{22}^{-1} \end{bmatrix} \tag{6.3.23}$$

where $\tilde{\mathbf{A}}_{11}$ and $\tilde{\mathbf{A}}_{22}$ are defined as

$$\begin{aligned} \tilde{\mathbf{A}}_{11} &= \mathbf{A}_{11} - \mathbf{A}_{12}\mathbf{A}_{22}^{-1}\mathbf{A}_{21} \\ \tilde{\mathbf{A}}_{22} &= \mathbf{A}_{22} - \mathbf{A}_{21}\mathbf{A}_{11}^{-1}\mathbf{A}_{12} \end{aligned} \tag{6.3.24}$$

Order-Update Recursions. Now, let us use the formula in (6.3.22) to obtain the inverse of $\mathbf{R}_{m+1}(n)$ by using the form in (6.3.20). First, we have

$$\begin{aligned} \tilde{\mathbf{A}}_{22} &= v(n) - \mathbf{V}_m^H(n)\mathbf{R}_m^{-1}(n)\mathbf{V}_m(n) \\ &= v(n) + \mathbf{b}_m^t(n)\mathbf{V}_m^*(n) = E_m^b(n) \end{aligned} \tag{6.3.25}$$

and

$$\mathbf{A}_{11}^{-1}\mathbf{A}_{12} = \mathbf{R}_m^{-1}(n)\mathbf{V}_m(n) = -\mathbf{b}_m(n) \tag{6.3.26}$$

Hence

$$\mathbf{R}_{m+1}^{-1}(n) \equiv \mathbf{P}_{m+1}(n) = \begin{bmatrix} \mathbf{P}_m(n) + \dfrac{\mathbf{b}_m(n)\mathbf{b}_m^H(n)}{E_m^b(n)} & \dfrac{\mathbf{b}_m(n)}{E_m^b(n)} \\ \dfrac{\mathbf{b}_m^H(n)}{E_m^b(n)} & \dfrac{1}{E_m^b(n)} \end{bmatrix}$$

or equivalently,

$$\mathbf{P}_{m+1}(n) = \begin{bmatrix} \mathbf{P}_m(n) & 0 \\ 0 & 0 \end{bmatrix} + \frac{1}{E_m^b(n)} \begin{bmatrix} \mathbf{b}_m(n) \\ 1 \end{bmatrix} [\mathbf{b}_m^H(n) \quad 1] \tag{6.3.27}$$

By substituting $n - 1$ for n in (6.3.27) and postmultiplying the result by $-\mathbf{Q}_m(n)$, we obtain the order update for $\mathbf{a}_m(n)$. Thus

$$\begin{aligned} \mathbf{a}_{m+1}(n) &= -\mathbf{P}_{m+1}(n-1)\mathbf{Q}_{m+1}(n) \\ &= \begin{bmatrix} \mathbf{P}_m(n-1) & 0 \\ 0 & 0 \end{bmatrix} \begin{bmatrix} -\mathbf{Q}_m(n) \\ \cdots \end{bmatrix} \\ &\quad - \frac{1}{E_m^b(n-1)} \begin{bmatrix} \mathbf{b}_m(n-1) \\ 1 \end{bmatrix} [\mathbf{b}_m^H(n-1) \quad 1]\mathbf{Q}_{m+1}(n) \\ &= \begin{bmatrix} \mathbf{a}_m(n) \\ 0 \end{bmatrix} - \frac{k_{m+1}(n)}{E_m^b(n-1)} \begin{bmatrix} \mathbf{b}_m(n-1) \\ 1 \end{bmatrix} \end{aligned} \tag{6.3.28}$$

where the scalar quantity $k_{m+1}(n)$ is defined as

$$k_{m+1}(n) = [\mathbf{b}_m^H(n-1) \quad 1]\mathbf{Q}_{m+1}(n) \tag{6.3.29}$$

The reader should observe that (6.3.28) is a Levinson-type recursion for the predictor coefficients.

To obtain the corresponding order update for $\mathbf{b}_m(n)$, we use the matrix inversion formula in (6.3.23) for the inverse of $\mathbf{R}_{m+1}(n)$, along with the form in (6.3.11). In this case we have

$$\begin{aligned} \tilde{\mathbf{A}}_{11} &= q(n) - \mathbf{Q}_m^H(n)\mathbf{R}_m^{-1}(n-1)\mathbf{Q}_m(n) \\ &= q(n) + \mathbf{a}_m^t(n)\mathbf{Q}_m^*(n) = E_m^f(n) \end{aligned} \tag{6.3.30}$$

and

$$\mathbf{A}_{22}^{-1}\mathbf{A}_{21} = \mathbf{R}_m^{-1}(n-1)\mathbf{Q}_m(n) = -\mathbf{a}_m(n) \tag{6.3.31}$$

Hence

$$\mathbf{P}_{m+1}(n) = \begin{bmatrix} \dfrac{1}{E_m^f(n)} & \dfrac{\mathbf{a}_m^H(n)}{E_m^f(n)} \\ \dfrac{\mathbf{a}_m(n)}{E_m^f(n)} & \mathbf{P}_m(n-1) + \dfrac{\mathbf{a}_m(n)\mathbf{a}_m^H(n)}{E_m^f(n)} \end{bmatrix}$$

or, equivalently,

$$\mathbf{P}_{m+1}(n) = \begin{bmatrix} 0 & 0 \\ 0 & \mathbf{P}_m(n-1) \end{bmatrix} + \frac{1}{E_m^f(n)} \begin{bmatrix} 1 \\ \mathbf{a}_m(n) \end{bmatrix} [1 \quad \mathbf{a}_m^H(n)] \tag{6.3.32}$$

Now, if we postmultiply (6.3.32) by $-\mathbf{V}_{m+1}(n)$, we obtain

$$\begin{aligned} \mathbf{b}_{m+1}(n) &= \begin{bmatrix} 0 & 0 \\ 0 & \mathbf{P}_m(n-1) \end{bmatrix} \begin{bmatrix} \cdots \\ -\mathbf{V}_m(n-1) \end{bmatrix} \\ &\quad - \frac{1}{E_m^f(n)} \begin{bmatrix} 1 \\ \mathbf{a}_m(n) \end{bmatrix} [1 \quad \mathbf{a}_m^H(n)]\mathbf{V}_{m+1}(n) \\ &= \begin{bmatrix} 0 \\ \mathbf{b}_m(n-1) \end{bmatrix} - \frac{k_{m+1}^*(n)}{E_m^f(n)} \begin{bmatrix} 1 \\ \mathbf{a}_m(n) \end{bmatrix} \end{aligned} \tag{6.3.33}$$

where

$$[1 \quad \mathbf{a}_m^H(n)]\mathbf{V}_{m+1}(n) = [\mathbf{b}_m^t(n-1) \quad 1]\mathbf{Q}_{m+1}^*(n) = k_{m+1}^*(n) \tag{6.3.34}$$

The proof of (6.3.34) and its relation to (6.3.29) are left as an exercise for the reader. Thus (6.3.28) and (6.3.33) specify the order-update equations for $\mathbf{a}_m(n)$ and $\mathbf{b}_m(n)$, respectively.

The order-update equations for $E_m^f(n)$ and $E_m^b(n)$ may now be obtained. From the definition of $E_m^f(n)$ given by (6.3.8) we have

$$E_{m+1}^f(n) = q(n) + \mathbf{a}_{m+1}^t(n)\mathbf{Q}_{m+1}^*(n) \tag{6.3.35}$$

By substituting from (6.3.28) for $\mathbf{a}_{m+1}(n)$ into (6.3.35), we obtain

$$\begin{aligned} E_{m+1}^f(n) &= q(n) + \left([\mathbf{a}_m^t(n) \quad 0] \begin{bmatrix} \mathbf{Q}_m^*(n) \\ \cdots \end{bmatrix} \right. \\ &\quad \left. - \frac{k_{m+1}(n)}{E_m^b(n-1)} [\mathbf{b}_m^t(n-1) \quad 1]\mathbf{Q}_{m+1}^*(n) \right) \\ &= E_m^f(n) - \frac{|k_{m+1}(n)|^2}{E_m^b(n-1)} \end{aligned} \qquad 6.3.36)$$

Similarly, by using (6.3.17) and (6.3.33), we obtain the order update for $E_{m+1}^b(n)$ in the form

$$E_{m+1}^b(n) = E_m^b(n-1) - \frac{|k_{m+1}(n)|^2}{E_m^f(n)} \tag{6.3.37}$$

The lattice filter is specified by two coupled equations involving the forward and backward errors $f_m(n, n-1)$ and $g_m(n, n-1)$, respectively. From the definition of the forward error in (6.3.1) we have

$$f_{m+1}(n, n-1) = x(n) + \mathbf{a}_{m+1}^t(n-1)\mathbf{X}_{m+1}(n-1) \tag{6.3.38}$$

Substituting for $\mathbf{a}_{m+1}^t(n-1)$ from (6.3.28) into (6.3.38) yields

$$\begin{aligned} f_{m+1}(n, n-1) &= x(n) + [\mathbf{a}_m^t(n-1) \quad 0]\begin{bmatrix} \mathbf{X}_m(n-1) \\ \cdots \end{bmatrix} \\ &\quad - \frac{k_{m+1}(n-1)}{E_m^b(n-2)}[\mathbf{b}_m^t(n-2) \quad 1]\mathbf{X}_{m+1}(n-1) \\ &= f_m(n, n-1) - \frac{k_{m+1}(n-1)}{E_m^b(n-2)} \\ &\quad \times [x(n-m-1) + \mathbf{b}_m^t(n-2)\mathbf{X}_m(n-1)] \\ &= f_m(n, n-1) - \frac{k_{m+1}(n-1)}{E_m^b(n-2)} g_m(n-1, n-2) \end{aligned} \tag{6.3.39}$$

To simplify the notation, we define

$$\begin{aligned} f_m(n) &= f_m(n, n-1) \\ g_m(n) &= g_m(n, n-1) \end{aligned} \tag{6.3.40}$$

Then (6.3.39) may be expressed as

$$f_{m+1}(n) = f_m(n) - \frac{k_{m+1}(n-1)}{E_m^b(n-2)} g_m(n-1) \tag{6.3.41}$$

Similarly, beginning with the definition of the backward error given by (6.3.13), we have

$$g_{m+1}(n, n-1) = x(n-m-1) + \mathbf{b}_{m+1}^t(n-1)\mathbf{X}_{m+1}(n) \tag{6.3.42}$$

Substituting for $\mathbf{b}_{m+1}(n-1)$ from (6.3.33) and simplifying the result, we obtain

$$g_{m+1}(n, n-1) = g_m(n-1, n-2) - \frac{k_{m+1}^*(n-1)}{E_m^f(n-1)} f_m(n, n-1) \tag{6.3.43}$$

or equivalently,

$$g_{m+1}(n) = g_m(n-1) - \frac{k_{m+1}^*(n-1)}{E_m^f(n-1)} f_m(n) \tag{6.3.44}$$

The two recursive equations in (6.3.41) and (6.3.44) specify the lattice filter illustrated in Fig. 6.23, where, for notational convenience, we have defined the *reflection coefficients* for the lattice as

$$\begin{aligned} \mathcal{K}_m^f(n) &= \frac{-k_m(n)}{E_{m-1}^b(n-1)} \\ \mathcal{K}_m^b(n) &= \frac{-k_m^*(n)}{E_{m-1}^f(n)} \end{aligned} \tag{6.3.45}$$

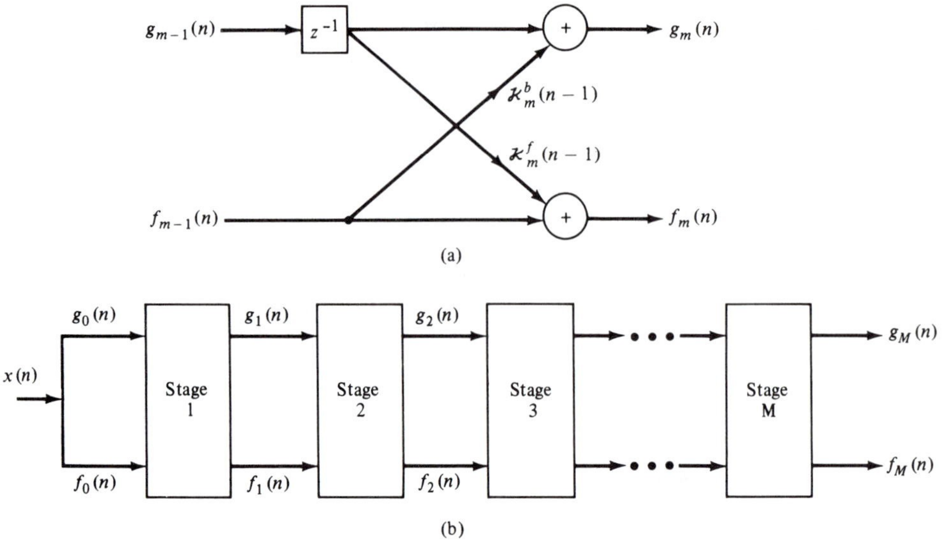

FIGURE 6.23 Least-squares lattice filter.

The initial conditions on the order updates are

$$f_0(n) = g_0(n) = x(n)$$

$$E_0^f(n) = E_0^b(n) = \sum_{l=0}^{n} w^{n-l}|x(l)|^2 \tag{6.3.46}$$

$$= wE_0^f(n-1) + |x(n)|^2$$

We note that (6.3.46) is also a time-update equation for $E_0^f(n)$ and $E_0^b(n)$.

Time-Update Recursions. Our goal is to determine a time-update equation for $k_m(n)$, which is necessary if the lattice filter is to be adaptive. This derivation will require time-update equations for the prediction coefficients. We begin with the form

$$k_{m+1}(n) = -\mathbf{V}_{m+1}^H(n)\begin{bmatrix} 1 \\ \mathbf{a}_m(n) \end{bmatrix} \tag{6.3.47}$$

The time-update equation for $\mathbf{V}_{m+1}(n)$ is

$$\mathbf{V}_{m+1}(n) = w\mathbf{V}_{m+1}(n-1) + x(n-m-1)\mathbf{X}_{m+1}^*(n) \tag{6.3.48}$$

The time update for the prediction coefficients is determined as follows. From (6.3.6), (6.3.7), and (6.2.63), we have

$$\begin{aligned} \mathbf{a}_m(n) &= -\mathbf{P}_m(n-1)\mathbf{Q}_m(n) \\ &= -\frac{1}{w}[\mathbf{P}_m(n-2) - \mathbf{K}_m(n-1)\mathbf{X}_m^t(n-1)\mathbf{P}_m(n-2)] \\ &\quad \times [w\mathbf{Q}_m(n-1) + x(n)\mathbf{X}_m^*(n-1)] \\ &= \mathbf{a}_m(n-1) - \mathbf{K}_m(n-1)[x(n) + \mathbf{a}_m^t(n-1)\mathbf{X}_m(n-1)] \end{aligned} \tag{6.3.49}$$

where $\mathbf{K}_m(n-1)$ is the Kalman gain vector at iteration $n-1$. But from (6.3.38) we have

$$x(n) + \mathbf{a}_m^t(n-1)\mathbf{X}_m(n-1) = f_m(n, n-1) \equiv f_m(n)$$

Therefore, the time update for $\mathbf{a}_m(n)$ is

$$\mathbf{a}_m(n) = \mathbf{a}_m(n-1) - \mathbf{K}_m(n-1)f_m(n) \tag{6.3.50}$$

In a parallel development to the above, using (6.3.15), (6.3.16), and (6.2.63), we obtain the time-update equations for the coefficients of the backward predictor, in the form

$$\mathbf{b}_m(n) = \mathbf{b}_m(n-1) - \mathbf{K}_m(n)g_m(n) \tag{6.3.51}$$

Now, from (6.3.48) and (6.3.50), the time-update equation for $k_{m+1}(n)$ is

$$\begin{aligned} k_{m+1}(n) &= -[w\mathbf{V}_{m+1}^H(n-1) + x^*(n-m-1)\mathbf{X}_{m+1}^t(n)] \\ &\quad \times \left(\begin{bmatrix} 1 \\ \mathbf{a}_m(n-1) \end{bmatrix} - \begin{bmatrix} 0 \\ \mathbf{K}_m(n-1)f_m(n) \end{bmatrix} \right) \\ &= wk_{m+1}(n-1) - w\mathbf{V}_{m+1}^H(n-1)\begin{bmatrix} 0 \\ \mathbf{K}_m(n-1) \end{bmatrix} f_m(n) \\ &\quad + x^*(n-m-1)\mathbf{X}_{m+1}^t(n)\begin{bmatrix} 1 \\ \mathbf{a}_m(n-1) \end{bmatrix} \\ &\quad - x^*(n-m-1)\mathbf{X}_{m+1}^t(n)\begin{bmatrix} 0 \\ \mathbf{K}_m(n-1) \end{bmatrix} f_m(n) \end{aligned} \tag{6.3.52}$$

But

$$\mathbf{X}_{m+1}^t(n)\begin{bmatrix} 1 \\ \mathbf{a}_m(n-1) \end{bmatrix} = [x(n)\ \mathbf{X}_m^t(n-1)]\begin{bmatrix} 1 \\ \mathbf{a}_m(n-1) \end{bmatrix} = f_m(n) \tag{6.3.53}$$

and

$$\begin{aligned} \mathbf{V}_{m+1}^H(n-1)\begin{bmatrix} 0 \\ \mathbf{K}_m(n-1) \end{bmatrix} &= \mathbf{V}_m^H(n-2)\mathbf{K}_m(n-1) \\ &= \frac{\mathbf{V}_m^H(n-2)\mathbf{P}_m(n-2)\mathbf{X}_m^*(n-1)}{w + \mu_m(n-1)} \\ &= \frac{-\mathbf{b}_m^H(n-2)\mathbf{X}_m^*(n-1)}{w + \mu_m(n-1)} \\ &= -\frac{g_m^*(n-1) - x^*(n-m-1)}{w + \mu_m(n-1)} \end{aligned} \tag{6.3.54}$$

where $\mu_m(n)$ is as defined in (6.2.62). Finally,

$$\mathbf{X}_{m+1}^t(n)\begin{bmatrix} 0 \\ \mathbf{K}_m(n-1) \end{bmatrix} = \frac{\mathbf{X}_m^t(n-1)\mathbf{P}_m(n-2)\mathbf{X}_m^*(n-1)}{w + \mu_m(n-1)} = \frac{\mu_m(n-1)}{w + \mu_m(n-1)} \tag{6.3.55}$$

Substituting the results of (6.3.53), (6.3.54), and (6.3.55) into (6.3.52), we obtain the desired time-update equation in the form

$$k_{m+1}(n) = wk_{m+1}(n-1) + \frac{w}{w + \mu_m(n-1)} f_m(n) g_m^*(n-1) \quad (6.3.56)$$

It is convenient to define a new variable

$$\alpha_m(n) = \frac{w}{w + \mu_m(n)} \quad (6.3.57)$$

Clearly, $\alpha_m(n)$ is real valued and has a range $0 < \alpha_m(n) < 1$. Then the time update equation (6.3.56) becomes

$$k_{m+1}(n) = wk_{m+1}(n-1) + \alpha_m(n-1) f_m(n) g_m^*(n-1) \quad (6.3.58)$$

Order Update for $\alpha_m(n)$. Although $\alpha_m(n)$ can be computed directly for each value of m and for each n, it is more efficient to use an order-update equation which is determined as follows. First, from the definition of $\mathbf{K}_m(n)$ given in (6.2.61), it is easily seen that

$$\alpha_m(n) = 1 - \mathbf{X}_m^t(n)\mathbf{K}_m(n) \quad (6.3.59)$$

To obtain an order-update equation for $\alpha_m(n)$, we need an order-update equation for the Kalman gain vector $\mathbf{K}_m(n)$. But $\mathbf{K}_{m+1}(n)$ may be expressed as

$$\begin{aligned}
\mathbf{K}_{m+1}(n) &= \mathbf{P}_{m+1}(n)\mathbf{X}_{m+1}^*(n) \\
&= \left(\begin{bmatrix} \mathbf{P}_m(n) & 0 \\ 0 & 0 \end{bmatrix} + \frac{1}{E_m^b(n)} \begin{bmatrix} \mathbf{b}_m(n) \\ 1 \end{bmatrix} [\mathbf{b}_m^H(n) \quad 1] \right) \quad (6.3.60) \\
&\quad \times \begin{bmatrix} \mathbf{X}_m^*(n) \\ x^*(n-m) \end{bmatrix} = \begin{bmatrix} \mathbf{K}_m(n) \\ 0 \end{bmatrix} + \frac{g_m^*(n,n)}{E_m^b(n)} \begin{bmatrix} \mathbf{b}_m(n) \\ 1 \end{bmatrix}
\end{aligned}$$

The term $g_m(n,n)$ may also be expressed as

$$\begin{aligned}
g_m(n,n) &= x(n-m) + \mathbf{b}_m^t(n)\mathbf{X}_m(n) \\
&= x(n-m) + [\mathbf{b}_m^t(n-1) - \mathbf{K}_m^t(n) g_m(n)]\mathbf{X}_m(n) \\
&= x(n-m) + \mathbf{b}_m^t(n-1)\mathbf{X}_m(n) - g_m(n)\mathbf{K}_m^t(n)\mathbf{X}_m(n) \quad (6.3.61) \\
&= g_m(n)[1 - \mathbf{K}_m^t(n)\mathbf{X}_m(n)] \\
&= \alpha_m(n) g_m(n)
\end{aligned}$$

Hence the order-update equation for $\mathbf{K}_m(n)$ in (6.3.60) may also be written

$$\mathbf{K}_{m+1}(n) = \begin{bmatrix} \mathbf{K}_m(n) \\ 0 \end{bmatrix} + \frac{\alpha_m(n) g_m^*(n)}{E_m^b(n)} \begin{bmatrix} \mathbf{b}_m(n) \\ 1 \end{bmatrix} \quad (6.3.62)$$

By using (6.3.62) and the relation in (6.3.59), we obtain the following order-update equation for $\alpha_m(n)$:

$$\alpha_{m+1}(n) = 1 - \mathbf{X}^t_{m+1}(n)\mathbf{K}_{m+1}(n) = 1 - [\mathbf{X}^t_m(n)\, x(n-m)]$$
$$\times \left(\begin{bmatrix} \mathbf{K}_m(n) \\ 0 \end{bmatrix} + \frac{\alpha_m(n) g^*_m(n)}{E^b_m(n)} \begin{bmatrix} \mathbf{b}_m(n) \\ 1 \end{bmatrix} \right)$$
$$= \alpha_m(n) - \frac{\alpha_m(n) g^*_m(n)}{E^b_m(n)} [\mathbf{X}^t_m(n)\, x(n-m)] \begin{bmatrix} \mathbf{b}_m(n) \\ 1 \end{bmatrix} \tag{6.3.63}$$
$$= \alpha_m(n) - \frac{\alpha_m(n) g^*_m(n)}{E^b_m(n)} g_m(n,n)$$
$$= \alpha_m(n) - \frac{\alpha^2_m(n)|g_m(n)|^2}{E^b_m(n)}$$

Thus we have obtained both the order-update and time-update equations for the basic least-squares lattice shown in Fig. 6.23. The basic equations are (6.3.41) and (6.3.44) for the forward and backward errors, usually called the *residuals;* (6.3.36) and (6.3.37) for the corresponding least-squares errors; the time-update equation (6.3.58) for $k_m(n)$; and the order-update equation (6.3.63) for the parameter $\alpha_m(n)$. Initially, we have

$$\begin{aligned} &E^f_m(-1) = E^b_m(-1) = E^b_m(-2) = \epsilon > 0 \\ &f_m(-1) = g_m(-1) = k_m(-1) = 0 \\ &\alpha_m(-1) = 1, \qquad \alpha_{-1}(n) = \alpha_{-1}(n-1) = 1 \end{aligned} \tag{6.3.64}$$

Joint Process Estimation. The last step in the derivation is to obtain the least-squares estimate of the desired signal $d(n)$ from the lattice. Suppose that the adaptive filter has $m + 1$ coefficients which are determined to minimize the average weighted squared error

$$\mathscr{E}_{m+1} = \sum_{l=0}^{n} w^{n-l} |e_{m+1}(l,n)|^2 \tag{6.3.65}$$

where

$$e_{m+1}(l,n) = d(l) - \mathbf{h}^t_{m+1}(n)\mathbf{X}_{m+1}(l) \tag{6.3.66}$$

The linear estimate

$$\hat{d}(l,n) = \mathbf{h}^t_{m+1}(n)\mathbf{X}_{m+1}(l) \tag{6.3.67}$$

which will be obtained from the lattice by using the residuals $g_m(n)$, is called the *joint process estimate*.

From the results of Section 6.2.4 we have already established that the coefficients of the adaptive filter that minimize (6.3.65) are given by the equation

$$\mathbf{h}_{m+1}(n) = \mathbf{P}_{m+1}(n)\mathbf{D}_{m+1}(n) \tag{6.3.68}$$

We have also established that $\mathbf{h}_m(n)$ satisfies the time-update equation given in (6.2.76).

Now let us obtain an order-update equation for $\mathbf{h}_m(n)$. From (6.3.68) and (6.3.27), we have

$$\mathbf{h}_{m+1}(n) = \begin{bmatrix} \mathbf{P}_m(n) & 0 \\ 0 & 0 \end{bmatrix} \begin{bmatrix} \mathbf{D}_m(n) \\ \cdots \end{bmatrix} + \frac{1}{E_m^b(n)} \begin{bmatrix} \mathbf{b}_m(n) \\ 1 \end{bmatrix} [\mathbf{b}_m^H(n) \quad 1]\mathbf{D}_{m+1}(n) \tag{6.3.69}$$

We define a complex-valued scalar quantity $\delta_m(n)$ as

$$\delta_m(n) = \left[\mathbf{b}_m^H(n) \quad 1\right]\mathbf{D}_{m+1}(n) \tag{6.3.70}$$

Then (6.3.69) may be expressed as

$$\mathbf{h}_{m+1}(n) = \begin{bmatrix} \mathbf{h}_m(n) \\ 0 \end{bmatrix} + \frac{\delta_m(n)}{E_m^b(n)} \begin{bmatrix} \mathbf{b}_m(n) \\ 1 \end{bmatrix} \tag{6.3.71}$$

The scalar $\delta_m(n)$ satisfies a time-update equation, which is obtained from the time-update equation for $\mathbf{b}_m(n)$ and $\mathbf{D}_m(n)$, given by (6.3.51) and (6.2.66), respectively. Thus

$$\begin{aligned} \delta_m(n) &= [\mathbf{b}_m^H(n-1) - \mathbf{K}_m^H(n)g_m^*(n) \quad 1][w\mathbf{D}_{m+1}(n-1) + d(n)\mathbf{X}_{m+1}^*(n)] \\ &= w\delta_m(n-1) + [\mathbf{b}_m^H(n-1) \quad 1]\mathbf{X}_{m+1}^*(n)d(n) \\ &\quad - wg_m^*(n)[\mathbf{K}_m^H(n) \quad 0]\mathbf{D}_{m+1}(n-1) - g_m^*(n)d(n)[\mathbf{K}_m^H(n) \quad 0]\mathbf{X}_{m+1}^*(n) \end{aligned} \tag{6.3.72}$$

But

$$[\mathbf{b}_m^H(n-1) \quad 1]\mathbf{X}_{m+1}^*(n) = x^*(n-m) + \mathbf{b}_m^H(n-1)\mathbf{X}_m^*(n) = g_m^*(n) \tag{6.3.73}$$

Also,

$$\begin{aligned} [\mathbf{K}_m^H(n) \quad 0]\mathbf{D}_{m+1}(n-1) &= \frac{1}{w + \mu_m(n)} [\mathbf{X}_m^t(n)\mathbf{P}_m(n-1) \quad 0] \begin{bmatrix} \mathbf{D}_m(n-1) \\ \cdots \end{bmatrix} \\ &= \frac{1}{w + \mu_m(n)} \mathbf{X}_m^t(n)\mathbf{h}_m(n-1) \end{aligned} \tag{6.3.74}$$

The last term in (6.3.72) may be expressed as

$$\begin{aligned} [\mathbf{K}_m^H(n) \quad 0] \begin{bmatrix} \mathbf{X}_m^*(n) \\ \cdots \end{bmatrix} &= \frac{1}{w + \mu_m(n)} \mathbf{X}_m^t(n)\mathbf{P}_m(n-1)\mathbf{X}_m^*(n) \\ &= \frac{\mu_m(n)}{w + \mu_m(n)} \end{aligned} \tag{6.3.75}$$

Upon substituting the results in (6.3.73) through (6.3.75) into (6.3.72), we obtain the desired time-update equation for $\delta_m(n)$ as

$$\delta_m(n) \equiv w\delta_m(n-1) + \alpha_m(n)g_m^*(n)e_m(n) \tag{6.3.76}$$

Order-update equations for $\alpha_m(n)$ and $g_m(n)$ have already been derived. With $e_0(n) = d(n)$, the order-update equation for $e_m(n)$ is obtained as follows:

$$
\begin{aligned}
e_m(n) &= e_m(n, n-1) = d(n) - \mathbf{h}_m^t(n-1)\mathbf{X}_m(n) \\
&= d(n) - [\mathbf{h}_{m-1}^t(n-1) \quad 0]\begin{bmatrix} \mathbf{X}_{m-1}(n) \\ \cdots \end{bmatrix} \\
&\quad - \frac{\delta_{m-1}(n-1)}{E_{m-1}^b(n-1)}[\mathbf{b}_{m-1}^t(n-1) \quad 1]\mathbf{X}_m(n) \qquad (6.3.77) \\
&= e_{m-1}(n) - \frac{\delta_{m-1}(n-1)g_{m-1}(n)}{E_{m-1}^b(n-1)}
\end{aligned}
$$

Finally, the output estimate $d(n)$ of the least-squares lattice is

$$\hat{d}(n) = \mathbf{h}_{m+1}^t(n-1)\mathbf{X}_{m+1}(n) \qquad (6.3.78)$$

But $\mathbf{h}_{m+1}^t(n-1)$ is not computed explicitly. By repeated use of the order-update equation for $\mathbf{h}_{m+1}(n)$ given by (6.3.71) in (6.3.78), we obtain the desired expression for $\hat{d}(n)$ in the form

$$\hat{d}(n) = \sum_{k=0}^{M-1} \frac{\delta_k(n-1)}{E_k^b(n-1)} g_k(n) \qquad (6.3.79)$$

In other words, the output estimate $\hat{d}(n)$ is a linear weighted sum of the backward residuals $g_k(n)$.

The adaptive least-squares lattice/joint-process (ladder) estimator is illustrated in Fig. 6.24. This lattice-ladder structure is mathematically equivalent

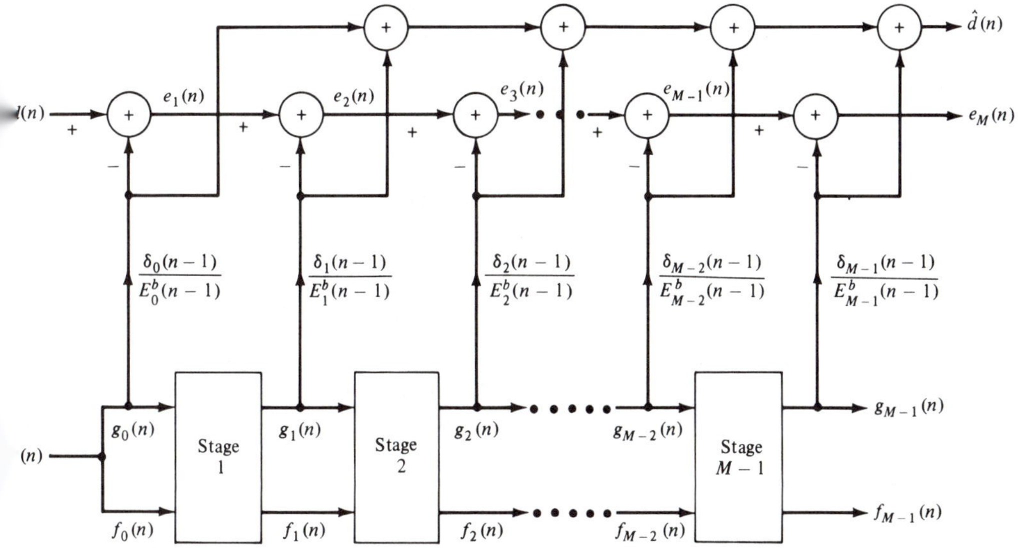

FIGURE 6.24 Adaptive RLS lattice-ladder filter.

to the RLS direct-form FIR filter. The recursive equations are summarized in Table 6.5. This is called the *a priori form* of the *RLS lattice-ladder algorithm,* to distinguish it from another form of the algorithm, called the *a posteriori form,* in which the coefficient vector $\mathbf{h}_M(n)$ is used in place of $\mathbf{h}_M(n-1)$ to compute the estimate $d(n)$. In many adaptive filtering problems, such as channel equalization and echo cancellation, the a posteriori form cannot be used, because $\mathbf{h}_M(n)$ cannot be computed prior to the computation of $d(n)$.

A number of modifications can be made to the "conventional" RLS lattice-ladder algorithm given in Table 6.5. Below we describe some of these modifications.

TABLE 6.5 A Priori Form of the RLS Lattice-Ladder Algorithm

Lattice predictor: Begin with $n = 1$ and compute the order updates for $m = 0, 1, \ldots, M-2$

$$k_{m+1}(n-1) = wk_{m+1}(n-2) + \alpha_m(n-2)f_m(n-1)g_m^*(n-2)$$

$$\mathcal{K}_{m+1}^f(n-1) = -\frac{k_{m+1}(n-1)}{E_m^b(n-2)}$$

$$\mathcal{K}_{m+1}^b(n-1) = -\frac{k_{m+1}^*(n-1)}{E_m^f(n-1)}$$

$$f_{m+1}(n) = f_m(n) + \mathcal{K}_{m+1}^f(n-1)g_m(n-1)$$

$$g_{m+1}(n) = g_m(n-1) + \mathcal{K}_{m+1}^b(n-1)f_m(n)$$

$$E_{m+1}^f(n-1) = E_m^f(n-1) - \frac{|k_{m+1}(n-1)|^2}{E_m^b(n-2)}$$

$$E_{m+1}^b(n-1) = E_m^b(n-2) - \frac{|k_{m+1}(n-1)|^2}{E_m^f(n-1)}$$

$$\alpha_{m+1}(n-1) = \alpha_m(n-1) - \frac{\alpha_m^2(n-1)|g_m(n-1)|^2}{E_m^b(n-1)}$$

Ladder filter: Begin with $n = 1$ and compute the order updates for $m = 0, 1, \ldots, M-1$

$$\delta_m(n-1) = w\,\delta_m(n-2) + \alpha_m(n-1)g_m^*(n-1)e_m(n-1)$$

$$\xi_m(n-1) = -\frac{\delta_m(n-1)}{E_m^b(n-1)}$$

$$e_{m+1}(n) = e_m(n) + \xi_m(n-1)g_m(n)$$

Initialization

$$\alpha_0(n-1) = 1, \quad e_0(n) = d(n), \quad f_0(n) = g_0(n) = x(n)$$

$$E_0^f(n) = E_0^b(n) = wE_0^f(n-1) + |x(n)|^2$$

$$\alpha_m(-1) = 1, \quad k_m(-1) = 0$$

$$E_m^b(-1) = E_m^f(0) = \epsilon > 0; \quad \delta_m(-1) = 0$$

Modified RLS Lattice Algorithms. The recursive equations in the RLS lattice algorithm given in Table 6.5 are by no means unique. Modifications can be made to some of the equations without affecting the optimality of the algorithm. However, some modifications result in algorithms which are more robust numerically when fixed-point arithmetic is used in implementation of the algorithms. We shall give a number of basic relationships that are easily established from the foregoing developments.

First, we have a relationship between the a priori error residuals and the a posteriori residuals:

A priori errors:

$$\begin{aligned} f_m(n, n-1) &\equiv f_m(n) = x(n) + \mathbf{a}_m^t(n-1)\mathbf{X}_m(n-1) \\ g_m(n, n-1) &\equiv g_m(n) = x(n-m) + \mathbf{b}_m^t(n-1)\mathbf{X}_m(n) \end{aligned} \tag{6.3.80}$$

A posteriori errors:

$$\begin{aligned} f_m(n,n) &= x(n) + \mathbf{a}_m^t(n)\mathbf{X}_m(n-1) \\ g_m(n,n) &= x(n-m) + \mathbf{b}_m^t(n)\mathbf{X}_m(n) \end{aligned} \tag{6.3.81}$$

The basic relations between (6.3.80) and (6.3.81) are

$$\begin{aligned} f_m(n,n) &= \alpha_m(n-1)f_m(n) \\ g_m(n,n) &= \alpha_m(n)g_m(n) \end{aligned} \tag{6.3.82}$$

These relations follow easily by using (6.3.50) and (6.3.51) in (6.3.81).

Second, we may obtain time-update equations for the least-squares forward and backward errors. For example, from (6.3.8) and (6.3.50) we obtain

$$\begin{aligned} E_m^f(n) &= q(n) + \mathbf{a}_m^t(n)\mathbf{Q}_m^*(n) \\ &= q(n) + [\mathbf{a}_m^t(n-1) - \mathbf{K}_m^t(n-1)f_m(n)] \\ &\quad \times [w\mathbf{Q}_m^*(n-1) + x^*(n)\mathbf{X}_m(n-1)] \\ &= wE_m^f(n-1) + \alpha_m(n-1)\,|f_m(n)|^2 \end{aligned} \tag{6.3.83}$$

Similarly, from (6.3.17) and (6.3.51) we obtain

$$E_m^b(n) = wE_m^b(n-1) + \alpha_m(n)\,|g_m(n)|^2 \tag{6.3.84}$$

Usually, (6.3.83) and (6.3.84) are used in place of the sixth and seventh equations in Table 6.5.

Third, we obtain a time-update equation for the Kalman gain vector, which is not explicitly used in the lattice algorithm, but which is used in the fast algorithms. For this derivation we also use the time-update equations for the forward and backward prediction coefficients given by (6.3.50) and (6.3.51). Thus we have

$$\begin{aligned}
\mathbf{K}_m(n) &= \mathbf{P}_m(n)\mathbf{X}_m^*(n) \\
&= \begin{bmatrix} 0 & 0 \\ 0 & \mathbf{P}_{m-1}(n-1) \end{bmatrix} \begin{bmatrix} x^*(n) \\ \mathbf{X}_{m-1}^*(n-1) \end{bmatrix} \\
&\quad + \frac{1}{E_{m-1}^f(n)} \begin{bmatrix} 1 \\ \mathbf{a}_{m-1}(n) \end{bmatrix} [1 \quad \mathbf{a}_{m-1}^H(n)] \begin{bmatrix} x^*(n) \\ \mathbf{X}_{m-1}^*(n-1) \end{bmatrix} \qquad (6.3.85) \\
&= \begin{bmatrix} 0 \\ \mathbf{K}_{m-1}(n-1) \end{bmatrix} + \frac{f_{m-1}^*(n,n)}{E_{m-1}^f(n)} \begin{bmatrix} 1 \\ \mathbf{a}_{m-1}(n) \end{bmatrix} \\
&\equiv \begin{bmatrix} \mathbf{C}_{m-1}(n) \\ c_{mm}(n) \end{bmatrix}
\end{aligned}$$

where, by definition, $\mathbf{C}_{m-1}(n)$ consists of the first $(m - 1)$ elements of $\mathbf{K}_m(n)$ and $c_{mm}(n)$ is the last element. From (6.3.60) we also have the order-update equation for $\mathbf{K}_m(n)$ as

$$\mathbf{K}_m(n) = \begin{bmatrix} \mathbf{K}_{m-1}(n) \\ 0 \end{bmatrix} + \frac{g_{m-1}^*(n,n)}{E_{m-1}^b(n)} \begin{bmatrix} \mathbf{b}_{m-1}(n) \\ 1 \end{bmatrix} \qquad (6.3.86)$$

By equating (6.3.85) to (6.3.86) we obtain the result

$$c_{mm}(n) = \frac{g_{m-1}^*(n,n)}{E_{m-1}^b(n)} \qquad (6.3.87)$$

and hence

$$\mathbf{K}_{m-1}(n) + c_{mm}(n)\mathbf{b}_{m-1}(n) = \mathbf{C}_{m-1}(n) \qquad (6.3.88)$$

By substituting from (6.3.51) into (6.3.88) for $\mathbf{b}_{m-1}(n)$ we obtain the time-update equation for the Kalman gain vector in (6.3.85) as

$$\mathbf{K}_{m-1}(n) = \frac{\mathbf{C}_{m-1}(n) - c_{mm}(n)\mathbf{b}_{m-1}(n-1)}{1 - c_{mm}(n)g_{m-1}(n)} \qquad (6.3.89)$$

There is also a time-update equation for the scalar $\alpha_m(n)$. From (6.3.63) we have

$$\begin{aligned}
\alpha_m(n) &= \alpha_{m-1}(n) - \frac{\alpha_{m-1}^2(n)\,|g_{m-1}(n)|^2}{E_{m-1}^b(n)} \\
&= \alpha_{m-1}(n)[1 - c_{mm}(n)g_{m-1}(n)]
\end{aligned} \qquad (6.3.90)$$

A second relation is obtained by using (6.3.85) to eliminate $\mathbf{K}_{m-1}(n)$ in the expression for $\alpha_m(n)$. Then

$$\begin{aligned}
\alpha_m(n) &= 1 - \mathbf{X}_m^t(n)\mathbf{K}_m(n) \\
&= \alpha_{m-1}(n-1)\left[1 - \frac{f_{m-1}^*(n,n)f_{m-1}(n)}{E_{m-1}^f(n)}\right]
\end{aligned} \qquad (6.3.91)$$

By equating (6.3.90) to (6.3.91) we obtain the desired time-update equation for $\alpha_m(n)$ as

$$\alpha_{m-1}(n) = \alpha_{m-1}(n-1)\left[\frac{1 - \dfrac{f^*_{m-1}(n,n)f_{m-1}(n)}{E^f_{m-1}(n)}}{1 - c_{mm}(n)g_{m-1}(n)}\right] \tag{6.3.92}$$

Finally, we wish to distinguish between two different methods for updating the reflection coefficients in the lattice filter and the ladder part, the *conventional (indirect) method* and the *direct method*. In the conventional (indirect) method,

$$\mathcal{K}^f_{m+1}(n) = -\frac{k_{m+1}(n)}{E^b_m(n-1)} \tag{6.3.93}$$

$$\mathcal{K}^b_{m+1}(n) = -\frac{k^*_{m+1}(n)}{E^f_m(n)} \tag{6.3.94}$$

$$\xi_m(n) = -\frac{\delta_m(n)}{E^b_m(n)} \tag{6.3.95}$$

where $k_{m+1}(n)$ is time-updated from (6.3.58), $\delta_m(n)$ is updated according to (6.3.76), and $E^f_m(n)$ and $E^b_m(n)$ are updated according to (6.3.83) and (6.3.84). By substituting for $k_{m+1}(n)$ from (6.3.58) into (6.3.93) and using (6.3.84) and the eighth equation in Table 6.5, we obtain

$$\begin{aligned}
\mathcal{K}^f_{m+1}(n) &= -\frac{k_{m+1}(n-1)}{E^b_m(n-2)}\left(\frac{wE^b_m(n-2)}{E^b_m(n-1)}\right) \\
&\quad - \frac{\alpha_m(n-1)f_m(n)g^*_m(n-1)}{E^b_m(n-1)} \\
&= \mathcal{K}^f_{m+1}(n-1)\left[1 - \frac{\alpha_m(n-1)|g_m(n-1)|^2}{E^b_m(n-1)}\right] \\
&\quad - \frac{a_m(n-1)f_m(n)g^*_m(n-1)}{E^b_m(n-1)} \\
&= \mathcal{K}^f_{m+1}(n-1) - \frac{\alpha_m(n-1)f_{m+1}(n)g^*_m(n-1)}{E^b_m(n-1)}
\end{aligned} \tag{6.3.96}$$

which is a formula for directly updating the reflection coefficient in the lattice. Similarly, by substituting (6.3.58) into (6.3.94) and using (6.3.83) and the eighth equation in Table 6.5, we obtain

$$\mathcal{K}^b_{m+1}(n) = \mathcal{K}^b_{m+1}(n-1) - \frac{\alpha_m(n-1)f^*_m(n)g_{m+1}(n)}{E^f_m(n)} \tag{6.3.97}$$

Finally, the ladder gain can also be updated directly according to the relation

$$\xi_m(n) = \xi_m(n-1) - \frac{\alpha_m(n)g^*_m(n)e_{m+1}(n)}{E^b_m(n)} \tag{6.3.98}$$

The RLS lattice-ladder algorithm that uses the direct update relations in (6.3.96) through (6.3.98) and (6.3.83) through (6.3.84) is listed in Table 6.6.

An important characteristic of the algorithm in Table 6.6 is that the forward and backward residuals are fed back to time-update the reflection coefficients in the lattice stage and $e_{m+1}(n)$ is fed back to update the ladder gain $\xi_m(n)$. For this reason, this RLS lattice-ladder algorithm has been called the *error-feedback form*. A similar form can be obtained for the a posteriori RLS lattice-ladder algorithm. For more details on the error-feedback form of RLS lattice-ladder algorithms, the interested reader is referred to the paper by Ling et al. (1986).

Fast RLS Algorithms. The two versions of the fast RLS algorithms given in the preceding section follow directly from the relationships we have

TABLE 6.6 Direct Update (Error-Feedback) Form of the A Priori RLS Lattice-Ladder Algorithm

Lattice predictor: Begin with $n = 1$ and compute the order updates for $m = 0, 1, \ldots, M-2$

$$\mathcal{K}^f_{m+1}(n-1) = \mathcal{K}^f_{m+1}(n-2) - \frac{\alpha_m(n-2)f_{m+1}(n-1)g^*_m(n-2)}{E^b_m(n-2)}$$

$$\mathcal{K}^b_{m+1}(n-1) = \mathcal{K}^b_{m+1}(n-2) - \frac{\alpha_m(n-2)f^*_m(n-1)g_{m+1}(n-1)}{E^f_m(n-1)}$$

$$f_{m+1}(n) = f_m(n) + \mathcal{K}^f_{m+1}(n-1)g_m(n-1)$$

$$g_{m+1}(n) = g_m(n-1) + \mathcal{K}^b_{m+1}(n-1)f_m(n)$$

$$E^f_{m+1}(n-1) = wE^f_{m+1}(n-2) + \alpha_{m+1}(n-2)|f_{m+1}(n-1)|^2$$

$$\alpha_{m+1}(n-1) = \alpha_m(n-1) - \frac{\alpha^2_m(n-1)|g_m(n-1)|^2}{E^b_m(n-1)}$$

$$E^b_{m+1}(n-1) = wE^b_{m+1}(n-2) + \alpha_{m+1}(n-1)|g_{m+1}(n-1)|^2$$

Ladder filter: Begin with $n = 1$ and compute the order updates $m = 0, 1, \ldots, M-1$

$$\xi_m(n-1) = \xi_m(n-2) - \frac{\alpha_m(n-1)g^*_m(n-1)e_{m+1}(n-1)}{E^b_m(n-1)}$$

$$e_{m+1}(n) = e_m(n) + \xi_m(n-1)g_m(n)$$

Initialization

$$\alpha_0(n-1) = 1, \quad e_0(n) = d(n), \quad f_0(n) = g_0(n) = x(n)$$

$$E^f_0(n) = E^b_0(n) = wE^f_0(n-1) + |x(n)|^2$$

$$\alpha_m(-1) = 1, \quad \mathcal{K}^f_m(-1) = \mathcal{K}^b_m(-1) = 0$$

$$E^b_m(-1) = E^f_m(0) = \epsilon > 0$$

obtained in this section. In particular, we fix the size of the lattice and the associated forward and backward predictors at $M - 1$ stages. Thus we obtain the first seven recursive equations in the two versions of the algorithm. The remaining problem is to determine the time-update equation for the Kalman gain vector, which was determined in (6.3.85) through (6.3.89). In version B of the algorithm, given in Table 6.3, we used the scalar $\alpha_m(n)$ to reduce the computations from $10M$ to $9M$. Version A of the algorithm, given in Table 6.2, avoids the use of this parameter. These algorithms have a computational complexity of $9M - 5$ and $8M + 6$. Since these algorithms provide a direct updating of the Kalman gain vector, they have been called *fast Kalman algorithms* [see Falconer and Ljung (1978) and Proakis (1989)].

Further reduction of computational complexity to $7M$ is possible by directly updating the following *alternative (Kalman) gain vector* [see Carayannis et al. (1983)] defined as

$$\tilde{K}_M(n) = \frac{1}{w} P_M(n - 1)\mathbf{X}_M^*(n)$$

Several fast algorithms using this gain vector have been proposed with complexities ranging from $7M$ to $10M$. Table 6.7 lists the FAEST (fast a posteriori error sequential technique) algorithm with a computational complexity $7M$ [for a derivation, see Carayannis et al. (1983, 1986) and Problem 6.8].

In general, the $7M$ fast RLS algorithms and some variations are very sensitive to round-off noise and exhibit instability problems [see papers by Falconer and Ljung (1978), Carayannis et al. (1983, 1986), and Cioffi and Kailath (1984)]. The instability problem in the $7M$ algorithms has been addressed by Slock and Kailath (1988, 1990) and modifications have been proposed that stabilize these algorithms. The resulting stabilized algorithms have a computational complexity ranging from $8M$ to $9M$. Thus their computational complexity is increased by a relatively small amount compared to the unstable $7M$ algorithms.

To understand the stabilized fast RLS algorithms, we begin by comparing the fast RLS algorithm given in Table 6.3 and the FAEST algorithm in Table 6.7. As indicated above, there are two major differences between these two algorithms. First, the FAEST algorithm uses the *alternative (Kalman) gain vector* instead of the *Kalman gain vector*. Second, the fast RLS algorithm computes the a priori backward prediction error $g_{M-1}(n)$ through FIR filtering using the backward prediction coefficient vector $\mathbf{b}_{m-1}(n - 1)$, while the FAEST algorithm computes the same quantity through a scalar operation by noticing that the last element of the alternative gain vector, $\tilde{c}_{MM}(n)$, is equal to $-wE^b_{M-1}g_{M-1}(n)$. Since these two algorithms are algebraically equivalent, the backward prediction errors calculated in different ways should be identical if infinite precision is used in the computation. Practically, when finite-precision arithmetic is used, the backward prediction errors computed using different formulas are only approximately equal to each other. In what follows we denote them by

TABLE 6.7 The FAEST Algorithm

$$f_{M-1}(n) = x(n) + \mathbf{a}^t_{M-1}(n-1)\mathbf{X}_{M-1}(n-1)$$

$$\tilde{f}_{M-1}(n,n) = \frac{f_{M-1}(n)}{\tilde{\alpha}_{M-1}(n-1)}$$

$$\mathbf{a}_{M-1}(n) = \mathbf{a}_{M-1}(n-1) - \tilde{\mathbf{K}}_{M-1}(n-1)\tilde{f}_{M-1}(n,n)$$

$$E^f_{M-1}(n) = wE^f_{M-1}(n-1) + f_{M-1}\tilde{f}^*_{M-1}(n,n)$$

$$\tilde{\mathbf{K}}_M(n) \equiv \begin{bmatrix} \tilde{\mathbf{C}}_{M-1}(n) \\ \tilde{c}_{MM}(n) \end{bmatrix} = \begin{bmatrix} 0 \\ \tilde{\mathbf{K}}_{M-1}(n-1) \end{bmatrix} + \frac{f^*_{M-1}(n)}{wE^f_{M-1}(n-1)} \begin{bmatrix} 1 \\ \mathbf{a}_{M-1}(n) \end{bmatrix}$$

$$g_{M-1}(n) = -wE^b_{M-1}(n-1)\tilde{c}^*_{MM}(n)$$

$$\tilde{\mathbf{K}}_{M-1}(n) = \tilde{\mathbf{C}}_{M-1}(n) + \mathbf{b}_{M-1}(n-1)\tilde{c}_{MM}(n)$$

$$\tilde{\alpha}_M(n) = \tilde{\alpha}_{M-1}(n-1) + \frac{|f_{M-1}(n)|^2}{wE^f_{M-1}(n-1)}$$

$$\tilde{\alpha}_{M-1}(n) = \tilde{\alpha}_M(n) + g_{M-1}(n)\tilde{c}_{MM}(n)$$

$$\tilde{g}_{M-1}(n,n) = \frac{g_{M-1}(n)}{\tilde{\alpha}_{M-1}(n)}$$

$$E^b_{M-1}(n) = wE^b_{M-1}(n-1) + g_{M-1}(n)\tilde{g}^*_{M-1}(n,n)$$

$$\mathbf{b}_{M-1}(n) = \mathbf{b}_{M-1}(n-1) + \tilde{\mathbf{K}}_{M-1}(n)\tilde{g}_{M-1}(n,n)$$

$$e_M(n) = d(n) - \mathbf{h}^t_M(n-1)\mathbf{X}_M(n)$$

$$\tilde{e}_M(n,n) = \frac{e_M(n)}{\tilde{\alpha}_M(n)}$$

$$\mathbf{h}_M(n) = \mathbf{h}_M(n-1) + \tilde{\mathbf{K}}_M(n)\tilde{e}_M(n,n)$$

Initialization: Set all vectors to zero

$$E^f_{M-1}(-1) = E^b_{M-1}(-1) = \epsilon > 0$$

$$\tilde{\alpha}_{M-1}(-1) = 1$$

$g^{(f)}_{M-1}$ and $g^{(s)}_{M-1}(n)$, respectively. The superscripts (f) and (s) indicate that they are computed using the filtering approach and scalar operation, respectively.

There are other quantities in the algorithms that can also be computed in different ways. In particular, the parameter $\alpha_{M-1}(n)$ can be computed from the vector quantities $\tilde{\mathbf{K}}_{M-1}(n)$ and $\mathbf{X}_{M-1}(n)$ as

$$\alpha_{M-1}(n) = 1 - \tilde{\mathbf{K}}^t_{M-1}(n)\mathbf{X}_{M-1}(n)$$

or from scalar quantities. We denote these values as $\tilde{\alpha}^{(f)}_{M-1}(n)$ and $\tilde{\alpha}^{(s)}_{M-1}(n)$, respectively. Finally, the last element of $\tilde{K}_M(n)$, denoted as $\tilde{c}^{(f)}_{MM}(n)$, may be computed from the relation

$$\tilde{c}^{(f)}_{MM}(n) = -\frac{g^{(f)}_{M-1}(n)}{wE^b_{M-1}(n-1)}$$

The two quantities in each of the three pairs $[g_{M-1}^{(f)}(n), g_{M-1}^{(s)}(n)]$, $[\alpha_{M-1}^{(f)}(n), \alpha_{M-1}^{(s)}(n)]$, and $[\tilde{c}_{MM}^{(f)}(n), \tilde{c}_{MM}^{(s)}(n)]$ are algebraically equivalent. Hence, either one of the two quantities or their linear combination of the form $k\beta^{(s)} + (1 - k)\beta^{(f)}$, where β represents any of the three parameters, are algebraically equivalent to the original quantities and may be used in the algorithm. Slock and Kailath (1988, 1991) found that by using the appropriate quantity or its linear combination in the fast RLS algorithm, it was sufficient to correct for the positive feedback inherent in the fast RLS algorithms. Implementation of this basic notion leads to the stabilized fast RLS algorithm given in Table 6.8.

We observe from Table 6.8 that the stabilized fast RLS algorithm employs constants k_i, $i = 1, 2, \ldots, 5$, to form five linear combinations of the three pairs of quantities indicated above. The best values of the k_i's found by Slock and Kailath resulted from computer search and are given as $k_1 = 1.5$, $k_2 = 2.5$, $k_3 = 1$, $k_4 = 0$, and $k_5 = 1$. When $k_i = 0$ or 1, we use only one of the quantities in the linear combination. Hence some of the parameters in the three pairs need not be computed. It was also found that the stability of the algorithm is only slightly affected if $\alpha_{M-1}^{(f)}(n)$ is not used. These simplifications result in the algorithm given in Table 6.9, which has a complexity of $8M$ and is numerically stable.

The performance of the stabilized fast RLS algorithms depends highly on proper initialization. On the other hand, an algorithm that uses $g_{M-1}^{(f)}(n)$ in its computations is not critically affected by proper initialization, although eventually, it will diverge. Consequently, we may initially use $g_{M-1}^{(f)}(n)$ in place of $g_{M-1}^{(s)}(n)$ or their linear combination for the first few hundred iterations, and then switch to the form for the stabilized fast RLS algorithm. By doing so, we obtain a stabilized fast RLS algorithm that is also insensitive to initial conditions.

Square-Root or Normalized Lattice Algorithm. Another type of LS lattice algorithm is called a *square-root* or *normalized lattice* algorithm. To derive the square-root/normalized LS lattice algorithm, we first define the *angle-and-power normalized* LS errors as

$$\tilde{f}_m(n) = \frac{f_m(n)\sqrt{\alpha_m(n-1)}}{\sqrt{E_m^f(n)}} = \frac{f_m(n,n)}{\sqrt{\alpha_m(n-1)}\sqrt{E_m^f(n)}} \tag{6.3.99}$$

$$\tilde{g}_m(n) = \frac{g_m(n)\sqrt{\alpha_m(n)}}{\sqrt{E_m^b(n)}} = \frac{g_m(n,n)}{\sqrt{\alpha_m(n)}\sqrt{E_m^b(n)}} \tag{6.3.100}$$

It is obvious that $\sqrt{E_m^f(n)}$ and $\sqrt{E_m^b(n)}$ perform power normalization. The terminology of *angle normalization* comes from the fact that $\alpha_m(n)$ is the cosine of the angle between the spaces spanned by the data vectors at $n - 1$ and the data vectors at n. Second, we define the normalized reflection coefficient $\rho_m(n)$ as

$$\rho_m(n) = \frac{k_m(n)}{\sqrt{E_{m-1}^b(n-1)}\sqrt{E_{m-1}^f(n)}} \tag{6.3.101}$$

TABLE 6.8 The Stabilized FRLS Algorithm

$$f_{M-1}(n) = x(n) + \mathbf{a}^t_{M-1}(n-1)\mathbf{X}_{M-1}(n-1)$$

$$f_{M-1}(n,n) = \frac{f_{M-1}(n)}{\tilde{\alpha}_{M-1}(n-1)}$$

$$\mathbf{a}_{M-1}(n) = \mathbf{a}_{M-1}(n-1) - \tilde{\mathbf{K}}_{M-1}(n-1)f_{M-1}(n,n)$$

$$\tilde{c}_{M1}(n) = \frac{f^*_{M-1}(n)}{wE^f_{M-1}(n-1)}$$

$$\begin{bmatrix} \tilde{\mathbf{C}}_{M-1}(n) \\ \tilde{c}^{(s)}_{MM}(n) \end{bmatrix} = \begin{bmatrix} 0 \\ \tilde{\mathbf{K}}_{M-1}(n-1) \end{bmatrix} + \tilde{c}_{M1}(n) \begin{bmatrix} 1 \\ \mathbf{a}_{M-1}(n) \end{bmatrix}$$

$$g^{(f)}_{M-1}(n) = x(n-M+1) + \mathbf{b}^t_{M-1}(n-1)\mathbf{X}_{M-1}(n)$$

$$\hat{c}^{(f)}_{MM}(n) = -\frac{g^{(f)*}_{M-1}(n)}{wE^b_{M-1}(n-1)}$$

$$\tilde{c}_{MM}(n) = k_4\tilde{c}^{(f)}_{MM}(n) + (1-k_4)\tilde{c}^{(s)}_{MM}(n)$$

$$\tilde{\mathbf{K}}_M(n) = \begin{bmatrix} \tilde{\mathbf{C}}_{M-1}(n) \\ \tilde{c}_{MM}(n) \end{bmatrix}$$

$$g^{(s)}_{M-1}(n) = -wE^b_{M-1}(n-1)\tilde{c}^{(s)*}_{MM}(n)$$

$$g^{(i)}_{M-1}(n) = k_i g^{(f)}_{M-1}(n) + (1-k_i)g^{(s)}_{M-1}(n), \quad i = 1, 2, 5$$

$$\tilde{\mathbf{K}}_{M-1}(n) = \tilde{\mathbf{C}}_{M-1}(n) + \mathbf{b}_{M-1}(n-1)\tilde{c}_{MM}(n)$$

$$\tilde{\alpha}_M(n) = \tilde{\alpha}_{M-1}(n-1) + \tilde{c}_{M1}(n)f_{M-1}(n)$$

$$\tilde{\alpha}^{(s)}_{M-1}(n) = \tilde{\alpha}_M(n) + g^{(5)}_{M-1}(n)\tilde{c}^{(s)}_{MM}(n)$$

$$\tilde{\alpha}^{(f)}_{M-1}(n) = 1 - \tilde{\mathbf{K}}^t_{M-1}(n)\mathbf{X}_{M-1}(n)$$

$$\tilde{\alpha}_{M-1}(n) = k_3\tilde{\alpha}^{(f)}_{M-1}(n) + (1-k_3)\tilde{\alpha}^{(s)}_{M-1}(n)$$

$$E^f_{M-1}(n) = wE^f_{M-1}(n-1) + f_{M-1}(n)f^*_{M-1}(n,n)$$

$$\left[\text{or, } \frac{1}{E^f_{M-1}(n))} = \frac{1}{w}\frac{1}{E^f_{M-1}(n-1)} - \frac{|\tilde{c}_{M1}(n)|^2}{\tilde{\alpha}^{(s)}_{M-1}(n)}\right]$$

$$g^{(i)}_{M-1}(n,n) = \frac{g^{(i)}_{M-1}(n)}{\tilde{\alpha}_{M-1}(n)}, \quad i = 1, 2$$

$$\mathbf{b}_{M-1}(n) = \mathbf{b}_{M-1}(n-1) + \tilde{\mathbf{K}}_{M-1}(n)g^{(1)}_{M-1}(n,n)$$

$$E^b_{M-1}(n) = wE^b_{M-1}(n-1) + g^{(2)}_{M-1}(n)\mathbf{g}^{(2)*}_{M-1}(n,n)$$

$$e_M(n) = d(n) - \mathbf{h}^t_M(n-1)\mathbf{X}_M(n)$$

$$e_M(n,n) = \frac{e_M(n)}{\tilde{\alpha}_M(n)}$$

$$\mathbf{h}_M(n) = \mathbf{h}_M(n-1) + \tilde{\mathbf{K}}_M(n)e_M(n,n)$$

TABLE 6.9 A Simplified SFRLS Algorithm

$$f_{M-1}(n) = x(n) + \mathbf{a}_{M-1}^t(n-1)\mathbf{X}_{M-1}(n-1)$$

$$f_{M-1}(n,n) = \frac{f_{M-1}(n)}{\tilde{\alpha}_{M-1}(n-1)}$$

$$\mathbf{a}_{M-1}(n) = \mathbf{a}_{M-1}(n-1) - \tilde{\mathbf{K}}_{M-1}(n-1)f_{M-1}(n,n)$$

$$\tilde{c}_{M1}(n) = \frac{f_{M-1}^*(n)}{wE_{M-1}^f(n-1)}$$

$$\tilde{\mathbf{K}}_M(n) \equiv \begin{bmatrix} \tilde{\mathbf{C}}_{M-1}(n) \\ \tilde{c}_{MM}(n) \end{bmatrix} = \begin{bmatrix} 0 \\ \tilde{\mathbf{K}}_{M-1}(n-1) \end{bmatrix} + \frac{f_{M-1}^*(n)}{wE_{M-1}^f(n-1)} \begin{bmatrix} 1 \\ \mathbf{a}_{M-1}(n) \end{bmatrix}$$

$$g_{M-1}^{(f)}(n) = x(n-M+1) + \mathbf{b}_{M-1}^t(n-1)\mathbf{X}_{M-1}(n)$$

$$g_{M-1}^{(s)}(n) = -wE_{M-1}^b(n-1)\tilde{c}_{MM}^*(n)$$

$$g_{M-1}^{(i)}(n) = k_i g_{M-1}^{(f)}(n) + (1-k_i)g_{M-1}^{(s)}(n), \quad i = 1, 2$$

$$\tilde{\mathbf{K}}_{M-1}(n) = \tilde{\mathbf{C}}_{M-1}(n) + \mathbf{b}_{M-1}(n-1)\tilde{c}_{MM}(n)$$

$$\tilde{\alpha}_M(n) = \tilde{\alpha}_{M-1}(n-1) + \tilde{c}_{M1}(n)f_{M-1}(n)$$

$$\tilde{\alpha}_{M-1}(n) = \tilde{\alpha}_M(n) + g_{M-1}^{(f)}(n)\tilde{c}_{MM}(n)$$

$$E_{M-1}^f(n) = wE_{M-1}^f(n-1) + f_{M-1}(n)f_{M-1}^*(n,n)$$

$$g_{M-1}^{(i)}(n,n) = \frac{g_{M-1}^{(i)}(n)}{\tilde{\alpha}_{M-1}(n)}, \quad i = 1, 2$$

$$\mathbf{b}_{M-1}(n) = \mathbf{b}_{M-1}(n-1) + \tilde{\mathbf{K}}_{M-1}(n)g_{M-1}^{(1)}(n,n)$$

$$E_{M-1}^b(n) = wE_{M-1}^b(n-1) + g_{M-1}^{(2)}(n)g_{M-1}^{(2)*}(n,n)$$

$$e_M(n) = d(n) - \mathbf{h}_M^t(n-1)\mathbf{X}_M(n)$$

$$e_M(n,n) = \frac{e_M(n)}{\tilde{\alpha}_M(n)}$$

$$\mathbf{h}_M(n) = \mathbf{h}_M(n-1) + \tilde{\mathbf{K}}_M(n)e_M(n,n)$$

It is easy to verify that all three quantities have magnitudes less than unity. Due to this property, the square-root/normalized LS lattice algorithm is suitable for fixed-point arithmetic implementation. Below we derive such an algorithm that is based on these three quantities.

Substituting (6.3.99), (6.3.100), and (6.3.101) into (6.3.58), we obtain

$$\begin{aligned} &\sqrt{E_{m-1}^b(n-1)}\sqrt{E_{m-1}^f(n)}\,\rho_m(n) \\ &= w\sqrt{E_{m-1}^b(n-2)}\sqrt{E_{m-1}^f(n-1)}\,\rho_m(n-1) \\ &\quad + \sqrt{E_{m-1}^b(n-1)}\sqrt{E_{m-1}^f(n)}\,\tilde{f}_{m-1}(n)\tilde{g}_{m-1}(n-1) \end{aligned} \tag{6.3.102}$$

or equivalently,

$$\rho_m(n) = \sqrt{\frac{wE^f_{m-1}(n-1)}{E^f_{m-1}(n)}}\sqrt{\frac{wE^b_{m-1}(n-2)}{E^b_{m-1}(n-1)}}\rho_m(n-1) + \tilde{f}_{m-1}(n)\tilde{g}_{m-1}(n-1) \tag{6.3.103}$$

From the time-update equation of $E^f_m(n)$ and $E^b_m(n)$ given by (6.3.83) and (6.3.84) it can be shown that

$$\frac{wE^f_{m-1}(n-1)}{E^f_{m-1}(n)} = 1 - \frac{\alpha_{m-1}(n-1)|f_{m-1}(n)|^2}{E^f_{m-1}(n)} = 1 - |\tilde{f}_{m-1}(n)|^2 \tag{6.3.104}$$

and

$$\frac{wE^b_{m-1}(n-1)}{E^b_{m-1}(n)} = 1 - \frac{\alpha_{m-1}(n)|g_{m-1}(n)|^2}{E^b_{m-1}(n)} = 1 - |\tilde{g}_{m-1}(n)|^2 \tag{6.3.105}$$

Then, by substituting (6.3.104) and (6.3.105) into (6.3.103), we obtain the time-update equation of $\rho_m(n)$ as

$$\rho_m(n) = \sqrt{1 - |\tilde{f}_{m-1}(n)|^2}\sqrt{1 - |\tilde{g}_{m-1}(n-1)|^2}\rho_m(n-1) + \tilde{f}_{m-1}(n)\tilde{g}_{m-1}(n-1) \tag{6.3.106}$$

To derive the order-update equations of the normalized forward and backward errors, we first write the a posteriori error order-update equations as

$$f_m(n,n) = f_{m-1}(n,n) - \frac{k_m(n)}{E^b_{m-1}(n-1)}g_{m-1}(n-1, n-1) \tag{6.3.107}$$

and

$$g_m(n,n) = g_{m-1}(n-1, n-1) - \frac{k_m(n)}{E^f_{m-1}(n)}f_{m-1}(n,n) \tag{6.3.108}$$

Then, by writing (6.3.107) in terms of normalized errors, we have

$$\begin{aligned}\sqrt{\alpha_m(n-1)}\sqrt{E^f_m(n)}\,\tilde{f}_m(n) &= \sqrt{\alpha_{m-1}(n-1)}\sqrt{E^f_{m-1}(n)}\,\tilde{f}_{m-1}(n) \\ &- \frac{\sqrt{E^f_{m-1}(n)}\sqrt{E^b_{m-1}(n-1)}\rho_m(n)}{E^b_{m-1}(n-1)}\sqrt{\alpha_{m-1}(n-1)}\sqrt{E^b_{m-1}(n-1)}\tilde{g}_{m-1}(n-1)\end{aligned} \tag{6.3.109}$$

After some simplification we obtain

$$\begin{aligned}\tilde{f}_m(n) &= \sqrt{\frac{\alpha_{m-1}(n-1)}{\alpha_m(n-1)}}\sqrt{\frac{E^f_{m-1}(n)}{E^f_m(n)}}\,\tilde{f}_{m-1}(n) \\ &\quad - \sqrt{\frac{\alpha_{m-1}(n-1)}{\alpha_m(n-1)}}\sqrt{\frac{E^f_{m-1}(n)}{E^f_m(n)}}\rho_m(n)\tilde{g}_{m-1}(n-1) \\ &= \sqrt{\frac{\alpha_{m-1}(n-1)}{\alpha_m(n-1)}}\sqrt{\frac{E^f_{m-1}(n)}{E^f_m(n)}}[\tilde{f}_{m-1}(n) - \rho_m(n)\tilde{g}_{m-1}(n-1)]\end{aligned} \tag{6.3.110}$$

From the order-update equation for $E_m^f(n)$ given by (6.3.36) it can be shown that

$$\frac{E_m^f(n)}{E_{m-1}^f(n)} = 1 - \frac{|k_m(n)|^2}{E_{m-1}^f(n)E_{m-1}^b(n-1)} = 1 - |\rho_m(n)|^2 \qquad (6.3.111)$$

From (6.3.63) we obtain

$$\frac{\alpha_m(n-1)}{\alpha_{m-1}(n-1)} = 1 - \frac{\alpha_{m-1}(n-1)|g_{m-1}(n-1)|^2}{E_{m-1}^b(n-1)} = 1 - |\tilde{g}_{m-1}(n-1)|^2 \qquad (6.3.112)$$

Then, by substituting (6.3.111) and (6.3.112) into (6.3.110), we obtain the desired result:

$$\tilde{f}_m(n) = \frac{\tilde{f}_{m-1}(n) - \rho_m(n)\tilde{g}_{m-1}(n-1)}{\sqrt{1 - |\rho_m(n)|^2}\sqrt{1 - |\tilde{g}_{m-1}(n-1)|^2}} \qquad (6.3.113)$$

Similarly, we can obtain the order-update equation for the normalized backward error as

$$\tilde{g}_m(n) = \frac{\tilde{g}_{m-1}(n-1) - \rho_m(n)\tilde{f}_{m-1}(n)}{\sqrt{1 - |\rho_m(n)|^2}\sqrt{1 - |\tilde{f}_{m-1}(n)|^2}} \qquad (6.3.114)$$

Equations (6.3.106), (6.3.113), and (6.3.114) form the square-root/normalized LS lattice algorithm. Note that the square-root/normalized LS lattice algorithm involves only three variables and is realized with only three equations. Thus it has a more compact form than the other forms of LS lattice algorithms. However, it requires many square-root operations, which are usually time consuming. This problem can be solved by using CORDIC processors, which compute a square-root operation in N clock cycles, where N is the number of bits of the computer word length. CORDIC processing is described in Section 7.3.4.

6.3.2 Gradient Lattice-Ladder Algorithm

The RLS lattice-ladder algorithms described in the preceding section are significantly more complicated than the LMS algorithm. However, they do result in superior performance, as we shall observe in the following section. In an attempt to simplify the computational aspects of this class of algorithms, yet retain many of their optimal properties, we consider a lattice-ladder filter structure in which the number of filter parameters is significantly reduced. In particular, the lattice-ladder filter structure is illustrated in Fig. 6.25. Each stage of the lattice is characterized by the output–input relations

$$\begin{aligned} f_m(n) &= f_{m-1}(n) - k_m(n)g_{m-1}(n-1) \\ g_m(n) &= g_{m-1}(n-1) - k_m^*(n)f_{m-1}(n) \end{aligned} \qquad (6.3.115)$$

where $k_m(n)$ is the reflection coefficient in the mth stage of the lattice, and $f_m(n)$ and $g_m(n)$ are the forward and backward residuals, respectively.

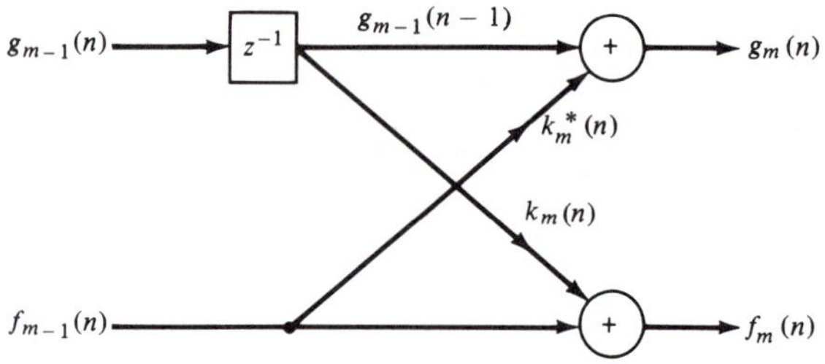

(a)

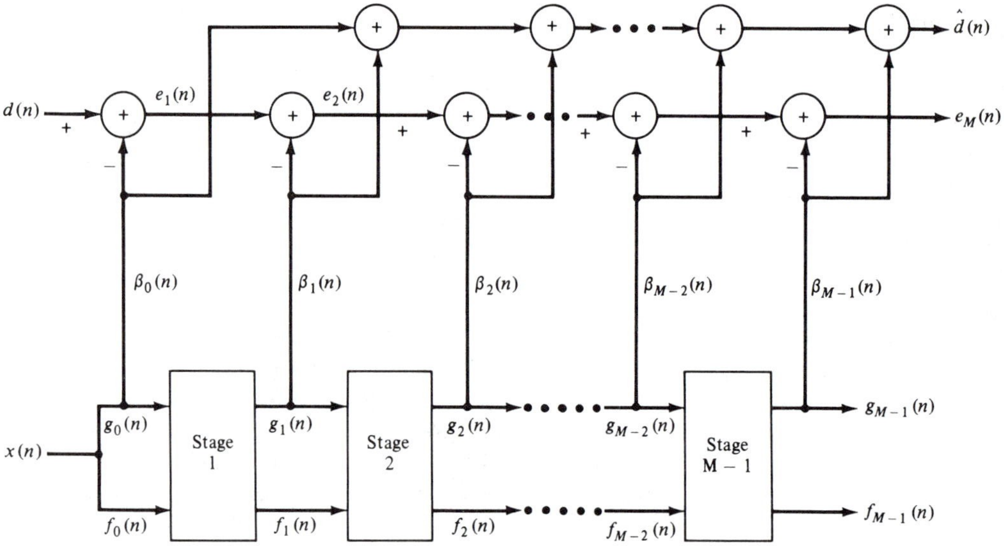

(b)

FIGURE 6.25 Gradient lattice-ladder filter.

This form of the lattice filter is identical to that obtained from the Levinson–Durbin algorithm, except that now $k_m(n)$ is allowed to vary with time so that the lattice filter adapts to the time variations in the signal statistics. In comparison with the RLS lattice filter, the lattice described by (6.3.115) is more restrictive, in that the forward and backward predictors have identical coefficients.

The lattice filter parameters $k_m(n)$ may be optimized according to the MSE criterion or by employing the method of least squares. Suppose that we adopt the MSE criterion and select the parameters to minimize the sum of the mean-square forward and backward errors,

$$\begin{aligned}\mathscr{E}_m &= E[|f_m(n)|^2 + |g_m(n)|^2]\\ &= E[|f_{m-1}(n) - k_m g_{m-1}(n-1)|^2 + |g_{m-1}(n-1) - k_m^* f_{m-1}(n)|^2]\end{aligned}$$

where we have dropped the time dependence on the parameters k_m for this optimization, since the statistics now are assumed to be time invariant. The minimization of $\mathscr{E}_m$ with respect to the filter parameters results in the solution

$$k_m = \frac{2E[f_{m-1}(n)g^*_{m-1}(n-1)]}{E[|f_{m-1}(n)|^2] + E[|g_{m-1}(n-1)|^2]} \tag{6.3.116}$$

Note that k_m has the form of a normalized correlation coefficient.

When the statistical properties of the signal are unknown, we adopt the least-squares criterion for determining $k_m(n)$. The performance index to be minimized is

$$\begin{aligned}\mathscr{E}_m^{\text{LS}} &= \sum_{l=0}^{n} w^{n-l}[|f_m(l)|^2 + |g_m(l)|^2] \\ &= \sum_{l=0}^{n} w^{n-l}[|f_{m-1}(l) - k_m(l)g_{m-1}(l-1)|^2 \\ &\quad + |g_{m-1}(l-1) - k_m(l)f_{m-1}(l)|^2]\end{aligned} \tag{6.3.117}$$

Minimization of $\mathscr{E}_m^{\text{LS}}$ with respect to $k_m(n)$ yields the solution

$$k_m(n) = \frac{2\sum_{l=0}^{n} w^{n-l} f_{m-1}(l)g^*_{m-1}(l-1)}{\sum_{l=0}^{n} w^{n-l}[|f_{m-1}(l)|^2 + |g_{m-1}(l-1)|^2]} \tag{6.3.118}$$

Clearly, (6.3.118) is the appropriate expression for estimating $k_m(n)$ in an adaptive filtering application.

In a recursive implementation of the computation in (6.3.118), the numerator and denominator terms may be updated in time as follows:

$$\begin{aligned}u_m(n) &= wu_m(n-1) + 2f_{m-1}(n)g^*_{m-1}(n-1) \\ v_m(n) &= wv_m(n-1) + |f_{m-1}(n)|^2 + |g_{m-1}(n-1)|^2\end{aligned} \tag{6.3.119}$$

Then

$$k_m(n) = \frac{u_m(n)}{v_m(n)} \tag{6.3.120}$$

Equivalently, $k_m(n)$ may be updated recursively in time according to the relation

$$k_m(n) = k_m(n-1) + \frac{f_{m-1}(n-1)g^*_m(n-1) + g^*_{m-1}(n-2)f_m(n-1)}{v_m(n-1)} \tag{6.3.121}$$

Following the form of the solution obtained in the RLS lattice, we form the output of the lattice in Fig. 6.25 as a linear combination of the backward residuals. Thus

$$\hat{d}(n) = \sum_{k=0}^{M-1} \beta_k(n) g_k(n) \tag{6.3.122}$$

where $\beta_k(n)$ are the weighting coefficients of the ladder part. The optimum values of the weighting coefficients are obtained by minimizing the MSE between the desired signal $d(n)$ and the estimate. Let $e_{m+1}(n)$ denote the error between $d(n)$ and the estimate at the output of the m-stage lattice. Then, with $e_0(n) = d(n)$, we have

$$\begin{aligned} e_{m+1}(n) &= d(n) - \sum_{k=0}^{m} \beta_k(n) g_k(n) \\ &= d(n) - \sum_{k=0}^{m-1} \beta_k(n) g_k(n) - \beta_m(n) g_m(n) \\ &= e_m(n) - g_m(n)\beta_m(n) \end{aligned} \tag{6.3.123}$$

The error in (6.3.123) may also be expressed in matrix form as

$$e_{m+1}(n) = d(n) - \boldsymbol{\beta}_{m+1}^t(n) \mathbf{G}_{m+1}(n) \tag{6.3.124}$$

where $\boldsymbol{\beta}_{m+1}(n)$ is the vector of ladder weights and $\mathbf{G}_{m+1}(n)$ is the vector of backward residuals.

If we assume for the moment that the signal statistics are stationary, we may drop the time dependence on the coefficient vector and select $\boldsymbol{\beta}_{M+1}$ to satisfy the orthogonality condition

$$E[e_M(n)\mathbf{G}_M^*(n)] = 0 \tag{6.3.125}$$

It we substitute from (6.3.124) into (6.3.125) and perform the expectation operation, we obtain

$$E[d(n)\mathbf{G}_M^*(n)] - E[\mathbf{G}_M^*(n)\mathbf{G}_M^t(n)]\boldsymbol{\beta}_M = 0$$

or equivalently,

$$\boldsymbol{\beta}_M = \{E[\mathbf{G}_M^*(n)\mathbf{G}_M^t(n)]\}^{-1} E[d(n)\mathbf{G}_M^*(n)] \tag{6.3.126}$$

An important property of the backward residuals in a lattice filter described by (6.3.115) is that they are orthogonal [see Makhoul (1978)],

$$E[g_k(n)g_j^*(n)] = \begin{cases} \mathscr{E}_k^b, & k = j \\ 0, & \text{otherwise} \end{cases} \tag{6.3.127}$$

Consequently, the matrix $E[\mathbf{G}_M^*(n)\mathbf{G}_M^t(n)]$ is diagonal and hence the optimum ladder gains are given as

$$\beta_m = \frac{1}{\mathscr{E}_m^b} E[d(n)g_m^*(n)] \tag{6.3.128}$$

There remains the problem of adjusting the ladder gains $\beta_m(n)$ adaptively. Since the desired β_m minimize the MSE between $d(n)$ and $\hat{d}(n)$, the error will be orthogonal to the backward residuals $g_n(n)$ in $d(n)$. This suggests a gradient algorithm of the form

$$\beta_m(n+1) = \beta_m(n) + \frac{e_m(n)g_m^*(n)}{\hat{\mathscr{E}}_m^b(n)} \tag{6.3.129}$$

where $\hat{\mathscr{E}}_m^b(n)$ is an estimate of $\mathscr{E}_m^b$, which may be computed recursively as

$$\hat{\mathscr{E}}_m^b(n) = w\hat{\mathscr{E}}_m^b(n-1) + |g_m(n)|^2 \tag{6.3.130}$$

However, the computation in (6.3.130) can be avoided. Since the forward and backward residuals have identical mean-square values, the variable $v_m(n)$ in (6.3.119), which represents the combined residual noise power in $f_m(n)$ and $g_m(n)$, is an estimate of $2\mathscr{E}_m^b$. Hence (6.3.129) is replaced by the recursive equation

$$\beta_m(n+1) = \beta_m(n) + \frac{2e_m(n)g_m^*(n)}{v_m(n)} \tag{6.3.131}$$

In summary, the adaptive lattice-ladder algorithm is listed in Table 6.10. Since the algorithm in (6.3.131) for updating the ladder gains is a gradient algorithm, this filter is called a *gradient lattice-ladder filter*. The factor $2/v_m(n)$ plays the role of the step size parameter.

This algorithm was originally proposed by Griffiths (1977), and considered for noise-canceling applications by Griffiths (1978) and for adaptive equalization by Satorius and Pack (1981) and Proakis (1989).

TABLE 6.10 Gradient Lattice-Ladder Algorithm

$$v_m(n) = wv_m(n-1) + |f_{m-1}(n)|^2 + |g_{m-1}(n-1)|^2$$

$$k_m(n) = k_m(n-1) + \frac{f_{m-1}(n-1)g_m^*(n-1) + g_{m-1}^*(n-2)f_m(n-1)}{v_m(n-1)}$$

$$f_m(n) = f_{m-1}(n) + k_m(n)g_{m-1}(n-1)$$

$$g_m(n) = g_{m-1}(n) + k_m^*(n)f_{m-1}(n)$$

$$e_{m+1}(n) = e_m(n) - g_m(n)\beta_m(n)$$

$$\hat{d}(n) = \boldsymbol{\beta}_M^t(n)\mathbf{G}_M(n)$$

$$\beta_m(n+1) = \beta_m(n) + \frac{2e_m(n)g_m^*(n)}{v_m(n)}$$

Initialization

$$f_0(n) = g_0(n) = x(n), \quad f_m(-1) = g_m(-1) = g_m(-2) = 0$$

$$e_0(n) = d(n), \quad e_m(0) = 0, \quad m > 1$$

$$v_m(-1) = \epsilon > 0$$

$$\beta_m(0) = 0$$

$$k_m(-1) = 0$$

6.3.3 Properties of Lattice-Ladder Algorithms

The lattice algorithms that we have derived in the two preceding sections have a number of desirable properties. In this section we consider the properties of these algorithms and compare them with the corresponding properties of the LMS algorithm and the RLS direct-form FIR filtering algorithms.

Convergence Rate. The RLS lattice-ladder algorithms basically have the same convergence rate as the RLS direct-form FIR filter structures. This characteristic behavior is not surprising since both filter structures are optimum in the least-squares sense. Although the gradient lattice algorithm retains some of the optimal characteristics of the RLS lattice, nevertheless, the former is not optimum in the least-squares sense, and hence its convergence rate is slower.

For comparison purposes, Figs. 6.26 and 6.27 illustrate the learning curves for an adaptive equalizer of length $M = 11$, implemented as a RLS lattice-ladder filter, as a gradient lattice-ladder filter, and a direct-form FIR filter using the LMS algorithm, for a channel autocorrelation matrix that has eigenvalue ratios of $\lambda_{max}/\lambda_{min} = 11$ and $\lambda_{max}/\lambda_{min} = 21$. From these learning curves we observe that the gradient lattice algorithm takes about twice as many iterations to converge as the optimum RLS lattice algorithm. Furthermore, the gradient lattice algorithm provides significantly faster convergence than does the LMS algorithm. For both lattice structures, the convergence rate does not depend on the eigenvalue spread of the correlation matrix.

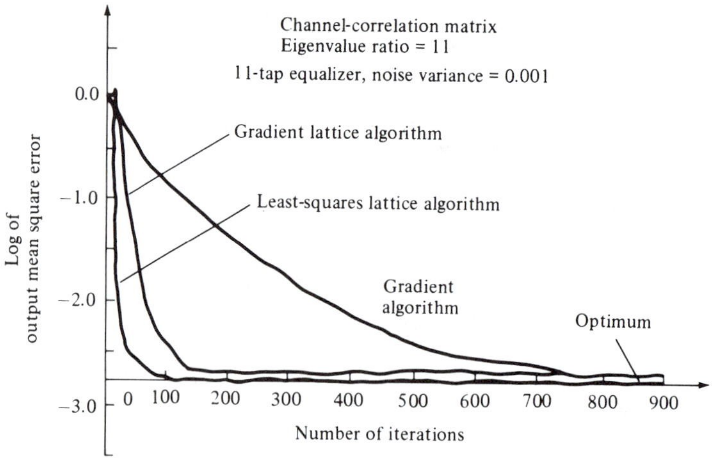

FIGURE 6.26 Learning curves for RLS lattice, gradient lattice, and LMS algorithm for adaptive equalizer of length $M = 11$. (From *Digital Communications* by John G. Proakis. © 1989 by McGraw-Hill Book Company. Reprinted with permission of the publisher.)

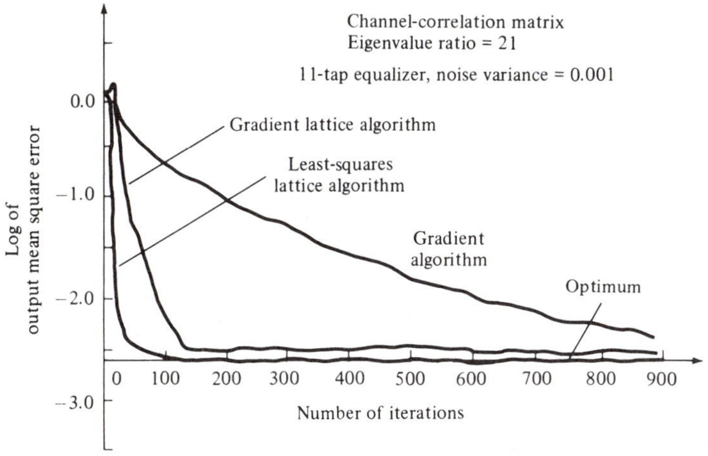

FIGURE 6.27 Learning curves for RLS lattice, gradient lattice and LMS algorithms for adaptive equalizer of length $M = 11$. (From *Digital Communications* by John G. Proakis. © 1989 by McGraw-Hill Book Company. Reprinted with permission of the publisher.)

Computational Requirements. The RLS lattice algorithms described in the preceding section have a computational complexity that is proportional to M. In contrast, the computational complexity of the RLS square-root algorithms have a complexity proportional to M^2. On the other hand, the direct-form fast algorithms, which are a derivative of the lattice algorithm, have a complexity proportional to M, and they are a little more efficient than the lattice-ladder algorithms.

In Fig. 6.28 we illustrate the computational complexity (number of complex multiplications and divisions) of the various adaptive filtering algorithms that we have described. Clearly, the LMS algorithm requires the smallest number of computations. The fast RLS algorithms in Tables 6.3 and 6.7 are the most efficient of the RLS algorithms shown, closely followed by the gradient lattice algorithm, then the RLS lattice algorithms, and finally, the square-root algorithms. Note that for small values of M, there is little difference in complexity among the rapidly convergent algorithms.

Numerical Properties. In addition to providing fast convergence, the RLS and gradient lattice algorithms are numerically robust. First, these lattice algorithms are numerically stable. The term *numerically stable* means that the output estimation error from the computational procedure is bounded when a bounded error signal is introduced at the input. Second, the numerical accuracy of the optimum solution is also relatively good compared to the LMS and the RLS direct-form FIR algorithms.

For purposes of comparison, we illustrate in Table 6.11 the steady-state average squared error or (estimated) minimum MSE obtained through computer simulation from the two RLS lattice algorithms and the direct-

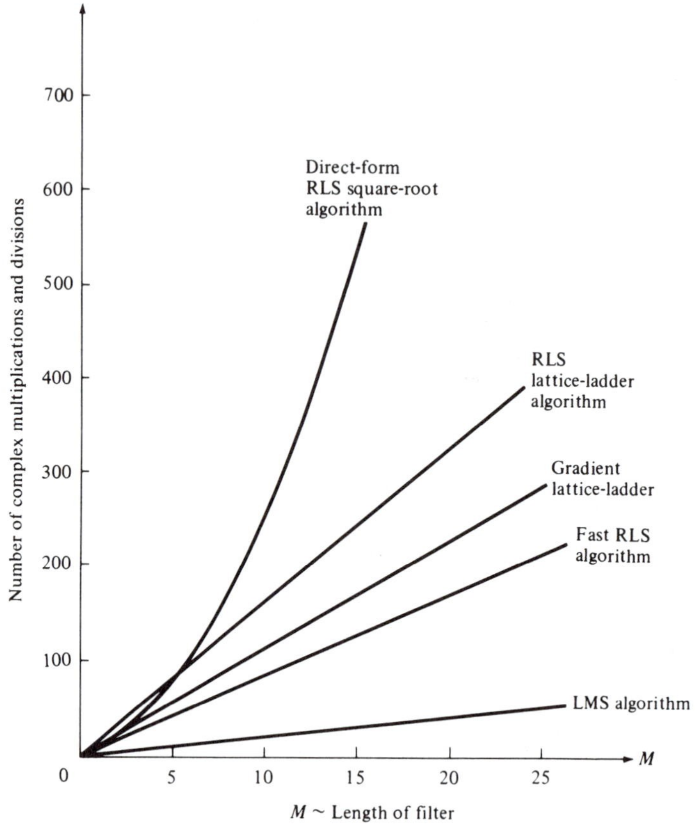

FIGURE 6.28 Computational complexity of adaptive filter algorithms.

form FIR filter algorithms described in Section 6.2. The striking result in Table 6.11 is the superior performance obtained with the RLS lattice-ladder algorithm, in which the reflection coefficients and the ladder gains are updated directly according to (6.3.96) through (6.3.98). This is the error-feedback form of the RLS lattice algorithm. It is clear that the direct updating of these coefficients is significantly more robust to round-off errors than are all the other adaptive algorithms, including the LMS algorithm. It is also apparent that the two-step process used in the conventional RLS lattice algorithm to estimate the reflection coefficients is not as accurate. Furthermore, the estimation errors that are generated in the coefficients at each stage propagate from stage to stage, causing additional errors.

The effect of changing the weighting factor w is illustrated in the numerical results given in Table 6.12. In this table we give the minimum (estimated) MSE obtained with the conventional and error-feedback forms of the RLS lattice algorithm. We observe that the output MSE decreases with an increase in the weighting factor when the precision is high (13 bits and 16 bits). This reflects the improvement in performance obtained by increasing

TABLE 6.11 Numerical Accuracy, in Terms of Output MSE for Channel with $\lambda_{max}/\lambda_{min} = 11$ and $w = 0.975$, MSE $\times 10^{-3}$

	Algorithm				
Number of bits (including sign)	RLS square root	Fast RLS	Conventional RLS lattice	Error feedback RLS lattice	LMS
16	2.17	2.17	2.16	2.16	2.30
13	2.33	2.21	3.09	2.22	2.30
11	6.14	3.34	25.2	3.09	19.0
9	75.3	[a]	365	31.6	311

[a] Algorithm did not converge.

the observation interval. As the number of bits of precision is decreased, we observe that the weighting factor should also be decreased in order to maintain good performance. In effect, with low precision, the effect of a longer averaging time results in a larger round-off noise. Of course, these results were obtained with time-invariant signal statistics. If the signal statistics are time variant, the rate of the time variations will also influence our choice of w.

In the gradient lattice algorithm, the reflection coefficients and the ladder gains are also updated directly. Consequently, the numerical accuracy of the gradient lattice algorithm is comparable to that obtained with the direct-update form of the RLS lattice.

Analytical and simulation results on numerical stability and numerical accuracy in fixed-point implementation of these algorithms can be found in the papers by Ling and Proakis (1984a), Ling et al. (1985, 1986), Ljung and Ljung (1985), and Gardner (1984).

Implementation Considerations. As we have observed, the lattice filter structure is highly modular and allows for the computations to be pipelined. Because of the high degree of modularity, the RLS and gradient lattice algorithms are particularly suitable for implementation in VLSI. As a result

TABLE 6.12 Numerical Accuracy, in Terms of Output MSE, of A Priori LS Lattice Algorithm with Different Values of the Weighting Factor w, MSE $\times 10^{-3}$

	Algorithm					
	$w = 0.99$		$w = 0.975$		$w = 0.95$	
Number of bits (with sign)	Conventional	Error feedback	Conventional	Error feedback	Conventional	Error feedback
16	2.14	2.08	2.18	2.16	2.66	2.62
13	7.08	2.11	3.09	2.22	3.65	2.66
11	39.8	3.88	25.2	3.09	15.7	2.78
9	750	44.1	365	31.6	120	15.2

of this advantage in implementation and the desirable properties of stability, excellent numerical accuracy, and fast convergence, we anticipate that in the near future, more and more adaptive filters will be implemented as lattice-ladder structures.

6.4 SUMMARY AND REFERENCES

We have presented adaptive algorithms for direct-form FIR and lattice filter structures. The algorithms for the direct-form FIR filter consisted of the simple LMS algorithm due to Widrow and Hoff (1960) and the direct-form, time-recursive least-squares (RLS) algorithms, including the conventional RLS form given by (6.2.72) through (6.2.76), the square-root RLS forms described by Bierman (1977), Carlson and Culmone (1979), and Hsu (1982), and the RLS fast Kalman algorithms, one form of which was described by Falconer and Ljung (1978) and other forms later derived by Carayannis et al. (1983), Proakis (1989), and Cioffi and Kailath (1984).

Of these algorithms, the LMS algorithm is simplest. It is used in many applications in which its slow speed of convergence is adequate. Of the direct-form RLS algorithms, the square-root algorithms have been used in applications where fast convergence is required. The algorithms have good numerical properties. The family of stabilized fast RLS algorithms is very attractive from the viewpoint of computational efficiency. Methods of avoiding instability due to round-off errors have been proposed by Hsu (1982), Cioffi and Kailath (1984), Lin (1984), Eleftheriou and Falconer (1987), and Slock and Kailath (1988, 1991).

The adaptive lattice-ladder filter algorithms derived in this chapter included the optimum RLS lattice-ladder algorithm, both the conventional form and the error-feedback form, and the gradient lattice-ladder algorithm. Only the a priori form of the lattice-ladder algorithm was derived, which is the form used most often in applications. In addition, there is an a posteriori form of the RLS lattice-ladder algorithm, both conventional and error-feedback types, as described by Ling et al. (1986). The error-feedback forms of the RLS lattice-ladder algorithm and the gradient lattice-ladder algorithm have excellent numerical properties and are particularly suitable for implementation in fixed-point arithmetic and in VLSI.

In the direct-form and lattice RLS algorithms we used exponential weighting into the past to reduce the effective memory in the adaptation process. As an alternative to exponential weighting we may employ finite-length uniform weighting into the past. This approach leads to the class of finite-memory RLS direct-form and lattice structures described in the papers by Cioffi and Kalaith (1985) and Manolakis et al. (1987).

Only single-channel adaptive filtering algorithms have been presented in this chapter. Multichannel RLS algorithms are treated in Chapter 7.

In addition to the various algorithms that we have presented in this chapter, there has been considerable research into efficient implementation of these algorithms using systolic arrays and other parallel architectures. For reference, the reader is referred to publications by Kung (1982) and Kung et al. (1985).

PROBLEMS

6.1 Use the least-squares criterion to determine the equations for the parameters of the FIR filter model in Fig. 6.2 when the plant output is corrupted by additive noise $w(n)$.

6.2 Determine the equations for the coefficients of an adaptive echo canceler based on the least-squares criterion. Use the configuration in Fig. 6.8 and assume the presence of a near-end echo only.

6.3 If the sequence $w_1(n)$, $w_2(n)$, and $w_3(n)$ in the adaptive noise-canceling system shown in Fig. 6.14 are mutually uncorrelated, determine the expected value of the estimated correlation sequences $r_{vv}(k)$ and $r_{yv}(k)$ contained in (6.1.26).

6.4 Prove the result in (6.3.34).

6.5 Derive the equation for the direct update of the ladder gain given by (6.3.98).

6.6 Derive the direct-update equation for the reflection coefficients in a gradient lattice algorithm given in (6.3.106).

6.7 Derive the time-update relations given in (6.3.104).

6.8 Derive the FAEST algorithm given in Table 6.7 by using the alternative Kalman gain vector

$$\tilde{\mathbf{K}}_M(n) = \frac{1}{w}\mathbf{P}_M(n-1)\mathbf{X}_M^*(n)$$

instead of the Kalman gain vector $\mathbf{K}_M(n)$.

6.9 Prove the orthogonality property of the backward residual errors given by (6.3.112).

6.10 The tap-leakage LMS algorithm proposed in the paper by Gitlin et al. (1982) may be expressed as

$$\mathbf{h}_M(n+1) = w\mathbf{h}_M(n) + \Delta e(n)\mathbf{X}_M^*(n)$$

where $0 < w < 1$, Δ is the step size, and $\mathbf{X}_M(n)$ is the data vector at time n. Determine the condition for the convergence of the mean value of $\mathbf{h}_M(n)$.

6.11 By using the alternative Kalman gain vector given in Problem 6.8, modify the a priori fast least-squares algorithms given in Tables 6.2 and 6.3, and thus reduce the number of computations.

6.12 Consider the random process

$$x(n) = gv(n) + w(n), \qquad n = 0, 1, \ldots, M - 1$$

where $v(n)$ is a known sequence, g is a random variable with $E[g] = 0$, and $E[g^2] = G$. The process $w(n)$ is a white noise sequence with

$$\gamma_{ww}(m) = \sigma_w^2\, \delta(m)$$

Determine the coefficients of the linear estimator for g, that is,

$$\hat{g} = \sum_{n=0}^{M-1} h(n)x(n)$$

which minimizes the mean-square error

$$\mathscr{E} = E[(g - \hat{g})^2]$$

6.13 Recall that an FIR filter can be realized in the frequency-sampling form with system function

$$\begin{aligned} H(z) &= \frac{1 - z^{-M}}{M} \sum_{k=0}^{M-1} \frac{H_k}{1 - e^{j2\pi k/M} z^{-1}} \\ &= H_1(z)H_2(z) \end{aligned}$$

where $H_1(z)$ is the comb filter and $H_2(z)$ is the parallel bank of resonators.

(a) Suppose that this structure is implemented as an adaptive filter using the LMS algorithm to adjust the filter (DFT) parameters H_k. Give the time-update equation for these parameters. Sketch the adaptive filter structure.

(b) Suppose that this structure is used as an adaptive channel equalizer in which the desired signal is

$$d(n) = \sum_{k=0}^{M-1} A_k \cos \omega_k n, \qquad \omega_k = \frac{2\pi k}{M}$$

With this form for the desired signal what advantages are there in the (LMS) adaptive algorithm for the DFT coefficients H_k over the direct-form structure with coefficients $h(n)$? [*Hint:* Refer to the paper by Proakis (1970).]

6.14 Consider the performance index

$$J = h^2 - 40h + 28$$

Suppose that we search for the minimum of J by using the steepest-descent algorithm

$$h(n + 1) = h(n) - \tfrac{1}{2}\Delta g(n)$$

where $g(n)$ is the gradient.

(a) Determine the range of values of Δ that provides an overdamped system for the adjustment process.

(b) Plot the expression for J as a function of n for a value of Δ in this range.

6.15 Consider the noise-canceling adaptive filter shown in Fig. 6.14. Assume that the additive noise processes are white and mutually uncorrelated with equal variances σ_w^2. Suppose that the linear system has a known system function

$$H(z) = \frac{1}{1 - \frac{1}{2}z^{-1}}$$

Determine the optimum weights of a three-tap noise canceler that minimizes the MSE.

6.16 Determine the coefficients a_1 and a_2 for the linear predictor shown in Fig. P6. 16, given that the autocorrelation $\gamma_{xx}(m)$ of the input signal is

$$\gamma_{xx}(m) = a^{|m|}, \qquad 0 < a < 1$$

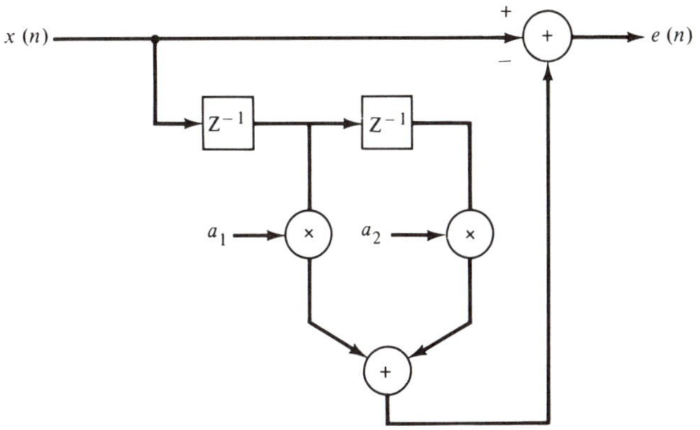

FIGURE P6.16

6.17 Determine the lattice filter and its optimum reflection coefficients corresponding to the linear predictor in Problem 6.16.

6.18 Consider the adaptive FIR filter shown in Fig. P6.18. The system $C(z)$ is characterized by the system function

$$C(z) = \frac{1}{1 - 0.9z^{-1}}$$

Determine the optimum coefficients of the adaptive FIR filter $B(z) = b_0 + b_1z^{-1}$ which minimize the mean-square error. The additive noise is white with variance $\sigma_w^2 = 0.1$.

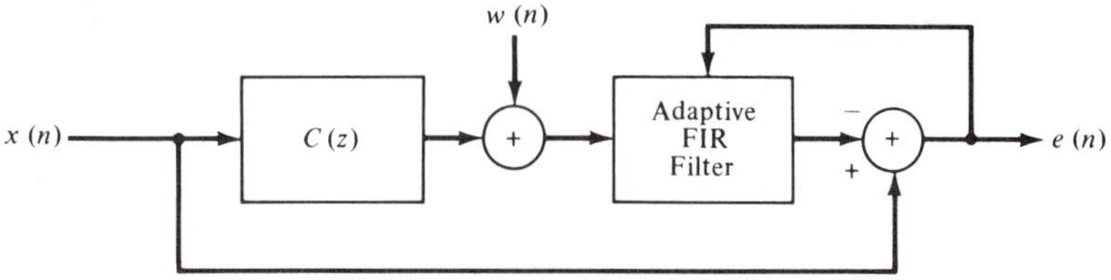

FIGURE P6.18

6.19 An $N \times N$ correlation matrix $\mathbf{\Gamma}$ has eigenvalues $\lambda_1 > \lambda_2 > \cdots > \lambda_N > 0$ and associated eigenvectors $\mathbf{v}_1, \mathbf{v}_2, \ldots, \mathbf{v}_N$. Such a matrix can be represented as

$$\mathbf{\Gamma} = \sum_{i=1}^{N} \lambda_i \mathbf{v}_i \mathbf{v}_i^H$$

(a) If $\mathbf{\Gamma} = \mathbf{\Gamma}^{1/2}\mathbf{\Gamma}^{1/2}$, where $\mathbf{\Gamma}^{1/2}$ is the square root of $\mathbf{\Gamma}$, show that $\mathbf{\Gamma}^{1/2}$ can be represented as

$$\mathbf{\Gamma}^{1/2} = \sum_{i=1}^{N} \lambda_i^{1/2} \mathbf{v}_i \mathbf{v}_i^H$$

(b) Using this representation, determine a procedure for computing $\mathbf{\Gamma}^{1/2}$.

COMPUTER EXPERIMENTS

6.20 Consider the adaptive predictor shown in Fig. P6.16.

(a) Determine the quadratic performance index and the optimum parameters for the signal

$$x(n) = \sin\frac{n\pi}{4} + w(n)$$

where $w(n)$ is white noise with variance $\sigma_w^2 = 0.1$.

(b) Generate a sequence of 1000 samples of $x(n)$ and use the LMS algorithm to adaptively obtain the predictor coefficients. Compare the experimental results with the theoretical values obtained in part (a). Use a step size of $\Delta \le \frac{1}{10}\Delta_{\max}$.

(c) Repeat the experiment in part (b) for $N = 10$ trials with different noise sequences and compute the average values of the predictor coefficients. Comment on how these results compare with the theoretical values in part (a).

6.21 An autoregressive process is described by the difference equation

$$x(n) = 1.26x(n-1) - 0.81x(n-2) + w(n)$$

(a) Generate a sequence of $N = 1000$ samples of $x(n)$, where $w(n)$ is a white noise sequence with variance $\sigma_w^2 = 0.1$. Use the LMS algorithm to determine the parameters of a second-order ($p = 2$) linear predictor. Begin with $a_1(0) = a_2(0) = 0$. Plot the coefficients $a_1(n)$ and $a_2(n)$ as a function of the iteration number.

(b) Repeat part (a) for 10 trials using different noise sequences and superimpose the 10 plots of $a_1(n)$ and $a_2(n)$.

(c) Plot the learning curve for the average (over the 10 trials) mean-square error for the data in part (b).

6.22 A random process $x(n)$ is given as

$$\begin{aligned} x(n) &= s(n) + w(n) \\ &= \sin(\omega_0 n + \phi) + w(n), \qquad \omega_0 = \pi/4, \quad \phi = 0 \end{aligned}$$

where $w(n)$ is an additive white noise sequence with variance $\sigma_w^2 = 0.1$.

(a) Generate $N = 1000$ samples of $x(n)$ and simulate an adaptive line enhancer (ALE) of length $L = 4$. Use the LMS algorithm to adapt the ALE.

(b) Plot the output of the ALE.

(c) Compute the autocorrelation $\gamma_{xx}(m)$ of the sequence $x(n)$.

(d) Determine the theoretical values of the ALE coefficients and compare them with the experimental values.

(e) Compute the frequency response of the linear predictor (ALE).

(f) Compute the frequency response of the prediction-error filter.

(g) Compute the experimental values of the autocorrelation $r_{ee}(m)$ of the output error sequence for $0 \le m < 10$.

(h) Repeat the experiment for 10 trials using different noise sequences and superimpose the frequency response plots on the same graph.

(i) Comment on the result in parts (a) through (h).

CHAPTER 7

RECURSIVE LEAST-SQUARES ALGORITHMS FOR ARRAY SIGNAL PROCESSING

In Chapter 6 we introduced the basic concepts in adaptive filtering, described the applications of adaptive filters, and developed several adaptive filtering algorithms. In this chapter we extend the development to two types of adaptive signal processing algorithms for least-squares (LS) adaptive estimation: namely, the LS estimation algorithms based on orthogonal transformations and order-recursive LS estimation algorithms.

Although all LS estimation algorithms solve the same set of equations, there are two reasons why we are interested in different types of LS estimation algorithms. First, the equivalence among different LS algorithms is exact only when infinite precision is used in computation. When finite-precision arithmetic is used in the implementation of the algorithms, the round-off error effects result in estimation errors that are generally different for different algorithms. The second reason for considering different types of LS estimation algorithms is concerned with the issues of efficiency and convenience of implementation. It is desirable to choose an algorithm that can be implemented efficiently. The issue of efficiency may be different for different types of implementations. For example, in commercially available digital signal processors, the use of many multiplications and accumulations (MACs) in a row is very efficient. On the other hand, in a systolic array implementation, modularity of an algorithm is preferable. The algorithms described in this chapter are considered from the viewpoint of computational efficiency and ease of implementation.

We refer to the orthogonal transformation-based LS algorithms and order-recursive LS algorithms described in this chapter as adaptive array signal-processing algorithms. The first reason for this terminology is that most of these algorithms, such as the LS algorithms based on the orthogonal transformations, were traditionally developed for and applied to adaptive radar antenna and sonar arrays. They are also called adaptive *spatial signal processing* algorithms, to distinguish these algorithms from algorithms for single time series. Second, these algorithms have modular structures and hence are suitable for implementation using systolic array processors. This feature makes the algorithms suitable for VLSI implementation, which results in a very high throughput. Consequently, these algorithms can be used in applications that require an extremely high sampling rate, such as radar signal processing.

7.1 QR DECOMPOSITION FOR LS ESTIMATION

The data vector $\mathbf{X}_M(n)$ in a spatial signal may be written in the general form

$$\mathbf{X}_M(n) = [x_1(n) \quad x_2(n) \quad \cdots \quad x_M(n)]^t \tag{7.1.1}$$

where $x_i(n)$, $1 \le i \le M$, may be viewed as representing the signal sequences of M sensors. From the data vectors $\mathbf{X}_M(l)$, $0 \le l \le n$, we construct an $(n + 1) \times M$ data matrix defined as

$$\mathbf{A}_M(n) = \begin{bmatrix} x_1(0) & x_2(0) & \cdots & x_M(0) \\ x_1(1) & x_2(1) & \cdots & x_M(1) \\ x_1(2) & x_2(2) & \cdots & x_M(2) \\ \vdots & \vdots & \vdots & \vdots \\ x_1(n) & x_2(n) & \cdots & x_M(n) \end{bmatrix} = \begin{bmatrix} \mathbf{X}_M^t(0) \\ \mathbf{X}_M^t(1) \\ \mathbf{X}_M^t(2) \\ \vdots \\ \mathbf{X}_M^t(n) \end{bmatrix} \tag{7.1.2}$$

$$= [\mathbf{a}_1(n) \quad \mathbf{a}_2(n) \quad \cdots \quad \mathbf{a}_M(n)]$$

where $\mathbf{a}_i(n)$, $i = 1, 2, \ldots, M$, are the column vectors of $\mathbf{A}_M(n)$. Our notation suggests that the dimension of the column vectors $\mathbf{a}_i(n)$ increases as new data are received.

Now, suppose that the data vectors are passed through an Mth-order linear combiner characterized by the coefficient vector $\mathbf{h}_M(n)$. As in the case of the adaptive FIR filter in Chapter 6, we may express the combiner output at time l, which is an estimate of the desired output $d(l)$, as

$$\hat{d}(l,n) = \mathbf{X}_M^t(l)\mathbf{h}_M(n)$$

and the estimation error between the desired output $d(l)$ and the actual output $\hat{d}(l,n)$ as

$$e_M(l,n) = d(l) - \hat{d}(l,n)$$

Let us use vector and matrix notation, which provides a more compact formulation of LS estimation. We define the desired signal vector as

$$\mathbf{d}(n) = [d(0) \quad \cdots \quad d(n-1) \quad d(n)]^t \tag{7.1.3}$$

and the error vector $\mathbf{e}_M(n)$ as

$$\mathbf{e}_M(n) \equiv \begin{bmatrix} e_M(0, n) \\ \vdots \\ e_M(n-1, n) \\ e_M(n, n) \end{bmatrix} = \mathbf{d}(n) - \mathbf{A}_M(n)\mathbf{h}_M(n) \tag{7.1.4}$$

Our objective is to determine the coefficient vector $\mathbf{h}_M(n)$ that minimizes the exponentially weighted sum of the magnitude-squared errors

$$\epsilon_M(n) = \sum_{l=0}^{n} w^{n-l}|e_M(l, n)|^2 \tag{7.1.5}$$

The weighted sum $\epsilon_M(n)$ can be written as the squared norm of the weighted error vector $\mathbf{e}_M(n)$. That is,

$$\epsilon_M(n) = \mathbf{e}_M^H(n)\mathbf{W}^2(n)\mathbf{e}_M(n) = \|\mathbf{W}(n)\mathbf{e}_M(n)\|^2 \tag{7.1.6}$$

where $\mathbf{W}(n)$ denotes the diagonal weighting matrix defined by $\mathbf{W}(n) = \text{diag}(\sqrt{w^n}, \sqrt{w^{n-1}}, \ldots, \sqrt{w}, 1)$, and $\|\cdot\|$ denotes the Euclidean norm of a vector.

The minimization of $\epsilon_M(n)$ with respect to $\mathbf{h}_M(n)$ yields the following matrix equation:

$$\mathbf{A}_M^H(n)\mathbf{W}^2(n)\mathbf{A}_M(n)\mathbf{h}_M(n) - \mathbf{A}_M^H\mathbf{W}^2(n)\mathbf{d}(n) = \mathbf{0} \tag{7.1.7}$$

The optimal coefficient vector $\mathbf{h}_M(n)$ is determined by solving (7.1.7). When $\mathbf{h}_M(n)$ satisfies (7.1.7), it is called the *LS estimator coefficient vector at time n* and the vector $\mathbf{e}_M(n)$ in (7.1.4) is called the *LS estimation error vector.*† We shall use the QR decomposition to obtain the LS solution.

Recall that for an arbitrary $N \times M$ matrix $\mathbf{A}$, $N > M$, there always exists an $N \times N$ orthogonal matrix $\mathbf{Q}$, such that $\mathbf{QA} = \begin{bmatrix} \mathfrak{R} \\ \mathbf{0} \end{bmatrix}$, where $\mathfrak{R}$ is an upper triangular square matrix and $\mathbf{0}$ is a zero matrix. Equivalently, we have $\mathbf{A} = \mathbf{Q}^H\begin{bmatrix} \mathfrak{R} \\ \mathbf{0} \end{bmatrix}$. The construction of $\mathbf{Q}$ and $\mathfrak{R}$ was described in Section 5.3. Hence let us assume that the orthogonal matrix $\mathbf{Q}(n)$ and the triangular matrix $\mathfrak{R}(n)$ form a QR decomposition of the data matrix $\mathbf{W}(n)\mathbf{A}_M(n)$,

$$\mathbf{Q}(n)\mathbf{W}(n)\mathbf{A}_M(n) = \begin{bmatrix} \mathfrak{R}(n) \\ \mathbf{0} \end{bmatrix} \tag{7.1.8}$$

By premultiplying (7.1.4) by $\mathbf{Q}(n)\mathbf{W}(n)$, we obtain

$$\mathbf{Q}(n)\mathbf{W}(n)\mathbf{e}_M(n) = \mathbf{Q}(n)\mathbf{W}(n)\mathbf{d}(n) - \begin{bmatrix} \mathfrak{R}(n) \\ \mathbf{0} \end{bmatrix}\mathbf{h}_M(n) \tag{7.1.9}$$

where

$$\mathfrak{R}(n) = \begin{bmatrix} r_{11}(n) & r_{12}(n) & r_{13}(n) & \cdots & r_{1M}(n) \\ & r_{22}(n) & r_{23}(n) & \cdots & r_{2M}(n) \\ & & r_{33}(n) & \ddots & \vdots \\ & \mathbf{0} & & \ddots & r_{M-1,M}(n) \\ & & & & r_{MM}(n) \end{bmatrix} \tag{7.1.10}$$

† To facilitate the discussion in this chapter, it is sometimes necessary to specify the data vectors and the desired signal vector that generate a certain estimation error vector. In such cases we define, for example, $\mathbf{e}_M(n)$ to be the *LS estimation error vector of* $\boldsymbol{d}(n)$ *based on the data vector set* $\boldsymbol{a}_i(n)$, $i = 1, 2, \ldots, M$, or, simply, *based on the data matrix* $\mathbf{A}_M(n)$.

As has been shown in Section 5.3, the optimal coefficient vector $\mathbf{h}_M(n)$ satisfies the equation

$$\mathcal{R}(n)\mathbf{h}_M(n) = \tilde{\mathbf{d}}_M(n) \tag{7.1.11}$$

where $\tilde{\mathbf{d}}_M(n)$ is a vector consisting of the top M elements of $\mathbf{Q}(n)\mathbf{W}(n)\mathbf{d}(n)$.

By factoring out the diagonal elements of $\mathcal{R}(n)$, we can express $\mathcal{R}(n)$ as

$$\mathcal{R}(n) = \mathbf{\Lambda}(n)\tilde{\mathcal{R}}(n) \tag{7.1.12}$$

where $\mathbf{\Lambda}(n)$ is a diagonal matrix, defined as $\mathbf{\Lambda}(n) = \text{diag}\{r_{11}(n), \ldots, r_{MM}(n)\}$ and $\tilde{\mathcal{R}}(n)$ is an upper triangular matrix with all its diagonal elements equal to unity,

$$\tilde{\mathcal{R}}(n) = \begin{bmatrix} 1 & \tilde{r}_{12}(n) & \tilde{r}_{13}(n) & \cdots & \tilde{r}_{1M}(n) \\ & 1 & \tilde{r}_{23}(n) & \cdots & \tilde{r}_{2M}(n) \\ & & 1 & \ddots & \vdots \\ & \mathbf{0} & & \ddots & \tilde{r}_{M-1,M}(n) \\ & & & & 1 \end{bmatrix} \tag{7.1.13}$$

where $\tilde{r}_{ij}(n) = r_{ij}(n)/r_{ii}(n)$. As a consequence, it follows that $\mathbf{h}_M(n)$ also satisfies

$$\tilde{\mathcal{R}}(n)\mathbf{h}_M(n) = \mathbf{\Lambda}^{-1}(n)\tilde{\mathbf{d}}_M(n) \tag{7.1.14}$$

From the results given in Section 5.3, it also follows that the matrices $\tilde{\mathcal{R}}^H(n)$, $\mathbf{\Lambda}^2(n)$, and $\tilde{\mathcal{R}}(n)$ form the LDU decomposition of the autocorrelation matrix $\mathbf{R}_M(n)$. It is more convenient to define a diagonal matrix $\mathbf{D}(n) \equiv \mathbf{\Lambda}^2(n)$. Then (7.1.14) may be expressed as

$$\tilde{\mathcal{R}}(n)\mathbf{h}_M(n) = \mathbf{D}^{-1/2}(n)\tilde{\mathbf{d}}_M(n) \tag{7.1.15}$$

It will be shown later that (7.1.15) is the basis for various QR-decomposition-based LS estimation algorithms that do not require square-root operations.

Time-Recursive Form of the QR Decomposition. In Section 5.3 we have shown how to use a QR decomposition to solve the LS estimation problem at time n using the data from 0 to n. Now, suppose that we have obtained the solution $\mathbf{h}_M(n-1)$ and we wish to update it upon receiving a new data vector $\mathbf{X}_M(n)$. Thus we seek a *time-recursive* implementation of LS estimation. Below we show *the time-recursive relation* for the QR-decomposition.

Let us assume that the QR decomposition of the exponentially weighted data matrix $\mathbf{W}(n-1)\mathbf{A}_M(n-1)$ at time $n-1$ has been computed as

$$\mathbf{Q}(n-1)\mathbf{W}(n-1)\mathbf{A}_M(n-1) = \begin{bmatrix} \mathcal{R}(n-1) \\ \mathbf{0} \end{bmatrix} \tag{7.1.16}$$

Now we demonstrate that computing the QR decomposition of the matrix $\mathbf{W}(n)\mathbf{A}_M(n)$ at time n is equivalent to determining the QR decomposition of the $(M + 1) \times M$ matrix $\begin{bmatrix} \sqrt{w}\,\mathcal{R}(n-1) \\ \mathbf{X}_M^t(n) \end{bmatrix}$. First, it is easy to show that $\mathbf{W}(n)\mathbf{A}_M(n)$ can be expressed as

$$\mathbf{W}(n)\mathbf{A}_M(n) = \begin{bmatrix} \sqrt{w}\,\mathbf{W}(n-1)\mathbf{A}_M(n-1) \\ \mathbf{X}_M^t(n) \end{bmatrix} \tag{7.1.17}$$

Second, from the matrix $\mathbf{Q}(n - 1)$ in (7.1.16), we construct a matrix $\mathbf{Q}'(n - 1)$ such that

$$\mathbf{Q}'(n-1) = \begin{bmatrix} \mathbf{Q}(n-1) & \mathbf{0} \\ \mathbf{0}^t & 1 \end{bmatrix} \tag{7.1.18}$$

Then it follows from (7.1.16) through (7.1.18) that

$$\mathbf{Q}'(n-1)\mathbf{W}(n)\mathbf{A}_M(n) = \begin{bmatrix} \mathbf{Q}(n-1)\sqrt{w}\,\mathbf{W}(n-1)\mathbf{A}_M(n-1) \\ \mathbf{X}_M^t(n) \end{bmatrix}$$

$$= \begin{bmatrix} \sqrt{w}\,\mathcal{R}(n-1) \\ \mathbf{0} \\ \mathbf{X}_M^t(n) \end{bmatrix} \tag{7.1.19}$$

Now, suppose that we construct an orthogonal matrix $\hat{\mathbf{Q}}(n)$ that performs the QR decomposition of the matrix on the right side of (7.1.19). Then we can use the orthogonal matrix $\hat{\mathbf{Q}}(n)\mathbf{Q}'(n - 1)$ to achieve the QR decomposition of the matrix $\mathbf{W}(n)\mathbf{A}_M(n)$. On the other hand, constructing $\hat{\mathbf{Q}}(n)$ is equivalent to finding an orthogonal matrix that performs the QR decomposition of the matrix $\begin{bmatrix} \sqrt{w}\,\mathcal{R}(n-1) \\ \mathbf{X}_M^t(n) \end{bmatrix}$, because the zeros at the middle of the matrix on the right side of (7.1.19) have no affect on the construction of $\hat{\mathbf{Q}}(n)$. Thus we have shown the equivalence between a data matrix and its R-factor when a new row data vector is added and a new QR decomposition is required. This method can be used for any QR-decomposition-based LS estimation algorithm when a new data vector is added after a QR decomposition has been constructed for data previously available.

Instead of adding one row of new data as described above, we may add a block of L rows of new data, $L > 1$, to the data matrix. In such a case, the equivalence between the data matrix and its R-factor is still valid. If exponential weighting is desired, it is convenient to weight the data on a block-by-block basis. Thus we perform *block-exponentially weighted* LS estimation. It should be pointed out that it is also possible to add L rows of data at a time and still obtain the same result as in the normal row-by-row exponentially weighted LS estimation. This will require proper preweighting of each of the new rows, and scaling the previous R-factor by $\sqrt{w^L}$.

7.2 GRAM–SCHMIDT ORTHOGONALIZATION FOR LS ESTIMATION

In Section 5.3 we presented the original Gram–Schmidt and modified Gram–Schmidt (MGS) algorithms. It was also shown that we can use these algorithms to perform QR decomposition of the autocorrelation matrix $\mathbf{R}_M(n)$. In this section we show how to use the modified Gram–Schmidt algorithm to solve the LS estimation problem. In particular, a time-recursive form of the MGS algorithm is derived. Its variations and a systolic array implementation are also presented.

7.2.1 Least-Squares Estimation Using the MGS Algorithm

In order to solve for the coefficient vector $\mathbf{h}_M(n)$, we need to compute the vector $\tilde{\mathbf{d}}_M(n)$, which consists of the top M elements of $\mathbf{Q}(n)\mathbf{W}(n)\mathbf{d}(n)$. It can be shown that the ith element of $\tilde{\mathbf{d}}_M(n)$, $\tilde{d}_i(n)$, $i = 1, 2, \ldots, M$, can be expressed as

$$\tilde{d}_i(n) = \frac{\mathbf{q}_i^H(n)\mathbf{W}(n)\mathbf{d}(n)}{\sqrt{\delta_i(n)}} = \frac{k_{id}(n)}{\sqrt{\delta_i(n)}} \tag{7.2.1}$$

and hence

$$\tilde{\mathbf{d}}_M(n) = \tilde{\mathbf{D}}^{-1/2}(n)\mathbf{k}_{Md}(n) \tag{7.2.2}$$

where $\tilde{\mathbf{D}}(n) = \operatorname{diag}[\delta_1(n), \delta_2(n), \ldots, \delta_M(n)]$ and $\mathbf{k}_{Md}(n) = [k_{1d}(n), k_{2d}(n), \ldots, k_{Md}(n)]^t$. Then the coefficient vector $\mathbf{h}_M(n)$ can be computed by solving

$$\mathcal{R}(n)\mathbf{h}_M(n) = \tilde{\mathbf{d}}_M(n) \tag{7.2.3}$$

From (5.3.72), we have the relationship

$$\mathcal{R}(n) = \mathbf{D}^{1/2}(n)\tilde{\mathcal{R}}(n) \tag{7.2.4}$$

Then, by using (7.2.2) and (7.2.4) in (7.2.3) we obtain the result

$$\begin{aligned}\tilde{\mathcal{R}}(n)\mathbf{h}_M(n) &= \tilde{\mathbf{D}}^{-1/2}(n)\tilde{\mathbf{d}}_M(n) = \tilde{\mathbf{D}}^{-1/2}(n)\tilde{\mathbf{D}}^{-1/2}(n)\mathbf{k}_{Md}(n) \\ &= \tilde{\mathbf{D}}^{-1}(n)\mathbf{k}_{Md}(n) \equiv \tilde{\mathbf{r}}_{Md}(n)\end{aligned} \tag{7.2.5}$$

The quantities k_{id} defined by (7.2.1) can be computed iteratively similar to (5.3.63) through (5.3.68), for $i = 1$ to M, as

$$\mathbf{e}^{(1)}(n) = \mathbf{W}(n)\mathbf{d}(n) \tag{7.2.6}$$

$$k_{id}(n) = \mathbf{q}_i^H(n)\mathbf{e}^{(i)}(n) \tag{7.2.7}$$

$$\tilde{r}_{id}(n) = \frac{k_{id}(n)}{\delta_i(n)} \tag{7.2.8}$$

$$\mathbf{e}^{(i+1)}(n) = \mathbf{e}^{(i)}(n) - \tilde{r}_{id}(n)\mathbf{q}_i(n) \tag{7.2.9}$$

The last vector $\mathbf{e}^{(M+1)}(n)$ computed in (7.2.9), denoted by $\mathbf{e}_W(n)$, can be written as

$$\begin{aligned}\mathbf{e}_W(n) &= \mathbf{W}(n)\mathbf{d}(n) - \sum_{k=1}^{M} \tilde{r}_{kd}(n)\mathbf{q}_k(n) \\ &= \mathbf{W}(n)\mathbf{d}(n) - [\mathbf{q}_1(n) \quad \mathbf{q}_2(n) \quad \cdots \quad \mathbf{q}_M(n)]\tilde{\mathbf{r}}_{Md}(n)\end{aligned} \tag{7.2.10}$$

Then we can combine (5.3.69) and (7.2.10) into the following matrix equation:

$$[\mathbf{W}(n)\mathbf{a}_1(n) \quad \cdots \quad \mathbf{W}(n)\mathbf{a}_M(n) \quad \mathbf{W}(n)\mathbf{d}(n)] = [\mathbf{q}_1(n) \quad \cdots \quad \mathbf{q}_M(n) \quad \mathbf{e}_W(n)]\overline{\mathfrak{R}}(n) \tag{7.2.11}$$

where

$$\overline{\mathfrak{R}}(n) = \begin{bmatrix} 1 \; \tilde{r}_{12}(n) & \cdots & \tilde{r}_{1M}(n) & \tilde{r}_{1d}(n) \\ 1 & \cdots & \tilde{r}_{2M}(n) & \tilde{r}_{2d}(n) \\ & \ddots & \vdots & \vdots \\ \mathbf{0} & & 1 & \tilde{r}_{Md}(n) \\ & & & 1 \end{bmatrix} = \begin{bmatrix} \tilde{\mathfrak{R}}(n) & \tilde{\mathbf{r}}_{Md}(n) \\ \mathbf{0}^t & 1 \end{bmatrix} \tag{7.2.12}$$

By comparing (7.2.10) with (5.3.69), we conclude that the $k_{id}(n)$'s can be computed together with the $k_{ij}(n)$'s by applying the MGS algorithm to the $M + 1$ column vectors of the augmented matrix $\overline{\mathbf{A}}_{M+1}(n) = [\mathbf{W}(n)\mathbf{A}_M(n), \mathbf{W}(n)\mathbf{d}(n)]$. The coefficient vector $\mathbf{h}_M(n)$ can be computed using (7.2.5). The MGS algorithm is summarized in Table 7.1.

7.2.2 Physical Meaning of the Quantities in the MGS Algorithm

The orthogonal vectors, $\mathbf{q}_i(n)$'s and the error vector $\mathbf{e}_W(n)$ have clear physical meanings. First, let us consider the error vector $\mathbf{e}_W(n)$. It follows from (7.2.11) that

$$[\mathbf{q}_1(n) \quad \mathbf{q}_2(n) \quad \cdots \quad \mathbf{q}_M(n)] = \mathbf{W}(n)\mathbf{A}_M(n)\tilde{\mathfrak{R}}^{-1}(n) \tag{7.2.13}$$

By substituting (7.2.13) into (7.2.10) and using (7.2.5), we obtain

$$\begin{aligned}\mathbf{e}_W(n) &= \mathbf{W}(n)\mathbf{d}(n) - \mathbf{W}(n)\mathbf{A}_M(n)\tilde{\mathfrak{R}}^{-1}(n)\tilde{\mathbf{r}}_{Md}(n) \\ &= \mathbf{W}(n)[\mathbf{d}(n) - \mathbf{A}_M(n)\mathbf{h}_M(n)]\end{aligned} \tag{7.2.14}$$

By comparing (7.2.14) with (7.1.4) we conclude that $\mathbf{e}_W(n)$ is the exponentially weighted error vector of $\mathbf{d}(n)$ that is estimated based on the data vector set $\{\mathbf{a}_i(n), i = 1, 2, \ldots, M\}$.

Similarly, it can be shown that the orthogonal vectors $\mathbf{q}_k(n)$, $k = 1, 2, \ldots, M$, are the exponentially weighted error vectors of $\mathbf{a}_k(n)$ that are estimated based on the data vector set $\{\mathbf{a}_i(n), i = 1, 2, \ldots, k - 1\}$, respectively. Another useful vector set $\{\mathbf{e}^{(k+1)}(n), k = 1, 2, \ldots, M\}$ is the set of exponentially weighted error vectors of $\mathbf{d}(n)$ that are estimated based on k data vectors, $\mathbf{a}_i(n)$, $i = 1, 2, \ldots, k$. We call $\mathbf{e}^{(k+1)}(n)$ an error vector

TABLE 7.1 Modified Gram–Schmidt (MGS) Algorithm

Initialization

$$\mathbf{e}^{(1)}(n) = \mathbf{W}(n)\mathbf{d}(n),\ \mathbf{q}_i^{(1)}(n) = \mathbf{W}(n)\mathbf{a}_i(n), \quad i = 1, 2, \ldots, M$$

$$\text{do } i = 1, 2, \ldots, M$$
$$\mathbf{q}_i(n) = \mathbf{q}_i^{(i)}(n)$$
$$\delta_i(n) = k_{ii}(n) = \mathbf{q}_i^H(n)\mathbf{q}_i(n)$$

$$\text{do } j = i + 1, i + 2, \ldots, M$$
$$k_{ij}(n) = \mathbf{q}_i^H(n)\mathbf{q}_j^{(i)}(n)$$
$$\tilde{r}_{ij}(n) = k_{ij}(n)/\delta_i(n)$$
$$\mathbf{q}_j^{(i+1)}(n) = \mathbf{q}_j^{(i)}(n) - \tilde{r}_{ij}(n)\mathbf{q}_i(n)$$
$$\text{end of loop } j$$

$$k_{id}(n) = \mathbf{q}_i^H(n)\mathbf{e}^{(i)}(n)$$
$$\tilde{r}_{id}(n) = k_{id}(n)/\delta_i(n)$$
$$\mathbf{e}^{(i+1)}(n) = \mathbf{e}^{(i)}(n) - \tilde{r}_{id}(n)\mathbf{q}_i(n)$$
$$\text{end of loop } i$$

of order k, and we call the MGS algorithm an *order-recursive* LS estimation algorithm, which is discussed further in Section 7.5.

Next let us examine the scalar quantities computed in the MGS algorithm. First we denote the lth elements of the error vectors $\mathbf{q}_i^{(k)}(n)$ and $\mathbf{e}^{(k)}(n)$ by $q_i^{(k)}(l,n)$ and $e^{(k)}(l,n)$, respectively. The first index, l, means that they are the lth elements in the vectors. The second index, n, indicates they are estimated using the optimum coefficients at time n. In particular, the last elements in these vectors, denoted by $q_i^{(k)}(n,n)$ and $e^{(k)}(n,n)$, have special importance. They are the LS estimation errors at time n using the optimal LS coefficients at time n. These most recent estimation errors are useful in many adaptive filtering and estimation problems, as we observed in the recursive estimation algorithms in Chapter 6. In such applications, the optimal estimation coefficient vector $\mathbf{h}_M(n)$ and the orthogonal vector set need not be computed explicitly as long as the estimation errors are obtained. These errors also play an important role in the *time-recursive* MGS algorithm to be described below.

It can be seen from (5.3.66) and Table 7.1 that $k_{ij}(n)$ is the dot product of the LS error vectors $\mathbf{q}_j^{(i)}(n)$ and $\mathbf{q}_i(n)$. This can be viewed as the cross-correlation between the LS error components $q_j^{(i)}(l,n)$ and $q_i(l,n)$. Note that both of the error vectors are estimated based on the same data vector set [i.e., $\mathbf{W}(n)\mathbf{a}_1(n)$ through $\mathbf{W}(n)\mathbf{a}_{i-1}(n)$]. Similarly, from (7.2.7) we view $k_{id}(n)$ as the cross-correlation between the LS errors $e^{(i)}(l,n)$ and $q_i(l,n)$, and $\delta_i(n)$ is the autocorrelation of $q_i(l,n)$, which is also the total energy of the error vector $\mathbf{q}_i(n)$. We can also define $\epsilon_w(n) \equiv \mathbf{e}_w^H(n)\mathbf{e}_w(n)$, which is the total energy in $\mathbf{e}_w(n)$.

7.2.3 Time-Recursive Form of the Modified Gram–Schmidt (RMGS) Algorithm

The original MGS algorithm is a block processing algorithm. It takes a block of data $\mathbf{X}_M(k)$ and $d(k)$, $k = 1, \ldots, n$, and computes a set of parameters $k_{ij}(n)$, $k_{id}(n)$, and $\delta_i(n)$, as well as the error vectors $\mathbf{e}^{(i)}(n)$ and $\mathbf{q}_i(n)$. When the LS estimator coefficient vector $\mathbf{h}_M(n)$ is required in the application, it can be computed from the parameters $k_{ij}(n)$, $k_{id}(n)$, and $\delta_i(n)$. In other estimation and filtering applications, the most recent LS estimation error $e(n,n)$, the last element of the error vector $\mathbf{e}_w(n)$, is the desired quantity. The orthogonal vector set is usually not used in the LS estimation solution.

In some applications it is desirable to obtain the most recent LS estimation error and/or the LS estimation coefficient vector at each time instant. In such applications the MGS algorithm is not the appropriate algorithm. For example, suppose that we have solved the LS problem by using the MGS algorithm and have computed all the required quantities at time $n - 1$. Then at time n we have a new data set $\mathbf{X}_M(n)$ and $d(n)$. To use the MGS algorithm to compute the new LS error $e(n,n)$ or the LS coefficient vector $\mathbf{h}_M(n)$, we have to repeat the entire computation. This is obviously computationally inefficient. Instead, we wish to take advantage of the previously computed parameters at time $n - 1$ [i.e., $k_{ij}(n - 1)$, $k_{id}(n - 1)$, and $\delta_i(n - 1)$] to reduce the computational burden in obtaining $e(n,n)$ or $\mathbf{h}_M(n)$. Hence we desire a time-recursive implementation of the MGS algorithm, which we call the *RMGS algorithm*.

The RMGS algorithm, derived by Ling et al. (1986), is given below. We first write

$$\mathbf{q}_j^{(1)}(n) = \mathbf{W}(n)\mathbf{a}_j(n) = \begin{bmatrix} \sqrt{w}\,\mathbf{W}(n-1)\mathbf{a}_j(n-1) \\ x_j(n) \end{bmatrix} = \begin{bmatrix} \sqrt{w}\,\mathbf{q}_j^{(1)}(n-1) \\ q_j^{(1)}(n,n) \end{bmatrix} \tag{7.2.15}$$

$j = 1, 2, \ldots, M + 1$. To simplify notation, let us treat the $M + 1$ column vector $\mathbf{d}(n)$ the same as the other M column vectors and denote it as $\mathbf{q}_{M+1}^{(1)}(n)$. According to the MGS algorithm given by Table 7.1, let us consider the first step (i.e., $i = 1$). From (7.2.15) it is easy to show that for $j = 1, 2, \ldots, M + 1$,

$$\begin{aligned} k_{1j}(n) &= \mathbf{q}_1^H(n)\mathbf{q}_j^{(1)}(n) = w\mathbf{q}_1^H(n-1)\mathbf{q}_j^{(1)}(n-1) + q_1^*(n,n)q_j^{(1)}(n,n) \\ &= wk_{1j}(n-1) + q_1^*(n,n)q_j^{(1)}(n,n) \end{aligned} \tag{7.2.16}$$

where $\mathbf{q}_1(n) = \mathbf{q}_1^{(1)}(n)$ and

$$\delta_1(n) = k_{11}(n) = w\delta_1(n-1) + |q_1(n,n)|^2 \tag{7.2.17}$$

Equation (7.2.16) shows that we can compute $k_{1j}(n)$ directly from $k_{1j}(n - 1)$, $q_1(n,n)$ and $q_j^{(1)}(n,n)$, the last elements of $\mathbf{q}_1(n,n)$ and $\mathbf{q}_j^{(1)}(n)$, respectively. The vectors $\mathbf{q}_1(n)$ and $\mathbf{q}_j^{(1)}(n)$ need not be computed explicitly. Thus, we obtain the *time-recursive* formula for $k_{1j}(n)$. Now, we are ready to compute the vectors $\mathbf{q}_j^{(2)}(n)$, $j = 2, 3, \ldots, M + 1$. By using the values $\delta_1(n)$ and $k_{1j}(n)$ obtained above and from (5.3.68) and (7.2.15), we obtain

$$\mathbf{q}_j^{(2)}(n) = \mathbf{q}_j^{(1)}(n) - \tilde{r}_{1j}(n)\mathbf{q}_1(n) = \begin{bmatrix} \sqrt{w}[\mathbf{q}_j^{(1)}(n-1) - \tilde{r}_{1j}(n)\mathbf{q}_1(n-1)] \\ q_j^{(1)}(n,n) - \tilde{r}_{1j}(n)q_1(n,n) \end{bmatrix} \tag{7.2.18}$$

where $\tilde{r}_{1j}(n) = k_{1j}(n)/\delta_1(n)$. This completes step 1.

At step 2, we first compute the correlations $k_{2j}(n)$ and $\delta_2(n)$. Using (7.2.16) and (7.2.17), we can write $\tilde{r}_{1j}(n)$ as

$$\begin{aligned} \tilde{r}_{1j}(n) &= \frac{k_{1j}(n-1)}{\delta_1(n-1)} + \frac{k_{1j}(n)\delta_1(n-1)/\delta_1(n) - k_{1j}(n-1)}{\delta_1(n-1)} \\ &= \tilde{r}_{1j}(n-1) + \frac{k_{1j}(n) - k_{1j}(n)/\delta_1(n)|q_1(n,n)|^2 - k_{1j}(n) + q_1^*(n,n)q_j^{(1)}(n,n)}{w\delta_1(n-1)} \\ &= \tilde{r}_{1j}(n-1) + \frac{q_1^*(n,n)[q_j^{(1)}(n,n) - \tilde{r}_{1j}(n)q_1(n,n)]}{w\delta_1(n-1)} \\ &= \tilde{r}_{1j}(n-1) + \frac{q_1^*(n,n)q_j^{(2)}(n,n)}{w\delta_1(n-1)} \end{aligned} \tag{7.2.19}$$

where we denote $q_j^{(1)}(n,n) - \tilde{r}_{1j}(n)q_1(n,n)$ by $q_j^{(2)}(n,n)$, which is also the last element of $\mathbf{q}_j^{(2)}(n)$. By substituting (7.2.19) into (7.2.18), we obtain

$$\begin{aligned} &\mathbf{q}_j^{(2)}(n) \\ &= \begin{bmatrix} \sqrt{w}\,[\mathbf{q}_j^{(1)}(n-1) - \tilde{r}_{1j}(n-1)\mathbf{q}_1(n-1) - \dfrac{q_1^*(n,n)q_j^{(2)}(n,n)}{w\delta_1(n-1)}\mathbf{q}_1(n-1)] \\ q_j^{(2)}(n,n) \end{bmatrix} \\ &= \begin{bmatrix} \sqrt{w}\,\mathbf{q}_j^{(2)}(n-1) \\ 0 \end{bmatrix} - q_j^{(2)}(n,n)\begin{bmatrix} \dfrac{q_1^*(n,n)\mathbf{q}_1(n-1)}{\sqrt{w}\,\delta_1(n-1)]} \\ 1 \end{bmatrix} \end{aligned} \tag{7.2.20}$$

From (7.2.20), it follows that

$$\begin{aligned} k_{2j}(n) &= \mathbf{q}_2^H(n)\mathbf{q}_j^{(2)}(n) \\ &= w\mathbf{q}_2^H(n-1)\mathbf{q}_j^{(2)}(n-1) + q_2^*(n,n)q_j^{(2)}(n,n) \\ &\quad \times \left[1 + \frac{|q_1(n,n)|^2\mathbf{q}_1^H(n-1)\mathbf{q}_1(n-1)}{w\delta_1^2(n-1)}\right] \\ &= wk_{2j}(n-1) + \left[1 + \frac{|q_1(n,n)|^2}{w\delta_1(n-1)}\right] q_2^*(n,n)q_j^{(2)}(n,n) \\ &= wk_{2j}(n-1) + \hat{\alpha}_1(n)q_2^*(n,n)q_j^{(2)}(n,n) \end{aligned} \tag{7.2.21}$$

where we have used the fact that $\mathbf{q}_1(n-1)$ is orthogonal to $\mathbf{q}_j^{(2)}(n-1)$, $j = 2, 3, \ldots, M+1$, and $\mathbf{q}_1^H(n-1)\mathbf{q}_1(n-1) = \delta_1(n-1)$. We have also defined the quantity $\hat{\alpha}_1(n) = 1 + |q_1(n,n)|^2/w\delta_1(n-1)$ in (7.2.21) to simplify notation. As a special case of $k_{2j}(n)$, we have

$$\delta_2(n) = k_{22}(n) = w\delta_2(n-1) + \hat{\alpha}_1(n)|q_2(n,n)|^2 \tag{7.2.22}$$

Due to the similarity of (7.2.16) and (7.2.17) with (7.2.21) and (7.2.22), the latter are called the time-recursive equations for $k_{2j}(n)$ and $\delta_2(n)$, respectively.

From (7.2.20) we obtain the vectors $\mathbf{q}_j^{(3)}(n) = \mathbf{q}_j^{(2)}(n) - \tilde{r}_{2j}(n)\mathbf{q}_2(n)$, where $\tilde{r}_{2j}(n) = k_{2j}(n)/\delta_2(n)$ and $j = 3, \ldots, M$, as

$$\mathbf{q}_j^{(3)}(n) = \begin{bmatrix} \sqrt{w}[\mathbf{q}_j^{(2)}(n-1) - \tilde{r}_{2j}(n)\mathbf{q}_2(n-1)] \\ 0 \end{bmatrix} - [q_j^{(2)}(n,n) - \tilde{r}_{2j}(n)q_2(n,n)]\begin{bmatrix} \dfrac{\mathbf{q}_1^*(n,n)\mathbf{q}_1(n-1)}{\sqrt{w}\,\delta_1(n-1)]} \\ 1 \end{bmatrix} \tag{7.2.23}$$

As in the derivation of (7.2.19), by using (7.2.21) and (7.2.22), we can express $\tilde{r}_{2j}(n)$ as

$$\begin{aligned} \tilde{r}_{2j}(n) &= \frac{k_{2j}(n-1)}{\delta_2(n-1)} + \frac{k_{2j}(n)\delta_2(n-1)/\delta_2(n) - k_{2j}(n-1)}{\delta_2(n-1)} \\ &= \tilde{r}_{2j}(n-1) + \frac{\hat{\alpha}_1(n)q_2^*(n,n)[q_j^{(2)}(n,n) - \tilde{r}_{2j}(n)q_2(n,n)]}{w\delta_2(n-1)} \\ &= \tilde{r}_{2j}(n-1) + \frac{q_2^*(n,n)q_j^{(3)}(n,n)}{w\delta_2(n-1)}\hat{\alpha}_1(n) \end{aligned} \tag{7.2.24}$$

where $q_j^{(3)}(n,n) = q_j^{(2)}(n,n) - \tilde{r}_{2j}(n)q_2(n,n)$. Then by substituting (7.2.24) into (7.2.23), we obtain

$$\begin{aligned} \mathbf{q}_j^{(3)}(n) &= \begin{bmatrix} \sqrt{w}\,[\mathbf{q}_j^{(2)}(n-1) - \tilde{r}_{2j}(n-1)\mathbf{q}_2(n-1)] \\ 0 \end{bmatrix} \\ &\quad - q_j^{(3)}(n,n)\begin{bmatrix} \dfrac{\hat{\alpha}_1(n)q_2^*(n,n)\mathbf{q}_2(n-1)}{w\delta_2(n-1)} \\ 0 \end{bmatrix} \\ &\quad - q_j^{(3)}(n,n)\begin{bmatrix} \dfrac{q_1^*(n,n)}{w\delta_1(n-1)}\mathbf{q}_1(n-1) \\ 1 \end{bmatrix} \\ &= \begin{bmatrix} \sqrt{w}\,\mathbf{q}_j^{(3)}(n-1) \\ 0 \end{bmatrix} - q_j^{(3)}(n,n)\begin{bmatrix} \displaystyle\sum_{k=1}^{2} \frac{\hat{\alpha}_{k-1}(n_1)q_k^*(n,n)\mathbf{q}_k(n-1)}{w\delta_k(n-1)} \\ 1 \end{bmatrix} \end{aligned} \tag{7.2.25}$$

where we define $\hat{\alpha}_0(n) = 1$. Now we have reached the end of step 2.

As in the derivation of (7.2.21), $k_{3j}(n) = \mathbf{q}_3^H(n)\mathbf{q}_j^{(3)}(n)$, where $\mathbf{q}_3(n) = \mathbf{q}_3^{(3)}(n)$ and hence

$$\begin{aligned} k_{3j}(n) &= wk_{3j}(n-1) + q_3^*(n,n)q_j^{(3)}(n,n) \\ &\quad \times \left[1 + \frac{|q_1(n,n)|^2}{w\delta_1(n-1)} + \frac{\hat{\alpha}_1^2(n)q_2(n,n)|^2}{w\delta_2(n-1)}\right] \\ &= wk_{3j}(n-1) + q_3^*(n,n)q_j^{(3)}(n,n)\hat{\alpha}_2(n) \end{aligned} \tag{7.2.26}$$

where

$$\hat{\alpha}_2(n) = 1 + \frac{|q_1(n,n)|^2}{w\delta_1(n-1)} + \frac{\hat{\alpha}_1^2(n)|q_2(n,n)|^2}{w\delta_2(n-1)} \tag{7.2.27}$$

In deriving (7.2.26), we have also used the fact that $\mathbf{q}_1(n-1)$ and $\mathbf{q}_2(n-1)$ are orthogonal to each other and both are orthogonal to $\mathbf{q}_j^{(3)}(n-1)$, $j = 3, 4, \ldots, M+1$.

By using the definition of $\hat{\alpha}_1(n)$ and (7.2.22), we obtain

$$\hat{\alpha}_2(n) = \hat{\alpha}_1(n)\left[1 + \frac{\hat{\alpha}_1(n)|q_2(n,n)|^2}{w\delta_2(n-1)}\right] = \frac{\hat{\alpha}_1(n)\delta_2(n)}{w\delta_2(n-1)} \tag{7.2.28}$$

or equivalently,

$$\frac{\hat{\alpha}_2(n)}{\hat{\alpha}_1(n)} = \frac{\delta_2(n)}{w\delta_2(n-1)} \tag{7.2.29}$$

Then, by using $k_{3j}(n)$ and $\delta_2(n)$, we compute $\mathbf{q}_j^{(4)}(n)$, for $j = 4, 5, \ldots, M+1$. This concludes step 3.

The results obtained above can be generalized for any step i. Let us assume that we have the vectors $\mathbf{q}_j^{(i)}(n)$, $j = i, i+1, \ldots, M+1$, as

$$\mathbf{q}_j^{(i)}(n) = \begin{bmatrix} \sqrt{w}\mathbf{q}_j^{(i)}(n-1) \\ 0 \end{bmatrix} - q_j^{(i)}(n,n)\begin{bmatrix} \displaystyle\sum_{k=1}^{i-1} \frac{\hat{\alpha}_{k-1}(n)q_k^*(n,n)\mathbf{q}_k(n-1)}{w\delta_k(n-1)} \\ 1 \end{bmatrix} \tag{7.2.30}$$

where $q_j^{(i)}(n,n)$ is the last element of $\mathbf{q}_j^{(i)}(n)$. By using the fact that the vectors $\mathbf{q}_k(n-1)$, $k = 1, 2, \ldots, i-1$, are orthogonal to each other and they are all orthogonal to $\mathbf{q}_j^{(i)}(n-1)$'s, $j = i, i+1, \ldots, M+1$, we can show that

$$k_{ij}(n) = wk_{ij}(n-1) + q_i^*(n,n)q_i^{(i)}(n,n)\hat{\alpha}_{i-1}(n) \tag{7.2.31}$$

where $q_i(n,n) \equiv q_i^{(i)}(n,n)$, and

$$\begin{aligned} \hat{\alpha}_{i-1}(n) &= 1 + \sum_{k=1}^{i-1} \frac{\hat{\alpha}_{k-1}^2(n)|q_{k-1}(n,n)|^2}{w\delta_k(n-1)} = \hat{\alpha}_{i-2}(n) + \frac{\hat{\alpha}_{i-2}^2(n)|q_{i-1}(n,n)|^2}{w\delta_{i-1}(n-1)} \\ &= \hat{\alpha}_{i-2}(n)\left[1 + \frac{\hat{\alpha}_{i-2}(n)|q_{i-1}(n,n)|^2}{w\delta_{i-1}(n-1)}\right] = \frac{\hat{\alpha}_{i-2}(n)\delta_{i-1}(n)}{w\delta_{i-1}(n-1)} \end{aligned} \tag{7.2.32}$$

As a special case of (7.2.31), we have

$$\delta_i(n) \equiv k_{ii}(n) = w\delta_i(n-1) + \hat{\alpha}_{i-1}(n)|q_i(n,n)|^2 \tag{7.2.33}$$

By using $k_{i,j}(n)$ and $\delta_i(n)$, we can compute the current errors

$$q_j^{(i+1)}(n,n) = q_j^{(i)}(n,n) - \tilde{r}_{i,j}(n)q_i(n,n), \qquad j = i+1, \ldots, M+1 \tag{7.2.34}$$

where

$$\tilde{r}_{i,j}(n) = \frac{k_{i,j}(n)}{\delta_i(n)} \tag{7.2.35}$$

The $(M + 1)$ column vector $\mathbf{d}(n)$ has been treated no differently than the other M columns. However, to make the algorithm more clear, we now use a special notation for the quantities related to this desired signal $\mathbf{d}(n)$. We use $k_{id}(n)$, $\tilde{r}_{id}(n)$, and $\mathbf{e}^{(i)}(n)$ instead of $k_{i,M+1}(n)$, $\tilde{r}_{i,M+1}(n)$, and $\mathbf{q}_{M+1}^{(i)}(n)$, respectively. For the special cases of (7.2.31), (7.2.35), and (7.2.34), for $i = 1, 2, \ldots, M+1$, and with $\mathbf{e}^{(1)}(n) = \mathbf{d}(n)$ we have

$$k_{id}(n) = wk_{id}(n-1) + q_i^*(n,n)e^{(i)}(n,n)\hat{\alpha}_{i-1}(n) \tag{7.2.36}$$

$$\tilde{r}_{i,d}(n) = \frac{k_{i,d}(n)}{\delta_i(n)} \tag{7.2.37}$$

and

$$e^{(i+1)}(n,n) = e^{(i)}(n,n) - \tilde{r}_{id}(n)q_i(n,n) \tag{7.2.38}$$

This concludes the derivation.

As shown previously, to solve the LS estimation problem at time n, we need only compute the matrices $\overline{\mathfrak{R}}(n)$ and $\tilde{\mathbf{D}}(n)$. The orthogonal vector set is not essential. It can be seen from (7.2.32) through (7.2.38) that to obtain $\overline{\mathfrak{R}}(n)$ and $\tilde{\mathbf{D}}(n)$ we need to compute the most recent elements in the orthogonal and intermediate vectors [i.e., $\mathbf{q}_i(n)$, $\mathbf{q}_j^{(i)}(n)$, and $\mathbf{e}^{(i)}(n)$] using the new data $x_i(n)$ and $d(n)$ and the quantities $k_{ij}(n-1)$ and $\delta_i(n-1)$ obtained at time $n-1$. Thus we obtain the *time-recursive form of the MGS algorithm or the RMGS algorithm*.

It is possible to implement the RMGS algorithm directly from $n = 1$ by initializing $\tilde{\mathbf{D}}(1)$ and $\overline{\mathfrak{R}}(n)$ to be a zero matrix and an identity matrix, respectively. During computation, if both $k_{ij}(n)$ and $\delta_i(n)$ are equal to zero, we let $\tilde{r}_{ij}(n) = 0$. However, it has been shown [Ling et al. (1986)] that the algorithm will behave better numerically by initializing the matrix $\tilde{\mathbf{D}}(1)$ to a small identity matrix $\delta\mathbf{I}$, where δ is a small positive number [i.e., $\delta_i(1) = \delta$, $i = 1, 2, \ldots, M$]. The price paid for better initial numerical behavior is a biased initial estimate of $\overline{\mathfrak{R}}(n)$ and $\tilde{\mathbf{D}}(n)$. The bias may be insignificant if we choose δ small enough. Furthermore, the bias will decay toward zero and become insignificant after a few iterations due to the exponential weighting.

The RMGS algorithm with such initialization is summarized in Table 7.2. Its computational complexity is about $1.5M^2 + 6.5M$ operations for every new data vector $\mathbf{X}_M(n)$. By one operation we mean one addition plus one multiplication or division.

As explained previously, to update $k_{ij}(n)$, $k_{id}(n)$, and $\delta_i(n)$, the RMGS algorithm computes the most recent LS errors $q_i(n,n)$ and $e^{(i)}(n,n)$. Therefore, the RMGS algorithm is most suitable for applications in which the most

TABLE 7.2 Time-Recursive Modified Gram–Schmidt (RMGS) Algorithm

Initialization before algorithm starts ($n = 0$)

$$\delta_i(0) = \delta,\ i = 1, 2, \ldots, M \text{ (}\delta\text{ is a small positive number)}$$

$$\tilde{r}_{ij}(0) = 0, \text{ for } i = 1, 2, \ldots, M, j = i + 1, \ldots, M$$

Initialization for every n

$$e^{(1)}(n,n) = d(n),\ \hat{\alpha}_0(n) = 1, \text{ and } q_i^{(1)}(n,n) = x_i(n)\ (i = 1, 2, \ldots, M)$$

$$\text{do } i = 1, 2, \ldots, M$$

$$q_i(n,n) \equiv q_i^{(i)}(n,n)$$

$$\delta_i(n) = w\delta_i(n-1) + \hat{\alpha}_{i-1}(n)|q_i(n,n)|^2$$

$$\hat{\alpha}_i(n) = \hat{\alpha}_{i-1}(n)[1 + \hat{\alpha}_{i-1}(n)|q_i(n,n)|^2/w\delta_i(n-1)]$$

$$[\text{or } \hat{\alpha}_i(n) = \hat{\alpha}_{i-1}(n)\delta_i(n)/w\delta_i(n-1)]$$

$$\text{do } j = i + 1, 2, \ldots, M$$

$$k_{ij}(n) = wk_{ij}(n-1) + q_i^*(n,n)q_j^{(i)}(n,n)\hat{\alpha}_{i-1}(n)$$

$$\tilde{r}_{ij}(n) = k_{ij}(n)/\delta_i(n)$$

$$q_j^{(i+1)}(n,n) = q_j^{(i)}(n,n) - \tilde{r}_{ij}(n)q_i(n,n)$$

$$\text{(end of loop } j\text{)}$$

$$k_{id}(n) = wk_{id}(n-1) + q_i^*(n,n)e^{(i)}(n,n)\hat{\alpha}_{i-1}(n)$$

$$\tilde{r}_{id}(n) = k_{id}(n)/\delta_i(n)$$

$$e^{(i+1)}(n,n) = e^{(i)}(n,n) - \tilde{r}_{id}(n)q_i(n,n)$$

$$\text{(end of loop } i\text{)}$$

recent estimation errors are the desired quantities. On the other hand, if the optimal coefficient vector $\mathbf{h}_M(n)$ is required explicitly, it can be computed by solving (7.2.5) with a modest amount of extra computation.

The error $e^{(i)}(n,n)$ generated at step i is the optimal LS estimation error at time n based on i input data samples $x_k(n)$, $k = 1, 2, \ldots, i$. We call $e^{(i)}(n,n)$ the ith-order LS estimation error at time n. Thus the RMGS algorithm is both time recursive and order recursive, as in the least-squares lattice algorithm, because the RMGS algorithm generates the LS estimation errors of all orders from 1 through M at every time instant n. These two algorithms are members of a family of order-recursive algorithms, discussed in detail in Section 7.5.

The auxiliary quantity $\hat{\alpha}_i(n)$ and, in particular, its reciprocal, denoted by $\alpha_i(n)$, plays an important role in different types of time-recursive LS estimation algorithms. Let us take a closer look at $\alpha_i(n)$. First from (7.2.32) we can write $\alpha_i(n)$ as

$$\begin{aligned}\alpha_i(n) &= \frac{1}{\hat{\alpha}_i(n)} = \frac{\alpha_{i-1}(n)w\delta_i(n-1)}{\delta_i(n)} \\ &= \frac{\alpha_{i-1}(n)[\delta_i(n) - \hat{\alpha}_{i-1}(n)|q_i(n,n)|^2]}{\delta_i(n)} \\ &= \alpha_{i-1}(n) - \frac{|q_i(n,n)|^2}{\delta_i(n)}\end{aligned} \tag{7.2.39}$$

We can further expand $\alpha_{i-1}(n)$ in terms of $\alpha_{i-2}(n)$, and so on. Thus we obtain

$$\alpha_i(n) = 1 - \sum_{k=1}^{i} \frac{|q_k(n,n)|^2}{\delta_k(n)} \tag{7.2.40}$$

On the other hand, by taking the last row of (7.2.13), and using the relation (7.2.4), it can be shown that

$$[q_1(n,n) \quad q_2(n,n) \quad \cdots \quad q_M(n,n)]\, \tilde{\mathbf{D}}^{-1/2}(n) = \mathbf{X}_M^t(n)\mathcal{R}^{-1}(n) \tag{7.2.41}$$

The squared norm of the vectors on both sides of (7.2.41) is

$$\sum_{k=1}^{M} \frac{|q_k(n,n)|^2}{d_k(n)} = \mathbf{X}_M^t(n)[\mathcal{R}(n)\mathcal{R}^H(n)]^{-1}\mathbf{X}_M^*(n) = \mathbf{X}_M^t(n)\mathbf{R}_M^{-1}(n)\mathbf{X}_M^*(n) \tag{7.2.42}$$

Similarly, we can show that

$$\begin{aligned}\sum_{k=1}^{i} \frac{|q_k(n,n)|^2}{d_k(n)} &= \mathbf{X}_i^t(n)[\mathbf{A}_i(n)\mathbf{W}^2(n)\mathbf{A}_i^H(n)]^{-1}\mathbf{X}_i^*(n) \\ &= \mathbf{X}_i^t(n)\mathbf{R}_i^{-1}(n)\mathbf{X}_i^*(n)\end{aligned} \tag{7.2.43}$$

where

$$\mathbf{W}(n)\mathbf{A}_i(n) = \mathbf{W}(n)[\mathbf{a}_1(n) \quad \mathbf{a}_2(n) \quad \cdots \quad \mathbf{a}_i(n)] \tag{7.2.44}$$

The scalar given by (7.2.42) is a real number and its value is between 0 and 1. It is called the *maximum likelihood factor* in the technical literature. By comparing (7.2.40) and (7.2.43), it is easy to see that

$$\alpha_i(n) = 1 - \mathbf{X}_i^t(n)\mathbf{R}_i^{-1}(n)\mathbf{X}_i^*(n) \tag{7.2.45}$$

It can be shown from (7.2.40) and (7.2.45) that

$$0 \le \alpha_i(n) \le \cdots \le \alpha_1(n) \le \alpha_0(n) = 1 \tag{7.2.46}$$

By comparing (7.2.46) and (6.3.59) it is easy to verify that the $\alpha_i(n)$ in both places are identically defined. Furthermore, the square root of $\alpha_i(n)$ has the geometric interpretation of $\cos\theta$, where θ is the angle between the spaces spanned by the column vectors of the matrices $\mathbf{W}(n-1)\mathbf{A}_i(n-1)$ and $\mathbf{W}(n)\mathbf{A}_i(n)$, respectively. This geometric interpretation explains why $\alpha_i(n)$ often appears in time-recursive LS algorithms.

7.2.4 Variations of the RMGS Algorithm

We have presented above a time-recursive form of the MGS (RMGS) algorithm. Although the basic RMGS algorithm discussed above has many attractive properties, we shall derive a few variations of the basic RMGS algorithm that are more appropriate for particular applications and may exhibit better numerical behavior. Furthermore, the RMGS algorithm can be realized by repeating a small set of basic equations and lends itself to modular implementation (e.g., implementations using a systolic array). These topics are discussed below.

A Priori Error RMGS Algorithm. As can be observed from Table 7.2, in order to compute the LS estimation errors at n [i.e., $q_j^{(i)}(n,n)$ and $e^{(i)}(n,n)$], we need to compute the correlations $k_{ij}(n)$ and $\delta_i(n)$, which can be computed only if the data vector $\mathbf{X}_M(n)$ and the desired signal $d(n)$ are available. As has been discussed in Section 6.3, in some applications, such as adaptive equalization for data communications, the desired signal $d(n)$ will not be available until the LS estimation errors and the estimate of $d(n)$ are computed. In such applications, instead of using $k_{ij}(n)$ and $\delta_i(n)$, we use the corresponding quantities at time $n-1$ [i.e., $k_{ij}(n-1)$ and $\delta_i(n-1)$] to compute the LS errors and the estimate of $d(n)$. Hence the LS estimation errors computed are the LS errors at time n by using the optimal coefficients at time $n-1$. These have been called *a priori errors* in the literature and can be expressed as $q_j^{(i)}(n, n-1)$ and $e^{(i)}(n, n-1)$, respectively. On the other hand, $q_j^{(i)}(n,n)$ and $e^{(i)}(n,n)$ are called *a posteriori errors*. In what follows we shall simply denote the a priori errors by $q_j^{(i)}(n)$ and $e^{(i)}(n)$, respectively.

By using the quantities computed at n, the a priori errors $q_j^{(i+1)}(n)$ are computed as

$$q_j^{(i+1)}(n) = q_j^{(i)}(n) - \tilde{r}_{i,j}(n-1)q_i(n) \tag{7.2.47}$$

$$e^{(i+1)}(n) = e^{(i)}(n) - \tilde{r}_{id}(n-1)q_i(n) \tag{7.2.48}$$

where $\tilde{r}_{ij}(n-1) = k_{ij}(n-1)/\delta_i(n-1)$ and $\tilde{r}_{id}(n-1) = k_{id}(n-1)/\delta_i(n-1)$. To compute the time recursion of $k_{ij}(n)$ and $\delta_i(n)$ using the a priori errors, we use the following relationship between the a priori errors and the a posteriori errors:

$$q_j^{(i)}(n,n) = \alpha_{i-1}(n)q_j^{(i)}(n) \tag{7.2.49}$$

Similarly, for $e^{(i)}(n)$ we have

$$e^{(i)}(n,n) = \alpha_{i-1}(n)e^{(i)}(n) \tag{7.2.50}$$

Proof of the relationships given by (7.2.49) and (7.2.50) is similar to that used to obtain (6.3.82). Actually, these relationships are true for any pair of corresponding LS a priori and a posteriori errors. We discuss this in more detail in Section 7.5.

By using (7.2.49) and (7.2.50) we can write the RMGS algorithm in terms of the a priori errors. The resulting algorithm, called the *a priori error RMGS algorithm,* is given in Table 7.3. As a direct consequence of (7.2.32), we have the order recursive relations

$$\alpha_i(n) = \frac{\alpha_{i-1}(n)w\delta_i(n-1)}{\delta_i(n)} \tag{7.2.51}$$

and

$$\begin{aligned}\alpha_i(n) &= \alpha_{i-1}(n)\left[\frac{\delta_i(n) - \alpha_{i-1}(n)|q_i(n)|^2}{\delta_i(n)}\right] \\ &= \alpha_{i-1}(n)\left[1 - \frac{\alpha_{i-1}(n)|q_i(n)|^2}{\delta_i(n)}\right]\end{aligned} \tag{7.2.52}$$

TABLE 7.3 A Priori Error RMGS Algorithm

Initialization before algorithm starts ($n = 0$)

$\delta_i(0) = \delta, \; i = 1, 2, \ldots, M$ (δ is a small positive number)

$\tilde{r}_{ij}(0) = 0, \text{ for } i = 1, 2, \ldots, M, j = i + 1, \ldots, M$

Initialization for every n

$e^{(1)}(n) = d(n), \; \delta_0(n) = 1, \text{ and } q_i^{(1)}(n) = x_i(n) \; (i = 1, 2, \ldots, M)$

$$
\begin{gathered}
\text{do } i = 1, 2, \ldots, M \\
q_i(n) \equiv q_i^{(i)}(n) \\
\delta_i(n) = w\delta_i(n-1) + \alpha_{i-1}(n)|q_i(n)|^2 \\
\alpha_i(n) = \alpha_{i-1}(n)[1 - \alpha_{i-1}(n)|q_i(n)|^2/\delta_i(n)] \\
[\text{or } \alpha_i(n) = \alpha_{i-1}(n)w\delta_i(n-1)/\delta_i(n)]
\end{gathered}
$$

$$
\begin{gathered}
\text{do } j = i + 1, 2, \ldots, M \\
q_j^{(i+1)}(n) = q_j^{(i)}(n) - \tilde{r}_{ij}(n-1)q_i(n) \\
k_{ij}(n) = wk_{ij}(n-1) + q_i^*(n)q_j^{(i)}(n)\alpha_{i-1}(n) \\
\tilde{r}_{ij}(n) = k_{ij}(n)/\delta_i(n) \\
\text{(end of loop } j)
\end{gathered}
$$

$$
\begin{gathered}
e^{(i+1)}(n) = e^{(i)}(n) - \tilde{r}_{id}(n-1)q_i(n) \\
k_{id}(n) = wk_{id}(n-1) + q_i^*(n)e^{(i)}\alpha_{i-1}(n) \\
\tilde{r}_{id}(n) = k_{id}(n)/\delta_i(n) \\
\text{(end of loop } i)
\end{gathered}
$$

From (7.2.48) we obtain the error

$$
e^{(M+1)}(n) = d(n) - \sum_{i=1}^{M} \tilde{r}_{id}(n-1)q_i(n) = d(n) - \hat{d}(n) \tag{7.2.53}
$$

It is clear from (7.2.53) that $\hat{d}(n) \equiv \Sigma_{i=1}^{M} \tilde{r}_{id}(n-1)q_i(n)$ is the estimate of $d(n)$. The a priori error form of the RMGS algorithm is particularly suitable for implementation of adaptive equalizers for data communications described in Section 6.1.

Direct Updating of the Coefficients Using an Error-Feedback Formula. In addition to the a priori error and a posteriori error RMGS algorithms [Ling et al. (1986)] it has been found that by modifying some of the equations of these algorithms, we can improve the numerical accuracy of the RMGS algorithm, especially when a short computer word length is used. The modified algorithms are algebraically equivalent to the original algorithm and thus are still optimal. Below we present a version of the RMGS algorithm that uses error feedback directly to update the coefficients $\tilde{r}_{ij}(n)$ and $\tilde{r}_{id}(n)$ instead of computing them as the quotient of $k_{ij}(n)$ and $\delta_i(n)$.

The error feedback for $\tilde{r}_{ij}(n)$ is easily obtained in a similar way to the derivation of (7.2.24). By using (7.2.49) we may express $\tilde{r}_{ij}(n)$ in terms of a priori errors as

$$\begin{aligned}
\tilde{r}_{ij}(n) &= \frac{k_{ij}(n-1)}{\delta_i(n-1)} + \frac{k_{ij}(n) - \delta_i(n)k_{ij}(n-1)/\delta_i(n-1)}{\delta_i(n)} \\
&= \tilde{r}_{ij}(n-1) + \frac{\alpha_{i-1}(n)q_i^*(n)q_j^{(i)}(n) - \alpha_{i-1}(n)|q_i^*(n)|^2k_{ij}(n-1)/\delta_i(n-1)}{\delta_i(n)} \\
&= \tilde{r}_{ij}(n-1) + \frac{\alpha_{i-1}(n)q_i^*(n)[q_j^{(i)}(n) - \tilde{r}_{ij}(n-1)q_i(n)]}{\delta_i(n)} \\
&= \tilde{r}_{ij}(n-1) + \frac{\alpha_{i-1}(n)q_i^*(n)q_j^{(i+1)}(n)}{\delta_i(n)}
\end{aligned} \tag{7.2.54}$$

This is the direct update equation for $\tilde{r}_{ij}(n)$. Similarly, we can obtain the direct update equation for $\tilde{r}_{id}(n)$ as

$$\tilde{r}_{id}(n) = \tilde{r}_{id}(n-1) + \frac{\alpha_{i-1}(n)q_i^*(n)e^{(i+1)}(n)}{\delta_i(n)} \tag{7.2.55}$$

The a priori error-feedback RMGS algorithm is given in Table 7.4. The name *error feedback* comes from the fact that the error $e^{(i+1)}(n)$ estimated by using the coefficient $\tilde{r}_{id}(n-1)$ is then used to time-update $\tilde{r}_{id}(n-1)$ to $\tilde{r}_{id}(n)$ and thus forms a negative-feedback loop. As a result, the error contained in $\tilde{r}_{id}(n)$, due to numerical precision in computations, will be compensated in the feedback loop.

It has been shown by computer simulation that the RMGS algorithm with error feedback exhibits superior numerical robustness. For purposes of comparison, in Table 7.5 we show the numerical accuracy of three LS estimation algorithms: the RMGS (Table 7.3), the RMGS with error feedback

TABLE 7.4 Error-Feedback A Priori Error RMGS Algorithm

Initiailziation before algorithm starts ($n = 0$)

$\delta_i(0) = \delta$, $i = 1, 2, \ldots, M$ (δ is a small positive number)

$\tilde{r}_{ij}(0) = 0$, for $i = 1, 2, \ldots, M$, $j = i + 1, \ldots, M$

Initialization for every n

$e^{(1)}(n) = d(n)$, $\alpha_0(n) = 1$, and $q_i^{(1)}(n) = x_i(n)$ ($i = 1, 2, \ldots, M$)

do $i = 1, 2, \ldots, M$

$q_i(n) \equiv q_i^{(i)}(n)$

$\delta_i(n) = w\delta_i(n-1) + \alpha_{i-1}(n)|q_i(n)|^2$

$\alpha_i(n) = \alpha_{i-1}(n)[1 - \alpha_{i-1}(n)|q_i(n)|^2/\delta_i(n)]$

[or $\alpha_i(n) = \alpha_{i-1}(n)w\delta_i(n-1)/\delta_i(n)$]

do $j = i + 1, 2, \ldots, M$

$q_j^{(i+1)}(n) = q_j^{(i)}(n) - \tilde{r}_{ij}(n-1)q_i(n)$

$\tilde{r}_{ij}(n) = \tilde{r}_{ij}(n-1) + q_i^*(n)q_j^{(i+1)}(n)\alpha_{i-1}(n)/\delta_i(n)$

(end of loop j)

$e^{(i+1)}(n) = e^{(i)}(n) - \tilde{r}_{id}(n-1)q_i(n)$

$\tilde{r}_{id}(n) = \tilde{r}_{id}(n-1) + q_i^*(n)e^{(i+1)}(n)\alpha_{i-1}(n)/\delta_i(n)$

(end of loop i)

TABLE 7.5 Comparison of Numerical Accuracy of RMGS and Square-Root LS Algorithms

	Variance of output error ($\times 10^{-3}$)		
Number of bits	RMGS	RMGS-EF	SQRT-LS
Floating point (ideal)	2.10	2.10	2.10
16	2.17	2.16	2.17
13	2.36	2.19	2.33
11	6.21	2.18	17.6
9	220	20.6	75.3

(Table 7.4), and the square-root least-squares Kalman (Table 6.1). The numbers shown are the mean-squared output error, obtained from a simulated linear equalizer using fixed-point arithmetic. It is clear from the table that the error-feedback form of the RMGS algorithm provides the best accuracy.

7.2.5 Implementation of the RMGS Algorithm Using VLSI Arrays and Its Relationship to the LS Lattice Algorithm

Every version of the RMGS algorithm described above is based on two sets of basic equations. For example, for the RMGS algorithm given in Table 7.1, the first set of equations consists of (7.2.32) and (7.2.33). The second set consists of (7.2.31), (7.2.34), and (7.2.35). Equations (7.2.36) through (7.2.38) are a special case of the second set. Similar classifications can be made for the a priori error and error-feedback RMGS algorithms. We can implement the first set of equations using an elementary processing unit (cell) and the second set by another elementary processing cell. We can construct a modular structure by cascading these two types of processing cells to implement the complete RMGS algorithm.

Figure 7.1 shows such a modular structure of the RMGS algorithm. In the figure each of the processing cells represented by double circles implements the first set of equations. For an M-order RMGS algorithm, we need M such cells, which are called *boundary cells,* for obvious reasons. The cells represented by single circles, called *internal cells,* implement the second set of equations. For this estimator, we need $M(M + 1)/2$ internal cells. Although the quantities given in the figure are for the a priori error form, the structure and the discussion given below are valid for any of the variations of RMGS algorithm. As shown in the figure, each boundary cell generates three quantities, $q_i(n)$, $t_i(n)$, and $\alpha_{i+1}(n)$, by using the inputs $q_i^{(i)}(n)$ and $\alpha_i(n)$ and its local variable $\delta_i(n)$. The first two quantities, $q_i(n)$ and $t_i(n)$, are sent to the internal cells on the same row. The third one, $\alpha_{i+1}(n)$, is sent to the next boundary cell along the diagonal line. The internal cells receive the quantity $q_i^{(j)}(n)$ from the internal cell located above and $q_i(n)$ and $t_i(n)$ from the boundary cell. After these quantities are processed, the internal cell sends the resulting quantity $q_i^{(j+1)}(n)$ to the cell located below. The local

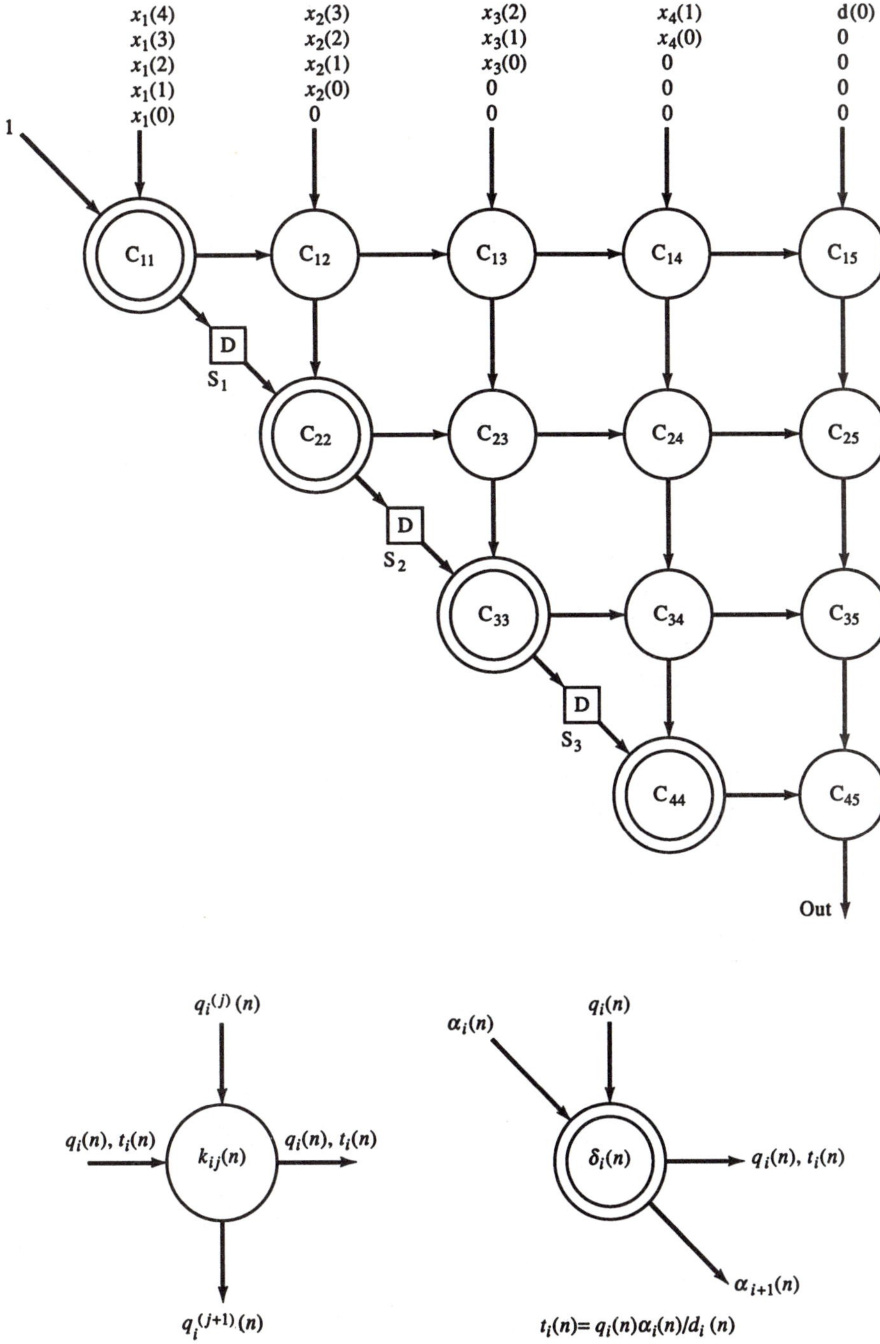

FIGURE 7.1 A triangular systolic array for RMGS algorithms.

variables $\delta_i(n)$ and $k_{ij}(n)$ in the internal and boundary cells are updated during processing. The modular structure of the RMGS algorithm lends itself to implementations using a VLSI *systolic array* and a *wavefront array* as described below.

A systolic array and a wavefront array are two digital signal processing architectures. By using parallel and pipelined processing with a large number of a few basic elementary processing cells, these two array architectures achieve a very high throughput and are suitable for VLSI realization. To be implemented using a systolic or wavefront array architecture, a DSP algorithm should be *modular* and *locally connected.* An algorithm is modular if it can be divided into a (large) number of a few types of identical computations each of which can be completed in a few steps. Thus a modular algorithm can be implemented using a repetition of a few types of elementary processing cells that are easy to design. An algorithm is called *locally connected* if each of its processing cells communicates only with the neighboring cells. This feature is important for the easier arrangement of data flow in VLSI design.

From earlier discussions it is clear that the RMGS algorithm is inherently modular. Only two types of cells are needed for its implementation. On the other hand, we note that the data generated in a boundary cell are used by all other cells in the same row. This type of data flow is called *broadcasting.* By definition, an algorithm requiring broadcasting is not locally connected. However, this problem can be solved by *localizing* the RMGS algorithm. Namely, after receiving data from the cell on its left, the internal cell stores the data while it processes the data. The stored data are then sent to the next cell on the right together with the data resulting from current processing. The RMGS algorithm becomes locally connected after such localization, and thus it is suitable for array implementation.

Systolic Array Implementation of the RMGS Algorithm. By definition, a systolic array is "*a network of processors that rhythmically compute and pass data through the system*" [Kung and Leiserson (1978)]. Each processor pumps data in and out each time under the control of a master clock and performs some short computation during the time period between two adjacent clocks. Thus a regular data flow is kept up in the network. The computation of the RMGS algorithm can be carried out in exactly such a fashion.

When the processing begins, during the first clock time interval, the first (leftmost) boundary cell C_{11} receives and processes the first data $x_1(0)$ from the first sensor, while all other processing cells are idle. This is indicated in Fig. 7.1 by showing that only the first element in the bottom row of the input data is nonzero. When the processing is completed, C_{11} generates $q_1(0)$, $t_1(0)$, and $\alpha_1(0)$. It sends out $q_1(0)$ and $t_1(0)$ to C_{12}, and $\alpha_1(0)$ to a storing/delay cell S_1. During the second clock time period, C_{11} receives $x_1(1)$ and processes it as described above and generates $q_1(1)$, $t_1(1)$, and $\alpha_1(1)$. In the meantime, C_{12} receives and processes $x_2(0)$, $q_1(0)$, and $t_1(0)$ and generates

$q_2^{(2)}(0)$. At the end of the second clock period, C_{11} sends $q_1(1)$ and $t_1(1)$ to C_{12} and sends $\alpha_1(1)$ to the storing cell S_1, while the stored value $\alpha_1(0)$ is sent to C_{22}. During the third clock period, C_{11} and C_{12} perform the same processing of new data as described above. The previously idle elements C_{22} and C_{13} start processing the new received data. At the end of the third period, the internal cell C_{13} sends the stored quantities $q_1(0)$ and $t_1(0)$ to C_{14} and the new generated quantity $q_3^{(2)}(0)$ to C_{23}. The boundary cell C_{22} generates $q_2(0)$ and $t_1(0)$, which are sent to C_{23}, and $\alpha_2(0)$, which is given to the storing cell S_2. The systolic array continues this process until all the cells are activated and the first output $q_M^{(M)}(0)$ is generated. From then on, one new output $q_M^{(M)}(k)$ is generated per clock interval. The data flow and processing order on a systolic RMGS array can be seen more clearly from Fig. 7.2, which shows the detail of the data flow and the processing in the first three columns of the array at time n. Since each processor performs only a small number of computations, the systolic array can achieve an extremely high overall throughput. We note that there is a delay between the time at which the data reach the array and the time at which the corresponding output is

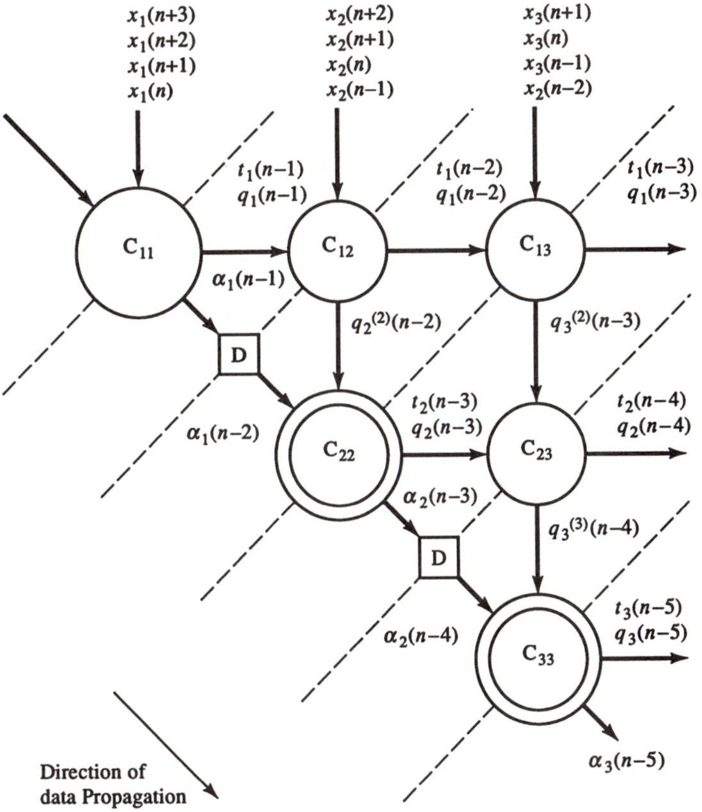

FIGURE 7.2 Data flow of a RMGS systolic array at time n.

generated. For the RMGS array described above, the latency is equal to $2M - 2$ master clock periods.

Wavefront Array Implementation of the RMGS Algorithm. The systolic array described above is governed by a global clock and can be viewed as a synchronous processing device. A wavefront array is data driven and is an asynchronous processing device. A cell in a wavefront array cannot start its processing until all the operands are available. Thus the arrival of data from neighboring processing cells is interpreted as a change of state and will initiate its processing. Data corresponding to the same time index reach a row of processing cells and propagate to a new row of cells after being processed. This phenomenon resembles a wavefront in wave propagation, which explains the origin of the term *wavefront array*. When the array size is not too large, the systolic array may be easier to implement under the control of a global clock. On the other hand, the wavefront array is advantageous for a large array because, without the need of a centralized clock, we eliminate the requirement of accurate timing, which will become increasingly difficult when the array size becomes large.

The operation of the RMGS algorithm using a wavefront array can be understood in the same way as the operation of the systolic array described above. The data flow is the same in both cases. The only difference is that the systolic array starts processing when a new clock is given, while the wavefront array starts processing when all the required data are available. In Fig. 7.2 we use the dotted lines to denote the "wavefronts" if the RMGS algorithm is implemented using a wavefront array.

As we have demonstrated, the RMGS algorithm is both time and order recursive and suited for VLSI modular array implementations. The order recursion is realized in the interconnection of processing cells and determines the structure of the VLSI arrays. On the other hand, the time updates are implemented inside these cells. The different versions (a priori form, error-feedback form, etc.) of the RMGS algorithm have the same order recursive structure, and hence they can be implemented by the same array structure. The difference between various versions of the RMGS algorithm is the way in which the time recursions are achieved. In other words, the basic equation sets implemented in the elementary processing cells are different among the various forms of the algorithm. Recognizing this fact greatly facilitates the evalation of the computational complexity in the implementation of different forms of the RMGS algorithm. We need only to calculate the numbers of operations needed by the two types of processing cells and then calculate the sum of these numbers multiplied by M and $M(M + 1)/2$, respectively. It is interesting to note that the error feedback RMGS not only behaves best numerically, but is also computationally more efficient.

It is interesting to compare the RMGS algorithm with the LS lattice algorithm. For example, for the error-feedback RMGS and LS lattice algorithms, we may compare Tables 7.4 and 6.5. It can be seen that there are only two types of basic equation sets in the LS lattice algorithm. These two types of basic equation sets are identical to the two types in the RMGS algorithm. Hence we conclude that the LS lattice algorithm can be implemented using the same basic processing cells as the RMGS algorithm but with a different configuration. Figure 7.3 shows the implementation of a LS lattice stage using these basic processing cells. In this figure, D represents a unit of delay. The similarity between these two algorithms suggests that a more fundamental relationship exists between them. This relationship is described in Section 7.5.

7.3 GIVENS ALGORITHM FOR TIME-RECURSIVE LS ESTIMATION

In Section 5.3 we demonstrated the use of Givens rotations to annihilate the elements in a column vector and showed that this method can be used to solve the LS problem through a QR decomposition. In this section we extend the solution of LS estimation based on Givens rotations to the time-

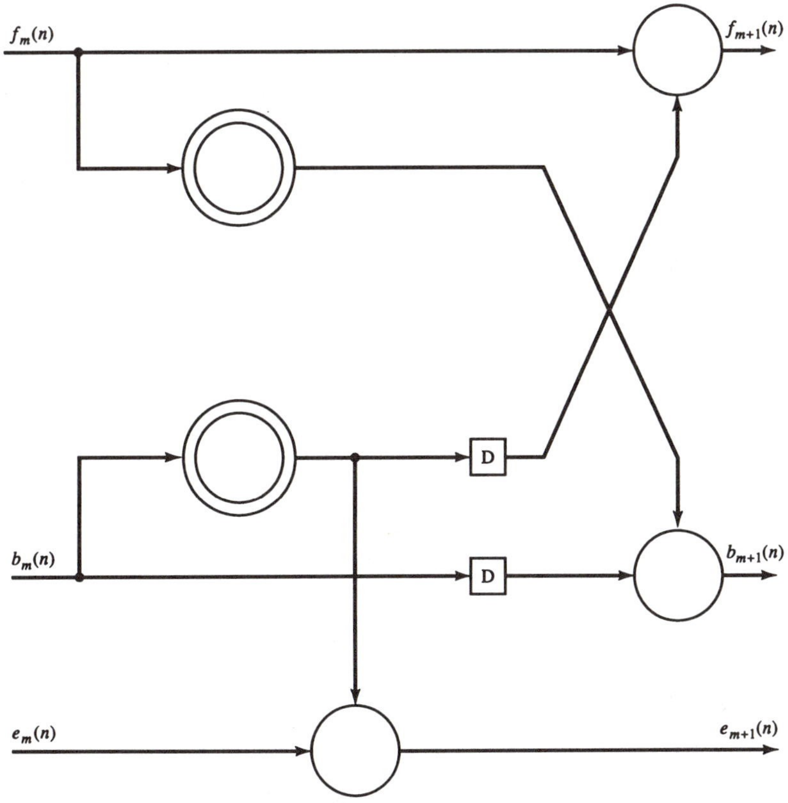

FIGURE 7.3 LS lattice stage using the RMGS elementary processing cells.

recursive form. Two types of Givens algorithms, one with square roots and one without square roots, are presented. The physical meanings of various quantities generated in the Givens algorithm are discussed by exploiting its relationship with the RMGS algorithm given in Section 7.2.3. The hardware approach of using a type of bit-iterative algorithm called CORDIC (coordinate rotation digital computation) for efficient implementation of Givens rotations is also discussed in this section.

7.3.1 Time-Recursive Givens Algorithm

We are interested in the case where we have a new row data vector $[\mathbf{X}_M^t(n), d(n)]$ appended to the original matrix $\sqrt{w}\ \mathbf{W}(n-1)\overline{\mathbf{A}}_M(n-1)$. Assuming that the QR decomposition has been computed for $\mathbf{W}(n-1)\overline{\mathbf{A}}_M(n-1)$, as was shown in Section 7.1, the R-factor of the matrix $\mathbf{W}(n)\overline{\mathbf{A}}_M(n)$ is the same as the R-factor of matrix the $\overline{\mathfrak{R}}(n)$ given by

$$\overline{\mathfrak{R}}(n) = \begin{bmatrix} \sqrt{w}\,\mathfrak{R}(n-1) & \sqrt{w}\,\tilde{\mathbf{d}}_M(n-1) \\ \mathbf{X}_M^t(n) & d(n) \end{bmatrix}$$

$$= \begin{bmatrix} \sqrt{w}\,r_{11}(n-1) & \sqrt{w}\,r_{12}(n-1) & \cdots & \sqrt{w}\,r_{1M}(n-1) & \sqrt{w}\,r_{1d}(n-1) \\ 0 & \sqrt{w}\,r_{22}(n-1) & \cdots & \sqrt{w}\,r_{2M}(n-1) & \sqrt{w}\,r_{2d}(n-1) \\ \vdots & \vdots & \vdots & \vdots & \vdots \\ 0 & 0 & \cdots & \sqrt{w}\,r_{MM}(n-1) & \sqrt{w}\,r_{Md}(n-1) \\ x_1(n) & x_2(n) & \cdots & x_M(n) & d(n) \end{bmatrix} \tag{7.3.1}$$

We can annihilate the vector $\mathbf{X}_M^t(n)$ in the last row of the matrix $\overline{\mathfrak{R}}(n)$ by using a series of M Givens rotations. First, we construct a Givens rotation matrix, $\hat{\mathbf{G}}^{(1)}(n)$, which operates on the first row and the last row of $\overline{\mathfrak{R}}(n)$ and annihilates the first element of $\mathbf{X}_M^t(n)$. Thus we have

$$\begin{bmatrix} c_1 & \mathbf{0}^t & s_1 \\ \mathbf{0} & \mathbf{I} & \mathbf{0} \\ -s_1^* & \mathbf{0}^t & c_1 \end{bmatrix} \begin{bmatrix} \sqrt{w}r_{11}(n-1) & \sqrt{w}\,r_{12}(n-1) & \cdots & \sqrt{w}\,r_{1M}(n-1) & \sqrt{w}\,r_{1d}(n-1) \\ \mathbf{0} & \vdots & \vdots & \vdots & \vdots \\ x_1(n) & x_2(n) & \cdots & x_M(n) & d(n) \end{bmatrix}$$

$$= \begin{bmatrix} r_{11}(n) & r_{12}(n) & \cdots & r_{1M}(n) & r_{1d}(n) \\ \mathbf{0} & \vdots & \vdots & \vdots & \vdots \\ 0 & x_2^{(2)}(n) & \cdots & x_M^{(2)}(n) & d^{(2)}(n) \end{bmatrix} \tag{7.3.2}$$

There are $M + 1$ elements in each of the two rows. We use the first pair to compute the Givens rotation parameters c_1 and s_1 and then apply the resulting Givens rotation on the rest of the elements. To be consistent with the notation that will be used later, we define $x_i^{(1)}(n) \equiv x_i(n)$ and $d^{(1)}(n) \equiv d(n)$.

Second, we apply a Givens rotation matrix $\hat{\mathbf{G}}^{(2)}(n)$ that operates on the second row and the last row of the rotated matrix $\hat{\mathbf{G}}^{(1)}(n)\overline{\mathfrak{R}}(n)$, to annihilate the second element of the last row:

$$\begin{bmatrix} 1 & 0 & \cdots & 0 \\ 0 & c_2 & \mathbf{0}^t & s_2 \\ \vdots & \mathbf{0} & \mathbf{I} & \mathbf{0} \\ 0 & -s_2^* & \mathbf{0}^t & c_2 \end{bmatrix} \begin{bmatrix} r_{11}(n) & r_{12}(n) & \cdots & r_{1M}(n) & r_{1d}(n) \\ 0 & \sqrt{w}\, r_{22}(n-1) & \cdots & \sqrt{w}\, r_{2M}(n-1) & \sqrt{w}\, r_{2d}(n-1) \\ \vdots & \vdots & \vdots & \vdots & \vdots \\ 0 & x_2^{(2)}(n) & \cdots & x_M^{(2)}(n) & d^{(2)}(n) \end{bmatrix}$$

$$= \begin{bmatrix} r_{11}(n) & r_{12}(n) & \cdots & r_{1M}(n) & r_{1d}(n) \\ 0 & r_{22}(n) & \cdots & r_{2M}(n) & r_{2d}(n) \\ \vdots & \vdots & \vdots & \vdots & \vdots \\ 0 & 0 & \cdots & x_M^{(3)}(n) & d^{(3)}(n) \end{bmatrix}$$

Because the first element of each of the rows is already zero, in this step there are only M nonzero elements in each row and we need to operate on $M - 1$ pairs of elements after the rotation parameters have been computed.

In general, we construct a Givens rotation matrix $\hat{\mathbf{G}}^{(i)}(n)$ that operates on the ith row and the last row of the matrix that has been transformed $i - 1$ times. Thus for the two rows of interest, the Givens rotation operating on these rows is expressed as

$$\begin{bmatrix} c_i & s_i \\ -s_i^* & c_i \end{bmatrix} \begin{bmatrix} 0 \cdots 0 & \sqrt{w}\, r_{ii}(n-1) & \sqrt{w}\, r_{i,i+1}(n-1) & \cdots & \sqrt{w}\, r_{iM}(n-1) & \sqrt{w}\, r_{id}(n-1) \\ 0 \cdots 0 & x_i^{(i)}(n) & x_{i+1}^{(i)}(n) & \cdots & x_M^{(i)}(n) & d^{(i)}(n) \end{bmatrix}$$

$$= \begin{bmatrix} 0 \cdots 0 & r_{ii}(n) & r_{i,i+1}(n) & \cdots & r_{iM}(n) & r_{id}(n) \\ 0 \cdots 0 & 0 & x_{i+1}^{(i+1)}(n) & \cdots & x_M^{(i+1)}(n) & d^{(i+1)}(n) \end{bmatrix} \tag{7.3.3}$$

After performing M such Givens rotations, we have eliminated the first M elements in the last row of matrix $\overline{\mathfrak{R}}(n)$, and thus it is transformed into a new triangular matrix. This process can be described by the equation

$$\hat{\mathbf{G}}^{(M)}(n) \cdots \hat{\mathbf{G}}^{(2)}(n)\hat{\mathbf{G}}^{(1)}(n) \begin{bmatrix} \sqrt{w}\, \mathfrak{R}(n-1) & \sqrt{w}\, \tilde{\mathbf{d}}(n-1) \\ \mathbf{X}_M^t(n) & d(n) \end{bmatrix}$$

$$= \begin{bmatrix} \mathfrak{R}(n) & \tilde{\mathbf{d}}(n) \\ \mathbf{0}^t & d^{(M+1)}(n) \end{bmatrix} \tag{7.3.4}$$

Hence in the entire process, we compute M Givens rotation matrices and apply them $M(M + 1)/2$ times in total. Then according to (7.1.11), the optimal LS coefficient vector at n is $\mathbf{h}_M(n) = \mathfrak{R}^{-1}(n)\tilde{\mathbf{d}}(n)$. The time-recursive LS estimation based on Givens rotations is summarized in Table 7.6.

Exact Initialization for Time-Recursive Givens Algorithm. In Section 5.3 we described how to construct the QR decomposition of the matrix

TABLE 7.6 Givens Algorithm

Initialization before algorithm starts ($n = 0$)

$$r_{ii}(0) = 0,\ i = 1, 2, \ldots, M$$
$$r_{ij}(0) = 0,\ i = 1, 2, \ldots, M,\ j = i, i+1, \ldots, M$$

Initialization for every n

$$d^{(1)}(n) = d(n) \text{ and } x_j^{(1)}(n) = x_i(n)\ (i = 1, 2, \ldots, M)$$

$$\text{do } i = 1, 2, \ldots, \min(M, n)$$
$$r_{ii}(n) = [wr_{ii}^2(n-1) + |x_i^{(i)}(n)|^2]^{1/2}$$
$$c_i = \sqrt{w}\, r_{ii}(n-1)/r_{ii}(n)$$
$$s_i = x_i^{(i)*}(n)/r_{ii}(n)$$

$$\text{do } j = i + 1, 2, \ldots, M$$
$$x_j^{(i+1)}(n) = c_i x_j^{(i)}(n) - s_i^* r_{ij}(n-1)$$
$$r_{ij}(n) = c_i r_{ij}(n-1) + s_i x_j^{(i)}(n)$$
$$\text{(end of loop } j)$$

$$d^{(i+1)}(n) = c_i d^{(i)}(n) - s_i^* r_{id}(n-1)$$
$$\tilde{r}_{id}(n) = c_i r_{ij}(n-1) + s_i d^{(i)}(n)$$
$$\text{(end of loop } i)$$

$\mathbf{W}(n)\overline{\mathbf{A}}_M(n)$ using Givens rotations. In the development above we showed how to append a new data vector to the R factor of $\mathbf{W}(n)\overline{\mathbf{A}}_M(n)$ and then compute the QR decomposition of the augmented matrix to achieve a time-recursive QR decomposition using Givens rotations. The time recursion may begin at $n = 0$ without performing the QR decomposition of the matrix $\mathbf{A}_M(n)$ first.

Now suppose that we begin the time recursions at $n = 1$ when we have two vectors $\mathbf{X}_M(0)$ and $\mathbf{X}_M(1)$. We transpose and stack these two vectors to form a matrix with two rows. Then we apply a 2×2 Givens rotation matrix to eliminate the first element of the row vector $\mathbf{X}_M(1)$:

$$\tilde{\mathbf{G}}(1)\begin{bmatrix} \sqrt{w}\,x_1(0) & \sqrt{w}\,x_2(0) & \cdots & \sqrt{w}\,x_M(0) \\ x_1(1) & x_2(1) & \cdots & x_M(1) \end{bmatrix}$$
$$= \begin{bmatrix} r_{11}(1) & r_{12}(1) & \cdots & x_{1M}(1) \\ 0 & x_2^{(2)}(1) & \cdots & x_M^{(2)}(1) \end{bmatrix} \tag{7.3.5}$$

For $n = 2$ we append vector $\mathbf{X}_M'(2)$ to the matrix at the right side of (7.3.5) to form a three-row matrix. By applying two Givens rotations to this three-row matrix, we eliminate the first two elements of $\mathbf{X}_M'(2)$. By continuing this process, we construct a triangular matrix at $n = M$. This procedure is called exact time-recursive initialization for LS estimation. The rest of the time-recursive operations are the same as those described above.

7.3.2 Givens Algorithm Without Square Roots

LS estimation based on Givens rotations as described above requires M square-root operations per time recursion. As in the Gram–Schmidt algorithm, we can avoid computing square roots if instead of computing the elements of matrix $\mathfrak{R}(n)$, we compute the elements of a diagonal matrix $\tilde{\mathbf{D}}(n)$ and an upper triangular matrix $\tilde{\mathfrak{R}}(n)$ that has unity diagonal elements. In other words, we compute the factor matrices of the LDU decomposition instead of Cholesky factors.

As has been shown in Section 7.1, we can express the matrix $\mathfrak{R}(n)$ as

$$\mathfrak{R}(n) = \mathbf{D}^{1/2}(n)\tilde{\mathfrak{R}}(n) \tag{7.3.6}$$

where $\tilde{\mathbf{D}}^{1/2}(n)$ is a diagonal matrix whose elements are $\sqrt{\delta_i(n)} \equiv r_{ii}(n)$, $i = 1, \ldots, M$, since $r_{ii}(n)$ are real and positive. The elements of $\mathfrak{R}(n)$, $\mathbf{D}^{1/2}(n)$ and $\tilde{\mathfrak{R}}(n)$, $r_{ij}(n)$, $\sqrt{\delta_i(n)}$, and $\tilde{r}_{ij}(n)$, have the following relationship:

$$r_{ij}(n) = \sqrt{\delta_i(n)}\tilde{r}_{ij}(n) \tag{7.3.7}$$

Furthermore, we may express the quantities $x_j^{(i)}(n)$ in the second row of (7.3.3) as

$$x_j^{(i)}(n) = \sqrt{\alpha_{i-1}(n)}\tilde{x}_j^{(i)}(n), \qquad j = i + 1, \ldots, M \tag{7.3.8}$$

where the auxiliary parameters $\alpha_i(n)$, $i = 1, \ldots, M$, are defined by

$$\alpha_0(n) = 1, \qquad \alpha_i(n) = \frac{\alpha_{i-1}(n)w\delta_i(n-1)}{\delta_i(n)} \tag{7.3.9}$$

By extending (7.3.7) and (7.3.8) to the $(M + 1)$-column of the matrix $\tilde{\mathfrak{R}}(n)$, we obtain

$$r_{id}(n) = \sqrt{\delta_i(n)}\tilde{r}_{id}(n) \tag{7.3.10}$$

and

$$d^{(i)}(n) = \sqrt{\alpha_{i-1}(n)}\tilde{d}^{(i)}(n) \tag{7.3.11}$$

Now (7.3.3) can be rewritten as

$$\begin{bmatrix} c_i & s_i \\ -s_i^* & c_i \end{bmatrix}$$
$$\times \begin{bmatrix} 0 \cdots 0 & \sqrt{w\delta_i(n-1)} & \sqrt{w\delta_i(n-1)}\tilde{r}_{i,i+1}(n-1) & \cdots & \sqrt{w\delta_i(n-1)}\tilde{r}_{i,M}(n-1) & \sqrt{w\delta_i(n-1)}\tilde{r}_{id}(n-1) \\ 0 \cdots 0 & \sqrt{\alpha_{i-1}(n)}\tilde{x}_i^{(i)}(n) & \sqrt{\alpha_{i-1}(n)}\tilde{x}_{i+1}^{(i)}(n) & \cdots & \sqrt{\alpha_{i-1}(n)}\tilde{x}_M^{(i)}(n) & \sqrt{\alpha_{i-1}(n)}\tilde{d}^{(i)}(n) \end{bmatrix}$$
$$= \begin{bmatrix} 0 & \cdots & 0 & \sqrt{\delta_i(n)} & \sqrt{\delta_i(n)}\tilde{r}_{i,i+1}(n) & \cdots & \sqrt{\delta_i(n)}\tilde{r}_{i,M}(n) & \sqrt{\delta_i(n)}\tilde{r}_{id}(n) \\ 0 & \cdots & 0 & 0 & \sqrt{\alpha_i(n)}\tilde{x}_{i+1}^{(i+1)}(n) & \cdots & \sqrt{\alpha_i(n)}\tilde{x}_M^{(i+1)}(n) & \sqrt{\alpha_i(n)}\tilde{d}^{(i+1)}(n) \end{bmatrix} \tag{7.3.12}$$

Since the Givens rotation annihilates the first nonzero element of the second row, it is easy to show that

$$\delta_i(n) = w\delta_i(n-1) + \alpha_{i-1}(n)|\tilde{x}_i^{(i)}(n)|^2 \tag{7.3.13}$$

$$c_i = \frac{\sqrt{w\delta_i(n-1)}}{\sqrt{\delta_i(n)}} \tag{7.3.14}$$

and

$$s_i = \frac{\sqrt{\alpha_{i-1}(n)}[\tilde{x}_i^{(i)}(n)]^*}{\sqrt{\delta_i(n)}} \tag{7.3.15}$$

From (7.3.12) and using (7.3.14) and (7.3.15), we have

$$\sqrt{\alpha_i(n)}\tilde{x}_j^{(i+1)}(n) = \frac{\sqrt{w\delta_i(n-1)}\sqrt{\alpha_{i-1}(n)}\tilde{x}_j^{(i)}(n)}{\sqrt{\delta_i(n)}} + \frac{\sqrt{\alpha_{i-1}(n)}\sqrt{w\delta_i(n-1)}\tilde{r}_{ij}(n-1)\tilde{x}_i^{(i)}(n)}{\sqrt{\delta_i(n)}} \tag{7.3.16}$$

and

$$\sqrt{\delta_i(n)}\tilde{r}_{ij}(n) = \frac{\sqrt{w\delta_i(n-1)}\sqrt{w\delta_i(n-1)}\tilde{r}_{ij}(n-1)}{\sqrt{\delta_i(n)}} + \frac{\tilde{x}_j^{(i)}(n)\sqrt{\alpha_{i-1}(n)}\sqrt{\alpha_{i-1}(n)}[\tilde{x}_i^{(i)}(n)]^*}{\sqrt{\delta_i(n)}} \tag{7.3.17}$$

After some algebra, the relationships in the elements of the matrix in (7.3.12) become

$$\tilde{x}_j^{(i+1)}(n) = \tilde{x}_j^{(i)}(n) - \tilde{r}_{ij}(n-1)\tilde{x}_i^{(i)}(n) \tag{7.3.18}$$

and

$$\tilde{r}_{ij}(n) = \tilde{c}_i\tilde{r}_{ij}(n-1) + \tilde{s}_i\tilde{x}_j^{(i)}(n) \tag{7.3.19}$$

where

$$\tilde{c}_i = \frac{w\delta_i(n-1)}{\delta_i(n)} = c_i^2 \tag{7.3.20}$$

$$\tilde{s}_i = \frac{\alpha_{i-1}(n)[\tilde{x}_i^{(i)}(n)]^*}{\delta_i(n)} \tag{7.3.21}$$

Similarly, we have

$$\tilde{d}^{(i+1)}(n) = \tilde{d}^{(i)}(n) - \tilde{r}_{id}(n-1)\tilde{x}_i^{(i)}(n) \tag{7.3.22}$$

and

$$\tilde{\mathbf{r}}_{id}(n) = \tilde{c}\tilde{r}_{id}(n-1) + \tilde{s}\tilde{x}_j^{(i-1)}(n) \tag{7.3.23}$$

Equations (7.3.9), (7.3.13), and (7.3.18) through (7.3.23) form the basis of the Givens LS estimation algorithm without square roots. The complete algorithm is given in Table 7.7. After we compute the matrices $\tilde{\mathbf{D}}(n)$ and $\tilde{\mathfrak{R}}(n)$, as well as vector $\tilde{\mathbf{r}}_{Md}(n)$ whose elements are $\tilde{r}_{id}(n)$, we can determine the optimal coefficient vector $\mathbf{h}_M(n)$ by using (7.2.5).

In applications where the LS estimation errors are the desired quantities, it is desirable to compute these estimation errors directly without computing $\mathbf{h}_M(n)$ explicitly. In Section 7.2 we have shown this can be achieved by using the RMGS algorithm. We have also shown that we can generate either a posteriori errors or a priori errors by using different forms of the RMGS algorithm. The same is true for the Givens algorithm. This fact was first demonstrated by McWhirter (1983). Below, we explore the relationships between the Givens algorithm and the RMGS algorithm.

TABLE 7.7 Givens Algorithm without Square Roots

Initialization before algorithm starts $(n = 0)$

$$\delta_i(0) = 0,\ i = 1, 2, \ldots, M$$
$$\tilde{r}_{i,j}(0) = 0,\ i = 1, 2, \ldots, M,\ j = i, i+1, \ldots, M$$

Initialization for every n

$$\tilde{d}^{(1)}(n) = d(n),\ \alpha_0(n) = 1, \text{ and } \tilde{x}_i^{(1)}(n) = x_i(n)\ (i = 1, 2, \ldots, M)$$

$$\text{do } i = 1, 2, \ldots, \min(M, n)$$
$$\delta_i(n) = w\delta_i(n-1) + \alpha_{i-1}(n)|\tilde{x}_i^{(i)}(n))|^2$$
$$\tilde{c} = w\delta_i(n-1)/\delta_i(n)$$
$$\tilde{s} = \alpha_{i-1}(n)[\tilde{x}_i^{(i)}(n)]^*/\delta_i(n)$$
$$\alpha_i(n) = \alpha_{i-1}(n)w\delta_i(n-1)/\delta_i(n)$$

$$\text{do } j = i+1, 2, \ldots, M$$
$$\tilde{x}_j^{(i+1)}(n) = \tilde{x}_j^{(i)}(n) - \tilde{r}_{i,j}(n-1)\tilde{x}_i^{(i)}(n)$$
$$\tilde{r}_{i,j}(n) = \tilde{c}\tilde{r}_{i,j}(n-1) + \tilde{s}\tilde{x}_j^{(i)}(n)$$
(end of loop j)
$$\tilde{d}^{(i+1)}(n) = \tilde{d}^{(i)}(n) - \tilde{r}_{id}(n-1)\tilde{x}_i^{(i)}(n)$$
$$\tilde{r}_{id}(n) = \tilde{c}\tilde{r}_{id}(n-1) + \tilde{s}\tilde{d}^{(i)}(n)$$
(end of loop i)

First let us examine the error-feedback a priori error RMGS algorithm and the Givens algorithm without square roots. As discussed before, the R-factor for QR decomposition of the same signal matrix $\mathbf{W}(n)\overline{\mathbf{A}}(n)$ is unique if its diagonal elements are real and positive. This is true for the resulting R-factors generated from the RMGS algorithm and the Givens algorithm. Therefore, the two R-factors are identical. Similarly, the matrix $\tilde{\mathbf{D}}(n)$ and $\tilde{\mathfrak{R}}(n)$ obtained from these two algorithms are also identical. Thus the corresponding quantities $\tilde{r}_{i,j}(n)$, $\tilde{r}_{id}(n)$, and $\delta_i(n)$ are the same in these two algorithms. Furthermore, the $\alpha_i(n)$ in these two algorithms are also the same quantity. This can easily be verified by comparing (7.3.9) with (7.2.32).

It is easy to see that (7.3.18) has exactly the same form as (7.2.47), except that it uses $\tilde{x}_j^{(i+1)}(n)$, $\tilde{x}_j^{(i)}(n)$, and $\tilde{x}_i^{(i)}(n)$ in place of $q_j^{(i+1)}(n)$, $q_j^{(i)}(n)$, and $q_i(n)$, respectively. We also note that the quantities $\tilde{x}_i^{(i)}(n)$ and $q_j^{(i)}(n)$ are both computed from the same order recursion given by (7.3.22) and (7.2.47). The initial values of both of the recursions are the same [i.e., $\tilde{x}_i^{(1)}(n) \equiv x_i(n) \equiv q_i^{(1)}(n)$], and the recursion coefficients $\tilde{r}_{ij}(n-1)$ are also the same in both equations. As a consequence, the corresponding quantities in these two equations are actually the same quantities.

By substituting (7.2.47) into (7.2.54) we obtain

$$\tilde{r}_{i,j}(n) = \tilde{r}_{i,j}(n-1) + \frac{\alpha_{i-1}(n)q_i^*(n)[q_j^{(i)}(n) - \tilde{r}_{ij}(n-1)q_i(n)]}{\delta_i(n)}$$
$$= \left[1 - \frac{\alpha_{i-1}(n)q_i^*(n)q_i(n)}{\delta_i(n)}\right]\tilde{r}_{i,j}(n-1) + \frac{\alpha_{i-1}(n)q_i^*(n)q_j^{(i)}(n)}{\delta_i(n)} \quad (7.3.24)$$

From (7.2.33) and (7.3.20) we obtain

$$1 - \frac{\alpha_{i-1}(n)q_i^*(n)q_i^{(i)}(n)}{\delta_i(n)} = \frac{[\delta_i(n) - \alpha_{i-1}(n)q_i^*(n)q_i^{(i)}(n)]}{\delta_i(n)} = \frac{w\delta_i(n-1)}{\delta_i(n)} = \tilde{c}_i \tag{7.3.25}$$

Since $q_j^{(i)}(n) = \tilde{x}_j^{(i)}(n)$ and $q_i(n) = \tilde{x}_i^{(i)}(n)$, (7.2.54) and (7.3.24) are actually the same equation and, as a result, (7.2.54) and (7.3.19) are equivalent. Similarly, we also observe that $e^{(i)}(n)$ in (7.2.48) is equal to $\tilde{d}^{(i)}(n)$ in (7.3.22). Thus we have shown that the Givens algorithm without square roots is algebraically equivalent to the a priori error RMGS algorithm. Their corresponding quantities are also equal. As a consequence, $\tilde{x}_j^{(i)}(n)$ and $\tilde{d}^{(i)}(n)$ are the a priori LS errors.

From (7.3.8) and (7.3.11), it can be shown that $x_j^{(i)}(n)$ and $d^{(i)}(n)$ are equal to $\tilde{x}_j^{(i)}(n)$ and $\tilde{d}^{(i)}(n)$ scaled by $\sqrt{\alpha_{i-1}(n)}$. It can also be shown from (7.2.49) and (7.2.50) that

$$x_j^{(i)}(n) = [q_j^{(i)}(n)q_j^{(i+1)}(n,n)]^{1/2} = \frac{q_j^{(i)}(n,n)}{\sqrt{\alpha_{i-1}(n)}} \tag{7.3.26}$$

$$d^{(i)}(n) = [e^{(i)}(n)e^{(i)}(n,n)]^{1/2} = \frac{e^{(i)}(n,n)}{\sqrt{\alpha_{i-1}(n)}} \tag{7.3.27}$$

It can be seen from (7.3.26) and (7.3.27) that $x_j^{(i)}(n)$ and $d^{(i)}(n)$ are the geometric means of the corresponding a priori error and a posteriori error. As we have mentioned in Section 7.2.3, $\sqrt{\alpha_{i-1}(n)}$ is equal to $\cos\theta$, where θ is the angle between the spaces spanned by $\{\mathbf{W}(n)\mathbf{a}_1(n), \ldots, \mathbf{W}(n)\mathbf{a}_{i-1}(n)\}$ and $\{\mathbf{W}(n-1)\mathbf{a}_{i-1}(n-1), \ldots, \mathbf{W}(n-1)\mathbf{a}_{i-1}(n-1)\}$, respectively. Thus we call $x_j^{(i)}(n)$ and $d^{(i)}(n)$ the *angle-normalized LS errors,* as defined in Lee et al. (1982). Since $\alpha_{i-1}(n)$ is a positive number that is smaller than but close to unity, in most cases, all three types of errors are equivalent to each other. Any one of them is as good as the others and it is not necessary to convert from one to another, in general. Therefore, the angle-normalized errors can also be directly used in applications requiring LS estimation errors.

In conclusion, we have shown that the Givens algorithm without square roots generates a priori LS estimation errors and the one with square roots generates angle-normalized errors. For applications that require only LS estimation errors, it is not necessary to compute the LS coefficient vector explicitly. We note that the Givens algorithms can also be implemented using either a systolic array or a wavefront array. This is clear from the close relationship between the RMGS algorithm and the Givens algorithms demonstrated above. A triangular array for the implementation of the Givens algorithms is given in Fig. 7.4. The details of such an implementation of the Givens algorithms are similar to our discussion in Section 7.2.5.

7.3.3 The CORDIC Approach to Givens Transformations

Above we have demonstrated the usefulness of the Givens transformation for solving least-squares estimation problems. Recall that the Givens

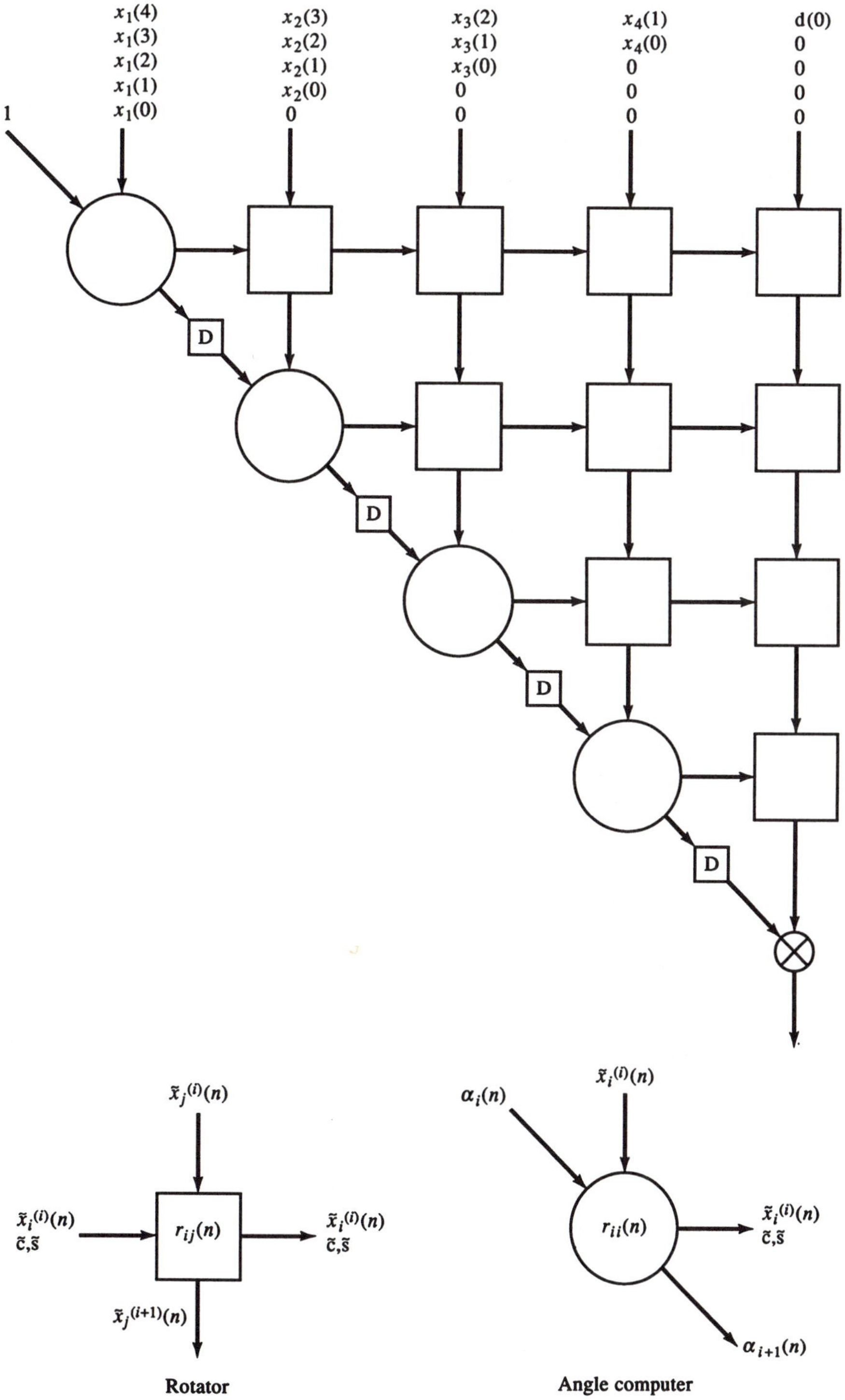

FIGURE 7.4 A triangular array for implementation of Givens algorithms.

transformation is an orthogonal matrix that performs plane rotations. We may construct a Givens rotation matrix to have the property that when we multiply a given vector or matrix by the Givens matrix, we force some specified element of the resulting vector or matrix to be zero. By repeating this process, we can realize a QR decomposition of a given data matrix and solve the LS estimation problem. Thus the operations needed for solving such a problem reduce to a series of plane rotations. Here we look into the details of this approach and present a hardware architecture for carrying out Givens transformations.

A typical Givens transformation matrix might be

$$G = \begin{bmatrix} 1 & & & & & & \\ & 1 & & & & & \\ & & \cos\phi & & & \sin\phi & \\ & & & 1 & & & \\ & & & & 1 & & \\ & & -\sin\phi & & & \cos\phi & \\ & & & & & & 1 \end{bmatrix}$$

We may use a Givens transformation matrix for either postmultiplication or premultiplication but we will use premultiplication examples in this section. Thus the typical Givens transformation matrix above can premultiply any matrix with exactly seven rows (or a seven-element column vector), resulting in a product matrix with exactly the same shape. In carrying out such a multiplication, rows 1, 2, 4, 5, and 7 of the original matrix would simply be copied into the product; only the third and sixth rows would involve actual computation. We could extract rows 3 and 6 to form a temporary matrix with two rows, then premultiply the temporary matrix by a 2×2 Givens transformation matrix

$$\tilde{G} = \begin{bmatrix} \cos\phi & \sin\phi \\ -\sin\phi & \cos\phi \end{bmatrix} \tag{7.3.28}$$

After this multiplication we would copy the two rows of the temporary product matrix into rows 3 and 6 of the full product matrix. Any Givens transformation, of whatever size or shape, reduces, in this way, to a 2×2 Givens transformation matrix premultiplying a matrix with two rows.

$$\begin{bmatrix} x_1' & x_2' & x_3' & \cdots & x_N' \\ y_1' & y_2' & y_3' & \cdots & y_N' \end{bmatrix} = \begin{bmatrix} \cos\phi & \sin\phi \\ -\sin\phi & \cos\phi \end{bmatrix} \begin{bmatrix} x_1 & x_2 & x_3 & \cdots & x_N \\ y_1 & y_2 & y_3 & \cdots & y_N \end{bmatrix}$$

The geometric interpretation of a Givens transformation is rotation. Suppose that x_i and y_i are real numbers. Then we would have (x_i, y_i) representing two-element vectors in some xy-plane and (x_i', y_i') would represent corresponding two-element vectors after rotating through some angle ϕ.

$$\begin{bmatrix} x_i' \\ y_i' \end{bmatrix} = \begin{bmatrix} x_i \cos\phi + y_i \sin\phi \\ y_i \cos\phi - x_i \sin\phi \end{bmatrix}$$

This interpretation makes it easy to see why a Givens transformation is orthogonal. The transpose of the matrix that rotates vectors clockwise by angle ϕ is the matrix that rotates vectors clockwise by angle $-\phi$.

$$\tilde{G}^{-1} = \begin{bmatrix} \cos(-\phi) & \sin(-\phi) \\ -\sin(-\phi) & \cos(-\phi) \end{bmatrix} = \begin{bmatrix} \cos\phi & -\sin\phi \\ \sin\phi & \cos\phi \end{bmatrix} = \tilde{G}^t$$

In geometric terms, to force any particular element y_l' to be zero we choose ϕ so that by rotating the input pair (x_l, y_l) through that angle we cause the output pair (x_l', y_l') to coincide with the x-axis:

$$\phi = \arctan\frac{y_l}{x_l} \tag{7.3.29}$$

although we could equally well use the angle $\pi - \phi$ instead.

Usually, we will want to make this happen with (x_1, y_1), the first of a string of two-element vectors, (x_i, y_i). We call this the *leader* of the string. When a Givens transformation is applied to a string in this way, the action on the leader is fundamentally different from the action on the other two-element vectors (followers). The action on the leader involves discovering the angle ϕ, while the action on the followers involves rotation only. The sequence of operations:

- Discover the angle that will rotate the leader (x_1, y_1) to the x-axis.
- Rotate all the followers (x_i, y_i) by that angle.

is used in many signal-processing applications, as well as in other computations. For this reason, an algorithm called CORDIC, which is an efficient way to perform such rotations, is of great interest. In the next subsection we explain the theory behind the CORDIC algorithm.

A Givens transformation makes mathematical sense even if the numbers processed are complex. The arctangent of a complex angle has mathematical meaning and a matrix whose elements are the cosine and sine of such a complex angle will zero out the y component of the leader, as in the real case. However, even in applications involving complex data, we will be able to limit ourselves to the much simpler case of real rotations. The CORDIC algorithm applies only to real rotations.

The CORDIC Algorithm. For certain special angles ϕ_i, namely those angles for which

$$\tan\phi_i = 2^{-i} \tag{7.3.30}$$

the rotation of the pair (x, y) through ϕ_i takes a simple form. In the general case we have

$$(x', y') = \cos\phi_i(x + y\tan\phi_i, y - x\tan\phi_i) \tag{7.3.31}$$

and for the special angles of (7.3.30) this becomes

$$(x', y') = \cos\phi_i(x + 2^{-i}y, y - 2^{-i}x) \tag{7.3.32}$$

Multiplications by powers of 2 are trivial in digital hardware. Therefore, we can rotate through one of these special angles ϕ_i using two multiplications instead of four. The two nontrivial multiplications both use the same constant $\cos \phi_i$. Note that a small change allows us to rotate through $-\phi_i$.

$$(x', y') = \cos \phi_i(x - 2^{-i}y, y + 2^{-i}x) \tag{7.3.33}$$

Let us collect these two cases together into one by introducing the control variable $\rho_i = \pm 1$. Then to rotate through the angle $\rho_i\phi_i$ we use

$$(x', y') = \cos \phi_i(x + \rho_i 2^{-i}y, y - \rho_i 2^{-i}x) \tag{7.3.34}$$

The nontrivial constant $\cos \phi_i$ is the same whether the rotation is by ϕ_i or by $-\phi_i$.

Now suppose that we want to rotate through the general angle ϕ, where we can express ϕ in terms of ϕ_i:

$$\phi = \sum_{i=0}^{\infty} \rho_i\phi_i, \qquad \rho_i = \pm 1 \tag{7.3.35}$$

Any angle in the range $-\pi/2 \leq \phi \leq \pi/2$ can be represented this way, although the representation may not be unique. Shortly we will present an algorithm that determines the ρ_i.

To rotate through a sum of angles we rotate through each angle in turn. When ρ_i is 1, we rotate counterclockwise, and when ρ_i is -1 we rotate clockwise. But there is an important simplification—we can collect together all the nontrivial multiplications into a single constant

$$K = \prod_{i=0}^{\infty} \cos \phi_i \tag{7.3.36}$$

and we have

$$(x^{(0)}, y^{(0)}) = K(x, y) \tag{7.3.37}$$

$$(x^{(1)}, y^{(1)}) = (x^{(0)} + \rho_0 2^0 y^{(0)}, y^{(0)} - \rho_0 2^0 x^{(0)}) \tag{7.3.38}$$

$$(x^{(2)}, y^{(2)}) = (x^{(1)} + \rho_1 2^{-1} y^{(1)}, y^{(1)} - \rho_1 2^{-1} x^{(1)}) \tag{7.3.39}$$

$$(x^{(3)}, y^{(3)}) = (x^{(2)} + \rho_2 2^{-2} y^{(2)}, y^{(2)} - \rho_2 2^{-2} x^{(2)}) \tag{7.3.40}$$

$$(x^{(4)}, y^{(4)}) = (x^{(3)} + \rho_3 2^{-3} y^{(3)}, y^{(3)} - \rho_3 2^{-3} x^{(3)}) \tag{7.3.41}$$

$$\vdots \qquad\qquad \vdots$$

$$(x', y') = (x^{(\infty)}, y^{(\infty)}) \tag{7.3.42}$$

We see that the CORDIC algorithm is composed of *stages*—most of the stages perform minirotations and one state performs a gain correction by the precomputed constant K. The gain correction stage can be the first, the last, or anywhere in the middle. For any angle we use, all the minirotations are employed but each is employed in either a clockwise or a counterclockwise direction. Although an infinite number of minirotations are called for in an exact realization of the CORDIC algorithm, it is practical to use a finite number of stages, in the same sense that it is practical to make a binary adder or multiplier with a finite number of stages—the higher-numbered stages contribute very little to the accuracy of the angle specification. The correction stage is multiplication by the fixed quantity K, not a general-purpose multiplier. The exact value of K depends only weakly on how many CORDIC stages are used (Table 7.8).

A CORDIC method therefore achieves rotation without using any of the trigonometric functions and without explicit multiplications. If we know in advance the angle by which we wish to rotate the pair (x, y), we can determine the set of controls

$$(\rho_i, i = 0, \ldots, i_{max})$$

which are each represented by a single bit. This may be thought of as representing the angle ϕ using digits ρ_i in an unconventional number system, a number system different from binary, decimal, or any of the radix systems that are commonly used. Each ρ_i can be stored in a flip-flop in the stage whose direction of rotation it is to control.

However, in the Givens transformation application we do not know the angle of rotation in advance. We are given a leader pair (x, y) and we must rotate that pair through the angle such that the resulting rotated pair takes the form $(x', 0)$: (In the early literature on the CORDIC algorithm this operation was called *vectoring*.) Then we must rotate some other pairs through the same angle. But we do not need to know the angle, as long as we can rotate by that angle. Therefore, what we really need for vectoring is an algorithm to determine the CORDIC controls ρ_i. A major advantage of the CORDIC algorithm is that the same circuit which is used for rotating may be used for vectoring.

Consider just the first CORDIC stage ($i = 0$), for which the special angle is either $\pi/4$ or $-\pi/4$. Since our purpose is to rotate the input $(x^{(0)}, y^{(0)})$ toward the x axis, if $y^{(0)}$ is above the axis we should rotate "down," and if $y^{(0)}$ is below the axis we should rotate "up." Therefore,

$$\rho_0 = \mathrm{sgn}(x^{(0)})\, \mathrm{sgn}(y^{(0)})$$

TABLE 7.8 Correction Constant Required when the Last Stage Rotates by Arctan 2^{-i}_{max}

i_{max}	K	i_{max}	K
0	0.707106781	8	0.607254479
1	0.632455532	9	0.607253321
2	0.613571991	10	0.607253031
3	0.608833912	11	0.607252959
4	0.607648256	12	0.607252941
5	0.607351770	13	0.607252936
6	0.607277644	14	0.607252935
7	0.607259112	15	0.607252935

Once we have determined ρ_0 we compute the effect of the first stage on $x^{(0)}$ and $y^{(0)}$ and pass $(x^{(1)}, y^{(1)})$ to the second stage. Here, again, our rule is to rotate "down" if $y^{(1)}$ is above the axis and "up" if $y^{(1)}$ is below the axis.

$$\rho_1 = \text{sgn}(x^{(1)})\,\text{sgn}(y^{(1)})$$

In this way, determination of the controls is quite simple.

$$\rho_i = \text{sgn}(x^{(i)})\,\text{sgn}(y^{(i)}),\ i = 0, \ldots, i_{\max}$$

These controls, once determined, are saved in the flip-flops of the specialized stages and used to control those stages for the succeeding (x, y) pairs which are to be rotated through the same angle.

Although we have presented this as a hardware description, it may equally well be considered as an algorithm for determining the control coefficients, ρ_i. The algorithm for determining the ρ_i is more carefully considered as Problem 7.7.

In Fig. 7.5 we show the concept of a CORDIC circuit made up of independent stages.† The inputs (x, y) are modified by minirotations as they proceed from stage to stage. This circuit has the virtue of natural pipelining. If registers are placed between the stages where there are dashed lines in Fig. 7.5, a new rotation problem, involving a new pair (x, y), can be started by the circuit as soon as the preceding pair has been latched at the output of the first stage, then yet another rotation may be started when the first two pairs have been latched at the output of the second and first stages, respectively, and so on. Note that rotation may follow vectoring in this pipelined fashion. Only an addition and a subtraction need to be performed in each stage. These operations can be carried out very rapidly in digital logic. Therefore, the rate at which a CORDIC circuit can begin new rotation problems is quite high. By contrast, the time required to complete any given rotation is proportional to the number of CORDIC stages provided.

CORDIC Solution of Least-Squares Problems. The CORDIC algorithm finds an especially attractive application in least-squares problems using the QR decomposition. Motivated by the treatment in Section 5.3.7, consider a set of equations in matrix form:

$$\begin{bmatrix} a_{11} & a_{12} & a_{13} & \cdots & a_{1N} \\ a_{21} & a_{22} & a_{23} & \cdots & a_{2N} \\ a_{31} & a_{32} & a_{33} & \cdots & a_{3N} \\ \vdots & \vdots & \vdots & & \vdots \\ a_{M1} & a_{M2} & a_{M3} & \cdots & a_{MN} \\ \vdots & \vdots & \vdots & & \vdots \end{bmatrix} \begin{bmatrix} h_1 \\ h_2 \\ h_3 \\ \cdots \\ h_N \end{bmatrix} \approx \begin{bmatrix} b_1 \\ b_2 \\ b_3 \\ \vdots \\ b_M \\ \vdots \end{bmatrix}$$

†In Fig. 7.5 the correction gain stage is not shown. Also, the controls ρ_i are shown as if they depended only on the $\text{sgn}(y^{(i)})$. The simplified figure is meant only to illustrate the pipelining aspect of CORDIC circuits. In fact, the controls depend on $\text{sgn}(x^{(i)})\,\text{sgn}(y^{(i)})$.

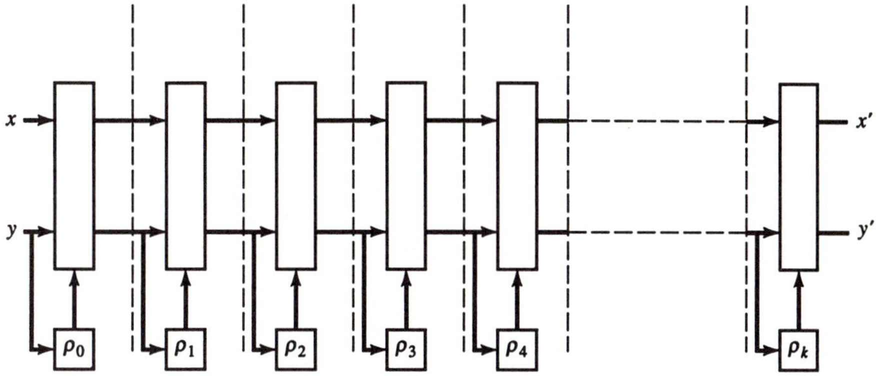

FIGURE 7.5 Pipelined CORDIC circuit.

which we may write even more compactly as

$$\left[\begin{array}{ccccc|c} a_{11} & a_{12} & a_{13} & \cdots & a_{1N} & b_1 \\ a_{21} & a_{22} & a_{23} & \cdots & a_{2N} & b_2 \\ a_{31} & a_{32} & a_{33} & \cdots & a_{3N} & b_3 \\ \vdots & \vdots & \vdots & & \vdots & \vdots \\ a_{M1} & a_{M2} & a_{M3} & \cdots & a_{MN} & b_M \\ \vdots & \vdots & \vdots & & \vdots & \vdots \end{array}\right] \begin{bmatrix} h_1 \\ h_2 \\ h_3 \\ \cdots \\ h_N \\ -1 \end{bmatrix} \approx \begin{bmatrix} 0 \\ 0 \\ 0 \\ \vdots \\ 0 \\ \vdots \end{bmatrix} \tag{7.3.43}$$

We abbreviate this as

$$\mathbf{Ah} \approx \mathbf{0} \tag{7.3.44}$$

Here $\mathbf{A}$ is given and our aim is to choose the unknowns $h_1, \ldots, h_N$ in such a way as to minimize the scalar quantity

$$\mathscr{E} = \|\mathbf{Ah}\|^2 = \mathbf{h}^H(\mathbf{A}^H\mathbf{A})\mathbf{h}$$

where $\mathbf{A}^H$ means simultaneous conjugation and transpose of $\mathbf{A}$.

This minimization problem depends on the given data $\mathbf{A}$ entirely through the matrix product $(\mathbf{A}^H\mathbf{A})$. Therefore, if the given data $\mathbf{A}$ were replaced by other data $\hat{\mathbf{A}}$ in such a way that

$$\hat{\mathbf{A}}^H\hat{\mathbf{A}} = \mathbf{A}^H\mathbf{A} \tag{7.3.45}$$

the minimization problem would discover the same answer $\mathbf{h}$.

We can change $\mathbf{A}$ to $\hat{\mathbf{A}}$ by premultiplying by a unitary matrix $\mathbf{Q}$ (e.g., a matrix $\mathbf{Q}$ with the property that $\mathbf{QQ}^H = \mathbf{I}$). If

$$\hat{\mathbf{A}} = \mathbf{QA}$$

then

$$\hat{\mathbf{A}}^H\hat{\mathbf{A}} = (\mathbf{A}^H\mathbf{Q}^H)(\mathbf{QA}) = \mathbf{A}^H(\mathbf{Q}^H\mathbf{Q})\mathbf{A} = \mathbf{A}^H\mathbf{A}$$

We are allowed to make such transformations repeatedly using a different unitary matrix **Q** in each transformation. This is like progressing through a series of problems

$$\begin{aligned} \mathbf{Ah} &\approx \mathbf{0} \\ (\mathbf{Q}_1\mathbf{A})\mathbf{h} &\approx \mathbf{0} \\ (\mathbf{Q}_2\mathbf{Q}_1\mathbf{A})\mathbf{h} &\approx \mathbf{0} \\ (\mathbf{Q}_3\mathbf{Q}_2\mathbf{Q}_1\mathbf{A})\mathbf{h} &\approx \mathbf{0} \\ \vdots \quad & \quad \vdots \end{aligned}$$

knowing that the **h** which solves any problem solves all the others.

Our strategy is to use Givens transformations to force many of the elements in the evolving A matrix to become zero. By such premultiplications, we can eventually arrive at a form of the problem where the configuration of nonzero elements in $\hat{\mathbf{A}}$ is as follows:

$$\left[\begin{array}{cccccc|c} \hat{a}_{11} & \hat{a}_{12} & \hat{a}_{13} & \cdots & \hat{a}_{1N} & & \hat{b}_1 \\ & \hat{a}_{22} & \hat{a}_{23} & \cdots & \hat{a}_{2N} & & \hat{b}_2 \\ & & \hat{a}_{33} & \cdots & \hat{a}_{3N} & & \hat{b}_3 \\ & & & \cdot & \cdot & & \vdots \\ & & & & \hat{a}_{NN} & & \hat{b}_N \\ \hline & & & & & & \hat{b}_{N+1} \\ & & & & & & \hat{b}_{N+2} \\ & & & & & & \vdots \\ & & & & & & \hat{b}_M \\ & & & & & & \vdots \end{array}\right] \begin{bmatrix} h_1 \\ h_2 \\ h_3 \\ \cdots \\ h_N \\ -1 \end{bmatrix} \approx \begin{bmatrix} 0 \\ 0 \\ 0 \\ \vdots \\ 0 \\ \vdots \end{bmatrix} \tag{7.3.46}$$

After this transformation the least-squares problem has a trivial solution. We want to choose **h** to minimize the norm of the column vector in (7.3.46). All but the first N elements are independent of **h**. The first N elements can be made equal to zero by a suitable choice of **h**. This clearly is the choice of **h** which minimizes the norm. Thus,

$$\left[\begin{array}{cccccc|c} \hat{a}_{11} & \hat{a}_{12} & \hat{a}_{13} & \cdots & \hat{a}_{1N} & & \hat{b}_1 \\ 0 & \hat{a}_{22} & \hat{a}_{23} & \cdots & \hat{a}_{2N} & & \hat{b}_2 \\ 0 & 0 & \hat{a}_{33} & \cdots & \hat{a}_{3N} & & \hat{b}_3 \\ \vdots & \vdots & \vdots & & \vdots & & \vdots \\ 0 & 0 & 0 & \cdots & \hat{a}_{NN} & & \hat{b}_N \end{array}\right] \begin{bmatrix} h_1 \\ h_2 \\ h_3 \\ \cdots \\ h_N \\ -1 \end{bmatrix} \approx \begin{bmatrix} 0 \\ 0 \\ 0 \\ \vdots \\ 0 \end{bmatrix} \tag{7.3.47}$$

Further, this choice of **h** can be made element by element in a simple way.

$$h_N = \frac{\hat{b}_N}{\hat{a}_{NN}}$$

$$h_{N-1} = \frac{\hat{b}_{N-1} - \hat{a}_{N-1,N} w_N}{\hat{a}_{N-1,N-1}}$$

$$h_{N-2} = \frac{\hat{b}_{N-2} - \hat{a}_{N-2,N-1} w_{N-1} - \hat{a}_{N-2,N} w_N}{\hat{a}_{N-2,N-2}}$$

$$h_{N-3} = \frac{\hat{b}_{N-3} - \hat{a}_{N-3,N-2} w_{N-2} - \hat{a}_{N-3,N-1} w_{N-1} - \hat{a}_{N-3,N} w_N}{\hat{a}_{N-3,N-3}}$$

$$\vdots$$

$$h_1 = \frac{\hat{b}_1 - \sum_{i=2}^{N} \hat{a}_{1i} h_i}{\hat{a}_{11}}$$

In the "equation" below, we use the symbol 0_m to identify the matrix element that we force to become zero in the mth such transformation. The other symbols a_{ij} and b_i in the equation are there as place keepers only. That is, they have the sense of variables in a computer program, and their values are changed by the successive transformations:

$$\left[\begin{array}{cccccc|c} a_{11} & a_{12} & a_{13} & a_{14} & \cdots & a_{1N} & b_1 \\ 0_1 & a_{22} & a_{23} & a_{24} & \cdots & a_{2N} & b_2 \\ 0_2 & 0_3 & a_{33} & a_{34} & \cdots & a_{3N} & b_3 \\ 0_4 & 0_5 & 0_6 & a_{44} & \cdots & a_{4N} & b_4 \\ 0_7 & 0_8 & 0_9 & 0_{10} & \cdots & a_{5N} & b_5 \\ \vdots & \vdots & \vdots & \vdots & \vdots & \vdots & \vdots \end{array}\right] \begin{bmatrix} h_1 \\ h_2 \\ h_3 \\ \cdots \\ h_N \\ -1 \end{bmatrix} \approx \begin{bmatrix} 0 \\ 0 \\ 0 \\ \vdots \\ 0 \\ \vdots \end{bmatrix}$$

As long as the data a_{ij} are real, we can force the necessary configuration of zeroed elements by Givens transformations. As we saw above, a Givens transformation always reduces to operations on a pair of rows extracted from the larger data matrix. Thus to introduce the first zero, which will occupy the a_{21} position, we need only begin with the first two rows of **A**

$$\begin{bmatrix} \cos\phi_1 & \sin\phi_1 \\ -\sin\phi_1 & \cos\phi_1 \end{bmatrix} \left[\begin{array}{cccccc|c} a_{11} & a_{12} & a_{13} & a_{14} & \cdots & a_{1N} & b_1 \\ a_{21} & a_{22} & a_{23} & a_{24} & \cdots & a_{2N} & b_2 \end{array}\right]$$

where we determine ϕ_1 using the pair (a_{11}, a_{21}) and rotate the other pairs accordingly. Note that we may accomplish this for real data by feeding the pair (a_{11}, a_{21}) into a CORDIC circuit as a leader pair, and then feeding the other general pairs (a_{1i}, a_{2i}) as followers. Because of the pipelining nature of a CORDIC circuit, we begin feeding (a_{12}, a_{22}) into the CORDIC while (a_{12}, a_{21}) is still within the circuit.

To introduce the second zero, which will occupy the a_{31} position, we use a Givens transformation that acts on rows 1 and 3—remember that our notation uses the subscripts as placekeepers, but we ought not forget that the values of a_{1i} in the first row are changed by the first Givens transformation. We feed rows 1 and 3 into a CORDIC circuit.

$$\begin{bmatrix} \cos\phi_2 & \sin\phi_2 \\ -\sin\phi_2 & \cos\phi_2 \end{bmatrix} \left[\begin{array}{cccccc|c} a_{11} & a_{12} & a_{23} & a_{14} & \cdots & a_{1N} & b_1 \\ a_{31} & a_{32} & a_{33} & a_{34} & \cdots & a_{3N} & b_3 \end{array}\right]$$

This operation is completely analogous to the first Givens transformation. At this point, our revised problem looks like this:

$$\left[\begin{array}{ccccc|c} a_{11} & a_{12} & a_{13} & \cdots & a_{1N} & b_1 \\ 0 & a_{22} & a_{23} & \cdots & a_{2N} & b_2 \\ 0 & a_{32} & a_{33} & \cdots & a_{3N} & b_3 \\ a_{41} & a_{42} & a_{43} & \cdots & a_{4N} & b_4 \\ \vdots & \vdots & \vdots & & \vdots & \vdots \\ a_{M1} & a_{M2} & a_{M3} & \cdots & a_{MN} & b_M \\ \vdots & \vdots & \vdots & & \vdots & \end{array}\right] \begin{bmatrix} h_1 \\ h_2 \\ h_3 \\ \cdots \\ h_N \\ -1 \end{bmatrix} \approx \begin{bmatrix} 0 \\ 0 \\ 0 \\ \vdots \\ 0 \\ \vdots \end{bmatrix}$$

The third zero, which will occupy the a_{32} position, is introduced by a CORDIC circuit which operates on rows 2 and 3.

$$\begin{bmatrix} \cos\phi_3 & \sin\phi_3 \\ -\sin\phi_3 & \cos\phi_3 \end{bmatrix} \left[\begin{array}{ccccc|c} 0 & a_{22} & a_{23} & \cdots & a_{2N} & b_2 \\ 0 & a_{32} & a_{33} & \cdots & a_{3N} & b_3 \end{array}\right]$$

Here the leader pair is (a_{22}, a_{32}). The initial pair of (0, 0) would remain (0, 0) after any possible rotation, so it can be left out of the computation.

Continuing, we rotate the first row against the fourth to force a zero in the position of a_{41}, the second row against the fourth to force a zero in the position of a_{42}, and the third row against the fourth to force a zero in the position of a_{43}.

Suppose that we have proceeded in this way with the data in the first $M - 1$ rows of the original matrix, where $M > N$, and we have zeroed out a trapezoid-shaped bite. The revised problem looks like this:

$$\left[\begin{array}{ccccc|c} a_{11} & a_{12} & a_{13} & \cdots & a_{1N} & b_1 \\ 0 & a_{22} & a_{23} & \cdots & a_{2N} & b_2 \\ 0 & 0 & a_{33} & \cdots & a_{3N} & b_3 \\ \vdots & \vdots & \vdots & & \vdots & \vdots \\ 0 & 0 & 0 & \cdots & a_{NN} & b_N \\ 0 & 0 & 0 & \cdots & 0 & b_{N+1} \\ \vdots & \vdots & \vdots & & \vdots & \vdots \\ 0 & 0 & 0 & \cdots & 0 & b_{M-1} \\ \hline a_{M1} & a_{M2} & a_{M3} & \cdots & a_{MN} & b_M \\ \vdots & \vdots & \vdots & & \vdots & \vdots \end{array}\right] \begin{bmatrix} h_1 \\ h_2 \\ h_3 \\ \cdots \\ h_N \\ -1 \end{bmatrix} \approx \begin{bmatrix} 0 \\ 0 \\ 0 \\ \vdots \\ 0 \\ \vdots \end{bmatrix} \qquad (7.3.48)$$

Again we remind the reader that the symbols a_{ij} and b_i are only placekeepers, and their values are not those of the original problem. However, all the quantities below the line are untouched and still have their original values.

For this and subsequent rows there are N elements which must become zeroes using N Givens transformations. The pattern then repeats from row to row. We zero out a_{M1} by rotating row M against row 1, then we zero out a_{M2} by rotating row M against row 2, . . . , and we zero out a_{MN} by rotating row M against row N.

This set of steps changes one row of raw data to a row of zeros, except for the last element, b_M, which is modified but need not be zeroed. The set of steps may be repeated for each new row until all the rows of data have been processed in this way. At that point we will have modified our least-squares problem sufficiently to see how to solve it, as explained above.

Each step consists of putting a pair of rows through a CORDIC circuit. One row comes from the triangular matrix and the other row comes from the new data. One output of the CORDIC circuit becomes a row of the modified triangular matrix. The other output is used in a succeeding CORDIC circuit with the next row of the triangular matrix. The array of N CORDIC circuits may be considered a systolic array, with each CORDIC circuit responsible for processing one row of the triangular matrix, which is retained "locally," while it passes the modified new row, whose leading element gets replaced by a zero, forward to the next in the chain of CORDIC circuits. This is shown in Fig. 7.6.

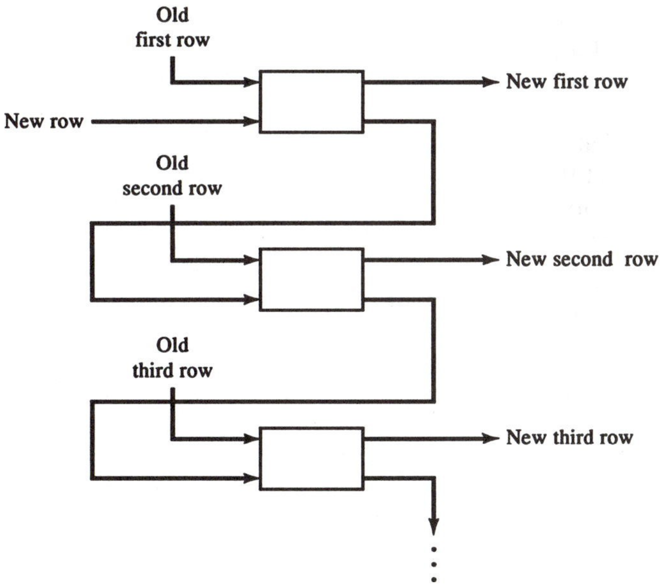

FIGURE 7.6 Systolic array of CORDICs to update a triangular matrix for one new row.

Systolic arrays can carry out large number-crunching problems very efficiently in many cases. They are characterized by these properties:

- Many operations are carried out simultaneously, using parallel processing.
- Data needed in each step are available either locally or in a physically adjacent processor.
- Data arrives where they are needed exactly when they are needed.

The foregoing description of CORDIC processing for the Givens transformations as they are used to triangularize an array of data for a least-squares problem is a good example of a systolic array. As soon as the first CORDIC in the chain has been fed all the data it needs for row M it is free to accept and process data for row $M + 1$. Therefore, the first CORDIC can be utilized as much as 100%. The second CORDIC can begin its work on row 2 of the triangular matrix and row M as soon as the first CORDIC has finished its work on the second element pair. The third CORDIC can begin its work as soon as the second CORDIC has finished its work on the third pair.

Unfortunately, this systolic array of CORDICs is not 100% efficient overall, for the simple reason that CORDICs near the end of the chain have less and less work to do. The last CORDIC, which is responsible for row N of the triangular matrix, only needs to do two rotations per new row. Overall the average CORDIC can be kept 50% occupied.

A scheme called *MUSE*, developed at Lincoln Laboratory, can achieve a 100% efficient use of CORDIC elements in this same problem. In the MUSE architecture, it is recognized that the total workload of the two CORDICs responsible for rows k and $N + 1 - k$, respectively, is constant. Therefore, one CORDIC is assigned the responsibility for updating both rows, alternately. A total of $N/2$ CORDICs is kept 100% occupied. Each CORDIC has access to memory sufficient to store two rows of the matrix, whose combined length is a constant ($N + 3$ words). To assure that data arrive at each CORDIC from either forward or backward along the chain of CORDICs at exactly the right time, the latency of the CORDIC circuit is chosen carefully, but all CORDICs in the system use the same latency.

Modification for Complex Data. In the preceding section, CORDIC circuits were proposed as a virtually ideal computing element for Givens transformations. However, when the data may be complex, the CORDIC approach is inadequate without modification. In the modification we propose, three CORDIC circuits are interconnected to form a *supercell* which does for complex data what one CORDIC circuit does for real data.

The issue with complex data is that the angle involved in a complex Givens transformation

$$\arctan \frac{y_l}{x_l}$$

although mathematically meaningful, cannot be expressed by (7.3.35).

But we are allowed to use other unitary transformations in the least-squares problem. In particular, we are allowed to premultiply our data matrix by another type of unitary matrix which makes the leading element of any row real. For example, to make the leading element of the first row of **A** become real, we multiply the entire first row of **A** by $e^{-j\theta}$, where $\theta = \arctan\,[\mathrm{Im}(a_{11})/\mathrm{Re}(a_{11})]$. We can embed this in a unitary matrix as

$$\begin{bmatrix} e^{-j\theta} & & & & \\ & 1 & & & \\ & & \ddots & & \\ & & & 1 & \\ & & & & 1 \end{bmatrix}$$

Multiplying by this matrix can also be accomplished by pushing data through a CORDIC circuit. The two inputs are the real and imaginary parts of the data, and the action of the CORDIC on the leader is to choose the angle to zero out the leader's imaginary part. For the followers, the action of a CORDIC circuit is to rotate the two-component vector $(\mathrm{Re}(a_{1i}), \mathrm{Im}(a_{1i}))$, which is actually the same as multiplying it by $e^{-j\theta}$.

Therefore, we can replace a typical step of the Givens approach by a more complicated step involving three substeps, as follows:

$$\begin{bmatrix} x_1'' & x_2'' & x_3'' & \cdots \\ y_1'' & y_2'' & y_3'' & \cdots \end{bmatrix} \Leftarrow \begin{bmatrix} e^{j\theta_x} & 0 \\ 0 & e^{j\theta_y} \end{bmatrix} \begin{bmatrix} x_1 & x_2 & x_3 & \cdots \\ y_1 & y_2 & y_3 & \cdots \end{bmatrix} \tag{7.3.49}$$

$$\begin{bmatrix} x_1' & x_2' & x_3' & \cdots \\ y_1' & y_2' & y_3' & \cdots \end{bmatrix} \Leftarrow \begin{bmatrix} \cos\phi & \sin\phi \\ -\sin\phi & \cos\phi \end{bmatrix} \begin{bmatrix} x_1'' & x_2'' & x_3'' & \cdots \\ y_1'' & y_2'' & y_3'' & \cdots \end{bmatrix} \tag{7.3.50}$$

$$\theta_x = \arctan\frac{\mathrm{Im}(x_1)}{\mathrm{Re}(x_1)} \tag{7.3.51}$$

$$\theta_y = \arctan\frac{\mathrm{Im}(y_1)}{\mathrm{Re}(y_1)} \tag{7.3.52}$$

$$\phi = \arctan\frac{y_1''}{x_1''} \tag{7.3.53}$$

In the above, the first substep makes the leading element of the first row real by forcing the first row through a CORDIC. Simultaneously, the second substep, expressed in the same matrix equation, (7.3.49), makes the leading element of the second row real by forcing the second row through a CORDIC.

The third substep is like a conventional Givens transformation involving a real angle ϕ. The setup of the angle uses leaders that are real numbers, so the angle may be determined by a CORDIC. The action on followers is to multiply the real Givens matrix by complex data. This means applying the Givens matrix independently to the real and imaginary parts of the data. The real and imaginary parts can be processed simultaneously and independently by two separate CORDICs if they can be contrived to use the same control variables ρ_i derived from the leaders of the real data. It would seem that the typical step requires four CORDIC circuits.

If we examine the work in updating the triangular matrix with a new row of data, it turns out that the typical step, combining the new row and the kth row of the old triangular matrix, can be accomplished with only three CORDICs instead of four. We force the *new row* through a CORDIC to make its leading element real. The leader of the kth row, a_{kk}, is already real—we can prove this by mathematical induction. Therefore, it is not necessary to provide a CORDIC to make a_{kk} real. Two CORDICs are still required to apply the Givens transformation to the real and imaginary parts of the data.

Altogether, three CORDIC circuits accomplish the update as follows:

- One CORDIC makes the leading element of the new row real.
- One CORDIC applies the Givens transformation to the real parts of two rows.
- Another CORDIC applies the Givens transformation to the imaginary parts of the same two rows.

The modification to handle complex data does not affect the general systolic organization of a system of CORDIC circuits. Figure 7.7 illustrates a systolic array of CORDICs to update a triangular matrix for one new row with complex data.

7.4 RECURSIVE LEAST-SQUARES ESTIMATION BASED ON THE HOUSEHOLDER TRANSFORMATION

In section 5.3 we described the use of the Householder transformation to perform QR decomposition. In this section we develop a time-recursive form for LS estimation using the Householder transformation. We shall describe an algorithm in a block time-recursive form.

7.4.1 Block Time-Recursive LS Estimation Using the Householder Transformation

The Householder transformation, introduced in Section 5.3, can also be adapted for time-recursive LS estimation. For such an application it is more efficient to have multiple new data vectors added to the data matrix at a time. Below we discuss the case where L rows of new data are added, so that we consider *block-exponentially weighted* LS estimation. Let us assume that we have obtained for R-factor of the matrix $\mathbf{W}_b(n-L)\bar{\mathbf{A}}(n-L)$, where n is an integer multiple of L and $\mathbf{W}_b(n)$ is the block-exponential weighting matrix, defined as

$$\mathbf{W}_b(n) = \begin{bmatrix} w^{(n-L)/2L}\mathbf{I}_{L\times L} & & & \mathbf{0} \\ & \ddots & & \\ & & w^{1/2}\mathbf{I}_{L\times L} & \\ \mathbf{0} & & & \mathbf{I}_{L\times L} \end{bmatrix} \tag{7.4.1}$$

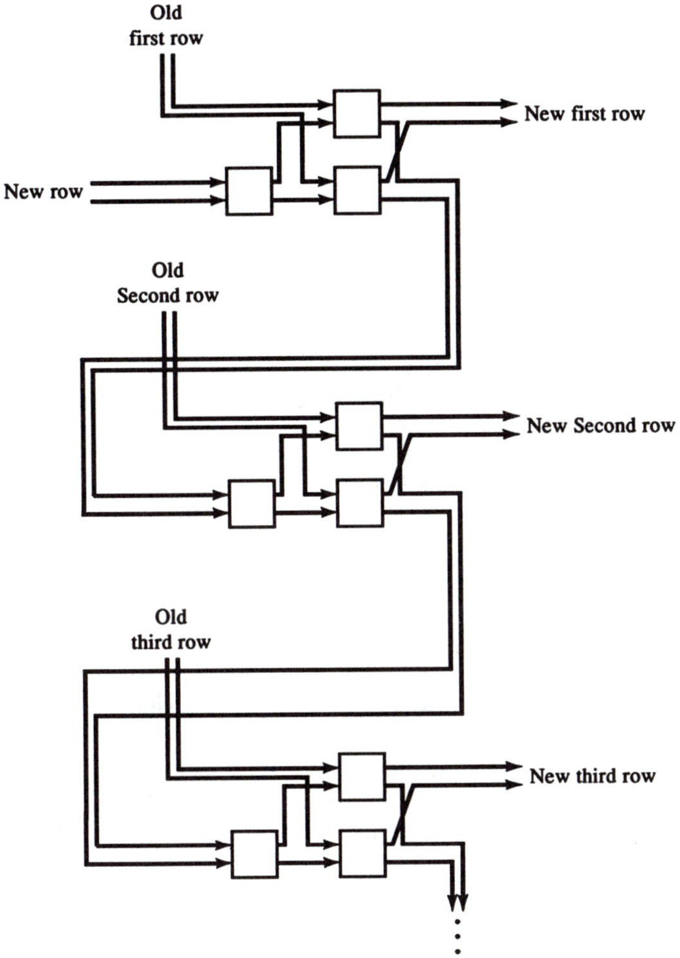

FIGURE 7.7 Systolic array of CORDICS to update a triangular matrix for one new row, with complex data.

where $\mathbf{I}_{L \times L}$ is an $L \times L$ identity matrix. To obtain the QR decomposition of the matrix $\mathbf{W}_b(n)\bar{\mathbf{A}}(n)$, we can apply the Householder transformation to the augmented matrix $\bar{\mathfrak{R}}_b(n)$, which is defined as

$$\bar{\mathfrak{R}}_b(n) = \begin{bmatrix} \sqrt{w}\mathfrak{R}(n-L) & \sqrt{w}\tilde{\mathbf{d}}_M(n-L) \\ \mathbf{X}^t_{M,L}(n) & \mathbf{d}_L(n) \end{bmatrix}$$

$$\equiv \begin{bmatrix} \sqrt{w}r_{11}(n-L) & \sqrt{w}r_{12}(n-L) & \cdots & \sqrt{w}r_{1M}(n-L) & \sqrt{w}r_{1d}(n-L) \\ 0 & \sqrt{w}r_{22}(n-L) & \cdots & \sqrt{w}r_{2M}(n-L) & \sqrt{w}r_{2d}(n-L) \\ \vdots & \vdots & \ddots & \vdots & \vdots \\ 0 & 0 & \cdots & \sqrt{w}r_{MM}(n-L) & \sqrt{w}r_{Md}(n-L) \\ \mathbf{x}_1^{(1)}(n) & \mathbf{x}_2^{(1)}(n) & \cdots & \mathbf{x}_M^{(1)}(n) & \mathbf{e}^{(1)}(n) \end{bmatrix} \tag{7.4.2}$$

where

$$\mathbf{x}_k^{(1)}(n) = [x_k(n - L + 1), \ldots, x_k(n - 1), x_k(n)]^t \tag{7.4.3}$$

for $k = 1, 2, \ldots, M$, and

$$\mathbf{e}^{(1)}(n) = [d(n - L + 1), \ldots, d(n - 1), d(n)]^t \tag{7.4.4}$$

Because of its special structure, it is less complex computationally to perform the QR decomposition of matrix $\bar{\mathfrak{R}}_b(n)$ through the Householder transformations than to perform the QR decomposition of an arbitrary $(M + L) \times (M + 1)$. The procedure for performing the QR decomposition of the matrix $\bar{\mathfrak{R}}_b(n)$ is given below.

From the first column of the matrix $\bar{\mathfrak{R}}_b(n)$, we construct the vector $\mathbf{b}_1$ given by (5.3.92). Since the first column $\mathbf{p}_1$ has $L + 1$ nonzero elements, $\mathbf{b}_1$ has only $L + 1$ nonzero elements, also. It can be written as

$$\mathbf{b}_1 = \begin{bmatrix} r_{11}(n - L) + [\text{sign of } r_{11}(n - L)] \times \sqrt{w|r_{11}(n - L)|^2 + \|\mathbf{x}_1^{(1)}(n)\|^2} \\ 0 \\ \vdots \\ 0 \\ \mathbf{x}_1^{(1)}(n) \end{bmatrix} \tag{7.4.5}$$

In constructing $\mathbf{b}_1$ we have assumed that $r_{11}(n - L)$ is real and selected $\sigma_1 = \pm 1$, where the sign of σ_1 is the same as the sign of $r_{11}(n - L)$. As indicated in Section 5.3, even though the Householder transformation does not guarantee the diagonal elements of the R-factor to be real, we can always convert them to real numbers by a pure angle rotation of the elements in each row. Once the diagonal elements become real, they will stay real in subsequent time-recursive Householder transformations.

After applying the Householder matrix $\mathbf{H}_1(n)$, which is constructed from $\mathbf{b}_1$, to the matrix $\bar{\mathfrak{R}}_b(n)$, we have

$$\mathbf{H}_1(n)\bar{\mathfrak{R}}_b(n) = \begin{bmatrix} r_{11}(n) & r_{12}(n) & \cdots & r_{1M}(n) & r_{1d}(n) \\ 0 & \sqrt{w}r_{22}(n - L) & \cdots & \sqrt{w}r_{2M}(n - L) & \sqrt{w}r_{2d}(n - L) \\ \vdots & \vdots & \ddots & \vdots & \vdots \\ 0 & 0 & \cdots & \sqrt{w}r_{MM}(n - L) & \sqrt{w}r_{Md}(n - L) \\ 0 & \mathbf{x}_2^{(2)}(n) & \cdots & \mathbf{x}_M^{(2)}(n) & \mathbf{e}^{(2)}(n) \end{bmatrix} \tag{7.4.6}$$

From (5.4.90) it follows that

$$r_{11}(n) = -\sigma_1\|\mathbf{v}_1\| = -[\text{sign of } r_{11}(n - L)] \times \sqrt{w|r_{11}(n - L)|^2 + \|\mathbf{x}_1^{(1)}(n)\|^2} \tag{7.4.7}$$

Note that $r_{11}(n)$ and $r_{11}(n - L)$ have different signs.

Since the application of the Householder matrix $\mathbf{H}_1(n)$ to the second through the $(M + 1) =$ columns of matrix $\bar{\mathfrak{R}}_b(n)$ only modify the top element and the bottom L elements in each column, we need only to consider these elements of interest. They can be computed as

$$r_{1k}(n) = \sqrt{w}r_{1k}(n - L) - g_{1k}[r_{11}(n - L) - r_{11}(n)] \tag{7.4.8}$$

and

$$\mathbf{x}_k^{(2)}(n) = \mathbf{x}_k^{(1)}(n) - g_{1k}\mathbf{x}_1^{(1)}(n) \tag{7.4.9}$$

where

$$\begin{aligned} g_{1k} &= \frac{r_{11}(n-L) - r_{11}(n)}{(\|\mathbf{b}_1\|^2/2)} \sqrt{w}r_{1k}(n-L) + \frac{[\mathbf{x}_1^{(1)}(n)]^H}{\|\mathbf{b}_1\|^2/2}\mathbf{x}_k^{(1)}(n) \\ &\equiv \zeta_1 r_{1k}(n-L) + \xi_1{}^H \mathbf{x}_k^{(1)}(n) \end{aligned} \tag{7.4.10}$$

Note that the scalar ζ_1 and the vector ξ_1 are common to all the columns and only need to be computed once. Since $r_{11}(n-L)$ and $r_{11}(n)$ have different signs, we will not lose precision in computing $r_{11}(n-L) - r_{11}(n)$. The quantity $\|\mathbf{b}_1\|^2/2$ in the denominators can be computed as

$$\begin{aligned} \frac{\|\mathbf{b}_1\|^2}{2} &= \frac{[r_{11}(n-L) - r_{11}(n)]^2 + \|\mathbf{x}_1^{(1)}(n)\|^2}{2} \\ &= \frac{r_{11}^2(n-L) + r_{11}^2(n) - 2r_{11}(n-L)r_{11}(n) + \|\mathbf{x}_1^{(1)}(n)\|^2}{2} \\ &= r_{11}^2(n) - r_{11}(n-L)r_{11}(n) = r_{11}(n)[r_{11}(n) - r_{11}(n-L)] \end{aligned} \tag{7.4.11}$$

Similarly, we construct the second Householder matrix $\mathbf{H}_2(n)$ to eliminate the bottom L elements of the second column of the matrix $\mathbf{H}_1(n)\bar{\mathfrak{R}}_b(n)$. This time we shall leave the first row untouched and only the elements in the second row and the bottom L rows are affected. In general, we construct the Householder matrices $\mathbf{H}_i(n)$, $i = 2, 3, \ldots, M$, to eliminate the bottom L elements of the ith column of the matrix $\mathbf{H}_{i-1}(n) \cdots \mathbf{H}_1(n)\bar{\mathfrak{R}}_b(n)$ while leaving the first $i-1$ rows untouched, and only the elements in the ith row and the bottom L rows are affected. The matrix $\mathbf{H}_i(n)$ is constructed the same way as $\mathbf{H}_1(n)$, by substituting $r_{ii}(n-L)$ and $\mathbf{x}_i^{(i)}(n)$ in place of $r_{11}(n-L)$ and $\mathbf{x}_1^{(1)}(n)$, respectively. Applying $\mathbf{H}_i(n)$ to $\mathbf{H}_{i-1}(n) \cdots \mathbf{H}_1(n)\bar{\mathfrak{R}}_b(n)$ results in the matrix

$$\mathbf{H}_i(n)\mathbf{H}_{i-1}(n) \cdots \mathbf{H}_1(n)\bar{\mathfrak{R}}_b(n)$$

$$= \begin{bmatrix} r_{11}(n) & r_{12}(n) & \cdots & r_{1i}(n) & r_{1i+1}(n) & \cdots & r_{1M}(n) & r_{1d}(n) \\ 0 & r_{22}(n) & \cdots & r_{2i}(n) & r_{2i+1}(n) & \cdots & r_{2M}(n) & r_{2d}(n) \\ \vdots & 0 & \ddots & \vdots & \vdots & \cdots & \vdots & \vdots \\ \vdots & \vdots & \ddots & r_{ii}(n) & r_{ii+1}(n) & \cdots & r_{iM}(n) & r_{id}(n) \\ \vdots & \vdots & \cdots & 0 & \sqrt{w}r_{i+1i+1}(n-L) & \cdots & \sqrt{w}r_{i+1M}(n-L) & \sqrt{w}r_{i+1d}(n-L) \\ \vdots & \vdots & \vdots & \vdots & 0 & \ddots & \vdots & \vdots \\ \vdots & \vdots & \cdots & \vdots & \vdots & 0 & \sqrt{w}r_{MM}(n-L) & \sqrt{w}r_{Md}(n-L) \\ 0 & 0 & & 0 & \mathbf{x}_{i+1}^{(i+1)}(n) & \cdots & \mathbf{x}_M^{(i+1)}(n) & \mathbf{e}^{(i+1)}(n) \end{bmatrix} \tag{7.4.12}$$

The modified scalars in the ith row and the vectors in the bottom row [i.e., $r_{id}(n)$, $\mathbf{e}^{(i)}(n)$, $r_{ik}(n)$'s, and $\mathbf{x}_k^{(i)}(n)$'s, $k = i + 1, \ldots, M$] are computed similarly to (7.4.7) through (7.4.11). Hence

$$r_{ii}(n) = -[\text{sign of } r_{ii}(n - L)] \times \sqrt{w|r_{ii}(n - L)|^2 + \|\mathbf{x}_i^{(i)}(n)\|^2} \qquad (7.4.13)$$

$$r_{ik}(n) = \sqrt{w}\, r_{ik}(n - L) - g_{ik}[r_{ii}(n - L) - r_{ii}(n)] \qquad (7.4.14)$$

and

$$\mathbf{x}_k^{(i+1)}(n) = \mathbf{x}_k^{(i)} \qquad {}_{ik}\ (n) - g\ \mathbf{x}_i^{(i)}(n) \qquad (7.4.15)$$

where

$$\begin{aligned} g_{ik} &= \frac{r_{ii}(n - L) - r_{ii}(n)}{|\mathbf{b}_i\|^2/2} \sqrt{w}\, r_{ik}(n - L) + \frac{[\mathbf{x}_i^{(i)}(n)]^H}{\|\mathbf{b}_i\|^2/2} \mathbf{x}_k^{(i)}(n) \\ &\equiv \zeta_i r_{ik}(n - L) + \xi_i^H \mathbf{x}_k^{(i)}(n) \end{aligned} \qquad (7.4.16)$$

By definition

$$\mathbf{b}_i = \begin{bmatrix} 0 \\ \vdots \\ r_{ii}(n - L) + [\text{sign of } r_{ii}(n - L)] \times \sqrt{w|r_{ii}(n - L)|^2 + \|\mathbf{x}_i^{(i)}(n)\|^2} \\ 0 \\ \vdots \\ 0 \\ \mathbf{x}_i^{(i)}(n) \end{bmatrix} \qquad (7.4.17)$$

Then

$$\frac{\|\mathbf{b}_i\|^2}{2} = r_{ii}^2(n) - r_{ii}(n - L) r_{ii}(n) = r_{ii}(n)[r_{ii}(n) - r_{ii}(n - L)] \qquad (7.4.18)$$

Note that the scalar ζ_i and the vector ξ_i in (7.4.16) are common to all the columns and only need to be computed once.

After constructing and applying the Householder matrices, $\mathbf{H}_i(n), \ldots, \mathbf{H}_M(n)$ to the matrix $\bar{\mathfrak{R}}_b(n)$, we complete its QR decomposition. That is,

$$\mathbf{H}_M(n) \cdots \mathbf{H}_1(n) \begin{bmatrix} \sqrt{w}\mathfrak{R}(n - L) & \sqrt{w}\tilde{\mathbf{d}}_M(n - L) \\ \mathbf{X}_{L,M}^t(n) & \mathbf{d}_L(n) \end{bmatrix} = \begin{bmatrix} \mathfrak{R}(n) & \tilde{\mathbf{d}}_M(n) \\ \mathbf{0} & \mathbf{e}^{(M+1)}(n) \end{bmatrix} \qquad (7.4.19)$$

The optimal LS coefficient at time n can be computed according to (7.1.11).

From (7.4.12), (7.4.17), and (7.4.18) it follows that we need $2L + 4$ CMACs plus one division and one square-root operation to construct one Householder matrix $\mathbf{H}_i(n)$, $i = 1, 2, \ldots, M$. It can be seen from (7.4.8) through (7.4.10) that applying $\mathbf{H}_i(n)$ to $\mathbf{H}_{i-1}(n) \cdots \mathbf{H}_i(n)\bar{\mathfrak{R}}_b(n)$ requires $(M - i + 1) \times (2L + 3)$ CMACs. In total we need $(L + 1.5) \times M^2 +$

$(3L + 5.5) \times M$ CMACs to perform the QR decomposition of the matrix $\bar{\mathfrak{R}}_b(n)$ in (7.4.12). This complexity is much less than that needed by using Householder matrices to perform the QR decomposition of a general $(M + L) \times (M + 1)$ matrix. The block time-recursive implementation of the Householder algorithm is given in Table 7.9.

When $L = 1$, we have a Householder transformation-based conventional (nonblock) time-recursive LS estimation algorithm. It can be shown that such an algorithm is equivalent to a Givens reflection-based algorithm. However, the nonblock time-recursive Householder QR decomposition algorithm is not as efficient as the algorithm based on Givens rotations with square roots, which requires about $2 \times M^2 + 5M$ CMACs to perform the same task. On the other hand, the block time-recursive Householder QR-decomposition algorithm is more efficient than the Givens algorithm for LS estimation when L is greater than or equal to 2. Moreover, both the Householder and the Givens algorithms can compress all the energy of a vector into one element. However, the algorithm using the Householder matrix is computationally more efficient if the dimension of the vectors is greater than 3.

Modular Implementation. The block time-recursive LS algorithm based on the Householder transformation can be implemented using a modular structure. From observation of (7.4.13) through (7.4.18) we note that different stages of the Householder transformation are implemented using the same

TABLE 7.9 Block Time-Recursive Householder Algorithm

Initialization before algorithm starts ($n = L$)

$$d_i(0) = 0, \; i = 1, 2, \ldots, M$$

$$r_{ij}(0) = 0, \; i = 1, 2, \ldots, M, \; j = i, i + 1, \ldots, M$$

Initialization for every n

$$\mathbf{d}^{(1)}(n) = [d(n - L + 1), \ldots, d(n - 1), d(n)]'$$

$$\text{and } \mathbf{x}_i^{(1)}(n) = \mathbf{x}_i(n) \; (i = 1, 2, \ldots, M)$$

do $i = 1, 2, \ldots, \min(M, n)$

$$r_{ii}(n) = -[\text{sign of } r_{ii}(n - 1)] \times [w r_{ii}^2(n - L) + \|\mathbf{x}_i^{(i)}(n)\|^2]^{1/2}$$

$$\psi_i = r_{ii}(n)[r_{ii}(n) - r_{ii}(n - L)]$$

$$\zeta_i = \sqrt{w}[r_{ii}(n - L) - r_{ii}(n)]/\psi_i$$

$$\xi_i = \mathbf{x}_i^{(i)}(n)/\psi_i$$

do $j = i + 1, 2, \ldots, M$

$$g_{ij}(n) = \zeta_i r_{ij}(n - L) + \xi_i^H \mathbf{x}_j^{(i)}(n)$$

$$\mathbf{x}_j^{(i+1)}(n) = \mathbf{x}_j^{(i)}(n) - g_{ij}(n)\mathbf{x}_i^{(i)}(n)$$

(end of loop j)

$$g_{id}(n) = \zeta_i r_{id}(n - L) + \xi_i^H \mathbf{d}^{(i)}(n)$$

$$\mathbf{d}^{(i+1)}(n) = \mathbf{d}^{(i)}(n) - g_{id}(n)\mathbf{x}_i^{(i)}(n)$$

(end of loop i)

set of equations with a different index. A systolic array implementation of the block time-recursive Householder algorithm has been given by Liu et al. (1990).

7.5 ORDER-RECURSIVE LS ESTIMATION ALGORITHMS

In this section we discuss a class of LS estimation algorithms that share a common characteristic—all are order recursive. In general, LS algorithms can be classified into two categories: fixed-order LS algorithms and order-recursive LS (ORLS) algorithms, where the order of an LS estimation algorithm is defined to be the dimension of the data vector in the estimation. For example, LS estimation based on $\mathbf{X}_M(n)$ is an Mth-order estimation. A fixed-order LS algorithm has a predetermined order. This order cannot be changed without reinitializing the entire algorithm. Examples of fixed-order algorithms are the RLS algorithms described in Section 6.2.4. On the other hand, an ORLS algorithm computes all LS estimates of order from 1 through N—the predetermined maximum order. Some ORLS algorithms have already been described [e.g., the LS lattice algorithm (Section 6.3.1), the time-recursive Gram–Schmidt (RMGS) algorithm (Section 7.2.2), and the Givens algorithm (Section 7.3.3)].

ORLS algorithms have many attractive properties, including the flexibility of selecting the optimal estimation order during operation, a modular structure suitable for systolic array implementation, and better numerical behavior. Due to these desirable properties, ORLS algorithms have attracted much attention in adaptive filtering and estimation. Much effort has been devoted to deriving different ORLS algorithms and to compare their numerical properties and computational complexities. As a result, a large number of ORLS algorithms have been derived. On the other hand, little effort has been made to investigate the relationships among the different types of ORLS algorithms.

In this section we provide a unified treatment of all existing ORLS algorithms. We view the ORLS algorithms from two independent aspects: their *structure* or how the order recursions are performed, and the way in which the *time updates* are performed. Such a treatment not only simplifies the understanding of ORLS algorithms but also provides a systematic way of constructing new ORLS algorithms. Although the emphasis will be on time-recursive LS algorithms, some of the conclusions also apply to block LS estimation algorithms.

7.5.1 Fundamental Relations Of Order-Recursive LS Estimation

The order-recursive property of LS estimation has a clear geometrical interpretation. It is directly related to the decomposition of projection in orthogonal subspaces of a Hilbert (metric) space. Although it is possible to understand the order-recursive LS estimation algorithms from a purely geometric point of view, such an approach requires the reader to have a deep understanding of Hilbert spaces and the operations in these spaces. Instead, in this section we show that the order-recursive LS estimation algorithms are actually the result of three basic relations that can be described algebraically. These relations, which are algebraic interpretations of the geometric method, preserve the power of the geometric approach while being easier to understand.

Preliminaries and Notation. In the Mth-order LS estimation problem described in Sections 5.3 and 7.1.1, our objective is to determine the LS residual error vector $\mathbf{e}_M(n)$. From (5.3.6) and (5.3.10) we know that $\mathbf{e}_M(n)$ satisfies the equation

$$\mathbf{e}_M(n) = \mathbf{d}(n) - \mathbf{A}_M(n)\mathbf{R}_M^{-1}(n)\mathbf{A}_M^H(n)\mathbf{W}^2(n)\mathbf{d}(n) = \mathbf{d}(n) - \mathbf{A}_M(n)\mathbf{h}_M(n) \quad (7.5.1)$$

where $\mathbf{R}_M(n)$ and $\mathbf{h}_M(n)$ are defined in (5.3.11) and (5.3.12).

To facilitate the discussion, we first introduce additional notation used in this section. A matrix and a vector are denoted by a boldface capital and lowercase character, respectively. A scalar is denoted by a nonboldface character. The letters e or E are used to denote quantities related to LS error, r and R denote correlations, and H or h denote LS estimation coefficients. These characters may have subscripts and superscripts. Superscripts denote the desired signal vector or matrix and subscripts denote the data matrix on which the LS estimation is based when the quantities represented are related to LS estimation errors. The meanings of subscripts and superscripts associated with other quantities are also defined and are illustrated by the following example.

We first partition the data matrix $\mathbf{A}_M(n)$ as

$$\mathbf{A}_M(n) = [\mathbf{X}(n){:}\mathbf{Y}(n)] \quad (7.5.2)$$

where $\mathbf{X}(n)$ and $\mathbf{Y}(n)$ are $(n + 1) \times (M - L)$ and $(n + 1) \times L$ matrices, respectively. The LS error vector of $\mathbf{d}(n)$ that is estimated based on $\mathbf{X}(n)$ can be denoted by $\mathbf{e}_\mathbf{x}^\mathbf{d}(n)$ and, as in (7.5.1), it satisfies the equation

$$\begin{aligned}\mathbf{e}_\mathbf{x}^\mathbf{d}(n) &= \mathbf{d}(n) - \mathbf{X}(n)[\mathbf{X}^H(n)\mathbf{W}^2(n)\mathbf{X}(n)]^{-1}\mathbf{X}^H(n)\mathbf{W}^2(n)\mathbf{d}(n) \\ &= \mathbf{d}(n) - \mathbf{X}(n)[\mathbf{R}^{\mathbf{XX}}(n)]^{-1}\mathbf{r}^{\mathbf{Xd}}(n) = \mathbf{d}(n) - \mathbf{X}(n)\mathbf{h}^{\mathbf{Xd}}(n)\end{aligned} \quad (7.5.3)$$

where, by definition, $\mathbf{R}^{\mathbf{XX}}(n) \equiv \mathbf{X}^H(n)\mathbf{W}^2(n)\mathbf{X}(n)$ is the autocorrelation matrix of $\mathbf{X}(n)$, $\mathbf{r}^{\mathbf{Xd}}(n) \equiv \mathbf{X}^H(n)\mathbf{W}^2(n)\mathbf{d}(n)$ is the cross-correlation vector between $\mathbf{X}(n)$ and $\mathbf{d}(n)$, and $\mathbf{h}^{\mathbf{Xd}}(n) \equiv [\mathbf{R}^{\mathbf{XX}}(n)]^{-1}\mathbf{r}^{\mathbf{Xd}}(n)$ is the LS coefficient vector $\mathbf{h}^{\mathbf{Xd}}(n)$ for estimation of $\mathbf{d}(n)$ based on $\mathbf{X}(n)$. Since $\mathbf{X}(n)$ and $\mathbf{d}(n)$ are simply the data matrix and vector but not LS errors, there are no subscripts associated with $\mathbf{R}^{\mathbf{XX}}(n)$, $\mathbf{r}^{\mathbf{Xd}}(n)$, and $\mathbf{h}^{\mathbf{dX}}(n)$. Later we shall need subscripts for the correlations and LS coefficients.

Similarly, we define the LS error matrix $\mathbf{E}_\mathbf{X}^\mathbf{Y}(n)$ of $\mathbf{Y}(n)$ that is estimated based on $\mathbf{X}(n)$:

$$\begin{aligned}\mathbf{E}_\mathbf{X}^\mathbf{Y}(n) &= \mathbf{Y}(n) - \mathbf{X}(n)[\mathbf{X}^H(n)\mathbf{W}^2(n)\mathbf{X}(n)]^{-1}\mathbf{X}^H(n)\mathbf{W}^2(n)\mathbf{Y}(n) \\ &= \mathbf{Y}(n) - \mathbf{X}(n)[\mathbf{R}^{\mathbf{XX}}(n)]^{-1}\mathbf{R}^{\mathbf{XY}}(n) = \mathbf{Y}(n) - \mathbf{X}(n)\mathbf{H}^{\mathbf{XY}}(n)\end{aligned} \quad (7.5.4)$$

To determine the $(n + 1) \times L$ LS error matrix $\mathbf{E}_{\mathbf{X}}^{\mathbf{Y}}(n)$ we use the matrix $\mathbf{Y}(n)$ as the desired signal and perform the estimation based on the data matrix $\mathbf{X}(n)$. By definition, the LS estimation coefficient matrix $\mathbf{H}^{\mathbf{XY}}(n)$ minimizes the trace of the matrix $[\mathbf{E}_{\mathbf{X}}^{\mathbf{Y}}(n)]^H\mathbf{W}^2(n)\mathbf{E}_{\mathbf{X}}^{\mathbf{Y}}(n)$. Then each column vector of $\mathbf{E}_{\mathbf{X}}^{\mathbf{Y}}(n)$ is the LS error vector for the corresponding column vector of $\mathbf{Y}(n)$ that is estimated from $\mathbf{X}(n)$. Thus $\mathbf{E}_{\mathbf{X}}^{\mathbf{Y}}(n)$ is orthogonal to $\mathbf{X}(n)$. Hence the computation of $\mathbf{E}_{\mathbf{X}}^{\mathbf{Y}}(n)$ is equivalent to the computation of L LS estimations given by (5.3.7), where the desired signal is a vector.

Based on these definitions and the examples given above, we can now state the *order-recursive relation for LS estimation.*

Order-Recursive Relation for LS Estimation (Decomposition of LS Estimation). The LS error vector of the desired signal vector $\mathbf{d}(n)$ that is estimated based on $[\mathbf{X}(n):\mathbf{Y}(n)] \equiv \mathbf{A}_M(n)$ can be computed as

$$\begin{aligned}\mathbf{e}_{[\mathbf{X}:\mathbf{Y}]}^{\mathbf{d}}(n) &= \mathbf{e}_{\mathbf{X}}^{\mathbf{d}}(n) - \mathbf{E}_{\mathbf{X}}^{\mathbf{Y}}(n)[\mathbf{E}_{\mathbf{X}}^{\mathbf{Y}^H}(n)\mathbf{W}^2(n)\mathbf{E}_{\mathbf{X}}^{\mathbf{Y}}(n)]^{-1}\mathbf{E}_{\mathbf{X}}^{\mathbf{Y}^H}(n)\mathbf{W}^2(n)\mathbf{e}_{\mathbf{X}}^{\mathbf{d}}(n) \\ &\equiv \mathbf{e}_{\mathbf{X}}^{\mathbf{d}}(n) - \mathbf{E}_{\mathbf{X}}^{\mathbf{Y}}(n)[\mathbf{R}_{\mathbf{X}}^{\mathbf{YY}}(n)]^{-1}\mathbf{r}_{\mathbf{X}}^{\mathbf{Yd}}(n) \qquad (7.5.5) \\ &\equiv \mathbf{e}_{\mathbf{X}}^{\mathbf{d}}(n) - \mathbf{E}_{\mathbf{X}}^{\mathbf{Y}}(n)\mathbf{h}_{\mathbf{X}}^{\mathbf{Yd}}(n)\end{aligned}$$

The error vector $\mathbf{e}_{\mathbf{X}}^{\mathbf{d}}(n)$ and the error matrix $\mathbf{E}_{\mathbf{X}}^{\mathbf{Y}}(n)$ in (7.5.5) have been defined in (7.5.3) and (7.5.4). Since $\mathbf{e}_{\mathbf{X}}^{\mathbf{d}}(n)$ and $\mathbf{E}_{\mathbf{X}}^{\mathbf{Y}}(n)$ are the LS errors estimated based on $\mathbf{X}(n)$, the autocorrelation matrix $\mathbf{R}_{\mathbf{X}}^{\mathbf{YY}}(n)$ and $\mathbf{r}_{\mathbf{X}}^{\mathbf{Yd}}(n)$ have the symbol $\mathbf{X}$ as their subscripts. For the same reason we have $\mathbf{X}$ in the subscript of $\mathbf{h}_{\mathbf{X}}^{\mathbf{Yd}}(n)$.

By comparing (7.5.5) and (7.1.4), it can be seen that (7.5.5) defines the LS estimation of $\mathbf{e}_{\mathbf{X}}^{\mathbf{d}}(n)$ that is based on $\mathbf{E}_{\mathbf{X}}^{\mathbf{Y}}(n)$, which can be considered as a data matrix having L columns. To generate $\mathbf{E}_{\mathbf{X}}^{\mathbf{Y}}(n)$ and $\mathbf{e}_{\mathbf{X}}^{\mathbf{d}}(n)$, we need to perform $L + 1$ $(M - L)$th-order LS estimations. Therefore, by using (7.5.5), we compute a *higher-order LS estimation through multiple lower-order LS estimations*. Thus we call (7.5.5) the *order-recursive relation* of LS estimation and its proof is given below.

Proof:

By substituting (7.5.3) and (7.5.4) into (7.5.5), we obtain, after some algebra,

$$\mathbf{e}_{[\mathbf{X}:\mathbf{Y}]}^{\mathbf{d}}(n) = \mathbf{d}(n) - [\mathbf{X}(n):\mathbf{Y}(n)]\begin{pmatrix}\mathbf{h}^{\mathbf{Xd}}(n) - \mathbf{H}^{\mathbf{XY}}(n)\mathbf{h}_{\mathbf{X}}^{\mathbf{Yd}}(n) \\ \mathbf{h}_{\mathbf{X}}^{\mathbf{Yd}}(n)\end{pmatrix} \qquad (7.5.6)$$

We observe that $\mathbf{e}_{[\mathbf{X}:\mathbf{Y}]}^{\mathbf{d}}(n)$ in (7.5.6) has the same form as $\mathbf{e}_{\mathbf{M}}(n)$ in (7.1.4) [i.e., both errors are obtained by subtracting a linear combination of the column vectors of $\mathbf{X}(n)$ and $\mathbf{Y}(n)$ from $\mathbf{d}(n)$]. To show that $\mathbf{e}_{[\mathbf{X}:\mathbf{Y}]}^{\mathbf{d}}(n)$ is indeed the LS estimation error of $\mathbf{d}(n)$ based on $[\mathbf{X}(n):\mathbf{Y}(n)]$, we need to show that $\mathbf{e}_{[\mathbf{X}:\mathbf{Y}]}^{\mathbf{d}}(n)$ is orthogonal (orthogonality principle) to $[\mathbf{X}(n):\mathbf{Y}(n)]$, that is, to show that

$$[\mathbf{e}_{[\mathbf{X}:\mathbf{Y}]}^{\mathbf{d}}(n)]^H\mathbf{W}^2(n)[\mathbf{X}(n):\mathbf{Y}(n)] = \mathbf{0}$$

Since both $\mathbf{e}_{\mathbf{X}}^{\mathbf{d}}(n)$ and $\mathbf{E}_{\mathbf{X}}^{\mathbf{Y}}(n)$ are LS errors based on $\mathbf{X}(n)$, it follows that the right side of (7.5.5) is orthogonal to $\mathbf{X}(n)$, and so is $\mathbf{e}_{[\mathbf{X}:\mathbf{Y}]}^{\mathbf{d}}(n)$. Furthermore, using (7.5.4) we have

$$\mathbf{Y}^H(n)\mathbf{W}^2(n)\mathbf{e}_{[\mathbf{X}:\mathbf{Y}]}^{\mathbf{d}}(n) = [\mathbf{E}_{\mathbf{X}}^{\mathbf{Y}}(n)]^H\mathbf{W}^2(n)[\mathbf{e}_{\mathbf{X}}^{\mathbf{d}}(n) - \mathbf{E}_{\mathbf{X}}^{\mathbf{Y}}(n)\mathbf{h}_{\mathbf{X}}^{\mathbf{Yd}}(n)] + [\mathbf{H}^{\mathbf{XY}}(n)]^H\mathbf{X}^H(n)\mathbf{W}^2(n)[\mathbf{e}_{\mathbf{X}}^{\mathbf{d}}(n) - \mathbf{E}_{\mathbf{X}}^{\mathbf{Y}}(n)\mathbf{h}_{\mathbf{X}}^{\mathbf{Yd}}(n)] \tag{7.5.7}$$

The second term on the right side of (7.5.7) is equal to zero according to the orthogonality principle, because both $\mathbf{e}_{\mathbf{X}}^{\mathbf{d}}(n)$ and $\mathbf{E}_{\mathbf{X}}^{\mathbf{Y}}(n)$ are LS estimation errors based on $\mathbf{X}(n)$. From (7.5.5) we can write the first term as

$$[\mathbf{E}_{\mathbf{X}}^{\mathbf{Y}}(n)]^H\mathbf{W}^2(n)\mathbf{e}_{\mathbf{X}}^{\mathbf{d}}(n) - [\mathbf{E}_{\mathbf{X}}^{\mathbf{Y}}(n)]^H\mathbf{W}^2(n)\mathbf{E}_{\mathbf{X}}^{\mathbf{Y}}(n)\mathbf{h}_{\mathbf{X}}^{\mathbf{Yd}}(n) = \mathbf{r}_{\mathbf{X}}^{\mathbf{Yd}}(n) - \mathbf{R}_{\mathbf{X}}^{\mathbf{YY}}(n)[\mathbf{R}_{\mathbf{X}}^{\mathbf{YY}}(n)]^{-1}\mathbf{r}_{\mathbf{X}}^{\mathbf{Yd}}(n) = \mathbf{0} \tag{7.5.8}$$

Since $\mathbf{e}_{[\mathbf{X}:\mathbf{Y}]}^{\mathbf{d}}(n)$ is orthogonal to both $\mathbf{Y}(n)$ and $\mathbf{X}(n)$, it is orthogonal to $[\mathbf{Y}(n):\mathbf{X}(n)]$. This completes the proof of the order-recursive relation for LS estimation.

As has been stated above, this relation is the basis of all ORLS algorithms. This relation allows us to simplify greatly the derivation of any ORLS algorithm, as we shall demonstrate below. To gain a better understanding of (7.5.5), we make the following remarks.

Remarks:

1. The order-recursive relation is summarized by the following equation:

$$\mathbf{e}_{[\mathbf{X}:\mathbf{Y}]}^{\mathbf{d}}(n) = \mathbf{e}_{\mathbf{X}}^{\mathbf{d}}(n) - \mathbf{E}_{\mathbf{X}}^{\mathbf{Y}}(n)\mathbf{h}_{\mathbf{X}}^{\mathbf{Yd}}(n) \equiv \mathbf{e}_{\mathbf{E}_{\mathbf{X}}^{\mathbf{Y}}}^{\mathbf{e}_{\mathbf{X}}^{\mathbf{d}}}(n)$$

   In words, the LS estimation error vector of $\mathbf{d}(n)$ based on the partitioned data matrix $[\mathbf{X}(n):\mathbf{Y}(n)]$ is equal to the LS estimation error vector of $\mathbf{e}_{\mathbf{X}}^{\mathbf{d}}(n)$ based on $\mathbf{E}_{\mathbf{X}}^{\mathbf{Y}}(n)$, where $\mathbf{e}_{\mathbf{X}}^{\mathbf{d}}(n)$ and $\mathbf{E}_{\mathbf{X}}^{\mathbf{Y}}(n)$ are LS estimation errors of $\mathbf{d}(n)$ and $\mathbf{Y}(n)$ based on $\mathbf{X}(n)$, respectively.
2. It is important to note that the LS estimation error given by (7.5.5) is meaningful only when the vector to be estimated [e.g., $\mathbf{e}_{\mathbf{X}}^{\mathbf{d}}(n)$] in the equation above and the data matrix [e.g., $\mathbf{E}_{\mathbf{X}}^{\mathbf{Y}}(n)$], on which the estimation is based, are both LS estimation errors based on the same data matrix [i.e., $\mathbf{X}(n)$]. If this condition is not satisfied, (7.5.5) is incorrect or meaningless.
3. The order recursion for LS estimation has a clear geometric meaning. It can be viewed as a decomposition of an orthogonal projection onto a linear space, into the projections onto its subspace and the orthogonal complement of its subspace. It is possible to prove (7.5.5) using a purely geometric approach based on this concept.
4. When $L = 1$ we call the LS estimation given by (7.5.5) a *scalar LS estimation*. Such an LS estimation has special importance because the auto- and cross-correlations are scalars. In the block implementation, we only need to compute the dot product of two vectors or multiply a vector by a scalar. We can totally avoid matrix or vector operations when implemented time recursively.

5. The lower-order LS estimations mentioned above can be further decomposed in two ways:
   (a) We can further partition the matrix $\mathbf{X}(n)$ into its components. The LS estimation errors $\mathbf{e}_{\mathbf{X}}^{\mathbf{d}}(n)$ and $\mathbf{E}_{\mathbf{X}}^{\mathbf{Y}}(n)$ can be computed based on the LS estimation errors that are based on component matrices.
   (b) we can also subdivide the estimation of $\mathbf{E}_{\mathbf{X}}^{\mathbf{Y}}(n)$. For example, we can partition the matrix $\mathbf{Y}(n)$ as $[\mathbf{Y}_1(n), \mathbf{Y}_2(n)]$. Instead of directly computing $\mathbf{E}_{\mathbf{X}}^{\mathbf{Y}}(n)$, we first compute $\mathbf{E}_{\mathbf{X}}^{\mathbf{Y}_1}(n)$ and $\mathbf{E}_{\mathbf{X}}^{\mathbf{Y}_2}(n)$. Then we compute $\mathbf{e}_{[\mathbf{X}:\mathbf{Y}_1]}^{\mathbf{d}}(n)$ and $\mathbf{E}_{[\mathbf{X}:\mathbf{Y}_1]}^{\mathbf{Y}_2}(n)$ from $\mathbf{E}_{\mathbf{X}}^{\mathbf{d}}(n)$, $\mathbf{E}_{\mathbf{X}}^{\mathbf{Y}_1}(n)$, and $\mathbf{E}_{\mathbf{X}}^{\mathbf{Y}_2}(n)$. Finally, $\mathbf{e}_{[\mathbf{X}:\mathbf{Y}]}^{\mathbf{d}}(n) \equiv \mathbf{e}_{[\mathbf{X}:\mathbf{Y}_1:\mathbf{Y}_2]}^{\mathbf{d}}(n)$ can be computed from $\mathbf{e}_{[\mathbf{X}:\mathbf{Y}_1]}^{\mathbf{d}}(n)$ and $\mathbf{E}_{[\mathbf{X}:\mathbf{Y}_1]}^{\mathbf{Y}_2}(n)$. By successively using such decompositions, we can eventually obtain ORLS algorithms by using only scalar LS estimations. In other words, the desired signal and data in all the estimations are vectors instead of matrices.
6. Although the notation for the partitioned matrix $\mathbf{A}_M(n) = [\mathbf{X}(n):\mathbf{Y}(n)]$ indicates that $\mathbf{X}(n)$ consists of the first $M - L$ column vectors and $\mathbf{Y}(n)$ consists of the last L column vectors of $\mathbf{A}_M(n)$, the relation given by (7.5.5) is valid under less restrictive conditions. Specifically, (7.5.5) is still valid if $\mathbf{X}(n)$ contains any $M - L$ column vectors of $\mathbf{A}_M(n)$ and $\mathbf{Y}(n)$ contains the rest. Furthermore, the data matrix $\mathbf{X}(n)$ is only required to have a set of $M - L$ column vectors, but the order of these vectors is not important in computing $\mathbf{e}_{\mathbf{X}}^{\mathbf{d}}(n)$ and $\mathbf{E}_{\mathbf{X}}^{\mathbf{Y}}(n)$.

Time Recursions for the Correlations in ORLS Estimation. To compute the correlations $\mathbf{R}_{\mathbf{X}}^{\mathbf{YY}}(n)$ and $\mathbf{r}_{\mathbf{X}}^{\mathbf{Yd}}(n)$ in (7.5.5) we need the LS error vector $\mathbf{e}_{\mathbf{X}}^{\mathbf{d}}(n)$ and the LS error matrix $\mathbf{E}_{\mathbf{X}}^{\mathbf{Y}}(n)$. However, if at time $n - 1$ we already have computed the correlation matrix $\mathbf{R}_{\mathbf{X}}^{\mathbf{YY}}(n-1)$ and vector $\mathbf{r}_{\mathbf{X}}^{\mathbf{Yd}}(n-1)$, it is possible to use only the last element of $\mathbf{e}_{\mathbf{X}}^{\mathbf{d}}(n)$, denoted by $e_{\mathbf{X}}^{\mathbf{d}}(n,n)$ and the last row vector of $\mathbf{E}_{\mathbf{X}}^{\mathbf{Y}}(n)$, denoted by $[\mathbf{e}_{\mathbf{X}}^{\mathbf{Y}}(n,n)]^t$ to compute $\mathbf{R}_{\mathbf{X}}^{\mathbf{YY}}(n)$ and $\mathbf{r}_{\mathbf{X}}^{\mathbf{Yd}}(n)$. Thus we avoid recomputing the entire error vector and matrix. This is given by the *time recursion of the correlations in ORLS estimation* shown below.

The autocorrelation matrix $\mathbf{R}_{\mathbf{X}}^{\mathbf{YY}}(n)$ and the cross-correlation vector $\mathbf{r}_{\mathbf{X}}^{\mathbf{Yd}}(n)$ can be computed as

$$\mathbf{R}_{\mathbf{X}}^{\mathbf{YY}}(n) = w\mathbf{R}_{\mathbf{X}}^{\mathbf{YY}}(n-1) + \frac{\mathbf{e}_{\mathbf{X}}^{\mathbf{Y}*}(n,n)\mathbf{e}_{\mathbf{X}}^{\mathbf{Y}t}(n,n)}{\alpha_{\mathbf{X}}(n)} \tag{7.5.9}$$

and

$$\mathbf{r}_{\mathbf{X}}^{\mathbf{Yd}}(n) = w\mathbf{r}_{\mathbf{X}}^{\mathbf{Yd}}(n-1) + \frac{\mathbf{e}_{\mathbf{X}}^{\mathbf{Y}*}(n,n)\,\mathbf{e}_{\mathbf{X}}^{\mathbf{d}}(n,n)}{\alpha_{\mathbf{X}}(n)} \tag{7.5.10}$$

where $\alpha_{\mathbf{X}}(n)$ is a scalar that is defined by

$$\alpha_{\mathbf{X}}(n) = 1 - \gamma_{\mathbf{X}}(n) \equiv 1 - \mathbf{x}^t(n)[\mathbf{R}^{\mathbf{XX}}(n)]^{-1}\mathbf{x}^*(n) \tag{7.5.11}$$

In (7.5.11) $\mathbf{x}^t(n)$ is the last row vector of the data matrix $\mathbf{X}(n)$.

Proof: Since $\mathbf{h}^{Xd}(n)$ are $\mathbf{H}^{XY}(n)$ in (7.5.3) and (7.5.4) are LS estimation coefficients, it can be shown that they satisfy time-recursive equations similar to (6.2.71) in the RLS algorithm. The relation in (6.2.71) was given in terms of the a priori error [e.g., $e_X^{\mathbf{d}}(n, n-1)$]. By using (6.3.82) we can write the relationship between the a priori error $e_X^{\mathbf{d}}(n, n-1)$ and a posteriori error $e_X^{\mathbf{d}}(n,n)$ as

$$e_X^{\mathbf{d}}(n,n) = e_X^{\mathbf{d}}(n, n-1)\alpha_X(n) \tag{7.5.12}$$

As in (6.2.71), the time recursion of $\mathbf{h}^{Xd}(n)$ is

$$\mathbf{h}^{Xd}(n) = \mathbf{h}^{Xd}(n-1) + \frac{[\mathbf{R}^{XX}(n)]^{-1}\mathbf{x}^*(n)e_X^{\mathbf{d}}(n,n)}{\alpha_X(n)} \tag{7.5.13}$$

The error vector $\mathbf{e}_X^{\mathbf{d}}(n)$ given by (7.5.3) can be written as

$$\mathbf{e}_X^{\mathbf{d}}(n) = \begin{bmatrix} \mathbf{d}(n-1) - \mathbf{X}(n-1)\mathbf{h}^{Xd}(n) \\ e_X^{\mathbf{d}}(n,n) \end{bmatrix} \tag{7.5.14}$$

By substituting (7.5.13) into (7.5.14) we obtain, after simplification,

$$\mathbf{e}_X^{\mathbf{d}}(n) = \begin{bmatrix} \mathbf{e}_X^{\mathbf{d}}(n-1) - \dfrac{\mathbf{X}(n-1)[\mathbf{R}^{XX}(n)]^{-1}\mathbf{x}^*(n)e_X^{\mathbf{d}}(n,n)}{\alpha_X(n)} \\ e_X^{\mathbf{d}}(n,n) \end{bmatrix} \tag{7.5.15}$$

As in (7.5.13) and (7.5.15), the coefficient matrix $\mathbf{H}^{XY}(n)$ satisfies the time-update equation

$$\mathbf{H}^{XY}(n) = \mathrm{w}\mathbf{H}^{XY}(n-1) + \frac{[\mathbf{R}^{XX}(n)]^{-1}\mathbf{x}^*(n)\mathbf{e}_X^{Yt}(n,n)}{\alpha_X(n)} \tag{7.5.16}$$

Then, we can write $\mathbf{E}_X^{Y}(n)$ in (7.5.4) as

$$\begin{bmatrix} \mathbf{E}_X^{Y}(n-1) - \mathbf{X}(n-1)[\mathbf{R}^{XX}(n)]^{-1}\mathbf{X}(n)\mathbf{e}_X^{Yt}(n,n)/\alpha_X(n) \\ \mathbf{e}_X^{Yt}(n,n) \end{bmatrix} \tag{7.5.17}$$

By using (7.5.15) and (7.5.17) and the fact that $\mathbf{e}_X^{\mathbf{d}}(n-1)$ and $\mathbf{E}_X^{Y}(n-1)$ are orthogonal to $\mathbf{X}(n-1)$, it follows that

$$\mathbf{r}_X^{Yd}(n) = \mathbf{E}_X^{Y^H}(n)\mathbf{W}^2(n)\mathbf{e}_X^{\mathbf{d}}(n) \tag{7.5.18}$$

$$= \mathrm{w}\mathbf{E}_X^{Y^H}(n-1)\mathbf{W}^2(n-1)\mathbf{e}_X^{\mathbf{d}}(n-1) + \mathbf{e}_X^{Y*}(n,n)\mathbf{e}_X^{\mathbf{d}}(n,n)\mathbf{x}^t(n)[\mathbf{R}^{XX}(n)]^{-1}$$

$$[w\mathbf{X}^H(n-1)\mathbf{W}^2(n-1)\mathbf{X}(n-1)][\mathbf{R}^{XX}(n)]^{-1}\mathbf{x}^*(n)\frac{1}{\alpha_X(n)} + \mathbf{e}_X^{Y*}(n)\mathbf{e}_X^{\mathbf{d}}(n,n)$$

We note that $\mathrm{w}\mathbf{E}_X^{Y^H}(n-1)\mathbf{W}^2(n-1)\mathbf{e}_X^{\mathbf{d}}(n-1) \equiv w\mathbf{r}_X^{Yd}(n-1)$. From (5.3.11) we have

$$[w\mathbf{X}^H(n-1)\mathbf{W}^2(n-1)\mathbf{X}(n-1)] \equiv w\mathbf{R}^{XX}(n-1)$$

$$= \mathbf{R}^{XX}(n) - \mathbf{X}^*(n)\mathbf{X}^t(n) \tag{7.5.19}$$

Substituting (7.5.19) into (7.5.18) and using the definition given by (7.5.11), we have

$$\begin{aligned}\mathbf{r}_{\mathbf{X}}^{\mathbf{Yd}}(n) &= w\mathbf{r}_{\mathbf{X}}^{\mathbf{Yd}}(n-1) + \left[1 + \frac{\gamma_{\mathbf{X}}(n)[1-\gamma_{\mathbf{X}}(n)]}{\alpha_{\mathbf{X}}^2(n)}\right]\mathbf{e}_{\mathbf{X}}^{\mathbf{Y}*}(n,n)\,\mathbf{e}_{\mathbf{X}}^{\mathbf{d}}(n,n) \\ &= w\mathbf{r}_{\mathbf{X}}^{\mathbf{Yd}}(n-1) + \frac{1}{\alpha_{\mathbf{X}}(n)}\mathbf{e}_{\mathbf{X}}^{\mathbf{Y}*}(n,n)\mathbf{e}_{\mathbf{X}}^{\mathbf{d}}(n,n)\end{aligned} \tag{7.5.20}$$

This is the time recursion for $\mathbf{r}_{\mathbf{X}}^{\mathbf{Yd}}(n)$. The time recursion of $\mathbf{R}_{\mathbf{X}}^{\mathbf{YY}}(n)$ can be proved similarly.

Order Recursion of the Maximum Likelihood Factors $\alpha_{\mathbf{X}}(n)$ and $\gamma_{\mathbf{X}}(n)$. The third relation that we need to complete the ORLS estimation is the order recursion of for $\gamma_{\mathbf{X}}(n)$ or $\alpha_{\mathbf{X}}(n)$. The desired relations are

$$\begin{aligned}\gamma_{[\mathbf{X}:\mathbf{Y}]}(n) &= [\mathbf{x}^t(n):\mathbf{y}^t(n)][\mathbf{R}^{[\mathbf{X}:\mathbf{Y}][\mathbf{X}:\mathbf{Y}]}(n)]^{-1}\begin{bmatrix}\mathbf{x}^*(n)\\ \mathbf{y}^*(n)\end{bmatrix} \\ &= \gamma_{\mathbf{X}}(n) + \mathbf{e}_{\mathbf{X}}^{\mathbf{Y}t}(n)[\mathbf{R}_{\mathbf{X}}^{\mathbf{YY}}(n)]^{-1}\mathbf{e}_{\mathbf{X}}^{\mathbf{Y}*}(n)\end{aligned} \tag{7.5.21}$$

$$\alpha_{[\mathbf{X}:\mathbf{Y}]}(n) = 1 - \gamma_{[\mathbf{X}:\mathbf{Y}]}(n) = \alpha_{\mathbf{X}}(n) - \mathbf{e}_{\mathbf{X}}^{\mathbf{Y}t}(n)[\mathbf{R}_{\mathbf{X}}^{\mathbf{YY}}(n)]^{-1}\mathbf{e}_{\mathbf{X}}^{\mathbf{Y}*}(n) \tag{7.5.22}$$

Their proof is relatively straightforward.

By using (7.1.9) and (7.5.2), we can rewrite the autocorrelation matrix $\mathbf{R}^{[\mathbf{X}:\mathbf{Y}][\mathbf{X}:\mathbf{Y}]}(n)$ as

$$\mathbf{R}^{[\mathbf{X}:\mathbf{Y}][\mathbf{X}:\mathbf{Y}]}(n) = \begin{bmatrix}\mathbf{X}^H(n)\mathbf{W}^2(n)\mathbf{X}(n) & \mathbf{X}^H(n)\mathbf{W}^2(n)\mathbf{Y}(n)\\ \mathbf{Y}^H(n)\mathbf{W}^2(n)\mathbf{X}(n) & \mathbf{Y}^H(n)\mathbf{W}^2(n)\mathbf{Y}(n)\end{bmatrix} \tag{7.5.23}$$

Then, by applying the partitioned matrix inversion identities given by (6.3.22) to the matrix on the right side of (7.5.23) and using (7.5.11), it follows that

$$\begin{aligned}[\mathbf{R}^{[\mathbf{X}:\mathbf{Y}][\mathbf{X}:\mathbf{Y}]}(n)]^{-1} &= \begin{bmatrix}[\mathbf{R}^{\mathbf{XX}}(n)]^{-1} & \mathbf{0}\\ \mathbf{0} & \mathbf{0}\end{bmatrix} \\ &\quad + \begin{bmatrix}-\mathbf{H}^{\mathbf{XY}}(n)\\ \mathbf{I}\end{bmatrix}[\mathbf{R}_{\mathbf{X}}^{\mathbf{YY}}(n)]^{-1}[-(\mathbf{H}^{\mathbf{XY}}(n))^H,\mathbf{I}]\end{aligned} \tag{7.5.24}$$

Finally, from (7.5.24) and (7.5.11) we obtain

$$\begin{aligned}\gamma_{\mathbf{X}:\mathbf{Y}}(n) &= [\mathbf{x}^t(n):\mathbf{y}^t(n)][\mathbf{R}^{[\mathbf{X}:\mathbf{Y}][\mathbf{X}:\mathbf{Y}]}(n)]^{-1}\begin{pmatrix}\mathbf{x}^*(n)\\ \mathbf{y}^*(n)\end{pmatrix} \\ &= \mathbf{x}^t(n)[\mathbf{R}^{\mathbf{XX}}(n)]^{-1}\mathbf{x}^*(n) + [\mathbf{y}^t(n) - \mathbf{x}^t(n)\mathbf{H}^{\mathbf{XY}}(n)] \\ &\quad [\mathbf{R}_{\mathbf{X}}^{\mathbf{YY}}(n)]^{-1}[\mathbf{y}^*(n) - [\mathbf{H}^{\mathbf{XY}}(n)]^{\mathbf{H}}\mathbf{x}^*(n)] \\ &= \gamma_{\mathbf{X}}(n) + \mathbf{e}_{\mathbf{X}}^{\mathbf{Y}t}(n,n)[\mathbf{R}_{\mathbf{X}}^{\mathbf{YY}}(n)]^{-1}[\mathbf{e}_{\mathbf{X}}^{\mathbf{Y}}(n,n)]^*\end{aligned} \tag{7.5.25}$$

This proves (7.5.21), and since $\alpha_{[\mathbf{X}:\mathbf{Y}]}(n) = 1 - \gamma_{[\mathbf{X}:\mathbf{Y}]}(n)$, it also proves (7.5.22).

7.5.2 Canonical Structures for Order-Recursive LS Estimation Algorithms

In this section we demonstrate the use of the basic relations for ORLS estimation given above to derive different ORLS estimation algorithms. First we note that the existing ORLS algorithms differ from each other in two aspects: (1) the method by which the order recursions are implemented, and (2) the way in which the time recursions are realized. We can investigate these two aspects independently. Let us begin with (1), the method by which the order recursions are implemented.

As has been discussed above, a higher-order LS estimation can be decomposed into multiple lower-order estimations. By continuously performing such decompositions, we can realize an LS estimation through multiple scalar LS estimations. Such realizations of LS estimation, when implemented in a time-recursive form, involves only scalar operations. All such scalar LS estimations of an ORLS algorithm are realized using the same set of equations given by (7.5.5), (7.5.20), and (7.5.22). Each such set of equations can be implemented in a small computation unit called a basic processing cell. Different ways of performing the decomposition result in different ORLS algorithms which have different ways of connecting the basic cells. As is known to date, only a few standard connections exist. We call these standard forms *canonical structures* of ORLS algorithms. It is also shown below that the structure of an ORLS algorithm depends on the structure the data matrix $\mathbf{A}_M(n)$, if it is Toeplitz or block Toeplitz, or equivalently, if the data vector $\mathbf{X}_M(n)$ satisfies a time-shifting or block-time-shifting property, as explained below. It also depends on the required output of the LS estimation. The structure of the ORLS algorithm is independent of how the time recursions are implemented. Different decompositions of LS are considered below.

Triangular Structure for General ORLS Estimation. We first consider the most general form for the input data given by (7.1.1) and (7.1.2). Since such input data do not have any special form, we must use a general decomposition method which results in an ORLS algorithm structure that can be used for solving a very general class of LS estimation problems. On the other hand, such an ORLS algorithm has a computational complexity proportional to M^2 per time iteration. That is, its complexity is $O(M^2)$. As a result, it is not as computationally efficient as some other ORLS algorithms that take advantage of some special structure of the input data.

To perform the general LS estimation in an order-recursive form, we first partition the data matrix $\mathbf{A}_M(n)$ into $\mathbf{A}_{M-1}(n)$ and $\mathbf{a}_M(n)$. Using the order-recursive relation and the notation given in Section 7.5.1, we can directly write

$$\mathbf{e}^{\mathbf{d}}_{\mathbf{A}_M}(n) \equiv \mathbf{e}^{\mathbf{d}}_{[\mathbf{A}_{M-1}:\mathbf{a}_M]}(n) = (n)\mathbf{e}^{\mathbf{d}}_{\mathbf{A}_{M-1}}(n) - \mathbf{e}^{\mathbf{a}_M}_{\mathbf{A}_{M-1}}(n) h^{\mathbf{a}_M\mathbf{d}}_{\mathbf{A}_{M-1}}(n) \tag{7.5.26}$$

Note that $h^{\mathbf{a}_M\mathbf{d}}_{\mathbf{A}_{M-1}}(n)$ is a scalar. We discuss its computation in more detail in the next section.

By partitioning $\mathbf{A}_{M-1}(n)$ into $\mathbf{A}_{M-2}(n)$ and $\mathbf{a}_{M-1}(n)$, we can compute $\mathbf{e}^{\mathbf{d}}_{\mathbf{A}_{M-1}}(n)$ and $\mathbf{e}^{\mathbf{a}_M}_{\mathbf{A}_{M-1}}(n)$ as in (7.5.26). Thus

$$\mathbf{e}^{\mathbf{d}}_{\mathbf{A}_{M-1}}(n) \equiv \mathbf{e}^{\mathbf{d}}_{[\mathbf{A}_{M-2}:\mathbf{a}_{M-1}]}(n) = \mathbf{e}^{\mathbf{d}}_{\mathbf{A}_{M-2}}(n) - \mathbf{e}^{\mathbf{a}_{M-1}}_{\mathbf{A}_{M-2}}(n) h^{\mathbf{a}_{M-1}\mathbf{d}}_{\mathbf{A}_{M-2}}(n) \qquad (7.5.27)$$

and

$$\mathbf{e}^{\mathbf{a}_M}_{\mathbf{A}_{M-1}}(n) \equiv \mathbf{e}^{\mathbf{a}_M}_{[\mathbf{A}_{M-2}:\mathbf{a}_{M-1}]}(n) = \mathbf{e}^{\mathbf{a}_M}_{\mathbf{A}_{M-2}}(n) - \mathbf{e}^{\mathbf{a}_{M-1}}_{\mathbf{A}_{M-2}}(n) h^{\mathbf{a}_{M-1},\mathbf{a}_M}_{\mathbf{A}_{M-2}}(n) \qquad (7.5.28)$$

In general, we partition $\mathbf{A}_{M-i+1}(n)$ into $\mathbf{A}_{M-i}(n)$ and $\mathbf{a}_{M-i+1}(n)$. The error vectors $\mathbf{e}^{\mathbf{d}}_{\mathbf{A}_{M-i+1}}(n)$ and $\mathbf{e}^{\mathbf{a}_k}_{\mathbf{A}_{M-i+1}}(n)$, $k = M - i + 2, \ldots, M$, can be computed through i scalar LS estimations from the error vectors $\mathbf{e}^{\mathbf{d}}_{\mathbf{A}_{M-i}}(n)$ and $\mathbf{e}^{\mathbf{a}_k}_{\mathbf{A}_{M-i}}(n)$, $k = M - i + 1, \ldots, M$, which are the LS error vectors of $\mathbf{d}(n)$, and $\mathbf{a}_k(n)$, $k = M - i + 1, \ldots, M$, based on $\mathbf{A}_{M-i}(n)$, respectively. By continuing the decomposition process, we finally reach the stage where we obtain the LS error vectors $\mathbf{e}^{\mathbf{d}}_{\mathbf{a}_1}(n)$ and $\mathbf{e}^{\mathbf{a}_k}_{\mathbf{a}_1}(n)$, $k = 2, \ldots, M$. These LS error vectors can be computed through M scalar LS estimations of the vectors $\mathbf{d}(n)$ and $\mathbf{a}_k(n)$, $k = 2, \ldots, M$ based on the data vector $\mathbf{a}_1(n)$. Thus we have shown that, in general, an Mth-order LS estimation can be computed through $M(M + 1)/2$ scalar LS estimations. The approach in obtaining such an algorithm can be viewed as a *top-down* design approach. To implement such an algorithm we must go from the bottom up. The structure for implementing such an algorithm has the form of a triangular array and is depicted in Figure 7.8. Each of the processing cells computes a scalar LS estimate that is computed according to (7.5.5).

The algorithm obtained above is a block LS estimation algorithm. Its time-recursive form can easily be obtained by computing only the most recent elements in the error vectors in different stages and incorporating (7.5.9), (7.5.10), and (7.5.22). It is easy to see from the discussion above and from Fig. 7.8 that the LS algorithm obtained above and its time-recursive form are exactly the same as the MGS and RMGS algorithms, respectively, which were described in Sections 5.3 and 7.2. We shall show that various implementations of this algorithm can be obtained by exploiting different, but algebraically equivalent, realizations of the basic processing cells.

Lattice-Ladder Structure for Time-Series Signal ORLS Estimation. The LS estimation problem often encountered in practice is the one treated in Chapter 6 where the data vector $\mathbf{X}_M(n)$ is a segment of samples of a single time-series signal,

$$\mathbf{X}_M(n) = [x(n), x(n-1), \ldots, x(n-M+1)]^t \qquad (7.5.29)$$

It can be seen that the data vector $\mathbf{X}_M(n)$ can be obtained by shifting the data vector at $n - 1$, $\mathbf{X}_M(n-1) = [x(n-1), \ldots, x(n-M)]^t$, by one position, thus dropping the oldest element $x(n - M)$ and adding a new

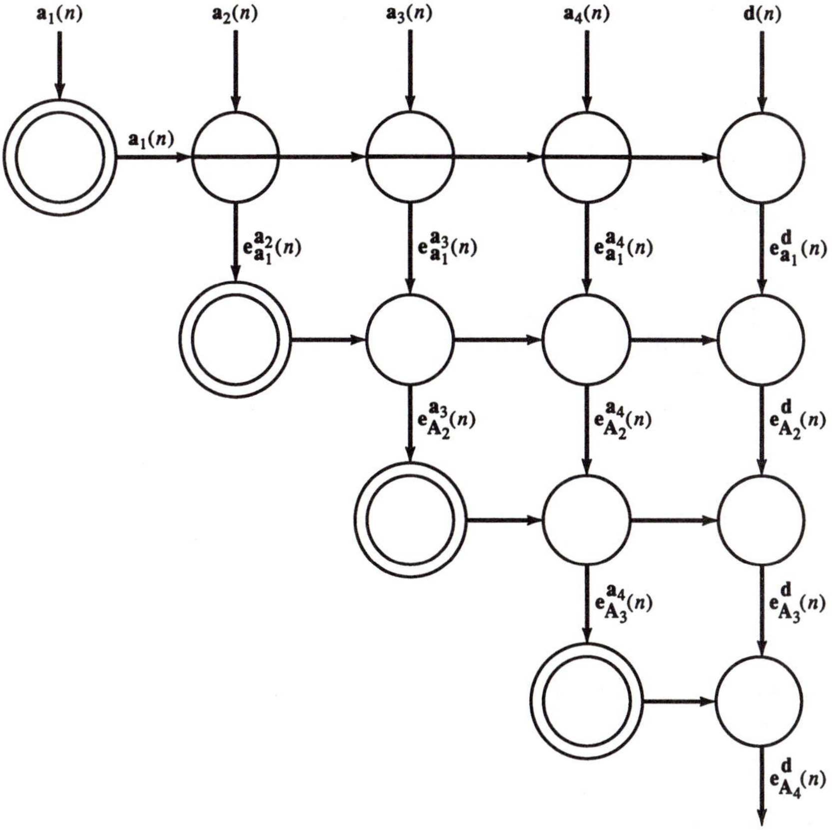

FIGURE 7.8 A triangular array for block ORLS estimation.

element $x(n)$. We say that the data vector satisfies a *shifting* property. For LS estimation with such input data vectors, it is possible to derive computationally more efficient ORLS algorithms that have a computational complexity proportional to M per time recursion, or O(M) complexity. Below we consider the simplest case for such ORLS algorithms, when the data sequence $x(k)$ is *prewindowed* [i.e., $x(k) = 0$ for $k < 0$].

In this case the ith column vector $\mathbf{a}_i(n)$ of the matrix $\mathbf{A}_M(n)$ is of the form

$$\mathbf{a}_i(n) = [0, \ldots, 0, x(0), x(1), \ldots, x(n - i + 1)]' \tag{7.5.30}$$

In other words, its first $i - 1$ elements are zero. Let us denote the submatrices of $\mathbf{A}_M(n)$ that consist of the first L columns and the second through $(L + 1)$-columns by $\mathbf{A}_L(n)$ and $\breve{\mathbf{A}}_L(n)$, respectively,

$$\mathbf{A}_L(n) = [\mathbf{a}_1(n), \mathbf{a}_2(n), \ldots, \mathbf{a}_L(n)] \tag{7.5.31}$$

and

$$\breve{\mathbf{A}}_L(n) = [\mathbf{a}_2(n), \mathbf{a}_3(n), \ldots, \mathbf{a}_{L+1}(n)] \tag{7.5.32}$$

Furthermore, by dropping the first zero element in $\mathbf{a}_{k-1}(n)$, we have

$$\mathbf{a}_{k-1}(n-1) = \mathbf{a}_k(n) \tag{7.5.33}$$

and similarly,

$$\mathbf{A}_L(n-1) = \breve{\mathbf{A}}_L(n) \tag{7.5.34}$$

To derive an ORLS algorithm for the time-series data through the decomposition approach, we first partition the data matrix $\mathbf{A}_M(n)$ into the matrix $\mathbf{A}_{M-1}(n)$ and vector $\mathbf{a}_M(n)$. Obviously, the desired LS error vector $\mathbf{e}^{\mathbf{d}}_{\mathbf{A}_M}(n)$ can be computed according to (7.5.26). In this case the error vector $\mathbf{e}^{\mathbf{a}_M}_{\mathbf{A}_{M-1}}(n)$ is called the $(M - 1)$-order *backward prediction error vector,* because $\mathbf{a}_M(n)$ is a time-delayed version of the column vectors of $\mathbf{A}_{M-1}(n)$.

By further partitioning the matrix $\mathbf{A}_{M-1}(n)$ into $\mathbf{A}_{M-2}(n)$ and $\mathbf{a}_{M-1}(n)$, the required error vector can be computed using (7.5.27). However, to derive a more efficient algorithm, we shall take a different approach in computing $\mathbf{e}^{\mathbf{a}_M}_{\mathbf{A}_{M-1}}(n)$. By partitioning the matrix $\mathbf{A}_{M-1}(n)$ as $[\mathbf{a}_1(n):\breve{\mathbf{A}}_{M-2}(n)]$, we have

$$\mathbf{e}^{\mathbf{a}_M}_{\mathbf{A}_{M-1}}(n) = \mathbf{e}^{\mathbf{a}_M}_{[\breve{\mathbf{A}}_{M-2}:\mathbf{a}_1]}(n) = \mathbf{e}^{\mathbf{a}_M}_{\breve{\mathbf{A}}_{M-2}}(n) - \mathbf{e}^{\mathbf{a}_1}_{\breve{\mathbf{A}}_{M-2}} n)h^{\mathbf{a}_1,\mathbf{a}_M}_{\breve{\mathbf{A}}_{M-2}}(n) \tag{7.5.35}$$

The error vector $\mathbf{e}^{\mathbf{a}_1}_{\breve{\mathbf{A}}_{M-2}}(n)$ is called the $(M - 2)$—order *forward prediction error vector*, because the column vectors of $\breve{\mathbf{A}}_{M-2}(n)$ are the delayed forms of $\mathbf{a}_1(n)$. From (7.5.33) and (7.5.34) we have $\mathbf{a}_M(n) = \mathbf{a}_{M-1}(n - 1)$ and $\breve{\mathbf{A}}_{M-2}(n) = \mathbf{A}_{M-2}(n - 1)$. It follows that

$$\mathbf{e}^{\mathbf{a}_M}_{\breve{\mathbf{A}}_{M-2}}(n) = \mathbf{e}^{\mathbf{a}_{M-1}}_{\mathbf{A}_{M-2}}(n-1) \tag{7.5.36}$$

which is the $(M - 2)$-backward prediction error vector at $n - 1$.

The equation for computing the backward errors, for $i = 1, \ldots, M - 2$, is similar to (7.5.35),

$$\mathbf{e}^{\mathbf{a}_{M-i}}_{\mathbf{A}_{M-i-1}}(n) = \mathbf{e}^{\mathbf{a}_{M-i}}_{[\breve{\mathbf{A}}_{M-i-2}:\mathbf{a}_1]}(n) = \mathbf{e}^{\mathbf{a}_{M-i}}_{\mathbf{A}_{M-i-2}}(n) - \mathbf{e}^{\mathbf{a}_1}_{\breve{\mathbf{A}}_{M-i-2}}(n)h^{\mathbf{a}_1,\mathbf{a}_{M-i}}_{\breve{\mathbf{A}}_{M-i-2}}(n) \tag{7.5.37}$$

We can also write the equation for computing the forward errors as

$$\mathbf{e}^{\mathbf{a}_1}_{\breve{\mathbf{A}}_{M-i-1}}(n) = \mathbf{e}^{\mathbf{a}_1}_{\breve{\mathbf{A}}_{M-i-2}:\mathbf{a}_{M-i}}(n) = \mathbf{e}^{\mathbf{a}_1}_{\breve{\mathbf{A}}_{M-i-2}}(n) - \mathbf{e}^{\mathbf{a}_{M-i}}_{\breve{\mathbf{A}}_{M-i-2}}(n)h^{\mathbf{a}_{M-i},\mathbf{a}_1}_{\breve{\mathbf{A}}_{M-i-2}}(n) \tag{7.5.38}$$

As in (7.2.36), we have

$$\mathbf{e}^{\mathbf{a}_{M-i}}_{\breve{\mathbf{A}}_{M-i-2}}(n) = \mathbf{e}^{\mathbf{a}_{M-i}}_{\mathbf{A}_{M-i-1}}(n-1) \qquad \text{for } i = 1, 2, \ldots, M - 3 \tag{7.5.39}$$

which is the $(M-i-2)$-backward prediction error vector at $n - 1$. Finally, the LS error vector of $\mathbf{d}(n)$ that is estimated based on $\mathbf{A}_M(n)$ can be computed order recursively as

$$\mathbf{e}^{\mathbf{d}}_{\mathbf{A}_{M-i}}(n) = \mathbf{e}^{\mathbf{d}}_{[\mathbf{A}_{M-i-1}:\mathbf{a}_{M-i}]}(n) = \mathbf{e}^{\mathbf{d}}_{\mathbf{A}_{M-i-1}} - \mathbf{e}^{\mathbf{a}_{M-i}}_{\mathbf{A}_{M-i-1}}(n)h^{\mathbf{a}_{M-i},\mathbf{d}}_{\mathbf{A}_{M-i-1}}(n) \tag{7.5.40}$$

This completes the derivation of the ORLS algorithm for a single time series signal.

This algorithm can be summarized as follows. To begin, we compute forward and backward error vectors $\mathbf{e}_{\mathbf{a}_2}^{\mathbf{a}_1}(n)$ and $\mathbf{e}_{\mathbf{a}_1}^{\mathbf{a}_2}(n)$, and $\mathbf{e}_{\mathbf{a}_1}^{\mathbf{d}}(n)$, the error vector of $\mathbf{d}(n)$ estimated based on $\mathbf{a}_1(n)$. Note that $\mathbf{A}_1(n) \equiv \mathbf{a}_1(n)$ and $\breve{\mathbf{A}}_1(n) \equiv \mathbf{a}_2(n) = \mathbf{a}_1(n-1)$. Assuming at time n that the backward errors $\mathbf{e}_{\mathbf{A}_{M-i-1}}^{\mathbf{a}_{M-i}}(n-1)$ are already available, we can use (7.5.38) through (7.5.40), for $i = M-2$ down to 1, to compute the three error vector sets. Finally, we use (7.5.40) for $i = 0$, to compute the desired error vector of $\mathbf{d}(n)$ based on $\mathbf{A}_M(n)$.

To perform the computations in the algorithm at time n, we need the backward prediction LS error vector at time $n-1$. As a consequence, this algorithm may not be used directly as an efficient block LS estimation algorithm because we need to compute all the LS error vectors for $k = n-M+1, \ldots, n-1, n$. On the other hand, we can use the time-recursive relations given in Section 7.5.1 to obtain an efficient time-recursive ORLS algorithm. To perform the computations in this algorithm at time n, we need only the last elements of the involved error vectors. These elements can be computed at each time n and only need to be stored for one time interval since they are used at time $n+1$.

The structure for the implementation of the ORLS algorithm described above is depicted in Fig. 7.9 It is obvious that the algorithm is the same as the LS lattice algorithm described in Section 6.3. The lattice structure is the most efficient time-recursive ORLS algorithm for time-series signals. Since both the LS lattice and the RMGS algorithm can be obtained using the decomposition for LS estimation, the basic processing cells of these two algorithms are the same and any variation in the implementation of the basic processing cells in one algorithm can be used without modification in the other algorithm. Recognizing this property greatly simplifies the investigation of different ORLS algorithms.

The lattice structure and the triangular array structure are probably the most useful structures for ORLS estimation. However, there are other ORLS algorithms that can be derived through the same approach based on the decomposition of LS estimation. We now briefly discuss a type of input data encountered in multichannel signal-processing applications which is a hybrid form of spatial signals and a single time-series signal.

Multichannel Lattice Structure. We consider the data vector $\mathbf{X}_M(k)$, where $M = KL$, which can be written as

$$\begin{aligned}\mathbf{X}_M(k) &= [x_1(k), \ldots, x_K(k), x_1(k-1), \ldots, x_K(k-1), \ldots, \\ &\qquad x_1(k-K+1), \ldots, x_K(k-K+1)]^t \qquad (7.5.41)\\ &= [\mathbf{x}^t(k), \mathbf{x}^t(k-1), \ldots, \mathbf{x}^t(k-\mathrm{K}+1)]^t\end{aligned}$$

The vectors $\mathbf{x}(k) \equiv [\mathbf{x}_i(k), \ldots, \mathbf{x}_L(k)]^t$ are L dimensional. Accordingly, we can write the data matrix $\mathbf{A}_M(n)$ as

$$\mathbf{A}_M(n) = [\mathbf{B}_1(n), \mathbf{B}_2(n), \ldots, \mathbf{B}_K(n)] \qquad (7.5.42)$$

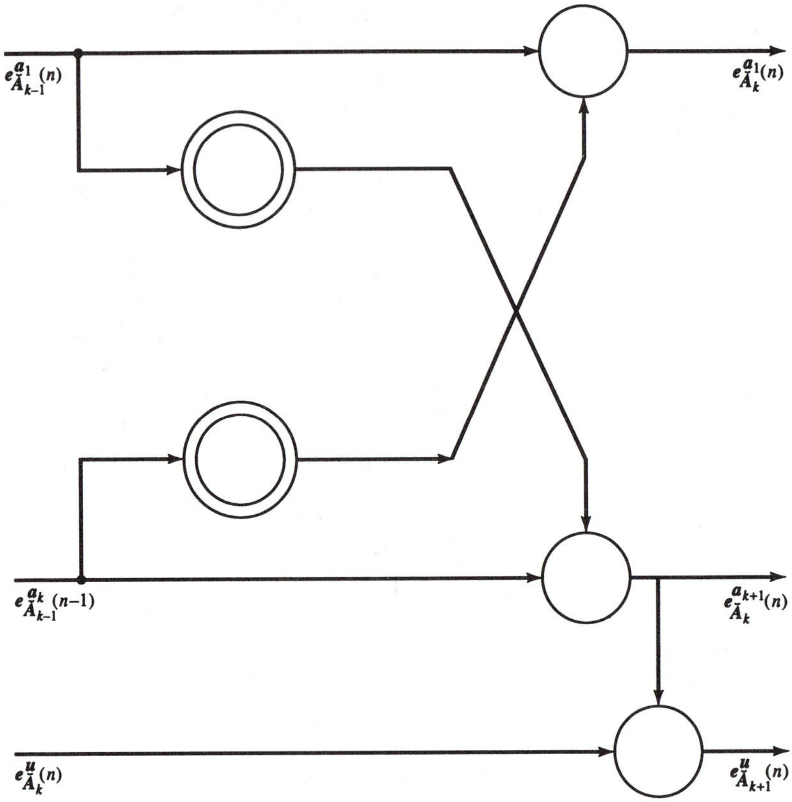

FIGURE 7.9 Efficient forward and backward error vector generation.

where $\mathbf{B}_i(n)$ are $(n+1) \times L$ matrices. By using $\mathbf{B}_i(n)$ in place of $\mathbf{a}_i(n)$ and following the same development of the LS lattice algorithm given above, we obtain a L-channel LS lattice algorithm that has $K - 1$ stages. Since $\mathbf{B}_i(n)$ are $(n + 1) \times L$ matrices, the forward and backward errors are also $(n + 1) \times L$ matrices and their auto- and cross-correlations are $L \times L$ matrices. To avoid matrix operations, we can use the result given in Remark 5 above, to further decompose the LS estimation inside each lattice stage. The result is an ORLS algorithm based only on scalar LS estimation.

We can adopt two approaches to perform further decomposition in each of the multichannel lattice stages. We can decompose the forward and backward errors in each lattice stage separately or jointly. The first approach results in the sequential processing implementation of multichannel lattice stages that was described by Ling et al. (1984c). The second approach results in an implementation of multichannel lattice stages that takes the form of a square array consisting of L^2 single-channel lattice stages that was described by Lev-Ari et al. (1987).

We have shown above that the structure of the ORLS algorithms are determined by the input data structure. We may derive more efficient ORLS algorithms by exploiting any special requirement on their outputs used in the particular application. One example is the ORLS implementation of a multi-input/multi-output LS estimation, which has the form of a trapezoidal array. This algorithm is described by Yuan et al. (1989). An alternative implementation that solves the problem was given by Gerlach (1986) using multiple MGS arrays. Although the latter was given in the context of statistical estimation, it can be modified to satisfy the exact least-squares criterion by using the time-recursive equations given by (7.5.9) and (7.5.10).

7.5.3 Variations of Basic Processing Cells of ORLS Algorithms

In the preceding section we have shown that ORLS algorithms can be derived from the order-recursion equation (7.5.5) presented in Section 7.5.1. The LS estimation coefficient vector $\mathbf{h}_{\mathbf{X}}^{\mathbf{Yd}}(n)$ can be obtained by using the time recursion of the correlations given by (7.5.9) and (7.5.10). The quantity $\alpha_{\mathbf{X}}(n)$ needed in these two equations can be computed order-recursively using (7.5.22). These four equations form the basic equation set needed to implement any of the ORLS algorithms discussed in this section. It is of interest to investigate alternative ways to implement these basic equations that result in some desired properties not provided by the basic equation set.

We have also shown that it is always possible to decompose the LS estimation problem recursively until it consists of only scalar LS estimations. Below, we shall only consider the scalar form of the basic equation set.

Correlation Quotient Forms. The correlation quotient form is the basic form discussed in Section 7.5.2. Below we restate it for the case where $L = 1$. When $L = 1$, $\mathbf{Y}(n)$ is an $n \times 1$ vector and the most recent element of $\mathbf{e}_{[\mathbf{X}:\mathbf{Y}]}^{\mathbf{d}}(n)$ can be computed as

$$e_{[\mathbf{X}:\mathbf{Y}]}^{\mathbf{d}}(n,n) = e_{\mathbf{X}}^{\mathbf{d}}(n,n) - \frac{r_{\mathbf{X}}^{\mathbf{Yd}}(n)}{r_{\mathbf{X}}^{\mathbf{YY}}(n)} e_{\mathbf{X}}^{\mathbf{Y}}(n,n) = e_{\mathbf{X}}^{\mathbf{d}}(n,n) - h_{\mathbf{X}}^{\mathbf{Yd}}(n) e_{\mathbf{X}}^{\mathbf{Y}}(n,n) \qquad (7.5.43)$$

where the correlations $r_{\mathbf{X}}^{\mathbf{Yd}}(n)$ and $r_{\mathbf{X}}^{\mathbf{YY}}(n)$ are scalars and can be computed according to (7.5.9) and (7.5.10) as

$$r_{\mathbf{X}}^{\mathbf{Yd}}(n) = w r_{\mathbf{X}}^{\mathbf{Yd}}(n-1) + \frac{e_{\mathbf{X}}^{\mathbf{Y}*}(n,n)\, e_{\mathbf{X}}^{\mathbf{d}}(n,n)}{\alpha_{\mathbf{X}}(n)} \qquad (7.5.44)$$

and

$$r_{\mathbf{X}}^{\mathbf{YY}}(n) = w r_{\mathbf{X}}^{\mathbf{YY}}(n-1) + \frac{|e_{\mathbf{X}}^{\mathbf{Y}}(n,n)|^2}{\alpha_{\mathbf{X}}(n)} \qquad (7.5.45)$$

The scalar factor $\alpha_X(n)$ is computed according to (7.5.22) as

$$\alpha_{[X:Y]}(n) = \alpha_X(n) - \frac{|e_X^Y(n,n)|^2}{r_X^{YY}(n)} \tag{7.5.46}$$

To initialize, we let $\alpha_{X=0}(n) = 1$, $e_{X=0}^Y(n,n) \equiv y(n)$, and $e_{X=0}^d(n,n) \equiv z(n)$.

In (7.5.43), the scalar LS coefficient $h_X^{Yd}(n)$ is expressed as the quotient of the cross-correlation $r_X^{Yd}(n)$ and the autocorrelation $r_X^{YY}(n)$. The errors $e_X^Y(n,n)$ and $e_X^d(n,n)$ used in (7.5.44) and (7.5.45) to compute these correlations are a posteriori errors. We call this form of the basic equation set the *a posteriori error correlation quotient form.*

The correlation quotient form can also be implemented using a priori errors. When the a priori errors are used, (7.5.43) becomes

$$e_{[X:Y]}^d(n) = e_X^d(n) - \frac{r_X^{Yd}(n-1)}{r_X^{YY}(n-1)} e_X^Y(n) = e_X^d(n) - h_X^{Yd}(n-1)e_X^Y(n) \tag{7.5.47}$$

where, by definition, $e_{[X:Y]}^d(n) \equiv e_{[X:Y]}^d(n,n-1)$, and $e_X^d(n)$ and $e_X^Y(n)$ are defined similarly. By using the relation between the a priori and a posteriori errors,

$$e_X^d(n) \equiv e_X^d(n,n-1) = \frac{e_X^d(n,n)}{\alpha_X(n)} \tag{7.5.48}$$

and

$$e_X^Y(n) \equiv e_X^Y(n,n-1) = \frac{e_X^Y(n,n)}{\alpha_X(n)} \tag{7.5.49}$$

and substituting them into (7.5.44), (7.5.45), and (7.5.46), we obtain the a priori error correlation quotient form.

Direct-Update (Error-Feedback) Forms. It has been found that the ORLS algorithms using the correlation quotient forms for time-updating are sensitive to round-off error. It is possible to use the error-feedback form, discussed in Sections 6.3 and 7.2.3, for directly time updating the LS coefficients, such as $h_X^{Yd}(n)$, in any of the ORLS algorithms to improve their numerical behavior. As in the derivation of (7.2.54) and (7.2.55), it can be shown that we can compute the LS coefficient $h_X^{Yd}(n)$ directly from $h_X^{Yd}(n-1)$ without using $r_X^{Yd}(n)$. Thus we have

$$h_X^{Yd}(n) = h_X^{Yd}(n-1) + \frac{e_{[X:Y]}^d(n)e_X^{Y*}(n)\alpha_X(n)}{r_X^{YY}(n)} \tag{7.5.50}$$

Equations (7.5.45) and (7.5.46) are still needed to complete the algorithm.

This form of the coefficient direct updating uses the a priori errors. It is also possible to derive a form using a posteriori errors. We leave this as an exercise for the reader.

Givens-Rotation-Based Forms. The relationship between the Givens algorithm and the RMGS algorithm has been shown in Section 7.3.3. Since the RMGS algorithm is a direct consequence of the basic relations of ORLS estimation, we can predict that the general order and time recursions of ORLS estimation can be realized by using only Givens rotations. Parallel to the derivation of (7.3.20) and (7.3.21), we can obtain

$$h_{\mathbf{X}}^{\mathbf{Y}\mathbf{d}}(n) = \tilde{c}h_{\mathbf{X}}^{\mathbf{Y}\mathbf{d}}(n-1) + \tilde{s}e_{\mathbf{X}}^{\mathbf{d}}(n) \tag{7.5.51}$$

where

$$\tilde{c} = \frac{wr_{\mathbf{X}}^{\mathbf{YY}}(n-1)}{r_{\mathbf{X}}^{\mathbf{YY}}(n)} \tag{7.5.52}$$

and

$$\tilde{s} = \frac{e_{\mathbf{X}}^{\mathbf{Y}*}(n)\alpha_{\mathbf{X}}(n)}{r_{\mathbf{X}}^{\mathbf{YY}}(n)} \tag{7.5.53}$$

Equations (7.5.47), (7.5.51) through (7.5.53), and a slightly modified version of (7.5.46) form a complete set equations for order and time recursions of ORLS estimation. It is the same as the basic equations of the Givens rotation without square roots.

The order and time recursions of ORLS estimation based on Givens rotations with square roots can be obtained by first defining $\check{e}_{[\mathbf{X}:\mathbf{Y}]}^{\mathbf{d}}(n) \equiv \sqrt{\alpha_{[\mathbf{X}:\mathbf{Y}]}(n)}e_{[\mathbf{X}:\mathbf{Y}]}^{\mathbf{d}}(n)$, $\check{e}_{\mathbf{X}}^{\mathbf{d}}(n) \equiv \sqrt{\alpha_{\mathbf{X}}(n)}e_{\mathbf{X}}^{\mathbf{d}}(n)$, $\check{e}_{\mathbf{X}}^{\mathbf{Y}}(n) \equiv \sqrt{\alpha_{\mathbf{X}}(n)}e_{\mathbf{X}}^{\mathbf{Y}}(n)$, $\check{r}_{\mathbf{X}}^{\mathbf{Y}\mathbf{d}}(n) \equiv h_{\mathbf{X}}^{\mathbf{Y}\mathbf{d}}(n)\sqrt{r_{\mathbf{X}}^{\mathbf{YY}}(n)} = r_{\mathbf{X}}^{\mathbf{Y}\mathbf{d}}(n)/\sqrt{r_{\mathbf{X}}^{\mathbf{YY}}(n)}$, and $\check{r}_{\mathbf{X}}^{\mathbf{YY}}(n) \equiv \sqrt{r_{\mathbf{X}}^{\mathbf{YY}}(n)}$. From the relationship between the Givens algorithms with and without square roots given in Section (7.3.3), we obtain the equation

$$\begin{bmatrix} c & s \\ -s^* & c \end{bmatrix}\begin{bmatrix} \sqrt{w}\check{r}_{\mathbf{X}}^{\mathbf{YY}}(n-1) & \sqrt{w}\check{r}_{\mathbf{X}}^{\mathbf{Y}\mathbf{d}}(n-1) \\ \check{e}_{\mathbf{X}}^{\mathbf{Y}}(n) & \check{e}_{\mathbf{X}}^{\mathbf{d}}(n) \end{bmatrix} = \begin{bmatrix} \check{r}_{\mathbf{X}}^{\mathbf{YY}}(n) & \check{r}_{\mathbf{X}}^{\mathbf{Y}\mathbf{d}}(n) \\ 0 & \check{e}_{[\mathbf{X}:\mathbf{Y}]}^{\mathbf{d}}(n) \end{bmatrix} \tag{7.5.54}$$

Where $c^2 + |s|^2 = 1$. From (7.5.54) it is clear that we can obtain the higher-order error and the new coefficients in the ORLS estimation through one Givens rotation.

Other Forms. Besides the few variations of the basic equation sets discussed above, there exist other forms of the basic equations which can be used in the implementation of ORLS algorithms. For example, the Householder transformation for block time-recursive implementation of LS estimation, discussed in Section 7.4.3, and the normalized, or square-root form, which has been discussed in the literature on LS lattice algorithms, can also be used the implementation of general ORLS estimation. The normalized form is especially suitable for fixed-point arithmetic implementation of the ORLS algorithms, because all its quantities have a magnitude that is less than 1. Exercises 7.11 and 7.12 address these two forms of ORLS implementation.

Different forms for the time-recursive implementation of the basic equations for the ORLS algorithms are summarized in Table 7.10. The different

TABLE 7.10 Variations of ORLS Basic Equation Set

Basic Equations with A Posteriori Errors

Correlation Quotient Form

$$r_X^{Yd}(n) = wr_X^{Yd}(n-1) + e_X^{Y*}(n,n)e_X^{d}(n,n)/\alpha_X(n)$$
$$r_X^{YY}(n) = wr_X^{YY}(n-1) + |e_X^{Y}(n,n)|^2/\alpha_X(n)$$
$$h_X^{Yd}(n) = r_X^{Yd}(n)/r_X^{YY}(n)$$
$$e_{[X:Y]}^{d}(n,n) = e_X^{d}(n,n) - h_X^{Yd}(n)e_X^{Y}(n,n)$$
$$\alpha_{[X:Y]}(n) = \alpha_X(n) - |e_X^{Y}(n,n)|^2/r_X^{YY}(n)$$

Error-Feedback Form

$$r_X^{YY}(n) = wr_X^{YY}(n-1) + |e_X^{Y}(n,n)|^2/\alpha_X(n)$$
$$h_X^{Yd}(n) = h_X^{Yd}(n-1) + e_X^{Y*}(n,n)[e_X^{d}(n,n) - h_X^{Yd}(n-1)e_X^{Y}(n,n)]/[\alpha_X(n)r_X^{YY}(n)]$$
$$e_{[X:Y]}^{d}(n,n) = e_X^{d}(n,n) - h_X^{Yd}(n)e_X^{Y}(n)$$
$$\alpha_{[X:Y]}(n) = \alpha_X(n) - |e_X^{Y}(n,n)|^2/r_X^{YY}(n)$$

Basic Equations with A Priori Errors

Correlation Quotient Form

$$e_{[X:Y]}^{d}(n) = e_X^{d}(n) - h_X^{Yd}(n-1)e_X^{Y}(n)$$
$$r_X^{Yd}(n) = wr_X^{Yd}(n-1) + e_X^{Y*}(n)e_X^{d}(n)\alpha_X(n)$$
$$r_X^{YY}(n) = wr_X^{YY}(n-1) + |e_X^{Y}(n)|^2\alpha_X(n)$$
$$h_X^{Yd}(n) = r_X^{Yd}(n)/r_X^{YY}(n)$$
$$\alpha_{[X:Y]}(n) = \alpha_X(n) - |e_X^{Y}(n)\alpha_X(n)|^2/r_X^{YY}(n)$$

Error-Feedback Form

$$e_{[X:Y]}^{d}(n) = e_X^{d}(n) - h_X^{Yd}(n-1)e_X^{Y}(n)$$
$$r_X^{YY}(n) = wr_X^{YY}(n-1) + |e_X^{Y}(n)|^2\alpha_X(n)$$
$$h_X^{Yd}(n) = h_X^{Yd}(n-1) + e_X^{Y*}(n)e_{[X:Y]}^{d}(n)\alpha_X(n)/r_X^{YY}(n)$$
$$\alpha_{[X:Y]}(n) = \alpha_X(n) - |e_X^{Y}(n)\alpha_X(n)|^2/r_X^{YY}(n)$$

Givens (without Square Roots)

$$e_{[X:Y]}^{d}(n) = e_X^{d}(n) - h_X^{Yd}(n-1)e_X^{Y}(n)$$
$$\tilde{c} = wr_X^{YY}(n-1)/r_X^{YY}(n)$$
$$\tilde{s} = e_X^{Y*}(n)\alpha_X(n/r_X^{YY}(n)$$
$$h_X^{Yd}(n) = \tilde{c}h_X^{Yd}(n-1) + \tilde{s}^*e_X^{d}(n)$$
$$\alpha_{[X:Y]}(n) = \tilde{c}\alpha_X(n)$$

continued

forms given are by no means exhaustive. It is possible to create other forms of ORLS algorithms by deriving new scalar LS estimation methods and applying these methods to different ORLS structures.

7.5.4 Systematic Investigation and Derivation of ORLS Algorithms

The most important conclusion that we have obtained from the discussion in the preceding three sections is that we can investigate variations of the basic equation set independently of their structures. The structures of ORLS algorithms are determined mainly by the input data structure. In other words, the form of the input data may lead to more efficient implementation of LS estimation. The structure may also be determined by the required output from the LS estimation. Once the structure is determined, we can

TABLE 7.10 Continued

Basic Equations with Angle-Normalzied Errors

Definition: $\breve{e}^{\mathbf{d}}_{[\mathbf{X}:\mathbf{Y}]}(n) = e^{\mathbf{d}}_{[\mathbf{X}:\mathbf{Y}]}(n)[\alpha_{[\mathbf{X}:\mathbf{Y}]}(n)]^{1/2}$; $\breve{e}^{\mathbf{d}}_{\mathbf{X}}(n) = e^{\mathbf{d}}_{\mathbf{X}}(n)[\alpha_{\mathbf{X}}(n)]^{1/2}$;

$\breve{e}^{\mathbf{Y}}_{\mathbf{X}}(n) = e^{\mathbf{Y}}_{\mathbf{X}}(n)[\alpha_{\mathbf{X}}(n)]^{1/2}$; $\breve{r}^{\mathbf{YY}}_{\mathbf{X}}(n) = [r^{\mathbf{YY}}_{\mathbf{X}}(n)]^{1/2}$

Givens (with Square Roots)

$\breve{r}^{\mathbf{YY}}_{\mathbf{X}}(n) = [w[\breve{r}^{\mathbf{YY}}_{\mathbf{X}}(n-1)]^2 + |\breve{e}^{\mathbf{Y}}_{\mathbf{X}}(n)|^2]^{1/2}$

$c = \sqrt{w}\breve{r}^{\mathbf{YY}}_{\mathbf{X}}(n-1)/\breve{r}^{\mathbf{YY}}_{\mathbf{X}}(n)$

$s = \breve{e}^{*\mathbf{Y}}_{\mathbf{X}}(n)/\breve{r}^{\mathbf{YY}}_{\mathbf{X}}(n)$

$\breve{r}^{\mathbf{Yd}}_{\mathbf{X}}(n) = c\sqrt{w}\breve{r}^{\mathbf{Yd}}_{\mathbf{X}}(n-1) + s\breve{e}^{\mathbf{d}}_{\mathbf{X}}(n)$

$\breve{e}^{\mathbf{d}}_{[\mathbf{X}:\mathbf{Y}]}(n) = c\breve{e}^{\mathbf{d}}_{\mathbf{X}}(n) - s^*\sqrt{w}\breve{r}^{\mathbf{Yd}}_{\mathbf{X}}(n-1)$

Householder (Time-Recursive Form)

$\breve{r}^{\mathbf{YY}}_{\mathbf{X}}(n) = -[\text{sign of } r_{ii}(n-1)] \times [w[\breve{r}^{\mathbf{YY}}_{\mathbf{X}}(n-1)]^2 + |\breve{e}^{\mathbf{Y}}_{\mathbf{X}}(n)|^2]^{1/2}$

$\psi = \breve{r}^{\mathbf{YY}}_{\mathbf{X}}(n)[\breve{r}^{\mathbf{YY}}_{\mathbf{X}}(n-1) - \breve{r}^{\mathbf{YY}}_{\mathbf{X}}(n)]$

$\zeta = \sqrt{w}[\breve{r}^{\mathbf{YY}}_{\mathbf{X}}(n-1) - \breve{r}^{\mathbf{YY}}_{\mathbf{X}}(n)]/\psi$

$\xi = \breve{e}^{\mathbf{Y}}_{\mathbf{X}}(n)/\psi$

$g = \zeta\breve{r}^{\mathbf{YY}}_{\mathbf{X}}(n-1) + \xi_i\breve{e}^{\mathbf{d}}_{\mathbf{X}}(n)$

$\breve{e}^{\mathbf{d}}_{[\mathbf{X}:\mathbf{Y}]}(n) = \breve{e}^{\mathbf{d}}_{\mathbf{X}}(n) - g\breve{r}^{\mathbf{Yd}}_{\mathbf{X}}(n-1)$

Basic Equations with Angle- and Energy-Normalized Errors

Definition: $\breve{\breve{r}}^{\mathbf{Yd}}_{\mathbf{X}}(n) = r^{\mathbf{Yd}}_{\mathbf{X}}(n)[r^{\mathbf{dd}}_{\mathbf{X}}(n)r^{\mathbf{YY}}_{\mathbf{X}}(n)]^{-1/2}$; $\breve{\breve{e}}^{\mathbf{d}}_{\mathbf{X}}(n) = e^{\mathbf{d}}_{\mathbf{X}}(n,n)[\alpha_{\mathbf{X}}(n)r^{\mathbf{dd}}_{\mathbf{X}}(n)]^{-1/2}$;

$\breve{\breve{e}}^{\mathbf{Y}}_{\mathbf{X}}(n) = e^{\mathbf{Y}}_{\mathbf{X}}(n,n)[\alpha_{\mathbf{X}}(n)r^{\mathbf{YY}}_{\mathbf{X}}(n)]^{-1/2}$; $\breve{\breve{e}}^{\mathbf{d}}_{[\mathbf{X}:\mathbf{Y}]}(n) = e^{\mathbf{d}}_{[\mathbf{X}:\mathbf{Y}]}(n,n)[\alpha_{[\mathbf{X}:\mathbf{Y}]}(n)r^{\mathbf{dd}}_{[\mathbf{X}:\mathbf{Y}]}(n)]^{-1/2}$

Square-Root Form

$\breve{\breve{r}}^{\mathbf{Yd}}_{\mathbf{X}}(n) = \breve{\breve{r}}^{\mathbf{Yd}}_{\mathbf{X}}(n-1)[1 - |\breve{\breve{e}}^{\mathbf{d}}_{\mathbf{X}}(n)|^2]^{1/2}[1 - |\breve{\breve{e}}^{\mathbf{Y}}_{\mathbf{X}}(n)|^2]^{1/2} + \breve{\breve{e}}^{\mathbf{Y}*}_{\mathbf{X}}(n)\breve{\breve{e}}^{\mathbf{d}}_{\mathbf{X}}(n)$

$\breve{\breve{e}}^{\mathbf{d}}_{[\mathbf{X}:\mathbf{Y}]}(n) = [\breve{\breve{e}}^{\mathbf{d}}_{\mathbf{X}}(n) - \breve{\breve{e}}^{\mathbf{Y}}_{\mathbf{X}}(n)\breve{\breve{r}}^{\mathbf{Yd}}_{\mathbf{X}}(n)][1 - |\breve{\breve{e}}^{\mathbf{Y}}_{\mathbf{X}}(n,n)|^2]^{-1/2}[1 - |\breve{\breve{r}}^{\mathbf{Yd}}_{\mathbf{X}}(n|^2]^{-1/2}$

use any of the variations of the basic equation set to implement the ORLS algorithm.

Since one form of the basic equation set can be applied to any of the ORLS structures, we can separate the investigation of the structure and the implementation of ORLS algorithms. From such viewpoint, the set of all existing ORLS algorithms is actually a Cartesian product of two much smaller sets, the set of structures and the set of time-updating (realization) methods. These two sets can be investigated separately, and by combining a pair of members, one from each set, we can form a valid ORLS algorithm. This relationship is summarized in the diagram in Fig. 7.10.

By using this approach we can simplify significantly the investigation of different ORLS algorithms. Furthermore, by combining variations of the basic equation set with different structures of the ORLS estimation, we can form various ORLS algorithms and create new algorithms. For example, by using the lattice structure and the Givens rotation for time and order updating, it is possible to obtain new LS lattice algorithms that are based on only Givens rotations [Ling (1989, 1991) and Proudler et al. (1989)]. Another possibility is combining the triangular array structure with the normalized, or square-root form of implementation which is discussed in Section 6.3 in the context of LS lattice algorithms. The normalized/square-

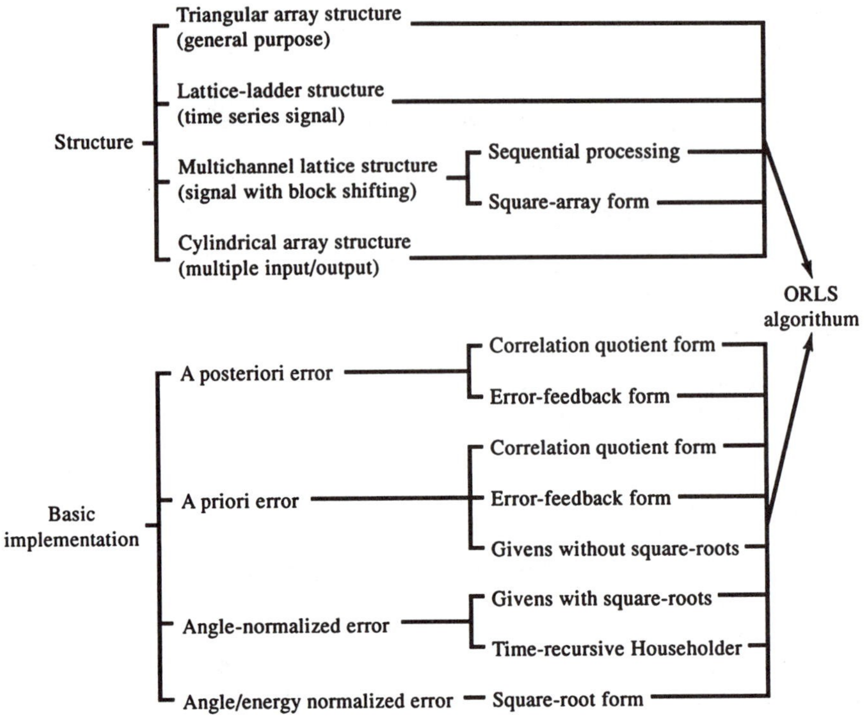

FIGURE 7.10 Various structures and implementations of ORLS algorithms.

root ORLS algorithms are suitable for fixed-point implementation of LS estimation of spatial signals.

In this section we have considered only the exponentially weighted growing memory ORLS algorithms. (In addition, for the LS lattice algorithms prewindowing is also required.) This form results in the simplest implementation of ORLS algorithms. There exist other more sophisticated forms of LS estimation algorithms. We shall not discuss these forms here but refer the reader to the references in the next section. The methodology used in this section applies to these forms of LS estimation with minor modification.

There also exist order-recursive estimation algorithms that are not *exact* least squares. For example, the so-called gradient lattice algorithm and the "escalator" algorithm by Ahmed and Youn (1980) are actually the approximate forms of the LS lattice and the RMGS algorithms. These *nonexact* LS algorithms are computationally more efficient than their exact LS counterparts. Some of these algorithms perform nearly as well as the LS algorithms in tracking nonstationary signal characteristics. However, in general, the LS algorithms have a faster initial convergence than that of gradient-based algorithms.

7.6 SUMMARY AND REFERENCES

In this chapter we have presented LS estimation algorithms based on orthogonal transformations and order-recursive LS estimation algorithms. Three orthogonalization methods discussed in Section 5.3—the modified Gram–Schmidt orthogonalization procedure, or simply the MGS algorithm, the Givens transformation, and the Householder transformation—are used for time-recursive LS estimation.

The LS estimation algorithms based on these three orthogonal transformation methods have been known for a long time in numerical analysis. It has been shown that these three algorithms have similar numerical behavior. Although we did not provide a detailed analysis on their numerical behavior, many publications have been devoted to this topic.

Rice (1966) was the first to point out the numerical pitfall of the classic Gram–Schmidt algorithm and the superior numerical properties of the MGS algorithm. The numerical behavior of the MGS algorithm was analyzed by Björck (1967). The time-recursive form of the MGS algorithm was proposed by Ling et al. (1984, 1986) and a similar algorithm was given by Kalson and Yao (1984).

The use of the Givens rotation for QR decomposition was attributed to Givens (1958). Gentleman (1973a) provides a detailed analysis of its round-off error. A variation of the original Givens algorithm that does not need square-root operations was proposed by Gentleman (1973b). The systolic array implementation of the Givens algorithm has attracted much attention due to the work of Gentleman and Kung (1981) and McWhirter (1983). More recently, there has been an increasing interest on more efficient LS estimation algorithms of time-series signals using Givens rotations. In particular, there is the work by Cioffi (1987, 1990) on fixed-order implementation of such algorithms, and by Ling (1989, 1991) and Proudler et al. (1989) on their lattice implementation.

The idea of using a Householder transformation for solving LS problems was proposed by Householder (1958). It was further elaborated by Golub (1965). Application of the Householder transformation to digital signal processing and the incorporation of different windows was treated by Rader and Steinhardt (1986). A systolic array implementation of a block time-recursive Householder algorithm is described in Liu et al. (1990). A Householder transformation-based algorithm for time-series signal processing has been proposed by Cioffi (1990).

Another class of algorithms discussed in this section is order-recursive LS estimation (ORLS) algorithms. This class of algorithms directly generate the LS estimation errors, but additional steps are required to generate the LS estimation coefficients (weights). As a result, these algorithms are most suitable in applications where the LS error, or equivalently, the estimate of the desired signal, is the needed result from the estimation.

The ORLS algorithms include a number of algorithms that we have discussed previously: the LS and gradient lattice algorithms, the multichannel lattice algorithms, the RMGS algorithm, and the Givens algorithm. Instead of investigating individual ORLS algorithms, we have shown that all the ORLS algorithms can be derived from a small set of basic relations in LS estimation. As a result, all of the ORLS algorithms can be implemented in modular forms that are based on a small number of basic equations for performing order and time recursions. From this point of view we have shown that it is possible to investigate independently the structure of ORLS algorithms and their implementation. The structure of an ORLS algorithm is determined by the property of the input data or the property of the required output. Any variation in the basic equation set can be applied to any of the ORLS structures to yield various ORLS algorithms. Such a unified treatment greatly simplifies the investigation of ORLS algorithms and facilitates the development of new ORLS algorithms. Due to their modular structure, ORLS algorithms are most suitable for VLSI based systolic and wavefront array implementations.

In addition to the references on the algorithms that we have mentioned previously, other related algorithms exist, such as the gradient type of order-recursive algorithms, covariance and normalized LS lattice algorithms, and finite memory algorithms. For a description of these algorithms, we refer readers to Ahmed and Youn (1980), Porat and Kailath (1983), Gerlach (1986), Manolakis et al. (1987), Yuen (1988), and Lev-Ari (1987).

PROBLEMS

7.1. The elements $\delta_i(n)$ of the diagonal matrix $\mathbf{D}(n)$ have the physical meaning of being the total energy of the LS error vector $\mathbf{q}_i(n)$. Show that

$$\delta_{i+1}(n) = \delta_{i+1}^{(i)}(n) - |\tilde{r}_{i,i+1}(n)|^2 \delta_i(n) = \delta_{i+1}^{(i)}(n) - \frac{|k_{i,i+1}(n)|^2}{\delta_i(n)}$$

where $\delta_{i+1}^{(i)}(n) = \mathbf{q}_{i+1}^{(i)H}(n)\mathbf{q}_{i+1}^{(i)}(n)$ is the total energy of the error vector $\mathbf{q}_{i+1}^{(i)}(n)$.

7.2. Show that $\mathbf{q}_k^{(j)}(n)$, $k = j, j + 1, \ldots, M$, in the MGS algorithm are the LS error vectors of $\mathbf{v}_j(n)$ estimated based on the vector set $\{\mathbf{v}_i(n), i = 1, 2, \ldots, j - 1\}$.

7.3. To show the effects of round-off errors when using different LS estimation algorithms we consider the following LS estimation problem: Let

$$\mathbf{A} = \begin{bmatrix} 1.0 & 1.5 \\ 1.01 & 1.5 \\ 1.0 & 1.5 \end{bmatrix} \quad \text{and} \quad \mathbf{d} = \begin{bmatrix} 2.0 \\ 1.5 \\ 2.5 \end{bmatrix}$$

Determine the optimal LS coefficient vector **h** that minimizes the length of the error vector $\mathbf{e} = \mathbf{d} - \mathbf{A}\mathbf{h}$, by:

(a) Solving the normal equations for the problem above using floating-point arithmetic with an accuracy of more than six digits (normal single-precision floating-point arithmetic).

(b) Solving the normal equation using floating-point arithmetic but only keep four effective digits in each step.

(c) Using the MGS algorithm with the same precision as part (b).

7.4. Prove the relationship between the a priori error and a posteriori error given by (7.2.49) and (7.2.50).

7.5. Solve the same LS problem given in Problem 7.3 using the Givens algorithm with and without square roots with floating-point arithmetic but keep only four effective digits in each step.

7.6. Repeat Problem 7.5, but this time use the Householder algorithm.

7.7. The special angles for which rotation is simple are $\phi_i = \arctan 2^{-i}$, $i = 0, 1, \ldots, \infty$. Prove that if $|\phi| \leq \phi_k$, a representation of ϕ exists of the form

$$\phi = \sum_{i=k+1}^{\infty} \rho_i \phi_i$$

Why is this sufficient to prove the convergence of the CORDIC algorithm to the proper angle in vectoring?

7.8. In (7.3.48) the new rows of the evolving matrix $\hat{\mathbf{A}}$ were not completely zeroed. The column of b_M could have been zeroed out using one more rotation per new row, when $M > N + 1$, ultimately making $\hat{\mathbf{A}}$ completely triangular. Show that if this modification is adopted, the final value of b_{N+1} must be minimum possible value of the norm of **Ah**.

7.9. A matrix of the form $\pm \begin{bmatrix} c & s \\ s^* & -c \end{bmatrix}$ is called a Givens reflection matrix, where c is a real number, s is a complex number, and $c^2 + |s|^2 = 1$. Show that when $L = 1$ the block time-recursive LS algorithm based on the Householder transformation derived in Section 7.4.1 is equivalent to the Givens algorithm with square roots using a Givens reflection matrix in place of a Givens rotation matrix, and the entries c and s are the same in both cases.

7.10. Derive the time-update equation of $h_{\mathbf{X}}^{\mathbf{Y}d}(n)$ in the a posteriori error-feedback form of the ORLS algorithm from the corresponding equation of the a priori error-feedback form.

7.11. Derive the Householder form of the ORLS basic equation set given in Table 7.10 using the result of the block time-recursive LS algorithm given in Section 7.4.1 for $L = 1$.

7.12. Derive the *angle- and energy-normalized error form* of the ORLS basic equation set given in Table 7.10.

Computer Experiment Simulation of an Adaptive Linear Equalizer:

7.13. The block diagram of an adaptive linear equalizer is given in the Fig. P7.13. The data generator generates a bipolar random sequence $a(n)$ with values of $+1$ and -1. The additive noise is white and Gaussian with a variance of σ^2. The channel is modeled by a three-tap FIR filter with tap coefficients of 0.3, 0.9, and 0.3. The delay is selected to be equal to 7 [i.e., the desired signal is $z(n) = a(n - 7)$]. The linear equalizer is an FIR filter with 11 tap coefficients.

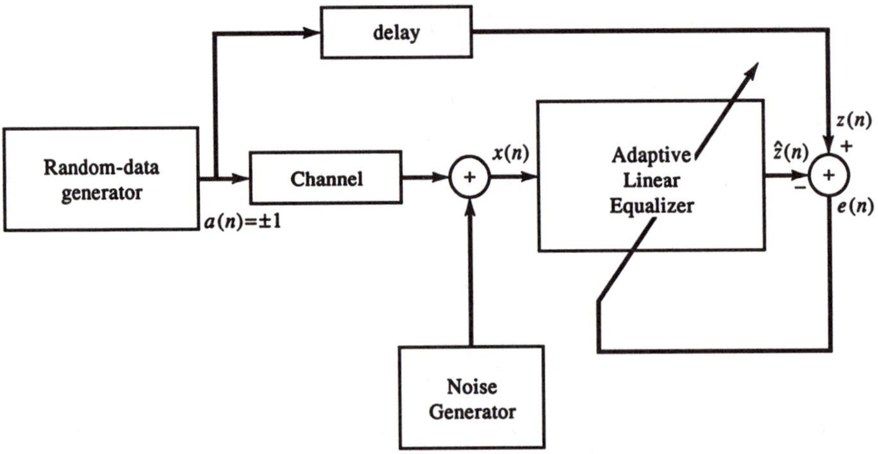

PROBLEM 7.13 (1) Implement the linear equalizer described above using the *a posteriori* and *a priori* error.

(a) Implement the linear equalizer described above using the a posteriori and a priori error forms of the RMGS algorithm. Plot the squared output errors for 500 samples (using a log y coordinate) and compare the behavior of these two types of errors.

(b) Implement the same linear equalizer using the Givens algorithms with and without square roots. Plot the squared output errors for 500 samples (using a log y coordinate). Compare the behavior of these two types of errors to each other and compare them with the plot generated in the previous experiment. Which types of errors best reflect the convergence of the LS estimation coefficients?

CHAPTER 8

POWER SPECTRUM ESTIMATION

In this chapter we are concerned with the estimation of the spectral characteristics of signals that are characterized as random processes. Many of the phenomena that occur in nature are best characterized statistically in terms of averages. For example, meteorological phenomena such as the fluctuations in air temperature and air pressure are best characterized statistically as random processes. Thermal noise voltages generated in resistors and electronic devices are additional examples of physical signals that are well modeled as random processes.

Due to the random fluctuations in such signals, we must adopt a statistical viewpoint, which deals with the average characteristics of random signals, as described in Chapter 1. In particular, the autocorrelation function of a random process is the appropriate statistical average that we will be concerned with for characterizing random signals in the time domain, and the Fourier transform of the autocorrelation function, which yields the power density spectrum, provides the transformation from the time domain to the frequency domain.

Power spectrum estimation methods have a relatively long history. For a historical perspective, the reader is referred to the paper by Robinson (1982) and the book by Marple (1986). Our treatment of this subject covers the classical power spectrum estimation methods based on the periodogram originally introduced by Schuster (1898), and the modern model-based or parametric methods that originated with the work of Yule (1927) and were subsequently developed by Bartlett (1948), Parzen (1957), Burg (1967), and others. We also describe the minimum variance spectral estimation method of Capon (1969) and methods based on eigenanalysis of the data correlation matrix.

8.1 ESTIMATION OF SPECTRA FROM FINITE-DURATION OBSERVATIONS OF SIGNALS

The basic problem that we consider in this chapter is estimation of the power density spectrum of a signal from observation of the signal over a finite time interval. As we will see, the finite record length of the data sequence is a major limitation on the quality of the power spectrum estimate. When dealing with signals that are statistically stationary, the longer the data record, the better the estimate that can be extracted from the data. On the other hand, if the signal statistics are nonstationary, we cannot select an arbitrarily long data record to estimate the spectrum. In such a case the length of the data record that we select is determined by the rapidity of the time variations in the signal statistics. Ultimately, our goal is to select as short a data record as possible that will allow us to resolve spectral characteristics of different signal components, contained in the data record, that have closely spaced spectra.

One of the problems that we encounter with classical power spectrum estimation methods based on a finite-length data record is distortion of the spectrum that we are attempting to estimate. This problem occurs in both the computation of the spectrum for a deterministic signal as well as in the estimation of the power spectrum of a random signal. Since it is easier to observe the effect of the finite length of the data record on a deterministic signal, we treat this case first. Thereafter, we consider only random signals and the estimation of their power spectra.

8.1.1 Computation of the Energy Density Spectrum

Let us consider the computation of the spectrum of a deterministic signal from a finite sequence of data. The sequence $x(n)$ is usually the result of sampling a continuous-time signal $x_a(t)$ at some uniform sampling rate F_s. Our objective is to obtain an estimate of the true spectrum from a finite-duration sequence $x(n)$.

Recall that if $x_a(t)$ is a finite energy signal,

$$E = \int_{-\infty}^{\infty} |x_a(t)|^2 \, dt < \infty$$

its Fourier transform exists and is given as

$$X_a(F) = \int_{-\infty}^{\infty} x_a(t) e^{-j2\pi F t} \, dt$$

From Parseval's theorem we have

$$E = \int_{-\infty}^{\infty} |x_a(t)|^2 \, dt = \int_{-\infty}^{\infty} |X_a(F)|^2 \, dF \tag{8.1.1}$$

The quantity $|X_a(F)|^2$ represents the distribution of signal energy as a function of frequency, and hence it is called the energy density spectrum of the signal,

$$S_{xx}(F) = |X_a(F)|^2 \tag{8.1.2}$$

as described in Chapter 1. Thus the total energy in the signal is simply the integral of $S_{xx}(F)$ over all F [i.e., the total area under $S_{xx}(F)$].

It is also interesting to note that $S_{xx}(F)$ may be viewed as the Fourier transform of another function, $R_{xx}(\tau)$, called the *autocorrelation function* of the finite energy signal $x(t)$, defined as

$$R_{xx}(\tau) = \int_{-\infty}^{\infty} x_a^*(t)x_a(t + \tau)\, dt \tag{8.1.3}$$

Indeed, it easily follows that

$$\int_{-\infty}^{\infty} R_{xx}(\tau)e^{-j2\pi F\tau}\, d\tau = S_{xx}(F) = |X_a(F)|^2 \tag{8.1.4}$$

so that $R_{xx}(\tau)$ and $S_{xx}(F)$ are a Fourier transform pair.

Now suppose that we compute the energy density spectrum of the signal $x_a(t)$ from its samples taken at the rate F_s samples per second. To ensure that there is no spectral aliasing resulting from the sampling process, the signal is assumed to be prefiltered, so that for practical purposes, its bandwidth is limited to B hertz. Then the sampling frequency F_s is selected such that $F_s > 2B$.

The sampled version of $x_a(t)$ is a sequence $x(n)$, $-\infty < n < \infty$, which has a Fourier transform (voltage spectrum)

$$X(\omega) = \sum_{n=-\infty}^{\infty} x(n)e^{-j\omega n}$$

or equivalently,

$$X(f) = \sum_{n=-\infty}^{\infty} x(n)e^{-j2\pi fn} \tag{8.1.5}$$

Recall that $X(f)$ may be expressed in terms of the voltage spectrum of the analog signal $x_a(t)$ as

$$X\left(\frac{F}{F_s}\right) = F_s \sum_{k=-\infty}^{\infty} X_a(F - kF_s) \tag{8.1.6}$$

where $f = F/F_s$ is the normalized frequency variable.

In the absence of aliasing, within the fundamental range $|F| \le F_s/2$, we have

$$X\left(\frac{F}{F_s}\right) = F_s X_a(F), \qquad |F| \le \frac{F_s}{2} \tag{8.1.7}$$

Hence the voltage spectrum of the sampled signal is identical to the voltage spectrum of the analog signal. As a consequence, the energy density spectrum of the sampled signal is

$$S_{xx}\left(\frac{F}{F_s}\right) = \left|X\left(\frac{F}{F_s}\right)\right|^2 = F_s^2\, |X_a(F)|^2 \tag{8.1.8}$$

We may proceed further by noting that the autocorrelation of the sampled signal, which is defined as

$$r_{xx}(k) = \sum_{n=-\infty}^{\infty} x^*(n)x(n+k) \tag{8.1.9}$$

has the Fourier transform

$$S_{xx}(f) = \sum_{k=-\infty}^{\infty} r_{xx}(k)e^{-j2\pi kf} \tag{8.1.10}$$

Hence the energy density spectrum may be obtained by Fourier transforming the autocorrelation of the sequence $\{x(n)\}$.

The relations above lead us to distinguish between two distinct methods for computing the energy density spectrum of a signal $x_a(t)$ from its samples $x(n)$. One is the *direct method*, which involves computing the Fourier transform of $x(n)$ and then

$$\begin{aligned} S_{xx}(f) &= |X(f)|^2 \\ &= \left| \sum_{n=-\infty}^{\infty} x(n)e^{-j2\pi fn} \right|^2 \end{aligned} \tag{8.1.11}$$

The second approach is called the *indirect method* because it requires two steps. First, the autocorrelation $r_{xx}(k)$ is computed from $x(n)$ and then the Fourier transform of the autocorrelation is computed as in (8.1.10) to obtain the energy density spectrum.

In practice, however, only the finite-duration sequence $x(n)$, $0 \le n \le N-1$, is available for computing the spectrum of the signal. In effect, limiting the duration of the sequence $x(n)$ to N points is equivalent to multiplying $x(n)$ by a rectangular window. Thus we have

$$\tilde{x}(n) = x(n)w(n) = \begin{cases} x(n), & 0 \le n \le N-1 \\ 0, & \text{otherwise} \end{cases} \tag{8.1.12}$$

From the basic Fourier transform properties, we recall that multiplication of two sequences is equivalent to convolution of their voltage spectra. Consequently, the frequency-domain relation corresponding to (8.1.12) is

$$\begin{aligned} \tilde{X}(f) &= X(f) * W(f) \\ &= \int_{-1/2}^{1/2} X(\alpha)W(f-\alpha)\,d\alpha \end{aligned} \tag{8.1.13}$$

Convolution of the window function $W(f)$ with $X(f)$ smooths the spectrum $X(f)$ provided that the spectrum $W(f)$ is relatively narrow compared to $X(f)$. But this condition implies that the window $w(n)$ be sufficiently long [i.e., N must be sufficiently large such that $W(f)$ is narrow compared to $X(f)$]. Even in $W(f)$ is narrow compared to $X(f)$, the convolution of $X(f)$ with the sidelobes of $W(f)$ results in sidelobe energy in $\tilde{X}(f)$ in frequency bands where the true signal spectrum $X(f) = 0$. This sidelobe energy is called *leakage*. The following example illustrates the leakage problem.

EXAMPLE 8.1.1

A signal with (voltage) spectrum

$$X(f) = \begin{cases} 1, & |f| \leq 0.1 \\ 0, & \text{otherwise} \end{cases}$$

is convolved with the rectangular window of length $N = 61$. Determine the spectrum of $\tilde{X}(f)$ given by (8.1.13).

Solution: The spectral characteristic $W(f)$ of a rectangular window is illustrated in Fig. 1.21. In general, the width of the main lobe of the window function is $\Delta\omega = 4\pi/N$ or $\Delta f = 2/N$. For $N = 61$, $W(f)$ is narrow compared to $X(f)$.

The convolution of $X(f)$ with $W(f)$ is illustrated in Fig. 8.1. We note that energy has leaked into the frequency band $0.1 < |f| \leq 0.5$, where $X(f) = 0$. A part of this is due to the width of the main lobe in $W(f)$, which causes a broading or smearing of $X(f)$ outside the range $|f| \leq 0.1$. However, the sidelobe energy in $\tilde{X}(f)$ is due to the presence of the sidelobes of $W(f)$, which are convolved with $X(f)$. The smearing of $X(f)$ for $|f| > 0.1$ and the sidelobes in the range $0.1 \leq |f| \leq 0.5$ constitute the leakage.

Just as in the case of FIR filter design, we can reduce sidelobe leakage by selecting windows that have low sidelobes. This implies that the windows

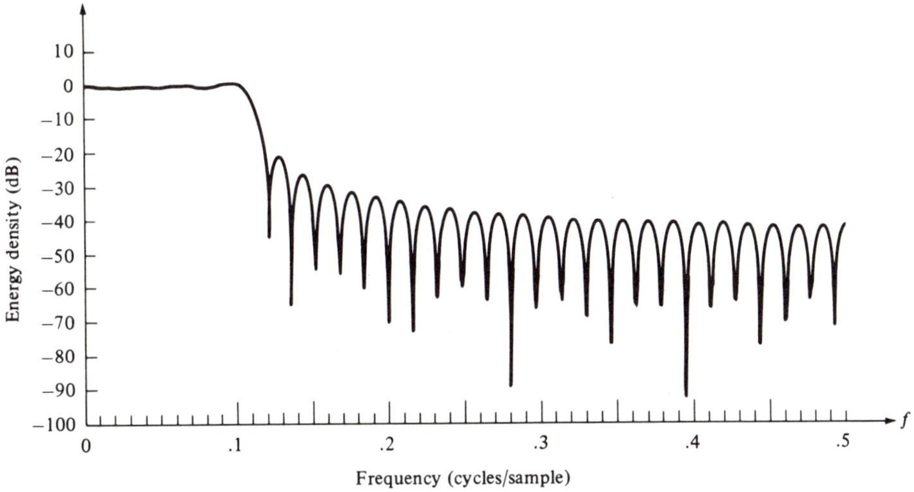

FIGURE 8.1 Spectrum obtained by convolving an $M = 61$ rectangular window with the ideal lowpass spectrum in Example 8.1.1

have a smooth time-domain cutoff instead of the abrupt cutoff in the rectangular window. Although such window functions reduce sidelobe leakage, they result in an increase in smoothing or broadening of the spectral characteristic $X(f)$. For example, the use of a Blackman window of length $N = 61$ in Example 8.1.1 results in the spectral characteristic $\tilde{X}(f)$ shown in Fig. 8.2. The sidelobe leakage has certainly been reduced, but the spectral width has been increased by about 50%.

Broadening of the spectrum being estimated due to windowing is particularly a problem when we wish to resolve signals with closely spaced frequency components. For example, as shown in Fig. 8.3, the signal with spectral characteristic $X(f) = X_1(f) + X_2(f)$ cannot be resolved as two separate signals unless the width of the window function is significantly narrower than the frequency separation Δf. Thus we observe that using smooth time-domain windows reduces leakage at the expense of a decrease in frequency resolution.

It is clear from the discussion above that the energy density spectrum of the windowed sequence $\tilde{x}(n)$ is an approximation of the desired spectrum of the sequence $\tilde{x}(n)$. The spectral density obtained from $\tilde{x}(n)$ is

$$S_{\tilde{x}\tilde{x}}(f) = |\tilde{X}(f)|^2 = \left| \sum_{n=0}^{N-1} \tilde{x}(n) e^{-j2\pi fn} \right|^2 \tag{8.1.14}$$

The spectrum given by (8.1.14) can be computed numerically at a set of N frequency points by means of the DFT. Thus

$$\tilde{X}(k) = \sum_{n=0}^{N-1} \tilde{x}(n) e^{-j2\pi kn/N} \tag{8.1.15}$$

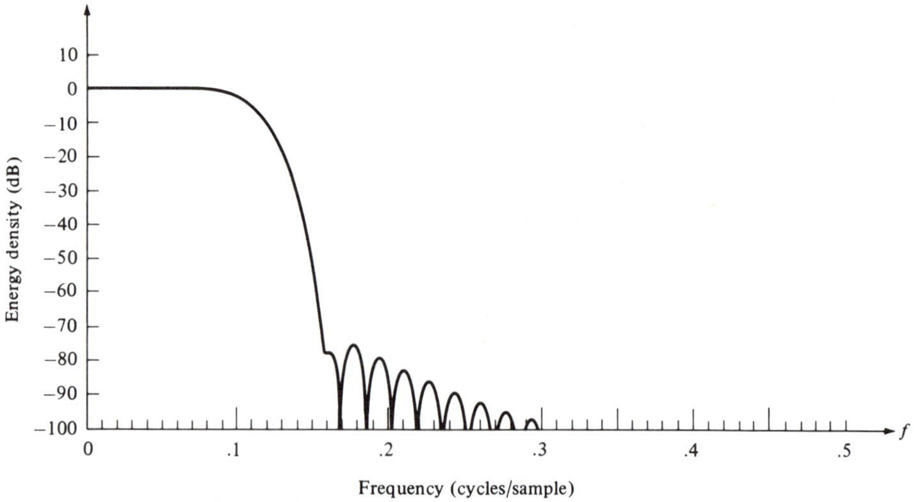

FIGURE 8.2 Spectrum obtained by convolving an $M = 61$ Blackman window with the ideal lowpass spectrum in Example 8.1.1.

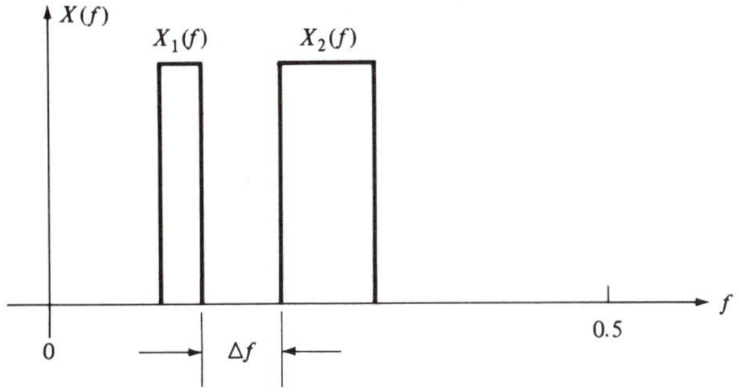

FIGURE 8.3 Two narrowband signal spectra.

Then

$$|\tilde{X}(k)|^2 = S_{\tilde{x}\tilde{x}}(f)|_{f=\frac{k}{N}} = S_{\tilde{x}\tilde{x}}\left(\frac{k}{N}\right) \tag{8.1.16}$$

and hence

$$S_{\tilde{x}\tilde{x}}\left(\frac{k}{N}\right) = \left|\sum_{n=0}^{N-1} \tilde{x}(n)e^{-j2\pi kn/N}\right|^2 \tag{8.1.17}$$

which is a distorted version of the true spectrum $S_{xx}(k/N)$.

8.1.2 Estimation of the Autocorrelation and Power Spectrum of Random Signals: The Periodogram

The finite energy signals considered in the preceding section possess a Fourier transform and were characterized in the spectral domain by their energy density spectrum. On the other hand, the important class of signals, characterized as stationary random processes, do not have finite energy and hence do not possess a Fourier transform. Such signals have finite average power and hence are characterized by a *power density spectrum*. If $x(t)$ is a stationary random process its autocorrelation function is

$$\gamma_{xx}(\tau) = E[x^*(t)x(t + \tau)] \tag{8.1.18}$$

where $E[\cdot]$ denotes the statistical average. Then, via the Wiener–Khinchin theorem, the power density spectrum of the stationary random process is the Fourier transform of the autocorrelation function,

$$\Gamma_{xx}(F) = \int_{-\infty}^{\infty} \gamma_{xx}(\tau)e^{-j2\pi F\tau}\, d\tau \tag{8.1.19}$$

In practice, we deal with a single realization of the random process from which we estimate the power spectrum of the process. We do not know the true autocorrelation function $\gamma_{xx}(\tau)$, and as a consequence we cannot compute the Fourier transform in (8.1.19) to obtain $\Gamma_{xx}(F)$. On the other hand, from a single realization of the random process we can compute the time-averaged autocorrelation function

$$R_{xx}(\tau) = \frac{1}{2T_0}\int_{-T_0}^{T_0} x^*(t)x(t+\tau)\,dt \tag{8.1.20}$$

where $2T_0$ is the observation interval. If the stationary random process is *ergodic* in the first and second moments (mean and autocorrelation function),

$$\begin{aligned}\gamma_{xx}(\tau) &= \lim_{T_0\to\infty} R_{xx}(\tau)\\ &= \lim_{T_0\to\infty}\frac{1}{2T_0}\int_{-T_0}^{T_0} x^*(t)x(t+\tau)\,dt\end{aligned} \tag{8.1.21}$$

This relation justifies the use of the time-averaged autocorrelation $R_{xx}(\tau)$ as an estimate of the statistical autocorrelation function $\gamma_{xx}(\tau)$. Furthermore, the Fourier transform of $R_{xx}(\tau)$ provides an estimate $P_{xx}(F)$ of the power density spectrum,

$$\begin{aligned}P_{xx}(F) &= \int_{-T_0}^{T_0} R_{xx}(\tau)e^{-j2\pi F\tau}\,d\tau\\ &= \frac{1}{2T_0}\int_{-T_0}^{T_0}\left[\int_{-T_0}^{T_0} x^*(t)x(t+\tau)\,dt\right]e^{-j2\pi F\tau}\,d\tau\\ &= \frac{1}{2T_0}\left|\int_{-T_0}^{T_0} x(t)e^{-j2\pi Ft}\,dt\right|^2\end{aligned} \tag{8.1.22}$$

The actual power density spectrum is the expected value of $P_{xx}(F)$ in the limit as $T_0\to\infty$,

$$\begin{aligned}\Gamma_{xx}(F) &= \lim_{T_0\to\infty} E[P_{xx}(F)]\\ &= \lim_{T_0\to\infty} E\left[\frac{1}{2T_0}\left|\int_{-T_0}^{T_0} x(t)e^{-j2\pi Ft}\,dt\right|^2\right]\end{aligned} \tag{8.1.23}$$

From (8.1.20) and (8.1.22) we again note the two possible approaches to computing $P_{xx}(F)$, the direct method as given by (8.1.22) or the indirect method, in which we obtain $R_{xx}(\tau)$ first and then compute the Fourier transform.

We shall consider the estimation of the power density spectrum from samples of a single realization of the random process. In particular, we assume that $x_a(t)$ is sampled at a rate $F_s > 2B$, where B is the highest frequency contained in the power density spectrum of the random process. Thus we obtain a finite-duration sequence $x(n)$, $0 \le n \le N-1$, by sampling

$x_a(t)$. From these samples we may compute the time-averaged autocorrelation sequence

$$r_{xx}(m) = \frac{1}{N - |m|} \sum_{n=0}^{N-|m|-1} x^*(n)x(n+m), \qquad m = 0\,1, \ldots, N-1, \quad (8.1.24)$$

where $r_{xx}(-m) = r_{xx}^*(m)$, and then compute the Fourier transform

$$P_{xx}(f) = \sum_{m=-N+1}^{N-1} r_{xx}(m)e^{-j2\pi fm} \qquad (8.1.25)$$

The normalization factor $N - |m|$ in (8.1.24) results in an estimate with mean value

$$\begin{aligned} E[r_{xx}(m)] &= \frac{1}{N - |m|} \sum_{n=0}^{N-|m|-1} E[x^*(n)x(n+m)] \\ &= \gamma_{xx}(m) \end{aligned} \qquad (8.1.26)$$

where $\gamma_{xx}(m)$ is the true (statistical) autocorrelation sequence of $x(n)$. Hence $r_{xx}(m)$ is an unbiased estimate of the autocorrelation function $\gamma_{xx}(m)$. The variance of the estimate $r_{xx}(m)$ is approximately

$$\text{var}[r_{xx}(m)] \approx \frac{N}{[N - |m|]^2} \sum_{n=-\infty}^{\infty} [|\gamma_{xx}(n)|^2 + \gamma_{xx}^*(n-m)\gamma_{xx}(n+m)] \quad (8.1.27)$$

which is a result given by Jenkins and Watts (1968). Clearly,

$$\lim_{N\to\infty} \text{var}[r_{xx}(m)] = 0 \qquad (8.1.28)$$

provided that

$$\sum_{n=-\infty}^{\infty} |\gamma_{xx}(n)|^2 < \infty$$

Since $E[r_{xx}(m)] = \gamma_{xx}(n)$ and the variance of the estimate converges to zero as $N \to \infty$, the estimate $r_{xx}(m)$ is said to be *consistent*.

For large values of the lag parameters m, the estimate $r_{xx}(m)$ given by (8.1.24) has a large variance, especially as m approaches N. This is due to the fact that fewer data points enter into the estimate for large lags. As an alternative to (8.1.24) we may use the estimate

$$\tilde{r}_{xx}(m) = \frac{1}{N} \sum_{n=0}^{N-|m|-1} x^*(n)x(n+m), \qquad m \geq 0 \qquad (8.1.29)$$

which has a bias of $|m|\gamma_{xx}(m)/N$, since its mean value is

$$\begin{aligned} E[\tilde{r}_{xx}(m)] &= \frac{1}{N} \sum_{n=0}^{N-|m|-1} E[x^*(n)x(n+m)] \\ &= \frac{N - |m|}{N} \gamma_{xx}(m) = \left(1 - \frac{|m|}{N}\right)\gamma_{xx}(m) \end{aligned} \qquad (8.1.30)$$

However, this estimate has a smaller variance, given approximately as

$$\operatorname{var}[\tilde{r}_{xx}(m)] \approx \frac{1}{N} \sum_{n=-\infty}^{\infty} [|\gamma_{xx}(n)|^2 + \gamma_{xx}^*(n-m)\gamma_{xx}(n+m)] \tag{8.1.31}$$

We observe that $r_{xx}(m)$ is *asymptotically unbiased*,

$$\lim_{N\to\infty} E[\tilde{r}_{xx}(m)] = \gamma_{xx}(m) \tag{8.1.32}$$

and its variance converges to zero as $N \to \infty$. Therefore, the estimate $\tilde{r}_{xx}(m)$ is also a *consistent estimate* of $\gamma_{xx}(m)$.

We shall use the estimate $\tilde{r}_{xx}(m)$ given by (8.1.29) in our treatment of power spectrum estimation. The corresponding estimate of the power density spectrum is

$$P_{xx}(f) = \sum_{m=-(N-1)}^{N-1} r_{xx}(m)e^{-j2\pi fm} \tag{8.1.33}$$

If we substitute for $r_{xx}(m)$ from (8.1.29) into (8.1.33), the estimate $P_{xx}(f)$ may also be expressed as

$$P_{xx}(f) = \frac{1}{N}\left|\sum_{n=0}^{N-1} x(n)e^{-j2\pi fn}\right|^2 = \frac{1}{N}|X(f)|^2 \tag{8.1.34}$$

where $X(f)$ is the Fourier transform of the sample sequence $x(n)$. This well-known form of the power density spectrum estimate is called the *periodogram*, which was originally introduced by Schuster (1898) to detect and measure "hidden periodicities" in data.

From (8.1.33) we obtain the average value of the periodogram estimate $P_{xx}(f)$ as

$$\begin{aligned} E[P_{xx}(f)] &= E\left[\sum_{m=-(N-1)}^{N-1} r_{xx}(m)e^{-j2\pi fm}\right] = \sum_{m=-(N-1)}^{N-1} E[r_{xx}(m)]e^{-j2\pi fm} \\ E[P_{xx}(f)] &= \sum_{m=-(N-1)}^{N-1} \left(1 - \frac{|m|}{N}\right)\gamma_{xx}(m)^{-j2\pi fm} \end{aligned} \tag{8.1.35}$$

The interpretation that we give to (8.1.35) is that the mean of the estimated spectrum is the Fourier transform of the windowed autocorrelation function

$$\tilde{\gamma}_{xx}(m) = \left(1 - \frac{|m|}{N}\right)\gamma_{xx}(m) \tag{8.1.36}$$

where the window function is the (triangular) Bartlett window. Hence the mean of the estimated spectrum is

$$\begin{aligned} E[P_{xx}(f)] &= \sum_{m=-\infty}^{\infty} \tilde{\gamma}_{xx}(m)e^{-j2\pi fm} \\ & \int_{-1/2}^{1/2} \Gamma_{xx}(\alpha)W_B(f-\alpha)\, d\alpha \end{aligned} \tag{8.1.37}$$

where $W_B(f)$ is the spectral characteristic of the Bartlett window. The relation (8.1.37) illustrates that the mean of the estimated spectrum is the convolution of the true power density spectrum $\Gamma_{xx}(f)$ with the Fourier transform $W_B(f)$ of the Bartlett window. Consequently, the mean of the estimated spectrum is a smoothed version of the true spectrum and suffers from the same spectral leakage problems which are due to the finite number of data points.

We observe that the estimated spectrum is asymptotically unbiased,

$$\lim_{N\to\infty} E\left[\sum_{m=-(N-1)}^{N-1} r_{xx}(m)e^{-j2\pi fm}\right] = \sum_{m=-\infty}^{\infty} \gamma_{xx}(m)e^{-j2\pi fm} = \Gamma_{xx}(f)$$

However, in general, the variance of the estimate $P_{xx}(f)$ does not decay to zero as $N \to \infty$. For example, when the data sequence is a Gaussian random process, the variance is easily shown to be (see Problem 8.4)

$$\text{var}[P_{xx}(f)] = \Gamma_{xx}^2(f)\left[1 + \left(\frac{\sin 2\pi fN}{N \sin 2\pi f}\right)^2\right] \tag{8.1.38}$$

which, in the limit as $N \to \infty$, becomes

$$\lim_{N\to\infty} \text{var}\,[P_{xx}(f)] = \Gamma_{xx}^2(f) \tag{8.1.39}$$

Hence, we conclude that the *periodogram is not a consistent estimate of the true power density spectrum* (i.e., it does not converge to the true power density spectrum).

In summary, the estimated autocorrelation $\tilde{r}_{xx}(m)$ is a consistent estimate of the true autocorrelation function $\gamma_{xx}(m)$. However, its Fourier transform $P_{xx}(f)$, the periodogram, is not a consistent estimate of the true power density spectrum. We observed that $P_{xx}(f)$ is an asymptotically unbiased estimate of $\Gamma_{xx}(f)$, but for a finite-duration sequence, the mean value of $P_{xx}(f)$ contains a bias, which from (8.1.37) is evident as a distortion of the true power density spectrum. Thus the estimated spectrum suffers from the smoothing effects and the leakage embodied in the Bartlett window. The smoothing and leakage ultimately limit our ability to resolve closely spaced spectra.

The problems of leakage and frequency resolution that we have described above, as well as the problem that the periodogram is not a consistent estimate of the power spectrum, provide the motivation for the power spectrum estimation methods described in Sections 8.2, 8.3, and 8.4. The methods described in Section 8.2 are classical, nonparametric methods, which make no assumptions about the data sequence. The emphasis of the classical methods is on obtaining a consistent estimate of the power spectrum through some averaging or smoothing operations performed directly on the periodogram or on the autocorrelation. As we will see, the effect of these operations is to further reduce the frequency resolution, while the variance of the estimate is decreased.

The spectrum estimation methods described in Section 8.3 are based on some model of how the data were generated. In general, the model-based methods that have been developed over the past two decades provide significantly higher resolution than the classical methods.

Additional methods are described in Sections 8.4 and 8.5. One of these methods, due to Capon (1969), is based on minimizing the variance in the spectral estimate. The methods described in Section 8.5 are based on an eigenvalue/eigenvector decomposition of the data correlation matrix.

8.1.3 Use of the DFT in Power Spectrum Estimation

As given by (8.1.14) and (8.1.34), the estimated energy density spectrum $S_{xx}(f)$ and the periodogram $P_{xx}(f)$, respectively, can be computed by use of the DFT, which in turn is efficiently computed by the FFT algorithm. If we have N data points, we compute as a minimum the N-point DFT. For example, the computation yields samples of the periodogram

$$P_{xx}\left(\frac{k}{N}\right) = \frac{1}{N}\left|\sum_{n=0}^{N-1} x(n)e^{-j2\pi nk/N}\right|^2, \qquad k = 0, 1, \ldots, N-1 \qquad (8.1.40)$$

at the frequencies $f_k = k/N$.

In practice, however, such a sparse sampling of the spectrum does not provide a very good representation or a good picture of the continuous spectrum estimate $P_{xx}(f)$. This is easily remedied by evaluating $P_{xx}(f)$ at additional frequencies. Equivalently, we may effectively increase the length of the sequence by means of zero padding and then evaluate $P_{xx}(f)$ at a more dense set of frequencies. Thus if we increase the data sequence length to L points by means of zero padding and evaluate the L-point DFT, we have

$$P_{xx}\left(\frac{k}{L}\right) = \frac{1}{N}\left|\sum_{n=0}^{N-1} x(n)e^{-j2\pi nk/L}\right|^2, \qquad k = 0, 1, \ldots, L-1 \qquad (8.1.41)$$

We emphasize that zero padding and evaluating the DFT at $L > N$ points does not improve the frequency resolution in the spectral estimate. It simply provides us with a method for interpolating the values of the measured spectrum at more frequencies. The frequency resolution in the spectral estimate $P_{xx}(f)$ is determined by the length N of the data record.

EXAMPLE 8.1.2

A sequence of $N = 16$ samples is obtained by sampling an analog signal consisting of two frequency components. The resulting discrete-time sequence is

$$x(n) = \sin 2\pi(0.135)n + \cos 2\pi(0.135 + \Delta f)n, \qquad n = 0, 1, \ldots, 15$$

where Δf is the frequency separation. Evaluate the power spectrum $P(f) = \frac{1}{N}|X(f)|^2$ at the frequencies $f_k = k/L$, $k = 0, 1, \ldots, L-1$, for $L = 16, 32, 64$, and 128 for values of $\Delta f = 0.06$ and $\Delta f = 0.01$.

Solution: By zero padding we increase the data sequence to obtain the power spectrum estimate $P_{xx}(k/L)$. The results for $\Delta f = 0.06$ are plotted in Fig. 8.4. Note that zero padding does not change the resolution, but it does have the effect of interpolating the spectrum $P_{xx}(f)$. In this case the frequency separation Δf is sufficiently large so that the two frequency components are resolvable.

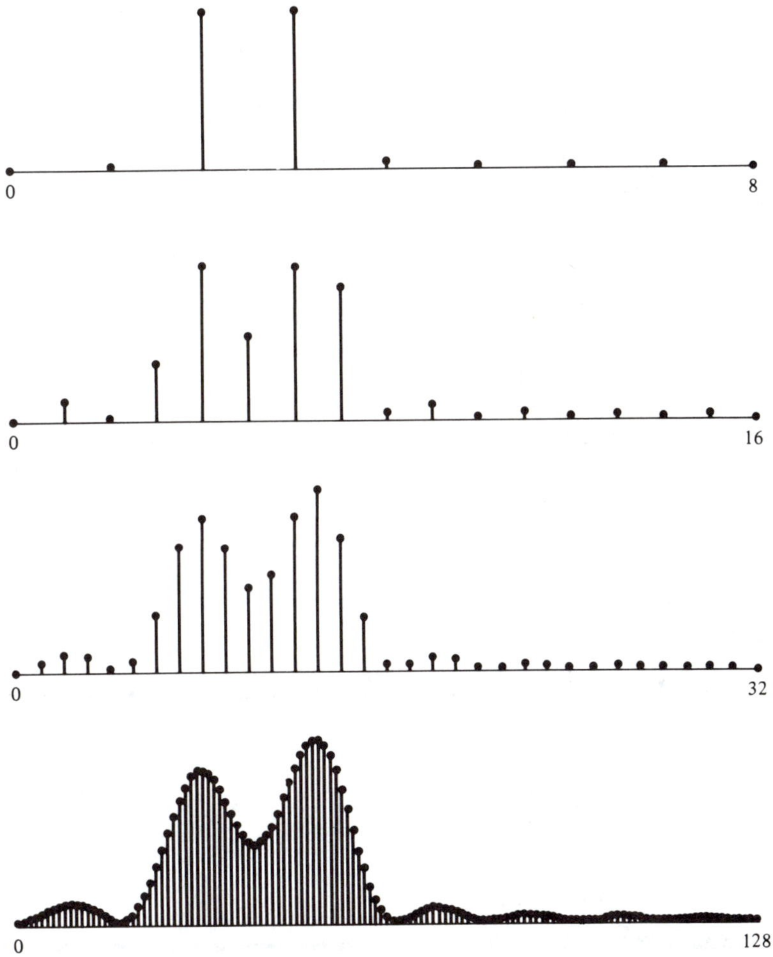

FIGURE 8.4 Spectra of two sinusoids with frequency separation $\Delta f = 0.06$.

The spectral estimates for $\Delta f = 0.01$ are shown in Fig. 8.5. In this case the two spectral components are not resolvable. Again, the effect of zero padding is to provide more interpolation, thus giving us a better picture of the estimated spectrum. It does not improve the frequency resolution.

When only a few points of the periodogram are needed, the Goertzel algorithm may provide a more efficient computation. Since the Goertzel algorithm may be interpreted as a linear filtering approach to computing the DFT, it is clear that the periodogram estimate can be obtained by passing the signal through a band of parallel tuned filters and squaring their outputs (see Problem 8.5).

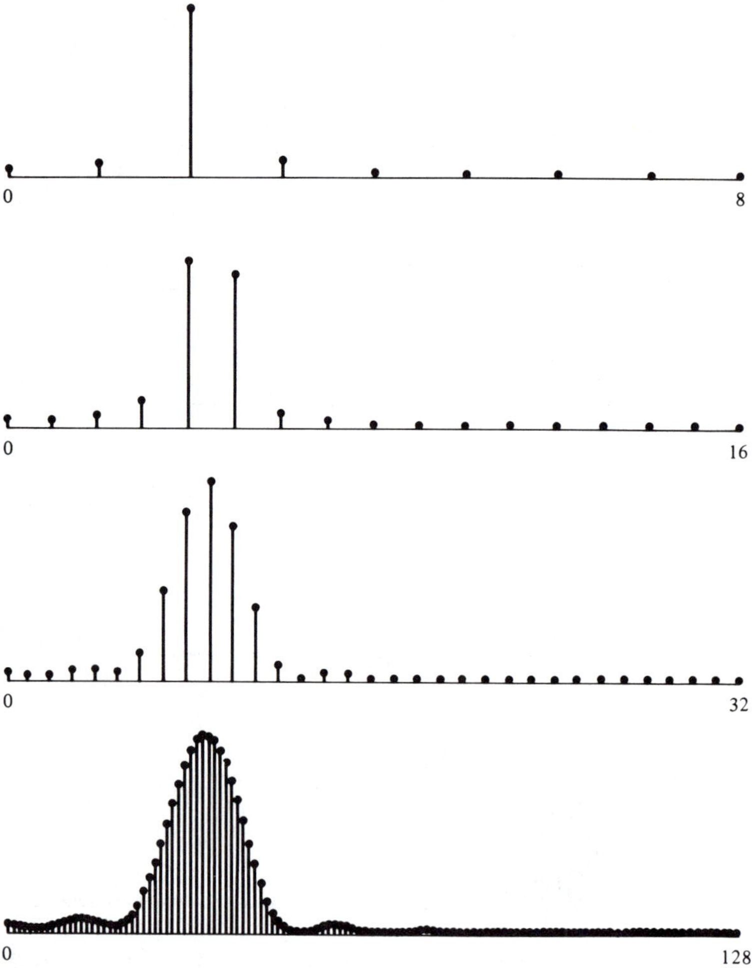

FIGURE 8.5 Spectra of two sinusoids with frequency separation $\Delta f = 0.01$.

8.2 NONPARAMETRIC METHODS FOR POWER SPECTRUM ESTIMATION

The power spectrum estimation methods described in this section are the classical methods developed by Bartlett (1948), Blackman and Tukey (1958), and Welch (1967). These methods make no assumption about how the data were generated and hence are called *nonparametric*.

Since the estimates are based entirely on a finite record of data, the frequency resolution of these methods is, at best, equal to the spectral width of the rectangular window of length N, which is approximately $1/N$ at the -3-dB points. We shall be more precise in specifying the frequency resolution of the specific methods. All the estimation techniques described in this section decrease the frequency resolution in order to reduce the variance in the spectral estimate.

First, we describe the estimates and derive the mean and variance of each one. A comparison of the three methods is given in Section 8.2.4. Although the spectral estimates are expressed as a function of the continuous frequency variable f, in practice, the estimates are computed at discrete frequencies via the FFT algorithm. The FFT-based computational requirements are considered in Section 8.2.5.

8.2.1 Bartlett Method: Averaging Periodograms

Bartlett's method for reducing the variance in the periodogram involves three steps. First, the N-point sequence is subdivided into K nonoverlapping segments, where each segment has length M. This results in the K data segments

$$x_i(n) = x(n + iM), \qquad \begin{aligned} i &= 0, 1, \ldots, K-1 \\ n &= 0, 1, \ldots, M-1 \end{aligned} \tag{8.2.1}$$

For each segment we compute the periodogram

$$P_{xx}^{(i)}(f) = \frac{1}{M}\left|\sum_{n=0}^{M-1} x_i(n)e^{-j2\pi fn}\right|^2, \qquad i = 0, 1, \ldots, K-1 \tag{8.2.2}$$

Finally, we average the periodograms for the K segments to obtain the Bartlett power spectrum estimate

$$P_{xx}^{B}(f) = \frac{1}{K}\sum_{i=0}^{K-1} P_{xx}^{(i)}(f) \tag{8.2.3}$$

The statistical properties of this estimate are easily obtained. First, the mean value is

$$\begin{aligned} E[P_{xx}^{B}(f)] &= \frac{1}{K}\sum_{i=0}^{K-1} E[P_{xx}^{(i)}(f)] \\ &= E[P_{xx}^{(i)}(f)] \end{aligned} \tag{8.2.4}$$

From (8.1.35) and (8.1.37) we have the expected value for the single periodogram as

$$
\begin{aligned}
E[P_{xx}^{(i)}(f)] &= \sum_{m=-(M-1)}^{M-1} \left(1 - \frac{|m|}{M}\right) \gamma_{xx}(m) e^{-j2\pi fm} \\
&= \frac{1}{M} \int_{-1/2}^{1/2} \Gamma_{xx}(\alpha) \left(\frac{\sin \pi(f-a)M}{\sin \pi(f-\alpha)}\right)^2 d\alpha
\end{aligned}
\tag{8.2.5}
$$

where

$$
W_B(f) = \frac{1}{M}\left(\frac{\sin \pi f M}{\sin \pi f}\right)^2 \tag{8.2.6}
$$

is the frequency characteristics of the Bartlett window

$$
w_B(m) = \begin{cases} 1 - \dfrac{|m|}{M}, & |m| \le M - 1 \\ 0, & \text{otherwise} \end{cases} \tag{8.2.7}
$$

From (8.2.5) we observe that the true spectrum is now convolved with the frequency characteristic $W_B(f)$ of the Bartlett window. The effect of reducing the length of the data from N points to $M = N/K$ points results in a window whose spectral width has been increased by a factor of K. Consequently, the frequency resolution has been reduced by a factor K.

In return for this reduction in resolution, we have reduced the variance. The variance of the Bartlett estimate is

$$
\begin{aligned}
\text{var}[P_{xx}^{B}(f)] &= \frac{1}{K^2} \sum_{i=0}^{K-1} \text{var}[P_{xx}^{(i)}(f)] \\
&= \frac{1}{K} \text{var}[P_{xx}^{(i)}(f)]
\end{aligned}
\tag{8.2.8}
$$

If we make use of (8.1.38) in (8.2.8), we obtain

$$
\text{var}[P_{xx}^{B}(f)] = \frac{1}{K} \Gamma_{xx}^2(f) \left[1 + \left(\frac{\sin 2\pi f M}{M \sin 2\pi f}\right)^2\right] \tag{8.2.9}
$$

Therefore, the variance of the Bartlett power spectrum estimate has been reduced by the factor K.

8.2.2 Welch Method: Averaging Modified Periodograms

Welch (1967) made two basic modifications to the Bartlett method. First, he allowed the data segments to overlap. Thus the data segments may be represented as

$$
x_i(n) = x(n + iD), \qquad \begin{aligned} n &= 0, 1, \ldots, M-1 \\ i &= 0, 1, \ldots, L-1 \end{aligned} \tag{8.2.10}
$$

where iD is the starting point for the ith sequence. Observe that if $D = M$, the segments do not overlap and the number L of data segments is identical to the number K in the Bartlett method. However, if $D = M/2$, there is

50% overlap between successive data segments and $L = 2K$ segments are obtained. Alternatively, we can form K data segments each of length $2M$.

The second modification made by Welch to the Bartlett method is to window the data segments prior to computing the periodogram. The result is a "modified" periodogram

$$\tilde{P}_{xx}^{(i)}(f) = \frac{1}{MU}\left|\sum_{n=0}^{M-1} x_i(n)w(n)e^{-j2\pi fn}\right|^2, \qquad i = 0, 1, \ldots, L-1 \tag{8.2.11}$$

where U is a normalization factor for the power in the window function and is selected as

$$U = \frac{1}{M}\sum_{n=0}^{M-1} w^2(n) \tag{8.2.12}$$

The Welch power spectrum estimate is the average of these modified periodograms,

$$P_{xx}^{W}(f) = \frac{1}{L}\sum_{i=0}^{L-1} \tilde{P}_{xx}^{(i)}(f) \tag{8.2.13}$$

The mean value of the Welch estimate is

$$\begin{aligned} E[P_{xx}^{W}(f)] &= \frac{1}{L}\sum_{i=0}^{L-1} E[\tilde{P}_{xx}^{(i)}(f)] \\ &= E[\tilde{P}_{xx}^{(i)}(f)] \end{aligned} \tag{8.2.14}$$

But the expected value of the modified periodogram is

$$\begin{aligned} E[\tilde{P}_{xx}^{(i)}(f)] &= \frac{1}{MU}\sum_{n=0}^{M-1}\sum_{m=0}^{M-1} w(n)w(m)E[x_i(n)x_i^*(m)]e^{-j2\pi f(n-m)} \\ &= \frac{1}{MU}\sum_{n=0}^{M-1}\sum_{m=0}^{M-1} w(n)w(m)\gamma_{xx}(n-m)e^{-j2\pi f(n-m)} \end{aligned} \tag{8.2.15}$$

Since

$$\gamma_{xx}(n) = \int_{-1/2}^{1/2} \Gamma_{xx}(\alpha)e^{j2\pi\alpha n}\, d\alpha \tag{8.2.16}$$

substitution for $\gamma_{xx}(n)$ from (8.2.16) into (8.2.15) yields

$$\begin{aligned} E[\tilde{P}_{xx}^{(i)}(f)] &= \frac{1}{MU}\int_{-1/2}^{1/2} \Gamma_{xx}(\alpha)\left[\sum_{n=0}^{M-1}\sum_{m=0}^{M-1} w(n)w(m)e^{-j2\pi(n-m)(f-\alpha)}\right] d\alpha \\ &= \int_{-1/2}^{1/2} \Gamma_{xx}(\alpha)W(f-\alpha)\, d\alpha \end{aligned} \tag{8.2.17}$$

where, by definition,

$$W(f) = \frac{1}{MU}\left|\sum_{n=0}^{M-1} w(n)e^{-j2\pi fn}\right|^2 \tag{8.2.18}$$

The normalization factor U ensures that

$$\int_{-1/2}^{1/2} W(f)\, df = 1 \tag{8.2.19}$$

The variance of the Welch estimate is

$$\text{var}[P_{xx}^{\text{W}}(f)] = \frac{1}{L^2} \sum_{i=0}^{L-1} \sum_{j=0}^{L-1} E[\tilde{P}_{xx}^{(i)}(f)\tilde{P}_{xx}^{(j)}(f)] - \{E[P_{xx}^{\text{W}}(f)]\}^2 \tag{8.2.20}$$

In the case of no overlap between successive data segments ($L = K$), Welch has shown that

$$\begin{aligned} \text{var}[P_{xx}^{W}(f)] &= \frac{1}{L}\,\text{var}[\tilde{P}_{xx}^{(i)}(f)] \\ &\approx \frac{1}{L}\,\Gamma_{xx}^2(f) \end{aligned} \tag{8.2.21}$$

In the case of 50% overlap between successive data segments ($I = 2K$), the variance of the Welch power spectrum estimate with the Bartlett (triangular) window, also derived in the paper by Welch, is

$$\text{var}[P_{xx}^{W}(f)] \approx \frac{9}{8L}\,\Gamma_{xx}^2(f) \tag{8.2.22}$$

Although we considered only the triangular window in the computation of the variance, other window functions may be used. In general, they will yield a difference variance. In addition, one may also overlap the data segments by either more or less than the 50% considered in this section, in an attempt to improve the relevant characteristics of the estimate.

8.2.3 Blackman and Tukey Method: Smoothing the Periodogram

Blackman and Tukey (1958) proposed and analyzed the method in which the sample autocorrelation sequence is windowed first, and then Fourier transformed to yield the estimate of the power spectrum. The rationale for windowing the estimated autocorrelation sequence $r_{xx}(m)$ is that for large lags, the estimates are less reliable because a smaller number ($N - m$) of data points enter into the estimate. For values of m approaching N, the variance of these estimates is very high and hence these estimates should be given a smaller weight in the formation of the estimated power spectrum. Thus the Blackman–Tukey estimate is

$$P_{xx}^{\text{BT}}(f) = \sum_{m=-(M-1)}^{M-1} r_{xx}(m)w(m)e^{-j2\pi fm} \tag{8.2.23}$$

where the window function $w(n)$ has length $2M - 1$ and is zero for $|m| \geq M$. With this definition for $w(n)$, the limits on the sum in (8.2.23) may be extended to $(-\infty, \infty)$. Hence the frequency-domain equivalent expression for (8.2.23) is the convolution integral

$$P_{xx}^{BT}(f) = \int_{-1/2}^{1/2} P_{xx}(\alpha)W(f - \alpha)\, d\alpha \tag{8.2.24}$$

where $P_{xx}(f)$ is the periodogram. It is clear from (8.2.24) that the effect of windowing the autocorrelation is to smooth the periodogram estimate, thus decreasing the variance in the estimate at the expense of reducing the resolution.

The window sequence $w(n)$ should be symmetric (even) about $m = 0$ to ensure that the estimate of the power spectrum is real. Furthermore, it is desirable to select the window spectrum to be nonnegative,

$$W(f) \geq 0, \qquad |f| \leq \tfrac{1}{2} \tag{8.2.25}$$

This condition will ensure that $P_{xx}^{BT}(f) \geq 0$ for $|f| \leq \frac{1}{2}$, which is a desirable property for any power spectrum estimate. We should indicate, however, that some popular window functions do not satisfy this condition. For example, despite their low sidelobe levels, the Hamming and Hann (or Hanning) windows do not satisfy the property in (8.2.25) and consequently, may result in negative spectrum estimates in some parts of the frequency range.

The expected value of the Blackman–Tukey power spectrum estimate is

$$E[P_{xx}^{BT}(f)] = \int_{-1/2}^{1/2} E[P_{xx}(\alpha)]W(f - \alpha)\, d\alpha \tag{8.2.26}$$

where from (8.1.37) we have

$$E[P_{xx}(\alpha)] = \int_{-1/2}^{1/2} \Gamma_{xx}(\theta)W_B(\alpha - \theta)\, d\theta \tag{8.2.27}$$

and $W_B(f)$ is the Fourier transform of the Bartlett window. Substitution of (8.2.27) into (8.2.26) yields the double convolution integral

$$E[P_{xx}^{BT}(f)] = \int_{-1/2}^{1/2}\int_{-1/2}^{1/2} \Gamma_{xx}(\theta)W_B(\alpha - \theta)W(f - \alpha)\, d\alpha\, d\theta \tag{8.2.28}$$

Equivalently, by working in the time domain, the expected value of the Blackman–Tukey power spectrum estimate is

$$\begin{aligned} E[P_{xx}^{BT}(f)] &= \sum_{m=-(M-1)}^{M-1} E[r_{xx}(m)]w(m)e^{-j2\pi fm} \\ &= \sum_{m=-(M-1)}^{M-1} \gamma_{xx}(m)w_B(m)w(m)e^{-j2\pi fm} \end{aligned} \tag{8.2.29}$$

where the Bartlett window is

$$w_B(m) = \begin{cases} 1 - \dfrac{|m|}{N}, & |m| < N \\ 0, & \text{otherwise} \end{cases} \tag{8.2.30}$$

Clearly, we should select the window length for $w(n)$ such that $M << N$ [i.e., $w(n)$ should be narrower than $w_B(m)$ in order to provide additional smoothing of the periodogram]. Under this condition, (8.2.28) becomes

$$E[P_{xx}^{\text{BT}}(f)] \approx \int_{-1/2}^{1/2} \Gamma_{xx}(\theta) W(f-\theta)\, d\theta \tag{8.2.31}$$

since

$$\int_{-1/2}^{1/2} W_B(\alpha-\theta) W(f-\alpha)\, d\alpha$$

$$= \int_{-1/2}^{1/2} W_B(\alpha) W(f-\theta-\alpha)\, d\alpha \approx W(f-\theta) \tag{8.2.32}$$

The variance of the Blackman–Tukey power spectrum estimate is

$$\text{var}[P_{xx}^{\text{BT}}(f)] = E\{[P_{xx}^{\text{BT}}(f)]^2\} - \{E[P_{xx}^{\text{BT}}(f)]\}^2 \tag{8.2.33}$$

where the mean may be approximated as in (8.2.31). The second moment in (8.2.33) is

$$E\{[P_{xx}^{\text{BT}}(f)]^2\} = \int_{-1/2}^{1/2}\int_{-1/2}^{1/2} E[P_{xx}(\alpha)P_{xx}(\theta)] W(f-\alpha) W(f-\theta)\, d\alpha\, d\theta \tag{8.2.34}$$

On the assumption that the random process is Gaussian (see Problem 8.5), we find that

$$E[P_{xx}(\alpha)P_{xx}(\theta)] = \Gamma_{xx}(\alpha)\Gamma_{xx}(\theta)\left\{1 + \left[\frac{\sin \pi(\theta+\alpha)N}{N \sin \pi(\theta+\alpha)}\right]^2 + \left[\frac{\sin \pi(\theta-\alpha)N}{N \sin \pi(\theta-\alpha)}\right]^2\right\} \tag{8.2.35}$$

Substitution of (8.2.35) into (8.2.34) yields

$$\begin{aligned} E\{[P_{xx}^{\text{BT}}(f)]^2\} = &\left[\int_{-1/2}^{1/2} \Gamma_{xx}(\theta) W(f-\theta)\, d\theta\right]^2 \\ &+ \int_{-1/2}^{1/2}\int_{-1/2}^{1/2} \Gamma_{xx}(\alpha)\Gamma_{xx}(\theta) W(f-\alpha) W(f-\theta) \\ &\left\{\left[\frac{\sin \pi(\theta+\alpha)N}{N \sin \pi(\theta+\alpha)}\right]^2 + \left[\frac{\sin \pi(\theta-\alpha)N}{N \sin \pi(\theta-\alpha)}\right]^2\right\} d\alpha\, d\theta \end{aligned} \tag{8.2.36}$$

The first term in (8.2.36) is simply the square of the mean of $P_{xx}^{\text{BT}}(f)$, which is to be subtracted out according to (8.2.33). This leaves the second term in (8.2.36), which constitutes the variance. For the case in which $N >> M$, the functions $\sin \pi(\theta+\alpha)N/N \sin \pi(\theta+\alpha)$ and $\sin \pi(\theta-\alpha)N/N \sin \pi(\theta-\alpha)$ are relatively narrow compared to $W(f)$ in the vicinity of $\theta = -\alpha$ and $\theta = \alpha$, respectively. Therefore,

$$\int_{-1/2}^{1/2} \Gamma_{xx}(\theta)W(f-\theta)\left\{\left[\frac{\sin \pi(\theta+\alpha)N}{N\sin \pi(\theta+\alpha)}\right]^2 + \left[\frac{\sin \pi(\theta-\alpha)N}{N\sin \pi(\theta-\alpha)}\right]^2\right\} d\theta$$
$$\approx \Gamma_{xx}(-\alpha)W(f+\alpha) + \Gamma_{xx}(\alpha)W(f-\alpha) \tag{8.2.37}$$

With this approximation, the variance of $P_{xx}^{\text{BT}}(f)$ becomes

$$\begin{aligned}\text{var}[P_{xx}^{\text{BT}}(f)] &\approx \frac{1}{N}\int_{-1/2}^{1/2} \Gamma_{xx}(\alpha)W(f-\alpha)[\Gamma_{xx}(-\alpha)W(f+\alpha) \\ &\quad + \Gamma_{xx}(\alpha)W(f-\alpha)]\, d\alpha \\ &\approx \frac{1}{N}\int_{-1/2}^{1/2} \Gamma_{xx}^2(\alpha)W^2(f-\alpha)\, d\alpha\end{aligned} \tag{8.2.38}$$

where in the last step, we made the approximation

$$\int_{-1/2}^{1/2} \Gamma_{xx}(\alpha)\Gamma_{xx}(-\alpha)W(f-\alpha)W(f+\alpha)\, d\alpha \approx 0 \tag{8.2.39}$$

We shall make one additional approximation in (8.2.38). When $W(f)$ is narrow compared to the true power spectrum $\Gamma_{xx}(f)$, (8.2.38) is further approximated as

$$\begin{aligned}\text{var}[P_{xx}^{\text{BT}}(f)] &\approx \Gamma_{xx}^2(f)\left[\frac{1}{N}\int_{-1/2}^{1/2} W^2(\theta)\, d\theta\right] \\ &\approx \Gamma_{xx}^2(f)\left[\frac{1}{N}\sum_{m=-(M-1)}^{M-1} w^2(n)\right]\end{aligned} \tag{8.2.40}$$

8.2.4 Performance Characteristics of Nonparametric Power Spectrum Estimators

In this section we compare the *quality* of the Bartlett, Welch, and Blackman and Tukey power spectrum estimates. As a measure of quality, we use the ratio of the square of the mean of the power spectrum estimate to its variance,

$$Q_A = \frac{\{E[P_{xx}^A(f)]\}^2}{\text{var}[P_{xx}^A(f)]} \tag{8.2.41}$$

where A = B, W, or BT for the three power spectrum estimates. The reciprocal of this quantity, called the *variability*, may also be used as a measure of performance.

For reference, the periodogram has a mean and variance

$$E[P_{xx}(f)] = \int_{-1/2}^{1/2} \Gamma_{xx}(\theta)W_{\text{B}}(f-\theta)\, d\theta \tag{8.2.42}$$

$$\text{var}[P_{xx}(f)] = \Gamma_{xx}^2(f)\left[1 + \left(\frac{\sin 2\pi f N}{N\sin 2\pi f}\right)^2\right] \tag{8.2.43}$$

where

$$W_B(f) = \frac{1}{N}\left(\frac{\sin \pi f N}{\sin \pi f}\right)^2 \tag{8.2.44}$$

For large N (i.e., $N \to \infty$)

$$\begin{aligned} E[P_{xx}(f)] &\to \Gamma_{xx}(f)\int_{-1/2}^{1/2} W_B(\theta)\,d\theta = w_B(0)\Gamma_{xx}(f) = \Gamma_{xx}(f) \\ \text{var}[P_{xx}(f)] &\to \Gamma^2_{xx}(f) \end{aligned} \tag{8.2.45}$$

Hence, as indicated previously, the periodogram is an asymptotically unbiased estimate of the power spectrum, but it is not consistent because its variance does not approach zero as N increases toward infinity.

Asymptotically, the periodogram is characterized by the quality factor

$$Q_P = \frac{\Gamma^2_{xx}(f)}{\Gamma^2_{xx}(f)} = 1 \tag{8.2.46}$$

The fact that Q_P is fixed and independent of the data length N is another indication of the poor quality of this estimate.

Bartlett Power Spectrum Estimate. The mean and variance of the Bartlett power spectrum estimate are

$$E[P^B_{xx}(f)] = \int_{-1/2}^{1/2} \Gamma(\theta) W_B(f-\theta)\,d\theta \tag{8.2.47}$$

$$\text{var}[P^B_{xx}(f)] = \frac{1}{K}\Gamma^2_{xx}(f)\left[1 + \left(\frac{\sin 2\pi f M}{M \sin 2\pi f}\right)^2\right] \tag{8.2.48}$$

and

$$W_B(f) = \frac{1}{M}\left(\frac{\sin \pi f M}{\sin \pi f}\right)^2 \tag{8.2.49}$$

As $N \to \infty$ and $M \to \infty$, while $K = N/M$ remains fixed, we find that

$$\begin{aligned} E[P^B_{xx}(f)] &\to \Gamma_{xx}(f)\int_{-1/2}^{1/2} W_B(f)\,df = \Gamma_{xx}(f) w_B(0) = \Gamma_{xx}(f) \\ \text{var}[P^B_{xx}(f)] &\to \frac{1}{K}\Gamma^2_{xx}(f) \end{aligned} \tag{8.2.50}$$

We observe that the Bartlett power spectrum estimate is asymptotically unbiased and if K is allowed to increase with an increase in N, the estimate is also consistent. Hence asymptotically, this estimate is characterized by the quality factor

$$Q_B = K = \frac{N}{M} \tag{8.2.51}$$

The frequency resolution of the Bartlett estimate, measured by taking the 3-dB width of the main lobe of the rectangular window is

$$\Delta f = \frac{0.9}{M} \tag{8.2.52}$$

Hence $M = 0.9/\Delta f$, and therefore the quality factor becomes

$$Q_B = \frac{N}{0.9/\Delta f} = 1.11N\,\Delta f \tag{8.2.53}$$

Welch Power Spectrum Estimate. The mean and variance of the Welch power spectrum estimate are

$$E[P_{xx}^{W}(f)] = \int_{-1/2}^{1/2} \Gamma_{xx}(\theta)W(f-\theta)\,d\theta \tag{8.2.54}$$

where

$$W(f) = \frac{1}{MU}\left|\sum_{n=0}^{M-1} w(n)e^{-j2\pi fn}\right|^2 \tag{8.2.55}$$

and

$$\text{var}[P_{xx}^{W}(f)] = \begin{cases} \dfrac{1}{L}\Gamma_{xx}^2(f) & \text{for no overlap} \\ \dfrac{9}{8L}\Gamma_{xx}^2(f) & \text{for 50\% overlap and triangular window} \end{cases} \tag{8.2.56}$$

As $N \to \infty$ and $M \to \infty$, the mean converges to

$$E[P_{xx}^{W}(f)] \to \Gamma_{xx}(f) \tag{8.2.57}$$

and the variance converges to zero, so that the estimate is consistent.

Under the two conditions given by (8.2.56) the quality factor is

$$Q_W = \begin{cases} L = \dfrac{N}{M} & \text{for no overlap} \\ \dfrac{8L}{9} = \dfrac{16N}{9M} & \text{for 50\% overlap and triangular window} \end{cases} \tag{8.2.58}$$

On the other hand, the spectral width of the triangular window at the 3-dB points is

$$\Delta f = \frac{1.28}{M} \tag{8.2.59}$$

Consequently, the quality factor expressed in terms of Δf and N is

$$Q_W = \begin{cases} 0.78N\,\Delta f & \text{for no overlap} \\ 1.39N\,\Delta f & \text{for 50\% overlap and triangular window} \end{cases} \tag{8.2.60}$$

Blackman–Tukey Power Spectrum Estimate. The mean and variance of this estimate are approximated as

$$\begin{aligned} E[P_{xx}^{\mathrm{BT}}(f)] &\approx \int_{-1/2}^{1/2} \Gamma_{xx}(\theta) W(f-\theta)\, d\theta \\ \operatorname{var}[P_{xx}^{\mathrm{BT}}(f)] &\approx \Gamma_{xx}^2(f) \left[\frac{1}{N} \sum_{n=-(M-1)}^{M-1} w^2(n) \right] \end{aligned} \tag{8.2.61}$$

where $w(n)$ is the window sequence, which is used to taper the estimated autocorrelation sequence. For the rectangular and Bartlett (triangular) windows we have

$$\frac{1}{N} \sum_{n=-(M-1)}^{M-1} w^2(n) = \begin{cases} 2M/N, & \text{rectangular window} \\ 2M/3N, & \text{triangular window} \end{cases} \tag{8.2.62}$$

It is clear from (8.2.61) that the mean value of the estimate is asymptotically unbiased. Its quality factor for the triangular window is

$$Q_{\mathrm{BT}} = 1.5 \frac{N}{M} \tag{8.2.63}$$

Since the window length is $2M - 1$, the frequency resolution measured at the 3-dB points is

$$\Delta f = \frac{1.28}{2M} = \frac{0.64}{M} \tag{8.2.64}$$

and hence

$$Q_{\mathrm{BT}} = \frac{1.5}{0.64} N\, \Delta f = 2.34 N\, \Delta f \tag{8.2.65}$$

These results are summarized in Table 8.1. It is apparent from the results we have obtained that the Welch and Blackman–Tukey power spectrum estimates are somewhat better than the Bartlett estimate. However, the differences in performance are relatively small. The main point is that the quality factor increases with an increase in the length N of the data. This characteristic behavior is not shared by the periodogram estimate. Furthermore, the quality factor depends on the product of the data length N and the frequency resolution Δf. For a desired level of quality, Δf can be

TABLE 8.1 Quality of Power Spectrum

Estimate	Quality Factor
Bartlett	$1.11N\,\Delta f$
Welch (50% overlap)	$1.39N\,\Delta f$
Blackman–Tukey	$2.34N\,\Delta f$

decreased (frequency resolution increased) by increasing the length N of the data, and vice versa.

8.2.5 Computational Requirements of Nonparametric Power Spectrum Estimates

The other important aspect of the nonparametric power spectrum estimates is their computational requirements. For this comparison we assume that the estimates are based on a fixed amount of data N and a specified resolution Δf. The radix-2 FFT algorithm is assumed in all the computations. We shall count only the number of complex multiplications required to compute the power spectrum estimate.

Bartlett Power Spectrum Estimate.

$$\text{FFT length} = M = \frac{0.9}{\Delta f}$$

$$\text{number of FFTs} = \frac{N}{M} = 1.11N\,\Delta f$$

$$\text{number of computations} = \frac{N}{M}\left[\frac{M}{2}\log_2 M\right] = \frac{N}{2}\log_2\frac{0.9}{\Delta f}$$

Welch Power Spectrum Estimate. (50% Overlap)

$$\text{FFT length} = M = \frac{1.28}{\Delta f}$$

$$\text{number of FFTs}\,\frac{2N}{M} = 1.56N\,\Delta f$$

$$\text{number of computations} = \frac{2N}{M}\left[\frac{M}{2}\log_2 M\right] = N\log_2\frac{1.28}{\Delta f}$$

In addition to the $\frac{2N}{M}$ FFTs there are additional multiplications required for windowing the data. Each data record requires M multiplications. Therefore, the total number of computations is

$$\text{total computations} = 2N + N\log_2\frac{1.28}{\Delta f} = N\log_2\frac{5.12}{\Delta f}$$

Blackman–Tukey Power Spectrum Estimate. In the Blackman–Tukey method, the autocorrelation $r_{xx}(m)$ can be computed efficiently via the FFT algorithm. However, if the number of data points is large, it may not be possible to compute one N-point DFT. For example, we may have $N = 10^5$ data points but only the capacity to perform 1024-point DFTs. Since the autocorrelation sequence is windowed to $2M - 1$ points where $M << N$, it is possible to compute the desired $2M - 1$ points of $r_{xx}(m)$ by segmenting the data into $K = N/2M$ records and computing $2M$-point DFTs and one $2M$-point IDFT via the FFT algorithm. Rader (1970) has described a method for performing this computation (see Problem 8.7).

If we base the computational complexity of the Blackman–Tukey method on this approach, we obtain the following computational requirements:

$$\text{FFT length} = 2M = \frac{1.28}{\Delta f}$$

$$\text{number of FFTs} = 2K + 1 = 2\left(\frac{N}{2M}\right) + 1 \approx \frac{N}{M}$$

$$\text{number of computations} = \frac{N}{M}[M \log_2 2M] = N \log \frac{1.28}{\Delta f}$$

We may neglect the additional M multiplications required to window the autocorrelation sequence $r_{xx}(m)$, since this is a relatively small number. Finally, there is the additional computation required to Fourier transform the windowed autocorrelation sequence. The FFT algorithm may be used for this computation with some zero padding for purposes of interpolating the spectral estimate. As a result of these additional computations, the number of computations given above is increased by a small amount.

From these results we conclude that the Welch method requires a little more computational power than do the other two methods. The Bartlett method apparently requires the smallest number of computations. However, the differences in the computational requirements of the three methods are relatively small.

8.3 PARAMETRIC METHODS FOR POWER SPECTRUM ESTIMATION

The nonparametric power spectrum estimation methods described in the preceding section are relatively simple, well understood, and easy to compute via the FFT algorithm. However, these methods require the availability of long data records to yield the necessary frequency resolution that is required in many applications. Furthermore, these methods suffer from spectral leakage effects due to windowing that is inherent in finite-length data records. Often, the spectral leakage masks weak signals that are present in the data.

From one point of view, the basic limitation of the nonparametric methods is the inherent assumption that the autocorrelation estimate $r_{xx}(m)$ is zero for $|m| \geq N$, as implied by (8.1.33). This assumption severely limits the frequency resolution and the quality of the power spectrum estimate that is achieved. From another viewpoint, the inherent assumption in the periodogram estimate is that the data are periodic with period N. Neither of these inherent assumptions is realistic.

In this section we describe power spectrum estimation methods that do not require such assumptions. In fact, these methods *extrapolate* the values of the autocorrelation for lags $m \geq N$. Extrapolation is possible if we have some a priori information on how the data were generated. In such a case, a model for the signal generation may be constructed with a number of parameters that can be estimated from the observed data. From the model and the estimated parameters we can compute the power density spectrum implied by the model.

In effect, the modeling approach eliminates the need for window functions and the assumption that the autocorrelation sequence is zero for $|m| \geq N$. As a consequence, *parametric* (model-based) power spectrum estimation methods provide better frequency resolution than the FFT-based, nonparametric methods described in the preceding section and avoid the problem of leakage. This is especially true in applications where short data records are available due to time-variant or transient phenomena.

The parametric methods considered in this section are based on modeling the data sequence $x(n)$ as the output of a linear system characterized by a rational system function of the form

$$H(z) = \frac{B(z)}{A(z)} = \frac{\sum_{k=0}^{q} b_k z^{-k}}{1 + \sum_{k=1}^{p} a_k z^{-k}} \tag{8.3.1}$$

The corresponding difference equation is

$$x(n) = -\sum_{k=1}^{p} a_k x(n-k) + \sum_{k=0}^{q} b_k w(n-k) \tag{8.3.2}$$

where $w(n)$ is the input sequence to the system and the observed data, $x(n)$, represent the output sequence.

In power spectrum estimation, the input sequence is not observable. However, if the observed data are characterized as a stationary random process, the input sequence is also assumed to be a stationary random process. In such a case the power density spectrum of the observed data is

$$\Gamma_{xx}(f) = |H(f)|^2 \Gamma_{ww}(f)$$

where $\Gamma_{ww}(f)$ is the power density spectrum of the input sequence and $H(f)$ is the frequency response of the model.

Since our objective is to estimate the power density spectrum $\Gamma_{xx}(f)$, it is convenient to assume that the input sequence $w(n)$ is a zero-mean, white noise sequence with autocorrelation

$$\gamma_{ww}(m) = \sigma_w^2 \delta(m)$$

where σ_w^2 is the variance (i.e., $\sigma_w^2 = E[|w(n)|^2]$). Then the power density spectrum of the observed data is simply

$$\Gamma_{xx}(f) = \sigma_w^2 |H(f)|^2 = \sigma_w^2 \frac{|B(f)|^2}{|A(f)|^2} \tag{8.3.3}$$

In Section 4.1 we described the representation of a stationary random process as given by (8.3.3).

In the model-based approach, the spectrum estimation procedure consists of two steps. Given the data sequence $x(n)$, $0 \leq n \leq N - 1$, we estimate the parameters a_k and b_k of the model. Then, from these estimates, we compute the power spectrum estimate according to (8.3.3).

Recall that the random process $x(n)$ generated by the pole–zero model in (8.3.1) or (8.3.2) is called an *autoregressive–moving average* (ARMA) *process* of order (p,q) and it is usually denoted as ARMA(p,q). If $q = 0$ and $b_0 = 1$, the resulting system model has a system function $H(z) = 1/A(z)$ and its output $x(n)$ is called an *autoregressive* (AR) *process* of order p. This is denoted as AR(p). The third possible model is obtained by setting $A(z) = 1$, so that $H(z) = B(z)$. Its output $x(n)$ is called a *moving-average* (MA) *process* of order q and denoted as MA(q).

Of these three linear models the AR model is by far the most widely used. The reasons are twofold. First, the AR model is suitable for representing spectra with narrow peaks (resonances). Second, the AR model results in very simple linear equations for the AR parameters. On the other hand, the MA model, as a general rule, requires many more coefficients to represent a narrow spectrum. Consequently, it is rarely used alone as a model for spectrum estimation. By combining poles and zeros, the ARMA model provides a more efficient representation from the viewpoint of the number of model parameters to represent the spectrum of a random process.

The decomposition theorem due to Wold (1938) asserts that any ARMA or MA process may be represented uniquely by an AR model of possibly infinite order and any ARMA or AR process may be represented by a MA model of possibly infinite order. In view of this theorem, the issue of model selection reduces to selecting the model that requires the smallest number of parameters which are also easy to compute. Usually, the choice in practice is the AR model. The ARMA model is used to a lesser extent.

Before describing methods for estimating the parameters in an AR(p), MA(q), and ARMA(p,q) models, it is useful to establish the basic relationships between the model parameters and the autocorrelation sequence $\gamma_{xx}(m)$. In addition, we relate the AR model parameters to the coefficients in a linear predictor for the process $x(n)$.

8.3.1 Relationships Between the Autocorrelation and the Model Parameters

In Section 4.1.2 we established the basic relationships between the autocorrelation $\gamma_{xx}(m)$ and the model parameters a_k and b_k.

For the ARMA(p,q) process, the relationship given by (4.1.18) is

$$\gamma_{xx}(m) = \begin{cases} -\sum_{k=1}^{p} a_k \gamma_{xx}(m-k), & m > q \\ -\sum_{k=1}^{p} a_k \gamma_{xx}(m-k) + \sigma_w^2 \sum_{k=0}^{q-m} h(k) b_{k+m}, & 0 \leq m \leq q \\ \gamma_{xx}^*(-m), & m < 0 \end{cases} \tag{8.3.4}$$

This relationship provides a formula for determining the model parameters a_k by restricting our attention to the case $m > q$. Thus the set of linear equations

$$\begin{bmatrix} \gamma_{xx}(q) & \gamma_{xx}(q-1) & \cdots & \gamma_{xx}(q-p+1) \\ \gamma_{xx}(q+1) & \gamma_{xx}(q) & \cdots & \gamma_{xx}(q-p+2) \\ \vdots & \vdots & & \\ \gamma_{xx}(q+p-1) & \gamma_{xx}(q+p-2) & \cdots & \gamma_{xx}(q) \end{bmatrix} \begin{bmatrix} a_1 \\ a_2 \\ \vdots \\ a_p \end{bmatrix} = - \begin{bmatrix} \gamma_{xx}(q+1) \\ \gamma_{xx}(q+2) \\ \vdots \\ \gamma_{xx}(q+p) \end{bmatrix} \tag{8.3.5}$$

may be used to solve for the model parameters a_k by using estimates of the autocorrelation sequence in place of $\gamma_{xx}(m)$ for $m \geq q$. This problem is discussed in Section 8.3.8.

Another interpretation of the relationship in (8.3.5) is that the values of the autocorrelation $\gamma_{xx}(m)$ for $m > q$ are uniquely determined from the pole parameters a_k and the values of $\gamma_{xx}(m)$ for $0 \leq m \leq p$. Consequently, the linear system model automatically extends the values of the autocorrelation sequence $\gamma_{xx}(m)$ for $m > q$.

If the pole parameters a_k are obtained from (8.3.5), the result does not help us in determining the MA parameters b_k, because the equation

$$\sigma_w^2 \sum_{k=0}^{q-m} h(k) b_{k+m} = \gamma_{xx}(m) + \sum_{k=1}^{p} a_k \gamma_{xx}(m-k), \qquad 0 \leq m \leq q$$

depends on the impulse response $h(n)$. Although the impulse response can be expressed in terms of the parameters b_k by long division of $B(z)$ with the known $A(z)$, this approach results in a set of nonlinear equations for the MA parameters.

If we adopt an AR(p) model for the observed data, the relationship between the AR parameters and the autocorrelation sequence given by (4.1.19) is

$$\gamma_{xx}(m) = \begin{cases} -\sum_{k=1}^{p} a_k \gamma_{xx}(m-k), & m > 0 \\ -\sum_{k=1}^{p} a_k \gamma_{xx}(m-k) + \sigma_w^2, & m = 0 \\ \gamma_{xx}^*(-m), & m < 0 \end{cases} \tag{8.3.6}$$

In this case, the AR parameters a_k are obtained from the solution of the Yule–Walker or normal equations

$$\begin{bmatrix} \gamma_{xx}(0) & \gamma_{xx}(-1) & \cdots & \gamma_{xx}(-p+1) \\ \gamma_{xx}(1) & \gamma_{xx}(0) & \cdots & \gamma_{xx}(-p+2) \\ \vdots & \vdots & & \vdots \\ \gamma_{xx}(p-1) & \gamma_{xx}(p-2) & \cdots & \gamma_{xx}(0) \end{bmatrix} \begin{bmatrix} a_1 \\ a_2 \\ \vdots \\ a_p \end{bmatrix} = - \begin{bmatrix} \gamma_{xx}(1) \\ \gamma_{xx}(2) \\ \vdots \\ \gamma_{xx}(p) \end{bmatrix} \tag{8.3.7}$$

and the variance σ_w^2 can be obtained from the equation

$$\sigma_w^2 = \gamma_{xx}(0) + \sum_{k=1}^{p} a_k \gamma_{xx}(-k) \tag{8.3.8}$$

The equations in (8.3.7) and (8.3.8) are usually combined into a single matrix equation of the form

$$\begin{bmatrix} \gamma_{xx}(0) & \gamma_{xx}(-1) & \cdots & \gamma_{xx}(-p) \\ \gamma_{xx}(1) & \gamma_{xx}(0) & \cdots & \gamma_{xx}(-p+1) \\ \vdots & \vdots & & \vdots \\ \gamma_{xx}(-p) & \gamma_{xx}(-p+1) & \cdots & \gamma_{xx}(0) \end{bmatrix} \begin{bmatrix} 1 \\ a_1 \\ \vdots \\ a_p \end{bmatrix} = \begin{bmatrix} \sigma_w^2 \\ 0 \\ \vdots \\ 0 \end{bmatrix} \tag{8.3.9}$$

Since the correlation matrix in (8.3.7), or in (8.3.9), is Toeplitz, it can be efficiently inverted by use of the Levinson–Durbin algorithm described in Chapter 4.

Thus all the system parameters in the AR(p) model are easily determined from knowledge of the autocorrelation sequence $\gamma_{xx}(m)$ for $0 \le m \le p$. Furthermore, (8.3.6) may be used to extend the autocorrelation sequence for $m > p$ once the a_k are determined.

Finally, we note that in a MA(q) model for the observed data, the autocorrelation sequence $\gamma_{xx}(m)$ is related to the MA parameters b_k by

$$\gamma_{xx}(m) = \begin{cases} \sigma_w^2 \sum_{k=0}^{q-m} b_k b_{k+m}, & 0 \le m \le q \\ 0, & m > q \\ \gamma_{xx}^*(-m), & m < 0 \end{cases} \tag{8.3.10}$$

which was established in Section 4.1. With the background established above, we will now describe the power spectrum estimation methods for the AR(p), ARMA(p,q), and MA(q) models.

8.3.2 Yule–Walker Method for the AR Model Parameters

In the Yule–Walker method we simply estimate the autocorrelation from the data and use the estimates in (8.3.7) to solve for the AR model parameters. In this method it is desirable to use the biased form of the autocorrelation estimate,

$$r_{xx}(m) = \frac{1}{N} \sum_{n=0}^{N-|m|} x^*(n)x(n+m) \tag{8.3.11}$$

to ensure that the autocorrelation matrix is positive semidefinite. The result will be a stable AR model. Although stability is not a critical issue in power spectrum estimation, it is conjectured that a stable AR model best represents the data.

The Levinson–Durbin algorithm described in Chapter 4 with $r_{xx}(m)$ substituted for $\gamma_{xx}(m)$ yields the AR parameters. The corresponding power spectrum estimate is

$$P_{xx}^{\mathrm{YW}}(f) = \frac{\hat{\sigma}_{wp}^2}{\left|1 + \sum_{k=1}^{p} \hat{a}_p(k)e^{-j\pi fk}\right|^2} \tag{8.3.12}$$

where $a_p(k)$ are estimates of the AR parameters obtained from the Levinson–Durbin recursions and

$$\hat{\sigma}_{wp}^2 = \hat{E}_m^f = r_{xx}(0)\prod_{k=1}^{p}[1 - |\hat{a}_k(k)|^2] \tag{8.3.13}$$

is the estimated minimum mean-square value for the pth-order predictor. An example illustrating the frequency resolution capabilities of this estimator is given in Section 8.3.9.

In estimating the power spectrum of sinusoidal signals via AR models, Lacoss (1971) showed that spectral peaks in an AR spectrum estimate are proportional to the square of the power of the sinusoidal signal. On the other hand, the area under the peak in the power density spectrum is linearly proportional to the power of the sinusoid. This characteristic behavior holds for all AR model-based estimation methods.

8.3.3 Burg Method for the AR Model Parameters

The Burg method for estimating the AR parameters may be viewed as an order-recursive, least-squares lattice method based on the minimization of the forward and backward errors in linear predictors, with the constraint that the AR parameters satisfy the Levinson–Durbin recursion.

To derive the estimator, suppose that we are given the data $x(n)$, $n = 0, 1, \ldots, N - 1$, and let us consider the forward and backward linear prediction estimates of order m, which are given as

$$\begin{aligned} \hat{x}(n) &= -\sum_{k=1}^{m} a_m(k)x(n-k) \\ \hat{x}(n-m) &= -\sum_{k=1}^{m} a_m^*(k)x(n+k-m) \end{aligned} \tag{8.3.14}$$

and the corresponding forward and backward errors $f_m(n)$ and $g_m(n)$ defined as $f_m(n) = x(n) - \hat{x}(n)$ and $g_m(n) = x(n-m) - \hat{x}(n-m)$, where $a_m(k)$, $0 \leq k \leq m - 1$, $m = 1, 2, \ldots, p$ are the prediction coefficients. The least-squares error is

$$\mathscr{E}_m = \sum_{n=m}^{N-1} [|f_m(n)|^2 + |g_m(n)|^2] \tag{8.3.15}$$

This error is to be minimized by selecting the prediction coefficients, subject to the constraint that they satisfy the Levinson–Durbin recursion given by

$$a_m(k) = a_{m-1}(k) + K_m a^*_{m-1}(m - k), \qquad \begin{matrix} 1 \le k \le m - 1 \\ 1 \le m \le p \end{matrix} \tag{8.3.16}$$

where $K_m = a_m(m)$ is the mth reflection coefficient in the lattice filter realization of the predictor. Recall that when (8.3.16) is substituted into the expressions for $f_m(n)$ and $g_m(n)$, the result is the pair of order-recursive equations for the forward and backward prediction errors given by (4.2.11).

Now, if we substitute from (4.2.11) into (8.3.15) and perform the minimization of $\mathscr{E}_m$ with respect to the complex-valued reflection coefficient K_m, we obtain the result

$$\hat{K}_m = \frac{-\sum_{n=m}^{N-1} f_{m-1}(n) g^*_{m-1}(n-1)}{\frac{1}{2}\sum_{n=m}^{N-1} [|f_{m-1}(n)|^2 + |g_{m-1}(n-1)|^2]}, \quad m = 1, 2, \ldots, p \tag{8.3.17}$$

The term in the numerator of (8.3.17) is an estimate of the cross-correlation between the forward and backward prediction errors. With the normalization factors in the denominator of (8.3.17), it is apparent that $K_m| < 1$, so that the all-pole model obtained from the data is stable. The reader should note the similarity of (8.3.17) with the statistical counterparts given by (4.2.39).

We note that the denominator in (8.3.17) is simply an estimate of the least-squares forward and backward errors, E^f_{m-1} and E^b_{m-1}, respectively. Hence (8.3.17) may be expressed as

$$\hat{K}_m = \frac{-\sum_{n=m}^{N-1} f_{m-1}(n) g^*_{m-1}(n-1)}{\frac{1}{2}[\hat{E}^f_{m-1} + \hat{E}^b_{m-1}]}, \qquad m = 1, 2, \ldots, p \tag{8.3.18}$$

where $\hat{E}^f_{m-1} + \hat{E}^b_{m-1}$ is an estimate of the total squared error $\mathscr{E}_m$. We leave as an exercise for the reader to verify that the denominator term in (8.3.18) can be computed in an order-recursive fashion according to the relation

$$\hat{E}_m = [1 - |K_m|^2]\hat{E}_{m-1} - |f_{m-1}(m-1)|^2 - |g_{m-2}(m-2)|^2 \tag{8.3.19}$$

where $\hat{E}_m \equiv E^f_m + E^b_m$ is the total least-squares error. This result is due to Andersen (1978).

To summarize, the Burg algorithm computes the reflection coefficients in the equivalent lattice structure as specified by (8.3.18) and (8.3.19), and the Levinson–Durbin algorithm is used to obtain the AR model parameters. From the estimates of the AR parameters we form the power spectrum estimate

$$P_{xx}^{\mathrm{BU}}(f) = \frac{\hat{E}_p}{\left|1 + \sum_{k=1}^{p} \hat{a}_p(k)e^{-j2\pi fk}\right|^2} \tag{8.3.20}$$

The major advantages of the Burg method for estimating the parameters of the AR model are: (1) it results in high-frequency resolution, (2) it yields a stable AR model, and (3) it is computationally efficient (due to the Levinson–Durbin algorithm).

The Burg method is known to have several disadvantages, however. First, it exhibits spectral line splitting at high signal-to-noise ratios [see Fougere et al. (1976)]. By *line splitting* we mean that the spectrum of $x(n)$ may have a single sharp peak, but the Burg method may result in two closely spaced peaks. For high-order models, the method also introduces spurious peaks. Furthermore, for sinusoidal signals in noise, the Burg method exhibits a sensitivity to the initial phase of a sinusoid, especially in short data records. This sensitivity is manifest as a frequency shift from the true frequency, thus resulting in a frequency bias that is phase dependent. For more details on some of these limitations the reader is referred to the papers of Chen and Stegan (1974), Ulrych and Clayton (1976), Fougere et al. (1976), Kay and Marple (1979), Swingler (1979a, 1980), Herring (1980), and Thorvaldsen (1981).

Several modifications have been proposed to overcome some of the more important limitations of the Burg method: line splitting, spurious peaks, and frequency bias. Basically, the modifications involve the introduction of a weighting (window) sequence on the squared forward and backward errors. That is, the least-squares optimization is performed on the weighted squared errors

$$\mathscr{E}_m^{\mathrm{WB}} = \sum_{n=m}^{N-1} w_m(n)\,[|f_m(n)|^2 + |g_m(n)|^2] \tag{8.3.21}$$

which, when minimized, results in the reflection coefficient estimates

$$\hat{K}_m = \frac{\sum_{n=m}^{N-1} w_{m-1}(n) f_{m-1}(n) g_{m-1}^*(n-1)}{\frac{1}{2}\sum_{n=m}^{N-1} w_{m-1}(n)\,[|f_{m-1}(n)|^2 + |g_{m-1}(n-1)|^2]} \tag{8.3.22}$$

In particular, we mention the use of a Hamming window used by Swingler (1979b), a quadratic or parabolic window used by Kaveh and Lippert (1983), the energy weighting method used by Nikias and Scott (1982), and the data-adaptive energy weighting used by Helme and Nikias (1983). These windowing and energy weighting methods have proved effective in reducing the occurrence of line splitting and spurious peaks, and are also effective in reducing frequency bias.

The Burg method for power spectrum estimation is usually associated with *maximum entropy spectrum estimation*, which is a criterion used by

Burg (1967, 1975) as a basis for the AR model in parametric spectrum estimation. The problem considered by Burg was how best to extrapolate from the given values of the autocorrelation sequence $\gamma_{xx}(m)$, $0 \leq m \leq p$, the values for $m > p$, such that the entire autocorrelation sequence is positive semidefinite. Since there are an infinite number of extrapolations that are possible, Burg postulated that the extrapolation be made on the basis of maximizing uncertainty (entropy) or randomness, in the sense that the spectrum $\Gamma_{xx}(f)$ of the process is the flattest of all spectra that have the given autocorrelation values $\gamma_{xx}(m)$, $0 \leq m \leq p$. In particular, when the process is Gaussian, the entropy per sample is proportional to the integral [see Burg (1975)],

$$\int_{-1/2}^{1/2} \ln \Gamma_{xx}(f)\, df \tag{8.3.23}$$

Burg found that the maximum of this integral subject to the $(p + 1)$ constraints

$$\int_{-1/2}^{1/2} \Gamma_{xx}(f) e^{j2\pi fm}\, df = \gamma_{xx}(m), \qquad 0 \leq m \leq p \tag{8.3.24}$$

is the AR(p) process for which the given autocorrelation sequence $\gamma_{xx}(m)$, $0 \leq m \leq p$, is related to the AR parameters by (8.3.6). This solution provides an additional justification for the use of the AR model in power spectrum estimation.

In view of Burg's basic work in maximum entropy spectral estimation, the Burg power spectrum estimation procedure is often called the *maximum entropy method* (MEM). We should emphasize, however, that the maximum entropy spectrum is identical to the AR-model spectrum only when the exact autocorrelation $\gamma_{xx}(m)$ is known. When only an estimate of $\gamma_{xx}(m)$ is available for $0 \leq m \leq p$, the AR-model estimates of Yule–Walker and Burg are not maximum entropy spectral estimates. The general formulation for the maximum entropy spectrum based on estimates of the autocorrelation sequence results in a set of nonlinear equations. Solutions for the maximum entropy spectrum with measurement errors in the correlation sequence have been obtained by Newman (1981) and Schott and McClellan (1984).

8.3.4 Unconstrained Least-Squares Method for the AR-Model Parameters

As described in the preceding section, the Burg method for determining the parameters of the AR model is basically a least-squares lattice algorithm with the added constraint that the predictor coefficients satisfy the Levinson recursion. As a result of this constraint, an increase in the order of the AR model requires only a single-parameter optimization at each stage. In contrast to this approach, we may use an unconstrained least-squares algorithm to determine the AR parameters.

To elaborate, we form the forward and backward linear prediction estimates given by (8.3.14) and their corresponding forward and backward errors. Then we minimize the sum of squares of both errors,

$$\begin{aligned}\mathscr{E}_m &= \sum_{n=m}^{N-1} [|f_m(n)|^2 + |g_m(n)|^2] \\ &= \sum_{n=m}^{N-1} \left[\left| x(n) + \sum_{k=1}^{m} a_m(k)x(n-k) \right|^2 + \left| x(n-m) + \sum_{k=1}^{m} a_m^*(k)x(n+k-m) \right|^2 \right]\end{aligned} \tag{8.3.25}$$

which is the same performance index as in the Burg method. However, we will not impose the Levinson–Durbin recursion in (8.3.16) for the AR parameters. The unconstrained minimization of $\mathscr{E}_m$ with respect to the prediction coefficients yields the set of linear equations

$$\sum_{k=1}^{m} a_m(k) r_{xx}(l,k) = -r_{xx}(l,0), \qquad l = 1, 2, \ldots, m \tag{8.3.26}$$

where, by definition, the autocorrelation $r_{xx}(l,k)$ is

$$r_{xx}(l,k) = \sum_{n=m}^{N-1} [x(n-k)x^*(n-l) + x(n-m+l)x^*(n-m+k)] \tag{8.3.27}$$

The resulting residual least-squares error is

$$E_m^{\text{LS}} = r_{xx}(0,0) + \sum_{k=1}^{m} \hat{a}_m(k) r_{xx}(0,k), \qquad m = 1, 2, \ldots, p \tag{8.3.28}$$

Hence the unconstrained least-squares power spectrum estimate is

$$P_{xx}^{\text{LS}}(f) = \frac{E_p^{\text{LS}}}{\left| 1 + \sum_{k=1}^{p} \hat{a}_p(k) e^{j2\pi fk} \right|^2} \tag{8.3.29}$$

The correlation matrix in (8.3.27), with elements $r_{xx}(l,k)$, is not Toeplitz, so that the Levinson–Durbin algorithm cannot be applied. However, the correlation matrix has sufficient structure which makes it possible to devise computationally efficient algorithms with computational complexity proportional to p^2. Marple (1980) devised such an algorithm, which has a lattice structure and employs Levinson–Durbin-type order recursions and additional time recursions. This algorithm is similar in form to the adaptive lattice algorithms described in Chapter 6 and will not be discussed further in this section. The interested reader is referred to the paper by Marple (1980).

The form of the unconstrained least-square method described above has also been called the *unwindowed data* least-squares method. It has been proposed for spectrum estimation in several papers, including the papers by Burg (1967), Nuttall (1976), and Ulrych and Clayton (1976). Its performance characteristics have been found to be superior to the Burg method, in the sense that the unconstrained least-squares method does not exhibit the same sensitivity to such problems as line splitting, frequency bias, and spurious peaks. In view of the computational efficiency of Marple's algorithm, which is comparable to the efficiency of the Levinson–Durbin algorithm, the unconstrained least-squares method is very attractive. With this method there is no guarantee that the estimated AR parameters yield a stable AR model. However, in spectrum estimation, this is not viewed as a problem.

8.3.5 Sequential Estimation Methods for the AR-Model Parameters

The three power spectrum estimation methods described in previous sections for the AR model may be classified as block processing methods. These methods obtain estimates of the AR parameters from a block of data, say $x(n)$, $n = 0, 1, \ldots, N - 1$. The AR parameters based on the block of N data points is then used to obtain the power spectrum estimate.

In situations where data are available on a continuous basis, we can still segment the data into blocks of N points and perform spectrum estimation on a block-by-block basis. This is often done in practice, for both real-time and non-real-time applications. However, in such applications, there is an alternative approach based on sequential (in time) estimation of the AR-model parameters as each new data point becomes available. By introducing a weighting function into past data samples, it is possible to deemphasize the effect of older data samples as new data are received. Alternatively, a sliding rectangular window may be used on the data.

The sequential estimation methods developed in Chapter 6 in the context of adaptive filtering are applicable to the estimation of the AR parameters. In particular, the sequential lattice methods, described in Chapter 6, directly and optimally estimate the prediction coefficients and the reflection coefficients in the lattice realization of the forward and backward linear predictors. The recursive equations for the prediction coefficients relate directly to the AR-model parameters. In addition to the order-recursive nature of these equations, as implied by the lattice structure, we also obtain time-recursive equations for the reflection coefficients in the lattice and for the forward and backward prediction coefficients.

The sequential recursive least-squares algorithms described in Chapter 6 are equivalent to the unconstrained least-squares, block processing method described in the preceding section. Hence the power spectrum estimates obtained by the sequential recursive least-squares method retain the desirable properties of the block processing algorithm described in Section 8.3.4. Since the AR parameters are being continuously estimated in a sequential estimation algorithm, power spectrum estimates may be obtained as often as desired, from once per sample to once every N samples. By properly weighting past data samples, the sequential estimation methods are particularly suitable for estimating and tracking time-variant power spectra resulting from nonstationary signal statistics.

The computational complexity of the sequential estimation methods described in Chapter 6 is proportional to p, the order of the AR process. As a consequence, the sequential estimation algorithms are computationally efficient and, from this viewpoint, may offer some advantage over the block processing methods.

In addition to the many references on sequential estimation methods in adaptive filtering given in Chapter 6, the paper by Griffiths (1975), Friedlander (1982), and Kalouptsidis and Theodoridis (1987) are particularly relevant to the spectrum estimation problem.

8.3.6 Selection of AR-Model Order

One of the most important aspects in the use of the AR model is the selection of the order p. As a general rule, if we select a model with too low an order, we obtain a highly smoothed spectrum. On the other hand, if p is selected too high, we run the risk of introducing spurious low-level peaks in the spectrum. We mentioned previously that one indication of the performance of the AR model is the mean-square value of the residual error, which, in general, is different for each of the estimators described above. The characteristic of this residual error is that it decreases as the order of the AR model is increased. We can monitor the rate of decrease and decide to terminate the process when the rate of decrease becomes relatively slow. It is apparent, however, that this approach may be imprecise and ill defined, and other methods should be investigated.

Much work has been done by various researchers on this problem and many experimental results have been given in the literature [e.g., the papers by Gersch and Sharpe (1973), Ulrych and Bishop (1975), Tong (1975, 1977), Jones (1976), Nuttall (1976), Berryman (1978), Kaveh and Bruzzone (1979), and Kashyap (1980)].

Two of the better known criteria for selecting the model order have been proposed by Akaike (1969, 1974). With the first, called the *final prediction error (FPE) criterion*, the order is selected to minimize the performance index

$$\text{FPE}(p) = \hat{\sigma}_{wp}^2 \left(\frac{N + p + 1}{N - p - 1} \right) \tag{8.3.30}$$

where $\hat{\sigma}_{wp}^2$ is the estimated variance of the linear prediction error. This performance index is based on minimizing the mean-square error for a one-step predictor.

The second criterion proposed by Akaike (1974), called the *Akaike information criterion* (AIC), is based on selecting the order that minimizes

$$\text{AIC}(p) = \ln \hat{\sigma}_{wp}^2 + \frac{2p}{N} \tag{8.3.31}$$

Note that the term $\hat{\sigma}_{wp}^2$ decreases, and hence $\ln \hat{\sigma}_{wp}^2$ also decreases, as the order of the AR model is increased. However, $2p/N$ increases with an increase in p. Hence a minimum value is obtained for some p.

An alternative information criterion, proposed by Rissanen (1983), is based on selecting the order that *minimizes the description length* (MDL), where MDL is defined as

$$\text{MDL}(p) = N \ln \hat{\sigma}_{wp}^2 + p \ln N \tag{8.3.32}$$

A fourth criterion has been proposed by Parzen (1974). This is called the *criterion autoregressive transfer* (CAT) function and it is defined as

$$\text{CAT}(p) = \left[\frac{1}{N}\sum_{k=1}^{p}\frac{1}{\bar{\sigma}_{wk}^2}\right] - \frac{1}{\hat{\sigma}_{wp}^2} \tag{8.3.33}$$

where

$$\bar{\sigma}_{wk}^2 = \frac{N}{N-k}\hat{\sigma}_{wk}^2 \tag{8.3.34}$$

The order p is selected to minimize CAT(p).

In applying the criteria given above, the mean should be removed from the data. Since $\hat{\sigma}_{wp}^2$ depends on the type of spectrum estimate we obtain, the model order is also a function of the criterion.

The experimental results given in the references cited above indicate that the model-order selection criteria do not yield definitive results. For example, Ulrych and Bishop (1975), Jones (1976), and Berryman (1978) found that the FPE(p) criterion tends to underestimate the model order. Kashyap (1980) showed that the AIC criterion is statistically inconsistent as $N \to \infty$. On the other hand, the MDL information criterion proposed by Rissanen is statistically consistent. Other experimental results indicate that for small data lengths, the order of the AR model should be selected to be in the range $N/3$ to $N/2$ for good results. It is apparent that in the absence of any prior information regarding the physical process that resulted in the data, one should try different model orders and different criteria and, ultimately, interpret the different results.

8.3.7 MA Model for Power Spectrum Estimation

As shown in Section 8.3.1, the parameters in a MA(q) model are related to the statistical autocorrelation $\gamma_{xx}(m)$ by (8.3.10). However,

$$B(z)B(z^{-1}) = D(z) = \sum_{m=-q}^{q} d_m z^{-m} \tag{8.3.35}$$

where the coefficients d_m are related to the MA parameters by the expression

$$d_m = \sum_{k=0}^{q-|m|} b_k b_{k+m}, \qquad |m| \le q \tag{8.3.36}$$

Clearly, then,

$$\gamma_{xx}(m) = \begin{cases} \sigma_w^2 d_m, & |m| \leq q \\ 0, & m > q \end{cases} \tag{8.3.37}$$

and the power spectrum for the MA(q) process is

$$\Gamma_{xx}^{\text{MA}}(f) = \sum_{m=-q}^{q} \gamma_{xx}(m)e^{-j2\pi fm} \tag{8.3.38}$$

It is apparent from these expressions that we do not have to solve for the MA parameters b_k to estimate the power spectrum. The estimates of the autocorrelation $\gamma_{xx}(m)$ for $|m| \leq q$ suffice. From such estimates we compute the estimated MA power spectrum, given as

$$P_{xx}^{\text{MA}}(f) = \sum_{m=-q}^{q} r_{xx}(m)e^{-j2\pi fm} \tag{8.3.39}$$

which is identical to the classical (nonparametric) power spectrum estimate described in Section 8.1.

There is an alternative method for determining b_k based on a high-order AR approximation to the MA process. To be specific, let the MA(q) process be modeled by an AR(p) model, where $p \gg q$. Then $B(z) = 1/A(z)$, or equivalently, $B(z)A(z) = 1$. Thus the parameters b_k and a_k are related by a convolution sum, which may be expressed as

$$\hat{a}_n + \sum_{k=1}^{q} b_k \hat{a}_{n-k} = \begin{cases} 1, & n = 0 \\ 0, & n \neq 0 \end{cases} \tag{8.3.40}$$

where $\hat{a}_n$ are the parameters obtained by fitting the data to an AR(p) model.

Although this set of equations may easily be solved for the b_k, a better fit is obtained by using a least-squares error criterion. That is, we form the squared error

$$\mathscr{E} = \sum_{n=0}^{p} \left[\hat{a}_n + \sum_{k=1}^{q} b_k \hat{a}_{n-k} \right]^2 - 1, \qquad \hat{a}_0 = 1, \quad \hat{a}_k = 0, \quad k < 0 \tag{8.3.41}$$

which is minimized by selecting the MA(q) parameters b_k. The result of this minimization is

$$\hat{\mathbf{b}} = -\mathbf{R}_{aa}^{-1}\mathbf{r}_{aa} \tag{8.3.42}$$

where the elements of $\mathbf{R}_{aa}$ and $\mathbf{r}_{aa}$ are given as

$$\begin{aligned} R_{aa}(|i-j|) &= \sum_{n=0}^{p-|i-j|} \hat{a}_n \hat{a}_{n+|i-j|}, \qquad i, j = 1, 2, \ldots, q \\ r_{aa}(i) &= \sum_{n=0}^{p-i} \hat{a}_n \hat{a}_{n+i}, \qquad i = 1, 2, \ldots, q \end{aligned} \tag{8.3.43}$$

This least squares method for determining the parameters of the MA(q) model is attributed to Durbin (1959). It has been shown by Kay (1988) that this estimation method is approximately maximum likelihood under the assumption that the observed process is Gaussian.

The order q of the MA model may be determined empirically by several methods. For example, the AIC for MA models has the same form as for AR models,

$$\mathrm{AIC}(q) = \ln \hat{\sigma}_{wq}^2 + \frac{2q}{N} \tag{8.3.44}$$

where $\hat{\sigma}_{wq}^2$ is an estimate of the variance of the white noise. Another approach, proposed by Chen (1972), is to filter the data with the inverse MA(q) filter and test the filtered output for whiteness.

8.3.8 ARMA Model for Power Spectrum Estimation

The Burg algorithm, and its variations, and the least-squares method described in the previous sections provide reliable, high-resolution spectrum estimates based on the AR model. An ARMA model provides us with an opportunity to improve on the AR spectrum estimate, perhaps, by using fewer model parameters.

The ARMA model is particularly appropriate when the data have been corrupted by noise. For example, suppose that the data $x(n)$ are generated by an AR system, where the system output is corrupted by additive white noise. The z-transform of the autocorrelation of the resultant signal may be expressed as

$$\begin{aligned}\Gamma_{xx}(z) &= \frac{\sigma_w^2}{A(z)A(z^{-1})} + \sigma_n^2 \\ &= \frac{\sigma_w^2 + \sigma_n^2 A(z)A(z^{-1})}{A(z)A(z^{-1})}\end{aligned} \tag{8.3.45}$$

where σ_n^2 is the variance of the additive noise. Therefore, the process $x(n)$ is ARMA(p,p), where p is the order of the autoregressive process. This relationship provides some motivation for investigating ARMA models for power spectrum estimation.

As we have demonstrated in Section 8.3.1, the parameters of the ARMA model are related to the autocorrelation by the equation in (8.3.4). For lags $|m| > q$, the equation involves only the AR parameters $\{a_k\}$. With estimates substituted in place of $\gamma_{xx}(m)$, we can solve the p equations in (8.3.5) to obtain a_k. For high-order models, however, this approach is likely to yield poor estimates of the AR parameters due to the poor estimates of the autocorrelation for large lags. Consequently, this approach is not recommended.

A more reliable method is to construct an overdetermined set of linear equations for $m > q$ and to use the method of least squares on the set of overdetermined equations, as proposed by Cadzow (1982). To elaborate, suppose that the autocorrelation sequence can be estimated accurately up to lag M, where $M > p + q$. Then we may write the following set of linear equations:

$$\begin{bmatrix} r_{xx}(q) & r_{xx}(q-1) & \cdots & r_{xx}(q-p+1) \\ r_{xx}(q+1) & r_{xx}(q) & \cdots & r_{xx}(q-p+2) \\ \vdots & \vdots & & \vdots \\ r_{xx}(M-1) & r_{xx}(M-2) & \cdots & r_{xx}(M-p) \end{bmatrix} \begin{bmatrix} a_1 \\ a_2 \\ \vdots \\ a_p \end{bmatrix} = - \begin{bmatrix} r_{xx}(q+1) \\ r_{xx}(q+2) \\ \vdots \\ r_{xx}(M) \end{bmatrix} \quad (8.3.46)$$

or equivalently,

$$\mathbf{R}_{xx}\mathbf{a} = -\mathbf{r}_{xx} \quad (8.3.47)$$

Since $\mathbf{R}_{xx}$ is of dimension $(M - q) \times p$ and $M - q > p$, we may use the least-squares criterion to solve for the parameter vector $\mathbf{a}$. The result of this minimization is

$$\hat{\mathbf{a}} = -(\mathbf{R}_{xx}^t\mathbf{R}_{xx})^{-1}\mathbf{R}_{xx}^t\mathbf{r}_{xx} \quad (8.3.48)$$

This procedure is called the *least-squares modified Yule–Walker method*. A weighting factor may also be applied to the autocorrelation sequence to deemphasize the less reliable estimates for large lags.

Once the parameters for the AR part of the model have been estimated as indicated above, we have the system

$$\hat{A}(z) = 1 + \sum_{k=1}^{p} \hat{a}_k z^{-k} \quad (8.3.49)$$

The sequence $x(n)$ may now be filtered by the FIR filter $\hat{A}(z)$ to yield the sequence

$$v(n) = x(n) + \sum_{k=1}^{p} \hat{a}_k x(n-k), \qquad n = 0, 1, \ldots, N-1 \quad (8.3.50)$$

The cascade of the ARMA(p,q) model with $\hat{A}(z)$ is approximately the MA(q) process generated by the model $B(z)$. Hence we may apply the MA estimate given in the preceding section to obtain the MA spectrum. To be specific, the filtered sequence $v(n)$ for $p \le n \le N - 1$ is used to form the estimated correlation sequences $r_{vv}(m)$, from which we obtain the MA spectrum

$$\hat{P}_{vv}^{\text{MA}}(f) = \sum_{m=-q}^{q} r_{vv}(m)e^{-j2\pi fm} \quad (8.3.51)$$

First, we observe that the parameters $\{b_k\}$ are not required to determine the power spectrum. Second, we observe that $r_{vv}(m)$ is an estimate of the autocorrelation for the MA model given by (8.3.10). In forming the estimate $r_{vv}(m)$, weighting (e.g., with the Bartlett window) may be used to deemphasize correlation estimates for large lags. In addition, the data may be filtered by a backward filter, thus creating another sequence, say $v^b(n)$, so that both $v(n)$ and $v^b(n)$ can be used in forming the estimate of the autocorrelation

$r_{vv}(m)$, as proposed by Kay (1980). Finally, the estimated ARMA power spectrum is

$$\hat{P}_{xx}^{\text{ARMA}}(f) = \frac{\hat{P}_{vv}^{\text{MA}}(f)}{\left|1 + \sum_{k=1}^{p} \hat{a}_k e^{-j2\pi fk}\right|^2} \tag{8.3.52}$$

An alternative method for determining the parameters b_k of the MA(q) process is the least-squares method of Durbin, described in the preceding section, where $\hat{\mathbf{b}}$ is obtained from (8.3.42).

The problem of order selection for the ARMA(p,q) model has been investigated by Chow (1972) and Bruzzone and Kaveh (1980). For this purpose the minimum of the AIC index

$$\text{AIC}(p,q) = \ln \hat{\sigma}_{wpq}^2 + \frac{2(p+q)}{N} \tag{8.3.53}$$

may be used, where $\hat{\sigma}_{wpq}^2$ is an estimate of the variance of the input error. An additional test on the adequacy of a particular ARMA(p,q) model is to filter the data through the model and test for whiteness of the output data. This would require that the parameters of the MA model be computed from the estimated autocorrelation, using spectral factorization to determine $B(z)$ from $D(z) = B(z)B(z^{-1})$.

For additional reading on ARMA power spectrum estimation, the reader is referred to the papers by Graupe et al. (1975), Cadzow (1981, 1982), Kay (1980), and Friedlander (1982).

8.3.9 Some Experimental Results

In this section we present some experimental results on the performance of AR and ARMA power spectrum estimates that were obtained with artificially generated data. Our objective is to compare the spectral estimation methods on the basis of their frequency resolution, bias, and their robustness in the presence of additive noise.

The data consist of either one or two sinusoids and additive Gaussian noise. The two sinusoids are spaced Δf apart. Clearly, the underlying process is ARMA(4,4). The results that are shown employ an AR(p) model for these data. For high signal-to-noise ratios (SNR) we expect the AR(4) to be adequate. However, for low SNR, a higher-order AR model is needed to approximate the ARMA(4,4) process. The results given below are consistent with this statement.

In Fig. 8.6 we illustrate the results for $N = 20$ data points based on an AR(4) model with SNR = 20 dB and $\Delta f = 0.13$. Note that the Yule–Walker method gives an extremely smooth (broad) spectral estimate with small peaks. If Δf is decreased to $\Delta f = 0.07$, the Yule–Walker method no longer resolves the peaks as illustrated in Fig. 8.7. Some bias is also evident in the Burg method. Of course, by increasing the number of data points the Yule–

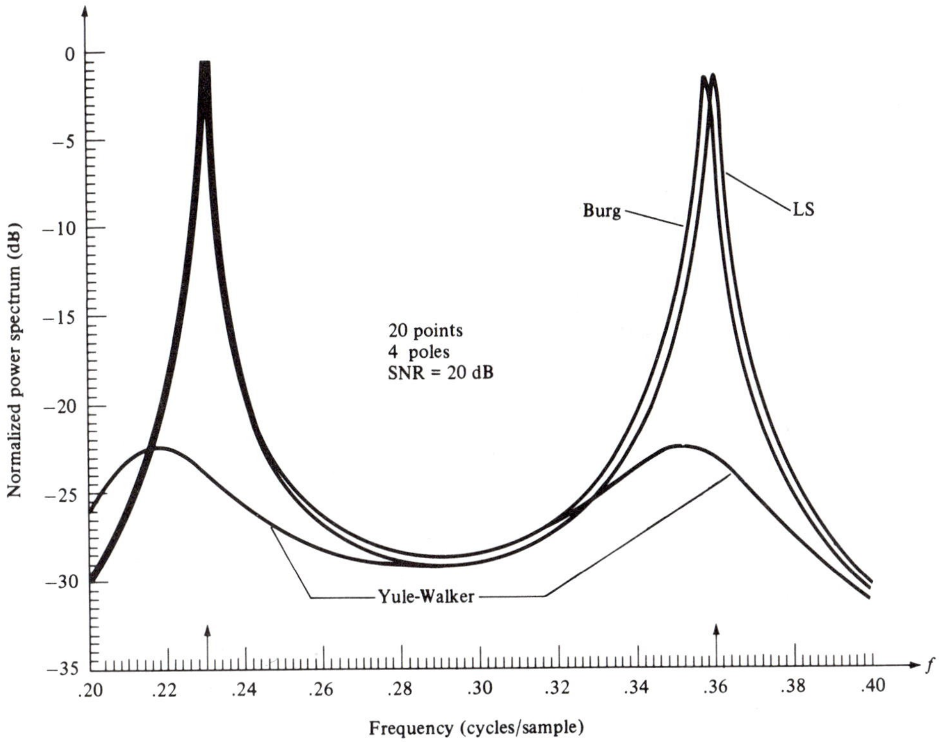

FIGURE 8.6 Comparison of AR spectrum estimation methods.

Walker method will eventually resolve the peaks. However, the Burg and least-squares methods are clearly superior for short data records.

The effect of additive noise on the estimate is illustrated in Fig. 8.8 for the least-squares method. The effect of filter order on the Burg and least-squares methods is illustrated in Figs. 8.9 and 8.10, respectively. Both methods exhibit spurious peaks when the order is increased to $p = 12$.

The effect of initial phase is illustrated in Figs. 8.11 and 8.12 for the Burg and least-squares methods. It is clear that the least-squares method exhibits less sensitivity to initial phase than the Burg algorithm.

An example of line splitting for the Burg method is shown in Fig. 8.13 with $p = 12$. It does not occur for the AR(8) model. The least-squares method did not exhibit line splitting under the same conditions. On the other hand, the line splitting for the Burg method disappeared with an increase in the number of data points N.

Figures 8.14 and 8.15 illustrate the resolution properties of the Burg and least-squares methods for $\Delta f = 0.07$ and $N = 20$ points at low SNR (3 dB). Since the additive noise process is ARMA, a higher-order AR model is required to provide a good approximation at low SNR. Hence the frequency resolution improves as the order is increased.

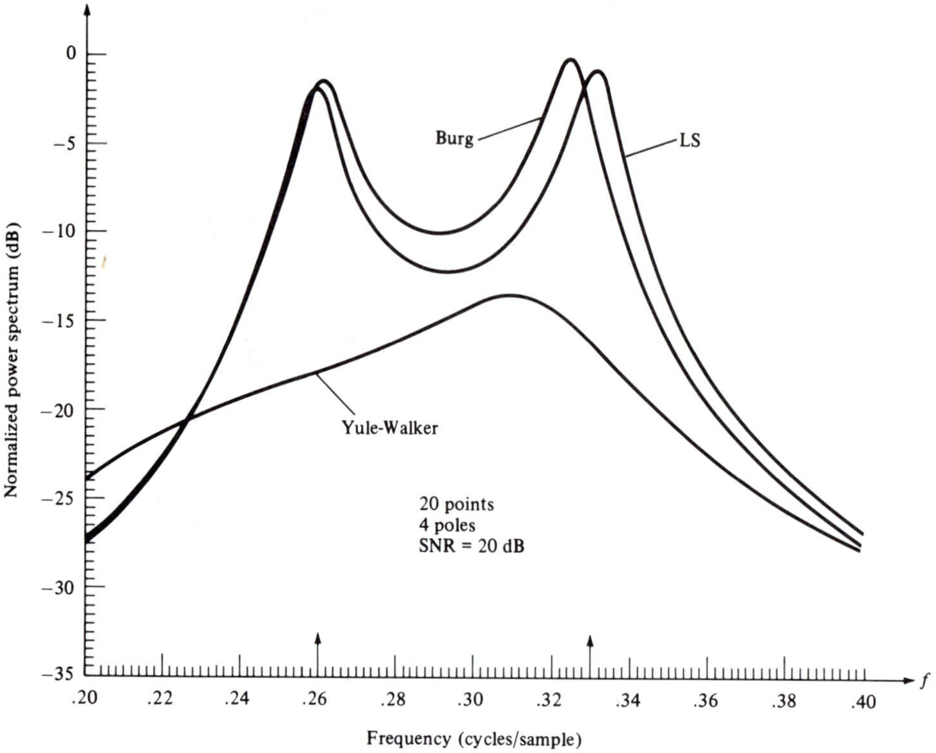

FIGURE 8.7 Comparison of AR spectrum estimation methods.

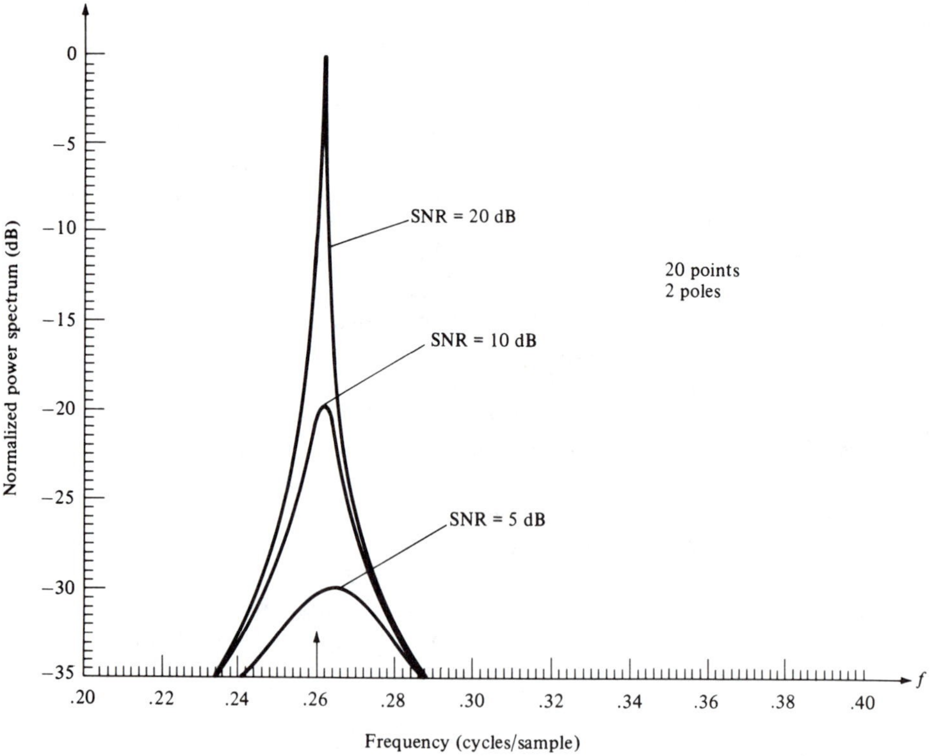

FIGURE 8.8 Effect of additive noise on LS method.

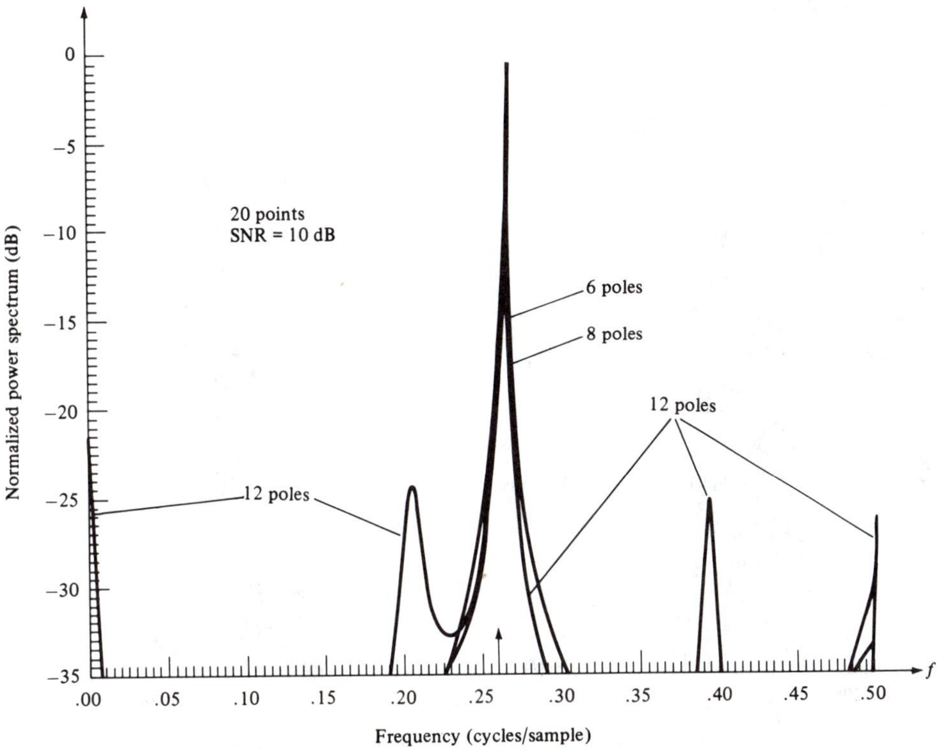

FIGURE 8.9 Effect of filter order on Burg method.

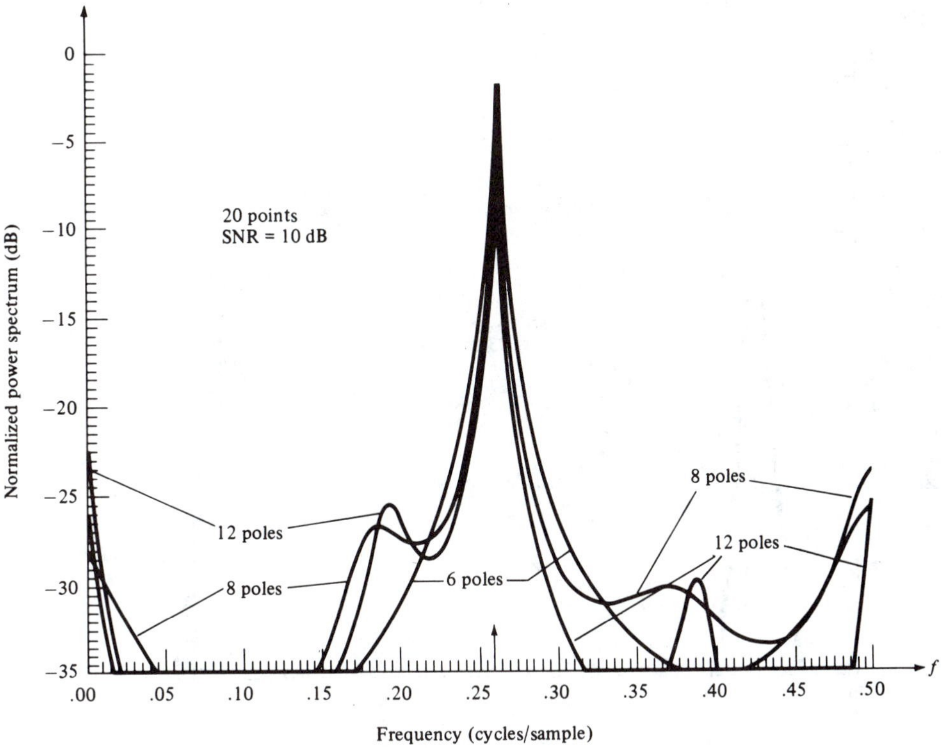

FIGURE 8.10 Effect of filter order on LS method.

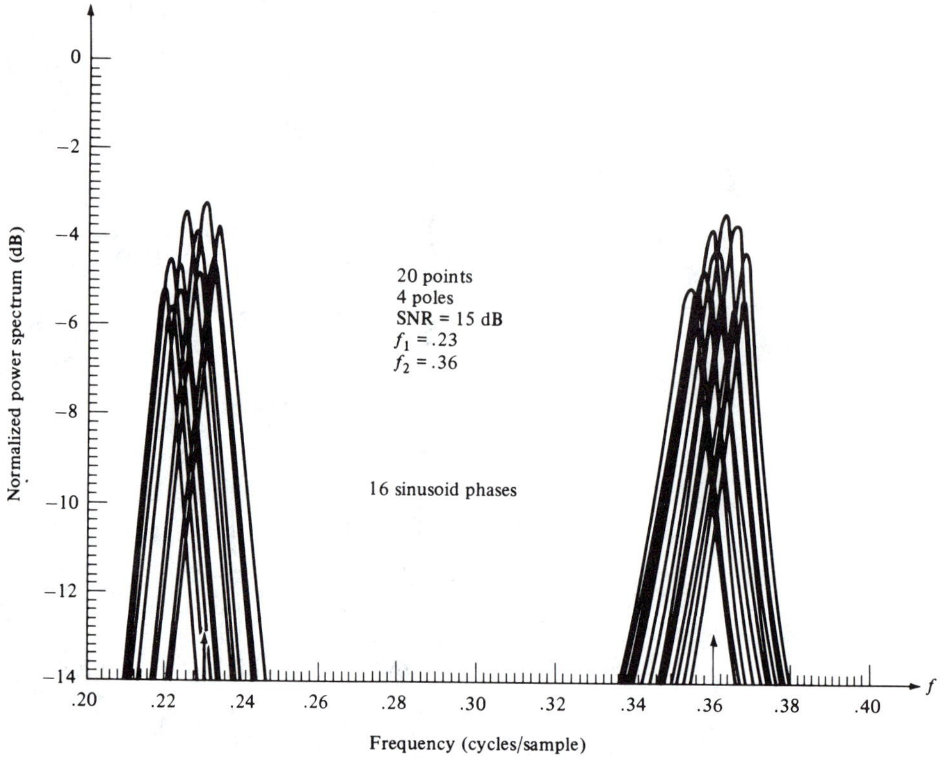

FIGURE 8.11 Effect of initial phase on Burg method.

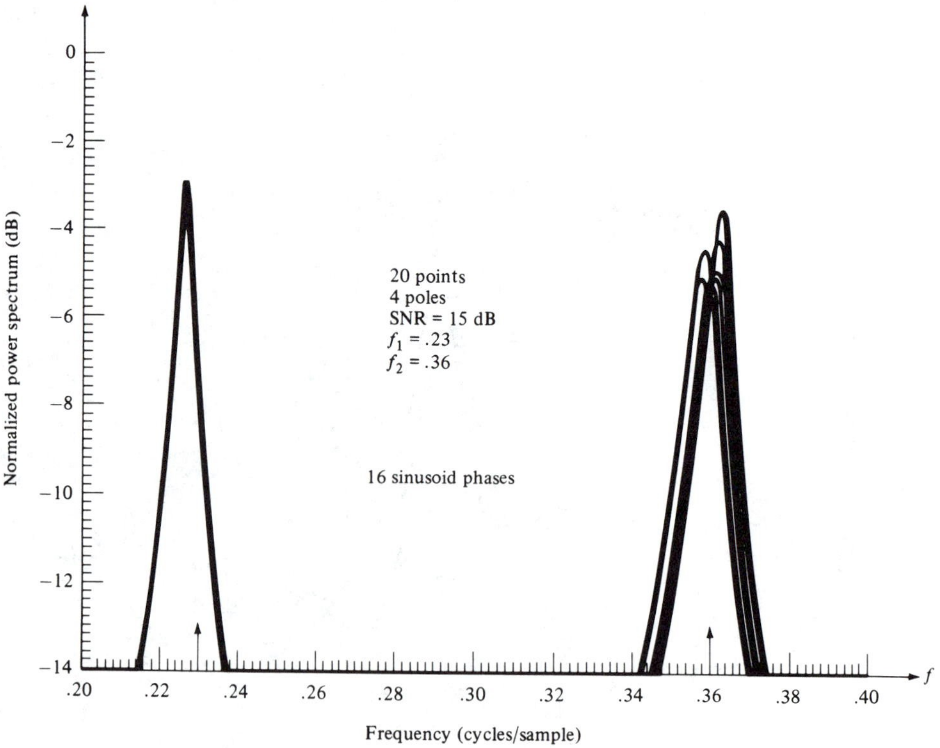

FIGURE 8.12 Effect of initial phase on LS method.

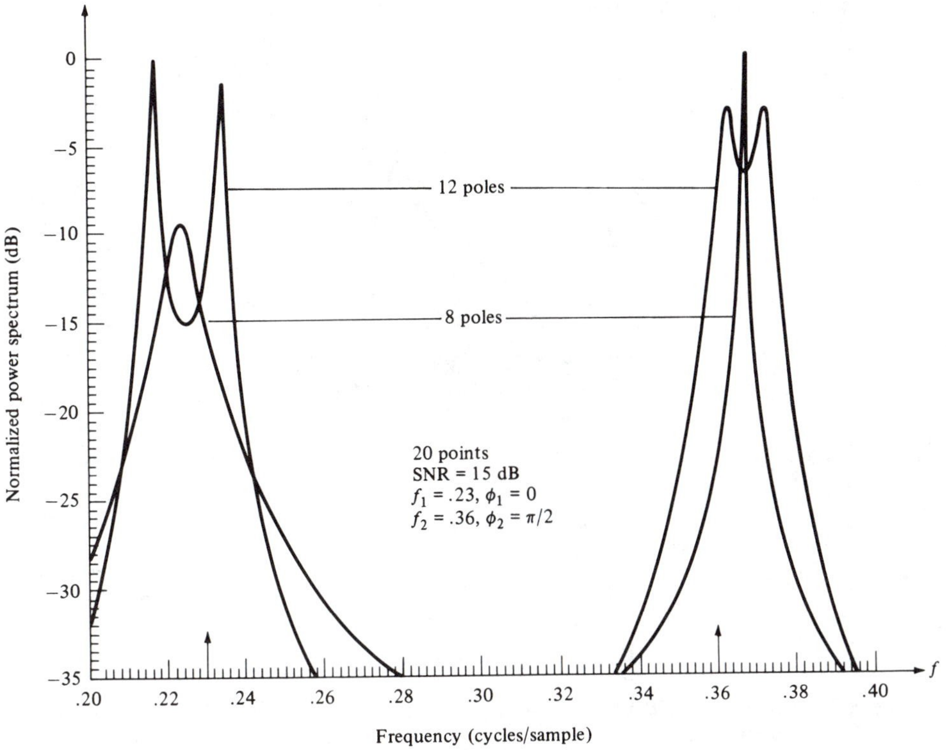

FIGURE 8.13 Line splitting in Burg method.

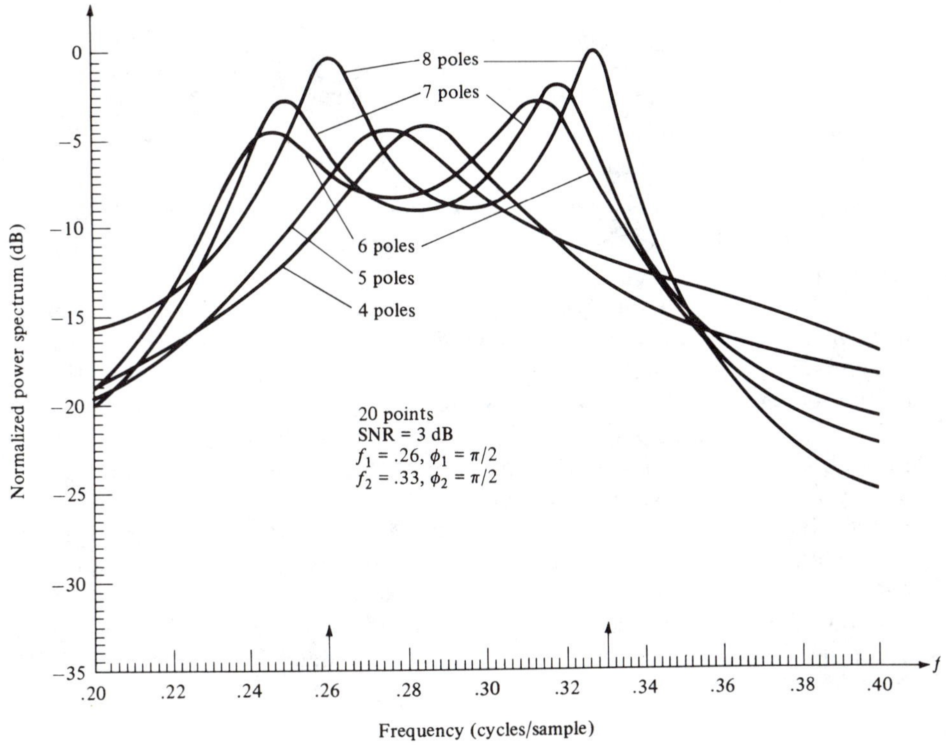

FIGURE 8.14 Frequency resolution of Burg method with $N = 20$ points.

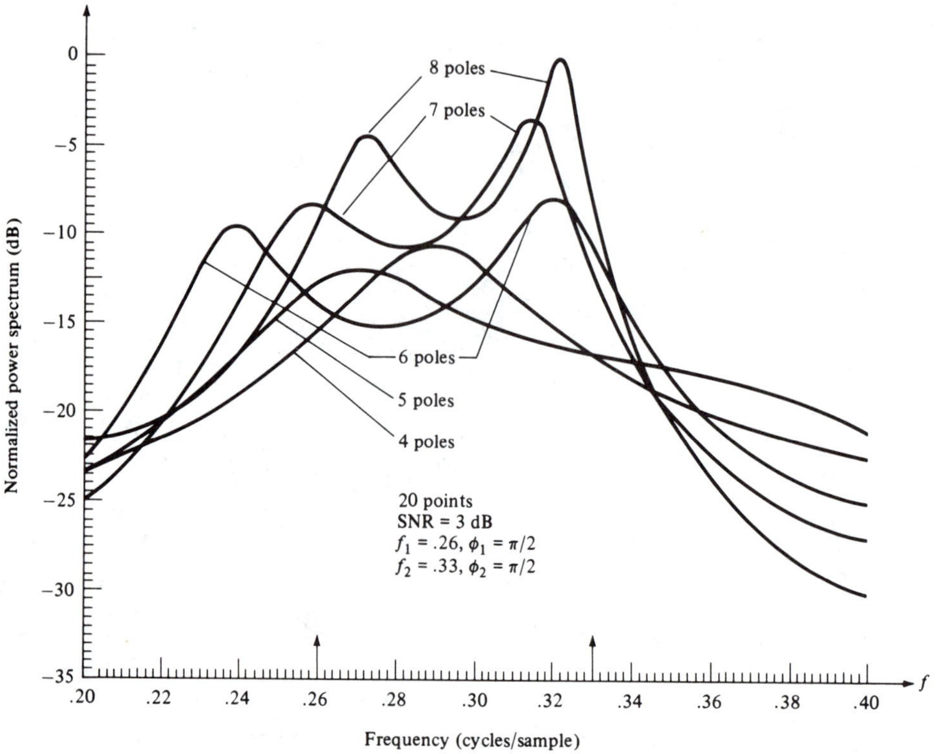

FIGURE 8.15 Frequency resolution of LS method with $N = 20$ points.

The FPE for the Burg method is illustrated in Fig. 8.16 for an SNR = 3 dB. For this SNR, the optimum value is $p = 12$, according to the FPE criterion.

The Burg and least-squares methods were also tested with data from a narrowband process, which was obtained by exciting a four-pole (two pairs of complex-conjugate poles) narrowband filter and selecting a portion of the output sequence for the data record. Figure 8.17 illustrates the superposition of 20 data records of 20 points each. We observe a relatively small variability. In contrast, the Burg method exhibited a much larger variability, approximately a factor of 2 greater compared to the least-squares method. The results shown in Fig. 8.6 through 8.17 are taken from Poole (1981).

Finally, we show in Fig. 8.18 the ARMA(10,10) spectral estimates obtained by Kay (1980) for two sinusoids in noise using the least-squares ARMA method described in Section 8.3.8, as an illustration of the quality of power spectrum estimation obtained with the ARMA model.

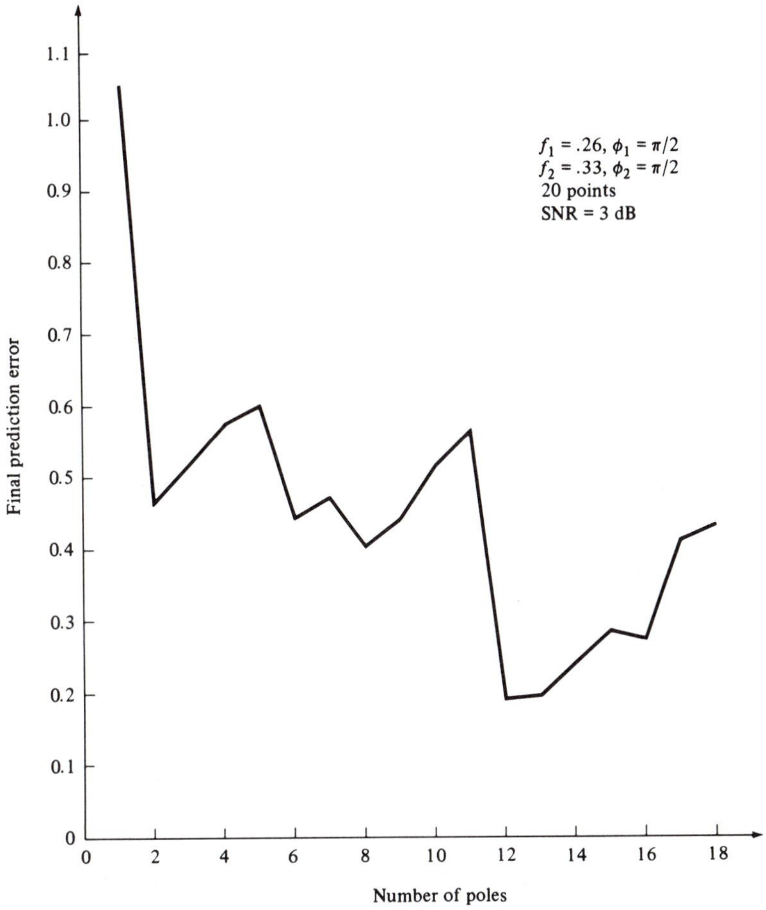

FIGURE 8.16 Final prediction error for Burg estimate.

8.4 MINIMUM-VARIANCE SPECTRAL ESTIMATION

Capon (1969) proposed a spectral estimation method that was intended for use in large seismic arrays for frequency–wave number estimation. It was later adapted to single-time-series spectrum estimation by Lacoss (1971), who demonstrated that the method provides a minimum variance unbiased estimate of the spectral components in the signal.

Following the development of Lacoss, let us consider an FIR filter with coefficients a_k, $0 \le k \le p$, to be determined. Unlike the linear prediction problem, we do not constrain a_0 to be unity. Then if the observed data $x(n)$, $0 \le n \le N - 1$, are passed through the filter, the response is

$$y(n) = \sum_{k=0}^{p} a_k x(n - k) \equiv \mathbf{X}^t(n)\mathbf{a} \tag{8.4.1}$$

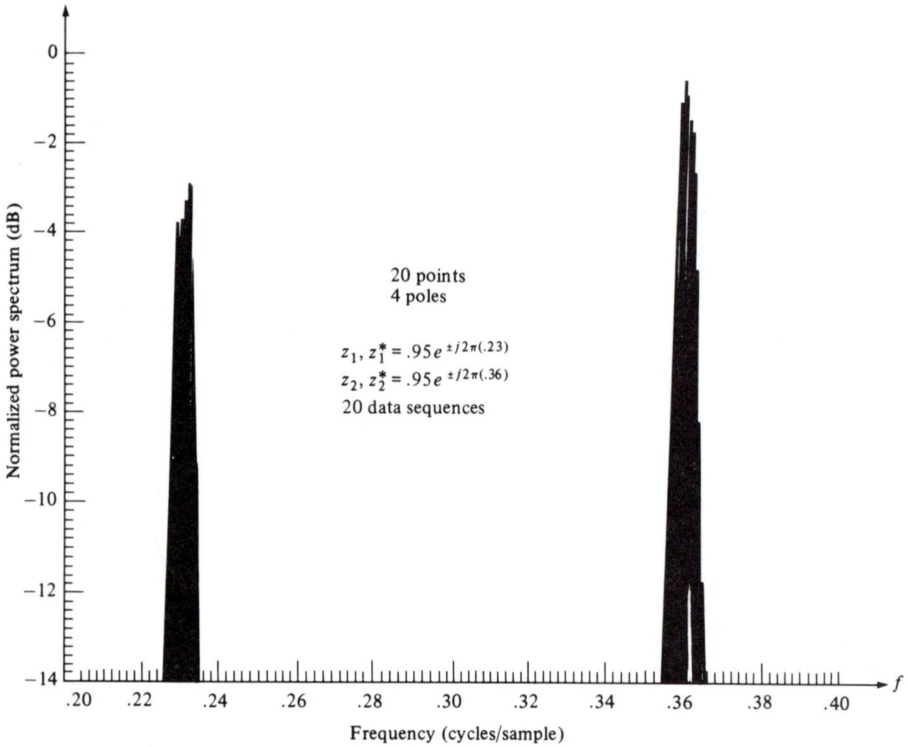

FIGURE 8.17 Effect of starting point in sequence on LS method.

where $\mathbf{X}^t(n) = [x(n) \quad x(n-1) \quad \cdots \quad x(n-p)]$ is the data vector and $\mathbf{a}$ is the filter coefficient vector. If we assume that $E[x(n)] = 0$, the variance of the output sequence is

$$\begin{aligned}\sigma_y^2 = E[|y(n)|^2] &= E[\mathbf{a}^{*t}\mathbf{X}^*(n)\mathbf{X}^t(n)\mathbf{a}] \\ &= \mathbf{a}^{*t}\mathbf{\Gamma}_{xx}\mathbf{a}\end{aligned} \tag{8.4.2}$$

where $\mathbf{\Gamma}_{xx}$ is the autocorrelation matrix of the sequence $x(n)$, with elements $\gamma_{xx}(m)$.

The filter coefficients are selected so that at the frequency f_l, the frequency response of the FIR filter is normalized to unity,

$$\sum_{k=0}^{p} a_k e^{-j2\pi k f_l} = 1$$

This constraint may also be written in matrix form as

$$\mathbf{E}^{*t}(f_l)\mathbf{a} = 1 \tag{8.4.3}$$

where $\mathbf{E}^t(f_l) = [1 \quad e^{j2\pi f_l} \quad \cdots \quad e^{j2\pi p f_l}]$.

By minimizing the variance σ_y^2 subject to the constraint (8.4.3), we obtain an FIR filter that passes the frequency component f_l undistorted, while

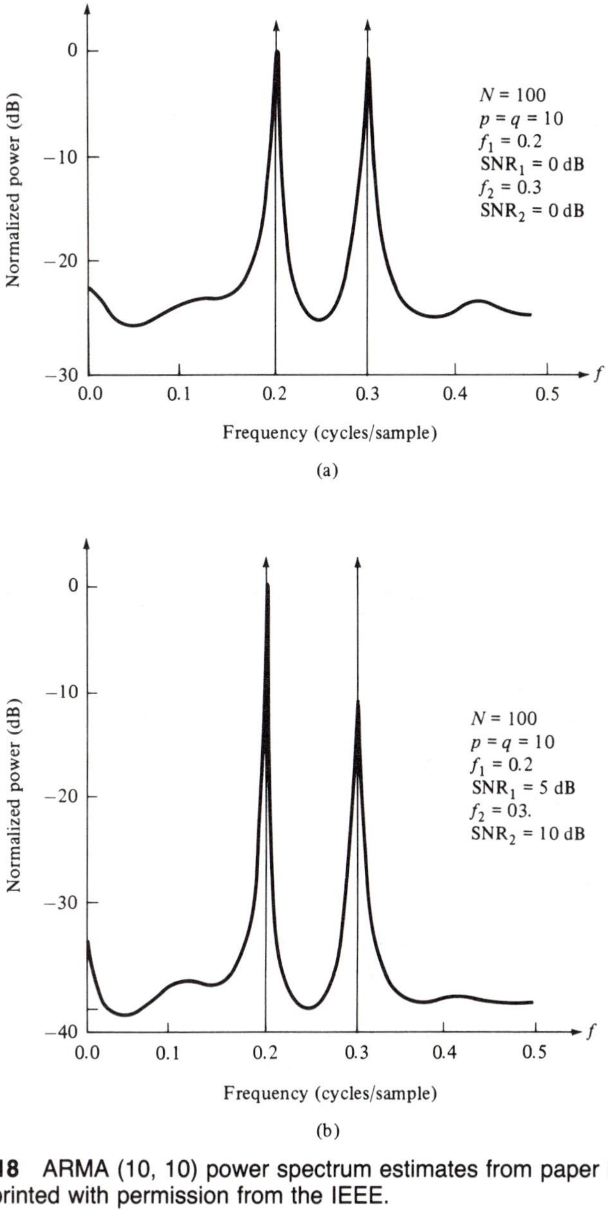

FIGURE 8.18 ARMA (10, 10) power spectrum estimates from paper by Kay (1980). Reprinted with permission from the IEEE.

components distant from f_l are severely attenuated. The result of this minimization is shown by Lacoss (1971) to lead to the coefficient vector

$$\hat{\mathbf{a}} = \frac{\mathbf{\Gamma}_{xx}^{-1}\mathbf{E}^*(f_l)}{\mathbf{E}^t(f_l)\mathbf{\Gamma}_{xx}^{-1}E^*(f_l)} \tag{8.4.4}$$

If **a** is substituted into (8.4.2), we obtain the minimum variance

$$\sigma^2_{min} = \frac{1}{\mathbf{E}^t(f_l)\mathbf{\Gamma}_{xx}^{-1}\mathbf{E}^*(f_l)} \tag{8.4.5}$$

The expression in (8.4.5) is the minimum variance power spectrum estimate at the frequency f_l. By changing f_l over the range $0 \leq f_l \leq 0.5$ we can obtain the power spectrum estimate. It should be noted that although $\mathbf{E}(f)$ changes with the choice of frequency, $\mathbf{\Gamma}_{xx}^{-1}$ is computed only once. As demonstrated by Lacoss (1971), the computation of the quadratic form $\mathbf{E}^t(f)\mathbf{\Gamma}_{xx}^{-1}\mathbf{E}^*(f)$ can be done with a single DFT.

With an estimate $\mathbf{R}_{xx}$ of the autocorrelation substituted in place of $\mathbf{\Gamma}_{xx}$, we obtain the minimum variance power spectrum estimate of Capon as

$$P_{xx}^{\mathrm{MV}}(f) = \frac{1}{\mathbf{E}^t(f)\mathbf{R}_{xx}^{-1}\mathbf{E}^*(f)} \tag{8.4.6}$$

It has been shown by Lacoss (1971) that this power spectrum estimator yields estimates of the spectral peaks which are proportional to the power at that frequency. In contrast, the AR methods described in Section 8.3 result in estimates of the spectral peaks which are proportional to the square of the power at that frequency.

The minimum variance method as described above is basically a filter bank implementation for the spectrum estimator. It differs basically from the filter bank interpretation of the periodogram in that the filter coefficients in the Capon method are optimized.

Experiments on the performance of this method compared with the performance of the Burg method have been done by Lacoss (1971) and others. In general, the minimum variance estimate in (8.4.6) outperforms the nonparametric spectral estimators in frequency resolution, but it does not provide the high-frequency resolution obtained with AR methods of Burg and the unconstrained least-squares method. Extensive comparisons between the Burg method and the minimum variance method have been made in the paper by Lacoss. Furthermore, Burg (1972) demonstrated that for a known correlation sequence, the minimum variance estimate is related to the AR model estimate through the equation

$$\frac{1}{\Gamma_{xx}^{\mathrm{MV}}(f)} = \frac{1}{p}\sum_{k=1}^{p}\frac{1}{\Gamma_{xx}^{\mathrm{AR}}(f,k)} \tag{8.4.7}$$

where $\Gamma_{xx}^{\mathrm{AR}}(f,k)$ is the AR spectral estimate obtained with an AR(k) model. Thus the reciprocal of the minimum variance estimate is equal to the average of the reciprocals of all spectra obtained with AR(k) models for $1 \leq k \leq p$. Since low-order AR models, in general, will not provide good resolution, the averaging operation in (8.4.7) reduces the frequency resolution in the spectral estimate. Hence we conclude that the AR power spectrum estimate of order p is superior to the minimum variance estimate of order p.

The relationship given by (8.4.7) represents a frequency-domain relationship between the Capon minimum variance estimate and the Burg AR estimate. A time-domain relationship between these two estimates can also be established as shown by Musicus (1985). This has led to a computationally efficient algorithm for the minimum variance estimate.

Additional references to the method of Capon and comparisons with other estimators can be found in the literature. We cite the papers of Capon and Goodman (1971), Marzetta (1983), Marzetta and Lang (1983, 1984), Capon (1983), and McDonough (1983).

8.5 EIGENANALYSIS ALGORITHMS FOR SPECTRUM ESTIMATION

In Section 8.3.8 we demonstrated that an AR(p) process corrupted by additive (white) noise is equivalent to an ARMA(p,p) process. In this section we consider spectrum estimation for signals consisting of sinusoidal components corrupted by additive white noise. The algorithms are based on an eigendecomposition of the autocorrelation matrix of the noise-corrupted signal.

First we note that a real sinusoidal signal can be generated via the second-order difference equation (AR (2) system)

$$x(n) = -a_1 x(n-1) - a_2 x(n-2) \tag{8.5.1}$$

where $a_1 = 2\cos 2\pi f_k$ and $a_2 = 1$, and initially, $x(-1) = -1$, $x(-2) = 0$. This system has a pair of complex-conjugate poles (at $f = f_k$ and $f = -f_k$) and thus generates the sinusoid $x(n) = \cos 2\pi f_k n$, for $n \geq 0$.

In general, a signal consisting of p sinusoidal components satisfies the difference

$$x(n) = -\sum_{m=1}^{2p} a_m x(n-m) \tag{8.5.2}$$

and corresponds to the system with system function

$$H(z) = \frac{1}{1 + \sum_{m=1}^{2p} a_m z^{-m}} \tag{8.5.3}$$

The polynomial

$$A(z) = 1 + \sum_{m=1}^{2p} a_m z^{-m} \tag{8.5.4}$$

has $2p$ roots on the unit circle, which correspond to the frequencies of the sinusoids.

Now suppose that the sinusoids are corrupted by a white noise sequence $w(n)$ with $E[|w(n)|^2] = \sigma_w^2$. Then we observe that

$$y(n) = x(n) + w(n) \tag{8.5.5}$$

If we substitute $x(n) = y(n) - w(n)$ in (8.5.2), we obtain

$$y(n) - w(n) = -\sum_{m=1}^{2p} [y(n-m) - w(n-m)]a_m$$

or equivalently,

$$\sum_{m=0}^{2p} a_m y(n-m) = \sum_{m=0}^{2p} a_m w(n-m) \tag{8.5.6}$$

where, by definition, $a_0 = 1$.

We observe that (8.5.6) is the difference equation for an ARMA(2p,2p) process in which both the AR and MA parameters are identical. This symmetry is a characteristic of the sinusoidal signals in white noise. The difference equation in (8.5.6) may be expressed in matrix form as

$$\mathbf{Y}^t\mathbf{a} = \mathbf{W}^t\mathbf{a} \tag{8.5.7}$$

where $\mathbf{Y}^t = [y(n) \quad y(n-1) \quad \cdots \quad y(n-2p)]$ is the observed data vector of dimension $(2p+1)$, $\mathbf{W}^t = [w(n) \quad w(n-1) \quad \cdots \quad w(n-2p)]$ is the noise vector, and $\mathbf{a} = [1 \quad a_1 \quad \cdots \quad a_{2p}]$ is the coefficient vector.

If we premultiply (8.5.7) by $\mathbf{Y}$ and take the expected value, we obtain

$$E[\mathbf{Y}\mathbf{Y}^t]\mathbf{a} = E[\mathbf{Y}\mathbf{W}^t]\mathbf{a} = E[(\mathbf{X} + \mathbf{W})\mathbf{W}^t]\mathbf{a}$$

$$\mathbf{\Gamma}_{yy}\mathbf{a} = \sigma_w^2\mathbf{a} \tag{8.5.8}$$

where we have used the assumption that the sequence $w(n)$ is zero mean and white and $\mathbf{X}$ is a deterministic signal.

The equation in (8.5.8) is in the form of an eigenequation,

$$(\mathbf{\Gamma}_{yy} - \sigma_w^2\mathbf{I})\mathbf{a} = 0 \tag{8.5.9}$$

where σ_w^2 is an eigenvalue of the autocorrelation matrix $\mathbf{\Gamma}_{yy}$. Then the parameter vector $\mathbf{a}$ is an eigenvector associated with the eigenvalue σ_w^2. The eigenequation in (8.5.9) forms the basis for the Pisarenko harmonic decomposition method.

8.5.1 Pisarenko Harmonic Decomposition Method

For p randomly phased sinusoids in additive white noise, the autocorrelation values are

$$\begin{aligned} \gamma_{yy}(0) &= \sigma_w^2 + \sum_{i=1}^{p} P_i \\ \gamma_{yy}(k) &= \sum_{i=1}^{p} P_i \cos 2\pi f_i k, \qquad k \neq 0 \end{aligned} \tag{8.5.10}$$

where $P_i = A_i^2/2$ is the average power in the ith sinusoid and A_i is the corresponding amplitude. Hence we may write

$$\begin{bmatrix} \cos 2\pi f_1 & \cos 2\pi f_2 & \cdots & \cos 2\pi f_p \\ \cos 4\pi f_1 & \cos 4\pi f_2 & \cdots & \cos 4\pi f_p \\ \vdots & \vdots & & \\ \cos 2\pi p f_1 & \cos 2\pi p f_2 & \cdots & \cos 2\pi p f_p \end{bmatrix} \begin{bmatrix} P_1 \\ P_2 \\ \vdots \\ P_p \end{bmatrix} = \begin{bmatrix} \gamma_{yy}(1) \\ \gamma_{yy}(2) \\ \vdots \\ \gamma_{yy}(p) \end{bmatrix} \tag{8.5.11}$$

If we know the frequencies f_i, $1 \le i \le p$, we may use this equation to determine the powers of the sinusoids. In place of $\gamma_{xx}(m)$, we use the estimates $r_{xx}(m)$. Once the powers are known, the noise variance can be obtained from as (8.5.10) as

$$\sigma_w^2 = r_{yy}(0) - \sum_{i=1}^{p} P_i \tag{8.5.12}$$

The problem that remains is to determine the p frequencies f_i, $1 \le i \le p$, which, in turn, require knowledge of the eigenvector **a** corresponding to the eigenvalue σ_w^2. Pisarenko (1973) observed [see Papoulis (1984) and Grenander and Szegö (1958)] that for an ARMA process consisting of p sinusoids in additive white noise, the variance σ_w^2 corresponds to the minimum eigenvalue of $\mathbf{\Gamma}_{yy}$, when the dimension of the autocorrelation matrix equals or exceeds $(2p + 1) \times (2p + 1)$. The desired ARMA coefficient vector corresponds to the eigenvector associated with the minimum eigenvalue. Therefore, the frequencies f_i, $1 \le i \le p$, are obtained from the roots of the polynomial in (8.5.4), where the coefficients are the elements of the eigenvector **a** corresponding to the minimum eigenvalue σ_w^2.

In summary, the Pisarenko harmonic decomposition method proceeds as follows. First we estimate $\mathbf{\Gamma}_{yy}$ from the data (i.e., we form the autocorrelation matrix $\mathbf{R}_{yy}$). Then we find the minimum eigenvalue and the corresponding minimum eigenvector. The minimum eigenvector yields the parameters of the ARMA($2p$,$2p$) model. From (8.5.4) we can compute the roots that constitute the frequencies f_i. By using these frequencies, we can solve (8.5.11) for the signal powers P_i by substituting the estimates $r_{yy}(m)$ for $\gamma_{yy}(m)$.

As we will observe below, the Pisarenko method is based on the use of a noise subspace eigenvector to estimate the frequencies of the sinusoids.

EXAMPLE 8.5.1

Suppose that we are given the autocorrelation values $\gamma_{yy}(0) = 3$, $\gamma_{yy}(1) = 1$ and $\gamma_{yy}(2) = 0$ for a process consisting of a single sinusoid in additive white noise. Determine the frequency, its power, and the variance of the additive noise.

Solution: The correlation matrix is

$$\mathbf{\Gamma}_{yy} = \begin{bmatrix} 3 & 1 & 0 \\ 1 & 3 & 1 \\ 0 & 1 & 3 \end{bmatrix}$$

The minimum eigenvalue is the smallest root of the characteristic polynomial

$$g(\lambda) = \begin{bmatrix} 3-\lambda & 1 & 0 \\ 1 & 3-\lambda & 1 \\ 0 & 1 & 3-\lambda \end{bmatrix} = (3-\lambda)(\lambda^2 - 6\lambda + 7) = 0$$

Therefore, the eigenvalues are $\lambda_1 = 3$, $\lambda_2 = 3 + \sqrt{2}$, and $\lambda_3 = 3 - \sqrt{2}$.

The variance of the noise is

$$\sigma_w^2 = \lambda_{\min} = 3 - \sqrt{2}$$

The corresponding eigenvalue is the vector that satisfies (8.5.9),

$$\begin{bmatrix} \sqrt{2} & 1 & 0 \\ 1 & \sqrt{2} & 1 \\ 0 & 1 & \sqrt{2} \end{bmatrix} \begin{bmatrix} 1 \\ a_1 \\ a_2 \end{bmatrix} = \begin{bmatrix} 0 \\ 0 \\ 0 \end{bmatrix}$$

The solution is $a_1 = -\sqrt{2}$ and $a_2 = 1$.

The next step is to use the value a_1 and a_2 to determine the roots of the polynomial in (8.5.4). We have

$$z^2 - 2z + 1 = 0$$

Thus

$$z_1, z_2 = \frac{1}{\sqrt{2}} \pm j\frac{1}{\sqrt{2}}$$

Note that $|z_1| = |z_2| = 1$, so that the roots are on the unit circle. The corresponding frequency is obtained from

$$z_i = e^{j2\pi f_1} = \frac{1}{\sqrt{2}} + j\frac{1}{\sqrt{2}}$$

which yields $f_1 = \frac{1}{8}$. Finally, the power of the sinusoid is

$$P_1 \cos 2\pi f_1 = \gamma_{yy}(1) = 1$$
$$P_1 = \sqrt{2}$$

and its amplitude is $A = \sqrt{2P_1} = \sqrt{2\sqrt{2}}$.

As a check on our computations, we have

$$\sigma_w^2 = \gamma_{yy}(0) - P_1$$
$$= 3 - \sqrt{2}$$

which agrees with $\lambda_{\min}$.

8.5.2 Eigendecomposition of the Autocorrelation Matrix for Sinusoids in White Noise

In the discussion above we assumed that the sinusoidal signal consists of p real sinusoids. For mathematical convenience we shall now assume that the signal consists of p complex sinusoids of the form

$$x(n) = \sum_{i=1}^{p} A_i e^{j(2\pi f_i n + \phi_i)} \tag{8.5.13}$$

where the amplitudes A_i and the frequencies f_i are unknown and the phases ϕ_i are statistically independent random variables uniformly distributed on $(0,2\pi)$. Then the random process $x(n)$ is wide-sense stationary with autocorrelation function

$$\gamma_{xx}(m) = \sum_{i=1}^{p} P_i e^{j2\pi f_i m} \tag{8.5.14}$$

where, for complex sinusoids, $P_i = A_i^2$ is the power of the ith sinusoid.

Since the observed sequence is $y(n) = x(n) + w(n)$, where $w(n)$ is a white noise sequence with spectral density σ_w^2, the autocorrelation function for $y(n)$ is

$$\gamma_{yy}(m) = \gamma_{xx}(m) + \sigma_w^2\delta(m), \qquad m = 0, \pm 1, \ldots, \pm(M-1) \tag{8.5.15}$$

Hence, the $M \times M$ autocorrelation matrix for $y(n)$ may be expressed as

$$\mathbf{\Gamma}_{yy} = \mathbf{\Gamma}_{xx} + \sigma_w^2\mathbf{I} \tag{8.5.16}$$

where $\mathbf{\Gamma}_{xx}$ is the autocorrelation matrix for the signal $x(n)$ and $\sigma_w^2\mathbf{I}$ is the autocorrelation matrix for the noise. Note that if select $M > p$, $\mathbf{\Gamma}_{xx}$, which is of dimension $M \times M$, is not of full rank because its rank is p. However, $\mathbf{\Gamma}_{yy}$ is full rank because $\sigma_w^2\mathbf{I}$ is of rank M.

In fact, the signal matrix $\mathbf{\Gamma}_{xx}$ may be represented as

$$\mathbf{\Gamma}_{xx} = \sum_{i=1}^{p} P_i \mathbf{s}_i \mathbf{s}_i^H \tag{8.5.17}$$

where H denotes the conjugate transpose and $\mathbf{s}_i$ is a signal vector of dimension M defined as

$$\mathbf{s}_i^t = [1, e^{j2\pi f_i}, e^{j4\pi f_i}, \ldots, e^{j2\pi(M-1)f_i}] \tag{8.5.18}$$

Since each vector (outer product) $\mathbf{s}_i\mathbf{s}_i^H$ is a matrix of rank 1 and since there are p vector products, the matrix $\mathbf{\Gamma}_{xx}$ is of rank p. Note that if the sinusoids were real, the correlation matrix $\mathbf{\Gamma}_{xx}$ will have rank $2p$.

Now, let us perform an eigendecomposition of the matrix $\mathbf{\Gamma}_{yy}$. Let the eigenvalues λ_i be ordered in decreasing value with $\lambda_1 \geq \lambda_2 \geq \lambda_3 \geq \cdots \geq \lambda_M$, and let the corresponding eigenvectors be denoted as $\{\mathbf{v}_i, i = 1, \ldots, M\}$. We assume that the eigenvectors are normalized so that $\mathbf{v}_i^H \cdot \mathbf{v}_j = \delta_{ij}$. In the absence of noise the eigenvalues λ_i, $i = 1, 2, \ldots, p$, will be nonzero while $\lambda_{p+1} = \lambda_{p+2} = \cdots = \lambda_M = 0$. Furthermore, it follows that the signal correlation matrix can be expressed as

$$\mathbf{\Gamma}_{xx} = \sum_{i=1}^{p} \lambda_i \mathbf{v}_i \mathbf{v}_i^H \tag{8.5.19}$$

Thus the eigenvectors $\mathbf{v}_i$, $i = 1, 2, \ldots, p$, span the *signal subspace* as the signal vectors $\mathbf{s}_i$, $i = 1, 2, \ldots, p$, do. These p eigenvectors for the signal subspace are called the *principal eigenvectors*, and the corresponding eigenvalues are called the *principal eigenvalues*.

In the presence of noise, the noise autocorrelation matrix in (8.5.16) may be represented as

$$\sigma_w^2 \mathbf{I} = \sigma_w^2 \sum_{i=1}^{M} \mathbf{v}_i \mathbf{v}_i^H \tag{8.5.20}$$

By substituting (8.5.19) and (8.5.20) into (8.5.16), we obtain

$$\begin{aligned} \mathbf{\Gamma}_{yy} &= \sum_{i=1}^{p} \lambda_i \mathbf{v}_i \mathbf{v}_i^H + \sum_{i=1}^{M} \sigma_w^2 \mathbf{v}_i \mathbf{v}_i^H \\ &= \sum_{i=1}^{p} (\lambda_i + \sigma_w^2) \mathbf{v}_i \mathbf{v}_i^H + \sum_{i=p+1}^{M} \sigma_w^2 \mathbf{v}_i \mathbf{v}_i^H \end{aligned} \tag{8.5.21}$$

This eigendecomposition separates the eigenvectors into two sets. The set $\{\mathbf{v}_i, i = 1, 2, \ldots, p\}$, which are the principal eigenvectors, span the signal subspace, while the set $\{\mathbf{v}_i, i = p + 1, \ldots, M\}$, which are orthogonal to the principal eigenvectors, are said to belong to the *noise subspace*. Since the signal vectors $\{\mathbf{s}_i, i = 1, 2, \ldots, p\}$ are in the signal subspace, it follows that the $\mathbf{s}_i$ are simply linear combinations of the principal eigenvectors and also are orthogonal to the vectors in the noise subspace.

In this context we see that the Pisarenko method is based on the estimation of the frequencies by using the orthogonality property between the vectors in the noise subspace and the signal vectors. For complex sinusoids, if we select $M = p + 1$ (for real sinusoids we select $M = 2p + 1$), there is only a single eigenvector in the noise subspace (corresponding to the minimum eigenvalue) which must be orthogonal to the signal vectors. Thus we have

$$\mathbf{s}_i^H \mathbf{v}_{p+1} = \sum_{k=0}^{p} v_{p+1}(k + 1) e^{-j2\pi f_i k} = 0, \qquad i = 1, 2, \ldots, p \tag{8.5.22}$$

But (8.5.22) implies that the frequencies f_i can be determined by solving for the zeros of the polynomial.

$$V(z) = \sum_{k=0}^{p} v_{p+1}(k + 1) z^{-k} \tag{8.5.23}$$

all of which lie on the unit circle. The angles of these roots are $2\pi f_i$, $i = 1, 2, \ldots, p$.

When the number of sinusoids is unknown, the determination of p may prove to be difficult, especially if the signal level is not much higher than the noise level. In theory, if $M > p + 1$, there is a multiplicity $(M - p)$ of the minimum eigenvalue. However, in practice the $(M - p)$ small eigenvalues of $\mathbf{R}_{yy}$ will probably be different. By computing all the eigenvalues it may be possible to determine p by grouping the $M - p$ small (noise) eigenvalues into a set and averaging them to obtain an estimate of σ_w^2. Then the average value may be used in (8.5.9) along with $\mathbf{R}_{yy}$ to determine the corresponding eigenvector.

8.5.3 MUSIC Algorithm

The multiple signal classification (MUSIC) method is also a noise subspace frequency estimator. To develop this method, let us first consider the "weighted" spectral estimate

$$P(f) = \sum_{k=p+1}^{M} w_k |\mathbf{s}^H(f)\mathbf{v}_k|^2 \qquad (8.5.24)$$

where $\{\mathbf{v}_k,\ k = p + 1, \ldots, M\}$ are the eigenvectors in the noise subspace, w_k are a set of positive weights, and $\mathbf{s}(f)$ is the complex sinusoidal vector

$$\mathbf{s}^t(f) = [1, e^{j2\pi f}, e^{j4\pi f}, \ldots, e^{j2\pi(M-1)f}] \qquad (8.5.25)$$

Note that at $f = f_i$, $\mathbf{s}(f_i) \equiv \mathbf{s}_i$, so that at any one of the p sinusoidal frequency components of the signal we have

$$P(f_i) = 0, \qquad i = 1, 2, \ldots, p \qquad (8.5.26)$$

Hence the reciprocal of $P(f)$ is a sharply peaked function of frequency and provides a method for estimating the frequencies of the sinusoidal components. Thus

$$\frac{1}{P(f)} = \frac{1}{\sum_{k=p+1}^{M} w_k |\mathbf{s}^H(f)\mathbf{v}_k|^2} \qquad (8.5.27)$$

Although theoretically $1/P(f)$ is infinite of $f = f_i$, in practice the estimation errors result in finite values for $1/P(f)$ at all frequencies.

The MUSIC sinusoidal frequency estimator proposed by Schmidt (1981) is a special case of (8.5.27) in which the weights $w_k = 1$ for all k. Hence

$$P_{\text{MUSIC}}(f) = \frac{1}{\sum_{k=p+1}^{M} |\mathbf{s}^H(f)\mathbf{v}_k|^2} \qquad (8.5.28)$$

The estimate of the sinusoidal frequencies are the peaks of $P_{\text{MUSIC}}(f)$. Once the sinusoidal frequencies are estimated, the power of each of the sinusoids may be obtained by solving (8.5.11).

8.5.4 ESPRIT Algorithm

ESPRIT (Estimation of Signal Parameters via Rotational Invariance Techniques) is yet another method for estimating frequencies of a sum of sinusoids by use of an eigendecomposition approach. As we will observe from the development given below, which is due to Roy et al. (1986), ESPRIT exploits an underlying rotational invariance of signal subspaces spanned by two temporally displaced data vectors.

We again consider the estimation of p complex-valued sinusoids in additive white noise. The received sequence is given by the vector

$$\begin{aligned}\mathbf{y}(n) &= [y(n), y(n+1), \ldots, y(n+M-1)]^t \\ &= \mathbf{x}(n) + \mathbf{w}(n)\end{aligned} \tag{8.5.29}$$

where $\mathbf{x}(n)$ is the signal vector and $\mathbf{w}(n)$ is the noise vector. To exploit the deterministic character of the sinusoids, we define the time-displaced vector $\mathbf{z}(n) = \mathbf{y}(n+1)$. Thus

$$\begin{aligned}\mathbf{z}(n) &= [z(n), z(n+1), \ldots, z(n+M-1)]^t \\ &= [y(n+1), y(n+2), \ldots, y(n+M)]^t\end{aligned} \tag{8.5.30}$$

With these definitions we may express the vectors $\mathbf{y}(n)$ and $\mathbf{z}(n)$ as

$$\begin{aligned}\mathbf{y}(n) &= \mathbf{S}\mathbf{a} + \mathbf{w}(n) \\ \mathbf{z}(n) &= \mathbf{S}\mathbf{\Phi}\mathbf{a} + \mathbf{w}(n)\end{aligned} \tag{8.5.31}$$

where $\mathbf{a} = [a_1, a_2, \ldots, a_p]^t$, $a_i = A_i e^{j\phi_i}$, and $\mathbf{\Phi}$ is a diagonal $p \times p$ matrix consisting of the relative phase between adjacent time samples of each of the complex sinusoids,

$$\mathbf{\Phi} = \text{diag}[e^{j2\pi f_1}, e^{j2\pi f_2}, \ldots, e^{j2\pi f_p}] \tag{8.5.32}$$

Note that the matrix $\mathbf{\Phi}$ relates the time-displaced vectors $\mathbf{y}(n)$ and $\mathbf{z}(n)$ and may be called a rotation operator. We also note that $\mathbf{\Phi}$ is unitary. The matrix $\mathbf{S}$ is the $M \times p$ Vandermonde matrix specified by the column vectors

$$\mathbf{s}_i^t = [1, e^{j2\pi f_i}, e^{j4\pi f_i}, \ldots, e^{j2\pi(M-1)f_i}], \qquad i = 1, 2, \ldots, p \tag{8.5.33}$$

Now the autocovariance matrix for the data vector $\mathbf{y}(n)$ is

$$\begin{aligned}\mathbf{\Gamma}_{yy} &= E[\mathbf{y}(n)\mathbf{y}^H(n)] \\ &= \mathbf{S}\mathbf{P}\mathbf{S}^H + \sigma_w^2\mathbf{I}\end{aligned} \tag{8.5.34}$$

where $\mathbf{P}$ is the $p \times p$ diagonal matrix consisting of the powers of the complex sinusoids,

$$\begin{aligned}\mathbf{P} &= \text{diag}[|a_1|^2, |a_2|^2, \ldots, |a_p|^2] \\ &= \text{diag}[P_1, P_2, \ldots, P_p]\end{aligned} \tag{8.5.35}$$

We observe that $\mathbf{P}$ is a diagonal matrix since complex sinusoids of different frequencies are orthogonal over the infinite interval. However, we should emphasize that the ESPRIT algorithm does not require $\mathbf{P}$ to be diagonal. Hence the algorithm is applicable to the case in which the covariance matrix is estimated from finite data records.

The cross-covariance matrix of the signal vectors $\mathbf{y}(n)$ and $\mathbf{z}(n)$ is

$$\mathbf{\Gamma}_{yz} = E[\mathbf{y}(n)\mathbf{z}^H(n)] = \mathbf{S}\mathbf{P}\mathbf{\Phi}^H\mathbf{S}^H + \Gamma_w \tag{8.5.36}$$

where

$$\mathbf{\Gamma}_w = E[\mathbf{w}(n)\mathbf{w}^H(n+1)] = \sigma_w^2 \begin{bmatrix} 0 & 0 & 0 & \cdots & 0 & 0 \\ 1 & 0 & 0 & \cdots & 0 & 0 \\ 0 & 1 & 0 & \cdots & 0 & 0 \\ \vdots & \vdots & \vdots & \vdots\vdots\vdots & \vdots & \vdots \\ 0 & 0 & 0 & & 1 & 0 \end{bmatrix} \equiv \sigma_w^2 \mathbf{Q} \qquad (8.5.37)$$

The auto and cross-covariance matrices $\mathbf{\Gamma}_{yy}$ and $\mathbf{\Gamma}_{yx}$ are given as

$$\mathbf{\Gamma}_{yy} = \begin{bmatrix} \gamma_{yy}(0) & \gamma_{yy}(1) & \cdots & \gamma_{yy}(M-1) \\ \gamma_{yy}^*(1) & \gamma_{yy}(0) & \cdots & \gamma_{yy}(M-2) \\ \vdots & \vdots & & \vdots \\ \gamma_{yy}^*(M-1) & \gamma_{yy}^*(M-2) & \cdots & \gamma_{yy}(0) \end{bmatrix} \qquad (8.5.38)$$

$$\mathbf{\Gamma}_{yz} = \begin{bmatrix} \gamma_{yy}(1) & \gamma_{yy}(2) & \cdots & \gamma_{yy}(M) \\ \gamma_{yy}(0) & \gamma_{yy}(1) & \cdots & \gamma_{yy}(M-1) \\ \vdots & \vdots & & \vdots \\ \gamma_{yy}^*(M-2) & \gamma_{yy}^*(M-3) & \cdots & \gamma_{yy}(1) \end{bmatrix} \qquad (8.5.39)$$

where $\gamma_{yy}(m) = E[y^*(n)y(n+m)]$. Note that both $\mathbf{\Gamma}_{yy}$ and $\mathbf{\Gamma}_{yz}$ are Toeplitz matrices. Based on this formulation, the problem is to determine the frequencies f_i and their power P_i from the autocorrelation sequence $\gamma_{yy}(m)$.

From the underlying model, it is clear that the matrix $\mathbf{SPS}^H$ has rank p. Consequently, $\mathbf{\Gamma}_{yy}$ given by (8.5.34) has $(M-p)$ identical eigenvalues equal to σ_w^2. Hence

$$\mathbf{\Gamma}_{yy} - \sigma_w^2\mathbf{I} = \mathbf{SPS}^H \equiv \mathbf{C}_{yy} \qquad (8.5.40)$$

From (8.5.36) we also have

$$\mathbf{\Gamma}_{yz} - \sigma_w^2\mathbf{\Gamma}_w = \mathbf{SP\Phi}^H\mathbf{S}^H \equiv \mathbf{C}_{yz} \qquad (8.5.41)$$

Now, let us consider the matrix $\mathbf{C}_{yy} - \lambda\mathbf{C}_{yz}$, which can be written as

$$\mathbf{C}_{yy} - \lambda\mathbf{C}_{yz} = \mathbf{SP}(\mathbf{I} - \lambda\mathbf{\Phi}^H)\mathbf{S}^H \qquad (8.5.42)$$

Clearly, the column space of $\mathbf{SPS}^H$ is identical to the column space of $\mathbf{SP\Phi}^H\mathbf{S}^H$. Consequently, the rank of $\mathbf{C}_{yy} - \lambda\mathbf{C}_{yz}$ is equal to p. However, we note that if $\lambda = \exp(j2\pi f_i)$, the ith row of $(\mathbf{I} - \lambda\mathbf{\Phi}^H)$ is zero, and hence the rank of $[\mathbf{I} - \mathbf{\Phi}^H \exp(j2\pi f_i)]$ is $p - 1$. But $\lambda_i = \exp(j2\pi f_i)$, $i = 1, 2, \ldots, p$, are the generalized eigenvalues of the matrix pair $(\mathbf{C}_{yy}, \mathbf{C}_{yz})$. Thus the p generalized eigenvalues $\{\lambda_i\}$ that lie on the unit circle correspond to the elements of the rotation operator $\mathbf{\Phi}$. The remaining $M - p$ generalized eigenvalues of the pair $\{\mathbf{C}_{yy}, \mathbf{C}_{yz}\}$, which correspond to the common null space of these matrices, are zero [i.e., the $(M - p)$ eigenvalues are at the origin in the complex plane].

Based on the mathematical relationships above we can formulate an algorithm (ESPRIT) for estimating the frequencies f_i. The procedure is as follows:

1. From the data, compute the autocorrelation values $r_{yy}(m)$, $m = 1, 2, \ldots, M$, and form the matrices $\mathbf{R}_{yy}$ and $\mathbf{R}_{yz}$ corresponding to estimates of $\mathbf{\Gamma}_{yy}$ and $\mathbf{\Gamma}_{yz}$.
2. Compute the eigenvalues of $\mathbf{R}_{yy}$. For $M > p$, the minimum eigenvalue is an estimate of σ_w^2.
3. Compute $\hat{\mathbf{C}}_{yy} = \mathbf{R}_{yy} - \hat{\sigma}_w^2\mathbf{I}$ and $\hat{\mathbf{C}}_{yz} = \mathbf{R}_{yz} - \hat{\sigma}_w^2\mathbf{Q}$, where $\mathbf{Q}$ is defined in (8.5.37).
4. Compute the generalized eigenvalues of the matrix pair $\{\hat{C}_{yy}, \hat{\mathbf{C}}_{yz}\}$. The p generalized eigenvalues of these matrices that lie on (or near) the unit circle determine the (estimate) elements of $\mathbf{\Phi}$ and hence the sinusoidal frequencies. The remaining $M - p$ eigenvalues will lie at (or near) the origin.

One method for determining the power in the sinusoidal components is to solve the equation in (8.5.11) with $r_{yy}(m)$ substituted for $\gamma_{yy}(m)$.

Another method is based on the computation of the generalized eigenvectors $\mathbf{v}_i$ corresponding to the generalized eigenvalues λ_i. We have

$$(\mathbf{C}_{yy} - \lambda_i\mathbf{C}_{yz})\mathbf{v}_i = \mathbf{SP}(\mathbf{I} - \lambda_i\mathbf{\Phi}^H)\mathbf{S}^H\mathbf{v}_i = \mathbf{0} \qquad (8.5.43)$$

Since the column space of $(\mathbf{C}_{yy} - \lambda_i \cdot \mathbf{C}_{yz})$ is identical to the column space spanned by the vectors $\{\mathbf{s}_j, j \neq i\}$ given by (8.5.33), it follows that the generalized eigenvector $\mathbf{v}_i$ is orthogonal to $\mathbf{s}_j$, $j \neq i$. Since $\mathbf{P}$ is diagonal, it follows from (8.5.43) that the signal powers are

$$P_i = \frac{\mathbf{v}_i^H\mathbf{C}_{yy}\mathbf{v}_i}{|\mathbf{v}_i^H\mathbf{s}_i|^2}, \qquad i = 1, 2, \ldots, p \qquad (8.5.44)$$

8.5.5 Order Selection Criteria

The eigenanalysis methods described in this section for estimating the frequencies and the powers of the sinusoids also provide information about the number of sinusoidal components. If there are p sinusoids, the eigenvalues associated with the signal subspace are $\{\lambda_i + \sigma_w^2, i = 1, 2, \ldots, p\}$, while the remaining $(M - p)$ eigenvalues are all equal to σ_w^2. Based on this eigenvalue decomposition, a test can be designed which compares the eigenvalues with a specified threshold. An alternative method also uses the eigenvector decomposition of the estimated autocorrelation matrix of the observed signal and is based on matrix perturbation analysis. This method is described in a paper by Fuchs (1988).

Another approach based on an extension and modification of the AIC criterion to the eigendecomposition method has been proposed by Wax and Kailath (1985). If the eigenvalues of the sample autocorrelation matrix are ranked so that $\lambda_1 \geq \lambda_2 \geq \cdots \geq \lambda_M$, where $M > p$, the number of sinusoids in the signal subspace is estimated by selecting the minimum value of MDL(p), given as

$$\text{MDL}(p) = -\log\left[\frac{G(p)}{A(p)}\right]^N + E(p) \tag{8.5.45}$$

where

$$G(p) = \prod_{i=p+1}^{M} \lambda_i, \qquad p = 0, 1, \ldots, M-1$$

$$A(p) = \left[\frac{1}{M-p}\sum_{i=p+1}^{M} \lambda_i\right]^{M-p} \tag{8.5.46}$$

$$E(p) = \tfrac{1}{2}p(2M-p)\log N$$

N: number of samples used to estimate the M autocorrelation lags

Some results on the quality of this order selection criterion are given in the paper by Wax and Kailath (1985). The MDL criterion is guaranteed to be consistent.

8.5.6 Experimental Results

In this section we illustrate via an example the resolution characteristics of the eigenanalysis-based spectral estimation algorithms and compare their performance with the model-based methods and nonparametric methods. The signal sequence is

$$x(n) = \sum_{i=1}^{4} A_i e^{j(2\pi f_i n + \phi_i)} + w(n)$$

where $A_i = 1$, $i = 1, 2, 3, 4$, ϕ_i are statistically independent random variables uniformly distributed on $(0, 2\pi)$, $w(n)$ is a zero-mean, white noise sequence with variance σ_w^2, and the frequencies are $f_1 = -0.222$, $f_2 = -0.166$, $f_3 = 0.122$, and $f_4 = 0.100$. The sequence $x(n)$, $0 \leq n \leq 1023$, is used to estimate the number of frequency components and the corresponding values of their frequencies for $\sigma_w^2 = 0.1, 0.5, 1.0$, and $M = 12$ (length of the estimated autocorrelation).

Figures 8.19, 8.20, 8.21, and 8.22 illustrate the estimated power spectra of the signal using the Blackman–Tukey method, the minimum variance method of Capon, the AR Yule–Walker method, and the MUSIC algorithm, respectively. The results from the ESPRIT algorithm are given in Table 8.2. From these results it is apparent that (1) the Blackman–Tukey method does not provide sufficient resolution to estimate the sinusoids from the data; (2) the minimum variance method of Capon resolves only the frequencies f_1 and f_2 but not f_3 and f_4; (3) the AR method resolves all frequencies for $\sigma_w^2 = 0.1$ and $\sigma_w^2 = 0.5$; and (4) the MUSIC and ESPRIT algorithms not

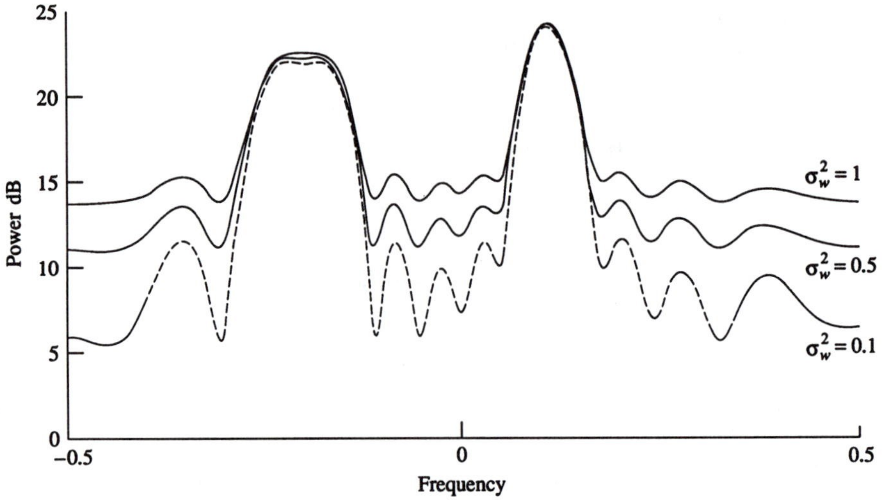

FIGURE 8.19 Power spectrum estimates from Blackman-Tukey method.

only recover all four sinusoids, but their performance for different values of σ_w^2 is essentially indistinguishable. We further observe that the resolution properties of the minimum variance method and the AR method are a function of the noise variance. These results clearly demonstrate the power of the eigenanalysis-based algorithms in resolving sinusoids in additive noise.

In conclusion, we should emphasize that the high-resolution, eigenanalysis-based spectral estimation methods described in this section, namely

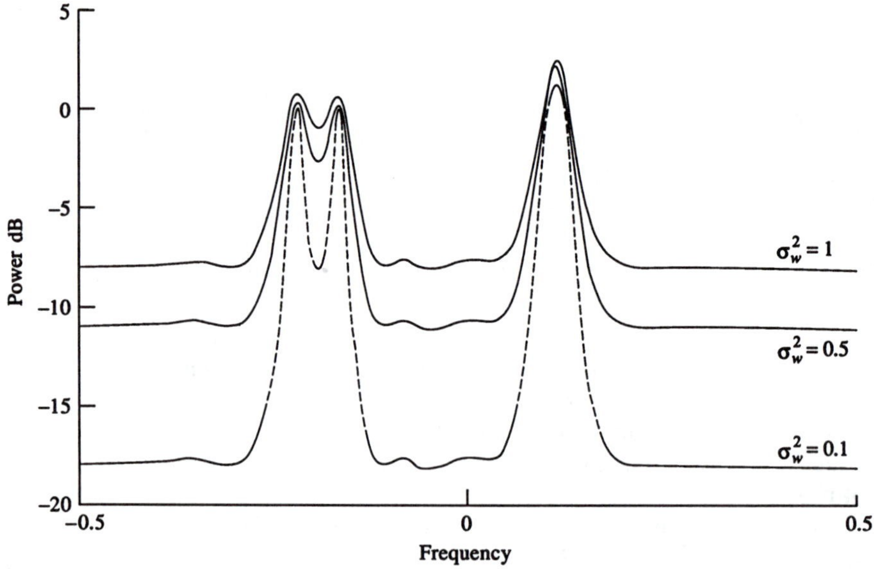

FIGURE 8.20 Power spectrum estimates from minimum variance method.

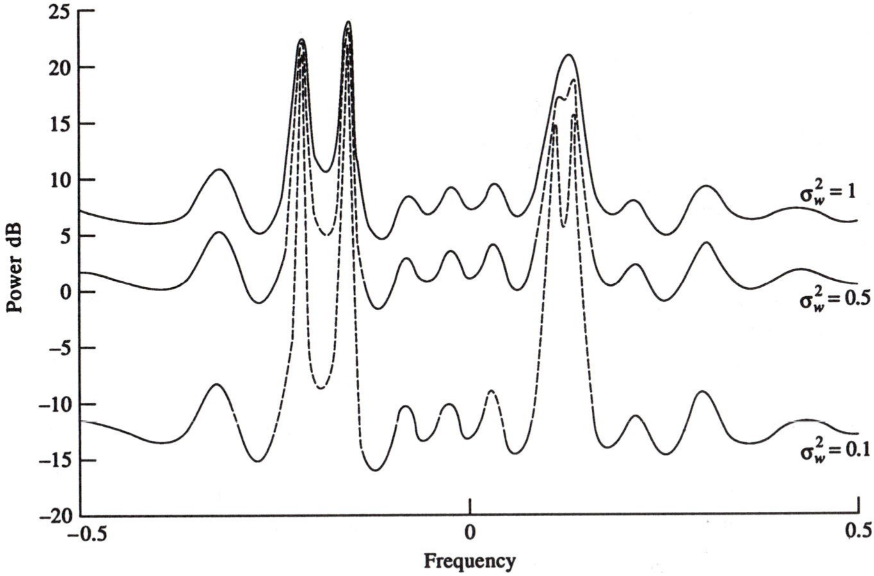

FIGURE 8.21 Power spectrum estimates from Yule-Walker AR method.

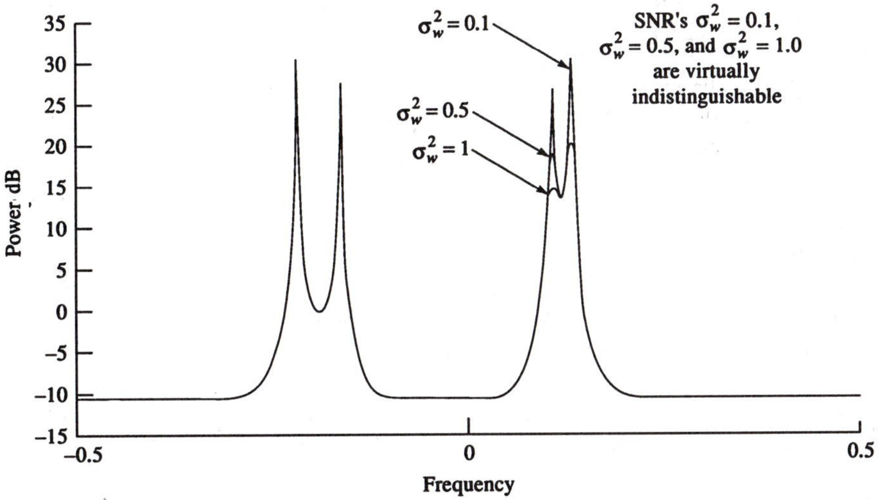

FIGURE 8.22 Power spectrum estimates from MUSIC algorithm.

TABLE 8.2 ESPRIT Algorithm

σ_w^2	$\hat{f}_1$	$\hat{f}_2$	$\hat{f}_3$	$\hat{f}_4$
0.1	−0.2227	−0.1668	−0.1224	−0.10071
0.5	−0.2219	−0.167	−0.121	0.0988
1.0	−0.222	−0.167	0.1199	0.1013
True values	−0.222	−0.166	0.122	0.100

MUSIC and ESPRIT, are not only applicable to sinusoidal signals, but apply more generally to the estimation of narrowband signals.

8.6 SUMMARY AND REFERENCES

Power spectrum estimation is one of the most important areas of research and applications in digital signal processing. In this chapter we have described the most important power spectrum estimation techniques and algorithms that have been developed over the past century, beginning with the nonparametric or classical methods based on the periodogram and concluding with the more modern parametric methods based on AR, MA, and ARMA linear models. Our treatment was limited in scope to single-time-series spectrum estimation methods, based on second moments (autocorrelation) of the statistical data.

The parametric and nonparametric methods that we have described have been extended to multichannel and multidimensional spectrum estimation. The tutorial paper by McClellan (1982) treats the multidimensional spectrum estimation problem, while the paper by Johnson (1982) treats the multichannel spectrum estimation problem. Additional spectrum estimation methods have been developed for use with higher-order cumulants that involve the bispectrum and the trispectrum. This topic is treated in Chapter 9.

As evidenced from our previous discussion, power spectrum estimation is an area that has attracted many researchers, and as a result, thousands of papers on this subject have been published in the technical literature. Much of this work has been concerned with new algorithms and techniques, and modifications of existing techniques. Other work has been concerned with obtaining an understanding of the capabilities and limitations of the various power spectrum methods. In this context the statistical properties and limitations of the classical nonparametric methods have been thoroughly analyzed and are well understood. The parametric methods have also been investigated by many researchers, but the analysis of their performance is difficult and, consequently, fewer results are available. Some of the papers that have addressed the problem of performance characteristics of parametric methods are those of Kromer (1969), Lacoss (1971), Berk (1974), Baggeroer (1976), Sakai (1979), Swingler (1980), and Lang and McClellan (1980).

In addition to the references already given in this chapter on the various methods for spectrum estimation and their performance, we should include for reference some of the tutorial and survey papers. In particular, we cite the tutorial paper by Kay and Marple (1981), which includes about 280 references, the paper by Brillinger (1974), and the Special Issue on Spectral Estimation of the *IEEE Proceedings*, September 1982. Another indication of the widespread interest in the subject of spectrum estimation and analysis is the recent publication of textbooks by Gardner (1987), Kay (1987), and Marple (1987) and the IEEE books edited by Childers (1978) and Kesler (1986).

Many computer programs as well as software packages that implement the various spectrum estimation methods described in this chapter are available. One software package is available through IEEE (*Programs for Digital Signal Processing*, IEEE Press, 1979); others are available commercially.

PROBLEMS

8.1 **(a)** By expanding (8.1.23), taking the expected value, and finally, taking the limit as $T_0 \to \infty$, show that the right-hand side converges to $\Gamma_{xx}(f)$.

(b) Prove that

$$\sum_{m=-N}^{N} r_{xx}(m)e^{-j2\pi fm} = \frac{1}{N}\left|\sum_{n=0}^{N-1} x(n)e^{-j2\pi fn}\right|^2$$

8.2 For zero-mean, jointly Gaussian random variables, X_1, X_2, X_3, X_4, it is well known [see Papoulis (1984)] that

$$E(X_1X_2X_3X_4) = E(X_1X_2)E(X_3X_4) + E(X_1X_3)E(X_2X_4) + E(X_1X_4)E(X_2X_3)$$

Use this result to derive the mean-square value of $r_{xx}(m)$, given by (8.1.27) and the variance, which is

$$\text{var}[r_{xx}(m)] = E[|r_{xx}(m)|^2] - |E[r_{xx}(m)]|^2$$

8.3 By use of the expression for the fourth joint moment for Gaussian random variables, show that

(a) $$E[P_{xx}(f_1)P_{xx}(f_2)] = \sigma_x^4\left\{1 + \left[\frac{\sin \pi(f_1 + f_2)N}{N \sin \pi(f_1 + f_2)}\right]^2 + \left[\frac{\sin \pi(f_1 - f_2)N}{N \sin \pi(f_1 - f_2}\right]^2\right\}$$

(b) $$\text{cov}[\mathbf{P}_{xx}(f_1)\mathbf{P}_{xx}(f_2)] = \sigma_x^4\left\{\left[\frac{\sin \pi(f_1 + f_2)N}{N \sin \pi(f_1 + f_2)}\right]^2 + \left[\frac{\sin \pi(f_1 - f_2)N}{N \sin \pi(f_1 - f_2)}\right]^2\right\}$$

(c) $$\text{var}[P_{xx}(f)] = \sigma_x^4\left\{1 + \left(\frac{\sin 2\pi fN}{N \sin 2\pi f}\right)^2\right\}$$

under the condition that the sequence $x(n)$ is a zero-mean white Gaussian noise sequence with variance σ_x^2.

8.4 Generalize the results in Problem 8.3 to a zero-mean Gaussian noise process with power density spectrum $\Gamma_{xx}(f)$. Then derive the variance of the periodogram $P_{xx}(f)$, as given by (8.1.38). (*Hint*: Assume that the colored Gaussian noise process is the output of a linear system excited by white Gaussian noise.)

8.5 Show that the periodogram values at frequencies $f_k = k/L$, $k = 0, 1, \ldots, L - 1$, given by (8.1.41) can be computed by passing the sequence through a bank of L IIR filters, where each filter has an impulse response

$$h_k(n) = e^{-j2\pi nk/N}u(n)$$

and then computing the magnitude-squared value of the filter outputs at $n = N$. Note that each filter has a pole on the unit circle at the frequency f_k.

8.6 Prove that the normalization factor given by (8.2.12) ensures that (8.2.19) is satisfied.

8.7 Let us consider the use of the DFT (computed via the FFT algorithm) to compute the autocorrelation of the complex-valued sequence $x(n)$,

$$r_{xx}(m) = \frac{1}{N} \sum_{n=0}^{N-|m|-1} x^*(n)x(n+m), \; m \geq 0$$

Suppose that the size M of the FFT is much smaller than that of the data length N. Specifically, assume that $N = KM$.

(a) Determine the steps needed to section $x(n)$ and compute $r_{xx}(m)$ for $-(M/2) + 1 \leq m \leq (M/2) - 1$, by using $4K$ M-point DFTs and one M-point IDFT.

(b) Now consider the three sequences $x_1(n)$, $x_2(n)$, and $x_3(n)$, each of duration M. Let the sequences $x_1(n)$ and $x_2(n)$ have arbitrary values in the range $0 \leq n \leq (M/2) - 1$, but are zero for $(M/2) \leq n \leq M - 1$. The sequence $x_3(n)$ is defined as

$$x_3(n) = \begin{cases} x_1(n) & 0 \leq \dfrac{M}{2} - 1 \\ x_2\left(n - \dfrac{M}{2}\right), & \dfrac{M}{2} \leq n \leq M - 1 \end{cases}$$

Determine a simple relationship among the M-point DFTs $X_1(k)$, $X_2(k)$, and $X_3(k)$.

(c) By using the result in part (b), show how the computation of the DFTs in part (a) can be reduced in number from $4K$ to $2K$.

8.8 The Bartlett method is used to estimate the power spectrum of a signal $x(n)$. We know that the power spectrum consists of a single peak with a 3-dB bandwidth of 0.01 cycle per sample, but we do not know the location of the peak.

(a) Assuming that N is large, determine the value of $M = N/K$ so that the spectral window is narrower than the peak.

(b) Explain why it is not advantageous to increase M beyond the value obtained in part (a).

8.9 Suppose that we have $N = 1000$ samples from a sample sequence of a random process.

(a) Determine the frequency resolution of the Bartlett, Welch (50% overlap), and Blackman–Tukey methods for a quality factor $Q = 10$.

(b) Determine the record lengths (M) for the Bartlett, Welch (50% overlap, and Blackman–Tukey methods.

8.10 Consider the problem of continuously estimating the power spectrum from a sequence $x(n)$ based on averaging periodograms with exponential weighting into the past. Thus with $P_{xx}^{(0)}(f) = 0$, we have

$$P_{xx}^{(m)}(f) = wP_{xx}^{(m-1)}(f) + \frac{1-w}{M}\left|\sum_{n=0}^{M-1} x_m(n)e^{-j2\pi fn}\right|^2$$

where successive periodograms are assumed to be uncorrelated and w is the (exponential) weighting factor.

(a) Determine the mean and variance of $P_{xx}^{(m)}(f)$ for a Gaussian random process.

(b) Repeat the analysis of part (a) for the case in which the modified periodogram defined by Welch is used in the averaging, with no overlap.

8.11 The periodogram in the Bartlett method may be expressed as

$$P_{xx}^{(i)}(f) = \sum_{m=-(M-1)}^{M-1}\left(1 - \frac{|m|}{M}\right) r_{xx}^{(i)}(m)e^{-j2\pi fm}$$

where $r_{xx}^{(i)}(m)$ is the estimated autocorrelation sequence obtained from the ith block of data. Show that $P_{xx}^{(i)}(f)$ may be expressed as

$$P_{xx}^{(i)}(f) = E^{*t}(f)R_{xx}^{(i)}E(f)$$

where

$$\mathbf{E}(f) = [1 \quad e^{j2\pi f} \quad e^{j4\pi f} \quad \cdots \quad e^{j2\pi(M-1)f}]^t$$

and therefore,

$$P_{xx}^{B}(f) = \frac{1}{K}\sum_{k=1}^{K} \mathbf{E}^{*t}(f)\mathbf{R}_{xx}^{(k)}E(f)$$

8.12 Derive the set of linear equations in (4.2.16) by substituting $a_m(k) = a_{mr}(k) + ja_{mi}(k)$ in (4.2.15) and differentiating the resulting equation with respect to $a_{mr}(k)$ and $a_{mi}(k)$, that is,

$$\frac{\partial \mathscr{E}_m^f}{\partial a_{mr}(k)} = 0 \qquad \frac{\partial \mathscr{E}_m^f}{\partial a_{mi}(k)} = 0$$

8.13 The set of linear equations in (4.2.16) may also be derived by invoking the orthogonality principle in mean-square estimation, which asserts that the mean-square error $\mathscr{E}^f_m$ is minimized by making the error $f_m(n)$ orthogonal to each of the data samples $x(n-l)$, $l = 1, 2, \ldots, m$ that are used to form the estimate.

$$E[f_m(n)x^*(n-l)] = 0 \qquad l = 1, 2, \ldots, m$$

(a) Demonstrate that (4.2.16) is easily derived by invoking the orthogonality principle.
(b) Derive the expression for the minimum mean-square error in (4.2.17) by substituting the optimum prediction coefficients in (4.2.15) and combining terms.
(c) Derive (4.2.17) by noting that

$$E^f_m = E[f_m(n)\hat{x}^*(n)]$$

8.14 Minimize (4.2.35) with respect to the prediction coefficients using the form of $g_m(n)$ given by (4.2.34). Also, prove (4.2.36).

8.15 Derive the recursive order-update equation given in (8.3.19).

8.16 Determine the mean and the autocorrelation of the sequence $x(n)$, which is the output of a ARMA(1, 1) process described by the difference equation

$$x(n) = \tfrac{1}{2}x(n-1) + w(n) - w(n-1)$$

where $w(n)$ is a white noise process with variance σ_w^2.

8.17 Determine the mean and the autocorrelation of the sequence $x(n)$ generated by the MA(2) process described by the difference equation

$$x(n) = w(n) - 2w(n-1) + w(n-2)$$

where $w(n)$ is a white noise process with variance σ_w^2.

8.18 An MA(2) process has the autocorrelation sequence

$$\gamma_{xx}(m) = \begin{cases} 6\sigma_w^2, & m = 0 \\ -4\sigma_w^2, & m = \pm 1 \\ -2\sigma_w^2, & m = \pm 2 \\ 0, & \text{otherwise} \end{cases}$$

(a) Determine the coefficients of the MA(2) process that have the foregoing autocorrelation.
(b) Is the solution unique? If not, give all the possible solutions.

8.19 An MA(2) process has the autocorrelation sequence

$$\gamma_{xx}(m) = \begin{cases} \sigma_w^2, & m = 0 \\ -\dfrac{35}{62}\sigma_w^2, & m = \pm 1 \\ \dfrac{6}{62}\sigma_w^2, & m = \pm 2 \end{cases}$$

(a) Determine the coefficients of the minimum-phase system for the MA(2) process.
(b) Determine the coefficients of the maximum-phase system for the MA(2) process.
(c) Determine the coefficients of the mixed-phase system for the MA(2) process.

8.20 Consider the linear system described by the difference equation

$$y(n) = 0.8y(n-1) + x(n) + x(n-1)$$

where $x(n)$ is a wide-sense stationary random process with zero mean and autocorrelation

$$\gamma_{xx}(m) = (\tfrac{1}{2})^{|m|}$$

(a) Determine the power density spectrum of the output $y(n)$.
(b) Determine the autocorrelation $\gamma_{yy}(m)$ of the output.
(c) Determine the variance σ_y^2 of the output.

8.21 We note that an AR(p) stationary random process satisfies the equation

$$\gamma_{xx}(m) + \sum_{k=1}^{p} a_p(k)\gamma_{xx}(m-k) = \begin{cases} \sigma_w^2, & m = 0 \\ 0, & 1 \le m \le p \end{cases}$$

where $a_p(k)$ are the prediction coefficients of the linear predictor of order p and σ_w^2 is the minimum mean-square prediction error. If the $(p+1) \times (p+1)$ autocorrelation matrix $\mathbf{\Gamma}_{xx}$ is positive definite, prove that:
(a) The reflection coefficients $|K_m| < 1$ for $1 \le m \le p$.
(b) The polynomial

$$A_p(z) = 1 + \sum_{k=1}^{p} a_p(k)z^{-k}$$

has all its roots inside the unit circle (i.e., it is minimum phase).

8.22 Consider the AR(3) process generated by the equation

$$x(n) = \tfrac{14}{24}x(n-1) + \tfrac{9}{24}x(n-2) - \tfrac{1}{24}x(n-3) + w(n)$$

where $w(n)$ is a stationary white noise process with variance σ_w^2.
(a) Determine the coefficients of the optimum $p = 3$ linear predictor.
(b) Determine the autocorrelation sequence $\gamma_{xx}(m)$, $0 \le m \le 5$.
(c) Determine the reflection coefficients corresponding to the $p = 3$ linear predictor.

8.23 An AR(2) process is described by the difference equation

$$x(n) = 0.81x(n-2) + w(n)$$

where $w(n)$ is a white noise process with variance σ_w^2,
(a) Determine the parameters of the MA(2), MA(4), and MA(8) models that provide a minimum mean-square error fit to the data $x(n)$.

(b) Plot the true spectrum and those of the MA(q), $q = 2, 4, 8$ spectra and compare the results. Comment on how well the MA(q) models approximate the AR(2) process.

8.24 An MA(2) process is described by the difference equation

$$x(n) = w(n) + 0.81w(n - 2)$$

where $w(n)$ is a white noise process with variance σ_w^2.

(a) Determine the parameters of the AR(2), AR(4), and AR(8) models that provide a minimum mean-square error fit to the data $x(n)$.

(b) Plot the true spectra m and those of the AR(p), $p = 2, 4, 8$, and compare the results. Comment on how well the AR(p) models approximate the MA(2) process.

8.25 The z-transform of the autocorrelation $\gamma_{xx}(m)$ of an ARMA(1, 1) process is

$$\Gamma_{xx}(z) = \sigma_w^2 H(z)H(z^{-1})$$

$$\Gamma_{xx}(z) = \frac{4\sigma_w^2}{9} \frac{5 - 2z - 2z^{-1}}{10 - 3z^{-1} - 3z}$$

(a) Determine the minimum-phase system function $H(z)$.

(b) Determine the system function $H(z)$ for a mixed-phase stable system.

8.26 Consider a FIR filter with coefficient vector

$$[1 \quad -2r\cos\theta \quad r^2]$$

(a) Determine the reflection coefficients for the corresponding FIR lattice filter.

(b) Determine the values of the reflection coefficients in the limit as $r \to 1$.

8.27 An AR(3) process is characterized by the prediction coefficients

$$a_3(1) = -1.25, \qquad a_3(2) = 1.3125, \qquad a_3(3) = -1$$

(a) Determine $\gamma_{xx}(m)$ for $0 \le m \le 3$.

(b) Determine the reflection coefficients.

(c) Determine the mean-square prediction error.

8.28 The autocorrelation sequence for a random process is

$$\gamma_{xx}(m) = \begin{cases} 1, & m = 0 \\ -0.5, & m = \pm 1 \\ 0.625, & m = \pm 2 \\ -0.6875, & m = \pm 3 \\ 0, & \text{otherwise} \end{cases}$$

Determine the system functions $A_m(z)$ for the prediction-error filters for $m = 1, 2, 3$, the reflection coefficients $\{K_m\}$, and the corresponding mean-square prediction errors.

8.29 **(a)** Determine the power spectra for the random processes generated by the following difference equations.

(1) $x(n) = -0.81x(n-2) + w(n) - w(n-1)$
(2) $x(n) = w(n) - w(n-2)$
(3) $x(n) = -0.81x(n-2) + w(n)$

where $w(n)$ is a white noise process with variance σ_w^2.

(b) Sketch the spectra for the processes given in part (a).
(c) Determine the autocorrelation $\gamma_{xx}(m)$ for the processes in (2) and (3).

8.30 The autocorrelation sequence for an AR process $x(n)$ is

$$\gamma_{xx}(m) = (\tfrac{1}{4})^{|m|}$$

(a) Determine the difference equation for $x(n)$.
(b) Is your answer unique? If not, give any other possible solutions.

8.31 Repeat Problem 8.28 for an AR process with autocorrelation

$$\gamma_{xx}(m) = a^{|m|} \cos \frac{\pi m}{2}$$

where $0 < a < 1$.

8.32 The Bartlett method is used to estimate the power spectrum of a signal from a sequence $x(n)$ consisting of $N = 2400$ samples.

(a) Determine the smallest length M of each segment in the Bartlett method that yields a frequency resolution of $\Delta f = 0.01$.
(b) Repeat part (a) for $\Delta f = 0.02$.
(c) Determine the quality factors Q_B for parts (a) and (b).

8.33 Prove that a FIR filter with system function

$$A_p(z) = 1 + \sum_{k=1}^{p} a_p(k) z^{-k}$$

and reflection coefficients $|K_k| < 1$ for $1 \le k \le p - 1$ and $|K_p| > 1$ is maximum phase [all the roots of $A_p(z)$ lie outside the unit circle].

8.34 A random process $x(n)$ is characterized by the power density spectrum

$$\Gamma_{xx}(f) = \sigma_w^2 \frac{|e^{j2\pi f} - 0.9|^2}{|e^{j2\pi f} - j0.9|^2 \, |e^{j2\pi f} + j0.9|^2}$$

where σ_w^2 is a constant (scale factor).

(a) If we view $\Gamma_{xx}(f)$ as the power spectrum at the output of a linear pole-zero system $H(z)$ driven by white noise, determine $H(z)$.
(b) Determine the system function of a stable system that produces a white noise output when excited by $x(n)$. This is called a *noise-whitening filter*.

8.35 The N-point DFT of a random sequence $x(n)$ is

$$X(k) = \sum_{n=0}^{N-1} x(n)e^{-j2\pi nk/N}$$

Assume that $E[x(n)] = 0$ and $E[x(n)x(n + m)] = \sigma_w^2\,\delta(m)$ [i.e., $x(n)$ is a white noise process].

(a) Determine the variance of $X(k)$.

(b) Determine the autocorrelation of $X(k)$.

8.36 A useful relationship is obtained by representing an ARMA(p,q) process as a cascade of a MA(q) followed by an AR(p) model. The input–output equation for the MA(q) model is

$$v(n) = \sum_{k=0}^{q} b_k w(n - k)$$

where $w(n)$ is a white noise process. The input–output equation for the AR(p) model is

$$x(n) + \sum_{k=1}^{p} a_k x(n - k) = v(n)$$

By computing the autocorrelation of $v(n)$, show that

$$\gamma_{vv}(m) = \sigma_w^2 \sum_{k=0}^{q-m} b_k^* b_{k+m} = \sigma_w^2 d_m$$

and hence the power spectrum for the MA(q) process is

$$\Gamma_{vv}(f) = \sigma_w^2 \sum_{m=-q}^{q} d_m e^{-j2\pi fm}$$

8.37 Determine the autocorrelation $\gamma_{xx}(m)$ of the random sequence

$$x(n) = A\cos(\omega_1 n + \phi)$$

where the amplitude A and the frequency ω_1 are (known) constants and ϕ is a uniformly distributed random phase over the interval $(0, 2\pi)$.

8.38 Suppose that the AR(2) process in Problem 8.23 is corrupted by an additive white noise process $v(n)$ with variance σ_v^2. Thus we have

$$y(n) = x(n) + v(n)$$

(a) Determine the difference equation for $y(n)$ and thus demonstrate that $y(n)$ is an ARMA(2, 2) process. Determine the coefficients of the ARMA process.

(b) Generalize the result in part (a) to an AR(p) process

$$x(n) = -\sum_{k=1}^{p} a_k x(n-k) + w(n)$$

and

$$y(n) = x(n) + v(n)$$

8.39 **(a)** Determine the autocorrelation of the random sequence

$$x(n) = \sum_{k=1}^{K} A_k \cos(\omega_k n + \phi_k) + w(n)$$

where the A_k are constant amplitudes, ω_k are constant frequencies, and ϕ_k are mutually statistically independent and uniformly distributed random phases. The noise sequence $w(n)$ is white with variance σ_w^2.

(b) Determine the power density spectrum of $x(n)$.

8.40 The harmonic decomposition problem considered by Pisarenko may be expressed as the solution to the equation

$$\mathbf{a}^{*t}\mathbf{\Gamma}_{yy}\mathbf{a} = \sigma_w^2\mathbf{a}^{*t}\mathbf{a}$$

The solution for $\mathbf{a}$ may be obtained by minimizing the quadratic form $\mathbf{a}^{*t}\mathbf{\Gamma}_{yy}\mathbf{a}$ subject to the constraint that $\mathbf{a}^{*t}\mathbf{a} = 1$. The constraint can be incorporated into the performance index by means of a Lagrange multiplier. Thus the performance index becomes

$$\mathscr{E} = \mathbf{a}^{*t}\mathbf{\Gamma}_{yy}\mathbf{a} + \lambda(1 - \mathbf{a}^{*t}\mathbf{a})$$

By minimizing $\mathscr{E}$ with respect to $\mathbf{a}$ show that this formulation is equivalent to the Pisarenko eigenvalue problem given in (8.5.9) with the Lagrange multiplier playing the role of the eigenvalue. Thus show that the minimum of $\mathscr{E}$ is the minimum eigenvalue σ_w^2.

8.41 The autocorrelation of a sequence consisting of a sinusoid with random phase in noise is

$$\gamma_{xx}(m) = P\cos 2\pi f_1 m + \sigma_w^2\,\delta(m)$$

where f_1 is the frequency of the sinusoidal, P its power, and σ_w^2 the variance of the noise. Suppose that we attempt to fit an AR(2) model to the data.

(a) Determine the optimum coefficients of the AR(2) model as a function of σ_w^2 and f_1.

(b) Determine the reflection coefficients K_1 and K_2 corresponding to the AR(2) model parameters.

(c) Determine the limiting values of the AR(2) parameters and (K_1, K_2) as $\sigma_w^2 \to 0$.

8.42 This problem involves the use of cross-correlation to detect a signal in noise and estimate the time delay in the signal. A signal $x(n)$ consists of a pulsed sinusoid corrupted by a stationary zero-mean white noise sequence. That is,

$$x(n) = y(n - n_0) + w(n), \qquad 0 \le n \le N - 1$$

where $w(n)$ is the noise with variance σ_w^2 and the signal is

$$y(n) = \begin{cases} A \cos \omega_0 n, & 0 \le n \le M - 1 \\ 0, & \text{otherwise} \end{cases}$$

The frequency ω_0 is known, but the delay n_0, which is a positive integer, is unknown, and is to be determined by cross-correlating $x(n)$ with $y(n)$. Assume that $N > M + n_0$. Let

$$r_{xy}(m) = \sum_{n=0}^{N-1} y(n - m)x(n)$$

denote the cross-correlation sequence between $x(n)$ and $y(n)$. In the absence of noise this function exhibits a peak at delay $m = n_0$. Thus n_0 is determined with no error. The presence of noise can lead to errors in determining the unknown delay.

(a) For $m = n_0$, determine $E[r_{xy}(n_0)]$. Also, determine the variance, $\text{var}[r_{xy}(n_0)]$, due to the presence of the noise. In both calculations, assume that the double-frequency term averages to zero. That is, $M \gg 2\pi/\omega_0$.

(b) Determine the signal-to-noise ratio, defined as

$$\text{SNR} = \frac{\{E[r_{xy}(n_0)]\}^2}{\text{var}[r_{xy}(n)_0)]}$$

(c) What is the effect of the pulse duration M on the SNR?

COMPUTER EXPERIMENTS

8.43 Generate 100 samples of a zero-mean white noise sequence $w(n)$ with variance $\sigma_w^2 = \frac{1}{12}$, by using a uniform random number generator.

(a) Compute the autocorrelation of $w(n)$ for $0 \le m \le 15$.

(b) Compute the periodogram estimate $P_{ww}(f)$ and plot it.

(c) Generate 10 different realizations of $w(n)$ and compute the corresponding sample autocorrelation sequences $r_k(m)$, $1 \le k \le 10$ and $0 \le m \le 15$.

(d) Compute and plot the average periodogram for part (c):

$$r_{\text{av}}(m) = \frac{1}{10} \sum_{k=1}^{10} r_k(m)$$

(e) Comment on the results in parts (a) through (d).

8.44 A random signal is generated by passing zero-mean white Gaussian noise with unit variance through a filter with system function

$$H(z) = \frac{1}{(1 + az^{-1} + 0.99z^{-2})(1 - az^{-1} + 0.98z^{-2})}$$

(a) Sketch a typical plot of the theoretical power spectrum $\Gamma_{xx}(f)$ for a small value of the parameter a (i.e., $0 < a < 0.1$). Pay careful attention to the value of the two spectral peaks and the value of $P_{xx}(\omega)$ for $\omega = \pi/2$.

(b) Let $a = 0.1$. Determine the section length M required to resolve the spectral peaks of $\Gamma_{xx}(f)$ when using Bartlett's method.

(c) Consider the Blackman–Tukey method of smoothing the periodogram. How many lags of the correlation estimate must be used to obtain resolution comparable to that of the Bartlett estimate considered in part (b)? How many data must be used if the variance of the estimate is to be comparable to that of a four-section Bartlett estimate?

CHAPTER 9

SIGNAL ANALYSIS WITH HIGHER-ORDER SPECTRA

This chapter is concerned with the definitions, properties, estimation methods, and applications of higher-order statistics and their associated Fourier transforms, known as *higher-order spectra*. Particular cases of higher-order spectra are the third-order spectrum, also called the bispectrum, and the trispectrum (fourth-order spectrum). We note that the power spectrum is a member of the class of higher-order spectra; it is a second-order spectrum. In the past 20 years we have witnessed an expansion of new power spectrum estimation techniques which have been applied to the design of advanced communications, sonar, radar, speech, biomedical, geophysical, and imaging systems.

9.1 THE USE OF HIGHER-ORDER SPECTRA IN SIGNAL PROCESSING

The information contained in the power spectrum is that which is present in the second-order statistics of a signal (i.e., the autocorrelation). Consequently, the power spectrum is sufficient for the complete statistical description of a Gaussian process with a known mean. Phase relationships among the various frequencies of the signal are suppressed in the autocorrelation domain because the signal under consideration is treated as a superposition of statistically uncorrelated harmonic components. However, there are practical applications in which one has to look beyond the second-order statistics of the process and extract signal phase information as well as information due to deviations from Gaussianity. Higher-order spectra, such as the bispectrum and the trispectrum, contain such information.

In general, there are three motivations behind the use of higher-order spectra in signal processing.

1. To suppress Gaussian noise of unknown spectral characteristics in detection, parameter estimation, and signal reconstruction problems

(the bispectrum can also suppress non-Gaussian noise having a symmetric probability density function).

2. To reconstruct the phase and magnitude response of signals or systems.
3. To identify a nonlinear system or to detect and characterize nonlinearities in time series.

The first motivation is based on the property that for Gaussian signals only, all higher-order spectra of order greater than two are identically zero. Hence in those signal-processing applications where the observed waveform consists of a non-Gaussian signal in additive Gaussian noise, there are certain advantages in detecting and/or estimating signal parameters in higher-order spectrum domains of the observed data. In particular, higher-order spectra may become high signal-to-noise ratio (SNR) domains in which one can perform detection, parameter estimation, or even entire signal reconstruction.

The second motivation is based on the fact that higher-order spectra preserve the true phase character of signals. For modeling time-series data in signal-processing problems, second-order statistics are used almost exclusively because they are usually based on least-squares optimization criteria. However, the autocorrelation domain suppresses phase information. An accurate phase reconstruction in the autocorrelation (or power spectrum) domain can be achieved only if the signal is minimum phase. On the other hand, non-minimum-phase signal reconstruction or system identification can be carried out in higher-order spectrum domains due to the ability of polyspectra to preserve both the correct magnitude and non-minimum-phase information.

Finally, higher-order spectra are useful when we try to identify the nonlinearity of a system operating under a random input. General relations are not available for arbitrary stationary random data passing through arbitrary nonlinear systems. As such, each type of nonlinearity has to be investigated as a special case. Higher-order spectra play an important role in detecting and characterizing the type of nonlinearity in a system from its output data.

Higher-order spectra have been applied to oceanography, geophysics, sonar, communications, biomedicine, speech processing, radio astronomy, image processing, fluid mechanics, economic time series, plasma physics, sunspot data, and a variety of other areas. Procedures have been developed based on cumulants for deconvolution and signal detection; for identification of nonlinear, non-minimum-phase, and spike-array processes; for parameter estimation, detection of quadratic phase coupling, and detection of aliasing in discrete-time signals. A useful bibliography on the subject that covers the period 1950–1980 was provided by Tryon (1980). Tutorial treatments of the subject are given in the papers by Nikias and Raghuveer (1987) and Mendel (1988, 1991). The statistics book by Rosenblatt (1985) is also a good reference.

9.2 DEFINITION AND PROPERTIES OF HIGHER-ORDER SPECTRA

In this section we first define moments, cumulants, and higher-order spectra of stationary random signals and then discuss their properties from a signal processing perspective.

9.2.1 Moments and Cumulants of Random Signals

Higher-order spectra of stationary random signals are defined in terms of cumulants. As such, they are also called *cumulant spectra*. Given a set of n real random variables $x_1, x_2, \ldots, x_n$, their joint cumulants of order $r = k_1 + k_2 + \cdots + k_n$ are defined as

$$c_{k_1 \cdots k_n} \equiv (-j)^r \frac{\partial^r \ln \Phi(\omega_1, \omega_2, \ldots, \omega_n)}{\partial \omega_1^{k_1} \partial \omega_2^{k_2} \cdots \partial \omega_n^{k_n}} \Bigg|_{\omega_1 = \omega_2 = \cdots = \omega_n = 0} \tag{9.2.1}$$

where

$$\Phi(\omega_1, \omega_2, \ldots, \omega_n) = E\{\exp[j(\omega_1 x_1 + \cdots + \omega_n x_n)]\} \tag{9.2.2}$$

is their joint characteristic function. The joint moments of order r of the same set of random variables are given by

$$\begin{aligned} m_{k_1 \cdots k_n} &\equiv E\,[x_1^{k_1} x_2^{k_2} \cdots x_n^{k_n}] \\ &= (-j)^r \frac{\partial^r \Phi(\omega_1, \omega_2, \ldots, \omega_n)}{\partial \omega_1^{k_1} \partial \omega_2^{k_2} \cdots \partial \omega_n^{k_n}} \Bigg|_{\omega_1 = \cdots = \omega_n = 0} \end{aligned} \tag{9.2.3}$$

Hence the joint cumulants can be expressed in terms of the joint moments of the set of random variables. For example, the first four moments of the random variable x_1 are

$$\begin{aligned} m_1 &= E[x_1], \qquad & m_2 &= E[x_1^2] \\ m_3 &= E[x_1^3], \qquad & m_4 &= E[x_1^4] \end{aligned} \tag{9.2.4}$$

and are related to its cumulants as follows:

$$\begin{aligned} c_1 &= m_1 \\ c_2 &= m_2 - m_1^2 \\ c_3 &= m_3 - 3m_2 m_1 + 2m_1^3 \\ c_4 &= m_4 - 4m_3 m_1 - 3m_2^2 + 12 m_2 m_1^2 - 6m_1^4 \end{aligned} \tag{9.2.5}$$

Consequently, the computation of the rth-order cumulant of x_1 requires knowledge of all its moments from the first order to the rth order (i.e., m_1, $m_2, \ldots, m_r$).

If $x(k)$, $k = 0, \pm 1, \pm 2, \ldots$, is a real-valued strictly stationary random process and its moments up to order n exist, then

$$\text{Mom}[x(k), x(k+\tau_1), \ldots, x(k+\tau_{n-1})] = E[x(k) \quad x(k+\tau_1) \quad \cdots \quad x(k+\tau_{n-1})] \tag{9.2.6}$$

will depend only on the time difference $\tau_1, \tau_2, \ldots, \tau_{n-1}$, and therefore we can write

$$m_n^x(\tau_1, \tau_2, \ldots, \tau_{n-1}) = E[x(k) \quad x(k+\tau_1) \quad \cdots \quad x(k+\tau_{n-1})] \tag{9.2.7}$$

For orders $n = 1, 2, 3, 4$ the cumulants $c_n^x(\tau_1, \ldots, \tau_{n-1})$ are related to the moments $m_n^x(\tau_1, \ldots, \tau_{n-1})$ of $x(k)$ as follows:

$$c_1^x = m_1^x = E\{x(k)\} \qquad \text{(mean value)} \tag{9.2.8}$$

$$c_2^x(\tau_1) = m_2^x(\tau_1) - (m_1^x)^2 \qquad \text{(covariance sequence)} \tag{9.2.9}$$

$$c_3^x(\tau_1,\tau_2) = m_3^x(\tau_1,\tau_2) - m_1^x[m_2^x(\tau_1) + m_2^x(\tau_2) + m_2^x(\tau_2 - \tau_1)] + 2(m_1^x)^3 \tag{9.2.10}$$

$$\begin{aligned} c_4^x(\tau_1,\tau_2,\tau_3) = {} & m_4^x(\tau_1,\tau_2,\tau_3) - m_2^x(\tau_1)\, m_2^x(\tau_3 - \tau_2) - m_2^x(\tau_2)\, m_2^x(\tau_3 - \tau_1) \\ & - m_2^x(\tau_3)\, m_2^x(\tau_2 - \tau_1) - m_1^x\, [m_3^x(\tau_2 - \tau_1, \tau_3 - \tau_1) \\ & + m_3^x(\tau_2,\tau_3) + m_3^x(\tau_1,\tau_3) + m_3^x(\tau_1, \tau_2)] \\ & + 2(m_1^x)^2\, [m_2^x(\tau_1) + m_2^x(\tau_2) + m_2^x(\tau_3) + m_2^x(\tau_3 - \tau_1) \\ & + m_2^x(\tau_3 - \tau_2) + m_2^x(\tau_2 - \tau_1)] - 6(m_1^x)^4 \end{aligned} \tag{9.2.11}$$

where $m_2^x(\tau)$ is the autocorrelation sequence.

If the process is zero mean ($m_1^x = 0$), it follows from (9.2.8) through (9.2.11) that the second- and third-order cumulants are identical to the second- and third-order moments, respectively. By setting $\tau_1 = \tau_2 = \tau_3 = 0$ in (9.2.9) through (9.2.11) and assuming that $m_1^x = 0$, we obtain

$$\begin{aligned} \gamma_2^x &= c_2^x(0) = E[x^2(k)] && \text{(variance)} \\ \gamma_3^x &= c_3^x(0,0) = E[x^3(k)] && \text{(skewness)} \\ \gamma_4^x &= c_4^x(0,0,0) = E[x^4(k)] - 3[\gamma_2^x]^2 && \text{(kurtosis)} \end{aligned} \tag{9.2.12}$$

The general relationship between the moments $m_2^x(\tau_1, \ldots, \tau_{n-1})$ and the cumulants $c_n^x(\tau_1, \ldots, \tau_{n-1})$ is given by Rosenblatt (1985). The best way to remember this relationship is through

$$c_n^x(\tau_1, \ldots, \tau_{n-1}) = m_n^x(\tau_1, \ldots, \tau_{n-1}) - m_n^G(\tau_1, \ldots, \tau_{n-1}) \tag{9.2.13}$$

where $m_n^G(\tau_1, \ldots, \tau_{n-1})$ is the nth-order moment of an equivalent Gaussian process that has the same mean and autocorrelation as the $x(k)$ process.

Moments and cumulants are symmetric functions in their arguments. The following three key properties distinguish cumulants from moments:

1. If $\{x(k), x(k + \tau_1), \ldots, x(k + \tau_{n-1})\}$ can be divided into any two or more groups that are statistically independent, their nth-order cumulants $c_n^x(\tau_1, \ldots, \tau_{n-1}) \equiv 0$, whereas $m_n^x(\tau_1, \ldots, \tau_{n-1}) \neq 0$.
2. If $x(k)$ and $y(k)$ are independent stationary random processes and $z(k) = x(k) + y(k)$, then

$$c_n^z(\tau_1, \ldots, \tau_{n-1}) = c_n^x(\tau_1, \ldots, \tau_{n-1}) + c_n^y(\tau_1, \ldots, \tau_{n-1}) \quad (9.2.14)$$

whereas

$$m_n^z(\tau_1, \ldots, \tau_{n-1}) \neq m_n^x(\tau_1, \ldots, \tau_{n-1}) + m_n^y(\tau_1, \ldots, \tau_{n-1}) \quad (9.2.15)$$

3. If the set of random variables $\{x(k), x(k + \tau_1), \ldots, x(k + \tau_{n-1})\}$ is jointly Gaussian, all its joint cumulants of order greater than the second ($n > 2$) are identically zero. This easily follows from (9.2.14).

9.2.2 Higher-Order Spectra (Cumulant Spectra)

Higher-order spectra of random signals are usually defined in terms of cumulants, and not moments, due to the above three properties of cumulants that moments do not share. Assuming that the cumulant sequence, $c_n^x(\tau_1, \ldots, \tau_{n-1})$ is absolutely summable, it follows that

$$\sum_{\tau_1=-\infty}^{\infty} \cdots \sum_{\tau_{n-1}=-\infty}^{\infty} \left|c_n^x(\tau_1, \ldots, \tau_{n-1})\right| < \infty \quad (9.2.16)$$

Then the nth-order cumulant spectrum $C_n^x(\omega_1, \ldots, \omega_{n-1})$, of $x(k)$ exists, it is continuous, and it is defined as the $(n - 1)$-dimensional Fourier transform of the nth-order cumulant sequence,

$$C_n^x(\omega_1, \omega_2, \ldots, \omega_{n-1}) = \frac{1}{(2\pi)^{n-1}} \sum_{\tau_1=-\infty}^{\infty} \cdots \sum_{\tau_{n-1}=-\infty}^{\infty} c_n^x(\tau_1, \tau_2, \ldots, \tau_{n-1}) \times \exp[-j(\omega_1\tau_1 + \cdots + \omega_{n-1}\tau_{n-1})] \quad (9.2.17)$$

where

$$|\omega_i| \leq \pi \text{ for } i = 1, 2, \ldots, n-1 \quad \text{and} \quad |\omega_1 + \omega_2 + \cdots + \omega_{n-1}| \leq \pi$$

In general, $C_n^x(\omega_1, \omega_2, \ldots, \omega_{n-1})$ is complex for $n > 2$ (i.e. it has magnitude and phase) and hence it may be expressed as

$$C_n^x(\omega_1, \ldots, \omega_{n-1}) = |C_n^x(\omega_1, \ldots, \omega_{n-1})| \exp\{j\psi_n^x(\omega_1, \ldots, \omega_{n-1})\} \quad (9.2.18)$$

The cumulant spectrum is also a periodic function with period 2π. The power spectrum, bispectrum, and trispectrum are special cases of the nth-order cumulant spectrum defined by (9.2.17). These are defined as follows.

Power Spectrum: $n = 2$

$$C_2^x(\omega) = \frac{1}{2\pi} \sum_{\tau=-\infty}^{\infty} c_2^x(\tau) \exp[-j\omega\tau], \qquad |\omega| \leq \pi \quad (9.2.19)$$

where $c_2^x(\tau)$ is the covariance sequence of $x(k)$. It is well known that $c_2^x(\tau) = c_2^x(-\tau)$, $C_2^x(\omega) = C_2^x(-\omega)$, and $C_2^x(\omega) \geq 0$ (real, nonnegative function).

Bispectrum: $n = 3$

$$C_3^x(\omega_1,\omega_2) = \frac{1}{(2\pi)^2} \sum_{\tau_1=-\infty}^{\infty} \sum_{\tau_2=-\infty}^{\infty} c_3^x(\tau_1,\tau_2) \exp\left[-j(\omega_1\tau_1 + \omega_2\tau_2)\right] \tag{9.2.20}$$

where $|\omega_1| \leq \pi$, $|\omega_2| \leq \pi$, $|\omega_1 + \omega_2| \leq \pi$, and where $c_3^x(\tau_1,\tau_2)$ is the third-order cumulant sequence of $x(k)$ described by (9.2.10). Symmetry conditions that follow from (9.2.10) are as follows:

$$\begin{aligned} c_3^x(\tau_1,\tau_2) &= c_3^x(\tau_2,\tau_1) = c_3^x(-\tau_2, \tau_1 - \tau_2) \\ &= c_3^x(\tau_2 - \tau_1, -\tau_1) = c_3^x(\tau_1 - \tau_2, -\tau_2) \\ &= c_3^x(-\tau_1, \tau_2 - \tau_1) \end{aligned} \tag{9.2.21}$$

As a consequence, the third-order cumulants have six symmetry regions in the plane (τ_1, τ_2), as illustrated in Fig. 9.1. One of these regions is an infinite wedge bounded by the lines $\tau_1 = 0$ and $\tau_1 = \tau_2$, where $\tau_1,\tau_2 \geq 0$.

The definition of the bispectrum and properties of third-order cumulants yield the following properties for the bispectrum:

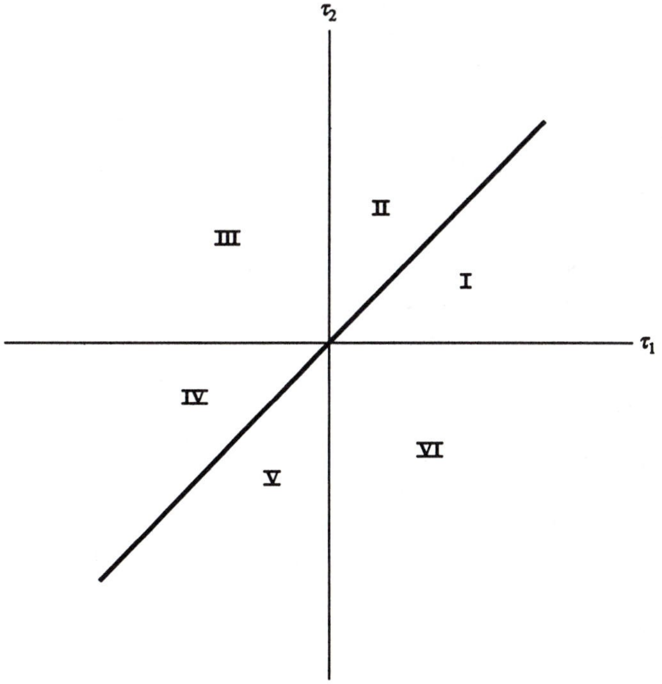

FIGURE 9.1 Symmetry regions of third-order cumulants of real stationary random signals.

$$\begin{aligned} C_3^x(\omega_1,\omega_2) &= C_3^x(\omega_2,\omega_1) = C_3^{x*}(-\omega_2, -\omega_1) \\ &= C_3^{x*}(-\omega_1, -\omega_2) = C_3^x(-\omega_1 - \omega_2, \omega_2) \\ &= C_3^x(\omega_1, -\omega_1 - \omega_2) = C_3^x(-\omega_1 - \omega_2, -\omega_1) \\ &= C_3^x(\omega_2, -\omega_1 - \omega_2) \end{aligned} \tag{9.2.22}$$

Thus knowledge of the bispectrum in the triangular region $\omega_2 \geq 0$, $\omega_1 \geq \omega_2$, $\omega_1 + \omega_2 \leq \pi$ is enough for a complete description of the bispectrum of real random signals.

Trispectrum: $n = 4$

$$C_4^x(\omega_1,\omega_2,\omega_3) = \frac{1}{(2\pi)^3} \sum_{\tau_1=-\infty}^{\infty} \sum_{\tau_2=-\infty}^{\infty} \sum_{\tau_3=-\infty}^{\infty} c_4^x(\tau_1,\tau_2,\tau_3) \times \exp[-j(\omega_1\tau_1 + \omega_2\tau_2 + \omega_3\tau_3)] \tag{9.2.23}$$

where $|\omega_1| \leq \pi$, $|\omega_2| \leq \pi$, $0 < |\omega_3| \leq \pi$, and $|\omega_1 + \omega_2 + \omega_3| \leq \pi$ and where $c_4^x(\tau_1,\tau_2,\tau_3)$ is the fourth-order cumulant sequence given by (9.2.11).

Many symmetry properties can be derived for the trispectrum, similar to those given in (9.2.22) for the bispectrum. Molle and Hinich (1990) point out that the trispectrum has 192 symmetry regions.

A normalized cumulant spectrum, or the nth-order coherency index, is a function that combines two completely different entities, namely the cumulant spectrum of order n, $C_n^x(\omega_1, \ldots, \omega_{n-1})$, and the power spectrum $C_2^x(\omega)$ of a process. It is defined as

$$P_n^x(\omega_1,\omega_2, \ldots, \omega_{n-1}) = \frac{C_n^x(\omega_1, \omega_2, \ldots, \omega_{n-1})}{[C_2^x(\omega_1) \; C_2^x(\omega_2) \; \cdots \; C_2^x(\omega_{n-1}) \; C_2^x(\omega_1 + \omega_2 + \cdots + \omega_{n-1})]^{1/2}} \tag{9.2.24}$$

The third order ($n = 3$) coherence index is also called the *bicoherence* (normalized bispectrum). The nth-order coherence index is very useful for the detection and characterization of nonlinearities in time series via phase relations of their harmonic components.

9.2.3 Linear Non-Gaussian Processes

Let us assume that $x(k)$ is the input to a linear time-invariant (LTI) system described by its impulse response $h(k)$ or equivalently, by the frequency response $H(\omega)$. The LTI system is assumed to be stable. Then it can be established that the nth-order cumulant spectra of $x(k)$ and the system output $y(k)$ are related by

$$C_n^y(\omega_1, \ldots, \omega_{n-1}) = H(\omega_1)H(\omega_2)\cdots H(\omega_{n-1}) H^*(\omega_1 + \cdots + \omega_{n-1})C_n^x(\omega_1, \ldots, \omega_{n-1}) \tag{9.2.25}$$

If we express the frequency response $H(\omega)$ as

$$H(\omega) = |H(\omega)| \exp[j\phi_h(\omega)] \tag{9.2.26}$$

then (9.2.25) can be expressed as

$$|C_n^y(\omega_1, \ldots, \omega_{n-1})| = |H(\omega_1)| \cdots |H(\omega_{n-1})| \\ |H^*(\omega_1 + \cdots + \omega_{n-1})| \, |C_n^x(\omega_1, \ldots, \omega_{n-1})| \tag{9.2.27}$$

and

$$\psi_n^y(\omega_1, \ldots, \omega_{n-1}) = \phi_h(\omega_1) + \phi_h(\omega_2) + \cdots + \phi_h(\omega_{n-1}) \\ - \phi_h(\omega_1 + \omega_2 + \cdots + \omega_{n-1}) \\ + \psi_n^x(\omega_1, \ldots, \omega_{n-1}) \tag{9.2.28}$$

In the special case where $x(k)$ is a non-Gaussian white process, its nth-order cumulant spectrum is given by

$$C_n^x(\omega_1, \omega_2, \ldots, \omega_{n-1}) = \frac{\gamma_n^x}{(2\pi)^{n-1}} \tag{9.2.29}$$

In this case (9.2.25) takes the special form

$$C_n^y(\omega_1, \ldots, \omega_{n-1}) = \frac{\gamma_n^x}{(2\pi)^{n-1}} H(\omega_1) \cdots H(\omega_{n-1}) \\ H^*(\omega_1 + \omega_2 + \cdots + \omega_{n-1}) \tag{9.2.30}$$

The magnitude of the n*th-order coherence index of linear non-Gaussian processes is constant* [i.e., $|P_n^y(\omega_1, \ldots, \omega_{n-1})|$ is constant for all frequencies]. Also, the nth-order cumulant spectrum is related to that of order $(n - 1)$ by the equation

$$C_n^y(\omega_1, \ldots, \omega_{n-2}, 0) = C_{n-1}^y(\omega_1, \ldots, \omega_{n-2}) \frac{H(0)}{2\pi} \frac{\gamma_n^x}{\gamma_{n-1}^x} \tag{9.2.31}$$

Hence the power spectrum of non-Gaussian linear processes may be reconstructed from the bispectrum up to a constant term,

$$C_3^y(\omega, 0) = C_2^y(\omega) \frac{H(0)}{2\pi} \frac{\gamma_3^x}{\gamma_2^x} \tag{9.2.32}$$

provided that $H(0) \neq 0$.

What makes higher-order spectra useful in non-minimum-phase system identification is that they contain phase information (except of course for the linear phase term). This fundamental property of higher-order spectra follows from (9.2.28).

EXAMPLE 9.2.1

Suppose that we have a first-order FIR system with impulse response

$$H(k) = \delta(k) - \alpha\delta(k - 1)$$

and frequency transfer function

$$H(\omega) = 1 - \alpha e^{-j\omega}$$

which is driven by a zero-mean non-Gaussian white noise $x(k)$ with variance γ_2^x and skewness γ_3^x. The output of the system is given by

$$y(k) = \sum_{i=0}^{1} h(i)x(k-i) = x(k) - \alpha x(k-1)$$

The power spectrum and bispectrum of $y(k)$ follow from (9.2.30). These are

$$C_2^y(\omega) = \frac{\gamma_2^x}{2\pi}|1 - \alpha e^{-j\omega}|^2$$

$$= \frac{\gamma_2^x}{2\pi}(1 + \alpha^2 - 2\alpha\cos\omega) \qquad \text{(power spectrum)}$$

and

$$C_3^y(\omega_1,\omega_2) = \frac{\gamma_3^x}{(2\pi)^2}(1 - \alpha e^{-j\omega_1})(1 - \alpha e^{-j\omega_2})(1 - \alpha e^{j(\omega_1+\omega_2)})$$

$$= \frac{\gamma_3^x}{(2\pi)^2}[(1 - \alpha^3) + \alpha^2 e(\omega_1,\omega_2) - \alpha e^*(\omega_1,\omega_2)] \qquad \text{(bispectrum)}$$

where $e(\omega_1,\omega_2) = e^{j\omega_1} + e^{j\omega_2} + e^{-j(\omega_1+\omega_2)}$. If we calculate

$$C_3^y(\omega,0) = \frac{\gamma_3^x}{(2\pi)^2}[(1 - \alpha^3) + \alpha^2 e(\omega,0) - \alpha e^*(\omega,0)]$$

$$= \frac{\gamma_3^x}{(2\pi)^2}[(1 - \alpha^3) + \alpha^2(1 + e^{j\omega} + e^{-j\omega}) - \alpha(1 + e^{-j\omega} + e^{j\omega})]$$

$$= \frac{\gamma_3^x}{(2\pi)^2}[(1 - \alpha^3 + \alpha^2 - \alpha) + (\alpha^2 - \alpha)\,2\cos\omega]$$

$$= \frac{\gamma_3^x}{(2\pi)^2}\cdot H(0)(1 + \alpha^2 - 2\alpha\cos\omega)$$

$$= \frac{\gamma_3^x}{\gamma_2^x}\frac{H(0)}{2\pi}C_2^y(\omega)$$

we see that (9.2.32) holds.

9.2.4 Nonlinear Processes

Higher-order spectra provide a means for detecting and quantifying nonlinearities in random signals. These signals arise when a nonlinear system is excited by a random input signal. For example, suppose that the signal

$$x(k) = A_1\cos(\lambda_1 k + \phi_1) + A_2\cos(\lambda_2 k + \phi_2) \tag{9.2.33}$$

where ϕ_1 and ϕ_2 are independent, identically and uniformly distributed (i.i.d) random variables, is the input to the quadratic nonlinear system

$$z(k) = x(k) + \epsilon x^2(k) \tag{9.2.34}$$

where ϵ is a nonzero constant. The signal $z(k)$ contains cosinusoidal terms in (λ_1, ϕ_1), (λ_2, ϕ_2), $(2\lambda_1, 2\phi_1)$, $(2\lambda_2, 2\phi_2)$, $(\lambda_1 + \lambda_2, \phi_1 + \phi_2)$, and $(\lambda_1 - \lambda_2, \phi_1 - \phi_2)$. Such a phenomenon, which gives rise to certain phase relationships of the same type as frequency relationships, is called *quadratic phase coupling*. In certain applications it is necessary to determine if peaks at harmonically related positions in the power spectrum are, in fact, phase coupled. Since the power spectrum suppresses all phase relationships, it cannot provide the answer. The third-order cumulants or the bispectrum, however, are capable of detecting and characterizing quadratic phase coupling. This is best illustrated in the following example.

Consider the random signals

$$x_1(k) = \cos(\lambda_1 k + \phi_1) + \cos(\lambda_2 k + \phi_2) + \cos(\lambda_3 k + \phi_3) \tag{9.2.35}$$

and

$$x_2(k) = \cos(\lambda_1 k + \phi_1) + \cos(\lambda_2 k + \phi_2) + \cos[\lambda_3 k + (\phi_1 + \phi_2)] \tag{9.2.36}$$

where $\lambda_3 = \lambda_1 + \lambda_2$ [i.e., $(\lambda_1, \lambda_2, \lambda_3)$ are harmonically related] and ϕ_1, ϕ_2, and ϕ_3 are i.i.d. uniformly distributed random variables. From (9.2.35) it is apparent that λ_3 is an independent harmonic component because ϕ_3 is an independent random-phase variable. However, λ_3 of $x_2(k)$ is a result of phase coupling between λ_1 and λ_2. From (9.2.35) and (9.2.36) we see that $E[x_1(k)] = E[x_2(k)] = 0$. Hence the autocorrelation sequences of the two signals are given by the expression

$$c_2^{x_1}(\tau_1) = c_2^{x_2}(\tau_1) = \tfrac{1}{2}[\cos(\lambda_1\tau_1) + \cos(\lambda_2\tau_1) + \cos(\lambda_3\tau_1)] \tag{9.2.37}$$

which implies that $x_1(k)$ and $x_2(k)$ have identical power spectra, consisting of impulses at λ_1, λ_2, and $\lambda_3 = \lambda_1 + \lambda_2$. The third-order cumulants of the signals are

$$c_3^{x_1}(\tau_1, \tau_2) = 0 \tag{9.2.38}$$

$$\begin{aligned} c_3^{x_2}(\tau_1,\tau_2) = \tfrac{1}{4}[&\cos(\lambda_2\tau_1 + \lambda_1\tau_2) + \cos(\lambda_3\tau_1 - \lambda_1\tau_2)] \\ &+ \cos(\lambda_1\tau_1 + \lambda_2\tau_2) + \cos(\lambda_3\tau_1 - \lambda_2\tau_2) \\ &+ \cos(\lambda_1\tau_1 - \lambda_3\tau_2) + \cos(\lambda_2\tau_1 - \lambda_3\tau_2) \end{aligned}$$

Therefore, the bispectrum of $x_3(k)$ is identically zero, whereas the bispectrum of $x_2(k)$ shows an impulse in the triangular region $\omega_2 \geq 0$, $\omega_1 \geq \omega_2$, and $\omega_1 + \omega_2 \leq \pi$. This impulse is located at (λ_1,λ_2) if $\lambda_1 \geq \lambda_2$.

Harmonically related peaks in the power spectrum (i.e., $\lambda_3 = \lambda_1 + \lambda_2$) may indicate the presence of quadratic nonlinearities in the data. However, the power spectrum suppresses phase relations of harmonic components and therefore fails to discriminate $x_1(k)$ from $x_2(k)$. On the other hand, we have demonstrated above that the bispectrum does preserve quadratic phase relations and therefore becomes a useful tool for detecting quadratic nonlinearities. Parametric methods for the detection of quadratic phase coupling were introduced by Raghuveer and Nikias (1985).

There are situations in practice where it is necessary to distinguish between a *linear* non-Gaussian process and a *nonlinear* process. Assuming that both linear and nonlinear processes have nonzero nth-order cumulants, a good test statistic was introduced by Hinich (1982) based on the nth-order coherence function defined in (9.2.24). If the non-Gaussian process is linear, its nth-order magnitude coherence function takes the form

$$|P_n^x(\omega_1, \ldots, \omega_{n-1})| = \frac{(2\pi)\gamma_n^x}{[2\pi\gamma_2^x]^{n/2}} \tag{9.2.39}$$

which is constant at all frequencies. Note that if the linear process is Gaussian, $\gamma_n^x = 0$ for all $n > 2$. If the values of $|P_n^x(\omega_1, \ldots, \omega_{n-1})|$ change with frequencies $(\omega_1, \ldots, \omega_{n-1})$, the process is said to be nonlinear. An example of a nonlinear process with frequency-dependent bicoherence, $|P_3^x(\omega_1, \omega_2)|$, is $x_2(k)$, described by (9.2.36).

9.3 CONVENTIONAL ESTIMATORS FOR HIGHER-ORDER SPECTRA

The problem met in practice is one of estimating higher-order spectra of a signal when a finite-length data record is available. There are two main approaches that can be used to estimate higher-order spectra: the conventional nonparametric method (Fourier type) and the parametric approach, which is based on autoregressive (AR), moving average (MA), and ARMA models.

The conventional nonparametric methods and their properties is the subject of discussion in this section. These methods may be classified into two classes, indirect and direct methods. While these methods are straightforward, limitations on statistical variance of the estimates, computer time, and memory impose severe problems in their implementation. In fact, the computations may be surprisingly expensive despite the use of fast Fourier transform (FFT) algorithms.

9.3.1 Indirect Method

Let $\{x(1)\}, x(2), \ldots, x(N)\}$ be the set of observed data. Then we proceed as follows:

1. Segment the data into K records of M samples each (i.e., $N = KM$).
2. Subtract the average value of each record from the data.
3. Assuming that $\{x^{(i)}(k), k = 0, 1, \ldots, M - 1\}$ is the data set per segment $i = 1, 2, \ldots, K$, obtain estimates of the higher-order moments

$$m_n^{(i)}(\tau_1, \ldots, \tau_{n-1}) = \frac{1}{M} \sum_{k=S_1}^{S_2} x^{(i)}(k) x^{(i)}(k+\tau_1) \cdots x^{(i)}(k+\tau_{n-1}) \quad (9.3.1)$$

$$n = 2, 3, \ldots, N; \quad i = 1, 2, \ldots, K$$

$$S_1 = \max(0, -\tau_1, \ldots, -\tau_{n-1})$$

$$S_2 = \min(M-1, M-1-\tau_1, M-1-\tau_2, \ldots, M-1-\tau_{n-1})$$

4. Average over all segments

$$\hat{m}_n^x(\tau_1, \ldots, \tau_{n-1}) = \frac{1}{K} \sum_{i=1}^{K} m_n^{(i)}(\tau_1, \ldots, \tau_{n-1}) \quad (9.3.2)$$

5. Generate the nth-order cumulant sequence $c_n^x(\tau_1, \ldots, \tau_{n-1})$, which, as we saw earlier, is a function of moments from second to nth order. However, for zero-mean signals we have

$$\begin{aligned} \hat{c}_2^x(\tau) &= \hat{m}_2^x(\tau) \\ \hat{c}_3^x(\tau_1,\tau_2) &= \hat{m}_3^x(\tau_1,\tau_2) \\ \hat{c}_4^x(\tau_1,\tau_2,\tau_3) &= \hat{m}_4^x(\tau_1,\tau_2,\tau_3) - \hat{m}_2^x(\tau_1)\hat{m}_2^x(\tau_3-\tau_2) \\ &\quad - \hat{m}_2^x(\tau_2)\hat{m}_2^x(\tau_3-\tau_1) - \hat{m}_2^x(\tau_3)\hat{m}_2^x(\tau_2-\tau_1) \end{aligned} \quad (9.3.3)$$

6. Generate the higher-order spectrum estimate

$$\begin{aligned} C_n^x(\omega_1, \ldots, \omega_{n-1}) &= \sum_{\tau_1=-L}^{L} \cdots \sum_{\tau_{n-1}=-L}^{L} c_n^x(\tau_1, \ldots, \tau_{n-1}) \\ &\times W(\tau_1, \ldots, \tau_{n-1}) \exp[-j(\omega_1\tau_1 + \cdots + \omega_{n-1}\tau_{n-1})] \end{aligned} \quad (9.3.4)$$

where $L < M - 1$ and $W(\tau_1, \ldots, \tau_{n-1})$ is a window function. Instead of a cumulant spectrum, a moment spectrum can be generated by (9.3.4) if we substitute by moment estimates (9.3.2) in place of the cumulants.

The multidimensional window function should satisfy the symmetry properties of higher-order moments or cumulants. Also, it should be zero outside the region of support of the estimated cumulants and have a nonnegative Fourier transform. Window functions that satisfy these constraints can be constructed from one-dimensional windows according to the relations

$$W(\tau_1, \ldots, \tau_{n-1}) = d(\tau_1) \; d(\tau_2) \; \cdots \; d(\tau_{n-1}) d(\tau_1 + \cdots + \tau_{n-1}) \quad (9.3.5)$$

where

$$\begin{aligned} d(\tau) &= d(-\tau) \\ d(\tau) &= 0, \qquad \tau > L \\ d(0) &= 1 \end{aligned} \quad (9.3.6)$$

$$D(\omega) = \sum_{\tau=-L}^{L} d(\tau) \exp(-j\omega\tau) \geq 0 \qquad \text{for all } \omega$$

We note, however, that not all one-dimensional windows satisfy the constraint $D(\omega) \geq 0$ for all ω. Two windows with good performance in terms of bias and variance are given as

$$d_0(\tau) = \begin{cases} \dfrac{1}{\pi}\left|\sin\dfrac{\pi\tau}{L}\right| + \left(1 - \dfrac{|\tau|}{L}\right)\left(\cos\dfrac{\pi\tau}{L}\right), & |\tau| \leq L \\ 0, & |\tau| > L \end{cases} \tag{9.3.7}$$

and

$$d_p(\tau) = \begin{cases} 1 - 6\left(\dfrac{|\tau|}{L}\right)^2 + 6\left(\dfrac{|\tau|}{L}\right)^3, & |\tau| \leq \dfrac{L}{2} \\ 2\left(1 - \dfrac{|\tau|}{L}\right)^3, & \dfrac{L}{2} \leq |\tau| \leq L \\ 0, & |\tau| > L \end{cases} \tag{9.3.8}$$

The first window achieves a bias that is about 18% smaller than that of the second window (Parzen window). However, the first window gives a variance which is about 26% larger than that of the Parzen window.

9.3.2 Direct Method

This class of conventional estimators is found to be very useful for the generation of moment spectra using FFT algorithms. It is similar to the Welch method for power spectrum estimation. Let $\{x(1), x(2), \ldots, x(N)\}$ be the available observation data for spectrum estimation. Let us assume that F_s is the sampling frequency and $\Delta_0 = F_s/N_0$ is the required spacing between frequency samples in the bispectrum domain, along the horizontal or vertical directions. Thus N_0 is the total number of frequency samples.

1. Segment the data into K segments of M samples each (i.e., $N = KM$) and subtract the average value of each segment from the corresponding data points. If necessary, add zeros at each segment to obtain a convenient length M for the FFT.
2. Assuming that $\{x^{(i)}(k), k = 0, 1, 2, \ldots, M - 1\}$ are the data of segment (i), generate the DFT coefficients

$$Y^{(i)}(\lambda) = \frac{1}{M}\sum_{k=0}^{M-1} x^{(i)}(k)\exp\left(\frac{-j2\pi k\lambda}{M}\right), \qquad \lambda = 0, 1, \ldots, \frac{M}{2}; \quad i = 1, 2, \ldots, K \tag{9.3.9}$$

3. In general, $M = M_1 \times N_0$, where M_1 is a positive integer (assumed to be an odd number); that is, $M_1 = 2L_1 + 1$. Since M is even and M_1 is odd, we compromise on the value of N_0 (closest integer). Generate the spectral estimates

$$\hat{M}_n^{(i)}(\lambda_1 \ldots, \lambda_{n-1})$$
$$= \frac{1}{\Delta_0^{n-1}} \sum_{k_1=-L_1}^{L_1} \cdots \sum_{k_{n-1}=-L_1}^{L_1}$$
$$Y^{(i)}(\lambda_1 + k_1) \cdots Y^{(i)}(\lambda_{n-1} + k_{n-1}) \tag{9.3.10}$$
$$Y^{(i)*}(\lambda_1 + \lambda_2 + \cdots + \lambda_{n-1} + k_1 + \cdots + k_{n-1})$$

for $i = 1, 2, \ldots, K$. For example, in the special case of the bispectrum where no frequency-domain average is performed (i.e., $M_1 = 1$, $L_1 = 0$, we have

$$M_3^{(i)}(\lambda_1,\lambda_2) = \frac{1}{\Delta_0^2} Y^{(i)}(\lambda_1) Y^{(i)}(\lambda_2) Y^{(i)*}(\lambda_1 + \lambda_2) \tag{9.3.11}$$

4. The moment spectrum estimate of the given data is obtained by averaging over the K pieces

$$M_n^x(\omega_1, \ldots, \omega_{n-1}) = \frac{1}{K} \sum_{i=1}^{K} M_n^{(i)}(\omega_1, \ldots, \omega_{n-1}) \tag{9.3.12}$$

where

$$\omega_i = \left(\frac{2\pi F_s}{N_0}\right)\lambda_i \tag{9.3.13}$$

Note that for zero-mean signals, $C_2^x(\omega) = M_2^x(\omega)$ and $C_3^x(\omega_1,\omega_2) = M_3^x(\omega_1,\omega_2)$. The nth-order cumulant spectrum is a function of all moment spectra from second order to nth order. This general relationship can be found in the text by Zurbenko (1986).

9.3.3 Statistical Properties of Conventional Estimators

In general, the indirect and direct methods for higher-order spectrum estimation give different estimates. However, it has been shown that both conventional estimates are asymptotically unbiased and consistent. Also, they have distributions that tend to a complex Gaussian distribution.

Let us first consider the case of the bispectrum. Assume that $C_2^x(\omega)$ and $C_3^x(\omega_1,\omega_2)$ are the true power spectrum and bispectrum of a strictly stationary zero-mean random process. Let $\hat{C}_3^x(\omega_1,\omega_2)$ be a consistent bispectrum estimate computed by indirect or direct conventional methods using a single realization of the random process of length N. The key result associated with these methods is that for sufficiently large record size M and total length N, both direct and indirect methods provide approximately unbiased estimates,

$$E[\hat{C}_3^x(\omega_1,\omega_2)] = C_3^x(\omega_1,\omega_2) \tag{9.3.14}$$

with asymptotic variances

$$\mathrm{var}[\mathrm{Re}\hat{C}_3^x(\omega_1,\omega_2)] = \mathrm{var}[\mathrm{Im}\,\hat{C}_3^x(\omega_1,\omega_2)] \approx \tfrac{1}{2}\sigma_3^2(\omega_1,\omega_2) \tag{9.3.15}$$

where

$$\sigma_3^2(\omega_1,\omega_2) = \begin{cases} \dfrac{1}{2\pi}\dfrac{VL^2}{MK} \quad C_2^x(\omega_1)C_2^x(\omega_2)C_2^x(\omega_1+\omega_2) & \text{(Indirect)} \\ \dfrac{1}{2\pi}\dfrac{N_0^2}{MK} \quad C_2^x(\omega_1)C_2^x(\omega_2)C_2^x(\omega_1+\omega_2) & \text{(Direct)} \end{cases} \tag{9.3.16}$$

for $0 < \omega_2 < \omega_1$, where K is the number of records, M the number of samples per record, and V the total energy of the bispectrum window, which is unity for a rectangular window; L is defined by (9.3.4) and $N_0 = M/(2L_1 + 1)$, where L_1 is defined by (9.3.10). From (9.3.16) it is apparent that if a rectangular window is used with the indirect method and $L = N_0$, the two conventional methods give approximately the same estimates.

Brillinger and Rosenblatt (1967) showed that for large M and N, the distribution of the error bicoherence, defined as

$$\frac{C_3^x(\omega_1,\omega_2) - \hat{C}_3^x(\omega_1,\omega_2)}{\sigma_3(\omega_1,\omega_2)} \tag{9.3.17}$$

is approximately complex Gaussian, with zero mean and unit variance. Another equally important large sample result that follows from the asymptotic results developed by Brillinger and Rosenblatt (1967) is that these statistics can be treated as independent random variables over the grid in the principal domain, if the grid width is larger than or equal to the bispectrum bandwidth; that is, $\hat{C}_3^x(\omega_j,\omega_k)$ and $\hat{C}_3^x(\omega_r,\omega_s)$ are independent for $j \neq r$ or $k \neq s$ if $|\omega_{j+1} - \omega_j| \geq 2\pi\Delta_0$ or $|\omega_{r+1} - \omega_r| \geq 2\pi\Delta_0$, where

$$\Delta_0 = \begin{cases} \dfrac{F_s}{L} & \text{(indirect)} \\ \dfrac{F_s}{N_0} & \text{(direct)} \end{cases} \tag{9.3.18}$$

The asymptotic independence and Gaussianity imply that the squared-magnitude bicoherence statistic

$$|P_3^x(\omega_1,\omega_2)|^2 = \frac{|C_3^x(\omega_1,\omega_2) - \hat{C}_3^x(\omega_1,\omega_2)|^2}{\sigma_3^2(\omega_1,\omega_2)} \tag{9.3.19}$$

is approximately a noncentral chi-square statistic with two degrees of freedom.

The extension of the bispectrum asymptotic results to higher-order spectra is somewhat straightforward. Conventional estimators are generally of high variance, and therefore a large number of records (K) is required to obtain smooth higher-order spectral estimates. From (9.3.2) and (9.3.12) it is apparent that the variance is reduced by increasing K. However, increasing the number of segments is demanding on computer time and may result in degradations due to potential nonstationarities in the data. Frequency-domain averaging over small rectangles, in addition to increasing computations, may increase the bias and does not help near bispectral peaks. In the case of "short" data records, K could be increased by using overlapping records.

9.3.4 Test for Aliasing (or Nonstationarity) with the Bispectrum

Aliasing will not occur in discrete-time signals if the following conditions hold: (1) the equivalent continuous-time signal is bandlimited at frequency F_0, and (2) the signal is sampled with sampling period T such that $1/T \geq 2F_0$. Aliasing is usually avoided in practice by filtering (lowpassing) the continuous-time signal to eliminate its frequency content above frequency F_0 and then sampling the filtered signal at or above twice the cutoff frequency F_0. However, there are applications, such as economics and social sciences, where we measure directly the discrete-time signal, and thus sampling designs for continuous-time signals are impossible. Hence it is of value to test the discrete-time signal for the presence of aliasing.

Hinich and Wolinsky (1988) introduced a test for aliasing using bispectral analysis. Their test is for stationary random signals that have a nonzero bispectrum. The test utilizes an often overlooked, fundamental property of the bispectrum principal domain. They point out correctly that there has been a surprisingly persistent confusion in the literature regarding the triangular form of the principal domain of the bispectrum of a signal. Assuming that $x(t)$ is a real zero-mean stationary continuous-time random signal, the principal domain of its bispectrum in the (f_1,f_2) plane is the cone $C = \{f_1,f_2\colon 0 \leq f_1, 0 \leq f_2 \leq f_1\}$ illustrated in Fig. 9.2. As such, the bispectrum cuts off at $f_1 = f_0$, $f_2 = \pm f_0$, and $f_1 + f_2 = \pm f_0$. Consequently, the continuous-time support set is the isosceles right triangle $\{f_1,f_2\colon 0 \leq f_1 \leq f_0, f_2 \leq f_1, f_1 + f_2 = f_0\}$.

The principal domain of the equivalent discrete-time sequence $x(nT)$, where $T = 1/2F_0$ is the triangle $\{f_1f_2\colon 0 \leq f_1 \leq 1/2T, f_2 \leq f_1, 2f_2 - f_2 = 1/T\}$ in the cone C. From Fig. 9.2 we see that this principal domain consists of two triangular regions, namely, OT $= \{f_1,f_2\colon f_2 \leq f_1, 1/2T \leq f_2 \leq 1/T - f_1\}$ and $IT = \{f_1,f_2\colon f_2 \leq f_1, 0 \leq f_1 + f_2 \leq 1/2T\}$. Hinich and Wolinsky (1988) showed that *when there is no aliasing in x(nT) its bispectrum is zero in the OT triangle*. This easily follows from the fact that the IT region is identical to the continuous-time support set of a signal that is bandlimited at frequency F_0.

Let $\hat{C}_3^x(\omega_1,\omega_2)$ denote a consistent estimator of the bispectrum $C_3^x(\omega_1,\omega_2)$ for a grid of equally spaced discrete frequencies given a realization of size N of $x(nT)$. This estimator can be computed by either indirect or direct conventional methods. The test for aliasing proceeds to form the magnitude-squared bicoherence

$$\Lambda(\omega_1,\omega_2) = \frac{|\hat{C}_3^x(\omega_1,\omega_2)|^2}{\sigma_3^2(\omega_1,\omega_2)} \qquad (9.3.20)$$

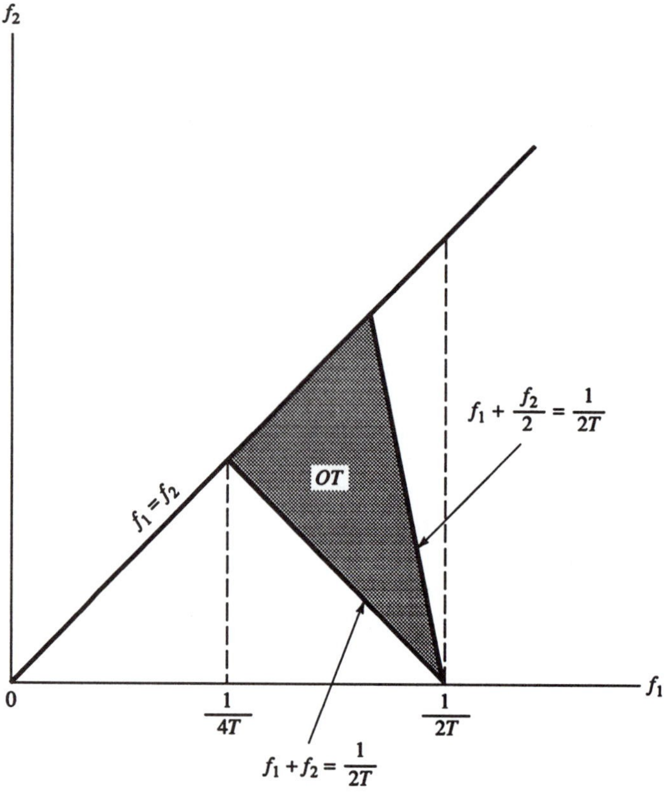

FIGURE 9.2 The continuous time and discrete-time principal domains of the bispectrum.

where $\sigma_3^2(\omega_1,\omega_2)$ is defined by (9.3.16), and to generate the detection statistic

$$\Lambda = \sum_{(\omega_1,\omega_2)} \Lambda(\omega_1,\omega_2) \qquad \text{for } (\omega_1,\omega_2) \in \text{OT} \tag{9.3.21}$$

With no aliasing, Λ is approximately central chi-squared with $2\hat{L}$ degrees of freedom, where $\hat{L}$ is the number of grid points in the OT triangular region. On the other hand, with aliasing, Λ is approximately noncentral chi-squared with $2\hat{L}$ degrees of freedom and positive noncentrality parameter.

Hinich and Wolinsky (1988) applied the test for aliasing on stock price time series corresponding to $N = 1000$ consecutive days. The resolution bandwidth in the principal domain was chosen as 0.03 (1 per day). There were $\hat{L} = 24$ points in the OT triangle. Their results overwhelmingly indicated that for a sampling period of $T = 1$ day, the data were aliased.

9.4 PARAMETRIC METHODS FOR HIGHER-ORDER SPECTRUM ESTIMATION

One of the widely used approaches in system identification and power spectrum estimation has been the construction of a white-noise-driven, linear time-invariant model from a given realization of a random signal. However, this approach was based primarily on a Gaussian assumption about the data and thus autocorrelation modeling. The main limitation associated with this assumption is that non-minimum-phase systems will be identified as being minimum phase when the input to the system is inaccessible. Consequently, the main motivation behind the use of non-Gaussian, white-noise-driven parametric models for higher-order spectrum estimation is to recover not only the magnitude but also the phase response of the system accurately.

Consider the real autoregressive moving average (ARMA) stable process $x(k)$ described by the linear difference equation

$$\sum_{i=0}^{p} a_i x(k-i) = \sum_{i=0}^{q} b_i w(k-i), \qquad a_0 = 1 \tag{9.4.1}$$

where $w(k)$ is a sequence of statistically independent, identically distributed, random variables with zero mean and $E[w(k)w(k+\tau_1)\cdots w(k+\tau_{n-1})] = \gamma_n^w \delta(\tau_1, \ldots, \tau_{n-1})$ (i.e., nth-order white). The higher-order spectra of the system input and output are related by

$$C_n^x(\omega_1, \ldots, \omega_{n-1}) = \frac{\gamma_n^w}{(2\pi)^{n-1}} H(\omega_1)\cdots H(\omega_{n-1}) \; H^*(\omega_1 + \omega_2 + \cdots + \omega_{n-1}) \tag{9.4.2}$$

where $H(\omega)$ is the transfer function of the ARMA system, given as

$$H(\omega) = \frac{\sum_{k=0}^{q} b_k \exp(-j\omega k)}{\sum_{k=0}^{p} a_k \exp(-j\omega k)}, \qquad a_0 = 1 \tag{9.4.3}$$

or equivalently,

$$H(\omega) = |H(\omega)| \exp[j\phi_h(\omega)] \tag{9.4.4}$$

If $w(k)$ is Gaussian, any real root (z_r) of $H(\omega)$ (pole or zero) can be replaced by its inverse $(1/z_r)$ and pairs of nonzero conjugate roots (z_0) by their paired conjugated inverse $(1/z_0^*)$ without changing the power spectrum $C_2^x(\omega)$ in (9.4.2) and therefore the probability structure of $x(k)$. For example, with real distinct roots there are 2^{p+q} ways of choosing the roots without changing $C_2^x(\omega)$. This implies that there are 2^{p+q} ways of choosing the phase $\phi_h(\omega)$ without changing the magnitude $|H(\omega)|$.

For classical system identification problems, least-squares estimation is used almost exclusively because it yields maximum likelihood estimates of the parameters of Gaussian white-noise-driven systems and because the equations obtained are usually in a linear form involving autocorrelation lags (or their estimates). However, the autocorrelation domain suppresses phase information, and therefore the aforementioned techniques are incapable of correctly identifying non-minimum-phase systems from their output sequence. An accurate phase reconstruction in the autocorrelation (or power spectrum) domain can be achieved only if the system is indeed minimum phase.

To put the system identification problem and its existing solutions into perspective, several comments are in order.

1. If the sequence $w(k)$ is Gaussian and $H(\omega)$ is minimum phase, autocorrelation-based methods will correctly identify both magnitude $|H(\omega)|$ and phase $\phi_h(\omega)$.
2. If the sequence $w(k)$ is Gaussian and $H(\omega)$ is non-minimum-phase, no procedure can correctly recover $\phi_h(\omega)$.
3. If the sequence $w(k)$ is non-Gaussian and $H(\omega)$ is non-minimum-phase, autocorrelation-based methods will correctly identify $|H(\omega)|$ but not $\phi_h(\omega)$.
4. If the process is non-Gaussian and $H(\omega)$ is non-minimum-phase, both $|H(\omega)|$ and $\phi_h(\omega)$ can be correctly estimated without a priori knowledge of the actual non-Gaussian distribution of $w(k)$ by exploiting the use of higher-order spectra (bispectrum or trispectrum) or higher-order cumulants of the system output sequence.

In this section we address the non-minimum-phase system identification problem in the bispectrum domain using MA, noncausal AR, and ARMA models. The methods described here can easily be extended to the trispectrum domain by using fourth-order cumulants to estimate the model parameters.

9.4.1 MA Methods

Let us assume that the sequence $x(k)$ is truly a MA(q) process which can be obtained from (9.4.1) by setting $p = 0$,

$$x(k) = \sum_{i=0}^{q} b_i w(k - i) \tag{9.4.5}$$

Our problem is to estimate the parameters b_i from the third-order cumulants (or moments) of the data. Hence we begin with

$$c_3^x(\tau,\tau) = E[x(k)x^2(k + \tau)] \tag{9.4.6}$$

and substitute (9.4.5) into (9.4.6). Thus we obtain

$$c_3^x(\tau,\tau) = \gamma_3^w \sum_{i=0}^{q} b_i b_{i+\tau}^2, \qquad \tau = -q, \ldots, 0, \ldots, q \tag{9.4.7}$$

Lii and Rosenblatt (1982) suggest two methods for the estimation of the MA coefficients based on (9.4.7): a nonlinear least-squares approach and a linear programming approach. Both methods employ estimates of the third moment, $\hat{c}_3^x(\tau,\tau)$, which is generated following the procedure described in Section 9.3.

The nonlinear least-squares approach solves the extremal problem

$$\text{minimize} \sum_{\tau=-q}^{q} \left(\hat{c}_3^x(\tau,\tau) - \gamma_3^w \sum_{i=0}^{q} b_i b_{i+\tau}^2 \right)^2 \tag{9.4.8}$$

with respect to the $q + 2$ unknowns $\{b_k\}$ and γ_3^w.

In the linear programming approach, one first uses a typical second-order method to estimate the coefficients of the MA process that will accurately reflect the autocorrelation structure of the data. Let us denote the resulting coefficients as $b_k^{(2)}$. Then the roots r_j, $j = 1,2, \ldots, q$, of the polynomial

$$B(z) = \sum_{k=0}^{q} b_k^{(2)} z^{-k} \tag{9.4.9}$$

have magnitude less than 1 (minimum phase). An accurate estimate of the distribution of roots can be obtained by taking the conjugated inverse of an appropriate number of r_j's. As pointed out earlier, there are 2^q possible sets of roots that yield the same autocorrelation sequence and 2^q distinct sets of third-moment sequences. Therefore, the linear programming method seeks to find the set of roots, and thus the coefficients b_i that minimize (9.4.8) among all possible sets of roots. Notice that if the roots are complex, the inverse complex conjugates are taken in pairs.

A different method for MA system identification based on forward and backward ARMA approximations was suggested by Nikias (1988). Assuming a generally mixed-phase system, (9.4.5) can be written as

$$B(z) = \sum_{i=0}^{q} b_i z^{-i} = I(z^{-1})O(z) \tag{9.4.10}$$

where $I(z^{-1})$ and $O(z)$ are polynomials with all their zeros, respectively, inside and outside the unit circle. By combining (9.4.10) and (9.4.5) we obtain

$$X(z) = I(z^{-1})O(z)W(z) \tag{9.4.11}$$

Hence

$$\frac{X(z)}{I(z^{-1})} = O(z)W(z) \tag{9.4.12}$$

which may be well approximated arbitrarily close by a stable forward ARMA model of the form

$$\sum_{i=0}^{p} c_i x(k-i) = \sum_{i=0}^{L_1} t_i w(k+i) \qquad (c_0 = t_0 = 1) \tag{9.4.13}$$

where

$$\sum_{i=0}^{p} c_i z^{-i} \approx \frac{1}{I(z^{-1})} \tag{9.4.14}$$

The AR coefficients c_i contain the minimum-phase component of the mixed-phase system. The model (9.4.13) satisfies the third-order recursive equation

$$\sum_{i=0}^{p} c_i c_3^x(-\tau + i, -\rho + i) = 0 \qquad \text{for } \tau > L_1, \quad \rho > L_2 \tag{9.4.15}$$

where $c_3^x(m,n)$ is the third-moment sequence of $x(k)$. From (9.4.15) an overdetermined system of equations is formed and solved via least squares or singular value decomposition (SVD). The minimum-phase component is then obtained from

$$|\hat{B}_I(\omega)| = \text{Magn}\left\{\frac{1}{\sum_{i=0}^{p} c_i \exp j(-\omega i)}\right\} \tag{9.4.16}$$

$$\hat{\phi}_I(\omega) = \text{Arg}\left\{\frac{1}{\sum_{i=0}^{p} c_i \exp j(-\omega i)}\right\} \tag{9.4.17}$$

Equation (9.4.11) can also be expressed as

$$\frac{X(z)}{O(z)} = W(z)I(z^{-1}) \tag{9.4.18}$$

and similarly, it be approximated arbitrarily close by a backward stable ARMA model of the form

$$\sum_{i=0}^{r} d_i x(n + i) = \sum_{k=0}^{L_2} u_k w(n - k), \qquad d_0 = 1 \tag{9.4.19}$$

The AR coefficients d_i contain the maximum-phase component of the mixed-phase system. The third-order recursion of (9.4.19) is given by

$$\sum_{i=0}^{r} d_i c_3^x(\tau - i, \rho - i) = 0, \qquad \text{for } \tau > L_2, \quad \rho > L_2 \tag{9.4.20}$$

which is solved for d_i using the pseudoinverse least-squares approach or SVD. The maximum-phase component of (9.4.10) is obtained from

$$|\hat{B}_O(\omega)| = \text{Magn}\left\{\frac{1}{\sum_{i=0}^{r} d_i \exp[j(\omega i)]}\right\} \tag{9.4.21}$$

$$\hat{\phi}_O(\omega) = \text{Arg}\left\{\frac{1}{\sum_{i=0}^{r} d_i \exp[j(\omega i)]}\right\} \tag{9.4.22}$$

The magnitude and phase of the MA system are easily obtained by combining the results of (9.4.16), (9.4.17), (9.4.21), and (9.4.22) as follows:

$$\hat{B}(\omega) = |\hat{B}_I(\omega)|\,|\hat{B}_O(\omega)| \tag{9.4.23}$$

$$\hat{\phi}_b(\omega) = \hat{\phi}_I(\omega) + \hat{\phi}_O(\omega) \tag{9.4.24}$$

Extension of this method to the trispectrum as well as to model order selection criteria can be found in the paper by Nikias and Pan (1988).

Nikias and Chiang (1988) have also suggested the use of a noncausal AR approximation to the MA system identification problem by rewriting (9.4.11) as

$$\frac{X(z)}{I(z^{-1})O(z)} = W(z) \tag{9.4.25}$$

or in terms of third-order cumulants, as

$$\sum_{i=-\infty}^{\infty} f_i c_3^x(m-i, n-i) = 0 \qquad \text{for } m > L_1 \quad \text{or} \quad m < -L_2 \quad \text{or} \quad n > L_1 \quad \text{or} \quad n < -L_2 \tag{9.4.26}$$

where L_1 and L_2 are the number of zeros of $B(z)$ inside the outside the unit circle, respectively, and $q = L_1 + L_2$. Methods for estimation of a finite number of f_i coefficients from cumulants as well as model-order selection criteria are described by Nikias and Chiang (1988). The estimated transfer function is obtained from

$$\hat{B}(\omega) \approx \frac{1}{\sum_{k=-M}^{M} f_k \exp(-j\omega_k)} \tag{9.4.27}$$

where M is chosen arbitrarily large.

Giannakis and Mendel (1989) obtained the following interesting relationship between the autocorrelation and third-order cumulants for a MA(q) process:

$$\sum_{i=0}^{q} b_i^2 c_2^x(m-i) = \frac{\gamma_2^w}{\gamma_3^w} \sum_{i=0}^{q} b_i c_3^x(m-i, m-i) \tag{9.4.28}$$

where $m = 1, 2, \ldots$. An overdetermined system of equations may be formed and solved for the q MA coefficients using least squares. Estimates are obtained for both b_i and b_i^2, and therefore different ways for combining these results to obtain final estimates for b_i are possible. An extension of the Giannakis–Mendel method was given by Friedlander and Porat (1988).

9.4.2 Noncausal AR Methods

Several methods have been suggested for determining the coefficients a_i of the AR model

$$\sum_{i=0}^{p} a_i x(k-i) = w(k), \qquad a_0 = 1 \tag{9.4.29}$$

where $w(k)$ is zero-mean, non-Gaussian, white with $\gamma_2^w \neq 0$ and $\gamma_3^w \neq 0$ (or $\gamma_4^w \neq 0$). If the AR model is causal and stable (e.g., minimum phase), the Yule–Walker approach with autocorrelation or any other AR power spectrum estimation technique can be used to compute the AR coefficients.

Huzii (1981) was the first to introduce a method for estimating the parameters of a noncausal AR model. From (9.4.29) we have

$$X(z)A_1(z^{-1})A_2(z) = W(z) \tag{9.4.30}$$

where $A_1(z^{-1})$ and $A_2(z)$ are polynomials with p_1 roots inside and p_2 outside the unit circle, respectively. Note that $p = p_1 + p_2$ and linear phase components are not included in (9.4.30). Let us define $\bar{A}_2(z^{-1})$ as the equivalent minimum phase polynomial of $A_2(z)$ [i.e., $|\bar{A}_2(z^{-1})| = |A_2(z)|$]. Huzii's method estimates first the AR coefficients of the spectrally equivalent model

$$\bar{A}(z^{-1}) = A_1(z^{-1})\bar{A}_2(z^{-1}) \tag{9.4.31}$$

using the Yule–Walker method with autocorrelations. By reflecting one or more poles to their reciprocal positions outside the unit circle, we obtain 2^p spectrally equivalent models to $\bar{A}(z^{-1})$ [i.e., $|A_i(z)| = |\bar{A}(z^{-1})|$ for $i = 1, 2, \ldots, 2^p$]. Which $A_i(z)$ is identical to $A_1(z^{-1})A_2(z)$? The answer is found by processing the data $x(k)$ through each one of the inverse filters $A_i(z)$ and testing for higher-order whiteness,

$$\begin{aligned} X_i(z) &= X(z)A_i(z) \\ &= \frac{W(z)}{A_1(z^{-1})A_2(z)} A_1(z^{-1})A_2^{(i)}(z) \\ &= W(z)\frac{A_2^{(i)}(z)}{A_2(z)} \end{aligned} \tag{9.4.32}$$

If $A_2^{(i)}(z) = A_2(z)$, then $x_i(k)$ is non-Gaussian white with variance and skewness identical to those of $\{w(k)\}$.

Tugnait (1987, 1988) has also suggested a number of methods for identifying a noncausal AR model from its output sequence. One method is to use Huzii's method to estimate $\bar{A}(z^{-1})$ first and then to filter the data $x(k)$ through the minimum-phase inverse filter $\bar{A}(z^{-1})$,

$$\begin{aligned} \bar{X}(z) &= X(z)\bar{A}(z^{-1}) \\ &= W(z)\frac{A_1(z^{-1})\bar{A}_2(z^{-1})}{A_1(z^{-1})A_2(z)} \\ &= W(z)\frac{\bar{A}_2(z^{-1})}{A_2(z)} \end{aligned} \tag{9.4.33}$$

or equivalently,

$$\begin{aligned} \bar{X}(z)A_2(z) &= W(z)\bar{A}_2(z^{-1}) \\ \sum_{i=0}^{p_2} a_{2i}\bar{x}(k+i) &= \sum_{i=0}^{p_2} \bar{a}_{2i}w(k-i) \qquad (a_{20} = 1) \end{aligned} \tag{9.4.34}$$

It follows from (9.4.34) that

$$\sum_{i=0}^{p_2} a_{2i} c_3^x(\tau - m - i, \tau - i) = 0 \qquad \text{for } \tau \geq p_2 + 1, \quad m > 0 \quad (9.4.35)$$

The coefficients a_{2i} can be estimated from (9.4.35) using the least-squares approach. Hence, knowing $\bar{A}(z^{-1})$ and $A_2(z)$, we can easily compute $A(z) = A_1(z^{-1})A_2(z)$ and thus $H(z) = 1/A(z)$.

A second method suggested by Tugnait is actually an extension of the Lii–Rosenblatt MA method to the noncausal AR case. Once $A(z^{-1})$ is estimated using the Yule–Walker method and the 2^p spectrally equivalent transfer functions $H_i(z) = 1/A_i(z)$ are generated, the optimum noncausal AR transfer function $H_0(z)$ is chosen to be the one that minimizes a squared-error cost function that represents the difference between the third-order cumulants calculated from (5.4.29), and the third-order cumulants estimated from the data. The cost function has been extended to include second-order cumulants also. In addition, both methods have been extended to accommodate noisy observation data.

9.4.3 ARMA Methods

Consider the ARMA model described by (9.4.1), which is assumed to be causal, stable, and generally non-minimum-phase. Consequently, some of the zeros of $H(\omega)$ in (9.4.3) may lie outside the unit circle. A number of methods have been suggested recently for the estimation of the a_i and b_i using higher-order cumulants of $\{x(k)\}$.

Lii (1982) introduced a method that is essentially based on four steps. First, the power spectrum of the data, $C_2^x(\omega)$, is estimated. Second, the phase $\phi_h(\omega)$ of the transfer function (9.4.4) is reconstructed from a conventional bispectrum estimate of the data. Third, the ARMA impulse response is generated using an inverse FFT algorithm. Finally, the model parameters are obtained from the impulse response via a Padé rational approximation. Therefore, this method is based on conventional bispectrum estimation techniques and also utilizes information that is present in the autocorrelation domain.

From (9.4.2) and (9.4.3) it follows that the frequency transfer function is given by

$$H(\omega) = \left[\frac{C_2^x(\omega)}{\gamma_2^w}\right]^{1/2} \exp[j\phi_h(\omega)] \qquad (9.4.36)$$

There is a large body of literature concerning the estimation of $C_2^x(\omega)$ and γ_2^w from the output data. In addition, the bispectrum conventional estimation methods have been described in Section 9.3. Thus the phase $\phi_h(\omega)$ is recovered from the phase of the estimated bispectrum (trispectrum). Therefore, having estimated $C_2^x(\omega)$, γ_2^w, and $\phi_h(\omega)$, the impulse response h_k of the ARMA model is obtained as described by Lii (1982) from

$$h_k = \frac{1}{2\pi} \int_{-\pi}^{\pi} H(\omega) \exp(j\omega k) \, d\omega \tag{9.4.37}$$

where $H(\omega)$ is given by (9.4.36). The ARMA parameters are computed utilizing the identity

$$\frac{B(z)}{A(z)} = H(z) = \sum_{k=0}^{\infty} h_k z^{-k} \tag{9.4.38}$$

Giannakis and Mendel (1989) have developed a method that uses autocorrelations and third- or fourth-order cumulants. The basic idea is to estimate the AR coefficients first, then form a residual MA time series, and finally, estimate the MA parameters by any one of the methods described in Section 9.4.1. The AR coefficients can be obtained either by using only autocorrelations and the Yule–Walker equations

$$c_2^x(\tau) + \sum_{i=1}^{p} a_i c_2^x(\tau - i) = 0 \qquad \text{for } \tau > q \tag{9.4.39}$$

or by using third-order cumulants in the equation

$$c_3^x(\tau,\tau) + \sum_{i=1}^{p} a_i c_3^x(\tau - i, \tau - i) = 0 \qquad \text{for } \tau > q \tag{9.4.40}$$

The residual MA time series is generated from the inverse filter equation

$$x(k) = \sum_{i=1}^{p} a_i x(k - i) \tag{9.4.41}$$

Giannakis and Swami (1987) introduced a method for computing ARMA parameters by applying a MA method twice. By combining (9.4.2) and (9.4.3) in the bispectrum domain, we obtain

$$C_3^x(\omega_1,\omega_2) = \frac{\gamma_3^w}{(2\pi)^2} \frac{B(\omega_1)B(\omega_2)B^*(\omega_1 + \omega_2)}{A(\omega_1)A(\omega_2)A^*(\omega_1 + \omega_2)} \tag{9.4.42}$$

or equivalently,

$$C_3^x(\omega_1,\omega_2)D(\omega_1,\omega_2) = \frac{\gamma_3^w}{(2\pi)^2} B(\omega_1)B(\omega_2)B^*(\omega_1 + \omega_2) \tag{9.4.43}$$

where

$$D(\omega_1,\omega_2) = A(\omega_1)A(\omega_2)A^*(\omega_1 + \omega_2) \tag{9.4.44}$$

Consequently, we have from (9.4.43) that

$$\sum_{i=0}^{p} \sum_{j=0}^{p} d(i,j) c_3^x(\tau - i, \rho - j) = 0 \qquad \text{for } \tau \text{ or } \rho > q \tag{9.4.45}$$

The coefficients $d(i,j)$ are computed from (9.4.45) using third-order cumulants and the least-squares approach. Since

$$d(i,j) = \sum_{k=0}^{p} a_k a_{k+i} a_{k+j} \tag{9.4.46}$$

it follows that

$$a_k = \frac{d(p,j)}{d(p,0)} \tag{9.4.47}$$

Having computed the AR coefficients in (9.4.47), we compute the inverse Fourier transform of (9.4.43). Thus we obtain

$$\sum_{i=0}^{p} \sum_{j=0}^{p} \sum_{k=0}^{p} a_i a_j a_k c_3^x(\tau + k - j, \rho + k - i) = b(\tau,\rho) \tag{9.4.48}$$

where

$$b(\tau,\rho) = \gamma_3^w \sum_{i=0}^{q} b_i b_{i+\tau} b_{i+\rho} \tag{9.4.49}$$

The MA coefficients are computed from $b(\tau,\rho)$ using (9.4.47), where $b_i = b(q,i)/b(q,0)$.

9.4.4 AR Methods for the Detection of Quadratic Phase Coupling

The motivation behind the use of AR models for the detection of quadratic phase coupling is to take advantage of the high-resolution capability and low variance estimates associated with AR techniques. The justification for the use of AR methods for detection of quadratic-phase coupling was given by Raghuveer and Nikias (1985) by proving that the third-order cumulant sequence of a process consisting of a sum of cosinusoids of which N pairs are coupled can be modeled exactly by a causal AR($6N$) model. For example, consider the signal

$$x(n) = \sum_{i=1}^{6} \cos(\lambda_i n + \phi_i) \tag{9.4.50}$$

where $\lambda_1 > \lambda_2 > 0$, $\lambda_4 > \lambda_5 > 0$, $\lambda_3 = \lambda_1 + \lambda_2$, $\lambda_6 = \lambda_4 + \lambda_5$, $\phi_1, \phi_2, \ldots, \phi_5$ are all independent, uniformly distributed over $(0,2\pi)$, and $\phi_6 = \phi_4 + \phi_5$. In (9.4.50), while $(\lambda_1, \lambda_2, \lambda_3)$ and $(\lambda_4, \lambda_5, \lambda_6)$ are at harmonically related positions, only the component at λ_6 is a result of phase coupling between those at λ_4 and λ_5, while the one at λ_3 is an independent harmonic component. The power spectrum of the process consists of impulses at λ_i for $i = 1, 2, \ldots, 6$. Looking at the spectrum, one cannot say if the harmonically related components are, in fact, involved in quadratic phase-coupling relationships. The third-order cumulant sequence $c_3^x(k,l)$ of $x(n)$ can easily be obtained as

$$c_3^x(k,l) = -\tfrac{1}{4}[\cos(\lambda_5 k + \lambda_4 l) + \cos(\lambda_6 k + \lambda_4 l) + \cos(\lambda_4 k + \lambda_5 l) + \cos(\lambda_6 k - \lambda_5 l) + \cos(\lambda_4 k - \lambda_6 l) + \cos(\lambda_5 k - \lambda_6 l)] \tag{9.4.51}$$

It is important to observe that in (9.4.51) *only the phase-coupled components appear.*

The third-order cumulant sequence $c_3^x(k,l)$ in (9.4.51) can be modeled exactly by a causal AR(6) model if its parameters take the values

$$\begin{aligned} a_1 &= -2(\cos\lambda_4 + \cos\lambda_5 + \cos\lambda_6) \\ a_2 &= 3 + 4(\cos\lambda_4\cos\lambda_5 + \cos\lambda_5\cos\lambda_6 + \cos\lambda_6\cos\lambda_4) \\ a_3 &= -4(\cos\lambda_4 + \cos\lambda_5 + \cos\lambda_6 + 2\cos\lambda_4\cos\lambda_5\cos\lambda_6) \\ a_4 &= a_2 \\ a_5 &= a_1 \\ a_6 &= 1 \end{aligned} \tag{9.4.52}$$

Assuming now that $x(n)$ is truly a pth-order AR(p) process, of the form

$$x(n) + \sum_{i=1}^{p} a_i x(n-i) = w(n) \tag{9.4.53}$$

the third-order cumulant sequence $c_3^x(\tau,\rho) = E[x(n)x(n+\tau)x(n+\rho)]$ satisfies the following third-order recursion (TOR):

$$c_3^x(-k,-l) + \sum_{i=1}^{p} a_i c_3^x(i-k, i-l) = \gamma_3^w \delta(k,l), \qquad (k,l) \geq 0 \tag{9.4.54}$$

where $\delta(k,l)$ is the two-dimensional unit impulse function. From (9.4.54), it follows that $2p+1$ third-moment values on the $r = \lambda$ line satisfy the matrix equation

$$\mathbf{R}_c \mathbf{a} = \boldsymbol{\beta} \tag{9.4.55}$$

where

$$\mathbf{R}_c = \begin{bmatrix} c_3^x(0,0) & c_3^x(1,1) & \cdots & c_3^x(p,p) \\ c_3^x(-1,-1) & c_3^x(0,0) & \cdots & c_3^x(p-1,p-1) \\ \vdots & & & \\ c_3^x(-p,-p) & c_3^x(-p+1,-p+1) & \cdots & c_3^x(0,0) \end{bmatrix}$$

$$\boldsymbol{\alpha} = [1, a_1, a_2, \ldots, a_p]^t \tag{9.4.56}$$

$$\boldsymbol{\beta} = [\gamma_3^x, 0, 0, \ldots, 0]^t$$

The matrix $\mathbf{R}_c$ is Toeplitz, but in general it is not symmetric.

Another representation of (9.4.54) is

$$c_3^x(-k,-l) + \sum_{i=1}^{p} a_i c_3^x(i-k, i-l) = \gamma_3^w \delta(k,l)$$

$$k = 0, 1, \ldots, L_1 \tag{9.4.57}$$

$$l = \begin{cases} 0, \ldots, k & \text{for } k < L_1 \\ 0, \ldots, L_2 & \text{for } k = L_1 \end{cases}$$

where L_1 and L_2 and chosen such that $L_2 \leq L_1$ and

$$p = 1 + L_2 + \frac{(L_1 - 1)(L_1 + 2)}{2} \tag{9.4.58}$$

The matrix corresponding to the equations in (9.4.57) does not possess the Toeplitz structure. However, this TOR approach draws information from samples over a finite area rather than just a portion of a straight line, and therefore it is more general than the case in (9.4.57).

Given data samples $\{x(1)\}, \ldots, x(n)\}$, third-order cumulants $c_3^x(\tau_1,\tau_2)$ are estimated first and used in place of the true values in (9.4.55) and (9.4.57). It is shown by Raghuveer and Nikias (1985) that if the process is in fact of the type given by (9.4.53), the TOR method provides consistent estimates of the AR parameters.

A second method for the estimation of AR parameters for quadratic-phase coupling, the constrained third-order mean (CTOM) method, was introduced by Raghuveer and Nikias (1986). Let us consider the estimate

$$\hat{q}_m(k,i) = x(m-i)x^2(m-k), \qquad i, k = 1, \ldots, p \tag{9.4.59}$$

We see that

$$E[\hat{q}_m(k,i)] = c_3^x(i-k, i-k) \tag{9.4.60}$$

If we were given samples of $c_3^x(\tau,\rho)$ itself, then to fit a pth-order AR model, we would be solving equations corresponding to (9.4.53); that is, we would have

$$E\left[\hat{q}_m(k,0) + \sum_{i=1}^{p} a_i \hat{q}_m(k,i)\right] = 0, \qquad k = 1, \ldots, p \tag{9.4.61}$$

We denote the quantity within the braces by $\hat{C}(m,k)$. Thus with true third-moment samples we would solve

$$E[\hat{C}(m,k)] = 0, \qquad k = 1, \ldots, p \tag{6.4.62}$$

We refer to $\hat{C}(m,k)$ as the third-order error process. With the given data samples we can obtain $N - p$ samples of $\hat{C}(m,k)$ for every value of k; that is, we can have $\hat{C}(m,k)$ for $m = p + 1, p + 2, \ldots, N$, and $k = 1, 2, \ldots, p$.

Instead of taking expectations, we now equate the sample mean of $\hat{C}(m,k)$ to zero to obtain the p linear equations to be solved for the parameters

$$\frac{1}{N-p} \sum_{m=p+1}^{N} \hat{C}(m,k) = 0, \qquad k = 1, \ldots, p \tag{9.4.63}$$

In matrix form we have

$$\hat{\mathbf{Q}}\mathbf{a} = \hat{\mathbf{q}} \tag{9.4.64}$$

where

$$\hat{\mathbf{Q}} = \begin{bmatrix} \hat{q}_{11} & \cdots & \hat{q}_{1p} \\ \vdots & & \\ \hat{q}_{p1} & \cdots & \hat{q}_{pp} \end{bmatrix} \quad \hat{\mathbf{a}} = [\hat{a}_1 \cdots \hat{a}_p]^t$$

$$\hat{\mathbf{q}} = [\hat{q}_{10} \cdots \hat{q}_{p0}]^t, \qquad \hat{q}_{ij} = \sum_{m=p+1}^{N} \hat{q}_m(i,j)$$

For simplicity of notation we considered an unbroken segment of N samples of data in outlining the CTOM approach. However, we may choose to divide the given data into records, form $\hat{C}(m,k)$ for each segment, average the $\hat{C}(m,k)$'s over all segments, and finally, equate the sample mean to zero to obtain the CTOM equations. It was shown by Raghuveer and Nikias (1986) that asymptotically, the CTOM method and the TOR method are equivalent for a given model order.

9.5 CEPSTRA OF HIGHER-ORDER SPECTRA

One of the early approaches for non-minimum-phase signal reconstruction has been homomorphic filtering based on the complex cepstrum or the differential cepstrum. However, the cepstrum approach requires that the input signal is an impulse train (not a stationary random process) and that it completely separates from the impulse response of the system in the cepstrum domain. In addition, the complex cepstrum approach requires the use of phase-unwrapping algorithms, whereas the differential cepstrum method may exhibit severe aliasing.

9.5.1 Preliminaries

Let us consider the ARMA process $x(k)$ described by (9.4.1), (9.4.3), and (9.4.4). Since the system is generally nonminimum phase and stable, its transfer function may also be written in terms of poles and zeros as

$$H(z) = AI(z^{-1})O(z)z^{-r} \tag{9.5.1}$$

where $I(z^{-1})$ is the minimum-phase component with poles c_i and zeros d_i inside the unit circle,

$$I(z^{-1}) = \frac{\sum_{i=1}^{L_1} (1 - d_i z^{-1})}{\sum_{i=1}^{p} (1 - c_i z^{-1})} \tag{9.5.2}$$

and $O(z)$ is the maximum phase component, defined as

$$O(z) = \prod_{i=1}^{L_2} (1 - e_i z) \tag{9.5.3}$$

The parameter A is a constant and r is a positive integer. Note that there is no specific reason for excluding maximum phase poles in (9.5.3). Similarly, the minimum-phase impulse response of the ARMA system is given by (causal part)

$$i(n) = \frac{1}{2\pi} \int_{-\pi}^{\pi} I(-\omega) \exp(j\omega n)\, d\omega, \qquad n \geq 0 \tag{9.5.4}$$

and the maximum-phase component (anticausal part) is

$$o(n) = \frac{1}{2\pi} \int_{-\pi}^{\pi} O(\omega) \exp(j\omega n)\, d\omega, \qquad n \leq 0 \tag{9.5.5}$$

From the system transfer function $H(z)$ in (9.5.1) and its impulse response components in (9.5.4) and (9.5.5), it follows that the system impulse response $h(n)$ is given by

$$h(n) = i(n) * o(n) \tag{9.5.6}$$

9.5.2 Complex Cepstrum and Differential Cepstrum

The differential cepstrum of $h(n)$ is defined by Polydoros and Fam (1981) as

$$h_d(n) \equiv Z^{-1}\left[\frac{1}{H(z)} \frac{\partial H(z)}{\partial z}\right] \tag{9.5.7}$$

and shown to satisfy the property

$$h_d(n) = i_d(n) + o_d(n) \tag{9.5.8}$$

where $i_d(n)$ and $o_d(n)$ are the differential cepstra of $i(n)$ and $o(n)$, respectively. On the other hand, the complex cepstrum of $h(n)$ is defined by Tribolet (1979) as

$$h_c(n) \equiv Z^{-1}[\ln H(z)] \tag{9.5.9}$$

and is related to the differential cepstrum by the expression

$$h_c(n) = -\frac{1}{n} h_d(n + 1), \qquad n \neq 0 \tag{9.5.10}$$

Polydoros and Fam (1981) have shown that the following recursive relations hold for $i(n)$ and $o(n)$:

$$i(n) = -\frac{1}{n}\sum_{k=2}^{n+1} i_d(k)i(n-k+1) \qquad \text{for } n \geq 1 \tag{9.5.11}$$

$$o(n) = -\frac{1}{n}\sum_{k=n+1}^{0} o_d(k)o(n-k+1) \qquad \text{for } n \leq -1 \tag{9.5.12}$$

where, initially, $i(0) = o(0) = 1$.

The system impulse response follows from (9.5.6). It should be pointed out that $i(n) \to 0$ as $n \to \infty$, as well as $o(n) \to 0$ as $n \to -\infty$.

9.5.3 Bicepstrum

Pan and Nikias (1988) have shown that the complex cepstrum or differential cepstrum coefficients can be computed directly from the higher-order cumulants of $x(k)$ without the need of phase unwrapping and without aliasing effects. We describe here the cepstrum of the bispectrum (bicepstrum) approach and its properties.

By combining (9.4.2) and (9.5.1) and ignoring the linear-phase term, the bispectrum of $x(k)$ is given by

$$\begin{aligned} C_3^x(z_1, z_2) = \gamma_3^w \frac{A^3}{(2\pi)^2} I(z_1^{-1})I(z_2^{-1})I(z_1 z_2) \\ \times O(z_1)O(z_2)O(z_1^{-1}z_2^{-1}) \end{aligned} \tag{9.5.13}$$

Thus the z-transform of the bicepstrum is defined as

$$\begin{aligned} C_x(z_1,z_2) = \ln[C_3^x(z_1,z_2)] &= \ln|A_3| + \ln I(z_1^{-1}) \\ &+ \ln I(z_2^{-1}) + \ln I(z_1 z_2) + \ln O(z_1) \\ &+ \ln O(z_2) + \ln O(z_1^{-1}z_2^{-1}) \end{aligned} \tag{9.5.14}$$

where $A_3 = \gamma_3^w A^3/(2\pi)^2$. The bicepstrum is obtained by computing the inverse z-transform of $C_x(z_1,z_2)$,

$$c_x(m,n) \equiv Z^{-1}[C_x(z_1,z_2)] = \begin{cases} \ln|A_3|, & m = 0, \quad n = 0 \\ -\frac{1}{n}A^{(n)}, & m = 0, \quad n > 0 \\ -\frac{1}{m}A^{(m)}, & n = 0, \quad m > 0 \\ -\frac{1}{m}B^{(-m)}, & n = 0, \quad m < 0 \\ \frac{1}{n}B^{(-n)}, & m = 0, \quad n < 0 \\ -\frac{1}{n}B^{(n)}, & m = n > 0 \\ \frac{1}{n}A^{(-n)}, & m = n < 0 \\ 0, & \text{otherwise} \end{cases} \tag{9.5.15}$$

where

$$A^{(k)} \equiv \sum_{i=1}^{L_1} d_i^k - \sum_{i=1}^{p} c_i^k$$
$$B^{(k)} = \sum_{i=1}^{L_2} e_i^k \tag{9.5.16}$$

are parameters that contain the minimum- and maximum-phase information, respectively. Pan and Nikias (1988) have shown that

$$i_d(n) = \begin{cases} A^{(n-1)}, & n \geq 2 \\ 0, & n \leq 1 \end{cases} \tag{9.5.17}$$

$$o_d(n) = \begin{cases} 0, & n \geq 1 \\ -B^{(1-n)}, & n \leq 0 \end{cases} \tag{9.5.18}$$

which implies that the parameters $A^{(k)}$ and $B^{(k)}$ correspond to the *differential* cepstrum coefficients of the system impulse response.

Since $C_x(z_1,z_2)$ is analytic in its region of convergence, which contains the unit surface, the following linear convolution (*) operation is valid:

$$c_3^x(m,n) * [-mc_x(m,n)] = -mc_3^x(m,n) \tag{9.5.19}$$

By substituting (9.5.15) into (9.5.19) we obtain the cepstral equation

$$\sum_{k=1}^{\infty} \{A^{(k)}[c_3^x(m-k,n) - c_3^x(m+k,n+k)] + B^{(k)}[c_3^x(m-k,n-k) - c_3^x(m+k,n)]\} = -mc_3^x(m,n) \tag{9.5.20}$$

which provides a *direct relationship* between parameters $A^{(k)}$ and $B^{(k)}$ and the third-order cumulants $c_3^x(m,n)$. Since $|d_i| < 1$, $|e_i| < 1$, and $|c_i| < 1$ for all i, we can always truncate the summation in (9.5.20) arbitrarily closely and obtain the approximate cepstral equation,

$$\sum_{i=1}^{p} \{A^{(i)}[c_3^x(m-i,n) - c_3^x(m+i,n+i)] + \sum_{j=1}^{q} B^{(j)}[c_3^x(m-j,n-j) - c_3^x(m+j,n)]\} \approx -mc_3^x(m,n) \tag{9.5.21}$$

Equation (9.5.21) may easily be written as an overdetermined system of equations with the cepstral parameters $A^{(i)}$ and $B^{(i)}$ as unknowns. A least-squares solution is then obtained for the cepstral parameters. The importance of the result given by (9.5.17) and (9.5.18) lies in its connection with the differential cepstrum and thus the complex cepstrum (9.5.9) of the system's impulse response.

An alternative method for computing the cepstrum coefficients in (9.5.15) that does not require phase unwrapping is based on the two-dimensional fast Fourier transform (FFT). From (9.5.19) we obtain

$$mc_x(m,n) = F^{-1}\left\{\frac{F[mc_3^x(m,n)]}{F[c_3^x(m,n)]}\right\} \tag{9.5.22}$$

where $F[\cdot]$ represents the two-dimensional Fourier transform. Therefore, $c_x(m,n)$ can be computed by using either the conventional bispectrum estimate (two-dimensional FFT computations) or the parametric bispectrum estimate.

Several properties of this approach have been given by Pan and Nikias (1988): (1) the minimum- and maximum-phase components of the impulse response are estimated separately; (2) the method is computationally attractive as it involves a solution of a linear system of equations; (3) it works for MA, AR, or ARMA signals (or systems); (4) it does not require model-order selection; (5) the length of the minimum and maximum impulse responses is determined by the algorithm itself based on a preselected threshold value; and (6) the method does not require a priori knowledge of the type of the model (AR, MA, or ARMA).

On the other hand, the computational complexity of the bicepstrum methods (LS- or FFT-based) rises when poles or zeros of the system come close to the unit circle. Also, the equations given in (9.5.21) require a priori knowledge or good estimates of the parameters p and q. If p and q are severely underestimated, the phase and magnitude information will not be recovered accurately. Procedures for choosing p and q are given in the paper by Pan and Nikias (1988).

9.5.4 Cepstrum of the Power Spectrum

From (9.4.2) we recall that the power spectrum is given by

$$C_2^x(\omega) = \frac{\gamma_2^w}{2\pi} H(\omega)H^*(\omega) \tag{9.5.23}$$

Therefore, the cepstrum of the power spectrum is defined as

$$p_x(m) = F^{-1}\{\ln C_2^x(\omega)\} \tag{9.5.24}$$

which can be shown to be equal to

$$p_x(m) = \begin{cases} \ln|A_2|, & m = 0 \\ -\dfrac{1}{m}[A^{(m)} + B^{(m)}], & m > 0 \\ \dfrac{1}{m}[A^{(-m)} + B^{(-m)}], & m < 0 \end{cases} \tag{9.5.25}$$

where $A^{(m)}$ and $B^{(m)}$ are given by (9.5.16) and $A_2 = \gamma_2^w A^2/2\pi$. The power cepstrum can be computed from

$$c_2^x(m) * [-mp_x(m)] = -mc_2^x(m) \tag{9.5.26}$$

either by forming and solving a linear system of equations or by using the one-dimensional FFT. Thus

$$p_x(m) = \frac{1}{m} F^{-1}\left\{\frac{F[mc_2^x(m)]}{F[c_2^x(m)]}\right\} \tag{9.5.27}$$

Note that $c_2^x(m)$ is the covariance sequence of the signal and $F[\cdot]$ denotes the Fourier transform.

9.5.5 Cepstrum of the Bicoherence

The complex cepstrum of the bicoherence is defined as the inverse Fourier transform of the complex logarithm of the bicoherence function (9.2.24). By combining (9.2.24), (9.2.27), and (9.2.28), we see that the bicoherence function is a function of the *phase of the bispectrum* only,

$$P_3^x(\omega_1,\omega_2) = A_4 \exp[j\psi_3^h(\omega_1,\omega_2)] \tag{9.5.28}$$

where $A_4 = \gamma_3^w/(\gamma_2^w)^{3/2}$. Thus the cepstrum of the bicoherence is given by

$$b_x(m,n) = F^{-1}\{\ln|A_4| + \psi_3^h(\omega_1,\omega_2)\} \tag{9.5.29}$$

or, as shown by Nikias and Liu (1990),

$$b_x(m,n) = \frac{1}{2}\begin{cases} \ln|A_4|, & m = 0, \quad n = 0 \\ -\frac{1}{m}[A^{(m)} - B^{(m)}], & m > 0, \quad n = 0 \\ -\frac{1}{m}[A^{(-m)} - B^{(-m)}], & m < 0, \quad n = 0 \\ -\frac{1}{n}[A^{(n)} - B^{(n)}], & m = 0, \quad n > 0 \\ -\frac{1}{n}[A^{(-n)} - B^{(-n)}], & m = 0, \quad n < 0 \\ \frac{1}{n}[A^{(m)} - B^{(m)}], & m = n > 0 \\ -\frac{1}{m}[A^{(-m)} - B^{(-m)}], & m = n < 0 \end{cases} \tag{9.5.30}$$

Clearly, the cepstrum of the bicoherence contains only the phase information of the system transfer function, $H(\omega)$.

There are two methods for computing $b_x(m,n)$. The first is based on the convolution formula

$$\begin{aligned} &c_3^x(m,n) * c_3^q(m,n) * [-mb_x(m,n)] \\ &= c_3^q(m,n) * [-mc_3^x(m,n)] - \tfrac{1}{2}c_3^x(m,n) * [-mc_3^q(m,n)] \end{aligned} \tag{9.5.31}$$

where $c_3^q(m,n)$ are the third-order moments of the autocorrelation sequence,

$$c_3^q(m,n) = F^{-1}\{C_2^x(\omega_1)\, C_2^x(\omega_2)\, C_2^x(\omega_1 + \omega_2)\} \tag{9.5.32}$$

The second method is via two-dimensional FFT, given by the formula

$$b_x(m,n) = \frac{1}{m}F^{-1}\left\{\frac{F[mc_3^x(m,n)]}{F[c_3^x(m,n)]} - \frac{1}{2}\frac{F[mc_3^q(m,n)]}{F[c_3^q(m,n)]}\right\} \tag{9.5.33}$$

where $F[\cdot]$ denotes the two-dimensional Fourier transform.

9.5.6 Summary of Cepstra and Key Observations

The complex cepstrum of the system inpulse response, defined in (9.5.9), is directly related to the $A^{(k)}$ and $B^{(k)}$ cepstral coefficients given in (9.5.16) as follows:

$$h_c(m) = \begin{cases} -\dfrac{A^{(m)}}{m}, & m > 0 \\ \dfrac{B^{(m)}}{m}, & m < 0 \end{cases} \tag{9.5.34}$$

By comparing (9.5.34) with (9.5.15), we see that the bicepstrum of $H(\omega)$ is indeed its complex cepstrum being repeated three times,

$$h_c(m) = c_x(m,0) = c_x(0,n) = c_x(m,m) \tag{9.5.35}$$

Thus (9.5.21) and (9.5.22) provide us with two different ways of computing the complex cepstrum of the signal directly from its third-order cumulants, *without* the need of phase unwrapping.

Another important observation is that the differences of cepstral coefficients $(A^{(m)} - B^{(m)})$ contain the phase information of $H(\omega)$, while their sums $(A^{(m)} + B^{(m)})$ contain the magnitude information. From (9.5.29) and (9.5.30), we obtain

$$b_x(m,0) = -\frac{1}{m}[A^{(m)} - B^{(m)}] \tag{9.5.36}$$

It has been shown by Petropulu and Nikias (1990) that the phase $\phi_h(\omega)$ of $H(\omega)$ is

$$\phi_h(\omega) = F[b_x(m,0)] \tag{9.5.37}$$

On the other hand, from (9.5.25), we obtain

$$p_x(m) = -\frac{1}{m}[A^{(m)} + B^{(m)}] \tag{9.5.38}$$

The magnitude $|H(\omega)|$ is related to the power spectrum via

$$p_x(m) = F^{-1}[\ln|H(\omega)|^2] \tag{9.5.39}$$

Thus we conclude that the complex cepstrum of the signal can be computed from second- and third-order statistics by using (9.5.36) through (9.5.39).

9.6 PHASE AND MAGNITUDE RETRIEVAL FROM THE BISPECTRUM

As we have observed, a knowledge of a higher-order spectrum ($n > 2$) of a linear non-Gaussian signal allows one to reconstruct both its magnitude and phase response (apart from a linear phase shift). In this section we describe phase and magnitude retrieval algorithms assuming that the phase and magnitude of the bispectrum are known, respectively. The extension of these algorithms to higher-order spectra (trispectrum) is straightforward.

Let us assume that the phase and magnitude of the bispectrum are given, respectively, by the expressions

$$\psi_3^x(\omega_1,\omega_2) = \phi_x(\omega_1) + \phi_x(\omega_2) - \phi_x(\omega_1 + \omega_2) \tag{9.6.1}$$

$$|C_3^x(\omega_1,\omega_2)| = |X(\omega_1)|\,|X(\omega_2)|\,|X(\omega_1 + \omega_2)| \tag{9.6.2}$$

where $\phi_x(\omega)$ is the phase response of the signal and $|X(\omega)|$ its magnitude. The problem is to reconstruct $\phi_x(\omega)$ ($|X(\omega)|$) from $\psi_3^x(\omega_1,\omega_2)$ ($|C_3^x(\omega_1,\omega_2)|$). An important observation is that a logarithmic operation on (9.6.2) yields

$$\log|C_3^x(\omega_1,\omega_2)| = \log|X(\omega_1)| + \log|X(\omega_2)| + \log|X(\omega_1 + \omega_2)| \tag{9.6.3}$$

Consequently, phase recovery algorithms from bispectra can also be used as magnitude recovery algorithms based on (9.6.3).

The relation in (9.6.1) is the governing identity and can take the discrete form

$$\psi_3^x(m,n) = \phi_x(m) + \phi_x(n) - \phi_x(m + n) \tag{9.6.4}$$

The phase retrieval problem is to reconstruct $\phi_x(m)$, $m = 0, 1, \ldots, N$ from $\psi_3^x(m,n)$. Brillinger (1967) originally suggested the recursive equation

$$\phi_x(\omega) = \frac{2\int_0^{\omega} \phi_x(\lambda)\, d\lambda - \int_0^{\omega} \psi_3^x(\lambda, \omega - \lambda)\, d\lambda}{\omega} \tag{9.6.5}$$

which was modified for digital computations, resulting in the expression

$$\phi_x(n) = \frac{2\sum_{i=0}^{n-1} \phi_x(i) - S(n)}{n - 1}, \qquad n = 2, 3, \ldots, N \tag{9.6.6}$$

where

$$S(n) = \sum_{i=0}^{n} \psi_3^x(i, n - i) \tag{9.6.7}$$

The term $n = 0$ corresponds to $\omega = 0$ and $n = N$ corresponds to $\omega = \pi$. Two initial conditions need to be specified, $\phi_x(0)$ and $\phi_x(1)$. The value of $\phi_x(0)$ may be zero or $\pm\pi$ and is determined from $\psi_3^x(0,0)$. Estimation of $\phi_x(1)$ is obtained from

$$\phi_x(1) = \sum_{n=2}^{N} \frac{S(n) - S(N - 1)}{n(n - 1)} + \frac{\phi_x(N)}{N} \tag{9.6.8}$$

where $\phi_x(N)$ can be set to zero or $k\pi$ (i.e., it is equivalent to a pure time delay).

Lii and Rosenblatt [Nikias and Raghuveer (1987)] introduced the recursive formula

$$\phi_x(n) = \sum_{i=0}^{n-1} \psi_3^x(i,1) + \phi_x(0) + n\phi_x(1) \tag{9.6.9}$$

where the initial conditions are determined as before. However, this algorithm is limited to the use of the bispectrum values along a straight line parallel to either ω_1 or ω_2 and therefore does not utilize all the available information. By defining

$$\begin{aligned} \mathbf{\Phi} &= [\phi_x(1), \phi_x(2), \ldots, \phi_x(N-1)]' \\ \mathbf{\Psi} &= [\psi_3^x(1,1), \psi_3^x(1,2), \ldots, \psi_3^x(2,2), \psi_3^x(2,3), \ldots, \psi_3^x(N/2,N/2)]' \end{aligned} \tag{9.6.10}$$

the Matsuoka–Ulrych method forms the following set of equations using (9.6.4):

$$\mathbf{A\Phi} = \mathbf{\Psi} \tag{9.6.11}$$

where $\mathbf{A}$ is a sparse coefficient matrix,

$$\mathbf{A} = \begin{bmatrix} 2 & -1 & 0 & 0 & 0 & \cdots & 0 \\ 1 & 1 & -1 & 0 & 0 & \cdots & 0 \\ 1 & 0 & 1 & -1 & 0 & \cdots & 0 \\ \vdots & \vdots & \vdots & \vdots & \vdots & & \vdots \\ 1 & 0 & 0 & 0 & 0 & \cdots & 1 \\ 0 & 2 & 0 & -1 & 0 & \cdots & 0 \\ 0 & 1 & 1 & 0 & -1 & \cdots & \\ \vdots & \vdots & \vdots & \vdots & \vdots & & \vdots \end{bmatrix} \tag{9.6.12}$$

of size $(N/2)^2 \times (N-1)$ for N even and $(N^2-1)/4 \times (N-1)$ for N odd. The unknown phase vector is obtained by using the least-squares solution

$$\mathbf{\Phi} = (\mathbf{A}'\mathbf{A})^{-1}\mathbf{A}'\mathbf{\Psi} \tag{9.6.13}$$

This algorithm is a nonrecursive method that utilizes all the bispectrum values available in the principal domain.

Additional phase retrieval algorithms have been suggested by Lohman and Wirnitzer (1984), Bartlett et al. (1984), and Pan and Nikias (1987). The performance evaluation of these algorithms in the trispectrum domain as well as their sensitivity due to initial condition estimates were studied by Pan and Nikias (1987).

Petropulu and Nikias (1992) introduced phase and magnitude retrieval algorithms based on the bicepstrum, which are simple and computationally attractive. Given the phase of the bispectrum, the algorithm proceeds to generate

$$d_\phi(m,n) = \begin{cases} \frac{1}{2}F^{-1}\{\psi_3^x(\omega_1,\omega_2\}, & m \neq 0 \\ 0, & m = 0 \end{cases} \tag{9.6.14}$$

and then

$$\phi_x(\omega) = F[d_\phi(m,0)] \tag{9.6.15}$$

An equivalent algorithm that employs the cepstrum of the bicoherence directly generates

$$d(m) = \begin{cases} j\dfrac{1}{2m}[A^{(|m|)} - B^{(|m|)}], & m \neq 0 \\ 0, & m = 0 \end{cases} \tag{9.6.16}$$

and then

$$\phi_x(\omega) = F[d(m)] \tag{9.6.17}$$

Let us note that all phase retrieval algorithms discussed in this section, except the algorithm described by (9.6.16) and (9.6.17), require that $\psi_3(\omega_1,\omega_2)$ be unwrapped. However, a simple two-dimensional phase unwrapping algorithm can be based on the bicepstrum, $c_x(m,n)$ and takes the form

$$\psi_3^x(\omega_1,\omega_2) = -jF[c_x(m,n)] - |C_3^x(\omega_1,\omega_2)| \tag{9.6.18}$$

In summary, the Brillinger and Lii–Rosenblatt algorithms are very sensitive to initial condition phase estimation errors. The Matsuoka–Ulrych algorithm requires matrix inversion. However, the inversion of the sparse matrix can be performed only once. The algorithm described by (9.6.14) and (9.6.15) recovers the phase with one two-dimensional FFT and one one-dimensional FFT operation.

9.7 SUMMARY AND REFERENCES

In this chapter we have introduced the motivation, definitions, properties, and estimation methods of higher-order spectra from a digital signal-processing perspective. In particular, we have summarized the conventional class of estimation techniques as well as parametric methods based on MA and causal and noncausal AR and ARMA models. We have introduced the concept of the cepstrum of higher-order spectra, its properties, and its computation. Finally, we have discussed phase and magnitude retrieval algorithms from the bispectrum.

The first tutorial paper on polyspectra was published in the statistics literature by Brillinger (1965). The definitions and properties of higher-order spectra, as well as conventional methods for their estimation, are treated in the books by Harris (1967), Rosenblatt (1985), and Zurbenko (1986). The first engineering tutorial paper on higher-order spectra, emphasizing digital signal-processing applications, was published by Nikias and Raghuveer (1987). The papers by Hinich (1982) and Hinich et al. (1988, 1990) provide tests for Gaussianity, linearity, and aliasing using the bispectrum.

There are numerous methods for higher-order spectrum estimation based on parametric models. MA models have been treated by Nikias et al. (1988), Giannakis and Mendel (1989), and Friedlander and Porat (1988). Huzzi (1981) and Tugnait (1987, 1988) have treated spectral estimation methods based on noncausal AR models. Methods based on ARMA models have been published by Lii (1982) and Giannakis and Swami (1987). The description of MA, AR, and ARMA methods based on higher-order statistics is the subject of the tutorial paper by Mendel (1991).

The quadratic phase coupling phenomenon has been studied by Raghuveer and Nikias (1986) using AR models with the bispectrum. Conventional methods for the detection and characterization of quadratic phase coupling are summarized in the tutorial paper by Nikias and Raghuveer (1987).

The complex cepstrum of a signal, its properties, and the description of phase unwrapping algorithms are treated by Tribolet (1979). The differential cepstrum and its properties are given in the paper by Polydoros and Fam (1981). The cepstrum of higher-order spectra, its properties, its computation, and several applications can be found in the papers by Pan and Nikias (1988), Petropulu and Nikias (1990), and Nikias and Liu (1990).

Finally, nonparametric methods for signal phase reconstruction from the bispectrum have been developed by Lohman and Wirnitzer (1984), Bartlett et al. (1984), Pan and Nikias (1987), and Petropulu and Nikias (1992).

PROBLEMS

9.1 Let x be a Gaussian random variable with zero-mean and variance σ_x^2. Show that its cumulants c_n^x of order $n > 2$ are all zero.

9.2 Let x and y be two independent random variables and $z = x + y$. Show that $c_n^z = c_n^x + c_n^y$ for $n \geq 2$. Also derive the relationship between m_1^x and the moments of x and y.

9.3 Let $y(n) = x(n) - x(n - 1)$, where $x(n)$ is a white, non-Gaussian, stationary random process with zero mean, variance γ_2^x, and skewness γ_3^x. Calculate the cumulants $c_2^y(\tau)$ and $c_3^y(\tau_1,\tau_2)$ and their corresponding power spectrum $C_2^y(\omega)$ and bispectrum $C_3^y(\omega_1,\omega_2)$. What is the value $c_3^y(0,0)$ [skewness of $y(n)$]?

9.4 Show the symmetry properties of third-order cumulants (9.2.2).

9.5 Suppose that $y(n) = a_1w(n) + a_2w(n - 1) + a_3w(n - 2)$, where $w(n)$ is a white, non-Gaussian, zero-mean stationary random process with variance γ_2^w and skewness γ_3^w. Determine the covariance and third-order cumulants of $y(n)$ for the following cases:

(a) $a_1 = 1$, $a_2 = -0.8$, $a_3 = 0.15$
(b) $a_1 = -0.5$, $a_2 = 1.15$, $a_3 = -0.3$
(c) $a_1 = 0.15$, $a_2 = -0.8$, $a_3 = 1$

9.6 Show that the third-order cumulants of $x_1(k)$ described by (9.2.35) are identical to zero.

9.7 Let $H(z) = (1 - az)(1 - bz^{-1})$, where $|a| < 1$ and $|b| < 1$. Derive closed-form expressions for the following:

(a) Complex cepstrum $h_c(n)$
(b) Differential cepstrum $h_d(n)$
(c) Bicepstrum $b_h(m,n)$
(d) Power cepstrum $P_h(n)$
(e) Cepstrum of bicoherence $b_h(m,n)$

References and Bibliography

AGARWAL, RAMESH C., and COOLEY, JAMES W. (1977). "New Algorithms for Digital Convolution, *IEEE Trans. ASSP*, vol. 25, pp. 392–410, October.

AHMED, A., and YOUN, D. H. (1980) "On a Realization and Related Algorithms of Adaptive Prediction," *IEEE Trans. ASSP*, vol. 28, pp. 493–497, October.

AKAIKE, H. (1969). "Power Spectrum Estimation Through Autoregression Model Fitting," *Ann. Inst. Math.*, vol. 21, pp. 407–419.

AKAIKE, H. (1974). "A New Look at the Statistical Model Identification," *IEEE Trans. Automatic Control*, vol. AC-19, pp. 716–723, December.

ANDERSEN, N. O. (1978). "Comments on the Performance of Maximum Entropy Algorithm," *Proc. IEEE*, vol. 66, pp. 1581–1582, November.

BAGGEROER, A. B. (1976). "Confidence Intervals for Regression (MEM) Spectral Estimates," *IEEE Trans. Information Theory*, vol. IT-22, pp. 534–545, September.

BARTELT, H. O., LOHMANN, A. W., and WIRNITZER, B. (1984). "Phase and Amplitude Recovery from Bispectrum," *Appl. Optics*, vol. 23, pp. 3121–3129, September.

BARTLETT, M. S. (1948). "Smoothing Periodograms from Time Series with Continuous Spectra," *Nature* (London), vol. 161, pp. 686–687, May.

BARTLETT, M. S. (1961). *Stochastic Processes*, Cambridge University Press, Cambridge.

BECKMAN, F. S. (1960). "The Solution of Linear Equations by the Conjugate Gradient Method," in *Mathematical Methods for Digital Computers*, A. Ralston and H. S. Wilf, Eds., Wiley, New York.

BERK, K. N. (1974). "Consistent Autoregressive Spectral Estimates," *Ann. Stat.*, vol. 2, pp. 489–502.

BERRYMAN, J. G. (1978). "Choice of Operator Length for Maximum Entropy Spectral Analysis," *Geophysics*, vol. 43, pp. 1384–1391, December.

BIERMAN, G. J. (1977). *Factorization Methods for Discrete Sequential Estimation*, Academic, New York.

BJÖRCK, A. (1967). "Solving Linear Least Squares Problems by Gram-Schmidt Orthogonalization," *BIT*, vol. 7, pp. 1–21.

BLACKMAN, R. B., and TUKEY, J. W. (1958). *The Measurement of Power Spectra*, Dover, New York.

BLAHUT, R. E. (1985). *Fast Algorithms for Digital Signal Processing*, Addison-Wesley, Reading, Mass.

BRENT, R. P., and LUK, F. T. (1985). "The Solution of Singular-Value and Symmetric Eigenvalue Problems on Multiprocessor Arrays," *SIAM J. Sci. Statist. Comput.*, vol. 6, pp. 69–84.

BRENT, R. P., LUK, F. T., and VAN LOAN, C. F. (1985). "Computation of the Singular

Value Decomposition Using Mesh-Connected Processors," *J. VLSI and Computer Systems*, vol. 1, pp. 242–270.

BRILLINGER, D. R. (1965). "An Introduction to Polyspectra," *Ann. Math. Statist.*, vol. 36, pp. 1351–1374.

BRILLINGER, D. R. (1974). "Fourier Analysis of Stationary Processes," *Proc. IEEE*, vol. 62, pp. 1628–1643, December.

BRILLINGER, D. R., and ROSENBLATT, M. (1967). "Asymptotic Theory of k-th Order Spectra," in *Spectral Analysis of Time Series*, B. Harris (ed.), pp. 153–188, Wiley, New York.

BRILLINGER, D. R., and ROSENBLATT, M. (1967). "Computation and Interpretation of k-th Order Spectra," in *Spectral Analysis of Time Series*, B. Harris (ed.), 189–232, Wiley, New York.

BROWN, J. L., JR. (1980). "First-Order Sampling of Bandpass Signals—A New Approach," *IEEE Trans. Information Theory*, vol. IT-26, pp. 613–615, September.

BROWN, R. C. (1983). *Introduction to Random Signal Analysis and Kalman Filtering*, Wiley, New York.

BRUZZONE, S. P., and KAVEH, M. (1980). "On Some Suboptimum ARMA Spectral Estimators," *IEEE Trans. Acoustics, Speech, and Signal Processing*, vol. ASSP-28, pp. 753–755, December.

BURG, J. P. (1967). "Maximum Entropy Spectral Analysis," *Proc. 37th Meeting of the Society of Exploration Geophysicists*, Oklahoma City, Okla., October. Reprinted in *Modern Spectrum Analysis*, D. G. Childers, Ed., IEEE press, New York.

BURG, J. P. (1968). "A New Analysis Technique for Time Series Data," NATO Advanced Study Institute on Signal Processing with Emphasis on Underwater Acoustics, August 12–23. Reprinted in *Modern Spectrum Analysis*, D. G. Childers, Ed., IEEE Press, New York.

BURG, J. P. (1972). "The Relationship Between Maximum Entropy and Maximum Likelihood Spectra," *Geophysics*, vol. 37, pp. 375–376, April.

BURG, J. P. (1975). "Maximum Entropy Spectral Analysis," Ph.D. dissertation, Department of Geophysics, Stanford University, Stanford, Calif., May.

CADZOW, J. A. (1979). "ARMA Spectral Estimation: An Efficient Closed-form Procedure," *Proc. RADC Spectrum Estimation Workshop*, pp. 81–97, Rome, N.Y., October.

CADZOW, J. A. (1981). "Autoregressive–Moving Average Spectral Estimation: A Model Equation Error Procedure," *IEEE Trans. Geoscience Remote Sensing*, vol. GE-19, pp. 24–28. January.

CADZOW, J. A. (1982). "Spectral Estimation: An Overdetermined Rational Model Equation Approach," *Proc. IEEE*, vol. 70, pp. 907–938, September.

CAPON, J. (1969). "High Resolution Frequency–Wavenumber Spectrum Analysis," *Proc. IEEE*, vol. 57, pp. 1408–1418. August.

CAPON, J. (1983). "Maximum-Likelihood Spectral Estimation," in *Nonlinear Methods of Spectral Analysis*, 2nd ed., S. Haykin, Ed., Springer-Verlag, New York.

CAPON, J., and GOODMAN, N. R. (1971). "Probability Distribution for Estimators of the Frequency–Wavenumber Spectrum, *Proc. IEEE*, vol. 58, pp. 1785–1786, October.

CARAISCOS, C., and LIU, B. (1984). "A Roundoff Error Analysis of the LMS Adaptive Algorithm," *IEEE Trans. Acoustics, Speech, and Signal Processing*, vol. ASSP-32, pp. 34–41, January.

CARAYANNIS, G., MANOLAKIS, D. G., and KALOUPTSIDIS, N. (1983). "A Fast Sequential Algorithm for Least-Squares Filtering and Prediction," *IEEE Trans. Acoustics, Speech, and Signal Processing*, vol. ASSP-31, pp. 1394–1402, December.

Carayannis, G., Manolakis, D. G., and Kalouptsidis, N. (1986). "A Unified View of Parametric Processing Algorithms for Prewindowed Signals," *Signal Processing*, vol. 10, pp. 335–368, June.

Carlson, N. A., and Culmone, A. F. (1979). "Efficient Algorithms for On-Board Array Processing," *Record 1979 International Conference on Communications*, pp. 58.1.1–58.1.5, Boston, June 10–14.

Chen, W. Y., and Stegen, G. R. (1974). "Experiments with Maximum Entropy Power Spectra of Sinusoids," *J. Geophys. Res.*, vol. 79, pp. 3019–3022, July.

Childers, D. G., ed. (1978). *Modern Spectrum Analysis*, IEEE Press, New York.

Chow, J. C. (1972). "On Estimating the Orders of an Autoregressive-Moving Average Process with Uncertain Observations," *IEEE Trans. Automatic Control*, vol. AC-17, pp. 707–709, October.

Chui, C. K., and Chen, G. (1987). *Kalman Filtering*, Springer-Verlag, New York.

Cioffi, J. M. (1990a). "The Fast Adaptive ROTOR's RLS Algorithm," *IEEE Trans. on ASSP*, vol. 38, No. 4, pp. 631–653, April 1990.

Cioffi, J. M. (1990b). "The Fast Householder RLS Adaptive Filter," *Proc. 1990 IEEE ICASSP*, pp. 1631–1634, April.

Cioffi, J. M. (1987). "The Fast QR Adaptive Filter," *Proc. 1987 IEEE ICASSP*, Dallas, Texas, April.

Cioffi, J. M. (1987). "Limited Precision Effects in Adaptive Filtering," *IEEE Trans. Circuits and Systems*, vol. CAS-34, pp. 821–833, July.

Cioffi, J. M., and Kailath, T. (1984). "Fast Recursive-Least-Squares Transversal Filters for Adaptive Filtering," *IEEE Trans. Acoustics, Speech, and Signal Processing*, vol. ASSP-32, pp. 304–337, April.

Cioffi, J. M., and Kailath, T. (1985). "Windowed Fast Transversal Filters Adaptive Algorithms with Normalization," *IEEE Trans. Acoustics, Speech, and Signal Processing*, vol. ASSP-33, pp. 607–625, June.

Crochiere, R. E. (1977). "On the Design of Sub-band Coders for Low Bit Rate Speech Communication," *Bell Syst. Tech. J.*, vol. 56, pp. 747–771, May–June.

Crochiere, R. E. (1981). "Sub-band Coding," *Bell Syst. Tech. J.*, vol. 60, pp. 1633–1654, September.

Crochiere, R. E., and Rabiner, L. R. (1975). "Optimum FIR Digital Filter Implementations for Decimation, Interpolation, and Narrowband Filtering," *IEEE Trans. Acoustics, Speech, and Signal Processing*, vol. ASSP-23, pp. 444–456, October.

Crochiere, R. E., and Rabiner, L. R. (1976). "Further Considerations in the Design of Decimators and Interpolators," *IEEE Trans. Acoustics, Speech, and Signal Processing*, vol. ASSP-24, pp. 296–311, August.

Crochiere, R. E., and Rabiner, L. R. (1981). "Interpolation and Decimation of Digital Signals—A Tutorial Review," *Proc. IEEE*, vol. 69, pp. 300–331, March.

Crochiere, R. E., and Rabiner, L. R. (1983). *Multirate Digital Processing*, Prentice-Hall, Englewood Cliffs, N.J.

Davenport, W. B., Jr. (1970). *Probability and Random Processes: An Introduction for Applied Scientists and Engineers*, McGraw-Hill, New York.

DeFatta, D. J., Lucas, J. G., and Hodgkiss, W. S. (1988). *Digital Signal Processing*, Wiley, New York.

Delsarte, P., and Genin, Y. (1986). "The Split Levinson Algorithm," *IEEE Trans. Acoustics, Speech, and Signal Processing*, vol. ASSP-34, pp. 470–478, June.

Delsarte, P., Genin, Y., and Kamp, Y. (1978). "Orthogonal Polynomial Matrices on the Unit Circle," *IEEE Trans. Circuits and Systems*, vol. CAS-25, pp. 149–160, January.

DURBIN, J. (1959). "Efficient Estimation of Parameters in Moving-Average Models," *Biometrika*, vol. 46, pp. 306–316.

DUHAMEL, P., and HOLLMANN, H. (1984). "Split-radix FFT Algorithm," *Electr. Letters*, vol. 1, pp. 14–16, January.

ELEFTHERIOU, E., and FALCONER, D. D. (1987). "Adaptive Equalization Techniques for HF Channels," *IEEE J. Selected Areas in Communications*, vol. SAC-5, pp. 238–247. February.

FALCONER, D. D., and LJUNG, L. (1978). "Application of Fast Kalman Estimation to Adaptive Equalization," *IEEE Trans. Communications*, vol. COM-26, pp. 1439–1446, October.

FLETCHER, R., and POWELL, M. J. D. (1963). "A Rapidly Convergent Descent Method for Minimization," *Comput. J.*, vol. 6, pp. 163–168.

FORSYTHE, G. E., and MOLER, C. B. (1967). *Computer Solution of Linear Algebraic Systems*, Prentice-Hall, Englewood Cliffs, N.J.

FOUGERE, P. F., ZAWALICK, E. J., and RADOSKI, H. R. (1976). "Spontaneous Line Splitting in Maximum Entropy Power Spectrum Analysis," *Phys. Earth Planet. Inter.*, vol. 12, 201–207, August.

FRIEDLANDER, B. (1982a). "Lattice Filters for Adaptive Processing," *Proc. IEEE*, vol. 70, pp. 829–867, August.

FRIEDLANDER, B. (1982b). "Lattice Methods for Spectral Estimation," *Proc. IEEE*, vol. 70, pp. 990–1017, September.

FRIEDLANDER, B., and PORAT, B. (1988). "Performance Analysis of MA Parameter Estimation Algorithms Based on High-Order Moments," *Proc. 1988 IEEE ICASSP*, pp. 2412–1415, New York, April.

FUCHS, J. J. (1988). "Estimating the Number of Sinusoids in Additive White Noise," *IEEE Trans. Acoustics, Speech, and Signal Processing*, vol. ASSP-36, pp. 1846–1853, December.

GANTMACHER, F. R. (1960). *The Theory of Matrices*, vol. I., Chelsea, New York.

GARDNER, W. A. (1984). "Learning Characteristics of Scholastic-Gradient-Descent Algorithms: A General Study, Analysis and Critique," *Signal Processing*, vol. 6, pp. 113–133, April.

GARDNER, W. A. (1987). *Statistical Spectral Analysis: A Nonprobabilistic Theory*, Prentice-Hall, Englewood Cliffs, N.J.

GARLAN, C., and ESTEBAN, D. (1980). "16 Kbps Real-Time QMF Sub-band Coding Implementation," *Proc. 1980 International Conference on Acoustics, Speech, and Signal Processing*, pp. 332–335, April.

GENTLEMAN, W. M., and KUNG, H. T. (1981). "Matrix Triangularization by Systolic Arrays," *Proc. SPIE*, vol. 298, Real-Time Signal Processing IV, pp. 19–26, August.

GENTLEMAN, W. M. (1973a). "Error Analysis of Q-R Decomposition by Givens Transformations," *Linear Algebra and Its Applications*, Vol. 10, pp. 189–197.

GENTLEMAN, W. M. (1973b). "Least Squares Computations by Givens Transformations Without Square Roots," *J. Inst. Math Applics*, No. 12, pp. 329–336, December.

GEORGE, D. A., BOWEN, R. R., AND STOREY, J. R. (1971). "An Adaptive Decision-Feedback Equalizer," *IEEE Trans. Communication Technology*, vol. COM-19, pp. 281–293, June.

GERLACH, K. (1986). "Fast Orthogonalization Networks," *IEEE Trans. Antennas and Propagat.*, vol. AP-34, March.

GERONIMUS, L.Y. (1958). *Orthogonal Polynomials* (in Russian) (English translation by Consultant's Bureau, New York, 1961).

GERSCH, W., and SHARPE, D. R. (1973). "Estimation of Power Spectra with Finite-

Order Autoregressive Models," *IEEE Trans. Automatic Control*, vol. AC-18, pp. 367–369, August.

GERSHO, A. (1969). "Adaptive Equalization of Highly Dispersive Channels for Data Transmission," *Bell Syst. Tech. J.*, vol. 48, pp. 55–70, January.

GIANNAKIS, G. B., and MENDEL, J. M. (1989). "Identification of Nonminimum Phase Systems Using Higher-Order Statistics," *IEEE Trans. Acoustics, Speech, and Signal Processing*, vol. ASSP-37, pp. 360–377, March.

GIANNAKIS, G. B., and SWAMI, A. (1987). "New Results on State-Space and Input-Output Identification of Non-Gaussian Processes Using Cumulants," *Proc. Conf. Int'l Soc. for Optical Eng.*, vol. 826, San Diego, CA.

GITLIN, R. D., and WEINSTEIN, S. B. (1979). "On the Required Tap-Weight Precision for Digitally Implemented Mean-Squared Equalizers," *Bell Syst. Tech. J.*, vol. 58, pp. 301–321, February.

GITLIN, R. D., and WEINSTEIN, S. B. (1981). "Fractionally-Spaced Equalization: An Improved Digital Transversal Equalizer," *Bell Syst. Tech. J.*, vol. 60, pp. 275–296, February.

GITLIN, R. D., MEADORS, H. C., and WEINSTEIN, S. B. (1982). "The Tap-Leakage Algorithm: An Algorithm for the Stable Operation of a Digitally Implemented Fractionally Spaced, Adaptive Equalizer," *Bell Syst. Tech. J.*, vol. 61, pp. 1817–1839, October.

GIVENS, W. (1958). "Computation of Plane Unitary Rotations Transforming a General Matrix to Triangular Form," *SIAM J. Appl. Math.*, vol. 6, pp. 26–50.

GIVENS, W. (1954). "Numerical Computation of the Characteristic Values of a Real Symmetric Matrix," Oak Ridge National Laboratory Report ORNL-1574, Oak Ridge, TN.

GOHBERG, I., ed. (1986). *I. Schür Methods in Operator Theory and Signal Processing*, Birkhauser Verlag, Stuttgart, Germany.

GOLUB, G. H., and VAN LOAN, C. F. (1989). *Matrix Computations*, Second Ed., Johns Hopkins University Press, Baltimore, MD.

GOLUB, G. H. (1965). "Numerical Methods for Solving Linear Least Squares Problems," *Numer. Math*, vol. 7, pp. 206–216.

GRAUPE, D., KRAUSE, D. J., and MOORE, J. B. (1975). "Identification of Autoregressive-Moving Average Parameters of Time Series," *IEEE Trans. Automatic Control*, vol. AC-20, pp. 104–107, February.

GRENANDER, O., and SZEGÖ, G. (1958). *Toeplitz Forms and Their Applications*, University of California Press, Berkeley, Calif.

GRIFFITHS, L. J. (1975). "Rapid Measurements of Digital Instantaneous Frequency," *IEEE Trans. Acoustics, Speech, and Signal Processing*, vol. ASSP-23, pp. 207–222, April.

GRIFFITHS, L. J. (1977). "A Continuously Adaptive Filter Implemented as a Lattice Structure," *Proc. ICASSP-77*, pp. 683–686, Hartford, Conn., May.

GRIFFITHS, L. J. (1978). "An Adaptive Lattice Structure for Noise Cancelling Applications," *Proc. ICASSP-78*, pp. 87–90. Tulsa, Okla., April.

HAYKIN, S. (1991). *Adaptive Filter Theory*, Sec. Ed. Prentice-Hall, Englewood Cliffs, N.J.

HELME, B., and NIKIAS, C. L. (1985). "Improved Spectrum Performance via a Data-Adaptive Weighted Burg Technique," *IEEE Trans. Acoustics, Speech, and Signal Processing*, vol. ASSP-33, pp. 903–910, August.

HELSTROM, C. W. (1984). *Probability and Stochastic Processes for Engineers*, Macmillan, New York.

HERRING, R. W. (1980). "The Cause of Line Splitting in Burg Maximum-Entropy Spectral Analysis," *IEEE Trans. Acoustics, Speech, and Signal Processing*, vol. ASSP-28, pp. 692–701, December.

HERRMANN, O., RABINER, L. R., and CHAN, D. S. K. (1973). "Practical Design Rules for Optimum Finite Impulse Response Lowpass Digital Filters," *Bell Syst. Tech. J.*, vol. 52, pp. 769–799, July–August.

HILDEBRAND, F. B. (1952). *Methods of Applied Mathematics*, Prentice-Hall, Englewood Cliffs, N.J.

HINICH, M. J., and WOLINSKY, M. A. (1988). "Test for Aliasing Using Bispectral Analysis," *J. American Statistical Association*, vol. 83(402), pp. 499–502, June.

HINICH, M. J. (1982). "Testing for Gaussianity and Linearity of a Stationary Time Series," *J. Time Series Analysis*, vol. 3, pp. 169–176.

HOUSEHOLDER, A. S. (1958). "Unitary Triangularization of a Non-Symmetric Matrix," *J. Assoc. Comput. Math.*, vol. 5, pp. 204–243.

HOUSEHOLDER, A. S. (1964). *The Theory of Matrices in Numerical Analysis*, Blaisdell, Waltham, Mass.

HSU, F. M. (1982). "Square-Root Kalman Filtering for High-Speed Data Received over Fading Dispersive HF Channels." *IEEE Trans. Information Theory*, vol. IT-28, pp. 753–763, September.

HSU, F. M., and GIORDANO, A. A. (1978). "Digital Whitening Techniques for Improving Spread Spectrum Communications Performance in the Presence of Narrowband Jamming and Interference," *IEEE Trans. Communications*, vol. COM-26, pp. 209–216, February.

HUZII, M. (1981). "Estimation of Coefficients of an Autoregressive Process by Using a Higher Order Moments," *J. Time Series Analysis*, vol. 2, pp. 87–93.

JAIN, V. K., and CROCHIERE, R. E. (1984). "Quadrature Mirror Filter Design in the Time Domain," *IEEE Trans. Acoustics, Speech, and Signal Processing*, vol. ASSP-32, pp. 353–361, April.

JENKINS, G. M., and WATTS, D. G. (1968). *Spectral Analysis and Its Applications*, Holden-Day, San Francisco.

JOHNSON, D. H. (1982). "The Application of Spectral Estimation Methods to Bearing Estimation Problems," *Proc. IEEE*, vol. 70, pp. 1018–1028, September.

JOHNSTON, J. D. (1980). "A Filter Family Designed for Use in Quadrature Mirror Filter Banks," *Proc. 1980 IEEE International Conference on Acoustics, Speech, and Signal Processing*, pp. 291–294, April.

JONES, R. H. (1976). "Autoregression Order Selection," *Geophysics*, vol. 41, pp. 771–773, August.

JONES, S. K., CAVIN, R. K., and REED, W. M. (1982). "Analysis of Error-Gradient Adaptive Linear Equalizers for a Class of Stationary-Dependent Processes," *IEEE Trans. Information Theory*, vol. IT-28, pp. 318–329, March.

KAILATH, T. (1974). "A View of Three Decades of Linear Filter Theory," *IEEE Trans. Information Theory*, vol. IT-20, pp. 146–181, March.

KAILATH, T. (1981). *Lectures on Wiener and Kalman Filtering*, 2nd Printing, Springer-Verlag, New York.

KAILATH, T. (1985). "Linear Estimation for Stationary and Near-Stationary Processes," in *Modern Signal Processing*, T. Kailath, ed., Hemisphere Publishing Corp., Washington, D.C.

KAILATH, T. (1986). "A Theorem of I. Schür and Its Impact on Modern Signal Processing," in Gohberg (1986).

KAILATH, T., VIEIRA, A. C. G., and MORF, M. (1978). "Inverses of Toeplitz Operators, Innovations, and Orthogonal Polynomials," *SIAM Rev.*, vol. 20, pp. 1006–1019.

KALMAN, R. E. (1960). "A New Approach to Linear Filtering and Prediction Problems," *Trans. ASME, J. Basic Eng.*, vol. 82D, pp. 35–45, March.

KALMAN, R. E., and BUCY, R. S. (1961). "New Results in Linear Filtering Theory," *Trans. ASME, J. Basic Eng.*, vol. 83, pp. 95–108.

KALOUPTSIDIS, N., and THEODORIDIS, S. (1987). "Fast Adaptive Least-Squares Algorithms for Power Spectral Estimation," *IEEE Trans. Acoustics, Speech, and Signal Processing*, vol. ASSP-35, pp. 661–670, May.

KALSON, S., and YAO, L. (1984). "Geometrical Approach to Generalized Least Squares Estimation with Systolic Array Processing, "*Proc. Twenty-Second Annual Allerton Conf. on Commu., Contr. and Comp.*, October.

KASHYAP, R. L. (1980). "Inconsistency of the AIC Rule for Estimating the Order of Autoregressive Models," *IEEE Trans. Automatic Control*, vol. AC-25, pp. 996–998, October.

KAVEH, M., and BRUZZONE, S. P. (1979). "Order Determination for Autoregressive Spectral Estimation," *Record of the 1979 RADC Spectral Estimation Workshop*, pp. 139–145, Griffin Air Force Base, Rome, N.Y.

KAVEH, M., and LIPPERT, G. A. (1983). "An Optimum Tapered Burg Algorithm for Linear Prediction and Spectral Analysis," *IEEE Trans. Acoustics, Speech, and Signal Processing*, vol. ASSP-31, pp. 438–444, April.

KAY, S. M. (1980). "A New ARMA Spectral Estimator," *IEEE Trans. Acoustics, Speech, and Signal Processing*, vol. ASSP-28, pp. 585–588, October.

KAY, S. M. (1987). *Modern Spectral Estimation*, Prentice-Hall, Englewood Cliffs, N.J.

KAY, S. M., and MARPLE, S. L., JR. (1981). "Spectrum Analysis: A Modern Perspective," *Proc. IEEE*, vol. 69, pp. 1380–1419, November.

KAY, S. M., and MARPLE, S.L., JR. (1979). "Sources of and Remedies for Spectral Line Splitting in Autoregressive Spectrum Analysis," *Proc. 1979 ICASSP*, pp. 151–154.

KESLER, S. B., ED. (1986). *Modern Spectrum Analysis II*, IEEE Press, New York.

KETCHUM, J. W., and PROAKIS, J. G. (1982). "Adaptive Algorithms for Estimating and Suppressing Narrow-Band Interference in PN Spread-Spectrum Systems," *IEEE Trans. Communications*, vol. COM-30, pp. 913–923, May.

KNUTH, DONALD. (1969). *The Art of Computer Programming*, vol. 2, Seminumerical Algorithms, pp. 260–266, Addison-Wesley Publ. Co., Reading, MA.

KRISHNA, H. (1988). "New Split Levinson, Schür, and Lattice Algorithms for Digital Signal Processing," *Proc. 1988 International Conference on Acoustics, Speech, and Signal Processing*, pp. 1640–1642, New York, April.

KROMER, R. E. (1969). "Asymptotic Properties of the Autoregressive Spectral Estimator," Ph.D. dissertation, Department of Statistics, Stanford University, Stanford, Calif.

KUNG, H. T. (1982). "Why Systolic Architectures?" *IEEE Computer*, vol. 15, pp. 37–46.

KUNG, S. Y., and HU, Y. H. (1983). "A Highly Concurrent Algorithm and Pipelined Architecture for Solving Toeplitz Systems," *IEEE Trans. Acoustics, Speech, and Signal Processing*, vol. ASSP-31, pp. 66–76, January.

KUNG, S. Y., WHITEHOUSE, H. J., and KAILATH, T., EDS. (1985). *VLSI and Modern Signal Processing*, Prentice-Hall, Englewood Cliffs, N.J.

KUNG, H. T., and LEISERSON, C. E. (1978). "Systolic Arrays (for VLSI)," Sparse Matrix Symposium, SIAM, pp. 256–282.

LACOSS, R. T. (1971). "Data Adaptive Spectral Analysis Methods," *Geophysics*, vol. 36, pp. 661–675, August.

LANG, S. W., and MCCLELLAN, J. H. (1980). "Frequency Estimation with Maximum Entropy Spectral Estimators," *IEEE Trans. Acoustics, Speech, and Signal Processing*, vol. ASSP-28, pp. 716–724, December.

LAWSON, C. L., and HANSON, R. J. (1974). *Solving Least Squares Problems*, Prentice-Hall, Englewood Cliffs, N.J.

LEE, D. T., MORF, M., and FRIEDLANDER, B. (1981). "Recursive Least-Squares Ladder Estimation Algorithms," *IEEE Trans. Acoustics, Speech, and Signal Processing*, vol. ASSP-29, pp. 627–641, June.

LEV-ARI, H. (1987). "Modular Architecture for Adaptive Multichannel Lattice Algorithms," *IEEE Trans. on ASSP*, vol. ASSP-35, pp. 543–552, April.

LEVINSON, N. (1947). "The Wiener RMS Error Criterion in Filter Design and Prediction," *J. Math. Phys.*, vol. 25, pp. 261–278.

LIEBOWITZ, L. (1976). "A Simplified Binary Arithmetic for the Fermat Number Transform," *IEEE Trans. ASSP*, vol. 24, pp. 356–359, October.

LII, K. S. (1982). "Non-Gaussian ARMA Model Identification and Estimation," *Proc. Bus. and Econ. Statistics*, ASA, pp. 135–141.

LII, K. S., and ROSENBLATT, M. (1982). "Deconvolution and Estimation of Transfer Function Phase and Coefficients for Non-Gaussian Linear Processes," *Ann. Statist.*, vol. 10, pp. 1195–1208.

LIN, D. W. (1984). "On Digital Implementation of the Fast Kalman Algorithm," *IEEE Trans. Acoustics, Speech, and Signal Processing*, vol. ASSP-32, pp. 998–1005, October.

LING, F. (1991). "Givens Rotation Based Least-Squares Lattice and Related Algorithms," *IEEE Trans. Signal Processing*, vol. 39, July.

LING, F. (1989). "Efficient and Robust Least-Squares Lattice Algorithms Based on Givens Rotation with Systolic Array Implementation," *Proc. 1989 IEEE ICASSP*, San Diego, CA., August.

LING, F. (1988a). "Order-Recursive Least-Squares Adaptive Algorithms—a Unified Framework," (invited paper), *IFAC Symposium on System Identification*, Beijing, China, August.

LING, F. (1988b). "Efficient and Robust Least-Squares Lattice Algorithms Based on Givens Rotation with Systolic Array Implementation," *Proc. 1989 IEEE ICASSP*, Scotland, UK., April.

LING, F., and PROAKIS, J. G. (1984a). "Numerical Accuracy and Stability: Two Problems of Adaptive Estimation Algorithms Caused by Round-Off Error," *Proc. ICASSP-84*, pp. 30.3.1–30.3.4, San Diego, Calif., March.

LING, F., and PROAKIS, J. G. (1984b). "Nonstationary Learning Characteristics of Least-Squares Adaptive Estimation Algorithms," *Proc. ICASSP-84*, pp. 3.7.1–3.7.4, San Diego, Calif., March.

LING, F., and PROAKIS, J. G. (1984c). "A Generalized Multichannel Least-Squares Lattice Algorithm with Sequential Processing Stages," *IEEE Trans. Acoustics, Speech, and Signal Processing*, vol. ASSP-32, pp. 381–389, April.

LING, F., MANOLAKIS, D., and PROAKIS, J. G. (1985). "New Forms of LS Lattice Algorithms and an Analysis of Their Round-Off Error Characteristics," *Proc. ICASSP-85*, pp. 1739–1742, Tampa, Fla., April.

LING, F., MANOLAKIS, D., and PROAKIS, J. G. (1986). "Numerically Robust Least-Squares Lattice-Ladder Algorithms with Direct Updating of the Reflection Coefficients," *IEEE Trans. Acoustics, Speech, and Signal Processing*, vol. ASSP-34, pp. 837–845, August.

LIU, K. J. R., HSIEH, S. F., and YAO, K. (1990). "Recursive LS Filtering Using Block Householder Transformation," *Proc. 1990 IEEE ICASSP*, pp. 1631–1634, April.

LJUNG, S., and LJUNG, L. (1985). "Error Propagation Properties of Recursive Least-Squares Adaptation Algorithms," *Automatica*, 21, pp. 157–167.

LOHMANN, A. W., and WIRNITZER, B. (1984). "Triple Correlations," *Proc. IEEE*, vol. 72, pp. 889–901, July.

LONG, G., LING, F., and PROAKIS, J. G. (1988). "Applications of Fractionally-Spaced Decision-Feedback Equalizers to HF Fading Channels," *Proc. MILCOM*, San Diego, CA., October.

LUCKY, R. W. (1965). Automatic Equalization for Digital Communications," *Bell Syst. Tech. J.*, vol. 44, pp. 547–588, April.

LUK, F. T. (1986). "A Triangular Processor for Computing Singular Values," *J. Lin. Alg. Applic.*, vol. 77, pp. 259–273.

MAGEE, F. R., and PROAKIS, J. G. (1973). "Adaptive Maximum-Likelihood Sequence Estimation for Digital Signaling in the Presence of Intersymbol Interference," *IEEE Trans. Information Theory*, vol. IT-19, pp. 120–124, January.

MAKHOUL, J. (1975). "Linear-Prediction: A Tutorial Review," *Proc. IEEE*, vol. 63, pp. 561–580, April.

MAKHOUL, J. (1978). "A Class of All-Zero Lattice Digital Filters: Properties and Applications." *IEEE Trans. Acoustics, Speech, and Signal Processing*, vol. ASSP-26, pp. 304–314, August.

MANOLAKIS, D., LING, F., and PROAKIS, J. G. (1987). "Efficient Time-Recursive Least-Squares Algorithms for Finite-Memory Adaptive Filtering," *IEEE Trans. Circuits and Systems*, vol. CAS-34, pp. 400–408, April.

MARKEL, J. D., and GRAY, A. H., JR. (1976). *Linear Prediction of Speech*, Springer-Verlag, New York.

MARPLE, S. L., JR. (1980). "A New Autoregressive Spectrum Analysis Algorithm," *IEEE Trans. Acoustics, Speech, and Signal Processing*, vol. ASSP-28, pp. 441–454, August.

MARPLE, S. L., JR. (1987). *Digital Spectral Analysis with Applications*, Prentice-Hall, Englewood Cliffs, N.J.

MARZETTA, T. L. (1983). "A New Interpretation for Capon's Maximum Likelihood Method of Frequency–Wavenumber Spectral Estimation," *IEEE Trans. Acoustics, Speech, and Signal Processing*, vol. ASSP-31, pp. 445–449, April.

MARZETTA, T. L., and LANG, S. W. (1983). "New Interpretations for the MLM and DASE Spectral Estimators," *Proc. 1983 ICASSP*, pp. 844–846, Boston, April.

MARZETTA, T. L., and LANG, S. W. (1984). "Power Spectral Density Bounds," *IEEE Trans. Information Theory*, vol. IT-30, pp. 117–122, January.

MAZO, J. E. (1979). "On the Independence Theory of Equalizer Convergence," *Bell Syst. Tech. J.*, vol. 58, pp. 963–993, May.

MCCLELLAN, J. H. (1982). "Multidimensional Spectral Estimation," *Proc. IEEE*, vol. 70, pp. 1029–1039, September.

MCCLELLAN, J. (1976). "Hardware Realization of a Fermat Number Transform," *IEEE Trans. ASSP*, vol. 24, pp. 216–225, June.

MCDONOUGH, R. N. (1983). "Application of the Maximum-Likelihood Method and the Maximum Entropy Method to Array Processing," in *Nonlinear Methods of Spectral Analysis*, 2nd ed., S. Haykin, Ed., Springer-Verlag, New York.

MCWHIRTER, J. G. (1983). "RLS Minimization Using a Systolic Array," *Proc. SPIE*, vol. 431, pp. 415–431, August.

MEDITCH, J. E. (1969). *Stochastic Optimal Linear Estimation and Control*, McGraw-Hill, New York.

MENDEL, J. M. (1988). "Use of Higher-Order Statistics in Signal Processing and System Theory: An Update," *Proc. SPIE Conf. on Advanced Algorithms and Architectures for Signal Processing III*, San Diego, Ca., August.

MENDEL, J. M. (1991). "Tutorial on Higher Order Statistics (Spectra) in Signal Processing and System Theory: Theoretical Results and Some Applications," *Proc IEEE*, vol. 79, pp. 278–305, March.

MOLLE, J. D., and HINICH, M. J. (1990). "The Trispectrum," *Proc. Workshop on Higher-Order Sopectral Analysis*, pp. 68–72, Vail, CO., June.

MORF, M., and LEE, D. T. (1979). "Recursive Least-Squares Ladder Forms for Fast Parameter Tracking," *Proc. 1979 IEEE Conference on Decision and Control*, San Diego, Calif., pp. 1362–1367, January.

MORF, M., VIEIRA, A., and LEE, D. T. (1977). "Ladder Forms for Identification and Speech Processing," *Proc. 1977 IEEE Conference Decision and Control*, pp. 1074–1078, New Orleans, La., December.

MORRIS, L. R. (1977). "Automatic Generation of Time Efficient Digital Signal Processing Software," *IEEE Trans. ASSP*, vol. 25, pp. 74–79, February.

MURRAY, W., ED. (1972). *Numerical Methods of Unconstrained Minimization*, Academic, New York.

MUSICUS, B. (1985). "Fast MLM Power Spectrum from Uniformly Spaced Correlations," *IEEE Trans. Acoustics, Speech, and Signal Proc.*, vol. ASSP-33, pp. 1333–1335, October.

NEWMAN, W. I. (1981). "Extension to the Maximum Entropy Method III," *Proc. 1st ASSP Workshop on Spectral Estimation*, pp. 1.7.1–1.7.6, Hamilton, Ontario, August.

NICHOLS, H. E., GIORDANO, A. A., and PROAKIS, J. G. (1977). "MLD and MSE Algorithms for Adaptive Detection of Digital Signals in the Presence of Interchannel Interference," *IEEE Trans. Information Theory*, vol. IT-23, pp. 563–575, September.

NIKIAS, C. L., and LIU, F. (1990). "Bicepstrum Computation Based on Second- and Third-Order Statistics with Applications," *Proc. 1990 ICASSP*, pp. 2381–2385, Albuquerque, NM., April.

NIKIAS, C. L. (1988). "ARMA Bispectrum Approach to Nonminimum Phase System Identification," *IEEE Trans. Acoustics, Speech, and Signal Processing*, vol. ASSP-36, pp. 513–524, April.

NIKIAS, C. L., and CHIANG, H. H. (1988). "Higher-Order Spectrum Estimation via Non-Causal Autoregressive Modeling and Deconvolution," *IEEE Trans. Acoustics, Speech, and Signal Processing*, vol. ASSP-36, pp. 1911–1913, December.

NIKIAS, C. L., and PAN, R. (1988). "ARMA Modeling of Fourth-Order Cumulants and Phase Estimation," *Circuits, Systems, and Signal Processing*, vol. 7, pp. 291–325.

NIKIAS, C. L., and RAGHUVEER, M. R. (1987). "Bispectrum Estimation: A Digital Signal Processing Framework," *Proc. IEEE*, vol. 75, pp. 869–891, July.

NIKIAS, C. L., and SCOTT, P. D. (1982). "Energy-Weighted Linear Predictive Spectral Estimation: A New Method Combining Robustness and High Resolution," *IEEE Trans. Acoustics, Speech, and Signal Processing*, vol. ASSP-30, pp. 287–292, April.

NUTTALL, A. H. (1976). "Spectral Analysis of a Univariate Process with Bad Data Points, via Maximum Entropy and Linear Predictive Techniques," *NUSC Technical Report TR-5303*, New London, Conn., March.

Oppenheim, A. V. (1978). *Applications of Digital Signal Processing*, Prentice-Hall, Englewood Cliffs, N.J.

Oppenheim, A. V., and Schafer, R. W. (1989). *Discrete-Time Signal Processing*, Prentice Hall, Englewood Cliffs, N.J.

Pan, N., and Nikias, C. L. (1987). "Phase Reconstruction in the Trispectrum Domain," *IEEE Trans. Acoustics, Speech, and Signal Processing*, vol. ASSP-35, pp. 895–897, June.

Pan, R., and Nikias, C. L. (1988). "The Complex Cepstrum of Higher-Order Cumulants and Nonminimum Phase Identification," *IEEE Trans. Acoustics, Speech, and Signal Processing*, vol. ASSP-36, pp. 186–205, February.

Papoulis, A. (1984). *Probability, Random Variables, and Stochastic Processes*, 2nd ed., McGraw-Hill, New York.

Parzen, E. (1957). "On Consistent Estimates of the Spectrum of a Stationary Time Series," *Am. Math. Stat.*, vol. 28, pp. 329–348.

Parzen, E. (1974). "Some Recent Advances in Time Series Modeling," *IEEE Trans. Automatic Control*, vol. AC-19, pp. 723–730, December.

Peacock, K. L., and Treitel, S. (1969). "Predictive Deconvolution—Theory and Practice," *Geophysics*, vol. 34, pp. 155–169.

Peebles, P. Z., Jr. (1987). *Probability, Random Variables, and Random Signal Principles*, 2nd ed., McGraw-Hill, New York.

Petropulu, A. P., and Nikias, C. L. (1992). "Signal Reconstruction from Phase of the Bispectrum" *IEEE Trans. Signal Processing*, vol. SP-40, March.

Petropulu, A. P., and Nikias, C. L. (1990a). "The Complex Cepstrum and Bicepstrum: Analytic Performance Evaluation and Comparisons," *IEEE Trans. Acoustics, Speech, and Signal Processing*, vol. ASSP-38, pp. 1246–1256, July.

Petropulu, A. P., and Nikias, C. L. (1990b). "Signal Reconstruction from the Phase of the Bispectrum," *Proc. 1990 IEEE ICASSP*, pp. 1567–1570, Albuquerque, NM., April.

Picinbono, B. (1978). "Adaptive Signal Processing for Detection and Communication," in *Communication Systems and Random Process Theory*, J. K. Skwirzynski, Ed., Sijthoff en Noordhoff, Alphen aan den Rijn, The Netherlands.

Pisarenko, V. F. (1973). "The Retrieval of Harmonics from a Covariance Function," *Geophys. J. R. Astron. Soc.*, vol. 33, pp. 347–366.

Polydoros, A., and Fam, A. (1981). "The Differential Cepstrum: Definition and Properties," in *Proc. IEEE Int. Symp. Circuits Syst.*, pp. 77–80, April.

Poole, M. A. (1981). *Autoregressive Methods of Spectral Analysis*, EE degree thesis, Department of Electrical and Computer Engineering, Northeastern University, Boston, May.

Porat, B., and Kailath, T. (1983). "Normalized Lattice Algorithms for Least-Squares FIR System Identification," *IEEE Trans. ASSP*, pp. 122–128.

Proakis, J. G. (1970). "Adaptive Digital Filters for Equalization of Telephone Channels," *IEEE Trans. Audio and Electroacoustics*, vol. AU-18, pp. 195–200, June.

Proakis, J. G. (1974). "Channel Identification for High Speed Digital Communications," *IEEE Trans. Automatic Control*, vol. AC-19, pp. 916–922, December.

Proakis, J. G. (1975). "Advances in Equalization for Intersymbol Interference," in *Advances in Communication Systems*, vol. 4, A. J. Viterbi, Ed., Academic, New York.

Proakis, J. G. (1989). *Digital Communications,* Second Ed., McGraw-Hill, New York.

PROAKIS, J. G., and MANOLAKIS, D. G. (1992). *Digital Signal Processing*, Second Ed., Macmillan, New York.

PROAKIS, J. G., and MILLER, J. H. (1969). "Adaptive Receiver for Digital Signaling Through Channels with Intersymbol Interference," *IEEE Trans. Information Theory*, vol. IT-15, pp. 484–497, July.

PROUDLER, I. K., et. al. (1989). "QRD-Based Lattice Filter Algorithm," *Proc. of SPIE'89*, San Diego, CA., August.

RABINER, L. R., and SCHAFER, R. W. (1978). *Digital Processing of Speech Signals*, Prentice-Hall, Englewood Cliffs, N.J.

RADER, C. M., and STEINHARDT, A. O. (1986). "Hyperbolic Householder Transformation," *IEEE Trans. Acoustics, Speech, and Signal Processing*, vol. ASSP-34, pp. 1589–1602, December.

RADER, C. M. (1970). An Improved Algorithm for High-Speed Auto-correlation with Applications to Spectral Estimation," *IEEE Trans. Audio and Electroacoustics*, vol. AU-18, pp. 439–441, December.

RADER, C. M., and BRENNER, N. M. (1976). "A New Principle for Fast Fourier Transformation," *IEEE Trans. Acoustics, Speech, and Signal Processing*, vol. ASSP-24, pp. 264–266, June.

RAGHUVEER, M. R., and NIKIAS, C. L. (1986). "Bispectrum Estimation via Parametric Modeling," *Signal Processing*, Special Issue on Modern Trends of Spectral Analysis, vol. 10, pp. 35–48, January.

RAGHUVEER, M. R., and NIKIAS, C. L. (1985). "Bispectrum Estimation: A Parametric Approach," *IEEE Trans. Acoustics, Speech, and Signal Processing*, vol. ASSP-33, no. 5, pp. 1213–1230, October.

RAMSTAD, T. A. (1984). "Digital Methods for Conversion Between Arbitrary Sampling Frequencies," *IEEE Trans. Acoustics, Speech, and Signal Processing*, vol. ASSP-32, pp. 577–591, June.

RICE, J. R. (1966). "Experiments on Gram-Schmidt Orthogonalization," *Math. Comp.*, vol. 20, pp. 325–328.

RISSANEN, J. (1983). "A Universal Prior for the Integers and Estimation by Minimum Description Length," *Ann. Stat.*, vol. 11, pp. 417–431.

ROBERTS, R. A., and MULLIS, C. T. (1987). *Digital Signal Processing*, Addison-Wesley, Reading, Mass.

ROBINSON, E. A. (1962). *Random Wavelets and Cybernetic Systems*, Charles Griffin, London.

ROBINSON, E. A. (1982). "A Historical Perspective of Spectrum Estimation," *Proc. IEEE*, vol. 70. pp. 885–907, September.

ROBINSON, E. A., and TREITEL, S. (1980). *Geophysical Signal Analysis*, Prentice Hall, Englewood Cliffs, N.J.

ROBINSON, E. A., and TREITEL, S. (1978). "Digital Signal Processing in Geophysics," in *Applications of Digital Signal Processing*, A. V. Oppenheim, Ed., Prentice-Hall, Englewood Cliffs, N.J.

ROSENBLATT, M. (1985). *Stationary Sequences and Random Fields*, Birkhauser, Boston, MA.

ROY, R., PAULRAJ, A., and KAILATH, T. (1986). "ESPRIT: A Subspace Rotation Approach to Estimation of Parameters of Cisoids in Noise," *IEEE Trans. Acoustics, Speech, and Signal Processing*, vol. ASSP-34, pp. 1340–1342, October.

SAFRANEK, R. J., MACKAY, K., JAYANT, N. S., and KIM, T. (1988). "Image Coding Based on Selective Quantization of the Reconstruction Noise in the Dominant

Sub-band," *Proc. 1988 IEEE International Conference on Acoustics, Speech, and Signal Processing*, pp. 765–768, April.

SAKAI, H. (1979). "Statistical Properties of AR Spectral Analysis," *IEEE Trans. Acoustics, Speech, and Signal Processing*, vol. ASSP-27, pp. 402–409, August.

SATORIUS, E. H., and ALEXANDER, J. T. (1978). "High Resolution Spectral Analysis of Sinusoids in Correlated Noise," *Proc. 1978 ICASSP*, pp. 349–351, Tulsa, Okla., April 10–12.

SATORIUS, E. H., and PACK, J. D. (1981). "Application of Least-Squares Lattice Algorithms to Adaptive Equalization, *IEEE Trans. Communications*, vol. COM-29, pp. 136–142, February.

SCHAFER, R. W., and RABINER, L. R. (1973). "A Digital Signal Processing Approach to Interpolation," *Proc. IEEE*, vol. 61, pp. 692–702, June.

SCHEUERMANN, H., and GOCKLER, H. (1981). "A Comprehensive Survey of Digital Transmultiplexing Methods," *Proc. IEEE*, vol. 69, pp. 1419–1450.

SCHMIDT, R. D. (1981). "A Signal Subspace Approach to Multiple Emitter Location and Spectral Estimation," Ph.D. dissertation, Department of Electrical Engineering, Stanford University, Stanford, Calif., November.

SCHMIDT, R. D. (1986). "Multiple Emitter Location and Signal Parameter Estimation," *IEEE Trans. Antennas and Propagation*, vol. AP 34, pp. 276–280, March.

SCHOTT, J. P., and MCCLELLAN, J. H. (1984). "Maximum Entropy Power Spectrum Estimation with Uncertainty in Correlation Measurements," *IEEE Trans. Acoustics, Speech, and Signal Processing*, vol. ASSP-32, pp. 410–418, April.

SCHÜR, I. (1917). "On Power Series Which Are Bounded in the Interior of the Unit Circle," *J. Reine Angew. Math.*, vol. 147, pp. 205–232, Berlin. For an English translation of the paper, see Gohberg 1986).

SCHUSTER, SIR ARTHUR. (1898). "On the Investigation of Hidden Periodicities with Application to a Supposed Twenty-Six-Day Period of Meterological Phenomena," *Terr. Mag.*, vol. 3, pp. 13–41. March.

SHANNON, C. E. (1949). "Communication in the Process of Noise," *Proc. IRE*, pp. 10–21, January.

SLOCK, D. T. M., and KAILATH, T. (1991). "Numerically Stable Fast Transversal Filters for Recursive Least Squares Adaptive Filtering," *IEEE Trans. Signal Processing*, vol. 39, pp. 92–114, January.

SLOCK, D. T. M., and KAILATH, T. (1988). "Numerically Stable Fast Recursive Least Squares Transversal Filters," *Proc. 1988 Int. Conf. Acoustics, Speech, and Signal Processing*, pp. 1364–1368, N.Y., April.

SMITH, M. J. T., and BARWELL, T. P. (1984). "A Procedure for Designing Exact Reconstruction Filter Banks for Tree Structured Subband Coders," *Proc. 1984 IEEE International Conference on Acoustics, Speech, and Signal Processing*, pp. 27.1.1–27.1.4, San Diego, March.

SMITH, M. J. T., and EDDINS, S. L. (1988). "Subband Coding of Images with Octave Band Tree Structures," *Proc. 1987 IEEE International Conference on Acoustics, Speech, and Signal Processing*, pp. 1382–1385, Dallas, April.

STEWART, G. W. (1973). *Introduction to Matrix Computations*, Academic Press, New York.

SWINGLER, D. N. (1979a). "A Comparison Between Burg's Maximum Entropy Method and a Nonrecursive Technique for the Spectral Analysis of Deterministic Signals," *J. Geophys. Res.*, vol. 84, pp. 679–685, February.

SWINGLER, D. N. (1979b). "A Modified Burg Algorithm for Maximum Entropy Spectral Analysis," *Proc. IEEE*, vol. 67, pp. 1368–1369, September.

SWINGLER, D. N. (1980). "Frequency Errors in MEM Processing," *IEEE Trans. Acoustics, Speech, and Signal Processing*, vol. ASSP-28, pp. 257–259, April.

SZEGÖ, G. (1967). *Orthogonal Polynomials*, 3rd ed., Colloquium Publishers, no. 23, American Mathematical Society, Providence, R. I.

THORVALDSEN, T. (1981). "A Comparison of the Least-Squares Method and the Burg Method for Autoregressive Spectral Analysis," *IEEE Trans. Antennas and Propagation*, vol. AP-29, pp. 675–679, July.

TONG, H. (1975). "Autoregressive Model Fitting with Noisy Data by Akaike's Information Criterion," *IEEE Trans. Information Theory*, vol. IT-21, pp. 476–480, July.

TONG, H. (1977). "More on Autoregressive Model Fitting with Noisy Data by Akaike's Information Criterion," *IEEE Trans. Information Theory*, vol. IT-23, pp. 409–410, May.

TRETTER, S. A. (1976). *Introduction to Discrete-Time Signal processing*, Wiley, New York.

TRIBOLET, J. M. (1979). *Seismic Applications of Homomorphic Signal Processing*, Prentice-Hall, Inc. Englewood Cliffs, N.J.

TRYON, P. V. (1981). "The Bispectrum and Higher-Order Spectra: A Bibliography," *NBS Technical Note 1036*.

TUFTS, D. W., and KUMARESAN, R. (1982). "Estimation of Frequencies of Multiple Sinusoids: Making Linear Prediction Perform Like Maximum Likelihood," *Proc. IEEE*, vol. 70, pp. 975–989, September.

TUGNAIT, J. K. (1988). "On Selection of Maximum Cumulant Lags for Noncausal Autoregressive Model Fitting," *Proc. 1988 IEEE ICASSP*, pp. 2372–2375, New York, N.Y., April.

TUGNAIT, J. K. (1987). "Fitting Noncausal Autoregressive Signal Plus Noise Models to Noisy Non-Gaussian Linear Processes," *IEEE Trans. Automat. Contr.*, vol. AC-32, pp. 547–552, June.

ULRYCH, T. J., and BISHOP, T. N. (1975). "Maximum Entropy Spectral Analysis and Autoregressive Decomposition," *Rev. Geophys. Space Phys.*, vol. 13, pp. 183–200, February.

ULRYCH, T. J., and CLAYTON, R. W. (1976). "Time Series Modeling and Maximum Entropy," *Phys. Earth Planet. Inter.*, vol. 12, pp. 188–200, August.

UNGERBOECK, G. (1972). "Theory on the Speed of Convergence in Adaptive Equalizers for Digital Communication," *IBM J. Res. Devel.*, vol. 16, pp. 546–555, November.

VAIDYANATHAN, P. P. (1987). "Quadrature Mirror Filter Banks, M-Band Extensions and Perfect Reconstruction Techniques", *IEEE ASSP Mag.*, vol. 4, pp. 4–20, July.

VAIDYANATHAN, P. P. (1990). "Multirate Digital Filters, Filter Banks, Polyphase Networks, and Applications: A Tutorial," *Proc. IEEE*, vol. 78, pp. 56–93, January.

VETTERLI, M. (1984). "Multi-dimensional Sub-band Coding: Some Theory and Algorithms," *Signal Processing*, vol. 6, pp. 97–112, April.

VETTERLI, M. (1987). "A Theory of Multirate Filter Banks," *IEEE Trans. Acoustics, Speech, and Signal Processing*, vol. ASSP-35, pp. 356–372, March.

VIEIRA, A. C. G. (1977). "Matrix Orthogonal Polynomials with Applications to Autoregressive Modeling and Ladder Forms," Ph.D. dissertation, Department of Electrical Engineering, Stanford University, Stanford, Calif., December.

WALKER, G. (1931). "On Periodicity in Series of Related Terms," *Proc. R. Soc.*, Ser. A, vol. 313, pp. 518–532.

WAX, M., and KAILATH, T. (1985). "Detection of Signals by Information Theoretic

Criteria," *IEEE Trans. Acoustics, Speech, and Signal Processing*, vol. ASSP-32, pp. 387–392, April.

WELCH, P. D. (1967). "The Use of Fast Fourier Transform for the Estimation of Power Spectra: A Method Based on Time Averaging over Short Modified Periodograms," *IEEE Trans. Audio and Electroacoustics*, vol. AU-15, pp. 70–73, June.

WIDROW, B. (1970). "Adaptive Filters," in *Aspects of Network and System Theory*, R. E. Kalman and N. DeClaris, Eds., Holt, Rinehart and Winston, New York.

WIDROW, B., and HOFF, M. E., JR. (1960). "Adaptive Switching Circuits," *IRE WESCON Conv. Rec.*, pt. 4, pp. 96–104.

WIDROW, B., MANTEY, P., and GRIFFITHS, L. J. (1967). "Adaptive Antenna Systems, *Proc. IEEE*, vol. 55, pp. 2143–2159, December.

WIDROW, B. ET AL. (1975). "Adaptive Noise Cancelling Principles and Applications," *Proc. IEEE*, vol. 63, pp. 1692–1716, December.

WIDROW, B., MCCOOL, J. M., LARIMORE, M. G., and JOHNSON, C. R., JR. (1976). "Stationary and Nonstationary Learning Characteristics of the LMS Adaptive Filters," *Proc. IEEE*, vol. 64, pp. 1151–1162, August.

WIENER, N. (1949). *Extrapolation, Interpolation and Smoothing of Stationary Time Series with Engineering Applications*, Wiley, New York.

WIENER, N., and PALEY, R. E. A. C. (1934). *Fourier Transforms in the Complex Domain*, American Mathematical Society, Providence, R.I.

WILKINSON, J. H. (1965). *The Algebraic Eigenvalue Problem*, Claredon Press, Oxford, England.

WINOGRAD, S. (1976). "On Computing the Discrete Fourier Transform," *Proc. Nat. Acad. Sci.*, vol. 73, pp. 105–106.

WINOGRAD, S. (1978). "On Computing the Discrete Fourier Transform," *Math. Comp.*, vol. 32, pp. 177–199.

WOLD, H. (1938). *A Study in the Analysis of Stationary Time Series*, reprinted by Almquist and Wichells Forlag, Stockholm, Sweden, 1954.

WOOD, L. C., and TREITEL, S. (1975). "Seismic Signal Processing," *Proc. IEEE*, vol. 63. pp. 649–661, April.

WOODS, J. W., and O'NEIL, S. D. (1986). "Subband Coding of Images," *IEEE Trans. Acoustics, Speech, and Signal Processing*, vol. ASSP-34, pp. 1278–1288, October.

YUEN, S. ET AL. (1988). "A Recursive Least-Squares Algorithm for Multiple Inputs and Outputs and a Cylindrical Systolic Implementation," *IEEE Trans. on ASSP*, vol. 36, pp. 1917–1923, December.

YOULA, D., and KAZANJIAN, N. (1978). "Bauer-Type Factorization of Positive Matrices and the Theory of Matrices Orthogonal on the Unit Circle," *IEEE Trans. Circuits and Systems*, vol. CAS-25, pp. 57–69, January.

YULE, G. U. (1927). "On a Method of Investigating Periodicities in Disturbed Series with Special References to Wolfer's Sunspot Numbers," *Philos. Trans. R. Soc. London*, ser. A, vol. 226, pp. 267–298, July.

ZURBENKO, I. G. (1986). *The Spectral Analysis of Time Series*, Chapter 6, North-Holland Series in Statistics and Probability, vol. 2, Elsevier Science Publishers, B. V.

Index